Ben Oakley

King's College

Cambridge

13 April 2012

The Oxford Handbook of
Music
Psychology

The Oxford Handbook of
Music
Psychology

Edited by
**Susan Hallam,
Ian Cross**
and
Michael Thaut

OXFORD
UNIVERSITY PRESS

OXFORD
UNIVERSITY PRESS

Great Clarendon Street, Oxford OX2 6DP

Oxford University Press is a department of the University of Oxford.
It furthers the University's objective of excellence in research, scholarship,
and education by publishing worldwide in

Oxford New York

Auckland Cape Town Dar es Salaam Hong Kong Karachi
Kuala Lumpur Madrid Melbourne Mexico City Nairobi
New Delhi Shanghai Taipei Toronto

With offices in

Argentina Austria Brazil Chile Czech Republic France Greece
Guatemala Hungary Italy Japan Poland Portugal Singapore
South Korea Switzerland Thailand Turkey Ukraine Vietnam

Oxford is a registered trade mark of Oxford University Press
in the UK and in certain other countries

Published in the United States
by Oxford University Press Inc., New York

© Oxford University Press, 2009

The moral rights of the authors have been asserted
Database right Oxford University Press (maker)

First published 2009

British Library Cataloguing in Publication Data
Data available

Library of Congress Cataloging-in-Publication Data

The Oxford handbook of music psychology/edied by Susan Hallam, Ian Cross, and
Michael Thaut

p. cm

Includes bibliographical references.

ISBN 978-0-19-929845-7

1. Music—Psychological aspects. 2. Music therapy. I. Hallam, Susan. II. Cross,
Ian. III. Thaut, Michael, 1952-

ML3830.09 2009

781'.11—dc22

2008046393

Typeset by Cepha Imaging Private Ltd., Bangalore, India
Printed in the United Kingdom
on acid-free paper by CPI Antony Rowe, Chippenham, Wiltshire.

ISBN 978-0-19-929845-7

10 9 8 7 6 5 4

Contents

*handwritten: * Look up ORIGINAL PAPERS in conjunction with topics.*

Contributors

Dr Bronwen Ackermann
School of Physiotherapy
Faculty of Health Sciences
The University of Sydney
Lidcombe NSW 2141
Australia

Professor Dr Eckart Altenmüller
Institut für Musikphysiologie und
Musiker-Medizin
Hohenzollernstr 47
30161 Hannover
Germany

Dr Richard Ashley
School of Music
Northwestern University
711 Elgin Road
Evanston IL 60208-1200
USA

Kristen T. Begosh
Department of Psychology, U-1020
University of Connecticut
406 Babbidge Road
Storrs CT 06269-1020
USA

Professor Emmanuel Bigand
LEAD-CNRS UMR 5022
Université de Bourgogne
Pôle AAFE
Esplanade Erasme, BP 26513
21065 Dijon Cedex
France

Tim Byron
MARCS Auditory Laboratories
University of Western Sydney
Locked Bag 1797
Penrith South DC NSW 1797
Australia

Dr Roger Chaffin
Department of Psychology,
U-1020
University of Connecticut
406 Babbidge Road
Storrs CT 06269-1020
USA

Professor Martin Clayton
The Music Department
Open University
Walton Hall
Milton Keynes MK7 6AA
UK

Professor Annabel J. Cohen
Department of Psychology
University of Prince Edward Island
550 University Avenue
Charlottetown PEI
Canada C1A 4P3

Dr Andrea Creech
Institute of Education
University of London
20 Bedford Way
London WCIH OAL
UK

Dr Ian Cross
Faculty of Music
University of Cambridge
11 West Road
Cambridge
CB3 9DP
UK

Dr Simone Dalla Bella
Department of Cognitive Psychology
University of Finance and Management in
Warsaw
Pawia 55 Street
01-030 Warsaw
Poland

Professor Jane W. Davidson
Department of Music
University of Sheffield
38 Taptonville Road
Sheffield S10 5BR
UK

Dr Shannon de l'Etoile
University of Miami
Frost School of Music
P O Box 248165
Coral Gables FL 33124
USA

Professor Alf Gabrielsson
Department of Psychology
Uppsala University
Box 1225
SE - 751 42 Uppsala
Sweden

Dr Helena Gaunt
Guildhall School of Music & Drama
Silk Street
Barbican
London EC2Y 8DT
UK

Dr Bruno L. Giordano
Centre for Interdisciplinary Research in Music,
Media and Technology
Schulich School of Music of McGill University
555 Sherbrooke Street West
Montreal QC
Canada H3A 1E3

Alinka Greasley
School of Psychology
Keele University
Keele
Staffordshire ST5 5BG
UK

Professor Timothy D. Griffiths
Auditory Group
Institute of Neuroscience
The Medical School
Newcastle University
Newcastle upon Tyne NE2 4HH
UK

Professor Susan Hallam
The Institute of Education
University of London
20 Bedford Way
London WC1H 0AL
UK

Professor David J. Hargreaves
Centre for International Research on Creativity
and Learning in Education (CIRCLE)
Roehampton University
Southlands College
Roehampton Lane
London SW15 5SL
UK

Professor Donald A. Hodges
Music Research Institute
University of North Carolina at Greensboro
P O Box 26170
Greensboro NC 27402-6170
USA

Professor David Huron
School of Music
1866 College Road
Ohio State University
Columbus OH 43210
USA

Dr Corene Hurt-Thaut
Assistant Professor of Music Therapy
Department of Music
Colorado State University
Fort Collins CO 80523
USA

Dr Jonathan Impett
School of Music
University of East Anglia
Norwich NR4 7TJ
UK

Dr Mari Riess Jones
Department of Psychology
Ohio State University and University
  of Santa Barbara California
5388 Traci Drive
Santa Barbara CA 93111
USA

Dr Harald Jørgensen
The Norwegian Academy of Music
PB 5190 Majorstua
N-0302 Oslo
Norway

Dr Patrik N. Juslin
Department of Psychology
Uppsala University
Box 1225
SE - 751 42 Uppsala
Sweden

Professor Dianna T. Kenny
Director, Australian Centre for Applied
Research in Music Performance
Sydney Conservatorium of Music
The University of Sydney
Australia

Dr Reinhardt Kopiez
Hochschule für Musik und Theater
Emmichplatz 1
D-30175 Hannover
Germany

Dr Alexandra Lamont
School of Psychology
Keele University
Keele
Staffordshire ST5 5BG
UK

Professor Andreas C. Lehmann
Hochschule für Musik
Hofstallstrasse 6-8
D-97070 Würzburg
Germany

Dr Anne Kathrin Leins
Abendsrothweg 71
D-20251 Hamburg
Germany

Topher R. Logan
Community School of the Arts
University of Connecticut, U-5195
3 Witryol Place
Storrs, CT 06269-5195
USA

Professor Stephen McAdams
Centre for Interdisciplinary Research
  in Music, Media and
  Technology
Schulich School of Music of
  McGill University
555 Sherbrooke Street West
Montreal QC
Canada H3A 1E3

Professor Raymond MacDonald
Department of Psychology
School of Life Sciences
Glasgow Caledonian University
George Moore Building
Cowcaddens Road
Glasgow G4 0BA
UK

Professor Gary McPherson
School of Music
University of Illinois
1114 W. Nevada Street
Urbana, IL 61801
USA

Professor Dorothy Miell
Department of Psychology
Faculty of Social Sciences
The Open University
Walton Hall
Milton Keynes MK7 6AA
UK

Professor Adrian C. North
School of Life Sciences
Heriot Watt University
Edinburgh EH14 4AS
UK

Professor Adam Ockelford
School of Education
Roehampton University
Roehampton Lane
London SW15 5PU
UK

Professor Richard Parncutt
Centre for Systematic Musicology
University of Graz
Merangasse 70
A-8010 Graz
Austria

Professor Aniruddh D. Patel
The Neurosciences Institute
10640 John Jay Hopkins Drive
San Diego CA 92121
USA

Dr Bénédicte Poulin-Charronnat
LEAD-CNRS UMR 5022
Université de Bourgogne
Pôle AAFE
Esplanade Erasme, BP 26513
21065 Dijon Cedex
France

Dr Frances H. Rauscher
Department of Psychology
University of Wisconsin Oshkosh
800 Algoma Boulevard
Oshkosh WI 54901
USA

Dr Gottfried Schlaug
Music and Neuroimaging Laboratory
Beth Israel Deaconess Medical Center
330 Brookline Avenue – Palmer 127
Boston MA 02215
USA

Dr Mark A. Schmuckler
Department of Psychology
University of Toronto Scarborough
1265 Military Trail
Scarborough ON
Canada M1C 1A4

Dr Sabine Schneider
Institut für Musikphysiologie und
Musiker-Medizin
Hohenzollernstr 47
30161 Hannover
Germany

Professor John Sloboda
School of Psychology
Keele University
Keele
Staffordshire ST5 5BG
UK

Professor Robert Snyder
Sound Department
School of the Art
Institute of Chicago
112 South Michigan Ave
Chicago IL 60604
USA

Professor Ralph Spintge
Director, Department of Pain Medicine
Sportklinik Hellersen
58515 Ludenscheid
Germany

Dr Thomas Stainsby
Department of Experimental Psychology
University of Cambridge
Downing Street
Cambridge CB2 3EB
UK

Dr Catherine Stevens
MARCS Auditory Laboratories
University of Western Sydney
Locked Bag 1797
Penrith South DC NSW 1797
Australia

Dr Lauren Stewart
Department of Psychology
Whitehead Building
Goldsmiths, University of London
New Cross
London SE14 6NW
UK

Professor Michael Thaut
School of the Arts
Center for Biomedical Research in music
Colorado State University
Fort Collins CO 80523
USA

Elizabeth Tolbert
Peabody Institute of the Johns
Hopkins University
1 East Mount Vernon Place
Baltimore, MD 21202
USA

Dr Laurel J. Trainor
Dept of Psychology, Neuroscience
& Behaviour
McMaster University
1280 Main Street W
Hamilton ON
Canada L8S 4K1

Professor Sandra E. Trehub
Department of Psychology
University of Toronto at Mississauga
3359 Mississauga Road N
Mississauga ON
Canada L5L 1C6

Dr Katharina von Kriegstein
Wellcome Department of Imaging
Neuroscience
Institute of Neurology
University College London
London WCIN 3BG
UK

Dr Jason D. Warren
Dementia Research Centre
Institute of Neurology
University College London
London WC1N 3BG
UK

Professor Peter R. Webster
School of Music
Northwestern University
711 Elgin Road, Room 119
Evanston IL 60208-1200
USA

Professor Graham Welch
The Institute of Education
University of London
20 Bedford Way
London WC1H 0AL
UK

John Whaley MSc
10291 Kismet Lane N
Stillwater, MN 55082
USA

Professor Barbara Wheeler
School of Music
University of Louisville
Louisville KY 40292
USA

Dr Aaron Williamon
Centre for the Study of Music
Performance (CSMP)
Royal College of Music
Prince Consort Road
London SW7 2BS
UK

Dr W. Luke Windsor
School of Music
University of Leeds
Leeds LS2 9JT
UK

Professor Robert J. Zatorre
Montreal Neurological Institute
McGill University
3801 University Street
Montreal, QC, Canada H3A2B4
and BRAMS laboratory
Montreal, QC
Canada

PART 1

The origins and functions of music

Edited by Ian Cross

CHAPTER 1

The nature of music and its evolution

Ian Cross

The theory of evolution in musicological context

The idea that the theory of evolution has anything to offer to our understanding of music provokes strong reactions (both positive and negative) and has swung in and out of favour amongst those who have thought and written about music over the last hundred and fifty years. For the last few decades of the nineteenth century and the first few of the twentieth, the theory of evolution was of huge significance for music theorists, historians and anthropologists as a means of exploring and explaining musical change, musical difference and musical value. From around the 1940s to the beginning of the 1990s, the theory of evolution more or less vanished from musical and musicological discourse: the term 'evolution' tends to co-occur with musical terms only in the titles of books and articles such as 'The evolution of twelve-tone music', 'of Beethoven's late style'—and so on. However, from around the late 1980s, the theory of evolution began to re-emerge as a valid and prospectively valuable way of thinking about important aspects of music. This chapter will outline aspects of 'classical' evolutionary theory before delineating some of the factors that have led to the fall and rise in the fortunes of evolutionary theory as applied to music. It will give an outline of current conceptions of the relationships between music and evolutionary theory, and will conclude by exploring some of the implications for music psychology of evolutionary views of music.

Dictionary definitions of the term 'evolution' include 'the appearance of events in due succession', and 'the gradual development of something into a more complex or better form'. Only with the publication of Darwin's *Origin of Species* in 1859 did the meaning in terms of which 'evolution' is now most widely understood take clear shape: 'the theoretical process[es] by which all species develop from earlier forms of life'. 'Classical' evolutionary theory starts by noting that not all members of any given population of animals will be identical; there will be minor differences of form and capacity between individual members, and if those differences allow an individual to exploit its environment better than other individuals, they will increase the likelihood that the individual will survive and reproduce. If those differences can be inherited, all members of the population that bear them will be similarly advantaged by being better adapted to their environment, becoming prevalent in the population over time and leading to a change in its make up and perhaps to speciation, the emergence of new species (roughly speaking, a discrete population of animals that do not interbreed with other populations of animals). This process of variation, leading to differential levels of survival and reproduction, leading to speciation, can be termed 'natural selection'. Natural selection, together with sexual selection (evident in processes governing mate choice and hence affecting likelihood of reproduction) constituted the foundations of Darwin's theory of evolution, which was intended to provide an explanation of the diversity of forms of life and their inter-relationships without invoking any creative agency other than the workings of observable physical and biological processes.

The theory of evolution was developed to account for the natural world, but was almost immediately co-opted into theory and debate about human society. For many it appeared to offer a scientific basis on which to erect social theory, particularly insofar as it could be interpreted as giving support to ideas of scientifically grounded distinctions between human races, and of the progressive development of human societies. After all, it seemed to many influential thinkers that the processes of evolution constituted a means of explaining the continual refinement of a species' abilities. What could be more natural, in the Victorian age of progress, than to suppose that differences in degrees of ability between species—with human races interpretable as distinct species, or at least, as being analogous to species—conformed to universal principles that could be summarized in the theory of evolution? With these teleological trappings the theory of evolution came to serve as one of the key features of much writing about music at the beginning of the twentieth century. The 'progressivist' notion of evolution seemed to provide a systematic framework that could account not only for stylistic change and development in music across Western musical history, but also a means of qualifying music from non-Western societies as being more, or less, developed in their relationships to refined and hence 'highly evolved' Western musical practice (for an overview see Rehding 2000).

It should be noted that Darwin's own writings in *The expression of the emotions in man and animals*, and in *The descent of man* on music as an evolved human capacity played almost no role in any of the early twentieth-century musicological writings that espoused evolutionary perspectives. Darwin viewed the human capacity for music as a likely precursor of the capacity for language, having its origins in the vocal expression of emotion and as having had utility in processes of sexual selection (see Cross 2007). Moreover, he was somewhat agnostic concerning whether or not music of different cultures or races had greater or lesser value, but in any case did not agree with the proposition that racial difference corresponded to any difference in innate, human, musical capacity; in other words, humans, to Darwin, were a single species (see Chapters 7 and 19 of *The descent of man* [Darwin 2004]).

As the twentieth century progressed, consideration of origins in the study of music moved away from any exploration of music's relationship to biology to re-focus on the historical relationships between contemporary Western musical theory and practice, on Western musical history, or on music's relationships with abstract domains such as mathematics. For these strands of thought evolution was simply irrelevant to their interests, which were viewed as primarily musicological, concerned with the explication of the historical and ontological roots of Western music. Moreover, the repellent consequences of the racialist theorizing that teleological interpretations of evolutionary theory had been called upon to sanction were all too evident in the aftermath of the Second World War.

In any case, within anthropology, an increasing tendency to focus on the cultural specificities of societies rather than on pancultural universalities or on any necessary concept of cultural progress diminished the apparent explanatory role of any biological foundation for culture and mind (see Shore 1996). By the middle of the twentieth century, exploration of music beyond the bounds of Western societies had come to concentrate on detailed ethnographic description and on attempts to understand the structures and functions of music in terms derived from the societies' own understandings of their music—in other words, in emic rather than etic terms. There is little evidence of evolutionary thinking as having had any significant impact on understanding music within societies or across cultures. Nevertheless, a vital feature of these ethnomusicological studies is the evidence they provide concerning the heterogeneity of music across different societies, a heterogeneity that problematizes the very notion of 'music' (see Chapter 4 this volume), and any evolutionary approach to understanding music requires at least an operational definition of what might constitute 'music'.

Evolutionary theory is first and foremost a theory about biology. It could be suggested that music has no existence that is independent of the discourse that frames it: that 'music' is simply a discursive category with an identity that is dependent on its opposition to the other categories of discourse that we employ in the linguistic taxonomies that we have developed—largely in the west—to describe or talk about types of human behaviours. This is a view that seems at least implicit in much musicological thinking of the recent past (see e.g. Korsyn 2003, p. 187). However, most ethnomusicologists would subscribe to the view that there is something that can be described as 'musical' that is evident in the patterns of thought and behaviour of all known societies (see Chapters 2 and 4 this volume). If this is indeed the case, given that humans share a common biology as members of a single species, then whatever constitutes 'music' across cultures may reflect some general processes of thought and behaviour that should, in principle, be a proper focus of exploration in terms of evolutionary theory.

'Music' as an object of evolutionary exploration

Music varies from society to society to the extent that one culture's music may not be recognizable as music by members of another culture. This applies both to the structural features of the music and to the functions that it may fulfil. As Stevens and Byron show in Chapter 2 of this volume, the cognitive processing of music across human societies exhibits many common characteristics. Some of these processing commonalities map onto structural musical features, such as the use of discrete pitch levels, unequal-stepped scales, octave equivalence, low-integer frequency ratios, and periodic pulses. Moreover, features such as hierarchical organization and temporal structures that are shaped so as to modulate the expectancies of those engaged with the music, also appear to be generic in music across cultures. It may be that some features, particularly those concerned with the experience of fine-grained pitch structures and periodic temporal structures, should be considered as proper to music. Nevertheless, at least some of these common structural regularities may not be evident in particular instances otherwise identifiable as music (a paradigmatic,

though controversial, case being Cage's *4'33'*), and at least some of the universal cognitive processes described in Chapter 2, such as the formation of hierarchical structures, and the implicit learning of expectancies, are operational in domains other than music. While arriving at an empirically grounded account of universal characteristics of musical processing and musical structure is essential in delineating what may constitute the foundations of music, it is not sufficient; it is also necessary to explore the extent to which there may be commonalities between people and across cultures in the ways in which music is manifested as social behaviour.

On the whole, ethnomusicologists have given surprisingly little consideration to the question of musical universals. Amongst the few significant exceptions are Bruno Nettl, Alan Merriam and John Blacking, who adopt somewhat different perspectives. Nettl (2005) takes a pragmatic approach, suggesting that etic (Western) and emic accounts should each feed in to determine what it is that ethnomusicologists should focus on as 'music'. Merriam (1964) suggests that 'music' can best be explored in terms of a tripartite model that embraces music as *sound* (what might conventionally be thought of as constituting music from a Western perspective), as *behaviour* (which embraces the musical—and 'non-musical'—acts of musicians, and the activities in which the production of music is embedded) and as *concept* (how people think about music in terms of its powers and its relations to other domains of human life). Blacking (1995), on the basis of his extensive fieldwork with the Venda peoples of southern Africa, and in particular, on his study of Venda children's music, claims that

> 'Music' is a primary modelling system of human thought and a part of the infrastructure of human life. 'Music'-making is a special kind of social action which can have important consequences for other kinds of social action.
>
> Blacking (1995, p. 223)

Blacking's claims appear to locate music as central to, and in some ways indissociable from, other domains of human behaviour. While the claim for music's centrality is not widely echoed in the ethnomusicological literature, the conception of music as embedded in broader suites of behaviour is more general, as Bohlman puts it:

> expressive practices do not divide into those that produce music and those that produce something else, say ritual or dance. Music accumulates its identities ... from the ways in which it participates in other activities.
>
> Bohlman (2000, p. 293)

For those engaged in understanding music as it manifests itself across different cultures and historical times, 'music' appears to be protean, and its identification in any consistent manner seems particularly intractable. Certainly, music cannot be defined in the terms in which it is conventionally conceived of in contemporary Western societies, as a consumable commodity constituted of complexly patterned sound that is produced by a class of specialists and engaged with through listening for primarily hedonic reasons. In many, perhaps most, non-Western cultures it involves overt action and active group engagement, and is employed not only in caregiver–infant interaction, entertainment and courtship but also in ritual, particularly at times of significant life transitions (such as the passage from adolescence to adulthood, from season to season, or from life to death). More often than not, music is an integral part of a wider range of everyday activities. If a category of behaviours that can be termed 'music' has any generality across cultures, it seems that it can best be characterized as active, as founded in interaction, and as permeated by many other aspects of social life (see also Chapter 4 this volume).

Given that, in the ethnomusicological view, music and other human activities seem almost amalgamated, are there any features that would serve to distinguish 'music' as a discrete category of human thought and behaviour? At first sight, music seems to possess few characteristics that are not shared with other domains of behaviour, notably dance and language. Music involves patterned action in time, as does dance. Music appears communicative, complex, generative and representational, as does language. The concept of music is amalgamated with that of dance in many—perhaps the majority of—cultures. This fact, together with the stress on

music as action in much of the ethnomusicological literature (see Chapter 2 this volume) suggests that it would be parsimonious to treat music and dance either as intrinsically related or simply as different manifestations of the same phenomenon.

Relationships between music and language are more difficult to disentangle, but perhaps the most significant factors that differentiate them are the types of structured interactions that they allow, and their contexts of use. Linguistic interactions are typically structured in time so as to coordinate the temporal succession of participants' contributions. Language possesses a generative complexity that allows for the production and reception of a potentially unlimited set of utterances: it is also directed towards the communication of representations of ideas, states of affairs, attitudes and affects that have relevance to their contexts of production and reception—language can signify or mean, unambiguously. While music seems to share some of these characteristics with language, at least two significant differences are apparent. Music may allow participants to act simultaneously rather than asynchronously as in language. In addition, music's meanings appear less stable and consensual than those of language (see Chapter 3 this volume).

Music's capacity to enable participants to act and to contribute to music-making simultaneously exploits the capacity of entrainment (Clayton et al. 2005). Entrainment here refers to the coordination in time of one participant's behaviours with those of another and involves the organization of the perception and behaviour of participants around temporal regularities that are inferred (generally non-consciously) from musical sounds and actions in the form of a periodic pulse or beat that is sensed by all participants (Clayton et al. 2005), being evidenced in continual processes of correction of errors by participants in alignment of action in both period and phase (see e.g. Repp 2001). Even engagement with music in apparently passive listening appears to rely on such entrainment processes, evidenced in periodic modulation of attentional load (see Chapter 8 this volume). It is notable that the capacity for entrainment may be unique to humans. While several species of cicadas and frogs do appear to entrain, they do so in ways that appear different from those implicated in human entrainment and the issue of the origins of entrainment in the hominid or hominin lineage remains to be investigated (see Bispham 2006; Cross *et al.* 2008, in press).

Language has an indisputable efficacy in human interaction, in large part by virtue of its capacities to mean. It is often supposed that music's meanings can be reduced to the emotions it represents, expresses or elicits (see Juslin and Sloboda 2001) which suggests that meaning in music is a poor or natural cousin of meaning in language. However, while it is undoubtedly the case that music is valued for its affective powers in all societies, music's meanings extend beyond its affective value; as Tolbert (2001) notes, music's meanings are equally embodied, natural or affective, and artificial or symbolic. In general, however, meaning in music appears to be less susceptible to consensual determination than is meaning in language; music certainly bears meaning, but the meanings that it can bear are more impenetrable and susceptible to change according to the contexts in which they are experienced than are those of language. As Blacking (1995 p. 237) notes, 'Not only can the "same" patterns of sound have different meanings in different societies; they can also have different meanings within the same society because of different social contexts', an attribute of music characterizable as 'floating intentionality' (Cross 1999).

So music is differentiable from language in its exploitation of the human capacity to entrain, in the probable scope of its generativity and in ways in which it can mean. In some respects this comparison could appear to objectify music as an impoverished version of language. However, music and language coexist in all societies and fulfil different (though perhaps complementary) functions in those societies. While language is capable of expressing semantically decompos-able propositions that have unambiguous reference, music cannot. Nevertheless, there are numerous social situations in which unambiguous reference in communicative acts is not a desideratum as it may precipitate conflict in attitudes or actions. Music's exploitation of the human capacity for entrainment allows participants to experience a sense of 'shared

intentionality', whilst under-specifying goals in ways that permit individuals to interact even while holding to personal meanings and goals that may actually be in conflict (Cross 2005). Music has a profoundly social efficacy (see Chapter 4 this volume), and it is possible to delineate music as a medium that is interactive, entraining, and that exhibits floating intentionality. Such a definition seems almost to exclude Western listening, which may often be passive and solitary rather than social. However, the object of listening—the music—can be conceived of as constituting a trace of human activity with which a listener may 'virtually' interact (see Clarke [2005] on 'subject-position' in music).

Music in recent evolutionary thought

In parallel with the development of broad conceptions of music, over the latter half of the twentieth century theories of evolution underwent a revolution, in part driven by developments in theoretical biology and by the rise of the science of genetics (see e.g. Maynard-Smith and Szathmáry 1995). Neo-Darwinian understandings of evolution elucidated the genetic mechanisms whereby organisms transmitted their characteristics from one generation to the next, as well as processes, in addition to natural and sexual selection, that could operate so as to shape an organism's fitness, or adaptedness, with respect to its environment. Processes of kin selection have been distinguished whereby genetic relatedness can be adduced to account for seemingly altruistic behaviours between members of social species as well as for the emergence of sterile animal castes (see e.g. Hölldobler and Wilson 1994). Processes of genetic drift have also been shown to be operational whereby random changes in the genetic make-up of a population come, over time, to lead to populations with quite different characteristics from the parent population (see Maynard Smith 1998). Other work has shown that processes of selection can *appear* to operate at the level of the group. Theories such as those proposed by Sober and Wilson (1998) support the notion of a role for relationships between social environment and individual fitness in profoundly social species such as humans. In a social species, behaviours that contribute towards survival and reproductive success may be determined as much by relations between members of the species (and by individual capacities to manage such relations) as by relations between individuals and their physical environments. All these developments provided substantial foundations for postulating that complex individual and social behaviours such as language and music, as well as the mental processes that underlie those behaviours, could be explored and understood in terms of evolutionary theory.

By the beginning of the last decade of the twentieth century, evolutionary psychology was coalescing as an identifiable and significant strand of research within both psychology and evolutionary theory. At first little attention was paid to music, but in 1997 one of its main protagonists, Steven Pinker, produced an evolutionary treatment of music that relegated it to the status of evolutionary by product. In *How the mind works*, Pinker devotes ten pages of his final chapter to considering music, because, in his words, he wishes to consider a mental faculty which 'shows the clearest signs of not being' [an evolutionary adaptation] to set against examples of mental faculties that are self-evidently adaptive, such as language. Pinker starts from the premise that 'as far as biological cause and effect are concerned, music is useless' (p. 528), noting that music is variable in its complexity from culture to culture, that while all tend to enjoy listening to music only a small subset of the population are practitioners, and that music communicates nothing but formless emotion. Hence music shows clear signs of being a 'technology', a human capacity developed and exploited for its own sake and at best evolutionarily neutral, rather than an adaptation. He suggests that this technology developed to exploit capacities that had arisen for largely adaptive reasons, claiming that 'music is auditory cheesecake, an exquisite confection crafted to tickle the sensitive spots of at least six of our mental faculties' (p. 534). However, the significance of Pinker's discussion of music is severely diminished by the lack of fit between his ethnocentric conception of music and that outlined above.

Pinker seems to subscribe to a thoroughly Westernized notion of music as a commodified set of complex sound patterns produced by the few and consumed by the many simply for pleasure, rather than as the complex and socially efficacious actions and structures that it is and has been both in the west and in other cultures, places and times.

Subsequently, another prominent evolutionary psychologist, Geoffrey Miller, presented an alternative evolutionary psychological account of music quite at variance with that of Pinker. For Miller, music constitutes a medium that is well-suited to demonstrate the 'protean', unpredictable and creative, properties of an individual, properties that are selectively advantageous and hence desirable in the determination of mate-choice. Music is well-suited to make manifest such properties as it combines 'ritualized rules of tonality, rhythmicity, melody and harmony and protean intentions and variations' (Miller 1997, p. 322). Hence protean individuals might well advertise their creative assets in musical display. Miller (in Wallin *et al.* 2000) seeks to support this argument by reference to a range of Western musical examples (including Jimi Hendrix) claiming that the sexual opportunities afforded by rock-star status are in line with the predictions of his theory. Although music is certainly used for courtship in most, if not all, societies, its roles are always more multifarious. Moreover, Miller's theory would predict that musical ability should exhibit, or at least should have exhibited, a significant sexual dimorphism. While this would be difficult to ascertain in our predecessor species, it is not the case with modern humans; while musical roles are often sexually differentiated, in most cultures musicality appears to be equally exhibited by both males and females. If anything, the manifestation of musicality that is perhaps most culturally widespread, in the form of the use of protomusical and musical forms of interaction between caregiver and infant, is primarily evidenced by females (see Dissanayake in Wallin *et al.* 2000). Moreover, as Fitch (2006) points out, the precocious capacities of human infants in music perception would suggest that musicality is a trait that is unlikely to have been sexually selected for, given that such traits tend to emerge only in sexual maturity in other species.

In contrast to the positions of both Miller and Pinker, the majority of recent evolutionary treatments of music have focused on its effects at the level of the group; music is viewed as having, and as having had, effects on inter-group and intra-group interaction, which are conceived of as having had evolutionary consequences. Hagen and Bryant (2003) propose that group musical displays allow groups to indicate to each other their cohesion and stability, affording groups which can engage successfully in such displays a means of deterring other, more fragmented, groups from attempting to compete for scarce resources. Merker (in Wallin *et al.* 2000) proposes a similar putative role for music as an indicator of coalition strength. Brown (2004) acknowledges music's prospective role in inter-group relations but emphasizes its functionality within groups. He develops the notion of music as efficacious at the level of the group, suggesting that music typically acts at to influence behaviours at the group level. He suggests that music acts to reinforce cooperative behaviour within the group by means of group ritual activities, promoting a sense of 'groupishness' that is likely to enhance prospects of group survival in addition to being effective in situations of inter-group conflict.

This focus on music's significance in promoting cooperative, within-group, behaviours, is mirrored by others. Kogan (1997) views music as significant in human evolution by virtue of its embeddedness in social interaction and its effect of the formation of group identity, as does Dunbar (2004), who suggests that its primary effect is in the consolidation of group bonds. Mithen's (2005) extensive treatment echoes Brown (in Wallin *et al.* 2000) in presenting a view of music and language as having common origins and in suggesting that music had an evolutionary efficacy in the formation of social bonds. Mithen concludes, however, that music is no more than an atavistic relic that may have been functional for earlier species of hominins but whose functions have come to be usurped by language—a view that contrasts significantly with that of most ethnomusicological evidence (see Chapter 4 this volume).

In a series of publications Cross (1999, 2005, 2008, in press) also subscribes to the notion that music has a bonding effect, but suggests in addition that music, by virtue of its polyvalent significances, can contribute positively to individual fitness within the group by facilitating communicative interactions that, were they to be conducted linguistically, might give rise to conflict, a view also presented in Morley (2002). Whilst proposing that music may have an impact on individual fitness outwith social contexts by virtue of its 'metaphorising' powers (Cross 1999), Cross notes that music's powers of entrainment, together with its 'floating intentionality', render it an extremely efficacious communicative medium in managing situations of social uncertainty (Cross 2008, in press, Cross and Woodruff 2008). Hence music can be regarded as possessing attributes that complement those of language, and it can be postulated that music and language are likely to have co-evolved as complementary aspects of the human communicative toolkit, differentiated only by the degree to which they are capable of specifying meaning unambiguously (see also Chapter 3 this volume).

Dissanayake (in Wallin *et al.* 2000) takes a rather more constrained notion of the 'group' that might have constituted the matrix for the evolution of human musicality; the mother–infant dyad. In alignment with the views of Trevarthen (1999), she views infant-directed speech (see Trehub 2003), the infant's responses, and the kinesthetically interactive context of mother–infant communication as forming protomusical behaviours that are oriented towards the (co-)regulation of emotion, as well as forming the basis for the infant's acquisition of prosodic, phonemic and social competence. In this her proposal is in line with that of Falk (2004), who suggests that complex, vocal and gestural mother–infant interactions of the type that can be categorized as motherese are an evolutionarily adaptive response to the emergence of bipedalism, at around the time of the chimp–hominin split (*c.* 5–7 million years ago).

Music and evolution—the evidence

These diverse evolutionary perspectives on music suggest that it can fruitfully be explored in terms of contemporary evolutionary theory.

The evidence would suggest that music has a significant role in human behaviour—that it is functional—and that it is distinguishable from other domains of human behaviour. The latter point suggests that music may have a distinct evolutionary track record, and its functionality implies that it may have been evolutionarily adaptive in the emergence of the human species (or at least, exaptive—that is, arising only as a consequence of the independent prior emergence of some adaptive capacity but having an impact on evolutionary fitness). This begs the questions of when might the capacities for music have arisen, and how they came to arise. In order to explore these issues we must turn to the archaeological evidence.

Music—and indeed, sound—in prehistory has received little attention in the archaeological literature. D'Errico *et al.* (2003) summarize much of what is known in the context of a re-evaluation of current archaeological approaches, particularly in the light of recent finds in southern Africa. They note that the earliest unequivocally musical artefact found to date is a bone pipe from Geissenklösterle in southern Germany, dating to *c.* 38 000 before the present (BP). A further sequence of bone pipes has been found at Isturitz in southern France (in contexts rich in parietal—cave—art), with dates ranging from 20 000 to 35 000 BP. The earliest of these dates more or less coincides with the arrival of modern humans in Europe and suggests that something like music was of high significance to those peoples. As D'Errico *et al.* (2003) comment, these artefacts are extremely sophisticated, exhibiting subtle design features that are analogous to those found in historic wind instruments; the time, effort and expertize devoted to their manufacture must have been considerable and suggests that music was likely to have been of considerable importance to a people who had just come to inhabit a new and potentially threatening environment. The use of musical artefacts will have been preceded by the expression of musical capacities by voice and body, and would appear likely to have an ancient provenance. The ubiquity of music in native American and Australian societies in forms that are not directly relatable to historic Eurasian or African musics strongly suggests that modern humans brought musicality with them out

of Africa. If this is the case we must look to evidence that will enable us to identify the time-depth of the capacity for music, or perhaps of different subcapacities that make up human musicality, which means turning to the prehistoric human fossil record.

A brief account of stages in human evolution might be useful at this point. The hominin (human) lineage last shared a common ancestor with chimpanzees and bonobos some 5–7 million years ago (mya). The earliest unambiguous members of the hominin line are found in Africa: *Ardipithecus ramidus*, at between 7 and 4.5 mya, and a range of *australopithecine* species, from around 4.2 to 2.4 mya). Both lineages were morphologically much more similar to chimps than to modern humans (having similar-size brains at <400 cc), and can be inferred to have had lifeways that closely resembled chimps—other than, in the case of the australopiths, at least partial bipedalism. Subsequently, the homo line proper appears with *Homo habilis* (ca 2.4–1.6 mya) and *Homo ergaster* or *erectus* (ca 1.9–0.2 mya), the latter line having a body build similar to modern humans and possessing brains of at least double the size of the australopiths; both *habilis* and *ergaster* made stone (lithic) tools, the latter making objects of some sophistication. *Homo heidelbergensis* (despite the name a predominantly African species, from around 0.6 to about 0.1 mya) shows a considerable increase in brain size (to around 1200 cc), and evidence of complex lifeways, including the making of non-lithic artefacts such as wooden spears. This last species was the ancestor of both *Homo neanderthalensis*, a mainly northern, highly cold-adapted, species (ca 0.2–0.03 mya) and *Homo sapiens*, ourselves who appear first in Africa some 200 000 years ago.

The fossil record from which we are able to construct this lineage of species suggests strongly that musicality does not emerge as a full-blown capacity, but rather that subcomponents of that capacity emerge at different times and probably in response to different selection pressures. Australopiths had funnel-shaped chests (as do chimps), which do not permit sufficiently fine control over phonation to make the subtly differentiated vocal sounds that would be required of music. Only with *ergaster* does the barrel-shaped chest of modern humans arise

(Frayer and Nicolay in Wallin *et al.* 2000), hence only with this species can we postulate the emergence of a capacity for control of fine-grained vocalizations (see also Morley 2002). However, it is only with *heidelbergensis*, around 0.5 mya, that vocal and auditory capacities characteristic of modern humans can unambiguously be claimed to be in place (Martinez *et al.* 2004). By contrast, the dating of the emergence of a capacity for entrainment, which appears central in musical behaviour, is highly debatable. As mentioned above, it has been postulated that amongst extant species, a capacity for entrainment is specific to humans (Bispham 2006; Cross *et al.* 2008, in press). If this is so then the capacity to entrain must have arisen at some point in the hominin lineage over the last 5–7 million years, but at present we can be no more specific than that.

In view of the close link between music and social behaviour, the dating of the emergence of a capacity for complex sociality is also relevant to the question of music in human evolution. A variety of species, particularly primates, exhibit complex social behaviours, but as Foley (1995) notes, none appears to be as socially flexible and inventive as humans and, probably, our immediate ancestor species. Given the likely continuity in lifeways between chimpanzees and australopithecines, it seems that a complex capacity for sociality comparable to that of modern humans is unlikely to have predated *habilis* or *ergaster*. It is likely that only with the appearance of *heidelbergensis*, with a brain size in the (low) modern human range and some evidence for behavioural complexity of a different order from *ergaster*, that the modern human range of complex social behaviours began to emerge. However, it is only with the arrival of modern humans that we find clear evidence for symbolic behaviours (Henshilwood and Marean 2003), which has been taken to indicate that only with modern humans do we see the appearance of something that would be recognizable as language. Overall, a reasonable initial hypothesis appears to be that many of the capacities for music emerge independently at different times in hominin evolution, but only with modern humans are we likely to find an integrated capacity for music together with language, as suggested by several researchers (including

Brown, Cross and Mithen). Whatever its precursors, it seems that modern musicality has very ancient roots.

Conclusions and directions for research

As should be evident, there is much about the relationships between human musicality and human evolution that remains unknown. If music is truly the product of distinct, and distinctly functional, human capacities, a better understanding of music in evolutionary terms should be of immense value in elucidating the significance and distinctness of music as cognitive process and as social behaviour. Much of what we know or infer is based on very sketchy evidence, and there is immense scope for empirical exploration.

As Stevens and Byron note in Chapter 3, most of the research on which our understanding of the universals of music processing is rooted in Western cultural practice and based on the responses of Western-encultured or formally trained participants. There is a pressing need to extend the scope of research on music cognition into non-Western musical domains. Similarly, ethnomusicological evidence, and the success of music as a therapeutic medium, suggests that music has profound efficacy in social context; research is urgently required that explores the cognitive and socially interactive correlates of that efficacy. Indeed, research into music as interactive behaviour in its own right is very much in its infancy. While a number of studies have explored musical interaction between formally trained western Musicians, and a few are beginning to investigate interaction amongst non-Western musicians (see Chapter 4 this volume and also Moran 2007), very little empirical research into either the generic foundations of musical interaction—though see Himberg (2006), or into musical interactions amongst encultured rather than formally trained participants, has been conducted.

One large-scale research programme that has aimed to identify key components of musicality in ways that might shed light on relationships between music and evolutionary process is that conducted by Peretz and her collaborators (see e.g. Peretz 2006), which has systematically sought to explore the nature, distribution within the population, and recently, genetic provenance, of the condition known as 'amusia': the incapacity to process musical information coherently. It appears that this condition is associable with an inability to process fine-grained pitch structures and relationships and that it is independent of deficits in other domains such as language and hence proper only to music (though see Patel *et al.* 2008). However, as with other studies that seek to explore any identifiable genetic bases for musicality (see e.g. Drayna *et al.* 2001), the vast majority of research has been conducted in listening tests using Western-encultured participants and musical materials that conform to western common-practice musical principles. As the issues addressed in this chapter and in Chapters 2 and 4, should make clear, it is imperative for the cognitive sciences to engage with music in all its cultural diversity in order to begin adequately to understand the nature of human musicality.

Moreover, as noted above, we know very little about the extent to which aspects of human musicality may be shared with other species. We have very little concrete evidence concerning the cross-specific generality of many capacities that appear central to human musicality, such as the capacity to entrain, or to differentiate between complex sonic and gestural structures, or to use complexly patterned sound and gesture to mediate interactions. There are very substantial ethological literatures (dealing with, for example, inter-individual and social functions of birdsong, and sonic communication amongst primates), as well as a few studies of animal behaviours in the presence of music (for an overview see Rickard *et al.* 2005). However, these literatures and studies require to be explored and extended in the light of questions concerning possible continuities between the capacities of non-human animal species and human musicality that are raised by an evolutionary perspective on music.

Over the last few years there has been a significant increase in the amount of attention devoted to the relationships between music and evolutionary theory. This chapter can only provide a sketch of the field, but those interested to know more should certainly explore Darwin

(1998) as well as the most significant publication in the field to date, the volume edited by Wallin *et al.* (2000). A more extended treatment of many of the issues raised in the present chapter is given in Cross (2007).

References

Bispham J (2006). Rhythm in music: what is it? Who has it? and Why? *Music Perception*, **24**(2), 125–134.

Blacking J (1995). *Music, culture and experience.* University of Chicago Press, Chicago, IL.

Bohlman P (2000). Ethnomusicology and music sociology. In D Greer, ed., *Musicology and sister disciplines*, 288–298. Oxford University Press, Oxford.

Brown S (2004). Evolutionary models of music: from sexual selection to group selection. In F Tonneau, and N Thompson, eds, *Perspectives in ethology 13: behavior, evolution and culture*, 231–281. Plenum Publishers, New York.

Clarke EF (2005). *Ways of listening: an ecological approach to the perception of musical meaning.* Oxford University Press, Oxford.

Clayton M, Sager R and Will U (2005). In time with the music: the concept of entrainment and its significance for ethnomusicology. *ESEM counterpoint*, **1**, 1–45.

Cross I (1999). Is music the most important thing we ever did? Music, development and evolution. In SW Yi, ed., *Music, mind and science*, 10–39. Seoul National University Press, Seoul.

Cross I (2005). Music and meaning, ambiguity and evolution. In D Miell, R MacDonald and D Hargreaves, eds, *Musical communication*, 27–43. Oxford University Press, Oxford.

Cross I (2007). Music and cognitive evolution. In RIM Dunbar and L Barrett, eds, *Handbook of evolutionary psychology*, 649–667. Oxford University Press, Oxford.

Cross I (2008, in press). The evolutionary nature of musical meaning. *Musicae Scientiae.*

Cross I, Bispham J, Himberg T and Swaine J (2008, in press). The evolution of musical rhythm. *Evolutionary Psychology.*

Cross I and Woodruff GE (2008). Music as a communicative medium. In R Botha and C Knight, eds, *The prehistory of language, Vol. 1*, 133–134. Oxford University Press, Oxford.

D'Errico F, Henshilwood C, Lawson G, Vanhaeren M, Tillier A-M, Soressi M *et al.* (2003). Archaeological evidence for the emergence of language, symbolism, and music—an alternative multidisciplinary perspective. *Journal of World Prehistory*, **17**(1), 1–70.

Darwin C (1859). *The origin of species.* John Murray, London.

Darwin C (1998). *The expression of the emotions in man and animals*, 3rd edn. HarperCollins Publishers, London.

Darwin C (2004). *The descent of man and selection in relation to sex*, 2nd edn. Penguin Books, London.

Drayna D, Manichaikul A, de Lange M, Snieder H and Spector T (2001). Genetic correlates of musical pitch recognition in humans. *Science*, **291**, 1969–1972.

Dunbar RIM (2004). *The human story*. Faber and Faber, London.

Falk D (2004). Prelinguistic evolution in early hominins: whence motherese? *Behavioral and Brain Sciences*, **27**(4), 491–541.

Fitch WT (2006). The biology and evolution of music: a comparative perspective. *Cognition*, **100**(1), 173–215.

Foley RA (1995). *Humans before humanity*. Blackwell, Oxford.

Hagen EH and Bryant GA (2003). Music and dance as a coalition signaling system. *Human Nature*, **14**(1), 21–51.

Henshilwood CS and Marean CW (2003). The origin of modern human behavior: critique of the models and their test implications. *Current Anthropology*, **44**(5), 627–651.

Himberg T (2006). Co-operative tapping and collective time-keeping—differences of timing accuracy in duet performance with human or computer partner. In M Baroni AR Addessi R Caterina and M Costa, eds, *Proceedings of the 9th international conference on music perception and cognition*, p. 377. ICMPC 2006, Bologna, Italy.

Hölldobler B and Wilson EO (1993). *Journey to the ants: a story of scientific exploration*. Harvard University Press, Cambridge, MA.

Juslin P and Sloboda JA (eds) (2001). *Music and emotion: theory and research*. Oxford University Press, Oxford.

Koelsch S, Kasper E, Sammler D, Schultze K, Gunter T and Frederici A (2004). Music, language and meaning: brain signatures of semantic processing. *Nature Neuroscience*, **7**(3), 302–307.

Kogan N (1997). Reflections on aesthetics and evolution. *Critical Review*, **11**(2), 193–210.

Korsyn K (2003). *Decentering music: a critique of contemporary music research*. Oxford University Press, Oxford.

Martinez I, Rosa M, Arsuaga J-L, Jarabo P, Quam R, Lorenzo C et al. (2004). Auditory capacities in Middle Pleistocene humans from the Sierra de Atapuerca in Spain. *Proceedings of the National Academy of Sciences*, **101**(27), 9976–9981.

Maynard Smith J (1998). *Evolutionary genetics*, 2nd edn. Oxford University Press, Oxford.

Maynard Smith J and Szathmáry E (1995). *The major transitions in evolution*. Oxford University Press, Oxford.

Merriam AP (1964). *The anthropology of music*. Northwestern University Press, Chicago, IL.

Miller GF (1997). Protean primates: the evolution of adaptive unpredictability in competition and courtship. In A Whiten and RW Byrne, eds *Machiavellian intelligence II: extensions and evaluations*, 312–340. Cambridge University Press, Cambridge.

Mithen S (2005). *The singing Neanderthals: the origins of music, language, mind and body*. Weidenfeld and Nicholson, London.

Moran NS (2007). *Measuring musical interaction*. Unpublished PhD thesis, Open University, Milton Keynes.

Morley I (2002). Evolution of the physiological and neurological capacities for music. *Cambridge Archaeological Journal*, **12**(2), 195–216.

Nettl B (2005). The study of ethnomusicology: thirty-one issues and concepts, 2nd edn. University of Illinois Press, Urbana and Chicago, IL.

Patel AD, Wong M, Foxton J, Lochy A and Peretz I (2008). Speech intonation perception deficits in musical tone deafness (congenital amusia). *Music Perception*, **25**(4), 357–368.

Peretz I (2006). The nature of music from a biological perspective. *Cognition*, **100**(1), 1–32.

Pinker S (1997). *How the mind works*. Allen Lane, London.

Rehding A (2000). The quest for the origins of music in Germany circa 1900. *Journal of the American Musicological Society*, **53**(2), 345–385.

Repp BH (2001). Phase correction, phase resetting, and phase shifts after subliminal timing perturbations in sensorimotor synchronization. *Journal of Experimental Psychology: Human Perception and Performance*, **27**(3), 600–621.

Rickard NS, Toukhsati SR and Field SE (2005). The effect of music on cognitive performance: insight from neurobiological and animal studies. *Behavioral and Cognitive Neuroscience Review*, **4**(4), 235–261.

Shore B (1996). *Culture in mind: cognition, culture, and the problem of meaning*. Oxford University Press, Oxford.

Sober E and Wilson D (1998). *Unto others: the evolution and psychology of unselfish behavior*. Harvard University Press, London.

Tolbert E (2001). Music and meaning: an evolutionary story. *Psychology of Music*, **29**, 89–94.

Trehub SE (2003). The developmental origins of musicality. *Nature Neuroscience*, **6**(7), 669–673.

Trevarthen C (1999). Musicality and the intrinsic motive pulse: evidence from human psychobiology and infant communication. *Musicae Scientiae, special issue: Rhythm, musical narrative, and the origins of human communcation*, 155–215.

Wallin N, Merker B and Brown S (eds) (2000). *The origins of music*. MIT Press, Cambridge, MA.

CHAPTER 2

Universals in music processing

Catherine Stevens and Tim Byron

Introduction and definitions

In this chapter we outline areas of musical processing that may be universal to humans. Music here refers to temporally structured human activities, social and individual, in the production and perception of sound organized in patterns that convey non-linguistic meaning. Music processing refers to the neural contribution in perception, cognition and production of music.

A universal in a domain of human activity such as music implies a static feature of a static environment. Not surprisingly, many ethnomusicologists have railed against a search for similarities at the expense of informative differences, and there is a logical problem with documenting definitive generalities rather than particular instances. The approach adopted here is to emphasize musical processing over content and discuss the psychological processes implicated in understanding and engaging in musical behaviour rather than the content of musical knowledge or action (cf. Harwood 1976; Meyer 1960). Our focus is on the principles by which the brain processes features of musical environments.

To call a process involved in the perception, cognition or production of music 'universal' does not necessarily mean that the process is found in all humans. When we refer to universality, we are using Nettl's (2005) concept of 'statistical universals'. Statistically universal music processing is universal to the great majority of adult humans and cultures.

However, there may be statistical outliers—which may take the form of all participants in a particular culture (see Everett [2005] for a culture that may be a statistical outlier in the field of linguistics). Additionally, some people may belong to a different statistical population; for example, those who have been described as having congenital amusia or infants who, for example, lack higher-order cognitive processes not developed until later in life.

Experimental studies of music cognition tend to focus on psychophysical features of Western post-Renaissance tonal music, and samples of participants from a restricted range of countries and cultures. Additionally, most experiments treat music as a purely auditory event and assume implicitly that the use of music in other cultures is similar to the use of music in Western cultures. Both assumptions are inaccurate. Vocal and instrumental music is also visual, motoric and kinaesthetic. All of the arts—oral literature/song poetry, visual arts and performing arts—are integrated, for example, in Australian Aboriginal song (Ellis 1984).

The universal music processes discussed here are hypotheses that require investigation and falsification in as many and varied cultural contexts as possible. The discussion begins with processes of grouping and segmentation, then statistically universal features of musical environments, and finally more general-purpose psychological processes. We illustrate some processes drawing on examples of production of song from particular Australian Aboriginal cultures.

Perceptual principles of grouping and segmentation

The perceptual organization principles of grouping by proximity, similarity, common fate, good continuation, and figure-ground, which appear to operate in the early stages of music perception (Deutsch 1999; Handel 1984; Trehub and Hannon 2006) are candidates for universals in music processing. Perceptual organization of this kind can be demonstrated in very young animals; general grouping rules override learned knowledge about the shape of objects. For example, in visual perception, camouflage exploits this principle (Bregman 1990). Auditory grouping processes are thought to (a) organize acoustic information into music events (simultaneous grouping); (b) connect events into musical streams (sequential grouping); and (c) chunk event streams into musical units (segmentational grouping). These perceptual processes develop earlier than knowledge about the meaning of the events that have been grouped together (McAdams 1989). The suggestion is that these processes may be a basic property of the mammalian nervous system, and thus a likely contender for a universal in music processing.

At the level of sequential grouping, there are several processes which contribute to the perception of grouping. A sequence of tones is perceived as a group or stream when the pitch distance between temporally adjacent tones is small (pitch proximity); tones with distant pitches are segregated into separate streams (Bregman 1990). Whether events are perceived as a group or stream is also influenced by timbre similarity, grouping by temporal proximity, grouping by good continuation, and grouping by amplitude similarity (Deutsch 1999). At the level of segmentational grouping, we may have a universal preference for musical elements that are grouped correctly, though what is defined as correct grouping may be culture-dependent. Experiments investigating segmentation of Western tonal music in 6- and 4½-month-old infants have shown that infants prefer correctly segmented pieces with relatively long notes and downward pitch contours, over incorrectly segmented pieces (e.g. Krumhansl and Jusczyk 1990; see also Nan et al. 2006). Infants' correct segmentation of music may occur because music bears a structural resemblance to speech, which infants have learned through exposure, and/or because downward contours and extended durations naturally mark the end of all auditory signals (Thompson and Schellenberg 2006). Grouping principles could be investigated in broader musical contexts. However, that they work from the bottom up suggests that such processes are universal. Grouping likely aids encoding and storage in memory, enables an understanding of new material, and facilitates transmission to others.

The processing of melodic contour, the ups and downs in pitch of a melody, has the hallmarks of universality. It has been argued that efficient computational recognition of melodies uses melodic contour as chunks (Trehub 2000), and it appears that the rises and falls of a melody are part of the framework by which working memory processes melody. An ability to discriminate between short melodies on the basis of melodic contour is present in Western infants (e.g. Jusczyk and Krumhansl 1993) and adults (e.g. Dowling 1978), and may share cognitive resources with the processing of prosodic information (Patel et al. 1998). Ethnomusicologists have used different melodic contour shapes (for example, arch shapes) to categorize different kinds of melodies from a culture into different kinds of song (e.g. Kolinski 1970), and to compare cultures based on their use of different kinds of melodic contours (Lomax 1968). In an exploratory ethnomusicological study by Arom and Fürniss (1993) Aka Pygmy musicians were reported to be able to discriminate between melodies on the basis of melodic contour. As the processing of melodic contour appears to be present in Western infants and adults, and can be used to distinguish music by different cultures, insofar as melody is universal, it is likely that the processing of melodic contour in memory is universal.

Features of musical environments and perceptual and cognitive constraints

Most discussions of universals in music from a psychological perspective consider the limits imposed by human perceptual and cognitive processes. The constraints that recur in the literature suggest consensus. However, results on which these accounts are based emanate, in the main, from psychophysical studies involving culturally narrow samples. Regarding pitch first and then time, patterns in musical environments related to human perceptual and cognitive limits that await further cross-cultural scrutiny include the following.

1 Perceptual fusion of harmonic spectra into pitches (Justus and Bharucha 2002).

2 The use of discrete pitch levels (Burns 1999).

3 The semitone as the smallest viable interval. As a semitone is six times larger than the smallest interval that most listeners are able to discriminate (McAdams 1989), human working memory and production limits rather than perceptual discrimination are likely to constrain retention of music constructed from finer-grained musical scales.

4 Musical scales with differently sized steps between consecutive tones. Unequal steps may confer a psychological advantage, allowing tones to have different functions within the scale, such as a reference tone (Balzano 1980).

5 The prevalence of small integer frequency ratios[1] possibly because of their efficiency in auditory perception, i.e., they facilitate encoding, retention of melodies, and enable detection of subtle violations (e.g. Schellenberg and Trehub 1996; but see Balzano 1982 for an alternative view). Such ratios apply not only to fundamental frequencies but also within spectra (Sethares 1998; Tenney 1988).

6 Tones and melodies that are separated by an octave being perceived as similar (Wright et al. 2000) although Carterette and Kendall (1999) note that the effect is subtle. The prevalence of octaves in the auditory environment is one possible explanation (Schwartz et al. 2003; Trainor 2006); a physiological basis is also debated (Burns 1999).

7 Perception of rhythmic groups of up to 5 seconds in duration—the approximate limit of auditory sensory memory (Darwin et al. 1972)—where inter-onset intervals are between 100 and 1500 ms; see Cowan (1984) for the limit exceeding 5 seconds.

8 A regular beat or periodic pulse that affords temporal coordination between performers and elicits a synchronized motor response from listeners (Drake and Bertrand 2001). Importantly, the concept and experience of beat may vary across cultures (Iyer 1998; Stobart and Cross 2000).

9 Small-integer ratios of durations being easier to process than more complex rhythms (Drake and Bertrand 2001). Regular rhythmic patterns may facilitate encoding and retention of gestural, spoken or sung material.

Higher-order processes in music cognition

Hierarchical organization and relational processing

So far, we have listed perceptual features of music and bottom-up perceptual constraints relating to music. However, higher-level cognitive processes are also engaged in music cognition, composition, improvisation, and performance in diverse cultural settings. The hierarchical organization of music, and relational processes in music, are possible universal processes in music cognition (see also Chapter 6 this volume).

Music is generally complex, generative, multilayered and hierarchical (Bharucha et al. 2006) although exceptions to hierarchical organization include the cyclical structures of Balinese gamelan music (Tenzer 2006) and minimalist music (e.g., compositions by Steve Reich). In general, streams of sound are structured hierarchically within and across dimensions; such structure likely confers a processing advantage. Bharucha et al. divide hierarchical representations into tonal hierarchies and event hierarchies. Tonal hierarchies organize tones within a key into stable and unstable pitches; some tones are perceived as more stable, thus more important, than others. Event hierarchies extend

---

[1] However, Will (1997) gives an example of a cultural context within which frequency differences rather than ratios might constitute the basis for melodic prediction and perception.

upward from smallest subdivisions of a beat, to beat level, then measure, phrase, period, and large-order forms.

Tonal hierarchies

Evidence of sensitivity to tonal hierarchies has also been established in Balinese music (Kessler *et al.* 1984), Scandinavian North Sami yoiks (Krumhansl *et al.* 2000), and Korean Court music (Nam 1998). These experiments sampled participants from within and outside those musical cultures. The basis of North Indian music, for example, is a set of melodic forms called the rāg that are built on a set of pitch scales called thāts. Tones within rāgs are organized hierarchically by importance, as in Western music. Castellano *et al.* (1984) demonstrated that both Indian and American students are sensitive to the hierarchical ordering of tones in rāgs.

Temporal hierarchies

The pulsation of some African musical styles is very different from the hierarchical concept of measure in Western classical music and the related concepts of metre, strong, and weak beats (Iyer 1998; Magill and Pressing 1997). Instead, this music is measured and is based on pulsations—a sequence of isochronous temporal units that can be realized as a beat. The beat is the analogue of the tactus of Western tonal music. In west African music, the main beat and its metric grouping are articulated in an indirect fashion—not with accentual reinforcement as in Western music, but with suggestion and complexity (Iyer 1998). The metre is encoded in the rhythm itself; it is unambiguous but culturally specific. Iyer provides examples of a standard bell pattern that would be heard phrased in three different ways by three different cultural groups.

Knowledge of temporal hierarchies is also attuned through experience. For example, Drake and Ben El Heni (2003) compared how Tunisian and French subjects synchronized tapping with music from those two contrasting musical cultures. Participants tapped more slowly and with more hierarchical levels with music of their own culture than with music of an unfamiliar musical culture. Musicians and non-musicians did not differ in a spontaneous synchronization task

although musicians could synchronize with significantly more hierarchical levels.

Clayton (1997), examining tal, a concept in North Indian (Hindustani) music broadly equivalent to metre, finds similarities and differences between tal and metre. Tal is a temporal framework acting as a background for rhythmic design; it is a periodic and hierarchic temporal framework which involves the interaction of two or more streams of pulsation. Rhythm in Indian music is interpreted with respect to tal; musically untrained Indian listeners would infer tal much as musically untrained Western listeners infer metre. While the conception of metre in Western culture may not be a musical universal, the hierarchical organization of temporal information may be a musical universal.

Examples of hierarchical structure in Australian Aboriginal song

In Central Australia the song series or songline is the largest scale traditional musical form (Barwick 1989). A song series describes the Dreaming journey of one or more ancestral beings. A song performance consists of a number of song items, each of about 30 seconds duration, interspersed with periods of informal discussion. Central Australian songs are characterized by several exact repetitions of a fixed word string or text set to an unvarying rhythmic pattern. The textual and rhythmic components are regarded as two facets of the same structure (Barwick 1989). Each rhythmically articulated text relates to a different stage of the journey described in the associated myth. It is set to a melodic contour said by performers to be the same throughout the series and to embody the essence of the ancestral being whose journey through the country creating and naming present-day geographical features is celebrated in the series. For a performance to be classified as a 'song' it must correctly interlock all three elements—melody, rhythm and text (Ellis 1983). Unison group performance is the ideal and is made possible by inexperienced performers joining in when they have grasped the text words and the appropriate rhythm; they follow melodic cues given by the song leader who performs solo for the first few syllables of each item and who cues changes of pitch within the melody slightly in advance of the group (Barwick 1989). The general melodic shape of the songs in the centre of Australia is, almost without exception, terraced (Ellis 1984); that is, a generally descending melodic line.

Performance involves the structuring of melodic contour according to various textual characteristics. Barwick (1989) argues that the melodic structure and rhythmic/textual structure are conceptually independent despite being performed in a song as an intermeshed sonic stream. Either element is able to be performed in isolation. Some evidence of this includes a) words to describe humming the sound of the Dreaming; b) rhythmically defined humming of verses in order to remember the words; c)wordless definitions of the melody; and d) instances of tapping out the rhythm of the words of a song (Barwick 1989). Thus memory for melody and rhythm is integrated but separable. Barwick describes hierarchical structures in both the melodic and rhythmic/textual dimension of central Australian song referring specifically to the *ngintaka* song series performed by Antakarinya, Yankunytjatjara and Pitjantjatjara people.

Melodic structure refers to the patterns of pitch relationships that recur in the different song items in a series, and the ways in which these recurring tonal patterns are organized into melodic sections, pitch areas, and main tones. In *ngintaka* songlines, there are three related forms of the basic melodic contour: a linear form, cyclical form, and a transposing cyclical form. Barwick describes and illustrates the hierarchical organization of the linear melodic form consisting of an introductory section, preliminary descent, main descent, and concluding section.

The rhythmic organization of the text of *ngintaka* is also hierarchical, reflecting organization of the pattern into text line pairs, text lines, rhythmic segments, and beating cells. The interdependence of melodic and temporal structures in *ngintaka* is reflected in the observation that the decision about which form of the melody to perform, its constitution in melodic sections, and tonal and durational realizations of the sections correlate with different properties of the text to be performed. The choice of linear, cyclical or transposing cyclical melodic form depends on rhythmic organization. Rhythm serves as

a mnemonic device for recall of the extramusical information that is associated with a particular song text (Ellis 1984). Barwick (1989) examines the 'point of fit' in combining melodic and rhythmic/textual structures:

> although an item of singing need neither begin nor end at significant boundaries in the rhythmic/textual cyclical, there is always at least one internal point in the sung item at which the major rhythmic/textual and melodic boundaries coincide.
>
> Barwick (1989, p. 19)

This meticulous musicological and structural analysis of *ngintaka* points to the role of *hierarchy* as both an organizational and perceptual process:

> choices relating to the upper levels of the melodic hierarchy (melodic form and section composition), which correlate with structures at the upper levels of the rhythmic/textual hierarchy (overall style of beating accompaniment and repetition organization), have ramifications that extend down to the smaller level decisions about movement around main tones. Performance of the music therefore requires a constant shifting of attention from one level of the system to another.
>
> Barwick (1989, p. 26)

Cognitive processes related to hierarchical organization, grouping and segmentation, expectancy, and entrainment are evident in this example from Australian Aboriginal song.

Development of musical expectancies and abstract implicit knowledge

Musical expectancies

A piece of music in a familiar genre generates expectations based on implicit knowledge about common features of the genre; variations in how these expectations are met or violated are important in determining emotional and aesthetic response to music (Meyer 1956; Tillmann *et al.* 2000). In Western tonal music, musical expectancies are shaped by rhythmic or metric structure (Large and Jones 1999), tonal and harmonic structure (Schmuckler 1989) and melodic structure (Cuddy and Lunney 1995). While it is unclear how broadly these principles apply cross-culturally, the tendency for large intervals to descend is evident in Australian Aboriginal music, Chinese folk songs, traditional Korean music, Ojibwa, Pondo, Venda, and Zulu songs (Huron 2006, although see Vos and Troost 1989), suggesting that melodic expectancies are important in emotional and aesthetic response to music in many cultures.

Differentiation of two kinds of expectations—schematic and veridical—solves a paradox of musical expectation (Bharucha 1994). A familiar piece of music contains no surprises—if the violation of expectations is aesthetically or emotionally important, a piece should become less aesthetically or emotionally interesting with each listen. This is not the case. Schematic expectations are automatic, culturally generic, and develop from assimilation of the music of a genre over years of experience. Veridical expectations refer to the actual next event in a familiar piece even though the event may be schematically unexpected. As schematic expectations are acquired from hearing many individual pieces the two kinds of expectancies will converge but, at times, will diverge, creating the continuing sense of violation in familiar pieces of music as described by Meyer (1956). The capacity to develop expectancies may be a universal process. Huron (2006) posits that implicit, statistical expectations are linked directly to emotional response, eliciting basic neurobiological responses. In his account, statistical learning (e.g., McMullen and Saffran 2004) underlies the development of musical expectations.

A small number of studies have examined expectations in music cross-culturally. Researchers have found listeners are sensitive to melodic expectancies in British folk songs, Webern Lieder, and Chinese pentatonic songs. On occasion, performance of American and Chinese participants has been compared and principles such as 'pitch proximity'—that a second pitch following a first pitch is likely to be close in pitch—and 'pitch reversal'—that listeners expect the direction of the melody to reverse—successfully predicted response patterns regardless of the musical style, or the

formal music training, and cultural background of the participants (Schellenberg 1997).

Krumhansl (2000; Krumhansl et al. 2000) conducted investigations of an indigenous music of the Scandinavian peninsula, the North Sami yoiks, which are quite distinct from Western tonal music. These experiments used North Sami yoiks as stimuli, with participants including North Sami, Finnish music students who had studied yoiks, and North American musicians unfamiliar with yoiks. Results suggested that Western listeners were most influenced by Western schematic expectations, and that veridical expectations were strongest for Sami participants. However, statistical models of melodic expectancies, specifically melodic continuations, appear robust in explaining melodic expectancies in listeners of North Sami, Finnish or North American cultures. While these findings warrant investigation in other cultures, they nonetheless suggest that melodic expectations are universal, insofar as music is melodic.

Implicit knowledge of musical structures

Abstract, implicit knowledge of musical structures and conventions is acquired by infants and children through mere exposure to a particular musical environment (Bigand et al. 2003). Some people explicitly learn the musical theory of their culture, but most acquire implicit knowledge of musical structures and conventions through incidental exposure to the environment.

Implicit learning and Australian Aboriginal song

The process of learning via exposure is evident in descriptions of the performance of Australian Aboriginal song. For example, Barwick (2002) discusses the way rhythmic mode in Church Lirrga songs of Wadeye in the Northern Territory is brought into relief by the juxtaposition of contrasting songs: 'The pairing of items in different tempo bands is one of the main ways in which learners become aware of the importance of this dimension of performance' (p. 81). The pairing of slow and fast songs is commonly found in northern Central Australia and the Kimberleys (Barwick 2002). Barwick (1989) alludes to the complexity of dimensions, relations and interrelations that are learned by an Aboriginal song leader:

> in addition to the mass of geographical and mythological detail to be mastered, leading a performance requires a high degree of sophisticated musical awareness, an awareness that is not taught directly, as in western educational practices, but is rather arrived at and internalized through repeated acts of performance.
>
> Barwick (1989, pp. 26–27)

Temporal expectancies, synchrony, and entrainment

Temporal entrainment is a domain-general mechanism and likely universal process in music perception and production (e.g., Clayton *et al.* 2005; Drake and Bertrand 2001; Fraisse 1982; see also Chapter 8 this volume). Entrainment occurs where two rhythmic processes interact with each other, eventually locking in to a common phase and/or periodicity. Such processes play a role in speech production (Goldstein *et al.* 2006) and models of joint action (e.g. Knoblich and Jordan 2003). Large and Jones (1999) argue that neural oscillators entrain to external events such as metres or rhythms. Because this entrainment process underlies temporal perception, periodic events (i.e., repeating rhythms, metre) facilitate the efficient allocation of limited attentional resources, and make synchronization activity (e.g., tapping along or musical activity) more accurate.

Non-periodic metres are common cross-culturally. 'Free rhythms' such as the Indian *alap* or the Turkish *taksim* are improvised and unmetred, while music with accelerating rhythms is found in Japanese Gagaku music and Tibetan monastic music (Huron 2006). The *aksak* metres (e.g., 3 + 2 + 2) of Bulgarian dances (Moelants 2006) and African rhythms are non-periodic. At first glance, non-periodic rhythms may be problematic for theories of entrainment. Jones argues that when there is no explicit pulse a listener might entrain to what they perceive as the median period length (Barnes and Jones 2000). Periodicity is not necessary for the formation of expectations, according to Huron (2006). Instead, listeners need to be experienced with the temporal structure of an event and some element of its temporal structure must be predictable. Regardless of whether accounts of entrainment or accounts of expectation are better at explaining the perception of temporal structure cross-culturally, some form of allocation of attentional resources based on the expectation of temporal information is likely to be universal.

Multimodal processes and integration

In many cultures, music and dance are inseparable. An analysis of the didjeridu-accompanied dance-song genre *Lirrga* from Wadeye in the Northern Territory of Australia, has shown that songs fall into named distinct tempo ranges which correlate with different metres in the vocal part resulting in rhythmic mode (Barwick 2002). The significance of rhythmic modes comes from their association with *dance* (Marett 2005). Thus, one universal process in music cognition might be movement perception and its development (Fraisse 1982; Friberg and Sundberg 1999).

Bharucha *et al.* (2006) have distinguished four primary facets of internal experiences of motion in music cognition: a fundamental sense of self-motion through space; perception of the motion of bodies, not necessarily one's own; movement elicited by abstract structures such as tonality; and a metaphorical, synaesthetic sense of motion. Movement in pitch, time, loudness, and timbre has been described as the interplay of tension and relaxation (Jackendoff and Lerdahl 2006). This metaphor of tension and relaxation may emerge as a universal quality in music cognition given further research cross-culturally.

Music is an example of a perception–action cycle (Janata and Grafton 2003; Keller *et al.* 2007); that is, streams of sensory information forming the basis of goal-directed actions. Evidence of neural simulation and mirroring continues to accumulate—seeing *or* hearing an intentional *action* gives rise to neural activity that is comparable with that underlying *performance* of the action (Keysers *et al.* 2003). Studies of music perception and performance are likely to shed new light on universal processes that are the result of tightly coupled sensorimotor systems.

Conclusion

There is much to do to test assumptions of contemporary theories of music cognition and to identify unique features of musical environments and musical processing. More than 30 years ago, Harwood (1976) called for an emphasis in research on musical processes rather than musical content and suggested that looking at how people learn to listen to and play their community's music is more informative than studying what it is they listen to or play. Researchers will need to be creative in applying a range of appropriate methods to music processing in non-Western cultures; these range from initial ethological and ethnographic phases, to analysis of everyday, multimodal musical events, through to the design of experiments that test particular hypotheses. Clarke and Cook (2004) detail methods for this endeavour. As Cole (1996) notes, such studies will need to 'maintain the integrity of the real-life situations [they are] designed to investigate, be faithful to the larger social and cultural contexts from which the subjects come, and be consistent with … participants' definitions' (p. 226). Interdisciplinary research that knits together the concerns and methods of the cognitive sciences with those of cultural anthropology, and that involves diverse materials, tasks, and cultural groups, is essential for explanatory and inclusive theories of music cognition, perception, and production.

Acknowledgments

Supported by an Australian Research Council Discovery Project grant (DP0771890) awarded to the first author and a University of Western Sydney Postgraduate Award held by the second author. We thank Nigel Nettheim, Roger Dean, Barbara Tillmann, Rudi Črnčec, Caroline Jones, and the MARCS Music and Movement Writing Group for helpful comments on an earlier draft. kj.stevens@uws.edu.au t.byron@uws.edu.au http://marcs.uws.edu.au

References

Arom S and Fürniss A (1993). An interactive experimental method for the determination of musical scales in oral cultures: application to the vocal music of the Aka Pygmies of Central Africa. *Contemporary Music Review*, **9**, 7–12.

Balzano GJ (1980). The group-theoretic description of 12-fold and microtonal pitch systems. *Computer Music Journal*, **4**, 66–84.

Balzano GJ (1982). The pitch set as a level of description for studying musical pitch perception. In M Clynes, ed., *Music, mind and brain: the neuropsychology of music*, 321–351. Plenum Press, New York.

Barnes R and Jones MR (2000). Expectancy attention and time. *Cognitive Psychology*, **41**, 254–311.

Barwick L (1989). Creative (ir)regularities: the intermeshing of text and melody in performance of Central Australian song. *Australian Aboriginal Studies*, **1989**/1, 12–28.

Barwick L (2002). Tempo bands, metre and rhythmic mode in Marri Ngarr 'Church Lirrga' songs. *Australasian Music Research*, **7**, 67–83.

Bharucha JJ (1994). Tonality and expectation. In R Aiello and JA Sloboda, eds, *Musical perceptions*, 213–239. Oxford University Press, New York.

Bharucha JJ, Curtis M and Paroo K (2006). Varieties of musical experience. *Cognition*, **100**, 131–172.

Bigand E, Poulin B, Tillmann B, Madurell F and D'Adamo D (2003). Sensory versus cognitive components in harmonic priming. *Journal of Experimental Psychology: Human Perception and Performance*, **29**, 159–171.

Bregman A (1990). *Auditory scene analysis*. The MIT Press, Cambridge, MA.

Burns EM (1999). Intervals, scales, and tuning. In D Deutsch, ed., *The psychology of music*, 215–264. Academic Press, San Diego, CA.

Carterette EC and Kendall RA (1999). Comparative music perception and cognition. In D Deutsch, ed., *The psychology of music*, 725–791. Academic Press, San Diego, CA.

Castellano MA, Bharucha JJ and Krumhansl CL (1984). Tonal hierarchies in the music of North India. *Journal of Experimental Psychology: General*, **113**, 394–412.

Clarke EF and Cook N (eds) (2004). *Empirical musicology: aims, methods, prospects*. Oxford University Press, Oxford.

Clayton M (1997). Metre and tal in North Indian music. Translated from Le metre et le tal dans la musique de l'Inde du Nord *Cahiers de Musiques Traditionelles*, **10**, 169–189. Trans. G. Goormaghtigh.

Clayton M, Sager R and Will U (2005). In time with the music: the concept of entrainment and its significance for ethnomusicology. *European Meetings in Ethnomusicology (ESEM Counterpoint 1)*, 3–75.

Cole M (1996). *Cultural psychology: a once and future discipline*. The Belknap Press of Harvard University Press, Cambridge, MA.

Cowan N (1984). On short and long auditory stores. *Psychological Bulletin*, **96**, 341–370.

Cuddy LL and Lunney CA (1995). Expectancies generated by melodic intervals: perceptual judgements of melodic continuity. *Perception and Psychophysics*, **57**, 451–462.

Darwin CJ, Turvey MT and Crowder RG (1972). An auditory analogue of the Sperling partial report procedure: evidence for brief auditory storage. *Cognitive Psychology*, **3**, 255–267.

Deutsch D (1999). Grouping mechanisms in music. In D Deutsch, ed., *The psychology of music*, 299–348. Academic Press, San Diego, CA.

Dowling WJ (1978). Scale and contour: two components of a theory of memory for melodies. *Perception and Psychophysics*, **14**, 37–40.

Drake C and Ben El Heni J (2003). Synchronizing with music: intercultural differences. *Annals of the New York Academy of Sciences*, **999**, 429–437.

Drake C and Bertrand D (2001). The quest for universals in temporal processing in music. In RJ Zatorre, I Peretz, eds, *The biological foundations of music: Annals of the New York Academy of Sciences, Vol. 930*, 17–27. The New York Academy of Sciences, New York.

Ellis CJ (1983). When is a song not a song? A study from Northern South Australia. *Bikmaus*, **4**, 136–144.

Ellis CJ (1984). The nature of Australian Aboriginal music. *The International Journal of Music Education*, **4**, 47–50.

Everett DL (2005). Cultural constraints on grammar and cognition in Pirahã: another look at the design features of human language. *Current Anthropology*, **46**, 621–634.

Fraisse P (1982). Rhythm and tempo. In D Deutsch, ed., *The psychology of music*, 149–180. Academic Press, New York.

Friberg A and Sundberg J (1999). Does music performance allude to locomotion? A model of final ritardandi derived from measurement of stopping runners. *Journal of the Acoustical Society of America*, **105**, 1469–1484.

Goldstein L, Byrd D and Saltzman E (2006). The role of vocal tract gestural action units in understanding the evolution of phonology. In MA Arbib, ed., *Action to language via the mirror neuron system*, 215–249. Cambridge University Press, Cambridge.

Handel S (1984). Using polyrhythms to study rhythm. *Music Perception*, **1**, 465–484.

Harwood DL (1976). Universals in music: a perspective from cognitive psychology. *Ethnomusicology*, **20**, 521–533.

Huron D (2006). *Sweet anticipation: music and the psychology of expectation*. The MIT Press, Cambridge, MA.

Iyer VS (1998). Microstructures of feel, macrostructures of sound: embodied cognition in West African and African-American musics. Unpublished doctoral dissertation, Technology and the Arts, University of California, Berkeley.

Jackendoff R and Lerdahl F (2006). The capacity for music: what is it, and what's special about it? *Cognition*, **100**, 33–72.

Janata P and Grafton ST (2003). Swinging in the brain: shared neural substrates for behaviors related to sequencing and music. *Nature Neuroscience*, **6**, 682–687.

Jusczyk PW and Krumhansl CL (1993). Pitch and rhythmic patterns affecting infants' sensitivity to musical phrase structure. *Journal of Experimental Psychology: Human Perception and Performance*, **19**, 627–640.

Justus TC and Bharucha JJ (2002). Music perception and cognition. In S Yantis, volume ed., and H Pashler, series ed. *Stevens' handbook of experimental psychology, Vol. 1: Sensation and perception*, 3rd edn, 453–492. Wiley, New York.

Keller PE, Knoblich G and Repp BH (2007). Pianists duet better when they play with themselves: on the possible role of action simulation in synchronization. *Consciousness and Cognition*, **16**, 102–111.

Kessler EJ, Hansen C and Shepard RN (1984). Tonal schemata in the perception of music in Bali and the West. *Music Perception*, **2**, 131–165.

Keysers C, Kohler E, Umiltà MA, Nanetti L, Fogassi L and Gallese V (2003). Audiovisual mirror neurons and action recognition. *Experimental Brain Research*, **153**, 628–636.

Knoblich G and Jordan JS (2003). Action coordination in groups and individuals: learning anticipatory control. *Journal of Experimental Psychology: Learning, Memory, and Cognition*, **29**, 1006–1016.

Kolinski M (1970). Review of 'Ethnomusicology of the Flathead Indians' by Alan P. Merriam. *Ethnomusicology*, **14**, 77–99.

Krumhansl CL (2000). Tonality induction: a statistical approach applied cross-culturally. *Music Perception*, **17**, 461–479.

Krumhansl CL and Jusczyk PW (1990). Infant's perception of phrase structure in music. *Psychological Science*, **1**, 70–73.

Krumhansl CL, Toiviainen P, Eerola T, Toiviainen P, Järvinen T and Louhivuori J (2000). Cross-cultural music cognition: cognitive methodology applied to North Sami yoiks. *Cognition*, **76**, 13–58.

Large E and Jones MR (1999). The dynamics of attending: how people track time-varying events. *Psychological Review*, **106**, 119–159.

Lomax A (1968). *Folk song style and culture*. American Association for the Advancement of Science, Washington, DC.

McAdams S (1989). Psychological constraints on form-bearing dimensions in music. *Contemporary Music Review*, **4**, 181–198.

McMullen E and Saffran JR (2004). Music and language: a developmental comparison. *Music Perception*, **21**, 289–311.

Magill JM and Pressing JL (1997). Asymmetric cognitive clock structures in West African rhythms. *Music Perception*, **15**, 189–222.

Marett A (2005). *Songs, dreamings, and ghosts: the Wangga of North Australia*. Wesleyan University Press, Middletown, CT.

Meyer LB (1956). *Emotion and meaning in music*. Chicago University Press, Chicago, IL.

Meyer LB (1960). Universalism and relativism in the study of ethnic music. *Ethnomusicology*, **4**, 49–54.

Moelants D (2006). Perception and performance of aksak metres. *Musicae Scientiae*, **X**, 147–172.

Nam U (1998). Pitch distributions in Korean Court music: evidence consistent with tonal hierarchies. *Music Perception*, **16**, 243–247.

Nan Y, Knösche TR and Friederici AD (2006). The perception of musical phrase structure: a cross-cultural ERP study. *Brain Research*, **1094**, 179–191.

Nettl B (2005). *The study of ethnomusicology: thirty-one issues and concepts*. University of Illinois Press, Champaign, IL.

Patel AD, Peretz I, Tramo M and Labreque R (1998). Processing prosodic and musical patterns: a neuropsychological investigation. *Brain and Language*, **61**, 123–144.

Schellenberg EG (1997). Simplifying the implication–realization model of melodic expectancy. *Music Perception*, **14**, 295–318.

Schellenberg EG and Trehub SE (1996). Natural musical intervals: evidence from infant listeners. *Psychological Science*, **7**, 272–277.

Schmuckler MA (1989). Expectation in music: investigation of melodic and harmonic processes. *Music Perception*, **7**, 109–150.

Schwartz DA, Howe CQ and Purves D (2003). The statistical structure of human speech sounds predicts musical universals. *The Journal of Neuroscience*, **23**, 7160–7168.

Sethares WA (1998). *Tuning, timbre, spectrum, scale.* Springer-Verlag, Berlin.

Stobart H and Cross I (2000). The Andean anacrusis? Rhythmic structure and perception in Easter songs of Northern Potosí, Bolivia. *British Journal of Ethnomusicology*, **9**, 63–94.

Tenney J (1988). *A history of consonance and dissonance.* Excelsior Music Publishing Co., New York.

Tenzer M (2006). Oleg Tumulilingan. Layers of time and melody in Balinese music. In M Tenzer, ed., *Analytical studies in world music*, 205–236. Oxford University Press, Oxford.

Thompson WF and Schellenberg EG (2006). Listening to music. In R Colwell, ed., *MENC handbook of musical cognition and development*, 72–123. Oxford University Press, Oxford.

Tillmann B, Bharucha JJ and Bigand E (2000). Implicit learning of tonality: a self-organizing approach. *Psychological Review*, **107**, 885–913.

Trainor LJ (2006). Innateness, learning and the difficulty of determining whether music is an evolutionary adaptation. *Music Perception*, **24**, 105–109.

Trehub SE (2000). Human processing predisposition and musical universals. In NL Wallin, B Merker, S Brown, eds, *The origins of music*, 427–448. The MIT Press, Cambridge, MA.

Trehub SE and Hannon EE (2006). Infant music perception: domain-general or domain-specific mechanisms? *Cognition*, **100**, 73–99.

Vos PG and Troost JM (1989). Ascending and descending melodic intervals: statistical findings and their perceptual relevance. *Music Perception*, **6**, 383–396.

Will U (1997). Two types of octave relationships in Central Australian vocal music? *Musicology Australia*, **XX**, 6–14.

Wright AA, Rivera JJ, Hulse SH, Shyan M and Neiworth JJ (2000). Music perception and octave generalization in rhesus monkeys. *Journal of Experimental Psychology: General*, **129**, 291–307.

CHAPTER 3

Music and meaning

Ian Cross and Elizabeth Tolbert

Introduction

What do we mean by 'meaning'? When we say that something has 'meaning', we are claiming that our original something points to, or is attached to, or can be used to infer the existence of, some other thing beyond itself. Some sort of relationship exists between our original entity or event and something beyond itself. Vernacularly, our original something has *significance*. Another simple way of putting it is that our original something *refers* to something else beyond itself. When we engage with music, we tend to feel that it has significance; it appears to mean something, even if that meaning is entirely personal to us. When we look at the ways in which music has been theorized and explored, the issue of musical meaning is often central, particularly when music is being explored in its social context (see Feld and Fox 1994). However, while music may have significance, by comparison with language it is very difficult to say what it is that music refers to, or indeed, whether music refers to anything else at all.

Contemporary methods of approaching the question of musical meaning have been shaped by a range of theories of meaning. Some theories hold that music is a species of art, which can only be understood as a phenomenon that is not susceptible to analysis in terms of general and formally expressible principles. Such theories tend to be predicated on the notion that recent and contemporary Western conceptions of music—in which music is produced by specialists for aural consumption by the many—are representative of music as a generic human phenomenon. Alternative views are found in literatures that aim to explore music as a social phenomenon (whether in Western or non-Western contexts), which tend to be pluralistic in the frameworks that they apply to articulate their understandings of meaning in music, drawing on semiotic, sociological and anthropological theories of meaning. Some influential theories that have emerged within analytical philosophy and that are prevalent in the study of linguistics seem to imply that meaning cannot properly be considered a property of music. In these theories meaning is held to be a property only of (formal) systems that are capable of embodying two types of meaning relation, *reference* and *sense* (see below), and that are thus capable of articulating complex propositions that are definable as true or false. The chapter will present an overview of theories of meaning that have been, and that may be, applicable to investigating music, particularly its cognitive dimensions.

Theories of meaning

Philosophers and logicians have devoted much attention to the problem of meaning—to analysing how it is that something means. In general, they have focused on meaning as it appears manifested through language. Their ideas, particularly in the form of theories of semantics, have tended to dominate conceptions of meaning within philosophy and within most sciences. Semantic theories generally aim to account for the relationships between the phenomena that constitute the objects of meaning and the expressions and sets of expressions that are used to articulate meanings.

One of the strongest influences on the development of recent and contemporary theories of the semantics of language has been the work of

Frege, who wrote at the end of the nineteenth century. Frege suggested that there are two necessary aspects of meaning that must be considered in any analysis; these he called *reference* and *sense*. Roughly speaking, the *reference* of a term is that which it denotes—that phenomenon in the world onto which it can be mapped. Its *sense* derives from the ways in which that original term relates to other terms that are interpretable as capable of bearing similar kinds of meanings. To give Frege's classic example, the expressions 'Morning Star' and 'Evening Star' have the same single reference—the planet Venus. But their senses differ in an obvious way, in that the sense of one is 'the star that appears in the morning', and that of the other 'the star that appears in the evening'. The senses of the two expressions arise by virtue of the meanings of the terms that are used to articulate them within the language system.

Hence in this view meaning is a consequence of the capacity of terms within a system to refer and at the same time be bounded by their relationships to other terms within a system of terms such as a formal logic (or a language when it is interpreted as having features that of the same type as those of a formal logic). These features enable terms within the system to be used to articulate propositions that may be evaluated as true or false—that have determinate *truth values*. Only in such systems can complex propositions be expressed and can their meaning be fully accounted for in terms of the elements that make up the complex propositions; only such systems have the capacity for *compositionality*, that of expressing semantically decomposable propositions. It has been suggested that only formal semantic theories founded on Frege's ideas, such as those of Montague or of Tarski, constitute 'genuine theories of meaning' (Scruton 1987). While these types of theories do not seem particularly pertinent to music (particularly in view of the difficulty that the ideas of reference, and of compositionality, pose for music), they are nonetheless highly relevant in that they have underpinned the development of theories of meaning throughout the twentieth century that has shaped much of the intellectual context in which any account of meaning in music has to be understood (for more detailed and technical considerations of Frege's ideas,

see Grayling 2000, Vol. 1, Chapter 2; Vol. 2, Chapter 12).

A rather different approach to meaning that has been widely applied to music derives from the work of CS Peirce (see Hoopes 1991), who proposed that meaning could be understood in terms of systems of signs, which can be defined as *natural* or *conventional* and can stand in a variety of relationships to that which the sign represents—its meaning. A sign may point beyond itself by virtue of some formal resemblance between the sign and that which is represented, and thus be *iconic*; it may have meaning because of some necessary connection between itself and what it indicates (as in the case of smoke indicating fire) or by virtue of repeated co-occurence, the relationship between sign and its meaning thus being *indexical*; and it may mean by virtue of arbitrary convention, its meaning being rooted in the *symbolic* domain. While Peirce's *semiotic* ideas have largely been neglected or rejected by philosophers and semantic theorists, they have played a role in several influential theories of meaning in music (e.g. Nattiez 1990). Nevertheless, music does not easily map onto the natural–conventional distinction that lies at the root of Peirce's original theories. Music has tended to be viewed as having an ambiguous status somewhere between the natural and the conventional, limiting the explicitness with which the bases for its meanings can be articulated in semiotic terms.

It may seem that meaning is simply a mapping from a term to its referent (and vice versa). However, for Peirce, the source of meaning is in the mind; in his theory, 'All thought is in signs' (Peirce quoted in Violi 1999). The idea that consideration of mind is necessary to theories of meaning lies at the heart of contemporary cognitive science and is central in much contemporary philosophy of meaning and language. Mental states and processes are said to exhibit *intentionality* or aboutness (Dennett 1987, 1995); they represent, or point to, phenomena beyond themselves. The idea of intentionality can be applied to understand the ways in which language can be interpreted as bearing meaning, by taking into account the ways in which we employ language to articulate the aboutness of our mental states.

A more radical account which explicitly sets out to provide an alternative to the idea that meaning can only be correctly defined in relation to the abstract properties of formal systems is found in *experientialist* approaches, of which the most developed is that of Lakoff and Johnson (Johnson 1987; Lakoff 1987). In this view, meaning is a property of the relationships between mind and world; however, it is best understood as mediated not by the principles of formal logic but by the embodied nature of our experiences of being in the world. Meaning is motivated by kinesthetic-image schemas, which are (Lakoff 1987, p. 267) 'relatively simple structures that constantly recur in our everyday bodily experience', and which may take forms such as 'CONTAINERS, PATHS, LINKS etc.' These body-image schemas constitute the preconceptual bases for the formation and combination of concepts, grounding meaning in our bodily experience of the world. A somewhat different approach to an experientialist theory of meaning is proposed by Jackendoff (1987, 2002), although directed more explicitly towards making sense of language structure and use. Experientialist theories, in particular those of Lakoff and Johnson, have been applied to understanding the nature of meaning in music, as we shall see.

Ideas such as reference and sense, natural and conventional signs, and intentionality can help account for different aspects of the ways in which something may be interpreted as bearing meaning. Yet music seems to pose particular problems for these ways of approaching meaning. Usually, we cannot use music to refer to a state of affairs in the world in the ways in which we can use language. In at least this respect, music certainly does not seem capable of bearing the types of meaning borne by language, which would suggest that an analysis of musical meaning in terms of sense and reference is unfeasible. Musical meaning also fits ambiguously with any distinction between natural and conventional signs, and it is also unclear how the notion of intentionality might be applied to clarify the aboutness of the mental states that arise when we engage in music.

In order to elucidate the ways in which meaning in music can be, and has been, explored in ways that are relevant to music (and to the psychology of music), it is necessary to consider what are the kinds of things that can be the objects of meaning. Are they states of affairs in the material world or in possible worlds (for which see Johnson-Laird 1983, p. 172)? Are they states of affairs in some abstract yet immanent domain, such as the theorems of formal logic and their validity—their truth values—within some logical system (Tarski 1956)? Are they states of affairs in some abstract yet immanent domain that *cannot* be described within the theorems of formal logic, such as the domain of the aesthetic (Sibley 1959)? Are they mental phenomena such as the thoughts, beliefs and desires of individuals (Dennett 1987), or the preconceptual schemas proposed by Lakoff and Johnson? Or are they social phenomena, such as cultural groupings, institutions, contracts or shared understandings (Bourdieu 1990)? At different times, theories of meaning have postulated all these types of phenomena as being potential or actual objects of meaning, and in one way or another, all have been applied to understanding the question of meaning in music over the history of Western thought.

Meaning in music in the western intellectual tradition

For the classical Greek philosophical tradition, music presented two conflicting faces. On the one side, music—and music, for the Greeks, was melodic—moved the passions (for good or ill), and was a fundamentally human activity, affecting our emotions by being stirring and martial, or beautiful and enticing. Its purposes could thus be considered as aligned with those of the science of rhetoric, which aimed to bend human minds and actions to the purposes of the orator. On the other side, music, in the theories erected on the basis of the measurement of aspects of the sounds that comprised it, embodied the natural laws of number and could thus be viewed as reflecting abstract and immanent aspects of the universe such as the principles of natural order, or the workings of the divine (James 1993).

This dichotomous view of music persisted through the first millennium CE, gaining in complexity as it was refracted through the multiple prisms of early Christian thought. Hence in the medieval world, music could be thought of as having meaning in at least two domains, the human and the divine. The tension between music as mirror of the heavenly world and music as mover of earthly passion was mediated by church doctrine and by the development of musical notations, through which polyphonic music that might be viewed as simply lascivious because of its sonorous beauty could alternatively be interpreted as reflecting the mathematical complexity of divine order (Sparshott and Goehr 2001).

By the later fifteenth century, music came to be seen in part as a foundationally human activity with its values and its meanings requiring to be expressed and interpreted in human rather than divine terms (Palisca 1985). Music's meanings were bound to the products and processes of human reason as well as to music's effects on human emotions, allowing for the possibility that music might express or bear types of meanings that were proper only to music as an art. By the later seventeenth and early eighteenth centuries, music's meanings had come to be largely theorized in terms of human passions or affects. Music's alignment with rhetoric was foregrounded (Sparshott 1998), as was the extent to which its forms mirrored those of the linguistic prosody, though the structures that music could articulate also became more important for their own sake. The values accorded to music and its meanings were largely those of rational pleasure, enjoyment founded on the exercise of reason; ostensibly rational principles (based in part on the development of the science of acoustics) were elaborated and adduced that were intended to account for the extent to which a piece of music had fulfilled its brief by expressing its meaning.

Through the eighteenth century the forms and the meanings of music changed radically. From being bound to the devices of rhetoric and hence to its purposes, music's forms became more and more intelligible in terms of theories of harmony, related to either, and sometimes to both, the findings of physical acoustics, and abstract principles of architectonic structure. Musical meaning thus no longer required any sort of justification by reference to the words that it could convey in song, or to the ways in which it conveyed those words (its 'prosody'); instrumental music came to be conceived of as

equally capable of bearing meaning in its own right. However, the effects of music on human passions were not completely displaced from consideration; as Thomas (1995, p. 5) notes, most of the writing on music by the philosophers of the mid- to late-eighteenth century had as a 'governing assumption' the idea 'that music was a kind of language'. Hence by the late eighteenth century, the objects of the meanings of music could be conceived of as private, being in the mind, or as public and social.

The aesthetic perspective

Towards the end of the eighteenth century a new way of understanding meaning in music emerged, one which had its precursors in the notion that music should be valued for its beauty but which sought to detach music's meaning from its social value and to valorize its experience as art as an end in itself. It developed in tandem with the emergence of the notion of music as being autonomous, or as having value in its own right. The ideas that underpin this approach have come to constitute the prevalent means of addressing questions of music's value and significance within the Western intellectual tradition of the last two centuries or so.

This new approach was first crystallized in ideas that were developed by Hume and by Kant, in proposing that both art and natural beauty can give rise to aesthetic experiences that are exclusive in that they are bound to felt response (in being logically dependent on pleasure and liking) but that are not reducible to any specific set of principles (as they cannot be induced second-hand by verbal description). Kant proposed that aesthetic contemplation is distinguished by being fundamentally 'disinterested', or free from concern with desire or any other purposive attitude. In current approaches the notion of the aesthetic is bound up with the notion that there are phenomena that can only be described as 'art', and various attempts have been made to demarcate the qualities that art must have in order to be art (see e.g. Wollheim 1980). The identity of art has been variously proposed as lying in its capacity for representation, its structural qualities, or in its capacities for expression. In expression-based approaches, works of art are viewed as the loci for aesthetic experience by virtue of encapsulating both emotional and rational qualities that may be more or less apparent to, or recuperable by, engaged audiences (see Davies 1994). In these theories, music's capacity to engender aesthetic experience does not rely on, and is not expressible in the same terms as, the capacity that language possesses of bearing meaning by expressing complex propositions that have determinable sense and reference (Dempster 1998).

Central to many expressivist analyses of musical meaning has been the idea that music's meaning is fundamentally emotional, though most of those who have sought to develop this approach have treated the relationship between music and emotion in ways that appear to have little connection with the scientific literature on music and affect. Two leading philosophers of music, Roger Scruton and Stephen Davies, both privilege the expressive dimensions of music in seeking to analyse its aesthetic qualities, though taking somewhat diverging paths. Davies (1994, 2003) proposes that a critical component of the aesthetic aspect of music is its engendering of an 'understanding response' in a listener, which requires the capacity to experience predictive coherence in the ongoing flow of a piece of music as heard. In addition to this aspect, music must be recognized as referring beyond itself in being expressive of emotion; music achieves this either by presenting the appearance of emotion (Davies 2003) or because we (1994, p. 277) 'experience the dynamic character of music as like the actions of a person'. The experience of music must involve both types of recognition to qualify as an appropriate aesthetic experience; only if both conditions are met will the music be understood, its 'meaning' grasped. Scruton (1987, 1997) suggests that music does not so much express emotion as embody it in a holistic way such that it is not possible to identify just which features of the music are directly responsible for this embodiment of emotion; he suggests that 'In responding to a piece of music we are being led through a series of gestures which gain their significance from the intimation of community' (1997, p. 357). However, for this aspect of meaning in music to be experienced, audiences must be capable of hearing the music *as* music. Thus for Scruton musical meaning is rooted in the metaphorical experience of

movement and is situated in *a* musical culture which aligns the intuitive capacities of audiences, composers and performers.

In theories of musical meaning that are grounded in aesthetic considerations, 'meaning' appears to take quite a different form from that which it holds in the types of semantic theories that can be applied to language. Meaning is immanent as a condition of felt response that depends on the qualities of the music as the object of listening and on the cultural capacities of its audiences. The factors that motivate musical meaning might be expressive, or might have their roots in the structural properties of Western music (particularly in the harmonic domain) that can be analysed in terms of patterns of tension and resolution. Just these types of factors were identified as the proper locus of meaning in music by Hanslick in the nineteenth century, and cognitively oriented theories of music's meaning as rooted in its structural properties have been proposed by theorists such as Lerdahl (see e.g. Lerdahl 2003). Nevertheless, the majority of philosophical approaches to understanding meaning in music have differentiated musical meanings from 'everyday' meanings by binding music's significances solely to the aesthetic domain. As Cook (2001) points out, such approaches stand in stark opposition to those which aim to locate, and to understand, music and its meanings in the social contexts in which it arises. Theories of this latter type have emerged from sociological and ethnomusicological explorations of music; they are central to approaches that adopt anthropological perspectives on the investigation of relationships between musical sounds, practices and concepts (Merriam 1964) in non-Western and, increasingly, in Western cultural contexts, to understand meaning in music.

Meaning in music in social and cultural context

The idea that music's meanings are inseparable from the social and cultural situations and circumstances in which they arise has become widely accepted in musicological (e.g. Kramer 1995), sociological (e.g. Martin 1995) and ethnomusicological (e.g. Bohlman 2000) circles.

Here, the ideas that underpin much philosophical writing on music—that music constitutes an autonomous and primarily aesthetic domain—are called into question or outright rejected, whether on the basis that such ideas are grounded in ethnocentric assumptions as to what constitutes music, or on the grounds that such approaches cannot deal adequately with the historical and dynamic aspects of engagement with music.

The consensus surrounding the notion that music is explicable only as in its social context, evaporates when addressing the question of what *forms* these meanings may take. As Titon and Slobin (1996, p. 1) note, while 'Music is universal its meaning is not.' Across cultures there is a vast range of ways in which music may be experienced or interpreted as bearing meaning; music's meaning can be understood as foundationally aesthetic, personal or social, or in terms of combinations of any or all of these domains. Within such approaches, as Feld and Fox (1994) point out, it is difficult to disentangle specifically musical meanings from the meanings of the activities of which music is a part. For example, in writing of Venda children's music, Blacking (1967, p. 31) notes that 'Many songs add to the meaning of a social event; they crystallize and confirm certain norms of behaviour'; hence the meaning of musical activities may be thought of as complementary to the specific circumstances that incorporate the music.

From such perspectives, meaning in music is multifarious and cannot be understood solely as a consequence of music's aesthetic dimension. As Clayton (Chapter 4 this volume) indicates, music may fulfil a multiplicity of the functions in different societies; taking this into account, its meanings can be best interpreted as adverting to emic conceptions of social facts and circumstances. Hence Feld (1982) is able to present a compelling account of the music of the Kaluli of Papua New Guinea as displayed in the *gisalo* funerary ceremony, where the musical component of the ceremony possesses a structure, identity, and efficacy in mourning that are inextricably bound both to its sacred connotations (it employs a motif derived from the song of the *muni*, a local bird which is the central numinous entity in the main Kaluli myth of 'the boy who turned into a *muni* bird' and thus joined the departed spirits) and to its place in the ecology of the local environment. Hence the meaning of the music is complex and local, in that it can only be understood by addressing it in the context of the belief systems and cultural practices within which it has a role. In other cultural contexts music's meanings may be interpreted as oriented towards more mundane ends, as when Blacking notes of Venda children's music that 'Knowledge of the children's songs is a social asset and in some cases a social necessity for a child who wishes to be an accepted member of his own age group'(1967, p. 31). Here, music is interpreted as fulfilling an instrumental function in the formation of social groups, its meanings somehow bound up in the emergence, or the maintenance (cf. Slobin 1993), of individual and group identities as social facts.

In parallel with reconceptualizations of the idea of musical meaning emerging from anthropological perspectives are sociologically motivated theories that have sought to ground musical meanings in the social and historical contexts of music, particularly in Western culture. These theories have tended to conceive of music as social construct of which the meanings can only be elucidated by analysis of the processes and conditions that pertain to the contexts within which music is produced and received. Influentially adumbrated by Adorno (1976), subsequent accounts have frequently aimed to address issues of hegemony and resistance (Born and Hesmondalgh 2000), and have led to radical accounts of meaning in familiar works of the classical canon such as the work of McClary (1991) on questions of gender in music, as well as to critical and subjectivist accounts of meaning (Kramer 1995).

Meaning in music has been conceptualized variously by philosophers, musicians, anthropologists and sociologists. While the aesthetic view of music's meaning has been predominant for the last two centuries, other conceptions of the bases for meaning in music have emerged that locate these in the relationship between music and social factors and forces. Many of these theories have been explored in the context of cognitive theories of music although, as we shall see, certain views of musical meaning present considerable obstacles to scientific theorization and investigation.

Theoretical and empirical approaches to meaning in the psychology of music

Most attempts to explore meaning empirically by way of music's aesthetic dimension have adopted a severely reduced notion of aesthetic engagement. As noted above, philosophical approaches view aesthetic judgement as dependent on, though not explicable solely in terms of, pleasure and liking; however, experimental approaches have tended to equate aesthetic judgement wholly with evaluative ratings of liking or pleasantness. The most influential theory in the field, that of Berlyne (1971), postulated an inverted U-shape function relating liking to stimulus complexity. Berlyne's theory has been empirically tested and found to account for aspects of the experience of music (North and Hargreaves 1995); however, other studies (Orr and Olsson 2005) have found no consistent relation between liking and complexity when factors such as musical style and level of musical expertize were taken into account.

There are fundamental difficulties in empirically exploring aesthetic experiences. In the first place, there is a lack of consensus as to the phenomenal and phenomenological correlates of aesthetic experience; do these inhere in the representative, the formal, or the expressive capacities of the artistic focus of aesthetic experience, or are they consequences of the capacities of the individual who has the experience? This lack of philosophical agreement is supplemented by the difficulties of implementing experimental designs that deal adequately with the issue of 'felt response' that is at the core of ideas of aesthetic experience. Perhaps some answers might be provided by neuroscientific approaches (see e.g. Blood and Zatorre [2001] in respect of intensely pleasurable responses to music), but even here what is being identified are not the phenomenological states that are the focus of philosophical aesthetics but neurophysiological states, albeit that these may have determinable correlates in behaviour and cognition.

Nevertheless, many recent accounts of aesthetic meaning in music tend to be rooted in the idea that music is expressive, particularly of the emotions. As is evident in the theories and empirical findings described in Chapter 35, most empirical approaches to emotion or affect in music explore the phenomenon within frameworks derived from cognitive and behavioural sciences. Emotions are viewed as dynamic mind–brain–body states that arise in response to the experience of environmental and social events (see e.g. Panksepp and Bernatzky 2002). From the perspective of the cognitive sciences, emotional responses to music tend to be viewed as belonging to subclasses of emotional responses in general rather than as being phenomenally in a category of their own (or even in a category together with responses to the expressivity of other art forms). Hence the types of meaning that psychological approaches understand as arising from emotional engagement with music do not appear to rest on the same types of premises as those that have been postulated by philosophers such as Davies or Scruton as pertinent to the workings of music's expressive powers.

While it might seem that psychological understandings of music's affective meaning should have precedence over the non-empirical ratiocinations of philosophers, it might instead be the case that philosophers have in fact identified good grounds for believing that music's expressivity cannot be understood simply by reference to general theories of emotional response. Indeed, the notion of 'disinterested pleasure' that is at the heart of Kant's conception of aesthetic engagement is one that seems almost to stand in opposition to the necessary interest that is implicit in psychological understandings of the experience of emotion. As yet, questions such as whether the affective states that music appears to elicit arise through empathic processes, as Davies (2001) suggests, or arise directly in response to objective properties of musical structures have not been the sustained focus of experimental investigation.

Affective dimensions of specifically musical meanings have, however, been explored fruitfully by empirical investigation from sociological and social–psychological perspectives. The work of DeNora (2000) suggests that music can be meaningful in being employed by listeners to do 'emotional work' in regulating their emotions and moods in everyday life. DeNora's findings are reinforced by those of Sloboda *et al.* (2001), who employed an innovative approach (the Experience Sampling Method) to sample the nature and significance of the experience of music in day-to-day life. They found that music was particularly significant in social and individual contexts in which personal choice of music was available, and that the efficacy of music in regulating emotion and mood was greatest in such contexts. Intertwined with the empirical study of the individual and social functionality of music's affective dimensions are explorations of the ways in which music is used in the formation and maintenance of senses of self and of group. A wide range of research is reported in MacDonald *et al.* (2002) that indicates that perhaps the primary motivation for engaging with music in the contemporary Western world is to facilitate the transactions involved in formulating, presenting and affirming the multiple dimensions of individual and group identities.

A very different account of musical meaning seems to emerge from some recent neuroscientific research. In an intriguing experiment, Koelsch *et al.* (2004) found that similar types of brain responses were elicited when words that were semantically incongruous were presented following either linguistic or musical contexts (for the latter type of context, that words that were used had been rated as either congruous or incongruous in respect of the musical excerpts in a preceding experiment). This would seem to indicate that musical meanings were being experienced as directly relatable to the meanings of individual words; in their words (ibid., p. 302) 'music can, as language, determine physiological indices of semantic processing'. This finding suggests that musical meanings may indeed be of a similar type to those of language, in stark contrast to most philosophical accounts of musical meaning. However, in a subsequent experiment (Steinbeis and Koelsch 2008) they suggest that the results of the earlier experiment arose because of imagery or association elicited in response to the music rather than through any intrinsically semantic properties of music. In the latter

experiment they find that the semantic unexpectedness of a sentence modulated the neural response to a simultaneously presented musical excerpt that contained an unexpected chord, but that the unexpectedness of the musical event had no effect on the processing of the sentence. They take this finding to indicate that tension–resolution patterns in harmony motivate cognitive and neural responses that are analogous with the contextual integration aspects of language processing, but do not call on representations of semantic knowledge. Hence they suggest that musical 'meaning' is best conceived of as being borne by the patterns of tension and resolution embodied in music, and is of a fundamentally different order from linguistic meaning.

This notion is somewhat problematized by research that applies the experientialist ideas of meaning developed by Johnson and Lakoff. Brower (2000) and Zbikowski (2002) present complex theories of the ways in which body-image schemas may be applied to understand the ways in which music may mean, illustrating their theories by reference to detailed analyses of structures in Western art music. They suggest that while the experience of musical meaning may well be mediated to patterns of tension and resolution, these patterns are themselves motivated by underlying body-image schemas that render the patterns coherent and comprehensible to listeners. Based on the results of a series of experiments and analyses, Larson (1998, 2002, 2004) has explored the extent to which experientialist ideas can account for listeners' experience of aspects of musical structure. Larson and Van Handel (2005) note that 'physical force schemas' appear to account well for listeners' judgements of musical pattern completion, supporting the idea that the types of musical meanings supposed to inhere in tension–relaxation structures in music are in fact grounded in experientialist schemas, a finding supported by subsequent experimental work by Martinez (2007).

Conclusions

One fact that becomes clear on surveying the literature on musical meaning is that there is no consensus as to how questions of musical meaning should best be addressed; indeed, certain philosophical perspectives call into question the idea that music can be claimed to have meaning at all. However, the majority cross-disciplinary view is that music is imbued with meaning, whether music is conceived of as aesthetic object, cultural commodity or social process, yet each discipline tends to propagate ideas of musical meaning that tend to lack the robustness to survive outside its borders. Perhaps it is the case that musical meanings are multifarious and that there is no single approach that can claim precedence for its own conceptions of those meanings. This heterogeneity of solutions to the question of musical meaning poses problems for the psychological sciences; as we have seen, quite different depictions of musical meaning emerge from the theoretical and empirical literature surveyed above. Again, it could be suggested that this is an inevitable outcome of the diffuseness of the concept that is being investigated; nevertheless, the diversity of psychological approaches do exhibit some common themes, although it is evident that there are some conceptions of meaning in music that have not been addressed.

Musical meanings in non-Western contexts have remained largely unexplored from psychological perspectives. This is unsurprising, given the relative dearth of studies of music cognition in non-Western cultures compared to the number of studies conducted in Western contexts. Yet the issue of musical meaning can only properly be addressed by the cognitive sciences when the types of meanings highlighted in numerous ethnomusicological studies are made the foci of psychological exploration. In addition, most empirical approaches to meaning in music take as the object of their investigation the processes that are involved in music listening. While this view is consonant with the ideas of music expressed within most philosophical and many sociological approaches (a notable exception in the latter domain being the work of Finnegan [1989]), ethnomusicological research indicates that music might be better conceived of as a mode of interaction rather than as the object of auditory perception. The psychological sciences need to find means of addressing the study of the meanings that are inherent or emergent in processes of musical interaction,

with a few studies beginning to indicate possible methods whereby this might be achieved (see e.g. Clayton 2007). Finally, the cognitive sciences of music will need to accommodate new approaches to meaning such as Millikan's (2004) 'teleosemantic' theory, which aims to account for meaning within an evolutionary framework (some theoretical groundwork in this area has been laid in Tolbert [2001] and in Cross and Woodruff [2008]).

The issue of musical meaning is unlikely to be accounted for by one generically applicable theory and is unlikely to be amenable to scientific exploration by any one method. This chapter has laid out some of the principal influences on the study of meaning in music and has suggested that some have had more impact on the scientific exploration of music's significance while others have been unduly neglected. Theoretical and empirical research into musical meaning is still at an early stage within the cognitive sciences; this chapter would suggest that it is important that multiple perspectives on meaning in music, particularly those emerging from the study of music in non-Western contexts, are taken fully into account in future explorations of musical meaning within the cognitive sciences.

References

Adorno T (1976). *Introduction to the sociology of music.* Seabury Press, New York.

Berlyne DE (1971). *Aesthetics and psychobiology.* Appleton-Century-Crofts, New York.

Blacking J (1967). *Venda children's songs: a study in ethnomusicological analysis.* Witwatersrand University Press, Johannesburg.

Blood AJ and Zatorre RJ (2001). Intensely pleasurable responses to music correlate with activity in brain regions implicated in reward and emotion. *Proceedings of the National Academy of Sciences*, **98**(20), 11818–11823.

Bohlman P (2000). Ethnomusicology and music sociology. In D Greer, ed., *Musicology and sister disciplines,* 288–298. Oxford University Press, Oxford.

Born G and Hesmondalgh D (eds) (2000). *Western music and others: difference, representation and appropriation in music.* University of California Press, Berkeley, CA.

Bourdieu P (1990). *The logic of practice.* Stanford University Press, Stanford, CA.

Brower C (2000). A cognitive theory of musical meaning. *Journal of Music Theory*, **44**(2), 323–379.

Clayton M (2007). Observing entrainment in music performance: video-based observational analysis of

Indian musicians' tanpura playing and beat marking. *Musicae Scientiae*, **11**(1), 27–60.

Cook N (2001). Theorizing musical meaning. *Music Theory Spectrum*, **23**(2), 170–195.

Cross I and Woodruff GE (2008). Music as a communicative medium. In R Botha, C Knight, eds, *The prehistory of language*, Vol. 1, 113–144. Oxford University Press, Oxford.

Davies S (1994). *Musical meaning and expression*. Cornell University Press, Ithaca, NY.

Davies S (2001). Philosophical perspectives on music's expressiveness. In P Juslin, JA Sloboda, eds, *Music and emotion: theory and research*, 23–44. Oxford University Press, Oxford.

Davies S (2003). *Themes in the philosophy of music*. Oxford University Press, Oxford.

Dempster D (1998). Is there even a grammar of music? *Musicae Scientiae*, **2**(1), 55–64.

Dennett D (1987). *The intentional stance*. MIT Press, Cambridge, MA.

Dennett D (1995). *Darwin's dangerous idea*. Penguin Books, London.

DeNora T (2000). *Music and everyday life*. Cambridge University Press, Cambridge.

Feld S (1982). *Sound and sentiment: birds, weeping, poetics and song in Kaluli expression*. Publications of the American Folklore Society. New series; 5. BZVDW, Philadelphia, PA.

Feld S and Fox AA (1994). Music and language. *Annual Review of Anthropology*, **23**, 25–53.

Finnegan R (1989). *The hidden musicians: music-making in an English town*. Cambridge University Press, Cambridge.

Grayling AC (ed.) (2000). *Philosophy: a guide through the subject*. Oxford University Press, Oxford.

Hoopes J (ed.) (1991). *Peirce on signs: writings on semiotic by Charles Sanders Peirce*. University of North Carolina Press, Chapel Hill, NC.

Jackendoff R (1987). *Consciousness and the computational mind*. MIT Press, Cambridge, MA.

Jackendoff R (2002). *Foundations of language: brain, meaning, grammar, evolution*. Oxford University Press, Oxford.

James J (1993). *The music of the spheres: music, science and the natural order of the universe*. Little, Brown and Co., London.

Johnson M (1987). *The body in the mind: the bodily basis of meaning, imagination and reason*. Chicago University Press, Chicago, IL.

Johnson-Laird PN (1983). *Mental models*. Cambridge University Press, Cambridge.

Juslin P and Sloboda JA (eds) (2001). *Music and emotion: theory and research*. Oxford University Press, Oxford.

Koelsch S, Kasper E, Sammler D, Schultze K, Gunter T and Frederici A (2004). Music, language and meaning: brain signatures of semantic processing. *Nature Neuroscience*, **7**(3), 302–307.

Kramer L (1995). *Music and postmodernist thought*. University of California Press, London.

Lakoff G (1987). *Women, fire and dangerous things*. University of Chicago Press, Chicago, IL.

Larson S (1998). Musical forces and melodic patterns. *Theory and Practice*, **22/23**, 55–71.

Larson S (2002). Musical forces, melodic expectation, and jazz melody. *Music Perception*, **19**(3), 351–385.

Larson S (2004). Musical forces and melodic expectations: comparing computer models and experimental results. *Music Perception*, **21**(4), 457–498.

Larson S and VanHandel L (2005). Measuring musical forces. *Music Perception*, **23**(2), 119–136.

Lerdahl F (2003). Two ways in which music relates to the world. *Music Theory Spectrum*, **25**(2), 367–373.

MacDonald, R Hargreaves D and Miell D (eds) (2002). *Musical identities*. Oxford University Press, Oxford.

Martin P (1995). *Sounds and society: themes in the sociology of music*. Manchester University Press, Manchester.

Martinez I (2007). The cognitive reality of prolongational structure in tonal music. Unpublished PhD thesis, Roehampton University, London.

McClary S (1991). *Feminine endings: music, gender and sexuality*. University of Minnesota Press, Minnesota, MN.

Merriam AP (1964). *The anthropology of music*. Northwestern University Press, Chicago, IL.

Millikan RG (2004). *Varieties of meaning: the 2002 Jean Nicod lectures*. MIT Press, Cambridge, MA.

Nattiez J-J (1990). *Music and discourse: toward a semiology of music*. Princeton University Press, Princeton, NJ.

North AC and Hargreaves DJ (1995). Subjective complexity, familiarity, and liking for popular music. *Psychomusicology*, **14**, 77–93.

Orr MG and Ohlsson S (2005). Relationship between complexity and liking as a function of expertise. *Music Perception*, **22**(4), 583–611.

Palisca C (1985). *Humanism in Italian Renaissance musical thought*. Yale University Press, New Haven, CT.

Panksepp J and Bernatzky G (2002). Emotional sounds and the brain: the neuro-affective foundations of musical appreciation. *Behavioural Processes*, **60**, 133–155.

Scruton R (1987). Analytical philosophy and the meaning of music. *Journal of Aesthetics and Art Criticism*, **46**, 169–176.

Scruton R (1997). *The aesthetics of music*. Clarendon Press, Oxford.

Sibley F (1959). Aesthetic concepts. *Philosophical Review*, **68**, 421–450.

Slobin M (1993). *Subcultural sounds: micromusics of the West*. Wesleyan University Press, Hanover, NH.

Sloboda JA, O Neill SA and Ivaldi A (2001). Functions of music in everyday life: an exploratory study using the Experience Sampling Method. *Musicae Scientiae*, **5**(1), 9–32.

Sparshott F (1998). Reflections on Affektenlehre and dance theory in the eighteenth century. *The Journal of Aesthetics and Art Criticism*, **56**(1), 21–28.

Sparshott F and Goehr L (2001). Philosophy of music: early Christian thought; medieval thought. In S Sadie, ed., *The new Grove dictionary of music and musicians*, Vol. 19, 608–611 Macmillan, London.

Steinbeis N and Koelsch S (2008). Shared neural resources between music and language indicate semantic processing of musical tension–resolution patterns. *Cerebral Cortex*, **18**, 1169–1178.

Tarski A (1956). *Logic, semantics. mathematics: papers from 1923 to 1938*, trans. J. H. Woodger. Oxford University Press, Oxford.

Thomas DA (1995). *Music and the origins of language: theories from the French Enlightenment*. Cambridge University Press, Cambridge.

Titon JT and Slobin M (1996). The music-culture as a world of music. In JT Titon, ed., *Worlds of music: an introduction to the music of the world's peoples*, 1–15. Schirmer Books, New York.

Tolbert E (2001). Music and meaning: An evolutionary story. *Psychology of Music*, **29**, 89–94.

Violi P (1999). Semiotics and cognition. In RA Wilson and FC Keil, eds, *The MIT encyclopedia of cognitive sciences*, 744–745 MIT Press, Cambridge, MA.

Wollheim R (1980). *Art and its objects*, 2nd edn. Cambridge University Press, Cambridge.

Zbikowski LM (2002). *Conceptualizing music: cognitive structure, theory and analysis*. Oxford University Press, Oxford.

CHAPTER 4

The social and personal functions of music in cross-cultural perspective

Martin Clayton

Introduction

In the grounds of an English country house, pop star Robbie Williams teases an audience of thousands before launching into his hit song 'Angels': the thousands sing along as one with his amplified voice, swaying from side to side in synchrony.[1] In the Peruvian Andes, weeks of silence are broken by a festival in which groups of men playing flutes or panpipes attempt to perform as one instrument, while fighting for the attention of the crowds in the town square of Conima (Turino 1993). In a healing ceremony held in Temiar village in Malaysia, a singing medium directs his voice into the back of a patient: he feels the spiritguide singing through him (Roseman 1991, pp. 80, 115). In a small concert hall in an industrial Bengali town, an audience member listens to a singer performing an evening raga and imagines an ideal landscape of gentle breeze, broad river and brilliant red sunset.[2]

Music's uses and contexts are so many and so various that the task of cataloguing its functions is daunting: how can we make sense of this diversity? These functions appear to range from the individual (music can affect the way we feel and the way we manage our lives)—to the social (it can facilitate the coordination of large numbers of people and help to forge a sense of group identity). I will argue that musical behaviour (within which category I include all kinds of listening as well as performance) also covers a vast middle ground in which relationships between self and other or between the individual and the collective are played out. This chapter surveys some of the extant literature on music's functions—referring to literature from ethnomusicology, anthropology, musicology, psychology, and sociology, and discussing a wide variety of musical contexts from around the world—and develops an argument emphasizing music's role in the management of relationships between self and other.

Approaches to the functions of music

Cross-cultural study of the functions of music reached a peak in the ethnomusicology of the 1950s and 1960s. The most concise and

[1] Robbie Williams, *What We Did Last Summer – Robbie Williams Live At Knebworth* (DVD, EMI, 2003). I would like to thank Laura Leante and Byron Dueck for their comments on a draft version of this chapter.
[2] This example is inspired by research Laura Leante, Tarun Kumar Nayak and I have been pursuing into audience attitudes and responses to raga performance.

comprehensive summary of this approach can be found in Merriam's *The Anthropology of Music* (1964), in which he distinguishes 'uses' from 'functions': ' "Use" . . . refers to the situation in which music is employed in human action; "function" concerns the reasons for its employment and particularly the broader purpose which it serves' (p. 210). This distinction is a productive one for my purposes here. A catalogue of the uses of music would list innumerable categories—to lull babies to sleep, to court, to accompany dancing, worship, weddings, funerals, aerobics classes, spirit possession ceremonies, and so on. A discussion of functions should ask what purpose the music serves in these events.

Merriam enumerates no fewer than ten principal functions (pp. 219–227):

1 Emotional expression

2 Aesthetic enjoyment

3 Entertainment

4 Communication

5 Symbolic representation

6 Physical response

7 Enforcing conformity to social norms

8 Validation of social institutions and religious rituals

9 Contribution to the continuity and stability of culture, and

10 Contribution to the integration of society.

His list is a useful device on which to hang a compilation of numerous case studies, but should not be taken as a thoroughly worked-out taxonomy: 'aesthetic enjoyment' and 'entertainment' receive little attention, and can be read as a concession to those who would separate Western music out as a special category; their relationship to the more communicative, expressive and social functions Merriam lists is not examined. Merriam himself admits to finding 'communication' difficult to assess, while his functions 5, 7, 8, 9 and 10 could, as Nettl points out, perhaps be combined into 'the statement that music functions as the symbolic expression of the main values, patterns, or themes of a culture' (1983, p. 15). Attali's take on this was somewhat different, figuring music as 'prophetic' of social change (1985); more

generally the issue of whether music *reflects* or *constitutes* a culture, or acts as a site for the *contestation* of cultural practice, has been a matter of debate.

Nettl also offers his own rating of the relative importance of Merriam's different functions in six very different cultures (1983, pp. 150–153). He uses the comparison to make the point that music has a range of different functions in his six chosen contexts, and that the balance between these functions varies cross-culturally. Another issue he raises is whether music has one overarching function or a multiplicity of overlapping functions, a question to which he devotes more thought. Although he has his own stab at the former—'The function of music in human society, what music ultimately does, is to control humanity's relationship to the supernatural, mediating between people and other beings, and to support the integrity of individual social groups' (p. 159)—he has at least as much sympathy for the 'many functions' argument. In this latter position we may find a parallel with Cross's more recent suggestion that music is effective precisely because of its ambiguity or 'floating intentionality', which enables it to 'serve as a medium for the maintenance of human social flexibility' (Cross 2005, p. 36). We might indeed argue that a single musical action can have multiple functions, and that it can perform these functions in different degrees for different participants. Two ethnomusicological examples will serve to reinforce this point. As Turino puts it in his study of Peruvian highland music:

Music, dance, and drama are especially apt media for *simultaneously* articulating and uniting widely divergent and even conflicting images and meanings. The achachk'umu dancers, for example, represent figures of power who are at once local, sacred, foreign, positive, human, negative, divine, animal, serious, and comical through a performance that is both lightly entertaining and deeply meaningful . . . The complex imagery within Conimeño performing arts and festivals articulates—perhaps more accurately than other semiotic practices, such as everyday speech—the complexity and tensions of history and life itself.

(p. 99, italics in original)

In her study of Prespa Albanian song, Sugarman refers this polysemy more explicitly to the topic of self and subjectivity:

> As a polysemic social practice, singing allows individuals to convey a range of messages that they might wish to make about themselves as social beings. Each rendition of each song thus serves as an embodied performance of *multiple aspects* of that performer's sense of self and of community.
>
> (1997, p. 3, italics added)

The comparative study of music's functions has received little attention in ethnomusicology since Nettl noted that 'the idea that we must find major, overriding functions for music seems to have come to a dead end' (1983, p. 150), although evolutionary, ethological and cognitive approaches have recently reopened the debate, and ethnomusicological literature continues to lend itself to cross-cultural schemes. This is demonstrated by ethologist Dissanayake in her list of 'Social functions served by ritual music', which I abbreviate here:

(D1) display of resources;

(D2) control and channelling of individual aggression;

(D3) facilitation of courtship;

(D4) establishment and maintenance of social identity through rites of passage;

(D5) relief from anxiety and psychological pain; and

(D6) promotion of group cooperation and prosperity.

The first three of these, she argues, can be traced back to the ritualization of animal behaviour, while the others, particularly (D4) and (D6) may be uniquely human (2006, pp. 43–49). These two categories, incidentally, are also the easiest to match with Merriam's list (functions 7–10): otherwise the different factors located by Dissanayake reflect a different disciplinary background more than they do any profound shift in the ethnomusicological research on which they draw.

Ethnomusicological studies have nonetheless made contributions that ought to influence discussions of music's functions. Amongst these are discussions of the role of music in inducing trance, possession and healing, and ecstatic listening (Rouget 1985; Roseman 1991; Friedson 1996; Racy 2003; Becker 2004); increasing awareness of the role of music in the negotiation of ideologies of gender and ethnicity (Koskoff 1989; Stokes 1994; Sugarman 1997; Moisala and Diamond 2000); and a greater focus on the use of music in maintaining and adapting cultural identity in migrant and diasporic cultures (Turino 1993; Shelemay 1998; Slobin 1993, 2003).

Durkheim's influence on ethnomusicology has also has been renewed in recent decades, his theories on the basis of religious thought in collective action inspiring reflections on music. As Durkheim wrote:

> [I]f collective life awakens religious thought on reaching a certain degree of intensity, it is because it brings about a state of effervescence which changes the conditions of psychic activity. Vital energies are over-excited, passions more active, sensations stronger.
>
> (1968, p. 422)

This idea of 'effervescence' or, as Stokes put it, 'the considerable surplus of affect [music-making and dance] generate in performance' (2008), offers a warning against defining music's functions too narrowly in terms of social efficacy. Durkheim suggested further that 'The life thus brought into being even enjoys so great an independence that it sometimes indulges in manifestations with no purpose or utility of any sort, for the mere pleasure of affirming itself' (p. 424). According to this view music is not limited to performing a function such as those on Merriam's and Dissanayake's lists: its power to arouse and excite becomes an end in itself. For some this might throw the whole issue of music's social 'function' into doubt, but it is important to separate motivation from effect here. The fact that participants may be motivated by the promise of a heightened state of arousal does not, for instance, preclude a musical event from influencing the way social relations are imagined: these effects may indeed be more profound if they are not brought to the surface and articulated.

Finally, while sociologists and social psychologists have discussed the deployment of musical resources in the realisation of individual identity (see below), ethnomusicologists have stressed both the variety of concepts of 'self' cross-culturally and the social constitution of the individual. Roseman draws on the notion of the 'sociocentric self', 'an interactive self that doesn't quite end at the boundaries of the individual' (1991, p. 46). In the case of the Temiar, whose sense of self seems to conform to this model, 'the beauty of interconnectedness with community and nature is offset by concern for the integrity of self', which requires a 'code of ritualized behaviour' for its management. The individual is implicated in the social and the social in the personal, then, and music—however we define it—provides tools for managing these interrelationships.

Defining musical behaviour

By 'music' we refer to an aspect of *human behaviour*; the creation of *organized sound* is an important part of that behaviour, whether conceived as an aim itself or as a means to another end; and this behaviour is *distinguishable from everyday speech communication*.[3] To start talking about the definition of music at this point may seem an odd strategy: nonetheless, the question of music's functions is inseparably tied up with that of its definition, and therefore it is important to revisit definition in this discussion. If my statement is accepted as a working definition, where do the boundaries of 'musical' behaviour lie? Is the recitation of poetry an instance of music? Auctioneering? Hunting calls? Bell-ringing? Birdsong?

In terms of the definition above the logical distinctions would be human vs non-human; organized sound vs noise; and music vs language. The first of these rules out birdsong—although Feld's analysis of the profound interconnectedness of bird calls, weeping and song in Kaluli culture in Papua New Guinea is a reminder that simple definitions are always challenged by the complexities of real life: non-human sounds are at least implicated in many conceptions of music (1990).

The distinction between music and noise lies not in the sound, but in the way human beings make use of it. A team of expert campanologists clearly make music; a bell accidentally sounding in the wind does not (even though the sound may be attractive); when Feld mixes his soundscape recordings into the 'compositions' of *The Time of Bells* (2004), he arguably nonetheless transforms non-musical sound into music.

To continue the same theme, a bell being struck to call people to a meal or meeting is probably not music—at least, not if heard merely as a signal that could have been replaced by a verbal instruction, just as a drum pattern *heard as a verbal message* is not for that listener music, but rather a form of language. Insofar as 'musical' sound can be substituted by words, it can be regarded as a form of language; conversely, almost all forms of vocalization can be said to have 'musical' qualities even when they are primarily linguistic in character. In each case, then, the boundaries of music can be seen to be less than clear cut.

For Rousseau both language and music originated together with the birth of human society (1998): the emergence of a single mode of vocal communication in the early stages of human development is echoed in more recent speculation (see the essays in Wallin *et al.* 2000), and child development studies suggest the same may be true ontogenetically. Vocal utterance is not the only source of musical behaviour, however. Just as important is a human tendency to rhythmic coordination and entrainment (Clayton *et al.* 2005). This can be observed in almost any kind of human activity—including walking and talking—but is particularly noticeable in forms of activity where rhythmic coordination makes physical work more efficient. Many examples of this can be found in the collaborative pounding of roots or grains, in which two or more people alternate strikes—a common activity in many parts of the world, and one which frequently incorporates a 'musical' dimension employing the sounds produced. In most kinds of musical behaviour, cross-culturally, these two elements (vocal utterance and coordinated action) are combined in some way—and if we regard most melodic instrumental music as a kind of extension of the voice (Cone 1974) then much if not

---

[3] This definition draws, of course, on Blacking's pithy 'humanly organized sound' (1973) and on Nettl's discussion of the issue (1983, pp. 15–25).

all music-making is founded on these two forms of behaviour.

Music as communicative medium

One thing that vocalization and coordinated action have in common is that both play a role in connecting individuals: they are both social. One of the ways in which speech and song may be distinguished, in fact, is in the kind of social relationships they presuppose. For Zuckerkandl, the fundamental distinction between speech and song is that speech involves communication from A to B, whereas song presupposes the merging of self and other into a social 'we':

> the tones—singing—essentially express not the individual but the group, more accurately, the individual in so far as he is a member of the group, still more accurately, the individual in so far as his relation to the others is not one of 'facing them' but of togetherness.
>
> (1973, p. 28)

As Miell, Macdonald and Hargreaves point out in their discussion of musical communication, transmission models have nonetheless predominated in music psychology. Their own model attempts 'to specify the main personal, musical and situational variables which give rise to a musical *performance*, [and similarly] to explain the *response* to music in a specific situation' (2005, p. 7): where the domains of performance and response meet they describe the 'spark' of communication (p. 18). In other fields authors have engaged similarly with the notion of 'transmission', whether considered to be from active performer to passive listener, or with active engagement on both sides of the equation. Nattiez's semiotic theory (1990) invokes three levels: instead of a unidirectional arrow from performer to listener, both relate to a 'neutral' middle level (located in the same place as Miell *et al.*'s 'spark' of communication). Feld plays down this neutral level and highlights the active and relational nature of meaning-making, allowing the listener greater autonomy in applying 'interpretive moves' (1994). Recent musicological writing has dealt with the ways in which music affords or contructs a 'subject position' for the listener, in effect constraining this act of interpretation while still allowing the listener some autonomy (Frith 1996, pp. 183ff; Cumming 2000; Dibben 2006). The ways in which real people deploy musical resources in managing their activities, identities and emotional states has been explored in music sociology, social psychology and ethnomusicology (Crafts *et al.* 1993; DeNora 2000; Hargreaves *et al.* 2002,), further elaborating the 'response' side of Miell *et al.*'s model. On the performance side of the equation, Swaine has argued that vocalization is a tool for an individual's emotional self-*regulation*,[4] with expression a secondary effect: the same could no doubt be said of much instrumental performance.

Transmission models clearly have explanatory power, especially when nuanced in the ways described above. No matter how good a fit they may be with some examples of musical behaviour, however, they are equally problematic in many others. I return to my example of Robbie Williams singing 'Angels': many in his audience know the song as well as the singer himself does; there is little, if any, new information to 'transmit'. In this case notions of interaction, intersubjectivity and encounter are surely more productive. If interaction is placed at the heart of our understanding of musical behaviour, the 'transmission' of information or affective states remains as a possibility but not a sine qua non.

Musical interaction can have other goals and other results, and these might include for instance—in the same or in other contexts—a loss or sublimation of ego or the promotion of fellow-feeling. Mithen argues for the evolutionary importance of collective music-making thus: 'Joint music-making served to facilitate cooperative behaviour by advertising one's willingness to cooperate, and by creating shared emotional states leading to "boundary loss"/"we-ness"/ "coupling"/"in-group bias"' (218); in ethnomusicology Keil stresses the 'participation' found in many social musical events (1994), while Blacking favoured the term 'fellow feeling', both drawing on Durkheim (see above). Friedson, in his study of spirit healing among the Tumbuka people of Malawi, argues that in this context

[4] See Cross *et al.* 2009, in press.

music can lead to a state of communion or communitas—'a relational quality of full unmediated communication, even communion, between definite and determinate entities'—(Turner and Turner 1978, p. 250, cited in Friedson 1996, p. 125), of intersubjectivity and the annihilation of interpersonal distance.

The notion of 'encounter', too, has been deployed by ethnomusicologists: for Averill, music is an index of encounter (2003), while for Bohlman (2002) encounter is the key organizing concept in his history of 'world music'. Where the notions of communion, group solidarity and fellow-feeling can lead people to write exclusively of social unity, that of 'encounter' leaves space for conflict, for exclusion and for maintaining a sense of alterity, which also have a place in musical performance. Turino's example quoted in my first paragraph shows how group identity and inter-group conflict—albeit of a relatively benign kind—can go hand in hand. Another example of this can be found in Afro-Brazilian Congado ritual, in which individual groups playing simultaneously strive to maintain a tight intra-group rhythmic coordination which indexes their group solidarity, while resisting entrainment with other co-present groups for the same reason (Lucas 2002; Clayton et al. forthcoming).

All of these approaches complicate the idea of music as a medium of communication, if the notion of information transfer or transmission is taken as defining 'communication'. Finnegan presents a different view, however, building on Birdwhistell's much broader definition of 'communication' as the 'dynamic aspect of human interconnection' (1968, p. 27, cited in Finnegan 2002, p. 32): following Finnegan's line allows us to continue to address music and language as complementary modes of human communication. Whether music indexes communication, communion or encounter makes a difference, of course: music is either a way for A to transfer information to B; how A and B affirm their collective identity; or simply what happens when A meets B. In fact it can be any and all of these things, and this flexibility is part of the point. If 'communication' encompasses information transfer, communion and encounter of all sorts, then we can freely describe music as part of man's communicatory toolbox, asking how it

relates to other related tools such as language and physical gesture.

My discussion above focused on the difficulty of defining boundaries such as those between music and language or between music and noise, but this does music something of a disservice: more positively, what defines music and what makes it a valuable analytical category cross-culturally? What would we lose if we argued the concept away? Ultimately, the phenomenon of people using organized sound in order to connect with each other—in ways which cannot be regarded simply as forms of language or information transfer, or completely explained in terms of verbal concepts—can be regarded as a single, generalizable idea, and a robust one no matter how ill-defined and porous its boundaries are.

Discussion: the functions of music

Music is not a single form of behaviour any more than it is a single kind of sonic product, but a composite of different forms of sound and behaviour. The behaviours we describe as 'musical' are founded principally on two distinct, yet interrelated phenomena: the human capacity for vocal utterance, and our innate tendency to mutually entrain our actions, especially those involving sound production and quasi-periodic behaviour. Neither of these factors can be reduced to the other, yet in practice most musical behaviour draws on both to varying degrees. Vocal utterance may also be considered as the origin of language, while music as coordinated action relates to other forms of group activity such as physical labour, marching and dance—the last of these frequently as inseparable from music as gesture is from speech. Musical behaviour generates humanly organized sound beyond the limits of normal speech communication: it is distinguishable from non-human sounds, from noise and from language, although each of these boundaries is inevitably fuzzy. In light of these discussions, I propose that musical behaviours tend to perform one or more of the following functions:

1   Regulation of an individual's emotional, cognitive or physiological state. Musical performance has physiological effects—singing

has implications for respiration and body posture, many instruments develop bimanual coordination skills, and so on. Given that physiological changes can influence emotional and cognitive states, it is not surprising that in many cultures musical behaviours are employed in the regulation of these states—involving mild effects such a temporary calming or excitation or more dramatic changes such as trance. Since music can be used in the regulation of emotional and cognitive states, again it is not surprising that performances are frequently taken as indexes of these states, and performers as expressing emotions. Music listening—whether in a live performance situation or to sound recordings—can be used in parallel ways as a tool for self-regulation (for example in managing mood), thanks to the role of mimesis and identification with the music's subjects (if the singer on the record is indicating an excited state, then to the extent that the listener sympathizes with the singer he or she may also become excited).

2   Mediation between self and other. Music has been used for centuries as a tool for interaction in instances where normal speech communication is found to be inadequate. Examples include the use of special forms of song or music to communicate with Gods, spirits or ancestors in ritual contexts. More mundane examples might include the use of song to communicate emotional states felt to be beyond the scope of everyday speech, or to communicate intimately with large numbers of people. Musicking can be both a powerful and an extremely flexible tool for modelling and mediating relations between self and other. These functions can be interpreted either as communication between the group and an external other (such as an ancestral spirit), or as a function of intragroup interaction. The 'other' could be the spirit or other entity felt to be singing through a performer (as in the case of the spirit guide described by Roseman above);[5]

it could be another being (human, divinity or spirit) addressed in song; or it could be another entity constructed and represented through song. In the last sense musicologists have drawn attention to the multiplicity of voices created through a musical performance (Cone 1974), and to the role—in opera in particular—of the play of identity and alterity (Abbate 1991; McClary 1992, pp. 29–43).

3   Symbolic representation. Although music seems in some respects to display ambiguity in specifying its referents, it can also be extremely efficient as a semiotic medium. Just as gesture can indicate the direction and velocity of a movement, or the shape, size and spatial disposition of objects with more precision than does the speech it accompanies (McNeill 1992), and facial expression can indicate emotional states more economically than can language, so too musical sound and action can specify aspects both of affect and of movement more precisely than words. Conventional musical signs as deployed in cinema or advertising, moreover, can specify their referents with unmatched precision and economy (Tagg and Clarida 2003). This play of signs has a different emphasis to that in language, perhaps because musical signs tend to be concerned with identity and alterity, bodily motion, and relationships between self and other. If world music is an index of encounter, as Bohlman argues, this music of encounter in fact relies on a degree of ambiguity between the perception of 'self' and 'other' (Leante 2004). Music can clearly evoke issues of alterity and identity without articulating an unambiguous message on the subject.

4   Coordination of action. Human beings display a tendency to entrain their physical actions, either to each other or to an external sound reference (such as a musical performance or recording): the fact that entrainment occurs even when resisted (Clayton 2007; Clayton *et al.* forthcoming) indicates the pervasiveness of the phenomenon in human interactions. The use of music to facilitate coordinated action hardly needs demonstration: what is

---

[5] Similarly, I have elsewhere quoted Indian singer Veena Sahasrabuddhe's view that her main relationship is an identification with the raga she sings rather than with her audience (Clayton 2005, p. 373).

striking is that in many instances the urge to coordinate action is accompanied by a development of 'fellow feeling', with the emergence or strengthening of bonds of shared mood or emotional state, and in some cases shared ideologies. As Dueck has argued, musical performance not only entertains existing groups, it plays a key role in constituting publics (2007); numerous examples have been described in which music is deployed in order to maintain, revive and/or to create a sense of 'tradition', or to facilitate a sense of identity amongst particular social groups—for instance in diaspora.

There may be examples in which one of these functions outweighs each of the others to such a degree that we may identify it as the principal function of music in that instance. Perhaps, as Nettl suggests, the balance between functions varies between cultures (or indeed between genres, or even between different moments in a single performance). Possibly more common, however, are instances in which several of these functions operate simultaneously. For instance, a popular song such as Robbie Williams's 'Angels' might (1) originate in an urge towards the regulation of an emotional state; and (2) be used in an act of communication between singer and audience that could not have been accomplished by speech alone. It (3) represents a particular pattern of feeling dynamically and precisely, and points to numerous referents, from the singer's public persona to English culture at the end of the twentieth century. Its singing at large public concerts (4) elicits a coordination of both action (singing along, swaying bodies in time with the music) and emotion on a massive scale; and bringing the matter full circle, individuals partaking in this communal experience can be seen to deploy their listening experience and participation as a means of emotional regulation. In this way, this and many other forms of musical behaviour simultaneously perform several distinct yet interrelated functions. This example may also remind us of Durkheim's 'effervescence': it is not simply that multiple functions are performed simultaneously, rather the very intensity of

experience provides a basis for its many effects and interpretations.

The four headings above are largely concerned with relations between the personal and the social—identity, alterity and mediation. Music is a tool for the discovery, manipulation and projection of individual identity; an individual's identity construction is however inherently social, implicating a variety of groups to which the individual feels he does or does not belong. Music is a tool for facilitating intimate interactions, and an index of such interactions: it therefore helps to bring social groups into being. Music is also a tool for constituting publics, for allowing social groups larger than the family, clan or village to create themselves and to include or exclude individuals. It can help to dissolve the boundary between self and other in a way speech generally does not; but music can also be deployed to reinforce boundaries and to distance or exclude. This is why it can be described as a flexible tool for managing relationships between self and other.

Like Merriam, I argue that underlying the bewildering variety of uses to which music is and has been put around the world we can define a finite set of global functions. My list is shorter and more synthetic than Merriam's, but this greater concision is offset by more emphasis on the idea that these functions can not be reduced to one: it is not simply that a particular writer, or the language itself, is incapable of specifying *the* function of music; rather, music frequently depends for its efficacy precisely on the indeterminacy of its 'true' or underlying function. We can say, nonetheless, that musical behaviour is deployed in the management of relations between self and other, and that it can and does perform this function at multiple levels simultaneously.

References

Abbate C (1991). *Unsung voices. Opera and musical narrative in the nineteenth century*. Princeton University Press, Princeton, NJ.

Attali J (1985). *Noise. The political economy of music*. University of Minnesota Press, Minneapolis, MN.

Averill G (2003). *Four parts, no waiting*. Oxford University Press, New York.

Becker J (2004). *Deep listeners: music, emotion and trancing*. Indiana University Press, Bloomington, IN.

Birdwhistell RL (1968). Communication. In DL Sills, ed. *International encyclopedia of the social sciences*, 17 Vols, Vol. 3, 24–29. Macmillan and Free Press, New York.

Blacking J (1973). *How musical is man?* University of Washington Press, Seattle, WA.

Bohlman PV (2002). *World music: a very short introduction.* Oxford University Press, Oxford.

Clayton M (2005). Communication in Indian raga performance. In D Miell, D Hargreaves, R MacDonald, eds. *Musical communication*, 361–381. Oxford University Press, Oxford.

Clayton M (2007). Observing entrainment in music performance: video-based observational analysis of Indian musicians' tanpura playing and beat marking. *Musicae Scientiae*, **11**(1), 27–60.

Clayton M, Lucas G and Leante L (forthcoming). Inter-group entrainment in Afro-Brazilian Congado ritual.

Clayton M, Sager R and Will U (2005). In time with the music: the concept of entrainment and its significance for ethnomusicology. *European Meetings in Ethnomusicology*, **11** (ESEM Counterpoint 1), 3–75.

Cone E (1974). *The composer's voice.* University of California Press, Berkeley, CA.

Crafts SD, Cavicchi D, Keil C and the Music in Daily Life Project (1993). *My music.* Wesleyan University Press, Hanover, NH and London.

Cross I (2005). Music and meaning, ambiguity and evolution. In D Miell, D Hargreaves, R MacDonald, eds *Musical communication*, 27–43 Oxford University Press, Oxford.

Cross I, Himberg T, Swaine J and Bispham J (2009, in press). Evolution and musical rhythm. *Evolutionary Psychology.*

Cumming N (2000). *The sonic self. Musical subjectivity and signification.* University of Indiana Press, Bloomington, IN.

DeNora T (2000). *Music in everyday life.* Cambridge University Press, Cambridge.

Dibben N (2006). Subjectivity and the construction of emotion in the music of Björk. *Music Analysis*, **25**, 171–197.

Dissanayake E (2006). Ritual and ritualization: musical means of conveying and shaping emotion in humans and other animals. In S Brown, U Volgsten, eds, *Music and manipulation. On the social uses and social control of music*, 31–56. Berghahn, New York and Oxford.

Dueck B (2007). Public and intimate sociability in First Nations and Metis fiddling. *Ethnomusicology*, **51**(1), 30–63.

Durkheim E (1968) [1915] *The elementary forms of the religious life.* George Allen and Unwin, London.

Feld S (1990) [1982]. *Sound and sentiment: birds, weeping, poetics and song in Kaluli expression*, revised edn. University of Pennsylvania Press, Philadelphia, PA.

Feld S (1994) [1984]. Communication, music and speech about music. In C Keil and S Feld eds, *Music grooves*, 77–95. University of Chicago Press, Chicago, IL.

Feld S (2004). *The time of bells.* Voxlox 104 (audio CD).

Finnegan R (2002). *Communicating. The multiple modes of human interconnection.* Routledge, London and New York

Friedson SM (1996). *Dancing prophets. Musical experience in Tumbuka healing.* University of Chicago Press, Chicago, IL.

Frith S (1996). *Performing rites: on the value of popular music.* Oxford University Press, Oxford.

Hargreaves D, Miell D and Macdonald R (2002). What are musical identities, and why are they important? In R Macdonald, D Hargreaves and D Miell, eds, *Musical identities*, pp 1–20. Oxford University Press, Oxford.

Keil C (1994) [1987]. Participatory discrepancies and the power of music. In C Keil and S Feld eds, *Music Grooves*, 96–108. University of Chicago Press, Chicago, IL.

Koskoff E (ed) (1989). *Women and music in cross-cultural perspective.* University of Illinois Press, Bloomington, IN.

Leante L (2004). Shaping diasporic sounds: identity as meaning in bhangra. *The World of Music*, **46**, 109–122.

Lucas G (2002). Musical rituals of Afro-Brazilian religious groups within the ceremonies of Congado. *Yearbook for Traditional Music*, **34**, 115–127.

McClary S (1992). *Georges Bizet, Carmen.* Cambridge University Press, Cambridge.

McNeill D (1992). *Hand and mind. What gestures reveal about thought.* University of Chicago Press, Chicago, IL.

Merriam A (1964). *The anthropology of music.* Northwestern University Press, Evanston, IL.

Miell D, Hargreaves D and MacDonald R (eds) (2005). *Musical communication.* Oxford University Press, Oxford.

Mithen S (2005). *The singing Neanderthals. The origins of music, language, mind and body.* Weidenfeld and Nicholson, London.

Moisala P and Diamond B (eds) (2000). *Music and gender.* University of Illinois Press, Bloomington, IN.

Nattiez J-J (1990). *Music and discourse. Toward a semiology of music*, trans. C Abbate. Princeton University Press, Princeton, NJ.

Nettl B (1983). *The study of ethnomusicology: twenty-nine issues and concepts.* University of Illinois Press, Bloomington, IN.

Racy AJ (2003). *Making music in the Arab world. The culture and artistry of Tarab.* Cambridge University Press, Cambridge.

Roseman M (1991). *Healing sounds from the Malaysian rainforest. Temiar music and medicine.* University of California Press, Berkeley and Los Angeles, CA.

Rouget G (1985). *Music and trance: a theory of the relations between music and possession.* University of Chicago Press, Chicago, IL.

Rousseau J-J (1998). *Essay on the origin of languages and writings related to music*, trans. J.T. Scott. University Press of New England, Hanover, NH.

Shelemay KK (1998). *Let jasmine rain down: song and remembrance among Syrian Jews.* University of Chicago Press, Chicago, IL.

Slobin M (1993). *Subcultural sounds: micromusics of the West.* Wesleyan University Press, Hanover, NH.

Slobin M (2003). The destiny of 'diaspora' in ethnomusicology. In M Clayton, T Herbert, R Middleton, eds, *The cultural study of music: a critical introduction*, 284–296. Routledge, New York and London.

Stokes M (1994). *Ethnicity, identity and music: the musical construction of place*. Berg, Oxford.

Stokes M (2008) Contemporary theoretical issues: communities and their musics. In C Pegg *et al. Ethnomusicology* §IV, **2**. *Grove Music Online,* http://www.oxfordmusiconline.com/Subscriber/article/grove/music/52178pg.

Sugarman JC (1997). *Engendering song: singing and subjectivity at Prespa Albanian weddings*. Chicago University Press, Chicago, IL.

Tagg P and B Clarida (2003). *Ten little title tunes*. The Mass Media Music Scholar's Press, New York and Montreal.

Turino T (1993). *Moving away from silence. Music of the Peruvian Altiplano and the experience of urban migration*. University of Chicago Press, Chicago, IL.

Turner VW and E Turner (1978). *Image and pilgrimage in Christian culture*. Columbia University Press, New York.

Wallin NL, Merker B and Brown S (eds) (2000). *The origins of music*. MIT Press, Cambridge, MA.

Zuckerkandl V (1973). *Man the musician. Sound and Symbol: Vol. 2*, Trans. Norbert Guterman. Bollingen Series 44/2. Princeton University Press, Princeton, NJ.

PART 2
Music perception

Edited by Ian Cross

CHAPTER 5

The perception of pitch

Thomas Stainsby and Ian Cross

Basic psychophysics of pitch perception

Pitch and frequency

While a musician may find a definition of pitch redundant, psychoacoustics—the scientific investigation of our perception of sound—nonetheless demands one. Although there is an intuitive understanding that pitch is related to frequency, it is important to understand that the two are not directly equatable. Pitch is a percept, measurable only by psychophysical investigation, and frequency is a physical quantity, which describes the periodic properties of a signal. Sounds that contain clearly measurable frequency content may not produce a clear or unambiguous sense of pitch, and the perceived pitch may also depend on other physical quantities such as intensity. The American National Standards Institute offers the following definition:

> Pitch [is] that attribute of auditory sensation in terms of which sounds may be ordered on a scale extending from low to high. Pitch depends primarily on the frequency content of the sound stimulus, but it also depends on the sound pressure and the waveform of the stimulus.
>
> ANSI (1994)

However, we require a more restricted definition for the present review. Frequencies below around 30 Hz and above around 5 kHz can lose their identities as *musical* pitches (Attneave and Olson 1971), while still sounding 'low' or 'high', respectively. Additionally, there is something more global about pitch than individual frequencies. Most sounds we hear are mixtures of components with many different simultaneous frequencies, yet our auditory system generally combines these into a single percept of one overall pitch. The mechanisms that group the individual frequency components into an overall pitch are also at work in processing combinations of notes arising from different instruments. Does the combined percept have a single overall sense of pitch, or perhaps a 'timbre' for that combination and instrumental voicing, or alternatively, is there a clear hierarchy with a given 'harmony' consisting of distinct individual pitches?

One solution is to offer definitions of pitch that require the ability to convey a musical melody (e.g. Attneave and Olson 1971; Burns and Viemeister 1976). A combination of this requirement and the ANSI definition meets an intuitive and informal definition that may satisfy most musicians, that 'pitch is the stuff that notes are made of'.

In this chapter's discussion of pitch, we begin with a brief introduction to the function of the auditory system. This considers what limitations there are on our ability to extract frequency information from the sounds reaching our ears, and provides an orientation for some of the mechanisms described in the later sections. A review is then offered of relevant psychoacoustic research—how do we construct a sense of pitch from the physical acoustic input? This leads to a consideration of higher auditory processing functions that include the mechanisms we use to interpret the complicated mixture of sounds around us and the relationships between pitch as it applies to music and how it is manifested in speech and language.

The only sound that has just one frequency component is termed a pure tone or sine tone,

Q:
What is
a pure
tone?

A: ↗

having a quality like that of a tuning fork. Its frequency spectrum has energy at only a single frequency, and its temporal wave form has the shape of a sine function. Although single pure tones are rare in nature, the concept is useful when we consider that real-world complex sounds and mixtures of sounds are made up of the sum of multiple pure tones such as these, termed *frequency components* or *partials*. We can then understand the task of the auditory system as being that of detecting and decoding such mixtures of frequency components, and interpreting this information to make sense of the sound world or *auditory scene* around us (Bregman 1990).

Before describing the mechanics of frequency coding, which occurs primarily in the inner ear, it is necessary to consider briefly the physiology of the auditory system. The acoustic wave from the outside world is captured and filtered by the outer ear, consisting of the pinna (external ear) and the ear canal. This stage of acoustic processing helps amplify the sound and encode information about the direction of sound sources. Subsequently, the sound is transmitted through the middle ear to the inner ear, consisting of the labyrinth (not considered here) and the cochlea, a small fluid-filled coil containing the sensory mechanisms that transform (transduce) mechanical energy into the electrical signals that are processed in the brain. The middle ear, which consists of the eardrum and the auditory ossicles (the three smallest bones in the body), is primarily concerned with the task of matching the impedance of the external air (its resistance to the passage of sound energy) to that of the fluid inside the cochlea. This maximizes the amount of energy transmitted—around 95 per cent would be reflected otherwise. It is not until the sound reaches the inner ear that frequency analysis and coding takes place. The cochlea in the inner ear is situated in the temporal bone of the skull, and is divided along its length (approximately 35 mm) by the basilar membrane (BM). The actual sensory transducers, the hair cells, are aligned along this membrane, in one row of inner hair cells (IHCs)—about 3500 in total—and three or four rows of outer hair cells (OHCs)—about 12 000 in total. The incoming sound sets up a travelling wave of vibration along the basilar membrane (von Békésy 1947).

primitive
processing

The IHCs in the vicinity of points of significant BM displacement are stimulated by the movement of their stereocilia (tiny hair-like projections grouped in bundles at the top of each hair cell) in the cochlear fluid, which in turn send electrical signals along the auditory nerve fibres that connect with, or *synapse* onto, each IHC. The OHCs fulfil a somewhat different function, which is described below.

The primary method of frequency coding is offered by the structure of the basilar membrane, which varies in width, thickness and stiffness along its length. As a result, each point of the membrane has a unique resonant frequency, i.e. the frequency at which it vibrates most easily. The base of the cochlea (closest to the middle ear) responds maximally to high frequencies (up to around 20 kHz), while the opposite, apical, end responds maximally to low frequencies (down to around 20 Hz). The frequency for which a given place on the basilar membrane shows a maximum response is termed its *characteristic frequency*. This leads us to understanding the first method of coding frequency, termed *place coding* or *tonotopic coding*. For each location on the BM showing maximum response to a characteristic frequency, there are a number of hair cells in the vicinity that will be maximally stimulated. There are roughly 30 000 auditory neurons that synapse onto the 3500 or so IHCs. With tonotopic coding, frequency can be represented by which neurons have been stimulated (i.e. they trace back to a specific localized region of the basilar membrane). Note that because there is a small region of maximum displacement rather than a point source, neural activity is not signalled in a single auditory neuron's response, but in the distribution of the responses of a population of probably hundreds or over a thousand neurons, a pattern of activity that is termed the *neural excitation pattern*. It should be noted that this does not imply that only one frequency will excite a discrete population of neurons; the mapping between frequencies and neurones is many-to-many, with a group of neurons responding to a limited range or band of frequencies, which will vary with signal intensity.

We can see that there is thus a limit to the specificity of frequency information derived from place coding; BM output in response to a single input frequency appears more like the output of a band-pass filter than the output of a sharply tuned system. This is enhanced by a second, active, tuning process, which is believed to be mediated by the OHCs in the vicinity of the peak of the travelling wave (Rhode 1971; Ruggero 1992; Robles and Ruggero 2001). These cells actively move and change shape in response to stimulation, thus increasing BM displacement, in turn causing greater stimulation of the IHCs. Because the action of the OHCs is quite localized, this spatially restricted amplification of travelling-wave displacement results in a sharpening of the excitation pattern around the characteristic frequency, and hence an improvement in frequency resolution.

Louder sounds generate a larger travelling wave, and hence a greater spread of excitation, than a quiet sound. Higher stimulus levels thus result in decreased frequency resolution, and increase the extent to which loud components 'mask' the quieter ones. This explains the loss of perceptible detail in sound mixtures at loud levels. The extent to which sounds mask each other in this way can be used to elucidate and quantify the concept of frequency selectivity (Fletcher 1940; Patterson 1976; Glasberg and Moore 1990), which can be defined as the ability to hear out the sinusoidal partials or components of a complex sound (Moore 2003). Sounds are said to fall within the same band-pass auditory filter when they are able to mask each other to a sufficient extent. Figure 5.1 shows how auditory filter bandwidth varies with centre frequency

(Glasberg and Moore 1990; Moore 2003). For frequency components to be 'heard out' and processed independently from each other, they need to fall within the passbands of different auditory filters. Once the centre frequency of one auditory filter has been defined, the next adjacent auditory filter needs be a certain distance along the basilar membrane to achieve the requisite independence of frequency selectivity. This is the logic behind the equivalent rectangular bandwidth (ERB) frequency scale (Glasberg and Moore 1990), which can be used to measure frequency in the perceptually relevant scale of auditory-filter bandwidth. Measured in this way, human hearing can be said to cover a range of a little fewer than 40 ERBs. Multiple frequencies falling within the same auditory filter cannot be resolved or processed independently, and only their combined effect is available to the auditory system.

The tonotopic organization and place frequency coding established in the cochlea are maintained up through higher centres in the auditory neural pathways. Progressively less is known about the nature of auditory processing and the function of particular structures as the auditory pathway ascends. A comprehensive review of the neurophysiology of pitch is provided in the chapter by Winter in Plack et al. (2005).

The second type of frequency coding, temporal coding, is achieved by an analysis of the behaviour of neural firings over time. That is, once the initial place coding of frequency has been achieved from the overall number of firings in a given population of neurons, further frequency information can be extracted from analysis of the period between successive spikes (more-or-less simultaneous bursts of energy produced by a group of neurones). However, such temporal information is only available for the coding of frequencies below approximately 5 kHz. Two factors contribute to this limitation on the frequencies that can be encoded by neural temporal coding. The first is the refractory period of an individual neuron. Once it has fired, a neuron is unable to fire again until it is metabolically 'recharged', which limits its firing to a maximum rate of 1 kHz. However, because stimulus frequency is being coded by populations of fibres, timing information averaged

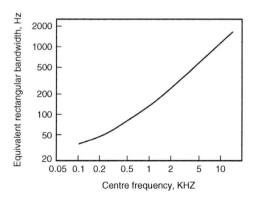

Fig. 5.1 Average auditory-filter width and the ERB scale (after Glasberg and Moore 1990). The solid line plots the calculated width of the auditory filter for a given centre frequency.

across multiple neurons can still code frequencies up to 5 kHz. At this point the second limiting factor is reached, that of the breakdown of phase locking (Rose *et al.* 1967; Palmer and Russell 1986). Phase locking is required for the information obtained from the timing of neural spikes to have any meaningful relationship to the stimulus frequency. The term refers to the ability of a neurone to fire at a predictable time point—phase—in the stimulus waveform cycle—e.g. at the maximum downward displacement of the basilar membrane's vibration. Once a neuron can no longer fire at a consistent phase of the stimulus, its response is random and hence noisy. Above 5 kHz, the stimulation period simply becomes too short for any neurons to fire at a predictable phase.

We can thus see that temporal coding should provide robust and reliable frequency information for lower frequencies. By contrast, all coding of frequencies above 5 kHz can only be achieved by place coding. Both types of coding are available over a good portion of the audible frequency range, meaning that the mechanisms of pitch perception can employ both types of frequency information in the majority of instances.

It is relatively straightforward to understand how the auditory system can derive pitch from pure tones. For such stimuli, the pitch is unambiguously related to the frequency. Place and temporal cues are fully congruent for these tones, which is not always the case for more complex stimuli. For these reasons, the pitch of any type of stimulus is often quantified by using the frequency of a pure tone that is subjectively matched to the complex tone as having the same pitch.

The relative contribution of place and temporal frequency coding to the perception of pitch for pure tones has been investigated by examining frequency discrimination data from different task types. This shows that place resolution is more or less constant across the usable frequency range, while for lower frequencies, temporal coding offers superior performance to that achievable from place coding alone (Sek and Moore 1995), yielding frequency discrimination thresholds of *c.* 3–4 Hz at 1 kHz. This observation is supported by the results of Attneave and Olson (1971), who found that while listeners could still detect changes in frequency above 5 kHz, the sense of pitch deteriorated to the point where melodies ceased to be recognizable. Musical practice is consistent with this in that C8, the highest note on a piano and the highest note of an orchestral instrument (the piccolo), has a fundamental frequency of 4176 Hz. Taken together, these facts suggest that temporal-frequency information is necessary for a sense of musical pitch.

The pitch of pure tones is not exclusively determined by frequency however. While an early study by Stevens (1935) found quite large interactions of pitch and level, subsequent studies (e.g. Terhardt 1974; Verschuure and van Meeteren 1975) have found similar but smaller effects. In summary, the pitch of pure tones above around 4000 Hz rises with an increase in level, while it falls with an increase in level for frequencies below about 2000 Hz. The magnitude of the effect in these ranges can be up to 5 per cent, but is less than 1 per cent for intermediate frequencies, and the magnitude and pattern of results is highly variable between individuals. The pitch of pure tones is also affected by duration. Moore (1973) showed that performance on frequency discrimination gets much better at all frequencies as tone duration increases. There is a sharp deterioration in performance for all durations at higher frequencies, where only place-frequency information is available.

Pitch of complex tones

The pitch of pure tones is a special case, in that it is not of primary importance to consider information across multiple auditory filters or channels. Sufficient temporal and place information can be obtained by attending primarily to only the single filter centred on the signal frequency (though at high levels there is increased spread of excitation to adjacent channels). However, the vast majority of sounds are complex, consisting of multiple frequency components across a number of channels, and it is in such circumstances that one of the most interesting aspects of pitch perception is manifested—the ability to derive an overall unitary percept from a mixture of frequency information. This skill is essential for the appreciation of music, given that a typical instrument will produce dozens of partials, yet we can assign a single pitch to this, and hence experience melody and harmony. In fact, an argument for the evolution of pitch perception is that it aids the segregation and identification of sound sources, such as the human voice, by helping to group related partials together, and in so doing assists us in interpreting the surrounding auditory scene (see chapter by Darwin, in Plack *et al.* 2005). While many complex sounds have harmonic spectra, ie. their partials have frequencies that are integer multiples of a common fundamental frequency, pitch can also be derived from stimuli that have inharmonic components (Schouten *et al.* 1962) or that contain only broadband noise in their spectra (Cramer and Huggins 1958; Burns and Viemeister 1976). There are also examples of pitches that arise from the input of different stimuli to each ear (Cramer and Huggins 1958; Houtsma 1972; Klein and Hartmann 1981).

A variety of models have been put forward over the years to explain how the auditory system derives a sense of pitch from such a range of stimuli. Related to the duality of place and temporal coding of frequency, pitch perception models tend to be divided into the *pattern matching* and *temporal* families (for overviews of these models see Houtsma 1995, see also the chapter by de Cheveigné in Plack *et al.* 2005). These models principally differ in the relative importance of frequency components that are resolved or unresolved by the auditory system. As described earlier, a component is said to be resolved if its place and temporal frequency information can be interpreted independently of any other components. Figure 5.2 (after Plack and Oxenham 2005) offers an illustration of the relationship between stimulus frequency spectrum, peripheral filtering, and the resultant excitation pattern and BM vibration. A range of studies (Plomp 1964; Plomp and Mimpen 1968; Moore and Ohgushi 1993) suggest that subjects are able to 'hear out' only the first five to eight components of a harmonic complex tone; these studies offer psychoacoustic evidence that beyond these harmonic numbers, the components remain unresolved by the auditory periphery.

The most common sounds we hear in music, such as sustained notes on strings, woodwinds,

brass, most keyboard instruments, and sung vowels, have harmonic spectra similar to the one shown in Figure 5.2 (although of course the relative amplitudes of the spectral components differ between instruments). Given that the pitch of such sounds usually corresponds to the fundamental frequency, it might be tempting to assume that the pitch is simply determined by this lowest frequency component. However, the phenomenon of the 'missing fundamental, robustly demonstrated by Schouten (1938), indicates that this is not the case. When higher harmonic components are present but not the fundamental, the pitch may remain the same as if the fundamental were physically present. In the example shown in Figure 5.2, imagine if the lowest component present were at 200 Hz, and all the other multiples of 100 Hz, i.e. 300 Hz, 400 Hz, 500 Hz, etc., remained. The pitch heard would still be 100 Hz, not 200 Hz. Schouten termed the pitch derived from the higher (non-fundamental) components the *residue pitch*, and it has also been called *periodicity pitch, virtual pitch*, or *low pitch* in the literature. Somehow, the global pattern of frequencies physically present is interpreted to create a pitch at a frequency that may not be physically present, and this effect is not a consequence of the existence of combination tones (Licklider 1956). Both pattern-matching and temporal models have been proposed as underlying the sensation of a unitary pitch experienced in respect of a complex tone.

The preceding discussion has considered the case in which a single sense of pitch is derived from simple or complex stimuli. However, much musical practice relies on the ability of the listener to perceive the relationship between simultaneous pitches. A fundamental aspect of this is the perception of consonance and dissonance. While musically trained listeners may have a specific concept of which intervals are more consonant than others, this assessment is heavily influenced by instruction in a particular musical culture. Of particular interest is the fact that even naive listeners have an intuitive sense of consonance as being the degree to which simultaneous notes sound pleasant, harmonious, or euphonious. This unlearned sense of consonance has been termed 'tonal consonance' by Plomp and Levelt (1965). They found that when simultaneously presented pure tones had very similar frequencies, a high degree of consonance was observed. However, dissonance increased rapidly as frequency difference was increased, reaching a maximum at around 25 per cent of the auditory-filter bandwidth. Further increases in frequency resulted in a progressive increase in consonance until a maximum was reached and maintained once the critical bandwidth was exceeded. Thus, sensory dissonance is related to the amount of interference between two tones within the same auditory filter. This same mechanism can account for the degree of consonance perceived when complex tones are

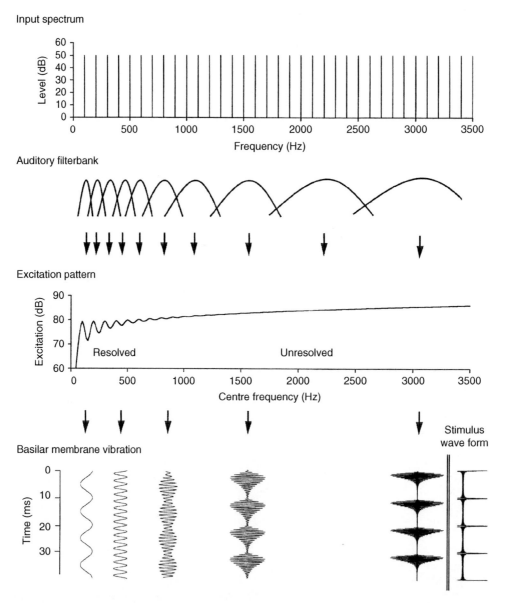

Fig. 5.2 A schematic illustration of the relationship between a harmonic complex stimulus, its analysis by the auditory filterbank, and the resulting excitation pattern and basilar membrane vibration (from Plack 2005).

presented simultaneously. Unlike the results seen with pure tones however, complex tones do not plateau at a level of maximum consonance once the critical bandwidth is exceeded. Rather, there are peaks in consonance when the fundamental frequencies possess simple integer ratios, e.g. 2:1 (octave), 2:3 (fifth), 3:4 (fourth), etc., as a consequence of the interactions between the individual partials of each tone complex. Dissonance is dependent on the roughness or interference of partials in various auditory filters, even if these are considerably above the filter centred on the fundamental frequency.

Higher-order processing and organization of pitch

When we experience pitch in music we do not experience single pitches, or arbitrary collections of individual pitches; we experience pitch *patterns*. We can conceptualize such pitch patterns in terms of the vertical dimension producing harmony, while the horizontal dimension produces melody. As Attneave and Olson (1971) put it, musical pitch is a morphophoric—pattern-bearing—medium. In general, the processes outlined above constrain but do not determine the types of patterns that we experience in musical pitch. In order to understand the experience of musical pitch we must take into account processes that operate on, and are in part driven by, the acoustic musical signal, *and* also processes that are mediated by central (largely cortical) mechanisms that have arisen through processes of development and learning. In other words, the perception of musical pitch relies on both bottom-up processes (driven by the musical signal) and top-down processes (arising from our evolutionary history and from individual, culturally situated, learning). The following section will focus on these top-down processes.

Grouping principles, stream formation and auditory scene analysis

The facility to extract musical patterns from the rich mixture of auditory information that reaches our ears has been termed *auditory scene analysis*

by Albert Bregman (Bregman 1990). Although Bregman developed much of his work in terms of the processing of all kinds of auditory stimuli (as evolutionary processes would have shaped us for optimally analysing all events around us), we can take music as a special case in which musical notes are the auditory events of interest. There are two ways in which auditory scene analysis, or auditory grouping, can function. In the case of a solo unaccompanied melody, there is the grouping process whereby we link the successive isolated notes to form one percept of contour. The same processes also allow us to disentangle the mixture of overlapping elements that occurs when multiple sounds are present. This ability to assign some elements to one inferred perceptual auditory source or 'stream', and others to a different stream, has been termed *auditory streaming*. Applied to the vertical dimension, we describe the grouping and parsing of elements that overlap in time as *simultaneous streaming*. It is this process that leads to the perception of harmony, when some frequency components are parsed into different simultaneous notes. The grouping and parsing of temporally non-overlapping notes, termed *sequential streaming*, is what gives rise to a perception of counterpoint. An extensive consideration of how these processes can be shown to generate the commonly accepted rules of harmony and voice-leading in Western music is provided by Huron (2001).

The principle of proximity states that notes are likely to be integrated into the same stream when they are close together in frequency or time. Most melodic writing conforms to a preference for movement by step or small intervals, an adherence to register, and minimal use of rests within a phrase. If other voices or parts are present, the same principles help prevent the notes of one voice being confused with those of others. Where larger melodic leaps do occur, it is very rare for the voice with the large leap to cross over the pitch of an adjacent voice. In the case of unaccompanied melodies, similar principles ensure the internal coherence of a single stream. The breakdown of such coherence, termed *stream segregation*, has been exploited by composers in the use of the technique of *compound melody* or *pseudo-polyphony*, whereby a single instrumental part can produce the percept of multiple simultaneous streams (a technique popular in much Baroque music: see the works for solo violin or cello by JS Bach). Such examples demonstrate that proximity in the frequency domain is not an independent determinant of streaming, however, as there is a strong interaction with the rate of note presentation. The illusion of multiple interleaved melodies breaks down when the tempo is slowed down sufficiently. Both Miller and Heise (1950) and van Noorden (1975) found that below a minimum pitch proximity of around one semitone, tone sequences were always perceived as integrated, independent of the rate of presentation up to a note inter-onset time of around 500 ms, beyond which larger pitch differences could lead to an integrated percept at these slower rates. The critical pitch difference was termed the *trill threshold* or the *fission boundary* in the two studies, respectively. Van Noorden also identified the *temporal coherence boundary*, which is the pitch difference above which stream segregation is always heard. Between the fission boundary and the temporal coherence boundary, there is a range of ambiguity where tone sequences can be perceived as either integrated or segregated, depending on context and the individual listener.

Two more principles derived from the Gestalt tradition that are relevant to stream formation in the auditory context are those of *common fate* and *good continuation*. These apply both at the level of discrete notes and of spectral components from sounds that may or not be overlapping in time. The principal of common fate groups events that have synchronous features. The principle of good continuation (Bregman and Dannenbring 1973) would lead listeners to group notes together that form a coherent line, and a logical melody. This would work in conjunction with the preference for linear, stepwise or small-interval motion described above.

A further strong streaming or grouping principle in the auditory domain is that of harmonicity. This is the tendency to group together frequency components that all consist of integer multiples of the same fundamental frequency (Moore *et al.* 1985). As many of the sound sources we commonly encounter are harmonic, e.g. sounds deriving from vibrating strings and air columns, it is a very useful cue for grouping components from the same source. The influence

of this phenomenon on contrapuntal writing and harmonic voice leading can be seen in the generally accepted practice of avoiding 'parallel fifths and octaves' between voices—such perfect consonances would be instances where all the resolved spectral components of both voices would be harmonically related, and hence an excessive degree or spectral fusion or grouping would result, leading to a loss of independence of the musical voices.

The broad principle of grouping by similarity does not rely on relatedness by pitch; it could work against a particular tendency of a pitch relationship to integrate or segregate a tone sequence. Examples of non-pitch similarity that influence streaming include timbre and temporal fine structure (Roberts *et al.* 2002; Stainsby *et al.* 2004a), level (Stainsby *et al.* 2004b), temporal envelope and apparent spatial location (Hartmann and Johnson 1991). In fact, Moore and Gockel (2002) argue that grouping by similarity can be so strong, that any perceptually salient acoustic attribute can induce streaming. Thus, the final effect of whether integration or segregation is perceived will be the result of the interaction of a number of, possibly competing, factors and the particular sensitivities of the individual listener.

Pitch in music, music-specific processes and constraints

It is evident that pitch is a continuous percept, which can take any value over a range of more than eight octaves. However, this is not the way musical traditions across many cultures use pitch. Instead, pitch is broken up into discrete piece-wise constant steps or quanta—the degrees of a scale. In Western music, the most common scales are the diatonic modes and the chromatic scale, while other musical cultures have their own individual scale systems, such as the *ragas* of North Indian music, *slendro* and *pelog* scales of Balinese gamelan music, or the *dastgah* of Persian music (Sadie 2001). The fact that musical traditions have adopted scales with discrete steps despite the fact that the most primary of all instruments, the human voice, is not bound by them, suggests that there is a perceptual requirement for such stepwise structuring of pitch. We can perceive frequency differences that are much smaller than the semitone by which we are bound in Western tonal music (Sek and Moore 1995). Many Arabic scales routinely use quarter-tone steps, yet this does not mean music is composed that uses a 24-step equal-interval scale (Burns 1999). Instead, it uses unequal step sizes, some smaller than the semitone and others larger, so that there are still approximately seven steps to the octave (similar to the Western seven-step diatonic modes). A plausible justification for this is the limited information-handling capacity of the human listener. Across a variety of sensory modes, continua are routinely divided into approximately seven categories (Miller 1956). Humans are intuitively good at having a meaningful 'feel' and reference for approximately seven degrees of a quantity, but errors increase markedly beyond this. The use of musical scales with discrete steps can thus be seen as a method of ensuring the robustness of melodies within a musical tradition.

Linked to the use of discrete steps for a sensory continuum is the phenomenon of *categorical perception*. This refers to the ability to assign the same label to a whole group of broadly similar yet still different stimuli, and the related step-like jump in assignment to the next available label as soon as a stimulus crosses a category boundary. The phenomenon was first described in the perception of speech sounds (Liberman *et al.* 1967), but has since also been demonstrated for non-speech sounds (Locke and Kellar 1973; Miller *et al.* 1976) and for musical pitches (Burns and Ward 1978). A musical example is the tendency to group a range of disparate tunings, some flat and some sharp, to the same note, such as a 'c', while with just a little increase in pitch, a note abruptly changes from being a 'sharp c natural' to being a 'flat c sharp'.

It can readily be seen why a categorical mode of perception is necessary in speech communication, to accommodate the whole range of acoustically diverse sounds that come from different speakers of differing age, sex, and accent. It is plausible that similar forces have shaped the selection of the dominant scales in general musical practice. For example, although Harry Partch (Sadie 2001) developed a whole range of instruments with 43-tone temperament, and Schoenberg advocated the equality of 12 equally

tempered semitones, diatonic melodies still dominate the common musical experience in Western performance practice. Admittedly however, there is also a mass of cultural and sociological factors that weigh on any purely perceptually driven evolution of musical fitness and acceptability in these cases.

If it is almost universal for music to be quantized into scale steps, the question arises as to what selects the particular intervals used. Nearly all the examples cited so far use intervals of non-equal size, so it is clear that we do not simply divide the octave neatly into seven equally tempered steps, as may at first appear a mathematically neat solution. The most plausible explanations are that melodic step sizes are selected for intervals that would work well in harmony with other voices, and that unequal step sizes enable listeners clearly to identify and differentiate between serial pattern structures. Harmonic intervals are preferred that maximize consonance, as discussed earlier (Plomp and Levelt 1965), and thus notes that would form such consonant intervals are preferred as scale degrees (Houtsma 1995). In the melodic domain, Trehub *et al.* (1999) showed that infants and adults showed a performance advantage in detecting mistunings in unequal-step scale melodies compared to those presented in equal-step scales.

It is interesting to note how pitch is generally used quite differently in music and language. Speech exhibits a variable pitch contour, with fundamental frequencies ranging over an octave (Fitzsimons *et al.* 2001). Variation in fundamental frequency shapes a phrase and gives clear emphasis to certain words. Meaning can be altered by placement of pitch accent, and whether an utterance is a statement or a question can be cued by the presence or absence of a rising pitch contour at the end of a sentence. This pragmatic function is probably the limit of pitch's contribution to many languages, particularly most European ones (Crystal 1969). However, pitch has explicit lexical significance in tonal languages, such as those found in South East Asia. As an example, Mandarin uses four tones, which when placed on the same combination of consonants and vowels, create words with totally different meanings. This is clearly a specific, categorical and semantic use of pitch, which goes beyond an auxiliary role of emphasis or clarification. Note however that the four tones of Mandarin are not equatable with four tones of a musical scale. They are categorized as much by contour as by absolute pitch height. The fact that these tones are not arranged in scale steps highlights an important difference between the uses of pitch in music and language. There is still something approximate about pitch in language—there are very broad perceptual categories for pitch and there would need to be a gross difference in pitch before a tone boundary in a tonal language were crossed. Similarly, for the role of intonation and emphasis in European languages, the actual deviation in fundamental frequency contour could be scaled significantly without a change in meaning; it is the shape of the contour that is most significant. Both of these factors clearly do not apply to music in the same way. Sensitivity to tuning is quite precise in music, as only a small deviation from a target pitch is required for a musical performance to be judged as being out of tune. Additionally, melodies cease to be identifiable when the interval range is significantly expanded or compressed (Moore and Rosen 1979). In summary, the use of pitch in music differs from that in speech by articulating complex, set patterns of contour, encoded by the robust categories of scale steps.

Summary and conclusion

This chapter began with description of the basic physiology and psychophysics that enable pitch to be derived from the acoustic stimulus reaching our ears. The fundamental means of coding frequency in the neural pathways of the auditory system are the dual systems of place coding and temporal coding. While a fairly straightforward relationship can be seen between the physical quantity of frequency and the perceptual quantity of pitch in the case of pure tones, the case is more complicated and can remain ambiguous in the case of complex tones. The auditory system can analyse a range of information from many frequency components to arrive at a unitary percept of overall pitch. The argument was presented that this is an essential skill as part of the process of auditory scene analysis, whereby perceptual representations of distinct

sound sources in our environment, so-called auditory streams, can be produced. The processes of auditory scene analysis and auditory streaming were further elucidated by a consideration of other grouping mechanisms such as common onset times, common fate, proximity and similarity. While on one level these processes group the spectral components of individual notes together, on a higher level they also group successive notes together to form melodies and counterpoint.

Finally, a consideration was presented of the different ways pitch is used in music and language. Music relies on the use of discrete, ordered sets of pitches called musical scales. The use of a finite set of discrete steps was argued to facilitate musical memory, melodic recognizability and robustness for transmission. By contrast, pitch in language can be seen to function in two main ways. In non-tonal languages, pitch contour is of primary importance, giving emphasis and inflexion, and distinguishing between a statement and a question. In tonal languages, tones differentiate lexical meaning, and as such absolute frequency values are more fundamental than in non-tonal languages. However, the use of tones in the former still differs significantly from that in music, as the categorical boundaries are significantly broader than in musical scales, and there is not the same use of specifically defined, intervallic steps along a musical scale.

References

ANSI (1994). *ANSI S1.1–1994. American National Standard Acoustical Terminology*. American National Standards Institute, New York.

Attneave F and Olson RK (1971). Pitch as a medium: a new approach to psychophysical scaling. *American Journal of Psychology*, **84**, 147–166.

Bregman AS (1990). *Auditory scene analysis: the perceptual organization of sound*. Bradford Books, MIT Press, Cambridge, MA

Bregman AS and Dannenbring G (1973). The effect of continuity on auditory stream segregation. *Perception and Psychophyics*, **13**, 308–312.

Burns EM (1999). Intervals, scales and tuning. In D Deutsch, ed., *The psychology of music*, 215–264. Academic Press, San Diego, CA.

Burns EM and Viemeister NF (1976). Nonspectral pitch. *Journal of the Acoustical Society of America*, **60**, 863–869.

Burns EM and Ward WD (1978). Categorical perception— phenomenon or epiphenomenon: evidence from experiments in the perception of melodic musical intervals. *Journal of the Acoustical Society of America*, **63**(2), 456–468.

Cramer EM and Huggins WH (1958). Creation of pitch through binaural interaction. *Journal of the Acoustical Society of America*, **30**, 413–417.

Crystal D (1969). *Prosodic systems and intonation in English*. Cambridge University Press, Cambridge.

Fitzsimons M, Sheahan N and Staunton H (2001). Gender and the integration of acoustic dimensions of prosody: implications for clinical studies. *Brain and Language*, **78**(1), 94–108.

Fletcher H (1940). Auditory patterns. *Reviews of Modern Physics*, **12**, 47–65.

Glasberg BR and Moore BCJ (1990). Derivation of auditory filter shapes from notched-noise data. *Hearing Research*, **47**, 103–138.

Hartmann WM and Johnson D (1991). Stream segregation and peripheral channeling. *Music Perception*, **9**, 155–184.

Houtsma AJM (1995). Pitch perception. In BCJ Moore, ed., *Hearing*, 267–295. Academic Press, Orlando, FL.

Huron D (2001). Tone and voice: a derivation of the rules of voice-leading from perceptual principles. *Music Perception*, **19**(1), 1–64.

Klein MA and Hartmann WM (1981). Binaural edge pitch. *Journal of the Acoustic Society of America*, **70**, 51–60.

Liberman AM, Cooper FS, Shankweiler DP and Studdert-Kennedy M (1967). Perception of the speech code. *Psychological Review*, **74**, 431–461.

Licklider JCR (1956). Auditory frequency analysis. In C Cherry, ed., *Information theory*, 253–268. Academic Press, New York.

Locke S and Kellar L (1973). Categorical perception in a non-linguistic mode. *Cortex*, **9**, 353–369.

Miller GA (1956). The magical number 7, plus or minus 2—some limits on our capacity for processing information. *Psychological Review*, **63**(2), 1–93.

Miller GA and Heise GA (1950). The trill threshold. *Journal of the Acoustical Society of America*, **22**, 637–638.

Miller JD, Wier CC, Pastore R, Kelly WJ and Dooling RJ (1976). Discrimination and labelling of noise-burst sequences with varying noise-lead times: an example of categorical perception. *Journal of the Acoustical Society of America*, **60**, 410–417.

Moore BCJ (1973). Frequency difference limens for short-duration tones. *Journal of the Acoustical Society of America*, **54**, 610–619.

Moore BCJ (2003). *An introduction to the psychology of hearing*. 5th edn. Academic Press, San Diego, CA

Moore BCJ, Glasberg BR and Peters RW (1985). Relative dominance of individual partials in determining the pitch of complex tones. *Journal of the Acoustical Society of America*, **77**, 1853–1860.

Moore BCJ and Gockel H (2002). Factors influencing sequential stream segregation. *Acta Acustica United with Acustica*, **88**, 320–333.

Moore BC J and Ohgushi K (1993). Audibility of partials in inharmonic complex tones. *Journal of the Acoustical Society of America*, **93**, 452–461.

Moore BCJ and Rosen SM (1979). Tune recognition with reduced pitch and interval information. *Quarterly Journal of Experimental Psychology*, **31**, 229–240.

Palmer AR and Russell IJ (1986). Phase-locking in the cochlear nerve of the guinea-pig and its relation to the receptor potential of inner hair-cells. *Hearing Research*, **24**(1), 1–15.

Patterson RD (1976). Auditory filter shapes derived with noise stimuli. *Journal of the Acoustical Society of America*, **59**, 640–654.

Plack CJ (2005). *The sense of hearing*. 1st edn. Lawrence, Erlbaum Associates, Mahwah, NJ.

Plack CJ and Oxenham AJ (2005). The psychophysics of pitch. In CJ Plack, AJ Oxenham, RR Fay and AN Popper, eds, *Pitch: neural coding and perception*, 7–55, Springer, New York.

Plack CJ, Oxenham AJ, Fay RR and Popper AN (eds) (2005). *Pitch: neural coding and preception perception*. Springer, New York.

Plomp R (1964). The ear as a frequency analyzer. *Journal of the Acoustical Society of America*, **36**, 1628–1636.

Plomp R and Levelt WJM (1965). Tonal consonance and critical bandwidth. *Journal of the Acoustical Society of America*, **38**, 548–560.

Plomp R and Mimpen AM (1968). The ear as a frequency analyzer II. *Journal of the Acoustical Society of America*, **43**, 764–767.

Rhode WS (1971). Observations of the vibration of the basilar membrane in squirrel monkeys using the Mössbauer technique. *Journal of the Acoustical Society of America*, **49**, 1218–1231.

Roberts B, Glasberg BR and Moore BCJ (2002). Primitive stream segregation of tone sequences without differences in F0 or passband. *Journal of the Acoustical Society of America*, **112**, 2074–2085.

Robles L and Ruggero MA (2001). Mechanics of the mammalian cochlea. *Physiological Reviews*, **81**, 1305–1352.

Rose JE, Brugge JF, Anderson DJ and Hind JE (1967). Phase-locked response to low-frequency tones in single auditory nerve fibers of the squirrel monkey. *Journal of Neurophysiology*, **30**, 769–793.

Ruggero MA (1992). Responses to sound of the basilar membrane of the mammalian cochlea. *Current Opinion in Neurobiology*, **2**, 449–456.

Sadie S (ed.) (2001). *The new Grove dictionary of music and musicians*. Macmillan, London. Also available online at http://www.oxfordmusiconline.com.

Schouten JF (1938). The perception of subjective tones. *Proceedings of the Koninklijke Akademie van Wetenschap*, **41**, 1086–1092.

Schouten JF, Ritsma RJ and Cardozo BL (1962). Pitch of the residue. *Journal of the Acoustical Society of America*, **34**, 1418–1424.

Sek A and Moore BCJ (1995). Frequency discrimination as a function of frequency, measured in several ways. *Journal of the Acoustical Society of America*, **97**, 2479–2486.

Stainsby TH, Moore BCJ and Glasberg BR (2004a). Auditory streaming based on temporal structure in hearing-impaired listeners. *Hearing Research*, **192**, 119–130.

Stainsby TH, Moore BCJ, Medland PJ and Glasberg BR (2004b). Sequential streaming and effective level differences due to phase-spectrum manipulations. *Journal of the Acoustical Society of America*, **115**, 1665–1673.

Stevens SS (1935). The relation of pitch to intensity. *Journal of the Acoustical Society of America*, **6**, 150–154.

Terhardt E (1974). Pitch of pure tones: its relation to intensity. In E Zwicker and E Terhardt, eds, *Facts and models in hearing*, 350–357. Springer, Berlin.

Trehub SE, Schellenberg EG and Kamenetsky SB (1999). Infants' and adults' perception of scale structure.

Journal of Experminetal Psychology: Human Perception and Performance, **25**(4), 965–975.

van Noorden LPAS (1975). Temporal coherence in the perception of tone sequences. Unpublished PhD thesis, Eindhoven University of Technology.

Verschuure J and van Meeteren AA (1975). The effect of intensity on pitch. *Acustica*, **32**, 33–44.

von Békésy G (1947). The variations of phase along the basilar membrane with sinusoidal vibrations. *Journal of the Acoustical Society of America*, **19**, 452–460.

CHAPTER 6

Tonal cognition

Emmanuel Bigand and Bénédicte Poulin-Charronnat

THE term *tonal music* can be applied to a large variety of musical styles in the West. This includes that of the four periods (Baroque, Classical, Romantic, and Modern) into which Western art-music is commonly divided, as well as other musical styles from popular traditions such as jazz, rock-pop music, reggae, and salsa. Pieces from these musical styles sound so different that it can be difficult to realize that they share some of the same features. The most basic is that they rest on a single set of 12 pitch classes, referred to as the chromatic scale, *c, c#/db, d, d#/eb, e, f, f#/gb, g, g#/ab, a, a#/bb, b.*[1] These 12 notes are recycled every octave leading to a large number of musical tones. However, the number of pitch classes (12) remains low, (see Chapter 5 this volume for more detailed information about the difference between *pitch height* and *pitch chroma*). This set of pitch classes is organized in subsets of seven tones referred to as diatonic scales. The fact that so many styles in West rest on a low number of pitch classes organized in small subsets of seven notes highlights the combinatory nature of Western music. The purpose of this chapter is to focus on this combinatory aspect. What type of organization in the tonal pitch structure allows producing so many different styles, and so many different pieces inside each style?

In order to address this issue, we start by considering the theoretical distinction between 'tonal' and 'event hierarchies'. The main features of tonal hierarchies are then summarized and we consider how these hierarchies may be parsimoniously represented. The influence of tonal hierarchies on music perception is then reviewed. To conclude this chapter, we briefly consider how tonal hierarchies contribute, along with other musical parameters, to the definition of an event hierarchy specific to a given piece.

Tonal and event hierarchies in Western music

A critical feature of Western music is its hierarchical organization (Lerdahl and Jackendoff 1983; Meyer 1973; Schenker 1935). This is not to say that all structures in Western music are of hierarchical nature. Associative relations (between thematic cells, for example) also contribute to musical structure. However, the possibility of organizing musical events in a hierarchy of structural importance has deep implications for the listeners. A simple way to understand the concept of hierarchy is to consider that musical events are not all of equal importance: some are structurally important, while others are primarily ornamental. Ornamental events have aesthetic and expressive qualities but they do not contribute to the structure of the piece per se. Removing the ornamental notes does not alter the perceptual identity of a melody, while removing structural tones would modify the melody greatly (Dibben 1994; Mélen and Deliège 1995). If musical events were strictly of equal importance, pieces would sound like monotonous strings of sounds. By contrast, the presence of a hierarchy confers dynamic qualities on musical pieces that have powerful psychological implications: ornamental events seem to 'go towards' events of structural importance, which in turn tend to 'go towards' events

---

[1] For convenience, musical notes will be represented by lower case letters in italics and chords by upper case letters.

hierarchically more important, and so on across the extent of a piece.

Like linguistic discourses, music is a time-oriented structure that progresses from a beginning to an end. If the music stops at some point before the end, most listeners will realize that it has been irregularly interrupted (Bigand 1993; Palmer and Kruhmansl 1987). In a related vein, playing a piece backwards would strongly alter its perceptual identity because the dynamic relationships between tones would be reversed. Let us consider the set of tones *b-c-d#-e-f#-g*. This set of tones is perceived as a melody in the key of C major when played forwards but as a melody in B major when played backwards (Bharucha 1984). In the former case, the tones *b*, *d#*, and *f#* are perceived as ornamental tones anchored on the structurally important tones of the C major chord (*c-e-g*). Playing the tune backwards reverses the relationships between musical events, and the tones *g*, *e*, and *c* are now perceived as ornamental tones anchored to the structurally more important tones of the B major chord (*f#-d#-b*). This change in perceptual organization may be metaphorically compared with the change in meaning that occurs when a sentence is read in a retrograde way (the boy calls the girl *versus* the girl calls the boy). In the first sentence, *the boy* is anchored to the verb *calls*. In the second sentence, *the girl* is anchored to that verb. In language, the main aspect of syntactic computation is to understand 'who is doing what to who'. Similarly, the core aspect of tonal cognition is to perceive 'which tones anchor which tones'. Solving such a problem reminds us of syntactic computation, because musical events can be deeply anchored to the overall structure of the piece: a given tone can be anchored to another one, which may be, in turn, anchored to another one, and so on. Organizing the pitch events of a piece into a single coherent structure, in such a way that the pitch events are heard in a hierarchy of relative importance, is the most fundamental aspect of tonal cognition for Western music (Lerdahl and Jackendoff 1983).

Where do hierarchies between events come from? Two types of hierarchies have been distinguished in music cognition (see Bharucha 1984; Krumhansl 1990; Lerdahl 1989). The term 'tonal hierarchy' was used to designate an atemporal schema of pitch regularities, specific to Western music, which is stored in long-term memory (see Chapter 2 this volume). It embodies the hierarchical relations that accrue to an entire tonal system beyond instantiation in any particular piece. It is atemporal in that it represents more or less permanent knowledge about the musical system rather than a response to a specific sequence of events. Tonal hierarchies thus designate the regularities in pitch that prevail for all styles of tonal music. By contrast an 'event hierarchy' is a hierarchy of specific pitch–time events inferred from the ongoing temporal sequence of musical events. In the next sections, we will focus on tonal hierarchies however, in conclusion, we will briefly consider how tonal hierarchies influence event hierarchies.

Tonal hierarchies: intra-key hierarchies and inter-key distances

The main aspects of tonal hierarchies can be summarized in the following way. From a set of 12 pitches, several subsets of seven pitches are defined, each defining a musical key. A musical key is defined in reference to a specific tone which is called the tonic tone and that gives its name to the key. Since there are 12 tones, there are 12 possible tonics. In Western music, some subsets of tones form major keys. Others form minor keys. For example, the C major key is made of the following tones: *c-d-e-f-g-a-b*. The C minor harmonic key is made of the tones, *c-d-eb-f-g-ab-b*. In both cases, the pitch *c* is the tonic. Major and minor correspond to two different scales of pitch intervals. For example, the set of pitch intervals separating the tones of the C major key is tone-tone-semitone-tone-tone-tone-semitone. This set defines a scale that is constant for all major keys. In a minor harmonic key, the scale is different: tone-semitone-tone-tone-semitone-one tone and a half-semitone. Applying these major and minor scales to each tone of the chromatic scale defines 24 major and minor keys.

The critical aspect of the tonal pitch system relates to the organization of pitches within keys (referred to as intra-key hierarchies), and to the organization that exists between the 24 major and minor keys (referred to as inter-key distances). Krumhansl and collaborators (see Krumhansl

1990, for a complete account) have investigated intra-key hierarchies with a 'probe tone' method, which consists of playing a test tone (the probe) after a musical context in a given key. Participants have to evaluate on a seven-point scale how the probe tone fits with the context. The 12 tones of the chromatic scale are presented as probe tones. It was found that all the probe tones did not received the same ratings of 'goodness of fit'. In major key contexts, the highest rating was given to the tonic note (the tone *c* in C major), followed by the fifth degree of the scale (*g*), and then the third degree (*e*), the fourth (*f*) and the remaining tones of the key (*d-a-b*). The tones that do not belong to the key (the 'non-diatonic tones'), received the lowest ratings. This set of values defined the C major key profile (Figure 6.1, top). The reader could easily obtain the profiles of all the other keys by translating these profiles to all the remaining tonics. As illustrated by Figure 6.1 (bottom), the ratings found when minor keys were used as context differed in an interesting way; the tonic remains the tone that fits the best with the key context, but then comes the third scale degree (*eb*), followed by the fifth and the sixth scale degrees (g and *ab*, respectively). The other diatonic tones received lower ratings, and the non-diatonic tones, the lowest. The minor key profile remains the same for all other minor keys but it has to be translated towards the tonic of the given key context. Important tones in these key

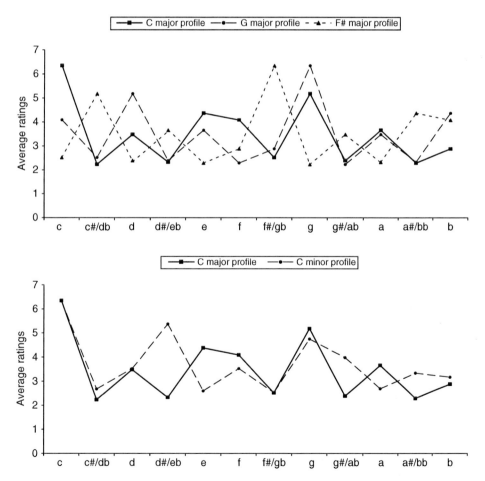

Fig. 6.1 Key profiles in the keys of C, G and F# major (top) and in the key of C major and C minor (bottom), after Krumhansl (1990).

profiles act as cognitive reference points that anchor all other events. In Western tonal music, the tonic is thus the most important cognitive reference point that anchors all the other tones (Schenker 1935).

Within a key, tones may be grouped to define larger musical units called chords. A chord is the simultaneous or sequential sounding of, at least, three different tones.[2] The three basic component tones of a perfect major or minor chord (also called a triad) are separated by one scale degree. For example, the C major triad is made of the tones *c-e-g*. The E minor triad is made of the tone *e-g-b*. The first interval defines the third of the chord. In a major chord, the third corresponds to a pitch interval of 4 semitones (*c-e*). In a minor chord, the third is made of a pitch interval of three semitones (*c-eb*). The second interval defines the fifth of the chord. Since there are seven tones per scale, there are seven chords in each key, some being major, others minor, and others diminished.[3] Over all the keys, there are 12 major, 12 minor, and 12 diminished chords. Chords are important events for Western music: they define harmonic frames from which thematic units derive. Vincent d'Indy (1900) metaphorically compared the themes of a musical piece to the actions of a drama, and the relationships between chords to the places where the actions occurred. This points up the fact that the relationships between chords (i.e., the harmony) are of considerable importance in defining the structure of a given piece.

In Western music, the relationships between chords are also of a hierarchical nature; some chords are structurally more important than others. Using the probe tone method, Krumhansl *et al.* (1982) investigated the hierarchies between chords. Goodness of fit ratings varied significantly with the chords: in major key context, chords build on the first scale degree (referred to as the

tonic chord) received the highest ratings, followed by the chords build on the fourth and fifth scale degrees (respectively referred to as subdominant and dominant chords). The other chords received lower ratings. Among all the major chords, those that did not belong to the key context received the lowest ratings. In other words, a harmonic hierarchy was found between chords.

The last main aspect of tonal hierarchies relies on the distance between the 12 major and 12 minor keys. Some keys share more tones and chords than others. For example, the key of C and G major share 6 tones and 4 chords, while the key of C major shares only 3 tones and no chord with the key of E major. These relationships are reflected on the chromatic circle of fifths (C-G-D-A-E-B-F#/Gb-C#/Db- G#/Ab-D#/Eb-A#/Bb-F). The higher the number of steps between two keys, the fewer the common tones and chords shared by the keys. Major keys share also tones and chords with minor keys. For example, C major and A minor share six tones and three chords. The number of tones and chords shared by keys contributes to define musical distances between the keys, with keys sharing numerous tones and chords being closer than others.

From a psychological point of view, the musical distances between keys is more complex that this simple computation. Krumhansl (1990) demonstrated that the perceptual distance between keys is expressed by the correlation that exists between the hierarchical profiles of the keys: the higher the correlation, the closer the keys. This finding suggests that keys are not only related because they share several tones, but also because hierarchically important tones in one key continue to be of importance in others. The hierarchical organization of tones and chords thus changes less between two related keys than between two distant ones. For example, the keys of C major and C minor are musically related although they do not share many tones and chords (four tones, and no chord). However, in both keys, the notes *c* and *g* act as the two most important reference points which anchor the other tones. In a similar way, the key of C major is close to its relative minor key (i.e., A minor). Indeed, the tones *c* and *e* that are hierarchically important in the former key continue to act as referential points in the latter. As a consequence, every major key (C, for example) is close to two minor keys (its parallel and relative minor keys; C

---

[2] The sounding of two sounds defines an interval, not a chord. More complex chords contained additional tones. For example, the famous dominant seventh chord is made of the tones *c-e-g-bb* in the F major key, and chords containing two or three ornamental tones are frequent in jazz and bossa nova (as in the major ninth chord *c-e-g-b-d*, or the minor ninth chord *d-f-a-c-e*).

[3] The C major key is made of the following chords: C major (*c-e-g*), D minor (*d-f-a*), E minor (*e-g-b*), F major (*f-a-c*), G major (*g-b-d*), A minor (*a-c-e*), and B diminished (*b-d-f*).

and A minor) and two major keys (those that are separated by one step on the circle of fifths: G and F major). Every major key is also indirectly close to the relative minor keys of the major keys that surround it (C major is close to E minor which is the relative minor of G major). The 12 major and 12 minor keys thus define a complex net of musical relationships (Figure 6.2, bottom).

Moving from one key to another results in a mental reorganization of the hierarchical values of tones and chords. This reorganization is as strong as the new key is distant from the previous one. These changes in cognitive reference points are experienced in an expressive way by listeners. Moreover, the expressive quality of a modulation (i.e., a change in key) is held to depend upon the distances between the two keys: the farther away the keys, the stronger the cognitive reorganization of reference points,

and the stronger the expressive effect. As the 12 major and 12 minor keys define a complex net of keys, an almost infinite number of ways exists to modulate from one key to another and to express different feelings for/in listeners.

Two models of tonal hierarchies

Notes, chords, and keys define three levels of entwined structures that allow Western composers to invent an infinite number of expressive musical pieces. An important issue for cognitive psychology is to capture in a single parsimonious model the creative power of such a musical system. In the present section, we will consider two models of Western pitch structures that derive from different scientific backgrounds.

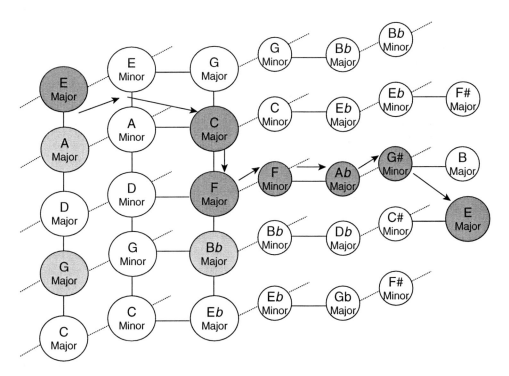

Fig. 6.2 Pitch class level (top) and regional level (bottom) of Lerdahl's tonal pitch space theory. The arrow illustrates the journey through pitch space of Chopin's E major prelude (adapted from Lerdahl 1991).

The Tonal Pitch Space Theory (TPST), initially described by Lerdahl (1988) and further developed in Lerdahl (1991, 1996, 2001) rests on a long tradition of representing the structure of Western music as a multidimensional space (Longuet-Higgins 1978; Krumhansl 1990; Shepard 1982). In such an approach, tonal hierarchies are represented in a space so that the distances between tones and chords from the instantiated tonic correspond to their relative hierarchical importance: the smaller the distances from the tonic, the stronger the importance. Lerdahl's TPST provides a formal means of quantifying the tonal distances maintained between any two events belonging to any key. Tonal hierarchy is represented in three embedded levels, the first two (pitch class and chordal level) representing the intra-key hierarchy, while the third (regional level) represents the distance between keys. The pitch class level expresses the relationships between the 12 pitch classes. It contains five sublevels corresponding to the chromatic level (1), the diatonic level (2), the triadic level (3), the fifth level (4) and the tonic level (5) (Figure 6.2, top). This basic space expresses Krumhansl and Kessler (1982)'s key profiles of Figure 6.1. In a given context (say, a C major chord in C major), the tonic tone (c) will be represented at all five levels. The dominant and the mediant tones (g and e) will be represented up to levels four and three, respectively. The diatonic tones are represented at level two and non-diatonic tones are represented at level one only. The level at which a given pitch class is represented thus expresses its importance in the tonal hierarchies of the key context. Hierarchies between pitch classes change as a function of context. For example, a C major chord in G major will produce a single change in pitch class (the f# will be now represented at level 2 and the f at level 1). The core idea of TPST is to quantify the tonal stability of each event (i.e., its place in the tonal hierarchy) by computing the number of changes in pitch classes it introduces in the context.

Let us consider the second level of the model, which involves the hierarchies between chords within a given key. The hierarchical values of the chords depend upon their distance to the tonic. This distance is measured in the model by the number of steps that separates the chords on the diatonic circle of fifths (C-G-D-A-E-B-F)

and the number of changes in pitch class created by the second chord. In C major, the G major chord stands one step apart from the C major chord on this circle, and it creates four changes in pitch classes by reference to the C major chord. As a consequence, its distance to the tonic chord equals five. Similarly, the tonal pitch space distance of the subdominant chord (F) is five, but the distance of the other chords, hierarchically less important, is higher (e.g., eight for the supertonic chord D minor). These distances express the local changes in hierarchies between tones that prevail when music moves from one chord to another. These changes are experienced by listeners as musical tensions (when the distance increases), or as musical relaxations (when the distance decreases) (Bigand *et al.* 1996). The set of distances traveled through pitch space by a musical sequence thus captures the dynamic quality of the sequence.

The two previous levels would suffice to account for intra-key hierarchies. The third level (regional level) deals with the distances between the 24 keys. The model accounts for key distances by measuring the number of changes in hierarchies between tones and chords consecutive to a shift towards a new key. Not surprisingly, the TPST computes small distances between keys that are one step apart on the chromatic circle of fifths (C, G, and F, for example, which have a distance of 7) and between keys that are related according to parallel and relative minor/major relations (C and C minor, C and A minor). The greatest distance computed by the TPST (30) is found between a given key and its augmented fourth key (C and F# major keys). The distance between two chords belonging to different keys depends upon the way the two chords are interpreted. Given that chords may belong to different keys, this distance can be reduced when the two chords are interpreted as chords of closely related keys. For example, the distance between a C major chord and a C# minor chord equals 30 if the latter chord is analysed as the tonic chord of the C# minor key. The same distance equals 23 if the C# minor chord is analyzed as a member of the E major key. By default, the model would compute the shortest distance. Figure 6.2 (bottom) illustrates how the 24 keys may be organized in a two-dimensional space. Circle of fifth relationships are represented on the vertical axis, and parallel/relative minor/major relationships are represented on the horizontal axis. Modulating to G, F, E, or C minor from the C major key would result in smaller movements than modulating to a musically less related key (e.g., A♭).

Lerdahl suggests that listening to music corresponds to a journey through pitch space. The arrows of Figure 6.2 illustrate a journey provided by the Chopin prelude in E major. The first part of the prelude remains in E major, with local movements from one chord to another. The second part introduces an intense journey from E to the A♭ major and a fast return to the main key of E. There seems no doubt that the expressive quality of this prelude comes from the velocity at which this journey from E to A♭ occurs during the second phrase (Bigand 2003). The TPST is a musical model of tonal hierarchies that has both theoretical and empirical roots, and that has received support from several empirical studies (Bigand and Parncutt 1999; Bigand *et al.* 1996; Krumhansl 1996; Lerdahl and Krumhansl 2007; Smith and Cuddy 2003; Vega 2003). The TPST is helpful in investigating challenging assumptions about tonal cognition and it has a number of psychological implications (see Bigand 2003). However, it may be viewed as a rather ad hoc complex model, difficult to implement in an automatic way in an artificial system, and of which the architecture is too abstract, as it stands, to correspond point by point to real cognitive processes.

An alternative account of tonal hierarchies that has roots in cognitive psychology and computational sciences has been proposed by Bharucha (1987). Following McClelland and Rumelhart's interactive model of lexical access (McClelland and Rumelhart 1981; Rumelhart and McClelland 1982), Bharucha defines a three-layer interactive model that links tones, chords, and keys. In this model, tone units are connected to all major and minor chords to which they belong (Figure 6.3a). These chords are, in turn, linked to each of the major key units to which they belong. An important musical limitation of the model is that only major and minor triads are represented, and that the model does not contain minor keys. However, the model captures interesting features of tonal hierarchies. For example, when a given triad is sounded (say the tones *c-e-g*), the activated tone units send activation towards all the chord units

to which they are connected (Figure 6.3b). At the second iteration, these chord units propagate activation towards the keys to which they are related, and backward to the tones they are connected to (Figure 6.3c). As a consequence, tone units that were not in the stimulus start to be activated. For example, the tone *a* receives some activation from the F and A major chords and the A minor chord that were stimulated by the tones *c* and *e*. At the third iteration, these new activations of the tones propagate towards the chord level. At the same time the activation of the key level spreads backward to the chord units (Figure 6.3d). Since the C major key was active, all the chords of the C major key now start to be stimulated. During the next iterations, all of these activations spread backward and forward up to a point of equilibrium where spreading activation is so small that it does not change the overall state of the network. The interesting point is that this model of MUSical ACTivation (MUSACT) nicely expresses tonal hierarchies. For example, after a C major triad, the most activated chord units correspond to the tonic chord (C), the dominant and subdominant chords (G and F). The activations decrease progressively as long as chords are musically distant from the C major chords. The pattern of activation found for the key units also reflects the inter-key distances. For example, after a perfect cadence in the C major key, the C major key unit is the most activated unit, and this activation decreases as a function of the musical distances from the C major key.

In this model the knowledge of tonal hierarchy is expressed by the pattern of activation that spreads automatically towards tone, chord, and key units. Closely related events lead to a highly correlated pattern of activation, distant events, to negative correlations. In a given context, the amount of activation found for each unit (tones or chords) represents their hierarchical importance in the context. MUSACT thus captures features of tonal hierarchies that are strongly similar to those accounted for by Lerdahl's TPST, but with a completely different architecture. In MUSACT, the tonal hierarchies are represented in a distributed way by the weights of the connections that link tones to major and minor chord units, and chord units to key units. The specific values of these weights were defined ad hoc in the pioneer work by Bharucha (1987),

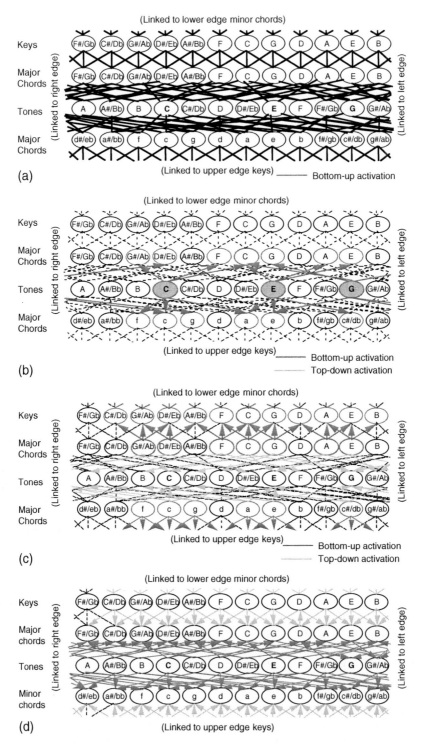

Fig. 6.3 Bharucha's MUSACT model. (a) When three tones are sounding, activation spread from tones to chord units (b), and then from chord to key and tone units (c), and from key units to chord and from tone to chord units (d) and so on up to equilibrium. See also colour plate section.

but it has been demonstrated that these weights may arise from a learning process that occurs automatically when the neural network is exposed to Western music (Tillmann *et al.* 2000).

Influences of tonal hierarchies on Western music perception

Much evidence has been collected demonstrating the influence of tonal hierarchies on music perception. For example, Francès (1958) required musicians to detect mistuned notes in piano pieces. This mistuning was performed in different ways. In one condition, some musical notes were mistuned in such a way that the pitch interval between the mistuned notes and those that anchored them was reduced. For example, the leading note (*b* in C major) which is hierarchically weakly important is generally anchored by the tonic note (*c* in C major). Francès mistuned the leading tone by increasing its fundamental frequency (F0) so that the pitch interval between the leading tone and the tonic was reduced. In the other experimental condition, this mistuning was performed in the opposite way. When played without a musical context, participants easily perceived both types of mistuning. Placed in a musical context, only the second type of mistuning (which conflicted with musical anchoring) was perceived. This outcome shows that the perceptual ability to perceive the shift of the F0 of a musical note is modulated by top-down processes that integrate the note into tonal hierarchies. More generally, performers such as violinists or cellists constantly adjust the fundamental frequency of the tones in order to make as clear as possible the way in which these tones are anchored by the hierarchically important tones of the context. This expressive intonation, which is entirely related to the tonal hierarchy, considerably increases a listener's comprehension of the musical discourse.[4]

Tonal hierarchies also influence the perception of melodic contour. Several experiments

demonstrate that discriminating a small change in a contour is more difficult when the standard and the comparison melodies are in distant, rather than close, keys (Dowling 1986). Several experiments run by Krumhansl and collaborators (see Krumhansl 1990) demonstrate the influence of tonal hierarchy on the perceptual distance of tones and chords and on their memorization. This influence can be summarized in terms of three contextual principles. The perceptual distance between two events (tones or chords) increases when these events are of hierarchical importance (contextual distance). The perceptual identity of two instances of a given event increases with its hierarchical importance (contextual identity). Two occurrences of the chord C would sound more similar if they occurred in a C major key context rather than in a distant key context (say, in an F# key context). Finally, the perceptual distance of two events depends on their sequential occurrence: the distance decreases when the hierarchically strong important event occurs after the other one (i.e., anchoring principle). It increases in the other case (contextual asymmetry). Krumhansl and collaborators demonstrate that these principles account for confusion errors in memory. For example, it is easier to detect that two occurrences of a seven chord sequence are identical when these chords belong to a single key (diatonic sequence; 69.3 per cent) than when they belong to different keys (55 per cent), illustrating the principle of contextual identity. When the second occurrence of the sequence contains a different chord, it is easier to detect the difference when the chord is changed for a chord belonging to another key than when it remains in the same key (86 per cent *versus* 56.9 per cent). This illustrates the principle of contextual distance. Finally, when the initial sequence is diatonic and the comparison sequence contains a non-diatonic chord, the change is easier to detect (86.8 per cent) than when the first sequence contains a non-diatonic chord that is replaced in the second sequence by a diatonic chord (61.3 per cent). This illustrates the principle of contextual asymmetry.

The influence of tonal hierarchy on the memorization of melody may be very impressive. In one experiment (Bigand 1997), participants were required to listen several times to a target melody

[4] The reader would find a remarkable demonstration of such expressive intonation in Casals' performances of the cello suite by Bach.

Fig. 6.4 Examples of standard and comparison melodies used in Bigand (1997).

such as the melody in A minor represented in Figure 6.4 (top). Participants were then presented with new melodies and were asked to evaluate how many pitches had been changed in comparison to the standard. Figure 6.4 (bottom) displays one of the comparison melodies used. As can be seen, it contains most of the tones of the standard. Only a few tones have been changed in order to instill the key of G major at the beginning of the melody. This new key context was assumed to modify the hierarchical weights of the melodic tones. Indeed, the *a* is no longer a tonic tone in this comparison melody, but a weakly important supertonic tone. The reader is invited to use the key profiles of Figure 6.1 to understand how much the hierarchical weights of the tones have been changed in the comparison melody. Not surprisingly, the participants (musically trained and untrained listeners) evaluate that about 66 per cent of the tones have been changed in the comparison melody, that is to say, much more than what has actually been done.

The influence of tonal hierarchies has been reported in several other studies in which participants were asked to evaluate the degree of completion or the degree of musical stability experienced at different points of a musical sequence. Ratings of completion or musical stability were higher when the music stopped on hierarchically important events (Bigand 1993, 1997; Palmer and Krumhansl 1987). A similar result was found for chord sequences (Bigand and Parncutt 1999; Bigand *et al.* 1996). In recent studies, a continuous measure of musical stability has been used, and data were found to correlate significantly with tonal hierarchy (Krumhansl 1996; Lerdahl and Krumhansl 2007). Other studies have investigated the influence of tonal hierarchies on the speed at which some musical features are processed. In Bharucha and Stoeckig's (1986) chord priming experiments, the participants were required to decide accurately but as fast as possible whether a target chord was in tune or out of tune. For the purpose of the experiment one component tone of the chord was slightly mistuned in half of the trials. The target chord was preceded by a chord prime. The critical point of the study was to assess whether the processing of the sensory consonance of the target chord would be modulated by the harmonic relationship of the two chords. The authors provided evidence that consonant target chords were more accurately and more quickly identified as consonant when they were preceded by a related prime (e.g., C and G chords) than by an unrelated prime (e.g., C and F# chords). An opposite finding was found for dissonant targets. Bharucha and Stoeckig argued that a given context primes the processing of chords that are musically related in the context, a finding which is reminiscent of semantic priming effects reported in language (McNamara 2005). Further experiments attempted to demonstrate that this priming effect in music occurs at a cognitive level and does not result from the overlap in harmonic spectra of both chords (Bharucha and Stoeckig 1987; Tekman and Bharucha 1998).

The influence of tonal hierarchies on perceptual expectancy in long musical contexts has also been investigated with the priming paradigm (Bigand and Poulin-Charronnat 2006, for a review). In our experiments, participants were presented with chord sequences (of 8 or 14 chords depending on the studies) that ended on a target chord. The target acted either as a tonic or as a subdominant chord depending upon the context. The chord preceding the target was always kept constant, except when the local and global harmonic contexts surrounding the target were simultaneously manipulated (Tillmann *et al.* 1998). In most of the studies, participants were required to indicate as quickly and as accurately as possible whether the target chord was consonant or dissonant. Dissonant targets contained a supplementary tone, a half tone above or below a triadic tone. In more recent studies, target chords were played with two different timbres which participants had to identify as fast and accurately as possible (Tillmann and Lebrun-Guillaud 2006). Processing the sensory consonance of the target or its harmonic spectra was always faster and easier when the target acted as a hierarchically important tonic chord. This effect is extremely robust since it has been replicated for relatively long chord sequences organized at three hierarchical levels (Bigand *et al.* 1999), for normal and scrambled musical sequences (Tillmann and Bigand 2001), for chord sequences that have extremely poor voice leading (Poulin-Charronnat *et al.* 2005a), and even when sensory priming was manipulated in order to favour the subdominant target (Bigand *et al.* 2003). Harmonic priming was also found to be stronger than repetition priming (Bigand *et al.* 2005), and to modulate the processing of linguistic information in sung music (Bigand *et al.* 2001; Poulin-Charronnat *et al.* 2005). Finally, it was observed for musically trained and untrained listeners (Bigand and Poulin-Charronnat 2006, for a review), as well as with young children (Schellenberg *et al.* 2005).

This large set of consistent data highlights the strength of tonal hierarchies on the formation of musical expectancies.

It is likely that tonal hierarchies influence several other aspects of music perception. In one recent study, we investigated how the tonal hierarchy influences emotional responses to music (Filipic and Bigand 2003). Participants were required to decide as fast and as accurately as possible whether two musical sequences expressed the same or different emotion. Musical sequences that were qualified as either sad or serene in Peretz *et al.*'s (1998) studies were used and the participants were informed that all stimuli fall into one of these two emotional categories. In half of the trials, the musical pieces were in the same keys. In the other half they were in distant keys. We found that emotional responses were faster and more accurate when both pieces were in the same key. This finding suggests that interpreting the tones in a tonal key context is a prerequisite for the recognition of the emotional value of the stimuli.

From tonal hierarchies to event hierarchies

The critical importance of the tonal hierarchy is to contribute to instilling an event hierarchy specific to a given piece. As formalized in Lerdahl and Jackendoff's Generative Theory of Tonal Music (1983), the tonal hierarchy provides the stability conditions that need to be integrated into rhythmic parameters (notably) in order to define the structural importance of each tone of the piece. The structural importance of a musical event thus depends upon its place in

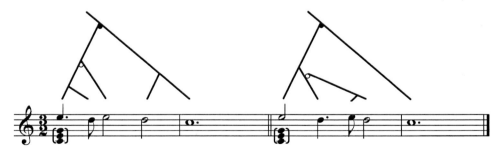

Fig. 6.5 Influence of tonal hierarchies and rhythm on event hierarchies. Inspired by Lerdahl and Jackendoff (1983) with the help of the first author.

tonal hierarchy and the rhythmic context in which it appears. A tonic note of a given melody would not always act as a structurally important tone. Depending upon the group of tones in which it appears as well as its duration and its metrical position, a tonic note may act as an ornamental event in the event hierarchy. Modifying the rhythm of a set of tones is enough to change the event hierarchy as expressed in the following example (Figure 6.5). The *e*, which is an important tone in the C major key context, may act as an important anchoring tone in some rhythmic contexts (Figure 6.5 left) but not in others (Figure 6.5 right). This point is most crucial as it means that the tonal hierarchy is considerably modulated by numerous other musical parameters such as rhythm, loudness, and timbre. These parameters are adjusted by the composer and the performer in numerous ways, leading to a quasi infinite number of possible event hierarchies. The combination of tonal and event hierarchies creates a great unity in a quasi-infinite variety of Western musical pieces.

References

Bharucha JJ (1984). Anchoring effects in music: the resolution of dissonance. *Cognitive Psychology*, **16**(4), 485–518.

Bharucha JJ (1987). Music cognition and perceptual facilitation: a connectionist framework. *Music Perception*, **5**(1), 1–30.

Bharucha JJ and Stoeckig K (1986). Reaction time and musical expectancy: priming of chords. *Journal of Experimental Psychology: Human Perception and Performance*, **12**(4), 403–410.

Bharucha JJ and Stoeckig K (1987). Priming of chords: spreading activation or overlapping frequency spectra? *Perception and Psychophysics*, **41**(6), 519–524.

Bigand E (1993). The influence of implicit harmony, rhythm and musical training on the abstraction of 'tension–relaxation schemas' in a tonal musical phrase. *Contemporary Music Review*, **9**, 128–139.

Bigand E (1997). Perceiving musical stability: the effect of tonal structure, rhythm and musical expertise. Journal of Experimental Psychology, *Human Perception and Performance*, **23**, 808–812.

Bigand E (2003). Travelling throught Lerdahl's tonal pitch space theory: a psychological perspective. *Musicae Scientiae*, **7**, 121–140.

Bigand E and Parncutt R (1999). Perceiving musical tension in long chord sequences. *Psychological Research*, **62**(4), 237–254.

Bigand E and Pineau M (1996). Context effects on melody recognition: a dynamic interpretation. *Current Psychology of Cognition*, **15**, 121–134.

Bigand E and Poulin-Charronnat B (2006). Are we 'experienced listeners'? A review of the musical capacities that do not depend on formal musical training. *Cognition*, **100**(1), 100–130.

Bigand E, Madurell F, Tillmann B and Pineau M (1999). Effect of global structure and temporal organization on chord processing. *Journal of Experimental Psychology: Human Perception and Performance*, **25**(1), 184–197.

Bigand E, Parncutt R and Lerdahl F (1996). Perception of musical tension in short chord sequences: The influence of harmonic function, sensory dissonance, horizontal motion, and musical training. *Perception and Psychophysics*, **58**(1), 124–141.

Bigand E, Poulin B, Tillmann B, Madurell F and D'Adamo DA (2003). Sensory versus cognitive components in harmonic priming. *Journal of Experimental Psychology: Human Perception and Performance*, **29**(1), 159–171.

Bigand E, Tillmann B, Poulin B, D'Adamo DA and Madurell F (2001). The effect of harmonic context on phoneme monitoring in vocal music. *Cognition*, **81**(1), B11–B20.

Bigand E, Tillmann B, Poulin-Charronnat B and Manderlier D (2005). Repetition priming: is music special? *Quarterly Journal of Experimental Psychology*, **58A**(8), 1347–1375.

D'Indy V (1900). *Traité de composition musicale*. Durand, Paris.

Dibben N (1994). The cognitive reality of hierarchic structure in tonal and atonal music. *Music Perception*, **12**, 1–25.

Dowling WJ (1986) Context effects on melody recognition: scale-step versus interval representations. *Music Perception*, **3**, 281–296.

Filipic S and Bigand E (2003). Emotion and cognition in music: which comes first ? In R Kopiez, AC Lehmann, I Wolther and C Wolf, eds, *Proceeding of the 5th Triennal ESCOM*, 231–233, 8–13 September, Germany.

Francès R (1958) *La perception de la musique*. Paris: Vrin [1984 The perception of music (Dowling trans.) Earlbaum, Hillsdale, NJ.

Krumhansl CL (1990). *Cognitive foundations of musical pitch*. Oxford University Press, New York.

Krumhansl CL (1996), A perceptual analysis of Mozart's piano sonata, K. 282: segmentation, tension and musical ideas. *Music Perception*, **13**, 401–432.

Krumhansl CL and Kessler EJ. (1982). Tracing the dynamic changes in perceived tonal organization in a spatial representation of musical keys. *Psychological Review*, **89**(4), 334–368.

Krumhansl CL, Bharucha JJ and Kessler EJ (1982). Perceived harmonic structure of chords in three related musical keys. *Journal of Experimental Psychology: Human Perception and Performance*, **8**(1), 24–36.

Lerdahl F (1988). Tonal pitch space. *Music Perception*, **5**(3), 315–349.

Lerdahl F (1989). Atonal prolongational structure. *Contemporary Music Review*, **4**, 65–87.

Lerdahl F (1991). Pitch-Space journeys in two Chopin Preludes (MR Jones and S Holleran, eds) *Cognitive bases of musical communication*, 171–91 APA, Washington, DC.

Lerdahl F (1996). Calculating tonal tension. *Music Perception*, **13**(3), 319–363.

Lerdahl F (2001). *Tonal pitch space theory*. Oxford University Press, Oxford.

Lerdahl F and Jackendoff R (1983). *A generative theory of tonal music*. The MIT Press, Cambridge, MA.

Lerdahl F and Krumhansl C (2007). Modeling tonal tension. *Music Perception*, **24**(4), 329–366.

Longuet-Higgins HC (1978). The perception of music. *Interdisciplinary Science Reviews*, **3**, 148–156.

McClelland JL and Rumelhart DE (1981). An interactive activation model of context effects in letter perception: Part 1. An account of basic findings. *Psychological Review*, **88**, 375–407.

McNamara TP (2005). *Semantic priming: perspectives from memory and word recognition*. [Psychology Press, New York].

Mélen M and Deliège I (1995). Extraction of cues or underlying harmonic structure: which guides recognition of familiar melodies? *European Journal of Cognitive Psychology*, **7**(1), 81–106.

Meyer LB (1973). *Explaining music*. University of California Press, Berkeley, CA.

Palmer C and Krumhansl CL (1987). Pitch and temporal contributions to musical phrase perception: effects of harmony, performance timing, and familiarity. *Perception and Psychophysics*, **41**(6), 505–518.

Peretz I, Gagnon L and Bouchard B (1998). Music and emotion: perceptual determinants, immediacy and isolation after brain damage. *Cognition*, **68**, 111–141.

Poulin-Charronnat B, Bigand E and Madurell F (2005a). The influence of voice leading on harmonic priming. *Music Perception*, **22**(4), 613–627.

Poulin-Charronnat B, Bigand E, Madurell F and Peereman R (2005b). Musical structure modulates semantic priming in vocal music. *Cognition*, **94**(3), B67–B78.

Rumelhart DE and McClelland JL (1982). An interactive activation model of context effects in letter

perception: Part 2. The context enhancement effect and some tests and extensions of the model. *Psychological Review*, **89**, 60–94.

Schellenberg EG, Bigand E, Poulin-Charronnat B, Garnier C and Stevens C (2005). Children's implicit knowledge of harmony in Western music. *Developmental Science*, **8**(6), 551–566.

Schenker H (1935). *Der freie Satz*. Universal Edition, Vienna.

Shepard RN (1982). Geometrical approximations to the structure of musical pitch. *Psychological Review*, **89**(4), 305–333.

Smith NA and Cuddy LL (2003). Perceptions of musical dimensions in Beethoven's Waldstein sonata: an application of Tonal Pitch Space theory. *Musicae Scientiae*, **7**, 7–34.

Tekman HG and Bharucha JJ (1998). Implicit knowledge versus psychoacoustic similarity in priming of chords. *Journal of Experimental Psychology: Human Perception and Performance*, **24**(1), 252–260.

Tillmann B and Bigand E (2001). Global context effect in normal and scrambled musical sequences. *Journal of Experimental Psychology: Human Perception and Performance*, **27**(5), 1185–1196.

Tillmann B and Lebrun-Guillaud G (2006). Influence of tonal and temporal expectations on chord processing and on completion judgments of chord sequences. *Psychological Research*, **70**(5), 345–358.

Tillmann B, Bharucha JJ and Bigand E (2000). Implicit learning of tonality: A self-organizing approach. *Psychological Review*, **107**(4), 885–913.

Tillmann B, Bigand E and Madurell F (1998). Local versus global processing of harmonic cadences in the solution of musical puzzles. *Psychological Research*, **61**(3), 157–174.

Vega DA (2003). A perceptual experiment on harmonic tension and melodic attraction in Lerdahl's tonal pitch space. *Musicae Scientiae*, **7**, 35–55.

CHAPTER 7

The perception of musical timbre[1]

Stephen McAdams and Bruno L. Giordano

TIMBRE is a misleadingly simple and vague word encompassing a very complex set of auditory attributes, as well as a plethora of psychological and musical issues. It covers many parameters of perception that are not accounted for by pitch, loudness, spatial position, duration, and various environmental characteristics such as room reverberation. This leaves a wealth of possibilities that have been explored over the last 40 years or so. We now understand timbre to have two broad characteristics that contribute to the perception of music: (1) it is a multifarious set of abstract sensory attributes, some of which are continuously varying (e.g. attack sharpness, brightness, nasality, richness), others of which are discrete or categorical (e.g., the 'blatt' at the beginning of a sforzando trombone sound or the pinched offset of a harpsichord sound), and (2) it is one of the primary perceptual vehicles for the recognition, identification, and tracking over time of a sound source (singer's voice, clarinet, set of carillon bells), and thus involves the absolute categorization of a sound (Hajda *et al.* 1997; McAdams 1993; Risset and Wessel 1999). The psychological approach to timbre has also included work on the musical implications of timbre as a set of form-bearing dimensions in music (McAdams 1989).

Timbre as a multidimensional set of auditory attributes

One of the main approaches to timbre perception attempts to characterize quantitatively the

ways in which sounds are perceived to differ. Early research on the perceptual nature of timbre focused on preconceived aspects such as the relative weights of different frequencies present in a given sound, or its 'sound color' (Slawson 1985). A voice singing a constant middle C while varying the vowel being sung, or a brass player holding a given note while varying the embouchure and mouth cavity shape would both vary the shape of the sound spectrum, which represents the level of each sound partial as a function of its frequency (cf. McAdams *et al.* 2004b). Helmholtz (1885/1954) invented some rather ingenious resonating devices for controlling spectral shape to explore these aspects of timbre. However, the real advances in understanding the perceptual representation of timbre had to wait for the development of multidimensional data analysis techniques in the 1960s and signal processing techniques in the 1970s. Plomp (1970) and Wessel (1973) first applied these to timbre perception.

Timbre space

Multidimensional scaling makes no preconceptions about the physical or perceptual structure of timbre. Listeners simply rate on a scale varying from very similar to very dissimilar all pairs from a given set of sounds. The sounds are usually equalized in terms of pitch, loudness, and duration so that only the timbre varies in order to focus listeners' attention on this attribute. The dissimilarity ratings are then fit to a distance model in which sounds with similar timbres are close together and those with dissimilar

---

[1] This chapter is an updated version of two previous summaries of musical timbre research (McAdams, 1999, 2003).

timbres are far apart. The graphic representation is called a 'timbre space'. The basic model is expressed in terms of continuous dimensions that are shared among the timbres, the underlying assumption being that all listeners use the same perceptual dimensions to compare the timbres. More complex models also include dimensions or features that are specific to individual timbres (called 'specificities') and different perceptual weights accorded to the dimensions and specificities by individual listeners or classes of listeners (Grey 1977; McAdams et al. 1995). Such techniques have been applied to synthetic sounds (Miller and Carterette 1975; Plomp 1970), resynthesized or simulated instrument sounds (Grey 1977; Krumhansl 1989; McAdams et al. 1995; Wessel 1979), recorded instrument sounds (Iverson and Krumhansl 1993; Lakatos 2000), and even dyads of recorded instrument sounds (Kendall and Carterette 1991).

Specificities are often found for complex acoustic and synthesized sounds. They are considered to represent the presence of a unique feature that distinguishes a sound from all others in a given context. For example, in a set of brass, woodwind, and string sounds, a harpsichord has a feature shared with no other sound: the return of the hopper which creates a slight 'thump' and quickly damps the sound at the end. This might appear as a strong specificity in the distance model (Krumhansl 1989; McAdams et al. 1995).

The models integrate individual and class differences as weighting factors on the different dimensions and the set of specificities. Some listeners pay more attention to spectral properties and ignore temporal aspects, whereas others have the inverse pattern. Such variability may reflect either differences in sensory processing or in listening and rating strategies. Interestingly, no study to date has demonstrated that such individual differences have anything to do with musical experience or training (McAdams et al. 1995). It may be that because timbre perception is so closely allied with the ability to recognize sound sources in everyday life, everybody is an expert to some degree.

Acoustic correlates of timbral dimensions

In many studies, independent acoustic correlates have been determined for the continuous dimensions by correlating the position along the perceptual dimension with a unidimensional acoustic parameter extracted from the sounds (e.g. Grey and Gordon 1978; Krimphoff et al. 1994). The most ubiquitous correlates derived from musical instrument sounds include spectral centroid (representing the relative weights of high and low frequencies and corresponding to timbral brightness: an oboe has a higher spectral centroid than a French horn), the logarithm of the attack time (distinguishing continuant instruments that are blown or bowed from impulsive instruments that are struck or plucked), spectral flux (the degree of evolution of the spectral shape over a tone's duration which is high for brass and lower for single reeds), and spectral irregularity (the degree of jaggedness of the spectral shape, which is high for clarinet and vibraphone and low for trumpet). A confirmatory study employing dissimilarity ratings on purely synthetic sounds in which the exact nature of the stimulus dimensions could be controlled was performed by Caclin et al. (2005). These authors confirmed the perception of stimulus dimensions related to spectral centroid, attack time and spectral irregularity, but did not confirm spectral flux.

The combination of a quantitative model of perceptual relations among timbres and the psychophysical explanation of the parameters of the model is an important step in gaining predictive control of timbre in several domains such as sound analysis and synthesis and intelligent search in sound databases (Peeters et al. 2000). Such representations are only useful to the extent that they are: (a) generalizable beyond the set of sounds actually studied, (b) robust with respect to changes in musical context, and (c) generalizable to other kinds of listening tasks than those used to construct the model. To the degree that a representation has these properties, it may be considered as an accurate account of musical timbre, characterized by an important feature of a scientific model, the ability to predict new empirical phenomena.

Timbre space models have been useful in predicting listeners' perception in situations beyond those specifically measured in the experiments, which suggests that they do in fact capture important aspects of timbre representation. Consistent with the predictions of a timbre model, Grey and Gordon (1978) found that by exchanging the spectral envelopes on pairs of sounds that differed primarily along the spectral dimension, these sounds switched positions in the space. Timbre space has also been useful in predicting the perception of intervals between timbres, as well as stream segregation based on timbre-related acoustic cues (see below).

Effects of pitch change on timbre relations

Marozeau and colleagues (2003) have shown that timbre spaces for recorded musical instrument tones are similar at different pitches (B3, C#4, Bb4). Listeners are also able to ignore pitch differences within an octave when asked to compare only the timbres of the tones. When the pitch variation is greater than an octave, interactions between the two attributes occur. Marozeau and de Cheveigné (2007) varied the brightness of a set of synthesized sounds, while also varying the pitch over a range of 18 semitones. They found that differences in pitch affected timbre relations in two ways:

1 Pitch shows up in the timbre space representation as a dimension orthogonal to the timbre dimensions (indicating simply that listeners were no longer ignoring the pitch difference), and

2 Pitch differences systematically affect the timbre dimension related to spectral centroid.

These results suggest a close relation between timbral brightness and pitch height. This link would be consistent with underlying neural representations that share common attributes, such as a tonotopic organization.

Timbre as a vehicle for source identity

The second approach to timbre concerns its role in the recognition of the identity of a musical instrument or, in general, of a sound-generating event. One reasonable hypothesis is that the sensory dimensions that compose timbre serve as indicators used in the categorization, recognition, and identification of sound events and sound sources (McAdams 1993; Handel 1995).

Research on musical instrument identification is relevant to this issue. Saldanha and Corso (1964) studied identification of isolated musical instrument sounds from the Western orchestra played with and without vibrato. They were interested in the relative importance of onset and offset transients, spectral envelope of the sustain portion of the sound, and vibrato. Identification of isolated sounds is surprisingly poor for some instruments. When attacks and decays were excised, identification decreased markedly for some instruments, particularly for the attack portion in sounds without vibrato. However, when vibrato was present, the effect of cutting the attack was less, identification being better. These results suggest that important information for instrument identification is present in the attack portion, but that in the absence of this information, additional information is still available in the sustain portion (although it is more important for some instruments than others), particularly when vibrato is present. The vibrato may increase our ability to extract information relative to the resonance structure of the instrument (McAdams and Rodet 1988).

Giordano (2005) analysed previously published data on the identification and dissimilarity ratings of musical tones. The goal of this study was to ascertain the extent to which tones generated with large differences in the mechanisms for sound production were recovered in the perceptual data. Across all identification studies, listeners frequently confused tones generated by musical instruments with a similar physical structure (e.g., clarinets and saxophones, both single-reed instruments), and seldom confused tones generated by very different physical systems (e.g., the trumpet, a lip-reed instrument, and the bassoon, a double-reed instrument). Consistently, the vast majority of previously published timbre spaces revealed that tones generated with similar resonating structures (e.g., string instruments vs wind instruments) or with similar excitation mechanisms (e.g., impulsive excitation as in piano tones vs sustained excitation as in flute tones) occupied the same region in the space. These results suggest that listeners can reliably identify large differences in the mechanisms of tone production, focusing on the timbre attributes used to evaluate the dissimilarity of musical sounds.

Several investigations on the perception of everyday sounds extend the concept of timbre beyond the musical context (see McAdams 1993; Handel 1995; Lutfi 2008 for reviews). Among them, studies on impact sounds provide information on the timbre attributes useful to the perception of the properties of percussion instruments: bar geometry (Lakatos *et al.* 1997), bar material (McAdams *et al.* 2004a), plate material (Giordano and McAdams 2006), and mallet hardness (Freed 1990). The timbral factors relevant to perceptual judgements vary with the task at hand. Spectral factors are primary for the perception of the geometry (Lakatos *et al.* 1997). Spectrotemporal factors (e.g., the rate of temporal change of the spectral centroid and of loudness) dominate the perception of the material of struck objects (McAdams *et al.* 2004a, Giordano and McAdams 2006) and of mallets (Freed 1990).

The perception of an instrument's identity in spite of variations in pitch may be related to timbral invariance, those aspects of timbre that remain constant with change in pitch and loudness. Handel and Erickson (2001) found that musically untrained listeners are able to recognize two sounds produced at different pitches as coming from the same instrument or voice only within a pitch range of about an octave. Steele and Williams (2006) found that musically trained listeners could perform this task at about 80 per cent correct even with pitch differences on the order of 2.5 octaves. These results suggest that there are limits to timbral invariance across pitch, but that they depend on musical training.

Its role in source identification and categorization is perhaps the more neglected aspect of timbre, and brings with it advantages and disadvantages for the use of timbre as a form-bearing dimension in music (McAdams 1989). One of the advantages is that categorization and identification of a sound source may bring into play perceptual knowledge (acquired by listeners implicitly through experience in the everyday world and in musical situations) that helps them track a given voice or instrument in a complex musical texture. Listeners do this easily and some research has shown that timbral factors may make an important contribution in voice tracking (Culling and Darwin 1993; Gregory 1994), which is particularly important in polyphonic settings.

The disadvantages may arise in situations in which the composer seeks to create melodies across instrumental timbres, e.g., the *Klangfarbenmelodien* of Schoenberg (1911/1978). Our predisposition to identify the sound source and follow it through time would impede a more relative perception in which the timbral differences were perceived as a movement through timbre space rather than as a simple change of sound source. For cases in which such timbral compositions work, the composers have often taken special precautions to create a musical situation that draws the listener more into a relative than into an absolute mode of perceiving.

Timbral intervals

If timbral interval perception can be demonstrated, it opens the door to musical operations on timbre sequences that are commonly used on pitch sequences (Slawson 1985). Another interest of this exploration is that it extends the use of the timbre space as a perceptual model beyond the dissimilarity paradigm.

Ehresman and Wessel (1978; Wessel 1979) took a first step forward in this direction, developing a task in which listeners were asked to make judgements on the similarity of intervals formed between pairs of timbres. The basic idea was that timbre intervals may have properties similar to pitch intervals; that is, a pitch interval is a relation along a well-ordered dimension that retains a degree of invariance under certain kinds of transformation, such as translation along the dimension, or what musicians call 'transposition'. What does transposition mean in a multidimensional space? A timbre interval can be considered as a vector in space connecting two timbres. It has a specific length (the distance between the timbres) and a specific orientation. Together these two properties define the amount of change along each dimension of the space that is needed to move from one timbre to another. If we assume these dimensions to be continuous and linear from a perceptual point of view, then pairs of timbres characterized by the same vector relation should have the same relative perceptual relation and thus embody the same timbre interval. Transposition thus consists of translating the vector anywhere else in the space as long as its length and orientation are preserved.

Ehresman and Wessel tested this hypothesis using a task in which listeners had to compare two timbral intervals (e.g. A–B vs C–D) and rank various timbre D's according to how well they fulfilled the analogy: timbre A is to timbre B as timbre C is to timbre D. They essentially found that the closer timbre D was to the ideal point defined by the vector model in timbre space (i.e. the ideal C–D vector was a simple translation of the A–B vector), the higher the ranking.

McAdams and Cunibile (1992) subsequently tested the vector model using the 3D space from Krumhansl (1989) (ignoring the specificities). Five sets of timbres at different places in timbre space were chosen for each comparison to test for the generality of the results. Both electroacoustic composers and non-musicians were tested to see if musical training and experience had any effect. All listeners found the task rather difficult to do, which is not surprising given that even professional composers have had almost no experience with music that uses timbre intervals in a systematic way. The main result is encouraging in that globally the data support the vector model, although this support was much stronger for composers than for non-musicians. However, when one examines in detail the five different versions of each comparison type, it is clear that not all timbre comparisons go in the direction of the model predictions.

One confounding factor is that the specificities on some timbres in this set were ignored. These, quite to the contrary, would necessarily distort the vectors that were used to choose the timbres, because the specificities are like an additional dimension for each timbre. As such, certain timbre intervals correspond well to what is predicted because specificities are absent or low in value, whereas others would be seriously distorted and thus not perceived as similar to other intervals due to moderate or high specificity values. What this line of reasoning suggests is that the use of timbre intervals as an integral part of a musical discourse runs the risk of being very difficult to achieve with very complex and idiosyncratic sound sources, because they will in all probability have specificities of some kind or another. The use of timbre intervals may, in the long run, be limited to synthesized sounds or blended sounds created through the combination of several instruments.

Timbre and musical grouping

An important way in which timbre can contribute to the organization of musical structure is related to the fact that listeners tend to connect perceptually sound events that arise from the same sound source. In general, a given source will produce sounds that are relatively similar in pitch, loudness, timbre and spatial position from one event to the next (cf. Bregman 1990; McAdams and Bregman 1979 for reviews). The perceptual connection of successive sound events into a coherent 'message' through time is referred to as auditory stream integration, and the separation of events into distinct messages is called auditory stream segregation (Bregman and Campbell 1971). One guiding principle that seems to operate in the formation of auditory streams is the following: successive events that are relatively similar in their spectrotemporal properties (i.e. in their timbres) may have arisen from the same source and should be grouped together; individual sources do not tend to change their acoustic properties suddenly and repeatedly from one event to the next. Early demonstrations of auditory streaming on the basis of timbre (Wessel 1979) suggest a link between the timbre–space representation and the tendency for auditory streaming on the basis of the spectral differences that were created (McAdams and Bregman 1979). Early researchers were convinced that it was primarily the spectral aspects of timbre (such as spectral centroid) that were responsible for auditory streaming and that temporal aspects (such as attack time) had little effect (Hartmann and Johnson 1991).

Recently the picture has changed significantly and several studies indicate an important role for both spectral and temporal attributes of timbre in auditory stream segregation (Moore and Gockel 2002). Iverson (1995) used sequences alternating between two recorded instrument tones with the same pitch and loudness and asked listeners to judge the degree of segregation. Multidimensional scaling of the segregation judgments treated as a measure of dissimilarity was performed to determine which acoustic attributes contributed to the impression of auditory stream segregation. A comparison with previous timbre–space work using the same sounds (Iverson and Krumhansl 1993) showed that both static acoustic cues (such as spectral centroid) and dynamic acoustic cues (such as attack time and spectral flux) were implicated in segregation. Other results consistent with this study have also been reported (Bey and McAdams 2003; Singh and Bregman 1997).

All of these results are important for auditory stream segregation theory on the one hand, because they show that several of a source's acoustic properties are taken into account when forming auditory streams. On the other hand, they are important for music-making (whether it be with computer or acoustic instruments), because they show that many aspects of timbre strongly affect the basic organization of the musical surface into streams. Different orchestrations of a given pitch sequence can completely change what is heard as melody and rhythm, as has been demonstrated by Wessel (1979). Timbre is also an important component in the perception of musical groupings, whether they are at the level of sequences of notes distinguished by changes in timbre (Deliège 1987) or of larger-scale musical sections delimited by marked changes in orchestration and timbral texture (Deliège 1989).

Timbre as a structuring force in music perception

Timbre perception is at the heart of orchestration, a realm of musical practice that has received relatively little experimental study. Instrumental combinations can give rise to new timbres if the sounds are perceived as blended, and timbre can play a role in creating and releasing musical tension.

Timbral blend

The creation of new timbres through orchestration necessarily depends on the degree to which the constituent sound sources fuse together or blend to create the newly emerged sound (Brant 1971; Erickson 1975). Sandell (1995) has proposed that there are three classes of perceptual goals in combining instruments:

1 timbral heterogeneity in which one seeks to keep the instruments perceptually distinct,

2 timbral augmentation in which one instrument embellishes another one that perceptually dominates the combination, and

3 timbral emergence in which a new sound results that is identified as none of its constituents.

Blend appears to depend on a number of acoustic factors such as onset synchrony of the constituent sounds and others that are more directly related to timbre, such as the similarity of the attacks, the difference in the spectral centroids, and the overall centroid of the combination.

Role of timbre in building and release of musical tension

Timbre can also contribute to larger-scale musical form and in particular to the sense of movement between tension and relaxation. This movement has been considered by many music theorists as one of the primary bases for the perception of larger-scale form in music. It has traditionally been tied to harmony in Western music and plays an important role in Lerdahl and Jackendoff's (1983) *A generative theory of tonal music*. Experimental work on the role of harmony in the perception of musical tension and relaxation (or inversely, in the sense of tension that accompanies a moment at which the music must continue and the sense of relaxation that accompanies the completion of the musical phrase) has suggested that auditory roughness is an important component of perceived tension (Bigand *et al.* 1996). Roughness is an elementary timbral attribute based on the sensation of rapid fluctuations in the amplitude envelope. It can be generated by proximal frequency components that beat with one another. Dissonant intervals tend to have more such beating than consonant intervals. As such, a fairly direct relation between sensory dissonance and roughness has been demonstrated (cf. Parncutt 1989; Plomp 1976 for reviews).

As a first step toward understanding how this operates in music, Paraskeva and McAdams (1997) measured the inflection of musical tension and relaxation due to timbral change. Listeners were asked to make judgments on a 7-point scale concerning the perceived degree of completion of the music at several points at which the music stopped. What results is a completion profile, which can be used to infer musical tension by equating completion with release and lack of completion with tension. Two pieces were tested: a fragment from the Ricercar from the *Musical Offering* for six voices by Bach (tonal) and the first movement of the *Six Pieces for Orchestra* by Webern (non-tonal). Each piece was played in an orchestral version (the Webern instrumentation was used for the Bach), and a direct transcription of this orchestral version for piano on a digital sampler. There were significant differences between the piano and orchestral versions, indicating a significant effect of timbre change on perceived musical tension. However, when they were significantly different, the orchestral version was always more relaxed than the piano version.

The hypothesis advanced by Paraskeva and McAdams (1997) for this effect was that the higher relaxation of the orchestral version might have been due to processes involved in auditory stream formation and the dependence of perceived roughness on the results of such processes (Wright and Bregman 1987). Roughness, or any other auditory attribute of a single sound event, is computed after auditory organization processes have grouped the bits of acoustic information together. Piano sounds have a rather sharp attack. If several notes occur at the same time in the score and are played with a piano sound, they will be quite synchronous. Because they all start at the same time and have similar amplitude envelopes, they will tend to be fused together and the computed roughness will result from the interactions of all the frequency components of all the notes.

The situation may be quite different for the orchestral version for two reasons. The first is that the same timing is used for piano and orchestra versions. In the latter, many instruments are used that have slow attacks whereas others have faster attacks. There could then be a great deal of asynchrony between the instruments in terms of perceived attack time (Gordon 1987). In addition, because the timbres of these instruments are often quite different, several different voices with different timbres arrive momentarily at a given vertical sonority, but the verticality is not perceived because the listener would more likely continue to track individual instruments horizontally. So the attack asynchrony and the decomposition of verticalities into horizontalities would concur to reduce the degree of perceptual fusion. Reduced fusion would mean greater segregation. Thus the roughness in the orchestral version would be computed on each individually grouped auditory event rather than on the whole sound mass. These individual roughnesses in the orchestral version would most likely be much less than that of the piano version. So once again, timbral composition can have a very tight interaction with auditory stream formation processes.

Conclusion

Musical timbre is a combination of continuous perceptual dimensions and discrete features to which listeners are differentially sensitive. The continuous dimensions often have quantifiable acoustic correlates. The timbre–space representation is a powerful psychological model that allows predictions to be made about timbre perception in situations beyond those used to derive the model in the first place. Timbre intervals, for example, can be conceived as vectors within the space of common dimensions. Timbre space also makes at least qualitative predictions about the magnitude of timbre differences that will provoke auditory stream segregation.

Timbre can play a role in larger-scale movements of tension and relaxation and thus contribute to the expression inherent in musical form. Under conditions of high blend among instruments composing a vertical sonority, timbral roughness is a major component of musical tension. However, it strongly depends on the way auditory grouping processes have parsed the incoming acoustic information into events and streams.

References

Bey C and McAdams S (2003). Post-recognition of interleaved melodies as an indirect measure of auditory stream formation. *Journal of Experimental Psychology: Human Perception and Performance*, **29**, 267–279.

Bigand E, Parncutt R and Lerdahl F (1996). Perception of musical tension in short chord sequences: the influence of harmonic function, sensory dissonance, horizontal motion, and musical training. *Perception and Psychophysics*, **58**, 125–141.

Brant H (1971). Orchestration. In J Vinton, ed., *Dictionary of contemporary music*, 538–546 EP Dutton, New York.

Bregman AS (1990). *Auditory scene analysis: the perceptual organization of sound*. MIT Press, Cambridge, MA.

Bregman AS and Campbell J (1971). Primary auditory stream segregation and perception of order in rapid sequences of tones. *Journal of Experimental Psychology*, **89**, 244–249.

Caclin A, McAdams S, Smith BK and Winsberg S (2005). Acoustic correlates of timbre space dimensions: a confirmatory study using synthetic tones. *Journal of the Acoustical Society of America*, **118**, 471–482.

Culling JF and Darwin CJ (1993). The role of timbre in the segregation of simultaneous voices with intersecting Fo contours. *Perception and Psychophysics*, **34**, 303–309.

Deliège I (1987). Grouping conditions in listening to music: an approach to Lerdahl and Jackendoff's grouping preference rules. *Music Perception*, **4**, 325–360.

Deliège I, (1989). A perceptual approach to contemporary musical forms. *Contemporary Music Review*, **4**, 213–230.

Ehresman D and Wessel DL (1978). Perception of timbral analogies. *Rapports de l'IRCAM*, vol. 13 IRCAM, Paris.

Erickson R (1975). *Sound structure in music*. University of California Press, Berkeley, CA.

Freed DJ (1990). Auditory correlates of perceived mallet hardness for a set of recorded percussive events. *Journal of the Acoustical Society of America*, **87**, 1236–1249.

Giordano BL (2005). Sound source perception in impact sounds. Unpublished doctoral dissertation. University of Padova, Italy.

Giordano BL and McAdams S (2006). Material identification of real impact sounds: effects of size variation in steel, glass, wood and plexiglass plates. *Journal of the Acoustical Society of America*, **119**, 1171–1181.

Gordon JW (1987). The perceptual attack time of musical tones. *Journal of the Acoustical Society of America*, **82**, 88–105.

Gregory AH (1994). Timbre and auditory streaming. *Music Perception*, **12**, 161–174.

Grey JM (1977). Multidimensional perceptual scaling of musical timbres. *Journal of the Acoustical Society of America*, **61**, 1270–1277.

Grey JM and Gordon JW (1978). Perceptual effects of spectral modifications on musical timbres. *Journal of the Acoustical Society of America*, **63**, 1493–1500.

Hajda JM, Kendall RA, Carterette EC and Harshberger ML (1997). Methodological issues in timbre research. In I Deliège and J Sloboda, eds, *Perception and cognition of music*, 253–306. Psychology Press, Hove.

Handel S (1995). Timbre perception and auditory object identification. In B Moore, ed., *Hearing*, 425–462. Academic Press, San Diego, CA.

Handel S and Erickson M (2001). A rule of thumb: the bandwidth for timbre invariance is one octave. *Music Perception*, **19**, 121–126.

Hartmann WM and Johnson D (1991). Stream segregation and peripheral channeling. *Music Perception*, **9**, 155–184.

Helmholtz HLF von (1885/1954). *On the sensations of tone as a physiological basis for the theory of music*. New York, from 1877 trans. by AJ Ellis of 4th German edn, republished 1954 by Dover, New York.

Iverson P (1995). Auditory stream segregation by musical timbre: effects of static and dynamic acoustic attributes. *Journal of Experimental Psychology: Human Perception and Performance*, **21**, 751–763.

Iverson P and Krumhansl CL (1993). Isolating the dynamic attributes of musical timbre. *Journal of the Acoustical Society of America*, **94**, 2595–2603.

Kendall RA and Carterette EC (1991). Perceptual scaling of simultaneous wind instrument timbres. *Music Perception*, **8**, 369–404.

Krimphoff J, McAdams S and Winsberg S (1994). Caractérisation du timbre des sons complexes. II: Analyses acoustiques et quantification psychophysique [Characterization of the timbre of complex sounds. II: Acoustic analyses and psychophysical quantification]. *Journal de Physique*, **4**(C5), 625–628.

Krumhansl CL (1989). Why is musical timbre so hard to understand? In S Nielzén and O Olsson, eds, *Structure and perception of electroacoustic sound and music*, 43–53. Excerpta Medica, Amsterdam.

Lakatos S (2000). A common perceptual space for harmonic and percussive timbres. *Perception and Psychophysics*, **62**, 1426–1439.

Lakatos S, McAdams S and Caussé R (1997). The representation of auditory source characteristics: simple geometric form. *Perception and Psychophysics*, **59**, 1180–1190.

Lerdahl F and Jackendoff R (1983). *The generative theory of tonal music*. MIT Press, Cambridge, MA.

Lutfi R (2008). Human sound source identification. In W Yost, A Popper and R Fay, eds, *Auditory perception of sound sources*, 13–42. Springer, New York.

Marozeau J, de Cheveigné A, McAdams S and Winsberg S (2003). The dependency of timbre on fundamental frequency. *Journal of the Acoustical Society of America*, **114**, 2946–2957.

Marozeau J and de Cheveigné A (2007). The effect of fundamental frequency on the brightness dimension of timbre. *Journal of the Acoustical Society of America*, **121**, 383–387.

McAdams S (1989). Psychological constraints on form-bearing dimensions in music. *Contemporary Music Review*, **4**(1), 181–198.

McAdams S (1993). Recognition of sound sources and events. In S McAdams and E Bigand, eds, *Thinking in sound: the cognitive psychology of human audition*, 146–198. Oxford University Press, Oxford.

McAdams S (1999). Perspectives on the contribution of timbre to musical structure. *Computer Music Journal*, **23**(2), 96–113.

McAdams S (2003). Perception of musical timbre. *Bulletin of Psychology and the Arts*, **4**, 39–42.

McAdams S and Bregman AS (1979). Hearing musical streams. *Computer Music Journal*, **3**(4), 26–43.

McAdams S and Cunibile JC (1992). Perception of timbral analogies. *Philosophical Transactions of the Royal Society, London*, series B, **336**, 383–389.

McAdams S and Rodet X (1988) The role of FM-induced AM in dynamic spectral profile analysis. In H Duifhuis, JW Horst, HP Wit, eds, *Basic issues in hearing*, 359–369. Academic Press, London.

McAdams S, Chaigne A and Roussarie V (2004a). The psychomechanics of simulated sound sources: material properties of impacted bars. *Journal of the Acoustical Society of America*, **115**, 1306–1320.

McAdams S, Depalle P and Clarke E (2004b). Analyzing musical sound. In E Clarke and N Cook, eds, *Empirical musicology: aims, methods, prospects*, 157–196. Oxford University Press, New York.

McAdams S, Winsberg S, Donnadieu S, De Soete G and Krimphoff J (1995). Perceptual scaling of synthesized musical timbres: common dimensions, specificities, and latent subject classes. *Psychological Research*, **58**, 177–192.

Miller JR and Carterette EC (1975). Perceptual space for musical structures. *Journal of the Acoustical Society of America*, **58**, 711–720.

Moore BCJ and Gockel H (2002). Factors influencing sequential stream segregation. *Acustica united with Acta Acustica*, **88**, 320–332.

Paraskeva S and McAdams S (1997). Influence of timbre, presence/absence of tonal hierarchy and musical training on the perception of tension/relaxation schemas of musical phrases. *Proceedings of the 1997 International Computer Music Conference, Thessaloniki*, 438–441. International Computer Music Association, San Francisco, CA.

Parncutt R (1989). *Harmony: a psychoacoustical approach*. Springer-Verlag, Berlin.

Peeters G, McAdams S and Herrera P (2000) Instrument sound description in the context of MPEG-7. *Proceedings of the 2000 International Computer Music Conference, Berlin*, 166–169. International Computer Music Association, San Francisco, CA.

Plomp R (1970). Timbre as a multidimensional attribute of complex tones. In R Plomp and GF Smoorenburg, eds, *Frequency analysis and periodicity detection in hearing*, 397–414. Sijthoff, Leiden.

Plomp R (1976). *Aspects of tone sensation: a psychophysical study*. Academic Press, London.

Risset J-C and Wessel DL (1999). Exploration of timbre by analysis and synthesis. In D Deutsch, ed., *The psychology of music*, 2nd edn, 113–168. Academic Press, San Diego, CA.

Saldanha EL and Corso JF (1964). Timbre cues and the identification of musical instruments. *Journal of the Acoustical Society of America*, **36**, 2021–2126.

Sandell GJ (1995). Roles for spectral centroid and other factors in determining 'blended' instrument pairings in orchestration. *Music Perception*, **13**, 209–246.

Schoenberg A (1911/1978). *Theory of harmony*. Original German publication, 1911 edn. University of California Press, Berkeley, CA.

Singh PG and Bregman AS (1997). The influence of different timbre attributes on the perceptual segregation of complex-tone sequences. *Journal of the Acoustical Society of America*, **120**, 1943–1952.

Slawson W (1985). *Sound color*. University of California Press, Berkeley, CA.

Steele K and Williams A (2006). Is the bandwidth for timbre invariance only one octave? *Music Perception*, **23**, 215–220.

Wessel DL (1973). Psychoacoustics and music: a report from Michigan State University. *PACE: Bulletin of the Computer Arts Society*, **30**, 1–2.

Wessel DL (1979). Timbre space as a musical control structure. *Computer Music Journal*, **3**(2), 45–52.

Wright JK and Bregman AS (1987). Auditory stream segregation and the control of dissonance in polyphonic music. *Contemporary Music Review*, **2**(1), 63–92.

CHAPTER 8

Musical time

Mari Riess Jones

THIS chapter presents perspectives on perception of metre and rhythm, with a focus on dynamic attending theory (DAT). Three major sections address, respectively, metre perception, rhythm perception, and the role of time markers.

Metre perception

Intuitively, metre perception refers to a listener's sensitivity to musical timing regularities, evident when 'keeping time' by tapping in synchrony with musical tones. Sometimes tones are clearly accented and contribute to *metric hierarchies*, as suggested in Figure 8.1(a). Here, an idealized hierarchy features accents that are increasingly stronger (i.e. more salient; thicker bars) on non-adjacent tones separated by increasingly longer

time spans. Metric hierarchies comprise overlapping (i.e., *embedded*) time spans; they can be distinguished from time spans between successive tones (i.e., *serial spans*). Whereas metric spans reflect temporal embeddings (Figure 8.1(a)), serial spans invite rhythmic grouping (Figure 8.1(b)). Conventional wisdom holds that metre and rhythm are distinct time structures, engaging different perceptual processes. In this chapter I question this dichotomy.

Let's begin with metre perception. First, we should differentiate metric information in a visual score from that which meets a listener's ears. A typical (Western) score spells out two hierarchical time spans: a measure and its subdivisions. Thus, a notated 4/4 metric signature defines the measure as a time level evenly subdivided into

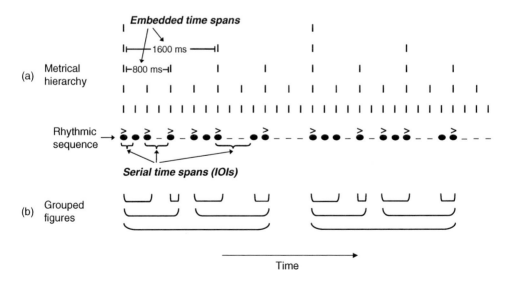

Fig. 8.1 Metric hierarchy, with embedding time spans (a); and rhythmic groups with serial (IOIs) time spans (b).

four quarter notes (a 4:1 embedded time ratio, Figure 8.1(a)), whereas a triple (3/4) metre implies a subdivision of three (a 3:1 ratio).

Yet, given an unfamiliar melody, a listener often does not 'know' its designated metre; people don't have scored bar lines in their heads. To understand metre perception in sound patterns, we must consider that listeners may infer several metric time levels. From this, challenging issues arise. For instance, listeners may selectively internalize aspects of a metric hierarchy by engaging a series of internal *beats* at one or more time levels. Stronger beats might be felt at points in a sound pattern where multiple objective accents align. Further, if an internal beat pattern persists, then beats are also felt at times where no objective accents exist, i.e., 'subjective accents'. Also, different listeners may focus upon different internal beat patterns as a referent level (tactus). In short, to understand metre perception, we must discover factors in sound patterns and in listeners that bias people to hear a pattern's time structure in a particular way.

Contemporary research on musical time began with classic work of Fraisse (1963), who focused on rhythmic groupings. He proposed that listeners rely on favoured *serial* time ratios to segment groups. Preferred ratios approximated 1:1 for within-group time spans and 2:1 for between-group serial time ratios. However, metric issues entered the picture when Povel

(1981) showed that metrical context modulates listeners preferences for 2:1 serial time ratios. Next, I describe theory and research surrounding two current psychological theories of metre perception, an encoding theory and a dynamic attending theory (DAT).

An encoding theory

Povel and Essens (1985) proposed that metre perception is governed by an internal clock. Metrical sequences, containing regular accents, readily induce a 'good' clock and lead to efficient encoding of serial time intervals, whereas non-metrical sequences, with irregular accents, do not. Examples of metrical and non-metrical monotone sequences, involving various inter-onset time intervals (IOIs), appear in Figures 8.1 and 8.2. Grouping accents (>) putatively occur on:

1 isolated tones;

2 the second tone of a two-tone group; and

3 initial and final tones in groups of three or more tones (Povel and Okkerman 1981).

This clock model has two stages. The first stage entails matching accents with internal clock ticks (i.e., beats). The best clock maximizes accent isochrony via minimizing mismatches (clock violations). Strong metric patterns (patterns 1 and 2, Figure 8.2), have accents (>) that coincide entirely with ticks (**O**) of the best clock,

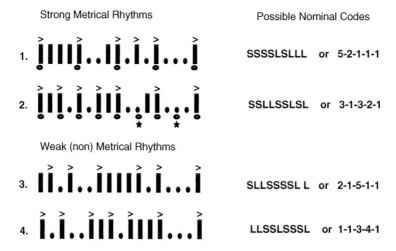

Fig. 8.2 Four patterns from Povel and Essens (1985). Grouping accents are >; clock ticks are **O**; negative clock evidence, s, is *.

namely the clock with fewest violations, i.e., least counter-evidence, C, where:

$$C = W \cdot s + u \qquad (1)$$

The W (W > 1.0) weights the number of clock ticks falling on a silence, s (*stars* in Figure 8.2) and u is the number of ticks on unaccented elements. Thus, for pattern 1, s = 0 and u = 0 whereas for pattern 2, s = 2 and u = 0. For both patterns, C is low reflecting strong metrical patterns.

The second stage features symbolic memory codes which are more economical for metric than for non-metric patterns. For non-metric patterns, codes reflect grouping properties (cf. Figure 8.2). Thus, although the non-metric pattern 3 lacks a good clock fit, its five groups produce nominal codes of Short or Long IOIs, or symbols of group sizes: 2–1–5–1–1. These codes reflect nominal segmentations, not interval time relationships. Others propose different coding strategies (e.g. Lerdahl and Jackendoff 1983; Temperley 2001).

Evidence for metric encoding

Povel and Essens required people to reproduce many metric and non-metric sequences. Consistent with clock model predictions, best temporal accuracy occurred with metrical sequences. Since 1985, this model has stimulated much research on metric encoding. However, conflicting reports surround its implications that highly metrical patterns elicit better temporal acuity (Handel 1992; Ross and Houtsma 1994; Handel 1998). Hebert and Cuddy (2002) found that both a metric frame (metrical sequences) and the presence of a rhythmic figure (non-metrical sequences) benefit time-change detection.

Much research on synchronized tapping appeals to motor control theory (see Repp 2005 for review). However, few (e.g. Palmer and Pfordresher 2003) consider metre perception. Some empirical examinations of synchronized and reproduction tapping do directly address clock model assumptions (e.g. McAuley and Semple 1999; Patel *et al.* 2005). McAuley and Semple questioned whether clock induction depends only on negative, i.e., counter-evidence (i.e., ticks at unaccented times). They formulated alternative versions of Equation 1, creating a

positive evidence model (P), weighting clock ticks coinciding with accents; and a hybrid model (H), weighting both positive and negative evidence. Musicians and non-musicians tapped to metrical sequences, indexed by C, P, and H. The Hybrid model best predicted musicians' behaviour, whereas Povel's C index best predicted non-musicians' performance. Thus, non-musicians appear to be affected by clock violations, consistent with Povel and Essens model, whereas musicians draw strength from confirmations as well as clock violations.

Patel *et al.* (2005) found that tapping to isochronous patterns at a fixed beat period of 800 ms was less variable with isochronous subdivisions of this period than with non-isochronous (rhythmic) ones. Although consistent with clock predictions, other findings involving subdivisions by 2 or 4 were more difficult for the clock model. These data converge with others (Essens 1986) to suggest that listeners rely on relationships among multiple time levels. Indeed, even very young children appear to use multiple time levels to differentiate duple from triple metre categories (Phillips-Silver and Trainor 2005; Trehub and Hannon 2006; Bergeson and Trehub 2006), although reports of children's preference for duple metre (2:1 ratios) (Drake 1993) were not confirmed.

Dynamic attending theory and the metric binding hypothesis

Dynamic attending theory (DAT) addresses 'in-the-moment' expectancies in listening. Its relevance to metre perception is discussed in this section, where I propose a new hypothesis: the *metric binding hypothesis*.

Entrainment is a biological process that realizes adaptive synchrony of *internal* attending oscillations with an *external* event. Different event timescales correspond to marked (i.e., accented) metric levels (Figures 8.1, 8.3). Time spans within a metric level can elicit a corresponding neural oscillation, which has a persisting internal periodicity (Pi), manifest as a *temporal expectancy*. It 'tunes into' recurrent time spans at a given level by adjusting its phase in response to temporal *expectancy violations* (φ) at that level.

Various DAT models share four assumptions (Large 1994; McAuley 1995; Large and Kolen 1995;

Large and Jones 1999). First, neural oscillations are *self-sustaining;* they persist over time, extrapolating the induced beat. Second, an oscillator's intrinsic period exhibits *stability;* a perturbation from an ill-timed tone only briefly disrupts a stable oscillation, which returns to its intrinsic period. Third, entraining oscillations exhibit *adaptivity,* the flip side of stability; an oscillator responds appropriately to event-generated expectancy violations by adjusting phase and period. Fourth, *multiple related oscillations* are activated by multiple time levels within metric and rhythmic events.

The metric binding hypothesis expands these assumptions. It adds learning principles to address training and enculturation that contribute to listeners' familiarity with metric categories. It holds: *whenever two or more neural oscillations are simultaneously active, over time their internal entrainments lead to binding and formation of a metric cluster.* A metric cluster comprises sets of co-occurring oscillations with interrelationships that persist due to acquired internal bindings. Entrainments among internal oscillations promote binding, which strengthens as a function of:

1 Duration of co-occurring oscillatory activity.

2 Phase coincidences, and,

3 Resonance (i.e., relatedness) among oscillator periods.

Figure 8.3 illustrates how metric clusters form. As a rhythmic pattern unfolds, it successively activates neural oscillations with periods (Pi) matching each of the lower-level IOIs. Initially recurrent IOIs, in this case, elicit an oscillation with a period of 200 ms, which is strongly coupled to these IOIs. However, this rhythm subsequently awakens oscillations with periods of 400 and 800 ms due to serial IOIs that follow. Oscillations of periods 400 and 800 ms find added support mainly from higher event time spans between non-adjacent tones. This analysis shows how rhythm and metre co-constrain oscillation activities. Once active, co-occurring internal oscillations mutually entrain.

I propose that, over time, internal entrainment leads to cluster binding and the formation of a persisting metric form (here duple metre). This is a mechanism for bootstrapping learning based on pattern relationships. It is constrained by binding principles such that learning is facilitated not only by longer total times of oscillator co-activity (e.g., Hebbian learning), but also by strong resonance and phase relations among active oscillations. The metric binding

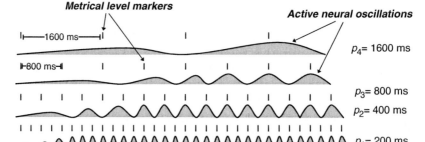

Multiple Neural Oscillations

Metrical level markers

Active neural oscillations

p_4= 1600 ms

p_3= 800 ms
p_2= 400 ms

p_1= 200 ms

Serial IOIs: 200, 200, 400, 400, 400, 400, 200, 200, 800, ...

A Metric Cluster

Multiple simultaneously-active oscillations *bind* as a function of: 1. Duration of simultaneous activity 2. Intrinsic period ratios (*pi/pj*)3. Coincidence of pulse peaks

Fig. 8.3 Multiple metric levels entrain corresponding neural oscillations. Rhythm (serial IOIs) also activates oscillations. This figure illustrates metric binding hypothesis principles.

hypothesis implies that: 'Oscillators that align together, bind together.'

Once acquired, metric clusters grant trained listeners attentional flexibility to activate oscillators for unmarked metric levels (Palmer and Krumhansl 1990) and to flexibly shift focal attending to different marked levels. In fact, Jones and Boltz (1989) proposed two attending modes, future-oriented and analytic attending, to reflect focal attending to higher and lower time levels, respectively.

Specialized entrainment models

Several DAT models formalize oscillator behaviours for different tasks; typically, a single oscillation exhibits three components: period; pulse, and phase. Some tasks rely on a single oscillation model, others on multiple oscillations.

The simplest oscillator model appears in Figure 8.4 entraining to an isochronous event (Large and Jones 1999). This single oscillation carries a concentration of attending energy, an attentional pulse. With rhythmically simple events, an oscillator's 'tuning' is reflected in a

steady narrowing of an attentional pulse about an expected phase point: $\phi = 0$. This entails continuous phase adjustments to minimize differences between momentarily expected phases and observed tone onsets. The goal is an attractor, defined by phase coincidence (synchrony), of expected and observed time points. Once attuned, an entrained oscillation persists to extrapolate beats (attentional pulses), each beat realizing an anticipated region in time (insert).

Metre perception is described with more complex models; at least two oscillations, entraining at different metric levels, are necessary (see Figure 8.3) (Large and Jones 1999; Large and Palmer 2002). Moreover, these oscillations can interact. To illustrate, consider pattern 2 (Figure 8.2). This rhythm differs from the rhythm of Figure 8.3 in containing lower order IOIs that elicit oscillations with periods: 200, 400, 600, 800 ms. That is, three oscillator periods (200, 400, 800 ms) nest neatly with higher metric levels (400, 800 ms, 1600 ms), but one does not (600 ms). Nevertheless, the metric binding hypothesis assumes internal entrainments

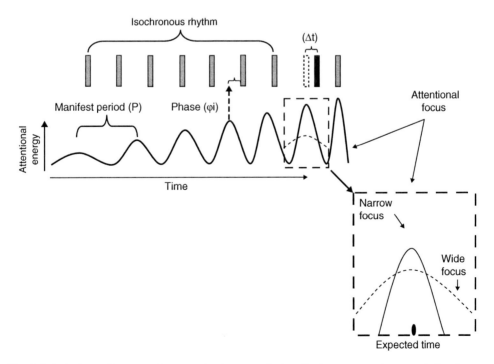

Fig. 8.4 A single oscillator entrains to an isochronous rhythm. Basic components are period, pulse (insert) and phase.

among active oscillations lead to common metric percepts for different rhythms. Binding among oscillations depends not only on the duration of joint oscillator activities, but also on resonance relations among these oscillations, namely period and phase relationships. Thus, for pattern 2, although the oscillator with an ill-fitting period (e.g., 600 ms), is initially active, it dies out due to poor resonance. The winning metric cluster for pattern 2 turns out to be identical to the metric cluster for the different rhythm of Figure 8.3. This analysis predicts that the 600 ms IOI (pattern 2, Figure 8.2) will be perceptually distorted to 'fit' the duple metre frame common to both rhythms. More generally, metric binding in multi-oscillator systems explains how various rhythmic instances are perceived as members of a common metric category.

The mathematics of multi-oscillator systems is complex. Nevertheless, resonance properties require some mention. When two oscillations are active, their periods form embedding ratios (e.g., 1:1, 2:1, 3:1, 1:2, 2:3; 3:2 etc.) that gauge overall stability of their interaction. Embedding ratios specify resonance states (i.e., attractors) that have different degrees of stability; this, in turn, predicts differential lasting qualities of metric clusters (Large and Kolen 1995; cf. London 2004). For instance, clusters based on duple metre ratios are predicted to be more stable than those based on complex ratios.

Finally, it is common to distinguish metre perception from rhythm perception, in that it reflects an acquired skill, whereas rhythm perception is attributed to innate Gestalt principles (Bregman 1990; Handel 1989). DAT does not incorporate this dichotomy. Rather, dynamical properties offer biological springboards that differentially constrain the learning of metric versus rhythmic time structures. DAT implies that unlearned biological responses (neural oscillations) are fundamental to time perception, whether metric or rhythmic. These biological dispositions (oscillatory entrainments) initially facilitate attending to event structure via activated oscillations. Next, stability differences among simultaneously active oscillations lead to differential learning of metric patterns versus non-metric and rhythmic patterns given the metric binding hypothesis.

Evidence for DAT

Evidence associated with various entrainment models of metre perception derives from both behavioral and biological sources.

Behavioural assessments of DAT

Experimental research often concerns responses to timing of metrically regular and irregular contexts. The most rigorous tests involve threshold judgements of timing and categorical time judgements (see Jones 2004 for a review).

Single oscillator entrainment models predict that lower-order serial IOIs of monotone rhythms are important, a finding confirmed by Demany and Semal (2002). These models also correctly predict that, in judging time intervals, listeners will distort unexpected time intervals to fit with a contextually expected beat span (Barnes and Jones 2000). Other entrainment models, which involve biologically preferred periods (McAuley 1995), also find support McAuley et al. (2006). Two oscillator entrainment models, used to describe metre perception, assume that one oscillation entrains to a higher metric level, marked by more salient accents, while another oscillation, with a shorter period, entrains to embedded event time spans, marked by less salient accents. Such a model was shown to correctly predict that greater metric regularity (within and between trials) enhances temporal acuity (Jones and Yee 1997; Large and Jones 1999).

Acuity thresholds are affected by tempo. London (2004) argued that such acuity limits affect metre identification, biasing listeners toward particular metres at certain tempi. Effectively, a perceived tactus corresponds to a lower metrical level in relatively slow patterns but a higher one in faster patterns (Handel and Oshinsky 1981; Parncutt 1994; Duke 1989).

McAuley et al. (2006) found that the limits of tempo perception (e.g. Weber's Law) depend upon entrainment constraints expressed by *entrainment regions*. An entrainment region is a range of tempi, surrounding a preferred event rate, that corresponds to good entrainment. Both the location and width of these regions were found to shift with age: children were shown to prefer narrow entrainment regions, surrounding a fast event rate (active oscillations with brief periods), whereas elderly listeners had broader entrainment regions centered on slower events (active oscillations with longer periods). Thus, perceived metre may modulate not only with tempo but also with age. Also see Drake and Botte (1993), Miller and McAuley (2005), Jones and McAuley (2005), and Parncutt (1994).

Biological assessments of DAT

Neurophysiological findings buttress entrainment theory (see Zanto *et al.* 2006). Consistent with DAT, electroencephalography (EEG) reveals neural oscillations that synchronize to periodic auditory stimuli in the musical range, i.e. 2 Hz (Will and Berg 2007).

Using event-related potentials (ERPs), Brochard *et al.* (2003) were the first to verify the presence of subjective accents, i.e., internalized beat patterns (Fraisse 1963; Woodrow 1932). They found ERP activity in the parietal cortex of non-musicians that reflected duple metre expectancies (see also Besson and Faita 1995; Janata 2001). Often ERP signal frequencies (0–10 Hz) reveal relatively long latency brain responses (e.g., P300), which may reflect a synthesis of higher frequency oscillations (Makeig *et al.* 2004). Indeed, fronto-cortical ERP recordings revealed two kinds of high frequency activities (Snyder and Large 2005):

1 An induced periodic response, in the Beta/ Gamma range (20–30Hz), prior to onsets of metrically expected tones;

2 A phase-locked evoked Gamma (30–60 Hz) response following tone onsets.

These findings confirm DAT distinctions between expectancies (oscillator period) and expectancy violations (phase corrections) (Janata 2001; Zanto *et al.* 2005).

A common question is: 'Are internal oscillations purely event driven?' (Iverson *et al.* 2006). Both behavioural and neurophysiological studies suggest the answer is 'No'. Combined manipulations of event structure with task and instructions (imagery, attentional set) suggest that event structure plays a role in facilitating or inhibiting listeners' compliance with instructions (Palmer and Krumhansl 1990; Klein and Jones 1996; Janata and Grafton 2003; Snyder and Large 2005; Iverson *et al.* 2006). Clearly, people rely upon both guided imagination and event structure to shape metric expectancies.

Rhythm

Rhythm is a serial figure based on an arrangement of discrete time intervals. It contrasts with metre, which is based upon embedded time intervals. In this section, I outline current limits on our understanding of rhythm perception.

Theoretical background

Many contemporary approaches to rhythm perception assume that it is psychologically distinct from metre perception (Figure 8.1(b) versus Figure 8.1(a)). Rhythm perception is assumed to depend upon temporal grouping principles, given by Gestalt rules of proximity, similarity, continuity, etc. In turn, Gestalt theory holds that rhythm perception is innate, based upon an automatic, primitive, universal process that is governed by hard-wired, domain-free, grouping principles. Thus, rhythm perception is considered inherently different from metre perception, which is viewed as an acquired skill, reflecting domain-specific musical rules.

The classic dichotomy of rhythm and metre perception is appealing for several reasons. First, it captures an experiential difference between serial (rhythmic) and embedded (metric) time structures. Second, reliance on Gestalt principles leads to coarse coding of serial time spans which correctly captures listeners' often fuzzy percepts of rhythmic time spans. By this account, the rhythmic figure of 400–200–200 ms invites lax encoding of proximal tones as 'groups', segmented by non-proximal tones (i.e., groups of 1 versus 3 tones; cf. Figure 8.2). Nominal codes of time intervals as either short (proximal) or long (non-proximal) yield a coarse rhythmic code, such as long–short–short for this figure. Third, nominal codes often accurately predict perceptual confusions among rhythms. For instance, the 400–200–200 ms figure has the same nominal code (long–short–short) as 500–100–200 ms, leading to observed confusions of such rhythms. In sum, Gestalt rules are intuitively compelling and coarse temporal groupings, nominally encoded, offer explanatory value.

In spite of the appeal of Gestalt theory, a rhythmic/metre dichotomy cloaks pitfalls. First, because Gestalt principles are hard-wired, this approach denies that listeners may blend innate with acquired responses to time structures. For instance, the two confusable rhythms (above) may be eventually differentiated as listeners acquire sensitivity to different temporal nesting properties. Second, by denying a role for learning, this approach discourages research on this topic. Indeed, Gestalt rules are often mistaken for final explanations when they are simply useful descriptions of phenomena that require explanation. Third, this dichotomy renders it difficult or impossible to address rhythmic priming of metre and vice versa.

DAT assumes that learning builds upon innate oscillatory brain activities. It offers a potential for explaining both metre and rhythm perception based on entrainment constraints associated with their respective time properties. Perceptual learning (i.e. the metric binding hypothesis) depends upon entrainments of innate oscillations elicited by an event's time spans. Although multiple time spans occur in both metric and non-metric rhythms (cf. Figure 8.1), they promote different learning paths. Relationships among saliently marked embedded time spans are typically orderly and aligned to highlight consistent ratio time relationships in metric patterns, whereas in rhythmic figures, time spans from grouping accents can offer unruly, misaligned, embeddings (especially in non-metric patterns) that obscure higher level temporal regularities. Because of this, metric patterns promote quicker binding of oscillators across embedded time levels than do rhythmic patterns. Rhythmic figures that lack consistent higher-order time spans cannot support effective entrainment of higher level oscillators; instead, loosely connected oscillations among IOI resolve to group segmentations. It follows that DAT can address rhythmic priming of metre and vice versa (Desain and Honing 2003). Nevertheless, despite its potential no DAT task model has formalized these ideas to rigorously explain serial segmentation in rhythmic patterns. In this regard DAT and Gestalt approaches share incomplete explanations of rhythm perception.

Empirical evidence on rhythm perception

Listeners can distinguish among theoretically confusable rhythms if timing differences are sufficiently large (Hebert and Cuddy 2002) or if patterns occur repeatedly (Handel 1992). Although poorly understood, listeners do learn to differentiate confusable rhythms having similar Gestalt grouping codes.

An important difference between DAT and Gestalt accounts is the latter's emphasis on nominal coding of rhythmic time spans. By contrast, DAT features roles for both interval (tempo) and ratio (metre/rhythm) time relationships. Critically, even in brief rhythmic sequences, listeners are sensitive to rhythmic categories with special serial time ratios (e.g., 1:1, 2:1) (e.g., Desain and Honing 2003). Using only two time intervals, incremental lengthening of the first interval (relative to the second) between serial ratios of 1:1 and 2:1 (and vice versa) revealed preferences for the simpler anchoring ratios, consistent with Fraisse's ideas. Not to be overlooked is research showing metric priming of such rhythms (Povel 1981; Clarke 1987; ten Hoopen et al. 2006)

Related findings accompany a *time-shrinking* phenomenon (Nakajima et al. 1992; Sasaki et al. 2002; Nakajima et al. 2004). Using brief two-interval patterns, Nakijima and his colleagues find that when a long time interval follows a short one, listeners underestimate it, revealing a gravitation to a preferred serial time ratio of 1:1. However, reversal of the two intervals fails to elicit time expansion. Generally, research on time distortions suggests that perception of rhythmic figures is influenced by stability of certain serial time ratios: 1:1, 2:1, 1:2. Interestingly, brain activities, measured by functional magnetic resonance imaging (fMRI), also appear to depend upon the simpler time ratios produced by listeners (i.e., stable anchoring ratios) and not stimulus ratios (Sakai et al. 1999).

Marking time and accent salience

All time patterns exist because *accents* mark constituent time spans. Accents 'call attention' to onsets of time spans. In this section I focus upon the neglected issue of *accent salience* (for different perspectives, see Krumhansl 2000; Clarke 1999).

Theoretical background

The dichotomy of rhythm and metre perception holds implications for understanding accents as time markers. Sometimes accents are drawn into this dichotomy through the assumption that codes for metre and rhythm are processed independently and/or stored in respectively separate modules. Thus, metric versus rhythmic accents may be distinguished by linking them, respectively, with different physical dimensions (e.g., time, intensity, pitch etc.). For instance, in some views metre is considered to be marked by intensity accents whereas rhythm is marked by duration accents. A related hypothesis holds that rhythm and metre percepts are not only dichotomous, but that both are independent of melodic features, e.g., pitch accents.

Complicating discussions of independence versus dependence of metre, rhythm and melody is the practice of differentiating musical accents a priori by dimensionality alone, e.g., as intensity, time, or pitch accents. This practice raises certain dilemmas. Consider this: if an accent effectively 'calls' attention to a point in time, then logically accents *cannot* be solely defined by their dimensions. Rather, accents must be contextually defined because they only occur in serial contexts. An accent gains its power as a *serial change*, regardless of dimension.

A large relative intensity change in a musical sequence is more attention-getting, i.e., more salient, than a small one. Thus, to compare accents of different types (i.e., dimensions) as effective markers of metre, it is important to equate them for salience.

Dynamic attending theory assumes that accents arise from local serial changes (Jones 1987). This broadens the definition of phenomenal accents of Lerdahl and Jackendoff (1983). Operationally, the salience of an accented tone increases with the:

1 Magnitude of its local serial change along a dimension of variation;

2 Number of simultaneous accents on it (i.e., all else equal, two co-occurring serial changes are stronger than one);

3 Surrounding variability (melodic, rhythmic, etc.) in global serial context (Ellis and Jones in press).

In DAT, various accent types mark time spans of both rhythm and metre. Further, if the perceptual impact of an accent, i.e. its salience, turns on the magnitude of a local serial change, then different accent types (pitch, time, etc.) can have equivalent salience. This idea is formalized in the concept of joint accent structure (JAS) (Jones 1987). A JAS reflects a temporal collaboration of different (salient) accent types that

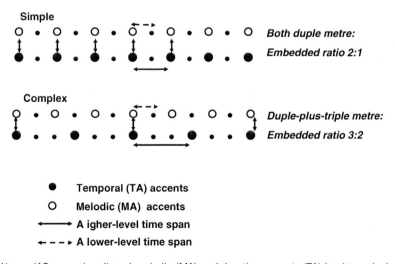

Fig. 8.5 Upper JAS example: aligned melodic (MA) and duration accents (TA) lead to a duple metre JAS pattern. Lower: misaligned accent sequences form a polyrhythmic JAS-based duple (MA) and triple (TA) patterns.

outline a common, higher order, time structure. As shown in Figure 8.5, structural interdependence of melodic (pitch change) and rhythmic (duration changes) accents is inherent in that a metric structure emerges from time spans marked by both melodic and rhythmic accents. One configuration reflects a simple combination of melodic accent and rhythmic accent sequences (duple metre embedding ratios of 2:1) where both melodic (MA) and temporal (TA) accents align; in the other, a more complex JAS combination results in misaligned accents (polyrhythmic ratios of 3:2). According to a metric binding hypothesis, the former is the more stable due to its resonance properties. Nevertheless, as experimental compositions, both JAS patterns reflect interdependence of melodic, rhythmic and metric structures.

Experimental evidence on marking time

Experimental evidence offers mixed support for hypotheses about perception of musical events containing melodic and temporal accents. Some favours a hypothesis that melody, rhythm and metre are perceived independently, whereas other evidence favours a perceptual dependency hypothesis. Such issues remain unresolved.

Research which relies upon established compositions is consistent with the idea that melody and metre are perceptually independent. For instance, listeners' inferred beats indicate a reliance on rhythmic (duration) over melodic accents (Snyder and Krumhansl 2001; Hannon *et al.* 2004). Hence, Huron and Royal (1996) question the effectiveness of melodic accents for marking metre. Yet evidence for this conclusion remains inconclusive. In part, this is because the salience of various accents is unknown, and in part it is because such correlational evidence precludes causal inferences. Furthermore, other evidence, based on experimental compositions, favours the alternative view. In these, melodic (pitch) and rhythmic (temporal) accents together appeared to determine listeners' sense of metre (Boltz and Jones 1986; Pfordresher 2003).

A resolution of this issue depends upon insuring comparable salience across accent types. For example, in specified musical contexts we must gauge whether a three semitone pitch leap

(melodic accent) is equal in salience to lengthening tone duration by 5 per cent or by 15 per cent (rhythm accents). Overall variability of surrounding melodic and rhythmic contexts must also be controlled.

A few studies have controlled accent salience. Windsor (1993) calibrated intensity accents, and confirmed that larger serial changes in intensity yielded clearer metric identifications. Ellis and Jones (in press) used melodic (MA) and temporal (TA) accents of calibrated equivalence in various sequences to create nine different JAS patterns; to appear in Figure 8.5 (i.e., 2:1 duple; 3:2 polyrhythm). Different JAS conditions combined duple and triple accent patterns in aligned (e.g., duple for TA and MA) and misaligned (e.g., duple TA and triple MA) ways. Listeners rated the metric clarity of all patterns. Results appear in Figure 8.6. In JAS patterns with aligned MAs and TAs, time spans should activate multiple aligned oscillations (for duple or triple metre), and thus here DAT correctly predicts stable metric clusters and high metric clarity. By contrast, in misaligned JAS patterns, with irregular high-level time spans, DAT correctly predicts lower clarity.

These findings reveal the importance of calibrating accent salience. Melodic and rhythmic accents, of comparable salience, lead to JAS

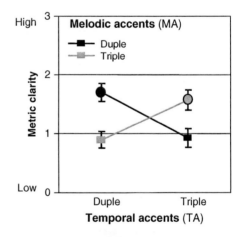

Fig. 8.6 Metric clarity ratings of average listeners. Melodic (MAs, dark lines) and temporal (TAs, light lines) accent patterns are either aligned (e.g., circles) or mis-aligned (squares) (Ellis and Jones in press).

patterns of different complexity when combined with embedding ratios of 2:1 versus 3:2. Listeners' ratings of these patterns supports the hypothesis that percepts of melody, rhythm and metre are not independent.

Summary

This chapter selectively reviews psychological research on perception of metre and rhythm. Its focus is upon the dynamics of attending to patterns in time. It considers how event timing, as outlined by salient accents in metre, rhythm, and even melodic structures, may guide attending in time, bootstrap learning, and influence time perception.

Acknowledgements

The author is grateful for the assistance of Robert Ellis.

References

Barnes R and Jones MR (2000) Expectancy, attention, and time. *Cognitive Psychology*, **41**, 254–311.

Bergeson TR and Trehub SE (2006) Infants' perception of rhythmic patterns. *Music Perception*, **23**, 345–360.

Besson M and Faita F (1995) An event-related potential (ERP) study of musical expectancy: comparison of musicians with nonmusicians. *Journal of Experimental Psychology: Human Perception and Performance*, **21**, 1278–1296.

Boltz M and Jones MR (1986) Does rule recursion make melodies easier to reproduce? If not, what does? *Cognitive Psychology*, 18, 389–431.

Bregman A (1990) *Auditory scene analysis*. MIT Press, Cambridge, MA.

Brochard R, Abecasis D, Potter D, Ragot R and Drake C (2003) The 'ticktock' of our internal clock: direct brain evidence of subjective accents in isochronous sequences. *Psychological Science*, **14**, 362–366.

Clarke EF (1987) Levels of structure in the organization of musical time. *Contemporary Music Review*, **2**, 211–238.

Clarke EF (1999) Rhythm and timing in music. In D Deutsch, ed., *The psychology of music*, 473–500. Academic Press, New York.

Demany L and Semal C (2002) Limits of rhythm perception. *Q J Exp Psychol A*, **55**, 643–657.

Desain P and Honing H (2003) The formation of rhythmic categories and metric priming. *Perception*, **32**, 341–365.

Drake C (1993) Reproduction of musical rhythms by children, adult musicians and adult nonmusicians. *Perception and Psychophysics*, **53**, 25–33.

Drake C and Botte M (1993) Tempo sensitivity in auditory sequences: evidence for a multiple-look model. *Perception and Psychophysics*, **54**, 277–286.

Duke RA (1989) Musicians' perception of beat in monotonic stimuli. *Journal of Research in Music Education*, **37**, 61–71.

Ellis RJ and Jones MR (in press) The role of accent salience and joint accent structure in meter perception. *Journal of Experimental Psychology: Human Perception and Performance*.

Essens PJ (1986) Hierarchical organization of temporal patterns. *Perception and Psychophysics*, **40**, 69–73.

Fraisse P (1963) *The psychology of time*. Harper and Row, New York.

Handel S (1989) *Listening: an introduction to the perception of auditory events*. MIT Press, Cambridge, MA.

Handel S (1992) The differentiation of rhythmic structure. *Perception and Psychophysics*, **52**, 497–507.

Handel S (1998) The interplay between metric and figural organization. *Journal of Experimental Psychology: Human Perception and Performance*, **24**, 1546–1561.

Handel S and Oshinsky JS (1981) The meter of syncopated auditory patterns. *Perception and Psychophysics*, **30**, 1–9.

Hannon EE, Snyder JS, Eerola T and Krumhansl CL (2004) The role of melodic and temporal cues in perceiving musical meter. *Journal of Experimental Psychology: Human Perception and Performance*, **30**, 956–974.

Hebert S and Cuddy LL (2002) Detection of metric structure in auditory figural patterns. *Percept Psychophys*, **64**, 909–918.

Huron D and Royal M (1993). What is melodic accent?. *Converging evidence from musical practice. Music Perception*, **13**, 489–516.

Iverson JR, Repp BH and Patel AD (2006) *Metrical interpretation modulates brain responses to rhythmic sequences*. The Neuroscience Institute, San Diego, CA.

Janata P (2001) Brain electrical activity evoked by mental formation of auditory expectations and images. *Brain Topogr*, **13**, 169–193.

Janata P and Grafton ST (2003) Swinging in the brain: shared neural substrates for behaviors related to sequencing and music. *Nat Neurosci*, **6**, 682–687.

Jones MR (1987). Dynamic pattern structure in music: recent theory and research. *Perception and Psychophysics*, **41**, 621–634.

Jones MR (2004) Attention and timing. In JG Neuhoff, ed., *Ecological psychoacoustics*, 45–89. Academic Press, San Diego, CA.

Jones MR and Boltz M (1989) Dynamic attending and responses to time. *Psychological Review*, **96**, 459–491.

Jones MR and Mcauley JD (2005) Time judgments in global temporal contexts. *Percept Psychophys*, **67**, 398–417.

Jones MR and Yee W (1997) Sensitivity to time change: the role of context and skill. *Journal of Experimental Perception and Psychophysics*, **32**, 693–709.

Klein JM and Jones MR (1996) Effects of attentional set and rhythmic complexity on attending. *Perception and Psychophysics*, **58**, 34–46.

Krumhansl CL (2000) Rhythm and pitch in music cognition. *Psychological Bulletin*, **126**, 159–179.

Large EW (1994) Dynamic representation of musical structure. Unpublished doctoral dissertation. Ohio State University, Columbus.

Large EW and Jones MR (1999) The dynamics of attending: how people track time-varying events. *Psychological Review*, **106**, 119–159.

Large EW and Kolen J (1995) Resonance and the perception of musical meter. *Connection Science*, **6**, 177–208.

Large EW and Palmer C (2002) Perceiving temporal regularity in music. *Cognitive Science*, **26**, 1–37.

Lerdahl F and Jackendoff R (1983) *A generative theory of tonal music*. MIT Press, Cambridge, MA.

London JM (2004) *Hearing in time: psychological aspects of musical meter*. Oxford University Press, New York.

Makeig S, Debener S, Onton J and Delorme A (2004) Mining event-related brain dynamics. *Trends Cogn Sci*, **8**, 204–210.

Mcauley JD (1995) *Perception of time phase: toward an adaptive oscillator model of rhythmic pattern processing*. Indiana University Press, Bloomington, IN.

Mcauley JD and Semple P (1999) The effect of tempo and musical experience on perceived beat. *Australian Journal of Psychology*, **51**, 176–187.

Mcauley JD, Jones MR, Holub S, Johnston HM and Miller NS (2006) The time of our lives: life span development of timing and event tracking. *J Exp Psychol Gen*, **135**, 348–367.

Miller NS and Mcauley JD (2005) Tempo sensitivity in isochronous tone sequences: the multiple-look model revisited. *Percept Psychophys*, **67**, 1150–1160.

Nakajima Y, Ten Hoopen G, Hilkhuysen G and Sasaki T (1992) Time-shrinking: a discontinuity in the perception of auditory temporal patterns. *Percept Psychophys*, **51**, 504–507.

Nakajima Y, Ten Hoopen G, Sasaki T, Yamamoto K, Kadota M, Simons M and Suetomi D (2004) Time-shrinking: the process of unilateral temporal assimilation. *Perception*, **33**, 1061–1079.

Palmer C and Krumhansl CL (1990) Mental representations for musical meter. *Journal of Experimental Psychology: Human Perception and Performance*, **16**, 728–741.

Palmer C and Pfordresher PQ (2003) Incremental planning in sequence production. *Psychol Rev*, **110**, 683–712.

Parncutt R (1994) A perceptual model of pulse salience and metrical accent in musical rhythms. *Music Perception*, **11**, 409–464.

Patel AD, Iversen JR, Chen Y and Repp BH (2005) The influence of metricality and modality on synchronization with a beat. *Exp Brain Res*, **163**, 226–238.

Pfordresher PQ (2003) The role of melodic and rhythmic accents in musical structure. *Music Perception*, **20**, 431–464.

Phillips-Silver J and Trainor LJ (2005) Feeling the beat: movement influences infant rhythm perception. *Science*, **308**, 1430.

Povel D-J and Essens P (1985) Perception of temporal patterns. *Music Perception*, **2**, 411–440.

Povel D-J (1981) Internal representation of simple temporal patterns. *Journal of Experimental Psychology: Human Perception and Performance*, **7**, 3–18.

Povel DJ and Okkerman H (1981) Accents in equitone sequences. *Percept Psychophys*, **30**, 565–72.

Repp BH (2005) Sensorimotor synchronization: a review of the tapping literature. *Psychon Bull Rev*, **12**, 969–992.

Ross J and Houtsma AJ (1994) Discrimination of auditory temporal patterns. *Percept Psychophys*, **56**, 19–26.

Sakai K, Hikosaka O, Miyauchi S, Takino R, Tamada T, Iwata NK and Nielsen M (1999) Neural representation of a rhythm depends on its interval ratio. *Journal of Neuroscience*, **19**, 10074–10081.

Sasaki T, Suetomi D, Nakajima Y and Ten Hoopen G (2002) Time-shrinking, its propagation, and Gestalt principles. *Percept Psychophys*, **64**, 919–931.

Snyder JS and Krumhansl CL (2001) Tapping to ragtime: cues to pulse finding. *Music Perception*, **18**, 455–489.

Snyder JS and Large EW (2005) Gamma-band activity reflects the metric structure of rhythmic tone sequences. *Cognitive Brain Research*, **24**, 117–126.

Temperley D (2001) *The cognition of basic musical structures*. MIT Press, Cambridge, MA.

Ten Hoopen G, Nakajima Y, Remin G, Massier, B, Rhebergen K and Holleman W (2006) Time-shrinking and categorical temporal ratio perception: evidence for a 1:1 temporal category. *Music Perception*, **24**, 1–22.

Trehub SE and Hannon EE (2006) Infant music perception: domain-general or domain-specific mechanisms? *Cognition*, **100**, 73–99.

Will U and Berg E (2007). Brain wave synchronization and entrainment to periodic acoustic stimuli. *Neuroscience Letters*, **424**, 55–60.

Windsor WL (1993) Dynamic accents and categorical perception of metre. *Psychology of Music*, **21**, 127–140.

Woodrow H (1932) The effects of rate of sequence upon the accuracy of synchronization. *Journal Experimental Psychology*, **15**, 357–379.

Zanto TP, Large EW, Fuchs A and Kelso JAS (2005) Gamma-band responses to perturbed auditory sequences: evidence for synchronization of perceptual processes. *Music Perception*, **22**, 535–552.

Zanot TP, Snyder JS and Large EW (2006) Neural correlates of rhythmic expectancy. *Advances in Cognitive Psychology*, **2**, 221–231.

CHAPTER 9

Components of melodic processing

Mark A. Schmuckler

Introduction

Melody is the most ubiquitous form of musical structure with which listeners come into contact on a daily basis. Mirroring the prevalence and importance of melody, research in music cognition has focused extensively on the processes involved in perceiving and remembering melodic structure. Despite these years of study, however, our understanding of pitch structure in melody can be described simply, with respect to the two components of tonality and pitch contour. Although the importance of these two components has been recognized over the years, it is only recently that workable models of these components have been proposed. This chapter describes such models of tonality and melodic contour, and discusses the role of these components in listeners' perceptions of and memory for melody.

Components of melodic processing

Melody is, with little doubt, the most ubiquitous form of musical structure with which people come into contact on a daily basis. Everywhere in our environment we are exposed to melody, from the songs we hear on the radio to the tunes we hum to ourselves. Additionally, melody is arguably the first clearly musical structure to which infants are exposed, through the prevalence of parental singing (e.g. Nakata and Trehub 2004, Rock et al. 1999; Shenfield et al. 2003). Finally, although cultures throughout the world vary in their respective musical structures, virtually all contain some form of melody (Eerola et al. 2006; Unyk et al. 1992).

Given its central role in music, it is no surprise that investigations of melody have occupied a similarly privileged position in music cognition. Such research has taken a variety of forms, ranging from explorations of how melodies are formed (i.e., what principles underlie the grouping of individual notes into a single perceptual object such as melody), to investigations of how melodies are themselves perceived (e.g., what does a listener truly experience upon hearing a melody) to how melodies are perceived in relation to one another (e.g., melodic categorization or similarity) to how melodies are remembered. Interestingly, although research on such questions has been extensive and insightful, there has been little explicit integration across these topics. Along these lines, one can ask whether there are any fundamental principles or organizational structures that function across these diverse aspects of melodic processing.

Fortunately, a close look at the literature on melodic processing implicates the operation of two basic organizational structures. Specifically, there is strong evidence for two fundamental components of melodic processing—a melody's tonal structure, and its melodic contour. Throughout a wealth of empirical findings these two components have time and again shown themselves to play a principal role in listeners' melodic processing, with tonality and contour continually influencing listeners' perceptions of and responses to melodies, as well as their sub-sequent memory for these melodies.

Recognition of the importance of tonality and contour in melody perception is not a new insight (e.g. Dowling 1978). In a classic paper, Dowling (1978) identified just these two components as critical in melodic processing, positing that melodic memory, and by implication melodic perception, is driven by a melody's tonality and contour. Over the years Dowling and others have continually demonstrated the importance of these components in melodic processing, employing a wide array of perceptual encoding, similarity, and memory paradigms.

Although our understanding of melodic processing has grown substantially since Dowling's (1978) original insights, nothing has yet arisen that would undermine the proposed fundamental role played by these two components. As such, tonality and contour are still considered to be the two primary characteristics of listeners' perceptions of melody (e.g. Krumhansl 2000; Schmuckler 2004). One way in which our knowledge has advanced, however, is in the establishment of models for formalizing the structure of these components. Such models allow for an explicit characterization of these parameters, and thus enable the generation of specific predictions for melodic processing based on the structure highlighted by these models.

Models of tonality and contour

Models of tonality

The impact of musical tonality, or the hierarchical organization of the chromatic set around a single reference pitch, on the processing of musical passages is one of the most thoroughly studied research topics in music cognition. Approached from musicological (e.g. Lerdahl 2001; Temperley 2001, 2007), psychological (e.g. Krumhansl 1990a, 2000), and neuroscientific perspectives (e.g. Janata et al. 2002; Koelsch and Siebel 2005), our knowledge of the impact of tonal structure on musical processing is immense.

In keeping with this focus, there have been a large number of models proposed to account for the psychological organization of tonality (Krumhansl and Kessler 1982; Shepard 1982;

Tillman et al. 2000), as well as explaining how listeners apprehend tonality in the first place. With reference to this latter goal, models describing the process of key-finding can be roughly divided into two categories (Huron and Parncutt 1993; Schmuckler and Tomovski 2005; Temperley and Marvin 2008)—those that posit the use of structural–functional information in key determination, and those that employ an event distribution strategy to key-finding.

The structural–functional models that have been proposed are diverse (e.g. Abe and Hoshino 1990; Brown 1988; Brown and Butler 1981; Butler 1990; Butler and Brown 1994; Holtzman 1977; Longuet-Higgins and Steedman 1971; Matsunaga and Abe 2005; Yoshino and Abe 2004), although all share an underlying assumption that there are particular local features or components of musical patterns that signal or indicate a specific musical key. Of these structural models, the most well-known are the approaches proposed by David Butler and Helen Brown (Brown 1988; Brown and Butler 1981; Butler 1990; Butler and Brown 1984, 1994) and by Jun-ichi Abe and colleagues (Matsunaga and Abe 2005; Yoshino and Abe 2004). Although a full review of these approaches cannot be considered here, Brown and Butler's 'intervallic rivalry theory' assumes that it is the presence of the rare intervals of the diatonic set (the minor seconds and the tritone), along with an additional disambiguating tone, that indicate the to-be-perceived tonality. Similarly, Abe and colleagues have posited that key-finding arises due to attempts to interpret the tones of a melodic pattern as members of a given diatonic set, and specifically the tonic triad (Abe and Hoshino 1990; Abe and Okada 2004; Matsunaga and Abe 2005; Yoshino and Abe 2004). Thus, both approaches explicitly look for certain structural and/or functional relations within musical events, and use the occurrence of these events to establish a key.

An alternative to this approach are distributional models of key-finding. Probably the best-known such model was proposed by Krumhansl and Schmuckler (1986a; see Krumhansl 1990a), who suggested that key-finding could be accomplished by matching the relative durations of the chromatic set in a piece of music with the hierarchies of perceived tonality stability of the chromatic set with reference to the 12 major and 12 minor tonalities (Krumhansl and Kessler 1982). Although numerous refinements to this model have been proposed (Huron and Parncutt 1993; Smith and Schmuckler 2004; Temperley 1999, 2001, 2002, 2007; Toiviainen and Krumhansl 2003), the basic premise of this approach has remained invariant.

Both models have, over the years, garnered an impressive degree of empirical support. Multiple studies have demonstrated the importance of certain structural relations in key-finding (Brown 1988; Brown and Butler 1981; Brown *et al.* 1994). In Brown and Butler (1981), for instance, listeners' key judgements in response to melodic trichords accorded well with the predictions of the rare interval hypothesis, with tonal judgements more consistent for trichords containing rare interval information than trichords in which the interval information was consistent with multiple keys. Similarly, multiple studies have demonstrated the importance of distributional information in key-finding (e.g., Schmuckler and Tomovski 2005; Toiviainen and Krumhansl 2003). Schmuckler and Tomovski (2005), for example, found that this model predicted listeners' tonal percepts for a range of materials, including very short initial excerpts of Bach and Chopin preludes, increasingly longer segments of Chopin preludes, and an entire Chopin prelude. In all of these cases, this approach modelled tonal percepts in terms of sensitivity to picking up the intended key of the passage, as well as in predicting errors in key-finding.

The simultaneous success of these different models raises the question of the relation between these approaches. Typically, these models have been viewed as fundamentally inconsistent with one another (Butler 1989; Krumhansl 1990b), although there have surprisingly been no attempts to explicitly compare these approaches. In one exception, reported by Schmuckler and Tomovski (2000), four variants of short musical excerpts were created that systematically manipulated the rare interval and distributional information available in these passages. Samples of these variants appear in Figure 9.1, and presents a series of passages in which distributional and rare interval information imply the same key (variant A), distribu-

tional but not rare interval information is specific to a given key (variant B), and distributional and rare interval information implicate different keys (variants C and D).

Using a probe tone and a tonic finding procedure, listeners' tonal percepts in response to these variants were assessed. Figure 9.2 summarizes the results from these studies, presenting the correlation between the averaged probe tone ratings and the C and G major tonal hierarchies and the percentage tonic choices for the target keys of C and G major (all data were ultimately transposed to these keys) for the variants. One clear finding is that tonal percepts matched the note distributions of the passages, a result seen most easily in variants C and D in which ratings and tonic choices aligned with predictions based on note distributions. There was, however, a subtle influence of rare interval information on tonal percepts. Specifically, Figure 9.2 also reveals a systematic weakening of tonal percepts when the two cues do not coincide. Thus, variant A, in which both sets of information indicated the same key, produced the strongest tonal percepts, followed by variant B, in which rare interval information was ambiguous, and finally variants C and D, in which the two sets of information diverged. Clearly the two types of information support each other in tonal perception.

Subsequent analyses support the idea that distributional and rare interval information converge in their tonal implications. For both processes to operate in musical contexts not built solely on the diatonic scale, it must be that the pattern of interval occurrences characterizing the diatonic set also represents the interval frequency of real musical contexts. In keeping with this idea, Table 9.1 presents an interval count for the four variants of the stimulus passages of this study, and reveals that the diatonic interval vector closely matches the interval content of these musical passages. Moreover, in a simulation study, 50 40-note melodies were randomly generated using note frequencies that either matched the tonal hierarchy, or were randomly organized (see Smith and Schmuckler 2004). Table 9.1 also presents the interval counts from this simulation, and demonstrates that randomly generated melodies containing note distributions similar to that found in tonal music also produce interval sets matching the

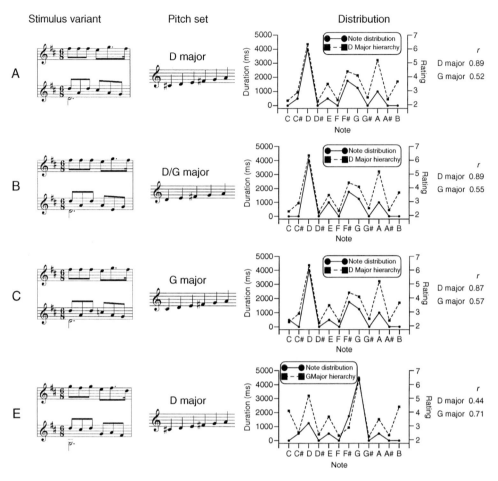

Fig. 9.1 Sample stimuli from Schmuckler and Tomovski (2000). The four variants correspond to passages in which both the pitch set and the note duration distribution strongly indicate the same key (variant A), the note distribution but not the pitch set indicates a single key (variant B), and the pitch set and note distributions indicate different keys (variants C and D).

diatonic interval vector. Together, these findings suggest that distributional and structural–functional approaches are really part of the same process, and that a complete description of tonality and key-finding will require both global distributional properties, along with more localized, structural–functional information, an idea that has been recognized by other researchers (Temperley and Marvin 2008).

Models of contour

In contrast to tonality, models of melodic contour have received less attention over the years. Of the contour models that do exist, it is also

(roughly) possible to divide them into two categories, the first based on local parameters of contour and the second on global contour information. In the first group are models focusing on the individual interval content of contour (Friedmann 1985, 1987; Marvin 1991, 1995; Marvin and Laprade 1987; Morris 1993; Quinn 1999), whereas the second group consists of procedures for characterizing the rises and falls within the contour, primarily through the use of time series analyes (Eerola and Bregman 2007; Eerola *et al.* 2001, 2006; Schmuckler 1999).

Again, both types of models have generated supporting experimental results. Quinn (1999),

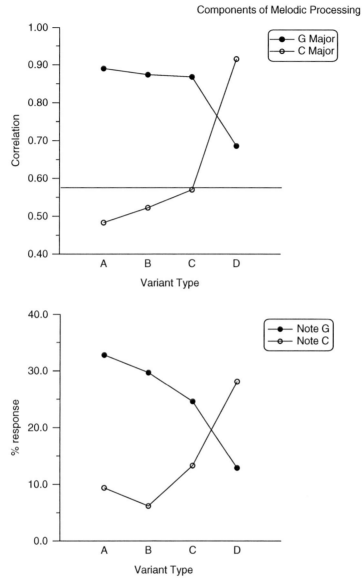

Fig. 9.2 Results from the two experiments of Schmuckler and Tomovski (2000). The top figure graphs the correlation between the averaged probe tone ratings and the tonal hierarchies for the target keys of G and C major across the four stimulus variants. The bottom figure graphs the percentage of times the notes G and C were chosen as the tonic tone, as a function of the four stimulus variants.

for instance, demonstrated that the perceived similarity of pairs of short melodies was predictable from comparability in the rise/fall relation between adjacent notes, and from non-adjacent notes separated by a single tone. Schmuckler (1999), in contrast, demonstrated that perceived contour similarity for pairs of melodies was predictable from the degree of overlap of the cyclic information of these contours, as quantified by a Fourier analysis of the contour code.

Table 9.1 The interval content of the diatonic set (Brown and Butler 1981), the stimulus variants of Schmuckler and Tomovski (2000), and of the simulation study using hierarchical and random organizations of pitch information (Smith and Schmuckler 2004). The final column shows the correlation between the interval vector of the diatonic set and the remaining interval vectors

Source	Interval vector						Correlation
	m2	M2	m3	M3	P4	TT	
Diatonic set	2	5	4	3	6	1	–
Variant A	212	352	303	301	534	58	$r(4) = 0.95**$
Variant B	140	378	325	253	521	0	$r(4) = 0.99**$
Variant C	145	341	328	297	508	36	$r(4) = 0.96**$
Variant D	195	296	244	281	567	57	$r(4) = 0.90**$
Hierarchical	98.1	131.9	120.4	114.7	170.0	43.0	$r(4) = 0.95**$
Random	137.6	128.7	137.7	111.4	114.2	50.1	$r(4) = 0.52$

** $p < .01$

Subsequent work (Schmuckler (2004 submitted) extended these findings to rhythmically complex melodies, using both direct and indirect similarity measures. Together, these findings suggest that melodic contour can be reliably characterized by both the individual interval relations within the contour as well as by more global contour parameters, although it is critical to recognize that these two approaches are not mutually exclusive. Schmuckler (2004) has hypothesized that the former approaches might be most applicable to short melodic contours, whereas the latter approach could be more powerful when applied to longer melodies.

Tonality and contour in melody perception

One advantage to the availability of tonal and contour models is that they provide a means for predicting aspects of melodic processing such as the perceptual organization of melodic form and melodic memory. The remainder of this chapter focuses on the role of contour and tonality in these aspects of melodic processing.

Tonality and contour in perceptual organization

Given the interest in tonality and contour, it is surprising that research on the role of these factors in the perceptual organization of melodies per se has been relatively neglected over the years.

Of the two, research on perceptual organization has looked more at the role of contour, and has (not surprisingly) found that this factor influences perceptual organization. Probably the most obvious aspect of perceptual organization in which contour has been examined is in stream segregation (Bregman 1990, 2005; Miller and Heise 1950; Van Noorden 1975). Unfortunately, a thorough review of this research is outside the purview of this chapter (see Bregman 1990, 2005; Carlyon 2004; Snyder and Alain 2007, for reviews). Even a cursory look at this topic, however, demonstrates that of the myriad of factors underlying stream segregation, one of the most important involves pitch proximity, and more critically in the current context, that the contour of pitch changes can drive stream segregation. For instance, Bregman and Dannenbring (1973) demonstrated that frequency glides, or tones with a continuous pitch contour, were grouped together into a single auditory stream, as opposed to discrete tones varying in pitch that grouped into separate streams; similar arguments have been advanced for pitch contour in the grouping of speech sounds (Darwin and Bethell-Fox 1977; Remez et al.1994).

Two well-known auditory perception illusions—Deutsch's (1975) scale illusion (Butler 1979; Deutsch 1975; Radvanysky et al. 1992), and the continuity illusion (Grossberg et al. 2004; Miller and Lickliter 1950; Tougas and Bregman 1990)—provide another example of contour influencing perceptual organization. In the scale illusion, listeners hear simultaneously sounded ascending and descending diatonic scales, with the tones of these scales alternated between the ears. Rather than hearing this pattern organized based on source localization (by ear) or as a prototypical musical pattern (the diatonic scale), listeners hear two simple melodies, the first consisting of an ascending and descending line and the second consisting of a descending and ascending line. In the continuity illusion, a sound of long duration that is interrupted by a sound of short duration is heard as continuing through the noise. However, when the continuous information involves a set of competing glides, listeners sometimes hear a pair of bouncing pitch glides, comparable to the percept in the scale illusion (Grossberg *et al.* 2004; Tougas and Bregman 1990).

In both cases, these percepts are typically ascribed to perceptual organization by pitch proximity, and possibly good continuation. An alternative, however, is that listeners are hearing two simple melodic contours, ones that, according to the Fourier analysis model, contain a large amount of power in the fewest number of cyclic frequency components. This observation suggests that the role of contour in perceptual organization might be more quantitatively predictable, with simplicity of the amplitude spectrum driving a specific organization. If true, this would provide an interesting formalization of the Gestalt law of *prägnanz* (Koffka 1935), or the idea that good patterns have few alternatives (Garner 1970).

Somewhat surprisingly, there are few studies demonstrating an explicit role for tonality on perceptual organization. One line of work related to this question involves research on the perception of polytonality (Krumhansl and Schmuckler 1986b; Thompson and Mor 1992). Krumhansl and Schmuckler (1986b), for instance, examined tonal percepts in Stravinsky's *Petroushka* (which instantiates the two tonal centres of C and F# major) using both selective and divided attention tasks, and demonstrated that listeners were unable to form two independent tonal percepts. Instead, percepts of this passage were a complex amalgamation of the two tonalities, similar in structure to a music-theoretic proposal by Van den Toorn (1983) based on the octatonic collection. Thompson and Mor

(1992), in contrast, did find that listeners perceived both keys of bitonal passages by Dubois and Milhaud, with the weights of these tonalities consistent with their relative importance in the musical score. Irrespective of an explanation for these divergent findings (which likely lies in the specifics of the musical contexts employed), this work does imply (indirectly) that tonal information can be a means of perceptually organizing melodic passages.

In a more explicit look at the role of tonality on perceptual organization, Dowling *et al.* (1987) had listeners identify nursery rhymes in which the melody notes were interspersed with distractor tones varying in their pitch overlap, temporal organization, and tonality, with the target. Interestingly, although pitch overlap and temporal organization influenced target identification, the tonal relation between target and distractors did not impact performance. In contrast, Bigand *et al.* (2000) had listeners attend to one of two French nursery rhythms, presented an octave apart, with these melodies played in the same key, a related key, or a distant key. These authors observed that varying tonal relations had no effect on detection of changes to the melodies (hits), although increasing tonal distance did lead to increased false alarms. Together, this work presents a mixed pattern, with some results consistent with the notion that tonality influences the perceptual organization of melodies, whereas other results indicated no such effect.

Recently, Vuvan and Schmuckler (2007) have further explored this question, employing the interleaved melody task of Bey and McAdams (2002) in which listeners hear a target melody followed by a pair of interleaved melodies, and must determine whether one of the interleaved melodies was the same as the target melody. In this study, the interleaved melodies varied in their average pitch spread (6, 9, 12, and 15 semitones), their inter-onset interval between sequential tones (80, 100, 120, and 140 msec), and in their tonalities (same, related, and unrelated; see Figure 9.3 for sample stimuli).

Figure 9.4 shows the averaged d' and bias scores for same/different judgment as a function of pitch spread and tonality (inter-onset interval had no effect in this study). Analyses of discrimination scores revealed a surprising pattern of

Fig. 9.3 Sample stimuli from Vuvan and Schmuckler (2007). The two interleaved comparison melodies could be in either the same key (e.g., C and C major), a related key (e.g., C and G major), or an unrelated key (e.g., C and F# major), and could be separated by an average of 6, 9, 12, or 15 semitones. The location and pitch of the changed notes in the target melody is notated by an 'X' adjacent to the note in the musical staff.

decreasing discrimination with increasing pitch spread, although this effect was likely due to a drop in performance at the largest pitch spread. More importantly, analyses of discrimination and bias revealed the worst performance for interleaved melodies having unrelated tonalities, followed by melodies with related tonalities, and finally by melodies with the same tonality. Although counterintuitive, this finding does converge with Krumhansl and Schmuckler (1986b) and Bigand *et al.* (2000), who both observed that divergent tonalities negatively impacted the formation of independent streams.

Tonality and contour in musical memory

Probably the most central arena in which tonality and contour have been recognized as critical factors in melodic processing involves memory for music. Unfortunately, a comprehensive review of work on this question cannot be presented here. Nevertheless, it is instructive to discuss, even if only superficially, some of the evidence demonstrating the importance of these factors in memory for music.

Research on the role of melodic contour in musical memory has a long history in music

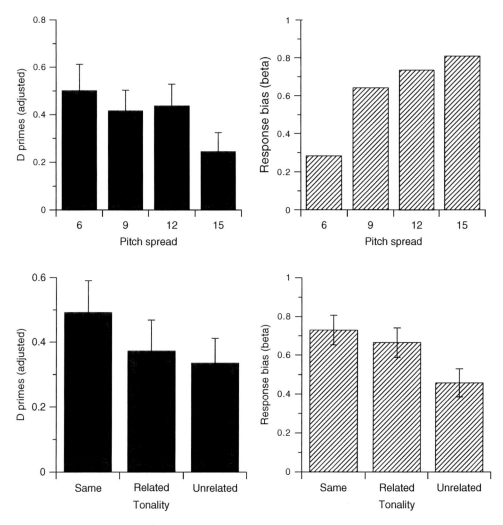

Fig. 9.4 D' and bias for same/different target-comparison judgements as a function of pitch spread (top) and tonality (bottom) in Vuvan and Schmuckler (2007).

cognition. In early classic work on this topic, Dowling and colleagues (Dowling 1971, 1972; Dowling and Fujitani 1971) demonstrated that listeners' short-term melodic memory was dramatically influenced by the melody's contour, with the ability to distinguish between a standard melody and a comparison melody transposed to a different starting pitch more difficult when the melodies shared a comparable melodic contour. Similarly, Dowling and Hollombe (1977) found that recognition of octave-scrambled familiar melodies (hence melodies available in long-term memory) was significantly enhanced

when these melodies retained their original melodic contour, relative to versions that violated this contour. These findings, and others like them, demonstrate that short-term melody recognition is strongly influenced by contour information (Croonen and Kop 1989; Cuddy et al. 1981; DeWitt and Crowder 1986; Dowling 1991; Dyson and Watkins 1984; Freedman 1999; Idson and Massaro 1978; Massaro et al. 1980; Watkins 1985).

There are, however, important limitations to the use of contour in melody recognition. Edworthy (1982, 1985), for instance, demonstrated that contour information becomes less precise in memory as melody length increases, a finding attributed to the growth of tonal information in memory. Moreover, multiple studies have demonstrated that contour information dominates memory following short delays, but decreases in potency after longer delays (Dowling 1991; Dowling *et al.* 1995). Dowling (1991), for instance, found that listeners frequently confused same contour, tonal melodies after short delays (e.g., 11 s) but not after long delays (e.g., 39 s). Most importantly, and as summarized by Dowling (1994), it is clear that although contour is crucial for melodic memory, it does not function independently, but rather, it is integrated with other key melodic features, such as tonality.

The evidence for tonal influences on melodic memory is also robust. One way in which tonality influences memory, and an effect comparable to the research just described, is that tonally strong melodies are better remembered than tonally weak or atonal melodies (Boltz 1991; Croonen 1994; Dowling 1991; Dowling *et al.* 1995; Halpern *et al.* 1998; Watkins 1985). Croonen (1994), for instance, demonstrated that listeners' accuracy in a standard-comparison melody task was significantly influenced by the tonality of the stimuli, with strongly tonal sequences better remembered than weakly tonal melodies.

A second, albeit less researched finding, involves the presence of key-distance effects in memory (Bartlett and Dowling 1980; Bharucha and Krumhansl 1983; Krumhansl *et al.* 1982; Krumhansl and Castellano 1983). Bartlett and Dowling (1980), for instance, had listeners' recognize comparison melodies that were exact transpositions of standard melodies from non-exact transpositions when the comparisons were in the same key, a related key, or an unrelated key. These researchers observed that it was harder to distinguish non-transposition comparisons from standards (i.e., higher false alarm rates) when the melodies were in the same or related keys, as opposed to unrelated keys. Interestingly, this effect did not occur for transpositions, suggesting that memory for melodies contains relatively separable stores for tonal information versus interval information.

Other evidence exists for key distance effects in musical memory, although not explicitly for melodic materials (Bharucha and Krumhansl 1983; Krumhansl *et al.* 1982; Krumhansl and Castellano 1983). Krumhansl *et al.* (1982), for instance, found that recognition memory for chords was influenced by the tonal context in which these chords were embedded, such that the key distance of the tonal context and the key of the to-be-remembered chords predicted the probability that a given chord would be recognized, as well as memory confusion errors and asymmetries in confusion errors. Accordingly, there is robust evidence for key distance effects in memory, both for melodic and harmonic sequences.

Conclusion

Melody has, over the years, been the focus of intensive investigation in research in music cognition. Somewhat ironically, despite these years of study our understanding of melodic structure can be described simply, with respect to two principal components—the underlying tonality of the melody, and the rising and falling pattern in pitch of the melody. The importance of these two components has, of course, been recognized since the beginning of the study of music in an experimental context, although it is only in recent years that formal models of these components have arisen. With the advent of these models, of course, has come the ability to make explicit predictions regarding how these components might predict listeners' melodic processing, including aspects such as perceptual organization and perceived similarity, as well as listeners' memory for melodic materials.

How might these models be applied to studying perceptual organization and melodic memory? One of the principal limitations of previous work examining tonality and contour in musical processing is that such research did not typically provide any formal characterization of the structure of these factors, and so could not make explicit predictions as to when such factors would play a role, or the relative strength of their role in such situations. For instance, contour relations between melodies were often characterized as being simply same or different, and tonality was typically determined on the basis of diatonicism of the melody.

Unfortunately, such characterizations ignore the idea that there are gradations to the degree to which melodies are related. Contour similarity studies (Eerola and Bregman 2007; Eerola *et al.* 2006; Eerola *et al.* 2001; Quinn 1999; Schmuckler 1999), for instance, have all convincingly demonstrated that one can compare melodic contours on a continuous, as opposed to dichotomous (e.g., same versus different), basis. Similarly, work in tonal perception (e.g., Smith and Schmuckler 2004; Takeuchi 1994) demonstrates that tonality is not simply all-or-none, but can be characterized in terms of degrees of tonal strength, with some passage more tonal than other passages.

As for perceptual organization and memory, the utility of directly assessing the relatedness between stimuli in their contour and tonal structure is obvious. Perceptual organization, for instance, either in the stability of a specific organization, or the ease with which differing groupings can be formed, should be predictable by the level of similarity between competing organizations. In fact, there is already evidence for this finding, in terms of the previous discussed possible explanations for the scale illusion, or in explaining the discrepancy between Krumhansl and Schmuckler's (1986b) and Thompson and Mor's (1992) research on the perception of multiple tonalities.

Similarly, memory for melodies should be predictable based on the measured degree of contour and tonal similarity between melodies. In the typical standard-comparison memory task, for instance, greater contour or tonal similarity between melodies should be reflected in decreased accuracy overall, and possibly in false alarm rates in particular. Again, there are findings indicative of just such effects. Schmuckler (1997, for instance, observed that listeners' memory for melodies was influenced by the expectedness of the melody's ending (better memory for highly expected endings) and the tonal coherence of that ending (better memory for more tonally coherent endings). Although none of this work explicitly employs assessments of tonality and contour as predictors for memory and memory confusions, it is nevertheless consistent with the notion that such factors can be quantified to make such predictions. Clearly, then, further work investigating the utility of tonal and contour models in predicting perceptual organization and melodic memory has a great deal of potential in providing insight into our understanding of melodic processing quite generally.

Acknowledgements

Preparation of this manuscript was supported by a grant from the Natural Sciences and Engineering Research Council of Canada to the author.

References

Abe J and Hoshino E (1990). Schema driven properties in melody cognition: experiments on final tone extrapolation by music experts. *Psychomusicology*, **9**, 161–172.

Abe J and Okada A (2004). Integration of metrical and tonality organization in melody perception. *Japanese Psychological Research*, **46**, 298–307.

Bartlett JC and Dowling WJ (1980). Recognition of transposed melodies: a key-distance effect in developmental perspective. *Journal of Experimental Psychology: Human Perception and Performance*, **6**, 501–515.

Bey C and McAdams S (2002). Schema-based processing in auditory scene analysis. *Perception & Psychophysics*, **64**, 844–854.

Bharucha JJ and Krumhansl CL (1983). The representation of harmonic structure in music: hierarchies of stability as a function of context. *Cognition*, **13**, 63–102.

Bigand E, McAdams S and Forêt S (2000). Divided attention in music. *International Journal of Psychology*, **35**, 270–278.

Boltz M (1991). Some structural determinants of melody recall. *Memory & Cognition*, **19**, 239–251.

Bregman AS (1990). *Auditory scene analysis: the perceptual organization of sound*. The MIT Press, Cambridge, MA.

Bregman AS (2005). Auditory scene analysis and the role of phenomenology in experimental psychology. *Canadian Psychology*, **46**, 32–40.

Bregman AS and Dannenbring GL (1973). The effect of continuity on auditory stream segregation. *Perception & Psychophysics*, **13**, 308–312.

Brown H (1988). The interplay of set content and temporal context in a functional theory of tonality perception. *Music Perception*, **5**, 219–249.

Brown H and Butler D (1981). Diatonic trichords as minimal tonal cue-cells. *In Theory Only*, **5**, 37–55.

Brown H, Butler D and Jones MR (1994). Musical and temporal influences on key discovery. *Music Perception*, **11**, 371–407.

Butler D (1979). A further study of melodic channeling. *Perception & Psychophysics*, **25**, 264–268.

Butler D (1989). Describing the perception of tonality in music: a critique of the tonal hierarchy theory and a proposal for a theory of intervallic rivalry. *Music Perception*, **6**, 219–241.

Butler D (1990). A study of event hierarchies in tonal and post-tonal music. *Music Perception*, **18**, 4–17.

Butler D and Brown H (1984). Tonal structure versus function: studies of the recognition of harmonic motion. *Music Perception*, **2**, 6–24.

Butler D and Brown H (1994). Describing the mental representation of tonality in music. In R Aiello, JA Sloboda, eds, *Musical perceptions*, 191–212. Oxford University Press, London.

Carlyon RP (2004). How the brain separates sounds. *Trends in Cognitive Sciences*, **8**, 465–471.

Croonen WLM (1994). Effects of length, tonal structure, and contour in the recognition of tone series. *Perception & Psychophysics*, **55**, 623–632.

Croonen WLM and Kop PFM (1989). Tonality, tonal scheme and contour in delayed recognition of tone sequences. *Music Perception*, **7**, 49–38.

Cuddy LL, Cohen AJ and Mewhort DJK (1981). Perception of structure in short melodic sequences. *Journal of Experimental Psychology: Human Perception and Performance*, **7**, 869–883.

Darwin CJ and Bethell-Fox CE (1977). Pitch continuity and speech source attribution. *Journal of Experimental Psychology: Human Perception and Performance*, **3**, 665–672.

Deutsch D (1975). Two-channel listening to musical scales. *Journal of the Acoustical Society of America*, **57**, 1156–1160.

DeWitt LA and Crowder RG (1986). Recognition of novel melodies after brief delays. *Music Perception*, **3**, 259–274.

Dowling WJ (1971). Recognition of inversions of melodies and melodic contours. *Perception & Psychophysics*, **9**, 348–349.

Dowling WJ (1972). Recognition of melodic transformations: inversion, retrograde, and retrograde inversion. *Perception & Psychophysics*, **12**, 417–421.

Dowling WJ (1978). Scale and contour: two components of a theory of memory for melodies. *Psychological Review*, **85**, 341–354.

Dowling WJ (1991). Tonal strength and melody recognition after long and short delays. *Perception & Psychophysics*, **50**, 305–313.

Dowling WJ (1994). Melodic contour in hearing and remembering melodies. In R Aiello, J Sloboda, eds, *musical perceptions* 173–190. Oxford University Press, Oxford.

Dowling WJ and Fujitani DS (1971). Contour, interval and pitch recognition in memory for melodies. *Journal of the Acoustical Society of America*, **49**, 524–531.

Dowling WJ and Hollombe AW (1977). The perception of melodies distorted by splitting into octaves: effects of increasing proximity and melodic contour. *Perception & Psychophysics*, **21**, 60–64.

Dowling WJ, Kwak S and Andrews MW (1995). The time course of recognition of novel melodies. *Perception & Psychophysics*, **57**, 150–158.

Dowling WJ, Lung KMT and Herrbold S (1987). Aiming attention in pitch and time in the perception of interleaved melodies. *Perception & Psychophysics*, **41**, 642–656.

Dyson MC and Watkins AJ (1984). A figural approach to the role of melodic contour in melody recognition. *Perception & Psychophysics*, **35**(5), 477–488.

Edworthy J (1982). Pitch and contour in music processing. *Psychomusicology*, **2**, 44–46.

Edworthy J (1985). Interval and contour in melody processing. *Music Perception*, **2**(3), 375–388.

Eerola T and Bregman M (2007). Melodic and contextual similarity of folk song phrases. *Musicae Scientiae, Discussion Forum*, **4A**, 211–233.

Eerola T, Himberg T, Toiviainen P and Louhivuori J (2006). Perceived complexity of Western and African folk melodies by Western and African listeners. *Psychology of Music*, **34**, 337–371.

Eerola T, Järvinen T, Louhivuori J and Toiviainen P (2001). Statistical features and perceived similarity of folk melodies. *Music Perception*, **18**, 275–296.

Freedman EG (1999). The role of diatonicism in the abstraction and representation of contour and interval information. *Music Perception*, **16**(3), 365–387.

Friedmann ML (1985). A methodology for the discussion of contour: its application to Schoenberg's music. *Journal of Music Theory*, **29**, 223–248.

Friedmann ML (1987). My contour, their contour. *Journal of Music Theory*, **31**, 268–274.

Garner WR (1970). Good patterns have few alternatives. *American Scientist*, **58**, 34–42.

Grossberg S, Govindarajan KK, Wyse LL and Cohen MA (2004). Artstream: a neural net model of auditory scene analysis and source segregation. *Neural Networks*, **17**, 511–536.

Halpern AR, Bartlett JC and Dowling WJ (1998). Perception of mode, rhythm and contour in unfamiliar melodies: effects of age and experience. *Music Perception*, **15**(4), 335.

Holtzman SR (1977). A program for key determination. *Interface*, **6**, 29–56.

Huron D and Parncutt R (1993). An improved model of tonality perception incorporating pitch salience and echoic memory. *Psychomusicology*, **12**, 154–171.

Idson WL and Massaro DW (1978). A bidimensional model of pitch in the recognition of melodies. *Perception & Psychophysics*, **24**, 551–565.

Janata P, Birk JL, Van Horn JD, Leman M, Tillman B and Bharucha JJ (2002). The cortical topography of tonal structures underling western music. *Science*, **298**, 2167–2170.

Koelsch S and Siebel WA (2005). Towards a neural basis of music perception. *Trends in Cognitive Sciences*, **9**(12), S78–S84.

Koffka K (1935). *Principles of gestalt psychology*. Harcourt, Brace and World, New York.

Krumhansl CL (1990a). *Cognitive foundations of musical pitch*. Oxford University Press, London.

Krumhansl CL (1990b). Tonal hierarchies and rare intervals in music cognition. *Music Perception*, **7**, 309–324.

Krumhansl CL (2000). Rhythm and pitch in music cognition. *Psychological Bulletin*, **126**, 159–179.

Krumhansl CL, Bharucha JJ and Castellano MA (1982). Key distance effects on perceived harmonic structure in music. *Perception & Psychophysics*, **32**, 96–108.

Krumhansl CL and Castellano MA (1983). Dynamic processes in music perception. *Memory & Cognition*, **11**, 325–334.

Krumhansl CL and Kessler EJ (1982). Tracing the dynamic changes in perceived tonal organization in a spatial representation of musical keys. *Psychological Review*, **89**, 334–368.

Krumhansl CL and Schmuckler MA (1986a). *Key-finding in music: an algorithm based on pattern matching to tonal hierarchies*. Paper presented at the 19th annual Mathematical Psychology Meeting, Cambridge, MA.

Krumhansl CL and Schmuckler MA (1986b). The petroushka chord: a perceptual investigation. *Music Perception*, **4**, 153–184.

Lerdahl F (2001). *Tonal pitch space*. Oxford University Press, Oxford.

Longuet-Higgins HC and Steedman MJ (1971). On interpreting Bach. *Machine Intelligence*, **6**, 221–241.

Marvin EW (1991). The perception of rhythm in non-tonal music: rhythmic contours in the music of Edgard Varèse. *Music Theory Spectrum*, **13**, 61–78.

Marvin EW (1995). A generalization of contour theory to diverse musical spaces: analytic applications to the music of dallapiccola and stockhausen. In EW Marvin, R Hermann, eds, *Concert music, rock and jazz since 1945: essays and analytic studies*, 135–171. University of Rochester Press, Rochester, NY.

Marvin EW and Laprade PA (1987). Relating musical contours: extensions of a theory for contour. *Journal of Music Theory*, **31**, 225–267.

Massaro DW, Kallman HJ and Kelly JL (1980). The role of tone height, melodic contour, and tone chroma in melody recognition. *Journal of Experimental Psychology: Human Perception and Performance*, **6**, 77–90.

Matsunaga R and Abe J (2005). Cues for key perception of a melody: pitch set along? *Music Perception*, **23**, 153–164.

Miller GA and Heise GA (1950). The trill threshold. *Journal of the Acoustical Society of America*, **22**, 167–173.

Miller GA and Lickliter JCR (1950). Intelligibility of interrupted speech. *Journal of the Acoustical Society of America*, **22**, 167–173.

Morris RD (1993). New directions in the theory and analysis of musical contour. *Music Theory Spectrum*, **15**, 205–228.

Nakata T and Trehub SE (2004). Infants' responsiveness to maternal speech and singing. *Infant Behavior and Development*, **27**, 455–464.

Quinn I (1999). The combinatorial model of pitch contour. *Music Perception*, **16**, 439–456.

Radvanysky GA, Hartmann WM and Rakerd B (1992). Structural alternations of an ambiguous musical figure: the scale illusion revisited. *Perception & Psychophysics*, **52**, 256–262.

Remez RE, Rubin PE, Berns SM, Pardo JS and Lang JM (1994). On the perceptual organization of speech. *Psychological Review*, **101**, 129–156.

Rock AML, Trainor LJ and Addison TL (1999). Distinctive messages in infant-directed lullabies and play songs. *Developmental Psychology*, **35**, 527–534.

Schmuckler MA (1997). Expectancy effects in memory for melodies. *Canadian Journal of Experimental Psychology*, **51**(4), 292–305.

Schmuckler MA (1999). Testing models of melodic contour similarity. *Music Perception*, **16**, 295–326.

Schmuckler MA (2004). Pitch and pitch structures. In J Neuhoff, ed., *Ecological psychoacoustics*, 271–315. Academic Press, San Diego, CA.

Schmuckler MA (submitted). Melodic contour similarity using folk melodies.

Schmuckler MA and Tomovski R (2000). *Tonal hierarchies and intervallic rivalries in musical key-finding*. Paper presented at the Society for Music Perception and Cognition, Toronto, ON.

Schmuckler MA and Tomovski R (2005). Perceptual tests of an algorithm for musical key-finding. *Journal of Experimental Psychology: Human Perception and Performance*, **31**, 1124–1149.

Shenfield T, Trehub SE and Nakata T (2003). Maternal singing modulates infants arousal. *Psychology of Music*, **31**, 365–375.

Shepard RN (1982). Geometrical approximations to the structure of musical pitch. *Psychological Review*, **89**, 305–333.

Smith NA and Schmuckler MA (2004). The perception of tonal structure through the differentiation and organization of pitches. *Journal of Experimental Psychology: Human Perception and Performance*, **30**, 268–286.

Snyder JS and Alain C (2007). Toward a neurophysiological theory of auditory stream segregation. *Psychological Bulletin*, **133**, 780–799.

Takeuchi A (1994). Maximum key-profile correlation (mkc) as a measure of tonal structure in music. *Perception & Psychophysics*, **56**, 335–346.

Temperley D (1999). What's key for key? The Krumhansl–Schmuckler key-finding algorithm reconsidered. *Music Perception*, **17**, 65–100.

Temperley D (2001). *The cognition of basic musical structures*. The MIT Press, Cambridge, MA.

Temperley D (2002). Bayesian models of musical structure and cognition. *Musicae Scientiae*, **8**, 1061–1069.

Temperley D (2007). *Music and probability*. MIT Press, Cambridge, MA.

Temperley D and Marvin EW (2008). Pitch class distribution and the identification of key. *Music Perception*, **25**, 192–212.

Thompson WF and Mor S (1992). A perceptual investigation of polytonality. *Psychological Research*, **54**, 60–71.

Tillman B, Bharucha JJ and Bigand E (2000). Implicit learning of tonality: a self-organizing approach. *Psychological Review*, **107**, 885–913.

Toiviainen P and Krumhansl CL (2003). Measuring and modeling real-time responses to music: the dynamics of tonality induction. *Perception*, **32**, 741–766.

Tougas Y and Bregman AS (1990). Auditory streaming and the continuity illusion. *Perception & Psychophysics*, **47**, 121–126.

Unyk AM, Trehub SE, Trainor LJ and Schellenberg EG (1992). Lullabies and simplicity: a cross-cultural perspective. *Psychology of Music*, **20**, 15–28.

Van den Toorn PC (1983). *The music of Igor Stravinsky*. Yale University Press, New Haven, CT.

Van Noorden LPAS (1975). Temporal coherence in the perception of tone sequences. University of Technology, Eindhoven.

Vuvan D and Schmuckler MA (2007). *Tonal influences on auditory stream segregation*. Poster presented at the Society for Music Perception and Cognition. Montreal, QC.

Watkins AJ (1985). Scale, key, and contour in the discrimnation of tuned and mistuned approximations to melody. *Perception & Psychophysics*, **37**, 275–285.

Yoshino I and Abe J (2004). Cognitive modeling of key intepretation in melodic perception. *Japanese Psychological Research*, **46**, 283–297.

CHAPTER 10

Memory for music

Bob Snyder

Introduction

This chapter will focus on musical memory: on how adult listeners form mental representations of music, and on how those representations affect music listening. The chapter will be divided into three sections, which will outline general concepts of memory, address research and theory about musical expectations, and consider listeners' ability to remember various aspects of music. The study of memory in music listening is relatively recent, although the scientific study of human memory dates back to the end of the nineteenth century (Ebbinghaus 1885/1964). The ways in which mind and brain are used in the perception and comprehension of music appear to be much in line with the way they are used in processing in other domains, although there are theories proposing that music is partly modularized in cognition and brain organization (Peretz and Zatorre 2005).

Memory in general

Let us start by defining some of the basic constructs that have been developed in the study of memory. Human memory is said to be *encoded*; events in the world (including events in the body and brain) may cause changes in the detailed micro-structure of the brain that persist over varying amounts of time. These changes are thought to take the form of differences in the strength of connections at gaps (*synapses*) between nerve cells (*neurons*). These connections regulate the flow of electrical charges between neurons. The term *encoding* indicates that these changes assume a form that is different from the things or events that cause them. This is true not only in the sense that neural connections arising through exposure to events in the real world are not the same as those events, but also in the sense that events are encoded in a previously existing context of their meaning to a particular person. In order to persist, a memory must, to some extent, be related to what an individual already knows.

Memory has been defined in different ways that refer to different *modes of functioning*, generally in relation to the time-spans over which it persists. Following research into very brief (250 msec) memory for visual images that yielded the concept of *iconic* memory (Sperling 1960), an analogous concept of a very brief auditory or 'echoic' memory was proposed (Crowder and Morton 1969). Echoic memory is posited as a very brief *sensory* image of an auditory stimulus that persists for a second or two at most; however, the distinction between echoic and auditory short-term memory is not always clear. (Crowder 1993).

A construct with a much more extensive history is that of short-term memory (STM). STM is said to exist on a time scale of seconds, ranging from approximately 4–30 seconds, though it is usually on the order of 4–8 seconds. STM has been referred to as the 'specious present' (James, 1890), and is the window of time within which the present moment of perception and thought are grasped. In addition to this *temporal* limit, STM may also have a *capacity* limit (Cowen 2005) on the actual number of items that can persist as STM at one time. This number was originally proposed by Miller (1956) as 7 ± 2, but has recently been scaled down to a usual maximum of 4 or less (Cowen 2005), although capacity can be increased by practice (Ericsson and Kintsch 1995). This is a very small number which seems to be contradicted by everyday experience.

Part of the explanation for this lies in the *associative* nature of human *long-term* memory; memories for items and events contiguous in space or time may become connected, and the occurrence or recall of one such item may *cue* the recall of an associated item.

The idea that memory is associative has a long provenance in western thought, from at least the mid-eighteenth century. Associations are now thought to consist of connections between networks of neurons in the brain (Hebb 1949), in that a group of items related by association can form a single consolidated item in long-term memory. This larger item can then be recalled (activated as STM) in its entirety, a process that can occur on multiple levels. In this way a kind of hierarchical compression occurs, which allows the most efficient use of the limited capacity of conscious STM; George Miller coined the term *chunking* for this process. A memory chunk is a group of 3–4 items related by association; a musical grouping consisting of 3–5 notes would be a chunk, and a phrase consisting of several of these groupings would be a higher-level chunk. It should be noted that the limitations of chunking are implicated in both the recall and the formation of memories. Chunks or prominent items in chunks can be used to cue other chunks, allowing for the recall of longer sequences. Memorability appears related to how 'chunkable' a sequence is, which will depend on the amount of repetition of items, and to boundaries formed by discontinuities or changes in a sequence; the more clearly a sequence can be subdivided in units of chunkable size, the more likely it is to be recalled. Chunking in music is often related to perceptual grouping processes (Bregman 1990; Lerdahl and Jackendoff 1983). The idea of chunking accounts for a great deal of how immediate human memory can have such a limited capacity, yet be so effective.

Everyday use of the term 'memory' refers not to short-term memory, but to *Long-Term memory* (LTM). LTM differs from STM in several ways. Long-term memories persist over a much longer time-period, even a lifetime, as their formation involves lasting structural change in the brain. Moreover, unlike STM, almost all the contents of long-term memory are not conscious at any given moment, although situational associations may cue memories into consciousness. There are distinctions within LTM that must be further considered. First, there is a distinction introduced by Tulving (Tulving 1972) between so-called *episodic* and *semantic* long-term memories: a distinction between memories of situations and events (*episodic* or autobiographical memory), and general knowledge of facts (*semantic* memory), the latter being more abstract and arising through the experience of repeated similar episodes (Schank 1982). Episodic memory is dynamic, and may be changed by the very act of remembering (Roediger *et al.* 2007, Chapter 8). These two types of memory appear to constitute two ends of a continuum extending from recollections of particular episodes through increasingly general models of types of situations to abstract knowledge representations that no longer have roots in any particular experiences. In music cognition research, *episodic* memory is typically tested in recognition or, more rarely, recall tasks. *Semantic* memory tests usually involve requiring participants to make judgments about types of events they judge likely in particular musical situations. This type of semantic memory is referred to as a *schema*, a general expectation about types and distributions of events (Bartlett 1932/1995; also see Gjerdingen 1988, pp. 3–10). Schemas appear to underlie structural regularities in music such as tonality and metre, as well as standardized musical forms.

A further distinction important for LTM is that between *explicit* and *implicit* memory (Cohen and Squire 1980), a distinction between memories that may be accessible to consciousness and those that are not. One of the major discoveries of the last one hundred fifty or so years about the human mind is that much of the activity of the brain and the mind is not available to awareness (Ellenberger 1970) but remains implicit, evidenced particularly in the acquisition of skills. Many kinds of physical skills, such as knowing how to ride a bicycle or produce a clear tone on a musical instrument, require memory for their execution, but those memories are not available to consciousness, and cannot be described verbally. More recently, another form of implicit long-term memory has been proposed—implicit *perceptual* representations (Mandler 2004). This form of memory is involved in unconscious statistical learning (Reber 1993) that keeps a record of regularities in the environment, and structures unconscious expectations about environmental events. Schemas are describable in terms of this kind of implicit memory, being involved in, e.g., the unconscious generation of expectations about musical events as a piece unfolds. Making such schemas *explicit* is one of the goals of the formal study of music. Implicit perceptual memory is the basis for much of *recognition* memory, though many types of activities involving memory may have both explicit and implicit components which are not easy to tease apart in experiment.

From a biological point of view, it seems that the primary function of LTM is not to construct highly detailed and accurate representations of the past, but to provide a generalized model of the world that will be useful to guide future behavior. Long-term schematic memories tend to be structured in terms of generalized *categories* (McAdams 1989; Snyder 2000). Musical long-term memories and expectations are thus often structured in terms of general categorical schemas such scale-steps, durational categories, etc. This means that listeners tend to not have exact detailed memories of music, but more generalized memories about the *kinds* of events that were heard; hence a listener's repertoire of categories of musical events (knowledge in memory) will affect what they can and do remember.

Short-term and long-term memory appear qualitatively different, yet there must be some mechanisms that allows the integration of information across both domains of memory. The idea of STM has thus been augmented by a more complex notion of 'working memory' (Baddeley 1986). Developing research on STM has revealed that most uses of this type of memory draw on long-term memory in various ways (e.g. Cowen 2005). Generally when we use STM, the contents of awareness draw on already existing knowledge, and this knowledge is in the form of long-term memories. In the most prevalent current theory of working memory (Baddely 1986), such memory consists of several parts, which are thought of as separate memory systems. These are a 'visuo-spatial sketchpad' (used for visualization), a 'phonological loop' (involved in speech production), and a 'central executive'(which sequences thinking and planning). This last is perhaps the least well-understood of the constructs associated with the concept of working memory. The originator of the idea, Baddeley, has himself recently suggested a new component, the episodic buffer (Baddeley 2003). There are probably other forms of working memory as well, for instance for motor movements, non-speech sounds, etc. (Jonides and Smith 1997, pp. 263–265). Some of the aspects of pitch memory mentioned below would qualify as forms of working memory. It may well be that the construct of working memory is an umbrella for a number of distinct memory phenomena that all have limits in the time range of several seconds; indeed, it may simply be a particular kind of persistence in many different processing systems in the brain (Crowder 1993).

At any given time, most of long-term memory is not accessible to consciousness. In order to explain certain kinds of memory phenomena, it has been suggested that there are degrees of unconsciousness, expressed in the construct of *activation* (Cowen 1988). The neural networks that are the basis for long-term memory can be active to a greater or lesser degree; at any particular moment, most will be inactive; some will be in a state of activity but not involved in current consciousness, while some will be active *and* involved in consciousness, a situation that will change from moment to moment. Memory can be *semi-activated* (Chafe 1994); memories at this lower degree of activation may be involved in mental activity, but not in consciousness. Experiments have shown that prior exposure to certain kinds of stimuli can affect later performance on another test, even when a participant is unaware of having experienced the original stimulus (Bornstein 1989). It seems that memory networks established by the original stimulus have been *primed* into semi-activity, which, although remaining below the level of consciousness, can affect ongoing thought and perception, providing a basis for *expectation*. An expectation (which may be more, or less, conscious) is thought to be a group of networks (a *schema*) that have been *cued* and *primed* into semi-activity by current ongoing experience. The concept of expectation is important here because it is a primary mode in which listeners utilize memory in listening to music, and because it is thought to be one of the sources of emotional responses to music (Meyer 1956; Huron 2006).

Musical expectations

Listeners acquire a variety of schematic expectations (manipulation of which may influence profoundly the affective experience of music) from repeated exposure to statistical relations between various elements in music. Bharucha (1994) makes a distinction between *schematic* expectations (based on a listener's knowledge in semantic memory of the style, genre, etc. of a heard piece) and *veridical* expectations (arising from repeated exposure to a particular piece of music, and hence a form of episodic memory); both types of expectation involve LTM. Huron (2006, p. 228) adds the notion of *dynamic* expectations, arising from local events in the ongoing music in the short-term, which would involve STM (this type of expectation would arise for instance when hearing a piece for the first time). Musical knowledge and/or training would affect all of these kinds of expectation.

In the domain of pitch, most musical cultures use *scales*, which are ways of dividing pitch space into a relatively small number of *degrees* or categories. It has been suggested that one motivation for this is the general limitations of STM mentioned above. In fact, most scales in use in musical cultures worldwide consist of 5–7 different pitches or scale degrees, a number of elements that is consistent with the suggestions about STM capacity made above (Dowling 1978). Within the Western musical traditions, a considerable amount of research has been conducted on listeners' expectations concerning scale degrees. Listeners are frequently able to infer the 'key' or tonal center (central scale degree) of music. This is thought to arise through learning based on the statistical distribution of the occurrence of particular scale-degrees in music (that listeners are able to learn the statistical relations between melodic pitches—even in a relatively short time—has been established in a series of experiments by Saffran *et al.* 1999). Building on classic research by Krumhansl (Krumhansl 1990), Aarden established that listeners' expectations for the occurrence of a particular scale-degree do in fact conform to the distribution of scale degrees in actual music (Aarden 2003 cited in Huron 2006), expectations varying from moment to moment as a piece unfolds.

In addition, listeners have some very general schematic expectations about types of *sequences* of melodic events. Huron and his colleagues have described four patterns of statistical learning in experienced listeners, resulting in several proposed types of very general melodic schemas (Huron 2006); several of these were previously hypothesized by Meyer (1956) and Narmour (1990). Listeners expect *pitch proximity*, expecting a pitched musical event to be followed by an event relatively close to it in pitch. This is thought to be statistical learning based on the fact that the majority of melodic intervals in actual music consist of pitches that are close (within a m3) together (Dowling and Harwood 1986, p. 155). Second, listeners expect *post-skip reversal*, the expectation that after a large melodic interval, there will be a change of direction of melodic motion (Meyer 1956, Narmour 1990). Third, musician listeners expect *step-inertia*, a tendency for a small pitch interval to be followed by another small pitch interval in the same direction (Meyer 1956, Narmour 1990). Fourth, listeners expect late phrase *pitch declination*—that a phrase will move down melodically at the end. Objectively, melodic phrases tend on average to have an arch-like shape, with a rise in pitch at the beginning, and a fall at the end. Interestingly, listeners seem to expect melodic phrases to fall at the end, but not to rise at the beginning.

Rhythmic expectations are rooted in the experience of *pulse* or *tactus*, a regular framework of time-points or *beats* that typically organize our perception of the timing of events in music. Beats will more-or-less coincide with events in the music, but are cognitive entities inferred from those events. Pulse can be defined as a kind of basic expectation about when events in music will happen (see chapter 8). The range of musically usable tempi within which musical pulse is experienced is from about 30 beats per minute (bpm) to about 300 bpm. A listener will typically infer a *basic tempo* that falls within a range of approx. 60–150 bpm (Fraisse 1982), the range within which participants are best able to maintain a steady beat in tapping experiments.

Current theories of pulse suggest that it arises from patterns of oscillation set up in the brain that *entrain* to the pulse of a piece of music, forming a dynamic memory within which unfolding temporal events are organized (Barnes and Jones 2000), and yielding a framework that guides immediate temporal expectations about when events are experienced as most likely to occur. This type of expectation is very local, existing on the time-scale of working memory. It is also robust, persisting in the face of small timing discrepancies or a temporary lack of confirming events in the music. Pulse may operate at multiple temporal levels that unfold at integer multiples and divisors of the basic pulse (Yeston 1976), but there is usually one level of pulse to which a listener will respond most strongly.

Much music, in addition to being organized around a regular pulse, is also organized at a higher time level into regular cycles of more, and less, accented beats (London 2004). This type of cyclical organization is referred to as *metre*; metrical organization is schematic, and generates expectations not only about when, but also what, kind of events will happen at what points in time. Like pulse, it is a cognitive structure that is inferred from actual events in music. Typical metrical cycles alternate between strong (accented) and weak beats. Metrical cycles in Western music exist within the span of STM, generally starting with a strong beat (downbeat), the most structurally important point in a metrical cycle. This is a point of metrical stability and closure and also the point where an event is most likely to occur (e.g. Huron, 2006, p. 178–9), being a focal point for temporal attending (Palmer and Krumhansl 1990; Jones *et al.* 2002). Just as the timing of events can deviate more or less from the expected beats of a pulse, the grouping of musical events can deviate more or less from the accent pattern of metre (Lerdahl and Jackendoff 1983). One typical way of creating a kind of metrical tension is by placing salient events, such as the first or last events of a grouping, on weak beats of the metre. Metrical organization can be ambiguous to a considerable degree, and many rhythmic sequences can be interpreted in several ways (Lee 1991).

Music and memory

Experiments conducted by Deutsch (1999) suggest that auditory *working memory* may consist of aspects of musical sounds, outputs of subsystems being combined in later stages of processing. Individual musical pitches use at least one of these subsystems. Listeners presented with two pitches that were the same or a half-step apart accurately judged pitches as the same or different when the pitches were up to 6 seconds apart in time, but accuracy decreased when other pitches were interpolated in the empty time interval. This *interference* effect was strongest when the intervening pitches were chosen from both the octaves above and below the comparison pitches, making the intervening pitch intervals very large, the large pitch intervals rendering difficult the formation of a memory framework to anchor the comparison pitches. Only interpolated sequences varying in pitch led consistently to memory interference , suggesting that memory for pitch is encoded by a specialized memory subsystem (Deutsch 1999). A few individuals (fewer than 1 in 1000) have an ability to accurately identify a pitch outside of any particular context, an ability referred to as 'absolute pitch' (AP). The basis for AP possession is still debatable, but it seems to be learned, learning occurring within a 'critical period' of development and being dependent on early musical training (Ward 1999; also Huron 2006 pp. 110–113, for a discussion). AP possessors are able to effortlessly encode their experience of musical pitch in the form of a (conceptual) pitch name, which resists interference much better than a sensory memory (Siegal 1970; see also Deutsch 2006).

A familiar melody can be presented at almost any tempo and at any pitch level and remain recognizable; hence memory encoding of familiar melodies is not an exact (episodic) copy of particular pitches and time intervals, but a higher-order abstraction (schema) of particular features of the melody. In addition to some surface-level aspects of the music, possible features encoded in memory include *interval, contour*, and *scale-step context* (position in a scale). Which of these features are more salient in melody recognition (as opposed to recall) has been tested in several ways. One technique for separating aspects of a remembered melody is octave scrambling, which destroys musical interval structure, but preserves the scale-step order of the pitches in a melody (Deutsch 1972). When familiar melodies are presented with their pitches randomly scrambled to different octaves, they are generally unrecognizable. However, if the contour (up and down pattern) of the melodic line is preserved, they are more frequently recognized (Dowling 1978).

Listeners are often unable to tell the difference between exact and contour-preserving transpositions of novel melodies (Dowling 1994), for both tonal and atonal melodies. However, the importance of contour versus interval seems to decline the more well-learned a melody is. This is in line with results of studies that have found that processes of memory formation in listening are highly dynamic, not just as a consequence of longer-term learning processes but also in the very process of real-time listening itself. As Dowling et al. (2002 p. 273) note, 'The processing of a phrase, once heard, continues automatically [in memory] even while the listener hears new phrases. What the listener can remember having heard continually changes during continued listening.' In a study of melodic recall (Sloboda 1985) it was concluded that recall of simple melodies 'was never note-for note perfect'. In recalling these melodies, participants produced small variations that were harmonically and metrically consistent with the originals (musically trained participants relying somewhat more than did untrained participants on harmonic structure). This study confirms the idea that episodic memory for melody typically consists of an underlying abstract schema in which not all of the surface detail is necessarily retained.

In the perception of melodic intervals, it seems that each culture creates a set of melodic intervals that become standard perceptual categories that detemine the tones occurring in its music (see Chapter 2). These intervals are categorical in that considerable leeway is allowed in what is considered an acceptable rendition of a particular interval. Exactly how much leeway is acceptable is itself a cultural variable (Arom et al. 1997), and perception of interval categories is much clearer to musically trained than to untrained listeners (Burns 1999).

Tonality—the organization of music around sets of pitches of which a central pitch is established by its frequent occurence and appearance at salient points—has significant ramifications for musical memory (see Chapter 6). Sets of pitches constitute scales; groups of pitch categories or scale 'steps' to which a passage or piece of music is limited. Both the central pitch and the steps of a scale have varying degrees of perceptual stability, serving as cognitive landmarks in establishing a framework for listeners (Krumhansl 1990). Knowledge of scale step categories is a kind of implicit memory acquired by members of a musical culture through exposure to its music (Burns 1999).

The above-mentioned stability may not be operative in the perception of music that does not conform to tonal principles; in the experience of atonal melodic sequences the anchoring effects of tonality cannot be operative, leading some authors to maintain that atonal music theory has little basis in human perception (Francès 1988; Lerdahl 1988). Experiments by Francès (Francès, 1988) using groups of musicians familiar, and unfamiliar, with atonal idioms, showed that both groups had great difficulty identifying varied repetitions of twelve-tone series, especially in an actual musical context. Further experiments (Krumhansl et al. 1987) indicate that the structures of twelve-tone music are slightly more transparent to musically trained listeners familiar with the style.

Rhythm can be defined as the articulation of events within the time limits of working memory. As noted above, to form a perceptible pattern the events that comprise a rhythm must seem connected together in the present. It is not yet entirely clear how rhythmic sequences are encoded in memory, various models proposing different levels of hierarchical coding. As mentioned above, listeners attempt to establish a framework for rhythms by inferring beats at a regular time interval from events in the music (Povel 1984). Most rhythm experiments involving memory are recall tests where listeners are asked to reproduce a heard rhythm. As with pitch, memory for duration appears to be a categorical phenomenon (Clarke 1987); out of many possible durations, memory seems to gravitate towards a few simple durational relationships, with considerable leeway as to what constitutes a particular duration. Foundational research by Fraisse (Fraisse 1982) established that when rhythmic patterns involve more than one duration, listeners tend to hear durations as either long or short, with long durations being over 400–600 msec. In addition, there appears to be a strong tendency for the long and short durations to be reproduced or remembered in a ratio of 2:1, a relationship that has been described as a durational schema (Povel 1981).

In general, listeners are better able to reproduce sequences of durations when they can be interpreted as having an underlying regular sequence of beats, often involving the use of one particular duration as the basis for the others (Povel 1984). It is also the case that sequences of durations are much easier to remember and reproduce when shorter durations are integral subdivisions of the longer durations. Although the perception and reproduction of rhythms is categorical, small within-category deviations of event onset times (nuances) can give performed rhythms a particular feel (Snyder 2000), referred to as expressive timing (Gabrielsson 1999). This means that a particular rhythmic pattern can be performed many ways without losing its identity as a pattern, as in swing in jazz (Collier and Collier 2002). This type of nuanced information is generally not a part of the episodic memory of rhythm in music; although subtle, such nuances are important parts of what makes rhythms dynamic and emotionally charged.

Long-term memory and musical form—hierarchical theories of long-term musical representation

Musical form can be defined as the timescale of musical phenomena that require some kind of long-term mental representation for their comprehension. The process of chunking can lead to hierarchical organization in LTM, and most theories of the structure of long-term representations of music use the concept of hierarchy to varying degrees, applied both to episodic memories and abstract schemas. Hierarchical levels in music may range from local groupings up to entire pieces.

When memory passes beyond the limits of STM, it is thought to persist in a more schematic form: to become a kind of reduction. Exactly what remains of actual musical details in musical LTM is an important question. Typically, theories of musical LTM reduction involve ideas

of hierarchies of structural importance (Deutsch and Feroe 1981; Lerdahl and Jackendoff 1983), in which certain events in music are structurally more important than others, and these constitute the *gist* of a listener's memory representation (see Chapter 6). These salient structurally important events can be said to constitute the 'deep' level of structure in music, more rapidly changing details forming the musical surface or foreground.

The musical surface is segmented into units of cognitively manageable size (chunks)—the actual groupings, phrases, etc. of the music. Typically in tonal music the proposed deep structural events occur on metrically strong beats, are of longer duration, and are located on an important scale degree (Serafine *et al.* 1989), although the metaphor of hierarchical depth may be more applicable to some types of music than to others (Fink 1999). It should also be noted that although the metaphor of deep and surface structure is also used in generative linguistics, music is not held, in general, to embody specific and definite semantic meaning (though see Chapter 3). Current models of musical representation differ considerably as to the importance, and indeed the cognitive reality of deeper levels of structure.

Two prominent theories of musical mental representation (LTM) are Lerdahl and Jackendoff's (1983) Generative Theory of Tonal Music (GTTM) and the 'Cue Abstraction' theory of Deliège (Deliège and Melen 1997). The GTTM is a hierarchical theory of *tonal* music, and involves four different types of reduction: segmentation analysis, metrical analysis, time-span reduction, and prolongational reduction. The first two act as 'inputs' to the formation of the latter two, which involve larger time-spans and constitute a reduction of the most important tonal events, and a tonal tension-release structure. The mental representations posited by the GTTM represent an idealized 'final state' of largely unconscious (semantic) knowledge by a 'perfect' experienced listener (Lerdahl and Jackendoff 1983, p. 3).

Cue-Abstraction theory is more general, and is proposed as applicable to a wider range of music than to classical tonal music. In this theory, units of memory may be created by any strikingly distinctive features in the surface of the music (called *cues*) over a range of time-spans, rather than just tonally significant events; these cues act as memory markers that represent larger segments of music. Cue abstraction theory proposes a simpler and looser hierarchality than the GTTM, a set of event hierarchies rather than tonal hierarchies. It privileges prominent surface details over deep structural events in the formation of musical LTM, and the importance of salience over tonal stability, though its operation at a range of time-spans allows it a degree of hierarchicality.

Because of the limitations of working memory, music can be immediately comprehended only on the time-scale of 5–8 sec. Hence the first step in a listener's construction of the form of a piece of music is the segmentation or chunking of the musical surface by identification of boundaries formed by points of change in the music. Many of the same factors that articulate musical units on lower levels such as phrases may also operate on higher structural levels; just as a musical phrase will be articulated by a change in the flow of events, a sectional boundary delineating a larger time-span may be articulated by an even stronger change, usually involving more musical parameters.

Both the GTTM and cue abstraction theory propose that segmentation is a foundation for the establishment of LTM representations, a proposal confirmed empirically by Deliège (1987). Experiments by Clarke and Krumhansl (1990) Krumhansl (1996), Deliège (1989), and Deliège *et al.* (1996) involving both classical and contemporary music established that listeners (both musicians and non-musicians) are often in considerable agreement about the location of major segmentation points in pieces of music.

Although an unconscious memory reduction is a theoretical entity, several experiments have been conducted to try to determine whether listeners have such representations. Building on an earlier experiment by Serafine (Serafine *et al.* 1989), experiments by Dibben (1994) and Bigand (1990) using composed reductions of short musical examples have produced some evidence of the cognitive reality of reductions in tonal music, at least on a modest time-scale. Dibben's results led her to conclude that cognitive representations of atonal music are associational rather than strictly hierarchical, echoing Imberty (1993).

Experiments by Deliège and others (Deliège and Melen 1997) established that listeners, both musicians and non-musicians, use surface features of music as memory cues. These experiments involved organizing randomly reordered segments of a previously heard piece on a timeline representing their original order (Deliège 1993; Clarke and Krumhansl 1990; Deliège and Melen 1997). Unlike segmentation experiments, where the performance of musicians and non-musicians are often comparable, in many of these experiments, musicians tended to do better than non-musicians, though for both groups judgments about segment location were more accurate near the beginning and end of pieces. Other experiments have explored the development of listeners' schemas for musical elements in particular pieces by requiring judgments about the similarity of fragments of music from the same piece. This approach proposes that thematic variants are categorized around abstract *prototypes* (generalized representations of thematic material) and that variants of a theme can be heard as similar (Zbikowski 1999). Deliège (2001) and Krumhansl (1991) performed experiments investigating listeners' ability to identify as yet unheard fragments of a partially heard piece. In both cases listeners were able to use what they had heard to identify unheard examples as being similar and as coming from the same piece. In a further experiment Deliège (1996) asked listeners (musicians and non-musicians) to compare a large set of small (1–2 measure) 'cells' from a Bach violin sonata to two different reference or 'prototype' cells. In general, listeners were able to identify the variants with the correct prototypes, although the non-musicians were found to have a narrower definition of similarity. From results of a similar experiment using pieces by Beethoven and Schoenberg, Lamont and Dibben (2001) concluded that the listeners had used *surface* features to relate fragments.

In summary, it appears that both musicians and non-musicians use surface features in constructing long-term mental representations of music. In effect, the existence and utility of larger-scale hierarchical memory reductions has not been firmly established, though most experiments on tonal structures have investigated relationships between events adjacent in time rather than those separated by large spans of music (see Chapter 6). The use of deep structural features in ordinary (not analytically oriented) listening has been called into question by the results of several experiments. These experiments have explored the question of the role of memory in the perception of an entire piece of music, in part by addressing the question of what sort of information seems to be available in memory over the total duration of a piece as it unfolds in time. The results of these experiments would suggest that, for most listeners, the types of relationships between constituent parts of a piece that are described in theories such as that of Lerdahl and Jackendoff are not accessible in memory.

Experiments by Cook (1987) and by West Marvin and Brinkman (1999) explored whether the initial key of a piece was still accessible in listeners' memories at the end of the piece. Both studies found some evidence that listeners were able to undertake this task successfully, but only for pieces shorter than ca 30 seconds. This supports the view that tonal closure may be perceived most strongly over short time-spans (Levinson, 1997 but see also Gjerdingen, 1999 for a critique of Cook's study). However, West Marvin and Brinkman also found that participants were unable to indicate that pieces that ended in keys other than the initial key were less 'tonally closed' than pieces which ended in their initial key.

The results of several other studies (e.g. Karno and Konecni 1992) support the view that long-range relationships between musical materials are neither particularly accessible nor stable in memory. Further experiments by Clarke and Krumhansl (1990) Deliège (1993), Deliège et al. (1996) and Deliège and Mélen (1997) explored the ability of musically trained and untrained listeners to remember the order in which events had occurred after hearings of classical and post-tonal pieces. Although listeners' judgments of location of segments and segment-order were roughly accurate, they were less so for segments toward the middle of pieces, although musically-trained participants appeared better able to use higher-level schematic knowledge to achieve greater accuracy. It has to be noted that the results of these experiments do not prove that large-scale musical relationships cannot be encoded in memory. It is still hypothetically possible that the memory processes of an expert listeners, or more likely, performers, are capable of dealing with musical relationships over large time-scales. However, for most listeners, it seems likely that memory does not accurately encode these longer-term, larger-scale, longer-duration, hierarchical relationships.

Conclusions

Much about musical memory still remains to be understood, indeed, explored. New fields of research are continuing to extend what is known, as well as throwing up new questions. The field of neuroscience and the methods of neuroimaging have already shown great promise in identifying the areas and networks in the brain that are implicated in memory for music. Frontal, parietal, and premotor cortical areas, together with the cerebellum, are associated with working memory for musical pitch, while processing and representation of musical meaning appear to rely on areas of the middle temporal gyrus and left anterior temporal areas (Koelsch and Siebel 2005). Similarly, the study of the effect of emotion on cognitive and memory processes is very much at an early stage, but can be expected to provide fruitful insights into the nature of musical memory. Many studies have shown that emotion, or affect, might be one of the most significant factors that determine how and what we remember (see Dolan 2002 for an overview), and given that music is strongly associated with the modulation of emotional state, it can be expected that the study of musical memory will provide critical evidence about the nature of human memory in general (see Juslin and Sloboda 2001).

References

Aarden B (2003). Dynamic melodic expectancy. PhD dissertation. School of Music, Ohio State University.

Arom S, Leothaud G and Voisin F (1997). Experimental ethnomusicology: an interactive approach to the study of musical scales. In I Deliège and J Sloboda, eds., Perception and cognition of music, 3–30, Psychology Press, Hove, East Sussex.

Baddeley A (1986). Working memory. Oxford University Press, New York.

Baddeley A (2003). Working memory and language: an overview. *Journal of Communication Disorders*, **36**, 189–208.

Barnes R and Jones MR (2000). Expectancy, attention, and time. *Cognitive Psychology*, **41**, 254–311.

Bartlett FC (1932). *Remembering*. Cambridge University Press, New York.

Bharucha J (1994). Tonality and expectation. In R Aiello with JA Sloboda, eds, *Musical perceptions*, 213–239. Oxford University Press, New York.

Bigand E (1990). Abstraction of two forms of underlying structure in a tonal melody. *Psychology of Music*, **18**(1), 45–59.

Bornstein RF (1989). Exposure and affect: overview and meta-analysis of research, 1968–1987. *Psychological Bulletin*, **106**(2), 265–289.

Bregman A (1990). *Auditory scene analysis*. MIT Press, Cambridge, MA.

Burns E (1999). Intervals, scales and tuning. In D Deutsch, ed., *The psychology of music*, 2nd Edn, 215–264. Academic Press, London.

Chafe W (1994). *Discourse, consciousness, and time*. University of Chicago Press, Chicago, IL.

Clarke E (1987). Categorical rhythm perception: an ecological perspective. In A Gabrielsson, ed., *Action and perception in rhythm and music*, 19–33. Royal Swedish Academy of Music, Stockholm.

Clarke E and Krumhansl C (1990). Perceiving musical time. *Music Perception*, **7**(3), 213–251.

Cohen NJ and Squire LR (1980). Preserved learning and retention of pattern analyzing skill in amnesia: dissociation of knowing how and knowing that. *Science*, **210**, 207–210.

Collier GL and Collier JL (2002). A study of timing in two Louis Armstrong solos. *Music Perception*, **19**(3), 463–483.

Cook N (1987). The perception of large-scale tonal closure. *Music Perception*, **5**(2), 197–206.

Cowen N (1988). Evolving conceptions of memory storage, selective attention, and their mutual constraints within the human information processing system. *Psychological Bulletin*, **104**, 163–191.

Cowen N (2005). *Working memory capacity*. Psychology Press, New York.

Crowder R (1993). Auditory memory. In S McAdams, E Bigand, eds, *Thinking in sound*, 113–140. Oxford University Press, Oxford.

Crowder R and Morton J (1969). Precategorical acoustic storage (PAS). *Perception and Psychophysics*, **5**, 365–373.

Deliège I (1987). Grouping conditions in listening to music: an approach to Lerdahl and Jackendoff's grouping preference rules. *Music Perception*, **4**, 325–360.

Deliège I (1989). A perceptual approach to contemporary musical forms. *Contemporary Music Review*, **4**, 213–230.

Deliège I (1993). Mechanisms of cue extraction in memory for musical time. *Contemporary Music Review*, **9**, 191–206.

Deliège I (1996). Cue abstraction as a component of categorization processes in music listening. *Psychology of Music*, **24**, 131–156.

Deliège I (2001) Prototype effects in music listening: an empirical approach to the notion of imprint. *Music Perception*, **18**, 371–407.

Deliège I, Mélen M, Stammers D and Cross I (1996). Musical schemata in real-time listening to a piece of music. *Music Perception*, **14**(2), 117–159.

Deliège I, Melen M (1997). Cue abstraction in the representation of musical form. In I Deliège and J Sloboda, eds, *Perception and cognition of music*, 387–412. Psychology Press, Hove, East Sussex.

Deutsch D (1972) Octave Generalization and tune recognition. *Perception and Psychophyics*, **11**, 411–412.

Deutsch D (1999). The processing of pitch combinations. In D Deutsch, ed., *The psychology of music*, 2nd Edn, 349–412. Academic Press, San Diego, CA.

Deutsch D (2006) The enigma of absolute pitch. *Acoustics Today*, **2**, 11–19.

Deutsch D and Feroe J (1981). The internal representation of pitch sequences in tonal music. *Psychological Review*, **86**, 503–22.

Dibben N (1994). The cognitive reality of hierarchical structure in tonal and atonal music. *Music Perception*, **12**(1), 1–26.

Dolan RJ (2002). Emotion, cognition and behavior. *Science*, **298**, 1191–1194.

Dowling WJ (1978). Scale and contour: two components of a theory for melodies. *Psychological Review*, **85**(4), 341–354.

Dowling WJ (1994). Melodic contour in hearing and remembering melodies. In R Aiello with JA Sloboda, eds, *Musical perceptions*, 173–190. Oxford University Press, New York.

Dowling WJ and Harwood DL (1986). *Music cognition*. Academic Press, San Diego, CA.

Dowling WJ, Tillmann B and Ayers D (2002). Memory and the experience of hearing music. *Music Perception*, **19**(2), 249–276.

Ebbinghaus H (1885) *Uber das Gedachtnis: Untersuchungen zur experimentellen Psychologie (1913) Memory, a contribution to experimental psychology*, trans. HA Ruger and CE Bussenius. New York: Teachers College, Columbia University. Reprint, 1964. Dover, New York.

Ellenberger HF (1970). *The discovery of the unconscious*. Basic Books, New York.

Ericsson KA and Kintsch W (1995). Long-term working memory. *Psychological Review*, **102**, 211–245.

Fink R (1999). Going flat: post-hierarchical music theory and the musical surface. In N Cook, M Everist, eds, *Rethinking music*, 102–137. Oxford University Press, New York.

Fraisse P (1982). Rhythm and tempo. In D Deutsch, ed., *The psychology of music*, 1st Edn, 149–181. Academic Press, San Diego, CA.

Francès R (1988). *The perception of music*, trans. WJ Dowling. Lawrence Erlbaum, Hillsdale, NJ.

Gabrielsson A (1999). The performance of music. In D Deutsch, ed., *The psychology of music*, 2nd Edn, 501–602. Academic Press, London.

Gjerdingen RO (1988). A classical turn of phrase. University of Pennsylvania Press, Philadelphia, PA.

Gjerdingen RO (1999). An experimental music theory? In N Cook and M Everist, eds, *Rethinking music*, 161–170. Oxford University Press, Oxford.

Hebb DO (1949) *The organization of behavior: a neuropsychological theory*. Wiley, New York.

Huron D (2006). *Sweet anticipation, music and the psychology of expectation*. MIT Press, Cambridge, MA.

Imberty M (1993). How do we perceive atonal music? Suggestions for a theoretical approach. *Contemporary Music Review*, 9, 322–337.

James W (1890/1950) *The principles of psychology*. (Reprint edition, 1950) Dover, New York.

Jones MR, Moynihan H, MacKenzie N and Puente J (2002). Temporal aspects of stimulus-driven attending in dynamic arrays. *Psychological Science*, 13(4), 313–319.

Jonides J and Smith EE (1997). The architecture of working memory. In M Rugg, ed., *Cognitive neuroscience*, 243–276. MIT Press, Cambridge, MA.

Juslin P and Sloboda JA (eds (2001)). *Music and emotion: theory and research*. Oxford University Press, Oxford.

Karno M and Konecni V (1992). The effects of structural interventions in the first movement of Mozart's Symphony in G Minor, K. 550 on aesthetic preference. *Music Perception*, 10(1), 63–72.

Koelsch S and Siebel WA (2005). Towards a neural basis of music perception. *Trends in Cognitive Sciences*, 9(12), 578–584.

Krumhansl CL (1990). Cognitive foundations of musical pitch. Oxford University Press, New York.

Krumhansl CL (1991). Memory for musical surface. *Memory and Cognition*, 19, 401–411.

Krumhansl CL (1996). A perceptual analysis of Mozart's piano sonata K. 282: segmentation, tension, and musical ideas. *Music Perception*, 13, 401–432.

Krumhansl CL, Sandell GJ and Sergeant DC (1987). The perception of tone hierarchies and mirror forms in twelve-tone serial music. *Music Perception*, 5, 31–78.

Lamont A and Dibben N (2001). Motivic structure and the perception of similarity. *Music Perception*, 18(3), 245–274.

Lee C (1991). The perception of metrical structure: experimental evidence and a model. In P Howell, R West and I Cross, eds, *Representing musical structure*, 59–128. Academic Press, London.

Lerdahl F (1988). Cognitive constraints on compositional systems. In JA Sloboda, ed., *Generative processes in music*, 231–259. Oxford University Press, Oxford.

Lerdahl F and Jackendoff R (1983). *A generative theory of tonal music*. MIT Press, Cambridge, MA.

Levinson J (1997). *Music in the moment*. Cornell University Press, Ithica, NY.

London J (2004). *Hearing in time: psychological aspects of musical metre*. Oxford University Press, Oxford.

Mandler J (2004). *The foundations of mind*. Oxford University Press, Oxford.

McAdams S (1989). Psychological constraints on the form-bearing dimensions in music. *Contemporary Music Review*, 4, 181–198.

Meyer LB (1956). *Emotion and meaning in music*. University of Chicago Press, Chicago, IL.

Miller GA (1956). The magical number seven, plus or minus 2: some limits on our capacity for processing information. *Psychological Review*, 63(2), 81–93.

Narmour E (1990). *The analysis and cognition of basic melodic structures*. University of Chicago Press, Chicago, IL.

Palmer C and C Krumhansl (1990). Mental representation for musical metre. *Journal of Experimental Psychology, Human Perception and Performance*, 16(4), 728–741.

Peretz I and Zatorre RJ (2005). Brain organization for music processing. *Annual Review of Psychology*, 56, 89–114.

Povel D (1981). Internal representation of simple temporal patterns. *Journal of Experimental Psychology: Human Perception and Performance*, 7(1), 3–18.

Povel D (1984). A theoretical framework for rhythm perception. *Psychological Research*, 45, 315–337.

Reber A (1993). *Implicit learning and tacit knowledge*. Oxford University Press, Oxford.

Roediger HL, Dudai Y and Fitzpatrick SM (2007). *Science of memory: concepts*. Oxford University Press, Oxford.

Saffran JR, Johnson EK, Aslin RN and Newport EL (1999). Statistical learning of tone sequences by human infants and adults. *Cognition*, 70, 27–52.

Schank R (1982). *Dynamic memory*. Cambridge University Press, Cambridge.

Serafine ML, Glassman N and Overbeeke C (1989). The cognitive reality of hierarchical structure in music. *Music Perception*, 6, 347–430.

Siegal JA (1970). Sensory and verbal coding strategies in subjects with absolute pitch. *Journal of Experimental Psychology*, 103, 37–44.

Sloboda J (1985). Immediate recall of melodies. In P Howell, I Cross, R West, eds, *Musical structure and cognition*, 143–168. Academic Press, London.

Snyder B (2000). *Music and memory*. MIT Press, Cambridge, MA.

Sperling G (1960). The information available in brief visual presentations. *Pyschological Monographs*, 74, 1–29.

Tulving E (1972). Episodic and semantic memory. In E Tulving and W Donaldson, eds, *Organization of memory*, 381–403. Academic Press, New York.

Ward WD (1999). Absolute pitch. In D Deutsch, ed. *The psychology of music*, 2nd edn, 265–298. Academic Press, New York.

West ME and Brinkman A (1999). The effect of modulation and formal manipulation on perception of tonic closure by expert listeners. *Music Perception*, 16(4), 389–407.

Yeston M (1976). *The stratification of musical rhythm*. Yale University Press, New Haven, CT.

Zbikowski L (1999). Musical coherence, motive, and categorization. *Music Perception*, 17(1), 5–42.

PART 3

Responses to music

Edited by Donald A. Hodges

CHAPTER 11

Bodily responses to music

Donald A. Hodges

BODILY responses are among the core, common experiences of music. To observe people at a rock concert or watching a marching band, is to observe heads nodding, feet tapping, and bodies swaying. Along with these observable behaviours are a host of reactions to music that occur beneath the skin, such as changes in heart rate, blood pressure, and blood chemistry. The experience of listening to music involves highly complex interactions among cognitive, affective, and bodily processes that take place within a personal–social–cultural context.

The purpose of this chapter is to explore bodily responses to music. At the outset, it is important to provide some operational definitions, as the terminology in the literature is not used uniformly. Following these definitions, the main body of the chapter will be devoted to reviews of research literature. Although various types of bodily responses to music are discussed in a linear, segmented fashion, it must be remembered that they occur in a holistic fashion.

Definition of terms

For simplicity, bodily responses are divided into physiological and physical responses. Behavioural responses might also be considered, but as they are dealt with in other chapters, they will not be discussed here. Even as these two categories are being defined, it is important to note that such operational definitions are somewhat arbitrary. Although experiences can be categorized for ease of understanding, the normal experience is one of integrated response, with no sharp boundaries between them. Given this caveat, for the purposes of this chapter the categories are defined as follows:

♦ *Physiological responses* include internal bodily processes, such as heart rate. Although occasionally these internal processes are reflected in observable changes, for the most part detection requires some type of monitoring device.

♦ *Physical responses* are external, readily observable, reflexive motor movements such as foot tapping. These responses occur naturally, without specific training. Physical responses that require training, for example training a new music student to tap a foot to keep the beat while performing, will not be covered in this chapter.

Physiological responses

What follows in the next section are extremely succinct reviews of the literature under the various physiological responses measured. Findings of research related to music listening responses are generally organized into those studies reporting increases, decreases, or no change in responses. This simplistic approach masks an underlying complexity that will be discussed in a concluding section. Because this concluding discussion will deal with general principles affecting more than one type of physiological response, comments in the brief review sections are kept to a minimum.

The effects of music on heart or pulse rate

A significant amount of research supports the position that listening to music can cause changes in heart rate (e.g. Bernardi *et al.* 2006; Blood and Zatorre 2001; Savan 1999). In general, stimulative music—characterized by fast, loud, staccato passages—tends to cause an increase in heart rate (HR) or pulse rate (PR), while sedative music—characterized by slow, soft, legato passages—tends to cause a decrease. However, some researchers found that any music, whether stimulative or sedative, tends to increase HR or PR (Krumhansl 1997; Rickard 2004).

In only a slightly fewer number of studies did researchers report that music caused no changes in HR or PR (e.g. Davis 1992; Gupta and Gupta 2005; Pujol 1994). In Iwanaga *et al.* (1996), HR did not change in response to stimulative music, but did decrease during sedative music.

The effects of performing music on heart rate are much less studied. Measurements of pulse rate in 24 orchestral musicians of the Vienna Symphony were made during rehearsals and public performances (Haider and Groll-Knapp 1981). Maximum pulse rates during performances reached 151 beats per minute. Pulse rates were up to 8 beats higher in concerts than during rehearsals and fluctuated widely depending on the character of the music being performed, with tempo being a salient feature. For example, during a Rachmaninoff symphony, one trumpet player went from a resting pulse rate of 68 to a peak of over 150. Often, peaks occurred just prior to an entrance. Abel and Larkin (1990) found that student musicians had increased heart rates in anticipation of a graded performance.

The effects of music on skin conductivity

Galvanic skin responses (GSR), now more often referred to as electrodermal activity or skin conductance, are temporary, primarily negative, fluctuations in the electrical resistance of the skin. Measured by a psychogalvanometer, usually attached to the fingers and/or palm of the hand, the GSR is a result of mental activity, most often of an affective nature (Venables 1987). An increase in GSR readings indicates a decrease in resistance, which in turn indicates an increase in arousal. Significant changes in GSR in response to music listening were found in numerous studies (e.g. Khalfa *et al.* 2002; Lundqvist *et al.* 2000; Rickard 2004). In other studies, no meaningful changes in GSR were found in response to music listening (Jellison 1975; Keller and Seraganian 1984).

The effects of music on blood pressure

Stimulative music increased blood pressure in Bernardi *et al.* (2006), Krumhansl (1997) and Pignatiello *et al.* (1989). In a number of studies, music decreased blood pressure; most often sedative music had this effect, though some stimulative music did so too (Lorch *et al.* 1994, Savan 1999). Noteworthy is the fact that self-selected music was found to be effective in lowering blood pressure (Geden *et al.* 1989; Oyama *et al.* 1987a; Updike and Charles 1987). Confounding these results are studies that reported no meaningful change in blood pressure as a result of listening to music (Gupta and Gupta 2005; Strauser 1997), which in some cases was self-selected (Geden *et al.* 1989; Schuster 1985). In a related study, music students experienced an increase in blood pressure in anticipation of a graded performance (Abel and Larkin 1990).

The effects of music on biochemical responses

A relatively new area of investigation has been the effect of music listening on hormone levels found in blood, urine, or saliva. The basis for this work is the field of psychoneuroimmunology, a field that explores interactions between nervous and immune systems (Hall 1989). The majority of published reports presented in Table 11.1 indicate meaningful changes in biochemicals in response to music listening or musical experiences.

Collectively, this line of research supports the central contention of psychoneuroimmunology, namely that mental and bodily responses are intertwined in a symbiotic relationship. This is well illustrated in three examples. Choral singers had increases in SigA of 159 per cent during rehearsal and 240 per cent during performance,

Table 11.1 Biochemical responses to music

Biochemical	Response to music	Sources
Secretory immunoglobulin A (SIgA)	Increased	Beck *et al*. 2000, Charnetski and Brennan 1998, Kreutz *et al*. 2004, Lane 1991, McCraty *et al*. 1996, Rider *et al*. 1991, Rider and Weldin 1990, Tsao *et al*. 1991
	Decreased	Miluk-Lolasa *et al*. 1994
	No change	Oyama *et al*. 1987a, Rider *et al*. 1985
Cortisol	Increased	Beck *et al*. 2000, Gerra *et al*. 1998, VanderArk and Ely 1992, 1993
	Decreased	Bartlett *et al*. 1993, Beck *et al*. 2000, Kreutz *et al*. 2004, Leardi *et al*. 2007, McKinney *et al*. 1997a, Tsao *et al*. 1991
	Increased in music majors but decreased in non-music majors	VanderArk and Ely 1992, 1993
Interleukin-1	Increased	Bartlett *et al*. 1993
Adrenocorticotropic hormone (ACTH)	Increased	Gerra *et al*. 1998
	Decreased	Oyama *et al*. 1987b
Neutrophils and lymphocytes	Decreased	Rider and Achterberg 1989
Norepinephrine	Increased	Gerra *et al*. 1998, Kumar *et al*. 1999, VanderArk and Ely 1992, 1993
Growth hormone	Increased	Gerra *et al*. 1998
Epinephrine	Increased	Kumar *et al*. 1999, VanderArk and Ely 1992, 1993
	No change	Gerra *et al*. 1998
Melatonin	Increased	Kumar *et al*. 1999
Serotonin	No change	Kumar *et al*. 1999
Prolactin	No change	Gerra *et al*. 1998, Kumar *et al*. 1999
Beta-endorphins	Increased	Gerra *et al*. 1998, Goldstein 1980
	Decreased	McKinney *et al*. 1997b
Dopamine	The release of dopamine in response to music, indicating a pleasure response, has been implicated by activations of mesolimbic structures involved in reward processing including the nucleus accumbens (NAc) and the ventral tegmental area (VTA), as well as the hypothalamus and insula (Blood and Zatorre 2001, Brown *et al*. 2004, Menon and Levitin 2005).	
Oxytocin	Although oxytocin has been mentioned in connection with lullabies and mother–infant bonding (Freeman 1995), such reporting is anecdotal and no published research studies have been identified.	
Genetic stress hormone markers	Participants in a recreational music-making programme experienced reversal in 19 of 45 genetic stress hormone markers (Bittman *et al*. 2005).	

with a corresponding decrease in cortisol of 30 per cent during rehearsal and an average increase of 37 per cent during performance (Beck *et al.* 2000). When patients with Alzheimer's disease underwent four weeks of music therapy sessions, melatonin, norepinephrine, and epinephrine all increased, while serotonin, and prolactin did not (Kumar *et al.* 1999). Among 18–19-year-olds, a meaningful increase was observed in beta-endorphins, ACTH, norepinephrine, growth hormone, and cortisol after listening to techno music (Gerra *et al.* 1998). Classical music induced an improvement in emotional state, but no meaningful changes in hormonal concentrations. This line of research is central to the practice of music medicine and is further explored in Chapter 49.

The effects of music on respiration

An increase in respiration or breathing rate was found in several studies (Blood and Zatorre 2001; Iwanaga and Moroki 1999). Ries (1969) correlated increases with preference and Haas *et al.* (1986) found that breathing rates entrained with musical rhythm. Researchers found no change in respiration rate as a result of listening to music (Davis 1992; Davis-Rollans and Cunningham (1987) and Iwanaga *et al.* (1996) found that respiration did not change to stimulative music but did decrease to sedative music.

The effects of music on finger, peripheral skin, or body temperature

Meaningful changes in skin temperature in response to music listening have been reported (Lundqvist *et al.* 2000; Rickard 2004). Beyond the fact that listening to music can affect temperature changes, there is very little consistency in results. In some studies, temperature increased—to sedative music (Kibler and Rider 1983; Peach 1984), to stimulative music (Lundqvist *et al.* 2000; Standley 1991), or to any music (Rickard 2004). In other cases, temperature decreased (Krumhansl 1997; Savan 1999). In only three reports did music not affect skin temperature (Guzzetta 1989; Kibler and Rider 1983; Zimmerman *et al.* 1988).

The effects of music on muscular tension

Muscular tension is most often measured by electromyography (EMG) and is related to tension-release patterns in music. The majority of studies found that muscular tension changes in response to music listening (Blood and Zatorre 2001; Rickard 2004). Only two published studies report no changes in EMG while listening to music (Davis and Thaut 1989; Scartelli 1984). Nielsen (1983, 1987; cited in Gabrielsson and Lindstrom 2001) reported that the more tension in the music, the harder subjects squeezed on a pair of tongs. Sears (1958) found that sedative music decreased tension more quickly than stimulative music increased tension. Carrick *et al.* (2007) found that listening to certain music had the potential to increase postural stability.

Chills

The following studies found that music listeners reported chills, often accompanied by shivers, tears, lump in the throat, or pilomotor (goosebump) responses (Craig 2005; Goldstein 1980; Panksepp 1995; Rickard 2004). Blood and Zatorre (2001) discovered that as the intensity of chills increased, so did blood flow to areas of the brain involved in mediating reward, motivation, emotion, and arousal. More than 80% of Sloboda's (1991) subjects reported having chills to music. Guhn *et al.* (2007) found that HR and skin conductance increased in musical passages that elicited the most chills. This confirmed findings by Craig (2005), Rickard (2004), and Panksepp (1995), but contrasted with Blood and Zatorre (2001).

The effects of music on blood volume

Two studies (Davis and Thaut 1989; Krumhansl 1997) found significant changes in blood volume in response to music listening, while two studies (Jellison 1975; Pignatiello *et al.* 1989) did not.

The effects of music on gastric motility

More formally known as peristalsis or gastric motility, stomach contractions move food along the alimentary canal. Presumably, music could speed up or slow down this process. Two studies (Chen *et al.* 2005; Demling *et al.* 1970) support the contention that music can affect gastric activity. Beyond that, there is no consensus on the relationship between type of music and its effect on digestion.

Miscellaneous studies

Blood-oxygen

Music had noticeably positive effects on blood oxygen saturation levels (Cassidy and Standley 1995) and varied according to the stimulation rates and intensity (Lovett *et al.* 1952).

Ankle jerk

Subjects' ankles jerked in response to music (Harrer and Harrer 1977).

Pupillary reflex

Music had a significant effect on pupillary reflex, with dilation occurring during stimulative music and constriction during sedative music (Slaughter 1954).

Zygomaticus activity

Happy/positive music elicited increased zygomaticus activity (smile muscle) compared to sad/negative music (Lundqvist *et al.* 2000; Witvliet and Vrana 2007).

General discussion of physiological responses to music

From this cursory review of research findings, it is apparent that there is overwhelming support for the notion that listening to music affects physiological responses. Furthermore, there is general, though by no means unanimous, support for the notion that stimulative and sedative music tend to increase and decrease physiological responses, respectively. The reason this relationship is not stronger is most likely due to personal preferences.

Music listening experiences are highly idiosyncratic, as each person possesses an individual history (e.g., amount of musical training) and personality, and each listening experience occurs in varying situations. One of Fridja's (1988) laws of emotion is the Law of Situational Meaning:

emotions arise in response to the meaning structures of a given situation; different emotions arise in response to different meaning structures (p. 349). Imagine, then, that one hears the same piece of music, say the slow movement of Bach's Concerto for Two Violins in d minor, BWV 1043, performed at a funeral and then a few weeks later at a wedding. Undoubtedly, the reactions would be significantly different.

As is evident from the foregoing reviews, there is not enough research on the effects of personal preference on physiological responses to clarify the issue and some of it is contradictory. For example, Iwanaga and Moroki (1999) found that type of music (i.e., stimulative or sedative) had a differing effect on heart rate, respiration rate, and blood pressure, but music preference did not. Nevertheless, the concept that personal preference is influential is firmly enough accepted to be utilized in the use of music in medical treatment (e.g., anxiolytic music for the treatment of pain and anxiety) (Spintge and Droh 1992; see Chapter 49 this volume for more details on medical applications and Chapter 15 for the role of preferences in general).

Once it is accepted that physiological processes change in response to music listening, what do such changes signify? Does an increase in heart rate, for example, necessarily indicate a positive response or could it just as easily indicate a negative response? Attaching specific physiological responses to specific emotional responses has not received much attention nor had much success. Increased smile muscle activity while listening to happy music as opposed to sad music is one of the few examples (Lundqvist *et al.* 2000). Carefully designed studies, with increased attention to personal preferences and idiosyncrasies, may lead to an enhanced understanding of the influence of music on physiological responses. Currently, the most advanced work is being conducted under the rubric of music medicine.

Physical responses

Anthropologists have documented that music and movement are linked in peoples all over the world (Blacking 1995). Many activities, such as dancing, marching, exercising, and working to music exhibit a synchronization and entrainment between auditory input and motor output (Brown *et al.* 2006). Our brains and bodies are wired to respond to sound and to rhythmic sounds in particular (Koepchen *et al.* 1992). Furthermore, entraining our bodies to musical rhythms brings pleasure (Levitin 2006). Listening to music activates the following brain regions in a sequential order:

1 the auditory cortex initially analyses sound;

2 frontal regions process musical structure;

3 the mesolimbic system, involved in arousal and pleasure, is activated and produces dopamine, further activating the nucleus accumbens; and

4 the cerebellum and basal ganglia process rhythm and meter leading to movement (Menon and Levitin 2005).

When we listen to music our bodies naturally respond with largely involuntary gestures, such as head nodding and foot tapping.

Audiomotor systems are interconnected such that musical patterns elicit and entrain strong motor responses (Baumann *et al.* 2007; Thaut 2003; Thaut *et al.* 1999). For example, subjects are able to finger tap synchronously with heard rhythms, even making adjustments when changes in tempo are below the threshold of detection (Tecchio *et al.* 2000). Such effects may be enhanced by mirror neurons (Nelissen *et al.* 2005; Rizzolatti *et al.* 1996). These are neurons in the brain that fire both when an action is performed and when it is observed in someone else. More recent work indicates that mirror neurons may also be triggered by auditory stimuli in what is called 'action-listening'. Lahav *et al.* (2007) demonstrated that non-pianists who learned to perform a brief excerpt and then who heard the same pattern without performing any physical action had activations in bilateral frontoparietal motor-related networks.

In the vast majority of musical experiences around the world, physical responses are a natural phenomenon. Only in a few situations, such as Western classical music concerts, is there an attempt to control these responses. One might speculate that the relatively immobile audience posture during Western classical music concerts, followed by a wild burst of applause after a performance judged to be stellar, might be, in part, a reflection of pent up physical responses.

Physical responses to music begin in the final trimester before birth (Parncutt 2006) and continue throughout infancy with the singing of lullabies, the playing of 'musical' games such as pat-a-cake and peek-a-boo, and the presence of crib mobiles and musical toys. Rhythmic and timing interactions between parent and child can be illustrated by the 'I'm gonna gitcha' game (Stern 1982). The parent chants: 'I'm gonna gitcha I'm gonna gitcha I'm gonna gitcha Gotcha!' At each repetition the pitch and loudness increase, while the amount of time between each repetition progressively elongates. Activities such as this are so important that they form the basis for acquiring cognitive expectancies and for interrelating cognition and affect (Beebe *et al.* 1982; Thaut *et al.* 2005).

The human body consists of multiple oscillators that create the rhythms that drive the body and control behaviour (Brown and Graeber 1982). These interaction rhythms are important to music and dance but are essential to all human interactions (Scheflen 1982). The intentional application of rhythmic entrainment to motor behaviours has been made with Parkinsonian and stroke patients, allowing them to regain walking, reaching, and grasping skills (see Chapter 49 this volume).

Conclusion

In the book entitled *How Musical is Man?*, Blacking (1973) eloquently captures the symbiotic relationship between music and human beings in the first and last chapters: 'Humanly organized sound' and 'Soundly organized humanity'. In the first chapter, Blacking contends that music is a product of human behaviour resulting from biological processes and cultural agreement. The brain's ability to imagine, create and perceive patterns of sounds combines with social conventions to give us music. Music, for Blacking, is 'sound that is organized into socially accepted patterns' (p. 25). Above all, music exists because human beings impose sonic order rather than accept passively the sounds that nature provides.

Having stressed that music is humanly organized sound, Blacking then counters with 'Soundly organized humanity'. He acknowledges that music affects bodily processes but concentrates his discussion primarily on the effects of music on social behaviours. Although the focus in the current chapter has, of course, been on the former, Blacking's main point is essentially the main point of this chapter: the music we create in turn affects us in profound ways. Even though the narrower focus of this chapter is on bodily responses, Blacking's larger view is also important to keep in mind. That is, bodily processes are influenced by the larger personal–social–cultural circumstances in which they occur. Lomax (1968), Merriam (1964) and many others have provided considerable field data from around the world to underscore the concept of music embedded in social context.

Main themes in this chapter are that bodily responses to music are among the core experiences of music. They are hugely complex, with a myriad of response types interwoven into the fabric of thoughts, feelings, and social context. Bodily responses are highly idiosyncratic as each person brings a unique self to a music listening situation. Researchers have made significant strides in ferreting out the details of these responses and in collaboration with practitioners have made progress in utilizing this knowledge, particularly in music therapy and music medicine applications. With all this, however, the richness and complexity of the human experience leaves much yet to be discovered.

While recognizing strides already made, the following ideas are offered as a means of advancing our knowledge of how humans react bodily to music to a new level of understanding:

◆ Greater consensus on terminology and standardization of protocol would be helpful. Some of the contradictory findings reported in the literature review must surely be due to these inconsistencies.

◆ Another explanation for contradictory findings may be that in some circumstances participants were emotionally responding to the music, while in others they were not (see Chapter 12 this volume for more discussion of this point). This is a confound that needs to be kept in mind in studies of bodily responses to music.

◆ Moving steadily toward more naturalistic musical experiences would be enlightening. Although it may appear as we as if are very far away from field studies, we may be closer than one might imagine. More than 25 years ago, members of the Vienna Symphony were monitored for heart rate and brain wave activity during rehearsals and public performances (Haider and Groll-Knapp 1981). Since then, ambulatory assessment has become a new and developing field. Using digital technology with hand-held PCs, researchers are now able to monitor such physiological responses as heart rate, blood pressure, blood glucose, and so on while subjects are engaged in routine activities (Fahrenberg 2001). Applying this technology to music listeners in all manner of naturalistic settings should be possible. In fact, in a recent experiment whose results are not yet known, a conductor, five members of a symphony orchestra, and fifteen audience members were all wired with sensors to record heart rate, muscle tension, respiration, and galvanic skin response during a performance (Dyer 2006). Findings may allow for comparisons of physiological responses as the music is expressed in conducting gestures, performer's reactions to those gestures, and audience responses to both.

◆ Paradoxically, we must pay increased attention to the idiosyncratic nature of responses while also gaining clarity in our understanding of corporate responses. Balancing personalized responses with the group dynamics involved in audience responses is a challenge that has not received much attention. For example, it is easy to imagine that one's bodily responses would be highly influenced by being one of thousands of wildly cheering fans at a rock concert.

◆ Advancing technologies are giving us an ability to gain increasingly refined views of bodily responses, particularly physiological responses, but this must not let us become myopic. Fine-grained details must be viewed within a social context.

None of these suggestions are made cavalierly. Surmounting inherent problems will be exceedingly difficult. Nevertheless, continuing to measure heart rate responses to 15 different 1-minute musical excerpts during a laboratory experiment is not likely to advance understanding much beyond what we already know. It will be most interesting to read a review of this literature at some point in the future to see what innovative strategies researchers have devised to bring deeper understanding to these most basic of human responses to music.

References

Abel J and Larkin K (1990). Anticipation of performance among musicians: physiological arousal, confidence, and state anxiety. *Psychology of Music*, **18**, 171–182.

Bartlett D, Kaufman D and Smeltekop R (1993). The effects of music listening and perceived sensory experiences on the immune system as measured by interleukin-1 and cortisol. *Journal of Music Therapy*, **30**(4), 194–209.

Baumann S, Koeneke S, Schmidt C, Meyer M, Lutz K and Jancke L (2007). A network for audio-motor coordination in skilled pianists and non-musicians. *Brain Research*, **1161**, 65–78.

Beck R, Cesario T, Yousefi A and Enamoto H (2000). Choral singing, performance perception, and immune system changes in salivary immunoglobulin A and cortisol. *Music Perception*, **18**(1), 87–106.

Beebe B, Gerstman L, Carson B, Dolinas M, Zigman A, Rosensweig H, Faughey K and Korma M (1982). Rhythmic communication in the mother-infant dyad. In M. Davis, ed., *Interaction rhythms: periodicity in communication behavior*, 79–100 New York: Human Sciences Press.

Bernardi L, Porta C and Sleight P (2006). Cardiovascular, cerebrovascular, and respiratory changes induced by different types of music in musicians and non-musicians: the importance of silence. *Heart*, **92**, 445–452.

Bittman B, Berk L, Shannon M, Sharaf M, Westengard J, Guegler K and Ruff D (2005). Recreational music making modulates the human stress response: a preliminary individualized gene expression strategy. *Medical Science Monitor*, **11**(2), BR231–40.

Blacking J (1973). *How musical is man?* University of Washington Press, Seattle WA.

Blacking J (1995). *Music, culture, and experience.* University of Chicago Press, Chicago, IL.

Blood A and Zatorre R (2001). Intensely pleasurable responses to music correlate with activity in brain regions implicated in reward and emotion. *Proceedings of the National Academy of Sciences of the United States of America*, **98**, 11818–11823.

Brown F and Graeber R (eds) (1982). *Rhythmic aspects of behavior.* Lawrence Erlbaum Associates, Hillsdale, NJ.

Brown S, Martinez M and Parsons L (2004). Passive music listening spontaneously engages limbic and paralimbic systems. *NeuroReport*, **15**(13), 2033–2037.

Brown S, Martinez M and Parsons L (2006). The neural basis of human dance. *Cerebral Cortex*, **16**(8), 1157–1167.

Carrick F, Oggero E and Pagnacco G (2007). Posturographic changes associated with music listening. *The Journal of Alternative and Complementary Medicine*, **13**(5), 519–526.

Cassidy J and Standley J (1995). The effect of music listening on physiological responses of premature infants in the NICU. *Journal of Music Therapy*, **32**(4), 208–227.

Charnetski C and Brennan F Jr (1998). Effect of music and auditory stimuli on secretory immunoglobulin A (IgA). *Perceptual Motor Skills*, **87**, 1163–1170.

Chen D, Xu X, Wang Z and Chen J (2005). Alteration of gastric myoelectrical and autonomic activities with audio stimulation in healthy humans. *Scandinavian Journal of Gastroenterology*, **40**(7), 814–821.

Craig D (2005). An exploratory study of physiological changes during 'chills' induced by music. *Musicae Scientiae: The journal of the European Society for the Cognitive Sciences of Music*, **9**(2), 273–285.

Davis C (1992). The effects of music and basic relaxation instruction on pain and anxiety of women undergoing in-office gynecological procedures. *Journal of Music Therapy*, **29**(4), 202–216.

Davis W and Thaut M (1989). The influence of preferred relaxing music on measures of state anxiety, relaxation, and physiological responses. *Journal of Music Therapy*, **26**(4), 168–187.

Davis-Rollans C and Cunningham S (1987). Physiologic responses of coronary care patients to selected music. *Heart-Lung*, **16**, 370–378.

Demling L, Tzschoppe M and Classen M (1970). The effect of various types of music on the secretory function of the stomach. *Digestive Diseases and Sciences*, **15**(1), 15–20.

Dyer R (2006). A new kind of experimental music. *Boston Globe*, 16 April.

Fahrenberg J (2001). Origins and developments of ambulatory monitoring and assessment. In J Fahrenberg, M Myrtek, eds, *Progress in ambulatory assessment. Computer-assisted psychological and psychophysiological methods in monitoring and field studies*, 578–614 Hogrefe and Huber, Seattle, WA.

Freeman W (1995). *Societies of brains: a study in the neuroscience of love and hate.* Lawrence Erlbaum Associates, Hillsdale, NJ.

Fridja N (1988). The laws of emotion. *American Psychologist*, **43**(5), 349–358.

Gabrielsson A and Lindström E (2001). The influence of musical structure on emotional expression. In P Juslin, J Sloboda, eds, *Music and emotion: theory and research*, 223–248 Oxford University Press, Oxford.

Geden E, Lower M, Beattie S and Beck N (1989). Effects of music and imagery on physiologic and self-report of analogued labor pain. *Nursing Research*, **38**(1), 37–41.

Gerra G, Zaimovic A, Franchini D, Palladino M, Giucastro G, Reali N, Maestri D, Caccavari R, Deslsignore R and Brambilla F (1998). Neuroendocrine responses of healthy volunteers to 'techno-music': relationships with personality traits and emotional state. *International Journal of Psychophysiology*, **28**(1), 99–111.

Goldstein A (1980). Thrills in response to music and other stimuli. *Physiological Psychology*, **3**, 126–129.

Guhn M, Hamm A and Zentner M (2007). Physiological and music-acoustic correlates of the chill response. *Music Perception*, **24**(5), 473–483.

Gupta U and Gupta B (2005). Psychophysiological responsivity to Indian instrumental music. *Psychology of Music*, **33**(4), 363–372.

Guzzetta C (1989). Effects of relaxation and music therapy on patients in a coronary care unit with presumptive acute myocardial infarction. *Heart Lung*, **18**, 609–616.

Haas F, Distenfeld S and Axen K (1986). Effects of perceived musical rhythm on respiratory patterns. *Journal of Applied Physiology*, **61**(1–3), 1185–1191.

Haider M and Groll-Knapp E (1981). Psychophysiological investigations into the stress experienced by musicians in a symphony orchestra. In M Piperek, ed., *Stress and music*, 15–34 Vienna: Wilhelm Braumüller.

Hall S (1989). A molecular code links emotions, mind and health. *Smithsonian*, **20**(3), 62–71.

Harrer G and Harrer H (1977). Music, emotion, and autonomic function. In M Critchley, R Henson, eds, *Music and the brain*, 202–216 William Heinemann Medical Books, London.

Iwanaga M, Ikeda M and Iwaki T (1996). The effects of repetitive exposure to music on subjective and physiological responses. *Journal of Music Therapy*, **33**(3), 219–230.

Iwanaga M and Moroki Y (1999). Subjective and physiological responses to music stimuli controlled over activity and preference. *Journal of Music Therapy*, **36**(1), 26–38.

Jellison J (1975). The effect of music on autonomic stress responses and verbal reports. In C Madsen, R Greer, C Madsen, eds, *Research in music behavior: modifying music behavior in the classroom*, 206–219 Teachers College Press, New York.

Keller S and Seraganian P (1984). Physical fitness level and autonomic reactivity to psychosocial stress. *Journal of Psychosomatic Research*, **28**(4), 279–287.

Khalfa S, Peretz I, Blondin J and Manon R (2002). Event-related skin conductance responses to musical emotions in humans. *Neuroscience Letters*, **328**, 145–149.

Kibler V and Rider M (1983). The effect of progressive muscle relaxation and music on stress as measured by finger temperature response. *Journal of Clinical Psychology*, **39**, 213–15.

Koepchen H, Droh R, Spintge R, Abel H-H, Klüssenforf D and Koralewski E (1992). Physiological rhythmicity and music in medicine. In R Spintge, R Droh, eds, *Music Medicine*, 39–70 MMB Music, St. Louis, MO.

Kreutz G, Bongard S, Rohrmann S, Hodapp V and Grebe D (2004). Effects of choir singing or listening on secretory immunoglobulin A, cortisol, and emotional state. *Journal of Behavioral Medicine*, **27**(6), 623–635.

Krumhansl C (1997). An exploratory study of musical emotions and psychophysiology. *Canadian Journal of Experimental Psychology*, **51**(4), 336–352.

Kumar A, Tims F, Cruess D and Mintzer M (1999). Music therapy increases serum melatonin levels in patients with Alzheimer's disease. *Alternative Therapies in Health and Medicine*, **5**(6), 49–57.

Lane D (1991). The effect of a single music therapy session on hospitalized children as measured by salivary immunoglobulin A, speech pause time, and a patient opinion Likert scale. *Pediatric Research*, **29**(4), 2:11A.

Lahav A, Saltzman E and Schlaug G (2007). Action representation of sound: audiomotor recognition network while listening to newly acquired actions. *Journal of Neuroscience*, **27**(2), 308–314.

Leardi S, Pietroletti R, Angeloni G, Necozione S, Ranalletta G and Del Gusto B (2007). Randomized clinical trial examining the effect of music therapy in stress response to day surgery. *British Journal of Surgery*, **94**(8), 943–947.

Levitin D (2006). *This is your brain on music.* Dutton, New York.

Lomax A (1968). *Folk song style and culture.* Transaction Books, New Brunswick, NJ.

Lorch C, Lorch V, Diefendorf A and Earl P (1994). Effect of stimulative and sedative music on systolic blood pressure, heart rate, and respiratory rate in premature infants. *Journal of Music Therapy*, **31**(2), 105–118.

Lovett Doust J and Schneider R (1952). Studies on the physiology of awareness: the effect of rhythmic sensory bombardment on emotions, blood oxygen saturation, and the levels of consciousness. *Journal of Mental Science*, **98**, 640–653.

Lundqvist L, Carlsson F and Hilmersson P (2000). Facial electromyography, autonomic activity, and emotional experience to happy and sad music. *Journal of Psychology*, **35**(3/4), 225.

McCraty R, Atkinson M, Rein G and Watkins A (1996). Music enhances the effect of positive emotional states on salivary IgA. *Stress Medicine*, **12**, 167–175.

McKinney C, Antoni M, Kumar M, Tims F and McCabe P (1997a). Effects of Guided Imagery and Music (GIM) therapy on mood and cortisol in healthy adults. *Health Psychology*, **16**(4), 390–400.

McKinney C, Tims F, Kumar A and Kumar M (1997b). The effect of selected classical music and spontaneous imagery on plasma beta-endorphin. *Journal of Behavioral Medicine*, **20**(1), 85–99.

Menon V and Levitin D (2005). The rewards of music listening: response and physiological connectivity of the mesolimbic system. *NeuroImage*, **28**(1), 175–184.

Merriam A (1964). *The anthropology of music.* Northwestern University Press, Chicago, IL.

Miluk-Kolasa B, Obminski Z, Stupnicki R and Golec L (1994). Effects of music treatment on salivary cortisol in patients exposed to pre-surgical stress. *Experimental and Clinical Endocrinology*, **102**, 118–120.

Nelissen K, Luppino G, Vanduffel W, Rizzolatti G and Orban G (2005). Observing others: multiple action representation in the frontal lobe. *Science*, **310**(5746), 332–336.

Oyama T, Sato Y, Kudo T, Spintge R and Droh R (1987a). Effect of anxiolytic music on endocrine function in surgical patients. In R Spintge, R Droh, eds, *Music in medicine*, 169–174 Springer-Verlag, Berlin.

Oyama T, Hatano K, Sato Y, Kudo R, Spintge R and Droh R (1987b). Endocrine effect of anxiolytic music in dental patients. In R Spintge and R Droh, eds, *Music in medicine*, 223–226 Springer-Verlag, Berlin.

Panksepp J (1995). The emotional sources of 'chills' induced by music. *Music Perception*, **13**(2), 171–207.

Parncutt R (2006). Prenatal development. In G McPherson, ed., *The child as musician*, 1–31 Oxford University Press, Oxford.

Peach S (1984). Some implications for the clinical use of music facilitated imagery. *Journal of Music Therapy*, **21**(1), 27–34.

Pignatiello M, Camp C, Elder S and Rasar L (1989). A psychophysiological comparison of the Velten and musical mood induction techniques. *Journal of Music Therapy*, **26**(3), 140–154.

Pujol K (1994). The effect of vibrotactile stimulation, instrumentation, and precomposed melodies on physiological and behavioral responses of profoundly retarded children and adults. *Journal of Music Therapy*, **31**(3), 186–205.

Rickard N (2004). Intense emotional responses to music: a test of the physiological arousal hypothesis. *Psychology of Music*, **32**(4), 371–388.

Rider M and Achterberg J (1989). Effect of music-assisted imagery on neutrophils and lymphocytes. *Biofeedback and Self-Regulation*, **14**(3), 247–257.

Rider M, Floyd J and Kirkpatrick J (1985). The effect of music, imagery, and relaxation on adrenal corticosteroids and the re-entrainment of circadian rhythms. *Journal of Music Therapy*, **22**(1), 46–58.

Rider M, Mickey C, Weldin C and Hawkinson R (1991). The effects of toning, listening, and singing on psychophysiological responses. In C Maranto, ed., *Applications of music in medicine*, 73–84 National Association for Music Therapy, Washington, DC.

Rider M and Weldin C (1990). Imagery, improvisation and immunity. *The Arts in Psychotherapy*, **17**, 211–216.

Ries H (1969). GSR and breathing amplitude related to emotional reactions to music. *Psychonomic Science*, **14**(2), 62.

Rizzolatti G, Fadiga L, Gallese V and Fogassi L (1996). Premotor cortex and the recognition of motor actions. *Cognitive Brain Research*, **3**(2), 131–141.

Savan A (1999). The effect of background music on learning. *Psychology of Music*, **27**(2), 138–146.

Scartelli J (1984). The effect of EMG biofeedback and sedative music, EMG biofeedback only, and sedative music only on frontalis muscle relaxation ability. *Journal of Music Therapy*, **21**(2), 67–78.

Scheflen A (1982). Preface: Comments on the significance of interaction rhythms. In M Davis, ed., *Interaction rhythms: periodicity in communicative behavior*, 13–22 Human Sciences Press, New York.

Schuster B (1985). The effect of music listening on blood pressure fluctuations in adult hemodialysis patients. *Journal of Music Therapy*, **22**(3), 146–153.

Sears W (1958). The effect of music on muscle tonus. In E Gaston, ed., *Music therapy, 1957*, 199–205 Allen Press, Lawrence, KS.

Slaughter F (1954). The effect of stimulative and sedative types of music on normal and abnormal subjects as indicated by pupillary reflexes. In M Bing, ed., *Music therapy*, 246–248 Allen Press, Lawrence, KS.

Sloboda J (1991). Music structure and emotional response: some empirical findings. *Psychology of Music*, **19**, 110–120.

Spintge R and Droh R (1992). Toward a research standard in musicmedicine/music therapy: a proposal for a multimodal approach. In R Spintge, R Droh, eds, *Musicmedicine*, 345–349 MMB Music, St. Louis, MO.

Standley J (1991). The effect of vibrotactile and auditory stimuli on perception of comfort, heart rate, and peripheral finger temperature. *Journal of Music Therapy*, **28**(3), 120–134.

Stern D (1982). Some interactive functions of rhythm changes between mother and infant. In M Davis, ed., *Interaction rhythms: periodicity in communicative behavior*, 101–117 Human Sciences Press, New York.

Strauser M (1997). The effects of music versus silence on measures of state anxiety, perceived relaxation, and physiological responses of patients receiving chiropractic interventions. *Journal of Music Therapy*, **34**(2), 88–105.

Tecchio F, Salustri C, Thaut M, Pasqualetti P and Rossini P (2000). Conscious and preconscious adaptation to rhythmic auditory stimuli: a magnetoencephalographic study of human brain responses. *Experimental Brain Research*, **135**, 222–230.

Thaut M (2003). Neural basis of rhythmic timing networks in the human brain. *Annals of the New York Academy of Sciences*, **999**, 364–373.

Thaut M, Kenyon G, Schauer M and McIntosh G (1999). The connection between rhythmicity and brain function. *IEEE Engineering in Medicine and Biology*, **18**, 101–108.

Thaut M, Peterson D and McIntosh G (2005). Temporal entrainment of cognitive functions: musical mnemonics induce brain plasticity and oscillatory synchrony in neural networks. *Annals of the New York Academy of Sciences*, **1060**, 243–254.

Tsao C, Gordon T, Maranto C, Lerman C and Murasko D (1991). The effects of music and directed biological imagery on immune response S-IgA. In C Maranto, ed., *Applications of music in medicine*, 85–121 National Association for Music Therapy, Washington, DC.

Updike P and Charles D (1987). Music Rx: physiological and emotional responses to taped music programs of preoperative patients awaiting plastic surgery. *Annals of Plastic Surgery*, **19**(1), 29–33.

VanderArk S and Ely D (1992). Biochemical and galvanic skin responses to music stimuli by college students in biology and music. *Perceptual and Motor Skills*, **74**, 1079–1090.

VanderArk S and Ely D (1993). Cortisol, biochemical and galvanic skin responses to music stimuli of different preference values by college students in biology and music. *Perceptual and Motor Skills*, **77**, 227–234.

Venables P (1987). Electrodermal activity. In R Gregory, ed., *The Oxford companion to the mind*, 213–214 Oxford University Press, Oxford.

Witvliet C and Vrana S (2007). Play it again Sam: repeated exposure to emotionally evocative music polarizes liking and smiling responses, and influences other affective reports, facial EMG, and heart rate. *Cognition and Emotion*, **21**(1), 3–25.

Zimmerman L, Pierson M and Marker J (1988). Effects of music on patient anxiety in coronary care units. *Heart-Lung*, **17**, 560–566.

CHAPTER 12

Emotional responses to music

Patrik N. Juslin

MUSIC has been linked to the emotions at least since Ancient Greece, and emotions do figure prominently in people's reported motives for listening to music. People use music to change emotions, to release emotions, to match their current emotion, to enjoy or comfort themselves, and to relieve stress. Yet, despite the ubiquity of music in everyday life today (see Chapter 40 this volume), emotional responses to music are still regarded as elusive. Why does music touch us so deeply? In this chapter, I will consider the best possible answers to this question that the psychology of music can currently provide. While music philosophers, musicologists, and aestheticians have written a lot about musical emotions (Budd 1985), psychologists have been slow to catch up due to both conceptual and methodological problems (Juslin and Sloboda 2001). Hence, this chapter will focus mainly on research carried out during the last decade.

It is important to make a distinction between *perception* and *induction* of emotions. We may simply perceive an emotion in the music, or we may actually feel an emotion in response to the music. This distinction is often, but not always, made in modern research. It is important to make the distinction for two reasons. First, the underlying mechanisms may be different depending on the process involved. Secondly, the types of emotions usually induced by music may be different from the types of emotions usually perceived in music. This chapter focuses on induction of emotions, whereas perception of emotions is discussed in Chapters 13 and 35.

The definition and measurement of emotions

A natural point of departure is to define the concept of emotion. Emotions belong to the field of affect. Based on an emerging consensus in the affective sciences (e.g. Davidson *et al.* 2003), *affect* is regarded as an umbrella term, which includes various affective phenomena such as preference, emotion, and mood. Affect simply refers to the fact that these phenomena are valenced—events are evaluated as positive or negative by the individual.

Although researchers do not agree on a precise definition of *emotions*, they agree about the characteristics. Emotions are described as brief (lasting minutes to a few hours) but intense responses to potentially important events or changes in the external or internal environment that involve certain subcomponents:

- cognitive appraisal (e.g., you appraise a situation as 'dangerous'),
- subjective feeling (e.g., you feel 'afraid'),
- physiological response (e.g., your heart starts to beat faster),
- expression (e.g., you shout),
- action tendency (e.g., you run away), and
- regulation (e.g., you try to calm yourself).

In principle, each of these six components can be used to measure emotions, though researchers debate the extent to which the components are 'synchronized' during an emotional response. Many researchers assume that people are always in *some* affective state. When the states are intense and involve salient stimuli, we tend to call them 'emotions', whereas when the same states are less intense, and their causes are not immediately apparent, we tend to call them 'moods'. The states have been conceptualized both as discrete categories and as dimensions such as valence and arousal.

Primary issues and methods

The fundamental issues to address in the study of music and emotion are: does music induce emotions? If so, which emotions does music typically induce? Under what circumstances do musical emotions commonly occur? How does music induce emotions? Are musical emotions different from other emotions? Could musical emotions have implications for our health? It is fair to say that music psychologists are only beginning to answer most of these questions.

There are several methods that may be used to investigate musical emotions, such as listening experiments (Waterman 1996), questionnaire studies (Juslin and Laukka 2004), diary studies (Sloboda *et al.* 2001), qualitative interviews (DeNora 2000) and brain imaging (Blood and Zatorre 2001). Since each method has both advantages and disadvantages, the best overall approach might be to combine various methods in a kind of 'method triangulation'. In addition, the componential approach to measurement of emotions is slowly gaining ground in music psychology; that is, music researchers increasingly realize the need to measure several emotion components to be able to draw valid conclusions about emotional responses (Scherer and Zentner 2001). However, such approaches are still available mainly in the laboratory. Field studies continue to rely mostly on self-report, even though there are techniques for ambulatory measurement of physiological responses that could be used (Fahrenberg and Myrtek 1996). As observed already by William James (1884), the physiological response may be the aspect that gives emotions their distinct phenomenological feeling, providing the 'heat' of the emotions: 'What kind of an emotion of fear would be left, if the feelings neither of quickened heartbeats nor of shallow breathing . . . were present, it is quite impossible to think' (pp. 193–

194). Thus, it is recommendable to complement self-reports of emotions with physiological measurements (see Chapter 11). Evidence suggests that more intense emotions to music tend to involve more pronounced physiological reactions (Rickard 2004), including 'chills' (Panksepp 1995).

Does music really induce emotions?

Although most musicians and listeners would seem to take the emotional powers of music for granted, it has been the matter of some controversy whether music really can evoke emotions (e.g. Kivy 1990). Strong empirical evidence has been slow to emerge, though an increasing number of studies have now obtained evidence in terms of different emotion components such as self-reported feeling (e.g. DeNora 2000; Gabrielsson 2001; Juslin and Laukka 2004; Pike 1972; Waterman 1996), physiology (e.g. Davis and Thaut 1989; Krumhansl 1997; Nyklíček *et al.* 1997; Vaitl *et al.* 1993), activation of brain regions similar to those of other emotions (e.g. Blood and Zatorre 2001, Brown *et al.* 2004; Menon and Levitin 2005), emotional expression (e.g. Sloboda 1991, Witvliet and Vrana 2007), action tendency (e.g. Fried and Berkowitz 1979; Harrer and Harrer 1977) and regulation (e.g. Becker 2001; Gabrielsson 2001). There is also preliminary evidence of synchronization among the various emotion components (Lundqvist *et al.* in press). Most of the evidence cited above was collected in Western societies, so cross-cultural studies are urgently needed.

It should be noted that many studies have relied only on self-report, which may be subject to *demand characteristics*, i.e., the total sum of cues that convey the researcher's hypothesis to the participant and thus may influence the participant's behaviour (Orne 1962). It is therefore promising that several studies have found effects of musically induced emotions on so-called implicit measures such as writing speed, word association, and decision time, which may be less sensitive to demand characteristics (Västfjäll 2002). The continued exploration and use of such indirect measures is recommended. Measuring emotions in the voice as a response to music is another hitherto unexplored approach (Juslin and Scherer 2005).

What is the prevalence of musical emotions?

To estimate the prevalence of musical emotions (i.e., the relative frequency of occurrence in the population of interest), it is necessary to capture the emotions as they spontaneously occur in daily life. The *experience sampling method* (ESM) is a useful tool in this context. Sloboda *et al.* (2001) conducted a pilot study to test the validity of the ESM with regard to music. Eight participants received an electronic pager and a diary. During a week, the pager was activated randomly once every two hours by a central computer. When they were paged, the participants were required to fill out the diary to describe the nature of any experiences of music that had occurred since the last paging. Findings suggested that music was heard during 44 per cent of the recorded episodes, that few of these episodes involved music listening as the main focus, and that music experiences tended to make the listeners more positive, more alert, and more focused in the present—particularly when personal choice over the music was involved. These results were replicated and extended in more extensive study, featuring 32 participants, by Juslin *et al.* (in press). Their participants were required to carry a small palmtop computer, which randomly gave off seven signals each day over a time period of two weeks. Music occurred in 37 per cent of the sampled episodes. In 64 per cent of the episodes that featured music, the participants reported that the music influenced how they felt. This is roughly similar to the retrospective, aggregated estimate provided in a survey study by Juslin and Laukka (2004), in which participants reported that they experienced emotions on average 55 per cent of the time they listened to music. Musical emotions were most frequent in the evening and during weekends. Overall, the results suggest that, although emotional responses to music are common, the occurrence of music does not itself necessarily guarantee that a listener will be moved by the music.

A much debated but little investigated issue is which emotions music can induce. Can music induce the full range of human emotions in listeners? In principle, depending on the specific music, the person listening, and the situation, it would indeed appear possible that music can induce just about any emotion that may be felt in other realms of human life. The wide range of emotions found in Gabrielsson's (2001; Table 19.1) study of strong experiences with music suggests that this is the case. However, given the rare nature of such experiences, a more interesting question is perhaps which emotions music *commonly* evokes in listeners. A handful of survey studies have provided preliminary estimates of the prevalence of particular emotions (Juslin and Laukka 2004 Table 4; Sloboda 1992 Table 1; Wells and Hakanen 1991 Table 1) and suggest that happiness, love, calm, sadness, excitement and nostalgia are relatively frequent emotional responses to music. However, these studies share two problems: they rely on retrospective and aggregated self-reports that may not be reliable and they do not directly compare musical with non-musical emotions, so that the 'uniqueness' of musical emotions can be assessed.

The previously mentioned ESM study by Juslin *et al.* (in press) provided estimates of occurrence of 14 emotional states in response to music as well as other stimuli during a 2-week period. Figure 12.1 shows the relative frequency (%) of emotions caused by music and emotions caused by other stimuli, respectively. As can be seen, emotions such as *calm–contentment, happiness–elation,* and *interest–expectancy* were generally common, whereas emotions such as *disgust–contempt* were not so common. A comparison of musical with non-musical emotion episodes indicated that *happiness–elation* and *nostalgia–longing* were significantly more frequent in episodes with musical emotions, whereas *anger–irritation, boredom–indifference,* and *anxiety–fear* were significantly more frequent in episodes with non-musical emotions. The remaining differences were not significant. Although the difficulties involved in translating experiences of emotions into verbal labels should be kept in mind, the results from both this and the above studies suggest that music may evoke a range of both basic and complex emotions, something that a satisfactory theory of musical emotions must be able to explain.

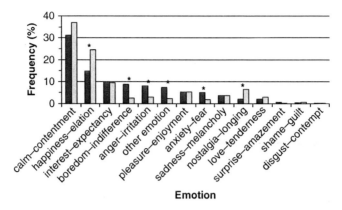

Fig. 12.1 The relative frequency (in percentages) of felt emotions for (a) non-musical emotion episodes (dark bars) and, (b) musical emotion episodes (light bars) during a 2-week period of experience sampling (from Juslin et al. in press). The number of response alternatives was limited by the computer software used. * p <.05.

Which factors influence musical emotions?

Factors that influence emotions in association with musical events have mostly been studied in an explorative fashion, and the factors may be grouped in terms of whether they are related to the music, the individual listener, or the situation.

Musical factors

Whereas the musical features involved in the expression and perception of different emotions are fairly well mapped by now (see Chapters 13 and 35), the features that induce emotions have been less investigated (though there might be some overlap depending on the induction mechanism, see later this chapter). I predict that it will be difficult to find direct and simple links between musical features and emotions. The musical features must rather be related to possible induction mechanisms. An excellent example is Sloboda's (1991) attempt to link emotional reactions to music to specific events in the music: 83 participants, aged 16–70, most of them performers, were asked to specify particular pieces of music to which they could recall having experienced various physical manifestations frequently associated with an emotion. Having identified such pieces, which came mainly from classical music, they were then asked to specify the exact location within the

music that provoked these reactions. Most participants reported whole pieces, movements, or sections of movements, which suggests an emotional response to the 'overall' character of the music (Table 3 in Sloboda 1991). Such a response might reflect 'emotional contagion' based on the emotional expression of the piece (Juslin and Västfjäll in press). However, roughly a third of the participants were able to locate their reaction within a theme or smaller unit. The data showed that musical events associated with 'tears' (i.e., crying, lump in the throat) commonly contained melodic appoggiaturas and melodic or harmonic sequences; events associated with 'shivers' (i.e., goose pimples, shivers down the spine) usually contained a new or unprepared harmony; and events associated with 'heart reactions' contained syncopations and prominent events occurring earlier than prepared for. The results were related to Meyer's (1956) notion that musical expectancies, and violations of these, play an important role in emotional responses to music.

Individual factors

Individual differences between listeners appear to be larger for induction of emotions than for perception of emotions, though little research has focused on individual differences in musical emotion induction. Still, research has revealed a number of factors in the individual that may potentially affect emotional responses to music, such as the listener's age, gender, personality, musical training, music preference and current mood (for a review, see Abeles and Chung 1996). Familiarity with the music tends to induce stronger emotional responses (Bartel 1992), which may explain why listeners respond stronger to self-selected than to experimenter-selected music (Harrer and Harrer 1977). Musical training might lead to less emotional involvement due to increasingly analytic listening (Harrer and Harrer 1977; but see also Lehmann 1997 for contradictory findings). Behne (1997) suggested that there may be different individual 'listening styles'. His proposals were based on cluster analyses of data from a questionnaire, which aimed to study musical experiences. Examples of such listening styles were 'emotional' ('I pay attention to what feelings are expressed through the music'), 'distancing' ('I try to follow the musical lines of a particular instrument'), 'sentimental' ('I remember things of the past'), and 'compensating' ('it makes me feel better').

Situational factors

Factors related to the situation of a musical event could be categorized in different ways. Gabrielsson (2001) divided them into 'physical factors' (e.g., acoustical and visual conditions, time, place), 'social factors' (e.g., listening alone or together with others, type of audience, co-performers), 'special occasions and circumstances' (e.g., vacation), and 'performance conditions' (e.g., music well-rehearsed or not). Only recently have researchers begun to explore the ways that music actually figures in the everyday life of ordinary people (Part 9 of this volume), but it is becoming increasingly clear that key to an understanding of musical emotions is to describe the complex interplay between the music, the listener, and the situation. Juslin et al. (in press) noted that emotional responses to music occurred in all kinds of locations, partly because the participants were able to bring their favourite music anywhere (thanks to devices such as mp3 players). However, the prevalence of specific emotions varied depending on the situation. For example, some emotions such as *happiness–elation*,

pleasure–enjoyment, and *anger–irritation* occurred frequently in 'social' settings, whereas others such as *calm–contentment, nostalgia–longing*, and *sadness–melancholy* occurred frequently in more 'solitary' settings. This highlights the need to use representative samples of situations in order to obtain accurate estimates of the prevalence of specific emotions.

How does music induce emotions?

Most scholars acknowledge that this is the primary issue (e.g., Dowling and Harwood 1986, p. 202). Yet a literature search reveals that few studies make any attempt to test a theory about the psychological mechanism that underlies emotional responses to music. In fact, apart from Meyer's (1956) treatise (arguably the most cited book on this subject ever), most theories of musical emotions focus on the expressive properties of music that allow listeners to *perceive* emotions (e.g., Clynes 1977; Cooke 1959; Juslin 2001; Langer 1957).

One problem with musical emotions is that the conditions for eliciting emotions appear to be different from those in everyday life: in the paradigmatic case, an emotion is evoked when an event is appraised as having the capacity to influence the goals of the perceiver. Since music would not appear to have any capacity to further or block goals in life, researchers have been forced to come up with an alternative explanation that makes more sense in a musical setting. (However, musical induction of emotions through a cognitive appraisal may occur sometimes, such as when our 'goal' to go to sleep at night is 'blocked' by a neighbour playing loud music.)

A theoretical framework

Building on the work of the pioneers in this field (Berlyne 1971; Meyer 1956) as well as on more recent research (Juslin and Sloboda 2001), Juslin and Västfjäll (in press) presented a theoretical framework featuring six mechanisms through which music can induce emotions. One could conceive of these mechanisms as consisting of a number of (more or less) distinct brain functions that developed gradually and in a specific order during evolution. Because the mechanisms depend on functions with different evolutionary origins, each mechanism should possess unique characteristics. The framework focuses on the following mechanisms:

Brainstem reflex refers to a process whereby an emotion is induced by music because one or more fundamental acoustical characteristics of the music are taken by the brainstem to signal a potentially important and urgent event. All other things being equal, sounds that are sudden, loud, dissonant, or feature fast temporal patterns induce arousal in the listener. Such responses reflect the impact of simple auditory sensations (i.e., music as *sound* in the most basic sense). The perceptual system is constantly scanning the immediate environment in order to discover potentially important changes or events. Sounds that meet certain criteria will thus lead to an increased activation of the central nervous system in the early stages of auditory processing. The precise physiological processes underlying such brainstem responses are not completely understood, although evidence suggests that they occur in close connection with the reticular formation of the brainstem and the intralaminar nuclei of the thalamus, which receive inputs from the auditory system. The brainstem is an ancient structure of the brain that sub-serves a number of sensory and motor functions including, but not limited to, auditory perception and the mediation and control of attention, emotional arousal, heart rate, breathing, and movement (Joseph 2000). It may thus influence physiological processes related to emotions (e.g., pulse, respiration), such that the listener's arousal level increases or decreases.

Evaluative conditioning (EC) refers to a process whereby an emotion is induced by a piece of music simply because this stimulus has often been paired with other positive or negative stimuli (De Houwer *et al.* 2001). For example, a particular piece of music may have occurred repeatedly together in time with a specific event that always makes you happy, such as meeting one of your friends. Over time, through repeated pairings, the music itself will eventually evoke happiness even in the absence of the friendly interaction. There are few studies of EC with music (but see Blair and Shimp 1992), though EC has a number of features that are interesting in regard to music. First, EC can occur even if

the participant is unaware of the contingency of the two stimuli. In fact, it has been found that EC can be both established and induce emotions without awareness (e.g. Martin *et al.* 1984). Secondly, EC appears to be fairly resistant to extinction, as compared to classical conditioning. Music often occurs in situations where music listening is not the main activity (Sloboda *et al.* 2001) and where subtle conditioning processes outside awareness might easily occur.

Emotional contagion refers to a process whereby an emotion is induced by a piece of music because the listener perceives the emotional expression of the music and then 'mimics' this expression internally (Juslin 2001). Emotional contagion has mostly been studied regarding facial expression (Hatfield *et al.* 1994), but Neumann and Strack (2000) also found evidence of contagion from emotional speech. Because music often features expressive acoustical patterns similar to those that occur in emotional speech (for a review, see Juslin and Laukka 2003), it has been argued that we get aroused by the voice-like aspects of music via a process in which a neural 'module' responds quickly and automatically to certain stimulus features, which leads us to mimic the perceived emotion internally (Juslin 2001). While the notion of emotional contagion via music admittedly remains somewhat speculative, a recent functional magnetic resonance imaging (fMRI) study by Koelsch *et al.* (2006) found that music listening activated brain areas related to a circuitry serving the formation of pre-motor representations for vocal sound production (no singing was observed among the participants). Koelsch *et al.* concluded that this could reflect a mirror-function mechanism, similar to the so-called 'mirror neurons' proposed as a possible explanation of emotional contagion via other non-verbal channels (Preston and de Waal 2002).

Visual imagery refers to a process whereby an emotion is induced in a listener because he or she conjures up visual images (e.g., of a beautiful landscape) while listening to the music. The emotions experienced are the result of an interaction between the music and these images. The precise nature of this process remains to be described, but listeners appear to conceptualize the musical structure through a metaphorical non-verbal mapping between the music and 'image-schemata' grounded in bodily experience (see Lakoff and Johnson 1980); for instance, hearing melodic movement as 'upward'. Listeners might respond to mental images much in the same way as they would to the corresponding stimuli in the 'real' world, for instance reacting with positive emotions to a beautiful nature scene. Mental imagery in relation to music has mostly been explored in the context of music therapy (Toomey 1996-1997). Helen Bonny developed a method, *guided imagery and music* (GIM), where a 'traveller' is invited to 'share' his or her images as they are experienced in real time during a programmed musical sequence (Bonny and Savary 1973). Characteristic of visual imagery as an induction mechanism is that the listener is able to influence the process to a considerable extent. Although images might come into the mind unbidden, often a listener may conjure up, manipulate, and dismiss images at will.

Episodic memory refers to a process whereby an emotion is induced in a listener because the music evokes a personal memory of a specific event in the listener's life (Baumgartner 1992). This has been referred to as the 'Darling, they are playing our tune' phenomenon (see Davies 1978). Research has revealed that music often evokes memories (Gabrielsson 2001; Sloboda 1992). When the memory is evoked, so too is the emotion associated with the memory. Such emotions may be intense, perhaps because the physiological response patterns to the original events are stored in memory along with the experiential contents. Many listeners use music to remind them of valued past events, suggesting that music may serve an important 'nostalgic' function in everyday life. Music plays a very prominent role in adolescents' lives in regard to the development of a self-identity (e.g., Saarikallio 2007). Hence, one could expect episodic memories associated with music to be particularly emotionally vivid and frequent with regard to music from young adulthood, as indeed seems to be the case. Schulkind *et al.* (1999) found that older adults preferred, knew more about, as well as had stronger emotional responses to music popular during their youth than to music popular later in life.

Musical expectancy refers to a process whereby an emotion is induced in a listener because a specific feature of the music violates, delays, or confirms the listener's expectations about the continuation of the music (Meyer 1956; see also Narmour 1992). For instance, the sequential progression of E-F# sets up the expectation that the music will continue with G#. If this does not happen, listeners familiar with the musical idiom may become surprised. The expectations are based on the listener's previous experiences of the same style of music. Although Meyer's theory is highly regarded, it has not stimulated much research on emotions (but see Sloboda 1991), perhaps because the theory is difficult to test. For instance, a musical piece may evoke several different musical expectations at different levels of the music, and these expectations may also be different for different listeners. However, support for Meyer's theory was found by Steinbeis *et al.* (2006), who used subjective and physiological measures to capture emotional responses to unexpected events in music (see Figure 12.2).

Only a few of the above mechanisms have been tested in regard to music, but one thing seems clear: there is no single mechanism that can account for all instances of musical emotion. A crucial goal for future research is to develop a process model of the induction process, though given the large number of mechanisms, such an endeavour is a formidable undertaking. A first step could be to specify the precise characteristics of each mechanism. By synthesizing theory and findings from different domains outside music, Juslin and Västfjäll (in press) were able to provide the first set of hypotheses that can help researchers to distinguish among the proposed mechanisms. The hypotheses concern characteristics such as the information focus, key brain regions, ontogenetic development, cultural impact, induced affect, induction speed, degree of volitional influence, and so forth (see Juslin and Västfjäll, in press, Table 4).

Implications of the framework

One implication of the novel framework is that it may resolve disagreements in the field. Specifically, apparent contradictions of different approaches may be reconciled by observing that they focus on different mechanisms. Hence, the framework may help to resolve previous disagreements about which emotions music can induce,

Fig. 12.2 Examples of musical stimuli used to induce emotions through the musical expectancy mechanism (from Steinbeis *et al*. 2006). (a) is a cadence from an excerpt of an original composition by JS Bach with an unexpected event enclosed within the box. (b) and (c) are identical to version (a) except for the harmonic events within the boxes, which were manipulated to be either more expected (b) or less expected (c) than the original. Reproduced by permission of the MIT Press.

how early musical emotions develop, whether listeners are active or passive in the causal process, how much time it takes to induce an emotion through music, and whether musical emotions are innate or learned responses—it depends on the mechanism concerned.

The most important implication of the proposed framework for future research in the field is that it will not be sufficient to induce and study musical emotions *in general*. In order for data to contribute in a cumulative fashion to our knowledge, researchers must try to specify as far as possible the mechanism involved in each study. Otherwise studies will produce results that are inconsistent or that cannot be given a clear interpretation. One example is provided by the recent flurry of research on the neuropsychological correlates of emotional responses to music (Peretz 2001). Numerous brain regions have been reported in previous studies of music and emotion (e.g., the thalamus, cerebellum, hippocampus, amygdala, prefrontal cortex, Broca's area, nucleus accumbens, visual cortex, and supplementary motor areas). However, different brain regions have been implicated in different studies for reasons that

are unclear. One likely explanation is that most studies have simply presented 'emotional music' to listeners without manipulating (or at least controlling for) the underlying induction mechanism. This makes it difficult to understand what the obtained neural correlates reflect in each study. Hence, Juslin and Västfjäll (in press) argue that musical emotions cannot be studied without respect to how they were evoked. An important task for the future is to develop standard paradigms and tasks that can reliably induce specific emotions in listeners through each of the mechanisms above.

Conclusions

The study of music and emotions is fraught with considerable controversy and disagreement. Current debates in the field revolve around such questions as which emotions music induces, whether there are uniquely musical emotions, and what the relationship is between perceived and induced emotions. An important direction for future research is to consider how emotions might be one of several features of an aesthetic response to music—the appreciation of music as 'art' (see Chapter 14 this volume). Real-world research has revealed that music is intentionally used by listeners to regulate their moods and emotions, and that positive emotions tend to dominate in their responses. The latter result has stimulated interest in effects of music on physical health and subjective well-being: can the emotional effects of music be used in health interventions that target biochemical substances, such as cortisol, oxytocin, dopamine, and serotonin? The development of such applications would obviously benefit from a better understanding of the underlying mechanisms. The framework discussed earlier may hopefully contribute to more hypothesis-driven approaches to exploring different mechanisms of musical emotions. Other possible applications of research on emotional responses to music include music therapy, film music, marketing, health care, and the gaming industry. In fact, several current applications of music presume its effectiveness in evoking emotions, yet we are only beginning to understand the mechanisms that make this possible. More often than not, music is intentionally designed to stir our emotions, exploiting whatever means available, and we have seen that music might induce emotions in many different ways. Hence, one answer to the question 'why does music move us?' is 'because we *want* music to move us and have designed it so that it will do it with the maximum effect'. However, rather than 'destroying the magic', an understanding of how music evokes emotions will only increase our never-ending fascination with music.

References

Abeles HF and Chung JW (1996). Responses to music. In DA Hodges, ed., *Handbook of music psychology*, 2nd edn, 285–342. IMR Press, San Antonio, TX.

Bartel LR (1992). The development of the cognitive–affective response test—music. *Psychomusicology*, **11**, 15–26.

Baumgartner H. (1992). Remembrance of things past: music, autobiographical memory, and emotion. *Advances in Consumer Research*, **19**, 613–620.

Becker J (2001). Anthropological perspectives on music and emotion. In PN Juslin and JA Sloboda, eds, *Music and emotion: theory and research*, 135–160. Oxford University Press, New York.

Behne KE (1997). The development of 'Musikerleben' in adolescence: how and why young people listen to music. In I Deliége, JA Sloboda, eds, *Perception and cognition of music*, 143–159. Psychology Press, Hove, UK.

Berlyne DE (1971). *Aesthetics and psychobiology*. Appleton Century Crofts, New York.

Blair ME and Shimp TA (1992). Consequences of an unpleasant experience with music: a second-order negative conditioning perspective. *Journal of Advertising*, **21**, 35–43.

Blood AJ and Zatorre RJ (2001). Intensely pleasurable responses to music correlate with activity in brain regions implicated in reward and emotion. *Proceedings of National Academy of Sciences*, **98**, 11818–11823.

Bonny HL and Savary LM (1973). *Music and your mind*. Station Hill, New York.

Brown S, Martinez MJ and Parsons LM. (2004). Passive music listening spontaneously engages limbic and paralimbic systems. *Neuroreport*, **15**, 2033–2037.

Budd M (1985). *Music and the emotions. The philosophical theories*. Routledge, London.

Clynes M (1977). *Sentics: the touch of emotions*. Doubleday, New York.

Cooke D (1959). *The language of music*. Oxford University Press, London.

Davidson RJ, Scherer KR and Goldsmith HH (eds) (2003). *Handbook of affective sciences*. Oxford University Press, New York.

Davies JB (1978). *The psychology of music*. Hutchinson, London.

Davis WB and Thaut MH (1989). The influence of preferred relaxing music on measures of state anxiety, relaxation, and physiological measures. *Journal of Music Therapy*, **26**, 168–187.

De Houwer J, Thomas S and Baeyens F (2001). Associative learning of likes and dislikes: a review of 25 years of research on human evaluative conditioning. *Psychological Bulletin*, **127**, 853–869.

DeNora T (2000). *Music in everyday life*. Cambridge University Press, Cambridge.

Dowling WJ and Harwood DL (1986). *Music cognition*. Academic Press, New York.

Fahrenberg J and Myrtek M (eds) (1996). *Ambulatory assessment: computer-assisted psychological and psychophysiological methods in monitoring and field studies*. Hogrefe, Seattle, WA.

Fried R and Berkowitz L (1979). Music that charms … and can influence helpfulness. *Journal of Applied Social Psychology*, **9**, 199–208.

Gabrielsson A (2001). Emotions in strong experiences with music. In PN Juslin and JA Sloboda, eds, *Music and emotion: theory and research*, 431–449. Oxford University Press, New York.

Harrer G and Harrer H (1977). Music, emotion, and autonomic function. In M Critchley and RA Henson, eds, *Music and the brain. Studies in the neurology of music*, 202–216. William Heinemann Medical Books, London.

Hatfield E, Cacioppo JT and Rapson RL (1994). *Emotional contagion*. Cambridge University Press, New York.

James W (1884). What is an emotion? *Mind*, **9**, 188–205.

Joseph R (2000). *Neuropsychiatry, neuropsychology, clinical neuroscience*. Academic Press, New York.

Juslin PN (2001). Communicating emotion in music performance: a review and a theoretical framework. In PN

Juslin and JA Sloboda, eds, *Music and emotion: theory and research*, 309–337. Oxford University Press, New York.

Juslin PN and Laukka P (2003). Communication of emotions in vocal expression and music performance: different channels, same code? *Psychological Bulletin*, **129**, 770–814.

Juslin PN and Laukka P (2004). Expression, perception, and induction of musical emotions: a review and a questionnaire study of everyday listening. *Journal of New Music Research*, **33**, 217–238.

Juslin PN, Liljeström S, Västfjäll D, Barradas G and Silva A (2008). An experience sampling study of emotional reactions to music: listener, music and situation. *Emotion*, **8**, 668–683.

Juslin PN and Scherer KR (2005). Vocal expression of affect. In JA Harrigan, R Rosenthal and KR Scherer, eds, *The new handbook of methods in nonverbal behavior research*, 65–135. Oxford University Press, New York.

Juslin PN and Sloboda JA (eds), (2001). *Music and emotion: theory and research*. Oxford University Press, New York.

Juslin PN and Västfjäll D (2008). Emotional responses to music: the need to consider underlying mechanisms. *Behavioral and Brain Sciences*, **31**, 559–575.

Kivy P (1990). *Music alone*. Cornell University Press, Ithaca, NY.

Koelsch S, Fritz T, von Cramon DY, Müller K and Friederici AD (2006). Investigating emotion with music: an fMRI study. *Human Brain Mapping*, **27**, 239–250.

Krumhansl CL (1997). An exploratory study of musical emotions and psychophysiology. *Canadian Journal of Experimental Psychology*, **51**, 336–352.

Lakoff G and Johnson M (1980). *Metaphors we live by*. University of Chicago Press, Chicago, IL.

Langer SK (1957). *Philosophy in a new key*, 3rd edn. Harvard University Press, Cambridge, MA.

Lehmann AC (1997). Affective responses to everyday life and music listening. *Psychology of Music*, **25**, 84–90.

Lundqvist L-O, Carlsson F, Hilmersson P, and Juslin PN (2008). Emotional responses to music: experience, expression, and physiology. *Psychology of Music*, OnlineFirst, October 15, doi:10.1177/0305735607086048.

Martin DG, Stambrook M, Tataryn DJ and Beihl H (1984). Conditioning in the unattended left ear. *International Journal of Neuroscience*, **23**, 95–102.

Menon V and Levitin DJ (2005). The rewards of music listening: response and physiological connectivity of the mesolimbic system. *Neuroimage*, **28**, 175–184.

Meyer LB (1956). *Emotion and meaning in music*. Chicago University Press, Chicago, IL.

Narmour E (1992). *The analysis and cognition of melodic complexity: the implication–realization model*. University of Chicago Press, Chicago, IL.

Neumann R and Strack F (2000). Mood contagion: the automatic transfer of mood between persons. *Journal of Personality and Social Psychology*, **79**, 211–223.

Nyklíček I, Thayer JF and Van Doornen LJP (1997). Cardiorespiratory differentiation of musically-induced emotions. *Journal of Psychophysiology*, **11**, 304–321.

Orne MT (1962). On the social psychology of the psychological experiment with particular reference to demand characteristics and their implications. *American Psychologist*, **17**, 776–783.

Panksepp J (1995). The emotional sources of 'chills' induced by music. *Music Perception*, **13**, 171–208.

Peretz I (2001). Listen to the brain: a biological perspective on musical emotions. In PN Juslin, JA Sloboda, eds, *Music and emotion: theory and research*, 105–134. Oxford University Press, New York.

Pike A (1972). A phenomenological analysis of emotional experience in music. *Journal of Research in Music Education*, **20**, 262–267.

Preston SD and de Waal FBM (2002). Empathy: its ultimate and proximate basis. *Behavioral and Brain Sciences*, **25**, 1–72.

Rickard NS (2004). Intense emotional responses to music: a test of the physiological arousal hypothesis. *Psychology of Music*, **32**, 371–388.

Saarikallio S (2007). Music as mood regulation in adolescence. *Doctoral dissertation*, University of Jyväskylä, Finland.

Scherer KR and Zentner MR (2001). Emotional effects of music: production rules. In PN Juslin and JA Sloboda, eds, *Music and emotion: theory and research*, 361–392. Oxford University Press, New York.

Schulkind MD, Hennis LK and Rubin DC (1999). Music, emotion, and autobiographical memory: they are playing our song. *Memory and Cognition*, **27**, 948–955.

Sloboda JA (1991). Music structure and emotional response: some empirical findings. *Psychology of Music*, **19**, 110–120.

Sloboda JA (1992). Empirical studies of emotional response to music. In Riess-Jones and S Holleran, eds, *Cognitive bases of musical communication*, 33–46. American Psychological Association, Washington, DC.

Sloboda JA, O'Neill SA and Ivaldi A (2001). Functions of music in everyday life: an exploratory study using the Experience Sampling Method. *Musicae Scientiae*, **5**, 9–32.

Steinbeis N, Koelsch S and Sloboda JA (2006). The role of harmonic expectancy violations in musical emotions: evidence from subjective, physiological, and neural responses. *Journal of Cognitive Neuroscience*, **18**, 380–1393.

Toomey L (1996–1997). Literature review: the Bonny method of guided imagery and music. *Journal of the Association for Music and Imagery*, **5**, 75–103.

Vaitl D, Vehrs W and Sternagel S (1993). Prompts— leitmotif—emotion: play it again, Richard Wagner. In N Birnbaumer and A Öhman, eds, *The structure of emotion: psychophysiological, cognitive, and clinical aspects*, 169–189. Hogrefe and Huber, Seattle, WA.

Västfjäll D (2002). A review of the musical mood induction procedure. *Musicae Scientiae*, Special Issue 2001–2002, 173–211.

Waterman M (1996). Emotional responses to music: implicit and explicit effects in listeners and performers. *Psychology of Music*, **24**, 53–67.

Wells A and Hakanen EA (1991). The emotional uses of popular music by adolescents. *Journalism Quarterly*, **68**, 445–454.

Witvliet CV and Vrana SR (2007). Play it again Sam: repeated exposure to emotionally evocative music polarizes liking and smiling responses, and influences other affective reports, facial EMG, and heart rate. *Cognition and Emotion*, **21**, 3–25.

CHAPTER 13

The relationship between musical structure and perceived expression

Alf Gabrielsson

THE relationship between structure and expression in music has been discussed by philosophers and music theorists ever since antiquity, but empirical research did not start until about one hundred years ago. Most of this research is limited to Western classical music.

Musical structure is an umbrella term for a host of factors such as tempo, loudness, pitch, intervals, mode, melody, rhythm, harmony and various formal aspects (e.g. repetition, variation, transposition). They are designated by different symbols in the common musical notation. Most symbols represent categories with allowance for performance variation within the respective category. Listeners' perception of expression is thus affected both by the composed/notated structure and by the actual performance. However, performance aspects will not be further discussed here as they are treated elsewhere in this volume (Part 7).

Listeners' perception of expression—for instance, to perceive sadness in the music—should be distinguished from listeners' own reactions (that is, feeling sad themselves); the latter are treated elsewhere (Chapter 12). However, the border between these two alternatives is sometimes blurred, and the relationship between them may vary (Evans and Schubert 2008; Gabrielsson 2002; Juslin and Laukka 2004; Kallinen and Ravaja 2006; Konečni *et al.* 2008).

Absolutism versus referentialism

Meyer (1956) made a distinction between absolutism and referentialism (other terms are formalism vs. expressionism, or autonomous vs. heteronomous music). Absolutism focuses on intra-musical relations; music is considered self-contained, refers only to itself. Referentialism implies, on the contrary, that music refers to extra-musical phenomena such as emotions, events, or characters.

Music critic Eduard Hanslick claimed that music consists of tone sequences which have no other content than themselves (Hanslick 1989, p. 162), and composer Igor Stravinsky held that 'if music appears to express something, this is only an illusion' (cited in Fisk 1997, pp. 280–281). However, the distinction between absolutism and referentialism is rather vague. Hanslick and Stravinsky later added several modifications to their seemingly dogmatic statements, and 'absolute meanings and referential meanings can and do coexist in one and the same piece of music' (Meyer 1956, p.1).

In the present chapter emphasis will be on *perceived* expression rather than expression somehow inherent in the music. The listener may apprehend music as 'pure' music (absolutism) or as expression of emotions, characters, events or whatever, and may very well alternate, consciously or unconsciously, between different approaches during the course of a piece. Focus will be on referential meaning, leaving questions about intra-musical relationships and structural listening to other chapters in this volume (Part 2); see Clarke (2005) for further comments on autonomous music and structural listening.

Expression of emotion

Among referential meanings, expression of emotion is the most common alternative. It has been discussed for centuries, as in the 'doctrine of the affections' (*Affektenlehre*) during the Baroque era and during Romanticism with its emphasis on expression of the subjective and emotional in music. Musicologist Deryck Cooke claimed that music is a language of emotions (1959, pp. 32–33), and philosopher Susanne Langer argued that 'music can *reveal* the nature of feelings with a detail and truth that language cannot approach' (1957, p. 235).

The following is a condensed review of empirical research on emotional expression in music. More complete reviews appear in Gabrielsson and Juslin (2003) and Gabrielsson and Lindström (2001).

Stimuli

Generally, subjects listened to pieces of music or other tonal stimuli and reported perceived expression. Stimuli were usually recordings of selected pieces of music, sometimes live music (e.g., Hevner 1935; Rigg 1937a), or synthesized tone stimuli. Using real music means good ecological validity but limits conclusions regarding the effects of separate structural factors since they are usually confounded in musical contexts. An alternative that allows more definite conclusions is to systematically vary one or more structural factors in short sound sequences (e.g., Scherer and Oshinsky 1977); however, the ecological validity is then limited. A further, commendable alternative is to systematically vary different structural factors (tempo, mode, form, etc.) in real pieces of music (e.g., Hevner 1935, 1936, 1937; Juslin 1997; Kamenetsky *et al.* 1997; Karno and Konečni 1992; Lindström 2006;

Peretz *et al.* 1998; Rigg 1940a, b; Schellenberg *et al.* 2000), and thus try to combine the advantages of the before-mentioned strategies.

Response format

Subjects reported perceived expression using:

(a) free phenomenological descriptions (e.g. Huber 1923; Tagg 2006) or free choice of descriptive terms/adjectives (Imberty 1979);

(b) choice among descriptive terms provided by the investigator (e.g. Gundlach 1935; Hevner 1935; Wedin 1972a);

(c) combination of free descriptions and choice among descriptive terms (Rigg 1937a);

(d) ratings of how well selected descriptive terms apply to the music in question (e.g. Gabrielsson 1973; Nielzén and Cesarec 1982; Tillman and Bigand 1996; Wedin 1969); Collier (2007) used ranking of emotion words;

(e) nonverbal methods, for instance, pressing a pair of tongs to indicate perceived tension (Nielsen 1983, 1987), finger pressure on a sentograph to study expression of different emotions (Clynes and Nettheim 1982; Gabrielsson and Lindström 1995; de Vries 1991); or

(f) various technical or computerized devices to allow continuous recording of perceived tension (e.g., Fredrikson 2000; Fredrikson and Coggiola 2003; Krumhansl 1996; Madsen 1998; Madsen and Fredrickson 1993) or various emotions (Krumhansl 1997; Schubert 2004).

Analysis

Free descriptions were subjected to content analysis. Listeners' choices among descriptive terms were analyzed regarding the frequency of chosen terms and inter-subject agreement. Ratings were usually analyzed by multivariate techniques, such as factor analysis, cluster analysis, multidimensional scaling or correspondence analysis in order to find a limited number of fundamental dimensions. Although the labels of these dimensions vary somewhat between different studies, they are in general interpretable in accordance with the valence-arousal model of emotion (Russell 1980; Russell and Feldman

Barrett 1999). There are also indications of a potency dimension (Kleinen 1968; cf. Osgood *et al.* 1957); a dimension related to body posture and gestures (Bigand *et al.* 2005); and a dimension reflecting stylistic differences between classical and popular music (Wedin 1969, 1972b). Further proposals include a distinction between energy arousal and tension arousal (Ilie and Thompson 2006; Schimmack and Grob 2000) and attempts to identify subtle dimensions beyond valence and activation (Collier 2007).

The relationship between the composed structure and perceived expression was studied by

(a) analyzing the musical score in relation to perceived expression (e.g. Gundlach 1935; Imberty 1979; Krumhansl 1996; Nielsen 1983; Thompson and Robitaille 1992);

(b) having musical experts judge the selected pieces with regard to structural properties (e.g. Kleinen 1968; Wedin 1972b);

(c) using various devices for measuring the acoustical properties of the music (e.g. Schubert 2004; Todd 1994); or

(d) using systematic manipulation of the musical stimuli and noting the effects on perceived expression (references given under Stimuli).

Expression of emotion: effects of separate musical factors

The effects of separate musical factors are summarized in Gabrielsson and Lindström (2001). The following is an abbreviated version of this summary, with some new references added.

Tempo, note density

Among factors affecting emotional expression, tempo—that is, perceived beat/pulse rate—is usually considered the most decisive.

Fast tempo may be associated with expressions of activity/excitement, happiness/joy/pleasantness, potency, surprise, flippancy/whimsicality, anger, uneasiness and fear.

Slow tempo may be associated with expressions of calmness/serenity, peace, sadness, dignity/solemnity, tenderness, longing, boredom, and disgust.

Both fast and slow tempo may thus be associated with many different expressions dependent on presence and level of other structural factors. However, in terms of the valence-arousal model, fast tempo is generally associated with high(er) activation, slow tempo with low(er) activation, while both of them may be associated with either positive or negative valence.

A related factor is note density, the number of notes per unit of time (e.g. per second). Tempo and note density may sometimes be additive—fast tempo combined with high note density results in still higher activation, slow tempo combined with low note density results in still lower activation—and may sometimes present an ambiguous picture as when high note density appears in combination with slow tempo (Gabrielsson 1988).

Mode, key

Major mode may be associated with happiness/joy, minor mode with sadness. Major mode may also be associated with expressions as graceful, serene, and solemn, minor mode with expressions as dreamy, dignified, tension, disgust, and anger.

While differences between fast and slow tempo are mainly associated with difference in activation, differences between major and minor mode are thus mainly associated with difference in valence, positive or negative. However, major mode is not a necessary condition for perceived happiness; a piece in minor mode in fast tempo may very well sound happy (e.g., the *Badinerie* in JS Bach's Second Suite for Orchestra). Using scales as stimuli, Collier and Hubbard (2001a) claim that pitch height and direction of pitch movement (contour) may be more important than mode for expression of happiness.

The common belief that certain keys are associated with certain moods has no empirical support (Powell and Dibben 2005).

Loudness

Loud music may be associated with expressions of intensity/power, excitement, tension, anger, and joy, soft music with softness, peace, tenderness, sadness, and fear. On the whole, loud music seems associated with high activation and potency, soft music with low activation and maybe submissiveness.

Large variations of loudness may suggest fear, small variations happiness or activity. Rapid changes in loudness may be associated with playfulness, pleading or fear, few or no changes with sadness, peace, and dignity.

Timbre/spectrum

Tones with many higher harmonics may suggest potency, anger, disgust, fear, activity, or surprise, thus usually high activation. Tones with few, low harmonics may be associated with pleasantness, boredom, happiness or sadness, and tones with suppressed higher harmonics may suggest tenderness and sadness, thus usually low(er) activation.

Pitch

High pitch may be associated with expressions as happy, graceful, serene, dreamy, exciting, surprise, potency, anger, fear, and activity. Low pitch may suggest sadness, dignity/solemnity, vigour, excitement, boredom, and pleasantness. Large pitch variation may be associated with happiness, pleasantness, activity, or surprise, small pitch variation with disgust, anger, fear, or boredom.

Intervals

For melodic (successive) intervals some results indicate that large intervals sound more powerful than small ones, the octave is perceived as positive and strong and the minor second as the most sad interval. For harmonic (simultaneous) intervals, results concerning consonance and dissonance are similar to corresponding results under Harmony.

Melody

Melodic range

Wide melodic range may be associated with joy, whimsicality, uneasiness, and fear, narrow range with expressions as sad, dignified, sentimental, tranquil, delicate, and triumphant.

Melodic direction (pitch contour)

Ascending melody may be associated with dignity, serenity, tension, happiness, fear, surprise, anger, and potency. Descending melody may be associated with expressions such as exciting, graceful, vigorous, sadness, boredom and pleasantness.

Melodic motion

Stepwise motion may suggest dullness, intervallic leaps excitement; stepwise motion leading to melodic leaps may suggest peacefulness (Thompson and Robitaille 1992). Activity (sense of instability and motion) may be conveyed by a greater occurrence of minor seconds, tritones, and intervals larger than the octave. Potency (vigour and power) may be expressed by a greater occurrence of unisons and octaves (Costa *et al.* 2004).

Harmony

Simple, consonant harmony may be associated with expressions as happy/gay, relaxed, graceful, serene, dreamy, dignified, serious, and majestic; complex and dissonant harmony with expression of excitement, tension, vigour, anger, sadness, and unpleasantness.

Tonality

Melodies composed to sound joyful, dull, and peaceful were tonal, while angry melodies could be atonal. Sad and angry melodies used chromatic harmony (Thompson and Robitaille 1992).

Rhythm

Regular/smooth rhythm may be perceived to express happiness, dignity, majesty, and peacefulness; irregular/complex rhythm may express amusement, uneasiness, and anger; varied rhythm may express joy. Firm rhythm may be associated with expressions of sadness, dignity, and vigour; flowing/fluent rhythm with expressions such as happy/gay, graceful, dreamy, and serene.

Articulation

Staccato may be associated with gaiety, energy, activity, fear, and anger, legato with sadness, tenderness, solemnity, longing, and softness.

Pauses

Perception of rests is dependent on musical context. Silences (rests) following tonal closure were identified more quickly and perceived as less tense than silences following music lacking such closure (Margulis 2007).

Musical form

High complexity (melodic/harmonic/rhythmic) is associated with tension or sadness, low complexity with relaxation, joy, or peace. High complexity combined with low dynamism may express melancholy and depression, high complexity combined with high dynamism may express anxiety and aggressiveness. Low complexity and average dynamism may be associated with positive emotions. Repetition, condensation, sequential development, and pauses may mean increased tension. Disruption of global form (changing the order of sections/movements in a musical work) may have little effect on (unknowing) listeners' perception of expression or general evaluation.

Expression as function of many factors

As seen above, each structural factor may influence many different expressions. This means, conversely, that each expression may depend on many different structural factors as displayed in the extensive Table 26.2 in Gabrielsson and Juslin (2003). This table provides a systematic exposition of how different expressions—happiness/joy/gaiety, sadness/gloom, tension, potency, activity/energy/excitement, relaxation/calm/softness/peace, solemnity/dignity, anger, fear, tenderness/love, boredom, disgust, and surprise—are affected by different structural features. To take but one example: perceived tension is related to dissonance, high sound level, ascending melody, increased note density, harmonic complexity, rhythmic complexity, lack of melody, and various formal properties such as repetition, condensation and sequential development.

Expression of emotion: summary and implications

The above review shows a complex picture. It seems that any structural factor may indicate a number of different emotional expressions.

Results seem most clear-cut regarding effects of tempo/speed, loudness, and timbre/spectrum: increase in any of them results in higher activation, decrease in lower activation (by increase in timbre is meant relatively more higher harmonics). Tempo and loudness, in particular, seem to reign over most other factors, and generally the activation dimension seems more salient and easier to judge than the valence dimension. The effects of pitch height seem more ambiguous than those of loudness or tempo; for instance, while the effects of fast tempo and/or high loudness are associated with high activation, high pitch may be associated with both high and low activation.

The most distinct results thus concern effects of basic variables in human audition (loudness, timbre, pitch) and motion (tempo/speed). With regard to more typical 'musical' variables results are less clear, or there is less research available. The typical major-happy and minor-sad associations may be overruled by interaction with tempo (as exemplified under Mode above) and do not appear until the age of 7–8 years (e.g., Gerardi and Gerken 1995). There are still only tentative results regarding perceived expression of different intervals, and their effects may be modulated by differences in tempo, loudness, and other factors (Gabrielsson and Lindström 2001, p. 243). There is further little research on perceived expression of different kinds of melodic and rhythmic progression and practically none regarding harmonic progression. Aspects of musical form are frequently discussed in relation to structural listening, but their influence on perceived expression is little investigated.

Perceived expression is never determined by a single factor but is a function of many factors which may work in additive or interactive ways. Several studies identify interactions *post hoc*; for instance, intensity x pitch height and pitch height × tempo interactions regarding valence (Ilie and Thompson 2006), scale direction x tempo regarding happiness (Collier and Hubbard 2001b), and triple interaction rhythm x contour x melodic progression in ratings of happiness (Lindström 2006). However, there are only a few studies planned to study the presence (or not) of specific interactions (e.g. Langner and Goebl 2003; Makris and Mullet 2003; Schellenberg *et al.* 2000).

Most studies have utilized music with the 'same' expression throughout, whereas an essential part of music's appeal lies in variation of emotional expression. Many of the most intense expressions are related to (sudden or gradual) changes in, say, loudness (e.g. crescendo, diminuendo), tempo (accelerando, ritardando), timbre, pitch level, rhythm, melodic and harmonic progression, or in various combinations of these factors. Therefore an important topic for continued research is refinement of techniques for continuous recording of expression (Schubert 2001, 2002, 2004; Vines *et al.* 2005). Free phenomenological descriptions may be used as a complement. However, certain subtleties in musical expression may never be captured in a strict scientific manner, nor be adequately verbalized; they may only be accessible in direct experience.

On the other hand some results indicate that listeners are able to perceive the 'correct' expression even in excerpts lasting only one second or less (Bigand *et al.* 2005; Peretz *et al.* 1998). It also seems that, on the whole, perceived emotional expression is not, or only marginally, influenced by differences in gender or musical experience (e.g. Bigand *et al.* 2005; Bigand and Poulin-Charronnat 2006; Fredrickson 2000; Kallinen 2005; Makris and Mullet 2003; Robazza *et al.* 1994; Wedin 1969); there are, however, some indications that women may find music more emotionally expressive than men (e.g. Kamenetsky *et al.* 1997)

Other referential meanings

Beyond emotions, music may also be perceived to express, reflect, or represent many other phenomena. (For discussion about definitions of expression, representation, or depiction, see Davies 1994; Scruton 1997).

Program music

Program music flourished during Romanticism, as in works by Berlioz, Liszt, and Richard Strauss. However, composers were aware of music's limited possibilities to represent objects and events and rather referred to the feelings associated with the program (Benestad 1978, p. 233).

Listeners who do not know the program are as a rule unable to provide a 'correct' description of the intended events or situations but are better at perceiving the intended emotional expression (e.g. Brown 1981; Rigg 1937b). However, Osborne's (1989) subjects seemed to capture several aspects of the representations and expressions in Richard Strauss' *Alpine Symphony*.

One may also speak of program music in another sense: programs made up by the listeners themselves. Listeners may perceive a narrative in music they listen to ('this music is about '). Delis *et al.* (1978) argued that listeners construct a story in relation to the music in order to better remember it.

Human character, personality, identity

In ancient Greece it was believed that music reflected human character and that these expressions would be imitated by the listener. Plato and Aristotle therefore gave advice concerning which modes, instruments, and rhythms ought to be used in education.

Clynes (1987, 1995) hypothesized that composers' character and 'presence' are reflected in unique patterns of timing and dynamics (composers' 'inner pulse'). Empirical tests regarding the existence of such patterns have provided mixed results (Clynes 1995; Repp 1990; Thompson 1989).

Tagg (2006) found striking differences between music perceived as 'male' or 'female'. In comparison with male tunes, female tunes were slower, more legato, had longer phrases, no repeated notes, static bass line, rare offbeats/syncopation, no brass or percussion, and the tonal idiom was classical/romantic compared to rock and jazz in male tunes. A 'male vs.female' factor, as well as some other human characteristics, was also observed in an exploratory study by Watt and Ash (1998). They claimed that music is assigned attributions that normally would be assigned to a person and went on to speculate that 'music creates a virtual person' (*ibid.* p. 49). In fact, many subjects perceive the music to reflect their own personality, how they think and feel; this provides a strong confirmation of their own identity (Gabrielsson and Lindström Wik 2003).

Music may reflect and be used to express not only personal but also social, cultural, and gender identity (e.g. Dibben 2002; Folkestad 2002; Martin 2006; Ruud 1997; Tarrant *et al.* 2002). Immigrants are eager to preserve their own music in the new country, and teenagers may use certain music to mark their belonging to youth culture in general or to a particular group of people.

Motion, dynamic forces

It is generally agreed that we may perceive motion in music. However, there is much discussion whether it refers to real motion, self-motion, virtual motion, or is entirely metaphorical. For discussions and overviews, see Bharucha *et al.* (2006, section 4), Clarke (2005), Eitan and Granot (2006), Jackendoff and Lerdahl (2006, section 4.3), and Shove and Repp (1995); see also Gjerdingen (1994) for a neural network model of apparent motion in music.

In music theory it is common to speak of tonal/harmonic motion in the sense that unstable tones/chords 'move' to (resolve to) stable tones/chords, typically in connection with perception of tension and release (e.g. Lerdahl and Krumhansl 2007). The concept of tension is thus related to structural listening but may also mediate emotional expression (Nielsen 1983).

Musicologist Ernst Kurth (1930) thought of music as a play of dynamic forces, gravitational forces between tones and chords, attracting or repelling each other; melody is perceived as a streaming force filled with kinetic energy. Larson and VanHandel (2005) defined three musical forces—musical gravity, musical magnetism, musical inertia—and operationalized them as short melodic patterns that were judged by listeners with regard to experienced 'strength' of the presented pattern completions. Results indicated that listeners' judgements were influenced by musical inertia and musical gravity.

While the above examples are mainly concerned with structural (intra-musical) listening, certain designations in scores (e.g. accelerando, ritardando, alla marcia, grazioso) refer to motion in a more concrete sense, and listeners find it natural to use motion labels as bouncing, dancing, flowing, rocking, swinging, and so on in descriptions of music (Gabrielsson 1973, 1988; Madison 2006). Tempo, articulation, and rhythm patterns seem obvious candidates underlying

such motion characters (*cf.* 'galloping rhythm', 'fluent rhythm ', 'uneven rhythm', etc.), but there is still little systematic research on what factors in musical structure affect perceived motion. Eitan and Granot (2006) asked subjects to describe imagined motion of a visualized person when listening to brief melodic figures varying in dynamics, pitch contour, pitch intervals, attack rate, motivic pace, and articulation. The manipulations affected several variables in the listeners' motion imagery, such as lateral and vertical direction, distance change, speed change, and energy level of motion.

It is also generally agreed that there is a close link between motion and emotion: 'Motion is heard in music, and that motion presents emotion characteristics' (Davies 1994, p. 229), 'musical affect arises in large part from its relation to physical patterns of posture and gesture' (Jackendoff and Lerdahl 2006, p. 65). Jackendoff and Lerdahl point out that many terms used for description of emotional expression are also used to describe gestures and postures and discuss possible underlying factors in musical structure and performance. (One may add that it is sometimes felt more natural and easier to describe music in terms of motion rather than emotion.) Here, then, is a domain awaiting pertinent empirical research.

Social conditions and organization

Philosopher Theodor W. Adorno speculated that music's formal properties may reflect organization and forces of society; for instance, tensions in society would be reflected in rupture of musical form (Benestad 1978, p. 329). While Adorno never sought empirical evidence, Lomax's (1968) large-scale investigation of folk song styles in 233 cultures throughout the world provides many examples of how music can reflect economic and social conditions and attitudes; for comments, see Dowling and Harwood (1986, p. 226).

Religious faith, transcendental phenomena

Music as expression of religious faith is a worldwide phenomenon. In Western music history, examples range from simple community singing to masterpieces such as J. S. Bach's passions, Handel's oratorios, or masses by Haydn, Mozart, and Beethoven.

Philosopher Arthur Schopenhauer regarded music as an expression of the Will, a never-ending striving toward existence that can never be quite fulfilled and therefore causes human suffering, and Friedrich Nietzsche viewed music as expression of Dionysian character and the will to life and power; see further in Benestad (1978) and Budd (1985).

Further comments on structure

There is only scattered research on structural variables connected with the referential meanings treated in this section. However, since many of these meanings—program music, motion, character, identity, religious faith—also have obvious emotional connotations, it is reasonable to expect that the structural variables underlying emotional expression are largely pertinent to them as well.

Finally, we should not forget that many people enjoy music simply for its expression of beauty. However, there seem to be no empirical investigations in music psychology directly focusing on structural factors underlying perceived beauty in music.

References

Benestad F (1978). *Musik och tanke. Huvudlinjer i musikestetikens historia från antiken till vår egen tid [Music and thought. Main lines in the history of musical aesthetics from antiquity to our time]*. Rabén and Sjögren, Stockholm.

Bharucha JJ, Curtis M and Paroo K. (2006). Varieties of musical experience. *Cognition*, **100**, 131–172.

Bigand E and Poulin-Charronnat B. (2006). Are we 'experienced listeners? A review of the musical capacities that do not depend on formal musical training. *Cognition*, **100**, 100–130.

Bigand E, Vieillard S, Madurell F, Marozeau J and Dacquet A (2005). Multidimensional scaling of emotional responses to music: the effect of musical expertise and of the duration of the excerpts. *Cognition and Emotion*, **19**, 1113–1139.

Brown R (1981). Music and language. In *Documentary report of the Ann Arbor symposium. National symposium on the applications of psychology to the teaching and learning of music*, 233–265. Music Educators National Conference, Reston, VA.

Budd M (1985). *Music and the emotions. The philosophical theories*. Routledge, London.

Clarke EF (2005). *Ways of listening. An ecological approach to the perception of musical meaning*. Oxford University Press, New York.

Clynes M (1987). What can a musician learn about music performance from newly discovered microstructure principles (PM, PAS)? In A Gabrielsson, ed., *Action and perception in rhythm and music*, 201–233. Publications issued by the Royal Swedish Academy of Music, No. 55, Stockholm.

Clynes M (1995). Microstructural musical linguistics: composers' pulses are liked most by the best musicians. *Cognition*, **55**, 269–310.

Clynes M and Nettheim N (1982).The living quality of music. Neurobiologic patterns of communicating feeling. In M Clynes, ed., *Music, mind, and brain. The neuropsychology of music*, 47–82. Plenum Press, New York.

Collier GL (2007). Beyond valence and activity in the emotional connotations of music. *Psychology of Music*, **35**, 110–131.

Collier GL and Hubbard TL (2001a). Musical scales and evaluations of happiness and awkwardness: effects of pitch, direction, and scale mode. *American Journal of Psychology*, **114**, 355–375.

Collier GL and Hubbard TL (2001b). Judgements of happiness, brightness, speed and tempo change of auditory stimuli varying in pitch and tempo. *Psychomusicology*, **17**, 36–55.

Cooke D (1959). *The language of music*. Oxford University Press, Oxford.

Costa M, Fine P and Ricci Bitti PE (2004). Interval distribution, mode, and tonal strength of melodies as predictors of perceived emotion. *Music Perception*, **22**, 1–14.

Davies S (1994). *Musical meaning and expression*. Cornell University Press, Ithaca, NY.

Delis D, Fleer J and Kerr P (1978). Memory for music. *Perception and Psychophysics*, **23**, 215–218.

Dibben N (2002). Gender identity and music. In RAR MacDonald, DJ Hargreaves and D Miell, eds, *Musical identities*, 117–133. Oxford University Press, Oxford.

Dowling WJ and Harwood DL (1986). *Music cognition*. Academic Press, Orlando FL.

Eitan Z and Granot RY (2006). How music moves: musical parameters and listeners' images of motion. *Music Perception*, **23**, 221–247.

Evans P and Schubert E (2008). Relationships between expressed and felt emotion in music. *Musicae Scientiae*, **12**, 75–99.

Fisk J (ed.) (1997). *Composers on music*. Northeastern University Press, Boston, MA.

Folkestad G (2002). National identity and music. In RAR MacDonald, DJ Hargreaves and D Miell, eds, *Musical identities*, 151–162. Oxford University Press, Oxford.

Fredrickson WE (2000). Perception of tension in music: musicians versus nonmusicians. *Journal of Music Therapy*, **37**(1), 40–50.

Fredrickson WE and Coggiola JC (2003). A comparison of music majors' and nonmajors' perceptions of tension for two selections of jazz music. *Journal of Research in Music Education*, **51**, 259–270.

Gabrielsson A (1973). Adjective ratings and dimension analysis of auditory rhythm patterns. *Scandinavian Journal of Psychology*, **14**, 244–260.

Gabrielsson A (1988). Timing in music performance and its relations to music experience. In JA Sloboda, ed., *Generative processes in music: the psychology of performance, improvisation, and composition*, 27–51. Clarendon Press, Oxford.

Gabrielsson A (2002). Emotion perceived and emotion felt: same or different? *Musicae Scientiae, Special Issue 2001–2002: Current Trends in the Study of Music and Emotion*, 123–147.

Gabrielsson A and Juslin PN (2003). Emotional expression in music. In RJ Davidson, KR Scherer and HH Goldsmith, eds, *Handbook of affective sciences*, 503–534. Oxford University Press, New York.

Gabrielsson A and Lindström E (1995). Emotional expression in synthesizer and sentograph performance. *Psychomusicology*, **14**, 94–116.

Gabrielsson A and Lindström E (2001). The influence of musical structure on emotional expression. In PN Juslin, JA Sloboda, eds, *Music and emotion: theory and research*, 223–248. Oxford University Press, New York.

Gabrielsson A and Lindström Wik S (2003). Strong experiences related to music: a descriptive system. *Musicae Scientiae*, **7**, 157–217.

Gerardi GM and Gerken L (1995). The development of affective responses to modality and melodic contour. *Music Perception*, **12**, 279–290.

Gjerdingen RO (1994). Apparent motion in music? *Music Perception*, **11**, 335–370.

Gundlach RH (1935). Factors determining the characterization of musical phrases. *American Journal of Psychology*, **47**, 624–644.

Hanslick E (1989/1854). *Vom musikalisch Schönen*. Breitkopf and Härtel, Wiesbaden.

Hevner K (1935). The affective character of the major and minor modes in music. *American Journal of Psychology*, **47**, 103–118.

Hevner K (1936). Experimental studies of the elements of expression in music. *American Journal of Psychology*, **48**, 246–268.

Hevner K (1937). The affective value of pitch and tempo in music. *American Journal of Psychology*, **49**, 621–630.

Huber K (1923). *Der Ausdruck musikalischer Elementarmotive [Expression in elementary musical motives]*. Johann Ambrosius Barth, Leipzig.

Ilie G and Thompson WF (2006). A comparison of acoustic cues in music and speech for three dimensions of affect. *Music Perception*, **23**, 319–329.

Imberty M (1979). *Entendre la musique*. Dunod, Paris.

Jackendoff R and Lerdahl F (2006). The capacity for music: what is it, and what's special about it? *Cognition*, **100**, 33–72.

Juslin PN (1997). Perceived emotional expression in synthesized performances of a short melody: capturing the listener's judgment policy. *Musicae Scientiae*, **1**, 225–256.

Juslin PN and Laukka P (2004). Expression, perception, and induction of musical emotions: a review and a questionnaire study of everyday listening. *Journal of New Music Research*, **33**, 217–238.

Kallinen K (2005). Emotional ratings of music excerpts in the western art music repertoire and their self-organization in the Kohonen neural network. *Psychology of Music*, **33**, 373–393.

Kallinen K and Ravaja N (2006). Emotion perceived and emotion felt: same and different. *Musicae Scientiae*, **10**, 191–213.

Kamenetsky SB, Hill DS and Trehub SE (1997). Effect of tempo and dynamics on the perception of emotion in music. *Psychology of Music*, **25**, 149–160.

Karno M and Konečni VJ (1992). The effects of structural interventions in the first movement of Mozart's Symphony in G minor K. 550 on aesthetic preference. *Music Perception*, **10**, 63–72.

Kleinen G (1968). *Experimentelle Studien zum musikalischen Ausdruck [Experimental studies on musical expression]*. Universität Hamburg, Hamburg.

Konečni VJ, Brown A and Wanic RA (2008). Comparative effects of music and recalled life-events on emotional state. *Psychology of Music*, **36**, 289–308.

Krumhansl CL (1996). A perceptual analysis of Mozart's Piano Sonata K. 282: segmentation, tension, and musical ideas. *Music Perception*, **13**, 401–432.

Krumhansl CL (1997). An exploratory study of musical emotions and psychophysiology. *Canadian Journal of Experimental Psychology*, **51**, 336–352.

Kurth E (1930/1947). *Musikpsychologie*. Verlag Krompholz, Bern.

Langer SK (1957). *Philosophy in a new key*, 3rd edn. Harvard University Press, Cambridge, Massachusetts.

Langner J and Goebl W (2003). Visualizing expressive performance in tempo–loudness space. *Computer Music Journal*, **27**(4), 69–83.

Larson S and VanHandel L (2005). Measuring musical forces. *Music Perception*, **23**, 119–136.

Lerdahl F and Krumhansl CL (2007). Modeling musical tension. *Music Perception*, **24**, 329–366.

Lindström E (2006). Impact of melodic organization on perceived structure and emotional expression in music. *Musicae Scientiae*, **10**, 85–117.

Lomax A (1968). *Folk song style and culture*. American Association for the Advancement of Science, Washington, DC.

Madison G (2006). Experiencing groove induced by music: consistency and phenomenology. *Music Perception*, **24**, 201–208.

Madsen CK (1998). Emotion versus tension in Haydn's Symphony No. 104 as measured by the two-dimensional continuous response digital interface. *Journal of Research in Music Education*, **46**, 546–554.

Madsen CK and Fredrickson WE (1993). The experience of musical tension: a replication of Nielsen's research using the continuous response digital interface. *Journal of Music Therapy*, **30**, 46–63.

Makris I and Mullet E (2003). Judging the pleasantness of contour-rhythm-pitch-timbre musical combinations. *American Journal of Psychology*, **116**, 581–611.

Margulis EH (2007). Silences in music are musical not silent: an exploratory study of context effects on the experience of musical pauses. *Music Perception*, **24**, 485–506.

Martin PJ (2006). Music, identity, and social control. In S Brown and U Volgsten, eds, *Music and manipulation. On the social uses and social control of music*, 57–73. Berghahn Books, New York.

Meyer LB (1956). *Emotion and meaning in music*. University of Chicago Press, Chicago, IL.

Nielsen FV(1983). *Oplevelse av musikalsk spænding [Experience of musical tension]*. Akademisk Forlag, Copenhagen. (Includes summary in English.)

Nielsen FV (1987). Musical 'tension' and related concepts. In TA Sebeok and J Umiker-Sebeok, eds, *The semiotic web 86. An international yearbook*, 491–513. Mouton de Gruyter, Berlin.

Nielzén S and Cesarec Z (1982). Emotional experience of music as a function of musical structure. *Psychology of Music*, **10**, 7–17.

Osborne JW (1989). A phenomenological investigation of the musical representation of extra-musical ideas. *Journal of Phenomenological Psychology*, **20**, 151–175.

Osgood CE, Suci GJ and Tannenbaum PH (1957). *The measurement of meaning*. University of Illinois Press, Urbana, IL.

Peretz I, Gagnon L and Bouchard B (1998). Music and emotion: perceptual determinants, immediacy, and isolation after brain damage. *Cognition*, **68**, 111–141.

Powell J and Dibben N (2005). Key-mood association: a self perpetuating myth. *Musicae Scientiae*, **9**, 289–311.

Repp BH (1990). Further perceptual evaluations of pulse microstructure in computer performances of classical piano music. *Music Perception*, **8**, 1–33.

Rigg MG, (1937a). Musical expression: an investigation of the theories of Erich Sorantin. *Journal of Experimental Psychology*, **21**, 442–455.

Rigg MG (1937b). An experiment to determine how accurately college students can interpret the intended meanings of musical compositions. *Journal of Experimental Psychology*, **21**, 223–229.

Rigg MG (1940a). The effect of register and tonality upon musical mood. *Journal of Musicology*, **2**, 49–61.

Rigg MG (1940b). Speed as a determiner of musical mood. *Journal of Experimental Psychology*, **27**, 566–571.

Robazza C, Macaluso C and D'Urso V (1994). Emotional reactions to music by gender, age, and expertise. *Perceptual and Motor Skills*, **79**, 939–944.

Russell JA (1980). A circumplex model of affect. *Journal of Personality and Social Psychology*, **39**, 1161–1178.

Russell JA and Feldman Barrett L (1999). Core affect, prototypical emotional episodes, and other things called emotion: dissecting the elephant. *Journal of Personality and Social Psychology*, **76**, 805–819.

Ruud E (1997). *Musikk og identitet [Music and identity]*. Universitetsforlaget, Oslo.

Schellenberg EG, Krysciak AM and Campbell RJ (2000). Perceiving emotion in melody: interactive effects of pitch and rhythm. *Music Perception*, **18**, 155–171.

Scherer KR and Oshinsky JS (1977). Cue utilization in emotion attribution from auditory stimuli. *Motivation and Emotion*, **1**, 331–346.

Schimmack U and Grob A (2000). Dimensional models of core affect: a quantitative comparison by means of structural equation modeling. *European Journal of Personality*, **14**, 325–345.

Schubert E (2001). Continuous measurement of self-report emotional response to music. In PN Juslin, JA Sloboda, eds, *Music and emotion: theory and research*, 393–414. Oxford University Press, New York.

Schubert E (2002). Correlation analysis of continuous emotional response to music: correcting for the effects of serial correlation. *Musicae Scientiae, Special issue 2001–2002: Current trends in the study of music and emotion*, 213–236.

Schubert E (2004). Modeling perceived emotion with continuous musical features. *Music Perception*, **21**, 561–585.

Scruton R (1997). *The aesthetics of music*. Oxford University Press, New York.

Shove P and Repp BH (1995). Musical motion and performance: theoretical and empirical perspectives. In J Rink, ed., *The practice of performance. Studies in musical interpretation*, 55–83. Cambridge University Press, Cambridge.

Tagg P (2006). Music, moving images, semiotics, and the democratic right to know. In S Brown and U Volgsten, eds, *Music and manipulation. On the social uses and social control of music*, 163–186. Berghahn Books, New York.

Tarrant M, North AC and Hargreaves DJ (2002). Youth identity and music. In RAR MacDonald, DJ Hargreaves, D Miell, eds, *Musical identities*, 134–150. Oxford University Press, Oxford.

Thompson WF (1989). Composer-specific aspects of musical performance: an evaluation of Clynes's theory of pulse for performances of Mozart and Beethoven. *Music Perception*, **7**, 15–42.

Thompson WF and Robitaille B (1992). Can composers express emotions through music? *Empirical Studies of the Arts*, **10**, 79–89.

Tillman B and Bigand E (1996). Does formal musical structure affect perception of musical expressiveness? *Psychology of Music*, **24**, 1–17.

Todd N (1994). The auditory 'primal sketch': a multiscale model of rhythmic grouping. *Journal of New Music Research*, **23**, 25–70.

Vines BW, Nuzzo RL and Levitin DJ (2005). Analyzing temporal dynamics in music: differential calculus, physics, and functional data analysis techniques. *Music Perception*, **23**, 137–152.

deVries B (1991). Assessment of the affective response to music with Clynes's sentograph. *Psychology of Music*, **19**, 46–64.

Watt RJ and Ash RL (1998). A psychological investigation of meaning in music. *Musicae Scientiae*, **2**, 33–53.

Wedin L (1969). Dimension analysis of emotional expression in music. *Swedish Journal of Musicology*, **51**, 119–140.

Wedin L (1972a). Multidimensional scaling of emotional expression in music. *Swedish Journal of Musicology*, **54**, 1–17.

Wedin L (1972b). A multidimensional study of perceptual–emotional qualities in music. *Scandinavian Journal of Psychology*, **13**, 241–257.

CHAPTER 14

Aesthetics

David Huron

Introduction

Aesthetics is commonly defined as the study of beauty, and its opposite, ugliness. Some philosophers conceive of aesthetics as applying solely to the arts or to artistic experience. However, most aesthetic philosophers construe the discipline as applying more broadly to beauty and ugliness in general. The term 'aesthetics' first appeared in a book by Alexander Baumgarten in 1735, yet philosophical discussions of beauty extend back thousands of years. Commentaries on 'good' and 'bad' music can be found in both ancient Greek and ancient Chinese sources.

Beginning in the 1960s, the field of cognitive science became increasingly influential in the philosophy of mind. While much of this influence relates to the nature of thought, reasoning, and consciousness, the impact of cognitive science has expanded to other areas of philosophy, including aesthetics. In this chapter, no effort will be made to provide a comprehensive survey of ideas related to musical aesthetics. Instead, it focuses more narrowly on how cognitive science has influenced—and continues to influence—modern thinking in musical aesthetics. This chapter concludes by arguing that cognitive neuroscience is poised to overtake philosophical aesthetics: rather than *influencing* aesthetic philosophy, aesthetic philosophy is receding to a sideline 'advisory' role, while cognitive science takes an unaccustomed leadership position.

Philosophical antecedents

In the West, the most influential writer on aesthetics has been the German philosopher Immanuel Kant (1724–1804). Kant laid out two pillars in

Western aesthetics. First, he distinguished aesthetic pleasure from other forms of pleasure. Aesthetic pleasure is not some other type of pleasure in disguise: for example, art is not the sublimation of food, sex, warmth, companionship, or some combination of other existing pleasures. Second, Kant argued that aesthetic emotions are 'disinterested'; when we experience an aesthetic pleasure, there are no utilitarian or ulterior motives underlying this experience. A mother's appreciation of the beauty of her daughter cannot be regarded as a purely aesthetic appreciation, since her experience is apt to be tainted by parental pride. Unlike garden-variety emotions, for Kant, aesthetic emotions serve no practical purpose.

In music, Kant's ideas were developed and extended by the famed Austrian music critic Eduard Hanslick (1825–1904). In *Vom Musikalisch-Schönen* (On the beautiful in music) (1854) Hanslick proposed a highly influential view that would later prove to be compatible with a core concept in cognitive science. Hanslick challenged the (then) prevailing beliefs that music somehow represents or expresses feelings. He proposed that sensation is imaginatively interpreted by the listener, and that this aesthetic contemplative process then leads to possible emotions. In short, aesthetic judgement precedes and leads to aesthetic feelings. Until recently, Hanslick's views have defined the principal parameters in debates concerning musical aesthetics. All major philosophers in the aesthetics of music have started by engaging with Hanslick's ideas: see for example Susanne Langer (1942), Peter Kivy (1990), Roger Scruton (1997), Jerrold Levison (1990, 2003) and Stephen Davies (1994).

Experimental antecedents

Most aesthetics scholars have followed a rationalist approach that emphasizes exegesis of existing theories and critical philosophical discussion. Independent of this philosophical tradition, aesthetics questions have also been addressed by empirically oriented scholars pursuing various avenues of scientific experimentation. In fact, the advent of experimental aesthetics coincides with the start of modern experimental psychology. One of the founders of modern experimental psychology, Wilhelm Wundt (1832–1920) carried out a number of experiments related to aesthetic experience. Wundt (1863) showed that arousal is related to stimulus complexity and proposed that aesthetic pleasure is evoked when the art object is optimally complex—neither too simple nor too complicated.

Aesthetics experiments were similarly carried out by another early experimental psychologist, Gustav Fechner (1801–1887). In his *Vorschule der Ästhetik* (Elementary aesthetics) Fechner suggested that 'half of aesthetics' originates in learned associations (1876, pp. 89–90). A lullaby may evoke feelings of comfort solely because of a learned association between the tune and formative experiences of being comforted by a caregiver. A German émigré to the United States, Max Meyer (1873–1967), carried out a key experiment showing that listeners prefer familiar music over unfamiliar music. Meyer (1903) showed that repeated listening to a novel musical work tends to increase reported satisfaction. While the Gestalt psychologists carried out relatively few experiments, they did produce a number of empirical demonstrations of various perceptual principles and suggested that these principles can be observed in both visual art and music (see, e.g. Koffka 1935).

A long-standing preoccupation in experimental musical aesthetics relates to the perception of consonance and dissonance. The ancient Greeks observed that euphonious sonorities appear to involve component tones whose frequencies are related by simple integer ratios. Both Hermann von Helmholtz (1877) and Carl Stumpf (1883) speculated about possible physiological origins for consonance and dissonance. Robert Lundin (1947) proposed that consonance and dissonance preferences are cultural in origin and arise primarily from the relative frequency of exposure to different sound combinations and the prevailing attitudes toward those sounds within a given social environment. By the 1970s, ample evidence pointing to both physiological and cultural factors influencing judgements of the euphoniousness of a sonority had accumulated. Regarding the physiological basis, a significant breakthrough occurred in the 1960s with the work of Donald Greenwood (1961) and Reinier Plomp and Willem Levelt (1965). These and subsequent researchers showed that at least some of the phenomenal experience musicians call 'dissonance' can be traced to mechanical interference within the organ of hearing. Regarding the influence of enculturation and familiarity on stimulus preference, mainstream psychology remained unaware of the pioneering work of Meyer and Lundin. Experimental research by Wilson (1975, 1979) and others unwittingly re-established what Zajonc (1980) later dubbed the 'mere exposure effect'. Over the past century, over 200 experiments have shown that familiarity has a marked impact on preference—especially when the listener is unaware that the sounds are familiar.

Among several notable empirically grounded volumes on the science of aesthetics, perhaps the most comprehensive attempt is found in the work of the Canadian psychologist Daniel Berlyne. In his 1971 book, *Aesthetics and psychobiology*, Berlyne extended Wundt's observations concerning the relationship between complexity, arousal, and pleasure. In particular, Berlyne linked Wundt's observations with contemporary neurophysiological research on pleasure. Berlyne proposed how the phenomenal experience of pleasure might be related to arousal and complexity. He distinguished two pleasure-inducing effects: one source of pleasure arises from moderate increases in arousal, while a second source of pleasure arises from inhibition or reduction of arousal from an uncomfortably high level. Together, these sources result in an inverted-U function when hedonic value (pleasure) is plotted against arousal level.

More recent experimental investigations by Vladimir Konečni and his colleagues have tested the common assumption that large-scale formal structures contribute to the aesthetic experience. For example, scrambling the order of variations in JS Bach's *Goldberg Variations* or the sections of a sonata-allegro movement by Mozart does not produce less aesthetically pleasing experiences for listeners (Gotlieb and Konečni 1985; Karno and Konečni 1992). Similarly, Nicholas Cook (1987) carried out an experiment suggesting that beginning and ending in the same key ('tonal closure') fails to evoke a greater sense of completion, coherence or pleasure for passages that are longer than roughly 2 minutes. Where Konečni and Cook have questioned existing ideas about form, other research has identified large-scale structures that occur cross-culturally. For example, Ollen and Huron (2004) carried out an analysis of patterns of musical repetition in music from 50 cultures, and found a cross-cultural preference for early repetition (e.g., AAABAABA rather than ABAABAAA). Huron (2006) noted that this pattern is consistent with the twin goals of pursing increasing predictability while avoiding habituation.

Despite a long history, the experimental tradition in aesthetics has had comparatively little influence among aesthetic philosophers. This is especially true in the case of musical aesthetics, where the influence of empirical approaches has been negligible or irrelevant. Among many music scholars, empirical ideas regarding musical pleasure have been regarded as naive, and indeed, some of the claims justify this wary reception.

Cognitive revolution

In contrast to the limited impact of experimental aesthetics on mainstream musical aesthetics, the cognitive revolution has proved to be an inspiration to a number of aesthetic philosophers (e.g., Raffman 1993; Madell 2002; Butler 2004; Robinson 2005). Before discussing the relationship between cognitive science and aesthetics, it is useful to distinguish two different conceptions of cognitive science.

Prior to the cognitive revolution, Anglo-American psychology was dominated by behaviourism, a perspective that emphasized sensation, motor behaviour, and learning. Influenced by linguistics and computer science, cognitive psychologists juxtaposed themselves against behaviourism by emphasizing the thoughtful and imaginative aspects of mental life. For example, rather than viewing emotions as types of reflexes, cognitive psychologists tended to view emotions as originating in cognitive appraisals (Arnold 1960; Averill 1980). That is, emotions were evoked by conscious or unconscious evaluations that depend on underlying conceptualizations. According to this view, judgement precedes emotion.

Until the mid 1990s, cognitive science was typically regarded as opposed to more biological approaches to understanding the mind. Early cognitive science also excluded or sidelined the role of affect or emotion. However, over the past two decades, the sciences of the mind have been converging into what Joseph LeDoux has referred to as 'the united kingdom of cognition and emotion' (1996, p. 39). Cognitive science has moved away from a strictly cognitivist perspective to embrace insights from ethology, evolutionary psychology, psychophysiology, genetics, biochemistry, and neuroimaging. The cognitive perspective remains an important component of contemporary cognitive science, but it no longer occupies the core to the exclusion of other perspectives. In short, cognitive science has become increasingly less cognitive.

This transformation of the field has repercussions for understanding the cognitive science of aesthetics. We can talk about two schools: the first might be called the 'old school' or *cognitivist* approach, while the second might be called the 'new school' or *cognitive neuroscience* approach. This distinction is important because there are two contrasting aesthetic traditions that both claim to be influenced by cognitive science.

The old school, or cognitivist view, has been especially congenial with Hanslick's formalist aesthetics. The traditional cognitivist view has been that cognitive appraisal precedes emotion: conscious or unconscious evaluation is the immediate source of evoked emotion. This view is consistent with Hanslick's argument that sensations are imaginatively interpreted, and that a contemplative process subsequently leads to possible emotions. Music evokes emotion only after passing through a cognitive/interpretive filter. Musical meaning and aesthetic evaluation precede musical affect.

This cognitivist view has become especially popular in literary aesthetics. British literary scholar Christopher Butler (2004), for example, has applied a cognitivist perspective in his compelling account of the pleasures evoked by narrative. However, such cognitivist approaches appear to be more useful in accounting for literature and representative art than for abstract art or instrumental music. For those art forms in which narrative content is foremost, the evoked pleasures do seem to align well with cognitive–appraisalist conceptions of emotion.

However, the cognitivist conception of emotion has been criticized by both psychologists and philosophers. Experimental studies have provided ample demonstrations that at least some emotions can be evoked without cognitive appraisals (Zajonc 1980; see Cornelius 1996, for review). Criticisms of a purely cognitivist perspective on emotions have been echoed by some music philosophers, notably Malcolm Budd (1985) and Geoffrey Madell (2002).

The existing experimental evidence suggests that emotions can be evoked with or without the involvement of cognitive appraisals. On the one hand, emotions can be evoked through conscious ruminations (as, for example, when jealousy is evoked by interpreting a telephone bill as suggesting that one's spouse has been talking to a former love-interest). However, emotions can also be evoked without the intervention of conscious thought (as in a startle response evoked by the slamming of a door or hearing a tone of voice suggestive of aggression).

Such unconscious/automatic responses can also be observed in behaviours that would normally be regarded as 'higher level' mental processes such as sympathy and empathy. Several philosophers (e.g. Roger Scruton) have argued that responding sympathetically to (say) grief is not the same as feeling grief. However, modern neuroscience appears to contradict this claim. Watching someone cut their finger can generate 'gut feelings' in the viewer that closely mimic the negative feelings experienced by the person whose finger is injured. The discovery of so-called 'mirror' neurons suggests that some complex emotions can be experienced with little or no cognitive mediation (Rizzolatti and Craighero 2004). In short, cognitive neuroscience implies that there exist both cognitive and non-cognitive pathways to the evoking of emotion.

Neo-hedonism

The idea that the principal appeal of art is the evoking of pleasure (hedonism) has not been a popular idea among Western aesthetics philosophers. However, recent cognitive neuroscience has given new life to this old idea. Perhaps the most important achievement of cognitive science has been the discovery that the mind, like the body generally, holds a series of specialized structures (Fodor 1983). A popular metaphor is that the mind is structured like a Swiss army knife. Many of the debates that have preoccupied aesthetics philosophers arise from the empirically incorrect assumption that the mind is unitary and homogeneous (see also Griffiths 1997). Since the mind is capable of propositional thinking, it is easy to suppose therefore that musical experience must arise from propositional thought; since the mind forms associations, musical experience must arise from deciphering associations, and so on.

In modern cognitive neuroscience, such claims are regarded as *cumulative* rather than mutually exclusive. For any given stimulus, the modular mind applies propositional, associational, representational, empathetic, narrative, and other mental processes simultaneously. While the experience of beauty and ugliness can involve cognitive appraisals, not all such experiences *require* cognitive appraisal. In short, the cognitive appraisals of the sort envisioned by Hanslick's followers are sufficient though not necessary conditions for the experience of musical beauty.

Plural pleasures

The idea of concurrent parallel mental processes has transformed our understanding of the phenomenon of pleasure. There are many behaviours that can evoke pleasure, such as scratching an itch, quenching a thirst, solving a puzzle, successfully predicting a future event, feeling virtuous, emptying one's bladder, conversing with a friend, receiving praise, putting cold hands in warm water, and so on. Physiologists have begun to trace the unique neurological pathways associated with different pleasures, from the pleasure of eating chocolate to the 'runner's high'.

Pleasure centres in the brain were discovered accidentally half a century ago by James Olds and Peter Milner (1954). In addition to these neuro-anatomical discoveries, a number of endogenous molecules have been implicated in the experience of pleasure. These include dopamine, oxytocin, serotonin, alpha-, beta-, and gamma-endorphins, alpha-, and beta-neoendorphin, dynorphin A and B, big dynorphin, methionine enkaphalin, leucine enkaphalin, and others (e.g. Pert 1997). Each endogenous molecule evokes a subtly different form of pleasure, and each is released under a number of unique circumstances. For example, oxytocin is released in various interpersonal situations associated with pleasure, including hugging, romantic eye contact, breast feeding, and sex.

In crafting a pleasurable event, people rarely confine themselves to evoking one form of pleasure. The most common pattern of behaviour is to combine several pleasures into a single experience: a person might drink a beer *and* smoke a cigarette *and* converse with friends *and* watch a football game—all at the same time. Current neuroscience indicates that the pleasures evoked by imbibing alcohol, inhaling nicotine, reinforcing social bonds, and prevailing over a perceived enemy have different neurological origins. Yet all may be evoked concurrently in the environment of the sports bar.

A useful metaphor for this hedonic pluralism is the dinner party. You might decide to cook an especially nice meal, but it is unlikely that you will stand alone at the kitchen counter feasting on your carefully prepared Coquille Saint Jacques. Instead, you will probably invite a friend to share in the meal (social pleasure), purchase flowers to embellish the table setting (visual pleasure), light scented candles (olfactory pleasure), put on recorded music (auditory pleasure), and so on. What begins as the crafting of a gustatory pleasure quickly expands into a multifaceted hedonic experience. When given the opportunity, we heap pleasure upon pleasure upon pleasure.

The discovery of multiple pleasure pathways has repercussions for philosophical debates concerning hedonism. Among aesthetic philosophers, the standard rebuttal of hedonism is that it suggests that all pleasurable experiences can be reduced to a single value (see e.g. Kagan 1998).

Hedonism implies that pleasures are interchangeable—implying, for example, that a sexual orgasm is equivalent to so many chocolate cookies. The most common argument against hedonism is that the positive emotions evoked by feeling virtuous are simply incommensurate with a sensory pleasure, such as viewing a flower. Geoffrey Madell summarizes this anti-hedonic argument by noting that the pleasure of listening to good music is phenomenologically different from the pleasure of gorging on junk food (2002 p. 89). However, two discoveries have given new life to the hedonic argument: (1) evolutionary psychologists have offered compelling arguments that all emotions (including jealousy, shame, pride, etc.) are evolutionary adaptations that promote survival and procreation, and (2) neurophysiologists have assembled evidence that the brain contains multiple pleasure systems. The neo-hedonic rejoinder to the classic objection to hedonism is that the biology of pleasure is not unidimensional and has multiple independent sources. Pleasures can be equated only when they engage the same endocrine or neurotransmitter pathways.

If pleasures are multidimensional, it is likely that musically evoked pleasure is itself multifaceted. Consider some of the ways by which sounds are thought to evoke pleasure:

◆ Listeners prefer stereo reproduction over monaural reproduction.

◆ Familiar sounds are preferred over unfamiliar sounds (Meyer 1903; Zajonc1980).

◆ Novelty-seeking is a rewarded behaviour in many circumstances (Berlyne 1971).

◆ Infant-directed singing has many features in common with infant-directed speech and these features are known to be preferred by infants (Unyk *et al.* 1992).

◆ The traditional practice of voice-leading is thought to capitalize on brain rewards for successful parsing of auditory scenes (Huron 2001).

◆ People experience pleasure from displays of extraordinary musical skill or virtuosity (Kubovy 1999).

◆ Experienced listeners regularly take pleasure in recognizing musical quotations or allusions to other works.

- Musically induced 'shivers' or frisson is reported by listeners as distinctly pleasurable (Sloboda 1991; Panksepp 1995; Gabrielsson and Lindstrom 1993; and others). Huron (2006) has suggested how such experiences might evoke pleasure.

- Listeners are consoled by and take pride in music whose style or genre is consistent with a sense of self-identity or social belonging.

This list represents only a partial catalogue of plausible pleasures that might be evoked (in various combinations) by music. As with studies investigating the specific pleasures involved in chocolate consumption or the 'runner's high', it seems likely that future research will trace the particular neurological pathways involved in each of the various forms of musically evoked pleasure. It appears that musical sounds are capable of activating multiple pleasure pathways in the brain. In the manner of the dinner party, musicians can assemble a unique mixture of pleasures into a single musical experience.

Indirect evidence in support of this 'plural pleasures' hypothesis can be found in an experiment by Avram Goldstein (1980). Goldstein exposed listeners to frisson-inducing musical passages and had them rate the pleasantness of the experience. Half of the listeners received an injection of an inert saline solution while the remaining listeners received injections of naloxone, an opiate receptor antagonist. Goldstein's results suggest a reduction in musically induced pleasantness for some of the naloxone-injected listeners compared with the control group. However, the pleasantness of the musical experience was not entirely eliminated, suggesting that musically induced pleasure is not restricted to neural mechanisms that result in the release of endogenous opiates. The implication is that there may be more than one way for music to evoke pleasure.

Evolutionary aesthetics

For Hanslick, the principal problem in musical aesthetics is explaining musical beauty rather than explaining musical feeling. For the psychologist, however, Hanslick's views imply an 'essentialist' conception of music. For Hanslick, the beauty is somehow *in* the music, rather than

evoked *by* the music. For most psychologists, there is nothing in the world that is objectively ugly or beautiful. Humans find darkness threatening and sunshine pleasant, but a bat will have the reverse experience. We enjoy the smell of roses more than the smell of a dead carcass, and are disgusted to discover that our pet dog has the opposite experience. In the words of Donald Symons (1992), 'Beauty is in the adaptations of the beholder.'

Feelings have a deep structure in evolution by natural selection. The feelings evoked on any given occasion can be traced to proximal causes; but the feelings themselves are generated by brain mechanisms that evolved so as to improve the organism's inclusive fitness. We love life and fear death because these feelings contribute to our survival. We fall in love and protect our children because these feelings contribute to reproductive success. According to current orthodoxy in biology and evolutionary psychology, the feelings evoked by art ought to be traceable to one or more underlying evolutionary mechanisms. This logic has led a number of scholars to offer evolutionary accounts of aesthetic experience (see Chapter 1).

Charles Darwin himself launched a history of speculation regarding the possible evolutionary benefits of music and art. In the past half century, new evolutionary aesthetics theories have appeared almost monthly. Evolutionary theories of art are both speculative and controversial. Part of the controversy arises from the ease of 'storytelling'. As Paul Griffiths has noted, 'adaptive hypotheses are too easy to form and too difficult to test' (1997, p. 71). While evolutionary theorizing appears to be an open invitation to unbridled speculation, as Jon Elster has noted, 'The first step toward finding a positive answer is telling a plausible story' (1989, p. 8).

In recent decades, many evolutionary stories regarding art have been proposed. Eibl-Eibesfeldt (1989), for example, has argued that people tend to prefer landscapes that resemble the primordial savanna environments of hominid evolution. Cross-cultural studies suggest that aesthetic preferences favour environmental conditions that have been conducive to survival, not in the contemporary world, but in the Pleistocene world of human evolution. Other theories have been proposed by Ellen Dissanayake (1988),

Nancy Aiken (1998) and others. In the case of music, possible evolutionary origins for music have been discussed by Geoffrey Miller (2000), Ian Cross (2001/2003), David Huron (2001/2003), and Steven Mithen (2006).

Most of the evolutionary accounts that have been offered regarding the origin of music propose a single function (such as sexual selection). This makes sense. If music does indeed have an evolutionary origin, it would have begun by conferring a single pre-eminent adaptive advantage. However, as we have seen above, there is a tendency to amalgamate multiple pleasures into a single human experience. Modern music-making is apt to engage a plethora of pleasure-evoking mechanisms and so it may prove difficult to untangle any presumed original purpose from the agglomerated mix of hedonic mechanisms assembled in modern music-making.

From a life sciences perspective, there are a limited number of stories that can be told that will reconcile art with biology. One story is that music and art might have originated as adaptive pleasures, where the art-related activity increased inclusive fitness in some (non-obvious) way. For example, music might have played an adaptive role through social bonding, sexual selection, or by facilitating language learning. In this case, we would have to conclude that Kant was wrong: aesthetic pleasures are indeed utilitarian. A second alternative story is that music-related behaviours might be non-adaptive forms of pleasure-seeking. Music might simply commandeer a pleasure pathway that is intended to serve some other purpose. In this case, music would be akin to nicotine or heroin addiction: Art is just a fancy way of tickling pleasure mechanisms that exist to reward other behaviors. A third alternative story is that music-related behaviours are biological 'spandrels'. That is, they are incidental artefacts that necessarily accompany other adaptive behaviours. Music might be akin to a benevolent form of sickle-cell anaemia (which is an artifact of a heterozygotic genetic strategy to protect against malaria infection). Music, for example, might simply be a non-functional artefact of brain mechanisms whose purpose is to promote language development.

For many people, none of these ideas is especially appealing. The idea that music is biologically ordained seems far-fetched and problematic. Similarly, the idea that music is a non-adaptive form of pleasure-seeking (like cocaine use) is equally unsavoury. Finally, the idea that music is a physiological accident (like the non-functioning appendix) is anti-climactic. While these ideas invite opinion, the origin or purpose of music is ultimately an empirical question that will be resolved only through future scientific research.

Conclusion

Cognitive science has brought into relief what appears to be a fundamental disagreement between modern psychology and traditional Western aesthetics. The bedrock of conventional Western aesthetics has been the notion, promulgated by Kant, that there are unique aesthetic pleasures that exist aside from utilitarian pleasures. Evolutionary psychologists and biologists argue that the brain mechanisms that generate emotions represent evolved adaptations.

Over the past two decades, a number of aesthetics philosophers have been inspired by the 'old school' cognitive revolution. In particular, early cognitive science lent credence to the contemplative–appraisalist view of musical aesthetics advocated by Hanslick. However, the subsequent development of cognitive science is raising significant challenges for aesthetic philosophy in general. From the perspective of modern cognitive neuroscience, the disembodied, non-utilitarian notion of aesthetic pleasure posited by Kant cannot easily be reconciled with biology (see also Huron 2006).

Over the course of history, many of the problems addressed under the rubric 'philosophy' have been ceded to newly emerging scientific disciplines. Questions formerly considered part of 'natural philosophy' have shifted to the realm of biology and geology. Cosmology was taken over by physics and astronomy, and questions regarding human behaviour passed to the domains of the social and behavioural sciences. If evolutionary psychologists are correct, then questions concerning the experience of beauty and ugliness may soon slip from the grasp of philosophy. Only time will tell whether we are witnessing the passing of the aesthetics baton from philosophy to empirical science.

References

Aitken NE (1998). *The biological origins of art*. Praeger, Westport, CT.

Arnold MB (1960). *Emotion and personality: vol. 1. psychological aspects*. Columbia University Press, New York.

Averill JR (1980). A constructivist view of emotion. In R Plutchik and H Kellerman, eds, *Emotion: theory, research and experience*, Vol. 1, 305–339. Academic Press, New York.

Berlyne DE (1971). *Aesthetics and psychobiology*. Appleton-Century-Crofts, New York.

Budd M (1985). *Music and the emotions: the philosophical theories*. Routledge, London.

Butler C (2004). *Pleasure and the arts: enjoying literature, painting, and music*. Oxford University Press, Oxford.

Cook N (1987). The perception of large-scale tonal closure. *Music Perception*, **5**(2), 197–206.

Cornelius R (1996). *The science of emotion: research and tradition in the psychology of emotion*. Prentice Hall, Upper Saddle River, NJ.

Cross I (2001/2003). Music, cognition, culture, and evolution. Annals of the New York Academy of Sciences, Vol. 930, 28–42. Reprinted in I Peretz and R Zatorre, eds, *The cognitive neuroscience of music*. Oxford University Press, Oxford.

Davies S (1994). *Musical meaning and expression*. Cornell University Press, Ithaca, NY.

Dissanayake E (1988). *What is art for?* University of Washington Press, Seattle, WA.

Eibl-Eibesfeldt I (1989). *Human ethology*. Aldine de Gruyter, Hawthorne, NY

Elster J (1989). *Nuts and bolts for the social sciences*. Cambridge University Press, Cambridge.

Fechner GT (1876). *Vorschule der Ästhetik*. Breitkopf and Härtel, Leipzig.

Fodor JA (1983). *Modularity of mind: an essay on faculty psychology*. MIT Press, Cambridge, MA.

Gabrielsson A and Lindstrom S (1993). On strong experiences of music. *Musikpsychologie: Jahrbuch der Deutschen Gesellschaft für Musikpsychologie*, **10**, 118–139.

Goldstein A (1980). Thrills in response to music and other stimuli. *Physiological Psychology*, **3**, 126–129.

Gotlieb H and Konečni VJ (1985). The effects of instrumentation, playing style, and structure in the Goldberg Variations by Johann Sebastian Bach. *Music Perception*, **3**, 87–102.

Greenwood D (1961). Critical bandwidth and the frequency coordinates of the basilar membrane. *Journal of the Acoustical Society of America*, **33**(4), 1513–1523.

Griffiths PE (1997). *What emotions really are: the problem of psychological categories*. University of Chicago Press, Chicago, IL.

Hanslick E (1854). *Vom Musikalish-Schönen*. Leipzig. Trans. Gustav Cohen as *The beautiful in music*. Bobbs-Merrill Co., New York 1957.

Helmholtz H von (1877). *Die Lehre von den Tonempfindungen als physiologische Grundlage für die Theorie der Musik*. Braunschweig: F. Vieweg. Trans. as *On the sensations of tone as a physiological basis for the theory of music*. P. Smith, New York 1948.

Huron D (2001). Tone and voice: a derivation of the rules of voice-leading from perceptual principles. *Music Perception*, **19**(1), 1–64.

Huron D (2001/2003). Is music an evolutionary adaptation? *Annals of the New York Academy of Sciences*, **930**, 43–61. Reprinted in I Peretz and R Zatorre, eds, *The cognitive neuroscience of music*. Oxford University Press, Oxford.

Huron D (2006). *Sweet anticipation: music and the psychology of expectation*. MIT Press, Cambridge, MA.

Kagan J (1998). *Three seductive ideas*. Harvard University Press, Cambridge, MA.

Karno M and Konečni VJ (1992). The effects of structural interventions in the first movement of Mozart's symphony in G minor K. 550 on aesthetic preference. *Music Perception*, **10**(1), 63–72.

Kivy P (1990). *Music alone: philosophical reflections on the purely musical experience*. Cornell University Press, Ithaca, NY.

Koffka K (1935). *Principles of Gestalt psychology*. Harcourt, Brace, New York.

Kubovy M (1999). On the pleasures of the mind. In D Kahneman, E Diener and N Schwarz, eds, *Well-being: the foundations of hedonic psychology*, 134–154. Russell Sage Foundation, New York.

Langer S (1942). *Philosophy in a new key*. Harvard University Press, Cambridge, MA.

LeDoux J (1996). *The emotional brain: the mysterious underpinnings of emotional life*. Touchstone Books, New York.

Levinson J (1990). *Music, art and metaphysics: essays in philosophical aesthetics*. Cornell University Press, Ithaca, NY.

Levinson J (ed.) (2003). Philosophical aesthetics: an overview. *The Oxford Handbook of Aesthetics*. Oxford University Press, Oxford.

Lundin RW (1947). Toward a cultural theory of consonance. *Journal of Psychology*, **23**, 45–49.

Madell G (2002). *Philosophy, music and emotion*. Edinburgh University Press, Edinburgh.

Meyer M (1903). Experimental studies in the psychology of music. *American Journal of Psychology*, **14**, 456–475.

Miller GF (2000). *The mating mind: how sexual choice shaped the evolution of human nature*. Doubleday, New York.

Mithen S (2006). *The singing Neanderthals: the origins of music, language, mind, and body*. Harvard University Press, Cambridge, MA.

Olds J and Milner P (1954). Positive reinforcement produced by electrical stimulation of the septal area and other regions of the rat brain. *Journal of Comparative and Physiological Psychology*, **47**, 419–428.

Ollen J and Huron D (2004). Listener preferences and early repetition in musical form. In SD Lipscomb, R Ashley, RO Gjerdingen and P Webster, eds, *Proceedings of the 8th International Conference on Music Perception and Cognition*, 405–407. Casual Productions, Evanston, IL.

Panksepp J (1995). The emotional sources of 'chills' induced by music. *Music Perception*, **13**(2), 171–207.

Pert C (1997). *The pleasure molecules*. Scribner, New York.

Plomp R and Levelt WJM (1965). Tonal consonance and critical bandwidth. *Journal of the Acoustical Society of America*, **37**, 548–560.

Raffman D (1993). *Language, music, and mind*. MIT Press, Cambridge, MA.

Rizzolatti G and Craighero L (2004). The mirror neuron system. *Annual Review of Neuroscience*, **27**, 169–192.

Robinson J (2005). *Deeper than reason: emotion and its role in literature, music and art*. Oxford University Press, Oxford.

Scruton R (1997). *The aesthetics of music*. Clarendon Press, Oxford.

Sloboda J (1991). Music structure and emotional response: some empirical findings. *Psychology of Music*, **19**(2), 110–120.

Stumpf C (1883). *Tonpsychologie*. S. Hirzel Verlag, Leipzig.

Symons D (1992). What do men want? *Behavioral and Brain Sciences*, **15**(1), 113–114.

Unyk AM, Trehub SE, Trainor LJ and Schellenberg EG (1992). Lullabies and simplicity: a cross-cultural perspective. *Psychology of Music*, **20**(1), 15–28.

Wilson WR (1975). Unobtrusive induction of positive attitudes. PhD dissertation, University of Michigan.

Wilson WR (1979). Feeling more than we can know: exposure effects without learning. *Journal of Personality and Social Psychology*, **37**, 811–821.

Wundt W (1863). *Vorlesungen über die Menschen- und Tierseele*. L. Voss, Leipzig.

Zajonc R (1980). Feeling and thinking: preferences need no inferences. *American Psychologist*, **35**, 151–175.

CHAPTER 15

Musical preferences

Alexandra Lamont and Alinka Greasley

THIS chapter explores our current understanding of why we like and choose to listen to the music that we do. We begin by carefully defining terms and considering methods, moving on to discuss the biological influences of arousal and other personality traits on music preference, questions of style discrimination, and finally the cultural influences of experience upon preference. The chapter evaluates existing models of music preference and considers further directions and challenges in the field.

Introduction

Liking for music in general is a strong human trait which can be as rewarding as food, sex, or drugs (e.g. Blood and Zatorre 2001; Panksepp and Bernatzky 2002). Certain features of music such as consonance are also liked from early infancy (Trainor and Heinmiller 1998), and these uniquely human preferences for music are not found in primates (Lamont 2005).

Research into liking for different kinds of music reveals a multitude of different concepts, sometimes used interchangeably. Over the last two decades, researchers have generally adopted Price's (1986) definition of preference as choosing or giving advantage to one thing over another. A relatively constant distinction has emerged between the concepts of *taste* (a relatively stable valuing) and *preference* (a shorter-term commitment), occupying opposite ends of a continuum (Abeles and Chung 1996). More recently, definitions of preference have also included specific notions of temporality: 'a person's liking for one piece of music as compared with another at a given point in time', while taste is held to reflect 'the overall patterning of an individual's preferences over longer time periods' (Hargreaves *et al.* 2006, p. 135). In practice, shorter-term experiences of preference inform longer-term judgements of taste and vice versa, in a cycle of reciprocal feedback (Hargreaves *et al.* 2006).

A further implicit distinction exists between research focusing on liking for specific pieces of music and that which explores liking for styles of music. Some theoretical explanations attempt to bring these two dimensions together (for example experimental aesthetics: see North and Hargreaves [2000a]). However, most of the research tends to confound responses to the piece and the style level, or to draw broader conclusions about style preference from research using specific pieces.

This chapter will thus adopt a broad definition of musical preference as referring to the music, whether style or piece, that people like and choose to listen to at any given moment *and* over time, highlighting these important dimensions throughout.

Methods of studying musical preferences

The moment of choice can be measured at a number of levels and using a diversity of measures (see also Abeles and Chung 1996). These measures can take place either in artificial laboratory settings, in more ecologically valid contexts, or somewhere in between (such as imagining a real-life setting and one's likely responses to it in the laboratory).

First, behavioural choices include listeners' psychophysiological responses to a given piece of music, short-term decisions about which piece to listen to, or real-life patterns of engagement with music over longer time spans as shown by concert attendance or music purchasing. Comparisons between two or more musical stimuli can be studied in infants, children and adults using preferential looking/listening paradigms (Trehub 2006) or variations on the Operant Music Listening Recorder (Greer *et al.* 1974; North and Hargreaves 2000b), which measures the amount of time a participant spends listening to different styles of music playing simultaneously through different channels. A further behavioural method involves playing extracts of music to participants and asking for different kinds of behavioural as well as verbal response (e.g. Marshall and Hargreaves 2007).

Secondly, choices can be expressed verbally in either spoken or written form, using rating scales or semantic differentials (either in response to a range of music provided or more abstractly in response to descriptions or names of types or pieces of music), individual preference nominations, or through interviews. The most common verbal report measure is the rating scale, typically requiring individuals to rate their preference for a list of predetermined musical styles on Likert scales. Several music preference scales have been developed, for example Litle and Zuckerman's (1986) Music Preference Scale, consisting of 60 established music categories from the US record industry, or Rentfrow and Gosling's (2003) Short Test of Musical Preferences, although these have not been used systematically throughout the literature. Another popular technique is in-depth interviewing of participants to uncover the richness and complexity of their everyday musical tastes (e.g. DeNora 2000).

The few studies combining different methods (e.g. Hargreaves 1988) show that different measures have different uses: self-report measures (particularly rating scales) are more suited to describing general long-term preferences, while behavioural measures seem more useful in discriminating between examples within a particular style. There thus tends to be a relatively low correlation between results, and verbal measures do not predict behaviour consistently. It is important to consider the choice of methods alongside research questions, and to consider how far methods limit the generalizability of results.

Arousal and biological influences on music listening behaviour

At a biological level, music that we prefer seems to affect us differently. Some physiological responses to familiar and unfamiliar music are similar (e.g. Craig 2005; Lai 2004), but Blood and Zatorre (2001) found that when listeners reported more intense 'chills' or highly pleasurable intense experiences, areas of the brain responsible for reward, emotion and arousal were more strongly activated. One explanation for music preference focuses on the notion of arousal as the underlying motivator for music listening behaviour.

Experimental aesthetics

Berlyne's psychobiological theory (1971), see also Chapter 14 this volume) argues that preference results from the interaction between an individual's level of arousal (held to be relatively stable) and the arousing properties of the music itself (more variable). Researchers have explored the musical characteristics which contribute to its arousal potential, including prototypicality, complexity, familiarity, tempo, and volume (North and Hargreaves 1995a, 1996b; Russell 1986). This research typically presents participants with simple, often artificially contrived and always experimenter-selected, musical stimuli and then measuring their verbal or behavioural preferences (North and Hargreaves 1997a, 2000b). Short-term preference for certain types of unfamiliar music can be consistently related to characteristics of that music. For example, North and Hargreaves (1995a) found a positive linear relationship between liking and familiarity for new age music, and an inverted U-shaped relationship between liking and subjective complexity of the musical examples.

This complements recent neuropsychological evidence about the arousing effects of music on the brain (see Chapter 11 this volume). It also assumes that preference expressed in an experimental setting for a given piece will be reflective of more generalized preference for a given musical style. Using Beatles songs performed in different musical styles, North and Hargreaves (1997b) found style was a more important determinant of liking than song: liking for *Yesterday* in a jazz style, for example, related more to listeners' liking for jazz than to their liking for *Yesterday*. This suggests there is some merit in using pieces as representative of given styles, but most research has not addressed this explicitly.

One strength of this approach in explaining preference is that listeners' individual ratings of familiarity and subjective complexity with the music are assessed within each study, thereby accounting for the effects of prior experience on liking. However, it is limited through the use of pieces of music that are typically and intentionally unfamiliar to the listeners, together with the assumption that preferences for a piece reflect more general durable style preferences. Furthermore, although Berlyne argued that familiarity and exposure should change individual preference, little research has explored changing preferences over time. The effects of repeated exposure have been studied over relatively short time spans, from hours to weeks (e.g. Peretz *et al.* 1998; Hargreaves 1984), yet developmental evidence suggests that stylistic preferences change in response to a complex set of experiential factors over the lifespan (e.g. Hargreaves and North 1999; see also Chapter 22 this volume). It is important not to over-interpret preferences expressed at a given moment in time as being representative of more enduring patterns of taste (see also Lamont and Webb in press).

Individual differences

Research has also explored the notion that different individuals have unique, preferred levels of arousal which explain their global music preferences for style. Temperament differences predict differences in preferential listening behaviour, even at 8 months of age. Trehub *et al.* (2002) found that infants who listened longer to a soothing version of a nursery song were rated by their mothers as calm and easy-going, while those who preferred a playful version of the same song were rated as highly active. Research with adults in this individual differences tradition typically employs established personality measures together with questionnaire-based music preference measures such as Litle and Zuckerman's Music Preferences Scale (1986), looking for correlations between the two.

Factors related to extraversion typically relate to preference for particularly arousing styles of music. For example, sensation seekers with high levels of optimal stimulation prefer more intense and/or complex styles of music like hard rock, soft rock, folk and classical music (Litle and Zuckerman 1986). Preference for highly arousing music such as heavy metal, rock, dance and rap correlates with high levels of resting arousal and sensation-seeking (McNamara and Ballard 1999). Preference for hard rock music is linked to excitement-seeking and extraversion (Pearson and Dollinger 2004), high levels of psychoticism and impulsiveness (Rawlings *et al.* 1995), and a relative dislike of other forms of music (Rawlings and Ciancarelli 1997). Conversely, preferences for 'softer' forms of music are associated with lower levels of psychoticism and extraversion (Rawlings *et al.* 1995). Pearson and Dollinger (2004) found that highly intuitive people showed a greater preference for classical, jazz, soul and folk music.

Some research has attempted to explain the connection between music preference and personality in relation to characteristics of the music rather than style labels. For example, Rentfrow and Gosling (2003) presented data indicating that music preferences can be organized into four independent dimensions:

1 Reflective and complex

2 Intense and rebellious

3 Upbeat and conventional, and

4 Energetic and rhythmic.

They then explored correlations between these dimensions and personality, self-views and cognitive ability ratings, finding a number of significant relationships. For example, people who preferred reflective and complex music also had active imaginations, valued aesthetic experiences, and viewed themselves as intelligent and tolerant; people who preferred upbeat and conventional music were more extrovert, agreeable, conservative, and less open to new experiences. They present a number of associations, some of which appear rather spurious (for example, why should people who like energetic rhythmic music be more likely to eschew conservative ideals?), but which they suggest may in time set the groundwork for a comprehensive theory of music preferences.

Rentfrow and Gosling's (2003) study reflects a comprehensive attempt to analyse the relationship between liking for music and aspects of personality. However, they note carefully that cultural and environmental influences also shape the music that an individual will like. Other personality researchers provide evidence that personality traits and music preferences are linked by a third factor of musical experience. For example, Rawlings and Ciancarelli (1997) found that preferences for popular and rock music, associated with extraversion and less openness to experience, were accompanied by a less intense interest in music and less musical training (see also Pearson and Dollinger 2004). This suggests that the influence of experience on personality and on music preference has yet to be fully explored.

The validity of the rating scale approach which has dominated this research depends on sufficient awareness of the differences between musical styles and style labels. Litle and Zuckerman's (1986) scale included specific stylistic examples for guidance, but both their examples and styles are culturally and historically specific (see Rawlings and Ciancarelli 1997). Rentfrow and Gosling (2003) derived their scale from empirical data about spontaneously nominated categories of liking, rated by judges and compared with industry categorization processes, and finally tested for familiarity: 29 out of 30 participants could provide preference ratings for the 14 items, which they suggest confirms their validity. However, no matter how carefully labels are constructed, the fundamental problem remains that rating scales reflect a reductionist approach. Qualitative approaches show that adults typically report preference for many different styles of music, which they often label idiosyncratically (Greasley and Lamont 2006). This sophistication and level of complexity presents an enduring challenge for the field.

Summary and evaluation of arousal-based explanations

In addition to the issues raised above, both experimental aesthetics and individual differences approaches focus exclusively on the intra-individual level. They thus remain unable to identify the nature of the relationship between

temperament and personality dimensions and musical preferences. For example, personality type may be a direct cause of musical preferences, or, as suggested above, may influence individuals' levels of engagement with music and musical activities which, in turn, affects their musical preferences. To our knowledge, none of the research has yet addressed these interactions. Finally, this emphasis on the intra-individual level neglects the social context in which the music listening is taking place.

Towards a more contextually grounded understanding of musical preferences

Konečni (1982) argued that experimental researchers often treat music as if it existed in a social vacuum, and that it is vital to consider social interactions, emotions, moods, and other environmental factors in order to understand music choices. This raises the necessity of explaining how listening behaviour changes as a function of its immediate social and non-social antecedents, concurrent cognitive activity and resultant emotional states.

More naturalistic research has drawn on real musical stimuli and attempted to simulate real-life situations to account for both the music and the listening context. For example, North and Hargreaves (1996a, b, c, 2000b) investigated the reciprocal relationship between listener and context. Specific musical variables (mostly arousal potential) were manipulated, but the experimental conditions were naturalistic settings such as yoga classes, aerobics classes, and a university cafeteria. Listeners preferred highly arousing music during periods of exercise and arousal-moderating music when relaxing.

However, although causal relationships can be established using experimental methodology, even these more naturalistic investigations appear to be treating the 'social' as an experimental variable. Sloboda (1999) argues that the continuing use of a traditional positivist paradigm (presenting listeners with music chosen by the experimenter, in an environment controlled and constructed by the experimenter) may be responsible for slow progress in the scientific understanding of responses to music. He argues that music listening is 'intensely situational' (p. 355) and thus context becomes central. This has led to another recent shift in approach towards a focus on capturing people's everyday musical practices and preference behaviour in the contexts in which they naturally occur.

Preferred music in everyday life

Studies have begun to investigate people's use of music in everyday contexts (Juslin and Laukka 2004; North et al. 2004; North and Hargreaves 2007; Sloboda et al. 2001). Typically using Experience Sampling Methodology (ESM), participants are contacted (via pagers or mobile telephones) at random intervals during the day and asked to complete response sheets about their music listening. Although these studies predominantly focus on the functions of music in everyday life, the results emphasize the concept of choice. People choose different types of music for different reasons (i.e., they have specific goals and purposes that music engagement fills), and their motivations for music listening are context-dependent. Personal favourites also change over time, and daily favourites reflect situational and emotional 'fit' while long-term favourites are more connected to personal life histories (Lamont and Webb in press). Sloboda et al. (2001) also found that greater personal choice was more likely to be associated with positive valued outcomes such as increased arousal, present-mindedness, and positivity. These findings underline the value of researching people's self-chosen uses of music (see also Chapter 40 this volume).

Reflecting on preferred music

An alternative approach is articulated by research that explores people's own music and the meaning of this to them as individuals, using social constructionist methods such as interviewing and ethnography. From such a perspective, music does not simply act as a stimulus on an individual, but rather its meaning and effects become stabilized through discourse, consumption practice, and patterns of use over time (DeNora 2000).

For example, Batt-Rawden and DeNora (2005) explored the therapeutic uses of music in everyday life using a unique methodology involving both researcher-chosen and participant-chosen music, repeated music listening over long time spans, and repeated in-depth interviews. This study led to a heightened awareness from participants of the ways in which they use music in everyday life (see also Carlton 2006; Sloboda et al. 2001). Greasley and Lamont (2006) also found differences between more and less engaged music listeners in terms of listening behaviour, preferences, and self-awareness. Less musically engaged adults lacked a strong commitment to any musical style, and were more likely to listen to an eclectic mix of music acquired from friends. Conversely, more musically engaged adults showed strong commitments to musical styles and a sense of necessity and urgency about buying or obtaining music. They expressed a detailed awareness of the styles they did and did not like listening to, and a thorough and explicit understanding of the effects that different styles of music would have on them.

Effects of musical preferences

We next consider the impact that musical preferences can have on other areas of life in two ways. The first relates to the use of *any* kind of preferred music to achieve certain non-musical goals. The second relates to the preference for *specific* kinds of music.

Preferred music listening has been shown to be particularly effective in achieving physical and psychophysiological goals, such as pain management and relief. It leads to enhanced control over, and effective distraction from, pain-inducing stimuli under laboratory conditions, when compared with non-preferred or experimenter-selected music (Mitchell et al. 2006; Mitchell and MacDonald 2006). Similar effects in reducing pain, anxiety and agitated behaviour have been found both in clinical settings (MacDonald et al. 2003; Siedliecki and Good 2006; Sung and Chang 2005) and in chronic pain in everyday life settings (Mitchell et al. 2007). Listening to preferred music rather than experimenter-chosen music or silence produces lower heart rate and perceived exertion and fatigue rates (Pothoulaki and Natsume 2006), and improves cognitive performance in driving simulation tasks (Cassidy 2006). Thus listening to preferred music has powerful effects on aspects of behaviour outside voluntary control as well as on mood and affect. In these cases, the nature of the musical stimulus has no bearing whatsoever on the physical and psychological effects.

Other uses of musical preferences are more closely tied to the particular music that an individual or a group shows preference for. During adolescence, musical preferences play an important role in the formation of identity through processes of in-group behaviour and impression management (Finnäs 1989; Tarrant *et al.* 2004). The social identity effect of musical preferences in bringing people together operates even when participants are unaware of precisely what musical preferences the in- and out-groups have (Bagakiannis and Tarrant 2006). Although specific music often has particular effects on different groups, these strong effects are more marked in adolescence; young adults are more willing to share and tolerate others' music, and this tolerance increases later in adulthood (Carlton 2006; Greasley and Lamont 2006). However, even in adulthood, musical preferences can be used in interpersonal perception to give messages about people's personalities (Rentfrow and Gosling 2006). This catalytic or self-directed effect of music in identity can be contrasted with the emblematic outward-directed effect of music, such as anthems, as symbols of national, ethnic, or cultural identity (Hammarlund 1990, cited in Folkestad 2002). In multicultural situations, the kind of music someone likes can play a significant role in the processes of adjustment to a new culture and retaining links to the old (Ilari 2006; O'Hagin and Harnish 2006).

Explaining and predicting music preferences

Although there has been a great deal of research exploring different facets of musical preference and taste, only two explicit models of music preference (LeBlanc 1982; Hargreaves *et al.* 2006) have attempted to tie these together.

LeBlanc's interactive theory of music preference (1982) is a complex and comprehensive attempt to represent the influence of 'input information' (the musical stimulus and the listener's cultural environment) and listener characteristics and behaviour. The approach is useful in formally identifying the large number of types of variables that fall into the three broad categories. For example, the listener's cultural environment includes the variables of media, peer group, family, educators and authority figures, and incidental conditioning. The model traces a trajectory through listener characteristics such as attention and mental processing through to a preference decision at a given moment, which then influences subsequent behaviour (e.g., acceptance and then repetition of the stimulus). While the detail is potentially useful, the fact that every variable potentially interacts with every other means, as LeBlanc concedes, that this is unlikely to serve as a usable predictive model. However, subsequent research has attempted to weight the relative contributions of the various factors, and LeBlanc *et al.* (2000) found that musical features accounted for more variation in children's expressed musical preferences, followed by 'culture' and finally age (see Chapter 22 this volume).

Hargreaves *et al.* (2006) developed a far simpler reciprocal feedback model of musical response, consisting of the interactions between the three broad variables of *music, listener,* and *situations and contexts* to evoke a given *response.* Drawing on experimental aesthetics, musical features include a reference system (genres, styles, etc.), collative variables (complexity, familiarity) and prototypicality. The listener is characterized in terms of individual differences (gender, age, personality) as well as musical knowledge, preference and taste, and identity. The listener's response to the music is also affected by physiological (engagement, arousal, active listening), cognitive (attention, expectation, discrimination) and affective (emotional, mood, liking) factors. Finally, situations and contexts include social and cultural contexts, everyday situations, and the presence or absence of others.

Both models express a tripartite division between music, listener, and context as well as a large number of interactions both between and within levels of analysis. However, culture should not be treated as a variable but rather as the medium through which all real-life experiences are mediated (Cole 1996; Lamont 2006). The models also say little about the outcome of musical preferences. LeBlanc's preference decision leading to rejection or acceptance (in the latter case resulting in freely chosen repetition and heightened attention) is simply linked back to the listener's cultural environment and musical stimulus input. Similarly, the concept of reciprocal feedback simply argues that listener and music, listener and situation, and situation and music 'interact'.

Discussion

Musical preferences serve a range of important functions for individuals and groups, and preferred music can play an important role in physical and psychological well-being. These clearly go beyond the simple behavioural outcome of repeated exposure, and have far-reaching effects ranging from the personal to the cultural.

While experimental research has addressed some important questions in relation to our understanding of musical preferences, there still remain many unanswered issues. The complexities lie largely in the interactive nature of musical preference. Even a single preference expressed at a given moment in time between one of two experimenter-selected pieces of music is likely to be affected by a host of factors, which will vary from individual to individual and may lead to a range of different outcomes. Attempting to isolate and examine these within a positivist approach can be a daunting and potentially fruitless challenge, which may explain why some of the more successful approaches to understanding musical preferences, both experimental and qualitative, appear rather content-free in terms of the *music* that is being preferred.

Furthermore, the complexity and flexibility in the ways that people categorize and label music is a critical issue for the field. As listeners argue about how particular pieces of music, particularly those they like, should be labelled into styles (Greasley and Lamont 2006), research asking participants to tick boxes of music preference categories is not likely to inform us significantly about the underlying meanings of those preferences, except, perhaps, in situations where the 'tick box' approach has validity, such as internet dating, cf. Rentfrow and Gosling

(2006). The particular categories employed are also likely to change rapidly along with changes in musical style (Hargreaves and North 1999), limiting comparability between different studies. An approach that prioritizes listeners' own constructions and interpretations of music circumvents some of these problems, and may prove more fruitful in explaining these less stable elements of musical preferences.

The temporal dimension of preference is another central issue, and while we have highlighted the temporal dimensions of decision-making throughout, it is harder to tease out practical implications for a theory of musical preferences. The two models of music preferences reviewed here adopt very different perspectives on temporality: LeBlanc systematically specifies the precise moment of choice but says less about the longer-term concomitants of that choice, whereas Hargreaves and colleagues attempt to capture longer-term dimensions while remaining vague about the choices which are being represented. A more considered explanation of the temporal dimension (where preferences originate, are shaped, grow, and die down—in essence, how reciprocal feedback actually works) is still required (cf. Lamont 2006).

Finally, adopting a cultural psychological approach of treating culture and context more thoroughly as a medium for musical preferences rather than a variable within a model may have the potential to address some of the unresolved issues in this field. Naturalistic and longitudinal methods of enquiry may be more valuable here. For example, interviewing people at home with their music collections (Greasley and Lamont 2006) enables them to interact with music in a far more contextualized manner, encouraging participants to reflect on the wide range of interacting factors influencing preference (see also Batt-Rawden and DeNora 2005).

To conclude, the privileged position of preferred music in individuals' lives is something that future research needs to be sensitive to. A colleague undergoing chemotherapy told us how she actively decided *not* to bring her favourite music into hospital, despite her specialist's exhortations that it would help alleviate her pain. She was concerned that over time listening to her favourite music in this context would lead to a negative association between the music and the treatment, thus 'spoiling' its potential as a source of pleasure (Chris Banks, personal communication). This kind of real-life engagement with music is not easily explained by inverted U-shapes or artificial distinctions between listener, music and context, yet it is such real-life challenges that future research must find better ways of explaining.

References

Abeles HF and Chung JW (1996). Responses to music. In DA Hodges, ed., *Handbook of music psychology*, 2nd edn, 285–342. IMR Press, San Antonio, TX.

Bakagiannis S and Tarrant M (2006). Can music bring people together? Effects of shared musical preference on intergroup bias in adolescence. *Scandinavian Journal of Psychology*, **47**, 129–136.

Batt-Rawden K and DeNora T (2005). Music and informal learning in everyday life. *Music Education Research*, **7**, 289–304.

Berlyne DE (1971). *Aesthetics and psychobiology*. Appleton-Century-Crofts, New York.

Blood AJ and Zatorre RJ (2001). Intensely pleasureable responses to music correlate with activity in brain regions implicated in reward and emotion. *Proceedings of the National Academy of Sciences*, **98**, 11818–11823.

Carlton L (2006). A qualitative analysis of everyday uses of preferred music across the life span. In M Baroni, AR Addessi, R Caterina and M Costa, eds, *Proceedings of the 9th International Conference on Music Perception and Cognition*, 582–583 University of Bologna, Bologna, Italy.

Cassidy G (2006). The effects of preferred music on driving game performance. In M Baroni, AR Addessi, R Caterina and M Costa, eds, *Proceedings of the 9th International Conference on Music Perception and Cognition*, 584–595 University of Bologna, Bologna, Italy.

Cole M (1996). *Cultural psychology: a once and future discipline*. Harvard University Press, Cambridge, MA.

Craig DG (2005). An exploratory study of physiological changes during 'chills' induced by music. *Musicae Scientiae*, **IX**(2), 273–287.

DeNora T (2000) *Music in everyday life*. Cambridge University Press, Cambridge.

Finnäs L (1989). A comparison between young people's privately and publicly expressed musical preferences. *Psychology of Music*, **17**, 132–145.

Folkestad G (2002). National identity and music. In RAR MacDonald, DJ Hargreaves and DE Miell, eds, *Musical identities*, 151–162. Oxford University Press, Oxford.

Greasley AE and Lamont AM (2006). Music preference in adulthood: why do we like the music we do? In M Baroni, AR Addessi, R Caterina and M Costa, eds, *Proceedings of the 9th International Conference on Music Perception and Cognition*, 960–966. University of Bologna, Bologna, Italy.

Greer RD, Dorow LG and Randall A (1974). Music listening preferences of elementary school children. *Journal of Research in Music Education*, **22**, 284–291.

Hargreaves DJ (1984). The effects of repetition on liking for music. *Journal of Research in Music Education*, **32**, 35–47.

Hargreaves DJ (1988). Verbal and behavioural responses to familiar and unfamiliar music. *Current Psychological Research and Reviews*, **6**, 323–330.

Hargreaves DJ and North AC (1999). Developing concepts of musical style. *Musicae Scientiae*, **III**(2), 193–216.

Hargreaves DJ, North AC and Tarrant M (2006). Musical preference and taste in childhood and adolescence. In GE McPherson, ed., *The child as musician*, 135–154. Oxford University Press, Oxford.

Ilari B (2006). Music and identity of Brazilian Dekasegi children and adults living in Japan. In M Baroni, AR Addessi, R Caterina and M Costa, eds, *Proceedings of the 9th International Conference on Music Perception and Cognition*, 123–130. University of Bologna, Bologna, Italy.

Juslin PN and Laukka P (2004). Expression, perception, and induction of musical emotions: a review and a questionnaire study of everyday listening. *Journal of New Music Research*, **33**, 217–238.

Konečni VJ (1982). Social interaction and music preference. In D Deutsch, ed., *The psychology of music*, 497–516. Academic Press, New York.

Lai H-L (2004). Music preference and relaxation in Taiwanese elderly people. *Geriatric Nursing*, **25**(5), 286–291.

Lamont A (2005). What do monkeys' music choices mean? *Trends in Cognitive Science*, **9**(8), 359–361.

Lamont A (2006). *Review of Musical Communication* (eds Miell, MacDonald and Hargreaves). *Musicae Scientiae*, **10**(2), 278–282.

Lamont A and Webb R (in press). Short- and long-term musical preferences: what makes a favourite piece of music? *Psychology of Music*.

LeBlanc A (1982). An interactive theory of music preference. *Journal of Music Therapy*, IXI(1), 28–45.

LeBlanc A, Jin YC, Chen-Hafteck L, Oliviera ADJ, Oosthuysen S and Tafuri J (2000). Tempo preferences of young listeners in Brazil, China, Italy, South Africa, and the United States. *Bulletin of the Council for Research in Music Education*, **147**, 97–102.

Litle P and Zuckerman M (1986). Sensation-seeking and music preferences. *Personality and Individual Differences*, **7**, 575–578.

MacDonald RAR, Mitchell LA, Dillon T, Serpell MG, Davies JB and Ashley EA (2003). An empirical investigation of the anxiolytic and pain-reducing effects of music. *Psychology of Music*, **31**, 187–203.

Marshall N and Hargreaves DJ (2007). Musical style discrimination in the early years. *Journal of Early Childhood Research*, **5**(1), 35–49.

McNamara L and Ballard ME (1999). Resting arousal, sensation-seeking, and music preference. *Genetic, Social and General Psychology Monographs*, **125**, 229–250.

Mitchell LA and MacDonald RAR (2006). An experimental investigation of the effects of preferred and relaxing music listening on pain perception. *Journal of Music Therapy*, **XLIII**(4), 295–316.

Mitchell LA, MacDonald RAR and Brodie EE (2006). A comparison of the effects of preferred music, arithmetic and humour on cold pressor pain. *European Journal of Pain*, **10**, 343–351.

Mitchell LA, Macdonald RAR, Knussen C and Serpell MG (2007). A survey investigation of the effects of music listening on chronic pain. *Psychology of Music*, **35**(1), 39–59.

North AC and Hargreaves DJ (1995a). Subjective complexity, familiarity, and liking for popular music. *Psychomusicology*, **14**, 77–93.

North AC and Hargreaves DJ (1995b). Eminence in pop music. *Popular Music and Society*, **19**, 41–66.

North AC and Hargreaves DJ (1996a). Situational influences on reported musical preferences. *Psychomusicology*, **15**, 30–45.

North AC and Hargreaves DJ (1996b). The effects of music on responses to a dining area. *Journal of Environmental Psychology*, **16**, 55–64.

North AC and Hargreaves DJ (1996c). Responses to music in aerobic exercise and yogic relaxation classes. *British Journal of Psychology*, **87**, 535–547.

North AC and Hargreaves DJ (1997a). Experimental aesthetics and everyday music listening. In DJ Hargreaves, AC North, eds, *The social psychology of music*, 84–101. Oxford University Press, Oxford.

North AC and Hargreaves DJ (1997b). Liking for musical styles, *Musicae Scientiae*, **I**(1), 109–128.

North AC and Hargreaves DJ (2000a). Collative variables versus prototypicality. *Empirical Studies of the Arts*, **18**, 13–17.

North AC and Hargreaves DJ (2000b). Musical preferences during and after relaxation and exercise. *American Journal of Psychology*, **113**, 43–67.

North AC and Hargreaves DJ (2007). Lifestyle correlates of musical preference: 1. Relationships, living arrangements, beliefs, and crime. *Psychology of Music*, **35**, 58–87.

North AC, Hargreaves DJ and Hargreaves JJ (2004). Uses of music in everyday life. *Music Perception*, **22**, 41–77.

O'Hagin IB and Harnish D (2006). Music as a cultural identity: a case study of Latino musicians negotiating tradition and innovation in northwest Ohio. *International Journal of Music Education*, **24**, 56–70.

Panksepp J and Bernatzky G (2002). Emotional sounds and the brain: the neuro-affective foundations of musical appreciation. *Behavioural Processes*, **60**, 133–155.

Pearson JL and Dollinger SJ (2004). Music preference correlates of Jungian types. *Personality and Individual Differences*, **36**, 1005–1008.

Peretz I, Gaudreau D and Bonnel AM (1998). Exposure effects on music preferences and recognition. *Memory and Cognition*, **26**(5), 884–902.

Pothoulaki M and Natsume M (2006). The effects of preferred music listening in college students and in renal failure patients. In M Baroni, AR Addessi, R Caterina and M Costa, eds, *Proceedings of the 9th International Conference on Music Perception and Cognition*, 586–587 University of Bologna, Bologna, Italy.

Price HE (1986). A proposed glossary for use in affective response. *Journal of Research in Music Education*, **34**, 151–159.

Rawlings D and Ciancarelli V (1997). Music preference and the five-factor model of the NEO Personality Inventory. *Psychology of Music*, **25**, 120–132.

Rawlings D, Hodge M, Sherr D and Dempsey A (1995). Toughmindedness and preference for musical excerpts, categories and triads. *Psychology of Music*, **23**, 63–80.

Rentfrow PJ and Gosling SD (2003). The do re mi's of everyday life: examining the structure and personality correlates of music preferences. *Journal of Personality and Social Psychology*, **84**(6), 1236–1256.

Rentfrow PJ and Gosling SD (2006). Message in a ballad: the role of musical preferences in interpersonal perception. *Psychological Science*, **17**(3), 236–242.

Russell PA (1986). Experimental aesthetics of popular music recordings: pleasingness, familiarity and chart performance. *Psychology of Music*, **14**, 33–43.

Siedliecki SL and Good M (2006). Effect of music on power, pain, depression and disability. *Journal of Advanced Nursing*, **54**(5), 553–562.

Sloboda JA (1999). Everyday uses of music listening: a preliminary study. In SW Yi, ed., *Music, Mind and Science*, 354–369. Western Music Institute, Seoul.

Sloboda JA, O'Neill SA and Ivaldi A (2001). Functions of music in everyday life: an exploratory study using the Experience Sampling Method. *Musicae Scientiae*, **V**, 9–32.

Sung H-C and Chang AM (2005). Use of preferred music to decrease agitated behaviours in older people with dementia: a review of the literature. *Journal of Clinical Nursing*, **14**(9), 1133–1140.

Tarrant M, North AC and Hargreaves DJ (2004). Adolescents' intergroup attributions: a comparison of two social identities. *Journal of Youth and Adolescence*, **33**, 177–185.

Trainor LJ and Heinmiller BM (1998). The development of evaluative responses to music: infants prefer to listen to consonance over dissonance. *Infant Behavior and Development*, **21**, 77–88.

Trehub SE (2006). Infants as musical connoisseurs. In GE McPherson, ed., *The child as musician: a handbook of musical development*, 33–49. Oxford University Press, Oxford.

Trehub SE, Nakata T and Bergeson T (2002). Infants' responsiveness to soothing and playful singing. Paper presented at the International Conference on Infant Studies, Toronto.

PART 4

Music and the brain

Edited by Aniruddh D. Patel

CHAPTER 16

The neurobiological basis of musical expectations

Laurel J. Trainor and Robert J. Zatorre

Introduction

As recently outlined by Huron (2006), we have evolved a brain that rewards accurate prediction. The evolutionary advantages of accurately predicting future events in the world are clear. Over half a century ago, Leonard Meyer (1956) presented his theory that emotional responses to music arise through expectations set up by musical patterns. However, for the most part, music is not about events in the world. What is the link between music and brain mechanisms for prediction? Meyer noted that some chords are more likely to follow other chords in Western musical structure: a melodic fragment sets up expectations for how it will continue. He proposed that low probability realizations give rise to physiological responses, such as changes in heart rate, breathing, and skin responses at an unconscious level, and thus spark emotional responses. Interpretation of the physiological responses in the context of the music gives rise to conscious emotional experience. Meyer proposed that most musical expectations were probably the result of familiarization with a particular musical genre. Indeed, a number of psychological studies have since asked Western listeners to rate their expectations of melodic continuations, and these studies show that people base their expectations on the rules of Western musical theory, whether or not they are explicitly aware of these rules (e.g. Krumhansl 1997; Tillmann *et al.* 2006; Tillmann and

Lebrun-Guillaud 2006; Unyk and Carlson 1987). On the other hand, Eugene Narmour (1990) presented his implication–realization model of musical expectation, which included a substantial set of innate, universal, bottom-up principles that should apply to all musical genres regardless of whether or not the listener is familiar with the genre. In testing people's expectations of various continuations of melodic patterns, Schellenberg (1997) was able to simplify Narmour's principle to two main ones. All else being equal, expect the next note to be proximate in pitch to the preceding note, and expect a reversal in pitch contour after relatively large intervals, but a continuation of pitch contour after relatively small intervals.

Recent neuroscientific work on musical processing is beginning to reveal the brain mechanisms by which expectations are set up and by which musical events are evaluated. In this chapter we will explore how the auditory system processes incoming information and generates perceptual representations that allow it to make predictions about future sound events from past context, and how music appears to make use of this general processing mechanism. We will focus on expectation formation in auditory cortex because this is where the most research has been done, but there is also evidence for prediction mechanisms at subcortical levels and at levels beyond sensory areas. We do not provide a complete review of the literature, but rather present a framework for thinking about the neurological basis of expectation and prediction in musical processing using selected examples.

Physiological measurement of auditory expectations: predicting *what* will happen next

When a neuron depolarizes or fires, the flow of sodium and potassium ions in and out of the cell membrane results in the creation of electrical field potentials. When a large number of neurons whose axons point in the same direction, as between cortical layers, depolarize at the same time, a field potential is created that is large enough to be measured in a non-invasive way using an array of sensors across the scalp. When the electroencephalogram (EEG) is measured in response to an event such as a sound, it is referred to as an event-related potential (ERP). When occasional changes are made to a stream of repetitions of one sound, or when a change is made to a category of sounds, a frontally negative component is superimposed on the ERP wave form (Figure 16.1) that peaks between 150 and 250 ms, depending on the type of change. This component is called the mismatch negativity, or MMN, because it occurs only when there is an occasional mismatch between the expected stimulus and the presented stimulus (Kujala *et al.* 2007; Näätänen *et al.* 2007; Picton *et al.* 2000). MMN is typically measured by subtracting the average response on the frequent standard trials from the average response on deviant trials (the occasional change trials). Although MMN can be influenced by attention, it occurs automatically and cannot be stopped by top-down conscious processing.

In the present context, MMN is of great interest because it reflects a process in the auditory system for predicting future sound events on the basis of the recent past, and the brain's reaction when those predictions are not fulfilled. We propose here that music fundamentally relies on expectation–realization processes, and that these processes are reflected in the MMN, whose main generators are in secondary auditory cortex (Schönwiesner *et al.* 2007). However, it should be kept in mind that there is a frontal contribution to the MMN response, that lower areas of the nervous system also employ expectation mechanisms (e.g., Csépe *et al.* 1989; Kraus *et al.* 1994; Ruusuvirta *et al.* 1995; Sonnadara *et al.* 2006b), and that some later ERP components reflecting conscious processing of music are also sensitive to expectations (e.g., Trainor *et al.* 2002; Desjardins *et al.* 1999).

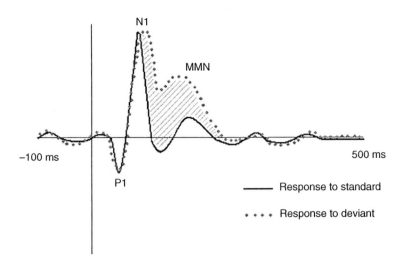

Fig. 16.1 Stylized rendition of the mismatch negativity event-related potential (MMN). Occasional deviants in a repeating stream of standard tones elicit an extra negativity (MMN) in the wave form of the deviants in comparison to standards. Note that negative deflections are depicted in the upwards direction.

Acoustic expectations reflected in the MMN response

Mismatch responses reflect a general mechanism in auditory cortex in that MMN has been measured in response to changes in virtually every basic sound feature. Across these different types of change, the larger the change, the larger and earlier the MMN tends to be, and the more rare the deviant, the larger the MMN. Occasional changes in the frequency or pitch of a tone elicit robust MMN (see below). Changes in timbre also elicit MMN (Tervaniemi *et al.* 1997b; Toiviainen *et al.* 1998), as do changes in duration, whether of a few milliseconds (e.g., Desjardins *et al.* 1999; Trainor *et al.* 2001, 2003a; Uther *et al.* 2003) or hundreds of milliseconds (e.g., Kaukoranta *et al.* 1989; Jaramillo *et al.* 2000). Changes in the spatial location of sounds produce MMN (e.g., Paavilainen *et al.* 1989; Sonnadara *et al.* 2006a). Interestingly, both increases and decreases in intensity elicit MMN (Näätänen *et al.* 1989; Näätänen 1992), and even the omission of an expected sound can elicit MMN (Raij *et al.* 1997; Tervaniemi *et al.* 1994), indicating that MMN is not the result of the recruitment of additional neurons required to process a new stimulus, but rather the reflection of expectation violation processes.

What makes the MMN response so interesting is that it is elicited not only in response to the basic sound features indicated above, but also to changes in more complex stimulus features. For example, a change in speech phoneme category in the presence of multiple exemplars of each category elicits MMN (Kujala *et al.* 2001), as does a change in the order of tones in a pattern (e.g., Tervaniemi *et al.* 1997a). Furthermore, the MMN response is sensitive to complex statistical properties of the input, such as the conjunction of simple features. When a number of standard stimuli are presented that vary in simple features such as frequency, intensity and location, the presentation of a sound with a novel combination of these features elicits MMN (Näätänen and Winkler 1999). MMN is also sensitive to abstract rules governing the conjunction of features. When many standard stimuli are presented that vary in frequency and intensity, but follow the rule that stimuli with higher frequency also tend to be more intense,

MMN is elicited when this rule is violated (e.g., with a high-frequency, low-intensity sound) (Paavilainen *et al.* 2003).

Interestingly, the mismatch response to each sound feature gives rise to a slightly different pattern of electrical activation across the scalp, suggesting that the location of the neurons generating the MMN is in a slightly different place for each feature (e.g., Giard *et al.* 1995). This suggests that there is not one central MMN mechanism that processes all types of expectations but rather that there are many MMN processors, each specialized for a different sound feature. Thus, expectations for future sound events, and the evaluation of the realization of these expectations, is a widespread type of processing that is applied in many different places in auditory cortex. Furthermore, as will be discussed below, there is evidence that more than one MMN process can occur at the same time. In the next section, we focus on MMN studies probing expectancies in musical contexts.

Expectations in musical contexts

Melody, the perceptual grouping of successive pitches into a coherent pattern, is central to musical structure. Although melodies are structured somewhat differently across different musical systems, there are universal features of melodies that probably evolved from basic constraints of the auditory system. One perceptually important feature is the contour, or up/down pattern of pitch changes without regard to the exact size of the pitch changes. Pitch contour is not specific to music as it is also important in the perception of linguistic information, playing a role in intonation, stress and, in the case of tone languages, lexical identity. However, melodies are also processed in terms of the exact size of the pitch intervals between tones, and unlike contour, interval processing does seem to be quite specific to music. In any particular musical system, pitch is not a continuous variable, but rather, only a small number of discrete intervals are used. For example, in the Western tonal musical system, the major scale defines one of the most common set of intervals used for composition. Other musical systems use different interval structures in their scales, but virtually all scales rely on octave equivalence and a small set of tones per octave (Dowling and Harwood 1986).

Melodic expectation arises in several ways. First, with a familiar melody, we can make predictions about the pitch of the next note that is expected based on a long-term memory representation. Second, when we hear music in a particular style, whether familiar or not, we can extract the statistical regularities and make predictions based on those. Third, whether or not a melody is familiar, we can make predictions about next notes that are based on our knowledge of universal melodic features. Fourth, we can use our culture-specific knowledge of what notes are likely to follow other notes in the music style with which we are familiar (Huron 2006; Hannon and Trainor 2007).

How might melodic expectations arise from the cortical system that handles pitch information? In order for expectations to develop, the system must first extract stable representations of the incoming input, and code relevant features in an invariant fashion (Whitfield 1985). The solution to this computational problem seems to lie in the hierarchical arrangement of sensory processing streams, which allow for different levels of abstraction to be computed at each level of processing. In the case of a melody, the interval information must be abstracted from individual tones which may vary in their fundamental frequency from one instance to another. In turn, the pitch of the individual tones must itself be computed in such a way as to achieve perceptual constancy, ignoring irrelevant variation in surface features. Substantial evidence now exists that pitch invariance is computed in an area of belt cortex lateral to primary cortex, in both monkeys (Bendor and Wang 2005), and humans (Zatorre 1988; Johnsrude et al. 2000; Griffiths et al. 1998; Penagos et al. 2004; Krumbholtz et al. 2003). This region then feeds information into more distal portions of the processing stream, both anterior and posterior to the pitch-sensitive region, where melodic features are processed (Zatorre 1985; Zatorre et al. 1994; Patterson et al. 2002). The hierarchy of processing must eventually make contact with long-term memory systems where both implicit knowledge about general patterns, and specific knowledge

about a particular musical piece, are stored. Expectations could thus arise from the interplay between the feedforward sensory abstraction mechanism, and the feedback received from stored internal representations.

MMN responses reflect musical expectations at a number of levels. Violation of both contour and interval expectations set up by a melodic context give rise to MMN, even in non-musicians. Saarinen et al. (1992) presented standard tone pairs where the pitches of the tones varied from trial to trial, but the pitch always rose from the first to the second tone. In deviant tone pairs the pitch fell from the first to second tone. Thus, despite the fact that standards varied in absolute pitch, the auditory cortex generated an expectation for rising contour. Tervaniemi et al. (2001) showed that contour expectations are also generated with a more complex inverted-U-shaped contour. Given that pitch contour is important in both speech and music, it is perhaps not surprising that the brain is set up to automatically predict contour based on current context in musicians and non-musicians alike. However, Trainor et al. (2002) showed that non-musicians also form expectations for particular intervals in the absence of absolute pitch information. Specifically, when presented with a standard 5-note melody that was transposed to different pitch levels (keys) on successive repetitions, occasional changes to the last note that altered the interval size but not contour led to robust MMN. Such mismatch responses are typically larger and earlier in musicians than in non-musicians (Figure 16.2), (Fujioka et al. 2004), indicating either genetic differences between musicians and non-musicians or the plastic effects of musical training. However, at the same time, these results suggest that even in the absence of musical training, auditory cortex automatically encodes music-specific melodic information and creates expectations for future events.

In polyphonic music, two or more melody lines occur at the same time. Fujioka et al. (2005) demonstrated that separate memory traces are formed for each melody, and that predictive processes within each stream can be measured with MMN. On 25 per cent of trials one note was raised by a tone or a semitone in one melody, and on another 25 per cent of trials one tone

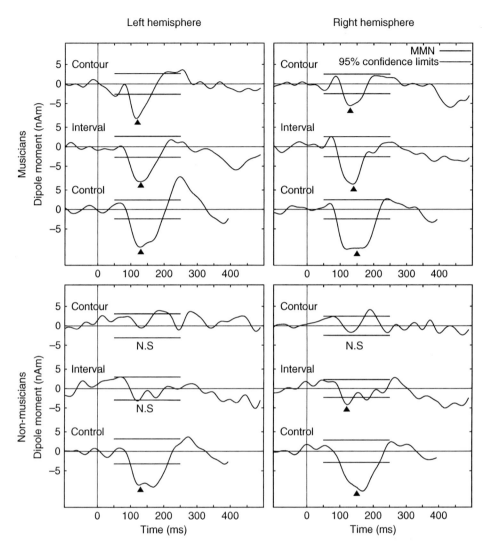

Fig. 16.2 MMN to occasional changes in the contour or interval of a melody. Source space wave forms in auditory cortex from MEG data are shown. Musicians are shown in the upper panel and non-musicians in the lower panel. In both groups, an MMN response can be seen to changes in pitch interval and to changes in pitch contour, but MMN amplitude is much larger in musicians than in non-musicians. MMN is also seen in the control condition where the pitch of a single repeating tone is occasionally changed. However, in the control condition there are no differences between musicians and non-musicians. Reprinted with permission from Fujioka *et al.* (2004).

was lowered by a tone or a semitone in the other melody. Thus, the overall deviance rate was 50 per cent, so if separate streams were not formed, no MMN response would be expected because standard and deviant trials were equally probable. However, significant MMN was found for changes in both melodies, indicating that the two melodies were encoded separately. In the case of two simultaneous melodies, as with single melodies (Fujioka *et al.* 2004), musicians showed more robust MMN responses than non-musicians. Interestingly, for both groups, high and low melodies were not encoded equally well, as MMN was larger for the higher voice, consistent with the compositional practice of putting the melody in the highest voice, and with people's superior perception of the highest voice (Crawley *et al.* 2002). In a follow up study, Fujioka *et al.* (2008) showed that the superiority of the higher voice is a very general phenomenon, also holding in the situation where each of the two voices consists of a single pitch. Finally, across a number of studies, no difference in MMN amplitude or latency was found for changes that went outside the key of a melody compared to changes that remained within the key (Trainor *et al.* 2001; Fujioka *et al.* 2004, 2005), suggesting that some aspects of culture-specific musical structure are processed beyond the auditory areas responsible for MMN generation.

While we have focused on the MMN as a neural correlate of musical expectancy, it is important to note that there are culture-specific aspects of musical expectancy which are processed in brain areas beyond the auditory regions responsible for MMN generation. For example, in Western musical structure chords follow each other according to genre-specific syntactic rules. Koelsch and his colleagues have demonstrated that a syntactically unexpected chord, such as a Neapolitan chord at the end of a cadence where a tonic chord is expected, gives rise to an early right anterior negativity (ERAN) (Koelsch *et al.* 2000; cf. Patel *et al.* 1998). ERAN is similar to MMN, but occurs somewhat later, is sensitive to harmonic expectations (Koelsch *et al.* 2001), and appears to involve inferior frontolateral cortex (Broca's area) (Maess *et al.* 2001). ERAN is also elicited by unexpected modulations in key (Koelsch *et al.* 2003). As with MMN responses to single and polyphonic melodies (Fujioka *et al.* 2004, 2005), ERAN responses to unexpected chords are present in both musicians and nonmusicians, although larger in musicians (Koelsch *et al.* 2002a). Furthermore, ERAN for unexpected chords is present even when other factors such as simple note repetition and degree of dissonance are controlled for (Koelsch *et al.* 2007; Leino *et al.* 2007). Finally, functional magnetic resonance imaging (fMRI) studies reveal that musical syntax activates a network of brain regions that resembles that for linguistic syntax (e.g., Koelsch *et al.* 2002b; cf. Patel 2003), suggesting further that music makes use of general processing properties of the cortex.

In summary, MMN and ERAN responses demonstrate that, for musical input, the brain is continually using the recent past to predict the future, and the magnitude of these responses reflects the degree to which these expectations are not fulfilled. MMN is sensitive to changes in acoustic features and patterns of sounds, and several MMN processes can occur simultaneously. ERAN is sensitive to culture-specific knowledge that is built up through exposure to a particular music system.

The early development of musical expectations in infants

ERP responses to sound are very immature in infancy, reflecting the protracted development of the auditory cortex that extends into the teenage years (Huttenlocher and Dabholkar 1997; Moore 2002; Moore and Guan 2001; Ponton *et al.* 2000; Shahin *et al.* 2004; Trainor *et al.* 2003). Despite this great immaturity, robust mismatch responses can be measured from infants, suggesting that infant MMN is among the first developing cortical responses to sound (Näätänen *et al.* 2007). We argued in the introduction that being able to accurately predict the future is of paramount importance to survival. From this perspective, it makes sense, then, that mismatch responses would be among the earliest cortical responses, as they may be essential for optimal wiring of the brain through experience.

In very young infants, the ERP wave form is dominated by a frontally positive, anterior-negative slow wave. Interestingly, when a repeating sound is changed in pitch (e.g., Leppänen *et al.* 1997), fine temporal structure (e.g., Trainor *et al.* 2003), or vowel category (Dehaene-Lambertz and Baillet 1998), the slow wave increases in positivity (see Figure 16.3). An adult-like MMN emerges around 4 months of age or so in response to sound feature changes (He *et al.* 2007a; Trainor *et al.* 2001, 2003a) (see Figure 16.3). The slow wave and adult-like MMN probably represent different processes as both can be seen in infants of intermediate age (He *et al.* 2007a). Furthermore, the MMN in 4-month-olds increases with larger pitch

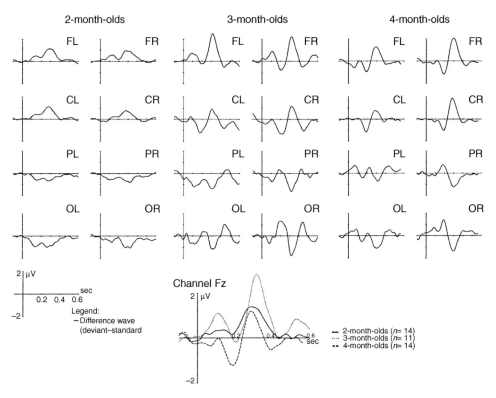

Fig. 16.3 Difference waves (deviant–standard) to occasional half-octave changes in the pitch of a repeating standard tone in 2-month-olds, 3-month-olds and 4-month-olds at different scalp locations: F, frontal; C, central; P, parietal; O, occipital; L, left; R, right. In 2-month-olds, a slow positive difference wave is seen. In 3- and 4-month-olds a faster negative response resembling adult MMN can be seen followed by a positivity resembling P3a in adults. Both components reverse polarity at the back of the head. MMN becomes larger with increasing age. Reprinted with permission from He *et al.* (2007).

changes and remains robust at fast presentation rates, similar to adult MMN (He *et al.* in press).

These mismatch responses allow investigation of the developmental origins of musical expectations. These studies are just beginning. To date, it is clear that a repeating tone of one pitch sets up expectations for future repetitions of that pitch in infants (e.g., Alho *et al.* 1990; Ceponiené *et al.* 2002; He *et al.* 2007a, in press; Leppänen *et al.* 1997; Morr *et al.* 2002). Furthermore, 4-month-olds show robust MMN responses to the pitch of occasional deviants with missing fundamental components, indicating that they integrate the frequency content of complex tones into a single percept (He and

Trainor 2007). Of most interest for musical processing, 4-month-olds also exhibit an MMN response when there is a change in a sequential pitch pattern (He *et al.* 2007b). Specifically, when the order of tones in a repeating two-tone sequence is occasionally reversed, a clear MMN is seen.

In sum, mismatch responses are among the earliest cortical responses to sound. The groundwork has now been established so that future studies can investigate in much more detail how musical expectations develop in the auditory cortex of human infants, and examine questions such as the effects of particular auditory experience on the development of these expectations.

Temporal expectations and auditory–motor interactions: predicting *when* events will occur

As music unfolds over time, the brain extracts rhythmic regularities and sets up expectancies for when events will occur as well as for what the events will be. Time structure in music involves two aspects. First, there is the sequence of sound events and silence durations, which is referred to as the *rhythmic pattern*. Second, when a pattern contains temporal regularities, listeners infer an underlying regular hierarchical beat structure (what you tap your foot to), called the *metrical structure*. Metrical structure is not given in the stimulus, and there may not actually be sound events on some beats; rather, metre is derived by the brain from temporal regularities in the rhythm pattern. Metrical structure is hierarchical, with the strong beats being spaced progressively further apart in time at higher levels of the hierarchy, such that you can clap or tap, for example, on every beat, every second beat, or every fourth beat of a rhythm pattern organized into binary groups. The strong expectancies set up by metrical structure are evident in that the sense of a beat can continue past the end of a piece of music. One plausible theory as to how this happens is that neural circuits in the brain act as oscillators that can adjust their phase and frequency to some extent in response to the input from rhythmic patterns (Large and Jones 1999). Evidence for the neurological instantiation of temporal expectancy comes from studies of the induced gamma band response. Gamma band activity is in the range of 40–80 Hz, and can be extracted from an EEG recording by doing a Fourier analysis. The evoked gamma-band response occurs shortly after the onset of a sound and is tightly time-locked to the sound onset (e.g., Ross *et al.* 2005). The induced gamma-band response, on the other hand, is only loosely time-locked to the sound, and therefore has a different phase on every trial (e.g., Tallon-Baudry *et al.* 1996). The induced gamma-band response appears to reflect processes of intrinsic temporal expectation as it can be measured at points in time where a sound is expected,

even if the sound event is not realized and there is only silence (Snyder and Large 2005). Furthermore, the induced gamma-band response is larger in musicians than in non-musicians, especially for sounds of their instrument of practice, and it also develops to a greater extent over the course of a year in young children taking music lessons compared to children not studying music (Shahin *et al.* 2008).

Temporal expectancies are important both in listening to music and in performing music (Large and Palmer 2002). A number of researchers have noted the close interaction between movement and auditory rhythm (Phillips-Silver and Trainor 2007, 2008; Trainor *et al.* in press; Repp 2005; Todd *et al.* 2007), even in infants (Phillips-Silver and Trainor 2005) and in non-human species (Todd *et al.* 2007). Indeed the close connection between music and dance suggests that musical rhythm might have evolved from rhythmic movement. A number of researchers, working on both speech and music, have postulated that *perception* of timing involves interactions between auditory and motor systems (Hickok and Poeppel 2004; Phillips-Silver and Trainor 2005, 2007, 2008; Repp 2005; Warren *et al.* 2005). This idea is related to research in vision, where similar neural responses exist both to observing an action and to performing the action (Rizzolatti and Craighero 2004).

A number of recent imaging studies dealing with musical perception and production suggest that the two processes may be closely intertwined; for instance, MEG data show that activity in the vicinity of the primary motor cortex could be evoked in pianists when they listened passively to well-known melodies (Haueisen and Knosche 2001). Two other fMRI studies (Bangert *et al.* 2006; Baumann *et al.* 2005) also reported that neural regions overlapped when pianists either listened to music without playing it, or played on a keyboard without any feedback; the overlap included the premotor cortex, supplementary motor area and the posterior auditory cortex. Increased motor excitability in the primary motor cortex of pianists has also been observed as they listened to a known piano piece, compared to a piece they were not trained on (D'Ausilio *et al.* 2006).

The phenomena are not limited to trained musicians, but can also be found amongst non-musicians. For example, a common pattern of EEG activity in auditory and motor areas was found in a task in which non-musicians were trained to play a simple melody on a keyboard (Bangert and Altenmuller 2003). The effect was only apparent when sound–movement mappings were congruent, and not when the learning did not result in a consistent assignment of key-presses to sounds. Similarly Lahav *et al.* (2007) used fMRI to show that premotor cortex and Broca's area were active when non-musicians heard melodies that they had previously learned to play, but not upon hearing equally familiar but motorically untrained melodies. Other studies have also noted premotor cortex activity during music listening under less specific circumstances, such as in melodic discrimination (Brown and Martinez 2007), or while listening to consonant musical excerpts (Koelsch *et al.* 2006). These effects have been interpreted as reflecting possible subvocal rehearsal, a phenomenon also suggested to occur during musical imagery tasks (Zatorre and Halpern 2005). Thus, it is now fairly well established that auditory–motor coactivation can be observed in musicians and in non-musicians, either spontaneously, or more specifically when there is a direct learned mapping between movement and sound.

Of most interest with respect to the involvement of auditory–motor interactions in the prediction of *when* events will happen, is the idea that interactions between posterior auditory cortices and premotor cortices might mediate the cognitive representations that are responsible for integrating feedforward and feedback information during performance and perception (Zatorre *et al.* 2007). Indeed, higher-order temporal organization (metricality) might emerge from the temporal predictions that are enabled by this system. Evidence for this comes from Chen *et al.* (2006) who found that the degree to which auditory input modulates motor behaviour and premotor cortex activity is enhanced by metrical saliency (the intensity of accented beats). In other words, increased predictability of auditory events in music leads to greater auditory–motor interaction. In a related study (Chen *et al.* 2008), a similar region

of premotor cortex was also found to be recruited as subjects reproduced progressively more complex rhythmic movements. These studies manipulated the abstract metrical structure of the rhythms, and therefore the organization of the movement sequences (i.e., their predictability). One hypothesis to account for these results is that what modulates premotor activity in these instances is not the direct mapping of sounds to movements, but rather, the selection of movements based on the auditory cue. The dorsal segment of premotor cortex would, according to this view, be involved in extracting higher-order features of the musical sound, including its rhythmic metrical structure, therefore allowing implementation of temporally organized actions. Listening to music may activate motor programmes directly associated with producing the music, for example when a musician knows the piece he or she is listening to; but perhaps more interesting, listening to music also appears to engage auditory–motor interactions that extract higher-order metrical information. This latter mechanism may be critical in setting up the temporal expectancies that are essential for musical understanding (Huron 2006). As such, the interplay between auditory processing streams and the premotor system could be thought of as the temporal counterpart of the pitch-based expectancies discussed above, which rely on the interplay between auditory and memory systems.

Future directions: understanding the neurobiology behind music expectations and emotional responses

In 1956, Meyer argued convincingly that music induces emotional experiences through physiological responses to musical expectations and the degree to which they are realized. In the present paper, we argue that music makes use of general brain mechanisms devoted to encoding the recent past, predicting the future, and dynamically adjusting the encoding of the recent past when the prediction is not accurate. We suggest, further, that such predictive processes are essential for adaptation, plasticity, and learning, because evaluation of the success of the prediction provides a learning signal by which neural networks can change in order to more accurately and usefully encode the sensory input. We provided extensive physiological evidence from EEG, fMRI and MEG studies that music makes use of these general-purpose mechanisms, and that musical structure constantly engages the brain in a game of prediction. Some aspects of musical prediction, such as using statistical properties of recent input, are probably relatively independent of specific experience with a musical system whereas others, such as predicting the next chord in a sequence, probably rely on experience with a specific musical system. In particular, the framework that we have presented, in which MMN responses to unexpected events occur automatically and without attention, can explain why a note or chord that is musically unexpected continues to evoke an emotional response even when we are familiar with the piece and know at a conscious level that the unexpected chord is coming.

Huron (2006) suggests that not only does the brain make predictions about the future, but that there are intrinsic reward systems for correct prediction. With less expected musical realizations, a physiological arousal occurs, but, after appraisal, it is evident that there are no 'bad' consequences from the poor prediction because music is not about events in the world. So the emotion we feel tends to be strong and positive. To date, there is little physiological data linking violation of musical expectation and emotional responses. However, one study revealed that subjective ratings of tension and emotion, electrodermal activity, and an early negativity in the ERP all increased more for very unexpected than for somewhat unexpected sound events (Steinbeis et al. 2006). It remains for future research, however, to uncover the pathways in the nervous system that link the perception of unexpected events with our emotional responses to them.

Acknowledgments

The writing of this chapter was supported by grants from the Natural Science and Engineering Research Council of Canada and the Canadian Institutes of Health Research.

References

Alho K, Sainio K, Sajaniemi N, Reinikainen K and Näätänen R (1990). Event-related brain potential of human newborns to pitch change of an acoustic stimulus. *Electroencephalography and Clinical Neurophysiology*, 77, 151–155.

Bangert M and Altenmuller EO (2003). Mapping perception to action in piano practice: a longitudinal DC-EEG study. *BMC Neurosci*, 4, 26.

Bangert M, Peschel T, Schlaug G, Rotte M, Drescher D, Hinrichs H et al. (2006). Shared networks for auditory and motor processing in professional pianists: evidence from fMRI conjunction. *Neuroimage*, 30(3), 917–926.

Baumann S, Koeneke S, Meyer M, Lutz K and Jancke L (2005). A network for sensory-motor integration: what happens in the auditory cortex during piano playing without acoustic feedback? *Annals of the New York Academy of Sciences*, 1060, 186–188.

Bendor D and Wang X (2005). The neuronal representation of pitch in primate auditory cortex. Nature, 436(7054), 1161.

Brown S and Martinez MJ (2007). Activation of premotor vocal areas during musical discrimination. Brain and Cognition, 63(1), 59.

Ceponiené R, Kushnerenko E, Fellman V, Renlund M, Suominen K and Näätänen R (2002). Event-related potential features indexing central auditory discrimination by newborns. *Cognitive Brain Research*, 13, 101–113.

Chen J, Penhune V and Zatorre R (2008). Moving in time: brain networks for auditory-motor synchronization are modulated by rhythm complexity and musical training. *Journal of Cognitive Neuroscience*, 20, 226–239.

Chen JL, Zatorre RJ and Penhune VB (2006). Interactions between auditory and dorsal premotor cortex during synchronization to musical rhythms. Neuroimage, 32(4), 1771–1781.

Crawley EJ, Acker-Mills BE, Pastore RE and Weil S (2002). Change detection in multi-voice music: the role of musical structure, musical training, and task demands. *Journal of Experimental Psychology: Human Perception and Performance*, 28, 367–378.

Csépe V, Karmos G and Molnár M (1989). Subcortical evoked potential correlates of early information processing: mismatch negativity in cats. In E Basar, TH Bullock, eds, *Springer series in brain dynamics*, vol. 2, 278–289. Springer Verlag, Berlin.

D'Ausilio A, Altenmuller E, Olivetti Belardinelli M and Lotze M (2006). Cross-modal plasticity of the motor cortex while listening to a rehearsed musical piece. *European Journal of Neuroscience*, 24(3), 955–958.

Dehaene-Lambertz G and Baillet SA (1998). A phonological representation in the infant brain. *NeuroReport*, 9, 1885–1888.

Desjardins RN, Trainor LJ, Hevenor SJ and Polak CP (1999). Using mismatch negativity to measure auditory temporal resolution thresholds. *NeuroReport*, **10**, 2079–2082.

Dowling WJ, Harwood DL (1986). *Music cognition*. Academic Press, Orlando, FL.

Fujioka T, Trainor LJ and Ross B (2008). Simultaneous pitches are encoded separately in auditory cortex: an MMNm study. *NeuroReport*, **19**, 361–366.

Fujioka T, Trainor LJ, Ross B, Kakigi R and Pantev C (2004). Musical training enhances automatic encoding of melodic contour and interval structure. *Journal of Cognitive Neuroscience*, **16**, 1010–1021.

Fujioka T, Trainor LJ, Ross B, Kakigi R and Pantev C (2005). Automatic encoding of polyphonic melodies in musicians and nonmusicians. *Journal of Cognitive Neuroscience*, **17**, 1578–1592.

Giard MH, Lavikainen J, Reinikainen K, Perrin F, Bertrand O, Thévenet M *et al.* (1995). Separate representation of stimulus frequency, intensity, and duration in auditory sensory memory. *Journal of Cognitive Neurosciences*, **7**, 133–143.

Griffiths TD, Buchel C, Frackowiak RS and Patterson RD (1998). Analysis of temporal structure in sound by the human brain. *Nature Neuroscience*, **1**(5), 422–427.

Hannon EE and Trainor LJ (2007). Music acquisition: effects of enculturation and formal training on development. *Trends in Cognitive Sciences*, **11**, 466–472.

Haueisen J and Knosche TR (2001). Involuntary motor activity in pianists evoked by music perception. *Journal of Cognitive Neuroscience*, **13**(6), 786–792.

He C and Trainor LJ (2007). Finding the pitch of the missing fundamental in infants. Presented at the 8th Conference of the Society for Music Perception and Cognition, Montreal, QC, Canada.

He C, Hotson L and Trainor LJ (2007a). Mismatch responses to pitch changes in early infancy. *Journal of Cognitive Neuroscience*, **19**, 878–892.

He C, Hotson L and Trainor LJ (2007b). Changes in melodic pattern perception over the first few months after birth: electrophysiological evidence. Presented at the 8th Conference of the Society for Music Perception and Cognition, Montreal, QC, Canada.

He C, Hotson L and Trainor LJ (in press). Maturation of cortical mismatch responses to occasional pitch change in early infancy: Effects of presentation rate and magnitude of change. *Neuropsycholgia*.

Hickok G and Poeppel D (2004). Dorsal and ventral streams: a framework for understanding aspects of the functional anatomy of language. *Cognition*, **92**(1–2), 67–99.

Huron D (2006). *Sweet anticipation: music and the psychology of expectation*. MIT Press, Cambridge, MA.

Huttenlocher PR and Dabholkar AS (1997). Regional differences in synaptogenesis in human cerebral cortex. *Journal of Comparative Neurology*, **387**, 167–178.

Jaramillo M, Paavilainen P and Näätänen R (2000). Mismatch negativity and behavioural discrimination in humans as a function of the magnitude of change in sound duration. *Neuroscience Letters*, **290**, 101–104.

Johnsrude IS, Penhune VB and Zatorre RJ (2000). Functional specificity in the right human auditory cortex for perceiving pitch direction. *Brain*, **123**, 155–163.

Kaukoranta E, Sams M, Hari R, Hämäläinen M and Näätänen R (1989). Reactions of human auditory cortex to changes in tone duration. *Hearing Research*, **41**, 15–22.

Koelsch S, Fritz T, von Cramon DY, Müller K and Friederici AD (2006). Investigating emotion with music: an fMRI study. *Human Brain Mapping*, **27**(3), 239–250.

Koelsch S, Gunter T, Schröger E and Friederici AD (2003). Processing tonal modulations: an ERP study. *Journal of Cognitive Neuroscience*, **15**, 1149–1159.

Koelsch S, Gunter TC and Friederici AD (2000). Brain indices of music processing: 'nonmusicians' are musical. *Journal of Cognitive Neuroscience*, **13**, 520–541.

Koelsch S, Gunter TC, Schröger E, Tervaniemi M, Sammler D and Friederici A (2001). Differentiating ERAN and MMN: an ERP study. *Neuroreport*, **12**, 1385–1389.

Koelsch S, Gunter TC, Yves D, von Cramon DY, Zysset S, Lohmann G and Friederici AD (2002b). Bach speaks: a cortical 'language-network' serves the processing of music. *Neuroimage*, **17**, 956–966.

Koelsch S, Jentschke S, Sammler D and Mietchen D (2007). Untangling syntactic and sensory processing: an ERP study of music perception. *Psychophysiology*, **44**, 476–490.

Koelsch S, Schmidt B-H and Kansok J (2002a). Effects of musical expertise on the early right anterior negativity: an event-related brain potential study. *Psychophysiology*, **39**, 657–663.

Kraus N, McGee T, Littman T and King C (1994). Nonprimary auditory thalamic representation of acoustic change. *Journal of Neurophysiology*, **72**, 1270–1277.

Krumbholz K, Patterson RD, Seither-Preisler A, Lammertmann C and Lutkenhoner B (2003). Neuromagnetic evidence for a pitch processing center in Heschl's gyrus. Cerebral Cortex, **13**(7), 765–772.

Krumhansl CL (1997). Effects of perceptual organization and musical form on melodic expectancies. In M Leman, ed., *Music, gestalt, and computing: studies in cognitive and systematic musicology*, 294–320. Springer Verlag, Berlin.

Kujala T, Karma K, Ceponiene R, Belitz S, Turkkila P, Tervaniemi M *et al.* (2001). Plastic neural changes and reading improvement caused by audio-visual training in reading-imparied children. *Proceedings of the National Academy of Sciences*, **98**, 10509–10514.

Kujala T, Tervaniemi M and Schröger E (2007). The mismatch negativity in cognitive and clinical neuroscience: theoretical and methodological considerations. *Biological Psychology*, **74**, 1–19.

Lahav A, Saltzman E and Schlaug G (2007). Action representation of sound: audiomotor recognition network while listening to newly acquired actions. *Journal of Neuroscience*, **27**(2), 308–314.

Large EW and Jones MR (1999). The dynamics of attending: how people track time-varying events. *Psychological Review*, **106**, 119–159.

Large EW and Palmer C (2002). Perceiving temporal regularity in music. *Cognitive Science*, **26**, 1–37.

Leino S, Brattico E, Tervaniemi M and Vuust P (2007). Representation of harmony rules in the human brain: further evidence from event-related potentials. *Brain Research*, **1142**, 169–177.

Leppänen PH, Eklund KM and Lyytinen H (1997). Event-related brain potentials to change in rapidly presented acoustic stimuli in newborns. *Developmental Neuropsychology*, **13**, 175–204.

Maess B, Koelsch S, Gunter T and Friederici AD (2001). 'Musical syntax' is processed in the area of Broca: an MEG-study. *Nature Neuroscience*, **4**, 540–545.

Meyer LB (1956). *Emotion and meaning in music*. University of Chicago Press, Chicago, IL.

Moore JK (2002). Maturation of human auditory cortex: implications for speech perception. *The Annals of Otology, Rhinology, and Laryngology*, **111**, 7–10.

Moore JK and Guan YL (2001). Cytoarchitectural and axonal maturation in human auditory cortex. *Journal of the Association for Research on Otolaryngology*, **2**, 297–311.

Morr ML, Shafer VL, Kreuzer JA and Kurtzberg D (2002). Maturation of mismatch negativity in typically developing infants and preschool children. *Ear and Hearing*, **23**, 118–136.

Näätänen R (1992). *Attention and brain function*. Lawrence Erlbaum Associates, Hillsdale, NJ.

Näätänen R and Winkler I (1999). The concept of auditory stimulus representation in neuroscience. *Psychological Bulletin*, **125**, 826–859.

Näätänen R, Paavilainen P, Alho K, Reinikainen K and Sams M (1989). Do event-related potentials reveal the mechanism of the auditory sensory memory in the human brain? *Neuroscience Letters*, **98**, 217–221.

Näätänen R, Paavilainen P, Rinne T and Alho K (2007). The mismatch negativity (MMN) in basic research of central auditory processing: a review. *Clinical Neurophysiology*, **118**, 2544–2590.

Narmour E (1990). *The analysis and cognition of basic melodic structures: the implication-realization model*. University of Chicago Press, Chicago, IL.

Paavilainen P, Degerman A, Takegata R and Winkler I (2003). Spectral and temporal stimulus characteristics in the processing of abstract auditory features. *NeuroReport*, **14**, 715–718.

Paavilainen P, Karlsson M-L, Reinikainen K and Näätänen R (1989). Mismatch negativity to change in the spatial location of an auditory stimulus. *Electroencephalography and Clinical Neurophysiology*, **73**, 129–141.

Patel AD (2003). Language, music, syntax, and the brain. *Nature Neuroscience*, **6**, 674–681.

Patel AD, Gibson E, Ratner J, Besson M and Holcomb P (1998). Processing syntactic relations in language and music: an event-related potential study. *Journal of Cognitive Neuroscience*, **10**, 717–733.

Patterson RD, Uppenkamp S, Johnsrude IS, Griffiths TD (2002). The processing of temporal pitch and melody information in auditory cortex. *Neuron*, **36**, 767–776.

Penagos H, Melcher JR, Oxenham AJ (2004). A neural representation of pitch salience in nonprimary human auditory ortex revealed with functional magnetic resonance imaging. *Journal of Neuroscience*, **24**(30), 6810–6815.

Phillips-Silver J and Trainor LJ (2005). Feeling the beat in music: movement influences rhythm perception in infants. *Science*, **308**, 1430.

Phillips-Silver J and Trainor LJ (2007). Hearing what the body feels: auditory encoding of rhythmic movement. *Cognition*, **105**, 533–546.

Phillips-Silver J and Trainor LJ (2008). Vestibular influence on auditory metrical interpretation. *Brain and Cognition*, **67**, 94–102.

Picton TW, Alain C, Otten L, Ritter W and Achim A (2000). Mismatch negativity: different water in the same river. *Audiology and Neuro Otology*, **5**, 111–139.

Ponton C, Eggermont JJ, Kwong B and Don M (2000). Maturation of human central auditory system activity: evidence from multi-channel evoked potentials. *Clinical Neurophysiology*, **111**, 220–236.

Raij T, McEvoy L, Mäkelä JP and Hari R (1997). Human auditory cortex is activated by omissions of auditory stimuli. *Brain Research*, **745**, 134–143.

Repp BH (2005). Sensorimotor synchronization: a review of the tapping literature. *Psychonomic Bulletin and Review*, **12**, 969–992.

Rizzolatti G and Craighero L (2004). The mirror-neuron system. *Annual Review of Neuroscience*, **27**, 169–192.

Ross B, Herdman AT and Pantev C (2005). Stimulus induced desynchronization of human auditory 40-hz steady-state response. *Journal of Neurophysiology*, **94**, 4082–4093.

Ruusuvirta T, Korhonen T, Penttonen M, Arikoski J and Kivirikko K (1995). Hippocampal event-related potentials to pitch deviances in an auditory oddball situation in the cat: experiment I. *International Journal of Psychophysiology*, **20**, 33–39.

Saarinen J, Paavilainen P, Schröger E, Tervaniemi M and Näätänen R (1992). Representation of abstract stimulus attributes in human brain. *NeuroReport*, **3**, 1149–1151.

Schellenberg EG (1997). Simplifying the implication–realization model of musical expectancy. *Music Perception*, **14**, 295–318.

Schönwiesner M, Novitski N, Pakarinen S, Carlson S and Tervaniemi M (2007). Heschl's gyrus, posterior superior temporal gyrus, and mid-ventrolateral prefrontal cortex have different roles in the activation of acoustic change. *Journal of Neurophysiology*, **97**, 2075–2082.

Shahin A, Roberts LE and Trainor LJ (2004). Enhancement of auditory cortical development by musical experience in children, *NeuroReport*, **15**, 1917–1921.

Shahin A, Roberts LE, Chau W, Trainor LJ and Miller LM (2008). *Musical training leads to the development of timbre-specific gamma band activity. NeuroImage*, **41**, 113–122.

Snyder JS and Large EW (2005). Gamma-band activity reflects the metric structure of rhythmic tone sequences. *Brain Research: Cognitive Brain Research*, **24**, 117–126.

Sonnadara RR, Alain C and Trainor LJ (2006a). Effects of spatial separation and stimulus probability on event-related potentials elicited by occasional changes in sound location. *Brain Research*, **1071**, 175–185.

Sonnadara RR, Alain C and Trainor LJ (2006b). Occasional changes in sound location enhance middle-latency-evoked responses. *Brain Research*, **1076**, 187–196.

Steinbeis N, Koelsch S and Sloboda JA (2006). The role of harmonic expectancy violations in musical emotions: evidence from subjective, physiological, and neural responses. *J Cognitive Neuroscience*, **18**, 1380–1393.

Tallon-Baudry C, Bertrand O, Delpuech C and Pernier J (1996). Stimulus specificity of phase-locked and non-phase-locked 40 Hz visual responses in human. *Journal of Neuroscience*, **16**, 4240–4249.

Tervaniemi M, Ilvonen T, Karma K, Alho K and Näätänen R (1997a). The musical brain: brain waves reveal the neurophysiological basis of musicality. *Neuroscience Letters*, **226**, 1–4.

Tervaniemi M, Rytkönen M, Schröger E, Ilmoniemi RJ and Näätänen R (2001). Superior formation of cortical memory traces for melodic patterns in musicians. *Learning and Memory*, **8**, 295–300.

Tervaniemi M, Saarinen J, Paavilainen P, Danilova N and Näätänen R (1994). Temporal integration of auditory information in sensory memory as reflected by the mismatch negativity. *Biological Psychology*, **38**, 157–167.

Tervaniemi M, Winkler I and Näätänen R (1997b). Pre-attentive categorization of sounds by timbre as revealed by event-related potentials. *NeuroReport*, **8**, 2571–2574.

Tillmann B and Lebrun-Guillaud G (2006). Influence of tonal and temporal expectations on chord processing and on completion judgments of chord sequences. *Psychological Research*, **70**, 345–358.

Tillmann B, Bigand E, Escoffier N and Lalitte P (2006). The influence of musical relatedness on timbre discrimination. *European Journal of Cognitive Psychology*, **18**, 343–358.

Todd NP, Cousins R and Lee CS (2007). The contribution of anthropometric factors to individual differences in the perception of rhythm. *Empirical Music Review*, **2**, 1–13.

Toiviainen P, Tervaniemi M, Louhivuori J, Saher M, Huotilainen M and Näätänen R (1998). Timbre similarity: convergence of neural, behavioral, and computational approaches. *Music Perception*, **16**, 223–241.

Trainor L, McFadden M, Hodgson L, Darragh L, Barlow J, Matsos L *et al.* (2003a). Changes in auditory cortex and the development of mismatch negativity between 2 and 6 months of age. *International Journal of Psychophysiology*, **51**, 5–15.

Trainor LJ, Gao X, Lei J, Lehtovarara K and Harris LR (in press). The primal role of the vestibular system in determining musical rhythm. *Cortex*.

Trainor LJ, McDonald KL and Alain C (2002). Automatic and controlled processing of melodic contour and interval information measured by electrical brain activity. *Journal of Cognitive Neuroscience*, **14**, 430–442.

Trainor LJ, Samuel SS, Galay L, Hevenor SJ, Desjardins RN and Sonnadara R (2001). Measuring temporal resolution in infants using mismatch negativity. *NeuroReport*, **12**, 2443–2448.

Trainor LJ, Shahin A and Roberts LE (2003b). Effects of musical training on auditory cortex in children. In G Avanzini, C Faienze, D Miciacchi, L Lopez and M Majno, eds, *Annals of the New York Academy of Sciences*, **999**, 506–513.

Unyk AJ and Carlson JC (1987). The influence of expectancy on melodic perception. *Psychomusicology*, **7**, 3–23.

Uther M, Jansen DHJ, Huotilainen M, Ilmoniemi RJ and Näätänen R (2003). Mismatch negativity indexes auditory temporal resolution: evidence from event-related potential (ERP) and event-related field (ERF) recordings. *Cognitive Brain Research*, **17**, 685–691.

Warren JE, Wise RJ and Warren JD (2005). Sounds do-able: auditory-motor transformations and the posterior temporal plane. *Trends in Neuroscience*, **28**(12), 636–643.

Whitfield I (1985). The role of auditory cortex in behavior. In A Peters and E Jones, eds, *Cerebral cortex*. Vol. 4, Association and Auditory Cortices, 329–351. Plenum Press, New York.

Zatorre RJ (1985). Discrimination and recognition of tonal melodies after unilateral cerebral excisions. *Neuropsychologia*, **23**, 31–41.

Zatorre RJ (1988). Pitch perception of complex tones and human temporal-lobe function. *Journal of the Acoustical Society of America*, **84**(2), 566–572.

Zatorre RJ and Halpern AR (2005). Mental concerts: Musical imagery and auditory cortex. *Neuron*, **47**, 9–12.

Zatorre RJ, Chen JL and Penhune VB (2007). When the brain plays music: auditory-motor interactions in music perception and production. *Nature Reviews Neuroscience*, **8**(7), 547–558.

Zatorre RJ, Evans AC and Meyer E (1994). Neural mechanisms underlying melodic perception and memory for pitch. *Journal of Neuroscience*, **14**, 1908–1919.

CHAPTER 17

Disorders of musical cognition

Lauren Stewart, Katharina von Kriegstein, Simone Dalla Bella,
Jason D. Warren and Timothy D. Griffiths

Introduction

The study of the neural underpinnings of musical perception and cognition has advanced greatly since Critchley and Henson published their edited volume *Music and the brain* (1977). Technical advances in functional neuroimaging and the development of theoretical models of musical processing (Peretz and Coltheart 2003) have allowed us to gain an understanding how musical processing occurs in the normal human brain. In parallel with this, the development of musical assessment tools such as the Montreal Battery for the Evaluation of Amusia (MBEA) (Peretz 2003) and the use of MRI to precisely define where lesions occur, allow us to determine which parts of these normal networks are critical for individual aspects of musical processing.

Here we present a comprehensive overview of case studies of acquired disorders of musical listening. The precise details of many of these published case studies are given in a previous review of disordered musical listening (Stewart *et al.* 2006). The current chapter draws general principles from those case studies, as well as presenting and commenting on a number of additional cases of disordered musical production.

Acquired deficits in musical listening

The identification of cases of acquired disorders of musical listening based on symptom profiles in individual patients constitutes the traditional 'symptom-led' approach. An alternative approach to the clinical study of musical deficits has been advocated, based on the study of cases selected on the basis of a particular brain lesion, rather than clinical symptoms: the 'lesion-led' approach. Tables 17.1 and 17.2 refer to symptom-led and lesion-led reports respectively. In the discussion that follows, lesion-led cases will be considered as an adjunct to our primary focus on symptomatic disorders of musical listening.

Examination of the individual cases listed in Table 17.1 demonstrates that a deficit in musical listening can arise as a consequence of a central disturbance of auditory processing: of all the musical listening deficits documented, none could be attributed to a peripheral hearing deficit. As Figure 17.1 shows, the brain lesions that produce deficits in musical listening are widely distributed, with a preponderance of locations in the right hemisphere. However, even though right-sided lesions are more commonly associated with deficits in pitch and other domains, left sided lesions can also produce deficits in these aspects of musical listening. The preponderance of right hemispheric lesions associated with musical listening deficits may, at least partially, reflect a sampling bias: individuals with left hemisphere damage are often aphasic and testing of non-linguistic skills is often difficult and rarely a priority. The majority of cases are attributable to cerebrovascular events, though other pathologies such as focal cerebral degeneration ('progressive amusia') are represented

Table 17.1 Acquired symptom-led reports

Brust 1980 (case 2) (1980)	Mendez and Geehan (MS) (1988)
Confavreux et al. (1992)	Murayama et al. (2004)
Di Pietro et al. (2004)	Patel et al. (CN) (1998)
Eustache et al. (cases 1, 2) (1990)	Patel et al. (IR) (1998)
Fries and Swihart (1990)	Peretz et al. (CN) (1994)
Fujii et al. (1990)	Peretz et al. (CN) (1996)
Griffiths et al. (1997)	Peretz et al. (IR) (1997)
Griffiths et al. (2004)	Peretz et al. (IR) (1998)
Griffiths et al. (2006)	Peretz and Gagnon (IR) (1999)
Habib et al. (1995)	Peretz et al. (IR) (2001)
Hattiangadi et al. (2005)	Piccirilli et al. (2000)
Hofman et al. (1993)	Satoh et al. (2005)
Johannes et al. (1998)	Schon et al. (2004)
Johkura et al. (1998)	Spreen et al. (1965)
Kohlmetz et al. (2003)	Tramo et al. (MS) (1990)
Lechevalier et al. (1984)	Tanaka et al. (1987)
Levin and Rose (1979)	Terao et al. (2005)
Mavlov (1980)	Tramo et al. (MS) (2002)
Mazzoni et al. (1993)	Uvstedt (case 9) (1937)
Mazzucchi et al. (1982)	Wilson et al. (2002)

(Confavreux et al. 1992). Because of the nature of these lesions, musical listening disorders are rarely 'pure': over half the cases are associated with disorders of speech perception, and approximately a third of cases with disorders of environmental sound perception. In most cases available data on speech processing are limited, preventing clear comment about the general association of directly related speech deficits (e.g. perceptual dysprosody) or other deficits in the speech domain. There is some evidence to suggest that the earlier stages of an acquired deficit in musical listening (e.g. less than one year after onset) tend to be accompanied by more deficits in listening to other classes of sounds suggesting a disorder in musical listening that can emerge as an isolated deficit following the recovery phase of a more generalized auditory agnosia.

Figure 17.1 shows that many areas are implicated in more than one function. However, it is clear that the necessary bases for music processing are separable: within the domain of music, relatively isolated deficits of pitch (Peretz et al. 1994), temporal (Mavlov 1980), timbral (Kohlmetz et al. 2003), mnemonic (Peretz 1996) and emotional (Griffiths et al. 2004) processing have all described. More fine-grained dissociations also occur: for instance, between pitch interval and pitch contour (Liegeois-Chauvel et al. 1998; Peretz 1990) and between rhythm and metre (Di Pietro et al. 2004; Wilson et al. 2002).

Pitch: interval

Deficits in the analysis of pitch intervals (the detection of a pitch change and/or the discrimination of the direction of a pitch change) are most strongly associated with lesions involving lateral Heschl's Gyrus (HG) and non-primary auditory cortical areas in Planum Temporale (PT) and the parieto-temporal junction (Figure 17.1). The detection of pitch differences and the discrimination of pitch direction are functionally

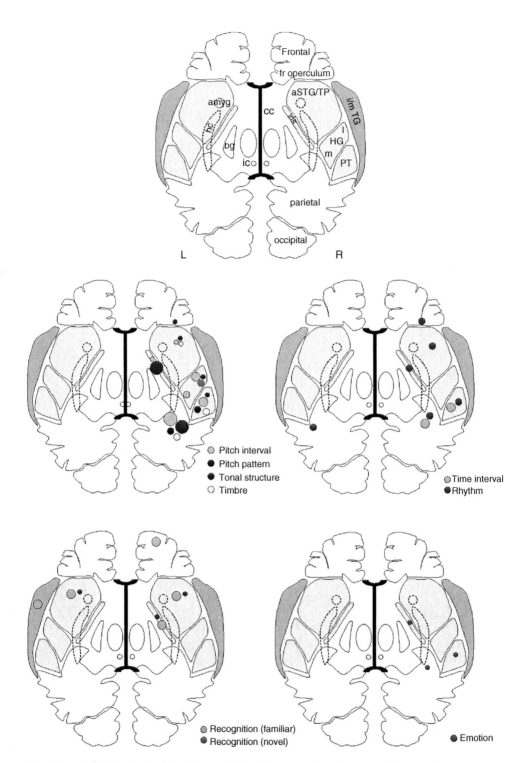

Fig. 17.1 Critical brain substrates for musical listening disorders. This data is based on the symptomatic cases of musical listening disorder (Table 17.1). The detailed analysis of these cases is

separable, but have been distinguished only infrequently in symptom-led studies. Where it has been specifically assessed, impaired pitch-difference detection is generally associated with involvement of subcortical structures and ascending auditory pathways or primary auditory cortex in medial HG (Habib *et al.* 1995, Hattiangadi *et al.* 2005, Terao *et al.* 2006, Tramo *et al.* 2002) while impaired pitch-direction discrimination is generally associated with involvement of lateral HG (Lechevalier *et al.* 1984, Tanaka *et al.* 1987, Terao *et al.* 2005, Tramo *et al.* 2002).

These data are congruent with evidence from temporal lobectomy series (Table 17.2). Right-lateral HG resection leads to deficits in the detection of pitch-change direction in pure tones (Johnsrude *et al.* 2000) and complex tones (Zatorre 1988) These findings, especially the latter, suggest that aspects of pitch perception, as opposed to the sensory representation of frequency- and time- domain properties of the stimulus, depend on the integrity of cortical areas beyond primary auditory cortex.

Pitch: pattern

Deficits in the analysis of pitch patterns, such as melodies, are common in acquired disorders of musical listening (Table 17.1). The deficits are most often associated with lesions posterior to HG, in PT and the parieto-temporal junction, and anterior to HG in anterior superior temporal gyrus (STG) (Figure 17.1). These lesions are more common on the right. Melody discrimination has also been widely assessed in the lesion-led literature (Table 17.2): right but not left temporal lobectomy impairs discrimination of pitch pattern, even where HG is not included (Milner 1962). However, inclusion of HG produces deficits in melody perception over and above those due to the resection of the temporal lobe anterior to it (Samson and Zatorre 1988, Zatorre 1985). In a study comparing resections involving posterior versus anterior STG (Liegeois-Chauvel *et al.* 1998), posterior resection was associated with more severe impairment of pitch pattern perception; this effect could not be attributed to involvement of HG. Right anterior temporal lobe resections have also been associated with impaired working memory for pitch (Zatorre and Samson 1991) which is likely to affect perception of long-term structure in melodies, and more specifically, discrimination tasks requiring comparisons between sequential stimuli.

Pitch contour (the pattern of 'ups' and 'downs' in a melody) and the associated absolute pitch values can be considered as corresponding to psychologically distinct 'global' and 'local' levels of pitch processing, respectively (Dowling and Harwood 1985). These levels can be probed by tasks which require discrimination of melodies with different pitch contour ('global' tasks) or different absolute pitch values with the same contour ('local' tasks), respectively. A 'pure' global task would require transposition

presented in supplementary Table 1 of Stewart *et al.* (2006). Five cartoons are shown, each depicting the brain in a schematic axial section that includes all key anatomical areas involved in music listening (identified on the top cartoon); the corpus callosum (black), superior temporal plane (light grey) and middle/inferior temporal gyri (dark grey areas, in exploded view) are coloured for ease of identification. Musical functions have been grouped as follows: pitch processing (pitch interval, pitch pattern, tonal structure, timbre); temporal processing (time interval, rhythm); musical memory (familiar and novel material); and emotional response to music. Each group of functions is assigned to a separate cartoon; individual functions are identified to the right of the corresponding cartoon. Raw data from Stewart *et al.* (2006) have been thresholded; the presence of a coloured circle corresponding to a particular function in a region indicates that at least 50 per cent of studies of the function implicate that region. The size of each circle is scaled according to the proportion of studies of the function implicating that region. Metre is not represented as no brain area was implicated in 50 per cent or more of cases. amyg, amygdala; aSTG, anterior superior temporal gyrus; bg, basal ganglia; cc, corpus callosum; fr, frontal; hc hippocampus; HG, Heschl's gyrus; i, inferior; ic, inferior colliculi; ins, insula; l, lateral; m, medial; PT, planum temporale; TG, temporal gyrus. See colour plate section. This figure is taken from Stewart L, Von Kriegstein K, Warren JD and Griffiths TD. Disorders of musical listening. *Brain* 2006, 129, 2533–2553, by permission of Oxford University Press.

Table 17.2 Acquired lesion-led reports

Resection cases	Stroke/other type of lesion
Gosselin et al. (2005)	Alcock et al. (2000)
Johnsrude et al. (2000)	Ayotte et al. (2000)
Kester et al. (1991)	Grossman et al. (1981)
Liegeois-Chauvel et al. (1998)	Kinsella et al. (1988)
Milner (1962)	Peretz (1990)
Samson and Zatorre (1988)	Prior et al. (1990)
Samson and Zatorre (1991)	Robin et al. (1990)
Samson and Zatorre (1992)	Samson et al. (2001)
Samson and Zatorre (1994)	Schuppert et al. (2000)
Samson et al. (2001)	Shapiro et al. (1981)
Samson et al. (2002)	Sidtis and Volpe (1988)
Shankweiler (1966)	Tramo and Bharucha (1991)
Warrier and Zatorre (2004)	
Zatorre (1985)	
Zatorre (1988)	
Zatorre and Halpern (1993)	
Zatorre and Samson (1991)	

between the melodies compared (like a shift in key) to prevent the use of any local information. However, this renders the task much harder for non-musicians and the MBEA does not employ it. Peretz (1990) showed that patients with right cerebral hemisphere strokes could process neither global nor local information in melodies, while patients with strokes involving the left hemisphere could process global but not local information. Isolated impairments of local processing were observed, but isolated impairments of global processing were not, leading Peretz to propose an influential hierarchical model of co-operation between the hemispheres. According to this model, the right hemisphere derives pitch contour which is then elaborated upon by the left hemisphere which fills in the detailed pitch structure. In the model, prior contour processing is necessary for absolute pitch values to be processed: lesions involving the right hemisphere therefore compromize the processing of both contour and the absolute values of pitch whereas lesions involving the left hemisphere prevent absolute pitch values being added to the contour provided by the right

hemisphere. This model was supported by the findings of a temporal lobectomy series (Liegeois-Chauvel et al. 1998). However, other neuropsychological and functional imaging evidence suggests that hemispheric differences are less clearcut (Schuppert et al. 2000, Stewart et al. 2008).

Pitch: tonal structure

Tonal structure refers to rule-based patterns of pitch determined by key. While both tonal and atonal pitch patterns exhibit global and local structure, tonal structure is specific to tonal music (i.e., most Western music composed before the twentieth century). The most widely used test of this type of processing is the key violation task in the MBEA, which assesses the ability of subjects to detect notes that are out of key. Deficits in tonal analysis have been associated with damage involving a predominantly right-sided network of non-primary auditory cortical areas including lateral HG, PT, parieto-temporal junction, insula, anterior STG and frontal operculum (Figure 17.1). The frontal opercular involvement is proportionately greater relative to its involvement in other aspects of pitch processing, but the number of studies is small.

Timbre

Timbral perception has a number of dimensions that can be related to different acoustic properties of the incoming sound, and lesions affecting any or all of these dimensions could in principle lead to a deficit of timbre perception. Many clinical studies include reports of perceptual alterations in the perceived quality of music (often described as unpleasant, 'flat' or 'mechanical' in nature) or inability to recognize musical instruments, which might represent specific deficits of timbre perception. However, timbre as a distinct functional component of music has only been assessed infrequently in the clinical literature. This evidence suggests that a network of areas in the right superior temporal lobe that overlaps closely with areas implicated in pitch-pattern analysis is critical for normal timbre perception (Figure 17.1). Timbral deficits have generally been observed in conjunction with pitch-pattern deficits, however timbral deficits with spared pitch-pattern perception have also been described after strokes involving right STG (Kohlmetz et al. 2003, Mazzucchi et al. 1982). The deficits may extend to the discrimination of timbre in voices and environmental sounds (Mazzucchi et al. 1982).

These findings from the symptom-led literature are mirrored by studies of temporal lobectomy series (Table 17.2). Right temporal lobectomy leads to deficits in the perception of timbral change when this is in the spectral dimension (Milner 1962, Samson and Zatorre 1994), temporal dimension (Samson and Zatorre 1994), or both (Samson et al. 2002). This last study also suggested a subtle effect of left temporal lobectomy deficit on the processing of timbre associated with melodies but not single notes.

Temporal structure: time interval, rhythm and metre

Like pitch perception, the perception of timing information in music can be analysed hierarchically: the lowest level of temporal processing that we consider here corresponds to the detection of simple durational differences in a tone or detection of a silent interval between two tones. These basic timing elements can be built into more complex structures embedded in metre and rhythm. Schuppert and colleagues (2000) propose a hierarchal scheme where metre and rhythm can be considered as global and local properties in the time domain. The symptom-led evidence implicates predominantly right-sided non-primary auditory cortical areas posterior to HG in the perception of time-interval differences, and bilateral areas widely distributed beyond HG in the perception of rhythm (Figure 17.1). Evidence from lesion-led studies broadly supports a bilateral organization: impaired durational processing has been described following right temporal lobectomy (Milner 1962) and impaired gap detection following left temporo-parietal strokes (Robin et al. 1990). Impaired detection of rhythmic violations has been described in left temporo-parietal stroke (Robin et al. 1990) and left hippocampal sclerosis (Samson et al. 2001), while other studies have not demonstrated laterality differences (Peretz, 1990, Schuppert et al. 2000, Shapiro et al. 1981). At least some of these apparent discrepancies in lateralization may reflect task effects: for example, the detection of rhythmic errors in familiar tunes (Prior et al. 1990, Samson et al. 2001) may require musical processing that is not required for the discrimination of simple rhythmic patterns.

Comparatively few studies of metrical processing have been conducted and evidence for a critical brain substrate remains inconclusive. This is likely to be due at least in part to the difficulty of assessing metre reliably, particularly in subjects without formal musical training. In the small symptom-led literature, impairments of metre perception have been associated with individual lesions widely distributed in both cerebral hemispheres. This pattern has been echoed in lesion-led studies. In temporal lobectomy series, Liegeois-Chauvel et al. (1998) found metrical impairments following left and right anterior temporal lobe resections, while Kester et al. (1991) found a specific decrement in performance following right but not left anterior temporal resection. Ayotte et al. (2000) and Peretz et al. (1990) both found that stroke patients with heterogeneous left and right hemisphere strokes were not impaired relative to neurologically normal control subjects, while Schuppert *et al.* (2000) found that both left and right hemispheric stroke patients were impaired relative to controls.

Memory: familiar and novel material

Impaired recognition of familiar tunes is described in a number of studies (Ayotte *et al.* 2000, Griffiths *et al.* 1997, Johannes *et al.* 1998, Lechevalier *et al.* 1984, Peretz *et al.* 1998, Peretz and Gagnon 1999, Peretz *et al.* 1994, Piccirilli *et al.* 2000, Satoh *et al.* 2005, Wilson *et al.* 2002). In all these cases, recognition problems were accompanied by impaired pitch-pattern perception. However, perception and recognition can sometimes dissociate. Patients may have intact perception but impaired recognition (Eustache *et al.* 1990 (case 1), Peretz 1996) or the converse (Eustache *et al.* 1990 (case 2); Schuppert *et al.* 2000).

Figures 17.1 demonstrates that deficits in the perception and recognition of familiar tunes may occur with damage in either cerebral hemisphere involving the anterior STG and insula (Lechevalier *et al.* 1984, Peretz *et al.* 1998, Peretz and Gagnon 1999, Peretz *et al.* 1994, Satoh *et al.* 2005). In the lesion-led literature, familiar-tune recognition was found to be deficient specifically in association with damage involving the right insula (Ayotte *et al.* 2000).

Impaired recognition of novel material is tested in the incidental memory test from the MBEA, which assesses implicit encoding and retrieval of novel musical material. Clinical impairments of musical incidental memory are associated with damage involving a bilateral network of areas that closely overlaps the network implicated in the recognition of familiar tunes (Figure 17.1), and extends into left middle and inferior temporal cortex. In temporal lobectomy series, incidental memory deficits have been described following both right and left anterior resections (Samson and Zatorre 1992, Zatorre 1985).

Emotion

Most people listen to music purely for the aesthetic pleasure it brings. A loss of enjoyment in musical listening is a common presenting complaint in clinical disorders of musical listening. In many cases, this loss of pleasure is accompanied by a perceptual derangement: 'like an out of tune child's dulcimer', (Griffiths *et al.* 1997), 'mechanical' (Griffiths *et al.* 2006), or 'instruments [may lose] their distinctive features of timbre and sound dull' (Piccirilli *et al.* 2000). Associated impairments of pitch-pattern perception (Habib *et al.* 1995) and generalized auditory agnosia (Mazzucchi *et al.* 1982) have been documented. The most consistent association of altered emotional response to music across studies is damage involving the right posterior temporal lobe and insula (Figure 17.1). However, few clinical studies have specifically assessed musical emotion.

Just as perception and recognition for musical material may dissociate, so too may perception and emotional response to music. Isolated deficits of musical emotional response have been described: the patient of Griffiths *et al.* (2004) had been used to experiencing an emotional transformation while listening to Rachmaninov preludes (the 'shiver down the spine' phenomenon) but this was lost following an infarction involving left amygdala and insula. In a temporal lobectomy series (Gosselin *et al.* 2005), patients who had undergone resections of the left or right medial temporal lobe, including the amygdala but sparing the STG, found fearful music less scary than a group of matched controls. Conversely, intact emotional response despite impaired music perception has also been observed (Lechevalier *et al.* 1984, Peretz *et al.* 1998, Peretz and Gagnon 1999). The patient of Peretz *et al.* (1998) still derived pleasure from music, and was able to classify tunes as happy or sad and to discriminate tunes based on emotional tone despite severe perceptual and recognition impairments.

Developmental deficits in musical listening

Case reports of lifelong tone deafness go back more than a century (Grant-Allen 1898), but it has only been in the last five years that the condition has undergone systematic investigation using the same tools that have been applied to acquired disorders of musical listening. The disorder was first characterized in this way by Peretz and colleagues using the MBEA and given the label 'congenital amusia' (Ayotte *et al.* 2002). This is not the same as what is commonly known as 'tone-deafness', a term which many people apply to themselves, mostly based on the belief that they cannot sing in tune (Sloboda *et al.* 2005, Cuddy *et al.* 2005). Infact, given normal brain development and opportunities for informal singing, the majority of the population can sing in tune (but see Bradshaw and McHenry 2005, Dalla Bella *et al.* 2007 for evidence that singing output may be impaired despite normal perception). Those with congenital amusia, on the other hand, cannot sing in tune, but this is likely to be a consequence of them having a true perceptual agnosia, in which the perception of music is abnormal in the presence of normal hearing and otherwise preserved cognition.

Pitch

Formal characterization of musical perception using the MBEA (Ayotte *et al.* 2002) demonstrates consistent deficits in the domain of pitch-pattern perception (pitch contour, absolute pitch value and key structure). Foxton *et al.* (2004) carried out tests in which types of pitch pattern that are more basic than melody are assessed. The group of subjects identified as having amusia using the MBEA were found to have abnormal perception of pitch change and pitch direction, the most striking changes being demonstrated for pitch direction. Most subjects in the amusic group had thresholds for the identification of pitch direction that were well above a semitone and likely relevant to the perception of Western music. This finding has been recently replicated in an independent group of amusic individuals (Griffiths *et al.* 2007). Given that pitch direction can be thought of as a 'building block' for contour (the pattern of 'ups' and 'downs' in a melody), this work suggests a fundamental deficit in pitch processing that is below the level of melody processing. However, the presence of such a causative deficit would predict that the deficit could be overcome by creating melodic sequences with large intervals. The fact that this is not the case (Foxton *et al.* 2004) argues against a simple low-level deficit in

pitch direction as a single causal mechanism for melodic deficits in amusia. However, it remains possible that an inability to analyse pitch direction leads to a failure to develop normal pitch-pattern perception.

Temporal structure

Subjects who have been recruited on the basis of lifelong musical difficulty and score below threshold on the pitch subtests of the MBEA may also have problems with 'following the beat' and with dancing, consistent with a deficit in the analysis of metre and rhythm. Hyde and Peretz (2003) found that although subjects with congenital amusia had a deficit in detection of pitch changes in an otherwise monotonic sequence, their detection of a change in the timing of a note in an otherwise regular sequence was normal. A subsequent study in a different group of amusics (Foxton *et al.* 2006) replicated the finding of normal detection of timing deviation within simple rhythms, but showed that when subjects were required to detect the same deviation in a melodic, as opposed to monotonic context, their performance was impaired. The results support a model in which the abnormal perception of pitch pattern in amusia also affects the perception of the temporal structure of music. It is also worth noting that the amusic individuals so far studied have been recruited using adverts that conceptualize musical difficulties in terms of tune rather than time. In contrast, a large number of individuals screened using an internet version of the scale and rhythm subtest of the MBEA (www.delosis.com/listening/home.html) suggest that certain individuals have specific difficulties with time, but not tune (unpublished observations). This is a potentially novel subtype of amusia with a distinct cognitive and neural basis.

Emotion

A recent questionnaire-based study (McDonald and Stewart 2008) shows that, as a group, those with developmental amusia do not implement music in their everyday lives in the same way as age, gender and training matched controls. They regard the presence of music in public places more negatively than controls and report significantly fewer emotional responses to music. However, there is considerable individual variation with respect to this. For instance, some amusics report enjoyment of music while others find it unpleasant. The dissociation between the perception of music and its self-reported emotional effects is consistent with evidence from normal functional imaging and clinical studies of acquired lesions that suggest distinct substrates for perception and appreciation but the reasons for such variability are presently unknown.

Neural substrate

The brain basis for congenital amusia has not been extensively investigated. These individuals do not have a history of neurological damage, and structural brain imaging using MRI reveals no gross structural differences. The technique of voxel-based morphometry allows structural MRI data from two or more groups of individuals (e.g. amusic versus non-amusic individuals) to be interrogated with regard to potential regional differences in grey and white matter density. Recent studies have demonstrated structural differences in the inferior frontal lobe and temporal cortex (Hyde *et al.* 2005, 2007; Mandell *et al.* 2007) and EEG studies of responses to pitch changes have demonstrated normal N1 responses to tones but abnormal N2-P3 responses at longer latency (Peretz *et al.* 2005). The N1 response arises from the PT whilst the longer latency responses have a number of more distributed generators. Congruent with the work based on structural MRI, this work suggests brain abnormalities in amusia that may occur in areas quite distinct from auditory cortex. Further studies will be required to ascertain the locus and nature of the abnormality in these developmental cases.

Acquired disorders of musical production

Music production deficits such as impaired singing (vocal amusia or oral-expressive amusia), or deficient music performance on an instrument (expressive instrumental amusia or musical apraxia) have been generally referred to as 'expressive amusia' (Benton 1977). Although cases of

musical production deficits have been described since the nineteenth century (reviewed in Benton 1977), there is a paucity of studies of instrumental amusia (Botez and Wertheim 1959; McFarland and Fortin 1982). For this reason, the following discussion will focus on acquired deficits in singing.

Impaired vocal performance (e.g., poor singing of well-known songs) consequent to brain damage has been documented in skilled professional singers and in nonmusicians (for reviews, see Ackermann *et al.* 2007; Gordon *et al.* 2006; Marin and Perry 1999). Early case reports indicate that lesions of the right-hemisphere fronto-insular cortex disrupt the ability to sing, hum or whistle a tune (Mann 1898, 1933; Jossmann 1926, 1927, cited in Benton 1977; Botez and Wertheim 1959). For example, Mann (1898 cited in Benton 1977) reported impaired abilities to sing and whistle songs in a professional singer following injury of the right frontal lobe. Despite the dramatic vocal expression disorder, the patient was still able to recognize familiar songs and did not show any signs of aphasia. Similar cases of musicians exhibiting poor singing in absence of language disorders and with relatively spared music perception and recognition were reported by Jossmann (1926, 1927) and Botez and Wertheim (1959). These findings are consistent with the observation that unilateral inactivation of the right hemisphere (i.e., with the Wada test, see Gordon and Bogen 1974) alter the ability to sing, hum or whistle a tune. Unfortunately, however, most of these case descriptions are anecdotal, thus lacking systematic assessment of music production and perception abilities.

More systematic studies of singing deficits (both symptom-led and lesion-led) are included in Tables 17.1 and 17.2. Confavreux *et al.* (1992) report on a patient who suffered focal cerebral degeneration of right-hemisphere regions involving the anterior temporal gyrus and the insula. Music perception abilities were relatively preserved in the presence of impaired singing and expressive aprosody in speech. More recently, Schön and collaborators (2004) presented the case of IP, a tenor singer with right hemisphere lesions distributed in the inferior frontal gyrus, posterior temporal lobe and inferior parietal lobe. IP is a pure case of vocal amusia exhibiting a specific deficit of in the production of musical intervals. In contrast, production of rhythm and contour were spared, as was musical perception and language abilities. In order to examine the role of the right and left hemispheres in pitch and rhythm vocal production, Alcock et al. (2000) examined vocal performance and music perception in a group study of patients with unilateral left- or right-hemisphere lesions. They found that left-hemisphere patients were mostly impaired in perceiving and reproducing rhythms, without difficulties in singing the correct pitch. Right-hemisphere patients, in contrast, had great difficulties in pitch production and perception tasks, with less marked rhythm processing disorders than left-hemisphere patients. Additional evidence confirming that the right hemisphere is engaged in pitch production comes from two recent single case studies in which acoustical measures of singing proficiency were obtained (Murayama et al. 2004; Terao et al. 2006). In sum, evidence from symptomatic case studies and lesion-led reports, in general, confirm what has been described in early reports, that the right hemisphere (mostly the frontal-insular regions) is central to vocal musical pitch production. In addition, vocal performance disorders can occur in a pure form in absence of perceptual and linguistic deficits, and may concern very specific aspects of music vocal production (e.g., interval production) while leaving other functions intact.

Further evidence indicating a predominant right-hemisphere involvement in vocal pitch performance comes from neuroimaging and TMS studies. In an fMRI study, Riecker et al. (2000) found that speech and singing without lyrics engage opposite hemispheres (at the level of anterior insula), with a left-hemisphere dominance for speaking and a right-hemisphere dominance for singing. A similar lateralization pattern was yielded by a PET study in which speaking and singing with words were contrasted (Jeffries et al. 2003). In addition, when TMS was applied over left-hemisphere regions traditionally related to speech production (e.g., near Broca's area) speech was disrupted; similar stimulation over homologous brain areas in the right hemisphere impaired singing, at least for some of the participants (Epstein et al. 1999; Lo and Fook-Chong 2004; Stewart et al. 2001).

A classical interpretation of these findings is that singing familiar songs engages right-hemisphere regions in contrast to propositional speech which engages the left-hemisphere. This account has gained credence from clinical reports that patients suffering from motor aphasia are still able to sing previously learned songs with well-articulated and linguistically intelligible words (e.g., Assal et al. 1977; Yamadori et al. 1977). However, the evidence is not clear-cut. Poor singing often emerges in association with linguistic deficits resulting from left-hemisphere damage (e.g. Benton 1977). Furthermore, bilateral hemispheric involvement in sung performance is substantiated by evidence that lesions in either of the two hemispheres impair sung performance (Kinsella et al. 1988; Prior et al. 1990), that both right- and left-hemisphere anesthetization interfere with singing (Borchgrevink 1980; Zatorre 1984), and that singing without words do no elicit any lip-opening asymmetry, as a measure of laterality (e.g., Cadalbert et al. 1994; Hough et al. 1994). Finally, clinical observations that motor aphasics can articulate words better when singing than when speaking were not fully corroborated by recent systematic studies (Hébert et al. 2003; Racette et al. 2006). In sum, it is likely that singing is characterized by less strict lateralization than is speech.

Conclusion

Like any cognitive faculty, music is multifaceted and the identification of the neural basis of any complex faculty must proceed, hand in hand, with an elucidation of its cognitive architecture. The past decade has seen an evolution in the theoretical models of musical processing, allowing the development of theoretically motivated instruments for the systematic evaluation of musical disorders. Such developments have allowed reports of musical disorders to evolve from historical anecdotes to systematic, verifiable accounts which can play a critical role in contributing to our understanding of the cognitive neuroscience of music.

Acknowledgements

L.S, T.D.G and J.W were supported by the Wellcome Trust. L.S. was additionally supported by the Economic and Social Research Council and J.W. received support from a EC grant to the APOPIS consortium. SDB received an integration grant from the European Commission.

References

Ackermann H, Wildgruber D and Riecker A (2006). Singing in the (b)rain: cerebral correlates. In E Altenmüller, M Wiesendanger, J Kesselring, eds, *Music, motor control and the brain*, 205–222. Oxford University Press, Oxford.

Alcock KJ, Wade D, Anslow P and Passingham RE (2000). Pitch and timing abilities in adult left-hemisphere dysphasic and right-hemisphere damaged subjects. *Brain and Language*, 75(1), 47–65.

Assal G, Buttet J and Javet RC (1997). Musical aptitude in aphasics. *Revue Medicale de la Suisse Romande*, 97(1), 5–12.

Ayotte J, Peretz I and Hyde K (2002). Congenital Amusia. A group study of adults afflicted with a music-specific disorder. *Brain*, 125, 238–251.

Ayotte J, Peretz I, Rousseau I, Bard C, Bojanowski M (2000). Patterns of music agnosia associated with middle cerebral artery infarcts. *Brain*, 123, 1926–1938.

Benton AL (1977) The amusias. In M Critchley and RA Henson, eds, *Music and the brain*, 378–397. William Heinemann, London.

Borchgrevink HM (1980) Cerebral lateralization of speech and singing after intracarotid amytal injection. In MT Sarno and O Hook, eds, *Aphasia. Assessment and Treatment*, 186–191. Stockholm: Almqvist and Wiksell

Botez MI and Wertheim N (1959) Expressive aphasia and amusia following right frontal lesion in a right-handed man. *Brain*, 82, 186–202.

Bradshaw E and McHenry MA (2005) Pitch discrimination and pitch-matching abilities of adults who sing inaccurately. *Journal of Voice*, 14(3), 431–439.

Brust JC (1980) Music and language: musical alexia and agraphia. *Brain*, 103, 367–392.

Cadalbert A, Landis T, Regard M and Graves RE (1994) Singing with and without words: hemispheric asymmetries in motor control. *Journal of Clinical and Experimental Neuropsychology*, 16(5), 664–670.

Confavreux C, Croisile B, Garassus P, Aimard G and Trillet M (1992). Progressive amusia and aprosody. *Archives of Neurology*, 49, 971–6.

Critchley M and Henson RA (eds) (1977) *Music and the brain. Studies in the neurology of music*. Heinemann, Oxford.

Cuddy LL, Balkwill L-L, Peretz I and Holden RR (2005). Neuropsychological assessment of musical difficulties: a study of 'tone deafness' among university students. Annals of the New York Academy of Sciences, 1060, 311–324.

Dalla Bella, S, Giguère J-F and Peretz I (2007) Singing proficiency in the general population. *Journal of The Acoustical Society of America*, 121, 1192–1189.

Di Pietro M, Laganaro M, Leemann B and Schnider A (2004). Receptive amusia: temporal auditory processing deficit in a professional musician following a left temporo-parietal lesion. *Neuropsychologia*, 42, 868–877.

Dowling WJ and Harwood DL (1985). Music and cognition. Academic Press, London.

Epstein CM, Meador KJ, Loring DW, Wright RJ, Weissmann JD, Sheppard S, Lah JJ, Puhalovich F, Gaitan L and Davey KR (1999) Localization and characterization of speech arrest during transcranial magnetic stimulation. *Clinical Neurophysiology*, 110(6), 1073–1079.

Eustache F, Lechevalier B, Viader F and Lambert J (1990). Identification and discrimination disorders in auditory perception: a report on two cases. *Neuropsychologia*, 28, 257–270.

Foxton JM, Dean JL, Gee R, Peretz I and Griffiths TD (2004) Characterization of deficits in pitch perception underlying tone deafness. *Brain*, 127, 801–110.

Foxton JM, Nandy RK and Griffiths TD (2006). Rhythm deficits in tone deafness. *Brain and Cognition*, 62(1), 24–29.

Fries W and Swihart AA (1990). Disturbance of rhythm sense following right hemisphere damage. *Neuropsychologia*, 28, 1317–23.

Fujii T, Fukatsu R, Watabe S, Ohnuma A, Teramura K, Kimura I *et al.* (1990) Auditory sound agnosia without aphasia following a right temporal lobe lesion. *Cortex*, 26, 263–268.

Gordon HW and Bogen JE (1974) Hemispheric lateralization of singing after intracarotid sodium amylobarbitone. *Journal of Neurology, Neurosurgery, and Psychiatry*, 37, 727–738.

Gordon RL, Racette A and Schön D (2006) Sensory-motor networks in singing and speaking: a comparative approach. In E Altenmüller, M Wiesendanger and J Kesselring, eds, *Music, motor control and the brain*, 223–238. Oxford University Press, Oxford.

Gosselin N, Peretz I, Noulhiane M, Hasboun D, Beckett C, Baulac M *et al.* (2005) Impaired recognition of scary music following unilateral temporal lobe excision. *Brain*, 128, 628–40.

Grant-Allen (1878). Note-deafness. *Mind*, 10, 157–167.

Griffiths TD, McDonald C, Kumar S, Deutsch D, Chinnery P and Stewart L (2007). Could a congenital disorder of musical perception ever be explained by a single gene? International Workshop on the Biology and Genetics of Music, Bologna, Italy.

Griffiths TD, Rees A, Witton C, Cross PM, Shakir RA and Green GG (1997). Spatial and temporal auditory processing deficits following right hemisphere infarction. A psychophysical study. *Brain*, 120, 785–794.

Griffiths TD, Warren JD and Jennings AR (2006). Dystimbria: a distinct musical syndome? Presented at the International Conference for Musical Perception and Cognition.

Griffiths TD, Warren JD, Dean JL and Howard D (2004). When the feeling's gone: a selective loss of musical emotion. *Journal of Neurology, Neurosurgery and Psychiatry*, 75, 344–345.

Grossman M, Shapiro BE and Gardner H (1981). Dissociable musical processing strategies after localized brain damage. *Neuropsychologia*, 19, 425–433.

Habib M, Daquin G, Milandre L, Royere ML, Rey M, Lanteri A *et al.* (1995) Mutism and auditory agnosia due to bilateral insular damage—role of the insula in human communication. *Neuropsychologia*, 33, 327–339.

Hattiangadi N, Pillion JP, Slomine B, Christensen J, Trovato MK and Speedie LJ (2005). Characteristics of auditory agnosia in a child with severe traumatic brain injury: a case report. *Brain and Language*, 92, 12–25.

Hébert S, Racette A, Gagnon L and Peretz I (2003). Revisiting the dissociation between singing and speaking in expressive aphasia. *Brain*, 126(8), 1838–1850.

Hofman S, Klein C and Arlazoroff A (1993). Common hemisphericity of language and music in a musician. A case report. *Journal of Communication Disorders*, **26**, 73–82.

Hough MS, Daniel HJ, Snow MA, O'Brien KF and Hume WG (1994) Gender differences in laterality patterns for speaking and singing. *Neuropsychologia*, **32**, 1067–1078.

Hyde KL and Peretz I (2003) Out-of-pitch but still in-time. An auditory psychophysical study in congenital amusic adults. *Annals of the New York Academy of Sciences*, **999**, 173–176.

Hyde KL, Lerch JP, Zatorre RJ, Griffiths TD, Evans AC and Peretz I (2007). Cortical thickness in congenital amusia: when less is better than more. *Journal of Neuroscience* **27**(47), 13028–13032.

Hyde KL, Zatorre RJ, Griffiths TD, Lerch JP and Peretz I (2005). Morphometry of the amusic brain: a two-site study. *Brain*, **129**, 2562–2570.

Jeffries KJ, Fritz JB and Braun AR (2003) Words in melody: an $H_2^{15}O$ PET study of brain activation during singing and speaking. *Neuroreport*, **15**(5), 749–754.

Johannes S, Jobges ME, Dengler R and Munte TF (1998). Cortical auditory disorders: a case of non-verbal disturbances assessed with event-related brain potentials. *Behavioural Neurology*, **11**, 55–73.

Johkura K, Matsumoto S, Hasegawa O and Kuroiwa Y (1998). Defective auditory recognition after small hemorrhage in the inferior colliculi. *Journal of Neurological Sciences*, **161**, 91–96.

Johnsrude IS, Penhune VB and Zatorre RJ (2000). Functional specificity in right human auditory cortex for perceiving pitch direction. *Brain*, **123**, 155–163.

Kester DB, Saykin AJ, Sperling MR, O'Connor MJ, Robinson LJ and Gur RC (1991). Acute effect of anterior temporal lobectomy on musical processing. *Neuropsychologia*, **29**, 703–708.

Kinsella G, Prior MR and Murray G (1988) Singing ability after right and left side brain damage. A research note. *Cortex*, **24**(1), 165–169.

Kohlmetz C, Muller SV, Nager W, Munte TF and Altenmuller E (2003). Selective loss of timbre perception for keyboard and percussion instruments following a right temporal lesion. *Neurocase*, **9**, 86–93.

Lechevalier B, Rossa Y, Eustache F, Schupp C, Boner L and Bazin C (1984). Un cas de surdit, corticale, pargnant en partie la musique. *Revue Neurologique*, **140**, 190–201.

Levin HS and Rose JE. (1979)Alexia without agraphia in a musician after transcallosal removal of a left intraventricular meningioma. *Neurosurgery*, **4**, 168–174.

Liegeois-Chauvel C, Peretz I, Babai M, Laguittin V and Chauvel P (1998). Contribution of different cortical areas in the temporal lobes to music processing. *Brain*, **121**, 1853–1867.

Lo YL and Fook-Chong S (2004). Ipsilateral and controlateral motor inhibitory control in musical and vocalization tasks. *Experimental Brain Research*, **159**(2), 258–262.

Mandell J, Schulze K and Schlaug G (2007) Congenital amusia: an auditory-feedback disorder? *Restorative Neurology and Neuroscience*, **25**, 323–334.

Marin OSM and Perry DW (1999) Neurological aspects of music perception and performance. In Deutsch D, ed. *Psychology of music*, 653–724. Academic Press, San Diego, CA.

Mavlov L (1980). Amusia due to rhythm agnosia in a musician with left hemisphere damage: a non-auditory supramodal defect. *Cortex*, **16**, 331–338.

Mazzoni (1993). A case of music imperception. *Journal of Neurology, Neurosurgery and Psychiatry*, 56, 322.

Mazzucchi A, Marchini C, Budai R and Parma M (1982). A case of receptive amusia with prominent timbre perception defect. *Journal of Neurology, Neurosurgery and Psychiatry*, **45**, 644–647.

McDonald C and Stewart L (2008) Uses and functions of music in congenital amusia. *Music Perception*, **25**(4), 345–355.

McFarland HR and Fortin D (1982) Amusia due to right temporoparietal infarct. *Archives of Neurology*, **39**(11), 725–727.

Mendez MF and Geehan GR (1988). Cortical auditory disorders:clinical and psychoacoustic features. *Journal of Neurology, Neurosurgery and Psychiatry*, **51**, 1–9.

Milner B (1962). Laterality effects in audition. In VB Mountcastle, ed., *Interhemispheric relations and cerebral dominance*, 177–195. Johns Hopkins University Press, Baltimore, MD.

Murayama J, Kashiwagi T, Kashiwagi A and Mimura M (2004). Impaired pitch production and preserved rhythm production in a right brain-damaged patient with amusia. *Brain and Cognition*, **56**, 36–42.

Patel AD, Peretz I, Tramo M and Labreque R (1998). Processing prosodic and musical patterns: a neuropsychological investigation. *Brain and Language*, **61**, 123–144.

Peretz I (1990). Processing of local and global musical information by unilateral brain-damaged patients. *Brain*, **113**, 1185–1205.

Peretz I (1996). Can we lose memory for music? A case of music agnosia in a non-musician. *Journal of Cognitive Neuroscience*, **8**, 481–496.

Peretz I, Coltheart M (2003). Modularity of music processing. *Nature Neuroscience*, **6**, 688–691.

Peretz I and Gagnon L (1999). Dissociation between recognition and emotion for melodies. *Neurocase*, **5**, 21–30.

Peretz I, Belleville S and Fontaine F (1997). Dissociations entre musique et langage apres atteinte cerebrale; un nouveau cas d'amusie sans aphasie. *Canadian Journal of Experimental Psychology*, **51**, 354–368.

Peretz I, Blood AJ, Penhune V and Zatorre R (2001). Cortical deafness to dissonance. *Brain*, **124**, 928–940.

Peretz I, Brattico E and Tervaniemi M (2005). Abnormal electrical brain responses to pitch in congenital amusia. *Annals of Neurology*, **58**, 478–482.

Peretz I, Gagnon L and Bouchard B (1998). Music and emotion: perceptual determinants, immediacy, and isolation after brain damage. *Cognition*, **68**, 111–141.

Peretz I, Champod A-S and Hyde KL (2003). Varieties of musical disorders. The Montreal Battery of Evaluation of Amusia. *Annals of the New York Academy of Sciences*, **999**, 58.

Peretz I, Kolinsky R, Tramo M, Labrecque R, Hublet C, Demeurize G *et al.* (1994) Functional dissociations following bilateral lesions of auditory cortex. *Brain*, **117**, 1283–1301.

Piccirilli M, Sciarma T and Luzzi S (2000). Modularity of music: evidence from a case of pure amusia. *Journal of Neurology, Neurosurgery and Psychiatry*, **69**, 541–545.

Prior M, Kinsella G and Giese J (1990). Assessment of musical processing in brain-damaged patients: implications for laterality of music. *Journal of Clinical and Experimental Neuropsychology*, **12**, 301–312.

Racette A, Bard, C and Peretz I (2006). Making non-fluent aphasics speak: sing along! *Brain*, **129**(10), 2571–2584.

Riecker A, Ackermann H, Wildgruber D, Dogil G and Grodd W (2000). Opposite hemispheric lateralization effects during speaking and singing at motor cortex, insula and cerebellum. *Neuroreport*, **11**, 1997–2000.

Robin DA, Tranel D and Damasio H (1990). Auditory perception of temporal and spectral events in patients with focal left and right cerebral lesions. *Brain and Language*, **39**, 539–555.

Samson S and Zatorre RJ (1988). Melodic and harmonic discrimination following unilateral cerebral excision. *Brain and Cognition*, **7**, 348–360.

Samson S and Zatorre RJ (1991). Recognition memory for text and melody of songs after unilateral temporal lobe lesion: evidence for dual encoding. *Journal of Experimental Psychology: Learning, Memory and Cognition*, **17**, 793–804.

Samson S and Zatorre RJ (1992). Learning and retention of melodic and verbal information after unilateral temporal lobectomy. *Neuropsychologia*, **30**, 815–826.

Samson S and Zatorre RJ (1994). Contribution of the right temporal lobe to musical timbre discrimination. *Neuropsychologia*, **32**, 231–240.

Samson S, Ehrle N and Baulac M (2001). Cerebral substrates for musical temporal processes. *Annals of the New York Academy of Sciences*, **930**, 166–178.

Samson S, Zatorre RJ and Ramsay JO (2002). Deficits of musical timbre perception after unilateral temporal-lobe lesion revealed with multidimensional scaling. *Brain*, **125**, 511–523.

Satoh M, Takeda K, Murakami Y, Onouchi K, Inoue K and Kuzuhara S (2005). A case of amusia caused by the infarction of anterior portion of bilateral temporal lobes. *Cortex*, **41**, 77–83.

Schön D, Lorber B, Spacal M and Semenza C (2004). A selective deficit in the production of exact musical intervals following right hemisphere damage. *Cognitive Neuropsychology*, **21**, 773–785.

Schuppert M, Munte TF, Wieringa BM and Altenmuller E (2000). Receptive amusia: evidence for cross-hemispheric neural networks underlying music processing strategies. *Brain*, **123**, 546–559.

Shankweiler D (1966). Effects of temporal lobe damage on the perception of dichotically presented melodies. *Journal of Comparative Physiology and Psychology*, **62**, 115–119.

Shapiro BE, Grossman M and Gardner H (1981). Selective musical processing deficits in brain damaged populations. *Neuropsychologia*, **19**, 161–169.

Sidtis JJ and Volpe BT (1988). Selective loss of complex-pitch or speech discrimination after unilateral lesion. *Brain and Language*, **34**, 235–245.

Sloboda JA, Wise KJ and Peretz I (2005). Quantifying tone deafness in the general population. *Annals of the New York Academy of Sciences*, **1060**, 255–261.

Spreen O, Benton AL and Fincham RW (1965). Auditory agnosia without aphasia. *Archives of Neurology*, **13**, 84–92.

Stewart L, Overath T, Warren JD, Foxton JM and Griffiths TD (2008) fMRI Evidence for a cortical hierarchy of pitch pattern processing. *PLoS ONE*, **3**(1), e1470. doi:10.1371/journal.pone.0001470.

Stewart L, Von Kriegstein K, Warren JD and Griffiths TD (2006) Disorders of musical listening. *Brain*, **129**, 2533–2553.

Stewart L, Walsh V, Frith U and Rothwell J (2001). Transcranial magnetic stimulation produces speech arrest but not song arrest. *Annals of the New York Academy of Sciences*, **930**, 433–435.

Tanaka Y, Yamadori A and Mori E (1987). Pure word deafness following bilateral lesions. *Brain*, **110**, 381–403.

Terao Y, Mizuno T, Shindoh M, Sakurai Y, Ugawa Y, Kobayashi S *et al.* (2005) Vocal amusia in a professional tango singer due to a right superior temporal cortex infarction. *Neuropsychologia*, **44**, 479–88.

Tramo MJ and Bharucha JJ (1991). Musical priming by the right hemisphere post-callosotomy. Neuropsychologia, 29, 313–325.

Tramo MJ, Bharucha JJ and Musiek FE (1990). Music perception and cognition following bilateral lesions of auditory cortex. *Journal of Cognitive Neuroscience*, **2**, 195–212.

Tramo MJ, Shah GD and Braida LD (2002). Functional role of auditory cortex in frequency processing and pitch perception. *Journal of Neurophysiology*, **87**, 122–139.

Ustvedt HI (1937). Ueber die Untersuchung der musikalischen Funktionen bei Patienten mit Gehirnleiden besonders bei Patienten mit Aphasie. *Acta Medica Scandinavica*, **86**, 1–186.

Warrier CM and Zatorre RJ (2004). Right temporal cortex is critical for utilization of melodic contextual cues in a pitch constancy task. *Brain*, **127**, 1616–1625.

Wilson SJ, Pressing JL and Wales RJ (2002). Modelling rhythmic function in a musician post-stroke. *Neuropsychologia*, **40**, 1494–1505.

Yamadori A, Osumi Y, Masuhara S and Okubo M (1977) Preservation of singing in Broca's aphasia. *Journal of Neurology, Neurosurgery and Psychiatry*, **40**(3), 221–224.

Zatorre RJ (1984). Musical perception and cerebral function: A critical review. *Music Perception*, **2**, 196–221.

Zatorre RJ (1985). Discrimination and recognition of tonal melodies after unilateral cerebral excisions. *Neuropsychologia*, **23**, 31–41.

Zatorre RJ (1988). Pitch perception of complex tones and human temporal-lobe function. *Journal of the Acoustical Society of America*, **84**, 566–572.

Zatorre RJ and Halpern AR (1993). Effect of unilateral temporal lobe excision on perception and imagery of songs. *Neuropsychologia*, **31**, 221–232.

Zatorre RJ and Samson S (1991). Role of the right temporal neocortex in retention of pitch in auditory short-term memory. *Brain*, **114**, 2403–2417.

CHAPTER 18

Music, musicians, and brain plasticity

Gottfried Schlaug

Musicians and non-musicians: their brains differ

Playing a musical instrument is an intense, multisensory and motor experience that is typically initiated at an early age and requires the acquisition and practice of a wide range of skills over the course of a musician's lifetime. Considering the early age at which they commence training and the continuous practice that maintaining such exacting skills demands over time, musicians make an ideal human model for studying the brain effects of acquiring highly specialized sensorimotor (Elbert *et al.* 1995; Amunts *et al.* 1997; Gaser and Schlaug 2003; Schlaug 2001; Schlaug *et al.* 2005; Hund-Georgiadis and von Cramon 1999; Meister *et al.* 2005; Bengtsson *et al.* 2005); auditory (Besson *et al.* 1994; Gaab and Schlaug 2003; Keenan *et al.* 2001; Pantev *et al.* 1998, 2001; Schlaug *et al.* 1995a, b; Schneider *et al.* 2002; Zatorre *et al.* 1998); auditory–spatial and visual–motor (Sergent *et al.* 1993; Münte *et al.* 2001); and auditory–motor (Lotze *et al.* 2003; Bangert *et al.* 2006; Zatorre *et al.* 2007) skills.

Strongest effects are found in primary domain regions

Several studies have found evidence for structural differences in brain regions that are directly involved with some of these skills, such as the primary auditory cortex and auditory association cortex (Schlaug *et al.* 1995a; Zatorre *et al.* 1998; Schneider *et al.* 2002; Gaser and Schlaug 2003) most likely related to important

skills of fine spectral and temporal discrimination and pitch categorization. Further examples include structural differences in primary sensorimotor cortex and closely related premotor and supplementary motor regions, which are essential for preparation, execution, and control of precise, independent finger movements (Elbert *et al.* 1995; Amunts *et al.* 1997; Gaser and Schlaug 2003; Bangert and Schlaug 2006), and in the midsagittal side of the corpus callosum (Schlaug *et al.* 1995b; Ozturk *et al.* 2002; Lee *et al.* 2003), which is likely related to interactions between both hemispheres necessary for independent movements of right and left hand. These structural between-group (musicians vs non-musicians) differences mirror structural changes seen in primary motor and cerebellar cortices of experimental animal models that have been subjected to long-term learning of complex motor skills over several months (Anderson *et al.* 2002). Micro-structural changes included increases in the number of synapses and glial cells, increased density of capillaries in primary motor cortex and the cerebellum, and new brain cells in the hippocampus after long-term motor training in adult rats (Black *et al.* 1990; Isaacs *et al.* 1992; Anderson *et al.* 1994; Kleim *et al.* 1996; Kempermann *et al.* 1997; van Praag *et al.* 1999). The sum of these micro-structural changes could amount to structural differences that are detectable on a macro-structural level (see Anderson *et al.* 2002; Bangert and Schlaug 2006).

Most cross-sectional studies comparing the brains of adult musicians with those of matched non-musicians, have used either age of commencement of musical training or intensity/duration of practice throughout a musician's career as predictors of regional differences suggesting that the longer and the more intensely musicians practiced, the more pronounced the between-group differences were (Elbert *et al.* 1995; Amunts *et al.* 1997; Schlaug 2001; Sluming *et al.* 2002; Schneider *et al.* 2002; Gaser and Schlaug 2003; Bangert and Schlaug 2006). Although these correlations suggest a causal relationship, it is still not a substitute for a longitudinal study proving that the between-group differences are due to training and are not related to genetic causes.

Relating structural differences to functional imaging correlates

Results of functional imaging studies are not always congruent with structural brain imaging studies. Although several studies have reported that musicians have more grey matter and greater cortical thickness in primary and auditory cortex (Heschl's gyrus) (Schneider *et al.* 2002; Gaser and Schlaug 2003), functional studies have actually shown stronger responses in secondary and tertiary auditory brain regions comparing musicians with non-musicians. Interestingly, non-musicians seem to show stronger activation of primary auditory regions (Besson *et al.* 1994; Trainor *et al.* 1999; Shahin *et al.* 2003; 2004; Gaab and Schlaug 2003; Bosnyak *et al.* 2004). Similar results were found in the motor system. Most functional imaging studies comparing musicians with non-musicians have shown that musicians have either less, or more focused activation in the primary motor cortex than non-musicians and more variable levels of activation in motor association regions such as the premotor and supplementary motor areas (Hund-Georgiadis and von Cramon 1999; Jancke *et al.* 2000; Krings *et al.* 2000; Haslinger *et al.* 2004; Meister *et al.* 2005). This contradiction between the pronounced between-group structural differences and within-group structural changes in primary auditory and motor cortices on one hand and the lower degree of functional activation of these regions on the other hand, has not been fully understood. Some argue that as a system becomes more

plastic and expands its representation, it may work more efficiently with fewer neurons and thus has less of a metabolic demand or less of a blood flow demand than a naive subject (a non-instrumentalist) might have while performing a behaviourally matched complex motor sequence (Hund-Georgiadis and Von Cramon 1999; Krings *et al.* 2000; Jancke *et al.* 2000; Koeneke *et al.* 2004; Meister *et al.* 2005).

Structural differences are also found in an extended network of multimodal sensorimotor integration regions

Structural brain differences comparing musicians with matched non-musician controls have also been found beyond primary domains in regions such as in the inferior frontal gyrus, the superior parietal lobe including the intraparietal sulcus, the inferior lateral temporal lobe, and the cerebellum (Sluming *et al.* 2002; Hutchinson *et al.* 2003; Gaser and Schlaug 2003), yet the functional role of these differences/changes in extra-primary domain regions is not fully understood. It is possible that parietal regions might play a role in multisensory encoding such as in the integration of auditory information with other sensory (e.g. visual) information. The prominent activation of the superior parietal lobule in musical sight-reading (Sergent *et al.* 1992) may be reflective of the sensorimotor transformation of a visuospatial representation (musical notation) to a pattern of intended movements and position of fingers on the keyboard. Stewart and colleagues (2003) were able to show that the superior parietal lobe (SPL) showed activity changes when comparing functional images obtained while musically naive subjects played melodies from notation before and after a 15-week training period that involved reading music and playing the keyboard. This is further support for the notion that the SPL is involved in the sensorimotor translation of visual–spatial representation into a motor programme.

Strong structural differences in the frontal lobe, particularly in the left inferior frontal gyrus (IFG), have been found in two independent studies (Sluming *et al.* 2002; Gaser and Schlaug 2003). The left IFG has also been found to be activated in various functional imaging studies using musical tasks. The interest in the inferior frontal lobule has been sparked further in recent years, as more studies have found this region to be a critical link in the auditory–motor network. However, the frontal lobe also plays a more general role in music-making which can range from integration of individual auditory events into larger units, making predictions about and recognizing alterations in sequential auditory–perceptual events, and in mapping actions to their associated sounds (Koelsch *et al.* 2002; Levitin and Menon, 2003; Lotze *et al.* 2003; Bangert and Altenmueller 2003; Bangert *et al.* 2006; Lahav *et al.* 2007; Zatorre *et al.* 2007).

It is possible that the specific and continuous engagement of this multimodal sensorimotor integration network and the induced changes in this network across a musician's career may be the neural basis for some of the cognitive enhancements attributed to musical training.

A form of cross-modal plasticity, induced by musical training, could affect extra-musical behavioural and cognitive tasks when those tasks engage regions that are altered through long-term music-making. Evidence for this hypothesis does already exist in the form of finding parietal activation with mathematical tasks (Chochon *et al.* 1999) that coincides with regions of activation induced by music making and musical sight-reading in particular (Sergent *et al.* 1992; Stewart *et al.* 2003), or the congruence of activations in the inferior parietal cortex with musical memory task and language tasks, both utilizing network components of the phonological loop (Gaab *et al.* 2003, 2006). Other examples include IFG activation while performing sequential, non-musical mental operations (Sluming *et al.* 2007) or while performing various speech and language tasks but also while performing musical tasks of auditory-motor mapping, integration of individual

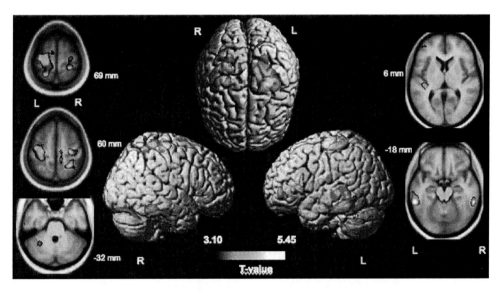

Fig. 18.1 A voxel-based morphometric study showing grey matter volume differences between three groups. Only voxels exhibiting a significant positive correlation between musician status (professional musician > amateur musician > non-musician) and increased grey matter volume are shown here, and those have been overlaid on the rendered cortical surface of a single subject. The distinction between professional and amateur musicians in this study was based on whether or not the keyboard player's main profession was being a musician (e.g., music teacher, performer). There was also a clear separation between both groups in terms of average practice intensity across their careers, with professional keyboard players having approximately double the amount of practice time than the group of amateur musicians. (This figure was adapted from Figure 1 in Gaser and Schlaug [2003]). See colour plate section.

auditory events into larger units, or making predictions about and recognizing alterations in structured musical sequences (Koelsch *et al.* 2002, 2005; Patel 2003; Tettamanti and Weniger 2006; Lahav *et al.* 2007).

Within-musician differences—stronger evidence for a causal effect

Further support for brain plasticity as an explanation for the anatomical differences between adult musicians and non-musicians comes from comparisons of musician groups that play different instruments. Pantev and colleagues (2001) found more pronounced cortical responses to trumpet and string tones in the respective players of those instruments, suggesting that perceptual markers of brain activity differ as a function of the instrument played and constantly heard (Pantev *et al.* 2001). In the absence of longitudinal data examining causal relationships, the search for structural brain differences within a heterogeneous group of musicians is a valuable alternative to support

the notion of structural brain adaptation. For example, string-players strongly differ from keyboard players in the specific fine motor (hand/finger) skills required for playing their instruments. While string players need highly developed fine motor skills of their left hand and more gross motor skills of the right, keyboard players require highly developed fine motor skills of both hands but with greater facilities in their right hand since the left hand frequently functions as more of an accompaniment in keyboard music. When comparing string and keyboard players, Bangert and Schlaug (2006) found gross anatomical differences in the precentral gyrus (Figure 18.2). Further, the majority of the adult keyboard players had an elaborate configuration (known as 'Omega Sign') of the precentral gyrus on the left more than in the right hemisphere, while most of the adult string players had this 'atypicality' only on the right. Although a genetic cause for the Omega Sign atypicality in this strongly right-handed group of musicians (i.e., a differential hemispheric expression favouring string playing in those who have a prominent

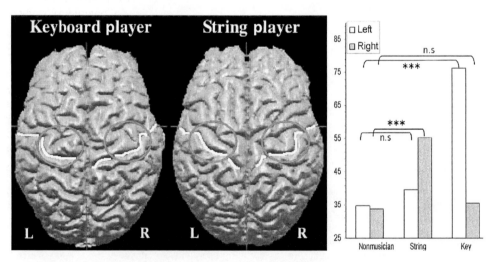

Fig. 18.2 Brain surface renderings of one typical keyboard and one typical string player. The central sulcus is marked with a white line. The portion of the precentral gyrus containing the gyral configuration similar to that of the inverted Greek letter 'Omega' is found within the red circles. In the two examples, a prominent omega sign can be seen on the left more than the right in the keyboard player, and only on the right in the string player. Across the entire group, we found significantly more prominent 'Omega signs' in the right hemisphere of string players compared to the right hemisphere of non-musicians and in the left hemisphere of keyboard players compared to the left hemispheres of both non-musicians and string players. See colour plate section.

Omega Sign in the right hemisphere and keyboard playing in those who have a prominent Omega Sign in their left hemisphere) cannot be completely ruled out, a correlation between the degree of the Omega Sign's prominence and the musicians' age at commencement of musical training, as well as with the cumulative amount of practice time accrued across the years strongly argues for a structural plasticity mechanism.

We also tested whether or not morphological differences between musicians and non-musicians (more elaborate motor cortex and larger midsagittal corpus callosum) have neurophysiological correlates. The larger midsagittal callosal size might reflect a more elaborate interaction between both hemispheres facilitating independent finger movements of both hands. Using transcranial magnetic stimulation (TMS), Ridding et al. (2000) found a reduced transcallosal inhibition and Nordstrom and Butler (2002) reported a reduced intracortical inhibition (ICI) and facilitation (ICF) in musicians. Although finding neurophysiological differences between musicians and non-musicians supports the notion that anatomical differences have neurophysiological correlates, these TMS results were counter-intuitive and contrary to what was expected. We used TMS to assess the interhemispheric interaction in a group of 21 right-handed adults (7 keyboard players, 7 string players and 7 non-musicians). We found that keyboard players have a stronger inhibition from the left to the right (LtoR) hemisphere while string players have a stronger inhibition from the right to the left (RtoL) hemisphere. The degree of inter-hemispheric inhibition (IHI) correlated with the size of the fourth and fifth segment (midbody) of the corpus callosum that contains fibres connecting primary sensorimotor cortex (Figure 18.3 c and d). Non-musicians showed similar IHI from either hemisphere. Since inhibitory interneurons in the primary motor cortex are known to mediate transcallosal inhibitory input to the homologous area in the opposite hemisphere, our results suggest that strengthening the activity of these inhibitory interneurons may be one mechanism by which different regions of the brain exert inhibitory control over those homologous regions in the opposite hemisphere. In addition, in within- and between-group comparisons,

string players had significantly greater intracortical facilitation (ICF) in (1) their right hemisphere than their left, and (2) the right hemisphere of non-musicians. The stronger ICF in string players' right hemisphere (controlling the left hand) most likely points to neural processes providing excitatory input to the corticospinal neurons involved in precise, fine motor control of the left hand (Nair et al. 2006).

Cognitive and brain changes when children learn to play a musical instrument

To determine whether the structural and functional differences seen in adult musicians reflect adaptations due to musical training during sensitive periods of brain development, or are instead markers of musical interest and/or aptitude that existed prior to training, it is necessary to examine children and/or adults before the onset of instrumental music training and compare them to a group of control subjects not planning to play and practice regularly on a musical instrument. For the past five years we have been conducting a longitudinal study of the effects of music training on brain development and cognition in young children (Overy et al. 2004; Norton et al. 2005; Koelsch et al. 2005; Schlaug et al. 2005). We have tested a large group of 5–7-year-old children prior to initiation of music lessons (baseline), approximately two-thirds of whom chose to take piano lessons and one third chose string lessons. We also tested a slightly smaller, untreated control group matched to the instrumental group in age, socio-economic status (SES), and verbal IQ. Each child underwent a battery of tests (for details see Norton et al. 2005). We found no pre-existing cognitive, auditory perceptual, motoric, or structural brain differences between the children that entered the instrumental group and those that entered the control group at baseline (Norton et al. 2005), thereby making it unlikely that children who choose to learn an instrument do so because they have an atypical brain. After an average follow-up interval of 15 months, we found significantly greater change scores in the instrumental group than in the control group in skills directly linked to

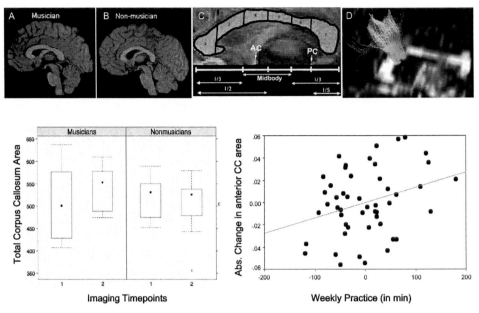

Fig. 18.3 Corpus callosum differences in adults (musicians vs non-musicians) and changes over time in children. (A) and (B) Show the midsagittal slice of an adult musician (A) and non-musician (B) showing a difference in the size of the anterior and midbody of the corpus callosum. (C) and (D) Show the major subdivisions of the corpus callosum and locations of the interhemispheric fibers connecting the motor hand regions on the right and left hemisphere through the corpus callosum. (E) and (F): The mean (dot inside box plots) midsagittal corpus callosum size of the 5–7-year-old children at baseline (time point 1) and after 15 months of musical training (time point 2) shows slightly opposite trends with the instrumental group showing an increase in the midsagittal corpus callosum area. The anterior portion of the corpus callosum (segments 1–4, see Fig. 18.3c) showed a significant correlation with the amount of weekly practice (p = 0.034; partial r^2 = 0.094). See colour plate section.

instrumental music training: fine motor skills and auditory discrimination skills including both rhythmic and melodic discrimination. At this time point, no significant between-group differences were seen in non-primary domains such as verbal and visuospatial skills (Forgeard *et al.* submitted). However, our analyses did reveal trends for between-group differences in several of the extra-primary domains or transfer domains (e.g., verbal skills), suggesting that a longer period of observation might lead to significant between-group differences in these transfer domains. Children with higher intensity of practice had stronger trends in these outcome variables. Brain imaging data also support this trend. There was a strong trend for a greater increase in midsagittal corpus callosum size in

the instrumental group than in the control group and there was a correlation between practice intensity and change in the anterior corpus callosum (Figure 18.3 e and f).

In addition to our longitudinal study of 5–7-year-old children learning to play a musical instrument, we also have preliminary data on a cross-sectional study of 9–11-year-old instrumentalists with an average of 4–5 years of music training and a group of non-musicians matched in age, handedness, and SES. Preliminary results from this cross-sectional study showed that the instrumentalists also performed significantly better in skills directly linked to instrumental music training: fine motor skills and auditory discrimination skills including both rhythmic and melodic discrimination. In addition, we found between-group differences in other domains such as verbal skills and visual pattern matching skills with the instrumentalists performing better on these tests. Furthermore, the 9–11-year-old instrumental group had significantly more grey matter volume that was regionally pronounced in the sensorimotor cortex bilaterally. These between-group differences suggest that a longer duration of musical training and also a longer duration of observation in longitudinal studies together with a higher practice intensity makes it more likely to find significant within-group and between-group structural changes.

There is a widespread view that learning to play a musical instrument in childhood stimulates cognitive development and leads to the enhancement of skills in a variety of extra-musical areas which is commonly referred to as transfer (Bangerter and Heath 2004; Bruer 1999). The most commonly observed form of transfer occurs when there is a close resemblance between the training domain and the transfer domain (typically referred to as 'near transfer'), (e.g., fine motor skills that develop while learning to play a musical instrument lead to increased speed and accuracy in typing). While near transfer effects are relatively common, it is notoriously difficult to demonstrate far transfer, where the resemblance between training and transfer domains is much less obvious (e.g., learning to read and perform with precision from musical rhythm notation and understanding fractions in math). Evidence of far transfer from instrumental music training has previously been claimed in the areas of verbal, spatial, mathematical, and IQ performance (Rauscher et al. 1993, 1997; Rauscher and Zupan 2000; Chan et al. 1998; Vaughn 2000; Hetland 2000; Ho et al. 2003; Schellenberg 2004; Fauvel et al. 2006). In a randomized experimental study, Schellenberg (2004) showed that a group of 6-year-olds who received keyboard or voice lessons for 36 weeks had significantly larger (although modest) increases in full-scale IQ and standardized educational achievement tests than matched groups of children receiving either drama lessons or no lessons. Schellenberg argued that music lessons simply function as additional schooling—requiring focused attention, memorization, and the progressive mastery of technical skills: it is well established that schooling increases IQ (Ceci and Williams 1997). In our 9–11-year-old cross-sectional comparison, we found differences in several but not all domains. The linear relationship between practice intensity and outcome variables in several far transfer domains strongly suggests a causal relationship, but is not absolute proof of it. The possibility of a causal link between music training and enhanced performance on transfer outcomes was confirmed for near transfer in our longitudinal study after a 15-month observation period. The trends that we observed in other domains suggest that a longer observation period and/or higher intensity of training and practice may be required in order to see effects in far transfer domains.

Making music specifically engages and changes a seeing-hearing-doing (mirror neuron) network

Musicians and non-musicians show strong differences in a functional brain network that is activated while listening to music. In addition to primary and secondary perceptual regions, this functional network also includes regions in the parietal and frontal lobes. Figure 18.4 shows this extensive functional network in a group comparison of adult musicians and non-musicians, and in 5–7-year-old children prior to music training, all of whom performed the same rhythmic discrimination task while their brain activity was being measured with functional magnetic resonance imaging (fMRI). Normal maturational changes can be seen in the comparison between the adult non-musicians and the musically naive children, while maturational changes modulated by musical experiences result in a different pattern of activation.

The additional regions activated in adult musicians include the parietal lobe (around the intraparietal sulcus), the posterior middle frontal gyrus (Brodmann area 6), and the inferior frontal gyrus (Brodmann areas 44, 45, and 47). In the paragraphs below, I will concentrate on discussing frontal lobe differences, since these regions show the most pronounced between-group differences.

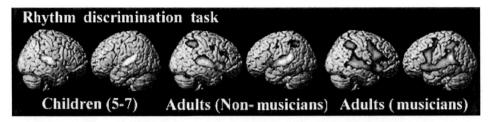

Fig. 18.4 Cerebral activation pattern of a rhythm discrimination task – modulated by maturation and experience. Statistical parametric images superimposed onto a surface rendering of a standardized anatomical brain depict significant activations during a rhythmic discrimination task in a group of 5–7-year-old, musically naive children, adult non-musicians, and adult musicians. The children showed prominent superior temporal gyrus activation on both sides. The adult groups show an extended pattern of activation involving polar and posterior planar regions of the superior temporal lobe as well as the parietal lobe, parts of the frontal lobe, and the cerebellum. Adult musicians differ from adult non-musicians by having less activation of the primary auditory cortex, but more activation of frontal regions bilaterally, particularly in the inferior frontal gyrus. See colour plate section.

Using functional imaging, it has been found that instrumental practice leads to the establishment of an auditory and visual–sensorimotor network (Bangert and Altenmueller 2003; Bangert et al. 2006). Listening to sounds of (and/or seeing) well-learned actions elicits involuntary activity in a network of brain regions (Haueisen and Knösche 2001; Kohler et al. 2002; Keysers et al. 2003; Hasegawa et al. 2004; Haslinger et al. 2005; Bangert et al. 2006; D'Ausilio et al. 2006; Lahav et al. 2007). A prominent component of this brain network is the posterior inferior frontal gyrus (IFG) (commonly referred to as Broca's region). It has been shown that the IFG is activated when one sees meaningful, goal-directed actions or hears action-related sounds including grasping food (Rizzolatti et al. 1996), imitating hand gestures (Buccino et al. 2004a), playing of guitar chords (Buccino et al. 2004b), hearing action words (Pulvermuller et al. 2005; Aziz-Zadeh et al. 2006), hearing instrumental sounds that are associated with motor actions (Lahav et al. 2007), as well as when the action is executed. These are functions and properties of a system that is commonly described as mirror neuron system. Mirror neurons were originally described by Rizzolatti et al. (1996) in region F5 in monkeys which is considered to be the precursor or homolog of Broca's region or the posterior IFG in humans (Rizzolatti and Arbib, 1998). 'Audiovisual' mirror neurons seem to encode the action abstractly, independent of the information source (auditory or visual) from which evidence regarding the presence of the action is taken (Keysers et al. 2003). These 'auditory–visual' mirror neurons exemplify high-level abstraction in the representation of actions—an identical neural system becomes activated whenever a particular action is heard, seen or performed. It is of particular interest that two, independent, voxel-based morphometric studies found more grey matter volume in the inferior frontal gyrus in musicians compared with non-musicians (Sluming et al. 2002; Gaser and Schlaug 2003; see also Figure 18.1) which in addition to parietal regions (supramarginal gyrus and superior parietal lobule) and more dorsal premotor regions constitute this network of multimodal–sensorimotor integration. Listening to, seeing notation for, and watching performances of music that one knows how to play, and actually playing that music all appear to engage this putative human mirror neuron system.

Conclusions

Making music not only engages primary auditory and motor regions and the connections between them, but also engages regions that integrate and connect areas involved in both auditory and motor operations as well as in the integration of other multisensory information.

Professional instrumentalists learn and repeatedly practice associatiing hand/finger movements with meaningful patterns in sound, and sounds and movements with specific visual patterns (notation) while receiving continuous multisensory feedback. Learning to associate actions with particular sounds leads to functional but also structural changes in frontal cortices. In considering the putative functions of the inferior frontal regions, including its hypothesized role as a supramodal hierarchical processor, auditory–motor mapping region, and hub of the mirror neuron system, it may not be surprising to see that some of the most pronounced differences between musicians and non-musicians, both structurally and functionally, are indeed, in the inferior frontal region. Training this network and changing it as a result of that training has a cross-modal effect on other behavioural/cognitive operations that draw on this network. This cross-modal plasticity in multimodal brain regions may explain some of the cognitive enhancements and/or far transfer effects that have been associated with long term instrumental music training.

Acknowledgements

The research discussed in this chapter was supported by grants from the National Science Foundation (NSF), the International Foundation for Music Research (IFMR), and The Grammy Foundation. Christian Gaser, Andrea Norton, Katie Overy, Ellen Winner, Andrew Norton, Camilla Rosam, and Marie Forgeard have contributed to the research presented in this chapter.

References

Amunts K, Schlaug G, Jäncke L, Dabringhaus A, Steinmetz H, Schleicher A and Zilles K (1997). Motor cortex and hand motor skills: structural compliance in the human brain. *Human Brain Mapp*, **5**, 206–215.

Anderson BJ, Eckburg PB and Relucio KI (2002). Alterations in the thickness of motor cortical subregions after motor skill learning and exercise. *Learn Mem*, **9**, 1–9.

Anderson BJ, Li S, Alcantara A, Isaacs KR, Black JE and Greenough WT (1994). Glial hypertrophy is associated with synaptogenesis following motor-skill learning but not with angiogenesis, following exercise. *Glia*, **11**, 73–80.

Aziz-Zadeh L, Wilson SM, Rizzolatti G and Iacoboni M (2006). Congruent embodied representations for visually presented actions and linguistic phrases describing actions. *Curr Biol*, **16**, 1818–1823.

Bangert M and Schlaug G (2006). Specialization of the specialized in features of external human brain morphology. *Eur J Neurosci*, **24**, 1832–1834.

Bangert M and Altenmüller EO (2003). Mapping perception to action in piano practice: a longitudinal DC-EEG study. *BMC Neurosci*, **4**, 26.

Bangert M, Peschel T, Rotte M, Drescher D, Hinrichs H, Schlaug G, Heinze HJ and Altenmüller E (2006). Shared networks for auditory and motor processing in professional pianists: evidence from fMRI conjunction. *NeuroImage*, **30**, 917–926.

Bangerter A and Heath C (2004). The Mozart effect: tracking the evolution of a scientific legend. *Br J Soc Psychol*, **43**, 605–623.

Bengtsson SL, Nagy Z, Skare S, Forsman L, Forssberg H and Ullen F (2005). Extensive piano practicing has regionally specific effects on white matter development. *Nat Neurosci*, **8**, 1148–1150.

Besson M, Gaita F and Requin J (1994). Brain waves associated with musical incongruities differ for musicians and non-musicians. *Neurosci Lett*, **168**, 101–105.

Black JE, Isaacs KR, Anderson BJ, Alcantra AA and Greenough WT (1990). Learning causes synaptogenesis whereas motor activity causes angiogenesis in cerebellar cortex of adult rats. *Proc Natl Acad Sci USA*, **87**, 5568–5572.

Bosnyak DJ, Eaton RA and Roberts LE (2004). Distributed auditory cortical representations are modified when non-musicians are trained at pitch discrimination with 40 Hz amplitude modulated tones. *Cereb Cortex*, **14**, 1088–1099.

Bruer J (1999). *The myth of the first three years*. Free Press, New York.

Buccino G, Binkofskik F and Riggio L (2004a). The mirror neuron system and action recognition. *Brain Lang*, **89**, 370–376.

Buccino G, Vogt S, Ritzl A, Fink GR, Zilles K, Freund HJ and Rizzolatti G (2004b). Neural circuits underlying imitation learning of hand actions: an event-related fMRI study. *Neuron*, **42**, 323–334.

Ceci SJ and Williams WM (1997). Schooling intelligence and income. *Am Psychol*, **52**, 1051–1058.

Chan AS, Ho Y and Cheung M (1998). Music training improves verbal memory. *Nature*, **396**, 128.

Chochon F, Cohen L, van de Moortele PF and Dehaene S (1999). Differential contributions of the left and right inferior parietal lobules to number processing. *J Cogn Neurosci*, **11**, 617–630.

D'Ausilio A, Altenmüller E, Olivetti Belardinelli M and Lotze M (2006). Cross-modal plasticity of the motor cortex while listening to a rehearsed musical piece. *Eur J Neurosci*, **24**, 955–958.

Elbert T, Pantev C, Wienbruch C, Rockstroh B and Taub E (1995). Increased cortical representation of the fingers of the left hand in string players. *Science*, **270**, 305–306.

Fauvel J, Flood R and Wilson R (2006). Music and mathematics: from Pythagoras to fractals. Oxford Press, New York.

Forgeard M, Winner E, Norton A, Overy K, Iyengar U, Goldstein TR and Schlaug G. Effects of fifteen months of instrumental music training: evidence for near transfer, submitted.

Gaab N and Schlaug G (2003). The effect of musicianship on pitch memory in performance matched groups. *NeuroReport*, **14**, 2291–2295.

Gaab N, Gaser C and Schlaug G (2006). Improvement-related functional plasticity following pitch memory training. *Neuroimage*, **31**, 255–263.

Gaab N, Gaser C, Zaehle T, Jäncke L and Schlaug G (2003). Functional anatomy of pitch memory—an fMRI study with sparse temporal sampling. *Neuroimage*, **19**, 1417–1426.

Gaser C and Schlaug G (2003). Brain structures differ between musicians and non-musicians. *J Neurosci*, **23**, 9240–9245.

Hasegawa T, Matsuki K, Ueno T, Maeda Y, Matsue Y, Konishi Y and Sadato N (2004). Learned audio-visual cross-modal associations in observed piano playing activate the left planum temporale. An fMRI study. *Cogn Brain Res*, **20**, 510–518.

Haslinger B, Erhard P, Altenmüller E, Hennenlotter A, Schwaiger M, Einsiedel H, Rummeny E, Conrad B and Ceballos-Baumann AO (2004). Reduced recruitment of motor association areas during bimanual coordination in concert pianists. *Human Brain Map*, **22**, 206–215.

Haslinger B, Erhard P, Altenmüller E, Schroeder U, Boecker H and Ceballos-Baumann AO (2005). Transmodal sensorimotor networks during action observation in professional pianists. *J Cogn Neurosci*, **17**, 282–293.

Haueisen J and Knösche TR (2001). Involuntary motor activity in pianists evoked by music perception. *J Cogn Neurosci*, **13**, 786–792.

Hetland L (2000). Learning to make music enhances spatial reasoning. *J Aesthetic Educ*, **34**, 179–238.

Ho YC, Cheung MC and Chan AS (2003). Music training improves verbal but not visual memory: cross-sectional and longitudinal explorations in children. *Neuropsychology*, **17**, 439–445.

Hund-Georgiadis M and von Cramon Y (1999). Motor-learning-related changes in piano players and non-musicians revealed by functional magnetic resonance signals. *Exp Brain Res*, **125**, 417–425.

Hutchinson S, Lee LHL, Gaab N and Schlaug G (2003). Cerebellar volume of musicians. *Cereb Cortex*, **13**, 943–949.

Isaacs KR, Anderson BJ, Alcantara AA, Black JE and Greenough WT (1992). Exercise and the brain: angiogenesis in the adult rat cerebellum after vigorous physical activity and motor skill learning. *J Cereb Blood Flow Metab*, **12**, 110–119.

Jäncke L, Shah NJ and Peters M (2000). Cortical activations in primary and secondary motor areas for complex bimanual movements in professional pianists. *Cogn Brain Res*, **10**, 177–183.

Keenan JP, Halpern AR, Thangaraj V, Chen C, Edelman RR and Schlaug G (2001). Absolute pitch and planum temporale. *Neuroimage*, **14**, 1402–1408.

Kempermann G, Kuhn HG and Gage FH (1997). More hippocampal neurons in adult mice living in an enriched environment. *Nature*, **386**, 493–495.

Keysers C, Kohler E, Umiltà MA, Nanetti L, Fogassi L and Gallese V (2003). Audiovisual mirror neurons and action recognition. *Exp Brain Res*, **153**, 628–636.

Kleim JA, Lussnig E, Schwarz ER, Comery TA and Greenough WT (1996). Synaptogenesis and fos expression in the motor cortex of the adult rat after complex motor skill acquisition. *J Neurosci*, **16**, 4529–4535.

Koelsch S, Fritz T, Schulze K, Alsop D and Schlaug G (2005). Adults and children processing music: an fMRI study. *Neuroimage*, **25**, 1068–1076.

Koelsch S, Gunter TC, v Cramon DY, Zysset S, Lohmann G and Friederici AD (2002). Bach speaks: a cortical 'language-network' serves the processing of music. *Neuroimage*, **17**, 956–966.

Koeneke S, Lutz K, Wüstenberg T and Jäncke L (2004). Long-term training affects cerebellar processing in skilled keyboard players. *Neuroreport*, **15**, 1279–1282.

Kohler E, Keysers C, Umiltà MA, Fogassi L, Gallese V and Rizzolatti G (2002). Hearing sounds, understanding actions: action representation in mirror neurons. *Science*, **297**, 846–848.

Krings T, Töpper R, Foltys H, Erberich S, Sparing R, Willmes K and Thron A (2000). Cortical activation patterns during complex motor tasks in piano players and control subjects. A functional magnetic resonance imaging study. *Neurosci Lett*, **278**, 189–193.

Lahav A, Saltzman E and Schlaug G (2007). Action representation of sound: audiomotor recognition network while listening to newly-acquired actions. *J Neurosci*, **27**, 308–314.

Lee DJ, Chen Y and Schlaug G. (2003). Corpus callosum: musician and gender effects. *NeuroReport*, **14**, 205–209.

Levitin DJ and Menon V (2003). Musical structure is processed in language areas of the brain: a possible role for Brodmann Area 47 in temporal coherence. *Neuroimage*, **20**, 2142–2152.

Lotze M, Scheler G, Tan HR, Braun C and Birbaumer N (2003). The musician's brain: functional imaging of amateurs and professionals during performance and imagery. *Neuroimage*, **20**, 1817–1829.

Meister I, Krings T, Foltys H, Boroojerdi B, Mueller M, Töpper R and Thron A (2005). Effects of long-term practice and task complexity in musicians and non-musicians performing cortical motor organization. *Human Brain Mapp*, **25**, 345–352.

Münte TF, Kohlmetz C, Nager W and Altenmüller E (2001). Neuroperception: superior auditory spatial tuning in conductors. *Nature*, **409**, 580.

Nair DG, von Bueren Jarchow A, Pascual-Leone A, and Schlaug G (2006). Differential inter-hemispheric inhibition in pianists and string players: TMS evidence. Human Brain Mapping Meeting, Florence, 2006.

Nordstrom MA and Butler SL (2002). Reduced intracortical inhibition and facilitation of corticospinal neurons in musicians. *Exp Brain Res*, **144**, 336–342.

Norton A, Winner E, Cronin K, Overy K, Lee D and Schlaug G (2005). Are there pre-existing neural, cognitive, or motoric markers for musical ability? *Brain Cogn*, **59**, 124–134.

Overy K, Norton A, Cronin K, Gaab N, Alsop D, Winner E and Schlaug G (2004). Imaging melody and rhythm processing in young children. *NeuroReport*, **15**, 1723–1726.

Oztürk AH, Tascioglu B, Aktekin M, Kurtoglu Z and Erden I (2002). Morphometric comparison of the human corpus callosum in professional musicians and non-musicians by using in vivo magnetic resonance imaging. *J Neuroradiol*, **29**, 29–34.

Pantev C, Oostenveld R, Engelien A, Ross B, Roberts LE and Hoke M (1998). Increased auditory cortical representation in musicians. *Nature*, **392**, 811–814.

Pantev C, Roberts LE, Schulz M, Engelien A and Ross B (2001). Timbre-specific enhancement of auditory cortical representations in musicians. *Neuroreport*, **12**, 169–174.

Patel AD (2003). Language, music, syntax and the brain. *Nat Neurosci*, **6**, 674–681.

Pulvermüller F, Shtyrov Y and Ilmoniemi R (2005). Brain signatures of meaning access in action word recognition. *J Cogn Neurosci*, **17**, 884–892.

Rauscher FH and Zupan MA (2000). Classroom keyboard instruction improves kindergarten children's spatial–temporal performance: a field experiment. *Early Childhood Research Quarterly*, **15**, 215–228.

Rauscher FH, Shaw GL and Ky KN (1993). Music and spatial task performance. Nature, 365, 611.

Rauscher FH, Shaw GL, Levine L, Wrigh E, Dennis W and Newcomb R (1997). Music training causes long-term enhancement of preschool children's spatial–temporal reasoning. *Neurol Res*, **19**, 2–8.

Ridding MC, Brouwer B and Nordstrom MA (2000). Reduced interhemispheric inhibition in musicians. *Exp Brain Res1*, **33**, 249–253.

Rizzolatti G and Arbib MA (1998). Language within our grasp. *TINS*, **21**, 188–194.

Rizzolatti G, Fadiga L, Gallese V and Fogass L (1996). Premotor cortex and the recognition of motor actions. *Cogn Brain Res*, **3**, 131–141.

Schellenberg EG (2004). Music lessons enhance IQ. *Psychol Sci*, **15**, 511–514.

Schlaug G (2001). The brain of musicians: a model for functional and structural adaptation. In R Zatorre and I Peretz, eds, The biological foundations of music. *Ann NY Acad Sci*, **930**, 281–299.

Schlaug G, Jäncke L, Huang Y and Steinmetz H. (1995a). In vivo evidence of structural brain asymmetry in musicians. *Science*, **267**, 699–671.

Schlaug G, Jäncke L, Huang Y, Staiger JF and Steinmetz H. (1995b). Increased corpus callosum size in musicians. *Neuropsychologia*, **33**, 1047–1055.

Schlaug G, Norton AC, Overy K and Winner E (2005). Effects of music training on the child's brain and cognitive development. *Ann NY Acad Sci*, **1060**, 219–230.

Schneider P, Scherg M, Dosch HG, Specht HJ, Gutschalk A and Rupp A (2002). Morphology of Heschl's gyrus reflects enhanced activation in the auditory cortex of musicians. *Nat Neurosci*, **5**, 688–694.

Sergent J, Zuck E, Terriah S and MacDonald B (1993). Distributed neural network underlying musical sight-reading and keyboard performance. *Science*, **257**, 106–109.

Shahin A, Bosnyak DJ, Trainor LJ and Roberts LE (2003). Enhancemment of neuroplastic P2 and N1c auditory evoked potentials in skilled musicians. *J Neurosci*, **23**, 5545–5552.

Shahin A, Roberts LE and Trainor LJ (2004). Enhancement of auditory cortical development by musical experience in children. *Neuroreport*, **15**, 1917–1921.

Sluming V, Barrick T, Howard M, Cezayirli E, Mayes A and Roberts N (2002). Voxel-based morphometry reveals increased gray matter density in Broca's area in male symphony orchestra musicians. *Neuroimage*, **17**, 1613–1622.

Sluming V, Brooks J, Howard M, Downes JJ and Roberts N (2007). Broca's area supports enhanced visuospatial cognition in orchestral musicians. *J Neurosci*, **27**, 3799–3806.

Stewart L, Henson R, Kampe K, Walsh V, Turner R and Frith U (2003). Brain changes after learning to read and play music. *NeuroImage*, **20**, 71–83.

Tettamanti M and Weniger D (2006). Broca's area: a supramodal hierarchical processor? *Cortex*, **42**(4), 491–494.

Trainor LJ, Desjardins RN and Rockel C (1999). A comparison of contour and interval processing in musicians and nonmusicians using event-related potentials. *Aust J Psychol*, **51**, 147–153.

Van Praag H, Christie BR, Sejnowksi TJ and Gage FH (1999). Running enhances neurogenesis, learning, and long-term potentiation in mice. *Proc Natl Acad Sci USA*, **96**, 13427–13431.

Vaughn K (2000). Music and mathematics: modest support for the oft-claimed relationship. *Journal of Aesthetic Education*, **34**, 149–166.

Zatorre RJ, Chen JL and Penhune VB (2007). When the brain plays music. Auditory-motor interactions in music perception and production. *Nature Reviews Neuroscience*, **8**, 547–558.

Zatorre RJ, Evans AC and Meyer E (1994). Neural mechanism underlying melodic perception and memory for pitch. *J Neurosci*, **14**, 1908–1919.

Zatorre RJ, Perry DW, Beckett CA, Westbury CF and Evans AC (1998). Functional anatomy of musical processing in listeners with absolute pitch and relative pitch. *Proc Natl Acad Sci USA*, **95**, 3172–3177.

CHAPTER 19

Music and the brain
Three links to language

Aniruddh D. Patel

Introduction

A major theme in the neuroscience of music over the past decade has been the existence of specialized cognitive and neural mechanisms involved in music processing (Peretz and Coltheart 2003). Research with brain damaged patients has been particularly important in demonstrating that music involves a neurocognitive system with many components, and that certain components can be selectively damaged without obvious effects on other cognitive abilities. These findings point to some degree of brain specialization for music, specialization that emerges even in the absence of any explicit musical training (Bigand and Poulin-Charronnat 2006).

One can recognize that music is a unique confluence of component abilities, yet still search for connections between music cognition and processes involved in other cognitive domains, such as language, visuospatial thinking, or mathematics. Such comparative work can be revealing about the mechanisms underlying music processing, and can provide new avenues for exploring how these mechanisms work in the brain.

The goal of this chapter is to acquaint the reader with some of the evidence for links between music and language, and to encourage further exploration along these lines (see Patel 2008 for a fuller treatment). The focus is on perceptual processes, and on links between mechanisms involved in the processing of instrumental music and of ordinary, day to day language.

Sensory encoding of sound

There is growing evidence that musical abilities and training have repercussions for language skills. For example, musical abilities predict unique variance in the ability to perceive and produce subtle phonetic contrasts in a second language (Slevc and Miyake 2006) and in the reading abilities of young children in their first language (Anvari *et al.* 2002). Furthermore, musical training enhances the ability to interpret affective prosody (Thompson *et al.* 2004). Are these benefits simply a non-specific consequence of musical training on attention and executive functioning, or are there more specific links between musical abilities and language processing? Support for the latter view has emerged recently via neuroscientific investigations of brainstem encoding of sound. These studies suggest that musical abilities and/or training sharpen the brain's encoding of linguistic sound at a very early stage of processing.

The human brainstem contains many subcortical processing nuclei, which perform a significant amount of neural processing before sound reaches the cortex. Importantly, these lower brain centres are connected to cortical areas via both bottom-up and top-down connections (cf. Figure 1 of Patel and Iversen 2007). The latter ('corticofugal') connections provide one possible mechanism by which long-term auditory experience may influence early brain responses to sound, via mechanisms of neural plasticity.

Wong *et al.* (2007) first demonstrated an influence of musical abilities on linguistic sound encoding. These researchers examined the processing of linguistic pitch contours in Mandarin Chinese syllables by musically trained and untrained native English speakers (neither of whom was familiar with Mandarin). The participants listened passively to Mandarin monosyllables with different lexical tones while their brainstem responses were recorded using electroencephalography (EEG). The researchers found that the musicians showed superior brainstem encoding of the linguistic pitch patterns. They also found a positive correlation between the quality of sensory encoding and amount of musical training, suggesting a role for musical experience (rather than innate differences between musicians and non-musicians) in shaping the sensory encoding of linguistic sound.

An impact of musical abilities on linguistic pitch processing seems intuitively plausible because music places strong demands on the control and/or perception of pitch. However, speech also makes extensive use of structured auditory patterns not based on pitch (e.g., timbre-based differences between phonemes). Do musical abilities have any impact on the sensory encoding of timbre-based aspects of language sounds? Recent results by Musacchia *et al.* (2007) address this issue. Like Wong *et al.* (2007), these researchers measured auditory brainstem responses to speech using EEG, but this time to a familiar English syllable ('da') with no salient pitch variation. They found that musicians had earlier brainstem responses than non-musicians to the onset of the syllable. Interestingly, when the syllable was presented as a multimodal event (sound + video of a face saying the syllable), the latency of the brainstem response was shortened for both musicians and non-musicians, but the musicians still showed an earlier response than the non-musicians. The authors suggest that this difference in response latency indicates that musicians had more synchronous neural responses to sound onset, which is a sign of a high-functioning peripheral auditory system.

The superior encoding of linguistic sounds by musicians may be one possible mechanism underlying the linguistic benefits of musical abilities (cf. Tallal and Gaab 2006; Patel and Iversen 2007). These findings may also be relevant to research which has examined the impact of musical training on the cortical processing of linguistic pitch patterns. These studies have examined how well individuals can detect a deviation in voice fundamental frequency (F0) at the end of a spoken utterance. Using EEG, these studies have focused on cortical event-related potentials (ERPs) which occur with a latency of a few hundred milliseconds after the onset of the deviant event. Research with French-speaking adults (Schön *et al.* 2004) and 8-year-old children (Magne *et al.* 2006) has shown that musically trained listeners are better at detecting such deviations, and show enhanced cortical ERPs to these events. In fact, even when listening to sentences in a foreign language (Portuguese), French adults with musical training are better at detecting such deviations, and show substantially shorter latency in their cortical ERPs to those deviations (Marques *et al.* 2007). One notable finding of this line of research is that the influence of musical training on cortical responses emerges remarkably quickly: 8-year-old children with just 8 weeks of musical training differ from their musically untrained counterparts in their cortical ERPs to intonational deviations in speech (Moreno and Besson 2006).

Further work is needed to clarify the relationship between subcortical and cortical enhancements to linguistic sound processing associated with musical training. Since connections in the auditory pathway flow both bottom-up and top-down, experimental studies are needed to disentangle patterns of cause and effect at different levels of the nervous system as the brain changes in response to musical training. Ideally, such studies would measure subcortical and cortical ERP responses to linguistic pitch patterns within the same individuals as they undergo musical training programmes, and relate these measures to behavioural performance on pitch-related language tasks. Baseline measures of brain responses to linguistic sound (prior to musical training) would be desirable, to show that differences between musically trained and untrained groups are not present prior to training (cf. Norton *et al.* 2005).

Processing of melodic contours

Humans readily recognize a pitch pattern transposed upward or downward in frequency (e.g., the same melody played on a piccolo or a tuba). This sensitivity to relative (vs absolute) pitch patterns seems commonplace to us, yet a cross-species perspective reveals that this is a rare ability (McDermott and Hauser 2005). Most birds and non-human primates, for example, gravitate to absolute pitch cues in identifying pitch sequences, and extensive training is often needed before sensitivity to relative pitch can be demonstrated.

This specialization in human brains for sensitivity to relative pitch may be related to the importance of relative pitch in spoken intonation. A listener needs to be able to hear the similarity of intonation patterns when spoken in different pitch registers. For example, a child learning English needs to understand that a rising pitch at the end of an intonation contour can signal a question, whether the utterance is produced by another child or by an adult (with a much lower average F0). Similarly, the child needs to learn that a salient pitch excursion on a word in a sentence signals that the speaker is trying to put focus on that word (as in 'give me the RED toy'), even though the precise size of the pitch excursion may differ from one speaker to the next. Thus speech intonation perception requires processing of melodic contour: the general patterns of up and down in a pitch sequence, independent of exact interval sizes or absolute pitch height (Dilley 2005).

Many experiments on music have shown that melodic contour is an important component of music perception. For example, Dowling and colleagues have shown that melodic contour (vs the pattern of precise intervals in a melody) plays a role in immediate memory for unfamiliar melodies among adults (e.g., Dowling *et al.* 1995). Furthermore, melodic contour is one of the first aspects of music to be discriminated by infants (Trehub *et al.* 1984), and 5-year-old children rely heavily on contour in melody perception (Schellenberg and Trehub 1999). Studies of patients with brain damage indicate that the right superior temporal gyrus plays an important role in musical melodic contour perception (Peretz and Zatorre 2005, but cf. Stewart *et al.* 2008).

Given the importance of melodic contour in both speech and music, it is natural to ask whether melodic contours are processed by similar brain mechanisms in the two domains. Early evidence for this idea was provided by Patel *et al.* (1998), who studied two individuals with acquired amusia subsequent to cortical brain damage. The amusics were tested for their ability to discriminate between sentences that differed only in their intonation contour. Two types of sentence pairs were tested. In 'statement–question' pairs, the intonation contours differed at the end of the sentence (e.g., 'He likes to drive fast cars' spoken with a pitch fall or rise on 'cars'). In 'focus–shift' pairs, the intonation contours differed within the sentence (e.g., 'Go in front of the bank, I said' spoken with a salient pitch accent on 'front' or 'bank'). The amusics were also tested for their ability to discriminate tone sequence analogues of intonation patterns. These analogues were created by replacing each syllable in a sentence with a tone whose pitch was fixed at the frequency midway between the highest and lowest F0 of the syllable. Discrete tones were used rather than gliding tones (which would mimic intonation contours more precisely) in order to make the stimuli more music-like. The salient finding from this study was that for both amusics, performance on the linguistic intonation task was very similar to performance on the tone sequence task, suggesting shared processing of melodic contours across the two domains. (One amusic, whose problem was primarily with recognition of familiar music, did well on both tasks, while the other amusic, who had more basic problems with perception and discrimination of musical patterns, did poorly on both tasks.) Examination of the lesion profiles of the amusics suggested that right inferior frontal brain areas were important for the task of remembering and discriminating melodic contours (cf. Zatorre *et al.* 1994).

In contrast to these findings, subsequent research with musically tone-deaf individuals painted a different picture. Before discussing this work, it is worth briefly describing musical tone deafness (or congenital amusia). Congenital amusia (henceforth, 'amusia') is not due to brain damage and appears to be developmental in origin. Amusic individuals report life-long problems with music perception. (Note that it is important to distinguish amusia from the informal label of 'tone-deafness' that many people apply to themselves, usually to indicate that they do not sing well, cf. Cuddy *et al.* [2005]). For example, amusics have difficulty judging if two melodies are the same or different, in detecting when music is out of key (including their own singing), and in recognizing what should be familiar tunes from their culture (Ayotte *et al.* 2002). These problems cannot be attributed to hearing loss, lack of exposure to music, or to any obvious non-musical social or cognitive impairments. The core deficit in this disorder concerns pitch processing (Foxton *et al.* 2004; Hyde and Peretz 2004). It appears that there is a genetic basis for this disorder (Drayna *et al.* 2001; Peretz *et al.* 2007), and evidence from neuroimaging has revealed specific structural differences between normal and amusic brains in right inferior frontal cortex and right superior temporal gryus, as well as in left frontal and temporal cortical areas (Hyde *et al.* 2007; Mandell *et al.* 2007).

Amusia presents an excellent opportunity to study the relationship between melodic contour processing in speech and music. Ayotte *et al.* (2002) first examined speech intonation perception in congenital amusia, using the stimuli and methods of Patel *et al.* (1998). The amusics had no problem discriminating sentences with different intonation contours. In contrast, they had difficulty discriminating the tone sequence analogs of intonation. These results suggested that amusics were unimpaired in speech intonation perception, and prompted Peretz and Coltheart (2003) to include melodic contour analysis as a domain-specific aspect of musical processing, not shared with speech.

Subsequent work, however, has re-opened the issue of speech intonation perception in amusia. Lochy *et al.* (2004) tested a group of amusics using methods very similar to those of Ayotte *et al.* (2002), but with different results. This time, about 30 per cent of the amusics had significant difficulty discriminating linguistic statements from questions, whereas they did well discriminating sentences with focus on different words. The critical difference between these tasks is that the statement-question task requires discriminating the direction of pitch movement on the same word (up versus down), whereas the focus-shift task simply requires detecting a salient pitch movement within a sentence, because different words bear the large

movement in the two members of a focus-shift pair. That is, sensitivity to the direction of pitch movement is irrelevant to the focus-shift task: as long as one can detect a pitch change, and can remember that this change happened on the same or different words in the two sentences, one can solve the task.

These findings were intriguing because psychophysical work on amusia has revealed a salient deficit for the perception of pitch direction (Foxton *et al.* 2004; Griffiths *et al.* 2007). That is, an amusic individual may be able to detect that pitch has changed, but not be able to discriminate an upward from a downward change. Lochy *et al.*'s findings suggest that such direction discrimination deficits may be relevant for speech intonation perception. Given the differences between the findings of Ayotte *et al.* (2002) and Lochy *et al.* (2004), it is important to determine which results replicate. Recently, Patel *et al.* (2008) replicated Lochy *et al.*'s findings with a different group of amusics, finding that about 30 per cent had problems with statement-question discrimination but not focus-shift discrimination. Notably, this replication occurred in a different language (English-speaking amusics, vs the French-speaking amusics of Lochy *et al.*). An important question raised by the results of Lochy *et al.* (2004) and Patel *et al.* (2008) is why only a subset of amusics (~30 per cent) exhibit intonation perception deficits. Does this subset have a qualitatively different kind of deficit from amusics without such problems, or are they simply at the end of a continuum such that all amusics would show intonation perception problems if pitch contrasts are made subtle enough? These questions await further research, but the current findings are sufficient to indicate that melodic contour processing in speech and music may in fact have overlapping neural substrates.

Syntactic processing

Music and language involve hierarchically structured sequences built from basic units via rich combinatorial principles. That is, both are syntactic systems. Native listeners have implicit knowledge of these combinatorial principles, knowledge which requires no formal training and which can readily be demonstrated via judgements of the well-formedness of novel sequences and via a range of implicit tasks (Bigand and Poulin-Charronnat 2006).

Despite these general similarities, however, it is also clear that musical and linguistic syntax differ in important ways. For example, fundamental grammatical categories in language (such as nouns and verbs) have no analogue in music, and the function of linguistic syntax in indicating 'who did what to whom' also has no musical parallel. Instead, (Western) musical syntax is based on selecting a set of seven discrete pitches within each octave and creating a musical 'key' by using these pitches in such a way that a hierarchy of structural importance is created among them. This leads to certain pitches and chords being perceived as more stable than others. These stable elements act as cognitive reference points, with one (the tonic note or chord) being the most stable (Krumhansl 1990). This syntax functions to build patterns of tension and resolution in musical sequences (Lerdahl and Jackendoff 1983, Lerdahl and Krumhansl 2007). Thus it is clear that musical syntax is not simply a trivial variant of linguistic syntax.

For many years, the evidence from neuroscience seemed to favour the independence of musical and linguistic syntax in the brain. Specifically, research on the neuropsychology of music provided clear cases of dissociations between linguistic and musical syntactic abilities following brain damage. For example, Peretz (1993) documented a case of a non-aphasic man with bilateral temporal lobe damage (due to strokes) who lost sensitivity to musical key, even though his basic perception of pitch patterns was intact. This is one of several well-documented cases of 'amusia without aphasia' (cf. Marin and Perry 1999).

Yet in direct contrast to these findings, neuroimaging research has pointed to overlap in the syntactic processing of language and music. An early study which directly compared brain responses to musical and linguistic syntactic processing in the same individuals was conducted by Patel et al. (1998). The researchers used ERPs to compare brain responses (from musicians) to linguistic syntactic and musical syntactic incongruities. The linguistic incongruities

involved manipulations of phrase structure in sentences, and the musical incongruities involved out-of-key chords in chord sequences. The linguistic incongruities generated a late positive ERP component known as the P600, previously known to be associated with syntactic processing in language (Osterhout and Holcomb 1993). The main finding of interest was that the out-of-key chords generated a P600 which was statistically indistinguishable from the 'linguistic' P600. The authors interpreted this to mean that processes involved in syntactic integration were shared across the two domains. In addition to the P600, out-of-key chords also elicited an early right anterior–temporal negativity (RATN) which had not been reported in previous neuroimaging studies of music. The functional significance of this component was not well understood, though it was thought to be involved in musical syntactic processing.

Subsequent ERP work by Koelsch et al. (2000) examined brain responses to out-of-key chords in non-musicians, and found an early right anterior negativity (ERAN), which had a shorter latency than the RATN and a more anterior and bilateral scalp distribution. Many subsequent studies by Koelsch and colleagues have found the ERAN to be reliably elicited by structurally unexpected chords, in both musicians and non-musicians, and in the absence of any task related to detecting these chords.[1] Furthermore, elicitation of the ERAN does not require the use of an out-of-key chord: it can also be elicited by a structurally unexpected chord from within the key of the preceding sequence. This rules out auditory sensory incongruity as the driving force behind the elicitation of this component (Koelsch et al. 2007).

What is the relationship between the ERAN and the RATN? As suggested by Koelsch and Siebel (2005), it seems likely that they represent the same underlying brain process, and that the earlier latency of the ERAN is related to the temporal predictability of the chord sequences

[1] Another ERP component that is often elicited by out-of-key chords is a negativity peaking around 500 ms after the onset of the target chord (the 'N500'). For possible links between mechanisms involved in this brain response and in language processing, see Steinbeis and Koelsch (2007).

that have typically been used in studies of the ERAN. That is, most such research has used isochronous sequences of chords, rendering the temporal onset of each successive chord quite predictable in time. In contrast, when more temporally variable musical contexts are used (as in Patel *et al.* 1998, and Koelsch and Mulder 2002), an early right negative component is elicited that is more similar to the RATN in latency and scalp distribution. Thus the precise latency and distribution of early right negativities to music is likely to be subject to rhythmic influences.

More interesting from the current standpoint are questions about the relationship of the ERAN to brain mechanisms involved in linguistic syntactic processing. Using MEG, Maess *et al.* (2001) localized the generators of the ERAN to Broca's area and its right hemisphere homologue, suggesting an overlap with language processing. Other research using functional magnetic resonance imaging (fMRI) also implicated Broca's area in the processing of syntactic (harmonic) structure in music (e.g. Tillmann *et al.* 2003). Yet the neuroimaging evidence for overlap between linguistic and musical syntax stood in sharp contrast to evidence from neuropsychology for dissociations between linguistic and musical syntactic abilities following brain damage, as discussed above. Thus it became clear that a theoretical framework was needed which could accommodate both the neuroimaging evidence (for overlap) and the neuropsychology evidence (for dissociation).

Patel (2003) proposed one such framework based on the idea that language and music have distinct and domain-specific syntactic representations (such as words and their syntactic features in language, and chords and their harmonic relations in music), but that activating these representations as part of online processing draws on a common pool of limited neural resources. This idea was termed the 'shared syntactic integration resource hypothesis' (SSIRH). The SSIRH posits that linguistic and musical syntactic representations are stored in distinct brain networks (and hence can be selectively damaged), whereas there is overlap in the networks which provide neural resources for the activation of stored syntactic representations. It was hypothesized that such resources

are needed when dealing with difficult structural integrations, because such integrations require the rapid and selective activation of items with low activation levels in representation networks (e.g., structurally unexpected words or chords).

How does this proposal map onto neural architecture? At the moment the answer to this question is not known. In its original formulation, the SSIRH combined the functional proposal outlined above with a rough localizationist proposal, namely that that neural resources reside in frontal brain regions, while syntactic representations reside in posterior regions. Hence syntactic processing is conceived of as involving the reciprocal interaction of frontotemporal regions (cf. Tyler and Marslen-Wilson 2007). Further research using localizationist techniques (such as fMRI) is needed to address this issue.

A principal motivation for developing the SSIRH was to generate predictions to guide future research into the relation of linguistic and musical syntactic processing. One salient prediction regards the interaction of musical and linguistic syntactic processing. In particular, because the SSIRH proposes that linguistic and musical syntactic integration rely on common neural resources, and because syntactic processing resources are limited (Gibson 2000), it predicts that tasks that combine linguistic and musical syntactic integration will show interference between the two. In particular, the SSIRH predicts that difficult harmonic integrations in music will interfere with concurrent difficult syntactic integration in language (Patel 2003). This idea can be tested in paradigms in which a harmonic and a linguistic sequence are presented together and the influence of harmonic structure on syntactic processing in language is studied.

Koelsch *et al.* (2005) conducted one such study, in which short sentences were presented visually in a word-by-word format simultaneously with musical chords, with one chord per word. In some sentences, the final word created a grammatical violation via a gender disagreement. (The sentences were in German, in which many nouns are marked for gender. An example of a gender violation used in this study is: 'Er trinkt den kühlen Bier', 'He drinks the[masculine] cool$_{masculine}$ beer$_{neuter}$.) The chord sequences were designed to strongly invoke a particular key, and the final chord could either be the tonic chord of that key or an unexpected out-of-key chord from a distant key (e.g., a D-flat major chord at the end of a C-major sequence). The participants (all non-musicians) were instructed to ignore the music and simply judge if the last word of the sentence was linguistically correct.

Koelsch *et al.* focused on early ERP negativities elicited by syntactically incongruous words and chords. Previous research on language or music alone had shown that the linguistic syntactic incongruities were associated with a left anterior negativity (LAN), while the musical incongruities were associated with an ERAN (Gunter *et al.* 2000; Koelsch *et al.* 2000). For their combined language–music stimuli, Koelsch *et al.* found that when sentences ended grammatically but were accompanied by an out-of-key chord, a normal ERAN was produced. Similarly, when chord sequences ended normally but were accompanied by a syntactically incongruous word, a normal LAN was produced. The question of interest was how these brain responses would interact when a sequence had simultaneous syntactic incongruities in language and music. The main finding was that the brain responses were not simply additive. Instead, there was an interaction: the LAN to syntactically incongruous words was significantly *smaller* when these words were accompanied by an out-of-key chord, as if the processes underlying the LAN and ERAN were competing for similar neural resources. In a control experiment, Koelsch *et al.* showed that this was not due to general attentional effects because the LAN was not influenced by a simple auditory oddball paradigm involving physically deviant tones on the last word in a sentence. Thus the study supported the prediction that tasks which combine linguistic and musical syntactic integration will show interference between the two processes. Further behavioural studies by Slevc *et al.* (in press) and Fedorenko *et al.* (in press) using simultaneous presentation of sentences and musical sequences have provided additional evidence for the interaction of linguistic and musical syntactic processing, even in the absence of any explicit music-related task

(cf. Patel in press for descriptions of these studies). Like the study of Koelsch *et al.* (2005), these studies have included control conditions to check that the interactions observed are not simply due to attentional factors.

One line of research which awaits exploration involves within-subjects comparisons of syntactic processing in language and music using fMRI. Such work could help localize shared resource networks for syntactic integration within specific regions of the brain.

Future directions

This chapter has discussed three points of contact between music and language processing in the brain. Many other areas of possible overlap await investigation, including the neural mechanisms involved in processing phrase boundaries, and the mechanisms involved in the affective appraisal of musical and linguistic sequences (for further discussion of these topics, see Patel 2008). Another little-explored area concerns the relationship between the neural mechanisms involved in the generation of novel linguistic and musical sequences (cf. Brown *et al.* 2006).

Conclusion

The extent to which music processing overlaps with mechanisms used in other cognitive domains is an active area of research and debate (e.g., Peretz 2006; Patel 2008). One fertile line of work that has grown out of this debate concerns relations between music and language processing. The evidence reviewed in this chapter suggests that music and language may have a number of common processes which act on distinct types of information, e.g., on musical melodies vs linguistic intonation contours, or on chord progressions vs sequences of words. Thus the distinction between the domain specificity of information vs the generality of processing is an essential conceptual tool for research that examines the relationship between music and other cognitive domains (cf. Massaro 1998 for an application of this distinction to the study of speech processing).

Comparative music–language research is still in its infancy. The ultimate promise of such work is not simply to resolve debates over modularity, but to gain a deeper understanding of the mechanisms humans use to make sense out of sound. This requires doing justice to both the differences and the similarities between the domains.

Acknowledgments

L. Robert Slevc, Lauren Stewart and Daniele Schön provided helpful comments. Supported by Neurosciences Research Foundation as part of its research programme on music and the brain at The Neurosciences Institute, where ADP is the Esther J. Burnham Senior Fellow.

References

Anvari S, Trainor LJ, Woodside J and Levy BA (2002). Relations among musical skills, phonological processing, and early reading ability in preschool children. *Journal of Experimental Child Psychology*, **83**, 111–130.

Ayotte J, Peretz I and Hyde K (2002). Congenital amusia: a group study of adults afflicted with a music-specific disorder. *Brain*, **125**, 238–251.

Bigand E and Poulin-Charronnat B (2006). Are we 'experienced listeners'? A review of the musical capacities that do not depend on formal musical training. *Cognition*, **100**, 100–130.

Brown S, Martinez MJ and Parsons LM (2006). Music and language side by side in the brain: a PET study of the generation of melodies and sentences. *European J Neuroscience*, **23**, 2791–2803.

Cuddy LL, Balkwill L-L, Peretz I and Holden RR (2005). A study of 'tone deafness' among university students. *Annals of the New York Academy of Sciences*, **1060**, 311–324.

Dilley L (2005). The phonetics and phonology of tonal systems. PhD dissertation, MIT.

Dowling WJ, Kwak S and Andrews MW (1995). The time course of recognition of novel melodies. *Perception and Psychophysics*, **57**, 136–149.

Drayna D, Manichaikul A, de Lange M, Snieder H and Spector T (2001). Genetic correlates of musical pitch recognition in humans. *Science*, **291**, 1969–1972.

Fedorenko E, Patel AD, Casasanto D, Winawer J and Gibson E (in press). Structural integration in language and music: Evidence for a shared system. Memory and Cognition.

Foxton JM, Dean JL, Gee R, Peretz I and Griffiths TD (2004). Characterisation of deficits in pitch perception underlying 'tone deafness'. *Brain*, **127**, 801–810.

Gibson E (2000). The dependency locality theory: a distance-based theory of linguistic complexity. In A Marantz, Y Miyashita and WO'Neil, eds, *Image, language, brain*, 95–126. MIT Press, Cambridge, MA.

Griffiths TD, Stewart L, McDonald C and Kumar A (2007) A selective deficit in pitch-direction perception in congenital amusia. *Society for Neuroscience Abstracts*, November.

Gunter TC, Friederici AD and Schriefers H (2000). Syntactic gender and semantic expectancy: ERPs reveal early autonomy and late interaction. *Journal of Cognitive Neuroscience*, **12**, 556–568.

Hyde K and Peretz I (2004). Brains that are out of tune but in time. *Psychological Science*, **15**, 356–360.

Hyde KL, Lerch JP, Zatorre RJ, Griffiths TD, Evans AC and Peretz I (2007). Cortical thickness in congenital amusia: when less is better than more. *Journal of Neuroscience*, **27**, 13028–13032.

Koelsch S and Mulder J (2002). Electric brain responses to inappropriate harmonies during listening to expressive music. *Clinical Neurophysiology*, **113**, 862–869.

Koelsch S and Siebel WA (2005). Toward a neural basis of music perception. *Trends in Cognitive Sciences*, **9**, 578–584.

Koelsch S, Gunter TC, Friederici AD and Schröger E (2000). Brain indices of music processing: 'non-musicians' are musical. *Journal of Cognitive Neuroscience*, **12**, 520–541.

Koelsch S, Gunter TC, Wittforth M and Sammler D (2005). Interaction between syntax processing in language and music: an ERP study. *Journal of Cognitive Neuroscience*, **17**, 1565–1577.

Koelsch S, Jentschke S, Sammler D and Mietchen D (2007). Untangling syntactic and sensory processing: an ERP study of music perception. *Psychophysiology*, **44**, 476–490.

Krumhansl CL (1990). *Cognitive foundations of musical pitch*. Oxford University Press, New York.

Lerdahl F and Jackendoff R (1983). *A generative theory of tonal music*. MIT Press, Cambridge, MA.

Lerdahl F and Krumhansl CL (2007). Modeling tonal tension. *Music Perception*, **24**, 329–366.

Lochy A, Hyde KL, Parisel S Van Hyfte S and Peretz I (April 2004). Discrimination of speech prosody in congenital amusia. Poster presented at the Cognitive Neuroscience Society, San Francisco.

Maess B, Koelsch S, Gunter T and Friederici AD (2001). Musical syntax is processed in Broca's area: an MEG study. *Nature Neuroscience*, **4**, 540–545.

Magne C, Schön D and Besson M (2006). Musician children detect pitch violations in both music and language better than nonmusician children: behavioral and electrophysiological approaches. *Journal of Cognitive Neuroscience*, **18**, 199–211.

Mandell J, Schulze K and Schlaug G (2007). Congenital amusia: an auditory-feedback disorder? *Restorative Neurology and Neuroscience*, **25**, 323–334.

Marin OSM and Perry DW (1999). Neurological aspects of music perception and performance. In D Deutsch, ed., *The psychology of music*, 2nd edn, 653–724. Academic Press, San Diego, CA.

Marques C, Moreno S, Castro SL and Besson M (2007). Musicians detect pitch violation in a foreign language better than nonmusicians: behavioral and electrophysiological evidence. *Journal of Cognitive Neuroscience*, **19**, 1453–1463.

Massaro D (1998). *Perceiving talking faces*. MIT Press, Cambridge, MA.

McDermott J and Hauser MD (2005). The origins of music: innateness, development, and evolution. *Music Perception*, **23**, 29–59.

Moreno S and Besson M (2006). Musical training and language-related brain electrical activity in children. *Psychophysiology*, **43**, 287–291.

Musacchia G, Sams M, Skoe E and Kraus N (2007) Musicians have enhanced subcortical auditory and audiovisual processing of speech and music. *Proceedings of the National Academy of Sciences, USA*, **104**, 15894–15898.

Norton A, Winner E, Kronin K, Overy K, Lee DJ and Schlaug G (2005) Are there neural, cognitive, or motoric markers for musical ability prior to instrumental training? *Brain and Cognition*, **59**, 124–34.

Osterhout L and Holcomb PJ (1993). Event-related potential and syntactic anomaly: evidence of anomaly detection during the perception of continuous speech. *Language and Cognitive Processes*, **8**, 413–437.

Patel AD (2003). Language, music, syntax, and the brain. *Nature Neuroscience*, **6**, 674–681.

Patel AD (2008). *Music, language and the brain*. Oxford University Press, New York.

Patel AD (in press). Language, music, and the brain: a resource-sharing framework. In M Rohrmeir, P Rebuschat, J Hawkins and I Cross, eds, *Language and music as cognitive systems*. Oxford University Press, Oxford.

Patel AD and Iversen JR (2007). The linguistic benefits of musical abilities. *Trends in Cognitive Sciences*, **11**, 369–372.

Patel AD, Gibson E, Ratner J, Besson M and Holcomb P (1998). Processing syntactic relations in language and music: an event-related potential study. *Journal of Cognitive Neuroscience*, **10**, 717–733.

Patel AD, Peretz I, Tramo M and Labrecque R (1998). Processing prosodic and musical patterns: a neuropsychological investigation. *Brain and Language*, **61**, 123–144.

Patel AD, Wong M, Foxton J, Lochy A and Peretz I (2008). Speech intonation perception deficits in musical tone deafness (congenital amusia). *Music Perception*, **25**, 357–368.

Peretz I (1993). Auditory atonalia for melodies. *Cognitive Neuropsychology*, **10**, 21–56.

Peretz I (2006). The nature of music from a biological perspective. *Cognition*, **100**, 1–32.

Peretz I and Coltheart M (2003). Modularity of music processing. *Nature Neuroscience*, **6**, 688–691.

Peretz I and Zatorre RJ (2005). Brain organization for music processing. *Annual Review of Psychology*, **56**, 89–114.

Peretz I, Cummings S and Dubé M-P (2007) The genetics of congenital amusia (or tone-deafness): a family aggregation study. *American Journal of Human Genetics*, **81**, 582–588.

Schellenberg EG and Trehub SE (1999). Redundancy, conventionality, and the discrimination of tone sequences: a developmental perspective. *Journal of Experimental Child Psychology*, **74**, 107–127.

Schön D, Magne C and Besson M (2004). The music of speech: electrophysiological study of pitch perception in language and music. *Psychophysiology*, **41**, 341–349.

Slevc LR and Miyake A (2006) Individual differences in second language proficiency: does musical ability matter? *Psychological Science*, **17**, 675–681.

Slevc LR, Rosenberg JC and Patel AD (in press). Making psycholinguistics musical: Self-paced reading time evidence for shared processing of linguistic and musical syntax. *Psychonomic Bulletin and Review*.

Steinbeis N and Koelsch S (2008). Shared neural resources between music and language indicate semantic processing of musical tension–resolution patterns. *Cerebral Cortex*, doi:10.1093/cercor/bhm149. **18**, 1169–1178.

Stewart L, Overeath T, Warren JD, Foxton JM and Griffiths TD (2008). fMRI evidence for a cortical hierarchy of pitch pattern processing. *PLoS ONE*, **3**(1), e1470. doi:10/1371/journal.pone.0001470.

Tallal P and Gaab N (2006). Dynamic auditory processing, musical experience and language development. *Trends in Neurosciences*, **29**, 382–370.

Thompson WF, Schellenberg EG and Husain G (2004). Decoding speech prosody: do music lessons help? *Emotion*, **4**, 46–64.

Tillmann B, Janata P and Bharucha JJ (2003). Activation of the inferior frontal cortex in musical priming. *Cognitive Brain Research*, **16**, 145–161.

Trehub SE, Bull D and Thorpe LA (1984). Infants' perception of melodies: The role of melodic contour. *Child Development*, **55**, 821–830.

Tyler L and Marslen-Wilson W (2008). Fronto-temporal brain systems supporting spoken language comprehension. Philosophical Transactions of the Royal Society, doi:10.1098/rstb/2007.2158. **363**, 1037–1054.

Wong PCM, Skoe E, Russo NM, Dees T and Kraus N (2007). Musical experience shapes human brainstem encoding of linguistic pitch patterns. *Nature Neuroscience*, **10**, 420–422.

Zattore RJ, Evans AC and Meyer E (1994). Neural mechanisms underlying melodic perception and memory for pitch. *Journal of Neuroscience*, **14**, 1908–1919.

PART 5

Musical development

Edited by David J. Hargreaves

CHAPTER 20

Prenatal development and the phylogeny and ontogeny of music

Richard Parncutt

Introduction

Prenatal musical development involves the acquisition of perceptual, cognitive, motor and emotional abilities and information that may influence later musical development. I argue in this chapter that research in this area can shed light on the origins of musical behaviours, not only in human prehistory (phylogeny) but also within the lifespan of an individual (ontogeny).

Ontogenetically, the infant is surprisingly sensitive to patterns of sound and movement that adults perceive as musical (Chapter 21 this volume). The origin and evolutionary function (if any) of this sensitivity is unclear. One possibility is that musical patterns are similar to perceptual patterns to which the fetus is regularly exposed before birth: the fundamental frequency trajectory of the mother's voice, its relationship to breathing, and the rhythm of her heartbeat and footsteps (Parncutt 1989, 1993).

In spite of a recent renaissance of research on the phylogeny (origins) of music (summarized by Mithen 2005), no theory currently enjoys broad acceptance. One possibility involves classical conditioning of the fetus during the third trimester by passive exposure to sounds, movements and hormonal changes within the mother's body (Parncutt, in press). Since (changes in) maternal emotional states regularly trigger both (changes in) the patterns of sound and movement to which the fetus is exposed and (changes in) blood hormone levels, the fetus may associate these with each other, giving emotional connotations to patterns of sound and movement.

The importance of the prenatal phase for general psychological development was emphasized by Smotherman and Robinson (1990) and by Hopkins and Johnson (2005). The fetus responds actively to changes in its intrauterine environment in ways that influence its later behavioural and biological development. The prenatal phase may be regarded as a *developmental niche* (cf. Super and Harkness 1986) with its own unique characteristics but also lying on the same developmental continuum as postnatal niches. Although no-one would question that sensation, emotion, cognition and motor abilities have prenatal origins (Hall and Oppenheim 1987), most empirical research about these abilities in the late twentieth century ignored the prenatal period, while at the same time repeatedly asking nature–nurture questions that can only be answered by studying the prenatal epigenesis[1] of behaviour.

---

[1] The word 'epigenesis' (rather than genesis) refers to the role of both nature (genetics) and nurture (environment), and the interaction between them, in the prenatal emergence of behaviour.

It is problematic to use the term 'music' in conjunction with fetal development. Neither the fetus nor the infant discriminates between music (including singing) and speech; *motherese*[2] (Papousek 1996), the playful vocal-gestural interaction between infants and carers, is a mixture of both. Because motherese is not music but may represent music's origin, the term *protomusic* is appropriate (cf. Fitsch 2006)—by analogy to *protolanguage*, the common ancestor of a group of related languages. For similar reasons, it is misleading to speak of 'womb music'[3] or of 'playing music to cows' (Uetake *et al.* 1997), since the sound patterns presented in such studies are not perceived as music (i.e. not as culturally situated) by the experimental participants. Those patterns may nonetheless have musically interesting physiological, behavioural or cognitive affects.

This chapter focuses on musically relevant psychological aspects of prenatal development: the development of perception, cognition and emotion, the relationships between them, and the musical and musicological implications of those relationships. The chapter begins by surveying relevant fetal sensory abilities: hearing, the vestibular sense of balance and acceleration, and the proprioceptive sense of body orientation and movement. All those senses are relevant for musical development, since in all known cultures music is inseparable from bodily movement and gesture, whether real (Blacking 1995) or implied (Tolbert 2001). The chapter goes on to consider what sounds and other stimuli are available to the fetus: what patterns are the earliest to be perceptually learned? It then considers psychological and philosophical issues of fetal attention, 'consciousness', learning and memory. The chapter closes with speculations about the possible role of prenatal development in the phylogeny of musical behaviours.

---

[2] I use the term *motherese* rathar than *infant-directed speech* to emphasize the two-way nature of this form of communication (including the active role of the infant) and the musically central role of women (especially in discussions of the phylogeny of music). Of course men (not only fathers) and women other than mothers can and should also speak motherese.

[3] E.g. 'Babies remember womb music', http://news.bbc.co.uk/2/hi/health/1432495.stm, viewed on 11 August 2007.

The ontogeny of music

Fetal auditory, vestibular and proprioceptive abilities

All human sensory systems begin to function before birth (Hepper 1992). The acoustical stimulation to which the fetus is exposed is more diverse and carries more information relative to corresponding discriminatory abilities than visual, tactile, olfactory or gustatory (biochemical) stimulation. In that sense, hearing may be regarded as the dominant sensory modality in the prenatal phase, and infancy as a transition from auditory to visual dominance.

The fetus can hear throughout the second half of gestation. Because the fetal inner ear is filled with fluid, much of the sound heard by the fetus is transmitted to the inner ear through the skull by bone conduction (Gerhardt *et al.* 1996; Sohmer *et al.* 2001). The cochlea begins to process sounds at about around 20 weeks gestation; the cochlea reaches adult size at 25 weeks, but continues to develop until birth (Bibas *et al.* 2008). Motor responses to sound begin during the same period (Joseph 2000). At 20 weeks, the fetus is sensitive to a narrow band of spectral frequencies around 300 Hz (Hepper and Shahidullah 1994). As the fetus develops, its auditory abilities—including the perceptible range of spectral frequencies, the discrimination of frequencies and rapid sequences of events, and the storage and recognition of pitch–time patterns—gradually improve and may approach adult levels at birth (Joseph 2000), even though brain myelination is not complete until several years later.

It is physically impossible for the fetus to localize sound sources (Parncutt 2006). First, the fetal head does not cast an acoustic shadow at the relatively low frequencies that are transmitted into the amniotic fluid. Second, interaural time differences are smaller for the fetus than for an adult due to the smaller head size and the faster speed of sound in liquid. The fetus therefore has no access to information about the direction from which sounds emanate. Prenatal sound is monophonic and omnidirectional.

The vestibular system (or organ of balance) begins to function at about the same time as the cochlea. The cochlea and vestibular system lie at opposite ends of the (bony/osseous) laby-rinth in the temporal bone or inner ear. The vestibular system consists of three semicircular canals that are sensitive to angular accelera-tions (rotation), and the saccule and utricle which each contain otoliths (dense structures) that are sensitive to gravity and linear accelera-tions (horizontal movement in the utricle, ver-tical in the saccule). The membranous labyrinth grows quickly and attains adult size by the mid-dle of the gestation period; the otic capsule ossifies between 18 and 24 weeks (Nemzek *et al.* 2000).

Fetal motility and proprioception

An overview of fetal motor development was given by de Vries and Hopkins (2005). Fetal motil-ity begins at about eight weeks' gestation, when the fetus begins to move through the amniotic fluid and to extend and flex its limbs. From then on, the movement repertoire of the fetus gradu-ally expands. Some movements may be regarded as adaptations to the prenatal environment, while others prepare the fetus for postnatal life. In the third trimester, different sleep–wake states are associated with different movement repertoires and different sizes and frequencies of movement. Movements are not confined to the limbs, but also include startles, breathing movements, jaw openings, sucking, swallowing, facial, tongue and laryngeal movements.

As movements develop, so too does *motor control*. Motor control generally involves an interaction between the neural signals that con-trol muscle activity and sensory feedback about the limb location and muscle tension. The spi-nal reflex arc begins to function during the first trimester, enabling motor signals to bypass the brain, speeding up motor reflexes.

Development of motor control occurs in par-allel with development of *proprioception*—the sense of the relative position and motion of parts of the body. Since musical meaning involves the perception of gesture (Tolbert 2001), which in turn depends on proprioception, the prenatal development of proprioception may be relevant for the later emergence of musical abilities.

Gestures also play an important role in moth-erese (Trevarthen 1985). As they get older, infants increasingly understand the meaning of

the physical and vocal gestures of their carers and learn to imitate them. It would be surprising if this striking postnatal development did not depend in some way on prenatal exposure to patterns of sound, movement and emotion.

The fetal auditory environment

The fetal auditory environment is rich and var-ied, and provides many opportunities for prena-tal perceptual learning. The fetus is exposed to sounds from both inside and outside the moth-er's body. Internal sounds include her voice, breathing, heartbeat, digestion, body move-ments, and footsteps (Lecanuet 1996). Of these, the voice is most often audible (Fifer and Moon 1994). The internal sounds tend to be louder than the external sounds: Richards *et al.* (1992) found the mother's voice to be about 8 dB louder to the fetus than the voices of her con-versational partners. The fetus is also exposed to patterns of movement that are coupled to sound patterns, such as when the mother walks.

Both internal and external sounds are muffled (low-pass filtered) as they pass through the mother's body and amniotic fluid. Spectral components in the approximate range 100–1000 Hz are attenuated relatively little and may even be slightly amplified, even if their original is external (Richards *et al.* 1992). When the fetus is exposed to speech, either internally from the mother or from an external source, muffling makes vowels more salient (audible) than con-sonants and the fundamental frequency contour more salient than spectral information (timbre, phonemes) (cf. Smith *et al.* 2003)—consistent with the important role of pitch contour in music perception (Dowling and Fujitani 1971).

Fetal 'consciousness'

The fetus is not conscious in the everyday sense of *reflective* consciousness, that is, the ability to reflect upon perceptual experience. It does how-ever have a range of abilities that may be consid-ered part of a broad definition of consciousness, including perception, cognition, and emotion; sleep–wake cycles (Nijhuis *et al.* 1982); prefer-ences; and attention. Newborns are capable of demonstrating preferences by the rate of suck-ing on a pacifier (DeCasper and Fifer 1980), suggesting that the fetus could also demonstrate preferences if a suitable empirical method could be developed. Kisilevsky *et al.* (2004) investigated the heart rate and movement of fetuses in response to a musical stimulus and observed a change at about 33 weeks, suggesting an ontogeny of attention.

According to the *levels of consciousness* approach (Zelazo 2003), adult reflective consciousness comprises separable components that are acquired at specific ages. The ability to label objects (including people) is acquired at the age of about 1 year, to distinguish self and from others at 2, to reflect about ideas or theories and apply rules at 3, and to reflect about self and others at 4. Since neither the newborn nor the fetus has any of these abilities, we may assert that the fetus is not conscious in the everyday sense. Attempts to ascribe consciousness to the fetus may be regarded as projections of adult reflective consciousness—animistic projection, anthropomorphism (Parncutt 2006).

Prenatal learning

Learning may be defined as acquisition of information that affects later behaviour. Fetal learning has been repeatedly demonstrated by the empirical paradigms of *habituation* and *classical conditioning*.

In habituation, an organism is exposed several times to the same stimulus and gradually stops reacting to it; in everyday language we would say the organism gets used to the stimulus or the stimulus becomes uninteresting for the organism. Leader *et al.* (1982) observed fetal habituation to a repeated vibrotactile stimulus at 22–30 weeks gestation. In a different habituation paradigm, Shahidullah and Hepper (1994) found that the fetus can discriminate between sounds at 35 weeks better than at 27 weeks.

Other empirical studies have demonstrated that the fetus is capable of associating stimuli with each other by classical conditioning. In that paradigm, stimuli are paired with each other in a temporal sequence, and after several such pairings the organism begins to expect the second stimulus as soon as the first is presented.

Classical conditioning may be regarded as the basic mechanism underlying *statistical learning*. All higher organisms are sensitive to statistical properties of their environment: given many occurrences of event A in different contexts, they learn the probability that it will be accompanied by (or co-occur with) event B, that is, the probability that event A predicts event B: conditional probability (Fiser and Aslin 2002). Saffran *et al.* (1996) demonstrated that 8-month-old infants can learn statistical properties of nonsense speech during only two minutes' exposure. Since statistical learning is such a fundamental means of picking up information about the environment for all organisms, we may safely assume that humans begin to learn statistically before birth.

Transnatal memory

Transnatal memory is postnatal retention of prenatally acquired information. If the above arguments concerning fetal (lack of) consciousness are correct, transnatal memory is always implicit, that is, not under any form of conscious control—unlike an adult's memory for a telephone number, which normally requires conscious effort.

Transnatal memory for stimulus patterns presented repeatedly to different fetal sensory modalites can last for weeks or months and may therefore be considered to be a form of long-term memory (Hepper 1991, 1992; Hopkins and Johnson 2005; Mastropieri and Turkewitz 2001). In experiments to measure the duration of transnatal memory, a given stimulus pattern is presented repeatedly before birth (e.g. a specific piece of music), or a pattern to which the fetus is naturally exposed (e.g. the mother's voice) is used as an experimental stimulus. When the same pattern is presented for the first time after birth, or in a specific new way, the reaction of the infant is observed and compared with its reaction to unfamiliar control stimuli.

Episodic memory involves memory for a specific event. The existence of *transnatal episodic memory* is suggested by reports of therapeutic patients in trance states who seem able to recall prenatal events or the experience of their own birth. Hartogh (2003) questioned the validity of such evidence. In general, memories are affected by relevant knowledge and by cultural and social context, and can easily be constructed (Harris et al. 1989). Since episodic memory in humans normally depends on language, and since prenatal episodic memory has no known evolutionary function, prenatal episodic memory is unlikely to exist. That does not necessarily prevent prenatal regression therapy from having a useful therapeutic function.

The phylogeny of musical behaviour

Recent research about the origins of music (summarized by Mithen 2005) has considered many scenarios. One involves prenatal exposure to the internal sounds and movements of the mother's body, which are associated with her changing physical and emotional state (Parncutt in press). The claim is that the associations between sound, movement and emotion upon which music is based are ultimately of prenatal origin.

Emotion

Strong emotions are generally associated with reflexes, instincts or drives that promote survival and reproduction (Tinbergen 1989), such as hunger, sex, fear, pain, disgust, jealousy, surprise, and anger. Music is exceptional in that it communicates strong emotions that are marked by changed states of consciousness and spiritual experiences (Gabrielsson and Lindström Wik 2003), although it has no clear survival value. A plausible theory of the origins of music should be consistent with this fundamental contradiction.

It is often supposed that music is emotional because it is associated with social behaviour and group survival (e.g., Dean and Bailes 2006). However, evolutionary theory primarily explains the behaviour of isolated pairs of individuals (e.g. reciprocal altruism) rather than groups considered as a whole (Boyd and Richerson 1988; Trivers 1971), and such an approach cannot easily explain music's *strong* emotionality and spirituality.

Musical emotions are associated with learned patterns of sound and movement. A possible source of those associations is motherese (Dissanayake 2000), whose vocabulary of gestural meanings evidently includes a universal component (Kuhl *et al.* 1997; Papousek 1996). The

question arises as to the origin of those gestural meanings.

Infant musical skills: innate or learned?

Another surprising thing about music is that all humans, including infants, possess basic musical skills. A plausible theory of the origins of music should be consistent with the documented musical abilities of infants. Trehub and Hannon (2006) proposed that

> infants' music perception skills are a product of general perceptual mechanisms that are neither music- nor species-specific. Along with general-purpose mechanisms for the perceptual foundations of music, we suggest unique motivational mechanisms that can account for the perpetuation of musical behavior in all human societies.
>
> Trehub and Hannon (2006, Abstract)

Prenatal associations between patterns of sound, movement and emotion could underlie such 'general perceptual mechanisms' and 'unique motivational mechanisms'. If so, they may explain the nature and origin of musical emotion.

Several sources of evidence suggest that the musical abilities of infants are at least partially inborn. Amusia can be inborn or genetically determined in a small proportion of the population (Ayotte *et al.* 2002). Children of deaf parents prefer infant-directed singing over adult-directed singing, suggesting an innate component—or at least an inborn preference for exaggeration (Masataka 1999). The development of musical ability is affected by prenatal testosterone levels (Sluming and Manning 2000).

Models of the interplay between genes and environments (Garcia Coll *et al.* 2004) suggest that behaviours and skills such as musicality are neither inborn nor innate, but a mixture of the two. Several empirical studies cited in this chapter are consistent with the prenatal learning of protomusical skills. For example, newborns respond to the emotional content of speech, but only in their maternal language, suggesting that their ability to recognize that emotion was acquired before birth (Mastropieri and Turkewitz 2001). The claim that musical skills are *largely* learned may be valid throughout the lifespan. In early life, the gestural vocabulary of motherese may be largely learned from prenatal exposure to the internal sounds of the mother's body. Later, musical expertise may depend primarily on the total accumulated duration of practice (Howe *et al.* 1998).

Fetal–maternal communication

Bonding (secure attachment) between primary caregiver and infant plays an important psychological and physiological role in early development (Schore 2001). The idea that maternal–infant bonding is an evolutionary adaptation is consistent with high rates of infant mortality among both non-human primate and human hunter-gatherer populations (>50%: Denham 1974). Maternal–infant bonding generally increases the chance of infant survival, but not necessarily of surviving infanticide or of preventing abandonment when chances of survival are particularly low (Hausfater 1984). Prenatally acquired knowledge about maternal emotional states may promote postnatal bonding and survival by helping the infant to communicate its needs appropriately (cf. Broad *et al.* 2006) and may in that sense be adaptive. Other factors being equal, the chance that an infant will survive to reproductive age will increase if infant demands on the mother or other carers do not radically exceed their momentary capabilities or resources.

Infant-mother bonding is two-way and reciprocal (Lee 2006): each party is at some level sensitive to the physical and emotional state of the other. Empirical research is beginning to document the infant's active perception of the mother: compare Stern's (2002) cognitive, psychoanalytic approach with Trevarthen's (1980) concept of intersubjective communication. To successfully monitor the mother's physical and emotional state, the infant must have prior knowledge about the relationship between maternal state and behaviour. The fetus has constant access to two reliable sources of information about the physical and emotional state of its mother: behavioural (sound and movement) and biochemical (blood hormone concentrations).

Regarding behavioural information, all patterns of sound and movement that are audible within the body in everyday situations, including vocalization, respiration, circulation, movement, footsteps and digestion, depend on physical and emotional state (Mastropieri and Turkewitz 2001). The human fetus has access to three behavioural sources of information about maternal state: sound patterns, linear and rotational acceleration of the fetal body, and relative movement of the fetal limbs. These are perceived by the fetal auditory, vestibular and proprioceptive systems respectively.

Regarding biochemical information, the hormones involved in the maternal–fetal interaction arise from three different sources: the placenta, maternal organs and fetal organs (Power and Schulkin 2005). The placenta and fetal membranes produce a large number of steroids that regulate and balance both maternal and fetal physiology. They include progesterone and oestrogen, which play a role in maintenance of pregnancy and support of the embryo/fetus (Albrecht *et al.* 2000); testosterone, which affects fetal development (Matt and MacDonald 1984); oestrogen, related to female secondary sex characteristics (Nelson and Bulun 2001); corticotropin-releasing hormone, which influences the duration of pregnancy (Hillhouse and Grammatopoulos 2002); relaxin, which facilitates birth (Klonisch *et al.* 1999); and placental lactogen (somatomammotropin), which influences nutrient (carbohydrate, lipid) levels in the maternal blood (Walker *et al.* 1991). In an evolutionary approach, hormonal manipulation of maternal nutrient supply represents an early stage of parent–offspring conflict (Wells 2003).

Hormone production in the mother involves a mixture of regular adult hormonal processes and processes specific to pregnancy. Regarding the former, externally caused stressors (flight-fight reaction) lead to stimulation of the adrenal gland, which secretes adrenaline (epinephrine) and noradrenaline (norepinephrine) into the blood, which in turn increases blood sugar, muscle tension, and blood pressure. Stress also causes the release of corticotropin-releasing hormone (CRH) and the production of glucocorticoids that affect immune responses (Elenkov *et al.* 1999). CRH is also associated with anxiety and depression (Steckler and Holsboer 1999), and cortisol is associated with fear and stress (Kalin *et al.* 1998). Oxytocin is more specific to reproduction and is associated with orgasm, birth and breastfeeding (Newton 1978).

That the fetus is sensitive to hormone concentrations in the maternal blood is clear from studies that demonstrate the effect of those concentrations during pregnancy on postnatal development. For example, postpartum concentrations of testosterone, estradiol, androstenedione and cortisol correlate with the children's later levels of physical aggression (Susman *et al.* 2001). Molecules that pass the blood–brain barrier include oxygen, carbon dioxide, alcohol, and steroid hormones, of which there are five main groups: progestagens, glucocorticoids, mineralocorticoids, androgens, and oestrogens (Pardridge and Mietus 1979). The permeability of the blood–brain barrier to steroid hormones depends on the molecule and involves different temporal delays (Zloković *et al.* 1988). The placenta is permeable to nutrients, oxygen, alcohol, antibodies and steroid hormones with different temporal delays of seconds, minutes or hours (Bajoria *et al.* 1998; Bajoria and Fisk 1998).

Thus, both evolutionary–biological and developmental–psychological approaches predict that the fetus perceives changes in patterns of sound and movement within the mother's body (behavioural information) following everyday changes in maternal state. The corresponding changes in maternal hormone levels are delayed by passage through the placental and fetal blood–brain barriers (biochemical information). The behavioural change thus predicts the biochemical change, allowing classical conditioning to occur—just as, in Pavlov's famous experiment, the footsteps of a master bringing food to a dog predict the appearance of the food.

Any stimulus can be associated with any other by classical conditioning, and all animals are capable of classical conditioning. The human fetus is no exception (Smotherman and Robinson 1990). The fetus must therefore learn to associate the behavioural information described above with the corresponding biochemical information. The theory of classical conditioning predicts that after several repetitions of such a sequence the fetus will begin to respond emotionally to the behavioural patterns—before the arrival of the biochemical information. While the time

interval between behavioural and biochemical information in this scenario is presumably of the order of minutes, classical conditioning may also occur for longer interstimulus intervals of the order of hours (Garcia *et al.* 1974).

Prenatal influences on postnatal behaviour

Prenatally established associations can influence postnatal behaviours and the development of musical culture in the context of *motherese, play* and *ritual*. In all three cases, *operant conditioning* (Skinner 1938) may be the underlying mechanism. Patterns of sound and movement that occur by accident in these behaviours may be similar to patterns of sound and movement that were prenatally linked to emotion. The triggering of associated emotions may reinforce the actions or behaviours that produced the patterns of sound, increasing their frequency of occurrence. Since motherese, play and ritual are social activities whose participants were subject to similiar prenatal conditioning processes, this theory predicts that such behaviours and associated emotions will generally be socially shared, enabling the development of music as a form of social behaviour.

On this basis, we might expect to find associations between sound, movement and emotion in all prenatally hearing animals. The reason why non-human animals are not musical in the human sense is presumably that only humans possess reflective consciousness, which emerged at least 60 000 years ago and enabled a cultural explosion (Mithen 2005). Reflective consciousness may be regarded as a co-requisite for the ability to conceptualize the past and future in relation to the present, which enables deliberate/intentional planning and action (Noble and Davidson 1996). According to this view, prenatal associations between sound, movement and emotion became 'music' when humans acquired the ability to deliberately manipulate shared emotions using sound—that is, to perform.

Conclusions

Recent research in music psychology has tended to avoid questions of prenatal development due to the practical and ethical difficulties associated with empirical investigations and the dubious quality of much of the available research literature. This period of restraint may be coming to an end as researchers realize that the prenatal period could be a source of answers to central questions in music psychology, and as developing empirical technologies make it increasingly possible to carry out methodologically sound empirical investigations.

The relevant empirical literature is expanding rapidly, but it is spread over many different disciplines, and many central issues remain to be critically addressed by independent research groups. The present theory presented on the origins of music may be internally consistent and logical, but further empirical work will be necessary to investigate the details of the hypothesized prenatal associations and their effect on postnatal behaviour.

Since our knowledge of music's emergence in the context of ritual will always be limited, any theory of music's phylogeny will always be speculative. The ontological question of how prenatal learning affects postnatal musical development will become increasingly accessible to empirical investigation, as non-invasive observational techniques improve. An improved understanding of the interaction between genes and environment in psychological development (e.g. Bakshi and Kalin 2000), combined with new approaches to fetal behaviour (such as preferences) and prenatal influences on postnatal behaviour (including transnatal memory), will lead to new insights that will confirm, complement, challenge or overthrow the ideas presented in this chapter.

References

Albrecht ED, Aberdeen GW and Pepe G J (2000). The role of estrogen in the maintenance of primate pregnancy. *American Journal of Obstetrics and Gynecology*, **182**, 432–438.

Ayotte J, Peretz I and Hyde K (2002). Congenital amusia: a group study of adults afflicted with a music-specific disorder. *Brain*, **125**, 238–251.

Bajoria R and Fisk NM (1998). Permeability of human placenta and fetal membranes to thyrotropin-stimulating hormone in vitro. *Pediatric Research*, **43**, 621–628.

Bajoria R, Peek MJ and Fisk NM (1998). Maternal-to-fetal transfer of thyrotropin-releasing hormone in vivo.

American Journal of Obstetrics and Gynecology, **178**, 264–269.

Bakshi VP and Kalin NH (2000). Corticotropin-releasing hormone and animal models of anxiety: gene–environment interactions. *Biological Psychiatry*, **48**, 1175–1198.

Bibas AB, Xenellis J, Michaels L, Anagnostopoulou S, Ferekidis E and Wright A (2008). Temporal bone study of development of the organ of Corti: correlation between auditory function and anatomical structure. *Journal of Laryngology and Otology*, http://journals.cambridge.org/.

Blacking J (1995). *Music, culture and experience: selected papers of John Blacking* (ed. R Byron). University of Chicago Press, London.

Boyd R and Richerson PJ (1988). The evolution of reciprocity in sizable groups. *Journal of Theoretical Biology*, **132**, 337–356.

Broad KD, Curley JP and Keverne EB (2006). Mother–infant bonding and the evolution of mammalian social relationships. *Philosophical Transactions of the Royal Society London: B Biological Sciences*, **361**(1476), 2199–2214.

de Vries JIP and Hopkins B (2005). Fetal movements and postures: what do they mean for postnatal development? In B Hopkins and SP Johnson, eds, *Prenatal development of postnatal functions*, 177–220. Greenwood, Westport, CT.

Dean RT and Bailes F (2006). Toward a sociobiology of music. *Music Perception*, **24**, 83–84.

DeCasper AJ and Fifer WP (1980). Of human bonding: newborns prefer their mothers' voices. *Science*, **208**, 1174–1176.

Denham WW (1974). Population structure, infant transport and infanticide among Pleistocene and modern hunter-gatherers. *Journal of Anthropological Research*, **30**, 191–198.

Dissanayake E. (2000). *Art and intimacy: how the arts began*. University of Washington Press, Seattle, WA.

Dowling WJ and Fujitani DS (1971). Contour, interval, and pitch recognition in memory for melodies. *Journal of the Acoustical Society of America*, **49**/2B, 524–531.

Elenkov IJ, Webster EL, Torpy DJ and Chrousos GP (1999). Stress, corticotropin-releasing hormone, glucocorticoids and the immune/inflammatory response: acute and chronic effects. *Annals of the New York Academy of Sciences*, **876**, 1–13.

Fifer WP and Moon CM (1994). The role of the mother's voice in the organization of brain function in the newborn. *Acta Paediatrica Supplement*, **397**, 86–93.

Fiser J and Aslin RN (2002). Statistical learning of new visual feature combinations by infants. *Proceedings of the National Academy of Sciences*, **99**(24), 15822–15826.

Fitsch WT (2006). The biology and evolution of music: a comparative perspective. *Cognition*, **100**, 173–215.

Gabrielsson A and Lindström Wik S (2003). Strong experiences related to music: a descriptive system. *Musicae Scientiae*, **7**, 157–217.

Garcia J, Hankins WG and Rusiniak KW (1974). Behavioral regulation of the milieu interne in man and rat. *Science*, **185**(4154), 824–831.

Garcia Coll C, Bearer EL and Lerner RM (eds) (2004). *Nature and nurture: the complex interplay of genetic and environmental influences on human behavior and development.* Erlbaum, Mahwah, NJ.

Gerhardt KJ, Huang X, Arrington KE, Meixner K, Abrams RM and Antonelli PJ (1996). Fetal sheep in utero hear through bone conduction. *American Journal of Otolaryngology*, **17**(6), 374–379.

Hall WG and Oppenheim RW (1987). Developmental psychobiology: prenatal, perinatal, and early postnatal aspects of behavioral development. *Annual Review of Psychology*, **38**, 91–128.

Harris RJ, Sardarpoor-Bascom F and Meyer T (1989). The role of cultural knowledge in distorting recall for stories. *Bulletin of the Psychonomic Society*, **27**, 9–10.

Hartogh T (2003). Prä- und perinatale Erinnerungen und ihr musiktherapeutischer Zugang: Eine kritische Analyse. *Musik-, Tanz- und Kunsttherapie*, **14**(4), 167–176.

Hausfater G (1984). Infanticide: comparative and evolutionary perspectives. *Current Anthropology*, **25**(4), 500–502.

Hepper PG (1991). An examination of fetal learning before and after birth. *Irish Journal of Psychology*, **12**, 95–107.

Hepper PG (1992). Fetal psychology: an embryonic science. In JG Nijhuis, ed., *Fetal behaviour*, 129–156. Oxford University Press, Oxford.

Hepper PG and Shahidullah BS (1994). Development of fetal hearing. *Archives of Disease in Childhood*, **71**, F81–F87.

Hillhouse EW and Grammatopoulos DK (2002). Role of stress peptides during human pregnancy and labour. *Reproduction*, **124**, 323–329.

Hopkins B and Johnson SP (2005). Prenatal development of postnatal functions. Greenwood, Westport, CT.

Howe MJA, Davidson JW and Sloboda JA (1998). Innate talents: reality or myth? *Behavioral and Brain Sciences*, **21**, 339–407.

Joseph R (2000). Fetal brain behavior and cognitive development. *Developmental Review*, **20**, 81–98.

Kalin NH, Larson C, Shelton SE and Davidson RJ (1998). Asymmetric frontal brain activity, cortisol, and behavior associated with fearful temperaments in Rhesus monkeys. *Behavioral Neuroscience*, **112**, 286–292.

Kisilevsky BS, Hains SM J, Jacquet A-Y, Granier-Deferre C and Lecanuet JP (2004). Maturation of fetal responses to music. *Developmental Science*, **7**, 550–559.

Klonisch T, Hombach-Klonisch S, Froehlich C, Kauffold J, Steger K, Huppertz B and Fischer B (1999). Nucleic acid sequence of feline preprorelaxin and its localization within the feline placenta. *Biology of Reproduction*, **60**, 305–311.

Kuhl PK, Andruski JE, Chistovich IA, Chistovich LA, Kozhevnikova EV, Ryskina VL *et al.* (1997). Cross-language analysis of phonetic units in language addressed to infants. *Science*, **277**, 684–686.

Leader LR, Baillie P, Martin B and Vermeulen E (1982). The assessment and significance of habituation to a repeated stimulus by the human fetus. *Early Human Development*, **7**, 211–219.

Lecanuet J-P (1996). Prenatal auditory experience. In I Deliège, JA Sloboda, eds, *Musical beginnings*, 3–34. Oxford University Press, Oxford.

Lee SY (2006). A journey to a close, secure, and synchronous relationship: infant–caregiver relationship development in a childcare context. *Journal of Early Childhood Research*, **4**, 133–151.

Masataka N (1999). Preference for infant-directed singing in 2-day-old hearing infants of deaf parents. *Developmental Psychology*, **35**, 1001–1005.

Mastropieri D and Turkewitz G (2001). Prenatal experience and neonatal responsiveness to vocal expressions of emotion. *Developmental Psychobiology*, **35**, 204–214.

Matt DW and MacDonald GJ (1984). In vitro progesterone and testosterone production by the rat placenta during pregnancy. *Endocrinology*, **115**, 741–747.

Mithen S (2005). *The singing Neanderthals: the origins of music, language, mind and body.* Weidenfeld and Nicholson, London.

Nelson LR and Bulun SE (2001). Estrogen production and action. *Journal of the American Academy of Dermatology*, **45**(3 Suppl), S116–124.

Nemzek WR, Brodie HA, Hecht ST, Chong BW, Babcook CJ and Seibert JA (2000). MR, CT, and plain film imaging of the developing skull base in fetal specimens. *American Journal of Neuroradiology*, **21**, 1699–1706.

Newton N (1978). The role of the oxytocin reflexes in three interpersonal reproductive acts: coitus, birth and breastfeeding. In L Carenza, L Zichella and P Pancheri, eds, *Clinical psychoneuroendocrinology in reproduction*, 411–418. Academic Press, New York.

Nijhuis JG, Prechtl HFR, Martin CB jr and Bots RSGM (1982) Are there behavioural states in the human fetus? *Early Human Development*, **6**, 177–195.

Noble W and Davidson I (1996). *Human evolution, language and mind.* Cambridge University Press, Cambridge.

Papousek M (1996). Intuitive parenting: a hidden source of musical stimulation in infancy. In I Deliège and J Sloboda, eds, *Musical beginnings*, 88–112. Oxford University Press, Oxford.

Pardridge WM and Mietus LJ (1979). Transport of steroid hormones through the rat blood–brain barrier. *Journal of Clinical Investigation*, **64**, 145–154.

Parncutt R (1989). *Harmony: a psychoacoustical approach.* Springer-Verlag, Berlin.

Parncutt R (1993). Prenatal experience and the origins of music. In T Blum, ed., *Prenatal perception, learning, and bonding*, 253–277. Leonardo, Berlin.

Parncutt R (2006). Prenatal development. In GE McPherson, ed., *The child as musician*, 1–31. Oxford University Press, Oxford.

Parncutt R (in press). Prenatal conditioning, the mother schema, and the origins of music and religion. *Musicae*

Scientiae (Special issue on Music and Evolution, Ed. O. Vitouch).

Power ML and Schulkin J (2005). Birth, distress and disease: placenta–brain interactions. Cambridge University Press, Cambridge.

Richards DS, Frentzen B, Gerhardt KJ, McCann ME and Abrams RM (1992). Sound levels in the human uterus. *Obstetrics and Gynecology*, **80**, 186–190.

Saffran JR, Aslin RN and Newport EL (1996). Statistical learning by 8-month-old infants. *Science*, **274**(5294), 1926–1928.

Schore AN (2001). Effects of a secure attachment relationship on right brain development, affect regulation, and infant mental health. *Infant Mental Health Journal*, **22**, 7–66.

Shahidullah S and Hepper PG (1994). Frequency discrimination by the fetus. *Early Human Development*, **36**, 13–26.

Skinner BF (1938). *The behavior of organisms*. Appleton-Century-Crofts, New York.

Sluming VA and Manning JT (2000). Second to fourth digit ratio in elite musicians: evidence for musical ability as an honest signal of male fitness. *Evolution and Human Behavior*, **21**, 1–9.

Smith SL, Gerhardt KJ, Griffiths SK, Huang X and Abrams RM. (2003). Intelligibility of sentences recorded from the uterus of a pregnant ewe and from the fetal inner ear. *Audiology and Neuro-Otology*, **8**, 347–353.

Smotherman WP and Robinson SR (1990). The prenatal origins of behavioral organization. *Psychological Science*, **1**, 97–106.

Sohmer H, Perez R, Sichel J-Y, Priner R and Freeman S (2001). The pathway enabling external sounds to reach and excite the fetal inner ear. *Audiology and Neurotology*, **6**, 109–116.

Steckler T and Holsboer F (1999). Corticotropin-releasing hormone receptor subtypes and emotion—suppression of pituitary ACTH release and peripheral inflammation. *Biological Psychiatry*, **46**, 1480–1508.

Stern DN (2002). *The first relationship: infant and mother*. Harvard University Press, Cambridge, MA.

Super CM and Harkness S (1986). The developmental niche: a conceptualization at the interface of child and culture. *International Journal of Behavioral Development*, **9**, 545–569.

Susman EJ, Schmeelk KH, Ponirakis A and Gariepy JL (2001). Maternal prenatal, postpartum, and concurrent stressors and temperament in 3-year-olds: a person and variable analysis. *Development and Psychopathology*, **13**, 629–652.

Tinbergen N (1989). *The study of instinct*. Oxford University Press, Oxford.

Tolbert E (2001). Music and meaning: an evolutionary story. *Psychology of Music*, **29**, 84–94.

Trehub SE and Hannon EE (2006). Infant music perception: domain-general or domain-specific mechanisms? *Cognition*, **100**, 73–99.

Trevarthen C (1980). The foundations of intersubjectivity: development of interpersonal and cooperative understanding in infants. In D Olson, ed., *The social foundations of language and thought*, 316–342. Norton, New York.

Trevarthen C (1985). Facial expressions in mother–infant interaction. *Human Neurobiology*, **4**, 21–32.

Trivers RL (1971). The evolution of reciprocal altruism. *Quarterly Review of Biology*, **46**, 35–57.

Uetake K, Hurnik JF and Johnson L (1997). Effect of music on voluntary approach of dairy cows to an automatic milking system. *Applied Animal Behaviour Science*, **53**, 175–182.

Walker WH, Fitzpatrick SL, Barrera-Saldana HA, Resendez-Perez D and Saunders GF (1991). The human placental lactogen genes: structure, function, evolution and transcriptional regulation. *Endocrine Reviews*, **12**, 316–328.

Wells JCK (2003). Parent–offspring conflict theory, signaling of need, and weight gain in early life. *Quarterly Review of Biology*, **78**, 169–202.

Zelazo PD (2003). The development of conscious control in childhood. *Trends in Cognitive Sciences*, **8**, 12–17.

Zlokoviĉ BV, Lipovac MN, Begley DJ, Davson H and Rakiĉ L (1988). Slow penetration of thyrotropin-releasing hormone across the blood–brain barrier of an in situ perfused guinea pig brain. *Journal of Neurochemistry*, **51**, 252–257.

CHAPTER 21

Music lessons from infants

Sandra E. Trehub

WHAT can we learn about music and about musicality from infants? Sceptics may question the possibility of deriving fruitful answers to such questions from immature beings whose hearing is deficient (relative to adults) and whose exposure to 'good' music, even conventional music, is limited. This chapter is aimed at less sceptical readers—those who are open to the possibility of *nature* making some contribution to our musical beginnings and to our subsequent development. It is organized as a series of lessons that emerge from empirical research over the past few decades.

Their world is alive with the sound of music

Preverbal infants hear a steady stream of incomprehensible but highly melodious speech. This speech, known variously as *motherese*, *parentese*, or infant-directed speech, is characterized by exaggerated prosody, including elevated pitch, expanded pitch contours, large dynamic range, and rhythmic regularity (Fernald 1991). The most striking aspects of maternal speech—its effusiveness and positive affective quality—are also the most difficult to quantify. At periodic breaks in the flow of mellifluous speech, infants sigh, yawn, gurgle or coo, all of which function as contributions to the dyadic conversation.

Research to date has largely emphasized the common melodic and rhythmic features in speech to infants, even across cultures (Fernald *et al.* 1989). It has become clear, however, that unique or person-specific musical features are also evident in speech to infants. In one study (Bergeson and Trehub 2007), sequences of intervals, or tunes, were transcribed from recordings of several mothers as they interacted with their infants (4–7 months of age) on different occasions. The observed intervals were unrelated to conventional musical intervals, but highly trained listeners agreed on the transcriptions. Mothers used a handful of tunes consistently, usually with different content, on different occasions. Moreover, each mother's tunes were distinct from those of every other mother, justifying their designation as *signature tunes* (Bergeson and Trehub 2007). It seems, then, that infants receive regular exposure to specific speech melodies in the context of interactions with their primary caregiver.

Aside from the musical speech that infants hear, they also hear a good deal of singing (Trehub *et al.* 1997). Mothers (and many fathers and grandparents) the world over sing to infants in the course of providing care (Trehub and Trainor 1998). For the most part, they use a distinct musical genre for this purpose—lullabies and play songs. Although music for adults often differs substantially from one culture to another, music for infants has many cross-cultural similarities. For example, lullabies from foreign musical cultures are readily recognizable as such (Trehub *et al.* 1992), perhaps by virtue of common features such as simplicity, repetitiveness, and falling pitch contours (Unyk *et al.* 1993).

Even more distinctive than the musical material for infants is the manner of singing to infants. Infant-directed singing is generally part of intimate interactions whose goals are playful, soothing, or emotion-sharing. Although songs have prescribed pitch intervals and rhythms, performances for infants share some features with maternal speech, such as elevated pitch, slurred articulation of words, and positive vocal tone (Trainor *et al.* 1997).

Casual listeners readily distinguish infant-directed from non-infant-directed versions of the same song by the same singer (Trehub *et al.* 1993b, 1997). Surprisingly, each mother seems to perform the same songs at nearly identical pitch level and tempo on different occasions (Bergeson and Trehub 2002), qualifying, perhaps, as *signature performances.*

Maternal performances are irresistible

Presumably, the maternal style of speech and singing would not have persisted across cultures and historical periods if it did not achieve its intended goals, for example, soothing or accelerating sleep in the case of lullabies and joyful engagement in the case of play songs. Over the past couple of decades, investigators have sought infants' perspective on the sounds they hear. To do so, they devised procedures for ascertaining whether infants prefer one type of speech or music to another. The essence of these procedures is to present contrasting material that is linked to infants' gaze toward one of two loudspeakers. For example, infants' gaze at one loudspeaker results in the presentation of one sound pattern, which continues to play until they look away. Their gaze at the other loudspeaker results in the presentation of a contrasting sound pattern until infants look away. This procedure continues for a specified period, after which total gaze duration for each selection is compared. If infants look significantly longer to hear one of the selections, the presumption is that they preferred it to the other. In this manner, one can estimate their relative interest in and attention to the material. In some cases, investigators videotape the sessions to document observable affective responses.

Procedures such as these have revealed greater infant attention and positive affect to melodious motherese than to conventional adult speech (Cooper and Aslin 1990; Fernald 1985; Werker

and McLeod 1989). In principle, familiarity with the maternal style could play a role in these preferences. Despite the popular notion that familiarity breeds contempt, the familiarity of music enhances its appeal (Szpunar *et al.* 2004).

Infants also prefer to listen to infant-directed than to non-infant-directed versions of the same song by the same singer (Trainor 1996). Evidence that 2-day-old infants with limited exposure to music or speech exhibit the same preference (Masataka 1999) rules out experiential factors. Prenatal exposure would have been minimal or absent for these particular infants because their deaf parents communicated by means of sign language. The findings are consistent with a *natural* or inborn preference for the maternal singing style and, in all likelihood, for the maternal speech style as well.

Young infants are poor at regulating their own state or arousal, so fussing and crying are frequent occurrences. At such times, caregivers intervene with non-verbal sounds (e.g., shush), singing, rocking, jiggling, feeding, or some combination of these. Singing is particularly effective at arresting, even preventing, such fussiness. Indeed, the effects of singing are evident in hormonal changes that reflect alterations in arousal or stress (Shenfield *et al.* 2003). Unfortunately, uninformed media reports and deceptive advertising—none of it based on solid scientific evidence—have convinced many parents that Mozart recordings are superior to their own humble performances. Such parents know that their songs 'work' in the sense of bringing comfort and joy to their offspring, but they worry that their performances lack the nutrients for the developing brain that are present in 'good' music.

More than meets the ear

The prevalence of recorded music makes it seem that music is a mere auditory phenomenon. For most of history, however, and for many remote communities in developing nations, music is commonly experienced through live performances in which the listener plays an active role. In such contexts, the performer's visual gestures are as critical as the sounds produced, and the audience typically moves in time with the music. Visual gestures (head and body motion), touch (e.g., holding, stroking), and movement (rocking, swaying) are also integral to mothers' sung and spoken performances. There are suggestions that motherese and maternal singing evolved as ways of keeping infants content when mothers' eyes and hands were required for food gathering or other work (Falk 2004). One prediction arising from this perspective is that mothers should intensify their vocal expressiveness when expressive means in other modalities are unavailable. In fact, there is evidence that mothers use a higher pitch level and wider pitch range (i.e., prosodic enhancement) when they are unable to touch their infants (Nakata and Trehub in preparation).

The consequences of hearing *and* seeing recordings of their mother talking or singing are potent (Nakata and Trehub 2004). Under these circumstances, infants become quite still and stare at their mother's image for extended periods. Interestingly, they remain engaged significantly longer during bimodal singing episodes than during comparable speech episodes.

Infants and adults often integrate information from different modalities, which influences their perception of what they hear, see or feel. For example, when infants are bounced to an ambiguous drumming rhythm (i.e., no accented beats) on every second beat, they subsequently prefer listening to an accented version in duple metre rather than triple metre (Phillips-Silver and Trainor 2005). If they are bounced on every third beat, they subsequently prefer the rhythm in triple metre. Simply watching an adult move on every second or third beat does not induce the preference. Similarly, adults' encoding of rhythms is influenced by their own movement but not by observations of others' movement (Phillips-Silver and Trainor 2007). Perhaps mothers' typical practice of moving with infants as they sing helps infants encode the rhythms of their songs.

Consonance matters

Much of the research on infant music perception has been done with auditory patterns that lack the expressive qualities of maternal performances, including the demonstrably potent qualities of the human voice (Vouloumanos and Werker 2004, 2007). Undoubtedly, instrumental and synthesized music are less interesting for infants but such materials enable precise control over various features, which makes it possible to specify the features noticed or preferred. Such research has revealed that, from the newborn period on, infants prefer consonant sequences of harmonic intervals to dissonant sequences (Masataka 2006; Trainor and Heinmiller 1998; Trainor et al. 2002). Infants remain calm while listening to consonant instrumental music, but they show a variety of negative reactions when dissonant intervals replace many of the consonant intervals (Zentner and Kagan 1996). Infants are also proficient at detecting melodic changes, big and small, but they are considerably more accurate in the context of sequences with consonant melodic intervals than those with dissonant intervals (Schellenberg and Trehub 1996). The perfect fifth interval, which is ubiquitous across musical cultures (Sachs 1943), seems to be especially important for infant listeners (Trainor and Trehub 1993).

Musical memories

There have been no attempts to assess infants' memory for the songs that mothers sing at home, but there is evidence that infants retain some aspects of music heard regularly. When infants are exposed to a Mozart sonata periodically during a 2-week period, they subsequently distinguish it from another Mozart sonata (Saffran et al. 2000). More limited at-home exposure to synthesized folk melodies enables infants to distinguish those melodies from others (Trainor et al. 2004). In circumstances such as the latter, infants retain information about relative pitch but not absolute pitch (Plantinga and Trainor 2005). The salience of the musical selection and performing style may affect what infants remember. For example, infants retain absolute features from expressively sung lullabies after 2 weeks of periodic exposure (Volkova et al. 2006). Their short-term memory for music is influenced by a number of factors including its tonality (Trehub et al. 1990), temporal regularity (Bergeson and Trehub 2006), and degree of consonance (Schellenberg and Trehub 1996, Trainor and Trehub 1993).

From universal to cultural tuning

For the first several months of life, infants approach music with open or universal ears.

Like their adult counterparts, they perceive the equivalence of melodies across changes in pitch level, or transposition (Chang and Trehub 1977; Trehub *et al.* 1987) and across changes in tempo (Trehub and Thorpe 1989). Unlike their adult counterparts, who are differentially sensitive to familiar diatonic scales, infants experience no more difficulty detecting changes to melodies based on the Javanese pelog scale than to those based on Western diatonic scales (Lynch *et al.* 1990). Similarly, they perform as well on invented scales as on the major scale, provided the invented scales incorporate the principle of unequal step size (Trehub *et al.* 1999). Although infants are surprisingly proficient at detecting melodic changes (Trehub 2000), they are unlike adults in their insensitivity to the implications of key membership or harmony (Trainor and Trehub 1992). The available evidence indicates that such sensitivity requires years of culture-specific exposure to music, emerging between 5 and 7 years of age (Trainor and Trehub 1994) and exhibiting further development thereafter (Lamont and Cross 1994).

Infants also exhibit universal principles of rhythm perception such as the grouping of notes based on similarities in pitch, loudness, timbre, and temporal proximity (Thorpe *et al.* 1988; Thorpe and Trehub 1989. When the flow of music is interrupted briefly, infants prefer such interruptions between musical phrases rather than within phrases, indicating that they grasp aspects of musical phrasing (Jusczyk and Krumhansl 1993).

Simple metres with isochronous timing (i.e., equal durations between strong beats) such as duple and triple metre are thought to be inherently simpler than the complex metres that are common in many parts of the world (e.g., Eastern Europe, South Asia, Africa). Recent evidence suggests otherwise. For example, 6-month-old infants detect timing changes as readily in Balkan music with simple metres as in Balkan music with complex metres (Hannon and Trehub 2005a). When North American adults are exposed to the same materials, they detect the changes only in the context of simple metres, but adults of Balkan origin detect both types of changes (Hannon and Trehub 2005a). These findings negate the view of inborn predispositions or preferences for simple metres. Instead,

they suggest that adults' long-term experience with Western rhythms interferes with their perception of foreign rhythms. By the time infants are 12 months of age, they exhibit adult-like difficulties with the complex metres (Hannon and Trehub 2005b). Unlike their adult counterparts, however, limited listening experience with complex metres is sufficient to overcome those difficulties. Not only does adults' experience interfere with their perception of foreign rhythms, it also interferes with their ability to learn such rhythms. Although passive listening is sufficient for 12-month-olds, adults may require more active listening, perhaps accompanied by movement. Guided moving to music, which influences adults' encoding of simpler rhythmic materials (Phillips-Silver and Trainor 2007), may help adults master the nuances of metrically complex music.

In sum

The story that emerges from infancy involves a rich musical environment, with mothers delivering performances that match the inclinations of their infants. Moreover, infants have predispositions or inborn preferences for musical features that are common across the world's cultures. Because musical systems across the world differ in notable respects, it makes sense that infants are open to the available alternatives. With increasing exposure to music, they gain expertise as listeners, but that expertise comes at the cost of diminished sensitivity to features that are irrelevant or infrequent in their own musical culture. Even when their listening skills begin to narrow in culturally appropriate ways, they remain flexible listeners and learners, which enables them to attain listening proficiency with foreign rhythms.

Much has been written about young children's ease of mastering the sounds of foreign languages and adults' difficulty in this regard. There may be parallels with regard to music, but the window of opportunity for music perception is unknown. Finally, there are hints that musical enculturation may occur more rapidly in the temporal domain than in the pitch domain. Evidence on the issue is limited, but it is consistent with the view that temporal processing is at the heart of listening to music and other auditory events (Large and Jones 1999).

Acknowledgements

The preparation of this paper was assisted by grants from the Social Sciences and Humanities Research Council and the Natural Sciences and Engineering Research Council of Canada.

References

Bergeson TR and Trehub SE (2002). Absolute pitch and tempo in mothers' songs to infants. *Psychological Science*, **13**, 72–75.

Bergeson TR and Trehub SE (2006). Infants' perception of rhythm patterns. *Music Perception*, **23**, 345–360.

Bergeson TR and Trehub SE (2007). Signature tunes in mothers' speech to infants. *Infant Behavior and Development*, **30**, 648–654.

Chang HW and Trehub SE (1977). Auditory processing of relational information by young infants. *Journal of Experimental Child Psychology*, **24**, 324–331.

Cooper RP and Aslin RN (1990). Preference for infant-directed speech in the first month after birth. *Child Development*, **61**, 1584–1596.

Falk D (2004). Prelinguistic evolution in early hominins: whence motherese? *Behavioral and Brain Sciences*, **27**, 491.

Fernald A (1985). Four-month-old infants prefer to listen to motherese. *Infant Behavior and Development*, **8**, 181–195.

Fernald A (1991). Prosody in speech to children: prelinguistic and linguistic functions. *Annals of Child Development*, **8**, 43–80.

Fernald A, Taeschner T, Dunn J, Papousek M, Boysson-Bardies B and Fukui I (1989). A cross-language study of prosodic modifications in mothers' and fathers' speech to preverbal infants. *Journal of Child Language*, **16**, 477–501.

Hannon EE and Trehub S (2005a). Metrical categories in infancy and adulthood. *Psychological Science*, **16**, 48–55.

Hannon EE and Trehub SE (2005b). Tuning in to musical rhythms: infants learn more readily than adults. *Proceedings of the National Academy of Sciences*, **102**, 12639–12643.

Jusczyk PW and Krumhansl CL (1993). Pitch and rhythmic patterns affecting infants' sensitivity to musical phrase structure. *Journal of Experimental Psychology: Human Perception and Peformance*, **19**, 627–640.

Lamont A and Cross I (1994). Children's cognitive representations of musical pitch. *Music Perception*, **12**, 27–55.

Large EW and Jones MR (1999). The dynamics of attending: how people track time-varying events. *Psychological Review*, **106**, 119–159.

Lynch MP, Eilers RE, Oller DK and Urbano RC (1990). Innateness, experience, and music perception. *Psychological Science*, **1**, 272–276.

Masataka N (1999). Preference for infant-directed singing in 2-day-old hearing infants of deaf parents. *Developmental Psychology*, **35**, 1001–1005.

Masataka N (2006) Preference for consonance over dissonance by hearing newborns of deaf parents and of hearing parents. *Developmental Science*, **9**, 46–50.

Nakata T and Trehub SE (2004). Infants' responsiveness to maternal speech and singing. *Infant Behavior and Development*, **27**, 455–464.

Nakata T and Trehub SE (in preparation). Melodious means of keeping in touch with infants.

Phillips-Silver J and Trainor LJ (2005). Feeling the beat: movement influences infant rhythm perception. *Science*, **308**, 1430.

Phillips-Silver J and Trainor LJ (2007). Hearing what the body feels: auditory encoding of rhythmic movement. *Cognition*, **105**, 533–546.

Plantinga J and Trainor LJ (2005). Memory for pitch: infants use a relative pitch code. *Cognition*, **98**, 1–11.

Sachs C (1943). *The rise of music in the ancient world: East and West*. Norton, New York.

Saffran JR, Loman MM and Robertson RRW (2000). Infant memory for musical experiences. *Cognition*, **77**, B15–B23.

Schellenberg EG and Trehub SE (1996). Natural intervals in music: a perspective from infant listeners. *Psychological Science*, **7**, 272–277.

Shenfield T, Trehub S and Nakata T (2003). Maternal singing modulates infant arousal. *Psychology of Music*, **31**, 365–375.

Szpunar KK, Schellenberg EG and Pliner P (2004). Liking and memory for musical stimuli as a function of exposure. *Journal of Experimental Psychology: Learning, Memory, and Cognition*, **30**, 370–381.

Thorpe LA and Trehub SE (1989). Duration illusion and auditory grouping in infancy. *Developmental Psychology*, **25**, 122–127.

Thorpe LA, Trehub SE, Morrongiello BA and Bull D (1988). Perceptual grouping by infants and preschool children. *Developmental Psychology*, **24**, 484–491.

Trainor LJ, (1996). Infant preferences for infant-directed versus noninfant-directed playsongs and lullabies. *Infant Behavior and Development*, **19**, 83–92.

Trainor LJ and Heinmiller BM (1998). The development of evaluative responses to music: infants prefer to listen to consonance over dissonance. *Infant Behavior and Development*, **21**, 77–88.

Trainor LJ and Trehub SE (1992). A comparison of infants' and adults' sensitivity to Western musical structure. *Journal of Experimental Psychology: Human Perception and Performance*, **18**, 394–402.

Trainor LJ and Trehub SE (1993). What mediates infants' and adults' superior processing of the major over the augmented triad? *Music Perception*, **11**, 185–196.

Trainor LJ and Trehub SE (1994). Key membership and implied harmony in Western tonal music: developmental perspectives. *Perception and Psychophysics*, **56**, 125–132.

Trainor LJ, Clark ED, Huntley A and Adams BA (1997). The acoustic basis of preferences for infant-directed singing. *Infant Behavior and Development*, **20**, 383–396.

Trainor LJ, Tsang CD and Cheung VHW (2002). Preference for sensory consonance in 2- and 4-month-old infants. *Music Perception*, **20**, 187–194.

Trainor LJ, Wu L and Tsang CD (2004). Long-term memory for music: infants remember tempo and timbre. *Developmental Science*, **7**, 289–296.

Trehub SE, (2000). Human processing predispositions and musical universals. In NL Wallin, B Merker and S Brown, eds The origins of music, 427–448. MIT Press, Cambridge MA.

Trehub SE and Thorpe LA (1989). Infants' perception of rhythm: categorization of auditory sequences by temporal structure. *Canadian Journal of Psychology*, **43**, 217–229.

Trehub SE and Trainor LJ (1998). Singing to infants: lullabies and play songs. *Advances in Infancy Research*, **12**, 43–77.

Trehub SE, Schellenberg EG and Kamenetsky SB (1999). Infants' and adults' perception of scale structure. *Journal of Experimental Psychology: Human Perception and Performance*, **25**, 965–975.

Trehub SE, Thorpe LA and Morrongiello BA (1987). Organizational processes in infants' perception of auditory patterns. *Child Development*, **58**, 741–749.

Trehub SE, Thorpe LA and Trainor LJ (1990). Infants' perception of *good* and *bad* melodies. *Psychomusicology*, **9**, 5–19.

Trehub SE, Unyk AM and Trainor LJ (1993a). Adults identify infant-directed music across cultures. *Infant Behavior and Development*, **16**, 193–211.

Trehub SE, Unyk AM and Trainor LJ (1993b). Maternal singing in cross-cultural perspective. *Infant Behavior and Development*, **16**, 285–295.

Trehub SE, Unyk AM, Kamenetsky SB, Hill DS, Trainor LJ, Henderson JL, *et al.*, (1997). Mothers' and fathers' singing to infants. *Developmental Psychology*, **33**, 500–507.

Unyk AM, Trehub SE, Trainor LJ and Schellenberg EG (1992). Lullabies and simplicity: a cross-cultural perspective. *Psychology of Music*, **20**, 15–28.

Volkova A, Trehub SE and Schellenberg EG (2006). Infants' memory for musical performances. *Developmental Science*, **9**, 583–589.

Vouloumanos A and Werker JF (2004). Tuned to the signal: the privileged status of speech for young infants. *Developmental Science*, **7**(3), 270–276.

Vouloumanos A and Werker JF (2007). Listening to language at birth: evidence for a bias for speech in neonates. *Developmental Science*, **10**, 159–164.

Werker JF and McLeod PJ (1989). Infant preference for both male and female infant-directed talk: a developmental study of attentional and affective responsiveness. *Canadian Journal of Psychology*, **43**, 230–246.

Zentner MR and Kagan J (1996). Perception of music by infants. *Nature*, **383**, 29.

CHAPTER 22

Music in the school years

Alexandra Lamont

Introduction

Music is ubiquitous in young children's experiences (see Chapter 21 this volume), but as children get older their experiences become more diverse. Defining the trajectories of musical development is thus complex; explaining them is still more challenging. Beginning by considering definitions of development, this chapter first provides a selective overview of existing evidence on children's responses to musical elements and secondly evaluates our understanding of musical development in culture and context.

What is musical development?

Despite much research interest, there is still no overarching consensus on what musical development is. Sloboda (1985) distinguished between two types of musical development: enculturation (generalized and effortless) and training (specialized, deliberate and conscious). Many researchers now consider the development of musical competence (Deliège and Sloboda 1996), further subdefined into activities such as 'singing, graphic representation of music, melodic perception, and composition' (Hargreaves 1996 p. 145) or 'skills, understandings and attitudes' (McPherson 2006, p. v). Runfola and Swanwick (2002) argue that any explanation of musical development must incorporate the three areas of production, performance, and perception (see also Hargreaves and Zimmerman 1992).

Other forms of development have more clearly defined goals: for example, literacy development has an end point of being able to read.

Becoming a musician is a more nebulous concept (MacDonald *et al.* 2002; Chapter 42 this volume), and not all children think of themselves as equally musical (Lamont 2002). Even research which adopts a relatively straightforward 'expertise' model of adult musicians has difficulty accounting for the diversity of findings in the musically more naive (Davidson 1994), and this may explain the imprecision in definitions. This chapter will take an inclusive approach to what musical development might encompass.

Developing musical understanding

First I review research on how children understand separate elements of music, individually (pitch/harmony, rhythm/metre, timbre) and in combination (structure, form, style), drawing on research that isolates and explores these experimentally and evidence from more ecologically valid tasks such as singing and composing.

Pitch, tonality, melody and harmony

Pitch includes tone chroma (individual notes), contour (high/low and patterns), and melodic and harmonic relationships between tones (tonality/tonal hierarchy) (see also Chapter 5 this volume). One early pitch capacity is absolute pitch, typically demonstrated by labelling individual pitches by note names. Absolute pitch is more easily acquired in early childhood (Takeuchi and Hulse 1993) and can be trained more rapidly in children aged 4–5 than those aged 13–15 (Crozier 1997). Crozier suggests that through music training which emphasizes relative pitch skills, children unlearn absolute pitch. A second capacity relates to the psycho-physical dimension of pitch height. Young children are unable to label pitch as 'high' and 'low', and much of their difficulty results from problems in analogical mapping between the musical and verbal concepts (Costa-Giomi and Descombes 1996). Although differences in pitch height can be perceived by infants (see Chapter 21), the terminology to describe the dimension of pitch height must be learned and takes time to stabilize.

Considering relationships between pitches, research has explored children's developing sense of tonality. Some studies find marked age differences: for example, Krumhansl and Keil (1982) showed an increasing sophistication in differentiation between and among diatonic and non-diatonic notes from 6 to 11 years (cf. Lamont and Cross 1994). Other studies find stable representations across this age range (Cuddy and Badertscher 1987), with children performing with less sophistication than musically trained adults. Training appears to accelerate the patterns of development found with age (Morrongiello and Roes 1990; Lamont 1998). Melodic expectancy studies using both perception and singing tasks show that for children aged 5–11 the best next note in a melody is one close in pitch, whereas a pitch reversal only emerges as a good next note at the age of 11 (Schellenberg et al. 2002). Preschoolers can detect mistunings to conventional tonal melodies (Trehub et al. 1986), but often fail to notice transpositions and contour-preserving changes as 'different' (Morrongiello et al. 1989), while out-of-harmony mistunings become detectable around the age of 7 (Trainor and Trehub 1994). In priming tasks, 6- and 11-year-olds make faster judgements about which vowel sound or instrument a target tone is sung or played on, or whether it is consonant or dissonant, when the target is a tonic chord (Schellenberg et al. 2005).

Converging evidence for developing pitch understanding comes from musical production tasks. Davidson (1985, 1994) shows a progression from contour schemes in songs at 3 years of age to fixed pitch reference points with older children.

Bamberger's (1986, 1991) research also highlights qualitatively different ways of understanding pitch in context. 6–11 year olds without musical training organize melodies figurally into shapes, while highly trained 11- and 12-year-olds can use pitch formally in an abstract manner. Children's melodic improvisations show a similar developmental sequence: children aged 6–7 only use the first five diatonic tones, at 8–9 prefer tones presented in the initial stimulus, and at 10–11 create improvisations emphasizing the tonic triad; the oldest children are most likely to end with a tonic chord (Paananen 2006a, b).

In summary, young children possess certain fundamental pitch capacities, such as the ability to respond to absolute pitch, which become more refined and culturally specified with age. By 6 or 7, children have developed an implicit understanding of Western tonality almost equivalent to that of adults, and use this in listening judgements and decisions about creating music. Furthermore, a shift from context-dependency to context-independency in pitch relationships occurs between 6 and 11 (Lamont and Cross 1994; Paananen 2006a). Musical training accelerates the development of understanding of pitch and tonality, although often does not change it radically. Finally, although some studies find differences between 11-year-olds and adults, very little research has explored development beyond the age of 11.

Tempo, timing, rhythm and metre

There has been less research on children's understanding of the temporal aspects of music, and existing studies use many different methodologies. In listening tasks, little difference is found according to age or music training in children's abilities to detect temporal irregularities (Drake et al. 2000) or to segment according to changes in tone duration or pause duration (Drake 1993) between 4 and 12 years. In general, children perform slightly less consistently or accurately than adults (Drake and Bertrand 2003). Production tasks also indicate little developmental difference in children's ability to synchronize (Drake et al. 2000) or to reproduce simple binary and regular rhythmic patterns (Drake and Gérard 1989) between 5 and 12 years, although they are less accurate than adults with ternary ratio rhythms and irregular patterns.

Evidence from children's invented notations of rhythms shows differences in understanding in middle childhood, moving from enactive action drawings to figural patterns and shapes; only children with training are able to focus on absolute durations and inter-onset intervals (Bamberger 1991). Children's compositions also show shifts from conventional metric patterns at age 5–8 to more speculative use of rhythm and metre at 9–11 (Swanwick and Tillman 1986; Brophy 2002; Paananen 2006c).

Certain fundamental features of temporal understanding are demonstrated relatively consistently across childhood, although others such as segmentation and the understanding (both perceptual and compositional) of more complex rhythmic ratios show gradual improvements with age and training. Again, although differences in understanding are found between children and adults, development beyond the age of 12 has not been explored.

Timbre

Very little research has been conducted on the development of timbre perception. One direct investigation of timbral sensitivity (Lowther 2004) finds rapid development between the ages of 3–8. Younger children make easy discriminations very accurately (e.g. comparing a triangle sound to a ratchet, or tuba to celeste), but are much less successful on more difficult comparisons (e.g. flute/clarinet). From children's qualitative responses, Lowther concludes that although performance increases with age, specific experiences of particular sounds are responsible for helping children make sense of timbral information.

Indirect information about timbre perception skills comes from research such as the priming paradigm used by Schellenberg et al. (2005, Experiment 2), finding that children aged 8–11 can discriminate between a piano and a trumpet. Despite the lack of concrete empirical evidence, timbre identification is often used as one indicator of exceptional musical ability in children, being presumed to indicate a high level of auditory discrimination (Shuter-Dyson 1999) linked to potential for learning.

Combinations of elements: musical structure and form

Brand (2000) has explored children's errors in learning to sing a new and unfamiliar song between the ages of 6 and 12. While older children learn the song more rapidly, all children irrespective of age or musical training make plausible errors in terms of song organization (e.g. more symmetrical phrases). Thus children attempt to organize the music they encounter into meaningful sections and familiar gestures, as in Davidson's 'pot-pourri' songs (1985). Oura and Hatano (1988) find 9–10-year-olds with around 5 years of musical experience can reproduce a novel melody as rapidly and accurately as trained adults (and more so than inexperienced adults). Thus familiar organizing principles such as tonality or repetition are seen to have been internalized and used in order to make sense of unfamiliar music.

Children's similarity judgements in terms of pitch and duration improve in accuracy between 5 and 11 years (Stevens and Gallagher 2004), although higher accuracy levels are found for pitch than duration. When given the opportunity to organize musical stimuli along the dimensions of pitch, contour, tempo, rhythm, timbre and loudness (Schwarzer 1997), young children focus on melody-unspecific features such as loudness (5–6-year-olds), tempo, and timbre (6–7-year-olds), while adults use more melody-specific features like contour. Children categorize short melodies analytically (using one musical element) rather than holistically (using combinations), and none of the younger children use pitch or contour relations. However, sorting tasks using real musical stimuli show that surface features such as dynamics and contour are commonly used, as well as underlying features such as tonal structure, by 10–11-year-olds (Koniari et al. 2001). Tonality can also be used to organize excerpts by younger children with musical training (Martin et al. 2003).

In a study directly comparing melody/tonality and rhythm/metre, Paananen (2006a) shows that children's improvisations at age 6–7 either focus on the surface (melodic/rhythmic figures) or deep (tonal or metrical hierarchy) structures, passing through a substage of beginning coordination between the two at 8–9 to a final substage of integration at 10–11. Children's invented notations also become more specific and detailed with age in relation to various musical dimensions (pitch, rhythm, timbre), illustrating how symbolization is tied to musical understanding (Fung and Gromko 2001; Bamberger 2006).

This evidence is somewhat conflicting because of the variety of tasks employed. When making simple comparison judgements to artificial musical stimuli (e.g. Stevens and Gallagher 2004), young children can focus on isolated musical elements (cf. Paananen 2006a). However, when using more complex stimuli or real music (e.g. Koniari et al. 2001), children are better able to combine musical elements. Although children aged 5–6 can use different musical elements and structures in complex tasks, older children are better able to deal with more complex underlying structures of music, and this is also sometimes dependent on formal training. It may take until adulthood to fully integrate different musical features (Schwarzer 1997), but research has not yet explored this beyond the age of 11.

Musical structure and emotion

Adults' perception of emotion relies on the structural features of tempo and mode in Western music (see Chapter 11 this volume). With happy and sad musical excerpts from real music contrasting in tempo and mode, 3–4-year-olds are unable to distinguish them on any basis; 5-year-olds recognize emotions based on tempo changes, while 6–8-year-olds perform similarly to adults in recognizing emotional changes due to both tempo and mode (Dalla Bella et al. 2001). In more naturalistic studies, children aged 3–5 can recognize music that adults judged as happy, sad, angry and fearful (Nawrot 2003), although they sometimes confuse fear and anger (Terwogt and van Grinsven 1991).

While Dalla Bella et al. (2001) note that it is remarkable that 6-year-olds demonstrate full knowledge of the rules governing happy and sad emotions in music, it should be recalled that these are 'basic' emotions and there is room for further sophisticated development. More research is required, along the lines of the recent study by Stachó (2006) indicating that children aged 3–6 are significantly less able to decode the emotional content of different musical performances.

Style discrimination

Musical preferences can be shown even before birth (see Chapter 20 this volume). Three-year-olds mainly prefer child-oriented music like nursery rhymes or television themes (Lamont 2008), and can also discriminate between different styles of classical and popular music given an appropriately sensitive methodology (Marshall and Hargreaves 2007). However, little research has directly explored the development of children's understanding of style (cf. Hargreaves et al. 2006).

Children appear to experience phases of 'open-earedness', such as middle childhood, where they tolerate a large amount of musical styles (Hargreaves 1982), and 'closed-earedness', such as adolescence, where their preferences are far more constrained (LeBlanc 1991). For example, Boal-Palheiros et al. (2006) find children aged 9–11 like very unfamiliar and complex music (Boulez, Ligeti and Stockhausen) more than those aged 12–14. In adolescence, a narrow range of musical preference forms an important part of self-identity (North et al. 2000; Stålhammar 2003). The 'rebound of open-earedness' in early adulthood (LeBlanc 1991, p. 37) coincides with a phase of seriously acquiring music (Greasley and Lamont 2006). Music preferences still convey messages about other individuals, although more subtle judgements can be made (Rentfrow and Gosling 2006).

The rapidly changing nature of popular musical styles presents an empirical challenge (cf. Hargreaves et al. 2006). Furthermore, developmental effects are understood to be moderated by a large number of other factors influencing preference (LeBlanc 1982) which relate to the music itself, to the listener, and to the context (Hargreaves et al. 2006) (see Chapter 15 this volume).

Production and performance skills

Although all children sing, children's singing skill takes time to stabilize (Welch 2006). Their vocal ranges at the start of school are relatively constrained, with large individual differences in skill (Leighton and Lamont 2006). Children's voices continue to change throughout childhood and adolescence, both continuously, for example the ability to sing in tune (Welch 1996) and qualitatively, for example physical changes in production capacity and vocal development in adolescence (Welch 1998).

Some children also learn to play an instrument, and the component skills are considered elsewhere (see Part 6 this volume; McPherson 2006). While research has revealed much about what is required to make progress with learning an instrument, there is still no real developmental perspective on this topic. McPherson and Davidson (2006) outline a set of learning principles for children of different ages (up to 5, 6–9, and 10 and above) but these are based more on common-sense suggestions (e.g. beginning at an early age, encouraging parents to sing and play musical games) than principled theorizing.

The process and product of children's compositions has been used to generate models of development (e.g. Barrett 1996; Davies 1992). Generally, children become more sophisticated and abstract in their musical compositions with age (Swanwick and Tillman 1986). Although it is often argued that creativity is not age-dependent or phase-related but rather dependent on context, some general changes can be charted (Burnard 2006). For example, early childhood is characterized by the importance of play, whereas middle childhood has wider social and educational influences, and adolescence prioritizes personal identity.

Finally, learning to read and write music is a highly culture-specific form of development (see Mills and McPherson 2006). Converting children's intuitive and invented notations into conventional Western staff notation is complex, and children often experience difficulties in matching sounds to symbols (McPherson and Gabrielsson 2002). Pedagogic approaches using meaningful wholes rather than individual isolated pitches are more effective in the earlier stages, perhaps reflecting children's musical understanding (Mills and McPherson 2006). However, arguably certain elements of music are better perceived analytically rather than holistically even by young children (cf. Schwarzer 1997) and so this approach may not be universally successful.

Theorizing development

A critical issue when considering all this research is the *causes* of differences in musical understanding. Adopting an individual differences approach, we would expect differences according to age, gender, and prior musical experience (over short and long time spans). Most research tends to seek, and generally finds, age-related differences. Some studies also include the effects of formal musical training. However, the field has not yet produced theoretical models of musical understanding which explain the range of musical behaviours coherently (cf. North and Hargreaves 2008; Runfola and Swanwick 2002). I next consider some of the challenges to theorizing musical development.

Musical development: one thing or many?

First, including different types of musical behaviour within a single theory presents a major theoretical challenge. As illustrated above, many differences in research findings can be ascribed to the particular tasks: building a composition requires different skills and poses different challenges to listening to two notes and deciding if they are the same or different, and explicit tasks also show slower rates of development than implicit ones (Schellenberg *et al.* 2005). To make progress on the relative 'rates' of development of different elements of music even within the field of musical understanding requires studies which explicitly include and compare these in real musical settings. For example, Stevens and Gallagher (2004) show that children can make better judgements based on pitch than duration, yet Schwarzer (1997) illustrated that when more potential musical elements are added children aged 5–6 choose neither of these dimensions. It is thus important that experimental demands do not unnecessarily constrain children's responses, and that researchers seek opportunities to allow children to demonstrate the full range of their understanding.

Should a theory of musical development be able to account for many different kinds of musical behaviour, including understanding alongside activities such as singing, playing instruments and composing? In developmental psychology, existing grand theories of general development (Piaget 1953; Vygotsky 1978) have largely been abandoned in favour of more specific models such as theories of cognitive development (e.g. Halford 1992; Siegler 1996). In music, the generalizability of theories or models hinges on a balance between precision and explanatory power. As in mainstream developmental psychology, the current state of the field is disparate and lacking coherence (see also North and Hargreaves 2008). Broader approaches, like Hargreaves and Galton's model of artistic competence (1992) or Swanwick and Tillman's developmental spiral (1986), can provide a useful description of similarities in stages of understanding (loosely tied to age) across different musical activities. However, these remain at a purely descriptive level. More constrained musical models of specific musical skills or understanding (e.g. Paananen 2006a, b; Stevens and Gallagher 2004; Welch 1996) seem to be more successful in explaining musical behaviour and predicting development in a limited number of domains. It may be that an overarching theory of musical development is still out of reach—at any rate, such a theory will need to be a great deal more flexible than those currently in circulation.

Where is musical development going, and how does it get there?

Considering the process of development itself, as illustrated above, very little research has systematically attempted to map cross-sectional patterns over large enough age spans or fine enough levels of detail to be able to explain the directions or the motors of change. There are two main reasons for this. First, from a theoretical perspective, debate continues over whether development progresses linearly or in a stepwise fashion towards one or multiple end points (Bamberger 2006; Hargreaves 1996; Mills 2005; Swanwick and Tillman 1986). Secondly, most research is not methodologically designed in such a way to enable these questions to be answered. Most studies compare children of different ages (sometimes including adults). Differences imply either quantitative change resulting from exposure or qualitative change resulting from different ways of thinking, while similarities indicate no development.

Furthermore, the period between 11–12 years of age and adulthood is rarely studied, and music training is rarely added as a developmental mechanism. As shown above, results seem highly dependent on the musical domain, the tasks administered, and the particular ages selected.

However, more interactive studies following children over short time spans highlight micro-level changes in their musical understanding. For example, Bamberger's (1991) detailed case study of an individual child's progress from a focus on the figural properties of melodies through to an awareness of formal features provides an insight into the process of change. This illustrates that the motor of change is the child's engagement and re-engagement with the musical material, in this case largely stimulated by a research/teaching intervention. Applying this kind of approach to more finely age- and experience-graded samples over longer time spans is necessary in order to be able to disentangle the theoretical questions of the relative contributions of age and experience which are becoming recognized as being so critical in musical development.

Natural development and cultural environments

The relative contribution of innately specified and culturally acquired aspects of musical development is another hotly debated issue. Much recent evidence supports the notion of certain aspects of musical understanding being innately specified, particularly considering elements like pitch in isolation. The cultural environment has been particularly weakly theorized in musical development: some simple approaches draw on connectionist principles to suggest that exposure predicts behaviour (Gruhn and Rauscher 2002), supported by evidence for linear patterns of development with age, for example in tonal sensitivity (Krumhansl and Keil 1982).

However, both natural and cultural approaches are rooted in a Western philosophical and psychological tradition where the individual child is either the 'motor' or the 'recipient' of development (cf. Burman 1994). For example, McPherson's explicit scope in exploring how biological, environmental, social, cultural and historical factors have shaped the acquisition of musical skill, understanding and attitudes (2006) treats the child as a recipient of culture. Vygotsky's (1978) approach placed a far greater emphasis on the specific social and cultural experiences that individuals encounter and which shape their individual development. Given the fundamentally social nature of music in society, a more complex formulation of the learning process is required which accounts for the child as an active participant in culture. This aspect of cultural environment has been weakly theorized even in models which attempt to account for experience (e.g. Swanwick and Tillman 1986; see Runfola and Swanwick 2002). Such a goal may be achieved following Gruhn and Rauscher's suggestion to focus research on the 'micro-structure of cognition' (2002, p. 446).

Concluding remarks: the importance of context

The research carried out to date on the development of musical understanding (pitch, tonality, rhythm, metre, form, structure and style) and of musical activities (singing, instrumental learning, composing, and improvising) reveals a complex pattern of evidence. The principal debates in the field hinge around the types and breadth of development being considered, and the influences of nature and culture, age and experience. I conclude with some suggestions for future directions relating to the importance of context.

Elsewhere (Lamont 2002) I have argued for the usefulness of contextually grounded theories such as Bronfenbrenner's (1979) ecological systems theory in understanding children's developing spheres of influence and levels of engagement with music, ranging from the micro contexts of home and school up to the macro contexts of dominant beliefs in society. In similar vein, Burnard (2006) adopts a systems view in understanding influences on children's developing creativity. She identifies a 'superculture' of children's musical creativity, incorporating the overlapping spheres of culture, society, in- and out-of-school contexts to specify various microcultures to be investigated. These approaches provide more formalized and thus practical ways of identifying and exploring the

significant contexts in children's and adolescents' lives which support and motivate many kinds of musical development.

A fuller consideration of context may also help address the empirical challenges of engagement and motivation for music. Not all children engage with music at school, with music tuition, or with music from different cultures or subcultures (e.g. Lamont et al. 2003; Stålhammar 2003). This provides a different impetus for developmental research. In addition to exploring the individual features of age and experience more systematically, it becomes vital to investigate the effects of different situations and settings on musical development of every kind. More flexible yet sensitive theories of musical development may offer solutions to these challenges, as well as informing us better about the ways in which children develop in and through music and the diversity of musical goals to which they aspire.

References

Bamberger J (1986). Cognitive issues in the development of musically gifted children. In RJ Sternberg and JE Davidson, eds, *Conceptions of giftedness*, 388–413. Oxford University Press, Oxford.

Bamberger J (1991). *The mind behind the musical ear*. Harvard University Press, Cambridge, MA.

Bamberger J (2006). What develops in musical development? In GE McPherson, ed., *The child as musician: a handbook of musical development*, 69–91. Oxford University Press, Oxford.

Barrett M (1996). Children's aesthetic decision-making: an analysis of children's musical discourse as composers. *International Journal of Music Education*, **28**, 37–62.

Boal-Palheiros G Ilari B and Monteiro F (2006). Children's responses to 20th century 'art' music, in Portugal and Brazil. In M Baroni, AR Addessi, R Caterina, M Costa, eds, *Proceedings of the 9th International Conference on Music Perception and Cognition*, 588–595. University of Bologna, Bologna, Italy.

Brand E (2000). Children's mental musical organisations as highlighted by their singing errors. *Psychology of Music*, **28**(1), 62–80.

Bronfenbrenner U (1979). *The ecology of human development*. Harvard University Press, Cambridge, MA.

Brophy TS (2002). The melodic improvisations of children aged 6–12: a developmental perspective. *Music Education Research*, **4**(1), 73–92.

Burman E (1994). *Deconstructing developmental psychology*. Routledge, London.

Burnard P (2006). The individual and social worlds of children's musical creativity. In GE McPherson, ed., *The child as musician: a handbook of musical development*, 353–374. Oxford University Press, Oxford.

Costa-Giomi E and Descombes V (1996). Pitch labels with single and multiple meanings: a study with French-speaking children. *Journal of Research in Music Education*, **44**(3), 204–214.

Crozier J (1997). Absolute pitch: practice makes perfect, the earlier the better. *Psychology of Music*, **25**(2), 110–119.

Cuddy LL and Badertscher BD (1987). Recovery of the tonal hierarchy: some comparisons across age and levels of musical experience. *Perception and Psychophysics*, **41**, 609–620.

Dalla Bella S, Peretz I, Rousseau L and Gosselin N (2001). A developmental study of the affective value of tempo and mode in music. *Cognition*, **80**(3), B1–B10.

Davidson L (1985). Tonal structures of children's early songs. *Music Perception*, **2**(3), 361–373.

Davidson L (1994). Song singing by young and old: a developmental approach to music. In R Aiello, with JA Sloboda, eds, *Musical perceptions*, 99–130. Oxford University Press, Oxford.

Davies C (1992). *Listen to my song. A study of songs invented by children aged 5–7 years. British Journal of Music Education*, **9**, 19–48.

Deliège I and Sloboda JA (eds) (1996). *Musical beginnings: origins and development of musical competence*. Oxford University Press, Oxford.

Drake C (1993). Influence of age and experience on timing and intensity variations in the reproduction of short musical rhythms. *Psychological Belgica*, **33**, 217–228.

Drake C and Bertrand D (2003). The quest for universals in temporal processing in music. In I Peretz, R Zatorre, eds, *The cognitive neuroscience of music*, 21–31. Oxford University Press, Oxford.

Drake C and Gérard C, (1989). A psychological pulse train: how young children use this cognitive framework to structure simple rhythms. *Psychological Research*, **51**, 16–22.

Drake C, Jones MR and Baruch C (2000). The development of rhythmic attending in auditory sequences: attunement, reference period, focal attending. *Cognition*, **77**, 251–288.

Fung CV and Gromko JE (2001). Effects of active versus passive listening on the quality of children's invented notations and preferences for two pieces from an unfamiliar culture. *Psychology of Music*, **29**(2), 128–138.

Greasley AE and Lamont A (2006). Music preference in adulthood: why do we like the music we do? In M Baroni, AR Addessi, R Caterina, M Costa, eds, *Proceedings of the 9th International Conference on Music Perception and Cognition*, 960–966. University of Bologna, Bologna, Italy.

Gruhn W and Rauscher F (2002). The neurobiology of music cognition and learning. In R Colwell, C Richardson, eds, *New handbook of research on music teaching and learning*, 445–460. Oxford University Press, Oxford.

Halford GS (1992). *Children's understanding: the development of mental models*. Erlbaum, Hillsdale, NJ.

Hargreaves DJ (1982). The development of aesthetic reactions to music. *Psychology of Music, Special Issue*, 51–54.

Hargreaves DJ (1996). The development of musical and artistic competence. In I Deliège, JA Sloboda, eds, *Musical beginnings: origins and development of musical*

competence, 145–170. Oxford University Press, Oxford.

Hargreaves DJ and Galton M (1992). Aesthetic learning: psychological theory and educational practice. In B Reimer, RA Smith, eds, *National Society for the Study of Education yearbook on the arts in education*, 124–150. NSSE, Chicago, IL.

Hargreaves DJ, North AC and Tarrant M (2006). Musical preference and taste in childhood and adolescence. In GE McPherson, ed., *The child as musician: a handbook of musical development*, 135–154. Oxford University Press, Oxford.

Hargreaves DJ and Zimmerman MP (1992). Developmental theories of music learning. In R Colwell, ed., *Handbook of research on music teaching and learning*, 377–391. Schirmer, New York.

Koniari D, Predazzer S and Mélen M (2001). Categorization and schematization processes used in music perception by 10- to 11-year old children. *Music Perception*, **18**(3), 297–324.

Krumhansl CL and Keil FC (1982). Acquisition of the hierarchy of tonal functions in music. *Memory and Cognition*, **10**, 243–251.

Lamont A (1998). Music, education, and the development of pitch perception: the role of context, age, and musical experience. *Psychology of Music*, **26**(1), 7–25.

Lamont A (2002). Musical identities and the school environment. In RAR MacDonald, DJ Hargreaves, DE Miell, eds, *Musical identities*, 41–59. Oxford University Press, Oxford.

Lamont A (2008). Young children's musical worlds: musical engagement in three-year-olds. Journal of Early Childhood Research, **6**(3), 247–261.

Lamont A and Cross I (1994). Children's cognitive representations of musical pitch. *Music Perception*, **12**, 27–55.

Lamont A, Hargreaves DJ, Marshall NA and Tarrant M (2003). Young people's music in and out of school. *British Journal of Music Education*, **20**(3), 229–241.

LeBlanc A (1982). An interactive theory of music preference. *Journal of Music Therapy*, **19**, 28–45.

LeBlanc A (1991). Effect of maturation/aging on music listening preference: a review of the literature. Paper presented to the Ninth National Symposium on Research in Music Behavior, Cannon Beach, Oregon, March 7–9.

Leighton GL and Lamont A (2006). Exploring children's singing development: do experiences in early schooling help or hinder? *Music Education Research*, **8**(3), 311–330.

Lowther D (2004). An investigation of young children's timbral sensitivity. *British Journal of Music Education*, **21**(1), 63–80.

MacDonald RAR, Hargreaves DJ and Miell DE (eds) (2002). *Musical identities*. Oxford University Press, Oxford.

Marshall N and Hargreaves DJ (2007). Musical style discrimination in the early years. *Journal of Early Childhood Research*, **5**(1), 35–49.

Martin N-J, Lamont A and Dibben N (2003). Children's perception of similarity relations in music. In R Kopiez, AC Lehmann, I Wolter and C Wolf, eds, *Proceedings of the 5th Triennial ESCOM Conference*, Hanover,

Germany, 586–590. Hanover University of Music and Drama, Hanover.

McPherson GE (ed.) (2006) *The child as musician: a handbook of musical development*. Oxford University Press, Oxford.

McPherson GE and Davidson JW (2006). Playing an instrument. In GE McPherson, ed., *The child as musician: a handbook of musical development*, 331–351. Oxford University Press, Oxford.

McPherson GE and Gabrielsson A (2002). From sound to sign. In R Parncutt, GE McPherson, eds, *The science and psychology of musical performance: creative strategies for music teaching and learning*, 99–115. Oxford University Press, Oxford.

Mills J (2005) *Music in the school*. Oxford University Press, Oxford.

Mills J and McPherson GE (2006). Musical literacy. In GE McPherson, ed., *The child as musician: a handbook of musical development*, 155–171. Oxford University Press, Oxford.

Morrongiello BA and Roes CL (1990). Developmental changes in children's perception of musical sequences: effects of musical training. *Developmental Psychology*, **26**, 814–820.

Morrongiello BA, Roes CL and Donnelly F (1989). Children's perception of musical patterns: effects of music instruction. *Music Perception*, **6**, 447–462.

Nawrot ES (2003). The perception of emotional expression in music: Evidence from infants, children, and adults. *Psychology of Music*, **31**(1), 75–92.

North AC and Hargreaves DJ (2008). *The social and applied psychology of music*. Oxford University Press, Oxford.

North AC, Hargreaves DJ and O'Neill SA (2000). The importance of music to adolescents. *British Journal of Educational Psychology*, **70**, 255–272.

Oura Y and Hatano G (1988). Memory for melodies among subjects differing in age and experience in music. *Psychology of Music*, **16**, 91–109.

Paananen P (2006a). Melodic improvisation at the age of 6–11 years: development of pitch and rhythm. *Musicae Scientiae*, XI(1), 89–119.

Paananen P (2006b) Harmonizing a tonal melody at the age of 6–15 years. In M Baroni, AR Addessi, R Caterina and M Costa, eds *Proceedings of the 9th International Conference on Music Perception and Cognition*, 484–488. University of Bologna, Bologna, Italy.

Paananen P (2006c). The development of rhythm at the age of 6–11 years: non-pitch rhythmic improvisation. *Music Education Research*, **8**(3), 349–368.

Piaget J (1953). *The origins of intelligence in children*. Routledge and Kegan Paul, London.

Rentfrow PJ and Gosling SD (2006). Message in a ballad: the role of musical preferences in interpersonal perception. *Psychological Science*, **17**(3), 236–242.

Runfola M and Swanwick K (2002). Developmental characteristics of music learners. In R Colwell, C Richardson, eds, *New handbook of research on music teaching and learning*, 373–397. Oxford University Press, Oxford.

Schellenberg EG, Adachi M, Purdy KT and McKinnon MC (2002). Expectancy in melody: tests of children and adults. *Journal of Experimental Psychology: General*, **131**(4), 11–537.

Schellenberg EG, Bigand E, Poulin-Charronat B, Garnier C and Stevens C (2005). Children's implicit knowledge of harmony in Western music. *Developmental Science*, **8**(6), 551–566.

Schwarzer G (1997). Analytic and holistic modes in the development of melody perception. *Psychology of Music*, **25**(1), 35–56.

Shuter-Dyson R (1999). Musical ability. In D Deutsch, ed. *The psychology of music*, 2nd edn, 627–651. Academic Press, New York.

Siegler RS (1996). *Emerging minds: the process of change in children's thinking*. Oxford University Press, Oxford.

Sloboda JA (1985). *The musical mind: the cognitive psychology of music*. Clarendon Press, Oxford.

Stachó L (2006). Interpretation of the emotional content of musical performance by 3- to 6-year-old children. In M Baroni, AR Addessi, R Caterina, M Costa, eds, *Proceedings of the 9th International Conference on Music Perception and Cognition*, 504–511. University of Bologna, Bologna, Italy.

Stålhammar B (2003). Music teaching and young people's own musical experience. *Music Education Research*, **5**(1), 61–68.

Stevens C and Gallagher M (2004). The development of mental models for auditory events: relational complexity and discrimination of pitch and duration. *British Journal of Developmental Psychology*, **22**, 569–583.

Swanwick K and Tillman J (1986). The sequence of musical development: a study of children's composition. *British Journal of Music Education*, **6**, 305–339.

Takeuchi AH and Hulse SH (1993). Absolute pitch. *Psychological Bulletin*, **113**(2), 345–361.

Terwogt MM and van Grinsven F, (1991). Musical expression of moodstates. *Psychology of Music*, **19**, 99–109.

Trainor LJ and Trehub SE (1994). Key membership and implied harmony in Western tonal music: developmental perspectives. *Perception and Psychophysics*, **56**, 125–132.

Trehub SE, Cohen AJ, Thorpe LA and Morrongiello BA (1986). Development of the perception of musical relations: semitone and diatonic structure. *Journal of Experimental Psychology: Human Perception and Performance*, **12**, 295–301.

Vygotsky LS (1978). *Mind in society: the development of higher psychological processes*. Harvard University Press, Cambridge, MA.

Welch GF (1996). The developing voice. In GF Welch, P White, and D Sergeant, *Singing development in early childhood. Final report to the Leverhulme Trust*. The Centre for Advanced Studies in Music Education, Roehampton Institute, London.

Welch GF (1998). Early childhood musical development. *Research Studies in Music Education*, **11**, 27–41.

Welch GF (2006). Singing and vocal development. In GE McPherson, ed. *The child as musician: a handbook of musical development*, 311–329. Oxford University Press, Oxford.

CHAPTER 23

The impact of music instruction on other skills

Frances H. Rauscher

Overview

As one can easily see from the chapters in this section of the Handbook, the area of children's musical development is diverse and exciting. The associated research programmes address some basic issues of human cognition and development, as well as some more applied concerns about children's musical understanding. The purpose of this chapter is to examine how making music may actually enhance children's abilities in other domains of reasoning. The goal is to integrate what is known about the area and to provide a substantive conclusion about the issue.

The Mozart effect

Our journey into the extra-musical benefits of music instruction must begin by clarifying what has been erroneously referred to as the 'Mozart effect'. The term 'Mozart effect' has been used to refer to the effects of music on children's behaviour, brain function, and overall intelligence. The phrase was initially introduced by the media in relation to a study using college students as subjects, not children (Rauscher et al. 1993). The study found that a composite score of three spatial tasks was higher for college students who first listened to a portion of a Mozart Sonata compared to 10 minutes of spoken relaxation instructions or silence. This facilitation lasted only 10–15 minutes. After a series of subsequent studies were unable to replicate

the research using a variety of spatial tasks (for review see Chabris 1999), further analyses revealed that the effect was carried by the spatial–temporal task only (Rauscher and Shaw 1998). A meta-analysis that included 36 studies concluded that the Mozart effect 'is limited to a specific type of spatial task … It is a moderate effect, and it is robust' (Hetland 2000a, p. 136). It is important to note that the original study made no mention of children's spatial abilities or general intelligence. To my knowledge, only three studies have examined the effect of listening to music on children's cognitive abilities, and the results are equivocal: one study found a significant effect (Ivanov and Geake 2003), whereas two studies did not (McKelvie and Low 2002; Schellenberg and Hallam 2005). The original report (Rauscher et al. 1993) was followed by an onslaught of media attention, with several articles extending the work to children and intelligence. Before long, the music industry began exploiting the findings. Compact discs with titles such as 'The Mozart Effect for Babies,' and even 'Mozart for Mutts' began appearing in music stores throughout North America and abroad. Indeed, there is very little research to suggest that children who listen to Mozart score higher on ability or intelligence tests than other children (see, for example, Rauscher and Hinton 2006). In fact, there is even evidence to support the notion that children who listen to popular music may score higher on a spatial–temporal task than children who listen to Mozart

(Schellenberg and Hallam 2005). From this and other studies, it appears that the Mozart effect is largely due to arousal or mood rather than to Mozart's music per se.

The effects of music instruction

This chapter, however, is not about the effects of listening to music. It is about the possible effects of music *instruction* on children's cognitive abilities. Before I begin to review the basic findings, however, two words of caution are warranted. First, several of the studies included in this chapter are *correlational*. A correlation between an intervention (e.g., music instruction) and an outcome measure (e.g., academic performance) offers no information about causality. Of course, two factors that are correlated may be causally related, although one cannot know how: A may cause B (music instruction may cause enhanced academic performance) or B may cause A (children with strong academic abilities may choose to study music). Two correlated factors may also be causally unrelated since a third factor may cause both. I therefore recommend a conservative approach to interpreting the findings of correlational studies.

Second, music should not be taught to students in order to improve their visuospatial or mathematical skills. As Hetland and Winner state,

> If the arts are given a role in our schools because people believe the arts cause academic improvement, then the arts will quickly lose their position if academic improvement does not result . . . The arts must be justified in terms of what the arts can teach that no other subject can teach.
>
> (2001, p. 3)

The studies presented here should not be used to advocate for school music programmes.

Let us now turn to the available research. Studies conducted over the past several decades have provided a wealth of information regarding the non-musical benefits of early music instruction. This line of research fits within the context of earlier discussions on the impact of early experience on children's intellectual development. During the eighteenth century the British empiricists, such as John Locke's *tabula rasa* view of the brain, linked intelligence to the natural powers of reason, implying that intelligence arises from experience and could be fostered in the right environment. In the nineteenth century, however, with the rise of rationalist science and, in particular, notions of natural selection and the study of heredity and genetics, attention was directed instead to the biological bases of intelligence. It was during this period that determinism and biological–maturational theories of intelligence took precedence. The 'nature vs nurture' debate was first articulated in the early twentieth century in terms rather similar to the framework it takes even today. Today, the debate concerning the nature of intelligence has focused on the complex effects of experience on the developing brain. New technologies, such as positron emission tomography (PET) and functional magnetic resonance imaging (fMRI) have taken current debate beyond the historically oppositional framework of nature or nurture, emphasizing instead that intellectual potential and achievement are the result of complex, only partially understood interactions between the physical body and experience. Thus, in many ways, the study of the effects of music instruction on intelligence is only the latest episode in a long-running controversy, and one with extensive historical roots.

One of the earliest studies to experimentally examine the effects of instrumental instruction on children's cognitive abilities was performed by Irving Hurwitz and his colleagues (Hurwitz *et al.* 1975). First-grade children were assigned to one of two groups. The experimental group received Kodály music lessons for five days each week for seven months. The control group did not receive music instruction. The Kodály method emphasizes the development of rhythmical and motor skills. The purpose of the study was to examine the effects of this method on children's sequencing and spatial skills and reading ability. Children were tested using a variety of sequencing and spatial tasks, as well as two tasks measuring general verbal intelligence. The experimental group scored significantly higher than the control group on three of the five sequencing tasks and four of the five spatial tasks. No significant differences between groups were found for either of the verbal measures. However, when the data were analysed according to sex, it was determined that the effect was carried by the boys in the study. Girls in the experimental and control groups did not differ on any of the items administered. To determine if reading ability was affected by Kodály music instruction, the authors compared the school records of children who received the instruction in the first grade to children who did not receive the instruction. Although there was no difference between the two groups on reading readiness at the beginning of the first grade, at the end of the first grade, after one academic year of Kodály instruction, the reading achievement scores of the children in the music group were significantly higher than those in the comparison group. When tested again at the end of the second grade, after two academic years of Kodály instruction, the Kodály group continued to score higher than the control group on reading achievement. Spatial and sequencing skills were not retested. Although the authors acknowledge that these positive results may have been due to the presence of a Hawthorne effect (wherein performance improves following any new intervention), they concluded that further research examining the mechanisms of transfer from music instruction to spatial abilities and reading achievement is warranted.

A more recent study also found that music instruction may improve spatial task performance (Rauscher *et al.* 1997). We assigned students from three preschools to music, computer, or no-instruction groups. The instruction groups received several months of instruction in either piano keyboard coupled with group singing sessions, group singing sessions only, or computer lessons. The purpose of the computer group was to control for the Hawthorne effect. Keyboard and computer lessons were provided individually each week for ten minutes, whereas group singing sessions occurred daily for 30 minutes. One hour each day was reserved for keyboard or computer practice. The children were tested using one spatial–temporal reasoning task and three spatial recognition tasks taken from the Wechsler Preschool and Primary Scale of Intelligence-Revised (WPPSI-R) (Wechsler 1989) before and after instruction began. The spatial–temporal task required the children to

arrange pieces of a puzzle to create a meaningful whole. Placing the pieces together in the correct order resulted in a higher score. The spatial recognition tasks involved matching, categorizing, and recognizing similarities of objects that were physically presented to the child. Sequential order is not relevant for these types of tasks. Although the pre-test scores of the four groups did not differ, children in the keyboard group scored significantly higher on the spatial–temporal task only. There were no differences between groups on the spatial–recognition tasks. The singing, computer and no-instruction groups did not improve significantly on any of the tests administered. It should be noted, however, that the musical experience of the children in the singing group was quite different from that of the keyboard group. The singing group did not receive individual instruction. A music instructor played the piano while the children simply sang along, whereas the keyboard group learned how to read music. One therefore cannot conclude from this study that vocal instruction would not affect spatial–temporal task performance.

In a related study, Gromko and Poorman (1998) examined the spatial–temporal task performance of children following seven months of weekly singing and songbell instruction. The children's spatial abilities were pre- and post-tested using five subtests of the WPPSI. A composite score was then computed from these five subtests. Results indicated that the music group's gain scores (post-test minus pre-test) were significantly higher than the control group's gain scores. The researchers concluded that music training affects the development of spatial intelligence in young children.

Several other studies have found improvement in children's spatial skills following music instruction (Bilhartz *et al.* 2000; Costa-Giomi 1999; Graziano *et al.* 1999; Orsmond and Miller 1999; Rauscher 2002; Rauscher and Zupan 2000; Zafranas 2004). A relatively recent meta-analysis synthesized the results of 15 independent studies and concluded that 'music instruction has ... been clearly shown to enhance at least one kind of spatial skill and may in the future be shown to enhance others' (Hetland 2000b, p. 226). However, other areas of intelligence may also be affected by music instruction. For example, Gardiner and his colleagues provided children with seven months of Kodály music instruction along with visual arts training (experimental group) (Gardiner *et al.* 1996). Their reading and maths scores were then compared to children who received the school's standard arts curriculum (control group). Although the pre-test scores of the experimental group were lower than the control group's grade averages for reading and maths, after the special arts training they scored equal to the control group in reading and above them in maths. The same result was found when the children were tested following an additional seven months of special arts training. Unfortunately, because the music and arts instruction were provided together, it is not possible to determine if the results were due to the music curriculum.

A recent study found that early music instruction emphasizing different musical skills produced different effects on cognitive performance (Rauscher *et al.* 2007). At-risk preschool children received piano, singing, rhythm, computer, or no instruction for two years. All children were pre- and post-tested using standardized intelligence, visuospatial, and auditory–perceptual tests. Although pre-test scores of the five groups did not differ, the three music groups scored significantly higher following instruction than the control groups on mental imagery tasks. The scores of the rhythm group, however, were significantly higher than all other groups on tasks requiring temporal cognition and mathematical ability. This suggests that the type of music instruction children receive has measurably different effects on cognition, with instruction in rhythm having the strongest impact on temporal and sequencing tasks.

Other studies have found advances in other abilities following music instruction. A positive relationship between reading and music instruction has been reported by several researchers (Anvari *et al.* 2002; Butzlaff 2000; Douglas and Willatts 1994). However, most of these studies were correlational rather than experimental and therefore cannot determine anything about causality. See Hurwitz *et al.* (1975), described above, for an experimental approach to understanding music's effects on reading. In two separate studies, Overy and her colleagues reported that fifteen weeks of rhythm-based music instruction improved the phonemic awareness and spelling abilities of dyslexic children (Overy 2000, 2003). In addition, one study reported that children who received music lessons for two or more years scored higher than controls on a mathematics achievement test (Cheek and Smith 1999). Two studies have found relationships between music instruction and verbal memory (Chan *et al.* 1998; Ho *et al.* 2003).

These diverse findings led Schellenberg (2004) to wonder if music instruction might affect general intelligence. This indeed appears to be the case: 144 six-year-olds were randomly assigned to four groups: two music-lesson groups (keyboard or voice) and two control groups (drama lessons or no lessons). Lessons were provided over a period of 36 weeks in groups of six. The Wechsler Intelligence Scale for Children (WISC-III) (Wechsler 1991), a test of general intelligence, was administered before and after the 36-week period. The keyboard and voice groups showed small but significant increases in IQ compared to children in the drama and no-lesson control groups combined. Schellenberg then examined differences across groups in individual WISC-III subtests, such as verbal comprehension and perceptual organization, and found significant advantage for the consolidated music group on 10 of 12 scales. Based on the number of experimental studies showing effects of keyboard instruction on spatial abilities, Catterall and Rauscher (2008) theorized that the students who received music instruction in Schellenberg's study might show greater improvement in the scales related to spatial ability than in other scales. To test this, we compared the verbal IQ and performance (i.e., spatial) IQ scores of the music and control groups separately. Since the numerical scales for verbal and performance IQ differ, we calculated the effect sizes associated with participating in music by dividing the music group's gain scores by the respective standard deviations of the control group's pre-test scores on the same measure. Music participation in Schellenberg's experiment showed an effect size of 0.45 on verbal IQ and a somewhat larger effect size (0.55) on performance IQ. An effect size of 0.30 is considered moderate but significant. Effect sizes above 0.50 are considered robust. These data suggest that the increase in general intelligence affected by music lessons was due to gains in visual–spatial intelligence more than to gains in verbal intelligence. We concluded that the impact of music on general intelligence may be driven by gains in spatial intelligence.

Neurophysiological mechanisms

Playing a musical instrument requires instantaneous examination of what has already occurred in the performance (e.g., up-bow vs down-bow; fingering) as well as thinking ahead to prepare for future challenges. Researchers over the past few decades have examined the brain bases for these highly specialized skills. One of the most remarkable features about the brain is its ability to reorganize as a function of experience. Based on William James' suggestion at the end of the nineteenth century that learning may alter synaptic connectivity (James 1890), Donald Hebb formulated an important and innovative theory that views the brain as a dynamic system (Hebb 1949). Hebb's theory is often paraphrased as 'neurons that fire together wire together', although this oversimplification of the nervous system should not be taken literally. The theory is commonly evoked to explain learning in which simultaneous activation of cells leads to pronounced increases in synaptic strength—a phenomenon known as Hebbian learning. The advent of brain imaging technology has permitted remarkable gains in our understanding of how an individual's brain develops and produces uniquely human capacities. Imaging studies suggest that different amounts and types of environmental input can alter cortical structure and function. Specifically, an increasing amount of research suggests that early music instruction influences the brain, perception, and cognition.

The effects of music instruction are evident in anatomical differences in the brains of musicians versus non-musicians. Studies have shown that extensive practice on a musical instrument can induce cortical reorganization, perhaps due to Hebbian learning rules. This reorganization may consequently produce functional changes in how the brain processes information relevant to the particular area of expertise. If the extensive practice occurs early in development, the alterations in brain function may become hard-wired and produce permanent changes in the way such information is processed. Such changes may represent the neural substrate of behavioural expertise. People who begin music instruction later may still develop considerable expertise, but perhaps without the cortical reorganization that occurs in those who begin earlier in life.

A study using structural magnetic resonance imaging reported that musicians who began instruction before age 7 had a larger cross-section of the anterior corpus callosum than non-musicians and musicians who began instruction after age 7 (Schlaug et al. 1995). No differences were found between non-musicians and musicians who began instruction after age 7, suggesting the importance of early music instruction for callosal plasticity. Schlaug and his colleagues proposed that the differences found reflect the need for greater interhemispheric communication of individuals performing complex bimanual motor sequences.

To examine differences in the motor cortex of musicians and non-musicians, researchers have examined the intrasulcal length of the posterior bank of the precentral gyrus (ILPG), a marker that roughly corresponds to the area of the motor cortex (Amunts et al. 1997). The researchers found a greater symmetry of the ILPG in the dorsal subregion of the motor cortex, a brain region that corresponds to the location of the functional hand motor area, of right-handed musicians (mostly pianists) compared to right-handed non-musicians. This symmetry is possibly due to a disproportionate increase in ILPG of the non-dominant (right) hemisphere as a function of the bimanual motor movements required for playing the piano. The ILPG was larger in both the left and right hemispheres in musicians than in non-musicians. The size of the ILPG in both hemispheres correlated positively with the age that music training commenced: pianists who began instruction at the earliest ages had the largest ILPGs.

A study using magnetoencephalography (MEG) provides further evidence for the influence of music instruction on plasticity. Dipole moments of the digits of the left hand were significantly larger in violinists compared to non-musicians (Elbert et al. 1995). Greater dipole moments can indicate either a larger cortical representation for that function or enhanced coherence of nerve impulses in that region. Right-hand representation did not differ between string players and non-musicians. The largest effects were found for those who began before age 12. A follow-up MEG study found auditory cortex dipole moments for piano tones were enlarged in musicians relative to non-musicians (Pantev *et al.* 1998). Again, there was a positive correlation between effect size and when participants initiated instruction.

Taken together, these studies and others suggest that early music training alters brain structure and/or function relevant to cognition. However, it remains unclear whether these differences between the brains of musicians and non-musicians existed prior to music instruction, or whether they occurred as a function of music instruction. To determine whether these differences reflect plasticity due to music training or instead are markers of musical interest or aptitude, it would be informative to conduct an imaging study of children before music instruction began and again following the onset of instruction. The brain scans of those children could then be compared with those of children who are not studying a musical instrument. This study is currently underway (Norton *et al.* 2005). Using magnetic resonance imaging (MRI), the brains of young children were scanned prior to the onset of instrumental music instruction. Children who would not be receiving music instruction were also scanned. Spatial, verbal, motoric, and music perception tasks were also administered. Preliminary data revealed no pre-existing differences of any kind between the experimental and control groups. The children will continue to be examined on a yearly basis. The lack of any pre-existing differences in brain structure and cognitive task performance suggests that the morphological and cognitive dissimilarities between musically trained and untrained individuals may be an outcome of music instruction.

Cognitive transfer

Transfer occurs when a person applies knowledge or skills that have been learned in one context to new contexts. Researchers interested in transfer were initially guided by theories that emphasized the similarities between the initial learning experience and later learning. Thorndike (1913) proposed that the amount of transfer that could occur between two domains was dependent upon the similarity of the elements of the domains. The more equivalent the elements of the two domains, the greater the likelihood of positive transfer. Thus, transfer is always a function of the relationship between what is learned and what is tested.

Psychologists draw a distinction between near and far transfer. Near transfer involves applying the same knowledge or skill in very similar circumstances, such as using one's car-driving skills to drive a truck. Far transfer implies a big leap. A chess master carrying the notion of control of the centre from chess to political or military settings would count as far transfer. Not only are political and military settings quite different in general from chess despite chess's underlying military metaphor, but the meaning of 'centre' plays out differently. In chess, it is the centre area of the board. In the military context, centre might mean a centre of command, communications, munitions, or supply, for example. Any of these would make tempting targets.

Salomon and Perkins (1989) point out two distinct mechanisms of transfer, the low road and the high road. Low-road transfer occurs when perceptual similarities of one situation to another trigger the making of a connection. For example, consider a professional figure-skater who switches to roller-blading. The familiar action of pushing off on one foot, then gliding, and then pushing off with the other foot evoke all the old figure-skating habits. Low-road transfer depends on abundant practice with the skill or knowledge in question to set up the perceptual triggering. It is a phenomenon of experience. Consequently, there is not much far low-road transfer. Far low-road transfer can occur, however, when the same skill gets practiced over a variety of circumstances, gradually stretching from one context to another until it achieves high generality.

High-road transfer, on the other hand, depends upon the learners' deliberate and mindful abstraction of a principle. The chess master that applies chess skills to a military setting is engaging in high-road transfer from chess to military strategy. In contrast to low-road processing, which is relatively spontaneous, high-road processing requires reflection. The transfer of musical skills to, for example, spatial–temporal tasks may therefore be an example of low-road far transfer. To determine if this is indeed the case one would need to somehow measure the overlap between the original domain of learning (e.g., playing a musical instrument) and the novel one (e.g., performing a spatial–temporal task). This undertaking would require a theory of how knowledge is represented and conceptually mapped across the domains.

Singley and Anderson (1989) argue that transfer between tasks is a function of the degree to which the tasks share *cognitive* elements. This hypothesis is hard to test experimentally until the task components are identified. Thus, a complete understanding of spontaneous transfer from music to another domain of reasoning (e.g., spatial–temporal reasoning or arithmetic) is possible only to the extent that the cognitive elements of the two domains can be identified. For example, the part–whole concept is a very important construct for many mathematical problems. This concept requires understanding the relationship between parts to wholes, such as when learning percentages, decimals, and fractions. In music, the part–whole concept is especially relevant in the conceptualization of rhythm. A literate musician is required to continually mentally subdivide the beat to arrive at the correct interpretation of rhythmic notation. The structure of the problem is essentially the same as any part–whole problem posed mathematically. Perhaps this relationship helps explain the finding that children who received instruction on rhythm instruments scored higher on part–whole mathematics problems than those who received piano or singing instruction (Rauscher *et al.* 2007). Further investigation into the components common to musical and mathematical knowledge will aid in the understanding of these possible transfer effects.

Schellenberg (2003) suggests that

> the ability to attend to rapidly changing temporal information, skills relevant to auditory stream segregation, the ability to detect temporal groups, sensitivity to signals of closure

and other gestalt cues of form, emotional sensitivity and fine motor skills ... should be particularly likely to transfer to a variety of nonmusical domains.

> (p. 444)

Likewise, Norton *et al.* (2005, p. 131) state that the

> skills such as decoding visual information into motor activity, memorizing extended passages of music, learning music structures and rules, learning to make fine auditory spectral and temporal discriminations, and learning to perform skilled bimanual finer movements

may all contribute to the transfer of musical knowledge to other cognitive abilities. For example, both music and mathematics employ and manipulate symbols, they both investigate and develop patterns (numerical in the case of math, and tonal or rhythmic for music), and they are both abstract constructions. A trained musician finds order in what is essentially arbitrarily organized sound, and has conceptually constructed a system of patterns, relationships, regularities, series, proportions, fractions, subdivisions, and ratios, represented and understood with a complex array of symbols. Thus, a deep structural level overlap between musicianship and mathematical knowledge could be expected in a number of areas. Research grounded in transfer theory has indeed shown relationships between music instruction and a variety of cognitively related skills (see, for example, Gromko 2004). Although studies specifically testing transfer as a mechanism are extremely difficult to implement due to an insufficient understanding of the overlap of the cognitive components inherent in the two domains, I suggest that transfer remains a potential explanation for improved cognitive abilities following music instruction.

Conclusion

Traditionally, school curricula have been characterized by hard boundaries between disciplines. The studies presented in this chapter suggest that curriculum reform could aim at the development of more permeable boundaries between disciplines, so that spontaneous transfer of skills and knowledge is facilitated. Zohar (1994) argues that thinking skills are likely to be enhanced if students receive explicit instruction to recognize the underlying logical structures of domains that underpin transfer. In addition to explicit teaching, it is possible that students' thinking and learning could be enhanced through analysis of the structural elements of disciplines that appear distinct on the surface but that are conceptually and logically similar at deep structural levels.

I conclude this chapter as I began it: with a word of caution. Although this area of study certainly seems worthy of further investigation in educational settings, we must be careful when applying the findings of music transfer to educational practice. Indeed, this research represents an excellent example of what has become known as a 'design experiment'. Design experiments are described as educational research experiments carried out in a complex learning context to determine how an innovation affects student learning and educational practice (Cobb *et al*. 2003). Real-life educational contexts are, in turn, excellent settings for experimental tests of an intervention. I believe such experiments represent a crucial research approach within the broader context of partnerships involving teachers, educational researchers, and scientists. I do not, however, advocate teaching music to students in order to improve their visuospatial or mathematical skills. The research base on studies showing enhancement of cognitive function following music instruction is still in its infancy, and there is certainly more to learn. The studies presented here are of scientific importance because they suggest that music and other areas of intelligence share common elements and may be psychologically and neurologically related. I believe researchers should continue to search for links between music instruction and cognitive performance, but that these studies should not be placed at the top of the advocacy agenda. In a recent *Boston Globe* article on arts education, Winner and Hetland (2007) state that

We don't need the arts in our schools to raise mathematical and verbal skills—we already target these in maths and language arts. We need the arts because in addition to introducing students to aesthetic appreciation, they teach other modes of thinking we value.

(2007, p. E1)

Music education should not have to prove its value by showing that it has non-musical outcomes.

References

Amunts K, Schlaug G, Jancke L, Dabringhaus A, Steinmetz H, Schleicher A and Zilles K (1997). Motor cortex and hand motor skills: structural compliance in the human brain. *Human Brain Mapping*, **5**, 206–215.

Anvari SH, Trainor LJ, Woodside J and Levy BZ (2002). Relations among musical skills, phonological processing, and early reading ability in preschool children. *Journal of Experimental Child Psychology*, **83**, 111–130.

Bilhartz TD, Bruhn RA and Olson JE (2000). The effect of early music training on child cognitive development. *Journal of Applied Developmental Psychology*, **20**, 615–636.

Butzlaff R, (2000). Can music be used to teach reading? *Journal of Aesthetic Education*, **34**, 167–178.

Carstens CB, Huskins E and Hounshell GW (1995). Listening to Mozart may not enhance performance on the Revised Minnesota Paper Form Board Test. *Psychological Reports*, **77**, 111–114.

Catterall JS and Rauscher FH (2008). Unpacking the impact of music on intelligence. In W Gruhn, FH Rauscher, eds, *Neurosciences in music pedagogy*, 171–201. Nova Science Publishers, New York.

Chabris C., (1999). Prelude or requiem for the 'Mozart effect'? *Nature*, **400**, 826–827.

Chan AS, Ho YC and Cheung MC (1998). Music training improves verbal memory. *Nature*, **396**, 128.

Cheek JM and Smith LR (1999). Music training and mathematics achievement. *Adolescence*, **34**, 759–761.

Cobb P, Confrey J, diSessa A, Lehrer R and Schauble L (2003). Design experiments in educational research. *Educational Researcher*, **32**(1), 9–13.

Costa-Giomi E (1999). The effects of three years of piano instruction on children's cognitive development. *Journal of Research in Music Education*, **47**, 198–212.

Douglas S and Willats P (1994). The relationship between musical ability and literacy skills. *Journal of Research and Reading*, **17**, 99–107.

Elbert T, Pantev C, Wienbruch C, Rockstroh B and Taub E (1995). Increased cortical representation of the fingers of the left hand in string players. *Science*, **270**, 305–307.

Gardiner MF, Fox A, Knowles F and Jeffrey D (1996). Learning improved by arts training. *Nature*, **381**, 284.

Graziano AB, Peterson M and Shaw GL (1999). Enhanced learning of proportional math through music training and spatial–temporal training. *Neurological Research*, **21**, 139–152.

Gromko JE (2004). Predictors of music sight-reading ability in high school wind players. *Journal of Research in Music Education*, **52**, 6–15.

Gromko J and Poorman A (1998). The effect of music training on preschoolers' spatial–temporal task performance. *Journal of Research in Music Education*, **46**, 173–181.

Hebb DO (1949). *The organization of behavior*. John Wiley and Sons, Chichester, UK.

Hetland L (2000a). Listening to music enhances spatial–temporal reasoning: evidence for the Mozart effect. *Journal of Aesthetic Education*, **34**, 105–148.

Hetland L, (2000b). Learning to make music enhances spatial reasoning. *Journal of Aesthetic Education*, **34**, 179–238.

Hetland L and Winner E (2001). The arts and academic achievement: what the evidence shows. *Arts Education Policy Review*, **102**, 3–6.

Ho YC, Cheung MC and Chan AS (2003). Music training improves verbal but not visual memory: cross-sectional and longitudinal explorations in children. *Neuropsychology*, **17**, 439–450.

Hurwitz I, Wolff PH, Bortnick BD and Kokas K (1975). Nonmusical effects of the Kodály music curriculum in primary grade children. *Journal of Learning Disabilities*, **8**, 167–174.

Ivanov VK and Geake JG (2003). The Mozart effect and primary school children. *Psychology of Music*, **31**(4), 405–413.

James W (1890). *Principles of psychology*. Holt, New York.

McKelvie P and Low J (2002). Listening to Mozart does not improve children's spatial ability: final curtains for the Mozart effect. *British Journal of Developmental Psychology*, **20**, 241–258.

Norton A, Winner E, Cronin K, Overy K, Lee DJ, Schlaug G., (2005). Are there pre-existing neural, cognitive, or motoric markers for musical ability? *Brain and Cognition*, **59**, 124–134.

Orsmond GI and Miller LK (1999). Cognitive, musical, and environmental correlates of early music instruction. *Psychology of Music*, **27**, 18–37.

Overy K (2000). Dyslexia, temporal processing, and music: the potential of music as an early learning aid for dyslexic children. *Psychology of Music*, **28**, 218–229.

Overy K (2003). Dyslexia and music: from timing deficits to musical intervention. *Annals of the New York Academy of Science*, **999**, 497–505.

Pantev C, Oostenveld R, Engelien A, Ross B, Roberts LE and Manfried H (1998). Increased auditory cortical representation in musicians. *Nature*, **392**, 811–813.

Rauscher FH (2002). Mozart and the mind: factual and fictional effects of musical enrichment. In J Aronson, ed., *Improving academic achievement: impact of psychological factors on education*, 269–278. Academic Press, New York.

Rauscher FH and Hinton SC (2006). The Mozart effect: music listening is not music instruction. *Educational Psychologist*, **41**, 233–238.

Rauscher FH and Shaw GL (1998). Key components of the 'Mozart effect'. *Perceptual and Motor Skills*, **86**, 835–841.

Rauscher FH and Zupan M (2000). Classroom keyboard instruction improves kindergarten children's spatial–temporal performance: a field experiment. *Early Childhood Research Quarterly*, **15**, 215–228.

Rauscher FH, LeMieux M and Hinton SC (2007). Lasting improvement of at-risk children's cognitive abilities following music instruction. Manuscript submitted for publication.

Rauscher FH, Shaw GL and Ky KN (1993). Music and spatial task performance. *Nature*, **365**, 611.

Rauscher FH, Shaw GL, Levine LJ, Wright EL, Dennis WR and Newcomb R (1997). Music training causes long-term enhancement of preschool children's spatial–temporal reasoning abilities. *Neurological Research*, **19**, 1–8.

Salomon G and Perkins DN (1989). Rocky roads to transfer: rethinking mechanisms of a neglected phenomenon. *Educational Psychologist*, **24**, 113–142.

Schellenberg EG, (2003). Does exposure to music have beneficial side effects? In R Peretz, RJ Zatorre, eds, *The cognitive neuroscience of music*, 430–448. Nova Science Press, New York.

Schellenberg EG, (2004). Music lessons enhance IQ. *Psychological Science*, **15**, 511–514.

Schellenberg EG and Hallam S (2005). Music listening and cognitive abilities in 10- and 11-year-olds: the Blur effect. *Annals of the New York Academy of Science*, **1060**, 1–8.

Schlaug G, Jancke L, Huang Y, Staiger JF and Steinmetz H (1995). Increased corpus callosum size in musicians. *Neuropsychologia*, **33**, 1047–1055.

Singley K and Anderson JR (1989). *The transfer of cognitive skill*. Harvard University Press, Cambridge, MA.

Thorndike EL, (1913). *Educational psychology*. Columbia University Press, New York

Wechsler D, (1989). *Wechsler Preschool and Primary Scale of Intelligence-Revised*. The Psychological Corporation, San Antonio, TX.

Wechsler D (1991). *Wechsler Intelligence Scale for children*, 3rd edn. The Psychological Corporation, San Antonio, TX.

Winner E and Hetland L (2007). *Art for our sake. Boston Globe*, 2 September.

Zafranas N (2004). Piano keyboard training and the spatial–temporal development of young children attending kindergarten classes in Greece. *Early Child Development and Care*, **174**, 199–211.

Zohar A (1994). Teaching a thinking strategy: transfer across domains and self-learning versus class-like setting. *Applied Cognitive Psychology*, **8**, 549–563.

PART 6

Learning musical skills

Edited by Susan Hallam

CHAPTER 24

Musical potential

Gary McPherson and Susan Hallam

Introduction

There is general agreement that music is a universal trait of humankind (Blacking 1995), that *Homo sapiens* as a species has the propensity for musical development, and that musical potential is as universal as linguistic ability (Wallin *et al.* 2000). An ongoing controversy persists however, concerning the extent of individual variability in musical potential and the extent to which observable differences in acquiring musical skills result from social contexts that facilitate learning, genetic factors, or interactions between the two. This chapter outlines key elements of these debates and also considers how 'musical potential' has been assessed.

The nature–nurture debate

Francis Galton (1876) pioneered the study of genetic influences on learning and development using evidence from twin studies to argue that traits leading to eminence were largely inherited. However, recent research suggests that there are complex interactions between the environment and genetic factors which influence observable behaviour, with genetic factors having a closer association with physical attributes than psychological factors, and that many dimensions of an individual's development, such as memory, language development and intelligence, can be enhanced through systematic practice and learning (Gross 2005). Research attempting to establish the extent of the heritability of musical potential has reached similar conclusions with no decisive evidence showing that it is directly dependent on aural acuity, intelligence, or other types of artistic ability (for reviews see Hodges 1996; Shuter-Dyson 1999).

A more plausible explanation is that musical development is the result of a range of gene combinations interacting with environmental stimulation in an interactive rather than additive manner (Ceci 1990). Evidence that the cerebral cortex has an amazing ability to self-organize in response to stimuli such as music supports this view (Rauschecker 2003). Cortical activation during music processing reflects personal musical experiences accumulated over time including listening to music, learning to play an instrument, formal instruction, and professional training resulting in multiple mental representations of music that are, in part, interchangeable and rapidly adaptive (Altenmuller 2003). While self-selection for musicianship by individuals with innate functional and structural brain differences cannot be completely ruled out, the evidence indicates that it is musical training that leads to changes in brain function and structure (Schlaug 2003). As genetic inheritance can clearly be enhanced by a musically enriched social context, considerable research is now focused on identifying the environmental factors that facilitate or impede musical development.

Musical savants and Williams syndrome

The most difficult phenomena to explain without resorting to some notion of inherited differences in musical potential are children at the extremes of neurodevelopment, for instance, musical savants, children with Williams syndrome, and child prodigies.

Savants have generally low cognitive functioning but are able to achieve at normal levels in some activities, especially those related to 'non-symbolic, artistic, visual and motor abilities' such as 'music, art, maths and various forms of calculating (such as calendar-counting)' (Gross 2005, p. 685). Many musical savants exhibit absolute pitch (Miller 1989) enabling them to make confident, rapid judgements about individual pitches and complex chords. They are also sensitive to rules reflecting harmonic relationships and the structure of musical compositions (Young and Nettelback 1995; Sloboda *et al.* 1985). Explaining these skills without resorting to genetic explanations is difficult. However, environmental influences should not be underestimated. Many savants have limited sight and language disorders, which may lead to increased development of auditory processing skills and the use of music as a means of communication. They also spend considerable time practising their skills.

Individuals with Williams syndrome have low measured intelligence and difficulties with mathematical and spatial reasoning but are more adept than might be expected in language and music, the development of the latter depending on access to appropriate musical opportunities. Levitin and colleagues (Levitin and Bellugi 1998; Levitin *et al.* 2003, 2007) have shown that these children are typically as musically accomplished, engaged and interested as ordinary children but display greater emotional responses to music, become interested at a younger age, spend more time listening to music, instinctively experience music much more fully than others, and possess a highly sensitive emotional attachment to music.

Musical prodigies

Prodigies are children who, from an early age, display exceptional talent. Famous examples include Mozart, Bach, Beethoven and Mendelssohn whose significant success in later life depended on having undertaken considerable focused and well-directed effort during their early years (McPherson and Williamon 2006). Ruthsatz and Detterman (2003) identified a recent example of a prodigy, a 6-year-old who despite having had no formal tuition acquired considerable musical skill by imitating other performers and improvising his own musical pieces. He could sing in two languages, had taught himself to play numerous instruments, had an Intelligence

Quotient (IQ) of 132, an extraordinary memory, and attained a high score on Gordon's (1982) music aptitude measure. His exceptional musical behaviours were self-motivated and spontaneous and he particularly liked entertaining people. His musical abilities were closely aligned with his extraordinary memory and high IQ, more so than with the time or type of practice he undertook. As we will see below, such early, specific situational behaviours that spark changes in cognitive development to allow a child to be able to direct extremely high levels of attention toward music are becoming of great interest to researchers.

The overt musical behaviours of savants and Williams syndrome individuals share some similarities with the behaviour of prodigies, even though their neurodevelopmental trajectories differ. Neuroconstructivists suggest that typical and atypical development can be viewed as different trajectories in a continuum of possibilities. An atypically developing trajectory affects the interactions of others with the child and the kind of experiences that the child seeks out, which further impact on the trajectory (Mareschal *et al.* 2007). For example, when parents believe that their child has musical ability, they are more inclined to provide musical resources and reward musical activity, which in turn supports increasing levels of expertise as the child engages more fully with music (McPherson, in press). These social dynamics result in the child developing particular neural structures that make further musical development much easier (Altenmüller and Gruhn 2002; Hodges 2006). Familial responses of this type may occur in relation to savants, Williams syndrome children, and prodigies.

Other research suggests that the typical 'rage to master' which characterizes prodigies can be explained as a result of domain-specific high attentional control that begins in infancy to produce a spontaneous version of deliberate practice (Vandervert and Liu in press). This view suggests that the high attentional control of prodigies originates and then accelerates connections between the cerebral cortex (where mental modelling construction and repetition occur) and the cerebellum (where model formation occurs), such that cerebellar control models feedback to the working memory areas of the cortex. In this way the child prodigy's working memory becomes faster, more concentrated, and more efficient (Vandervert 2007). This explains the behaviour of these individuals in terms of 'the *reciprocal* learning relationships between the anticipatory, *adaptive* cognitive-affective and attentional modelling functions of the cerebellum and those of the cerebal cortex' (Vandervert and Liu in press).

Shavinina (in press) proposes that extreme levels of giftedness occur as a result of stimulation and activation early in life when the developing child selectively responds in ways that heighten his or her cognitive, emotional, and social sensitivities. Such sensitive periods in these children's early years provide the foundations for giftedness in that they accelerate the gifted child's mental development through the actualization of intellectual potential and cognitive experience (Shavinana 2007). Cognitive experience of this type provides the psychological basis from which highly gifted children are able to develop their creative, metacognitive, and extracognitive (i.e., feelings, beliefs, intellectual values, intuition) abilities.

The above explanations support an interactive, dynamic model of how exceptional achievement in music develops as a result of environmental forces acting together with innate potentials at critical moments in a child's development. The following sections attempt to frame these conceptions within specific areas of musical engagement.

The role of learning in the development of musical expertise

Research undertaken within the expertise paradigm has also challenged previously accepted notions that high-level achievement depends exclusively on inherited ability. The basic premise of this theory is that time spent on 'deliberate practice' underpins the development of high-quality expert performance. For instance, it has been established that classical Western musicians need to have accrued up to 16 years of practice to achieve levels that will lead to international standing in playing an instrument. Such individuals usually begin playing at a very

early age and over succeeding years increase the amount of practice undertaken, sometimes up to as much as 50 hours a week by adolescence (Sosniak 1985).

Ericsson and colleagues (1993) have suggested a monotonic relationship between 'deliberate practice' (which they define as goal-oriented, structured and effortful practice that is influenced by motivation, resources and attention) and an individual's acquired performance (for review see Chapter 25 this volume, Lehmann and Gruber 2006). This is supported by evidence that musicians with the highest levels of expertise accumulate considerably more hours of practice than their less successful peers, although there are substantial individual (Jørgensen 2002; Sloboda *et al.* 1996), instrumental and genre differences (Kopiez 1998; Gruber *et al.* 2004; Jørgensen 2002).

While researchers agree that practice is important in facilitating the development of expertise, several studies question the simplicity of a monotonic relationship. Sloboda and Howe (1991) found that students identified as having greater ability by their teachers had spread their practice across each of their instruments and therefore undertaken less practice on their main instrument. Wagner (1975) found that increased practice did not lead to any greater improvement in performance over an eight-week period, and Zurcher (1972) found no relationship between total practice time and performance achievement.

Reported correlations between achievement and time spent practising vary between 0.25 (Doan 1973 and 0.67 (Hallam 1998a). In the Hallam study, the correlation rose to 0.84 when years of time learning was correlated with achievement, as opposed to time spent practising. It seems therefore, that the overall length of time over which learning has taken place may be as important as the actual amount of practice in determining level of expertise. This was especially evident in a causal model developed by McPherson *et al.* (1997) which shows a strong association between the length of time learning and taking lessons and high school musicians' ability to sight-read and perform music that they had rehearsed over the previous weeks and months.

Accumulated practice from the time of beginning learning to the present does not seem to predict the quality of performance at any point in time (Hallam 1998a; Williamon and Valentine 2000). Other factors such as teachers' ratings of musical ability, self-esteem, and involvement in extra-curricular music activities are better predictors of achievement (Hallam 2004). A longitudinal study with beginning instrumentalists also showed that accumulated practice only partly explains children's ability to perform rehearsed music and sight-read and none of their ability to memorize music, play by ear, or improvise. McPherson (2005) showed that accumulated practice explained between 9 and 32 per cent of the variance in the learner's ability to perform rehearsed repertoire over their first three years of learning, and even less for their sight-reading ability. Other skills, such as the sophistication of the mental strategies which the young players adopted to guide their playing, were more important (see also Chapter 25 this volume).

To date, much of the research has failed to take account of the amount of time spent acquiring musical skills through listening to music, engaging in playful musical activity, and participating in group activities where learning and consolidation of skills occurs in an informal learning context (e.g. Kokotsaki and Hallam 2007). In addition, research has neglected those who may have undertaken considerable amounts of practice but have dropped out of music instruction. There are complex relationships between prior knowledge, motivation, effort and perceived efficacy which influence decisions to continue or discontinue learning (Hallam 1998a; Sloboda et al. 1996). When a child begins to learn an instrument, prior musical knowledge affects facility of learning and the time needed to achieve mastery. While undertaking additional practice may compensate for a lack of prior knowledge, this has a time cost and requires perseverance. If a task proves too challenging, then a child may perceive that the effort required to succeed is too great and may give up learning altogether (Hurley 1995). Difficulties may also be evident when a child perceives that he or she does not have sufficient ability. Such perceptions often lead to a loss of self-esteem, loss of motivation, less practice, and a downward spiral leading to the termination of lessons (Austin et al. 2006; Chandler et al. 1987).

Another way to understanding individual differences is to focus on the personal beliefs held by learners and their parents. Parental and child ability conceptions are recognized as having a major impact on motivation and the desire of children to continue learning, especially when faced with obstacles (Austin et al. 2006). Indeed, McPherson's (in press) review of literature on mother–child interactions shows that parental ability conceptions can be self-fulfilling. McPherson and Davidson (2002) interviewed mothers before and after their child commenced learning an instrument. Those who held fixed views that their child may not have sufficient ability to succeed musically tended to provide less support for practice than mothers whose view was more malleable. They were also more likely to encourage their child to pursue other activities when they came to believe that their child was not coping. These fixed views of musical potential explained why some of the unsuccessful learners came to feel that they did not have sufficient ability to cope with learning music. Some mothers actually gave up on their child as a potential musician much sooner than the child.

The development of general musical skills

The impact of parents and the home environment is of profound importance in the development of children's musical potential (McPherson, in press). The general milieu of the environment to which a child is exposed and the opportunities parents and significant others provide are among the most critical factors for realizing children's musical potential (McPherson and Williamon 2006)(see also Chapter 28 this volume).

The seeds of musical potential are sown early because the human auditory system is functional 3–4 months before birth. After 28 to 30 weeks of gestation, foetuses can reliably react to external sounds, such that their heart rates vary as a result of exposure to music (Parncutt 2006). The process of musical enculturation therefore begins from the point at which brain development starts to become influenced by auditory stimulation. These processes gain momentum in the minutes after birth when a mother and infant will imitate each other's vocalizations in ways that show a shared emotional experience that some believe is the very basis of musicality (Trevarthen and Malloch 2002).

In the immediate months after an infant is born, the complex skills required for understanding and analysing music within any particular culture start to develop as a result of ongoing exposure to music. Even though each infant will experience many different levels of exposure, the perceptual and motor control needed to sing an intended pitch and the self-monitoring necessary to notice pitch or rhythmic differences can be accelerated by training (Trehub 2006). Wide individual differences exist regarding the extent to which preschool children engage in singing. For some, it is a part of almost all activities, while others sing only occasionally (Sundin 1997). Even though their exposure to music will have been markedly different, all children will have typically developed a surprising array of internal schemata for particular types of music long before they reach school or begin formal music instruction.

Measuring musical potential

Historically, the developers of musical aptitude tests have held varying views regarding the heritability of musical ability. Seashore (1938a, Seashore *et al.* 1938) believed that musical ability was a set of loosely related basic aural discrimination skills, which had a genetic basis and did not change over time. Wing (1981), Drake (1957) and Bentley (1966) shared Seashore's view of musical ability as being inherited, although they differed in their conceptions of the nature of that ability and how it might be assessed.

More recent tests, based on measurements involving tonal (melody, harmony), rhythm (tempo, metre), and preference (phrasing, balance, style) aptitudes, have been devised by Gordon (1965, 1979, 1982). Gordon (2007) suggests that students rarely display high (or low) aptitudes in all seven aptitudes and that all are based on the ability to 'audiate'; a term he has coined to describe how individuals give meaning to music that is heard or imagined.

The rationale underlying all of these approaches is that 'musicality' has its basis in aural perception. However, the predictive reliability of all of these measures is generally low (Hodges and Haack 1996). While alternative, more active measures for selecting pupils for learning to play an instrument have been adopted by teachers, these have tended not to be formalized. Perhaps the most common of these has been selection based on the child's ability to sing. However, the relationship between developmental tonal aptitude and use of the singing voice may also be very small (Rutkowski 1996). Researchers now generally recognize that aural skills alone are insufficient to predict future success across the full range of musical activities, especially those involving motor skills (Gilbert 1981) and creativity (Vaughan 1977; Webster 1988).

Recent conceptions of musical potential

McPherson and Williamon (2006) adapted Gagné's (2003) *differentiated model of giftedness and talent* to music as a means of defining the natural innate abilities, intrapersonal factors, and environmental catalysts that might impact on the development of musical skills. This conception defines *gifts* (e.g., intellectual, creative, socio-affective, sensorimotor) as natural innate potentials to achieve and *talent* as observable skills. The framework proposes that at least eight distinct types of musical talents (performing, improvising, composing, arranging, analysing, appraising, conducting, music teaching) can be developed through systematic practice and training. Moreover, although physical and mental dexterity, musicality, motor memory and auditory memory are all evident in the first few weeks of formal musical training, each needs to be refined and developed further through extensive practice and learning for children to develop their musical talents. Another key element of the theory is that some types of talents can go unnoticed or, as in the case of composing, develop later than others. By including a range of non-performance based outcomes of musical involvement, the model represents a broader conception of musical potential than has been evident in the past.

As an extension, McPherson (1993, 1996) distinguishes between visual (i.e., sight-reading, performing rehearsed music from notation), aural (i.e., playing from memory and by ear) and creative (i.e., improvising) aspects of music performance. When considering these in relation to groups of children of differing ages and abilities, he found that different musical skills are involved in developing each of these ways of performing music, that there is not an automatic transfer between the three orientations, and that each needs to be developed separately and in combination to maximize potential. This is rarely the case in most formal learning situations, where visual forms of performance often dominate at the expense of other orientations.

From an even wider perspective, Hallam (1998b) suggests that learning to play a musical instrument depends on the development of a wide range of different professional and personal skills. Some of these may be required for all musical activities, and others are applied more selectively to particular tasks (see Table 24.1). In order to become a successful musician, individuals need to develop social skills (being able to work with other musicians, promoters, the public); planning and organizational skills (planning practice schedules, programmes, travel

Table 24.1 Musical skills

Aural skills required for:	Developing rhythmic accuracy and a sense of pulse;
	Good intonation;
	The facility to know how music will sound without having to play it;
	Improvisational skills.
Cognitive skills required in the processes of:	Reading music;
	Transposition;
	Understanding keys;
	Understanding harmony;
	Understanding the structure of music;
	The memorization of music;
	Composing;
	Understanding different musical styles and their cultural and historic contexts.
Technical skills required for developing:	Instrument specific skills;
	Technical agility;
	Articulation;
	Expressive tone quality.
Musicianship skills are concerned with:	Being able to play expressively;
	Being able to project sound;
	Developing control;
	Conveying meaning.
Performance skills include:	Being able to communicate with an audience;
	Communicating with other performers;
	Being able to coordinate a group;
	Presenting to an audience.
Learning skills are concerned with:	Being able to learn, monitor and evaluate progress independently.

arrangements); and time management skills (being punctual, meeting deadlines). These are clearly required for developing expertise in a range of professions and while necessary are not exclusively 'musical'.

Actualization of musical potential

In the modern world, children have greater access to music through the media and are able to learn music in a multitude of different ways from the past. Technological developments have resulted in changes to the way music is perceived and valued within society, such that mere aural perception is no longer regarded as the defining aspect of musical ability.

Haroutounian (2000), in analysing the level of importance attached to particular criteria in identifying musically able children, suggests that the general behaviours of 'sustained interest' and 'self-discipline' are more important than music-specific characteristics which are normally regarded as indicative of musical ability. Similarly, Hallam and Prince (2003) asked a sample of musicians, student musicians, educators, and the general public to define musical ability. They reported that 71 per cent of the respondents viewed musical ability as being able to play a musical instrument or sing. This finding suggests that musical ability is often identified on the basis of developing practical skills. Overall, 28 per cent of the sample mentioned aural skills as indicative of musical ability, 32 per cent included listening and understanding, 24 per cent having an appreciation of music, and 15 per cent being responsive to music. The integration of a range of skills was cited by only 9 per cent of respondents. Personal qualities including motivation, personal expression, immersion in music, total commitment, and metacognition (being able to learn how to learn) were cited most often by musicians. Unsurprisingly, the musicians gave more complex responses, with many more elements in their explanations.

Further work by Hallam and Shaw (2003) using rating scales to illicit responses to a set of statements about musical ability showed that it was conceptualized in relation to rhythmic ability, organization of sound, communication,

motivation, personal characteristics, the integration of a range of complex skills, and performing in a group. Having a musical ear ranked lower in responses than might have been expected given its prominent position with regard to musical ability historically. The high ratings given to motivation and personal commitment demonstrate their importance in developing high-level skills. Overall, the conceptions of musical ability generated by the research were complex and multifaceted, and they reflected the wide range of expert achievement that occurs in the music professions of the developed world.

Conclusions

The extent to which genetic endowment underpins or limits all subsequent musical development has and continues to be fiercely debated (see Hallam 2006; McPherson and Williamon 2006; *High Ability Studies* Volume 18; *Behavioral and Brain Sciences* Volume 21), although there is general consensus that human beings as a species are pre-programmed to acquire a wide range of musical skills. We argue that what children are born with *enables* rather than *constrains* what they will eventually be able to achieve. While a range of generalized abilities may come into play when learning music, a host of environmental and personal catalysts work in combination with teaching and learning processes to develop particular types of talent. These talents form the basis of the many varied ongoing professional, amateur, and informal forms of meaningful engagement that individuals can have with music.

In developed countries, where formal schooling has taken over some of the traditional roles of the family, tests of musical aptitude have been devised to facilitate the identification of children who might benefit from music instruction, or to provide a base line for catering for individual differences after instruction has commenced. In our view, the rationale that underpins approaches based exclusively on aural acuity is questionable, especially given current methodologies and technologies which do not enable us to state with any certainty whether observed differences in musical ability in children are the result of genetic inheritance or learning.

As noted by Kemp and Mills (2002), musical potential is a complex phenomenon that involves many factors. While aural abilities are undeniably important, they do not provide the basis from which to accurately assess a child's current or future musical potential. Instead, musical potential is best thought of as malleable and ever-changing, and a dimension of human experience that takes many forms and occurs at many different levels. As a species-specific behaviour, music is inextricably linked to our basic human design (Welch and Adams 2003), therefore all children are inherently musical and deserve access to the types of informal and formal experiences that will maximize their own, individual musical potential.

References

Altenmüller E and Gruhn W (2002). Brain mechanisms. In R Parncutt and GE McPherson, eds, *The science and psychology of music performance: creative strategies for teaching and learning*, 63–81. Oxford University Press, New York.

Altenmuller EO (2003). How many music centres are in the brain? In I Peretz and R Zatorre, eds, *The cognitive neuroscience of music*, 346–356. Oxford University Press, Oxford.

Austin J, Renwick J and McPherson GE (2006). Developing motivation. In GE McPherson, ed., *The child as musician: a handbook of musical development*, 213–238. Oxford University Press, Oxford.

Bentley A. (1966). *Measures of musical abilities*. NFER-NELSON, Windsor, England.

Blacking J (1995). *Music, culture, and experience*. University of Chicago Press, Chicago, IL.

Ceci SJ (1990). *On intelligence … more or less: a bio-ecological treatise on intellectual development*. Prentice Hall, Englewood Cliffs, NJ.

Chandler TA, Chiarella D and Auria C (1987). Performance expectancy, success, satisfaction and attributions as variables in band challenges. *Journal of Research in Music Education*, **35**, 249–258.

Doan GR (1973). An investigation of the relationships between parental involvement and the performance ability of violin students. Unpublished Doctoral dissertation, Ohio State University, Columbus, OH.

Drake RM (1957). *Manual for the Drake musical aptitude tests*, 2nd edn. Science Research Associates, Chicago, IL.

Ericsson KA, Krampe RT and Tesch-Romer C (1993). The role of deliberate practice in the acquisition of expert performance. *Psychological Review*, **100**, 363–406.

Gagné F (2003). Transforming gifts into talents: the DMGT as a developmental theory. In N Colangelo and GA Davis, eds, *Handbook of gifted education*, 3rd edn, 60–74. Allyn and Bacon, Boston, MA.

Galton F (1876). The history of twins as a criterion of the relative powers of nature and nurture. *Royal Anthropological Institute of Great Britain and Ireland Journal*, **6**, 391–406.

Gilbert JP (1981). Motoric music skill development in young children: a longitudinal investigation. *Psychology of Music*, **9**(1), 21–25.

Gordon EE (1965). *Musical aptitude profile*. GIA, Chicago, IL.

Gordon EE (1979). *Primary measures of music audiation*. GIA, Chicago, IL.

Gordon EE (1982). *Intermediate measures of music audiation*. GIA, Chicago, IL.

Gordon EE (2007). *Learning sequences in music: a contemporary music learning theory*. GIA: Chicago, IL.

Gross E (2005). *Psychology: the science of mind and behaviour*, 5th edn. Hodder Arnold, London.

Gruber H, Degner S and Lehmann AC (2004). Why do some commit themselves in deliberate practice for many years—and so many do not? Understanding the development of professionalism in music. In M Radovan and N Dordevic, eds, *Current issues in adult learning and motivation*, 222–235. Slovenian Institute for Adult Education, Ljubljana.

Hallam S (1998a). The predictors of achievement and drop out in instrumental music tuition, *Psychology of Music*, **26**, 116–132.

Hallam S (1998b). *Instrumental teaching: a practical guide to better teaching and learning*. Heinemann, Oxford.

Hallam S (2004). How important is practicing as a predictor of learning outcomes in instrumental music? In SD Lipscomb, R Ashley RO Gjerdingen and P Webster, eds, *Proceedings of the 8th international conference on music perception and cognition*, 3–7 August 2004, 165–168. Northwestern University, Evanston, IL.

Hallam S (2006). Musicality. In G McPherson, ed., *The child as musician: a handbook of musical development*, 93–110. Oxford University Press, Oxford.

Hallam S and Prince V (2003). Conceptions of musical ability. *Research Studies in Music Education*, **20**, 2–22.

Hallam S and Shaw J (2003). Constructions of musical ability. *Bulletin of the Council for Research in Music Education*, Special Issue, 19th International Society for Music Education Research Seminar, Gothenburg, Sweden, School of Music, University of Gothenberg, August 3–9 2002, **153/4**, 102–107.

Haroutounian J (2000). Perspectives of musical talent: a study of identification criteria and procedures. *High Ability Studies*, **11**, 137–160.

Hodges DA (1996). Human musicality. In DA Hodges, ed., *Handbook of music psychology*, 29–68. IMR Press, San Antonio, TX.

Hodges DA (2006). The musical brain. In GE McPherson, ed., The child as musician: a *handbook of musical development*, pp 51–68. Oxford University Press, Oxford.

Hodges DA and Haack PA (1996). The influence of music on human behavior. In DA Hodges, ed., *Handbook of music psychology*, 469–555. IMR Press, San Antonio, TX.

Hurley CG (1995). Student motivations for beginning and continuing/discontinuing string music tuition. *The*

Quarterly Journal of Music Teaching and Learning, **6,** 44–55.

Jørgensen H. (2002). Instrumental performance expertise and amount of practice among instrumental students in a conservatoire. *Music Education Research,* **4,** 105–119.

Kemp AE and Mills AE (2002). Musical potential. In R Parncutt and GE McPherson, eds, *The science and psychology of music performance: creative strategies for teaching and learning,* 3–16. Oxford University Press, Oxford.

Kokotsaki D and Hallam S (2007). Higher education music students' perceptions of the benefits of participative music making. *Music Education Research,* **9,** 93–109.

Kopiez R. (1998). Singers are late beginners. Sangerbiographien aus Sicht der Expertiseforschung. Ein Schwachstellenanalyse. [Singers biographies from the perspective of research on expertise. An analysis of weaknesses] In H Gembris R Kraemer and G Maas, eds, *Singen als Gegenstand der Grundlagenforschung,* 37–56. Wissner, Augsberg.

Lehmann AC and Gruber H (2006). Music. In KA Ericsson, N Charness, PJ Feltovich and RR Hoffman, eds, *The Cambridge handbook of expertise and expert performance,* 457–470. Cambridge University Press, Cambridge.

Levitin DJ, Bellugi U. (1998). Musical abilities in individuals with Williams syndrome. *Music Perception,* **15,** 357–89.

Levitin DJ, Cole K, Chiles M, Lai Z, Lincoln A and Bellugi U (2007). Characterizing the musical phenotype in individuals with Williams syndrome. *Child Neuropsychology,* **10,** 223–247.

Levitin DJ, Menon V, Schmitt JE, *et al.* (2003). Neural correlates of auditory perception in Williams syndrome: an iMRI study. *Neuroimage,* **18,** 74–82.

Mareschal D, Johnson MH, Sirois S, Spratling MW, Thomas MSC and Westerman G (2007) *Neuroconstructivism: how the brain constructs cognition. Volume 1.* Oxford University Press, Oxford.

McPherson GE (1993). Factors and abilities influencing the development of visual, aural and creative performance skills in music and their educational implications. Doctor of Philosophy, University of Sydney, Australia. Dissertation Abstracts International, 54/04-A, 1277. (University Microfilms No. 9317278.)

McPherson GE (1996). Five aspects of musical performance and their correlates. *Bulletin of the Council for Research in Music Education,* **127,** 115–121.

McPherson GE (2005). From child to musician: skill development during the beginning stages of learning an instrument. *Psychology of Music,* **33,** 5–35.

McPherson GE (in press). The role of parents in children's musical development. *Psychology of Music.*

McPherson GE and Davidson JW (2002). Musical practice: mother and child interactions during the first year of learning an instrument. *Music Education Research,* **4,** 143–158.

McPherson GE and Williamon A (2006). Giftedness and talent. In GE McPherson, ed., *The child as musician: a handbook of musical development,* 239–256. Oxford University Press, Oxford.

McPherson GE, Bailey M and Sinclair K (1997). Path analysis of a model to describe the relationship among five types of musical performance. *Journal of Research in Music Education,* **45,** 103–129.

Miller LK (1989). *Musical savants: exceptional skill in the mentally retarded.* Erlbaum, Hillsdale, NJ.

Parncutt R (2006). Prenatal development. In GE McPherson, ed., *The child as musician: a handbook of musical development,* 1–32. Oxford University Press, Oxford.

Rauschecker JP (2003). Functional organization and plasticity of auditory cortex. In I Peretz and R Zatorre, eds, *The cognitive neuroscience of music,* 357–365. Oxford University Press, Oxford.

Ruthsatz J and Detterman DK (2003). An extraordinary memory: the case study of a musical prodigy. *Intelligence,* **31,** 509–518.

Rutkowski J (1996). The effectiveness of individual/small group singing activities on kindergartners' use of singing voice and developmental music aptitude. *Journal of Research in Music Education,* **44,** 353–368.

Schlaug G (2003). The brain of musicians. In I. Peretz and R. Zatorre, eds, *The cognitive neuroscience of music,* 366–381. Oxford University Press, Oxford.

Seashore CE (1938, reprinted 1960). *Psychology of music.* Dover, New York.

Seashore CE, Lewis L and Saetveit JG (1938). *Seashore measures of musical talents.* Psychological Corporation, New York.

Shavinina LV (2007). On the advancement of the expert performance approach via a deep understanding of giftedness. *High Ability Studies,* **18,** 79–82.

Shavinina LV (in press). When child prodigies, unique representations, and the extracognitive combine: toward a cognitive–developmental theory of giftedness. In LV Shavinina, ed., *The international handbook on giftedness.* Amsterdam: Springer Science and Business Media.

Shuter-Dyson R (1999). Musical ability. In D Deutsch, ed., *The psychology of music,* 627–651. Harcourt Brace and Company, New York.

Sloboda J, Hermelin B and O'Connor N (1985). An exceptional musical memory. *Musical Perception,* **3,** 155–170.

Sloboda JA and Howe MJA (1991). Biographical precursors of musical excellence: an interview study. *Psychology of Music,* **19,** 3–21.

Sloboda JA, Davidson JW, Howe MJA and Moore DG (1996). The role of practice in the development of performing musicians. *British Journal of Psychology,* **87,** 287–309.

Sosniak LA (1985). Learning to be a concert pianist. Developing talent in young people. In BS Bloom, ed., *Developing talent in young people,* 19–67. Ballantine, New York.

Sundin B (1997). Musical creativity in childhood—a research project in retrospect. *Research Studies in Music Education,* **9,** 48–57.

Trehub SE (2006). Infants as musical connoisseurs. In GE McPherson, ed., *The child as musician: a handbook of musical development,* 33–49. Oxford University Press, Oxford.

Trevarthen C and Malloch S (2002). Musicality and music before three: human vitality and invention shared with pride. *Zero to Three*, September, 10–18.

Vandervert LR (2007). Cognitive functions of the cerebellum explain how Ericsson's deliberate practice produces giftedness. *High Ability Studies*, **18**, 89–92.

Vandervert LR and Liu H (in press). How working memory and the cognitive cerebellum collaboratively produce the child prodigy. In LV Shavinina, ed., *The international handbook on giftedness*. Amsterdam: Springer Science and Business Media.

Vaughan MM (1977). Measuring creativity: its cultivation and measurement. *Bulletin of the Council for Research in Music Education*, **50**, 72–77.

Wagner MJ (1975). The effect of a practice report on practice time and musical performance. In CK Madsen, RD Greer and CH Madsen Jr, eds, *Research in music behaviour*, 125–130. Teachers College Press, New York.

Wallin N, Merker B and Brown S (2000). *The origins of music*. The MIT Press, Cambridge, MA.

Webster PR (1988). New perspectives on music aptitude and achievement. *Psychomusicology*, **7**, 177–194.

Welch GF and Adams P. (2003). *How is music learning celebrated and developed?* British Educational Research Assocation (BERA), Southwell, UK.

Williamon A and Valentine E (2000). Quantity and quality of musical practice as predictors of performance quality. *British Journal of Psychology*, **91**, 353–376.

Wing HD (1981). *Standardised tests of musical intelligence*. National Foundation for Educational Research, Windsor.

Young L and Nettelbeck T (1995). The abilities of a musical savant and his family. *Journal of Autism and Developmental Disorders*, **25**, 231–247.

Zurcher W (1972). The effect of model-supportive practice on beginning brass instrumentalists. In CK Madsen, RD Greer and CH Madsen, eds, *Research in music behavior: modifying music behavior in the classroom*, 125–130. Teachers College Press, New York.

CHAPTER 25

Practising

Harald Jørgensen and Susan Hallam

Introduction

Practice is central to the development of all aspects of musical expertise. The musician not only needs to consider the development of technical skills but must also develop musical interpretation, may have to play or sing from memory, rehearse and perform in cooperation with other musicians, improvise, and contend with stage fright. These elements require aural, technical, cognitive, communication, performance and learning skills. These complex skills cannot be acquired, improved and maintained by simple repetitive practice.

Effective practice has been defined by Hallam (1997c) as 'that which achieves the desired end-product, in as short a time as possible, without interfering negatively with longer-term goals' (p. 181). This definition assumes that effective practice might take many forms and implies that the musician requires considerable meta-cognitive skills to facilitate the completion of task requirements or, in the case of the novice, appropriate support. Practising may be addressed from a psychological viewpoint as an act of learning, where theories of psychomotor learning and motor programmes are relevant, and it may also be viewed as 'self-teaching' (Jørgensen 2004). The multifaceted nature of practice has been encapsulated in models which provide a framework for understanding its relationships with creativity and performance (see Hallam 1997c; Chaffin and Lemieux 2004).

Empirical research on practice has a history that dates back to the beginning of the twentieth century, although the majority of research has been undertaken in the last 25 years. Its focus has been almost exclusively in relation to the training of classical musicians and the individual practitioner.

The quantity of practice

Practitioners and researchers agree that there are two important variables relating to practice that determine progress and attainment: the *quality* and *quantity* of practice in interaction with prior knowledge and skills. In the following section we will concentrate on the quantity of practice, returning to quality issues in the section on practice strategies.

Time spent practising

Research on time spent practising has addressed three different aspects: the initial starting age; the accumulated amount of practice from initial starting age to the present; and the amount of practice at one particular time or during a limited period of time. A major challenge to this type of research is the difficulty in obtaining reliable and valid measures of the amount of practice undertaken (Madsen 2005).

Despite these difficulties some broad trends have emerged. First, most of those who reach a high level of expertise on an instrument have made an *early start*, on either their major instrument or another instrument. This phenomenon has been demonstrated on a broad range of instruments (Jørgensen 2001; Sosniak 1985). Pianists and violinists tend to be particularly early starters, aged from 3–8 years old, while brass and woodwind performers start a little later with their major instrument (Jørgensen 2001). Starting to play at an early age, when physically the body is more flexible, may be important. Certainly, Wagner (1988) has demonstrated that pianists' hands can change physically if they begin playing when very young.

Another trend is that time spent in practice usually increases as age and expertise develops, with most young people practising almost every day (Sloboda *et al.* 1996). There is evidence that the increase in practice time is greater for those who go on to become professional rather than amateur musicians. However, after entrance to the profession, duration of regular practice time is observed to decrease as pressures of rehearsals and public performance increase (Krampe 1994).

Since many students start early and gradually increase the amount of time that they practise, it follows that many of them have *accumulated a large amount of practice time* by their late teens, and that expert performers have invested several thousand hours of practice over a period of 15–16 years before reaching a high performance level in their twenties (Sosniak 1985). Accumulated practice time has also been found to relate to the performance of rehearsed music in novice players aged 7–9 years, although use of specific strategies seems to be more important when children engage in sight-reading, playing from memory, playing by ear, or improvising (McPherson 2005).

Most research on the amount of practice has not differentiated between instruments or has focused on only one instrument. An exception to this is a study by Jørgensen (1997). He found that the keyboard students in a conservatoire invested most time in practice, 25–30 hours a week, followed by strings, woodwind, brass and voice. There were also differences between specific instruments within these groups. Violinists, for instance, tended to practise more than double bass players, and trumpet players practised more than tuba players. Lammers and Kruger (2006), in a study of American and Japanese students, reported similar results. Physiological restrictions related to the instrument's physical and technical demands (Jørgensen 1997) and the nature and extent of the repertoire are probably important factors determining amount of practice.

Assessment, whether formal in examinations, or informal in a lesson, has an impact on practice time. Hallam (2001) reported that 95 per cent of the novices and advanced students in her study increased their practice time in weeks preceding examinations. Practice activity increases as the number of lessons received increases (Sloboda *et al.* 1996), and there is an increase in practice time the day after a weekly lesson

(Lehmann and Ericsson 1998). Not surprisingly the quantity of practice decreases during holidays, even for students in a specialized music school (Sloboda *et al.* 1996).

Research on the relationship between *amount of practice at a particular time and general achievement level* at this time has considered a range of different instruments and age groups with varying outcomes (see Chapter 24 this volume and Jørgensen and Hallam in preparation). The different age groups and levels of expertise, lengths of time period studied, as well as the variety of instruments included in the studies may partly explain why the results are different from study to study. All of the studies have found a positive correlation between amount of practice at a particular point of time and general achievement, although Ericsson *et al.* (1993) found no difference in length of weekly practice between the 'best' and the 'good' violin students. The difference between the 'best' and 'good' violinists was in amount of accumulated practice.

Ericsson and colleagues (1993) suggested a monotonic relationship between 'deliberate practice' and an individual's acquired performance. Similarly, Sloboda *et al.* (1996, p. 308) stated that 'We believe that we have established, beyond any reasonable doubt, that amount of relevant practice is a key variable in determination of music performance expertise.' However, there are substantial individual differences in the relationship between the quantity of practice and attainment (Ericsson *et al.* 1993; Sloboda *et al.* 1996; Jørgensen 2002), suggesting that attainment is not exclusively a question of quantity of practice, but also of quality, which is a result of individual engagement with and knowledge of practice strategies.

Two studies have related amount of current practice to more specific areas of achievement, with conflicting results. Williamon and Valentine (2000) looked at practice and performance among piano students from under 11 to more than 24 years in four levels of skill on one composition, and found that pianists at higher levels of expertise spent more time in each practice session, but that quantity of practice was not significantly related to quality of performance as rated by experienced teachers. Wagner (1975), with college students, assessed performance on 'a selection which best represented their level of musicianship at that time', and found a positive relationship between amount of practice and 'level of musicianship'.

A specific issue is the time spent practising a single composition. To date, research has focused on the memorization of piano music by professional musicians, students with high levels of expertise (Chaffin and Imreh 1997), or pianists with a broad range of skill levels (Williamon and Valentine 2000). The findings illustrate how time-consuming the memorization process can be, depending on the complexity of the piece. Lehmann and Ericsson (1998) studied a university student preparing for her degree recital, memorizing eight unfamiliar pieces by Haydn, Prokofiev and Debussy. She spent a total of 531 hours practising to prepare for a concert with a total playing time of 37 minutes.

Motivation and drop out

Evidence from students who have dropped out suggests that there are complex relationships between time spent practising, prior knowledge, motivation, and perceived efficacy (Hurley 1995). The amount of practice undertaken predicts whether students will drop out (Sloboda et al. 1996; Hallam 1998), although other factors such as socio-economic status, self-concept in music, reading achievement, scholastic ability, measured musical ability, maths achievement, and motivation are also predictors (McCarthy 1980; Klinedinst 1991; Hallam 1998).

McPherson and McCormick (2006) found that self-efficacy was the best predictor of performance. The role of psychological characteristics (rather than musical talent or expertise) was also observed by McNamara et al. (2006) in their study of a group of internationally renowned musicians. They found that some characteristics were generic (e.g. dedication, planning and commitment), while others were particularly evident at transition points in their career, i.e. perseverance and adaptability in the transition from study to entry into the music profession.

The quality of practice

Quality is an elusive matter. The concept of 'deliberate practice' defined as goal-oriented,

structured, and effortful, was introduced by Ericsson and colleagues (1993) to address the issue of quality. They also outlined constraints which might determine the quantity and quality of practice—motivation, resources, attention. Much of the research exploring issues relating to the quality of practice has focused on the strategies that musicians adopt when practising. Jørgensen (2004) has proposed four strategy types, i.e. planning strategies; strategies for the conduct (execution) of practice; strategies to evaluate practice; and meta-strategies. A similar conception is that of practice as self-regulated learning (McPherson and Zimmerman 2002), where the practitioner is recommended to engage in forethought, performance/volitional control, and self reflection.

Planning strategies

The organization of practice

Instrumentalists and singers are expected to *practise regularly*. Several management strategies have been observed in relation to this. Some students in higher music education practise at the same time every day (Duke et al. 1997), while others integrate practice into a daily or weekly plan (Jørgensen 1997). Most students, however, try to fit in practice sessions between other activities without any preconceived plan. The morning may be the best time for high levels of concentration (Lehmann and Ericsson 1998). Ericsson and colleagues (1993) found that conservatoire students at the highest levels of expertise practised in the morning, took naps in the afternoon, and then put in more practice in the evening. For novice students the regularity of practice may be more related to one specific day a week (Hallam 2001), or a specific period of the day, i.e. 'before bedtime' (Pitts et al. 2000b). Sloboda et al. (1996) showed that the students in a selective specialist music school distributed their repertory practice evenly to morning, afternoon and evening sessions.

Practice may be most effective when it is organized in sequential and logical manner (Barry 1992). At the start of practice sessions many musicians use warm-up exercises, although there is considerable individual variation in the extent to which these are perceived to be necessary (Hallam 1995a). Technical exercises often follow with repertory work left until last (Duke *et al.* 1997). Sloboda *et al.* (1996) showed that the students in a selective specialist music school practised more than 40 per cent of their scales in the morning session. For conservatoire students, there are pronounced differences between instruments in the relative amount of warming up exercises, technical work, and repertory practice (Jørgensen 1998).

Setting goals and adopting appropriate approaches for particular tasks

Ericsson *et al.* (1993) concluded that a well-defined task was one of four requirements for effective learning through practice, although the evidence suggests that novices and more accomplished students often fail to formulate goals for practice activities and mastering specific tasks (Jørgensen 1998). The nature of particular learning tasks inevitably affects the goals set and the ways in which they are undertaken. McPherson (2005) stressed the importance of helping students to develop task-appropriate strategies for such diverse tasks as practising notated repertoire, playing from memory, sight-reading, playing by ear, and improvising.

Musicians seem to approach practising particular repertoire in different ways. Miklaszewski (1995) observed that professional musicians spent a much shorter time learning a late romantic miniature than three contemporary variations. Lehmann and Ericsson (1995) suggest that the increasing technical demands of twentieth-century music have influenced the nature of practice. Research on sight-reading and improvisation suggests that time spent engaged in these activities is the key element in their development to expert levels (see Chapter 32 this volume).

Developing interpretation

A specific task in formulating goals is the 'performance plan', and the way interpretation is planned and developed through practice sessions. Some musicians plan interpretation at the outset, based on a study of the score or from ideas gleaned from listening to a wide range of music and different interpretations of the same piece (Hallam 1995b; Lisboa *et al.* 2005); primarily letting the expressive ideas guide the technical work (Chaffin *et al.* 2003). A second approach is to develop a performance plan after mastering most of the technical challenges (Nielsen 2001). Experienced performers also report taking the audience perspective into account when developing expressive ideas (Oura and Hatano 2001).

Strategies for the conduct of practice

Variable practice

Schema theory suggests that motor programmes, including those required for playing a musical instrument, are strengthened by increased variability in practice (for instance, practising a passage with different articulations, at different tempos, or a technique using different examples), rather than repetition of the same actions. This facilitates transfer to other tasks (Schmidt 1976). The evidence for the effectiveness of this is mixed (see Hallam 1997c for a review).

Part–whole strategies

Particularly relevant to the acquisition of musical skill is the question of *part–whole transfer* of training. Given a reasonably short piece of music to practise, observational studies have shown that many novice pupils play through the music without stopping to focus on difficult sections, and usually repeat the whole piece several times (see Hallam 1997b; Renwick and McPherson 2002). Some novice and advanced students use a combined approach, starting with the whole and stopping to practise difficult sections en route (Hallam 1997b; Miklaszewski 1989). This gives the performer an overview of the music, and the opportunity to identify and select parts which require more intense work while relating the parts to longer sections or the whole (Chaffin and Imreh 1997; Nielsen 1997). Sections for concentrated work are selected on the basis of a range of criteria including those relating to the formal structure and motor aspects of the performance (Miklaszewski and Sawicki 1992); new or related elements (Nielsen 1999), and the visual layout of the music and its harmonic progression (Williamon and Valentine 2000). As practice progresses and the music is increasingly mastered technically, the sections worked on become longer (Chaffin and Imreh 1997; Nielsen 1999), although attention to detail and work on small sections may continue throughout practice sessions. It is clear from these examples that the relationship between practising a piece in its entirety, focusing on parts, and mastery is complex. For different tasks whole or part strategies may be more appropriate.

Transfer of learning

Exercises are sometimes used to address *specific challenges* within a given composition (Hallam 1995; Nielsen 1999), but the alternative and more common solution is to practise difficult sections within the music being learnt. Transfer of learning in music needs to be considered in relation to particular tasks and different timescales. In the short term, practice seems to be most effective when it relates specifically to the task being undertaken, with the conditions for learning and performance being as similar as possible.

Strategies for increasing tempo

When passages need to be played at speed, Drake and Palmer (2000) observed three approaches adopted by students at different levels of expertise. Beginners tended to stick to one tempo throughout practice sessions, novices increased tempo gradually until they reached a limit, while the most accomplished students gradually increased tempo over each practice session. Research on the efficiency of these approaches has been equivocal probably due to the ambiguity of concepts such as 'slow', 'fast', and 'in performance tempo'; differences between beginners and experts; the way strategies relating to tempo are often combined with other strategies; and the length and complexity of music involved. Since the adoption of these strategies involves motor and muscular considerations, the observation by Winold *et al.* (1994), that fast and slow speeds of movement seem to be controlled in different ways is important.

Mental practice

Mental practice, where the learner thinks through the procedures without actually playing, has been compared with playing practice in several studies, with conflicting results (Kopiez 1990; Ross 1985). This is hardly surprising, taking into account that:

- the studies differ in the length, familiarity and complexity of the music used;
- 'mental strategy' has been operationalized differently;

- the length of time using the strategies has differed; and
- familiarity with the use of mental strategies has varied between those taking part in the studies. The conclusion by Ross (1985), that a combination of mental and physical practice is most effective because mental practice allows concentration on the cognitive aspects of music performance without the distractions of exercising motor control, is probably sound.

Strategies for preparing for performance

Even if the music is well prepared, performance anxiety may jeopardize all prior efforts, particularly where the performer has to play from memory. The most common strategy for overcoming performance nerves is to be well-prepared and over-learn, investing more time than is required for basic mastery (Lehman and Ericsson 1998) (see Chapters 31, 33 and 36 this volume for issues relating to planning, memorization and anxiety).

Strategies to evaluate practice

Monitoring the effectiveness of practice

To monitor the effectiveness of practice it is particularly important that appropriate schema against which to evaluate progress are developed. Hallam (1997a) found that 60 per cent of beginners, novices and advanced students when learning a new piece left errors uncorrected. She observed that errors once made tended to become permanent and were left uncorrected. Only when students had considerable expertise and had well-developed schema were errors consistently corrected. Whitaker (1996), studying performers, arrangers, conductors and composers also established the necessity of possessing a mental template that served as the focus for all learning and performance activities. In contrast to professionals, many students have been found to be unable to generate auditory schemata from written notation (Grøndahl 1987). These skills need to be developed until at expert level current information about progress can be utilized to develop more sophisticated mental representations. Several external remedies and techniques have been used in the process of developing schemata. Some studies have reported that to use a tape with a recording of the music is an efficient strategy (Puopolo 1971; Zurcher 1975), although others have found no effect of a recorded model (Anderson 1981; Linklater 1997).

Meta-strategies

Metacognitive strategies are concerned with the planning, monitoring and evaluation of learning. There are considerable differences between beginners, novices and experts in their knowledge and deployment of different practising and self-regulating strategies (Hallam 1997b; Pitts *et al.* 2000a, b) as well as individual differences among musicians and novices at the same level of competence (Nielsen 1997, 1999, 2001; Austin and Berg 2006). Hallam (1997b) demonstrated that professional musicians had well-developed metacognitive skills, including self-awareness of strengths and weaknesses, extensive knowledge regarding the nature of different tasks and what would be required to complete them satisfactorily, and strategies which could be adopted in response to perceived needs. This not only encompassed technical matters, interpretation and performance but also issues relating to learning itself, concentration, planning, monitoring and evaluation. Novices demonstrated less metacognitive awareness, the amount and structure of their practice tending to be determined by external commitments, e.g. examinations. There are differences in students' practising strategies and metacognitive skills, the former being inextricably intertwined with the acquisition of expertise. Skilled musicians are more likely to monitor and control their playing by focusing their attention on what they are practising and how it can be improved.

Among monitoring strategies, the monitoring of concentration is regarded by many music students as crucial to practice. Attempting to improve undergraduate students' concentration, Madsen and Geringer (1981) required them to keep a record of their practice, rate each practice session for productivity over an 8-week period and complete a distraction index. This increased observed attentiveness and performance although the index was time-consuming to complete. Nielsen (2001) suggests that students

can enhance self-guidance by covertly or overtly describing how to proceed, giving comments on progress, noting concentration lapses and changes in motivation. Focus is crucial to avoid mindless repetition. The regulation of strategies requires deliberate effort, task selection, speed and intensity.

Rehearsing in small groups

Research on rehearsals in small groups has shown that there is no single best strategy for rehearsing repertoire (Davidson and King 2004). Individual ensembles find their own best ways of working. Berg (2000) found that high school student ensembles adopted four main activities, initiating, performing, orienting and assisted learning. Professional groups usually have a draft plan of the material to be covered across a series of rehearsals with room for extra sessions should they be needed (Goodman 2000). Group cohesiveness centres around the music (Davidson and Good 2002) but trust and respect are crucial for the functioning of groups working together continuously over long periods of time, e.g. string quartets (Young and Colman 1979). To be successful in the long term rehearsals have to be underpinned by strong social frameworks (for a full review see Davidson and King 2004).

The role of the learning environment in practice

The impact that institutional learning environments have on practice has been little studied, although research at conservatoire level in Norway (Jørgensen 1997) reported that music education students and church music students practiced more than expected, probably due to the predominant performance values in a conservatoire.

Instrumental teachers are an important influence on practice. Research on the way that they teach about practising has had mixed results. Jørgensen (2000), in research with beginning conservatoire students in Norway, reported that 40 per cent indicated that their previous teachers had invested 'little' or 'no' effort in teaching them how to practise. However, in the USA, teachers have reported that they always or almost always include instructions about practice in their lessons (Barry and McArthur 1994). Students do seem to be able to learn how to use expert practising strategies (Barry 1992) and having done so report more positive attitudes towards practising, are more likely to engage in practice planning and problem identification, are better able to select appropriate performance goals, and are able to formulate more cognitively complex goals (Kenny 1992). This suggests that there can be benefits in teaching about practice.

Conclusions

Over the last 25 years our understanding of the nature of practice and its importance in the development of expertise has increased enormously. We know that both the quantity and quality of practice contribute to the level of expertise attained, and that the individual's ability to adopt more effective practising strategies is inextricably linked with their level of expertise. There has also been a recognition that musicians exhibit considerable diversity in the ways that they practise and that these can lead to equally successful outcomes. Despite the considerable progress made there are still areas where we know little. In relation to the quantity of practice there is a need for more studies that address the interaction between instrument, age, level of expertise and amount of practice within a range of different contexts. In relation to the quality of practice there is a need for studies exploring:

- how practice plans and goals are formulated and the way that these influence practice and subsequently performance;
- skill transfer between warming up exercises, technical studies, and repertory practice and the impact of these on performance;
- the effectiveness of aural models of what is to be learned and other types of feedback;
- concentration in practice, and how self-regulating techniques and meta-cognitive skills can be developed;
- the relationships between learning approaches, motivation and practice efficiency;
- how best to teach practice strategies at all levels of expertise;

- the way that social interaction in groups, including non-verbal communication, affects performance;
- the ways in which practice is undertaken on a variety of different tasks, e.g. sight reading, improvisation and in different genres, e.g. popular music, jazz, and world musics.

Such research will not only increase our understanding but also contribute towards enhancing learning and teaching.

References

Anderson JN (1981). Effects of tape recorded aural models on sight-reading and performance skills. *Journal of Research in Music Education*, **29**, 23–30.

Austin JR and Berg MH (2006). Exploring music practice among sixth grade band and orchestra students. *Psychology of Music*, **34**, 535–558.

Barry NH (1992). The effects of practice strategies, individual differences in cognitive style, and gender upon technical accuracy and musicality of student instrumental performance. *Psychology of Music*, **20**, 112–123.

Barry NH and McArthur V (1994). Teaching practice strategies in the music studio: a survey of applied music teachers. *Psychology of Music*, **22**, 44–55.

Berg MH (2000). Thinking for yourself: the social construction of chamber music experience. In RR Rideout, SJ Paul, eds. *On the sociology of music: vol 2. Papers from the Music Education Symposium at the University of Oklahoma*, 91–112. University of Massachusetts Press, Amherst, MA.

Chaffin R and Imreh G (1997). Pulling teeth and torture: musical memory and problem solving. *Thinking and Reasoning*, **3**, 315–336.

Chaffin R, Imreh G, Lemieux A and Chen C (2003). Seeing the big picture: piano practice as expert problem solving. *Music Perceotion*, **20**, 465–490.

Chaffin R and Lemieux AF (2004). General perspectives on achieving musical excellence. In A Williamon, ed., *Musical excellence: strategies and techniques to enhance performance*, 19–40. Oxford University Press, Oxford.

Davidson JW and Good JMM (2002). Social and musical co-ordination between members of a string quartet: an exploratory study. *Psychology of Music*, **30**, 186–201.

Davidson J and King EC (2004). Strategies for ensemble practice. In A Williamon, ed. *Musical Excellence*, 105–122. Oxford University Press, Oxford.

Drake C and Palmer C (2000). Skill acquisition in music performance: relations between planning and temporal control. *Cognition*, **74**, 1–32.

Duke RA, Flowers PJ and Wolfe DE (1997). Children who study with piano with excellent teachers in the United States. *Bulletin of the Council for Research in Music Education*, **132**, 51–84.

Ericsson KA, Krampe RT and Tesch-Romer C (1993). The role of deliberate practice in the acquisition of expert performance. *Psychological Review*, **100**, 363–406.

Goodman E (2002). Ensemble performance. In J Rink, ed., *Musical performance: a guide to understanding*, 153–167. Cambridge University Press, Cambridge.

Grøndahl D (1987). *Thinking processes and structures used by professional pianists in keyboard learning.* Hovedfagsewksamen in Music Education, The Norwegian State Academy of Music, Oslo.

Hallam S (1995a). Professional musicians' orientations to practice: implications for teaching. *British Journal of Music Education*, **12**, 3–19.

Hallam S (1995b). Professional musicians' approaches to the learning and interpretation of music. *Psychology of Music*, **23**, 111–128.

Hallam S (1997a). The development of memorisation strategies in musicians: implications for instrumental teaching. *British Journal of Music Education*, **14**, 87–97.

Hallam S (1997b). Approaches to instrumental music practice of experts and novices: implications for education. In H Jorgensen and A Lehman, eds, *Does practice make perfect? Current theory and research on instrumental music practice*, 89–108. NMH-publikasjoner 1997:1, Norges musikkhgskole, Oslo.

Hallam S (1997c).What do we know about practising? Towards a model synthesising the research literature. In H Jorgensen and A Lehman, eds, *Does practice make perfect? Current theory and research on instrumental music practice*, 179–231. NMH-publikasjoner 1997:1. Norges musikkhgskole, Oslo.

Hallam S (1998). Predictors of achievement and drop out in instrumental tuition. *Psychology of Music*, **26**, 116–132.

Hallam S (2001). The development of expertise in young musicians: strategy use, knowledge acquisition and individual diversity. *Music Education Research*, **3**, 7–23.

Hurley CG (1995). Student motivations for beginning and continuing/discontinuing string music tuition. *The Quarterly Journal of Music Teaching and Learning*, **6**, 44–55.

Jørgensen H (1997). Time for practicing? Higher level students' use of time for instrumental practicing. In H Jørgensen and AC Lehmann, eds, *Does practice make perfect? Current theory and research on instrumental music practice*, 123–140. Norges musikkhøgskole, Oslo.

Jørgensen H (1998). *Planlegges øving?* (Is practice planned?). Norwegian Academy of Music, Oslo.

Jørgensen H (2000). Student learning in higher instrumental education: who is responsible? *British Journal of Music Education*, **17**, 67–77.

Jørgensen H (2001).Instrumental learning: is an early start a key to success? *British Journal of Music Education*, **18**, 227–239.

Jørgensen H (2002). Instrumental performance expertise and amount of practice among instrumental students in a conservatoire. *Music Education Research*, **4**, 105–119.

Jørgensen H (2004). Strategies for individual practice. In A Williamon, ed., *Musical excellence*, 85–104. Oxford University Press, Oxford.

Jørgensen H and Hallam S (in preparation) How important is the quantity of practice in attainment?

Kenny WE (1992). The effect of metacognitive strategy instruction on the performance proficiency and attitude toward practice of beginning band students. Unpublished doctoral dissertation, University of Illinois, Urbana-Champaign, IL.

Klinedinst RE (1991). Predicting performance achievement and retention of fifth-grade instrumental students. *Journal of Research in Music Education*, **39**, 225–238.

Kopiez R (1990). *Der Einfluss kognitiver Strukturne auf das Erlernen eines Musikstucks am Instrument.* (The influence of cognitive structures on the learning of instrumental music.) Peter Lang, Frankfurt.

Krampe RT (1994). *Maintaining excellence: cognitive-motor performance in pianists differing in age and skill level* (Studien und Berichte/MPI fur Bildungsforschung 58). Sigma, Berlin.

Lammers M and Kruger M (2006). Brass and woodwind student practice habits in Norway, Japan and the United States. *NACWPI Journal*, **54**, 4–13.

Lehmann AC and Ericsson KA (1995). The relationship between historical constraints of musical practice and increase of musicians' performance skills. Paper presented at the 7th European conference on Developmental Psychology, Poland. 1995, 23–27 August.

Lehmann AC and Ericsson KA (1998). Preparation of a public piano performance: the relationship between practice and performance. *Musicae Scientae*, **2**, 67–94.

Linklater F (1997). Effects of audio- and videotape models on performance achievement of beginning clarinettists. *Journal of Research in Music Education*, **45**, 402–414.

Lisboa T, Williamon A, Zicari M and Eiholzer H (2005). Mastery through imitation: a preliminary study. *Musicae Scientiae*, **19**, 75–110.

Madsen C (2005). A 30-year follow-up study of actual applied music practice versus estimated practice. *Journal of Research in Music Education*, **52**, 77–88.

Madsen C K and Geringer JM (1981). The effect of a distraction index on improving practice attentiveness and musical performance. *Bulletin of the Council for Research in Music Education*, **66–67**, 46–52.

McCarthy JF (1980). Individualised instruction, student achievement and drop out in an urban elementary instrumental music program. *Journal of Research in Music Education*, **28**, 59–69.

MacNamara A, Holmes P and Collins D (2006). The pathway to excellence: the role of psychological characteristics in negotiating the challenges of musical development. *British Journal of Music Education*, **23**, 285–302.

McPherson GE (2005). From child to musician: skill development during the beginning stages of learning an instrument. *Psychology of Music*, **33**, 5–35.

McPherson GE and McCormick J (2006) Self-efficacy and performing music. *Psychology of Music*, **34**, 321–336.

McPherson GE and Zimmerman BJ (2002). Self-regulation of musical learning. In R Colwell and C Richardson, eds, *The new handbook of research on music teaching and learning*, 348–372. Oxford University Press, Oxford.

Miklaszewski K (1989). A case study of a pianist preparing a musical performance. *Psychology of Music*, **17**, 95–109.

Miklaszewski K (1995). Individual differences in preparing a musical composition for public performance. In M Manturzewska, K Milaszewski and A Bialkowski, eds, *Psychology of music today: proceedings of the international seminar of researchers and lecturers in the psychology of music*, 138–147. Fryderyk Chopin Academy of Music, Warsaw.

Miklaszewski K and Sawicki L (1992). Segmentation of music introduced by practicing pianists preparing compositions for public performance. In R Dalmonte and M Baroni, eds, *Secudo convegno Europeo di analasi musicale* [Proceedings of the second European conference on musical analysis], 113–121. University of Trento Press, Trento.

Nielsen SG (1997). Self-regulation of learning strategies during practice: a case study of a church organ student preparing a musical work for performance. In H Jorgensen and AC Lehmann, eds, *Does practice make perfect? Current theory and research on instrumental music practice*, 109–122. Norges Musikkogskole, Oslo.

Nielson SG (1999). Learning strategies in instrumental music practice. *British Journal of Music Education*, **16**, 275–91.

Nielsen SG (2001). Self-regulating learning strategies in instrumental music practice. *Music Education Research*, **3**, 155–167.

Oura Y and Hatano G (2001). The constitution of general and specific mental models of other people. *Human Development*, **44**, 144–159.

Pitts S, Davidson J and McPherson GE (2000a). Developing effective practising strategies: case studies of three young instrumentalists. *Music Education Research*, **2**, 45–56.

Pitts S, Davidson JW and McPherson GE (2000b). Models of success and failure in instrumental learning: case studies of young players in the first 20 months of learning. *Bulletin of the Council for Research in Music Education*, **146**, 51–69.

Puopolo V (1971). The development and experimental application of self-instructional practice materials for beginning instrumentalists. *Journal of Research in Music Education*, **19**, 342.

Renwick JM and McPherson GE (2002). Interest and choice: student-selected repertoire and its effect on practising behaviour. *British Journal of Music Education*, **19**, 173–188.

Ross SL (1985). The effectiveness of mental practice in improving the performance of college trombonists. *Journal of Research in Music education*, **33**, 221–230.

Schmidt RA (1976).The schema as a solution to some persistent problems in motor learning theory. In GE Stelmach, ed., *Motor control: issues and trends*, 41–65. Academic Press, New York.

Sloboda JA, Davidson JW, Howe MJA and Moore DG (1996). The role of practice in the development of performing musicians. *British Journal of Psychology*, **87**, 287–309.

Sosniak LA (1985). Learning to be a concert pianist. Developing talent in young people. In BS Bloom, ed., *Developing talent in young people*, 19–67. Ballantine, New York.

Wagner MJ (1975). The effect of a practice report on practice time and musical performance. In CK Madsen, RD Greer and CH Madsen Jr, eds, *Research in music behaviour*, 125–130. Teachers College Press, New York.

Wagner C (1988). The pianist's hand: anthropometry and biomechanics. *Ergonomics*, **31**, 97–131.

Whitaker NL (1996). A theoretical model of the problem solving and decision making of performers, arrangers, conductors and composers. *Bulletin of the Council for Research in Music Education*, **128**, 1–14.

Williamon A and Valentine E (2000). Quantity and quality of musical practice as predictors of performance quality. *British Journal of Psychology*, **91**, 353–376.

Winold H, Thelen E and Ulrich BD (1994). Coordination and control in the bow arm movements of highly skilled cellists. *Ecological Psychology*, **6**, 1–31.

Young VM and Coleman AM (1979).Some psychological processes in string quartets. *Psychology of Music*, **7**, 12–16.

Zurcher W (1975). The effect of model-supportive practice on beginning brass instrumentalists. In CK Madsen, RD Greer and CH Madsen Jr, eds, *Research in Music Behaviour*, 125–30. Teachers College Press, New York.

CHAPTER 26

Individuality in the learning of musical skills

Helena Gaunt and Susan Hallam

Introduction

Historically, research concerned with individual differences in music has tended to focus on how musicians as a group differ from non-musicians, and the key characteristics which differentiate between musicians. This chapter outlines what we know about the way that individual characteristics including sex differences, physiological characteristics, age, personality, and cognitive and learning styles impact on engagement with and approaches to learning music. Issues relating to musical ability are explored in Chapter 24. The way that elements of the musical and wider environment influence the nature of engagement with music are also considered, excepting the role of the family, which is the focus of Chapter 28, and the school, which is the focus of Chapter 22. This chapter concludes by presenting theoretical frameworks which may serve to guide future research in elucidating the way that different environments interact in a reiterative manner with the individual leading, to different musical engagement outcomes.

Individual characteristics

Sex differences

In the past women have adopted roles in music which have been subservient to those of men, despite the fact that no reliable sex differences have been found in a range of measures of musical ability (Shuter-Dyson and Gabriel 1981; Hallam 2004), that girls tend to perform better in school music examinations (DES 1991; Agak 2002), and that girls report more positive attitudes towards music and musical activities (Crowther and Durkin 1982), and more positive competence beliefs and values for instrumental music than boys (Eccles *et al.* 1993).

Paradoxically, despite the dominance of men in the music professions music is regarded as a 'feminine' subject (Colley *et al.* 1994), although boys are more interested in and confident about music when it is linked to technology (Hanley 1998; Ho 2001) or when musical instruments depend on technology (Hallam *et al.* 2006). Girls are perceived to be interested and successful in singing, playing classical music and in dealing with notation while boys are perceived to have greater confidence in improvisation and composition. Girls are also perceived to be more persistent and more successful with instrumental study, have a broader listening repertoire, and are open to a wider range of musical styles (Green 1997; Hargreaves *et al.* 1995). Singing, in particular, is designated as a feminine activity (Green 1997; Hanley 1998) and although the proportions vary across studies and cultures, in most countries girls are more likely to learn to play a musical instrument than boys (Sheldon and Price 2005; Hallam *et al.* 2006). There are also gender differences in the particular instruments that boys and girls play. Early studies in Western cultures revealed that drums, trombone and trumpet tended to be played more by boys, while flute, violin and clarinet have tended to be played by girls (Abeles and Porter 1978). Despite the increasing equality of women in Western cultures, stereotypical choice of instruments continues (Sinsel *et al.* 1997; Sheldon and Price 2005; Hallam *et al.* 2006) and exists in non-Western cultures (Ho 2001), although girls are selecting a wider variety of instruments to play along the feminine–masculine continuum than boys (Zervoudakes and Tanur 1994). These gender instrumental stereotypes are shared by parents (Abeles and Porter 1978; Delzell and Leppla 1992).

Presenting instruments to children aurally and visually without players can encourage boys to select more feminine instruments (Abeles and Porter 1978) as can changing the sex-role model playing the instrument (Bruce and Kemp 1993). However, where children choose to play an instrument which is considered inappropriate for their gender they may experience bullying or loss of popularity in school (Howe and Sloboda 1992). Children have clear ideas about which instruments are likely to lead to bullying if they are played (O'Neill and Boulton 1995).

Gendered engagement with different music genres changes over the lifespan. McKeage (2004) found that more girls participated in playing jazz in high school than in college. The women's decisions to discontinue were affected by primary instrument selection, institutional obstacles that narrowed participation options, feeling more comfortable in traditional ensembles, and an inability to connect jazz participation to career options.

Physiological demands of different instruments

Physiology plays an important role in the nature of individual engagement with music. For instance, there are considerable differences in relation to the human voice (Thurman and Welch 2000; Harris *et al.* 1998). The pitch range of a human voice varies with sex and age, the voice tending to become stronger and less agile somewhere in the third decade of life, as the laryngeal cartilages start to ossify (Welch and Sundberg 2002). Different instruments also make different physiological demands both in

terms of how a basic sound is produced and the coordination required to play patterns of notes. For instance, singers and wind players rely to a considerable extent on refined muscular control of the respiratory system to make and vary the dynamic and timbre of the sound they make, while string players use both arms and hands for independent tasks which then have to be coordinated to control pitch, articulation and the quality of sound. These physiological requirements may inhibit the take up of some instruments by some individuals and also have implications for the stage of physical development at which learning them can begin.

Whilst instruments are versatile in their potential for musical expression, some within particular genres take on specific roles which impact on the individual player's experience of the music and participation. For example, in jazz, the role of rhythm section players is considered substantially different from 'front line' players who take the lead and play solos, but are not taking the 'whole tune' (MacDonald and Wilson 2005).

Age

Age affects the development of musical skills in a number of ways, through physical development, levels of cognitive skill and approaches to learning, and changing musical taste and motivation. Gembris and Davidson (2002) suggested that between the ages of 0 and 10, musical development in instrumental lessons may be limited by general sensorimotor as well as mental and emotional developmental processes. This is less the case with singing, which plays an almost universal role in childhood and is closely linked to the acquisition of language (Davidson 1994), although a fully professional singing voice in the Western classical tradition develops more slowly than proficiency in instrumental disciplines, and is rarely mature before the age of 30.

Sensorimotor abilities peak in adolescence and early adulthood, but then start to decrease, making facility harder to maintain as an instrumentalist. A crucial period of development amongst professional musicians (other than singers) has been identified as between 12 and 16 years. Sensorimotor ability is high, and cognitive skills are sufficiently developed to enable independent practice to be increased significantly (Ericsson *et al.* 1993). Taking up a complex instrument as an adult is more difficult physically and tends not to yield the same results in terms of dexterity and instrumental control. On the other hand, knowledge and experience of music continue to grow throughout life, and professional classical musicians have articulated how they have used this resource to compensate for reduced technical facility as the speed of cognitive processing and kinaesthetic response decrease (Coffman 2002). The ability to use and manipulate musical symbols also changes over time, gradually becoming more sophisticated (Davidson and Scripp 1992; Gembris 2002). Coffmann (2002) outlines the different learning strategies adopted at different ages, with adult learners often showing particularly high levels of motivation including personal motivations (self-expression, recreation, self-improvement, use of leisure time), musical motivations (professed love of music, performing for one's self and others, learning more about music) and social motivations (meeting new people, being with friends, having a sense of belonging). Adopting an alternative classification, Gates defines adult learners as dabblers, recreationists, hobbyists, amateurs, apprentices, and professionals (Gates 1991).

Adult beginners may have higher expectations of themselves than children, and experience greater disappointment if they do not achieve their aspirations (Cope 2002). Some prefer informal and self-directed, critically reflective and collaborative modes of learning (Brookfield 1983, 1987), although in formal lessons they may rely on the teacher's expertise and analysis of their playing (Chen 1996). These differences seem to depend on the particular context of learning and may not be related to age per se.

The culture of our childhood determines the types of musical traditions with which we engage and as a result the specific musical schemata which develop and are reinforced over time. Those brought up within a Western culture may be able to distinguish fine pitch differences in Western tonality but be unable to distinguish similar pitch differences within the Javanese pelog scale (Lynch *et al.* 1990). Similarly, children exposed to Western music show no preference for consonance over dissonance up to the age of five, but by the age of nine or ten have developed this (Zenatti 1993).

Personality

The musical temperament of Western classical musicians has been reported to be dominated by introversion, independence, sensitivity and anxiety. Kemp (1996) describes the professional musician as a bold introvert who directs energy inwards and appears outwardly reserved. The nature of solitary practice encourages autonomy, and independence of thought, although introversion while supporting the long hours of practice required may also induce anxiety. High levels of imagination, sensitivity and intuition are reflected in high levels of pathemia (extreme sensitivity) (Kemp 1996) while the presence of suspiciousness and low self-sentiment have been reported as potential contributing factors for the increase of anxiety. Kemp (1996) has suggested that musicians become so committed to music that many fail to separate their personal identities from their identity as musicians. Student performers tend to relate their self-esteem to how they perform (Dews and Williams 1989; Tobacyk and Downs 1986) and in musicians it is difficult to discriminate between self-esteem and self-efficacy (Smith *et al.* 2000). Kemp (1996) has argued that identification of musical achievement with personal value results in either 'prima donna' behaviour observed in high self-esteem performers that perceive themselves to be successful, or negative self-perceptions in performers with low self-esteem who have heightened apprehension, self-criticism and perceptions of incompetence. The competitive nature of the classical music profession provides a context which may encourage these trends. However, the personal characteristics of non-Western musicians in non-competitive environments have not been studied making it impossible to draw conclusions about causality, although comparisons have been made between those engaged in different aspects of Western music.

Research has been undertaken in relation to orchestral players, keyboard players, composers and singers (Davies 1978; Wilson 1984) as well as popular musicians (Wills and Cooper 1988). The findings suggest that string players are introverted, imaginative and radical, while brass players are more extraverted and have lower levels of self-discipline and intelligence in comparison to other performing groups. Percussionists also tend towards extroversion. These findings suggest that the extent of practice required for these different instruments (typically more for string players) and their role in the orchestra (more prominent for brass, wind and percussion players) either attracts people with personality characteristics suited to these roles or that these characteristics develop in response to the particular demands being made of them by their chosen roles in the music profession. Similar issues are raised with regard to keyboard players who have been described as extroverted, warmhearted, group-dependent, highly conscientious and self-sentimental, conservative and low in anxiety, and singers who are generally considered as extraverted, independent and sensitive (Kemp 1996).

There may also be complex relationships between personality, practising and performance. Kemp (1996) suggested that the relatively high levels of introversion exhibited by musicians in comparison with the general population might assist them in undertaking repetitive practice, while Hallam (2001a) observed that there appeared to be a relationship between concentration in practice and arousal levels in performance in professional musicians. Those who described themselves as effective, focused learners experienced higher arousal levels in performance which were often problematic.

Cognitive and learning styles, and approaches to learning

In adult learners it has generally been accepted that some individual characteristics are more stable than others. Personality and cognitive styles are perceived as more consistent over time, while learning styles and approaches to learning have tended to be perceived as more responsive to particular learning contexts (Curry 1987). The relationships between these have been relatively little researched in music. Such research as there is has tended to explore whether there are differences between musicians in the way that they learn, with a particular focus on practice and interpretation. Differences have been found in learning styles, conceptions of

and approaches to practice, and the length of time taken by professional musicians to learn repertoire.

Two main approaches to interpretation have been identified: analytic holist (taking a wide view of what is to be learned, considering the connections between disparate ideas, making wide use of analogy and illustration, developing ideas from listening extensively to music, planning interpretation in advance of learning) and intuitive serialist (developing interpretation as music is learned, using intuition rather than analysis, avoiding extensive listening to minimize undue influence on ideas), with versatile learners adopting either serialist or analytic strategies as necessary (Hallam 1995a). Musicians also adopt differential approaches to practising, adopting either technical, musical or mixed approaches, the latter depending on the nature of the specific task. Approaches to practising relate to some extent to the styles of interpretation described above. No musicians adopting an analytic holist approach adopted a technical approach to practice, and no musicians adopting an intuitive serialist approach adopted a musical approach to practice. Versatile learners tended to adopt a mixed approach (Hallam 1995b).

Changes in approach have also been identified as expertise develops. Reid (2001) identified five conceptions of learning amongst students learning to play an instrument or sing in a higher education context. At level 1 (instruments) the students focused their attention on the technical aspects of learning and learned by copying their teachers. At level 2 (elements) the students shared similar concerns with those at level 1 but also focused on some musical elements. Students whose conceptions were at the level of musical meaning (level 3) focused on the meaning found in the music and learned by reflecting and adapting their teacher's advice. At level 4 (communicating) the focus of learning shifted to learning to communicate musical meaning and the students learned by experimenting with different styles of playing music using the teacher as only one source. At the final level (express meaning) students focused on expressing personal meanings through the music. These findings reflect those of Hallam (1995a) who identified nine levels of intellectual development in relation to the development of interpretation.

Some of the research has suggested that the adoption of particular approaches to learning leads to particular learning outcomes, while other findings suggest that similarly high-quality performing standards can be attained regardless of the approach adopted (Hallam 1995a, b; Miklaszewski 1995). These differences may depend on the context of performance.

Environmental influences on individuality

Characteristics of musical cultures

Historically, ethnicity determined the nature of the cultural background within which the individual grew up, although with increasing globalization this is now less the case. The impact of ethnicity on the nature of musical participation is determined by the complex interactions between the particular ethnic group to which the individual belongs and the extent to which its cultural traditions have remained intact, adapted, or been superseded by those of the wider global culture. Differences between musical cultures are evident in three ways, each of which can impact on the differences between musicians. These differences concern the music itself including genre, the kinds of behavior associated with making, teaching and listening to the music (the use of notation, aural traditions, relationship between composition and performance, the role of improvisation, formal or informal learning and teaching, group versus individual tuition) and ideas about music and its place in society (Lundquist 2002). Within each musical culture these dimensions form a dynamic system.

Different genres of music are associated with different expectations of performance. In some genres participation in performance is regarded as normal for all players, and the performance context is often dynamic and unpredictable (Cope 2002). In classical Western music the ultimate goal of learning to play an instrument has been viewed as being able to perform in public, although this can be interpreted in many ways from playing in a school concert to performing as an international soloist. Few players achieve the latter (Cope and Smith 1997). Within this tradition technical competence is highly prized, whereas in folk cultures, musicians can regard themselves as competent to play within their chosen musical and social context with relatively little technical expertise (Cope 2002). In popular music, the use of regular recording and listening back to it as a means of reflecting on and evaluating progress and the musical product is increasingly used, and a relationship between this and the development of critical reflection and self-evaluation of musical skills has been suggested (Boespflug 1999; Lebler 2006). This contrasts with the process of exchange between teacher and student which dominates apprenticeship in Western and Indian classical music.

In musical cultures where participation in music-making through singing, playing and dance is integral to social participation, the nature of the support provided for learning in music is a normal part of daily life, embedded in the community, and resulting in young and old alike acquiring an extensive repertoire and often able to play several instruments (see Blacking 1967; Walker 2006). Within the Western classical tradition, where an individual typically spends more time in isolated practice of an instrument, support for learning tends to be more dependent on individual family members, teachers and particular contexts of music-making. In this environment, lifelong commitment to music (involving intrinsic motivation) in adults has been shown to depend on childhood conditions which were supportive of music (see Chapter 28).

Within Western, post-industrial societies, the role of music has changed dramatically in the last 150 years as a result of changing patterns in work, leisure and social interaction; the development of technology, the recording industry and mass media; and improvements in the standard of living. In the UK, for example, many opportunities for music-making in community centres and within family settings have been replaced by a more solitary consumption of recorded music (Zillmann and Gan 1997), although alongside this there are often more opportunities for engagement with music within education (Hallam *et al.* 2005).

Socio-economic status

Socio-economic status is an important determinant of the type of music with which individuals engage (North and Hargreaves 2007) and plays a key role in musical enculturation. It also impacts on the extent of active engagement in music (Brandstrom 2000) and dropout from instrumental music lessons (McCarthy 1980; Klinedinst 1991). This may be due in part to financial considerations as it can be expensive to provide instruments, pay for tuition, support concert attendance, and create appropriate facilities for practice. Children from middle class backgrounds are more likely to engage with classical music than those from poorer backgrounds.

The way forward: theoretical approaches conceptualizing interactions between the individual and the environment

Research to date exploring individuality in relation to engagement with and learning in music has tended to neglect consideration of the complex interactions which occur between the individual and their environment. Key to developing understanding of these interactions are biosocial models and systems theory. Below we describe two such models: an ecological systems approach to human development and a biosocial model of interaction.

An ecological systems model of human development

Bronfenbrenner (1979) proposed an ecological model of human development, in which the notion of situations or environments is conceptualized as a series of nested structures, each structure itself being a system interacting with other systems (see Figure 26.1). At the centre Bronfenbrenner conceptualized a micro-system consisting of an individual in their immediate environment. For a teenager teaching himself the guitar informally in a pop group the micro-system might include the teenager, the group, and those family members having a direct impact on the individual's musical development. The meso-system refers to the individual's interactions in a wider group of settings.

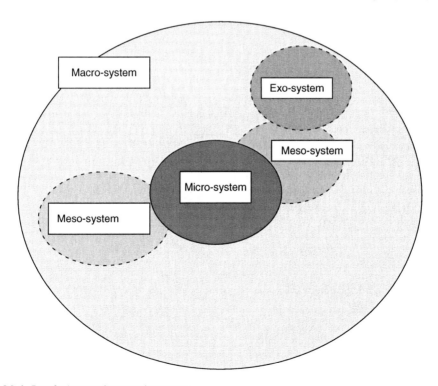

Fig. 26.1 Bronfenbrenner's nested systems.

In the example described above, a meso-system could consist of the teenager's experiences relating to extra-curricular activities at school or through participation in a youth group which facilitated musical activities. Bronfenbrenner also suggests that the individual might be influenced by activity in what he termed an exo-system, a system in which the individual does not interact with others directly but in which another person close to the individual interacts. In the example above, this might be the influence of a parent's working life on a child. For instance, a parent working long hours in an entrepreneurial role might stimulate the teenager to become more committed to the pop group because it offered the potential for commercial success, while also providing an activity in the parent's absence. Finally, all three systems are nested within a macro-system defined as a particular subculture in which particular beliefs, values and ideologies of the lower order systems will be embodied, for instance, a Western culture. An important characteristic of the ecological model is the premise that the interconnections between the different systems within the model are critical to individual development and as important as events taking place within any one system.

A biosocial model of interaction

Adopting a different perspective, Hettema and Kenrick (1992) outline six categories of interaction: static person–environment mesh (the individual is situated in an unchanging environment); choice of environments by persons (the individual selects new environments which meet their needs); choice of persons by environments (typified by a variety of selection processes, for instance in education and the work place);

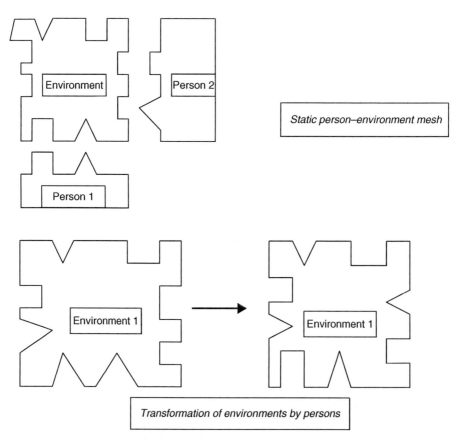

Fig. 26.2 A static person–environment mesh and transformation of environment by person mesh (adapted from Hettema and Kenrick 1992).

transformation of environments by persons (individuals through their actions change environments, for instance, through leadership or disruption); transformation of persons by environments (individuals are socialized into new environments); and person–environment transactions or mutual transactions in which both persons and environments change over time (Hettema and Kenrick 1992). Each category represents different degrees of fit between the individual and the environment. Two examples are given in Figure 26.2. Such interactions influence the development of individuals and the environments within which they find themselves.

A combined model

An example of how the two models may operate simultaneously is shown in Figure 26.3. The presented scenario is based on a teenager teaching themselves the guitar in a pop group formed with a group of friends. Combining the two models highlights the dynamic relationships between the individual and the environment, and suggests the need for research approaches which attempt to develop a framework for understanding the multilayered factors involved in the acquisition of musical skills and the complex relationships between them.

Conclusions

Much of the research exploring individuality has neglected consideration of the dynamic interactions between the individual and their environment which determine the nature of particular behaviours. To increase our understanding of musical learning studies need to take account of the interactions between different elements, map the relationships between micro-, meso-, exo- and macro-systems, and explore the ways that individuals negotiate their relationships with the musical environments to which they have access. Ideally, this would be through longitudinal research which documented individuals' engagement with music through the lifecourse in different learning and performance

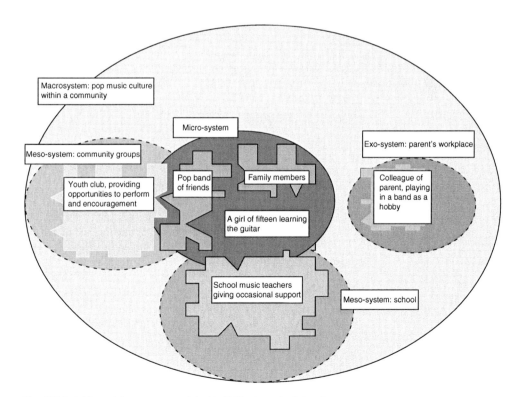

Fig. 26.3 A biosocial systems model of individual musical development.

cultures and contexts. However, findings drawn from small-scale cross-sectional studies could be drawn together to map the impact of a range of factors contributing to our understanding of commonality and difference in the way that systems influence learning and development.

Research also needs to contextualize findings within recent global changes. The rapid development of technology and sound recording, and the expansion of the mass media have created a huge increase in music consumption, and have dictated standards of production and of 'performance' which make no allowances for the errors which may occur in 'live' performance. There has also been increased recognition of the value of active engagement with music to the individual's intellectual functioning and well-being (see Chapters 23 and 44). As a result, in the developed world, through educational and community initiatives, there has been an emphasis on music for all rather than a select few. In the longer term this will provide greater research opportunities to explore systemic interactions and their influence on a range of learning outcomes.

References

Abeles HF and Porter SY (1978).The sex-stereotyping of musical instruments. *Journal of Research in Music Education*, **26**, 65–75.

Agak H (2002). Gender difference and academic achievement in music among Form Four students in Kenya 1991–1994. *Bulletin of the Council for Research in Music Education*, **153**, 94–101.

Blacking J (1967). *Venda children's song: study in ethnomusicological analysis.* University of Chicago, Chicago, IL.

Boespflug G (1999). Popular music and the instrumental ensemble. *Music Educators Journal*, **May**, 33–37.

Brandstrom S (2000). For whom is music school intended? *Bulletin of the Council for Research in Music Education*, **147**, 36–39.

Bronfenbrenner U (1979). *The ecology of human development.* Harvard University Press, Cambridge, MA.

Brookfield S (1983). *Adult learners, adult education and the community.* Teachers College Press, New York.

Brookfield S (1987). *Developing critical thinkers.* Jossey-Bass, San Francisco, CA.

Bruce R and Kemp A (1993). Sex stereotyping in children's preferences for musical instruments. *British Journal of Music Education*, **10**, 213–217.

Chen H (1996). An investigation of self-directed learning among non-music major adult piano learners in one-to-one piano instruction. Dissertation abstracts international 57(7), 2929A (UMI No. AAT96–35962).

Coffman D (2002). Adult education. In R. Colwell, C. Richardson, eds, *The new handbook of research on music teaching and learning*, 199–209. Oxford University Press, Oxford.

Colley A, Comber C and Hargreaves DJ (1994). Gender effects in school subject preferences: a research note. *Educational Studies*, **20**, 13–18.

Cope P (2002). Informal learning of musical instruments: the importance of social context. *Music Education Research*, **4**, 93–104.

Cope P and Smith H (1997). Cultural context in musical instrument learning. *British Journal of Music Education*, **14**, 283–289.

Crowther R and Durkin K (1982). Sex- and age-related differences in the musical behaviour, interests and attitudes towards music of 232 secondary school students. *Educational Studies*, **8**, 131–139.

Curry L (1987). *Integrating concepts of cognitive or learning style: a review with attention to psychometric standards.* Canadian College of Health Service Executives, Ottawa, Ontario.

Davidson L (1994). Song singing by young and old: a developmental approach to music. In R Aiello, ed., *Musical perceptions*, 99–130. Oxford University Press, New York.

Davidson L, Scripp L (1992). Surveying the coordinates of cognitive skills in music. In R Colwell, C Richardson, eds, *The new handbook of research on music teaching and learning*, 392–413. Schirmer Books, New York.

Davies JB (1978). *The psychology of music.* Hutchinson, London.

Delzell JK and Leppla DA (1992). Gender association of musical instruments and preferences of fourth-grade students for selected instruments. *Journal of Research in Music Education*, **40**, 93–103.

Department of Education and Skills (1991). *Music for ages 5 to 14: proposals of the Secretary of State for Education and Science and Secretary of State for Wales.* HMSO, London.

Dews CLB and Williams MS (1989). Student musicians' personality styles, stresses and coping patterns. *Psychology of Music*, **17**, 37–47.

Eccles J, Wigfield A, Harold RD, Blumenfeld P (1993). Age and gender differences in children's self- and task perceptions during elementary school. *Child Development*, **64**, 830–47.

Ericsson KA, Krampe RT and Tesch-Romer C (1993). The role of deliberate practice in the acquisition of expert performance. *Psychological Review*, **100**, 363–406.

Gates JT (1991). Music participation: theory, research, and policy. *Bulletin of the Council for Research in Music Education*, **109**, 1–35.

Gembris H (2002). The development of musical abilities. In R Colwell and C Richardson, eds, *The new handbook of research on music teaching and learning*, 487–508. Oxford University Press, Oxford.

Gembris H., Davidson JW (2002) The role of the environment in musical development. In R Parncutt, GE McPherson, eds, *The science and psychology of musical performance*, 17–30. Oxford University Press, New York.

Green L (1997). *Music, gender and education*. Cambridge University Press, New York.

Green L (2001). *How popular musicians learn: a way ahead*. Ashgate, Aldershott.

Hallam S (1995a). Professional musicians' approaches to the learning and interpretation of music. *Psychology of Music*, **23**, 111–128.

Hallam S (1995b). Professional musicians' orientations to practice: implications for teaching. *British Journal of Music Education*, **12**, 3–19.

Hallam S (2001a). The development of metacognition in musicians: implications for education. *The British Journal of Music Education*, **18**, 27–39.

Hallam S (2004). Sex differences in the factors which predict musical attainment in school aged students. *Bulletin of the Council for Research in Music Education*, **161**, 107–117.

Hallam S, Rogers L and Creech A (2005). *Survey of local authority music services 2005. Research report 700*. Department for Education and Skills, London.

Hallam S, Rogers L and Creech A (2008). Gender differences in musical instrument choice. *International Journal for Music Education*, **26**, 7–19.

Hanley B (1998). Gender in secondary music education in British Columbia. *British Journal of Music Education*, **15**, 51–6.

Hargreaves DJ, Comber C and Colley A (1995). Effects of age, gender and training on musical preferences of British secondary school students. *Journal of Research in Music Education*, **43**, 242–250.

Harris T, Harris S, Rubin JS, Howard DM (1998). *The voice clinic handbook*. Whurr, London.

Hettema J and Kenrick DT (1992). Models of person-situation interactions. In GV Caprara, GL Van Heck, eds, *Modern personality psychology: critical reviews and new directions*, 393–417. Harvester Wheatsheaf, New York.

Ho W-C (2001). Musical learning: differences between boys and girls in Hong Kong Chinese co-educational schools. *British Journal of Music Education*, **18**, 41–54.

Howe MJA and Sloboda J (1992). Problems experienced by talented young musicians as a result of the failure of other children to value musical accomplishments. *Gifted Education*, **8**, 16–18.

Kemp AE (1996). *The musical temperament: psychology and personality of musicians*. Oxford University Press, Oxford.

Klinedinst RE (1991). Predicting performance achievement and retention of fifth-grade instrumental students. *Journal of Research in Music Education*, **39**, 225–238.

Lebler D (2006). Student as master? Reflections on a learning innovation in popular music pedagogy. Paper presented at the International Society for Music Education World Conference, Kuala Lumpur, Malaysia, 17–21 July, 2006.

Lundquist BR (2002). Music, culture, curriculum and instruction. In R Colwell and C Richardson, eds, *The new handbook of research on music teaching and learning*, 626–647. Oxford University Press, Oxford.

Lynch MP, Eilers RE, Oller DK and Urbano RC (1990). Innateness, experience, and music perception. *Psychological Science*, **1**, 272–276.

MacDonald RAR and Wilson GB (2005). Musical identities of professional jazz musicians: a focus group investigation. *Psychology of Music*, **33**, 395–417.

McCarthy JF (1980). Individualised instruction, student achievement and drop out in an urban elementary instrumental music program. *Journal of Research in Music Education*, **28**, 59–69.

McKeage KM (2004). Gender and participation in high school and college instrumental jazz ensembles. *Journal of Research in Music Education*, **52**, 343–356.

Miklaszewski K (1995). Individual differences in preparing a musical composition for public performance. In M Manturzewska, K Miklaszewski and A Biatkowski, eds, *Psychology of music today*, 138–147. Fryderyk Chopin Academy of Music, Warsaw.

North AC and Hargreaves DJ (2007). Lifestyle correlates of musical preference: a. Relationships, living arrangements, beliefs and crime. *Psychology of Music*, **35**, 58–87.

O'Neill SA and Boulton MJ (1995). Is there a gender bias towards musical instruments: a function of gender? *Psychology of Music*, **24**, 171–183.

Reid A (2001). Variation in the way that instrumental and vocal students experience learning music. *Music Education Research*, **3**, 25–40.

Sheldon DA and Price HE (2005). Sex and instrumentation distribution in an international cross-section of wind and percussion ensembles. *Bulletin of the Council for Research in Music Education*, **163**, 43–51.

Shuter-Dyson R and Gabriel S (1981). *The psychology of musical ability*, 2nd edn. Methuen, London.

Sinsel TJ, Dixon WE and Blades-Zeller E (1997). Psychological sex type and preferences for musical instruments in fourth and fifth graders. *Journal of Research in Music Education*, **45**, 390–401.

Smith A M, Maragos A and Van Dyke A (2000). Psychology of the musician. In R Tubiana, PC Amadio, eds, *Medical problems of the instrumentalist musician*, 135–170. Martin Dunitz Ltd, London.

Thurman L and Welch G (2000). *Body mind and voice: foundations of voice education*. The VoiceCare Network, St. John's University, Minnesota, MN.

Tobacyk JJ and Downs A (1986). Personal construct threat and irrational beliefs as cognitive predictors of increases in musical anxiety. *Journal of Personality and Social Psychology*, **51**, 779–82.

Walker R (2006) Cultural traditions. In GE McPherson, ed., *The child as musician: a handbook of musical development*, 439–460. Oxford University Press, Oxford.

Welch GF and Sundberg J (2002). Solo voice. In R Parncutt, G McPherson, eds, *The science and psychology of music performance: creative strategies for teaching and learning*, 253–268. Oxford University Press, Oxford.

Whitchurch GG and Constantine LL (1993). Systems theory. In PG Boss, WJ Doherty, R Laroosa, WR Schumm, S Steinmetz, eds, *Source book of family theories: a contextual approach*, 325–352. Plenum Press, New York.

Wills G and Cooper CL (1988). *Pressure sensitive: popular musicians under stress*. Sage, London.

Wilson GD (1984). The personality of opera singers. *Personality and Individual Differences*, **5**, 195–201.

Zenatti A (1993). Children's musical cognition and taste. In TJ Tighe, WJ Dowling, eds, *Psychology of music: the understanding of melody and rhythm*, 177–196. Erlbaum, Hillsdale, NJ.

Zervoudakes J and Tanur J (1994). Gender and musical instruments: winds of change. *Journal of Research in Music Education*, **42**, 58–67.

Zillmann D and Gan S-L (1997). Musical taste in adolescence. In DJ Hargreaves, AC North, eds, *The social psychology of music*, 161–187. Oxford University Press, Oxford.

CHAPTER 27

Motivation to learn

Susan Hallam

The historical perspective

Human motivation is extremely complex. Historically, numerous theories have developed in attempts to explain it. These, to varying degrees, emphasize motivation as deriving from within the individual, within the environment, or as a complex interaction between the two mediated by cognition. The most recent theories emphasize the way that our perceptions of events are determined by our construction of them, these interpretations subsequently influencing our self-esteem, self-efficacy and motivation. They acknowledge the capacity of individuals to determine their own behaviour, whilst also recognizing the role of the environment in rewarding or punishing particular behaviours influencing subsequent cognitions and later actions. There has also been increasing recognition that motivation operates at different levels and across different timescales (for more detail of generic theories of motivation and earlier reviews of motivation in relation to music see Asmus 1994; O'Neill and McPherson 2002; Hallam 2002; Austin *et al.* 2006).

Much of the early research on motivation in music was not embedded within any specific motivational research paradigm or theoretical position, although expectancy-value models which have been proposed to explain motivation for particular tasks in education (e.g., Eccles 1983) have provided a framework for some recent work. The research has also focused almost exclusively on motivation to learn and continue to play an instrument. There has been little interest in motivation to listen to music, compose, or engage in other musical activities.

A framework for understanding motivation in music

In this chapter, I set out a model which attempts to integrate the various theoretical approaches to understanding motivation, embedded within a broadly systemic approach as proposed by Bronfenbrenner (1979), which suggests that the process of human development depends on mutual accommodation which occurs throughout the life-course between an individual and the various systems which they or others close to them encounter in their environment (see Chapter 26 for details).

Figure 27.1 sets out a framework which illustrates the complex interactions which occur over time in relation to motivation. Certain aspects of our individuality are predetermined, for instance, our biological temperament, our sex, and our age. These are shaped through interaction with the environment to develop our personality, gender identity, cognitive processes, and our self-perceptions. We are motivated because we desire social approval, particularly from those we admire and respect. Such praise from others is internalized, raises self-esteem, and enhances confidence. Some environmental influences are internalized to such an extent that they come to affect the individual's functioning over time in a fairly consistent way. Individuals set themselves goals, which determine their behaviour. These goals are influenced by individual and self-perception characteristics as well as environmental factors. Where the environment satisfies individual needs and

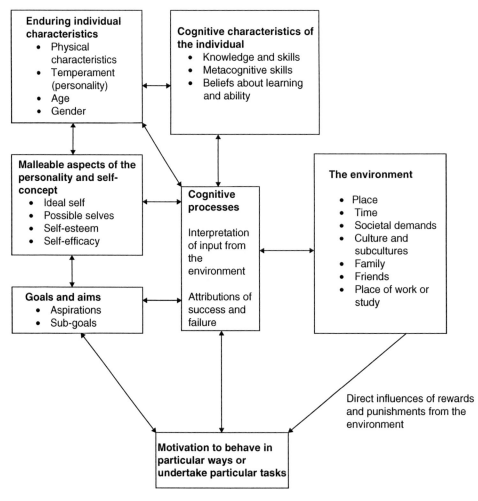

Fig. 27.1 Interactions between individual and environmental factors in determining motivation.

facilitates personal goals motivation is likely to be enhanced. Where the environment presents obstacles, the individual may give up or be spurred on to greater efforts to overcome them, perhaps by finding a more conducive environment. Behaviour is the end link in the chain, but at the time of enactment it too can be influenced and changed by environmental factors. There is interaction between the environment and the individual at every level and in the long and short term. Individuals can act upon the environment to change it, or seek out new environments more conducive to their needs (Hettema and Kenrick 1992). The model recognizes the importance of cognitive factors and self-determination in behaviour. While we have needs and desires we are aware that we need to consider the consequences of our actions before we attempt to satisfy them. Cognition plays a role in the ways in which we attempt to enhance our self-esteem, leading us to attribute our success or failure to causes which will allow us to maintain a consistent view of ourselves. When a learner has completed a learning task successfully this will have an impact on self-esteem and motivation which will be carried forward to subsequent learning tasks. Conversely, when learning outcomes are negative, motivation may be impaired. In the following sections I provide a more detailed account of what we know about each of the elements outlined in the model as they relate to motivation in music.

Individual characteristics

Enduring individual characteristics: physical, gender and personality factors

Chapter 26 considers many elements of individuality which may influence the nature of engagement with music including physical, gender, and personality characteristics. These are not discussed further here. The focus in this section is the complex and multifaceted nature of motivation to become actively involved in music-making, which includes the way that it intrinsically acts to meet needs which vary between individuals in relation to their personality characteristics. For instance, Motte-Haber (1984) has suggested a range of internal motives including the desire for achievement, curiosity, and self-actualization, while Nagel (1987) stressed the need for personal fulfilment met by the emotion-inducing quality of music, satisfaction of a positive social response within performance settings, exploration of aggressive drives through the exploitation of the motor skills entailed in musical performance, and some voyeuristic and exhibitionist desires. Persson (1993; Persson et al.1996) studying pianists also emphasized the importance of hedonic drive, while acknowledging the role of social and achievement motives. Gellrich and colleagues (1986) identified three achievement-related motives: a general achievement motivation; a specifically music-oriented achievement orientation; and a sensual–aesthetic motive, the pleasure and joy of playing certain pieces of music. Musicians it seems derive considerable personal fulfilment from the act of making music, in addition to the social rewards that it offers. The balance between these motives may change over time as individuals progress through their musical careers (Sosniak 1985; Harnischmacher 1997; Manturzewska 1990) and may contribute to determining individual career trajectories.

The diversity of individual motivation has been explored in relation to amateur musicians in addition to professionals. Some amateurs view music as personal amusement, while for others it constitutes serious leisure only distinguishable from the work of professionals because it is not their livelihood (Gates 1991). For some music is a key element of their identity (Pitts 2005) and they invest huge energy and creativity in it (Finnegan 1997). Their amateur status suggests that they find their musical activities intrinsically motivating, although social interaction can also be an important motivator.

Malleable aspects of the personality and self-concept

An individual's identity or self-concept represents the way they thinks about themself and their relationships with others (Rogers 1961) (see Chapter 43) and plays a crucial role in motivation. Behaviour is influenced by the individual's interpretation of situations and events; their expectations; and the goals that they have set for themselves related to their identity. Music self-concept has been shown to be linked to motivation, interest, and participation in school and out of school musical activities (Austin 1991) and develops early as quite young children are able to assess how well they can complete particular musical tasks (Greenberg 1970). However, being good at something does not necessarily transfer to interest in it. Asmus and Harrison (1990) working with non-music major college students found no relationship between music motivation and aptitude. They argued that the drive for music stems from love of music.

Children's self-concept in relation to music at school and the value that they place on music appear to decline as they get older, the latter more than for reading and mathematics (Wigfield et al. 1997; Mota 1999). However, those adolescents who are actively engaged in music-making through playing an instrument favour this activity over almost all others. Being a musician becomes an important element of their identity. As children progress through school they become increasingly aware of their own capabilities through making comparisons and receiving feedback from others. Where comparisons are made with high-attaining others self-concept is likely to be deflated. This process is influenced by the context of learning, whether it is supportive or critical.

Self-efficacy beliefs based on our evaluation of the likelihood of our success in relation to particular tasks or areas of work also play a part in determining whether particular goals will be pursued and subsequently achieved (Bandura 1982). McPherson and McCormick (1999, 2006) studied 190 pianists aged 9–18 before taking an examination and found that self-efficacy prior to entering the examination predicted their examination result more strongly than any other factors. Bandura (1989) suggested that motivation for an activity is at its peak when strong self-efficacy beliefs are combined with some moderate uncertainty about the outcome, i.e. when a person feels competent but challenged. However, for intrinsic motivation to flourish, feelings of self-determination are also necessary. So even if an activity is challenging and a person feels themselves to be highly competent, they will not display high levels of intrinsic motivation unless the activity is perceived as self-determined (Ryan and Deci 2000). Evidence of the links between intrinsic motivation, self-determination, and the use of self-regulating practising strategies support this (Austin *et al.* 2006). Renwick and McPherson (2002) demonstrated how a 12-year-old practised with heightened attention, persistence and enhanced strategy use when working on a piece which she had chosen herself as opposed to one chosen by the teacher. The extent to which learners value what they are doing predicts engagement across many different facets of musical practice (O'Neill 1999) and contributes to prediction of examination results more strongly than weekly practice or anxiety (McPherson and McCormick 2000).

Goals and aims

The goals and aims that individuals strive to attain are related to their identity, self-concept, self-efficacy and what they believe is possible for them. These take account of both context and cognition. If an individual perceives themselves as successful and attributes this success to high ability they may come to include in their self-concept a 'positive possible future self in that domain' (Markus and Ruvolo 1989). Possible selves can be powerful motivators, providing long-term goals and encouraging the setting up of interim goals which need to be achieved en route. If an individual does not have a positive possible self as a musician (professional, amateur

or listener) in the long, medium, or short term they are unlikely to maintain their interest in music. This is illustrated by McPherson and McCormick (2000) who found that for many children playing an instrument was no different from participating in a team sport, taking up a hobby, or pursuing other interests. Very few saw it as something that could possibly lead to a future career. MacNamara and colleagues (2006) also showed that career planning was in evidence in the very earliest stages of learning for nine professional musicians along with dedication, commitment, determination and a willingness to make sacrifices. Self-belief became increasingly important as they encountered more critical appraisal and greater competition as they progressed (MacNamara *et al.* 2006). However, goals can sometimes conflict with each other and their fulfilment can be disrupted by others (Harnischmacher 1995). Individuals may have to make trade-offs between goals at different levels and undertake some activities to attain a particular goal which they may not find particularly enjoyable. For instance, young people wishing to become professional musicians do not always enjoy practising alone and may require parental support and encouragement to do so (Howe and Sloboda 1991).

Cognition: individual characteristics and processes

All modern theories of motivation take account of cognition—an acceptance that much of our behaviour is mediated by our thoughts about and perceptions of events (Kelly 1955). This process is influenced, in part, by locus of control, the extent to which individuals perceive that they have control over situations (Rotter 1966). While prior knowledge and skills in a domain are powerful determinants of performance in that domain, our beliefs about our current capabilities also play a part. Also important are our beliefs about the nature of learning. In mainstream education a distinction has been made between performance and learning goals (Elliott and Dweck 1988), the former concerned with gaining positive judgements of competence as compared with others and avoiding negative ones, the latter with increasing mastery, reflecting the desire to learn new skills, master new tasks or understand new things.

In learning in music, the relationship between these goals is complex. For instance, in studies of band students, Austin (1988, 1991) found that those assigned to a competitive condition exhibited levels of motivation and performance achievement comparable to those in a non-competitive condition, while Schmidt (2005) reported that instrumental students defined their success in relation to mastery and cooperative orientations, placing less emphasis on competitive and ego orientations. The context of active participation in music seems to influence the goals adopted, some contexts supporting the development of both types of goals. Sandene (1998) found that students' goal orientations were related to the perceived motivational climate in the classroom with overt teacher behaviours, in particular the ratio of positive to negative feedback, being particularly important.

To succeed in music clearly requires mastery behaviour to sustain the motivation for many hours of practice. For instance, O'Neill (1997), studying beginner instrumentalists, found that children who experienced mastery-oriented behaviour after experiencing failure on a problem-solving task made more progress on their instrument than children who initially displayed helpless behaviour. Research from other domains has shown a relationship between students' theories of intelligence and their goal choices. Where students hold an entity theory of intelligence (fixed and immutable) they are more likely to adopt performance goals, while those holding an incremental view of intelligence are more likely to choose a learning goal (Dweck and Leggett 1988). There is potential for exploring these relationships in novice, expert, amateur and professional musicians (see also Austin *et al.* 2006).

Individuals are motivated to establish, maintain and promote a consistent and usually positive self-image, so they develop a variety of coping strategies to maintain self-worth, some of which may be self-defeating, for instance, reducing effort (Covington 1984). How individuals attribute successes and failures is important in maintaining self-esteem (Weiner 1986). The causes of success or failure can be seen as stable

or unstable; controllable or uncontrollable and internal or external. Overall, five major attribution categories have been found in music: effort, musical background, classroom environment, musical ability, and affect for music (Asmus 1986a), although findings specifically related to performance in an examination also included effort in preparation, effort in the examination, nervousness, luck, and task difficulty (McPherson and McCormick 2000). Musical ability and effort are the most frequently cited attributions by music students (Austin and Vispoel 1998). Highly motivated music students tend to make effort attributions, while students with low motivation cite ability (e.g. Austin and Vispoel 1998). These findings seem to be broadly consistent across grade levels (Asmus 1986b; McPherson and McCormick 2000), school settings, and music populations, although there is some evidence that ability attributions become more frequent as children get older (Arnold 1997; Asmus 1986b). Harter (1985) proposes that what is important in maintaining self-esteem and motivation is beneffectance. This involves attributing successful outcomes to internal causes and unsuccessful outcomes to external ones. This is likely to be important in sustaining motivation in musical activities. Considering the effect of attributing success or failure to the use of particular learning strategies, Vispoel and Austin (1993) found that explaining failure in terms of the adoption of less than optimal learning strategies was effective in improving these and increasing effort.

Metacognition (the term given to our knowledge of our own learning) is relevant for motivation insofar as it indicates our awareness of our own strengths and weaknesses and the ways in which we learn best, and may be implicated in the way that we manage our attributions. Metacognitive strategies are concerned with the planning, monitoring and evaluation of learning and performance. For most musicians life is dominated by public performance and preparation for it. As practice is not always intrinsically motivating, developing strategies for managing motivation is crucial. Preparing for public performance necessitates giving priority to practice (Manturzewska 1969), mobilizing arousal specifically for performance (Bochkaryov 1975) and managing anxiety (Hamann 1982). These all depend on the development of appropriate metacognitive skills.

The environment

The environment is crucial in determining the opportunities that individuals have to engage with music and the extent to which they will be supported while doing so. Music is not valued equally in all cultures. In some it is viewed as decadent and is forbidden. In others it is highly valued and those involved in its composition or execution are highly revered members of society. Economic, demographic and political factors can have a major impact on the opportunities that may be available for musical engagement (Simonton 1997). Over time the value placed on music can change, and within any particular culture different types of music may be valued by specific subgroups. We know very little about how these cultural and societal factors mediate motivation to engage with music or the type of activity selected. In the Western world some individuals learn to play an instrument because it is expected by their family or school. Others start by chance because tuition is on offer in school or their friends have decided to play.

Although most individuals are involved in full time education when they take up a musical instrument, there has been almost no research on the relationship between the institutional learning environment and motivation to engage with music. There is some evidence that in a conservatoire environment there are relationships between institutional and departmental expectations and the amount of time spent practising which are mediated by the dominating value system (Jorgensen 1997), and that in mainstream education support within schools from generalist classroom teachers and the senior management team impacts on the extent to which instrumental teaching is effective (Hallam and Prince 2000). Teachers play an important role in motivating students and can contribute towards pupils' attitudes and subsequent attainment (Szubertowska 2005). Where teachers motivate pupils to engage with music, identities as musicians develop leading to more positive attitudes towards school music and teachers (Lamont 2002). In adolescence the peer group is very powerful and can bring negative pressure to bear in relation to engagement with some types of music (Finnas 1987; 1989). To withstand this musical identities need to be well developed. The influence of early teachers who are viewed as warm and sympathetic seems to be particularly important in this respect (Sosniak 1985; Sloboda and Howe 1991). Relatively uncritical encouragement in the early stages of engagement with music encourages the development of a positive musical identity. Once this is established later teachers provide high-status role models with whom the young musician can identify and emulate (Manturzewska 1990).

There is considerable evidence that parents have a vital influence on children's motivation for involvement with music and the acquisition of musical skill (see Chapter 28). In the early years the family are likely to be the main source of musical stimulation and may be key to engendering future interest in music. The age at which children first sing is related to the number of musical behaviours initiated by the parents (Howe et al. 1995) and the development of perfect pitch seems to occur with particularly systematic exposure to music in early childhood (Sergeant 1969). The influence of parents can also contribute to the choice of instrument to be played (Fortney et al. 1993) and their ongoing support plays a crucial role in whether children persist and commit to musical engagement in the long term. While the literature as a whole indicates that having a highly supportive and encouraging home background is important, it is clearly not essential. Highly effective individuals in a range of domains have been found to have histories marked by severe frustration, deprivation and traumatic experiences (MacKinnon 1965). Another important contributor to motivation is the relationship between teachers, parents and learners (see Chapter 28). The most motivated students are those who work in harmony with their teachers and parents.

Direct influences of rewards and punishments from the environment

Intrinsic motivation is a crucial aspect of developing self-identity as a musician. This may take several forms, but one key element is enjoyment of the experience of engagement with music. Tasks that are intrinsically motivating share certain structural and emotional characteristics (Csikszentmihalyi 1990), offering a level of challenge that is in balance with a person's current skills (Good and Brophy 1991). When this occurs an individual derives pleasure from the work and tends to continue with it. This is known as a state of flow. If the task is too easy the person becomes bored. If the work demands skills beyond the capabilities of the individual anxiety is created. Csikszentmihalyi and colleagues (1993) have shown that students experience a state of flow most often when participating in chosen activities such as music as opposed to academic-oriented activities or when interacting with peers. Custodero (1999) observed 4- and 5-year-old children in a music classroom over 8 weeks and flow experience was associated with high self-concept or skill, perceived challenge, and active engagement.

Not all musical activities are intrinsically motivating for all people. For instance, novice and professional musicians exhibit diversity in motivation to practise. Many students require parental encouragement to practise (Howe and Sloboda 1991) or other rewards including playing favourite pieces of music or pleasing teachers. Practising for love of the instrument is rare (Harnischmacher 1995). A study of the motivation of beginner instrumentalists found that where the children remained enthusiastic about continuing to play their involvement centred around the instrument itself and the repertoire that they were learning, with less motivated children referring to participation in a band, or the opinions of their parents and friends as shaping their own attitudes (Pitts *et al.* 2000).

Lack of motivation

For a full understanding of musical motivation, the study of drop-outs is important. Those ceasing to play tend to do less practice, have attained less (Sloboda *et al.* 1996; Hallam 1998) and perceive themselves as less musically able, receiving less family encouragement and having greater strengths in other recreational activities (Frakes 1984). The time costs of playing an instrument are too great in relation to the rewards that they

receive (Hurley 1995). Overall, no single explanatory factor emerges in explaining drop-out but several have been identified including lower socio-economic status, poor ability to understand instructions, and poor self-concept in relation to reading music, maths, reading achievement, and general scholastic attainment (Klinedinst 1991; Hallam 1998). Research to date has tended to focus on participation in formal music tuition in the Western classical tradition. Different factors may apply to those dropping out of other musical activities.

Future research directions

The evidence presented above suggests that motivation to be involved in active music-making is determined by complex interactions between the individual and the environment within which they find themselves. Some of the environmental effects, in particular those relating to early musical experiences, learning outcomes, self-efficacy and subsequently self-esteem are internalized by the individual in such a way that they become part of that individual's characteristics, rendering it both impossible and pointless to disentangle them. Once internalized they impact on motivation to continue to be involved in music. The individual's commitment to and involvement in music-making can also affect their environment and the people in it. Families may make changes to support their musical offspring, friends may be influenced to participate in making music. The transaction is bidirectional. The nature of the music profession, which is extremely competitive, means that only the highly motivated will have sufficient determination to succeed, although many more may become highly skilled amateurs.

The research to date has mainly, although not exclusively, related to school-aged students and the types of tuition on offer in those contexts. There is a need for research exploring issues of motivation in different learning contexts, informal and formal, and for learners of different ages and across different types of music. Related to this is the question of drop-out at higher levels of expertise than have so far been considered, for instance, those who study music in higher education, who do not then go on to make their living from musical activities, or indeed those who become professional musicians and then leave the profession early. In addition, most of the research has focused on motivation to become a musician. Listening to music plays an important part in the daily lives of most people in the Western world but there is little research relating to those individuals for whom listening to music is a passion, who have extensive collections of recorded music and are extremely knowledgeable about music without necessarily actively participating in making it. There is also a need to explore why music plays little part in the lives of some people.

References

Arnold JA (1997). A comparison of attributions for success and failure in instrumental music among sixth-, eighth-, and tenth grade students. *Update: Applications of Research in Music Education*, **15**, 19–23.

Asmus EP (1986a). Achievement motivation characteristics of music education and music therapy students as identified by attribution theory. *Bulletin of the Council for Research in Music Education*, **86**, 71–85.

Asmus EP (1986b). Student beliefs about the causes of success or failure in music: a study of achievement motivation. *Journal of Research in Music Education*, **34**, 262–278.

Asmus EP and Harrison CS (1990). Characteristics of motivation for music and musical aptitude of undergraduage nonmusic majors. *Journal of Research in Music Education*, **38**, 258–268.

Asmus EP (1994). Motivation in music teaching and learning. *The Quarterly Journal of Music Teaching and Learning*, **5**, 5–32.

Austin JR (1988). The effect of music contest format on self-concept, motivation, and attitude of elementary band students, *Journal of Research in Music Education*, **36**, 95–107.

Austin JR (1991). Competitive and non-competitive goal structures: an analysis of motivation and achievement among elementary band students. *Psychology of Music*, **19**, 142–158.

Austin JR, Renwick J and McPherson GE (2006). Developing motivation. In GE McPherson, ed., *The child as musician: a handbook of musical development*, 213–238. Oxford University Press, Oxford.

Austin JR and Vispoel WP (1998). How American adolescents interpret success and failure in classroom music: relationships among attributional beliefs, self-concepts and achievement. *Psychology of Music*, **26**, 26–45.

Bandura A (1982). Self-efficacy mechanism in human agency. *American Psychologist*, **37**, 122–147.

Bandura A (1989). Self-regulation of motivation and action through internal standards and goal systems. In LA Pervin, ed., *Goal concepts in personality and social psychology*, 19–86. Erlbaum, Hillsdale, NJ.

Bochkaryov LL (1975). The psychological aspects of musicians' public performance. *Voprosy Psikhologii*, **21**, 68–79.

Bronfenbrenner U (1979). *The ecology of human development*. Harvard University Press, Cambridge, MA.

Covington M. (1984). The motive for self-worth. In R Ames and C Ames, eds, *Research on motivation in education: student motivation*, 77–111. Academic Press, New York.

Csikszentmihalyi M (1990). *Flow: the psychology of optimal experience*. Harper Row, New York.

Csikszentmihalyi M, Rathunde K and Whalen S (1993). *Talented teenagers: the roots of success and failure*. Cambridge University Press, Cambridge.

Custodero LA (1999). Construction of musical understandings: the cognition–flow interface. Paper presented at the Cognitive Processes of Children Engaged in Music Activity Conference, Champaign, Urbana, IL, June, 1999.

Dweck CS and Leggett EL (1988). A social cognitive approach to motivation and personality. *Psychological Review*, **95**, 256–373.

Eccles J (1983). Expectancies, values and academic behaviours. In JT Spence, ed., *Achievement and achievement motives*, 75–146. Freeman, San Francisco, CA.

Elliott ES and Dweck CS (1988). Goals: An approach to motivation and achievement. *Journal of Personality and Social Psychology*, **54**, 5–12.

Finnas L (1987). Do young people misjudge each other's musical taste? *Psychology of Music*, **15**, 152–166.

Finnas L (1989). A comparison between young people's privately and publicly expressed musical preferences. *Psychology of Music*, **17**, 132–145.

Finnegan R (1997). Music, performance and enactment. In H Mackay, ed., *Consumption and everyday life*, 114–158. Sage/Open University, London.

Fortney PM, Boyle JD and DeCarbo NJ (1993). A study of middle school band students' instrumental choices. *Journal of Research in Music Education*, **41**, 28–39.

Frakes L (1984). Differences in music achievement, academic achievement and attitude among participants, dropouts and non-participants in secondary school music. Unpublished Phd thesis, University of Iowa.

Gates JT (1991). Music participation: theory, research and policy. *Bulletin of the Council for Research in Music Education*, **109**, 1–35.

Gellrich M, Osterwold M and Schulz J (1986). Leistungsmotivation bei Kindern im Instumentalunterricht. Bericht uber eine erkundungsstudie. (Children's performance motivation in instrumental teaching.) *Musikpsychologie*, **3**, 33–69.

Good TL and Brophy JE (1991). *Educational psychology*. Longman, New York.

Greenberg M (1970). Musical achievement and self-concept. *Journal of Research in Music Education*, **18**, 57–64.

Hallam S (1998). Predictors of achievement and drop out in instrumental tuition. *Psychology of Music*, **26**, 116–132.

Hallam S (2002). musical motivation: towards a model synthesising the research. *Music Education Research*, **4**, 225–244.

Hallam S and Prince V (2000). *Research into instrumental music services, research report RR229*. Department for Education and Employment, London.

Hamann DL (1982). An assessment of anxiety in instrumental and vocal performances. *Journal of Research in Music Education*, **30**, 77–90.

Harnischmacher C (1995). Spiel oder Arbeit? Eine Pilotstudie zu, instrumentalen Ubeverhalten von Kindern und Jugendlichen. In Gembris H, Kraemer RD and G Maas, eds, *Musikpadagogosche Forschungsberichte 1994*, 41–56. Wisner, Augsburg.

Harnischmacher C (1997) The effects of individual differences in motivation, volition, and maturational processes on practice behaviour of young instrumentalists. In Jorgensen H and Lehman A, eds, *Does practice make perfect? Current theory and research on instrumental music practice*, 71–88. Norges musikkh gskole, Oslo.

Harter S (1985) Competence as a dimension of self-evaluation: toward a comprehension model of self-worth. In R Leahy, ed., *The development of the self*, 55–118. Academic Press, New York.

Hettema J and Kenrick DT (1992). Models of person-situation interactions. In G-V Caprar and GL Van Heck, eds, *Modern personality psychology: critical reviews and directions*, 393–417. Harvester Wheatsheaf, New York.

Howe MJA, Davidson JW, Moore DM and Sloboda JA (1995). Are there early childhood signs of musical ability? *Psychology of Music*, **23**, 162–76.

Howe MJA and Sloboda JA (1991). Young musicians' accounts of significant influences in their early lives 1. The family and the musical background. *British Journal of music Education*, **8**, 39–52.

Hurley CG (1995). Student motivations for beginning and continuing/discontinuing string music tuition. *The Quarterly Journal of Music Teaching and Learning*, **6**, 44–55.

Jorgensen H (1997). Time for practising? Higher level music students' use of time for instrumental practising. In H Jorgensen and A Lehman, eds, *Does practice make perfect? Current theory and research on instrumental music practice*, 123–140. Norges musikkh gskole, Oslo.

Kelly GA (1955). *The psychology of personal constructs*. Norton, New York.

Klinedinst RE (1991). Predicting performance achievement and retention of fifth-grade instrumental students. *Journal of Research in Music Education*, **39**, 225–238.

Lamont A (2002). Musical identities and the school environment. In RAR MacDonald, DJ Hargreaves and D Miell, eds, *Musical identities*, 41–59. Oxford University Press, Oxford.

MacKinnon DW (1965). Personality and the realization of creative talent. *American Psychologist*, **20**, 273–281.

MacNamara A, Holmes P and Collins D (2006). The pathway to excellence: the role of psychological characteristics in negotiating the challenges of musical development. *British Journal of Music Education*, **23**, 285–302.

Manturzewska M (1969). *Psychologiczne Warunki Osiagniec Pianistycznych (Psychological conditions and piano achievement)*. Ossolineum, Warsaw.

Manturzewska M (1990). A biographical study of the life-span development of professional musicians. *Psychology of Music*, **18**, 112–139.

Markus H and Ruvolo A (1989). Possible selves: personalized representations of goals. In LA Pervin, ed., *Goal concepts in personality and social psychology*, 211–242. Lawrence Erlbaum Associates, Hillsdale, NJ.

McPherson GE and McCormick J (1999). Motivational and self-regulated learning components of musical practice. *Bulletin of the Council for Research in Music Education*, **141**, 98–102.

McPherson GE and McCormick J (2000). The contribution of motivational factors to instrumental performance in a performance examination. *Research Studies in Music Education*, **15**, 31–39.

McPherson GE and McCormick J (2006). Self-efficacy and performing music. *Psychology of Music*, **34**, 322–336.

Mota G (1999). Young children's motivation in the context of classroom music: an exploratory study about the role of music content and teaching style. *Bulletin of the Council for Research in Music Education*, **141**, 119–123.

Motte-Haber H de la (1984). Die Bedeutung der Motivation fur den Instrumentalbericht (The significance of motivation in instrumental reports). *Zeitschrift fur Musikpadagogik*, **51**, 51–54.

Nagel JJ (1987). An examination of commitment to careers in music: implications for alienation from vocational choice. Unpublished doctoral dissertation, University of Michigan, Ann Arbor, MI.

O'Neill SA (1997). The role of practice in children's early musical performance achievement during the early years of learning a musical instrument. In H Jørgensen and A Lehmann, eds, *Does practice make perfect? Current theory and research on instrumental music practice*, 3–70. Norges Musikkhogskole, Oslo.

O'Neill SA (1999). The role of motivation in the practice and achievement of young musicians. In SW Yi, ed., *Music, mind and science*, 420–433. Seoul National University Press, Seoul.

O'Neill SA and McPherson GE (2002). Motivation. In R Parncutt and GE McPherson, eds, *The science and psychology of musical performance: creative strategies for teaching and learning*, 31–46. Oxford University Press, Oxford.

Persson RS (1993). The subjectivity of musical performance: an exploratory music–psychological real world enquiry into the determinants and education of musical reality. Unpublished doctoral dissertation, School of Human and Health Sciences, Huddersfield University, Huddersfield, UK.

Persson RS, Pratt G, Robson C (1996). Motivational and influential components of musical performance: a qualitative analysis. In AJ Cropley and D Dehn, eds, *Fostering the growth of high ability: European perspectives*, 287–301. Ablex, Norwood, NJ.

Pitts SE (2005). *Valuing musical participation*. Ashgate, Aldershot.

Pitts SE, Davidson JW and McPherson GE (2000). Models of success and failure in instrumental learning: case studies of young players in the first 20 months of learning. *Bulletin of The Council for Research In Music Education*, **146**, 51–69.

Renwick JM and McPherson GE (2002). Interest and choice: student-selected repertoire and its effect on practising behaviour. *British Journal of Music Education*, **19**, 173–188.

Rogers CR (1961). *On becoming a person*. Houghton Mifflin, Boston, MA.

Rotter JB (1966). Generalised expectancies for internal versus external control of reinforcement. *Psychological Monograph*, 80 (Whole No. 609).

Ryan RM and Deci EL (2000). Self-determination theory and the facilitation of intrinsic motivation, social development, and well being. *American Psychologist*, **55**, 68–78.

Sandene BA (1998). An investigation of variables related to student motivation in instrumental music. *Dissertation Abstracts International*, **58**, 3870A. (UMI No. 9811178.)

Schmidt CP (2005). Relations among motivation, performance achievement, and music experience variables in secondary instrumental music students. *Journal of Research in Music Education*, **53**, 134–147.

Sergeant D (1969). Experimental investigation of absolute pitch. *Journal of Research in Music Education*, **17**, 135–43.

Simonton DK (1997). Products, persons, and periods: histrometric analyses of compositional creativity. In DJ Hargreaves and AC North, eds, *The social psychology of music*, 107–122. Oxford University Press, Oxford.

Sloboda JA, Davidson JW, Howe MJA and Moore DG (1996). The role of practice in the development of performing musicians. *British Journal of Psychology*, **87**, 287–309.

Sloboda JA and Howe MJA (1991). Biographical precursors of musical excellence: an interview study. *Psychology of Music*, **19**, 3–21.

Sosniak LA (1985). Learning to be a concert pianist. In BS Bloom, ed., *Developing talent in young people*, 19–67. Ballentine, New York.

Szubertowska E (2005). Education and the music culture of Polish adolescence. *Psychology of Music*, **33**, 317–330.

Vispoel WP and Austin JR (1993). Constructive response to failure in music: the role of attribution feedback and classroom goal structure. *British Journal of Educational Psychology*, **63**, 110–129.

Weiner B (1986) *An attributional theory of motivation and emotion*. Springer-Verlag, New York.

Wigfield A, Eccles JS, Yoon KS, Harold RD, Arbreton AJA, Freedman-Doan C and Blumenfield PC (1997). Changes in children's competence beliefs and subjective task values across the elementary school years: a 3-year study. *Journal of Educational Psychology*, **89**, 451–469.

CHAPTER 28

The role of the family in supporting learning

Andrea Creech

Introduction

Powerful images of musicians' parents have been immortalized in accounts of the lives of many iconic figures in Western music. Parents have been depicted as exerting enormous influence on their children's musical development, as in the cases of Mozart (Solomon 1994), Clara Schumann (Galloway 2002), and more recently, Yehudi Menuhin (Menuhin 1977) and Jacqueline du Pré (Easton 1989), to name but a few. At the other end of the spectrum are exceptional accounts of musicians who attained high levels of expertise and musical intelligence without parental support, as in the case of Louis Armstrong (Collier 1983). Kyle Pruett (2003, p. 154) invites us to conjure up our 'most enduring stereotype of the musician's parent. Then consider the opposite pole. Next, reflect on the intermediaries.' This chapter will attempt to respond to Pruett's challenge by considering these 'intermediaries' and suggesting the ways in which parents may most constructively support their children's musical development.

Years of educational research, theory and wisdom sustain the view that parents play a key role in their children's academic achievement, educational aspirations, well-being and motivation (Baker 1997; Grolnick *et al.* 2002; Gonzalez De Hass *et al.* 2005). Researchers have concluded that young children and adolescents alike experience improved student outcomes when their parents are actively involved at home and in the school context (Henderson and Berla 1994).

In the domain of music, and specifically relating to the acquisition of expertise on musical instruments, the question of how families can best support their children's interest has been a preoccupation of many researchers. Positive relationships between musical home environments and the musical responsiveness of children from these homes have been reported (Kirkpatrick 1962; Shelton 1965; Wermuth 1971), and these findings have been elucidated by more recent research that has found children's musical development to be influenced by parental musical background (Bloom and Sosniak 1981; Klinedinst 1991), socio-economic background (Klinedinst 1991), parent support for practice and lessons (Doan 1973; Brokaw 1982; Sloboda and Howe 1991; Zdzinski 1992; Davidson *et al.* 1995), parental goals, aspirations and values (Sosniak 1985; Addison 1990; Davidson and Scott 1999), parental self-efficacy (Creech 2001), family interaction patterns (Davidson and Borthwick 2002), and parent–teacher–pupil relationships (Manturzewska 1990; Creech 2006; Hallam 1998). It has been acknowledged that the conditions which facilitate the development of musical gifts and talents involve considerable investment of time and financial resources as well as parental belief and philosophical commitment (Chadwick 1996). The process of facilitating developing talents is seen by Feldhusen (2001) as a long-range one in which parents work together with pupils and teachers. This growing body of research suggests that the ways parents might support their children in persisting with learning musical instruments and developing musical expertise are diverse and complex.

The advent of the Japanese Suzuki method of violin teaching, which came to the West during the 1960s holding as a central tenet the importance of the parent as 'home teacher', played a powerful role in highlighting the issue of parent participation in the realm of children's instrumental learning. The Suzuki method, however, cannot claim sole ownership of the concept of parent–teacher–pupil partnership in instrumental learning; it has been demonstrated through biographical evidence (Lochner 1950; Weschler-Vered 1986; Milstein and Volkov 1990; Lewis and Staryk 2000; Stern and Potok 1999; Menuhin 1977) that parents, across cultures and historical time frames, have chosen to involve themselves integrally in the process of their children's acquisition of musical expertise. Empirical studies into the role of parents in instrumental learning (Doan 1973; Brokaw 1982; Sosniak 1985; Sloboda and Howe 1992; Davidson *et al.* 1996; Creech 2001, 2006; McPherson and Renwick 2001; Welch *et al.* 2006) have indicated that parental involvement in their children's musical development is not unusual; parents from diverse backgrounds and with children learning by a range of teaching methods and representing a number of instruments and musical genres, have supported their children in pursuit of musical excellence.

Parent involvement has been defined as 'the dedication of resources by the parent to the child within a given domain' (Grolnick 1997, p. 538). Grolnick conceptualizes parent involvement as comprising behavioural support, cognitive/intellectual support, and personal support. This chapter will begin with a brief discussion of the ways in which these three types of parental support have been found to influence children's musical development, with an emphasis given to the latter category of personal support, an area of parental involvement that has been shown in the domain of music to have far-reaching consequences for pupils, parents and teachers alike (Pruett 2003; Creech 2006). A discussion of whether interpersonal relating styles determine the extent to which parents engage in various types of involvement will follow, paying particular attention to the findings of a recent investigation into the influence of interpersonal relationships on learning outcomes (Creech 2006). Based on these findings a typological approach will be taken, with parental support of their children's musical development discussed within

the framework of six distinct types of parent–pupil–teacher partnerships in instrumental learning.

Behavioural support

Overt manifestations of parental support, including participatory activities and modelling the importance of the subject area, are included under the umbrella of *behavioural support* (Grolnick 1994). Parent participation in school activities has been found to be a positive predictor of primary school-aged children's school engagement (Izzo *et al.* 1999), and helping with homework is one of a number of parent practices that has been found to have a positive relationship with secondary students' academic engagement (Steinberg *et al.* 1992).

In the domain of instrumental learning parents may offer behavioural support in the form of monitoring and participating in practice, attending lessons and adopting the role of home teacher. In an experimental study involving beginning band students (aged 11–12) Brokaw (1982) found that

> while it was not surprising to discover a strong relationship between the amount of time a student spends practising and the student's achievement in performance … the amount of time spent by parents in supervising home practice is even a better predictor of successful achievement in the initial stages of development.
>
> (1982, p. 97)

Previously, Doan (1973) had produced similar results, in his study of 11-and 12-year-old violin students. Amongst a number of factors, parental supervision of practice and parent attendance at the child's concerts were identified by Doan as being significantly correlated to student achievement on the violin (1973, p. 79).

Other research has helped to elucidate Doan and Brokaw's findings. In a study of American concert pianists, Sosniak (1985) found that although many of the parents of her cohort had little musical background, their role of stimulating and supporting practice had been vital in sustaining their children's growth in musical competence throughout a first phase of early formal instruction and second phase of systematic acquisition of knowledge and skills. Sloboda and Howe (1991) concurred with Sosniak when they found that high-achieving 8–18-year-old students in a specialist music school had benefited from the support and encouragement of parents who, with little formal knowledge of music, took responsibility for helping with home practice and for encouraging their children to gain and maintain good practice habits. Beginning band pupils, aged 7–9, were found by McPherson and Renwick (2001) to be helped by parents in developing self-regulated learning, particularly during the first year of learning. Davidson *et al.* (1995) demonstrated that parental commitment to assisting, encouraging and supporting the child in the early stages of learning was a more important predictor of successful musical outcomes than any specialist knowledge on the part of the parent. 'Without the positive involvement of the parent in the process, the highest levels of achievement are likely to remain unattainable' (1995, p. 44).

Zdzinski (1992), in a study involving teenage woodwind players, demonstrated that the effects of behavioural support upon musical achievement may differ with student age. This view was supported by the findings from a more recent study involving 337 violin pupils and their parents (Creech 2006) where a considerable drop in monitoring and assisting with practicing, providing feedback during practice sessions and attending instrumental lessons was found amongst the parents of 13–14-year-olds, as compared to those with children up to the age of 12. Furthermore, when parents were grouped according to levels of behavioural support it was evident that high levels of participatory activities during adolescent years was significantly associated with inhibited pupil–teacher accord and with limitations on the child's autonomous learning. These findings support the evidence reported by Ginsburg *et al.* (1993) who found decreased pupil autonomy amongst early adolescents whose parents operated a regime of homework surveillance.

The ages of 12–18 have been described as the mid-life crisis of young musicians, when the need to acquire or disown the interest in music becomes paramount (Bamberger 1987). This is the point at which behavioural support may become less helpful, while an increasing emphasis on cognitive/intellectual support and personal support may become more valuable to the developing musician.

Parents who have engaged in considerable behavioural support during the early years of their children learning musical instruments face a special challenge of managing the transition to pupil–parent independence, in relation to the instrumental learning. Creech (2006) reported that this transition to independent pupil learning and the shift of emphasis from behavioural support to cognitive/intellectual and personal support sometimes involved the difficult risk that their child would make the choice to discontinue, a choice that carried implications of rejection of parental values. In addition, for many parents this shift entailed the loss of a role they had constructed for themselves, and despite being supportive of their children becoming independent learners many reluctantly surrendered their participation in practice and lessons. Teenage children often took the lead, 'encouraging' parents to relinquish their home teacher role by making it clear that this type of parental input was not welcome. Teachers too sometimes took the initiative, asking parents to cease attending lessons in order to allow a more independent relationship to flourish between pupil and teacher. The most successful transitions were experienced by parents whose children had established strong and positive relationships with their teachers, remaining receptive to parental interest yet taking responsibility for learning without external motivation provided by parents.

Cognitive/intellectual support

Exposing the child to cognitively stimulating activities and materials and engaging in intellectually domain-specific activities in the home have been found to comprise an important area of parental support (Grolnick 1994). Kulieke and Olszewski-Kubilius (1989) demonstrated that families of gifted children engaged in this form of support by espousing values relating to persistence and achievement in the subject area and by facilitating the progress of their children along particular domain-specific paths. Some evidence suggests that children internalize their parents' values and educational aspirations;

Marchant (2001) reported that the perceptions held by early adolescents of their parents' values had a strong association with motivation and attainment. Whether adolescents are likely to incorporate the parents' orientation and persevere on these paths has been found by Smith (1991) to be dependent on parent–adolescent communication regarding educational aims, together with perceived agreement between the two parents.

According to Csikszentmihalyi et al. (1993, p. 174) high levels of cognitive/intellectual support and challenge have a positive effect on teenagers across all talent areas. Parents of these accomplished children typically:

- Devote great amounts of time and energy to meeting the needs of their children
- Set high standards
- Encourage productive use of time
- Provide challenging opportunities
- Make sure lessons and materials are available
- Set aside areas of the home where child can work privately.

In the context of instrumental learning, parents offering this type of support provide the opportunities and materials that will assist the development of their children's musical intelligence, including arranging instrumental lessons, attending professional concerts with their children, listening to and discussing music in the home, encouraging participation in extra-curricular musical activities, and providing a quality instrument.

Evidence from a study investigating parental influence on the musical development of musically involved young Australians (Chadwick 1996) suggests that parents who perceived their children to be exhibiting characteristics of musical giftedness provided high levels of cognitive support for home-based musical activities. It has been suggested that children flourish when parents follow their lead and provide the wherewithal for in-depth exploration of their particular interests (Silverman 1992). Chadwick (2000) elucidates this view, suggesting that opportunities to engage in challenging and rigorous musical activities from an early age enhance normative musical development and provide a foundation for the development of musical expertise.

Creech (2006) reported that parents of violin pupils aged 13–18 who had persisted with learning for seven or more years and had attained relatively high levels of expertise on their instruments (beyond grade five, practising six or more hours per week) engaged in higher levels of music-specific cognitive/intellectual support than those with children below the age of 13 and in the beginning stages of playing. In the same study, when 337 parent–pupil pairs were grouped according to parent scores for cognitive/intellectual support, increased pupil enjoyment and parent satisfaction were found in the groups where the parents offered the greatest amount of this type of support. Cognitive/intellectual support was also found to be associated with increased professional satisfaction on the part of the teachers and with pupil–teacher influence, whereby pupils demonstrated independent learning, contributing to setting goals and effecting changes in the learning agenda.

Personal support

A growing body of evidence demonstrates that high levels of personal support represents a key area of parent involvement associated with sustaining a child's musical well-being (Pruett 2003; Creech 2006).

Education researchers have found that children in all age groups, including secondary school students, value their parents' help, interest and support, and that parental influence on children's behaviour remains extensive in adolescence (Brown et al. 1993; Crozier 1999). However, Crozier emphasizes the need for pupils to have some control over parents' involvement, highlighting the importance of negotiation rather than imposition of psychological control characterized by intrusive or manipulative controlling/surveillance measures (Crozier 1999; Baumrind 2005). Crozier here touches on the issue, so stark in adolescence, of the delicate balance between dimensions of 'agency' (the drive for independence) and 'communion' (the need to be engaged with others), which has been identified both in the literature relating to parenting style (Baumrind 1989; Brown et al. 1993; Noack 1998) and that concerned with interpersonal style (Van Tartwijk et al. 1998) and relationships (Birtchnell 1993; Tubbs 1984; Noller et al. 2001).

Steinberg *et al.* (1992) demonstrated that teenage students were most likely to benefit from parental involvement activities that included attending school programmes and extra-curricular activities and maintaining an interest in student progress when these forms of parental support were offered within a parenting style characterized by acceptance, warmth, democracy, and some degree of student autonomy. While Ginsburg and Bronstein (1993) found that behavioural support in the form of surveillance and monitoring of homework was associated with an extrinsically motivated orientation on the part of their children, they also noted that when parents provided encouragement and praise the children were more likely to demonstrate curiosity and an intrinsic interest in challenging learning tasks. It has been suggested that emotional support offered by parents in the form of interest and enthusiasm for their children's learning establishes 'a foundation for socializing children's motivation to learn' (Gonzalez-DeHass *et al.* 2005, p. 111). Furthermore, there is strong evidence that regardless of social class parental involvement in the form of home interest, support and discussion has a major impact on educational outcomes (Sui-Chu and Willms 1996; McNeal 2001).

Researchers and theorists argue that 'people function most cohesively and confidently in contexts in which they experience significant others as being both caring and autonomy-supportive' (Noack 1998, p. 227) and achieving a successful balance in this respect is a key factor in providing personal support for children's musical development.

In a musical context, biographical evidence gathered from finalists in the German 'Jugend Musiziert' music competition demonstrated that these young expert musicians had typically benefited from supportive and motivating relationships with their mothers (Bastian 1989). More recently, personal support was found to be associated with persistence with learning and musical attainment as well as with increasing pupil enjoyment of music and motivation (Creech 2006). Those parents with the highest scores for personal support were interested in understanding their child's point of view and prepared to compromise when their personal goals or expectations conflicted with those of

the child, subscribing to the stated aim of supporting the child in whatever course of action was chosen (i.e. to continue or not with musical studies). These parents were deeply interested in their children's learning, and were involved with their child learning an instrument to the extent that they considered this endeavour to have been a life-changing experience for themselves. A predominant view amongst these parents was that their children should develop independent learning skills and yet continue to feel supported by their parents. Strong pupil–teacher rapport was valued and this together with admiration of the teacher appeared to make it relatively easy for parents to become progressively less directly involved in the learning partnership (Creech 2006).

The potential for conflict

Considering the potential for conflict amongst those involved with musical instrument learning, particularly over practice, musical preferences, and time commitment expectations, it is perhaps rather surprising that little research to date has been directly concerned with this issue.

The emotional demands made on parents by their musical children can be considerable. The parent–child relationship is particularly vulnerable when adolescents reach the aforementioned musical mid-life crisis (Bamberger 1987) and as young musicians become increasingly susceptible to performance anxiety and the fear of negative judgement (Robson 1987). Clearly it is important for children to sustain a sense of being emotionally supported by their parents even in the face of disagreements. Research with gifted children and their families advocates family meetings as a forum where conflicts and power struggles may be resolved via shared responsibility and negotiation (Silverman 1992).

While parents of young musicians have been found to make frequent references to reluctant practising and to parent–pupil conflict these issues did not, as many parents fear, inevitably diminish either their children's persistence with learning or their own personal satisfaction (Creech 2006). Strategies that parents have identified as being successful in dealing with this potential battleground include simply leaving the room, discussions at times other than practice time, lowering expectations of daily practice, challenging the child, and offering praise as a reward. Parents did not acknowledge that material rewards would be a useful strategy to resolve conflict over practice, and considered the most successful strategy to have been allowing the child to choose when and how much to practise, within parameters negotiated with the teacher (Creech 2006).

Pruett identifies transcultural qualities of 'good enough parenting' (Pruett 2003, p. 155), amongst which the challenges of personal support are encapsulated. Included on his list are sensitivity to children and their ever-changing needs, the ability to make children feel loved, adored and enjoyed, devotion to sustaining strong values, affirmation of the child's uniqueness while expecting competence, and sustaining an abiding presence through thick and thin. Research in the domain of music supports the enduring importance of these qualities, suggesting that pupils function best when they perceive the adults as both caring and supportive of autonomy and when they are able to engage in ongoing mutual interaction with adults who continue to have a stake in their development and to act as their advocate (Noack 1998; Manturzewska 1990; Creech 2006).

Parent–pupil–teacher interaction: a typological approach

Any discussion of the parental role in children's musical development must take into account the interpersonal context. Systems theory provides a framework in which this context, comprising parents, teachers and pupils, may be conceptualized as a micro-system characterized by *holism*, whereby a human system is understood as the sum of its individual members, and *exchange*, whereby any change in one member of the system produces change throughout the system (Becvar and Becvar 1996). O'Neill (1996) argues that the parent–pupil–teacher relationship in the context of musical instrument learning can justifiably be conceptualized as a micro-system because all three participants experience new patterns of action and communication as a direct result of their interaction, and because

many motivational issues can be understood and possibly resolved when considered as a function of the micro-system. From this perspective parental support may be seen as part of the functioning of the parent–teacher–pupil system, influenced by the parent's position on a *control–responsiveness* axis, in relation to teacher and pupil.

Control and responsiveness

Baumrind (2005) suggests that the extent to which parents engage in supportive behaviour is associated with interpersonal qualities she labels as responsiveness and demandingness (interpreted here as *control*). A study by Marchant (2001) involving 230 early adolescents measured parental style using these two dimensions and provided evidence that children's school achievement is indeed influenced by interpersonal relationships amongst teachers, parents and pupils. Trusty and Lampe (1997) investigated the dimension of parent control and suggest that this interpersonal dynamic, when manifested in the context of relationships where parents offer cognitive and personal support in the form of discussing school, current events or troubling issues with their teenagers, is associated with an internal locus of control on the part of the young people whereby they experience pride and satisfaction for their successes. However, Ginsburg and Bronstein (1993) investigated the impact of behavioural support on student motivation and found that when parents monitored, enforced or helped with homework in a controlling fashion their early adolescent children showed less autonomy, satisfaction, persistence and intrinsic motivation related to their schoolwork. Garland (2005) discuss control as a dimension that varies from controlling to autonomy-supportive behaviour, and puts forth the view that while the former encourages children's obedience and compliance the latter promotes choice, self-reliance and participation in decision-making.

Baumrind's model of demandingness—responsiveness interpersonal relating style is reflected in Birtchnell's relating theory (2001) whereby interaction is conceptualized on a horizontal closeness–distance axis intersecting with a vertical upperness–lowerness axis. Birtchnell does not priviledge different positions on his interpersonal model, pointing out that while closesness holds people together, distance provides the space to become autonomous, and while upperness allows the opportunity for people to exert influence on others, lowerness enables individuals to benefit from the care and leadership of others.

Categories of parent–teacher–pupil interaction

The models proposed by Baumrind and Birtchnell resemble Leary's model for interpersonal interaction (1957) that served as the basis for the examination of parent control and responsiveness in the context of their relationships with their children who were learning the violin and with their children's instrumental teachers (Creech 2006). Parent control, on the vertical axis, was found to comprise underlying dimensions that were (1) perceived teacher leadership, (2) parent–teacher communication, (3) parent isolation within the learning partnership, (4) parent ambition and (5) parent preponderance. Responsiveness, on the horizontal axis, comprised (1) perceived teacher

approachability, (2) teacher–parent intimidation, (3) parent–pupil reciprocity and (4) parent–teacher acquiescence.

Six distinct clusters of parent–teacher–pupil interaction types, determined by dimensions of control and responsiveness, were found amongst the parent–teacher–pupil trios. A model (Figure 28.1) representing these six types of learning partnerships demonstrates that clusters one, two and three may be conceptualized as primary dyad plus a third party, while cluster four is represented as two primary dyads connected by one common member. Cluster five is characterized by very little communication between any two of the three individuals, while cluster six is characterized by reciprocity amongst all three participants.

Differences amongst the clusters of parent–teacher–pupil interaction types

Parent support

Significant differences were found between the parents of each cluster with respect to the types

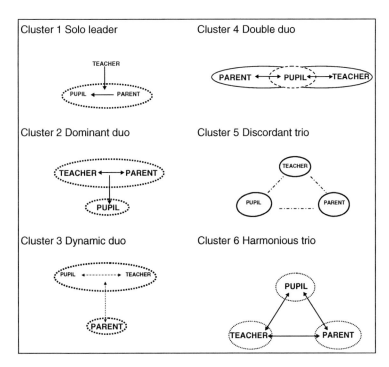

Fig. 28.1 Parent–teacher–pupil interaction types.

of support they were most likely to engage in. Parents in the *dynamic duo* and *discordant trio* clusters, characterized by a distant and powerless parent–teacher relation, offered the least amount of support, overall. Those occupying the *solo leader* cluster, where the parent took responsibility for ensuring that parent and pupil together followed the directive teacher, were found to offer the most behavioural support. The highest levels of cognitive/intellectual support were offered by parents occupying the *dominant duo* cluster, characterized by parents who adopted a predominant and controlling role in relation to both pupil and teacher. The *harmonious trio* cluster, where parents balanced ambitions for their children with responsiveness in relation to both teacher and pupil, had parents who engaged in the most personal support (Figure 28.2).

Pupil age

As pupils matured parent–pupil–teacher trios tended to gravitate towards the *dynamic duo* (pupil–teacher relationship becoming the primary dyad and parents becoming less influential), adding to the body of evidence showing that while parent–child relationships are typically hierarchical, family relationships undergo transformations towards more egalitarian patterns during adolescence (Noack 1998). While younger pupils were more likely to occupy the categories of *solo leader* and *dominant duo* where the basis for teacher–parent cooperation was the perceived dependency of the child, during the adolescent years pupils ceased to be dependent on the parent for motivation and structure (Johnson 1991). It was evident that some parents became isolated third parties (*dynamic duo*) while others shifted from an emphasis on behavioural

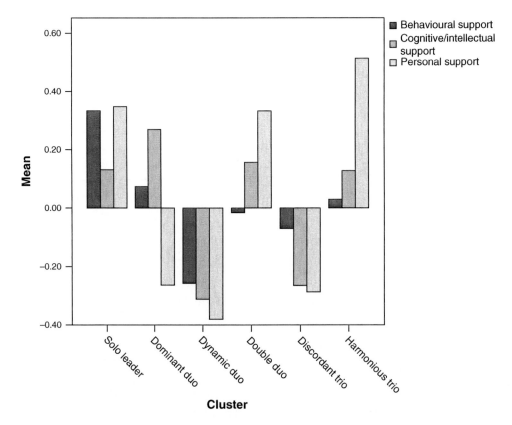

Fig. 28.2 Parent support according to parent–teacher–pupil interaction type (standardized scores).

support to personal and cognitive/intellectual support, continuing to support their children at home but becoming remote from the teacher (*double duo*). Still others (likely to be found in the *harmonious trio*) achieved a balance of agency and communion with their children and teachers within a relationship characterized by continued moderate behavioural support together with an emphasis on both cognitive/intellectual and personal support.

Persistence with learning

Numbers occupying the *discordant trio* category decreased sharply after three years of study, suggesting that characteristics of this type may have led to pupil drop-out, or alternatively to changes to other teachers. Conversely, there was a large increase in numbers occupying *harmonious trios*, after three years of study. The numbers in the *dynamic duo* category remained stable and were not sensitive to years of study, while numbers occupying *dominant duo* and *double duo* categories declined after six years of study. Thus it would seem that the balance of parent support achieved by those in *harmonious trios*, which included moderate behavioural support, higher levels of cognitive/intellectual support and a great deal of personal support, may be associated with their children's perseverance on the instrument.

Few pupils occupying the *discordant trio* cluster progressed beyond grade five, while the *dominant duo* and *harmonious trio* clusters contained greater proportions of pupils who had attained a minimum of grade four. Parents occupying these two clusters, while differing in respect of personal support, were similar in that they demonstrated high parent–teacher acquiescence and perceptions of strong teacher leadership but low teacher–parent intimidation and isolation.

The *harmonious trio* and the *solo leader* were the clusters where the greatest proportion of pupils did in excess of three hours practice per week. Parents in these two clusters were most similar in that they perceived strong leadership on the part of the teachers and also offered a great deal of personal support to their children. Again, parental perception of teacher leadership seems to be a key factor in sustaining persistence with learning.

Pupil learning outcomes

Differences amongst the clusters of interaction types were evident in respect of pupil learning outcomes including enjoyment of music, personal satisfaction, motivation, self-efficacy and self-esteem. Overall the *discordant trio* produced the least positive outcomes while the *harmonious trio* produced the most consistently positive outcomes for pupils. With reference to the former this finding adds to earlier research that suggests where parents place a low value on the subject matter, have low expectations of success, do not have the wherewithal to help their children at home and/or are intimidated by teachers the result can be a downward spiral of mutual distrust, lack of communication and absence of shared purpose amongst parents, teachers and pupils alike (Bandura 1997; Hurley 1995). In contrast, the findings in respect of the latter elucidate earlier research that has proposed a model of parent–professional–child partnership whereby parents lie at the heart of a system which advances the child's development while professionals take primary responsibility for advancement of knowledge and skills (Henry 1996). Furthermore, these findings support the view that pupils function best when they perceive the adults as both caring and supportive of autonomy and when they are able to engage in ongoing mutual interaction with adults who continue to have a stake in their development and to act as their advocate (Noack 1998; Manturzewska 1990).

Summary: the versatile parent

Effective and supportive parental involvement in instrumental learning requires parents to be versatile, adept at moving between the close and distant positions on the responsiveness axis and between directive and acquiescent positions on the control axis of the model for interpersonal dimensions. This involves providing much practical assistance and personal support during the early years of learning yet seeking and following the teacher's advice in musical matters and allowing the child and teacher the space to develop an autonomous relationship. It also involves remaining resilient in the face of reluctant practising while remaining as the child's interested and supportive advocate, long after practical help has ceased to be appropriate or welcomed by the teacher and pupil. Most importantly, parents should not become uninvolved in their children's learning in the name of agency, nor disempower their children in the name of communion. Specifically, positive outcomes may be achieved when parents (a) elicit their children's views regarding appropriate parental involvement, (b) negotiate with their children over practising issues, within parameters set by the teacher, (c) provide a structured home environment for practice, (d) take an interest in promoting good teacher-pupil rapport, (e) communicate with the teacher in relation to the child's progress, and (f) remain as a supremely interested audience.

Returning to the systems framework, the versatile parent may be conceptualized as one part of a dynamic interpersonal system, influenced by and having a reciprocal influence on the characteristics of both teacher and pupil. There is much scope for future research in relation to this point, particularly concerning (a) how parent–teacher–pupil systems evolve over time and (b) the processes by which these interpersonal systems may underpin teaching and learning outcomes.

References

Addison R (1990). parents' views on their children's musical education in the primary school: a survey. *British Journal of Music Education*, 7, 133–141.

Baker A (1997). Parent involvement in children's education: a critical assessment of the knowledge base. *Annual Meeting of the American Education Research Association*, Eric Document Reproduction Service, New York.

Bamberger J (1987). The mind behind the musical ear. Presented at the Biology of Music Making Conference, Denver, CO.

Bandura A (1997). *Self-efficacy: the exercise of control*. W.H. Freeman and Company, New York.

Bastian HG (1989). *Leben fur musik. Eine Biographie-Studie uber musikalisch (Hoch-) Begabungen*. Schott, Mainz.

Baumrind D (1989). Rearing competent children. In W Damon, ed., *Child development today and tomorrow*, 349–378. Jossey-Bass, London.

Baumrind D (2005). Patterns of parental authority and adolescent autonomy. *New Directions for Child and Adolescent Development*, 108, 61–69.

Becvar D and Becvar R (1996). *Family therapy: a systemic integration*. Allyn and Bacon, Boston, MA.

Birtchnell J (1993). *How humans relate: a new interpersonal theory*. Psychology Press, Hove, East Sussex.

Birtchnell J (2001). Relating therapy with individuals, couples and families. *Journal of Family Therapy*, 23, 63–84.

Bloom B and Sosniak L (1981). Talent development. *Educational Leadership*, November, 86–94.

Brokaw JP (1982). The extent to which parental supervision and other selected factors are related to achievement of musical and technical-physical characteristics by beginning instrumental music students. Unpublished PHD Dissertation; Music, University of Michigan, Michigan, USA.

Brown BB, Mounts N, Lamborn SD and Steinberg L (1993). Parenting practices and peer group affiliation in adolescence. *Child Development*, 64, 467–482.

Chadwick F (1996). *Gifted education: proceedings from the 1996 national conference in Adelaide, South Australia*. Australian Association for the Education of the Gifted and Talented, Adelaide.

Chadwick F (2000). An Australian perspective on talent development in music: the influence of environmental catalysts upon the provision of opportunities for learning, training, and practice in the musical domain. Unpublished PhD thesis; University of New South Wales, Sydney.

Collier JL (1983). *Louis Armstrong: an American genius*. Oxford University Press, Oxford.

Creech A (2001). Play for me: An exploration into motivations, issues and outcomes related to parental involvement in their children's violin study. Unpublished MA dissertation; Music, University of Sheffield, Sheffield.

Creech A (2006). Dynamics, harmony and discord: a systems analysis of teacher-pupil-parent interaction in instrumental learning. Unpublished PhD thesis; Institute of Education, University of London, London.

Crozier G (1999). Parent involvement: who wants it? *International Studies in Sociology of Education*, 9, 111–130.

Csikszentmihalyi M, Rathunde K and Whalen S (1993). *Talented teenagers: the roots of success and failure*. Cambridge University Press, Cambridge.

Davidson J and Borthwick SJ (2002). Family dynamics and family scripts: a case study of musical development. *Psychology of Music*, 30, 121–136.

Davidson J, Howe M, Moore D and Sloboda J (1996). The role of parental influences in the development of musical performance. *British Journal of Developmental Psychology*, 14, 399–412.

Davidson J, Howe M and Sloboda J (1995). the role of parents and teachers in the success and failure of instrumental learners. *Bulletin of the Council for Research in Music Education*, 127, 40–44.

Davidson J and Scott S (1999). Instrumental learning with exams in mind: a case study investigating teacher, student and parent interactions before, during and after a music examination. *British Journal of Music Education*, 16, 79–95.

Doan G (1973). An investigation of the relationships between parental involvement and the performance ability of violin students. Unpublished PhD Dissertation; Music, Ohio State University, Ohio, USA.

Easton C (1989). *Jacqueline du Pré: a biography*. Da Capo Press, Cambridge, MA.

Feldhusen JF (2001). *Talent development in gifted education*. ERIC Clearinghouse on Disabilities and Gifted Education, Arlington, VA.

Galloway J (2002). *Clara*. Jonathan Cape, London.

Garland S (2005). Perceived threat, controlling parenting, and children's achievement orientations. *Motivation and Emotion*, **29**, 103–120.

Ginsburg GS and Bronstein P (1993). Family factors related to children's intrinsic/extrinsic motivational orientation and academic performance. *Child Development*, **64**, 1461–1474.

Gonzalez-DeHass AR, Willems PP and Doan Holbein MF (2005). Examining the relationship between parental involvement and student motivation. *Educational Psychology Review*, **17**, 99–123.

Grolnick W (1994). Parents' involvement in children's schooling: a multidimensional conceptualization and motivational model. *Child Development*, **65**, 237–252.

Grolnick W (1997). Predictors of parent involvement in children's schooling. *Journal of Educational Psychology*, **89**, 538–548.

Grolnick W, Gurland S, DeCourcey W and Jacob K (2002). Antecedents and consequences of mothers autonomy support: an experimental investigation. *Developmental Psychology*, **38**, 143–155.

Hallam S (1998). The predictors of achievement and dropout in instrumental tuition. *Psychology of Music*, **26**, 116–132.

Henderson AT and Berla N (1994). *A new generation of evidence: the family is critical to student achievement*. National Committee for Citizens in Education, Columbia, MD.

Henry M (1996). *Young children, parents, and professionals: enhancing the links in early childhood*. Routledge, London.

Hurley CG (1995). Student motivations for beginning and continuing/discontinuing string music instruction. *The Quarterly Journal of Music Teaching and Learning*, VI, 44–55.

Izzo CV, Weissberg RP, Kasprow WJ and Fendrich M (1999). A longitudinal assessment of teacher perceptions of parent involvement in children's education and school performance. *American Journal of Community Psychology*, **27**, 817–839.

Johnson D (1991). Parents, students and teachers: a three-way relationship. *International Journal of Educational Research*, **15**, 171–181.

Kirkpatrick W (1962). Relationships between the singing ability of pre-kindergarten children and their home environment. Unpublished PhD thesis; University of Southern California, Los Angeles.

Klinedinst R (1991). Predicting performance achievement and retention of fifth-grade instrumental students. *Journal of Research in Music Education*, **39**, 225–238.

Kulieke MJ and Olszewski-Kubilius P (1989). The influence of family values and climate on the development of talent. In JL VanTassel-Baska and P Olszewski-Kubilius, eds, *Patterns of influence on gifted learners*, 40–59. Teachers College Press, New York.

Leary T (1957). *Interpersonal diagnosis of personality: a functional theory and methodology for personality evaluation*. Ronald Press Company, New York.

Lewis T and Staryk S (2000). *Fiddling with life: the unusual journey of Steven Staryk*. Mosaic Press, Canada.

Lochner LP (1950). *Fritz Kreisler*. Paganiniana Publications Inc., Neptune City, NJ.

Manturzewska M (1990). A biographical study of the life-span development of professional musicians. *Psychology of Music*, **18**, 112–139.

Marchant GJ (2001). Relations of middle school students' perceptions of family and school contexts with academic achievement. *Psychol Schools*, **38**, 505–519.

McNeal RB (2001). Differential effects of parental involvement on cognitive and behavioural outcomes by socioeconomic status. *Journal of Socio-Economics*, **30**, 171–179.

McPherson G and Renwick J (2001). A longitudinal study of self-regulation in children's musical practice. *Music Education Research*, **3**, 169–186.

Menuhin Y (1977). *Unfinished journey*. Macdonald and Jane's Publishers Ltd, London.

Milstein N and Volkov S (1990). *From Russia to the West*. Henry Holt and Co., New York.

Noack P (1998). School achievement and adolescents' interactions with their fathers, mothers, and friends. *European Journal of Psychology of Education*, XIII, 503–513.

Noller P, Feeney JA and Peterson C (2001). *Personal relationships across the lifespan*. Psychology Press, Hove, East Sussex.

O'Neill S (1996). Factors influencing children's motivation and achievement during the first year of instrumental music tuition. Unpublished PhD thesis; Keele University, Keele, UK.

Pruett K (2003). First patrons: parenting the musician. Presented at the 21st Annual Symposium on the Medical Problems of Musicians and Dancers, Aspen, Colorado.

Robson B (1987). Post-performance depression in arts students. *Medical Problems of Performing Artists*, **2**, 137–141.

Shelton J (1965). The influence of home musical environment upon musical response of first grade children. Unpublished PhD dissertation; George Peabody College for Teachers, Vanderbilt University, Nashville TN.

Silverman L (1992). *How parents can support gifted children*. Council For Exceptional Children, Reston, VA.

Sloboda J and Howe M (1991). Biographical precursors of musical excellence: an interview study. *Psychology of Music*, **19**, 3–21.

Sloboda J and Howe M (1992). Transitions in the early musical careers of able young musicians: choosing instruments and teachers. *Journal of Research in Music Education*, **40**, 283–294.

Smith TE (1991). Agreement of adolescent educational expectations with perceived maternal and paternal educational goals. *Youth and Society*, **23**, 155–174.

Solomon M (1994). *Mozart: a life*. Hutchinson, London.

Sosniak LA (1985). Learning to be a concert pianist. In BS Bloom, ed., *Developing talent in young people*, 19–67. Ballantine, New York.

Steinberg L, Lamborn SD and Darling N (1992). Impact of parenting practices on adolescent achievement: authoritative parenting, school involvement, and encouragement to succeed. *Child Development*, **63**, 1266–1281.

Stern I and Potok C (1999). *My first 79 years*. Alfred A. Knopf, New York.

Sui-Chu EH and Willms JD (1996). Effects of parental involvement on eighth-grade achievement. *Sociology of Education*, **69**, 126–141.

Trusty J and Lampe RE (1997). Relationship of high-school seniors' perceptions of parental involvement and control to seniors' locus of control. *Journal of Counselling Development*, **75**, 375–384.

Tubbs SL (1984). *A systems approach to small group interaction*. Random House, New York.

Van Tartwijk J, Brekelmans M and Wubbels T (1998). Students' perceptions of teacher interpersonal style: the front of the classroom as the teacher's stage. *Teaching and Teacher Education*, **14**, 607–617.

Welch G, Duffy C, Potter J and Whyton T (2006). *Investigating musical performance (IMP): comparative studies in advanced musical learning*. Institute of Education, University of London, Funded by the ESRC/TLRP, grant reference RES-139–25–0258.

Wermuth R (1971). Relationship of musical aptitude to family and student activity in music, student interest in music, socioeconomic status, and intelligence among caucasian and negro middle school students. Unpublished PhD Dissertation; Ohio State University, Ohio, USA.

Weschler-Vered A (1986). *Jascha Heifetz*. Schirmer Books, New York.

Zdzinski S (1992). Relationships among parental involvement, music aptitude, and musical achievement of instrumental music students. *Journal of Research in Music Education*, **40**, 114–125.

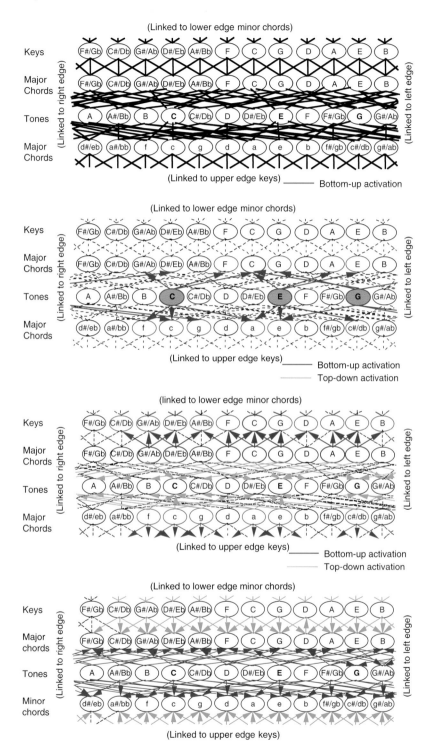

Plate 1 Bharucha's MUSACT model. (a) When three tones are sounding, activation spread from tones to chord units (b), and then from chord to key and tone units (c), and from key units to chord and from tone to chord units (d) and so on up to equilibrium. See Chapter 6, p 66, for further details.

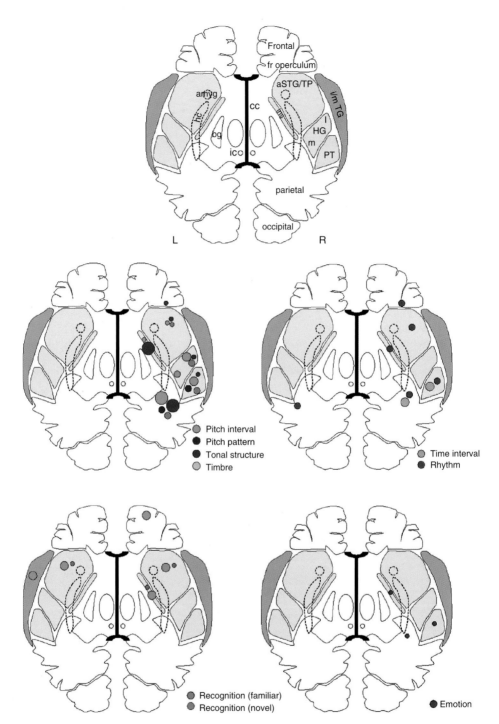

Plate 2 Critical brain substrates for musical listening disorders. Schematic cartoons based on symptomatic cases of musical listening disorder. For each musical listening function, the presence of a circle indicates that at least 50% of studies reviewed involved damage to the corresponding brain region. The size of the circle scales with the proportion of studies in which such a link was evident. See Chapter 17, p 186, for further details. Key: amyg, amygdala; aSTG, anterior superior temporal gyrus; bg, basal ganglia; cc, corpus callosum; fr, frontal; hc hippocampus; HG, Heschl's gyrus; i, inferior; ic, inferior colliculi; ins, insula; l, lateral; m, medial; PT, planum temporale; TG, temporal gyrus

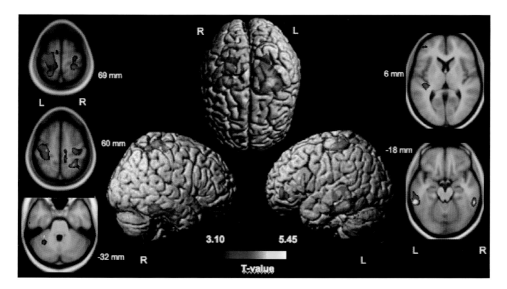

Plate 3 A voxel-based morphometric study showing grey matter volume differences between three groups. Only voxels exhibiting a significant positive correlation between musician status (professional musician > amateur musician > non-musician) and increased grey matter volume are shown here, and those have been overlaid on the rendered cortical surface of a single subject. (This figure was adapted from Figure 1 in Gaser and Schlaug [2003]). See Chapter 18, p 199, for further details.

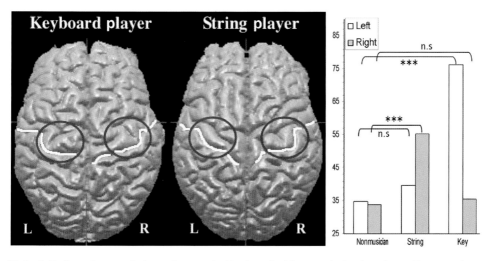

Plate 4 Brain surface renderings of one typical keyboard and one typical string player. The central sulcus is marked with a white line. The portion of the precentral gyrus containing the configuration similar to that of the inverted Greek letter 'Omega' is found within the red circles. In the two examples, a prominent omega sign can be seen on the left more than the right in the keyboard player, and only on the right in the string player. See Chapter 18, p 200, for further details.

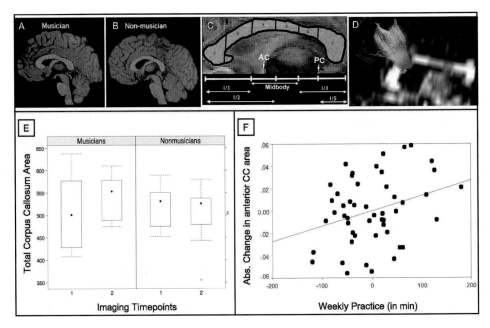

Plate 5 Corpus callosum differences in adults (musicians vs non-musicians) and changes over time in children. (A) and (B) show the midsagittal slice of an adult musician (A) and non-musician (B) showing a difference in the size of the anterior and midbody of the corpus callosum. (C) and (D) show the major subdivisions of the corpus callosum and locations of the interhemispheric fibers connecting the motor hand regions on the right and left hemisphere through the corpus callosum.

(E) and (F) show the mean (dot inside box plots) midsagittal corpus callosum size of the 5–7-year-old children at baseline (time point 1) and after 15 months of musical training (time point 2) shows slightly opposite trends with the instrumental group showing an increase in the midsagittal corpus callosum area. The anterior portion of the corpus callosum (segments 1–4, see Fig. 18.3c) showed a significant correlation with the amount of weekly practice (p = 0.034; partial r2 = 0.094). See Chapter 18, p 202, for further details.

Plate 6 Cerebral activation pattern of a rhythm discrimination task – modulated by maturity and experience. Statistical parametric images superimposed onto a surface rendering of a standardized anatomical brain depict significant activations during a rhythmic discrimination task in a group of 5–7-year-old, musically naive children, adult non-musicians, and adult musicians. The children showed prominent superior temporal gyrus activation on both sides. The adult groups show an extended pattern of activation involving polar and posterior planar regions of the superior temporal lobe as well as the parietal lobe, parts of the frontal lobe, and the cerebellum. Adult musicians differ from adult non-musicians by having less activation of the primary auditory cortex, but more activation of frontal regions bilaterally, particularly in the inferior frontal gyrus. See Chapter 18, p 204, for further details.

CHAPTER 29

The role of the institution and teachers in supporting learning

Graham Welch and Adam Ockelford

Introduction

Musical behaviour and development are natural by-products of the interface between intrapersonal maturational processes and an individual's enculturation into locally dominant sound worlds (e.g. Hallam and Lamont 2004; Welch 2006a) and are basic to human design. They are not dependent on the input of an institution or a 'teacher' as such, but are related to the evolution of generative skills in a sonic environment— our natural propensity to 'continually create, recreate and develop new ideas and materials' (Hallam and Lamont 2004, p. 243). Within such environments, there are various 'institutions' (including cultural settings as well as educational establishments) and 'teachers', i.e. people who have a role in musical learning, with both exemplified in the peer-to-peer popular music skill development of musicians and adolescents (Green 2001; Tarrant *et al.* 2002). Other examples are found in the interweaving of indigenous musics with the rituals of daily life, such as in the *iorram* or rowing songs of the Isle of Mull (Macnab 1970) and as practised by the Northern Ewe children of Eastern Ghana (Agawu 1995).

> *6.00 a.m.* The day's work has begun in earnest. In one home, girls are pounding dried cassava in a mortar to make *kokonte*. In another, they are pounding recently harvested rice in order to remove the husks. As with other forms of daily pounding ... the work ... is made a little less routine by incorporating some rhythmic interest. In place of a regularly spaced alternation between two pounders ... a variant may be introduced. Pounder 1 keeps a steady pace while Pounder 2 pushes her strokes closer to Pounder 1's. Here as elsewhere in Northern Ewe culture, work merges into play and reemerges into work.
>
> Agawu (1995, p. 12)

Contemporary explanations for the mechanism for the process of learning in social and cultural settings often draw on the work of Vygotsky, Luria and Leont'ev in the first half of the twentieth century (cf. Bannon 1997; Cole 1999), as well as being related to systems theory—the interlinking of relationships within some form of organization—(von Bertalanffy 1968), and social ecology theory—the nurturing of development within social contexts (Bronfenbrenner 1979). The early Russian investigators and those who developed their work subsequently (such as the Finnish researcher Engeström) explored how learning and development are the product of inter- and intrapersonal behaviours that are shaped by cultural artefacts (e.g., literature), alongside tools (including psychological tools, e.g., language and other symbol systems), expectations, 'rules'/conventions and norms. The internalization of artefacts is also seen to facilitate the agency of the individual, such that the artefacts themselves are modified through personal use, enabling the possibility of consequent change within the culture. Thus there is an ongoing mediation process in how individuals interact with the world around them and make sense of their reality.

A key concept in this view of culturally based learning is 'activity', which has been defined as 'the engagement of a subject toward a certain goal or objective' (Ryder 2005). One widely cited model of activity within a system is provided by Engeström (1999, 2001) (see Figure 29.1). In his interrelated system of elements as applied to education, the 'subject' (the learner) is supported in reaching the 'object' (the intended learning outcome) through interaction with various 'mediating artifacts' (such as language and other symbol systems) (a conceptualization strongly associated with the work of Vygotsky). This process is seen as being embedded in a social context that provides support for the activity through the subject and intended outcome being located within a 'community' that has 'rules' (expectations for behaviour) and also the likelihood of a 'division of labour' (diversity of effort). Because of the possibility of tensions within the activity system, it may be that the actual outcome is at variance with the intended object (i.e. that there are unintended outcomes—as explored below).

If the activity system is seen in relation to learning within an institution (such as a school or social collective, for example, the family) in which certain people either adopt or are expected to have, roles as 'teachers', then it is possible to envisage how the theorized activity system might be able to support the intended learning in music (or fail to). The world of music has certain characteristics:

◆ There are many different musical genres and subgenres;

◆ Each has its own customary view of what counts as musical learning, or at least the outcomes of musical learning in relation to performance, as well as the traditions (custom and practice) in how learning is usually fostered in relation to the genre's characteristic features, as exemplified in the 'institutions' of India, for example the tradition of musical households or *Gharanas* (Farrell 2001) and Japan, for example the culture schools managed by major business and voluntary organizations (Murao and Wilkins 2001);

◆ In many diverse musics, there is evidence of the high status accorded to the accomplished expert who demonstrates solo mastery over the sonic material;

◆ Certain cultures, such as China, Afghanistan and India, continue to have strong traditional music genres. These are characterized by expertise transmission within families across several (or many) generations (Jones 1995; Doubleday and Baily 1995; Farrell 1997). In such traditional cultures, the 'teacher' is in

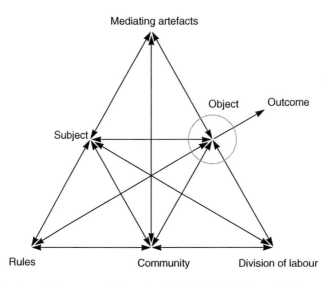

Fig. 29.1 The structure of a human activity system (Engeström 2001b, p. 136).

a master/apprentice relationship with the 'pupil' within a strong local community, often fostered by pupils playing for each other in the presence of the master.

Aspects of the role of institutions and teachers in the process by which musical expertise is learned and demonstrated are illustrated in the four examples that follow (see below). The first relates to musical development in a special education context, the second to advanced music learning in higher education, the third to the relatively new music education world of the female cathedral chorister and the fourth to pupils' experiences of lower secondary school classrooms in England. In the first three cases, the intention is to suggest how the teacher and institution support the activity of learning within a social context, whilst the last demonstrates that not all music learning in within an institution is necessarily positive or as intended.

The role of institutions and teachers in supporting musical learning: four examples

Example one: supporting musical learning in a young prodigious musical savant

Derek Paravicini is a musical savant, now in his late twenties, who is well known to the public through success on the concert platform as a jazz and popular pianist on both sides of the Atlantic. His early life was very difficult, and the initial development of his musical expertise was highly unconventional (Ockelford 2007).

Derek was born premature at 26 weeks, weighing a little over 700 g. In the fight for survival that followed, he lost his sight through retinopathy of prematurity, and developed unspecified neurological impairments that meant he grew up with severe learning difficulties. His family were upper-class and employed the services of an experienced Nanny to care for him and to oversee his upbringing. Neither she, nor anyone else, expected Derek to develop musically in a way that was at all out of the ordinary (there was no history of exceptional musical development in the family). However, following the diagnosis of Derek's blindness a few weeks after returning home from hospital, Nanny decided that sound was likely to play an important part in his life. So she sang to him constantly and surrounded him with sound-making toys. Just like any other baby's, Derek's environment was also perfused with music from the TV, radio and other incidental sources.

Derek was attracted to music as a potential source of stimulation and order in the world around him, and unbeknown to Nanny or his family, his ability to process musical sounds developed rapidly and precociously. Desperate to find an activity that would keep the 1-year-old Derek gainfully occupied, Nanny gave him his grandfather's little electric keyboard to play with. From the start, Derek loved the sounds that it produced and discovered that he could imitate some of the musical sounds that he had came into contact with. With no intervention on the part of Nanny or his family, and with no visual model to guide him, Derek taught himself how to get his hands and fingers in the right places at the right times to recreate some of the snatches of melody and harmony that were familiar to him. This situation—Stage 1 in the journey of Derek's musical learning—is summarized in terms of Engeström's model in Figure 29.2.

One day, after about six months of self-directed exploration at the keyboard, Nanny heard Derek play a version of 'Cockles and Mussels'—using both hands, with a tune and rudimentary accompaniment. His repertoire soon widened, and Derek's relationship with Nanny, his extended family and friends took a new course with the addition of this unexpected but welcome dimension. Still there was no *formal* intervention or guidance, though, from those around Derek in terms of supporting his learning. In the months and years that followed, Derek continued to chart his own, unique, autodidactic course (Stage 2: Figure 29.3).

At the age of five, Derek came to the attention of the second author (AO), who was then teaching in a school for the blind in south-west London. Derek's raw talent was evident, as were his technical eccentricities—including the use of his knuckles, hands and even the occasional

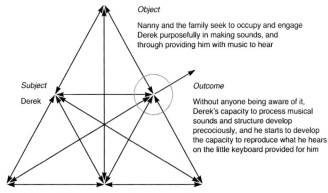

Derek's capacity to process musical sounds and structure develop precociously, and he starts to learn to play by ear without the awareness of those around him

Mediating artefacts

- Tapes of music in a range of genres
- Nanny singing nursery rhymes, other songs and hymns
- Music in the wider environment - TV, radio, etc
- Derek's grandfather's little electric keyboard

Object

Nanny and the family seek to occupy and engage Derek purposefully in making sounds, and through providing him with music to hear

Subject

Derek

Outcome

Without anyone being aware of it, Derek's capacity to process musical sounds and structure develop precociously, and he starts to develop the capacity to reproduce what he hears on the little keyboard provided for him

Rules, assumptions, expectations and drivers

- There are no formal rules operating in relation to Derek's learning to process musical sound
- Nanny assumes that, as a blind child, Derek should be stimulated with sound, including music
- Unable to grasp many everyday concepts and given the semantic nature of language, Derek's attracted to the rule-bound, self-referencing nature of musical sounds, for which his blindness and learning difficulties do not present a barrier to processing
- With regard to his grandfather's keyboard, he is driven purely by the internal motivation of realising that he can reproduce in sound what he hears, and relishing that ability
- Derek is unaware of the assumptions and expectations of those around him

Community

Family
Nanny

Division of labour

- Nanny and the family surround Derek with music (both wittingly and unwittingly)
- Nanny provides Derek with a range of soundmakers including his grandfather's little electric organ
- Externally, Derek appears merely to be a recepient of the stimulation that is provided; internally, though, his mind is working to develop the capacity to process musical sound
- Through his own heuristic efforts, Derek starts to teach himself to play by ear
- Those around him are unaware of what he is doing, and do not intervene in, support or guide his efforts

Fig. 29.2 Stage 1, 0–21 months.

judicious dip of his nose which enabled him to reproduce sonorities that were beyond the reach of his limited span (around a fifth on the standard-sized keyboard). In AO's view, while Derek's achievements up to that point were remarkable, particularly given his blindness and severe developmental delay, it was essential that he should come to accept the intervention of another, to guide his further musical development and realize his creative intent. However, Derek had never experienced anything approaching a conventional 'teacher–pupil' relationship, and he was not remotely inclined even to share *his* piano with anyone else, let alone engage in a structured learner–teacher dyad. Hence, a large part of AO's effort for the first six months of working with Derek was

directed towards showing him that interaction through music could be productive and, above all, enjoyable. Gradually, involving an initial degree of physical intervention, Derek did come to appreciate that discourse through the medium of musical improvisation was possible and could indeed be a source of great pleasure.

Engaging in social discourse through sound could not alone solve Derek's technical challenges, however, and a final stage in AO's early relationship with him was necessary, whereby Derek would allow AO to show him—physically—how to hold his hands and use his fingers in conventional patterns that would facilitate his technical development. Clearly, Derek had no concept of the goals that AO was pursuing, so it was critical that he enjoyed being guided

Derek develops his ability to play the keyboard with the awareness and encouragement of those around him

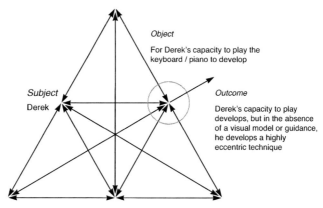

Mediating artefacts

- Derek's grandfather's little electric keyboard
- Subsequently, his father's Yamaha organ and a piano
- Tapes of music in a range of styles, including some that are chosen deliberately for him to emulate
- Nanny's singing
- Other music in the wider environment

Object
For Derek's capacity to play the keyboard / piano to develop

Subject
Derek

Outcome
Derek's capacity to play develops, but in the absence of a visual model or guidance, he develops a highly eccentric technique

Rules, assumptions, expectations and drivers

- There remain no formal rules of Derek's engagement with music, although the music he hears and reproduces is structured in a highly rule-bound way
- When they realise that he can play, people's assumptions about Derek change radically - though no-one understands how he is able to do what he does
- Gradually, expectations grow that Derek will be able to play on demand
- Derek becomes aware of these expectations and is motivated by the positive response his playing engenders and the expectations of those around him

Community
Family
Nanny
Friends

Division of labour

- Nanny provides Derek with a range of music to learn
- Derek learns to play pieces, purely through his own efforts
- Those around him provide the motivation through recognition of his achievements, which he enjoys

Fig. 29.3 Stage 2, 21–66 months.

through the daily ritual of technical exercises, scales and arpeggios that AO devised for him. Luckily, Derek relished the one-to-one attention and the orderliness of his practice routine, and the pattern of highly formalized intervention with AO continued throughout his childhood on a daily basis (Stage 3; Figure 29.4).

There is much to learn from Derek's story: most obviously, the fact that an individual can be motivated to pursue musical learning to a highly advanced level at an early age with no direct intervention or encouragement on the part of others, and with no global sense of moving towards the goal of becoming a competent performer (see also Ockelford 2008, Ockelford

et al. 2006). Beyond this, however, it is also the case that Derek, as someone with severe learning difficulties, could, initially through a discourse comprising nothing but musical sounds, develop a relatively conventional teacher–pupil relationship, that eventually enabled him as an adult to have a career as an internationally recognized musician.

Example two: supporting musical learning in higher education

Higher education (HE), on the other hand, is a relatively (often highly) selective educational environment that seeks to advance already competent

Derek and AO develop an unconventional though effective 'teacher-pupil' relationship that enables Derek to learn through verbal guidance and physical intervention

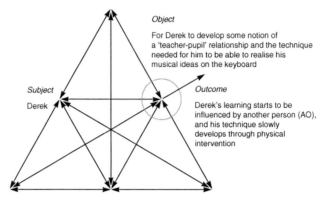

Mediating artefacts
- Derek's piano
- Weekly sessions with AO
- Teaching tapes, made by AO
- Daily sessions with Nanny, using the tapes, as reinforcement

Object

For Derek to develop some notion of a 'teacher-pupil' relationship and the technique needed for him to be able to realise his musical ideas on the keyboard

Subject

Derek

Outcome

Derek's learning starts to be influenced by another person (AO), and his technique slowly develops through physical intervention

Rules, assumptions, expectations and drivers

- AO tries to inculcate the ground rules of a teacher-pupil relationship by playing 'copy' games with Derek in sound, showing him that potentially this is a two-way thing: that discourse is possible through music
- Derek comes to enjoy the discourse, and comes to appreciate its reciprocity: accepting the influence of another through sound and realising that he can influence someone else
- Derek has enough awareness of the rules of teacher-pupil interaction to allow AO to guide him technically (necessary since Derek cannot see or understand what is required)

Community

AO
Nanny

Division of labour

- AO has sessions with Derek, at first allowing him to take the lead, showing him that a non-verbal discourse in sound is possible
- Derek increasingly allows AO to take the lead in that discourse
- AO physically guides Derek in the acquisition of technique through excercises, scales and arpeggios; something that continues for many years
- Derek accepts and comes to expect the guidance from AO
- Nanny continues to support between sessions

Fig. 29.4 Stage 3, from 66 months.

musical skill levels in young people who normally exhibit (or report) little or no disability (though see for example Lerner and Straus 2006).

Within the spectrum of HE in music, there are observable similarities and differences in the way that the activity of music learning is processed. These are particularly related to context, such as the age and gender of performers, their principal musical genre and the particular HE location. For example, an ongoing study of advanced music learning and teaching in four UK higher education institutions (HEIs) is investigating how classical, popular, jazz and Scottish traditional musicians deepen and develop their learning about performance in undergraduate, postgraduate and wider music community contexts (Welch *et al.* 2006). In the first year of the study, a specially designed, web-based questionnaire was used to survey 244 musicians across the four HEIs. In addition to demographic information, participants provided self-reports about their earliest engagement with music (including first instrumental or vocal lessons), secondary and tertiary education, as well as significant musical experiences and influences. The participants were questioned about the perceived relevance of a range of musical skills and activities, experience of performance and general life anxiety, how they spent their time in an average week, the pleasure that they derived from engagement in musical activities, various self-views (musical self-efficacy, self-esteem,

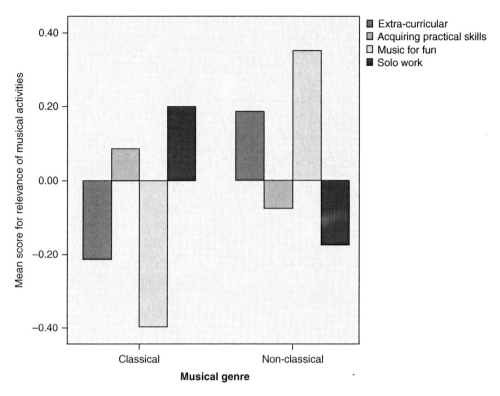

Fig. 29.5 Classical and other-than-classical-musicians' mean scores for categories of musical activities (*extra-curricular*: listening to music from own and outside of own genre, acquiring general musical knowledge, engaging in professional conversations, networking; *acquiring practical skills*: practising alone, practising with others, taking lessons, solo and group performance, listening to music from own genre; *music for fun*: playing for fun alone or with other; *solo work*: mental rehearsal, giving lessons, solo performance). (Creech *et al.* 2008, p223)

self-regulation), group membership and their beliefs about the nature of expertise in musical performance and teaching.

The resultant data analyses suggest that all musicians attached great importance to achieving a high overall standard of performance, although they had different perspectives on the processes by which this might be achieved (Creech *et al.* 2008). For example, in terms of the performance expectations of their particular musical 'community' and its requisite 'tools' and 'rules' (*pace* Engeström), classical musicians ranked the ability to improvise as the least important musical skill, but perceived sight-reading to be very important. In contrast, in relation to the performance expectations of *their* particular communities, the other-than-classical musicians (jazz, popular, Scottish traditional) tended to

assign the least importance to the ability to sight-read, but placed greater emphasis on playing from memory and improvisation. Although all musicians recognized the value of practice, the community of classical musicians tended to place greater emphasis on practising alone, whereas other-than-classical musicians attached greater relevance to making music for fun, networking and extra-curricular activities such as listening to a diverse range of musics and engaging in professional conversations with peers (see Figure 29.5). Nevertheless, both classical and other-than-classical groups considered musical expertise to involve the possession of global musical skills that could be transferred to other musical genres (Papageorgi *et al.* in press).

An exploration of underlying processes that might explain the similarities and differences between these two groups implicated both institutions (whether home, school or elsewhere) and teachers (including parents, private tutors and teachers in educational institutions). Other-than-classical musicians reported that they typically began to engage with music of any kind at a later age than their classical musician peers (non-classical: $\overline{X}$ = 8.4 years, classical: $\overline{X}$ = 6.6 years). Similarly, they began formal learning on their first instrument at a later age (non-classical: $\overline{X}$ = 12 years, classical: $\overline{X}$ = 8.8 years). Notwithstanding the nature of their early musical experiences, all the participant musicians, irrespective of genre, were able to achieve the requisite baseline skill levels for entry to higher education and beyond. Nevertheless, contexts were not identical. Classical musicians reported that their most important musical influences (past and present) were parents, instrumental/vocal teachers, significant musical events, professional colleagues and previous membership of county (regional) music ensembles. In contrast, other-than-classical musicians claimed to be particularly influenced by well-known performers, as well as university or college lecturers and informal groups of friends (Creech *et al.* 2007). Across all musicians, irrespective of genre, higher education tutors, whether lecturers in particular aspects of music or specialist solo instrumental and vocal teachers, were reported to be significant agents in a communal process of advanced music learning.

Overall, participant classical musicians rated themselves higher in terms of perceived musical expertise. The basis for this difference is likely to relate to (1) the comparative longevity of classical musical cultures in HE, (2) other aspects of participants' group-based self-views and (3) differences in participants' cumulative years of study. For example, interviews with senior academics in the participant HEIs revealed that:

1 Classical music had been established for much longer in their academic programmes compared to the three selected other-than-classical genres (jazz, popular and Scottish traditional). Concomitantly, classical music teaching and learning and assessment practices were reported to be more firmly embedded, rehearsed, formalized and understood within their particular communities;

2 It may be that (as reported earlier) other-than-classical musicians have idealized views of expertise that relate to how they see themselves in comparison to the individual quality of star performers in their chosen genre rather than some more generic HE measure of performance;

3 It is also the case that the participant musicians in other-than-classical genres typically begin to engage with music at a later age and, as a consequence, were more likely to have expert role models from outside their peers and teachers, having had relatively less time to be immersed in their musical genre.

As an example of differences *within* a musical genre in relation to age and experience, the same data set suggests that portfolio career classical musicians who engage in both performance and teaching are more likely to be able to identify successful teaching strategies than their younger, undergraduate peers. Furthermore, the activity of teaching, allied to extensive solo performance experiences, are likely to reduce levels of performance anxiety.

Example three: supporting female music learning in a UK cathedral setting

Male choristers have participated in UK cathedrals since their inception in 597AD at Canterbury. In comparison, it was not until 1991 that Salisbury became the first old cathedral foundation to admit girls on the same basis as boys. The political impact and success of their initiative (although foreshadowed by other religious institutions earlier in the twentieth century but without the same publicity) has led to a growing (sometimes grudging) acceptance of female choristers within the previously all-male culture. By 2006, a majority of cathedrals had choristers of both sexes for the first time in their long history, even though it continues to be relatively rare for the two sexes to sing together, other than at special festival events (Welch 2007).

One of the cited reasons for the longevity of the all-male cathedral music tradition was that young females were regarded as being unable to sing with the same 'pure' quality of vocal timbre demonstrated by the young male voice in the performance of the cathedral sacred music repertoire. This belief does have some basis in the physical realities of child voice acoustics, even though research has demonstrated its fallibility. First, there are slight differences in the relative sizes of girls' and boys' vocal anatomy, the male being slightly larger throughout childhood and into adolescence (cf. Welch and Howard 2002) and these could be expected to generate perceptible disparities in acoustic outputs. Secondly, with regard to untrained children's voices, there is increasingly perceptible psycho-acoustic differentiation between the sexes as they progress through childhood (Sergeant *et al.* 2005; Sergeant and Welch in press), with observable gender-related differences in their sung spectra. However, the power of the musical activity system in the cathedral is such that formal induction of girls into its performance expectations

can generate changes in their basic vocal behaviour such that any gender differences are reduced significantly and often become imperceptible. A series of perceptual studies from the mid 1990s onwards has demonstrated that membership of a cathedral choir can allow girls to be trained to produce sounds that are 'boy-like' in character in order to match the customary, male-biased, performance expectations of the musical repertoire (Sergeant and Welch 1997; Howard and Welch 2002; Welch 2006; Welch and Howard 2002).

Detailed longitudinal case study data from one cathedral suggests that the activity of becoming a female chorister is closely linked to the customary tripartite relationship in music (Small 1999) between the physical setting, people (performers and listeners) and the way that the musical soundscape constrains the variety

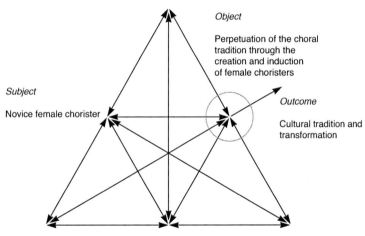

Mediating artefacts

- Rehearsal practices (Undercroft, Nave)
- Nature and structure of cathedral services
- Artefacts and discourse of sacred music
- Acoustic environment
- Choral sound of senior choristers

Object

Perpetuation of the choral tradition through the creation and induction of female choristers

Subject

Novice female chorister

Outcome

Cultural tradition and transformation

Rules, assumptions, expectations and drivers

- Rules for membership of choir
- Sung performances
- Cathedral worship
- Regulated pattern of the extended day (practice, school, rehearsal, performance)

Community

Cathedral communities (within the cathedral and across cathedrals—clerical, musical, voluntary, worshippers, tourists)

Division of labour

- Hierarchical roles within choir (musical and non-musical)
- Performance practices (group, solo, sides—Decani, Cantoris)
- Boys, girls, men
- Organist and Deputy roles

Fig. 29.6 An example of the activity system that frames the development of the novice (female) cathedral chorister (Welch 2007, p. 29).

of possible musical outcomes. The induction process for both young males and females involves the novice chorister (probationer) being required to learn, practise, rehearse and perform music systematically many times each week across the school and ecclesiastical year, whilst standing between and listening to the vocal models of established senior performers (head chorister, deputy head chorister, senior corner girls), supported by group-based (communal) teaching by a highly experienced church musician (organist and choir director or deputy), in order to master a ritualized repertoire (such as the *Introit*, *Psalms*, *Response Settings* and *Anthem* for Evensong) that involves both choral and solo performance: see Figure 29.6 for how this experience can be framed within an activity system (Welch 2007).

The acoustic features of the rehearsal and performance spaces within the chancel and choir of the cathedral also shape the learning experience, with features of the choristers' sound amplified by the high stone vaulting of the nave and adjacent spaces and fed back to the performers. The collective and ritual nature of the performance is reinforced by the addition of adult male voices (for most services) and the organ. It is not surprising, therefore, that females are able to perform the established religious repertoire in customary fashion, given the interrelated expectations of the musical learning process and the longevity of the performance practices within the culture that are handed down across generations of cathedral musicians (and where it is extremely rare for a new director to be appointed from outside the tradition).

Example four: supporting music learning in the lower secondary school

In contrast to the above, it is possible that institutions and teachers can also hinder as well as support learning in music. For example, notwithstanding recent improvements in the quality of music education across all four curriculum 'stages' in English schools, embracing the ages 5–16 (Welch 2006b), there is often a particular disparity in the individual experiences of pupils in the lower secondary school (ages 12–14). Although the independent school inspection

body, OfSTED,[1] has reported a steady improvement in lower secondary school music teaching since 2001, the overall quality in the other school age phases (both older and younger) has often been reported as higher. The reasons for these systematic differences are likely to relate to:

1 The organization of the timetable in primary schools where one class teacher tends to take all curriculum subjects and, therefore, is in a better position to know each individual child across a school year and to match music teaching to individual need,

2 English National Curriculum music learning expectations of primary school children are lower (in terms of the complexity of musical behaviours) than in secondary schools; this may encourage more positive judgements from school inspectors (who are themselves unlikely to be primary music specialists);

3 Upper secondary school music (ages 14–16) is optional, catering for a small minority of pupils (between 7–9 per cent) who have opted to study music for a further two years to examination at age 16; and

4 Lower secondary school music is compulsory for all pupils—a period of intense personal development in their musical identity (Tarrant *et al.* 2002).

Nevertheless, some secondary schools have been able to counter this trend, even in contexts where 'success' in school examinations may not be the norm. For example, a recent analysis of data from secondary schools in one part of inner London with a high Black African-Caribbean (BAC) population found that up to 62% of such pupils were opting to study music (with an average across schools of 24%). This was much higher than the non-BAC groups in the same schools (average 8%) (Spence 2006). Furthermore, these pupils went on to achieve higher grades in their 16+ examinations for music than in their other

---

[1] The Office for Standards in Education (OfSTED) assesses the quality of music teaching on behalf of the Government. This is a non-ministerial Government department that reports directly to the UK Parliament. OfSTED is headed by a senior civil servant and is required to inspect and report on the quality of education in schools and in initial teacher education.

subjects, such as English, mathematics and science. A recurrent theme from interviews with these young people was that lesson content had greater enjoyment when it drew on music that they knew, liked and/or could play. They also reported greater liking of teachers who showed respect for them and their music. Such positive emotional engagement appears to be reflected in their relative success in school music.

Further insights in why some young people are 'successful' at school music and some are not are reported in a study of lower secondary school music (Saunders 2006). Pupils in the final year of compulsory music education in England (Year 9, age 13+) have to make a decision about whether or not to continue their school music studies. Coding and analyses of the transcripts of interviews with 44 pupils in one school revealed that pupils tended to see themselves in one of five categories (see Table 29.1).

Only one of the five groups is fully engaged with school music (termed the 'traditional Western musician'), in part because of their formal instrumental performance skills and an ability to identify successfully with the content of the school music curriculum. However, four other groups of pupils have alternative, less positive perspectives. Some see themselves as non-musicians; some have self-taught instrumental skills, but do not identify with school music, even though they are accomplished musicians ('alternative Western musician'); some are accomplished musicians in a traditional sense, but believe that school music is irrelevant and a possible threat to their musician status ('disengaged traditional Western musician'); and some find that the mismatch between their musical skills and the skills needed for the school curriculum is intimidating to their self-concept as a musician ('disengaged alternative Western

Table 29.1 Pupils' self-identified grouping related to classroom music in Year 9 (age 13+) of lower secondary school

Pupil identity related to school music	Example key characteristics
Traditional Western musician	Strong engagement with all music; good family support
	Successful experience of formal learning of an instrument
	Peer group status as a 'musician'
Western non-musician	Strong engagement with music outside school; limited family support
	Limited instrumental skill; immediate peer group do not identify with school music; peer group recognition as a 'non' musician
Alternative Western musician	Strong engagement with all music; family support
	Informally/self-taught instrumental skills; school music seen as irrelevant; peer group status as a 'musician'
Disengaged traditional Western musician	Strong engagement with music outside school
	Formally taught instrumental skills, family support variable
	Peer group do not identify with school music
	Music curriculum seen as a 'threat' to musician status within peer group
Disengaged alternative Western musician	Strong engagement with music outside school
	Informally or self-taught instrumental skills; family support limited
	Peer group share counter culture of musical identity
	'Musician' status threatened by lack of success

musician'). When interviewed, a significant number of young people consider themselves (wrongly) to be unsuitable for continuing music studies. Yet virtually all connect successfully with music outside school, as consumers, listeners, and/or practitioners. Unless pupils identify and find success with school music (e.g. Spence 2006), they are likely to disengage. Subsequent research and analyses of pupil interviews in three other schools has confirmed these findings (Saunders 2008). Comments from individual pupils demonstrate the kinds of diversity in their experiences of music in school:

It's my favourite lesson of the whole week and well, I wish we could do a bit more of it really.

I think the stuff at lunchtimes and for the shows is really good, but that lessons aren't anywhere near as exciting as that. I suppose that's because we can't all sing and play like them though.

Music at school is pants; it's just not any good. It's all duff music. I mean, who listens to this stuff?

I'm learning from my brother and his mate taught him, so when we get together, it's a bit scrappy, but we're getting better. I don't do it that much in class cos Miss wants us working on the keyboards and I'm not great at that.

Collectively, these comments illustrate the underlying positive connection that these young people have with music, although not necessarily the kinds of music (and musical practices) found in school. Adolescence is a period characterized by the emergence of strong musical identities (Zillman and Gan 1997), often with a clear perception of boundaries between different musics as young people use music to negotiate positions for themselves within their group identities (O'Neill and Green 2001). It is not surprising, therefore, that school music has such a mixed reception during this age phase.

Conclusion

Overall, the various examples cited above are an indication of how learning and teaching in music are shaped by processes outside the individual, not least because of the influences of group membership (allied to age and gender), performance expectations and practices, and professional and institutional cultures. The process of individual induction into the characteristics of a particular musical culture by teachers and institutions influences the formation of identities in music (cf. MacDonald *et al.* 2002), for better or for worse, at least in terms of dominant models within the culture. Indeed, the development of music teachers themselves can be seen within an activity system, i.e. the teacher's understanding of their role is developed both by informal personal reflection of the experience of performance and their own learning and, more systematically, through their own induction process by attendance at a specialist pedagogically focused institution.

References

Agawu K (1995). *African rhythm*. Cambridge University Press, Cambridge.

Bannon L (1997). *Activity theory*. Retrieved 24 October 2005 from http://wwwsv.cict.fr/cotcos/pjs/TheoreticalApproaches/Actvity/ActivitypaperBannon.htm

Bronfenbrenner U (1979). *The ecology of human development: experiments by nature and design*. Harvard University Press, Cambridge, MA.

Cole M (1999). Cultural psychology: some general principles and a concrete example. In Y Engeström, R Miettinen and R-L Punamäki, eds, *Perspectives on activity theory*, 87–106. Cambridge University Press, Cambridge.

Creech A, Papageorgi I, Duffy C, Morton F, Haddon L, Potter J, de Bézenac C, Whyton T, Himonides E and Welch GF (2008). Investigating musical performance: commonality and diversity amongst classical and other-than-classical musicians. *Music Education Research*, **10**(2), 215–234.

Doubleday V and Baily J (1995). Patterns of musical development among children in Afghanistan. In EJ Fernea, ed., *Children in the muslim Middle East*, 431–444. University of Texas Press, Austin, TX.

Engeström Y (1999). Activity theory and individual and social transformation. In Y Engeström, R Miettinen, R-L Punamäki, eds, *Perspectives on activity theory*, 19–38. Cambridge University Press, Cambridge.

Engeström Y (2001). *Expansive learning at work: toward an activity-theoretical reconceptualisation. With a commentary by Michael Young*. Learning Group, Occasional Paper No 1. Institute of Education, London.

Farrell G (1997). *Indian music and the West*. Clarendon Press, Oxford.

Farrell G (2001). India. In DJ Hargreaves and AC North, eds, *Musical development and learning: the international perspective*, 56–72. Continuum, London.

Green L (2001). *How popular musicians learn*. Ashgate, Aldershot.

Hallam S and Lamont A (2004). Learners: their characteristics and development. *Psychology of Music*, **32**(3), 243–252.

Howard DM and Welch GF (2002). Female chorister development: a longitudinal study at Wells, UK. *Bulletin of the Council for Research in Music Education*, **153**(4), 63–70.

Jones S (1995). *Folk music of China: living instrumental traditions*. Clarendon Press, Oxford.

Lerner N and Straus JN (eds) (2006). *Sounding off: theorizing disability in music*. Routledge, New York.

Mcnab PA (1970). *The Isle of Mull*. (David and Charles), Newton Abbot.

MacDonald R, Hargreaves DJ and Miell D (eds) (2002). *Musical identities*. Oxford University Press, Oxford.

Murao T and Wilkins B (2001). Japan. In DJ Hargreaves, AC North, eds, *Musical development and learning: the international perspective*, 87–101. Continuum, London.

Ockelford A (2007). *In the key of genius: the extraordinary life of Derek Paravicini*. Hutchinson, London.

Ockelford A (2008). *Music for children and young people with complex needs*. Oxford University Press, Oxford.

Ockelford A, Pring L, Welch GF and Treffert D (2006). *Focus on music: exploring the musical interests and abilities of blind and partially-sighted children with septo-optic dysplasia*. Institute of Education/RNIB, London.

O'Neill S and Green L (2001). Social groups and learning in music education. In BERA Music Education Review Group, *Mapping music education research in the UK*, 26–31. British Educational Research Association, Macclesfield.

Papageorgi I, Creech A, Duffy C, Potter J, Whyton T, Morton F, Haddon L, de Bézenac C, Himonides E and Welch GF (in press). Investigating musical performance: the development and prediction of expertise in advanced musical learners. *Psychology of Music*.

Ryder M (2005) *What is activity theory?* Retrieved 24 October 2005 from http://carbon.cudenver.edu/~mryder/itc_data/act_dff.html.

Saunders J (2006). Music learning in year 9: the pupils' perspective. *NAME Magazine*, **18**, 9–11.

Saunders J (2008). The music classroom: pupil experience and engagement during adolescence. Unpublished PhD thesis. Institute of Education, University of London, London.

Sergeant DC, Sjölander PJ and Welch GF (2005). Listeners' identification of gender differences in children's singing. *Research Studies in Music Education*, **24**, 28–39.

Sergeant DC and Welch GF (1997). Perceived similarities and differences in the singing of trained children's choirs. *Choir Schools Today*, **11**, 9–10.

Sergeant DC and Welch GF (in press). Age-related changes in long-term average spectra of children's voices. *Journal of Voice*. Published online July 2007, available at: http://www.jvoice.org.inpress.

Small C (1999). Musicking—the meanings of performing and listening. A lecture. *Music Education Research*, **1**(1), 9–21.

Spence S (2006). Black Caribbean children and school music: expectation and achievement. *NAME Magazine*, **18**, 12–15.

Tarrant M, North AC and Hargreaves DJ (2002). Youth identity and music. In R MacDonald, DJ Hargreaves and D Miell, eds, *Musical identities*, 134–150. Oxford University Press, Oxford.

Welch GF (2006a). The musical development and education of young children. In B Spodek, O Saracho, eds, *Handbook of research on the education of young children*, 251–267. Lawrence Erlbaum Associates Inc., Mahwah, NJ.

Welch GF (2006b). What research into music teacher education tells us about the contexts and challenges for teacher education. *Proceedings, Beijing International Forum on Music Education* 2006, 84–97. 15–17 May, Beijing: NAMM/CSME/ISME/CNU. [Chinese version, 98–113.]

Welch GF (2006c). Singing and vocal development. In G McPherson, ed., *The child as musician: a handbook of musical development*, 311–329. Oxford University Press, Oxford.

Welch GF (2007). Addressing the multifaceted nature of music education: an activity theory research perspective. *Research Studies in Music Education*, **28**, 23–38.

Welch GF, Duffy C, Potter J and Whyton T (2006). *Investigating musical performance (IMP): comparative studies in advanced musical learning*. Institute of Education, University of London, funded by the ESRC/TLRP, grant reference RES-139–25–0258. http://www.tlrp.org/proj/Welch.html.

Welch GF and Howard DM (2002). Gendered voice in the cathedral choir. *Psychology of Music*, **30**, 102–120.

Welch GF, Ockelford A, Zimmermann S-A, Carter F-C and Himonides E (2006). Sounds of intent: initial mapping of musical behaviours and development in profoundly disabled children. In M Baroni, AR Addessi, R Caterina and M Costa, eds, *Proceedings, 9th International Conference on Music Perception and Cognition*, 274–275. Bologna University Press, University of Bologna, Bologna.

Welch GF, Ockelford A, Carter F-C, Zimmermann S-A and Himonides E (in press). Sounds of intent: mapping musical behaviour and development in children and young people with complex needs. *Psychology of Music*.

von Bertalanffy L (1968) *General system theory: foundations, development, applications*. George Braziller, New York.

Zillman D and Gan S (1997). Musical taste in adolescence. In DJ Hargreaves and AC North, eds, *The social psychology of music*, 161–187. Oxford University Press, Oxford.

PART 7

Musical performance

Edited by Richard Parncutt

CHAPTER 30

Measurement and models of performance

W. Luke Windsor

Introduction

Rationale and overview

This chapter describes and evaluates the ways in which both the measurement and modelling of performances have contributed to the emerging discipline of music psychology. What is intended is a tutorial guide covering major issues, techniques and findings in this area, along with enough context and exemplification to meet this end. Therefore, only a representative sample of references to the literature will be made, and although it is hoped that the chapter might serve as a bibliographical starting point for the researcher, apologies are made in advance for any omissions of literature that might have been central to another's view of this field. Moreover, although the discriminability of measured changes in expressive parameters is an important issue for music psychology this chapter must restrict itself to consideration of measurements themselves, and direct comparisons between such measurements and the predictions made by models.

Measuring performance

Hardware for measuring performances

Mechanical devices for measurement

It is not until the invention of the Piano Camera and its application to a psychology of performance by Seashore and colleagues (see Seashore 1938) that an accurate manner of registering the action of piano keys and pedals in relation to both timing and velocity was obtained. Shaffer, who published a number of studies of music performance in the early 1980s (see e.g., Shaffer 1981, 1984; Shaffer et al. 1985), used a modified grand piano using photo-electric cells to register the movement of the hammers. The development of a number of commercial MIDI compatible grand and upright pianos which also utilize photocells has meant that specialist instrumentation is no longer needed for such research. Although the only study (Goebl and Bresin 2003) which addresses recording accuracy on recent Yamaha and Bosendorfer pianos finds considerable evidence for timing errors (especially for the Yamaha instrument) many of the errors are smaller than the errors associated with MIDI itself. However, if exceptionally fine-grained timing microstructure in performance is an issue for the researcher care must be taken to ensure that such recording inaccuracy is not, for example, mistaken for performance variance: some of the errors measured by Goebl and Bresin were five times larger than the errors one might expect from MIDI transmission of data.

Movement and physiological transduction

Recent published work on body movement in performance (and its control) has begun to demand and apply sophisticated techniques that measure and analyse bodily or instrumental movement (see e.g., Askenfelt 1986; Clarke and Davidson 1998; Wanderley and Vines 2006), muscular activity (see e.g. Fjellman-Wiklund et al. 2004a, b), or even electrical activity in the central or peripheral nervous system (see e.g., Kelso *et al.* 1992).

Acoustic instrumentation

Hardware for the acquisition and digitization of sound is available within most computer architectures, either off the shelf, or using third-party solutions. Given that analysing representations of the acoustic wave form of sounds allows for the analysis of timing, intensity, frequency and derivatives of these parameters (such as spectral envelope) is potentially of interest to anyone researching the psychology of performance who wishes to eschew keyboard instruments as data sources, and for the analysis of acoustic recordings of historical interest, such hardware is a vital resource. Moreover, although it may create other measurement issues, it avoids the potentially distorting influence of mechanical measurement.

Software and techniques for measuring and analysing performances

The main purposes of computer software in this context are to (1) transform and record measurements into a particular numerical form, (2) convert between different data formats, (3) apply mathematical functions to deliver visual, numerical or statistical analyses of a data set. To illustrate different software solutions (and demonstrate how they are designed to integrate with hardware choices and particular research questions) two examples will be offered. Whilst not intended as comprehensive, these will give some indications of the range of issues faced when choosing measurement and analysis software.

The first example measures timing and dynamics in commercial recordings of piano performance (Repp 1998, 1999). The main research questions addressed here are what features of inter-onset timing and dynamic variation are shared between performances of the same piece, and how these vary between individual performers, groups of performers and whether sociocultural factors account for this variance. Repp's measurement approach here is fairly direct: the timing of onsets was obtained through the 'visual and auditory cues' provided by a commercial wave form editor. Where there

were performance asynchronies (as in chordal events) the onset of the highest pitch was chosen (Repp 1998). Although a partly perceptual measure, this is in direct contrast to some musicological studies of tempo variability (such as Bowen 1996) which involve analysis of the researcher's finger taps at the beat or bar level (indeed there are no psychological studies which use this approach, perhaps because it may suffer from any number of known of unknown perceptuomotor biases or inaccuracies). Neither does Repp utilize automated or semi-automated onset detection software such as that developed by Moelants and Rampazzo (1997) or Dixon (2001), which other researchers have found useful when analysing timing in audio recordings (see e.g., Moelants 2000). For dynamics, measurements of peak sound level in dB were obtained using the automatic peak-picking function in the Signalyze program, using the prior analysis of timing as a guide. Repp then uses a combination of general spreadsheet and statistical software to organize, display and analyse these measurements, converting onset times into inter-onset intervals, and applying standard statistical techniques such as principle components analysis (to identify a small number of common traits), and correlation or analysis of variance (to test whether these vary with the chosen sociocultural variables).

The second example (Windsor *et al.* 2006) analyses inter-onset timing in a dataset of MIDI encoded piano performances, provided at a single sitting by an expert pianist. Here, the extraction of onset timings was achieved by a Yamaha Disklavier, which was connected to a computer running a commercial sequencer package. These MIDI files were converted into a textual format with time expressed in seconds, and were annotated with structural information (such as the beginnings and endings of bars and phrases at different hierarchical levels) in order that the onset timing could be modelled, using the POCO performance research environment (see Honing 1990). Statistical techniques were applied to fit the timing data optimally to the musical structure using a third-party add-on to POCO (SAPA) which shared the same LISP programming environment, and a commercial statistics package was used to display the results in tabular and graphical form.

Future developments in analysis techniques in the form of functional data analysis of time-varying parameters, which might include measurements of body movement and tempo, might offer useful opportunities to relate such continuous time-varying measures to each other (see e.g., Vines *et al.* 2005, 2006). Such techniques can be applied where sampling rates in the two domains to be compared are unrelated, or where one wishes to compare measurements taken from performances with different global tempi.

Analytical methods and discoveries

Psychological studies of performance that derive from measurements exhibit a strong bias towards the measurement and analysis of onset timing. Dynamic variation has also been studied fairly extensively, but perhaps because of the relative ease with which onset times can be derived from performances, most studies are happy to focus on one or more aspects of timing. It is also the case that despite some attempts to model the relationship between parameters such as timing and dynamics (see e.g., Todd 1992) the relationship between the different variables that make up a performance is still little understood (although see Sloboda 1983; Drake and Palmer 1993).

Contributions of measurement to a psychology of performance

Motor programming

Music provides a rich context for studying the control of timing: the performer must often follow instructions from a score or match their movements to a co-performer (or ensemble), and the timing of their actions must be rhythmically organized to reflect the musical structure. The main observation in relation to timing control in music performance is that a serial timekeeper mechanism controls the production of fine-grained units in performance, whereas the timing of larger hierarchical units may be continuously modulated by a rate parameter (Shaffer *et al.* 1985; Vorberg and Wing 1996). These directly controlled units are often argued to be at the beat level in the metrical hierarchy: Shaffer (e.g. 1981, 1984) applied covariance

analysis at different hierarchical levels (note, beat, bar) to attempt to identify negatively covarying intervals. Although such analyses normally rely on stationary time-series and may be distorted by drift or systematic tempo changes—which is often removed (Vorberg and Wing 1996, pp. 197–199) which are present in musical performances of this kind, Palmer (1997, p. 130) concludes that such results 'suggest that temporal precision in performance is influenced by the structure of the sequence—in particular, the salience of the beat level or tactus'.

The next issue that arises from this is how such a timing mechanism interacts with the actual events to be performed. The theory of motor programming (see e.g., Schmidt 1985; Gentner 1987) suggests that in a musical context an individual performance is derived from a mental representation of sequence of actions, often organized hierarchically: if one adds to this (as in Shaffer *et al.* 1985) the concept of a controlling internal timekeeper one has a recipe for generating an infinite number of performances from a single motor programme, with the timing of one hierarchical level directly controlled. Given that it is clear that performances by the same performer are surprisingly consistent in timing microstructure (see e.g., Gabrielsson 1987), even when recorded at different times (see e.g. Shaffer 1984; Clynes and Walker 1986), can show remarkable durational similarity, and that patterns of expressive timing reflect the hierarchical metrical and phrase structure of the music (see e.g. Shaffer 1981; Clarke 1988; Palmer 1989), it has become common to assume that for memorized performance at least, each performance given by an individual is related to a common motor programme, and that such motor programmes are structured in such a way as to reflect musical concerns. One theoretical question this raises is the extent to which such programmes are invariant given different overall rates (or global tempi). Deviations from proportional invariance are widely observed (Clarke 1982; MacKenzie and van Eerd 1990; Desain and Honing 1994; Windsor *et al.* 2001; Timmers *et al.* 2002; Repp *et al.* 2002; Windsor *et al.* 2006), and may reflect changes in perceptual or rhythmic grouping at different tempi or failures to transfer learning across tempi (Palmer 1997).

Coordination: within and between performers

Although there is an unfortunate concentration on solo performance in the music–psychological literature, there is a growing body of empirical data which relates to the psychological processes governing within- and between-performer coordination. Evidence from studies of chord asynchrony (see e.g. Rasch 1988; Shaffer 1984; Palmer 1989) shows that melody lead is widespread, again providing evidence that timing in music performance is governed by structural understanding.

Shaffer (1984) argued that synchronization in expert ensemble performance is not achieved by coordinating actions at the level of individual events or even the lowest level of nominal isochrony (beat) or tactus, but at the level of the bar. His data certainly suggest that timing control, whether in a solo or ensemble situation, is most clearly observable at these intermediate structural levels. He (1984) argues that just as a single pianist may coordinate two separate time-keepers for each hand using a single motor programme, so too may two or more performers integrate their performance using such a shared plan. It is also further evidence that musical structures and expressive strategies are formally linked: being able to predict patterns of timing relies on a shared conception not only of musical structure but on the resulting interpretative decisions.

Rhythm and timing

It has long been observed that musical performances of notated scores do not preserve their canonic durations (Seashore 1938), and there are a number of hypotheses that claim to explain this discrepancy. Some researchers explain such deviations from the metronome as expressive, either of underlying musical structures (Clarke 1988) or of extra-musical content (such as emotion or mood) (see e.g., Palmer 1989; Juslin and Madison 1999). Others attempt to show that many such deviations are the result of compensation for perceptual biases or due to motor noise (Penel and Drake 1998). Even simple rhythmic patterns are not performed metronomically, with adjacent intervals exhibiting assimilation (such that intervals are played

more equal than they are notated) or contrast (such that similar intervals are made more different) and also context-dependent effects relative to the position of long and short intervals within a sequence and the number of events to be performed (Gabrielsson 1974; Repp et al. 2002). Interestingly, the latter of these two studies (which partly confirms earlier work by Fraisse (1956) shows that in a musical context, three note rhythms are rather unlike two note rhythms in that the patterns of assimilation change with tempo, and these changes bring increasing ratio-simplification of the two long-er intervals (and little change to the shorter interval).

Expression, communication and signification

The deviations from nominal score durations (and from small whole number ratios) evident in measurements of performances, along with patterns of dynamics, timbre and vibrato, have suggested that performers may be using such means to express, communicate or signify either intra-musical or extra-musical content. Such an approach is best exemplified by Palmer (1989) and the work of Shaffer, Clarke and Todd (see above). Within this perspective it is possible to find in the literature copious examples of measurements which suggest rule-following expressive behaviour. Expressive timing and dynamics seem to be linked to phrase and metrical structure in predictable ways: many studies (see Clarke 1988; Palmer 1997; Clarke 1999; Gabrielsson 1999 for reviews) have argued on the basis of empirical evidence that the location, and extent of deviations from metronomic performance can be predicted from analyses of phrase structure, metrical structure and voice prominence: hence, it has become accepted that such features may be generative in nature, mapping structural features through a system of rules onto patterns of articulation, rubato, and the like.

Such a generalizing tendency begs the question of the extent to which performances differ, and the underlying reasons for these differences. It is clear that different structural interpretations or intended moods or emotions leads to different performance outcomes, and this is observed in work on emotion (Juslin 2000) as it is in work which varies structural interpretation (such as Clarke 1988; Palmer 1989; Clarke and Windsor 2000). This is precisely what a generative rule-based explanation of expression in performance would predict. However, large-scale comparison of multiple performances of the same music (e.g., Repp 1998, 1999) suggests that even where performers may share a structural interpretation (and leaving aside differences in intended characterization) there may be significant differences between performers which are as yet hard to explain in any formal manner. Using principal components analysis, Repp here identifies traits in interpretation that suggest different strategies in relation to the same musical structure. It is clear that here is another way in which performers can choose to differ from one another. Precisely how such choices are made is little understood, although work which looks at the development of performances in a more longitudinal manner (such as Chaffin and Imreh 2002) might help deliver some answers.

Algorithmic and statistical modelling of performance

Hypothesis testing and simulation

Models of performance fall into two main categories by motivation: either they seek to test a hypothesis about behaviour, or they seek to simulate that behaviour. As Desain *et al.* (1998) argue, it is possible to fit the output of models with very different assumptions to the same data, and it may be necessary to pay close attention to the architecture of the individual models to judge whether they can be distinguished in terms of their psychological veracity. Moreover, as Honing (2006) demonstrates persuasively, models that fit data well do not always tell us more about the behaviour modelled: they may fit trivial aspects of the data precisely because they do not account for important features in the data which are hard to model. Honing gives two additional criteria to goodness of fit: *simplicity* and *surprise*, arguing that whereas some models will over-generalize to all sorts of behaviour, some will only fit a narrow range of behaviour and are therefore a priori better as they are more falsifiable.

Data-driven and theory-driven simulation

Whereas Gabrielsson (1999, pp. 550–557) distinguishes between models based on measurements and models based in intuitions, it is perhaps more useful here to propose a methodological distinction between data-driven and theory-driven simulations of human data (or a continuum, given that models nay combine the two approaches). Although the one example he gives of a model based on measurements (Todd 1985, 1989, 1992, 1995; see also Windsor and Clarke 1997; Clarke and Windsor 2000) was partly based on measurements it is more accurate to suggest that this is a theory-driven model which was then compared and refined through comparison with measurements of human performances. The model is actually driven by an extremely rigid application of a generative understanding of music performance. Similarly theoretically driven, although based on a rather loose set of intuitions (based largely on informal empirical investigation characterized as 'analysis by synthesis') is the model developed by Friberg and others (see e.g. Friberg 1991; Sundberg 1988).

The alternative to starting from rule-like algorithmic approaches which are then tested against data is to take measurements and to attempt to fit them to hypotheses using statistical means. This is the approach taken by Palmer (e.g. 1989) where hypotheses about the effects of musical structure and performance intentions on rubato, asynchrony and dynamics are tested using standard linear modelling techniques familiar to experimental psychology. Such approaches (based as they are on small numbers of performers and one or two pieces) may present problems of generalization, and do not require the researcher to make specific predictions about the precise effect that, for example, voicing has on asynchrony.

Performance modelling: psychological relevance

In this final subsection on modelling an attempt will be made to evaluate the extent to which such models not only capture general principles of performance, but also whether their architecture in any way represents psychologically plausible processes (see Desain *et al.* 1998). To this end, four examples will be reviewed briefly. Unfortunately, space does not allow for detailed consideration of the performance modelling approaches taken by Clynes (Clynes 1983) nor that of Mazzola and colleagues (Mazzola 2002): both share some features with one or more of the approaches described below, and are important contributions in their own right.

The first model considered here is most commonly know as *Director Musices*, and has been described in detail in many publications (see e.g. Sundberg 1988; Friberg 1991). Interestingly, just as Todd's approach (e.g., 1992 and see above) both benefits from and is limited by its theoretical simplicity, its ad hoc construction is probably closer to psychological reality than many more systematic models. It is clear that performers combine many different expressive strategies in a performance (see e.g., Palmer, 1989) and that these are often independent (Repp 1999). Nonetheless, such diverse rules make evaluation of the model as a whole, or its independent parameters, extremely tricky, although it has been fit to real performance data with some success (see e.g. Sundberg *et al.* 2003; Zanon and de Poli 2003a, b; Widmer and Goebl 2004). The recent attempt to complement the generative rules in *Director Musices* with models of various types of noise, emotional intent and physical motion (Juslin *et al.* 2002) may indeed make this problem even more pronounced (Widmer and Goebl 2004, p. 206).

Although there have been some successful attempts to fit the different versions of Todd's generative model to actual data (e.g. Todd 1989), 1992) and other more equivocal results (Windsor and Clarke 1997; Clarke and Windsor 2000; see also Widmer and Goebl 2004), Todd's admission in later work that two different models of tempo change might be required for the model to fit different rubato depths (Todd 1995 rather weakens this model's elegance and explanatory power. The model, especially in its earliest form, is an extremely powerful example of how to translate psychologically plausible theories into a coherent algorithm. This model takes a small number of assumptions (about the representation of musical structure and the mapping of structure to expression) which relate well to empirical and theoretical ideas of the time.

Widmer and Tobudic (2003) combine some aspects of curve-fitting, which are similar to Todd's approach, to machine-learning techniques. Widmer and Goebl (2004) suggest that this is a way of combining 'local timing and dynamic deviations' with tempo and dynamic curves associated with phrasing. Such an approach is elegant and clearly effective in terms of fitting real data, accounting for these different levels and types of expression, and doing so without excessive numbers of parameters. Instead it adapts to a training set of performances using fitting and machine-learning. Both of these features make this questionable as a psychologically plausible model, although the rules that it discovers may reflect or describe the outcomes of underlying psychological processes. Hence, this model reflects its background in artificial intelligence (AI), where the outcomes may offer more in terms of the development of machine simulation than they do to the realm of psychology.

Such potential problems are also evident for the final and most recent model to be considered, described in Windsor *et al.* (2006). However, here it is an analytical bias that is evident. The overall degree of fit achieved is high, but the authors focus on the way in which the fitting technique decomposes a complex time-series into different components, and how this can be used to answer empirical questions related to proportional invariance over tempo. The model itself might have some degree of psychological plausibility, but only if the components have an independence in the motor or memory systems of the performer, and it is not at present clear how this might be assessed. In conclusion, this approach, although it looks on the surface to resemble that of Todd, is much closer to the approaches taken in standard statistical testing in experimental psychology.

Measurement and modelling of performance in context

Psychological work on performance such as that described above has had little impact on research and practice within the field of music. Where measurement of performance is evident there seems to be little interest in or account taken of psychological findings. Repp's work on diversity and commonality (1998, 1999) is hardly known outside the music–psychological community, despite its potential musicological importance), different measurement techniques are employed (as in Bowen 1996), and modelling of performance often seems irrelevant to either musicological or pedagogical research. In some ways this is unsurprising, as music psychology comes with many concerns foreign to the wider study or practice of music. However, there are some indications that a psychological approach to measuring and modelling performance might offer insights and techniques of wider value.

For example, a number of recent projects involving measurement and or modelling have gained funding or produced results which are relevant to, or aimed at, performance pedagogy. In Uppsala, Juslin and colleagues have attempted to use empirical and modelling techniques as part of a project aiming to develop methods of teaching expressivity (see e.g., Juslin *et al.* 2004). Similarly, Desain and colleagues are currently working on a project which both utilizes existing understanding of expression and real-time visualization techniques for learning expression (Brandmeyer *et al.* 2006). Similar goals underlie work by Goebl and Widmer (2006). In a rather different way, research in the development of expert performance has begun to adopt the empirical measurement techniques described here: for example Chaffin and Imreh (2002) have addressed issues of learning and memory in performance through detailed analysis of recorded performances.

Measurement and modelling have provided the psychology of music with substantial insights into the processes underlying music performance. One can safely assume that these insights will be extended given the attention paid to this area by researchers. However, it is disappointing to note that work on expression in music, and one might take as an example that on tempo rubato, is being simultaneously studied both by musicologists and psychologists, without much reference to each others' work. Although the goals of psychology and musicology may be different, both seek to explain and describe musical behaviours in their different ways, and one might hope for more cross-fertilization of methodologies and knowledge. This might simply extend to seeing more reference to historical

and cultural context in work on performance within a psychological context (such as in Repp 1998, 1999; Windsor *et al.* 2001) or more methodological exactitude in work carried out in a musicological context (although see Bowen 1996; Fabian 2003). More than this, however it calls for researcher collaborations between these two disciplines (see e.g., Fabian and Schubert 2003) or indeed researchers that are sufficiently experienced in both fields.

References

Askenfelt A (1986). Measurement of bow motion and bow force in violin playing. *Journal of the Acoustical Society of America*, **80**, 1007–1015.

Bowen Jose A (1996). Tempo, duration and flexibility: techniques in the analysis of performance. *Journal of Musicological Research*, **16**(2), 1–47.

Brandmeyer A, Hoppe D, Sadakata M, Timmers R and Desain P (2006) Practice space: a platform for real-time visual feedback in music instruction. *Proceedings of the 9th International Conference on Music Perception and Cognition* (ICMPC9), Bologna, Italy.

Chaffin R and Imreh G (2002). Practicing perfection: piano performance as expert memory. *Psychological Science*, **13**(4), 342–349.

Clarke EF (1982). *Timing in the performance of Erik Satie's Vexations. Acta Psychologica, 50*, 1–19.

Clarke EF (1988). Generative principles in music performance. IN JA Sloboda, ed., *Generative processes in music: the psychology of performance, improvisation, and composition*, 1–26. Clarendon Press, Oxford.

Clarke EF (1999). Rhythm and timing in music. In D Deutsch, ed., *The psychology of music*, 473–500. Academic Press, New York.

Clarke EF and Davidson JW (1998). The body in performance. In W Thomas, ed., *Composition–performance–reception. Studies in the creative process in music*, 74–92. Ashgate Press, Aldershot.

Clarke EF and Windsor WL (2000). Real and simulated expression: a listening study. *Music Perception, 17*(3), 1–37.

Clynes M (1983). Expressive microstructure in music, linked to living qualities. In J Sundberg, ed., *Studies of music performance*, 76–181. Royal Swedish Academy of Music, Stockholm.

Clynes M and Walker J (1986). Music as time's measure. *Music Perception, 4*, 85–119.

Desain P and Honing H. (1994). Does expressive timing in music performance scale proportionally with tempo? *Psychological Research, 56*, 285–292.

Desain P, Honing H, Van Thienen H and Windsor L (1998). Computational modeling of music cognition: problem or solution? *Music Perception, 16*(1), 151–166.

Dixon S (2001). Automatic extraction of tempo and beat from expressive performances. *Journal of New Music Research*, **30**(1), 39–58.

Drake C and Palmer C (1993). Accent structures in music performance. *Music Perception,* **10**(3), 343–378.

Fabian D (2003). *Bach performance practice 1945–1975: A comprehensive review of sound recordings and literature.* Ashgate, Aldershot.

Fabian D and Schubert E (2003). Expressive devices and perceived musical character in 34 performances of Variation 7 from Bach's Goldberg Variations. *Musicae Scientiae,* Special Issue 2003–2004, 49–68.

Fjellman-Wiklund A, Grip H, Karlsson JS and Sundelin G (2004a). *EMG trapezius muscle activity pattern in string players: Part I—is there variability in the playing technique? International Journal of Industrial Ergonomics,* **33**, 347–356.

Fjellman-Wiklund A, Grip H, Karlsson JS and Sundelin G (2004b). *EMG trapezius muscle activity pattern in string players: Part II—influences of basic body awareness therapy on the violin playing technique. International Journal of Industrial Ergonomics,* **33**, 357–367.

Fraisse P (1956). *Les structures rhythmiques.* Editions Universitaires, Louvain.

Friberg A (1991). Generative rules for music performance: a formal description of a rule system. *Computer Music Journal,* **15**(2), 56–71.

Gabrielsson A (1974). Performance of rhythm patterns. *Scandinavian Journal of Psychology,* **15**, 63–72.

Gabrielsson A (1987). Once again: the theme from Mozart's piano Sonata in A Major (k. 331). In A Gabrielsson, ed., *Action and perception in rhythm and music,* 81–104. Royal Swedish Academy of Music, Stockholm.

Gabrielsson A (1999). The performance of music. In D Deutsch, ed., *The psychology of music,* 501–602. Academic Press, New York.

Gentner DR (1987). Timing of skilled motor performance: tests of the proportional duration model. *Psychological Review,* **94**(2), 255–276.

Goebl W and Bresin R (2003). Measurement and reproduction accuracy of computer-controlled grand pianos. *Journal of the Acoustical Society of America,* **114**(4), 2273–228.

Goebl W and Widmer G (2006). Unobtrusive practice tools for pianists. *In Proceedings of the 9th International Conference on Music Perception and Cognition* (ICMPC9), 209–214. Bologna.

Honing H (1990). POCO: an environment for analysing, modifying, and generating expression in music. In *Proceedings of the 1990 International Computer Music Conference,* 364–368. International Computer Music Association, San Francisco,CA.

Honing H (2006). Computational modeling of music cognition: a case study on model selection. *Music Perception,* **23**(5), 365–376.

Juslin PN (2000). Cue utilization in communication of emotion in music performance: relating performance to perception. *Journal of Experimental Psychology: Human Perception and Performance,* **26**, 1797–1813.

Juslin PN and Madison G (1999). The role of timing patterns in recognition of emotional expression from musical performance. *Music Perception,* **17**(2), 197–221.

Juslin PN, Friberg A and Bresin R (2002). Toward a computational model of expression in performance: the GERM model. *Musicae Scientiae,* Special Issue 2001–2002, 63–122.

Juslin PN, Friberg A, Schoonderwaldt E and Karlsson J (2004). Feedback learning of musical expressivity. In A Williamson, ed., *Enhancing musical performance: a resource for performers, teachers, and researchers,* 247–270. Oxford University Press, New York.

Kelso JAS, Bressler SL, Buchanan S, Deguzman GC, Ding M, Fuchs A and Holroyd T (1992). A phase transition in human brain and behavior. *Physics Letters A,* **169**(3), 134–144.

MacKenzie CL and Van Eerd DL, (1990). Rhythmic precision in the performance of piano scales: motor psychophysics and motor programming. In M. Jeannerod, ed., Attention and performance XIII, 375–408. Lawrence Erlbaum Associates, Hillsdale, NJ.

Mazzola G (2002). *The topos of music, geometric logic of concepts, theory, and performance.* Birkhäuser, Basel.

Moelants D (2000). Statistical analysis of written and performed music. A study of compositional principles and problems of coordination and expression in punctual serial music. *Journal of New Music Research,* **29**(1), 37–60.

Moelants D and Rampazzo C (1997). A computer system for the automatic detection of perceptual onsets in a musical signal. In A. Camurri, ed., *KANSEI—the technology of emotion,* 141–146. AIMI-DIST, Genovo.

Palmer C (1989). Mapping musical thought to musical performance. *Journal of Experimental Psychology: Human Perception and Performance,* **15**(12), 331–346.

Palmer C (1997). Music performance. *Annual Review of Psychology,* **48**, 115–138.

Penel A and Drake C (1998). Sources of timing variations in music performance: a psychological segmentation model. *Psychological Research,* **61**, 12–32.

Rasch RA (1988). Timing and synchronisation in ensemble performance. In JA Sloboda, ed., *Generative processes in music,* 70–90. Oxford University Press, Oxford.

Repp BH (1998). A microcosm of musical expression: I. Quantitative analysis of pianists' timing in the initial measures of Chopin's Etude in E major. *Journal of the Acoustical Society of America,* **104**, 1085–1100.

Repp BH (1999). A microcosm of musical expression: II. Quantitative analysis of pianists' dynamics in the initial measures of Chopin's Etude in E major. *Journal of the Acoustical Society of America,* **105**(3), 1972–1988.

Repp BH Windsor WL, Desain PWM., (2002). Effects of tempo and timing of simple musical rhythms. *Music Perception,* **19**(4), 565–594.

Schmidt RA (1985). The search for invariance in skilled movement behavior. *Research Quarterly for Exercise and Sport,* **56**(2), 188–200.

Seashore CE (1938). *Psychology of music.* McGraw-Hill, New York.

Shaffer LH (1981). Performances of Chopin, Bach and Bartok: studies in motor programming. *Cognitive Psychology,* **13**, 326–376.

Shaffer LH (1984). Timing in solo and duet piano performances. *The Quarterly Journal of Experimental Psychology, 36A*, 577–595.

Shaffer LH, Clarke EF and Todd NPM (1985). Metre and rhythm in piano playing. *Cognition, 20*, 61–77.

Sloboda JA (1983) The communication of musical metre in piano performance. *Quarterly Journal of Experimental Psychology A, 35*, 377–396.

Sundberg J (1988). Computer synthesis of music performance. In JA Sloboda, ed., *Generative processes in music: the psychology of performance, improvisation, and composition*, 52–69. Clarendon Press, Oxford.

Sundberg J, Friberg A and Bresin R (2003). Attempts to reproduce a pianist's expressive timing with director musices performance rules. *Journal of New Music Research, 32*(3), 317–325.

Timmers R, Ashley R, Desain PWM, Honing HJ and Windsor WL (2002). Timing of ornaments in the theme of Beethoven's Paisiello variations: empirical data and a model. *Music Perception, 20*(1), 3–33.

Todd NP (1985). A model of expressive timing in tonal music. *Music Perception, 3*, 33–58.

Todd NP (1989). Towards a cognitive theory of expression: the performance and perception of rubato. *Contemporary Music Review, 4*(1), 405–416.

Todd NP (1992). The dynamics of dynamics: a model of musical expression. *Journal of the Acoustical Society of America, 91*, 3540–3550.

Todd NP McA. (1995). The kinematics of musical expression. *Journal of the Acoustical Society of America, 97*, 1940–1949.

Vines BW, Krumhansl CL, Wanderley MM and Levitin DJ (2006). *Cross-modal interactions in the perception of musical performance. Cognition, 101*, 80–113.

Vines BW, Nuzzo RL and Levitin DJ (2005). Analyzing temporal dynamics in music: differential calculus, physics, and functional data techniques. *Music Perception, 23*, 139–154.

Vorberg D and Wing AM (1996). Modeling variability and dependence in timing. In H Heuer and SW Keele, eds, *Handbook of perception and action II: motor skills*, 181–262. Academic Press, London.

Wanderley MM and Vines B (2006). Ancillary gestures of clarinettists. In A Gritten and E King, eds, *Music and gesture: new perspectives on theory and contemporary practice*, Ashgate Press, Aldershot.

Widmer G and Goebl W (2004). Computational models of expressive music performance: the state of the art. *Journal of New Music Research, 33*(3), 203–216.

Widmer G and Tobudic A (2003). Playing Mozart by analogy: learning multi-level timing and dynamics strategies. *Journal of New Music Research, 32*(3), 259–268.

Windsor WL and Clarke EF (1997). Expressive timing and dynamics in real and artificial musical performances: using an algorithm as an analytical tool. *Music Perception, 15*(2), 127–152.

Windsor WL, Aarts R, Desain P, Heijink H and Timmers R (2001) The timing of grace notes in skilled musical performance at different tempi: a preliminary case study. *Psychology of Music, 29*, 149–169.

Windsor WL, Desain PWM, Penel A and Borkent M (2006). A structurally guided method for the decomposition of expression in music performance. *Journal of the Acoustical Society of America, 119*(2), 1182–1193.

Zanon P and De Poli G (2003a). Time-varying estimation of parameters in rule systems for music performance. *Journal of New Music Research, 32*(3), 295–316.

Zanon P and De Poli G (2003b). Estimation of parameters in rule systems for expressive rendering in musical performance. *Computer Music Journal, 27*(1), 29–46.

CHAPTER 31

Planning and performance

Eckart Altenmüller and Sabine Schneider

Introduction

Performing music at a professional level is probably the most demanding of human accomplishments. Making music requires the integration of multimodal sensory and motor information and precise monitoring of the performance via auditory feedback. In the context of Western classical music, musicians have to reproduce highly controlled movements almost perfectly with a high reliability. These specialized sensorimotor skills require extensive training periods over many years, starting in early infancy and passing through stages of increasing physical and strategic complexities. The superior skills of musicians are mirrored in plastic adaptations of the brain on different timescales.

In the first section of this chapter we introduce essential general information for musical readers concerning the organization of cortical, subcortical and cerebellar motor systems in the brain. The electrophysiological correlates of motor planning and motor expectation will be briefly mentioned, as they provide a deeper understanding of the time course of anticipation and retrieval of motor programmes in music performance. In the second section, brain processes during acquisition of skilled movements in music-making will be addressed and the dynamics of neuronal networks will be demonstrated. Because these processes rely on plastic adaptations of brain networks and anatomical brain structures, the interplay of increasing precision of movements and plastic changes in the brain will be explained. In the third section, new findings on practice strategies and performance

quality will be reported. Brain imaging measures collected during mental practice or listening tasks suggest that both motor and auditory cortical areas are active during musical thought processes. Motor-based brain representations are found in behavioural studies on performers' musical interpretations, transfer of learning from one musical task to another, mental practice effects, and anticipatory movements. Implications from these behavioural tasks suggest that an accurate auditory and motor representation underlies successful performance from memory. In the fourth section, the causes of degradation of skilled movements in professional musicians will be addressed. This disorder, termed focal dystonia, is due to maladaptive brain plasticity with fusion of brain representations of adjacent digits in somatosensory brain regions. Such a fusion and blurring of receptive fields of the digits results in a loss of control, because skilled motor actions are necessarily bound to intact somatosensory feedback input. Prolonged practice and pain syndromes due to overuse can precipitate dystonia, which is developed by about 1 per cent of professional musicians and usually ends their career. Finally, we will end the chapter with an outlook and add some comments concerning the significance of results of brain research in order to improve practice habits and performance in musicians.

Introduction

There can be no doubt that making music is one of the most demanding tasks for the human central nervous system. It involves the precise execution of very fast and, in many instances, extremely complex physical movements that must be coordinated with continuous auditory feedback. Practice is required to develop these skills and carry out these complex tasks. Perhaps the most important study on practice to emerge during the past couple of decades was undertaken by Ericsson and his colleagues in 1993 with students at the Berlin Academy of Music. Ericsson *et al.* proposed the concept of 'deliberate practice' as a means of studying goal-oriented, structured and effortful facets of practice in which motivation, resources and attention determine the amount and quality of practice undertaken. They argued that a major distinction between professional and amateur musicians (and perhaps successful versus un-successful learners) is the amount of deliberate practice undertaken during the many years required to develop instrumental skills to a high level (Ericsson and Lehmann 1996). They proposed that highly skilled musicians exert a great deal more effort and concentration during their practice than less skilled musicians, and are more likely to plan, image, monitor and control their playing by focusing their attention on what they are practising and how it can be improved.

Motor skills are best acquired by massed practice involving countless repetitions, whereas aural skills are typically refined through a broad variety of listening experiences. Both types of skills are not represented in isolated brain areas however, but rather depend on the multiple connections and interactions established during training within and between the different regions of the brain. The general ability of our central nervous system to adapt to changing environmental conditions and newly imposed tasks during its entire life span is referred to as *plasticity*. In music, planning, learning through experience and training are accompanied by development and changes which not only take place in the brain's neuronal networks as a result of a strengthening of neuronal connections but also in its overall gross structure. Unfortunately, it is still not completely understood how practice habits and sensorimotor maturation influence each other. With respect to brain plasticity it is known that music practice enhances myelination, grey matter growth and fibre formation

of brain structures involved in the specific musical task (for a review see Münte *et al.* 2002).

There are two main reasons why researchers believe that these effects on brain plasticity are more pronounced in instrumental music performers than in other skilled activities. First, musical training usually starts very early, sometimes before age six when the adaptability of the central nervous system is highest, and second, musical activities are strongly linked to positive emotions, which are known to enhance plastic adaptations. We would be wise to keep in mind however, that the methodologies currently used in contemporary brain research might produce a bias. As an example, it could be argued that the results demonstrated for group investigations of classical instrumentalists are due to these musicians having a similar acculturation due to the canonical nature of their training. Classical pianists tend to study etudes of Hanon, Czerny and Chopin, and the similarity of their training may produce uniform brain adaptations which in turn then dominate any individual changes. In other pursuits such as the visual arts, creative writing, architecture and composing music, individualized training may produce more diverse effects that may be masked within group statistics.

Neuroanatomy and neurophysiology of motor systems involved in planning and performance

Playing a musical instrument requires highly refined motor skills that are acquired over many years of extensive training, and that have to be stored and maintained as a result of further regular practice. Auditory feedback is needed to improve and perfect performance. Performance-based music-making therefore, relies primarily on a highly developed auditory–motor integration capacity, which can be compared to the phonological loop in speech production. In addition, somatosensory feedback constitutes another basis of high-level performance. Here, the kinaesthetic sense, which allows for control and feedback of muscle- and tendon-tension as well as joint positions which enable continuous monitoring of finger-, hand- or lip-position in the frames of body and instrument coordinates (e.g., the keyboard, the mouthpiece), is especially important. In a more general context, the motor system of music performance can be understood as a subspecialty of the motor systems for planned and skilled voluntary limb movements.

Planned voluntary skilled limb movements involve four cortical regions in both hemispheres: the *primary motor area* (M1) located in the *precentral gyrus* directly in front of the central sulcus; the *supplementary motor area* (SMA) located anterior to the M1 of the frontal lobe and the inner (medial) side of the cortex; the *cingulate motor area* (CMA) below the SMA and above the corpus callosum on the inner (medial) side of the hemisphere; and the *premotor area* (PMA), which is located adjacent to the lateral aspect of the primary motor area (see Figure 31.1).

SMA, CMA and PMA can be described as *secondary motor areas*, because they are used to process movement patterns rather than simple movements. In addition to the cortical regions, the motor system includes the subcortical structures of the basal ganglia, and the cerebellum. The sensory areas are necessary in order to maintain the control of movements. Their steady

kinaesthetic feedback information is required for any guided motor action. The sensory areas are located in the *primary somatosensory area* (S1) behind the central sulcus in the parietal lobe. This lobe is involved in many aspects of movement processing. It is an area where information from multiple sensory regions converges. In the posterior parietal area, the body coordinates in space are monitored and calculated and visual information is transferred into body coordinates. As far as musicians are concerned, this area is prominently activated during tasks involving multisensory integration, for example during sight-reading and the playing of complex pieces of music (Haslinger *et al.* 2005).

The *primary motor area* (M1) represents the movements of body parts in a separate but systematic order. The representation of the leg is located on the top and the inner side of the hemisphere, the arm in the upper portion, and the hand and mouth in the lower portion of M1. This representation of distinct body parts in corresponding brain regions is called *somatotopic* or *homuncular order*. Just as the *motor homunculus* is represented upside down, so too is the *sensory homunculus* on the other side of the central sulcus. The proportions of both—the motor

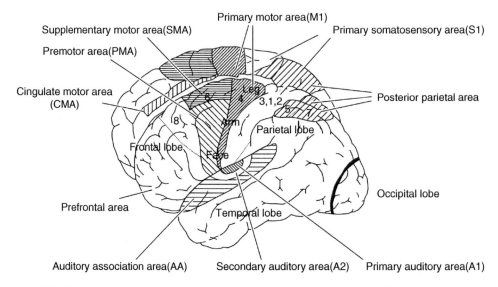

Fig. 31.1 Brain regions involved in sensory and motor music processing. The left hemisphere is shown in the foreground (lower right); the right hemisphere in the background (upper left). The numbers relate to the respective Brodmann's areas, a labelling of the cortical areas according to the fine structure of the nervous tissue.

and the sensory homunculus—are markedly distorted because they are determined by the density of motor and sensory innervations of the respective body parts. For example, control of fine movements of the tongue requires many more nerve fibres transmitting the information to this muscle as compared to the muscles in the back. Therefore, the hand, the lips and the tongue require almost two-thirds of the neurons in this area. However, as further explained below, the representation of the body parts may be modified by usage. Moreover, the primary motor area does not simply represent individual muscles: multiple muscular representations are arranged in a complex way so as to allow the execution of simple types of movements rather than the activation of a specific muscle. This is a consequence of the fact that a two-dimensional array of neurons in M1 has to code for three-dimensional movements in space (Gentner and Classen 2006). Put more simply, our brain does not represent muscles but rather movements.

The *supplementary motor area* (SMA) is mainly involved in the coordination of the two hands, in the sequencing of complex movements and in the triggering of movements based on internal cues. It is particularly engaged when the execution of a sequential movement depends on internally stored and memorized information. The SMA can be subdivided into two distinct functional areas. In the anterior SMA, it would seem that the planning of complex movement patterns is processed. The posterior SMA seems to be predominantly engaged in two-handed movements and, in particular, in the synchronization of both hands during complex movement patterns.

The function of the *cingulate motor area* (CMA) is still under debate. Electrical stimulation and brain imaging studies demonstrate its involvement in movement selection in situations when movements are critical to obtain reward or punishment. This points towards close links between the cingulate gyrus and the emotion-processing limbic system. From what we know therefore, it would seem that the CMA plays an important role in mediating cortical cognitive functions and limbic–emotional functions. The *premotor area* (PMA) is primarily engaged when externally stimulated behaviour is being planned and prepared. It is involved in

the learning, execution and recognition of limb movements and seems to be particularly concerned with processing of visual information which is necessary for movement planning.

The *basal ganglia*, located deep inside the cerebral hemispheres, are interconnected reciprocally via the thalamus to the motor and sensory cortices, thus constituting a loop of information flow between the cortex and the basal ganglia. They are indispensable for any kind of voluntary actions that are not highly automated. Their special role consists in the control of voluntary action by selecting appropriate motor actions and by comparing the goal and course of those actions with previous experience. In the basal ganglia, the flow of information between the cortex and the limbic emotion system, in particular the amygdala, converges. It is therefore assumed that the basal ganglia process and control the emotional evaluation of motor behaviour in terms of expected rewards or punishment. Finally, the *cerebellum* contributes essentially to the timing and accuracy of fine-tuned movements.

Observing planning in the brain

During the last two decades, knowledge of brain regions involved in complex tasks such as playing a musical instrument has increased enormously. This is mainly due to the development of novel technologies that allow non-invasive assessment of the intact brain's function. A pioneering step was the observation of movement-related brain potentials reflecting planning and movement preparation in the brain. These brain potentials can be extracted from the ongoing electrical activity of neuronal populations in the cerebral cortex using electroencephalography (EEG). The most prominent activation is the so callled Bereitschaftspotential (see Figure 31.2).

The Bereitschaftspotential (BP) is a ramp-like brain activation which precedes any self-paced voluntary motor activity, starting 2000 to 1000 ms prior to movement onset. There is still some debate on the structures in the brain generating the BP. It seems that the first part of the ramp-like shift is produced in the SMA, reflecting the planning of a movement. The subsequent part of the shift is probably generated in the primary

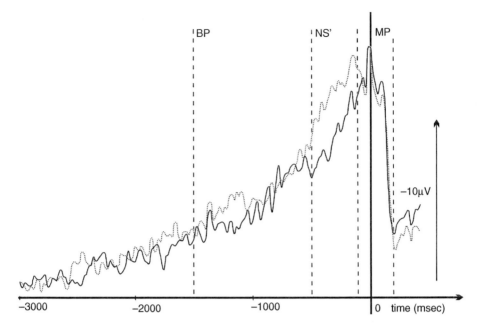

Fig. 31.2 Typical Bereitschaftspotential (BP) in healthy pianists and in pianists suffering from focal dystonia (dotted line) prior to scale playing (Time 0). Brain activation starts about 3 seconds prior to movement onset, reflecting planning and preparation. The proper BP starts 1.5 prior to movement onset and is generated in the supplementary motor cortex. The negative slope (NS′) 500 ms prior to movement onset is generated in the anterior part of the primary motor cortex. The motor potential (MP) finally corresponds to activation of the motor neurons in the pyramidal tract. After movement onset, brain activation is reset, yielding a sudden positive shift in brain activation. Note that pianists suffering from pianists' dystonia have larger amplitudes especially in the NS′ component of the Bereitschaftspotential (modified from Peschel and Altenmüller 2004).

motor areas, reflecting the activation of motor neurons directly linked to muscles via the spinal cord (for a concise review see Altenmüller *et al.* 2004).

Traditionally, the BP was related to the intentional decision processes of willed action. In intriguing experiments Libet *et al.* (1983) demonstrated that the BP starts about 350 ms prior to conscious awareness of the intention to act. When the subjects 'vetoed' their decision to act, the BP, which had normally developed prior to this 'veto', collapsed and no movement occurred. Libet (1985) concluded that voluntary acts can be initiated by unconscious cerebral processes before conscious intention appears but that conscious control over the actual motor performance of the acts remain possible. This experimental design has had a long and often controversial history. After all, it has remained

unclear whether the urge to act, and the action itself, represent actual differences in brain states (Eagleman 2004).

EEG measures such as the BP-recordings have an excellent temporal resolution, reflecting the electrical activity of neurons in the range of milliseconds. Therefore these methods are suitable to investigate the rapid neuronal interactions which constitute the basis of motor planning and performance.

Other imaging tools such as positron emission tomography (PET), and functional magnetic resonance imaging (fMRI) allow the functional assessment and the precise localization of active brain regions. However, these methods have the disadvantage of a relatively poor time resolution, allowing the monitoring of neuronal activation during planning and performance in the range of seconds, but not of milliseconds.

Additionally, new imaging techniques, derived from MRI) technology, demonstrate minute changes in brain structure with precision. Voxel-based morphometry (VBM) for example, provides detailed information of the thickness of the grey matter in the layers of neurons in the cerebral cortex. Using this technique, cross-sectional studies have demonstrated differences in grey matter volume in the range of cubic millimeters as a result of musical training (Gaser and Schlaug 2003). Diffusion tensor imaging (DTI), on the other hand, is a way to assess direction and volume of fibre tracts in the white matter of the brain. In pianists this method has shown changes in myelination of the callosal body which connects the two brain hemispheres (Bengtsson *et al.* 2005).

Learning to plan: the acquisition of fine motor skills

Our knowledge concerning the regions and mechanisms of the brain involved in sensorimotor learning is still incomplete. Overall, musicians appear to process new incoming stimuli more effectively compared to non-musicians. According to newly emerging evidence (for a review see Halsband and Lange 2006) all structures involved in motor control participate in the acquisition of new sensorimotor skills. The cerebellum is involved in the selection, the sequence and the timing of movements and the basal ganglia play a crucial role in procedural learning and automation of movements.

It has been known for some time that the activity in the SMA and in the premotor area of the brain are enhanced as a result of increasing complexity of finger movement sequences (Roland *et al.* 1980). Using fMRI, Karni and colleagues (1995) investigated adult subjects' learning of complex finger sequences which are similar to those necessary for piano playing. After 30 minutes of practice the representation of the fingers in the primary motor cortex increased. However, without further training, this effect diminished after one week with the hand representation returning to its previous size. In contrast, continuous practice resulted in a stable enlargement of the hand area in the pri-

mary motor cortex. This effect was specific for the daily trained sequence of complex finger movements, and did not occur when the subjects improvised complex finger movements which were not subsequently repeated. Parallel to the enlargement of the hand area in the primary motor cortex, the size of the cerebellar hand representation diminished, suggesting that the cerebellum plays an important role only in the initial phase of motor learning.

The above mentioned study does not take into account one special quality of musicianship, namely the strong coupling of sensorimotor and auditory processing required for performing music. Practicing an instrument involves assembling, storing, and constantly improving complex sensorimotor programmes through prolonged and repeated execution of motor patterns under the controlled monitoring of the auditory system. In a cross-sectional experiment, strong linkages between auditory and sensorimotor cortical regions as a result of many years of practice have been reported (Bangert *et al.* 2006). Using fMRI, professional pianists were asked to listen to simple piano tunes without moving their fingers or any other body part. Figure 31.3(a) demonstrates the increase in activation of professional pianists in comparison to non-musicians. There is an impressive activation of the motor cortex demonstrating the subconscious or automated auditory–motor co-activation.

Furthermore, in a longitudinal study, it was possible to show that the formation of such neuronal multisensory connections needs less than six weeks of regular piano training (Bangert and Altenmüller 2003). This demonstrates how dynamically brain adaptations accompany musical learning processes.

Activation of motor co-representations can occur in trained pianists not only by listening to piano tunes, but also by observing a pianist's finger movements while watching a video. In Figure 31.3(b) the increases in brain activation of trained pianists are shown whilst they are observing video sequences of a moving hand at the piano as compared to the activation of musically naive subjects (Haslinger *et al.* 2005). Besides the motor hand area in the primary motor cortex, secondary auditory cortices in the temporal lobe and the cerebellum are activated. This neuronal network corresponds to a '*mirror*

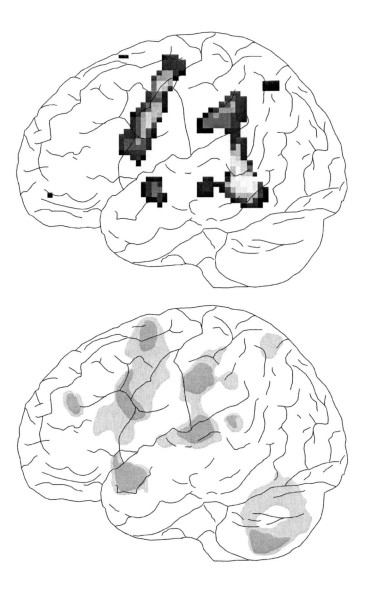

Fig. 31.3 (a) Additional brain activity (grey zones) of skilled pianists compared to non-pianists when listening to piano tunes without moving their fingers. The primary motor cortex of the precentral area and auditory association areas are lighting up, demonstrating an unconscious co-representation of heard tunes as movement patterns (modified from Bangert *et al.* 2006). (b) Additional brain activity (grey zones) of skilled pianists compared to non-pianists when observing pianist movements in a soundless video. Again, the precentral area and auditory association areas are lighting up demonstrating the mirror system: the observed movements are unconsciously activated, albeit the subjects did not move their fingers. Furthermore the auditory areas are activated demonstrating a visual–auditory co-representation of seen movements. This effect demonstrates impressively the powerful human imitation system, and may be utilized by teachers when demonstrating at the instrument (modified from Haslinger *et al.* 2005).

neuron network'. As a consequence of musical practice, it follows that careful demonstration at the instrument may enhance learning. Such a teaching method based on demonstration and imitation is widely used at all levels of musical training, and would appear to be particularly effective in cases where teachers demonstrate an action or series of actions that are carefully and methodically observed by the student.

Practicing through listening and/or observation can be considered as special cases of *mental training*. Narrowly defined, mental training is understood as the vivid imagination of movement sequences without physically performing them. As with observation of actions, principally the same brain regions are active as if the imagined action is performed; that is, the primary motor cortex, the supplementary motor cortex and the cerebellum (Kuhtz-Buschbeck *et al.* 2003). In a study investigating mental training of finger movement sequences of different complexities, brain activation increased along with the degree of difficulty of the imagined motor task. Furthermore, when continuing mental practice over a period of several days, the involved brain regions showed plastic adaptations. Although these adaptations are less dramatic than if the motor tasks were practiced physically, mental training produced a clear improvement in task performance as assessed in finger tapping tests.

Plasticity of sensory motor systems: musicians' brains are different

During the past decade, brain imaging has provided important insights into the enormous capacity of the human brain to adapt to complex demands. These adaptations are referred to as *brain plasticity* and do not only include the connections or firing rates of neurons—the 'software' of our brain—but also the 'hardware', namely the fine structure of nervous tissue and even the visible gross structure of brain anatomy. Brain plasticity is best observed in complex tasks with high behavioural relevance for the individual such that they cause strong emotional and motivational activation. Plastic changes are more pronounced in situations where the task or activity is intense and the earlier

in life it has been developed. Obviously, the continued activities of accomplished musicians provide the prerequisites of brain plasticity in an ideal manner. It is therefore not astonishing that the most dramatic brain plasticity effects have been demonstrated in professional musicians (for a review see Münte *et al.* 2002).

Our understanding of the molecular and cellular mechanisms underlying these adaptations is far from complete. Brain plasticity may occur on different time axes. For example, the efficiency and size of synapses may be modified in a time window of seconds to minutes, the growth of new synapses and dendrites may require hours to days. An increase in grey matter density, which mainly reflects an enlargement of neurons, needs at least several weeks. White matter density also increases as a consequence of musical training. This effect is primarily due to an enlargement of myelin cells: the myelin cells, wrapped around the nerve fibres (axons) are contributing essentially to the velocity of the electrical impulses travelling along the nerve fibre tracts. Under conditions requiring rapid information transfer and high temporal precision these myelin cells grow and as a consequence nerve conduction velocity increases. Finally, brain regions involved in specific tasks may also be enlarged after long-term training due to the growth of structures supporting the nervous function, for example, in the blood vessels that are necessary for the oxygen and glucose transportation to sustain nervous function.

Comparison of the brain anatomy of skilled musicians with that of non-musicians shows that prolonged instrumental practice leads to an enlargement of the hand area in the motor cortex (Amunts *et al.* 1997) and to an increase in grey matter density corresponding to more and/or larger neurons in the respective area (Gaser and Schlaug 2003). These adaptations appear to be particularly prominent in all instrumentalists who have started to play prior to the age of ten and correlate positively with cumulative practice time. Furthermore, in professional musicians, the normal anatomical difference between the larger, dominant (mostly right-) hand area and the smaller, non-dominant (left-) hand area is less pronounced when compared to non-musicians. These results suggest that functional adaptation of the gross structure of the brain occurs during training at an early age.

Similar effects of specialization have been found with respect to the size of the corpus callosum. Professional pianists and violinists tend to have a larger anterior (front) portion of this structure, especially those who have started prior to the age of seven (Schlaug *et al.* 1995). Since this part of the corpus callosum contains fibres from the motor and supplementary motor areas, it seems plausible to assume that the high demands on coordination between the two hands, and the rapid exchange of information may either stimulate the nerve fibre growth—the *myelination* of nerve fibres that determines the velocity of nerve conduction—or prevent the physiological loss of nerve tissue during ageing.

In summary, when training starts at an early age (before about seven years), these plastic adaptations of the nervous system affect brain anatomy by enlarging the brain structures that are involved in different types of musical skills. When training starts later, it modifies brain organization by rewiring neuronal webs and involving adjacent nerve cells to contribute to the required tasks. These changes result in enlarged cortical representations of, for example, specific fingers or sounds within existing brain structures. In the following section, the behavioural correlates of the maladaptive plastic changes, leading to a loss of motor control of highly skilled movements, will be focused on.

Focal dystonia: when planning goes wrong

Approximately 1 in 100 professional musicians suffer from a loss of voluntary control of their extensively trained, refined, and complex sensorimotor skills—a condition generally referred to as focal dystonia, violinist's cramp, or pianist's cramp. In most cases, focal dystonia is so disabling that it prematurely ends the artist's professional career (Altenmüller 2003). Subtle loss of control in fast passages, finger curling (cf. Figure 31.4), lack of precision in forked fingerings in woodwind players, irregularity of trills, sticking fingers on the keys, involuntary flexion of the bowing thumb in strings, impairment of control of the embouchure in woodwind and brass

players in certain registers, are the various symptoms that can mark the beginning of the disorder. At this stage, most musicians believe that the reduced precision of their movements is due to a technical problem. As a consequence, they intensify their efforts, but this often only exacerbates the problem.

Males, classical musicians of a younger age and instrumentalists such as guitarists, pianists and woodwind players are among the most commonly affected by focal dystonia. The majority of patients have solo positions and often they have a perfectionist, control-type personality. About 20 per cent of such patients report a history of chronic pain syndromes or over-use injury. Preventing these musicians from developing chronic over-use and tendinitis will most probably prevent them from developing focal dystonia (Jabusch and Altenmüller 2006). However, once focal dystonia is established, the cure of the pain syndrome will generally not eliminate the pathological movement pattern.

Thus far the aetiology of focal hand dystonia is not completely understood, but is probably multifactorial. Without going into the details, most studies of focal dystonia reveal abnormalities in three main areas: (a) reduced inhibition in the motor system at cortical, subcortical and spinal levels (b) reduced sensory perception and integration; and (3) impaired sensorimotor integration. The latter changes are mainly believed to originate from dysfunctional brain plasticity. There is growing evidence for an abnormal cortical processing of sensory information as well as degraded representation of motor functions in patients with focal dystonia. A study with trained monkeys demonstrated that chronic over-use and repetitive strain injury in highly stereotyped movements can actively degrade the cortical representation of the somatosensory information that guides the fine motor hand movements in primates (Byl *et al.* 1996). A similar degradation of sensory feedback information and concurrent fusion of the digital representations in the somatosensory cortex was confirmed in a brain activation study conducted in musicians with focal dystonia, although these musicians had no history of chronic pain (Elbert *et al.* 1998). Therefore, additional factors such as a genetic predisposition and certain susceptibility appear to play an

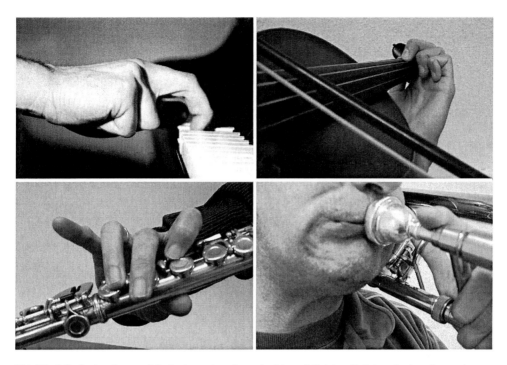

Fig. 31.4 Typical patterns of dystonic posture in a pianist, a violinist, a flutist and a trombone player.

important role in the development of focal dystonia (Schmidt *et al.* 2006). Interestingly, in musicians suffering from focal dystonia the BP is markedly larger as compared to healthy musicians (see Figure 31.2). This 'overshoot' in brain activation prior to movement execution seems to be linked to the core deficit in focal dystonia, the defective inhibition of motor output.

Unfortunately, there is no simple cure for the condition. Retraining may be successful in a minority of cases, but usually requires several years to succeed. Symptomatic treatment with temporary weakening of the cramping muscles by injecting Botulinum-toxin has proven to be helpful in other cases; however, since the injections need to be applied regularly every three to five months during the professional career, it presents no solution for young patients. Thus, the challenge is to prevent young musicians from such a disorder. Reasonable practice schedules, economic technique, prevention of over-use and pain, mental practice, avoidance of exaggerated perfectionism and psychological support with respect to self-confidence are the components of such a prevention programme.

Conclusions: some implications for practice

In the preceding paragraphs we have demonstrated the neurobiological foundations of planning, motor learning and practice. Here we will summarize the data in order to formulate some practical rules which might be useful for the daily work of instrumentalists.

As with all skilled human motor activities, effective planning, movement preparation and practising are largely based on procedural knowledge. How to practise and when to stop practising is best learned by experience. Practising can be considered as a self-organizing process, which frequently starts with uneconomical activation of large neuronal pools in the sensorimotor brain regions. Optimizing the movement patterns occurs under continuous sensory feedback from the ears, the eyes, the muscles, tendons, joints, and from the skin. The integration of this information into movement patterns is the most important step in procedural learning. It is mainly based on the formation of neuronal networks; for example, the connections between auditory and motor areas and in a step-wise reduction of cortical activity and augmentation of subcortical activity in the basal ganglia and the cerebellum.

When playing a musical instrument, the central nervous system is mainly involved in processing a huge amount of incoming information from the ears and eyes, and from the sensory organs in muscles, tendons, joints, and skin. The consolidation of the networks necessary for programming movement sequences occurs mainly in the breaks after playing and during sleep. As a consequence, the more complex a task is, the shorter the practice time that should be scheduled in one session and the longer the breaks should be planned. Sleep is another factor supporting procedural memory formation. Therefore, sufficient sleep should be encouraged, especially when an instrumentalist of any ability level is working hard to master new repertoire.

Generally, a practice session should be terminated when signs of fatigue appear. It is important to consider that over-practice (practice into bodily or mental fatigue) not only leads to no improvement, but to an active worsening of motor programmes. This is due to a blurring of central nervous system sensorimotor representations, when muscular fatigue appears. Furthermore, a lack of attention causes a higher probability of uneconomical movements or production of false notes which, as a consequence, are stored in the procedural memory.

The human mirror system is a powerful tool to facilitate skill learning. Auditory and visual cues presented to students activate their sensorimotor representations and can lead directly to the formation of motor programmes. This is the basis of imitation learning. On the other hand, sloppy and careless demonstrations may produce a negative effect for students, decreasing their sensorimotor programmes as they adopt bad habits modelled by their teacher. Teachers should therefore demonstrate skills in a variety of ways in order to ensure that their students are able to comprehend the difference between effective and ineffective performance techniques.

We would like to conclude our chapter with a general remark: processes involved with instrumental musical training are probably the most complex of all human activities. Importantly,

these are not restricted to the sensorimotor brain circuits but also involve emotion, memory and imagination. The best trained musicians with the best working sensorimotor networks will not move their listeners if imagination, colour, fantasy and emotion are not a part of their artistic expression. These qualities are often not trained solely within a practice studio, but depend on and are possible linked to experiences from daily life, to human relationships, to a rich artistic environment and to empathy and emotional depth. These factors, which profoundly influence the aesthetic quality of a music performance, are at present far from being accessible to any neuroscientific research.

Acknowledgments

The authors thank Gary McPherson for his valuable comments on an earlier version of the manuscript. Both authors are generously supported by a grant of the German Research Foundation (Al 269/7–1).

References

Altenmüller E (2003). Focal dystonia: advances in brain imaging and understanding of fine motor control in musicians. *Hand Clin*, **19**, 523–538.

Altenmüller E, Münte TF and Gerloff Ch (2004). Neurocognitive functions and the EEG. In E Niedermeyer and F Lopes da Silva, eds, *Electroencephalography*, 5th Edn, 661–682. Lippincott Williams, Baltimore, MD.

Amunts K, Schlaug G, Jäncke L, Steinmetz H, Schleicher A, Dabringhaus A and Zilles K (1997). Motor cortex and hand motor skills: structural compliance in the human brain. *Human Brain Mapping*, **5**, 206–215.

Bangert M and Altenmüller E (2003). Mapping perception to action in piano practice: a longitudinal DC-EEG-study. *BMC Neuroscience*, **4**, 26–36.

Bangert M, Peschel T, Rotte M, Drescher D, Hinrichs H, Schlaug G, Heinze HJ and Altenmüller E (2006). Shared networks for auditory and motor processing in professional pianists: evidence from fMRI conjunction. *NeuroImage*, **15**, 917–926.

Bengtsson SL, Nagy Z, Skare S, Forsman L, Forssberg H and Ullen F (2005). Extensive piano practicing has regionally specific effects on white matter development. *Nature Neuroscience*, **8**, 1148–1150.

Byl NN, Merzenich MM and Jenkins WM (1996). A primate genesis model of focal dystonia and repetitive strain injury: I. Learning-induced dedifferentiation of the representation of the hand in the primary somatosensory cortex in adult monkeys. *Neurology*, **47**, 508–520.

Eagleman DM (2004). The where and when of intention. *Science*, **303**, 1144–1146.

Elbert T, Candia V, Altenmüller E, Rau H, Rockstroh B, Pantev C and Taub E (1998). Alteration of digital representations in somatosensory cortex in focal hand dystonia. *NeuroReport*, **16**, 3571–3575.

Ericsson KA, Krampe RT and Tesch-Römer C (1993). The role of deliberate practice in the acquisition of expert performance. *Psychological Review*, **100**, 363–406.

Ericsson KA, Lehmann AC (1996). Expert and exceptional performance: evidence of maximal adaptation to task constraints. *Annual Review of Psychology*, **47**, 273–305.

Gaser C and Schlaug G (2003). Brain structures differ between musicians and non-musicians. *Journal of Neuroscience*, **23**, 9240–9245.

Gentner R and Classen J (2006). Modular organization of finger movements by the human central nervous system. *Neuron*, **52**, 731–742.

Halsband U and Lange RK (2006). Motor learning in man: a review of functional and clinical studies. *J Physiol Paris*, **99**, 414–424.

Haslinger B, Erhard P, Altenmüller E, Schroeder U, Boecker H and Ceballos-Baumann AO (2005). Transmodal sensorimotor networks during action observation in professional pianists. *Journal of Cognitive Neuroscience*, **17**, 282–293.

Jabusch HC and Altenmüller E (2006). Epidemiology, phenomenology and therapy of musician's cramp. In E Altenmüller, J Kesselring and M Wiesendanger eds, *Music, motor control and the brain*, 265–282. Oxford University Press, Oxford.

Karni A, Meyer G, Jezzard P, Adams MM, Turner R and Ungerleider LG (1995). Functional MRI evidence for adult motor cortex plasticity during motor skill learning. *Nature*, **377**, 155–158.

Kuhtz-Buschbeck JP, Mahnkopf C, Holzknecht C, Siebner H, Ulmer S and Jansen O (2003). Effector-independent representations of simple and complex imagined finger movements: a combined fMRI and TMS study. *European Journal of Neuroscience*, **18**, 3375–3387.

Libet B (1985). Unconscious cerebral initiative and the role of conscious will in voluntary action. *The Behavioural and Brain Sciences*, **8**, 529–566.

Libet B, Gleason CA, Wright EW and Pearl D (1983). Time of conscious intention to act in relation to onset of cerebral activity (readiness-potential). *Brain*, **106**, 623–642.

Münte TF, Altenmüller E and Jäncke L (2002). The musician's brain as a model of neuroplasticity. *Nature Neuroscience*, **3**, 473–478.

Peschel T and Altenmüller E (2004). Pathologische bewegungskorrelierte kortikale Potentiale (MRCPs) bei Musikern mit aktionsinduzierter fokaler Dystonie. *Klin Neurophysiologie*, **34**, 96–106.

Roland PE, Larsen B, Lassen NA and Skinhoj E (1980). Supplementary motor area and other cortical areas in the organization of voluntary movements in man. *Journal of Neurophysiology*, **43**, 118–136.

Schlaug G, Jäncke L, Huang Y and Steinmetz H (1995). Increased corpus callosum size in musicians. *Neuropsychologia*, **33**, 1047–1055.

Schmidt A, Jabusch HC, Altenmüller E, Hagenah J, Brüggemann N, Hedrich K, Saunders-Pullman R, Bressman SB, Kramer PL and Klein C (2006). Dominantly transmitted focal dystonia in families of patients with musicians' cramp. *Neurology*, **67**, 691–693.

CHAPTER 32

Sight-reading

Andreas C. Lehmann and Reinhard Kopiez

Introduction

Anyone who wants to perform the works of traditional Western music, and approach other musical styles using a similar performance practice, will most likely have to master music notation. Many musical cultures rely on a system of symbols to store and teach complex musical styles that are not, or only partly, grounded in improvisation. While the beginning music reader has to overcome the same problems as all readers do when learning to read other texts, namely going from a tedious matching of symbols to sounds to meaning, the expert reader has automatized the process of encoding and transforming the signs into embodied action.

For our purposes, we will call sight-reading the execution—vocal or instrumental—of longer stretches of non- or under-rehearsed music at an acceptable pace and with adequate expression. Some people also label this 'playing by sight' or 'prima vista'. Another related set of activities might be called music or note reading: for example, the following of a score with the aim of studying a piece while the music is playing, or the studying of a new piece of music away from the instrument prior to physically practising it. Both activities may even be accompanied by the sounding out of some notes on an instrument. However, the characteristic goal of sight-reading is the authentic performance, or as Mozart once phrased it, 'to play the piece . . . so as to make believe that it had been composed by the one who plays it' (letter from 1778 cited in Crofton and Fraser 1985, p. 111). Similar to improvisation, sight-reading requires the instant adaptation to new constraints, which places it among those that motor scientists refer to as open skills (as opposed to closed skills that

require reproduction of well-rehearsed motions, such as swimming, figure skating or playing a well-rehearsed piece of music). Today, studio musicians and accompanists must be able to sight-read, and many orchestra musicians have done it on a regular basis for centuries. It is this kind of un- or under-rehearsed performance that we are concerned with because it forms a well-defined and discrete skill comparable to that of playing by ear or improvising.

When and under what conditions does sight-reading emerge as a skill in a culture? Music archaeology tells us about some forms of notation from ancient Egypt and Greece and other cultures which have developed coding systems for music that mainly serve mnemonic purposes (e.g. Bent *et al.* 2008). The Western model of notation started to develop in the ninth century in order to code multivoice vocal and later instrumental music. In a musical culture (regardless of geographical place and historical time) in which music is solely improvised, sight-reading is not necessary, yet music reading skills may still be used for learning to play an instrument (e.g. in India). When composers and performers assume specialized roles and performers are expected to perform a fixed repertoire, then sight-reading may be required to limit rehearsal times or if the repertoire changes frequently (e.g. in the Baroque era). While the nineteenth century still saw renowned performers play other composers' pieces from the score, canonization of the repertoire, the developing art of interpretation, and rising audience expectations has since then led to a performance practice based on memorized performance by solo performers of the piano and violin. Our modern performance traditions have come to favour polished performances and relegated sight-reading to a useful craft, generally not worthy of public notice or competition (we know only of the Karl Bergemann sight-reading competition, Hanover, Germany).

Obviously, most orchestral, chamber, and studio musicians play from the score and so do many performers of contemporary art music. There are a few known solo pianists who have used scores even for standard repertoire. It is unclear whether musicians perform better with or without the score, but the audience is likely to expect memorized performances. Also, using the score requires page-turning or the presence of a music stand which may be disturbing for the audience and the performer and might detract from the sounding music. A music stand may obstruct the view and hinder gestural freedom and the positive influence of expression that is conveyed through the body (cf. Lehmann *et al.* 2007, pp. 173–174).

In marked contrast to the public neglect and low prestige of sight-reading among performers stands the steady interest of music psychologists and pedagogues in this skill (for reviews see Sloboda 1984; Lehmann and McArthur 2002; Lehmann *et al.* 2007, Chapter 6). Starting with the early music psychology experiments of the 1920s (published in Jacobsen 1941) and the development of sight-reading tests (Watkins 1942, and the Watkins–Farnum Performance Scale), all aspects of skills relating to sight-reading attracted renewed interest in the 1970s (e.g. Sloboda 1974, 1976, 1977) and have continued to do so (cf. Lehmann and Ericsson 1993, 1996; Kopiez and Lee 2006, 2008 for the acquisition of sight-reading skills) up until recent psychophysiological studies (e.g. Schon and Besson 2005; Yumoto *et al.* 2005). It is important for research that we measure individuals' ability to perform at first sight under standardized conditions. Optimally, those conditions should mirror real-life conditions encountered by expert sight-readers (Lehmann and Ericsson 1993).

In this chapter we will briefly look at how notation is perceived and then move on to the structure of sight-reading while taking into account the real-time conditions under which it takes place. This will include a discussion of perceptual and problem-solving issues. Finally we will outline the course of skill acquisition with its characteristic differences between novices and experts, and present a model of sight-reading performance.

Perception of music notation and sight-reading

To begin, we have to understand how the eye operates when we try to acquire information in everyday life. Contrary to what most people believe, the eye does not function like a movie camera. Rather, its operation can be likened to that of a flashlight in the dark being turned on and off at short intervals. Roughly four to five times a second the eye moves around the visual field in discrete jumps (saccades) with short resting points (fixations). The saccades take about 15–50 msecs, the fixations about 150–200 msecs. At this point it becomes clear that a conscious attending to every eighth note in a piece at MM = 120 would be almost impossible. During each fixation, the external image is projected on the retina at the back of the eye. Wile the retina is comparably large, we are able to receive a sharp image only from a narrow part in the middle. This round central part is called the fovea centralis, and whatever surrounds it will produce the somewhat blurry parafoveal image. Hence, the field of vision that will be perceived in great clarity only averages 0.5–2°, which corresponds to the size of an inch at a reading distance of about 30 inches (75 cm), or the area covered by a pointed-up thumb with extended arm. The parafoveal vision includes 10° of the field of vision (e.g. Rayner and Pollatsek 1989). The role of preview benefits and parafoveal-on-foveal effects are currently a hot topic in word-reading research. It is from such individual snapshots that our brain fashions what we experience as a large and steady picture of the outside world. Unfortunately, the eye movements cannot be allocated wilfully but are in fact guided by preconscious processes and drawn by outside stimuli. For example, movements and boundaries in the visual field attract attention, just as do human faces, but our cognition also guides the eye movements. For example, when a car disappears behind another we are likely to scan the plausible location of its reappearance, and we search the face of a person for cues to his or her mood. Today, we know that information gathered from one or several fixations is integrated in meaningful units or chunks of information which are the basis for further processing. Since the location and duration of fixations is indicative of the processing underlying music reading, eye movements offer important insights into the workings of the musical mind. To explain the structure of sight-reading, we have to account for how much and which information is retrieved from the page and how it is assembled into meaningful units that are sequentially programmed and executed.

The problem in surveying the results of eye movement in sight-reading is that the research methodologies are not standardized with regard to complexity of stimulus, tempo of performance, and so forth. Unlike in text-reading research where many studies appear within a few years using the same paradigm, the time lag between publications on sight-reading is large and findings are often difficult to integrate. By and large, the earliest studies (Jacobsen 1941) established what subsequent studies have confirmed, namely that eye movement patterns are dependent on the level of expertise: beginners had many fixations, long pauses during fixations, and unsystematic reading of note combinations; intermediate musicians had about as many fixations as there were notes, and they read chords in systematic fashion from bottom to top; experts showed fewer fixations than notes and also systematic reading of chords (from top to bottom). Saccades can point forward in reading direction but also backwards (regressively)—for example to the current point of performance. This is most likely done to double-check things that have been read already or result from attention being detracted to performance errors (not a very efficient strategy). With increasing experience, the sight-reader experiences a reduction in the number of regressive fixations. Kinsler and Carpenter (1995), who strangely claimed that 'a thorough search of the literature failed to find any account whatsoever of the eye movements used to read music' (p. 12), studied eye movements during performance of notated rhythms. Their results showed that slower tempi lead to more and shorter fixations. One problem in research with self-selected

performance tempo is that slower tempi necessarily result in more fixations. Lannert and Ullman (1945) found a 0.45 correlation between tempo and accuracy, and we can never be sure if participants have traded off faster tempi for more fixations and thus ensure a more accurate performance. Equal speeds can only be achieved by using a pacing-voice methodology (Lehmann and Ericsson 1993).

That notational input has an influence on the eye movements was mentioned previously (cf. systematic vertical reading of chords). Notational variants (e. g., eighth notes with or without connecting bars) resulted in person-specific eye movements, and eighth notes (with connecting bars) tended to be looked at in pairs while quarter notes were attended to individually (Kinsler and Carpenter 1995). Truitt *et al.* (1997, also Goolsby 1994) questioned why fixations often landed between notes, and we suggest that readers tend to construct intervals rather than reading every note. Weaver (1943) found that polyphonically structured music was read in horizontal zigzagging patterns that tended to follow melodic lines in the different voices, whereas homophonic music resulted in zigzagging up and down motions. However, a critical look at his stimuli unveils that notation and structure were hopelessly confounded, e.g. no attempt was made to notate polyphonic stimuli in alternative (more homophonic looking) ways. none of the stimuli was polyphonic, yet it notated as if homophonically structured. Regardless of the shortcomings, we can say that experience and structure of input modify viewing patterns.

Once the information has been retrieved during one or several fixations, it is stored and assembled in meaningful units in anticipation of the motor performance. Here also it was found that experience allowed for larger temporal range of planning (Drake and Palmer 2000). The extent and nature of the buffering of information is part of the memory system to be discussed in the next section.

Memory processes

The amount of information stored temporarily from a particular sequence of fixations or during a certain timespan can be assessed by experiments that allow sight-readers only limited visual access to the score by either very brief (tachisto-scopic) display, by limiting the period of time during which the score is visible, or by using a computer that follows the fixations with a 'moving window' technique that permits variable pre-view. By this we can measure aspects of memory, namely the perceptual and the eye–hand span. The perceptual span denotes the distance between the current point of performance and the far-thest distance the person is looking ahead. Using a moving window technique, Truitt *et al.* (1997) found that a preview of two beats leads to a slower tempo, larger variability in note dura-tions, and errors. Subjects performed better with previews between two and four beats or, ideally, with previews to the end of the next bar. Furneaux and Land (1999) found the number of notes to be about four for experts and two for novices. Unlike Truitt *et al.* (1997) who found the time between fixation and performance to stand at 0.5 secs, Furneaux and Land (1999) documented between 0.7–1.3 seconds, depend-ent on the tempo. Similar results have been found in studies on typewriting (Gentner 1988). This narrow preview is at odds with the phe-nomenological experience of sight-readers who claim a much larger preview. With multiple fix-ations that can go anywhere in the piece, musi-cians construct motor programmes that rely on more than mere visual input of the foveal area (see below for further details). This leads to the larger eye–hand spans that can be measured when withdrawing the notation unexpectedly (Sloboda 1977). Sloboda found that meaningful musico-structural units influenced the length of the eye–hand span. For example, a larger dis-tance from the next phrase boundary tended to stretch the eye–hand span; a shorter caused it to shrink. Hiding a longer piece of music at arbi-trary points might still allow for cumulative effects of the previously sight-read material, whereas the method of briefly displaying dis-jointed snippets of information for several hun-dred milliseconds does not. We know that the reading context influences patterns of fixation (Bekkering and Neggers 2002). If we consider that repeated trials lead to better sight-reading accuracy and that better sight-readers have a better recall for material after a single trial (Lehmann and Ericsson 1993), we have to con-sider the effects of long-term working memory

typically found among experts (Ericsson and Kintsch 1995). This privileged access to long-term memory allows expert readers to store briefly presented material in long-term memory with-out extensive rehearsal.

Inner hearing

Some authors have claimed that inner hearing and audiation processes may be important in sight-reading, and independent tests of audia-tion, imagery, and pattern matching are posi-tively associated with sight-reading ability (e.g. Kornicke 1995; Waters *et al.* 1998; Kopiez and Lee 2006). These processes would suggest that the mental representation of music nota-tion involves the building of melodic and other expectancies by the performer. Recent electro-physiological studies have confirmed this point. In studies in which listeners followed a visually presented score that was accompanied by the corresponding sounds, discrepancies between the printed score and auditory events resulted in a recorded mismatch negativity about 150 msec after the dissociation in the vicinity of Heschl's gyrus, where auditory pitch detection is located (Schon and Besson 2005; Yumoto *et al.* 2005). This means that performers are likely able to know if their sounds match the score or not. Whether or not auditory images are used for planning of movements may depend on the musician. For example, Banton (1995) found that sight-reading without auditory feedback led to only slightly more mistakes than normal feed-back; however, omitting visual access to the keys resulted in markedly poorer performance. A clas-sic experiment by Allport *et al.* (1972) revealed that pianists could repeat words that were pre-sented while sight-reading at the piano, which suggests that auditory feedback is not necessary. However, it may be used to create expectations.

Sight-reading as problem-solving

We already mentioned that not all notes can be focused on and that problem-solving processes will have to complement the incomplete visual input. In fact, everyday experiences teach us that some pieces are able to be sight-read more easily than others, which suggests that those processes may be more or less easily accomplished. Ortmann in 1934 (cited in Clifton 1986) showed with brief presentation times of stimuli, 400 msec and 2 sec, respectively, that diatonically organized music, smaller intervals, and sequences that were congruent with tonal expectations were more easily read than others. This suggests—and this conclusion is backed by much research in other domains—that we tend to form meaningful units that are influenced by our previous knowledge, and hence, expectations. Kinsler and Carpenter (1995) found that repeated renditions of the same piece were accompanied by a reduced amount of ocular movements. Presumably, larger chunks were formed, more previous knowledge was brought to the task, and the visual input functioned as a retrieval cue to a known motor programme (just like playing well-rehearsed music from notation).

What happens when our expectations are not met by the printed score? In a clever study (Sloboda 1976), pianists performed a classically sounding piece of music in which several notes had been altered by a half or whole step to violate tonal expectations. These violations were either introduced in the beginning, middle or the end of a phrase, and they were evenly distributed across the left- and right-hand part. Participants were asked to play exactly what was written. As the researcher expected, many of the artificial alterations were erroneously corrected to sound tonal again, middle positions being more likely corrected, and a repeated trial led to even more such corrections. These alterations may be termed proof-reader's errors. Sloboda (1974) asked music experts to judge mistakes made by sight-readers with regard to their musical adequacy. In keeping with our expectations, the errors were plausible alternatives to or reductions of the written music. Expectations are powerful: one can ask pianists to fill in blanks in an unfamiliar piece while sight-reading it, and they will generate successful inferences (i.e. improvise) based solely on the context of the piece, their stored knowledge, and current expectations (Lehmann and Ericsson 1996). Fine et al. (2006) showed that singers also made more mistakes when sight-reading tonally modified Bach chorals compared to unmodified ones and that they were also hindered by modified notes in other voices' parts.

Sight-reading is more than pressing the right notes at the right time; it also involves adding musical expression. Although no specific studies have been done so far, we suggest that expression is added algorithmically according to a likely grammar of musical expression (e.g. Friberg et al. 2006). Most interestingly, merely counting up the number of correct notes in a sight-reading task correlates highly with expert ratings of the same performance (Lehmann and Ericsson 1993), suggesting that better sight-readers integrate musical expression and correct notes on the fly. This may be due to a larger temporal range of planning. Only when the performer knows what is ahead can meaningful musical expression be added (e.g. slowing at the end of a phrase).

In essence, problem-solving or reconstructive processes during sight-reading are considerable if we consider how few fixations are available and how much material needs to be covered. Obviously, those processes function more effectively in better sight-readers. While plausible expectations are constantly being constructed and will usually facilitate performance, in rare instances they may lead the sight-reader astray and cause errors that unveil the underlying mediating processes.

Acquiring the skill

Sight-reading is such a specialized skill that it is futile to look for specific inborn traits that may cause individual differences in sight-reading skill. Among musicians observable individual differences in sight-reading ability are great and need to be explicated. Several variables have attracted the interest of researchers: all sorts of training variables, intelligence, other musical skills, musical ability, general indicators of memory, and reading performance.

The most promising predictors so far have been training variables. Kornicke (1995) and Banton (1995) found that higher self-rated experience as an accompanist or more regular sight-reading practice was related to more accurate sight-reading in the authors' studies. In Kornicke's study, a cumulative index of experience from several scales correlated reliably ($r = 0.4$) with sight-reading achievement. In a regression analysis the best predictor was the estimated number of pieces sight-read. Lehmann and Ericsson

(1996) assessed first, the size of repertoire that pianists possessed to accompany soloists and ensembles and second, accumulated duration of accompanying experience. Both indicators accounted independently for individual differences in sight-reading: a larger accompanying repertoire and more accompanying experience led to better sight-reading performance under standardized conditions. One could conclude from this that experience with the representative situation (real-time demands, short or no preparation time, etc.) as well as the knowledge base acquired through the performance of many pieces facilitates future performance. In general, among the participants of the study the experience as accompanist started a few years after the onset of piano training. They reported playing progressively more difficult accompanying piano parts, commensurate with their parallel increase in pianistic skills. Counter to many musicians' intuitions, this explains nicely why positive correlations are found between general instrumental skills and sight-reading at pre-professional levels (McPherson 1995, 2005).

A similar study on the acquisition of sight-reading skills included different levels of musical complexity (Kopiez and Lee 2006, 2008). In their experiment, subjects sight-read pieces of five levels of difficulty. Sight-reading performance was assessed along with indicators of psychomotor speed (tapping speed, trill speed), elementary cognitive skills (reaction time, speed of information processing [number connection test]), general cognitive skills (tests of short-term and working memory and general mental capacity), and expertise-related indicators (inner hearing, practice times for piano alone and accompanying, starting ages). The best single predictors for the overall score across all five levels of difficulty were trill speed between the third and fourth fingers, sight-reading experience up to age 15, scores on the number connection test, and inner hearing (Kopiez and Lee 2008). While those results emphasize the impact of experience and efficient perceptual encoding, they also suggest that pianistic abilities play a role. The authors also analysed their results separately for the individual levels of complexity (Kopiez and Lee 2006, see Figure 32.1) and showed convincingly that performance at different levels of difficulty was mediated by different combinations of predictors. Hence, those factors that contribute to better performance at lower levels of difficulty may not be the same as those which mediate superior performance at higher levels.

Many educational studies and reviews have offered suggestions on how to improve sight-reading (e.g. Lehmann and McArthur 2002, pp. 147–148; McPherson 2005) and insightful teachers have developed graded material to train sight-reading systematically. However, some advice might be more useful than other: for example, training eye movements by rolling your eyes or similar exercises are certainly futile—you would simply get better at rolling your eyes. Rather, young performers should get accustomed to playing their instrument without constantly looking at it (e.g. piano) to free up their vision to look at the score while still finding their way on the instrument. Performing under real-time conditions also precludes stuttering, i.e. stopping at every mistake and correcting it, but rather 'faking' one's way through the score, i.e. trying to infer plausible content. This can only be done if the student has ample experience with a certain style of music and can build up suitable expectations about how the music might continue. It is here also that knowledge of music theory can be applied. One has to acknowledge that a stable and deliberate interpretation may not be possible at first sight but that attending to dynamic and articulatory signs along with applying simple rules of expression (e.g. creating phrase arches of tempo and loudness) will generate a musically sounding first impression.

Summary

Sight-reading provides a complex problem-solving situation with an intricate interplay of bottom-up mechanisms (driven by the input stimulus of the score and auditory feedback) and top-down processes (driven by expectations and cognitions). It is conceivable that limitations on the general playing of an instrument or a lack of technical proficiency exist that may consequentially impact the ability to sight-read: One can never sight-read beyond the level of rehearsed performance, but how close to it one sight-reads seems to be very much a matter of training. Sight-reading ability at lower skill levels may partly emerge from general instrumental skill

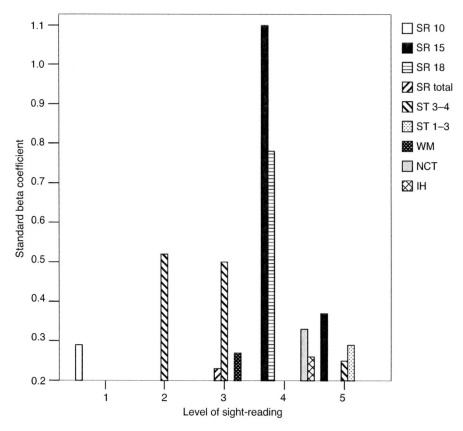

Fig. 32.1 Significant predictors of sight-reading performance, separate for five levels of stimulus difficulty 1=easy, 5=difficult (data from Kopiez and Lee 2006). Predictors: SR, sight-reading experience up to age 10, 15, 18 or total up to the time of the experiment; ST, speed trilling between fingers 1–3 or 3–4 of right hand; WM, working memory in a number task; NCT, speeded number connection test; IH, inner hearing using an embedded melody paradigm.

increase whereas expert sight-reading necessitates extensive deliberate efforts to improve performance. By engaging in many hours of related experience, for example as an accompanist (in the case of pianists), sight-readers develop particular cognitive adaptations, such as efficient encoding, building of expectations and plausible inferencing, and memory skills. These help them cope with the real-time demands of reconstructing on the fly the score along with a preliminary expressive interpretation.

References

Allport DA, Antonis B and Reynolds P. (1972). On the division of attention: a disproof of the single channel hypothesis. *Quarterly Journal of Experimental Psychology*, **24**(2), 225–235.

Banton LJ (1995). The role of visual and auditory feedback during the sight reading of music. *Psychology of Music and Music Education*, **23**, 3–16.

Bekkering H and Neggers FW (2002). Visual search is modulated by action intentions. *Psychological Science*, **13**(4), 370–374.

Bent ID *et al.* (22 Apr. 2008). Notation. Grove music online, http://www.oxfordmusiconline.com/subscriber/article/grove/music/20114pg1.

Clifton JV (1986). Cognitive components in music reading and sight-reading performance. Doctoral dissertation, University of Waterloo, Ontario.

Crofton I and Fraser D (1985). *Dictionary of musical quotations*. Schirmer, New York.

Drake C and Palmer C. (2000). Skill acquisition in music performance: relations between planning and temporal control. *Cognition*, **74**(1), 1–32.

Ericsson K and Kintsch W (1995). Long-term working memory. *Psychological Review*, **102**(2), 211–245.

Fine P, Berry A and Rosner B (2006). The effect of pattern recognition and tonal predictability on sight-singing ability. *Psychology of Music*, **34**(4), 431–447.

Friberg A, Bresin R and Sundberg J (2006). Overview of the KTH rule system for musical performance. *Advances in Cognitive Psychology*, **2**(2–3), 145–161.

Furneaux S and Land MF (1999). The effects of skill on the eye–hand span during musical sight-reading. *Proceedings of the Royal Society. Biological Sciences*, **266**(1436), 2435–2440.

Gentner D (1988). Expertise in typewriting. In M Chi, R Glaser and M Farr, eds, *The nature of expertise*, 1–21. Erlbaum, Hillsdale, NJ.

Goolsby TW (1994). Profiles of processing: eye movements during sight reading. *Music Perception*, **12**(1), 97–123.

Jacobsen OI (1941). An analytical study of eye-movements in reading vocal and instrumental music. *Journal of Musicology*, **3**, 1–22.

Kinsler V and Carpenter RH (1995). Saccadic eye movements while reading music. *Vision Research*, **35**, 1447–1458.

Kopiez R and Lee JI (2006). Towards a dynamic model of skills involved in sight reading music. *Music Education Research*, **8**(1), 97–120.

Kopiez R and Lee JI (2008). Towards a general model of skills involved in sight reading music. *Music Education Research*, **10**(1), 41–62.

Kornicke LE (1995). An exploratory study of individual difference variables in piano sight-reading achievement. *Quarterly Journal of Music Teaching and Learning*, **6**(1), 56–79.

Lannert V and Ullman M (1945). Factors in the reading of piano music. *American Journal of Psychology*, **58**, 91–99.

Lehmann AC and McArthur VH (2002). Sight-reading. In R Parncutt and G McPherson, eds, *Science and psychology of music performance*, 135–150. Oxford University Press, Oxford.

Lehmann AC and Ericsson KA (1996). Performance without preparation: structure and acquisition of expert sight-reading and accompanying performance. *Psychomusicology*, **15**(1/2), 1–29.

Lehmann AC and Ericsson KA (1993). Sight-reading ability of expert pianists in the context of piano accompanying. *Psychomusicology*, **12**(2), 182–195.

Lehmann AC, Sloboda JA and Woody RH (2007). *Psychology for musicians: understanding and acquiring the skills*. Oxford University Press, New York.

McPherson GE (1995). The assessment of musical performance: development and validation of five new measures. *Psychology of Music*, **23**, 142–161.

McPherson GE (2005). From child to musician: skill development during the beginning stages of learning an instrument. *Psychology of Music*, **33**, 5–35.

Rayner K and Pollatsek A (1989). *The psychology of reading*. Erlbaum, Hillsdale, NJ.

Schon D and Besson M (2005). Visually induced auditory expectancy in music reading: a behavioral and electrophysiological study. *Journal of Cognitive Neuroscience*, **17**(4), 694–705.

Sloboda JA (1974). The eye–hand span. An approach to the study of sight reading. *Psychology of Music*, **2**, 4–10.

Sloboda JA (1976). The effect of item position on the likelihood of identification by interference in prose reading and music reading. *Canadian Journal of Psychology*, **30**, 228–236.

Sloboda JA (1977). Phrase units as determinants of visual processing in music reading. *British Journal of Psychology*, **68**, 117–124.

Sloboda JA (1984). Experimental studies of music reading: a review. *Music Perception*, **2**, 222–236.

Truitt FE, Clifton C, Pollatsek A and Rayner K (1997). The perceptual span and the eye–hand span in sight-reading music. *Visual Cognition*, **4**(2), 134–161.

Waters AJ, Townsend E and Underwood G (1998). Expertise in musical sight-reading: a study of pianists. *British Journal of Psychology*, **89**, 123–149.

Watkins JG (1942). *Objective measurement of instrumental performance*. Columbia University Teachers College, New York.

Weaver HE (1943). A study of visual processes in reading differently constructed musical selections. *Psychological Monographs*, **55**, 1–30.

Yumoto M, Matsuda M, Itoh K, Uno A, Karino S, Saitoh O, Kaneko Y, Yatomi Y and Kaga K (2005). Auditory imagery mismatch negativity elicited in musicians. *Neuroreport*, **16**(11), 1175–1178.

CHAPTER 33

Performing from memory

Roger Chaffin, Topher R. Logan and Kristen T. Begosh

WHAT is the difference between 'learning' a new piece of music and 'memorizing' it? Both involve memory, but of different kinds. The memories that develop spontaneously while learning a new piece take the form of *associative chains* in which each passage cues the memory of what comes next. Deliberate memorization transforms the motor and auditory chains, making them *content addressable*. A memory is content addressable if you can ask yourself, e.g., 'How does the third repetition of the main theme go?', and the music comes to mind. Associative chains have a major weakness: to reach any link in the chain you have to start at the beginning. For a musician, this becomes a problem when something goes wrong in performance. Besides the embarrassment of starting over, there is the agony of wondering whether memory will fail again in the same place. Content-addressable memories avoid this problem. They can be located directly by thinking of the relevant location in the piece. In a memorized performance, content-addressable memory provides a safety net that permits recovery in case the associative chain breaks and the performance is disrupted.

Associative chains and content-addressable memories are learned in different ways and have different properties. Content-addressable memories are more likely to be explicit (conscious) and to involve declarative (language-based) knowledge *that* such-and-such is the case, whereas associative chains are more likely to be implicit (unconscious) and to involve procedural (motor-based) knowledge of *how* to do

something. To memorize a piece of music for performance, the musician must smoothly integrate the two kinds of memory.

English has only the one term 'memory' to refer to these two very different mental processes. In everyday talk, musicians make the distinction by referring to 'learning' and 'memorizing'. There is the potential for confusion here. For example, how should we understand musicians who say that they do not memorize, for whom memorization is 'something that just happens' (André-Michel Schub), 'a subconscious process' (Harold Bauer), that is 'very simple' (Walter Gieseking), 'like breathing' (Jorge Bolet); how should we understand Jorge Bolet, when he says that he memorized Liszt's *Mephisto Waltz* in 75 minutes (Chaffin *et al.* 2002, Chapter 3)?

For the musician, the relevant question is whether memory will be reliable on stage. Jorge Bolet probably did not mean that he was ready to go on stage and perform. Professional performers may sometimes find themselves in the position of having to perform at short notice, but they do not normally choose to. It is risky. What happens if something goes wrong? If the memory is in the form of an associative chain, then the only recourse is to start again at the beginning of the chain. This kind of catastrophic memory failure is an unfortunate staple of student recitals. Students often make the mistake of assuming that because they can get through a piece without the score in the studio, they can do the same in live performance. They do not appreciate that the associative chain is just the first step; much more work is needed to create a reliable, content-addressable memory.

Experienced performers know better; they give themselves a safety net. Memory failures are inevitable in live performance. A performer may go for years without a problem but, with enough performances, eventually it will happen. The important thing is to recover gracefully. Experienced performers do not stop and go back to the beginning. They go on. They have a mental map of the piece that allows them to keep track of where they are as the performance unfolds. The map provides landmarks where they can restart the performance if necessary (Chaffin *et al.* 2002, Chapter 9). When something goes wrong, the expert jumps to the next landmark and the performance continues. Most of the time, the audience is not even aware that anything went wrong. Memorization is the creation of this safety net.

Our account of memory for performance builds on the standard view of memory described by Bob Snyder in Chapter 10 of this volume (also Ginsborg 2004). We focus on the role of serial chaining and content addressability. Two areas of the episodic memory literature are particularly relevant to our discussion: oral traditions and expert memory. In oral traditions, materials such as children's rhymes and folk songs are handed down from one generation to another without the benefit of written records, often for hundreds of years. We will draw on David Rubin's (1995, 2006) analysis of this phenomenon and on his *basic system theory of episodic memory* to describe the role of different types of memory (auditory, motor, visual, emotional, structural, and linguistic) in associative chaining.

The second area of psychological research that we will draw on is the study of expert memory. The history of music is filled with examples of extraordinary feats of memory and these are often exhibited as evidence that the musician in question possessed some special gift or talent. For example, the young Mozart's writing out of Allegri's *Miserere* from memory was seen, at the time and ever since, as evidence of his genius (Chaffin *et al.* 2002, p. 66). The conclusion of careful study by psychologists is that such feats are *not* the product of a special talent for memorization but are the entirely predictable result of years of training and the effective use of retrieval schemes (Ericsson and Charness 1994). Expert memorists develop retrieval strategies to make their memories content addressable so that they can find the information they need when they need it (Ericsson and Kintsch 1995). We will use Anders Ericsson's theory of expert memory to explain how experienced performers memorize, as opposed to simply learn, a new piece.

Associative chaining

Music performance relies heavily on associative chaining: what you are playing reminds you of what comes next. In this respect, memory for music is similar to memory for rhymes, songs, and poems. In each case, the task of memorization is made easier by the fact that what comes next is heavily constrained by what precedes it (Rubin 1995, 2006). For example:

There was a young man of Japan,

Whose limericks never would ____.

The possibilities for the next word in this little verse are constrained by syntax to verbs, by semantics to verbs that can take 'limericks' as agent, and by rhyme to words that end in '__an'. These multiple constraints narrow the possibilities. One does not have to have heard this limerick before to know that the missing word is 'scan'.

The role of schemas[1]

How do we know that the second line must rhyme with the first? We recognize it as a limerick. Even if the word 'limerick' were not explicitly mentioned in the second line, we would recognize the characteristic formulaic opening and 'Te dee-ya, te dee-ya, te-dum' rhythm. Rapid recognition of this sort is a normal feature of memory: it is the same when we recognize a strawberry, a rain storm, or a birthday party. Information in long-term memory is represented in the form of *schemas* that summarize our previous experience and tell us what to expect. The schema for

---

[1] The Latin root of 'schema' dictates a plural form 'schema' or 'schemata'. We prefer the more regular, colloquial form 'schemas'. All three forms are in common use in the psychological literature.

limericks tells us that the second line will rhyme with the first. Similarly, schemas tell us to eat strawberries, use umbrellas when it rains, and give presents at birthday parties.

Contrary to popular belief, memory is not a vast storehouse containing exact records of a myriad of original events (Mandler 1984). Memories for specific events (episodic memories) are *reconstructed* at each remembering on the basis of schematic (semantic) knowledge representing generic memories. Schemas allow us to economically recall our past in enormous detail, but this ability has a price. When we take the trouble to check, many of the details turn out to be wrong. The same schematic frameworks that allow us to remember are also a source of distortion. We remember the gist, and fill in the details, systematically misremembering in the process.

Given the general fallibility of memory, musicians' routine reliance on rote memory seems remarkable. How is accurate recall possible, if memory for a piece must be reconstructed from generic musical schemas each time it is played? We would expect performances to be full of mistakes as the musician replaces the exact notes provided by the composer with the musical gist based on generic knowledge of harmonic, melodic, metric, and rhythmic patterns.

The answer comes from studies of how memory functions in oral traditions (Rubin 1995, 2006). In non-literate cultures, oral traditions such as ballads, epic poems, and religious enactments often remain stable across centuries, indicating that memories for their performance have been transmitted, more or less verbatim, from one generation to the next across many years. How is this done? Like everyone else, the memories of bards, minstrels, and storytellers are reconstructed at each performance (Rubin 1995, 2006). Their performances *do* vary, but they are sufficiently consistent that the distortion is minimal, even across generations. This surprising level of accuracy is a product of *multiple constraints*. In every oral tradition studied, the material follows strict formal constraints on rhyme, rhythm, and alliteration. Our example of the limerick illustrates how these constraints operate. The multiple constraints of grammar, meaning, metre and rhyme reduce the possibilities available.

In music, similar constraints are provided by melody, harmony, metre, and rhythm. In addition, repetition is normally much more pronounced in music than in language and provides additional local constraints (Huron 2006, p. 229–231). All of these constraints combine to make the task of memory reconstruction easier. Knowing how different composers use the various conventions of each musical genre makes constraints more specific, and so memorization is easier for experts than for novices (Williamon and Valentine 2002). In song, the constraints of the musical and literary forms combine, making memorization easier when words or music are learned together rather than separately (Ginsborg and Sloboda 2007).

Multiple memory systems

Another feature that music shares with the materials transmitted in oral traditions is that it is recalled as part of a *performance*. Performance calls on the many different cognitive and bodily systems involved in action, each of which lays down its own memory traces, subject to its own schemas. These provide multiple retrieval cues, making memory for performance more robust than memory for text (Rubin 1995, 2006). On the basis of cognitive and neurological evidence, Rubin (2006) has proposed a model of memory in which multiple memory systems contribute to episodic memories. We will restrict our description to those systems most relevant to musical performance: auditory, motor, visual, emotional, narrative, and linguistic memory. A memorized performance is generated through the interaction of the information available in each system. For example, musicians find it easier to play a piece of music they have memorized than to write it out because playing provides memory cues from the motor system that are absent when writing out the score (Chaffin and Logan 2006). Just as in the limerick example, the multiple retrieval cues from the different systems interact to reduce the range of possibilities.

Auditory memory

The history of Western music is replete with stories of musicians who were able to hear entire works in their heads (Deutsch and Pierce 1992). Psychological studies confirm this ability in people with or without musical training, and have begun to specify the form in which the auditory information is stored (Halpern 1992). These studies confirm that people can 'hear' a melody in their heads, usually without accompanying imagery from other modalities, suggesting that the ability is based on an independent auditory memory (Reisberg 2001, Chapter 11). Neuropsychological studies provide further confirmation of the existence of a separate auditory subsystem (e.g. Fornazzari *et al.* 2006). In performance, auditory memory tells the musician what comes next, providing cues to elicit the music from memory, while also letting the musician know that things are on track (Finney and Palmer 2003).

We demonstrated one important way that auditory memory helps constrain recall when we showed how the rhythmic and rhyming schema for limericks narrow the range of possibilities for recall. In a similar vein, Rubin (2006) argued that the organization of ballads into stanzas with invariant metric and rhyming schemas has been largely responsible for the preservation of an oral tradition in North Carolina that is directly traceable to European ballads of the Middle Ages. In similar ways, schemas for standard rhythmic, melodic and harmonic patterns allow musicians to remember music better than non-musicians (Halpern and Bower 1982). Auditory memory appears to contain information about both pitch contour (relative pitch) as well as pitch category (absolute pitch), since people can sometimes recall music in the same key as the original (Dowling 1978; Halpern 1989).[2]

Motor memory

Motor memory allows actions to be executed automatically by providing kinaesthetic memory of the sensory feedback from joints, muscles, and touch receptors. Although motor skills have been studied since the earliest days of experimental psychology (Adams 1987), the contribution of the motor system to memory was neglected by early cognitive theories of memory, entering mainstream cognitive theorizing only with the distinction between procedural (motor)

and declarative (conceptual) memory (Anderson 1978; Squire 1987). More recently, the discovery of 'mirror neurons' in the motor system that respond to seeing the corresponding action performed by another (Rizzolatti and Craighero 2004) has reaffirmed earlier claims that the motor and sensory systems are intimately linked (Liberman and Mattingly 1985). The motor system is still largely treated as a completely separate system (Rosenbaum 2005), however, and the study of its contribution to memory is still in its infancy, under the rubric of 'embodied cognition' (Glenberg 1997).

Musicians talk about motor memory as being 'in the hands'. Perhaps the most important feature of motor memory for musicians is that it is implicit (unconscious). Musicians know *that* they can play a particular piece (declarative knowledge), but the knowledge of *how* to play can only be exhibited by actually playing (procedural knowledge). This is a source of anxiety, and may lead to over-practice. Playing seems to be the only way to reassure oneself that memory for a piece is intact. Mental practice provides an alternative but requires explicit memory. To make motor memory explicit, actions must be recoded in propositional form so that they can be rehearsed in working memory as a thought of the general form, 'Next, do this'. This kind mental instruction is a form of *linguistic memory*, discussed below.

Motor memory provides the clearest examples of associative chaining in memory; each action in the series cues the next. This is what makes motor memories implicit: to be accessed, they must be performed. Actions can, of course, be cued in other ways. People stand up for national anthems, shake hands when introduced, and remember to stop at the grocery store on the way home from work. This last example is different from the others, because the action is directed by a cue that we provide for ourselves. The cue is a thought in working memory, e.g., 'Take this exit'. This is the same kind of self-cuing that makes mental rehearsal possible. Chaffin, Imreh & Crawford (2002) introduced the term *performance cues* to refer to the use of this kind of cue in music performance. Setting up performance cues is the main work involved in memorizing for performance and is described below in the sections on *expert memory* and *performance cues*.

---

[2] Remembering pitch contour requires the use of spatial imagery which Rubin (2006) identifies as a separate basic system.

Visual memory

Visual memory of the score is used mainly in the early stages of memorizing, while visual memory of the hands on the instrument becomes more important in the later stages. The role of visual memory for the score is evident in the difficulty that some musicians experience when working with a different edition of a score from the one they used to initially learn a piece (e.g. Chaffin *et al.* 2002, p. 37). A new score is difficult to work with because the visual information it provides is different from the musician's visual memory. It is common to remember the location of a passage on the page, a form of spatial imagery. Student musicians frequently use the spatial organization of music by pages rather than the formal structure of the piece to organize their practice (Williamon and Valentine 2000).

As in the general population, there are large individual differences between musicians in their subjective experience of visual memory. Some musicians report having 'photographic' memories, while others say that their visual memories are poor or unhelpful. For example, Myra Hess described how she could 'see' and 'read' the printed page when playing from memory, whereas Alfred Brendel reported that his memory was 'not visual at all' (Chaffin *et al.* 2002, pp. 37–41). These reports probably reflect real differences in the detailed information available in visual memory (Reisberg 2001, Chapter 11). Reports of visual images are misleading, however, in two ways. First, mental images are *not* pictures. Images are not neutral, objective depictions of reality but are organized interpretations that reflect the way that the original was understood. To discover whether you misread a note you cannot inspect your mental image of the score, you have to go back and look at the real thing. Second, people who report having no visual memory still have spatial memories which are stored in a separate system. While spatial memory does not provide a vivid subjective experience, it does provide information about the location of notes on the page.[3]

So a person could experience no visual imagery but still be disrupted by using a different edition of a score.

Emotional memory

Memories for emotional events are formed more easily and are less likely to be forgotten than non-emotional memories (Bower 1981; Talmi *et al.* 2007). This is as true for music as any other material (Schulkind *et al.* 1999). The positive effects of emotion on memory are disrupted by damage to neural areas involved in emotion (Greenberg and Rubin 2003). Together, these findings are the basis for identifying emotional memory as a separate system.[4] It seems clear that the performer's visceral response to the music contributes to musical memory. We have observed that musicians find it difficult to play from memory when asked to perform without expression and surmise that playing without expression eliminates emotional cues that normally contribute to the retrieval of the music from memory.

Structural memory

We suggest that structural memory is the musical equivalent of Rubin's *narrative memory*: memory for the overall sequential organization and goal structure of a story or biography. Memories for events are organized by schemas that connect temporal series of discrete actions through narrative structures based on the goals of the actors involved (Mandler 1984). Although often expressed in language, narrative structure can be expressed in a variety of forms including pictures, cartoons, silent films, dreams, dance, and mime (Rubin 2006). In the Western classical tradition, the same kind of narrative structure is responsible for the hierarchical organization of a piece into sections and subsections based on melodic, harmonic, and metrical structures. In preparing a piece of music, experienced musicians analyse these structural properties and use them to organize both their practice and their memories (Chaffin and Imreh 1997,

[3] We have not followed Rubin (2006) in singling out spatial imagery as a separate form of memory because in music performance it appears to operate across modalities, binding together representations in the auditory, motor, and visual systems

[4] This is an oversimplification since emotion is a complex and varied phenomenon that draws on multiple neural systems (Rubin 2006).

2002; Chaffin *et al.* 2002; Hallam 1995; Williamon and Valentine 2002).

In 'programme' music, narrative organization is explicitly applied to music. Despite the resistance of critics to providing a storyline for every piece of music, the ease with which music lends itself to this kind of treatment suggests that musical and narrative structure share common roots. We suggest that they stem from the same cognitive system; musical form and the storyline of a musical programme are both manifestations the underlying ability to identify large-scale structural relations between events.

An important difference between narrative and musical structure is that the former seems to be easier to perceive. Even young children are sensitive to narrative structure (Nelson and Fivush 2004), whereas sensitivity to musical structure develops slowly with musical training (Williamon and Valentine 2002) and is not always found, even with experienced musicians (Chapter 10 this volume, pp 113–115). The difference may be due to the fact that in our culture people generally have a lot more experience telling stories than they do playing music.

Linguistic memory

The mental instructions that experienced performers use to remind themselves what to do at key points in a performance are a form of *linguistic memory* (Chaffin *et al.* 2002).[5] These instructions do not necessarily involve words. They are stored in an abstract 'subject-predicate' (propositional) form that usually points to other modalities (motor, auditory, visual, and emotional memories). However, their propositional form means that they can normally be glossed in words, e.g., 'Hold back' or 'Now, like this' (Englekamp 2001).

An important characteristic of linguistic memories is that they can be rehearsed in working memory, where they can serve to direct other mental processes. When the activity of

other cognitive systems is re-described in language, the inner speech that results provides a means of mental control that can be used to implement plans and strategies (Reisberg 1992, p. viii; Rubin 2006).[6] Rehearsing a mental instruction in working memory broadcasts it throughout the nervous system, automatically activating other systems and coordinating their activity (Barrs 1988).[7] As we noted above, this ability can be used for mental rehearsal or to recover if the associative chain of a memorized performance breaks.

Content-addressable memory

Associative chaining works well so long as the chain is intact. If the performance stops, however, the chain is broken, and then memory failure is complete and catastrophic. The performer can only go back to the beginning and start over. To avoid such ignominy, experienced performers prepare a safety net that provides other options; they prepare multiple starting points.

When you want to sing happy birthday, you simply think, 'Happy Birthday', and start singing. The verbal label acts as a retrieval cue for the start of the song and the rest is then cued by associative chaining. Now imagine that you want to start at the last line. Most of us cannot do this immediately. We have to start at the beginning and run through. Once we have the last line in working memory, however, we can easily set up a new starting point by thinking, 'Start of the last line' as we sing. A few repetitions to strengthen the associative link between the new cue and singing the last line and we have a new starting point. Any time we want to start at the last line, we can now simply think, 'Start of the last line' and start singing.

We have set up a new performance cue, making this place in the music content addressable (Chaffin *et al.* 2002). Simply thinking of the cue now activates the memories needed to start singing.

[5] The first author has previously referred to both linguistic and structural memory as 'conceptual' or 'declarative' memory (e.g., Chaffin *et al.* 2002; Chaffin and Imreh, 2002). The present terminology represents a refinement of that classification.

[6] The important role of inner speech in mental control has been noted by many psychologists including Pavlov, Watson, Vygotsky, and Piaget.

[7] The process of directing and monitoring our own mental operations in this way may be responsible for uniquely human qualities of conscious experience (Dennett 1991).

The performance cue lacks the multidimensional richness of the associative chain, where the next link was cued by sound, action, and emotion. What it lacks in richness, it makes up for in flexibility. You can now think of the passage at any time, without running through the whole piece from the beginning.

We will focus on two aspects of this strategy. First, when applied to a long piece of music, the strategy of creating multiple starting points has many similarities with how experts memorize in other domains that have nothing to do with music. We will describe these similarities in the next section. Second, there is a risk involved in setting up additional starting points. Thinking about what you are doing can interfere with skilled performance, a phenomenon known as *choking* (Beilock and Carr 2001). We will describe how experienced musicians avoid this problem in the section on *performance cues*.

Expert memory

Experts in any domain memorize with a facility that seems superhuman (Gobet and Simon 1996). Musicians are no exception; as we have already noted, their biographies are full of tales of amazing memory feats. The abilities of other expert memorists have been attributed to the use of highly practiced retrieval strategies by skilled memory theory (Chase and Ericsson 1982) and its extension, long-term working memory theory (Ericsson and Kintsch 1995). These theories are based on the study of domains such as chess boards (Chase and Simon 1973), digit strings (Thompson *et al.* 1993), and dinner orders (Ericsson and Oliver 1989) that are very different from music performance: structural and linguistic memory are primary and associative chaining of motor and auditory memories play minor roles. Despite the differences, the principles of expert memory established in these domains apply to music performance because experienced musicians also rely on structural and linguistic memory to provide a safety net in case the chain of motor and auditory memories breaks (Chaffin and Logan 2006).

The feats of expert memorists can be explained in terms of three principles: meaningful encoding of novel material, use of a well-learned retrieval structure, and extended practice to decrease the time needed for retrieval from long-term memory (Ericsson and Kintsch 1995). The same three principles apply to expert music performance (Chaffin *et al.* 2002; Krampe and Ericsson 1996). First, experts' knowledge of their domain of expertise allows them to make use of schematic knowledge already stored in memory to organize information into larger chunks (Tulving 1962). For a musician, these include familiar patterns like chords, scales, and arpeggios, whose practice forms an important part of every musician's training (Halpern and Bower 1982). Second, expert memory in any domain requires a retrieval scheme to organize the cues that provide access to the chunks of information in long-term memory (Ericsson and Oliver 1989). For a musician, the formal structure of the music conveniently provides a ready-made hierarchical organization to serve as a retrieval scheme. For example, Figure 33.1 shows how the hierarchical organization of JS Bach's Italian Concerto (Presto) into movements, sections, subsections, and bars was used by a pianist to organize her memory for the piece (Chaffin *et al.* 2002). The third principle of expert memory is that prolonged practice is required to bring the speed of operation of a memory retrieval scheme like the one in Figure 33.1 up to the speed needed to guide behaviour (Ericsson and Kintsch 1995). For the musician, this involves practising memory retrieval until it is rapid and reliable enough to keep pace with the performance.

Rapid memory retrieval is important in music performance to prevent the hands from 'running away' as the retrieval of procedural knowledge by associative chaining outpaces the slower, content-addressable retrieval of declarative knowledge. The smooth integration of the two systems creates 'long-term working memory' (Ericsson and Kintsch 1995). Practice is needed so that the performance cue for what comes next arrives in working memory at just the right moment, before the corresponding motor sequences, but not so far in advance as to distract from the execution of the preceding passage and cause 'choking'.

The interplay of the two retrieval systems is illustrated in Figure 33.2. The figures shows the two routes by which memory for a piece of music

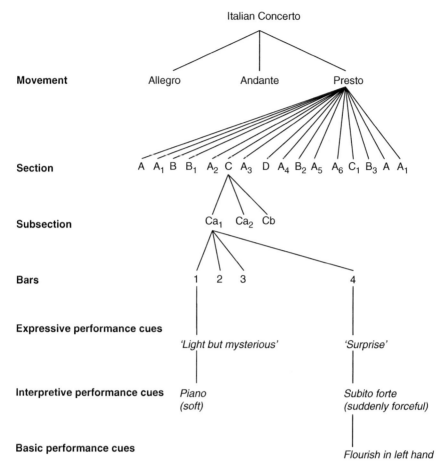

Fig. 33.1 Hypothetical hierarchical retrieval scheme 'unpacked' for Section C of the Presto from the Italian Concerto by JS Bach. Main themes (sections) are represented by capital letters. Section C is 'unpacked' into subsections (Ca1, Ca2, Cb). Subsection Ca1 is further 'unpacked' into its performance cues. (From Chaffin R., Imreh G., & Crawford M. (2002). *Practicing perfection: Memory and piano performance*. Erlbaum, Mahwah NJ, p. 200. Copyright © 2002. Adapted with permission).

can be retrieved. At the bottom of the figure are the serial associations set up while learning to play the piece. These associations, based on schema for rhythm, meter, harmony, and melody, directly link each passage with the next. Each passage is cued only by the preceding passage. Direct, content-addressable access is provided by a second retrieval system, shown at the top of the figure. Here, a hierarchical retrieval organization, similar to that in Figure 33.1, provides direct access to any section of the piece. Performance cues embedded in this organization provide possible 'starting points' in case things go wrong in performance.

Performance cues

One of the main challenges in memorizing for performance is to integrate the two retrieval systems. As one pianist put it in talking about her learning the Italian Concerto (Presto) by JS Bach:

My fingers were playing the notes just fine. The practice I needed was in my head. I had to learn to keep track of where I was. It was a matter of learning exactly what I needed to be thinking of as I played, and at exactly what point so that as I approached a switching point I would automatically think

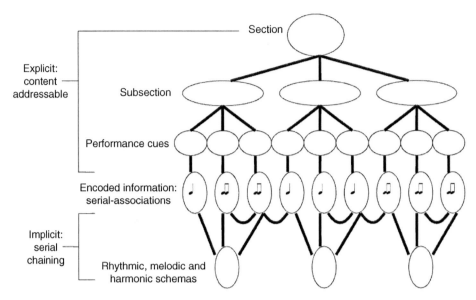

Fig. 33.2 Model of episodic memory for music performance showing separate retrieval organizations for access by content address and by serial associative chaining. (From Ericsson K. A., & Kintsch W., Long-term working memory. Psychological Review, 102, 211–245. Copyright © 1995, The American Psychological Association. Adapted with permission).

about where I was, and which way the switch would go.

Chaffin et al. (2002, p. 224)

The musician was talking about the need to practice performance cues. Performance cues are landmarks in the mental map of a piece that an experienced musician maintains in working memory during performance. Because they can be accessed both by serial cuing and directly, by address, they provide a safety net in case serial cuing breaks down. Careful preparation of performance cues makes it possible for soloists to reliably perform challenging works from memory on the concert stage. By repeatedly paying attention to performance cues during practice, the musician ensures that that they become an integral part of the performance, coming to mind effortlessly as the music unfolds. The performer remains mindful of these aspects of the performance while allowing others to be executed automatically. When things go smoothly, performance cues are a source of spontaneity and variation in highly polished performances (Chaffin *et al.* 2007). When things go wrong, they provide places at which the soloist can recover and go on.

Performance cues point to different types of memory according to which aspect of the music they address.[8] *Structural* cues are critical places in the formal structure, such as section boundaries. *Expressive* cues represent musical feelings, e.g., excitement.[9] *Interpretive* cues refer to musical gestures, such as changes of tempo or dynamics. *Basic* cues point to motor memory for critical details of technique, e.g., a fingering that sets the hand up for what follows. Musicians are likely to agree on the musical structure of a piece.[10] They are likely to differ, however, on other cues that are more specific to the performer or instrument. For example, basic performance cues for a cellist include decisions about intonation, bowing, and changing string that are not relevant for a pianist (Chaffin *et al.*

[8] The organization of cues into types here is descriptive and somewhat arbitrary. Other descriptive organizations are possible.
[9] Musical structure and expression are necessarily linked, but expressive cues do not always coincide with structural boundaries (Chaffin *et al.* 2008).
[10] The musical structure of some pieces may, however, be understood in more than one way, e.g., Ginsborg *et al.* (2006).

2008). For solo works, the only performance cues required are those for the individual musician, while for ensemble performance the musicians must also establish shared performance cues to coordinate their actions (Ginsborg *et al*. 2006).

Performance cues are content addressable through their location in the hierarchical organization of the piece (see Figure 33.1). In learning a new piece, the musician moves up and down the hierarchy, attending to each level of organization and each type of cue in turn (Chaffin *et al*. 2006; Williamon *et al*. 2002). Like experts in other fields, who approach a new problem by looking at the 'big picture', experienced musicians approach the task of learning a new piece by getting an overall artistic image of how the music should sound, focusing on structural and expressive cues (Neuhaus 1973; Chaffin *et al*. 2003). Beyond this commonality, the order in which different types of performance cue are practiced appears to depend on the individual, piece, and situation. What all the experienced performers that have been studied to date have in common is that they practice performance cues. This provides them with a safety net for times when associative cuing fails (Chaffin and Logan 2006).

Conclusion

Though it has a long history in Western classical music, playing from memory is often a source of great anxiety for performers. Pianist Janina Fialkowska talked of the 'terror of forgetting'. Lazar Berman reported that, 'Every time I play in front of an audience, it is a very important and difficult affair, both physically and spiritually. I am never sure that it is going to end well' (Chaffin *et al*. 2002, Chapter 3). Anton Rubenstein wrote that fear of memory failure 'inflicted upon me tortures only to be compared with those of the Inquisition' (Rubenstein 1969, p. 18).

Given the costs involved in playing from memory and its long tradition, stretching back 175 years, it might be expected that musicians would have developed a systematic understanding of the problems involved. This has not happened (Aiello and Williamon 2004). Individual musicians know a great deal about strategies for memorization (Hallam 1995, 1997), but this knowledge is conveyed from teacher to student through an apprenticeship system of training that makes it unavailable for systematic analysis. Memorization is viewed as an individual and mysterious process. It is up to each person to find their own method (Ginsborg 2002). This is regrettable and unnecessary. Memory varies no more from one person to another than any other trait or capacity. Beneath a superficial diversity, the cognitive and neurological systems involved in memory are common to all human beings. In this chapter we have described those aspects that are most relevant to performing music from memory.

Acknowledgements

We thank Mary Crawford, Jane Ginsborg, and Aaron Williamon for helpful comments on previous versions of this chapter.

References

Adams J (1987). Historical review and appraisal of research on the learning and transfer of human motor skills. *Psychological Bulletin*, **101**, 41–74.

Aiello R and Williamon A (2004). Memory. In R Parncutt and GE McPherson, eds, *The science and psychology of music performance*, 167–182. Oxford University Press, New York.

Anderson JR (1978). Arguments concerning representations for mental imagery. *Psychological Review*, **85**, 249–277.

Baars BJ (1988). *A cognitive theory of consciousness*. Cambridge University Press, Cambridge University Press.

Beilock SL and Carr TH (2001). On the fragility of skilled performance: what governs choking under pressure? *Journal of Experimental Psychology: General*, **130**, 701–725.

Bower GH (1981). Mood and memory. *American Psychologist*, **36**, 129–148.

Chaffin R and Imreh G (1997). 'Pulling teeth and torture': musical memory and problem solving. *Thinking and reasoning*, **3**, 315–336.

Chaffin R and Imreh G (2002). Practicing perfection: piano performance as expert memory. *Psychological Science*, **13**, 342–349.

Chaffin R, Imreh G and Crawford M (2002). *Practicing perfection: memory and piano performance*. Erlbaum, Mahwah, NJ.

Chaffin R, Imreh G, Lemieux AF and Chen C (2003). 'Seeing the big picture': piano practice as expert problem solving. *Music Perception*, **20**, 465–490.

Chaffin R, Lemieux A and Chen C (2006). Spontaneity and creativity in highly practiced performance. In I Deliège and GA Wiggins, eds, *Musical creativity: multidisciplinary research in theory and practice*, 200–218. Psychology Press, London.

Chaffin R, Lemieux A and Chen C (2007). 'It's different every time I play': spontaneity in highly prepared musical performance. *Music Perception*, **24**, 455–472.

Chaffin R, Lisboa T, Logan T and Begosh KT (in press). Preparation for cello performance: The role of performance cues. *Music Psychology*.

Chaffin R and Logan T (2006). Practicing perfection: how concert soloists prepare for performance. *Advances in Cognitive Psychology*, **2**, 113–130.

Chase W and Ericsson KA (1982). Skill and working memory. In GH Bower, ed., *The psychology of learning and motivation*, 1–58. Academic Press, New York.

Chase W and Simon H (1973). Perception in chess. *Cognitive Psychology*, **4**, 55–81.

Dennett DC (1991). *Consciousness explained*. Little, Brown and Co., New York.

Deutsch D and Pierce JR (1992). The climate of auditory imagery and music. In D Reisberg, ed., *Auditory imagery*, 237–260. Earlbaum, Hillsdale, NJ.

Dowling WJ (1978). Scale and contour: two components of a theory of memory for melodies. *Psychological Review*, **85**, 341–354.

Englekamp J (2001). *Memory for action*. Psychology Press, Hove, England.

Ericsson KA and Charness N (1994). Expert performance: its structure and acquisition. *American Psychologist*, **49**, 725–747.

Ericsson KA and Kintsch W (1995). Long-term working memory. *Psychological Review*, **102**, 211–245.

Ericsson KA and Oliver WL (1989). A methodology for assessing the detailed structure of memory skills. In AM Colley, JR Beech, eds, *Acquisition and performance of cognitive skills*, 193–215. John Wiley and Sons, Oxford.

Finney SA and Palmer C (2003). Auditory feedback and memory for music performance: sound evidence for an encoding effect. *Memory and Cognition*, **31**, 51–64.

Fornazzari L, Nadkarni S and Miranda D (2006). Preservation of episodic musical memory in a pianist with Alzheimer disease. *Neurology*, **66**, 610–611.

Ginsborg J (2002). Singing by heart: memorisation strategies for the words and music of songs. In JW Davidson, ed., *The music practitioner: exploring practices and research in the development of the expert music performer, teacher and listener*, 149–160. Ashgate Press, London.

Ginsborg J (2004). Strategies for memorizing music. In A Williamon, ed., *Musical excellence: strategies and techniques to enhance performance*, 123–142. Oxford University Press, Oxford.

Ginsborg J, Chaffin R and Nicholson G (2006). Shared performance cues in singing and conducting: a content analysis of talk during practice. *Psychology of Music*, **34**, 167–194.

Ginsborg J and Sloboda J (2007). Singers' recall for the words and melody of a new, unaccompanied song. *Psychology of Music*, **35**, 421–440.

Glenberg AM (1997). What memory is for? *Behavioral and Brain Sciences*, **20**, 1–55.

Greenberg DL and Rubin DC (2003). The neuropsychology of autobiographical memory. *Cortex*, **39**, 687–728.

Hallam S (1995). Professional musicians' approaches to the learning and interpretation of music. *Psychology of Music*, **23**, 111–128.

Hallam S (1997). The development of memorization strategies in musicians: implications for education. *British Journal of Music Education*, **14**, 87–97.

Halpern AR (1989). Memory for the absolute pitch of familiar songs. *Memory and Cognition*, **17**, 572–581.

Halpern AR (1992). Musical aspects of auditory imagery. In D Reisberg, ed., *Auditory imagery*, 1–27. Erlbaum, Hillsdale, NJ.

Halpern AR and Bower GH (1982). Musical expertise and melodic structure in memory for musical notation. *American Journal of Psychology*, **95**, 31–50.

Huron D (2006). *Sweet anticipation: music and the psychology of expectation*. MIT Press, Cambridge, MA.

Krampe RT and Ericsson KA (1996). Maintaining excellence: deliberate practice and elite performance in young and older pianists. *Journal of Experimental Psychology: General*, **125**, 331–359.

Liberman AM and Mattingly IG (1985). The motor theory of speech perception revised. *Cognition*, **21**, 1–36.

Mandler G (1984) *Stories, scripts, and scenes: aspects of schema theory*. Erlbaum, Hillsdale, NJ.

Nelson K and Fivush R (2004). The emergence of autobiographical memory: a social cultural developmental theory. *Psychological Review*, **111**, 486–511.

Neuhauss H (1973). *The art of piano playing*. Praeger Publishers Inc., New York.

Reisberg D (1992). *Auditory imagery*. Erlbaum, Hillsdale, NJ.

Reisberg D (2001). *Cognition: exploring the science of the mind*, 2nd edn. WW Norton, New York.

Rizzolatti G and Craighero L (2004). The mirror-neuron system. *Annual Review of Neuroscience*, **27**, 169–192.

Rosenbaum DA (2005). The Cinderella of psychology: the neglect of motor control in the science of mental life and behavior. *American Psychologist*, **60**, 308–317.

Rubin DC (1995). *Memory in oral traditions: the cognitive psychology of epic, ballads, and counting-out rhymes*. Oxford University Press, New York.

Rubin DC (2006). The basic-system model of episodic memory. *Perspectives on Psychological Science*, **1**, 277–311.

Rubinstein A (1969). *Autobiography of Anton Rubinstein: 1829–1889*, trans. A. Delano. Haskell House Publishers, New York (Original work published 1890).

Schulkind MD, Hennis LK and Rubin DC (1999). Music, emotion, and autobiographical memory: they're playing your song. *Memory and Cognition*, **27**, 948–955.

Squire LR (1987). *Memory and brain*. Oxford University Press, New York.

Talmi D, Schimmack U, Paterson T and Moscovitch M (2007). The role of attention and relatedness in emotionally enhanced memory. *Emotion*, **7**, 89–102.

Thompson CP, Cowan TM and Frieman J (1993). *Memory search by a memorist*. Erlbaum, Hillsdale, NJ.

Tulving E (1962). Subjective organization in free recall of 'unrelated' words. *Psychological Review*, **69**, 344–354.

Williamon A and Valentine E (2000). Quantity and quality of musical practice as predictors of performance quality. *British Journal of Psychology*, **91**, 353–376.

Williamon A and Valentine E (2002). The role of retrieval structures in memorizing music. *Cognitive Psychology*, **44**, 1–32.

Williamon A, Valentine E and Valentine J (2002). Shifting the focus of attention between levels of musical structure. *European Journal of Cognitive Psychology*, 493–520.

CHAPTER 34

Movement and collaboration in musical performance

Jane W. Davidson

Introduction

The body has a crucial role in the production and perception of musical performance that has been recognized for centuries. Indeed, the Ancient Greeks recognized the centrality of the body in all artistic performance expression, revealing that there was little to distinguish between the physical coordination required in music and dance. Speaking of all human activity, ethnomusicologist John Blacking (1977) argued in *The Anthropology of the Body* that a detailed understanding of the body set within the individual's cultural context can reveal subtle details about that person and how they interact within society. Increasingly since the 1970s scholarship has paid more attention to the role of the body in artistic activity, providing useful theories relating to how embodied thoughts and actions allow us to know and understand the world we inhabit through artistic performance activities like music and dance. For example, by the 1990s, in the area of critical musicology, Susan McClary's (1991) *Feminine endings* usefully addressed the function of the body through groundbreaking studies of popular artists, especially female artists like Madonna and kd Lang. She illustrated how it was as much our knowledge of these women as pop stars that influenced our experience of them, as it was their physical appearance and stage persona alongside the expressive affect experienced in their musical expressions that contributed to the performance: their bodies

were recognized as a very special site of social exchange, thus highlighting the physical, social and cultural nexus.

Research in the field of music psychology on the body has reflected some of the recent social anthropology and critical musicology trends, and so has developed a strand of socially focused enquiry. These ideas have been central to the work of the current author and will be explored in this chapter. Generally, however, the origins of modern psychology of music work on the body has tended to focus more on the bodily control aspects of playing, such as how movements assemble to execute a musical task. Intriguingly, these motor programming studies have been interfaced with some studies on music learning so that evidence for the emergence of these skills has occurred. Further perceptual enquiries and movement tracking studies have explored the body movements used for expressive musical effects. Also, applied research projects for pedagogical results have explored the use of bodily movement and movement metaphors to enhance understanding of musical expressivity for performers, with parallels being drawn between movement effort and flow to depict qualities in the musical semantics. Finally, within the group music context, studies of the identification of types of bodily movement used for interpersonal collaboration, including the coordination of musical and extra-musical material (musical and general social dynamics), and how this information helps to develop efficient collaborations have been undertaken. Thus, there has been a broad range of investigation, although the overall volume of work to date has been relatively small. In this chapter all the areas of existing enquiry will be explored. Though not comprehensive, the aim of this chapter is to explore the key existing music psychology investigations on this topic. It begins with research on motor programming, moving to more social aspects of performance and bodily movement, and finishing by considering musical collaborations.

Motor programming

We know that the assemblage of all the subcomponent actions required for a musician's movement activity is a highly complex process. Recent writing by Jäncke (2006) explains that the movements musicians use emerge from 'a concatenation of mechanical and neural factors'. Though such movements have been of interest for many decades, understanding how the movement plans are organized has been a challenge to researchers (see Lashley 1951; Bernstein 1967; Wing 2002). There is an underlying 'degrees of freedom' problem that relates to understanding the vast potential array of muscle and nerve impulses that create actions. Since Bernstein (1967) suggested that motor programmes (memory representations) operate for classes of movements rather than individual movements, theories to account for movement systems have ranged from the brain operating as a central executive to control movements, to proposals where movement control arises in an open system where the movements are themselves self-organizing (see Dahl 2004 for a more detailed explanation of these ideas). Ideas have been broad-ranging: for example, it could be that movements trigger one another in a *chain* or a *chain complex* (sequential or in parallel), a *radial net* (this is, where one action may drive several others of equal weighting), a *hierarchy* (here one or more actions trigger more actions at the next level down through the branches of the hierarchy) or a *heterarchy* (multiple feedback loops across the hierarchical structure) (see Wing 2002 for details). The current reality is that we do not have a clear single theory to understand how the movements are organized.

For the musician, an understanding motor programming itself is not essential, however, knowing that the activity of the body involved in playing a piece of music depends on generating and embedding these motor programmes in memory by rehearsal is essential. Indeed, musicians need to rehearse their physical actions until they achieve fluency, or an incompressible minimum time to execute them. We know that it can take years for a professional musician to reach fluency. Sloboda and colleagues (1994) found this to be in the range of 3 hours of practice a day across the 10 childhood years of learning. Intriguingly, and offering support for the positive effects of rehearsal, researchers have revealed that practice results in enlarged representations of somatosenory and auditory cortex (Pantev *et al.* 2001), as well as the motor areas in their brains (Altenmüller and Gruhn 2002). Moreover, since these programmes are established in memory, thought practice can have benefit on physical skill, though it is not as profitable as actual physical practice (Palmer 2006). Additionally, Dalla Bella and Palmer (2004) have shown that pianists move their fingers approximately three to four events ahead of time, suggesting that an early retrieval for action is required, motor activity being an anticipatory and unfurling behaviour in performance.

The development of the motor programmes for economy leads to automaticity. In a complex physical activity like musical performance, automaticity is absolutely necessary because it offers fluency. This automaticity varies from the basic assemblage of the body to execute a single musical note through to rapid sequences of notes, often containing subtle musical effects such as counterpoint or inner voicings to be played out for expressive effects. In essence, the expert's performance movements are seemingly effortless and necessarily effortless: in achieving a high degree of automation (unconscious processing) in the action, the expert performer's conscious thought is relatively 'free' to deal with moment by moment modifications that may be necessary as the music is being performed. The novice, by contrast, requires full conscious attention on the biomechanical activity. Movements often seem cumbersome, the novice not being able to achieve the actions to fluent effect. This means that the novice is not able to consider other performance-related concerns, for example adapting to new situations such as encountering a piano with a sticking key (see Lehmann and Davidson 2002 for more details).

Of course automaticity is required not only for movement fluency, but for the link between eye and hand if the musician is reading music, or between co-performers and timing, dynamic and overall expressive markings or ideas if the performance is to be coordinated and varying along the same dimensions for all players at all times. Clearly automaticity is a complex and multilayered skill. The layers of complexity were demonstrated in terms of musical timing by Shaffer (1984), who showed that when carrying out an activity like keyboard performance, there are specific timing effects that result as a consequence of the task demand. He noted, for example, that the typing performance by touch typists had specific timing profiles for certain combinations of letters. It is certain that the individual performer's body and instrument itself adds to this situation. For instance, a small pianist will have to develop his or her representations for playing a sequence of loud, large hand-span chords in a manner that will be slightly different from a larger person, even if the technicalities of playing the piano are based on the same principles and similar thought processes. Additionally, the musical systems developed within a specific culture and the types of sonic outputs created (e.g., Indian rag scales or Western tonality) are related to the ergonomics of the musical instrument used (Baily 1985). Wiesendanger *et al.* (2006) have shown that the bowing arm of the string player is highly constrained by the dynamical principles that operate between the bow and string and the arm controlling the bowing action. We can see the interaction of bodily constraints, ergonomics and cultural context within Western art music when a composition is played on different instruments of the same family; for instance, on a harpsichord versus the piano, or even from one piano to another. The differences in the size and shape of the instrument, plus the force required to play it, inevitably shape the physical approach required, and this in turn is influenced by the stylistic requirements of the music to be played—e.g., Baroque versus contemporary.

Shaffer also examined piano keyboard performances, noting that the timing profiles were additionally related to musical structure features, with, for example, a slowing always occurring at phrase boundaries. So, besides the requirements of achieving motor programming automaticity in order to execute sounds on instruments, it has been demonstrated that each music performer does not play in a purely mechanically efficient manner. The performer also has a set of representations that draw on knowledge and experience of musical style. Furthermore, as will be shown in the next section and throughout this chapter, cultural appropriateness also impacts significantly on how the movements are assembled and presented.

Body movements for musically expressive effects

Solo performers

A study by Davidson (1993) demonstrated that when the same piece of music was played with different expressive intentions (deadpan or withheld expression, with usual expression, and with exaggerated expression), the performers moved their bodies in identifiably different ways. Detailed tracking of a pianist's movements (Davidson 1994) showed that although the hands, arms, head and torso followed similar movement contours (those required to execute the music) across performances, there were significant differences in the scale of the movements. This suggested that the more highly expressive the piece, the larger and more ample the movements. The lesser the expressive intention, the smaller the movement. This finding seems to be rather like those seen in the actions of a speaker who frames and articulates speech, where big ideas or highly expressive or emotional states use much larger gestures than more constrained states (Kendon 1980).

From movement tracking data collected, it seems that it was impossible for the performers to use their bodies in a completely 'deadpan' manner. The same was found to be true of the musical sound, with some expressive feature of the music still being articulated, e.g., making slower and more pronounced movements at the boundary points, and surging forwards at a rising crescendo.

Such a finding would correspond with the idea that a musician's body is both generating and reacting to the sounds it is producing.

It is important to note that the performers observed in a series of studies from 1991 to 2007 (see Davidson 1993, 1994, 1995, 1997, 2002, 2006, 2007) demonstrated that the performers bodies moved in a rhythmical pulsing/swaying movement. Sometimes this was more or less apparent, but once movement tracks were made, the swaying could be traced across whatever piece was being played. For pianists, cellists, and tuba players this swaying occurred around the balancing point (fulcrum) of their sitting position; and for instrumentalists who were standing, this swaying was articulated from the balancing position of the weight over the feet, knees, and hips. An explanation for this movement was that the players were pivoting their bodies around a fulcrum through which all expressive information was being articulated. Such conclusions were drawn from extensive observations and detailed analyses of the performance movements generated. Indeed, it was discovered that within the overall swaying there were more local indications of the same sort of action (e.g., a rotating wrist) which conveyed very similar types of information (observers could detect from any single body part the expressive intention). It was concluded, therefore, that a physical centre or fulcrum to express mental representations relating to expressive intention may exist, and that these are then revealed in the body a hierarchical manner: overall movement sway, local body part movement (see in particular, Davidson and Correia 2002; Davidson 2005).

However, in addition to the overall performance movement—which seemed to be a combination of basic biomechanical action integrated with overall information about the music's general expressive intention—it was also discovered that musicians peppered their performances with many specific postures and gestures that had qualities akin to the types of non-verbal communication that accompany speech, e.g., those metaphorical and illustrative features which both generate and react to ideas being expressed (Kendon 1980). For example, head nodding in a series of rapid gestures that seem to mirror the music as it repeats a specific figure

or sequence, potentially illustrating the repetition within the musical material. Other gestures seemed to have iconic value, that is, where some feature of the musical action was being described. For example, pianists creating the contour of the music being played by tracing this form in the air with the left hand whilst playing the notes with the right hand. This arguably is done to 'draw out' the smooth legato line that is being attempted in the music.

The specifically identifiable gestures used by individual instrumentalists seems to be rather limited in number, yet what these gestures had the potential to express appeared to be endlessly variable, depending on the context in which they are used. Indeed, Davidson's (2007) assessment of the pianist's movement vocabulary showed that the movements were limited so less than 20 movement types, and these happened to appear across all sorts of musical styles. Indeed, one style of music (Beethoven, for example) an emphatic 'wiggle' of the torso might illustrate an ornament in the music in one context, yet in another context (CPE Bach) this could signal the start of a long legato passage.

These gestures were person-specific, the 'wiggle' being specific to a case study pianist. Some of the other movements seemed more related to illustrative gestural purposes—e.g., nodding for emphasis—and there was a high degree of individual variability in how many of these gestures were used (Davidson 2005).

Since there are some schools of pedagogy which appear to focus only on the efficiency of the action of playing, it might be asked if these postures and gestures are really necessary for the optimal expression of the musical ideas in performance. A study by Davidson and Dawson (1995) requested that pianists should learn an especially composed piece which did not require any range movement as it was constrained to the central two octaves, yet when completely free to move, the pianists made quite extravagant movements in their performances, including both sways and identifiable gestures. Some were asked to learn the piece in a restraining harness to restrict them from moving around, though they were free to reach the keyboard and play all the notes required. In this condition, the performances were never as musically expressive or indeed as visually 'pleasing' as the freely learned pieces. This indicates that freedom of movement is obviously important in the generation of musical expression.

So far, the indications have been that the gestural and postural movements used help to articulate the musical expression, and that movement gestures have roles of metaphorical function to articulate the musical sounds. It is possible to take these ideas one step further to suggest that musical material itself operates like a virtual person—a social inter-actor—with the performer. So, in a score-indicated fortissimo, a violinist may nod her head as she plays loudly. This action could be an illustration of the force of the movement required, or she may be 'agreeing' with the force of the musical sounds by nodding in 'agreement', as if interacting with another person. These are all speculative ideas, but it is feasible that the music itself operates on the performer like a partner in a conversation, except that in the case of a musical performance the performer both generates and reacts to the musical narrative.

Music pedagogy

It is important to note that the idea of movement and metaphor being crucial to musical meaning is featured in several schools of music pedagogy. Dalcrozian Eurythmics, for example, uses movement coordination such as groups of children bouncing balls in unison as a means of illustrating to them how musical material needs to be coordinationed and musical phrases shaped (see Gell 1997, 2005). Guile (in preparation) has undertaken a Laban technique for dance training and has employed his concepts, such as Effort, into the music learning context. Undertaking extensive training programmes with children, she has found that demonstrating actions with effort characteristics such as 'dabbing' and 'punching', children are able to imbue their musical performance with expressive/emotional characters not otherwise present. At a more advanced level, Pierce (1994) has drawn on movement concepts to assist tertiary level and professional performers to optimize the expressive features of playing.

Thus far, the gestures and movements we have considered all relate to musical material itself, and deal only with the soloist. This ignores the significant influence that co-actors and audience may have on performance movement.

Co-performance

An attempt to understand which postures and gestures are used by co-performers, Davidson and Coulam (2006) studied singers working with an accompanist. It was shown that a co-performing accompanist preferred collaborating with the singers who coordinated musical detail through non-verbal means using the sorts of metaphoric devices mentioned above. However, in addition to these, illustrative gestures such as clicking fingers to set a tempo, and using a series of regulatory head nods and arm gestures to control when and how the players should develop an idea or stop were also used. Such non-verbal means were preferred over talking (Davidson 2005). Indeed, when interviewed after rehearsal and performance activity, the co-performers spoke about 'reading the signs' between them as being crucial to the successful ensemble. Thus, in order to optimize the non-verbal material, gaze and eye contact were very important. Intriguingly, the performers were conscious that they needed to look at one another frequently to make sure that their bodies could coordinate to make the precise musically timed expressive effects.

Durrant (1994) has researched conductors, especially choral conductors, and noted that they use culturally embedded emblems quite extensively, but these are often very elaborate codes (e.g. we need to 'know that a "V" sign with the index and middle finger means "Victory"'), and part of the rehearsal period is concerned with choristers learning and then speeding up on decoding what these emblems signify. As the emblems are usually complex signs to short-circuit a lot of spoken instruction, they typically combine technical and expressive instruction. For example, using the hand at the side of the head in a rotational gesture to indicate the notion of creating 'space' for the singing voice to sound and accompanying this with a sharp downward pointed gesture to indicate the vocal attack on the sound. Although there is very limited formal research, Davidson (1997) has hypothesized that the most successful conductors on the international professional circuit are those who not only focus on non-verbal interaction, but who are also efficient in their use of illustrators and regulators and keep emblems to a minimum, given the time involved in learning their meanings.

Clearly, co-performers need to be able to decipher intention within and between musical parts in order to achieve a fluent performance. Therefore it is necessary to understand the nature of their collaboration and the effect it has on creating a musical performance.

Co-performer collaboration: from rehearsal to performance

Van Knippenberg and Hogg (2003) discuss that any form of group interaction necessarily gives rise to individual as well as group outcomes. It is these outcomes that motivate people to join and continue in groups. Davidson and Good (2002) discovered that collaborative activities between string quartet members depended in almost equal measure upon: first, the dynamics of musical content and its coordination (achieving entrances and exits etc.) in order to get the performance to cohere; and, secondly, those dynamics of a more personal nature (for example, the first violinist making a head nodding gesture of approval to the second violinist after executing a particularly well-accomplished passage) in order to make the social group cohere. In their data, Davidson and Good saw a power struggle emerging in the rehearsal activity observed. This was based principally on sexual politics—one flirtatious male amongst three more or less admiring females—and it was noted that the flirtation was apparent in the use of non-verbal gestures. The male second violinist teased the first violinist about her lack of clarity, imitating in a bold and exaggerated bowing arm the sudden jerkiness of her regulatory gesture to say 'start the music, now!' The example served also to show how multifunctional the role of non-verbal communication can be in the rehearsal. Additionally, the example shows that individual agendas—even if at odds with the musical goals—can still be expressed, and a coherent musical outcome achieved. Indeed, we are all aware of some famous ensembles who do

not get along socially, yet are able to rehearse and perform in an excellently coordinated manner by sticking solely to the musical task.

Recalling the string quartet study and the video data obtained, it was intriguing to observe that when there was a lull in the playing activities of the rehearsal, the cellist moved away from the group sitting arrangement to place herself at the edge of the room, away from a flirtatious social interaction between the first and second violinists. The viola player sat in her traditional position but looked away, shifting her body position as if to exclude herself from the interaction. This type of behaviour has been examined within non-verbal communication research and is known as 'proxemics'—the use of personal space.

The field of proxemics was first studied by Hall (1963), and it was soon discovered that humans have a desire to maintain certain spatial 'zones' or safe distances from one another dependent on circumstance, cultural norm and individual variability. At an everyday level, we are all sensitive to someone who stands too close for comfort or is too far away or avoids eye contact. Music-making is no exception. Finding an appropriate place to stand or sit and assessing performance distance seems crucial.

Williamon and Davidson (2002) found that in the collaboration of a piano duo, where the players sit within one another's personal space (the brief overlapping arms are often required), practice brought an increase in the quantity of non-verbal interaction from first meeting through to a performance. The most used movement was a slight head and eye indication for regulation. Also, and again intriguingly, during the course of the rehearsals, the movement styles of the two individuals altered. The player who moved the most moderated his movements by reducing the quantity of his bodily movements somewhat, while the more conservative player produced more movement. It was as if they began to move as one, rather than two individuals, once they were within the same zone. Evidently, the social dimension was found in that they sensed that they were performing this 'together', as one 'unit'.

Davidson and Good (2002) also noticed this movement unifying effect in the string quartet especially when it played Britten's 'Rhapsody'; the players found it much easier to achieve the canonical musical entries if they were all ebbing and flowing in exactly the same manner, leaning across into one another's movement pathway.

The current author has researched many types of musical interaction and collaboration, and for her one of the most revelatory experiences has been to work with blind musicians. Over a number of years she has run workshops on rehearsal, performance and stage presentation classes in association with the Royal National Institute for Blind People UK (RNIB). In this work, she has become highly sensitive to the importance of proxemics. Clearly, for practical reasons, blind people may need to pace out distances between stage activities, or be advised how best to position themselves in relation to co-players and audience for the advantage of all. These practicalities aside, blind people also demonstrate how important 'safe' distance zones for interactions are for all. As opera singing student Victoria Oruwari comments in a personal communication, blind people can feel 'invaded' as sighted people stand too close for comfort ('they often stand close in attempt to be better understood'). Sighted people also employ a range of non-verbal touching behaviours in their everyday social encounters as they chat (tapping on the shoulder, nudging with the elbow) which are behaviours blind people do not participate in ('Why do they do all that poking and prodding?'). This information has important implications for rehearsal and performance. Achieving a good distance between sighted and blind players for extra-musical feedback, for instance picking up cues from breath and the sounds of movements (shift of foot position, turn of torso *etc.*) all provide information for the blind musician, without engaging in verbal explanation, or worse still uninvited touch. However, the same could be said of any social interaction. These are codes that we need to respect. Keeping a respectful or appropriate distance is essential, just as it is to be sufficiently close to share in musical and necessary social exchange.

Actions including and beyond words

As explored above, movements in musical rehearsal and performance clearly aid in the achievement of musical coherence and can enhance social unity. Studying chamber musicians, Goodman (2002) and Murninghan and Conlon (1991) found that non-verbal communication during rehearsal often solved problems where talk had failed. By simply playing and sorting out coordination 'on the hoof', drawing on non-verbal means of communication, there was often no need to discuss a particular point at all. Or alternatively, when a verbal disagreement about musical interpretation emerged, playing the piece through in several different manners would often lead to a decision being made, again without verbal discussion. These findings are supported in the much larger context of a Western symphony orchestra. It is well-reported that in rehearsals, where there is a conductor, this person leads (Atik 1994). The musical ensemble research indicates that too much talking either from the conductor or in the form of questions from an individual player disrupts the flow of the music in rehearsals (see Weeks 1996; Yarborough 1975; Durrant 1994; Price and Byo 2002). That is, if too much questioning is permitted from one individual, it is likely to lead to interference as other members may become irritated or distracted.

Focusing on the key requisites of ensemble performance, Davidson and Goodman (2004) highlighted that specific moment by moment information needs to be processed and responded to in an ongoing manner, in order to accommodate a co-player's sudden change of tempo or coping with a memory slip. Such a capacity to deal with these matters clearly depends on former exposure to such situations and so also relies on previous knowledge of similar situations. Most powerfully, it depends on an opening of ears and eyes to hear and see cues.

What of these cues? Are they of the form and quantity normally encountered in social conversation? Goodman's work (see Goodman 2002; Davidson and Goodman 2004) has drawn on Bales's (1950, 1999) small group behaviour framework. It shows that in terms of both speech and gesture used in rehearsals of two cello and piano duos, the high amount of agreement indicated in the performers' discourses exceeded a suggested 'normal' social upper limit, suggesting that the performers gave mainly positive socio-emotional reactions (perhaps stronger than witnessed in other small group scenarios). Indeed, in addition to the illustrative, regulatory and emblematic gestures described above, it has been both observed and discussed (Davidson and Coulam 2006; Davidson 2007) that performers—whether singers or instrumentalists—who make non-verbal signals which revealed unconscious processes of self-stimulation, e.g. rubbing the ear lobe in a gentle manner, or flicking the finger tips in a particularly soft but repetitive manner. These—completely unconsciously produced movements—have been regarded as important factors in determining performance quality, for those performers who were rated highest by their collaborating accompanist used more of these self-stimulating adaptors, the movements seeming to offer knowledge of the performer's 'intimate' socio-emotional states.

Are there elite examples of exceptional performance communication?

In building relations, rehearsing and developing an ensemble, it seems that there are elite profiles. Murninghan and Conlon (1991) studied more or less successful string quartets. They noted that the most successful took account specifically of the opinions and behaviours of the second violinist, who could easily feel like the lesser partner to the first violinist. This finding fits well with group behaviour theory that individuals need to adapt to meet the group demand (see Davidson 1997).

The ensemble achieved between siblings might offer insights or examples of special collaborative and communicative advantage, all members having a deep knowledge of one another in terms of abilities, personalities and movement style (adaptive and personal as well as external and more projected behaviours). Examining the Irish pop band, The Corrs, it was surprising to find that the three sisters who perform in the ensemble were quite idiosyncratic, being influenced by the types of musical instruments, the musical tasks they occupied within the band and their personalities (see Kurosawa and Davidson 2005). For example, Andrea was much more extrovert, and employed many

more illustrative and display behaviours. Sharon focused on communicating the narrative of the song, her manner was smaller and less demonstrative than Andrea. Caroline was the most reticent and rather than communicative with her sisters and the audience, most of her movements had a regulatory function. Even when performing the same song, Caroline and Sharon use their bodies differently, with Caroline using more emblematic gestures, gaze and general facial expression, and Sharon using regulators and illustrators.

To try to gain insight into these differences, biographical information was collected. It emerged that Caroline is reported to be the most shy, as well as being the youngest sibling. Also, she plays drums, instruments which fully engage the limbs and which operate within the tight constraint of 'keeping the musical pulse', so she may have developed a general performance style which relies entirely on coordinating and regulating rather than exploring expressive content. By contrast, the violin, played by Sharon, has far more movement possibilities, the arms, hands and fingers arguably being used through their mechanical action through the bow and on the strings to create the musical expression. Finally, Andrea is the most clearly defined as a lead vocalist, and perhaps has more freedom for bodily expression as well as being more used to having attention focused on her. So, according to the case study of The Corrs, it would seem that the observed collaboration and movements of the performers reveal aspects of personality and reflect the type of instrument as well as the hierarchy of prominence of position within their ensemble.

Performers certainly seem to manage multiple social tasks: they have to construct the correct ambience in the rehearsal situation, they have to develop their musical material for the audience: whilst they have to interact with their co-performers to coordinate the performance task, they also have to communicate with and sometimes interact with the audience. Frith (1996) observes that a performance involves thoughts and actions to create the performance which relate to: the occasion itself (e.g., 'star-like' postures and gestures of being the 'stage persona'); the music to be performed (the musical material's narrative content; e.g., 'living' out the qualities of the character depicted in a song); and the individual performer's true states (current mood, sense of self, etc.). This suggests that there is the potential for a tension between the information contained in the music (its own narrative content), the performer's real state (the individual performers on stage, presenting their own personalities), and behaviours they may engage in to present the music and themselves to their co-performers and audience. It would seem that that performers would need to be efficient at managing these aspects in combination.

Successive studies of popular, jazz, classical and traditional Cantonese opera singers (Davidson 2001, 2002; Davidson and Lai 2007 revealed that above all other musical performers, singers clearly adopt the different roles Frith outlines. The roles were revealed, as indicated with The Corrs, in the very different types of behaviours and communication, much being revealed in bodily movement. For instance, Annie Lennox literally 'showed off' to her audience using provocative sexual body postures. The countertenor Michael Chance created a sense of poise and 'performance occasion' by making a large and slow sweeping forward arm movements over the course of the whole introduction to a Bach solo cantata. The Chinese opera singer Amy Wu held an emblematic stance drawing a focused attention to her raised hand which then flickered, illustrating the 'flame of the red candle' (the title of the song) and presenting the story in a bold and dramatic manner to her audience, yet showed her personal shyness and vulnerability in timid small bows and sideways glances after she had finished performing.

With few existing music research models in this area, it is necessary to turn to another field of psychological research, sports psychology, to pursue the implications of such findings in more detail. There has been some investment of research in sports to understand the personal attributes of elite-level performing athletes (see Vealey *et al.* 1998). Subtle theoretical work by Beauchamp *et al.* (2003) has shown that these performers display an acute understanding of 'self', coupled with the capacity to establish very quickly the patterns of behavioural preference of their collaborators—being highly empathic, they are able to embrace the collaborator's (team member) or audience's perspective in performance.

So, working within specific traditions, the 'good' music performer is likely to be someone who can indeed play to the demands of both co-performer and audience. The Jungian concepts of being able to think, feel, sense and intuit are presented by Beauchamp and colleagues as being of central importance to the elite performer, with extraverted attitudes of thought (taking action and seeking order) being associated with feelings of being outgoing, and with sensing preferences for the here and now combining with intuitions including creative work, but also having those reflective, sensitive characteristics apparent. Ronglan (2007), who undertook a season-long in-depth case study of an elite women's handball team to look at the process within the team to build for cooperation and collaboration, showed the same types of characteristics to be crucial to success, with personal enthusiasm, willpower, and persistence being stressed as highly desirable attitudes—but also empathy and patience towards others. In sports, such research has been used to assist in developing suitable training programmes to build performer strategy for collaborative team work and solo excellence. There is, of course, such scope in music though frameworks have not been established to undertake such investigations or training programmes. We can look to extremely successful music performer examples, however, to see whether their case fits the theoretical propositions.

Consider Robbie Williams, arguably one of the most loved performers in the world today. His concerts are hugely popular, and investigating the content of his performer–co-performer and audience exchanges in some detail, it is possible to see that a principal concern for him is to create a coherence between himself and the musicians and to engage the audience actively in the performance. An analysis of Williams' singing the song 'She's the one' at the Knebworth Music Festival in 2004 by Davidson (2006) shows that he gestures warmly to his band, making empathic movements in time with their accompaniment and spends time engaging with them on stage. He also runs to greet his audience on a special performance 'catwalk' which stretches out into the crowd. Crucially, the audience 'know Robbie' through extensive exposure on video. The audience 'knows' how he moves and gestures when he adopts his stage persona.

The crowd even begins to make Robbie's own emblematic gestures ahead of him, anticipating the unfurling narrative of the song he is performing. Despite the thousands in the crowd, they whole audience is found to sway, swirl, dance and sing in perfect unison with their idol. Thus, the pop audience has a special kind of attunement to Robbie's stage persona in the performance. Of course much has been learned in viewing preceding music videos, but it is clear that all of this has been translated into the audience's own expectation and knowledge of Williams' and his stage movements. Yet there is more to Robbie than this the 'cheeky chappy' persona. The crowd also seems to have an empathy with Robbie himself—his authenticity and vulnerability. How is this achieved? Robbie connects with individual members within the whole audience, and without showing self-consciousness, he carries out small personal adjustments behaviours such as fiddling with his earpiece. He also speaks to the audience as it if were a single person. Robbie seems to be the consummate musical communicator.

Of course, each individual performance is a unique confluence of new interactive elements, and familiarity with such experiences prepares co-performers for likely scenarios and outcomes: but does the presence of an audience change the quality of musician behaviour?

Movements for audience effect

We know that physical gestures are not prerequisites to understanding either speech or music, such as in a phone conversation or music played on a CD recording. However, since we make fewer gestures when there is no face-to-face contact in both speech and music, it would seem that whilst some gestures are specifically oriented towards generating the music, a proportion would seem to be used for audience communication effects. Differences between musical and audience concerns are demonstrated in the evidence found in the biography of case the Canadian pianist, Glenn Gould.

Early in his career, Gould performed in all the top classical concert venues including Carnegie Hall. Later in his career, he decided to give up public performance, focusing solely on recording

studio performances. Delalande (1990) made a study of Gould's performances taken from rare film footage of both periods. What is striking is that in the recording of the studio playing, Gould's movements are highly repetitive and often quite disturbing to watch. By contrast, those of the public recitals have smooth, flowing movements. Thus, there is some evidence that in the studio case, Gould's concerns were entirely focused on the music, whereas in the public context, he was taking into account the audience's presence.

Not every social tradition permits the same social concerns to develop in collaborative performance, however. In Japanese classical music, for example, performers are not supposed to make any extraneous gestures or facial expressions to detract from the emotional content of the music, thus giving relatively few social cues to the audience or indeed their co-performers about their outer expression (Malm 2000).

Studying Indian classical music, Clayton *et al.* (2004) have shown that performers not only use movement gestures to highlight features of the music in a metaphorical way, but they use gestures that are often almost immediately adopted by both their co-performers and audiences. Fascinatingly, a performer may initiate one gesture, such as a head shaking movement, which is then mirrored by another player in the ensemble, and then passed on to members of the audience. The result is that all participants in the event mutually 'tune-in' to the shared moment. It is as if by collaborating in the production of the gestures they are being active participants in the making of the music itself.

Generally, in Western classical music performance, audiences are far more passive, sitting quietly and acknowledging the performance activity with hand clapping, but never as part of the performance itself. In jazz, audiences do take on more of a performance-focused role, toe-tapping and dancing in response to the music. Similar evidence occurs in other culture—Balinese music drama (e.g., McIntosh 2006a, b). However, as the earlier example of Robbie Williams demonstrated, pop performance offers one of the greatest forums where performer and audience can share in a directed but often mutual 'tuning-in' social interaction. We see in the case of Williams that he offers both the self-stimulating adaptors—the movements seeming to offer knowledge of the performer's 'intimate' states—alongside the projected 'public' states of 'display' (showing off) and emblematic gesture.

Conclusions

It has been demonstrated throughout this chapter that playing a piece of music requires a high-level interaction of developed cognitive and action processes; thus a range of internal representations in memory are necessary. The ability to use mental representations is determined by knowledge and experience. The capacity to generate representations seems to be limitless, with opportunities for learning permitting refinement, adaptation and addition. It is possible to summarize the key points explored as follows:

For performers:

◆ The body and bodily movement is inherently bound up with the mental representations required to develop musical performance skills

◆ Musical performance skills involve the biomechanical aspects of playing the music fluently and also expressively

◆ Technical achievement and expression combine to produce movements with overall fluency, and also local specifically identifiable gestures which are not necessary for note execution, but are essential for the communicative aspects of performance

◆ These gestures have functions, a first level being to give the music an immediate and communicative purpose for the performer as they create the music product (generating and responding to the musical sounds in a interactional manner between themselves and the music)

◆ A second level of function is to provide co-performer cues for regulation of musical content and expression of immediate and perhaps idiosyncratic expressive content

◆ The movements used to generate these stimuli draw from individual movement repertoires, some of which reveal intimate personal states, others of which are for much more direct communicative ends, e.g., end the phrase *now!*

◆ The original of these movements is likely to be similar to that of non-verbal communication in speech

◆ The social and cultural origin of the performance tradition out of which a performance is being produced influences the extent and types of communicative movement produced.

For audiences:

◆ The movements permit accurate perception of musical intention

◆ The movements offer possibilities for sharing and participation.

Needless to say, understanding bodily movement is a key area for further enquiry for both performers and audiences. Much research still needs to be done to detail systematically the types and functions of all movement in musical performance. Yet however limited our present knowledge, it is obvious that psychological investigations have given musicians and their audiences insights into how crucial bodily movement is to the execution and interpretation of musical performance, and this research area continues to grow.

References

Altenmüller E and Gruhn W (2002) Brain mechanisms. In R Parncutt and GE McPherson, eds, *The science and psychology of music performance: creative strategies for teaching and learning*, 63–82. Oxford University Press, Oxford.

Atik Y (1994). The conductor and the orchestra: interactive aspects of the leadership process. *Leadership and Organisation Development Journal*, **13**, 22–28.

Bailes RF (1950) A set of categories for the analysis of small group interaction. *American Sociological Review*, **15**, 257–263.

Bales RF (1999). *Social interaction systems: theory and measurement*. Transaction Publishers, London.

Baily J (1985) Music structure and human movement. In P Howell, I Cross and R West, eds, *Musical Structure and Cognition*, 237–258. Academic Press, London.

Beauchamp M, Lee KE, Haxby JV and Martin A (2003) fMRI response to video and point-light displays of moving humans and manipulable objects. *Journal of Cognitive Neuroscience*, **15**(7), 991–1001.

Bernstein N (1967) *Coordination and regulation of movement*. Pergamon, London.

Blacking J (1977) *The anthropology of the body*, ASA Monograph 15, edited volume. Academic Press, London.

Clayton M, Sager R and Will U (2004) In time with the music: the concept of entrainment and its significance for ethnomusicology. *ESEM Counterpoint*, **1**, 1–45, 70–74.

Dahl S (2004). Playing the accent—comparing striking velocity and timing in an ostinato rhythm performed by four drummers. *Acta Acustica*, **90**(4), 762–776.

Dalla-Bella S and Palmer C (2004). Tempo and dynamics in piano performance: the role of movement and amplitude. In SD Liscomb, R Ro Gjerdingen and P Webster, eds, *Proceedings of the international conference on music perception and cognition*, 256–257. Causal Productions, Adelaide.

Davidson JW (1993). Visual perception of performance manner in the movements of solo musicians. *Psychology of Music*, **21**, 103–113.

Davidson JW (1994). What type of information is conveyed by the body movements of solo musician performers? *Journal of Human Movement Studies*, **6**, 279–301.

Davidson JW (1997). The social psychology of performance. In DJ Hargreaves, AC North, eds, *The social psychology of music*, 209–226. Oxford University Press, Oxford.

Davidson JW (2001) The role of the body in the production and perception of solo vocal performance: a case study of Annie Lennox. *Musicae Scientiae*, **V**(2), 235–256.

Davidson JW (2002) The performer's identity. In R MacDonald, D Miell and DJ Hargreaves, eds, *Musical identities*, 97–116. Oxford University Press, Oxford.

Davidson JW (2005) Bodily communication in musical performance. In D Miell, DJ Hargreaves and R Macdonald, eds, *Musical communication*, 215–238. Oxford University Press, New York.

Davidson JW (2006) 'She's the One': multiple functions of body movement in a stage performance by Robbie Williams. In A Gritten and E King, eds, *Music and gesture*, 208–226. Ashgate, Aldershot.

Davidson JW (2007). Qualitative insights into the use of expressive body movement in piano performance. *Psychology of Music*, **35**(3), 381–401.

Davidson JW and Correia JS (2002) Body movement in performance. In R Parncutt and GE McPherson, eds, *The science and psychology of music performance: creative strategies for teaching and learning* 237–250. Oxford University Press, Oxford

Davidson JW and Coulam A (2006) Exploring jazz and classical solo singing performance behaviours: a preliminary step towards understanding performer creativity. In G Wiggins and I Deliège, eds, *Musical creativity: current research in theory and practice*, 181–199. Oxford University Press, New York

Davidson JW and Dawson JC (1995). The development of expression in body movement during learning in piano performance. *Conference Proceedings of Music Perception and Cognition Conference*, p. 31. University of California, Berkeley, June.

Davidson JW and Good JMM. (2002) Social and musical coordination between members of a string quartet: an exploratory study. *Psychology of Music*, **30**, 86–201.

Davidson JW and Goodman E (2004) E. Strategies for ensemble performance. In A Williamon, ed., *Musical excellence: strategies and techniques to enhance performance*, 105–122. Oxford University Press, Oxford.

Davidson JW and Lai V (2007) Shanghai street: art in and of a city. *International Journal of Arts in Society*, **1**(7), 109–119.

Delalande F (1990) Human movement and the interpretation of music. Paper presented at the Second International Colloquium on the Psychology of Music, Ravello, Italy.

Durrant C (1994). Towards an effective communication: a case for structured teaching of conducting. *British Journal of Music Education*, **11**, 56–76.

Frith S (1996) *Performance rites*. Oxford University Press, Oxford.

Gell H (1997) *Lessons in music through movement*. CIRCME, University of Western Australia.

Gell H (2005) *Dalcroze Eurythmics: music through movement: a hundred lessons and thousands of ideas for early childhood*. Callaway Centre, University of Western Australia.

Goodman E (2002) Ensemble performance. In J Rink, ed., *Musical performance: a guide to understanding*, 153–167. Cambridge University Press, Cambridge.

Guile LM (in preparation) Laban's concept of effort applied to musical expression. Work for PhD dissertation, University of Sheffield, UK.

Hall ET (1963). A system for the notation of proxemic behaviour. *American Anthropologist, Selected papers in methods and techniques*, **63**(5), 1003–1026.

Jäncke L (2006) From cognition to action. In E Altenmüller, M Wiesendanger and J Kesselring, eds, *Music, motor control and the brain*, 25–37. Oxford University Press, Oxford.

Kendon A (1980) Gesticulation and speech: two aspects of the process. In MR Key, eds, *The relation between the verbal and nonverbal communication*, 207–228. Mouton, The Hague.

Kurosawa K and Davidson JW (2005) Non-verbal interaction in popular performance: The Corrs. *Musicae Scientiae*, **9**(1), 111–136.

Lashley KS (1951) The problem of serial order in behaviour. In LA Jeffress, ed., *Cerebral mechanisms in behaviour*, 118–142, Wiley, New York.

Lehmann AC and Davidson JW (2002) Taking an acquired skills perspective on music performance. In R Colwell, C Richardson, eds, *Second handbook on music teaching and learning*, 542–560. Oxford University Press, Oxford.

Malm WP (2000) *Traditional Japanese music and musical instruments*. Kodansha International, Tokyo.

McClary S (1991) *Feminine endings: music, gender and sexuality* University of Minnesota Press, Minneapolis, MN.

McIntosh J (2006a). Moving through tradition: children's practice and performance of dance, music and song in South-Central Bali, Indonesia. Unpublished PhD dissertation, Queen's University Belfast.

McIntosh J (2006b). How singing, dancing and playing shape the ethnographer: research with children in a

Balinese dance studio. *Anthropology Matters*, **8**(2), 1–17. Available at: http://www.anthropologymatters. com/journal/2006 2/mcintosh_2006_how.pdf.

Murninghan JK and Conlon DE (1991). The dynamics of intense work groups: a study of British string quartets. *Administrative Science Quarterly*, **36**, 165–186.

Palmer C (2006) The nature of memory for music performance skills. In E Altenmüller, M Wiesendanger and J Kesselring, eds, *Music, motor control and the brain*, 109–123. Oxford University Press, New York.

Pantev C, Engelien A, Candia V and Elebert T (2001). Representational cortex of musicians: plastic alterations in response to music. *Annals of the New York Academy of Sciences*, **930**, 300–314.

Pierce A (1994) Developing Schenkerian hearing and performing. *Integral*, **8**, 51–123.

Price HE and Byo JL (2002). Rehearsing and conducting. In R Parncutt and GE McPherson, eds, *The science and psychology of musical performance: ceative strategies for teaching and learning*, 335–351. Oxford University Press, Oxford.

Ronglan LT (2007). Building and communicating collective efficacy: a season-long in-depth study of an elite sport team. *The Sport Psychologist*, **21**, 8–93.

Shaffer LH (1984) Timing in solo and duet piano performance. *Quarterly Journal of Experimental Psychology*, **36**, 577–595.

Sloboda JA, Davidson JW, Howe MJ A and Moore DG (1994). The role of practice in the development of expert musical performance. *British Journal of Psychology*, **87**, 287–309.

Van Knippenberg D and Hogg MA (2003). A social identity model of leadership effectiveness in orgnisations. *Research in Organisational Behaviour*, **25**, 243–296.

Vealey RS, Hayashi SW, Garner-Holman M and Giacobbi P (1998). Sources of sport-confidence: conceptualisation and instrument development. *Journal of Sport and Exercise Psychology*, **20**, 54–80.

Weeks P (1996). A rehearsal of a Beethoven passage: an analysis of correction talk. *Research on Language and Social Interaction*, **29**, 247–290.

Wiesendanger M, Baader A and Kazennikov O (2006) Fingering and bowing in violinists: a motor control approach. In E Altenmüller, M Wiesendanger, J Kesselring, eds, *Music, motor control and the brain*, 109–123. Oxford University Press, New York.

Williamon RA and Davidson JW (2002) Exploring co-performer communication. *Musicae Scientiae*, **VI** (1), 1–17.

Wing A (2002) Voluntary timing and brain function: an information processing approach. *Brain and Cognition*, **48**, 7–30.

Yarborough C (1975). Effect of magnitude of conductor behaviour on students in mixed choruses. *Journal of Research in Music Education*, **23**, 134–146.

CHAPTER 35

Emotion in music performance

Patrik N. Juslin

[handwritten margin notes: interpretation often leads to expression — deliberate, innate, articulation]

THERE are several features that we have come to expect from an expert perform-ance: technical mastery, confidence, origi-nality, flexibility, and a true understanding of the musical style. Yet the feature that both perform-ers and listeners appear to regard as the most important is that the performer is expressive. The most loved artists are commonly the ones that are able to express and evoke emotions in listeners.

[handwritten margin notes: re-exciting expectation is there]

It should be noted at the outset that there are several ways in which emotion might enter into the performance of music: emotions might influ-ence a performer's motivation, choice of reper-toire, interpretation, and concentration, as well as the precise nature of the performance. However, there is little systematic knowledge about most of these processes. Previous studies have mainly concerned how performers express emotions, and this chapter will thus focus on this question, though with brief detours to related topics.

[handwritten margin note: type of workterform]

First, I provide working definitions of key concepts (e.g., expression, communication), and consider how performers conceive of these issues. Then I review up-to-date evidence on how performers express emotions. Finally, I propose directions for future research.

Conceptual foundations

Music performance, virtually by definition, requires a performer and a piece of music. The term *interpretation* usually refers to the individ-ualistic shaping of the piece according to the musical ideas of the performer (Palmer 1997). This may or may not involve an intention to

'express' something (e.g., an idea, an emotion) beyond the musical structure, although such expression is usually achieved through the way in which the structure is articulated.

Expression will be used in this chapter to refer to a particular set of perceptual qualities that reflect psychophysical relationships between 'objective' properties of the music (patterns of information) and 'subjective' impressions of the listener (e.g., perceiving certain emotions). Sometimes the perception of an expressive per-formance evokes an emotion in the listener, but this is not required for the listener to hear the music as expressive. We may be able to perceive that a performer is playing expressively, yet we remain untouched by the performance.

Expression has often been treated as a homo-geneous category of which there is more or less (Marchand 1975). However, a careful review of the literature suggests that performance expres-sion is better conceived of as a multidimensional phenomenon that can be decomposed into vari-ous subcomponents. Drawing on previous research, I have proposed that performance expression derives from five primary sources, referred to as the GERMS model (Juslin 2003):

◆ *Generative rules (G)* that mark the structure in a musical manner (Clarke 1988). By means of variations in such parameters as timing, dynamics, and articulation, a performer is able to convey group boundaries, metrical accent, and harmonic structure.

◆ *Emotional expression (E)* that serves to com-municate emotions to listeners (Juslin 1997a).

By manipulating overall features of the performance such as mean tempo, a performer is able to play the same structure with different emotional characters.

- *Random fluctuations (R)* that reflect human limitations in motor precision (Gilden 2001). It has been revealed in several studies that even expert performers who try to play perfectly even time intervals show small, involuntary fluctuations in the timing of their performance.

- *Motion principles (M)* that hold that tempo changes should follow natural patterns of human movement, or biological motion, in order to obtain a pleasing shape (Shove and Repp 1995).

- *Stylistic unexpectedness (S)* that reflects a performer's deliberate attempts to 'deviate' from stylistic expectations concerning performance conventions to add tension and unpredictability to the performance (Meyer 1956, p. 206).

In reality, all components occur together in complex interactions, though for specific purposes (e.g., research, teaching), it can be useful to consider them separately (Juslin 2003).

In this chapter, I will focus on emotional expression (for a working definition of emotion, see Chapter 12 this volume), whilst acknowledging that the other aspects are also important (see Chapters 30–34 this volume). In one sense the term 'emotional expression' is misleading: it is only occasionally that performers are truly expressing their own emotions during the performance—perhaps because optimal performance requires a certain psychological state (e.g., relaxed concentration) that is incompatible with experiencing certain emotions. More typically, what the performer presents in a music performance is not the emotion itself, but rather its expressive form—derived from other forms of non-verbal communication. Still, the term 'emotional expression' is now widely established, and has been used in both cases where the expression is 'spontaneous' (genuinely felt) and where it is 'symbolic' (portrayed). I will therefore retain the term in this chapter.

The notion of expression does not require that there is a correspondence between what a listener perceives in the performance and what the performer intends to express. In contrast, the concept of *communication* requires that there is both a performer's intention to express a specific emotion and recognition of this emotion by a listener. The listener may, additionally, come to experience or feel the emotion in question, but this is not required for it to qualify as a case of communication. For a discussion of emotional reactions to music, see Chapter 12.

Performers' views

Issues concerning expression, communication, and emotions tend to invite controversy. However, while philosophers, musicologists, psychologists, and educators commonly express strong views on these issues, it is surprisingly rare that the performers or listeners themselves are consulted. Thus, before reviewing findings from basic research on these issues, it may be appropriate to consider recent findings on performers' views. Lindström *et al.* (2003) carried out a questionnaire study, featuring 135 expert performers from music conservatoires in three countries (England, Italy, Sweden). Open-ended responses to the question 'In your view, what does it mean to play expressively?' were content-analysed and divided into categories. The results revealed that the musicians (both classical and popular) defined 'playing expressively' largely in terms of 'communicating emotions' (44 per cent) and 'playing with feeling' (16 per cent). The two response categories were not always easy to distinguish, although the first focused more on conveying something to an audience, whereas the second focused more on the performer's own feelings. A third group (34 per cent) provided answers in terms of 'a focus on the music itself' (e.g., 'conveying the structure'). Of particular interest is that 83 per cent of the performers reported that they consciously try to express specific emotions in their music performances 'always' or 'often'.

These results were confirmed and extended by Minassian *et al.* (2003), who conducted a survey study, including 53 expert performers of classical music, in order to explore what factors were associated with an 'optimal' performance. Performances judged as optimal tended to be those where the performer had a clear intention to communicate (usually an emotional 'message'), was emotionally engaged with the music, and believed the message had been received by the audience. Interview studies have further indicated that performers in pursuit of a professional performing career are more inclined to think of music as a vehicle for communication than performers in pursuit of a non-music career (Burland and Davidson 2004), and that many performers value music as a form of emotional outlet (Gullberg and Brändström 2004).

Research paradigms

There is an immense number of historical treatises that feature very detailed descriptions or prescriptions concerning the performance practices that may be used to enhance emotional expression (Bach 1778/1985; Buelow 1983; Mattheson 1739/1954). Most of these writings, however, are based on speculation, intuition, folk theory, or personal experience –which may or may not be correct.

Systematic attempts to investigate emotional expression—as manifested in performance features (e.g., timing, timbre) rather than features of particular pieces of music (e.g., melody, mode)—developed only in the mid-1990s. Most investigations used the so-called *standard paradigm* (a term borrowed from studies of vocal expression of affect; e.g., Juslin and Scherer 2005): this means that musicians are asked to play brief melodies to express various emotions chosen by the researcher. The resulting performances are first recorded and then evaluated in listening experiments to check whether listeners can recognize the intended expression. Each performance is further analysed to study what acoustic means each performer used to achieve each emotional expression. The basic assumption is that because the melody remains the same in different emotional expressions, whatever effects that are found in listeners' judgements or acoustic measures should mainly be the result of the performer's expressive intention. Having performers play the same piece with different emotional expressions might appear 'unnatural' from a musical point of view. However, this design is necessary to secure the internal validity of the experiments: if different emotions are expressed by different melodies, it is impossible to know whether the obtained effects on listener judgements or performance measures are due to the melody, the performance, or some interaction between the two.

However, there is no denying that this is a fairly artificial set-up, even though musicians sometimes do try alternative interpretations of the same piece (Lindström *et al.* 2003). Hence, it is paramount to try other approaches to investigating emotional expression in performances, such as analysing existing recordings of performances (Siegwart and Scherer 1995), observing a performer from the preparation of a piece to a concert performance (Clarke *et al.* 2005), or investigating listeners' responses to performance in a real concert using questionnaire (Thompson 2006).

Can performers communicate emotions accurately to listeners?

It might appear strange to talk about accuracy of communication in a musical context. However, it is reasonable to assume that most performers are concerned about whether their interpretation is perceived by the audience in the manner that they intended it. The performer may, for instance, wish to highlight an emotional character in the piece. The degree to which performer and listeners 'agree' about the expression of the performance can pragmatically be seen as a measure of the accuracy of the communication. Listeners' judgements can be indexed in terms of adjective ratings (Juslin 1997a), forced choice (Juslin 1997b, Experiment 1), free labelling (Juslin 1997c), or continuous response (Sloboda and Lehmann 2001).

Juslin and Laukka (2003) reviewed 41 studies of emotional expression in performance. The studies covered a wide range of musical styles such as classical music, folk music, Indian ragas, jazz, pop, rock, children's songs, and free improvisations. The most common style was classical music (17 studies = 41 per cent). The number of emotions studied ranged from 3 to 9 (M = 4.98), and typically included happiness, sadness, anger, fear, and tenderness. Twelve musical instruments and twelve nationalities were included. Most studies used professional performers and the performances were mostly monophonic to facilitate acoustic measurements.

Juslin and Laukka conducted a meta-analysis of communication accuracy featuring 29 studies, which indicated that performers are able to

[margin handwritten notes: BASIC EMOTIONS]

communicate 'basic emotions' (happiness, anger, sadness, fear, and tenderness) to listeners with an accuracy approximately as high as in facial and vocal expression of emotions. Overall decoding accuracy was equivalent to a 'raw' proportion correct of $P_c = 0.70$, in a forced-choice task with five response alternatives. Across studies, sadness and anger were the emotions that were communicated with the highest level of accuracy, and this pattern was found for both music performance and vocal expression. The available evidence suggests that the communication proceeds in terms of fairly broad emotion categories, whereas finer distinctions within these categories are hard to communicate reliably—at least, without some additional context. In general, commonly postulated 'basic' emotions are easier to communicate than 'complex' emotions. For explanations, see p. 385–386.

The accuracy depends on a number of variables (e.g., the piece, the response format, the procedure), yet perception of emotions in music is robust in that listeners' judgements are only marginally influenced by musical training, age, and gender of the listener (see Gabrielsson and Juslin 2003). That musical training is not required to express (Yamasaki 2002) or recognize (Juslin 1997a) emotion in music performance suggests that general mechanisms of perception of emotions are involved—which is supported by the finding that abilities to decode emotions in music performance are correlated with measures of emotional intelligence (e.g., Resnicow et al. 2004). Developmental studies of perception of emotions in music have not clearly separated performance features (e.g., tempo, timbre) from compositional features (e.g., melody, harmony), but preliminary evidence from several studies indicates that that children as young as 3 or 4 years old are able to decode 'basic emotions' from music with better than chance accuracy (for a review, see Juslin and Laukka 2003, p. 788). The ability appears to improve with age, but declines again in old adults (Laukka and Juslin 2007).

How are different emotions communicated?

Most of the processes that underlie communication of emotions in music are implicit—which

helps to 'mystify' the nature of expression (see Juslin et al. 2004). One of the pioneers in research on emotional expression in music more generally (e.g., Chapter 13), Kate Hevner (1935), observed:

> If the great artist could speak to the audience verbally as effectively as he does musically, our efforts would be unnecessary, but seldom he expresses himself except through the medium of his art, and when he does, it is usually not in the terms calculated to be most useful and helpful.
>
> (p. 204)

Hence, psychologists are forced to explore the mechanisms by means of acoustic measurements, commonly carried out using computer software. Table 35.1 presents a summary of the most important acoustic parameters and also explains how they are measured. In the following, I shall refer to these parameters as *cues* (bits of information) that together make up the code used to communicate various emotions. Researchers have recently developed computer algorithms that can help to speed up the otherwise complicated and time-consuming process of manually analysing the cues (Friberg et al. 2007).

Code description

*[margin handwritten note: * ACOUSTIC CUES OBJECTIVE CHARACTER IN MUSIC THAT CAN BE MANIPULATED]*

Table 35.2 shows a summary of cues that are correlated with specific emotions in musical expression. For completeness, the table includes cues that are commonly part of the musical structure (for further discussion of structural features, see Chapter 13). However, those cues that can usually be controlled or modulated by the performer are set in italics. While Table 35.2 is limited to a few emotion categories (i.e., those that have been explored most frequently in previous research), one can easily imagine how the categories can be combined or 'mixed' in various ways, and also how the expression can be altered during a performance. Some of the cues shown in Table 35.2 may be common knowledge to most performers, whereas other cues are less obvious. The number of cues available depends on the instrument used. Other things being equal, the communication will be more reliable the more cues that are available. The results suggest that tempo, sound level, timbre and

[margin handwritten note: SUBJECT TO VARIATION (from genre to instrument)]

Table 35.1 Definition and measurement of primary acoustic cues in emotional expression in music performance

Acoustic cues	Perceived correlate	Definition and measurement
Pitch		
Fundamental frequency (F0)	Pitch	Acoustically, F0 is defined as the lowest periodic cycle component of the acoustic wave form. One can distinguish between the macro pitch level of particular musical pieces, and the micro intonation of the performance. The former is often given in the unit of the semitone, the latter is given in terms of deviations from the notated macro pitch (e.g., in cents).
F0 contour	Intonation contour	Sequence of F0 values. In music, intonation refers to manner in which the performer approaches and/or maintains the prescribed pitch of notes, in terms of deviations from precise pitch.
Vibrato	Vibrato	Periodic changes in the pitch (or loudness) of a tone. Depth and rate of vibrato can be measured manually from the F0 trace (or amplitude envelope).
Intensity		
Intensity	Loudness	Intensity is a measure of the energy in the acoustic signal. Usually measured from the amplitude of the acoustic wave form. The standard unit used to quantify intensity is a logarithmic transformation of the amplitude called the decibel (dB).
Attack	Rapidity of tone onsets	Attack refers to the rise-time or rate of rise of the amplitude of individual notes. Usually measured from the acoustic wave form.
Temporal features		
Tempo	Velocity of music	The mean tempo of a performance is obtained by dividing the total duration of the performance until the onset of its final note by the number of beats, and then calculating the number of beats per minute (bpm).
Articulation	Proportion of sound to silence in successive notes	The mean articulation of a performance is typically obtained by measuring two durations for each tone—the duration from the onset of a tone until the onset of the next tone (dii), and the duration from the onset of a tone until its offset (dio). These durations are used to calculate the successive dio:dii ratio (the articulation) of each tone. These values are averaged across the performance and expressed as a percentage. A value around 100% refers to legato articulation; a value around 70% or lower refers to staccato articulation.
Timing	Tempo and rhythm variation	Timing variations are usually described as 'deviations' from the nominal values of a musical notation. Overall measures of the amount of deviations in a performance may be obtained by calculating the number of notes whose deviation is less than a given percent of the note value. Another index of timing changes concerns so-called durational contrasts between 'long' and 'short' notes in rhythm patterns. Contrasts may be played with 'sharp' durational contrasts (close to or larger than the nominal ratio) or with 'soft' durational contrasts (a reduced ratio).

Continued

Table 35.1 Definition and measurement of primary acoustic cues in emotional expression in music performance (*continued*)

Acoustic cues	Perceived correlate	Definition and measurement
Timbre		
High-frequency energy	Timbre	Refers to the relative proportion of total acoustic energy above versus below a certain cut-off energy in the frequency spectrum of the sound wave. In music performance, timbre is in part a characteristic of the specific instrument. However, different techniques of playing may also influence the timbre of many instruments, such as the guitar.
The singer's formant	Timbre	The singer's formant refers to a strong resonance around 2500—3000 Hz, and adds brilliance and carrying power to the voice. It is attributed to a lowered larynx and widened pharynx, which forms an additional resonance cavity.

Table 35.2 Summary of cues correlated with specific emotions in musical expression

Emotion	Cues
Happiness	*fast tempo*, *small tempo variability*, major mode, simple and consonant harmony, *medium-high sound level*, *small sound level variability*, high pitch, much pitch variability, wide pitch range, ascending pitch, perfect 4th and 5th intervals, *rising micro intonation*, *raised singer's formant*, *staccato articulation*, *large articulation variability*, smooth and fluent rhythm, *bright timbre*, *fast tone attacks*, *small timing varibility*, *sharp contrasts between 'long' and 'short' notes*, *medium-fast vibrato rate*, *medium vibrato extent*, *micro-structural regularity*
Sadness	*slow tempo*, minor mode, dissonance, *low sound level*, *moderate sound level variability*, low pitch, narrow pitch range, descending pitch, *'flat' (or falling) intonation*, small intervals (e.g., minor 2nd), *lowered singer's formant*, *legato articulation*, *small articulation variability*, *dull timbre*, *slow tone attacks*, *large timing variability (e.g., rubato)*, *soft contrasts between 'long' and 'short' notes*, pauses, *slow vibrato*, *small vibrato extent*, *ritardando*, *micro-structural irregularity*
Anger	*fast tempo*, *small tempo variability*, minor mode, atonality, dissonance, *high sound level*, *small loudness variability*, high pitch, moderate pitch variability, ascending pitch, major 7th and augmented 4th intervals, *raised singer's formant*, *staccato articulation*, *moderate articulation variability*, complex rhythm, sudden rhythmic changes (e.g., syncopations), *sharp timbre*, *spectral noise*, *fast tone attacks/decays*, *small timing variability*, *accents on tonally unstable notes*, *sharp contrasts between 'long' and 'short' notes*, *accelerando*, *medium-fast vibrato rate*, *large vibrato extent*, *micro-structural irregularity*
Fear	*fast tempo*, *large tempo variability*, minor mode, dissonance, *low sound level*, *large sound level variability*, *rapid changes in sound level*, high pitch, ascending pitch, very wide pitch range, large pitch contrasts, *staccato articulation*, *large articulation variability*, jerky rhythms, *soft timbre*, *very large timing variability*, pauses, *soft tone attacks*, *fast vibrato rate*, *small vibrato extent*, *micro-structural irregularity*
Tenderness	*slow tempo*, major mode, consonance, *medium-low sound level*, *small sound level variability*, low pitch, fairly narrow pitch range, *lowered singer's formant*, *legato articulation*, *small articulation variability*, *slow tone attacks*, *soft timbre*, *moderate timing variability*, soft contrasts between long and short notes, accents on tonally stable notes, *medium-fast vibrato*, *small vibrato extent*, *micro-structural regularity*

pitch are the most powerful cues in terms of their effects on listeners' ratings (see Juslin 1997b; Juslin and Madison 1999; Scherer and Oshinsky 1977). Certain instruments might be more effective in communicating certain emotions than others depending on their specific timbre (Behrens and Green 1993; Bunt and Pavlicevic 2001). The focus on 'basic emotions' is sometimes criticized, though findings from survey studies of both music performers (Lindström *et al.* 2003) and listeners (Juslin and Laukka 2004) suggest that they regard these emotions as the ones that are easiest to express via music, and they thus represent a natural point of departure from which more 'complex' emotions may gradually be investigated. See Juslin *et al.* (2004, Table 13.2) for examples of complex emotions.

Expressive patterns and ornamentation

Most studies in the field so far have focused on cues that are applied in much the same way, and to much the same extent, throughout a piece. Indeed, experiments suggest that 'overall' levels of cues, such as mean tempo, explain considerably more variance in listeners' emotion ratings than does variability (e.g. Madison 2000). However, there exist patterns of changes in tempo and dynamics that are characteristic of particular emotions. Listening tests using systematic manipulations of synthesized (Juslin 1997b) or real performances (Juslin and Madison 1999) indicate that such patterns may be used by a listener to decode the emotional expression. What is it in these patterns that conveys the relevant information? One clue comes from the study by Lindström (1999), who found that performers accentuated different aspects of the melodic structure of a piece depending on the intended expression; thus, for example, if a certain note in the melodic structure was regarded as especially 'happy', then the performers emphasized this note in happiness expressions, but de-emphasized it in sadness expressions.

Another structure-related aspect of emotional expression in performances that has been little investigated is *ornamentation*, the use of expressive features that are not necessary to the melodic or harmonic line, but only serve to decorate that line.

Historical performance treatises feature extensive discussions of ornaments, and they may be especially important in Baroque music (e.g. Bach 1778/1985; Neumann 1978). Standard ornaments include the trill (a rapid alternation between two notes), the mordent (a rapid, single alternation between two notes), the glissando (a continuous slide upwards or downwards between two notes), and the appoggiatura (a grace note which delays the next note of the melody, taking half or more of its written time value). A first attempt to investigate the use of ornaments in the expression of specific emotions was made by Timmers and Ashley (2007). They analysed performances of fragments from Handel's G-minor sonata for recorder and basso continuo (HWV 360) by a flutist and a violinist and found that the use of ornaments varied according to the intended expression. Figure 35.1 shows examples of the ornaments use to express the various emotions.

Synthesis of emotional expression

Performance analyses have shown that performers can use a number of cues to express particular emotions. However, these analyses do not prove that listeners actually *use* the same cues in their judgements. To take just one example, the above study of ornaments showed that a performer used ornaments differently to express various emotions, but it did not prove that a listener could actually utilize any of these ornaments to decode the intended expression. Thus, to test the validity of hypotheses about expressive cues derived from performance studies, it is necessary to conduct listening experiments with synthesized performances. Note that there are two different approaches to synthesis of emotional expression in performance that can answer different questions. Based on a distinction introduced by Brunswik (1956), I have called them *representative design* and *systematic design* (Juslin 1997b).

Representative design means that one tries to recreate the emotional expressions of real music performances by programming a computer to perform in accordance with the emotion-specific patterns of acoustic cues obtained in previous studies (Table 35.2). Ideally, the patterns used to synthesize the emotional expression should be 'representative' of real performances in the

Fig. 35.1 Examples of ornaments used by a flutist and a violinst in music performances intended to express 'basic emotions' (from Timmers and Ashley 2007). Reprinted by permission of the University of California Press.

sense that they display similar statistical characteristics (e.g., cue intercorrelations, means, and standard deviations). Preliminary studies have shown that one can program a computer to communicate emotions with the same level of accuracy as a human performer (Juslin 1997b, Experiment 1; see also Bresin and Friberg 2000). However, such synthesized performances do not sound as musically satisfying as human performances do, perhaps because they lack other expressive features, such as marking of structure, biological motion, and random fluctuations, that are also important (Juslin *et al.* 2002). A representative design is useful when comparing the decoding accuracy of real and synthesized performances, although it cannot prove that the implementation of an individual cue is correct, or even that listeners are using the cue.

To be able to unambiguously attribute variance in a listener's judgements of emotions to individual acoustic cues, one needs to use a systematic design, or more specifically a factorial design. Such a design removes all the intercorrelations among cues, and renders it possible to ascertain the effectiveness of individual cues. Notably, only some of the performance cues in Table 35.2 have been tested in this way (Juslin 1997b, Experiment 2; see also Scherer and Oshinsky 1977). The lack of independent cue manipulation may explain why some early studies of emotional expression in music reported that some cues were associated with opposing emotional expressions.

A theoretical approach

Origin of the code

Juslin (1997a, 2000, 2001) proposed that the acoustic code used in emotional expression in

The Theory

music performance reflects two primary factors. The first factor is innate patterns for vocal expressions of 'basic emotions'. According to this notion—partly inspired by Herbert Spencer (1857)—the origin of the 'expressive code' is to be found in involuntary and emotion-specific physiological changes associated with emotional reactions, which strongly influence different aspects of voice production (for a review of the relationships among emotion, physiology, and voice, see Juslin and Scherer 2005). This notion was later named 'Spencer's law' by Juslin and Laukka (2003), who also offered strong empirical support from an extensive meta analysis of parallels between vocal and musical expression of emotions. One implication of this finding is that 'basic emotion' categories will be privileged, because of their biological preparedness for effective communication. This is not to deny that more precise emotional contents can also be conveyed under certain circumstances (e.g., through social or musical convention).

The second factor governing emotional expression in performance is social learning of various forms. This is a life-long process, beginning with the early interaction between mother and infant. (In fact, this 'imprinting' process might begin even prior to birth; see Chapter 20.) For example, when mothers talk to their infants, if they want to calm their infant, they reduce the tempo and intensity of their speech, and talk with slowly falling pitch contours, whereas if they want to express disapproval towards some unfavourable activity, they employ brief, sharp, and staccato-like contours (Papoušek 1996). Although the code used by mothers seems to be universal, the expressive style of the mother modulates the expressive style of the infant. This modulation of expressive skills continues throughout life, as one accumulates experience and learns links between cues and extra-musical phenomena, such as movement (see Chapter 34).

Nature of the code: modelling the communicative process

Studies of emotional expression in music performance present some puzzling findings, which can only be explained if the nature of the communication process is explored in greater detail. For instance, how can the communicative process usually be successful despite the fact that different instruments offer different cues, and that there are so wide individual differences among performers in expressive style? One way of capturing the crucial characteristics of the communicative process is to conceptualize it in terms of a variant of Egon Brunswik's (1956) *lens model*, as first suggested and implemented by Juslin (1995, 2000).

The modified lens model (Figure 35.2) captures how a performer 'encodes' (i.e., expresses) emotions by means of a set of acoustic cues (e.g., variations of tempo, sound level, or timbre) that are probabilistic (i.e., uncertain) and partly redundant. The emotions are 'decoded' (i.e., recognized) by listeners, who utilize these same cues to 'infer' the expression. The cues are probabilistic in that they are not perfectly reliable indicators of the intended expression. For example, a fast tempo is not a perfectly reliable indicator of happiness expressions, because a fast tempo occurs also in anger expressions. Thus, relationships among cues and emotions are merely correlational—they do not have a one-to-one mapping. Consequently, performers and listeners have to combine the cues for reliable communication to occur. However, this is not just a matter of pattern matching, because cues contribute in an additive fashion to listeners' judgements—each cue is neither necessary, nor sufficient, but the larger the number of cues used, the more reliable the communication. The redundancy among cues partly reflects how sounds are produced on musical instruments (e.g., a harder string attack produces a tone that is both louder and sharper in timbre). A mathematical formulation of the relationships among the various parts of the lens model, *the lens model equation*, was first formulated by Hursch et al. (1964). When applied to music performance (Juslin 2000), it allows one to explain the success (or not) of the communicative process by decomposing it into different components (e.g., the consistency of cue utilization, the degree to which the performer's cue utilization is matched to the listeners' cue utilization). Such a decomposition is highly useful if one wants to improve the communicative process (for evidence, see Juslin et al. 2006).

Although the lens model may appear simple, it has a crucial implication for research on

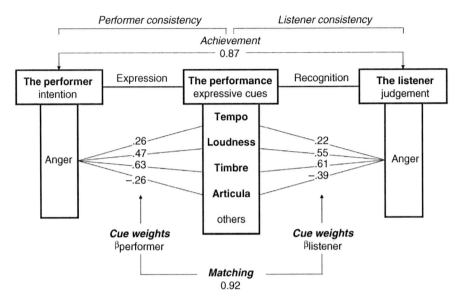

Fig. 35.2 Modified lens model of communication of emotions in music performance (adapted from Juslin 1995). *Achievement* (r_a) refers to the relationship between the performer's intention (e.g., intending to express sadness) and the listener's judgement (e.g., perceiving sadness). It is a measure of how well the performer succeeds in communicating an emotion to listeners. *Cue weight* (β_1, β_2, β_3 ...) refers to the strength of the relationship between a cue (e.g., tempo), on the one hand, and a performer's intentions or listeners' judgements, on the other. *Matching* (G) refers to the degree of similarity between the performer's and the listeners' use of acoustic cues, respectively. *Consistency* (R_e and R_s) refers to the degree of consistency with which the performer and listeners, respectively, are able to use the cues.

communication: if the cues are redundant to some extent, more than one way of using the cues may lead to a similarly high level of decoding accuracy, because different cues may substitute for one another—so-called *vicarious functioning*. Hence, Brunswik's lens model may explain why there is accurate communication of emotions even when the cues are used inconsistently across different performers or pieces of music. Multiple cues that are partly redundant yield a robust communicative system that is forgiving towards deviation from optimal cue utilization. Therefore, researchers should not expect acoustic cues in expressive performances to conform rigidly to the patterns shown in Table 35.2; the communicative system is so robust that perfect consistency is not required. Robustness comes with a price, however. The redundancy of the cues means that the same information is conveyed by many cues. This limits the information capacity, which is another

reason why 'basic emotion' categories are the easiest to convey.

The 'original' version of the lens model was limited to performance cues (Juslin 2000), but listeners' perception of emotions may also be affected by interactions between composer and performer cues. Hence, we have suggested an *expanded lens model* (Juslin and Lindström 2003; see Figure 35.3) in which both composer cues and performance cues are included to make it possible to explore their relative contributions. Furthermore, important interactions between performer and composition cues are included as separate predictors in the regression model. An experimental study based on this framework, using synthesized and systematically varied pieces of music, showed that about 75–85 per cent of the variance in listeners' emotion ratings could be explained by a linear combination of the main effects alone. Moreover, results suggested that the interactions between

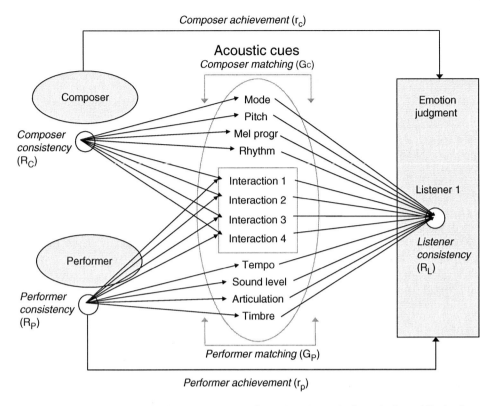

Fig. 35.3 Extended lens model of communication of emotions in music (from Juslin and Lindström 2003).

composer and performer cues made small—although not negligible—contributions to the predictive power. That the cues contribute primarily in an additive fashion to judgements is partly why the communicative process is so robust, because additive cues may compensate for one another in ways that multiplicative cues cannot.

Directions for future research

As revealed by this review, researchers have made much progress in understanding how music performers are able to communicate emotions via music performances. However, there are several limitations that need to be addressed in future research. One limitation is that the studies thus far have focused mainly on Western music (but see Balkwill and Thompson 1999; Clayton 2005). Hence, it remains to be seen how much of the results will generalize to other musical cultures. Even within the current culture, more research is required to examine more subtle, style-specific aspects of expression that contribute to the communicative process (e.g., ornamentation). Another important future direction is to study more closely how the different aspects of expression (e.g., structure marking, emotional expression, motion) interact with one another (Juslin *et al.* 2002). So far, the components have been studied either separately, or as if they all consisted of a homogeneous single entity. Closer collaboration among performance researchers within different subspecialties represents a promising avenue towards a deeper understanding of performance expression in all its complexity. One further topic that currently receives increasing attention is the influence of other perceptual channels. While most studies of expression in music performance have focused only on auditory features, it seems that visual features of the performer can also make important contributions to the perceived expression of the music in live settings (see Dahl and Friberg 2007; Thompson *et al.* 2005). Finally, much current work concerns applications of findings in music education (Juslin *et al.* 2006), therapy (Bunt and Pavlicevic 2001), the gaming industry (Livingstone and Brown 2005), ring signals in mobile phones (Bresin and Friberg 2001), and automatic analysis of emotions in music (Friberg *et al.* 2007) which might be used in content-based music searches at the Internet (Wieczorkowska *et al.* 2005).

References

Bach CPE (1778/1985). *Essay on the true art of playing keyboard instruments*, trans. WJ Mitchell. Eulenburg Books, London.

Balkwill L-L and Thompson WF (1999). A cross-cultural investigation of the perception of emotion in music: psychophysical and cultural cues. *Music Perception*, **17**, 43–64.

Behrens GA and Green SB (1993). The ability to identify emotional content of solo improvisations performed vocally and on three different instruments. *Psychology of Music*, **21**, 20–33.

Bresin R and Friberg A (2000). Emotional coloring of computer-controlled music performance. *Computer Music Journal*, **24**, 44–62.

Bresin R and Friberg A (2001). Expressive musical icons. In J Hiipakka, N Zakarov and T Takala, eds, *Proceedings of the International Conference on Auditory Display (ICAD) 2001*, 141–143. ICAD, Espoo, Finland.

Brunswik E (1956). *Perception and the representative design of experiments*. University of California Press, Berkeley, CA.

Buelow GJ (1983). Johann Mattheson and the invention of the Affektenlehre. In GJ Buelow and HJ Marx, eds, *New Mattheson studies*, 393–407. Cambridge University Press, Cambridge.

Bunt L and Pavlicevic M (2001). Music and emotion: perspectives from music therapy. In PN Juslin and JA Sloboda, eds, *Music and emotion: theory and research*, 181–201. Oxford University Press, Oxford.

Burland K and Davidson JW (2004). Tracing a musical life transition. In JW Davidson, ed., *The music practitioner*, 225–249. Ashgate, Aldershot.

Clarke EF (1988). Generative principles in music performance. In JA Sloboda, ed., *Generative processes in music: the psychology of performance, improvisation, and composition*, 1–26. Clarendon Press, Oxford.

Clarke EF, Cook N, Harrison B and Thomas P (2005). Interpretation and performance in Bryn Harrison's *être-temps*. *Musicae Scientiae*, **9**, 31–74.

Clayton M (2005). Communication in Indian raga performance. In D Miell, DJ Hargreaves and R MacDonald, eds, *Musical communication*, 361–381. Oxford University Press, Oxford.

Dahl S and Friberg A (2007). Visual perception of expressiveness in musicians' body movements. *Music Perception*, **24**, 433–454.

Friberg A, Schoonderwaldt E and Juslin PN (2007). CUEX: an algorithm for automatic extraction of expressive tone parameters in music performance from acoustic signals. *Acta Acustica united with Acustica*, **93**, 411–420.

Gabrielsson A and Juslin PN (2003). Emotional expression in music. In RJ Davidson, KR Scherer and HH Goldsmith, eds, *Handbook of affective sciences*, 503–534. Oxford University Press, Oxford.

Gilden DL (2001). Cognitive emissions of 1/f noise. *Psychological Review*, **108**, 33–56.

Gullberg A-K and Brändström S (2004). Formal and non-formal music learning amongst rock musicians. In J Davidson, ed., *The music practitioner*, 161–174. Ashgate, Aldershot.

Hevner K (1935). Expression in music: a discussion of experimental studies and theories. *Psychological Review*, **42**, 186–204.

Hursch CJ, Hammond KR and Hursch JL (1964). Some methodological considerations in multiple-cue probability studies. *Psychological Review*, **71**, 42–60.

Juslin PN (1995). Emotional communication in music viewed through a Brunswikian lens. In G Kleinen, ed., *Music and expression: Proceedings of the Conference of DGM and ESCOM, Bremen, 1995*, 21–25. University of Bremen, Bremen, Germany.

Juslin PN (1997a). Emotional communication in music performance: a functionalist perspective and some data. *Music Perception*, **14**, 383–418.

Juslin PN (1997b). Perceived emotional expression in synthesized performances of a short melody: capturing the listener's judgment policy. *Musicæ Scientiæ*, **1**, 225–256.

Juslin PN (1997c). Can results from studies of perceived expression in musical performances be generalized across response formats? *Psychomusicology*, **16**, 77–101.

Juslin PN (2000). Cue utilization in communication of emotion in music performance: relating performance to perception. *Journal of Experimental Psychology: Human Perception and Performance*, **26**, 1797–1813.

Juslin PN (2001). Communicating emotion in music performance: a review and a theoretical framework. In PN Juslin and JA Sloboda, eds, *Music and emotion: theory and research*, 309–337. Oxford University Press, Oxford.

Juslin PN (2003). Five facets of musical expression: a psychologist's perspective on music performance. *Psychology of Music*, **31**, 273–302.

Juslin PN, Friberg A and Bresin R (2002). Toward a computational model of expression in music performance: the GERM model. *Musicæ Scientiæ*, Special Issue 2001–2002, 63–122.

Juslin PN, Friberg A, Schoonderwaldt E and Karlsson J (2004). Feedback-learning of musical expressivity. In A Williamon, ed., *Musical excellence: strategies and techniques for enhancing performance*, 247–270. Oxford University Press, Oxford.

Juslin PN, Karlsson J, Lindström E, Friberg A and Schoonderwaldt E (2006). Play it again with feeling: Computer feedback in musical communication of emotions. *Journal of Experimental Psychology: Applied*, **12**, 79–95.

Juslin PN and Laukka P (2003). Communication of emotions in vocal expression and music performance: different channels, same code? *Psychological Bulletin*, **129**, 770–814.

Juslin PN and Laukka P (2004). Expression, perception, and induction of musical emotions: a review and a questionnaire study of everyday listening. *Journal of New Music Research*, **33**, 217–238.

Juslin PN and Lindström E (2003). Musical expression of emotions: modeling composed and performed features. Paper presented at 5th Conference of the European Society for the Cognitive Sciences of Music (ESCOM), Hanover, Germany, September 2003.

Juslin PN and Madison G (1999). The role of timing patterns in recognition of emotional expression from musical performance. *Music Perception*, **17**, 197–221.

Juslin PN and Scherer KR (2005). Vocal expression of affect. In JA Harrigan, R Rosenthal and KR Scherer, eds, *The new handbook of methods in nonverbal behavior research*, 65–135. Oxford University Press, New York.

Juslin PN and Sloboda JA (eds) (2001). *Music and emotion: theory and research*. Oxford University Press, Oxford.

Laukka P and Juslin PN (2007). Similar pattern of age-related differences in emotion recognition from speech and music. *Motivation and Emotion*, **31**, 182–191.

Lindström E (1999). Expression in music: interaction between performance and melodic structure. Paper presented at the Meeting of the Society for Music Perception and Cognition, Evanston, USA, 14–17 August, 1999.

Lindström E, Juslin PN, Bresin R and Williamon A (2003). 'Expressivity comes from within your soul': a questionnaire study of music students' perspectives on expressivity. *Research Studies in Music Education*, **20**, 23–47.

Livingstone SR and Brown AR (2005). Dynamic response: real-time adaption for music emotion. In Y Pisan, ed., *Proceedings of the Second Australasian Conference on Interactive Entertainment*, 105–111. Creativity and Cognition Studios Press, Sydney.

Madison G (2000). Properties of expressive variability patterns in music performance. *Journal of New Music Research*, **29**, 335–356.

Marchand DJ (1975). A study of two approaches to developing expressive performance. *Journal of Research in Music Education*, **23**, 14–22.

Mattheson J (1739/1954). *Der volkommene Capellmeister*. Bärenreiter Verlag, Basel.

Meyer LB (1956). *Emotion and meaning in music*. University of Chicago Press, Chicago, IL.

Minassian C, Gayford C and Sloboda JA (2003). Optimal experience in musical performance: a survey of young musicians. Paper presented at the Meeting of the Society for Education, Music, and Psychology Research, London, March 2003.

Neumann F (1978). *Ornamentation in Baroque and post-Baroque music: with special emphasis on JS Bach*. Princeton University Press, Princeton, NJ

Palmer C (1997). Music performance. *Annual Review of Psychology*, **48**, 115–138.

Papoušek M (1996). Intuitive parenting: a hidden source of musical stimulation in infancy. In I Deliége and JA Sloboda, eds, *Musical beginnings. Origins and development of musical competence*, 89–112. Oxford University Press, Oxford.

Resnicow JE, Salovey P and Repp BH (2004). Is recognition of emotion in music performance an aspect of emotional intelligence? *Music Perception*, **22**, 145–158.

Scherer KR and Oshinsky JS (1977). Cue utilisation in emotion attribution from auditory stimuli. *Motivation and Emotion*, **1**, 331–346.

Shove P and Repp BH (1995). Musical motion and performance: theoretical and empirical perspectives. In J Rink, ed., *The practice of performance*, 55–83. Cambridge University Press, Cambridge.

Siegwart H and Scherer KR (1995). Acoustic concomitants of emotional expression in operatic singing: the case of Lucia in Ardi gli incensi. *Journal of Voice*, **9**, 249–260.

Sloboda JA and Lehmann AC (2001). Tracking performance correlates of changes in perceived intensity of emotion during different interpretations of a Chopin piano prelude. *Music Perception*, **19**, 87–120.

Spencer H (1857). The origin and function of music. *Fraser's Magazine*, **56**, 396–408.

Thompson S (2006). Audience responses to a live orchestral concert. *Musicae Scientiae*, **10**, 215–244.

Thompson WF, Graham P and Russo FA (2005). Seeing music performance: visual influences on perception and experience. *Semiotica*, **156**, 203–227.

Timmers R and Ashley R (2007). Emotional ornamentation in performances of a Handel sonata. *Music Perception*, **25**, 117–134.

Wieczorkowska A, Synak P, Lewis R and Zbigniew WR (2005). Extracting emotions from music data. *Lecture Notes in Computer Science*, **3488**, 456–465.

Yamasaki T (2002). Emotional communication in improvised performance by musically untrained players. In T Kato, ed., *Proceedings of the 17th International Congress of the International Association of Empirical Aesthetics*, 521–524. IAEA, Osaka.

CHAPTER 36

Optimizing physical and psychological health in performing musicians

Dianna T. Kenny and Bronwen Ackermann

Introduction

Performing musicians face a number of physical, social and psychological challenges that must be mastered if their musical career is to be both rewarding and sustainable. However, musicians are at high risk of physical and psychological strain and injury in the execution of their art. Physical and psychological stressors exert reciprocal and synergistic effects on the musician, and careful analysis of the intrinsic characteristics of the performer and the extrinsic demands on the musician must be made in order to develop appropriate interventions. In this chapter we provide an overview of the risks and challenges facing musicians with the aim of developing awareness and understanding of how to prevent and manage these challenges. The chapter is divided into two sections: physical challenges and psychological challenges, focusing on music performance anxiety. In each section, we outline the key issues and then provide an overview of evidence-based treatment.

Physical health issues

Musicians are like athletes because both require superior sensorimotor integration (Alternmuller et al. 2000), neuro-musculoskeletal skill and many hours of training and practice to achieve mastery (Tubiana 2000). Several large epidemiological studies have shown high physical injury rates among musicians (Manchester 2006).

Performer-related risk factors for injury include poor posture, poor physical condition, inadequate instrument set-up, long hours of playing, insufficient rest breaks and inefficient movement patterns (or poor technique) (Ackermann and Adams 2004a).

Although musicians may suffer injury from non-performance related causes such as lifting and carrying awkward or heavy instruments and suitcases (when on tour), demanding work schedules, sitting on poorly designed orchestral chairs, temperature variations (Manchester 2006), demanding repertoire and poor visibility of music scores (Horvath 2002), the majority of musicians' injuries are over-use injuries (Dawson et al. 1998) with soft-tissue symptoms predominating (Pascarelli and Hsu 2001).

Musicians of all ages and levels of skill are vulnerable to injury, but the risk increases as hours of playing increases. The neck, upper limbs and lower back (Fjellman-Wiklund et al. 2003) are vulnerable with upper limb over-use injuries comprising 75–85 per cent of all injuries (Slade et al. 1999). Strains of the muscle–tendon unit predominate, with other common problems including inflammatory disorders such as tenosynovitis, arthritic problems and hypermobility (also called double-jointedness) i.e. joints that stretch more than normal (Dawson 2002). People with hypermobile joints may be more easily injured and may be more at risk of developing problems from muscle over-use, as muscles must work harder to control joint movement.

Injury types vary according to instrument type, gender (Engquist *et al.* 2004), years of performing, repertoire, hours of practice and age (Warrrington *et al.* 2002). Older musicians more typically develop degenerative conditions (i.e. conditions that have a gradual deterioration in the structure of a body part with a consequent loss of the part's ability to function) while younger musicians suffer more from performance-related musculoskeletal pain (Warrington *et al.* 2002).

Effective training for any athletic pursuit, including music performance, involves a fine balance between working hard enough to continually improve performance, while simultaneously resting enough to avoid incurring an over-use injury, a task assisted by specifically designed cross-training programmes (Marieb 2001). Muscle fatigue, which may arise from central (brain) or peripheral (muscle) fatigue (Gandevia 2001) due to over-practising without adequate rest breaks (Ackermann and Adams 2004a) may be a factor in developing altered movement patterns that can be a precursor to injury. Exercise aimed at conditioning muscles may reduce the effect of muscle fatigue by increasing muscle cross-sectional area and creating neural adaptations that lead to an improved ability to recruit motor units (Herbert 1993).

Types of injuries

Muscle/tendon injuries

Muscles are the primary source of force needed for the performance of motor skills such as instrumental playing. An occupational over-use injury may result from insufficient muscle tolerance to cope with the quality, quantity and rate of task demands (Hagberg *et al.* 1997). Dynamic postures are less likely to cause pain than static postures due to the short rests that occur between the bursts of activity of muscles involved in dynamic movements (Vergara and Page 2002). Some strategies for musicians within task-constraints are possible for small-scale movements that can allow these dynamic motions to occur (Rolland 1974). Pablo Casals intentionally practised relaxing between phrases, no matter how difficult the material, to minimize the build up of adverse muscle tension (Ma 1986).

Joint injuries

Joint injuries in musicians are degenerative, likely to be related to repetitive use, but more specifically to regional overload. For example, the right thumb of a clarinettist carries the whole weight of the instrument and shows early degenerative changes (Chesky *et al.* 2000). Ergonomic devices such as a neck strap to carry the weight of the clarinet may effectively reduce strain on the thumb, although long-term effects of transmitting this load through the neck are unclear (Chesky *et al.* 2000).

Nerve compression disorders

Nerve compression syndromes in musicians are related to the demands and nature of musicians' work, such as sustained awkward positions, sustained muscle contraction pressure, or the compression arising from having to support the instrument itself (Spinner and Amadio 2000). Common nerve-entrapment disorders include symptoms from compression of the ulna nerve at the elbow, the median nerve at the wrist, cervical radiculopathies, occasional digital neuropathies and symptomatic thoracic outlet syndrome (Schuele and Lederman 2004).

Central nervous system disorders

The most common performance-related condition of the central nervous system (CNS) affecting musicians is focal dystonia, a movement dysfunction syndrome thought to be due to disruptions between central sensory processing and motor output (Chen and Hallett 1998). Focal dystonias involve abnormal, often twisting movements that tend to affect performers in a similar way, with the left ring finger the main reported site of the dysfunction in violinists (Hochberg and Hochberg 2000). While a definitive cause remains unclear, the amount of movement repetition is a major factor in developing dystonias (Hochberg and Hochberg 2000), and these are potentially more potent if abnormal biomechanical factors are present (Wilson 2000).

Treatment

Treatment, assessment and management procedures are still largely based on clinical experience rather than scientific research (Schuele and Lederman 2004). A primary goal of treatment is not only relief of symptoms but restoration of function, addressing both local and general effects of an injury (Herring and Kibler 1998). Psychological factors may be involved in the genesis or maintenance of physical problems. Spahn *et al.* (2001) found significant rates (25%) of somatization and somatoform disorders in musicians presenting to hand surgery clinics. Most of their sample (75%) did not attribute their current physical problems to psychosocial factors, even though there was no identified organic cause for their physical problems. The authors concluded that psychosomatic aspects play a decisive role in somatic problems of musicians and that these should be addressed in treatment to avoid unwarranted medical interventions.

Rest and rehabilitation

There is no benefit from prolonged rest for soft tissue injuries in the majority of cases (Nash *et al.* 2004). Scott (1997) defines the term rest for soft tissue injuries with the mnemonic 'Resume Exercise below Soreness Threshold', and emphasizes the importance of continuing to play in a reduced and careful fashion wherever possible without causing aggravation of the injury. Guidelines for rehabilitating sports overuse injuries stress the importance of relative rest, where overall fitness is maintained even in the acute stage of an injury while rehabilitating the injured part back to performance requirements (Herring and Kibler 1998). Relative rest can be achieved if necessary with the assistance of splints or ergonomic aids.

Poor muscle balance around the shoulder girdle is frequently considered to be a cause of upper limb symptoms in the musician, and restoring a good balance of muscle condition as well as strengthening postural muscles in this area is an important part of rehabilitation (Chamagne 2000).

Retraining

Retraining is used for the treatment of both neurological and musculoskeletal conditions occurring in musicians. Some treatment approaches for focal dystonia include splinting with specific exercises (Candia *et al.* 1999), postural and movement retraining strategies (Chamagne 2000), proprioceptive and sensory retraining techniques (Ackermann and Adams 2005), and

the slow-down exercise regime involving task-specific music drills (Sakai 2006). Movement patterns can be re-trained by restoring good muscle balance and functioning of the arm as a whole kinetic chain unit to correct any underlying mechanical inefficiencies (Dreyer and Boden 1999).

Manual therapy

Trigger point therapy may be useful for soft tissue problems, particularly when palpation of active trigger points reproduces the musicians' symptoms (Davies 2002). Joint mobilization techniques of the cervical spine, thoracic spine, forearm, wrist and hand are necessary to restore full functional range of movement for musicians following an injury (Kember 1998).

Prevention of playing-related injuries

Prevention is the best form of management for occupational over-use injuries (Melhorn 1998). Key factors in injury prevention include awareness of correct postural requirements, technique and biomechanics involved in playing one's instrument, and maintaining overall good physical condition that is achieved by warming up, stretching (Zaza 1994) and strength and endurance training (Marieb 2001).

Posture

Correct posture minimizes stress applied to each joint. Poor posture, defined as a 'faulty relationship of the various segments of the body, producing increased stress on supporting structures' (Aaras *et al.* 2001), is a major risk for injury because musicians have to maintain awkward, relatively static postures over extended time periods (Brandfonbrener 2000). Musicians must maintain their posture within physiological boundaries, even with asymmetrical instruments such as the violin and flute, with good proximal muscle support and weight balance to avoid injury and to allow optimal fine control of movements during performance (Tubiana *et al.* 1989). The musical instrument should be considered as an extension of the musicians' body (Dommerholt 2000).

Ideal sitting posture alignment occurs with hips and knees at 90° of flexion, with a 10° backward inclination of a supportive back on the chair (Kendall *et al.* 1993), or a level seat and a back-rest set back 20° to minimize lumbar loadings (Bonney and Corlett 2002). Sitting should also be balanced between sides by weight-bearing evenly on both sides, as excessive weight-bearing on one side may lead to lateral stresses on the lumbar discs (Cailliet 1990).

Technique, biomechanics and physical condition

Within a technique or movement pattern on a musical instrument, early more rigid movements are replaced by efficient movements within anatomical and task constraints as the skill is mastered (Sparrow and Newell 1998). Musicians working under pressure may be so focused on achieving a musical goal that a distortion of technique or posture occurs, and these aberrations may then become established in the motor programme, causing a subconscious alteration in technique (Wilson 2000). These physical adaptations do not represent the players' normal technique and may lead to maladaptive changes including muscle misuse or more serious neurological disorders such as focal dystonia (Wilson 2000). Excessive muscle tension also accompanies mechanical inefficiencies in performance (Ma 1986).

Warming up and stretching

Regular stretching improves flexibility (Wilkinson 1992), and musicians benefit from instrument-specific stretching programmes (Markison 1998). Stretching should be performed regularly to maintain adequate range for performance demands (Norris 1993). Stretching prior to performance only may not be sufficient to minimize injury risk (Pope *et al.* 2000). General warming-up and cooling-down routines are recommended (Markison 1998). Players using instrumental warm-up strategies may protect themselves against the development of a playing-related injury (Zaza and Farewell 1997).

Strength or endurance conditioning

Poor physical condition is a predisposing factor to playing-related injuries (Ackermann and Adams 2004a). Instrument-specific strength and endurance training is effective in reducing injury frequency and intensity as well as reducing

the perceived exertion associated with practising their instrument (Ackermann *et al.* 2002). In contrast, participating in unsupervised general sports was not found to provide any benefits in terms of injury prevention for musicians (van Hees 1997).

Ergonomic aids and advice

Various ergonomic interventions aimed at reducing physical load include hand splint adaptations for the trombone to assist with reach difficulties (Quarrier and Norris 2001), development of polymer drumsticks with reduced vibration characteristics (Zaza *et al.* 2000), a neck strap to carry the weight of the clarinet and bassoon may effectively reduce strain on the thumb (Chesky *et al.* 2000), and many other designs such as angle-headed flutes, key extensions on wind instruments, and remodelling of viola or guitar bodies (Norris 2000). Instruction on good lifting technique is important for musicians who may injure their lower back as a result of carrying heavy or awkward-shaped instruments (Fjellman-Wiklund *et al.* 2003).

Psychological health issues

Stressors experienced by musicians

Sternbach (1995) described the working conditions of professional musicians as generating a 'total stress quotient' that far exceeds that observed in other professions. Like elite athletes, performing artists must maintain their skills at peak form, endure many hours of solitary, repetitive practice, constantly self-evaluate their performances and subject their public performances to close scrutiny. They are required to work in a pattern akin to shift work, be available to travel to performance venues, leave their families while on tour, adjust to changing time zones, live at close quarters with colleagues and peers, and cope with financial insecurity. For these reasons, it can be difficult to differentiate between the occupational and physical stressors discussed in the previous section and psychological problems that can arise in individual musicians that may require individualized psychological intervention.

Frequently reported psychosocial issues while on tour or working on contract with interstate and overseas orchestras include loneliness, homesickness, sexual frustration and relationship breakdown. Occupational issues include language barriers, unfamiliar backstage arrangements at concert venues and variable quality of dressing rooms. In addition to these psychological and occupational stressors, there is the physical stress associated with moving instruments and luggage, setting up on different stages, adjusting to differently shaped chairs at every venue, sleeping in different beds with different pillows, coping with jet lag, general fatigue and lack of sleep. New injuries or pains are frequently reported by professional musicians on tour, as a direct result of these factors (Ackermann 2002).

Individuals vary in their capacity to cope with such stressful working conditions. However, since not all performers suffer the same degree of psychological distress or indeed report the same levels of occupational stress, individual differences in a range of psychological characteristics are likely to account for variations in the degree to which musicians experience symptoms. For example, the difficulty in coping may be compounded for those who are also highly anxious, who lack confidence in their abilities and who engage in unhelpful strategies to deal with their anxieties, such as the regular consumption of alcohol, and licit (e.g. beta blockers) or illicit (e.g. marijuana) drugs. Since music performance anxiety is one of the most commonly reported psychological stressors in musicians, the remainder of this chapter will focus on music performance anxiety, its manifestations, consequences and treatment.

Anxiety in public performance

Performance anxiety is a group of disorders that affect individuals in a range of performance settings, such as examinations, competitions and public speaking. Solo and orchestral instrumentalists (van Kemenade *et al.* 1995) and solo and choral vocal artists (Kenny *et al.* 2004) all report experiencing music performance anxiety. Music performance anxiety is also observed in young musicians (Kenny and Osborne 2006), and children and adolescents show a similar constellation of symptoms to college level music students and professional musicians (Osborne *et al.* 2005).

Students of classical music report higher levels of performance anxiety than students of Jazz (Kaspersen and Gotestam 2002). Like all performance anxieties, music performance anxiety occurs on a continuum of severity from 'normal everyday healthy aspects of stress and anxiety that are intrinsic to the profession' (Brodsky 1996, p. 91) to the severely debilitating symptoms of stage fright.

The phenomenology and determinants of music performance anxiety

Performance anxiety may occur as an isolated disorder, affecting only one specific part of a person's life, such as public speaking, test-taking or music performance. However, for a significant minority of those suffering performance anxieties, other comorbid disorders may be present, the most common of which is generalized anxiety disorder, which appears to co-occur in about one third of those presenting with severe performance anxiety (Sanderson *et al.* 1990). Generalized anxiety disorder is characterized by excessive, uncontrollable and often irrational worry about everyday concerns and is disproportionate to the actual source of worry. People with generalized anxiety disorder may have a long history of chronic worry and apprehension in most facets of their lives, not just in performance situations (American Psychological Association 2000).

Others may qualify for a diagnosis of social phobia (social anxiety) if the performer demonstrates significant impairment in interactions with others as well as in the performance setting and who otherwise meet the criteria for social phobia presented in DSM-IV-TR (American Psychological Association 2000). About 10–15% of those with a social phobia also meet criteria for clinical depression (Kessler *et al.* 1999). For a subgroup of music performance anxiety sufferers, there may be underlying psychological conflicts that need to be identified and resolved before the symptoms abate (Lazarus and Abramovitz 2004).

Two distinct aspects of performance anxiety have been identified—cognitive anxiety and somatic anxiety (Martens *et al.* 1990). High cognitive anxious individuals generally display a consistent style of thinking about their performance that includes the following characteristics:

1 stronger negative expectancies before the event

2 stronger negative bias in their retrospective self-evaluations of performance

3 stronger expectation that their performance will be judged negatively by their examiners/audience

4 stronger concerns about the consequences of a poor performance

5 heightened responsiveness to changes in reactions of judges or audience

6 failure to derive comfort from evidence that they have handled the situation skilfully (Wallace and Alden 1997).

Somatic anxiety refers to the experiencing of a cluster of physical symptoms during an anxiety-provoking activity such as performing in front of an audience. It is characterized by muscle tension, agitation, and other phenomena such as trembling, sweating, dry mouth, shallow breathing and 'buttlerflies in the stomach' that are associated with the 'fright–fight–flight' response, first described by Cannon (1915) and subsequently by many researchers (Friedman and Silver 2007). These symptoms occur as a result of arousal of the sympathetic nervous system via the release of the hormone epinephrine (adrenaline) and to a lesser extent norepinephrine from the medulla of the adrenal glands (Gleitman *et al.* 2004).

Music performance anxiety and performance quality

Performance quality is determined by a number of interacting factors, including the ability of the performer and the level of achievement attained as a musician (Fortune 2007), the degree to which the performance repertoire has been mastered (Wilson 2002), the fit between technical ability and task difficulty (Fehm and Schmidt 2006), the circumstances of the performance, for example, whether the performance will be evaluated by expert judges, audience characteristics (Brotons 1994), and the type and severity of anxiety experienced (Wang 2002).

To date, Wilson (2002) has offered the most comprehensive model of music performance anxiety that incorporates the performer's trait anxiety, or their constitutional and learned tendency to become anxious in response to socially stressful situations; the degree of task mastery achieved; and degree of situational stress, such that high anxiety is more likely to be experienced in situations where social or environmental pressures are high. Performance anxiety may exert either an enhancing or detrimental effect on performance depending upon the interaction between these three factors (Fehm and Schmidt 2006). For example, an individual with high trait anxiety will perform best with an easy, well-prepared piece in a relaxed environment, whereas an individual with low trait anxiety will perform better if the piece is challenging and performed in an evaluating environment, such as an exam or competition.

Optimizing music performance

An optimal performance is determined by a complex interaction between person characteristics, task characteristics and performance setting. These include adequate preparation, achievement of task mastery such that the complex motor tasks required to perform the task have been (over) learnt to the point of being automatic (Oliveira and Goodman 2004), familiarization with the performance venue and adequate rehearsal with other performers in the case of ensemble performance. When all of these characteristics occur at an optimal level, the performer is said to be 'in the zone' (Young and Pain 1999) or to have achieved a state of 'flow' (Marr 2000). Another construct to describe peak performance, borrowed from sport psychology, is the 'individualized zone of optimal functioning' (IZO) (Hanin 1986), that is, the performer has achieved the optimal level of pre-performance anxiety that results in a peak performance. 'Optimal' pre-performance anxiety is a good predictor of performance quality (Turner and Raglin 1991).

Although one would expect highly anxious individuals to experience performance breakdown or impaired performance quality more often than low-anxiety performers, this is not usually the case (Strahan and Conger 1998).

Even in situations where the highly anxious do perform less well than the less anxious, social or artistic performance catastrophes are rare. There are a number of possible explanations for this. First, people display highly individual ways of responding to stressful situations. Very small changes in context or task-expectancy can change a person's appraisal of a situation as anxiety-provoking or not (Bandura 1991). Secondly, those situations that could produce a catastrophe are indeed rare, even for highly anxious individuals. Thirdly, highly anxious professional performers are likely to engage in a number of pre-performance compensatory activities, such as over-learning, additional rehearsals, or visiting the venue before the performance to ensure that their performance can withstand the additional anxiety they know they will experience during the performance (Kenny *et al.* 2004).

Treatments for music performance anxiety

Many treatment programmes have been developed to assist the anxious or stressed musician. However, most of the available treatments have not been adequately assessed as to their effectiveness. These include:

1 Prescription pharmacological interventions such as antidepressants, benzodiazepines, beta-adrenergic receptor blockers, and busipone.

2 Meditative interventions (autogenic training, (self-) hypnosis, meditation, yoga)

3 Physiological and physically based interventions (aerobic exercise, Alexander technique, biofeedback, Feldenkrais, massage)

4 Relaxation therapies e.g. progressive muscle relaxation training

5 Cognitive and cognitive behavioural interventions: assertiveness training, attention-focusing techniques, cognitive behaviour therapy (cognitive restructuring), multimodal behavioural therapy, coping skills training, exposure therapy, goal setting, lifestyle changes (e.g. development of non-musical hobbies and interests), imagery (distraction and focused), mental rehearsal, stress inoculation, systematic desensitization and systematic rehearsal

6 Music therapy (music enhanced relaxation techniques; group therapy for musicians)

7 Psychotherapy (Nagel 2004).

Space permits only a brief overview, update and summary of the most commonly used and researched treatments and their effectiveness—the cognitive and behavioural therapies. A detailed review and analysis of other treatments for performance anxiety can be found in Kenny (2005).

Cognitive, behavioural and cognitive behaviour therapies

Behaviour is determined by a combination of thoughts, feelings and past and present behaviours (Turkington *et al.* 2006). Three groups of therapies—behavioural (van de Wiel *et al.* 2007), cognitive (Willner, 2006) and cognitive behavioural (Butler *et al.* 2006)—are all based on the same principles, but use the available therapeutic techniques in different amounts. Behavioural therapies focus primarily on changing the dysfunctional behaviours that arise when people feel anxious. One of the main targets of behavioural therapies for anxiety disorders is excessive muscle tension, which is treated with deep muscle relaxation training (Conrad and Roth 2007) and systematic desensitization (Pagoto *et al.* 2006), a procedure in which the person is encouraged to imagine the feared or anxiety provoking situation in graded steps, called the fear hierarchy, until they can visualize the situation without experiencing the muscle tension that used to accompany the visualizations. Once the fear hierarchy has been mastered in the therapist's office (imaginal desensitization), people are encouraged to apply their new skills in the actual, anxiety-provoking situation (called *in vivo* desensitization) (Choy *et al.* 2007). This allows for behavioural exposure, i.e. repeatedly practising the task in the feared situation until the associated anxiety is reduced to manageable levels. For this to be effective, the task must have been mastered so that the performer can ensure successful performance in the more stressful situation (Rauch and Foa 2006).

Cognitive therapy focuses on mental states such as thoughts, feelings and images (Willner 2006). Dysfunctional cognitions, those that create emotional distress or maladaptive responses, can be the result of cognitive deficits (i.e. difficulties with problem solving) (van Winkel *et al.* 2006), and/or errors or biases in information processing (Joormann *et al.* 2007). Cognitive therapy changes faulty thinking patterns that give rise to maladaptive behaviours, such as excessive muscle tension, avoidance of the feared situation, or impaired performance. In this therapy, people learn a skill called cognitive restructuring, a process whereby people replace negative, unproductive, catastrophic thinking with more rational, useful ways of understanding their problem situations (Murphy *et al.* 2007). Based on changed thinking patterns, people are often able to reassess or reappraise their feared situations in ways that reduce the perceived threat.

Cognitive behavioural therapy (CBT) is a combination of behavioural and cognitive interventions (Turkington *et al.* 2006). CBT uses educational and psychological interventions that are based on the idea that changing negative thinking patterns and behaviours can have a powerful effect on a person's emotions, which in turn can change behaviour in situations in which the negative emotions arose. Like all new learning, CBT requires commitment, practice and application in situations outside the therapy office (Yovel and Safren 2007). CBT is focused and directive, usually of short duration and is action-oriented,—it relies on the client's record-keeping, active participation, application and evaluation (Rees *et al.* 2005).

A more recent variant of CBT, multimodal behavioural therapy (Lazarus and Abramovitz 2004) proposes a multimodal approach to treatment that involves the assessment and management of any combination of seven components: behaviour, affect, sensations, imagery, cognition, interpersonal relationships, and drugs/biological factors. Research is needed to assess whether this more comprehensive approach will produce better results for the anxious musician.

Prevention of music performance anxiety

Parenting style is important in the prevention of anxiety and depression in children (Barlow 2000). Parents who are responsive, unobtrusive, not overly protective, and who give children age-appropriate opportunities to exercise control over their environment foster a sense of control and mastery in their children that provides protection against the development of anxiety (Gar *et al.* 2005).

Most forms of performance anxiety are difficult to treat and anxiety levels after treatment rarely reduce to those of non-anxious people (Kenny 2005). The best form of treatment is to prevent its occurrence. Sound pedagogy, appropriate parental support and expectations, and the learning of self-management strategies early in one's musical education can help to mitigate the effects of entering a highly stressful profession.

Children should be offered frequent, low-stress opportunities to perform almost from the beginning of their musical training. These performances should be presented in a positive, non-judgemental way, so that young performers can learn that performance is an integral, enjoyable and manageable part of their musical education. Children should not be prematurely thrust into competitive environments whose focus is evaluation (such as auditions or competitions) and when they are, students need to be well prepared for the performance both musically and psychologically. Repertoire should be well within the technical capacity and interpretive abilities of the student and the material should be well-learned. Sensible pre-performance routines should be established that attend to the performer's physical well-being (having adequate diet and sleep), psychological well-being (developing positive self-statements and realistic self-appraisal capacity) and musical demands (adequate practice, appropriate level of complexity, cognitive and physical capacity commensurate with the musical demands). These strategies will enhance the student's sense of competence and control so that when confronted with critical performances, a strong sense of a competent self will guide a self-actualized performance.

References

Aaras A, Horgen G, Bjorset HH, Ro O and Walsoe H (2001). Musculoskeletal, visual and psychosocial stress in VDU operators before and after multidisciplinary ergonomic interventions. A 6-year prospective study—part II. *Applied Ergonomics*, **32**, 559–571.

Ackermann B (2002). Managing the musculoskeletal health of musicians on tour. *Medical Problems of Performing Artists*, **17**(2), 63–67.

Ackermann B and Adams R (2004a). Perceptions of causes of performance-related injuries by music health experts and injured violinists. *Perceptual and Motor Skills*, **99**, 669–678.

Ackermann B and Adams R (2005). Finger movement discrimination in focal hand dystonia: a cellist case study. *Medical Problems of Performing Artists*, **20**(1), 77–81.

Ackermann B, Adams R and Marshall E (2002). Strength or endurance training for undergraduate music majors at a university. *Medical Problems of Performing Artists*, **17**(1), 33–41.

Altenmueller E, Gruhn W, Liebert G and Parlitz D (2000). The impact of music education on brain networks: evidence from EEG studies. *International Journal of Music Education*, **35**, 47–53.

American Psychiatric Association (2000). *Diagnostic and Statistical Manual (DSM-IV-TR)*. American Psychiatric Association, Washington, DC.

Bandura A (1991). Self-efficacy conception of anxiety. In S Schwarzer, RA Wicklund, eds, *Anxiety and self-focused attention*, 89–110. Harwood Academic Publishers, Amsterdam, Netherlands.

Barlow H (2000). Unravelling the mysteries of anxiety and its disorders from the perspective of emotion theory. *American Psychologist*, **55**(11), 1245–1263.

Bonney R and Corlett E (2002). Head posture and loading of the cervical spine. *Applied Ergonomics*, **33**, 415–417.

Brandfonbrener A (2000). Epidemiology and risk factors. In R Tubiana and P Amadio, eds, *Medical problems of the instrumentalist musician*, 171–194. Martin Dunitz Ltd, London.

Brodsky W (1996). Music performance anxiety reconceptualised: a critique of current research practices and findings. *Medical Problems of Performing Artists*, **11**, 88–98.

Brotons M (1994). Effects of performing conditions on music performance anxiety and performance quality. *Journal of Music Therapy*, **31**, 63–81.

Butler AC, Chapman JE, Forman EM and Beck AT (2006). The empirical status of cognitive-behavioral therapy: a review of meta-analyses. *Clinical Psychology Review*, **26**, 17–31.

Cailliet R (1990). Abnormalities of the sitting postures of musicians. *Medical Problems of Performing Artists*, **5**(4), 131–135.

Candia V, Elbert T, Altenmueller E, Rau H, Schafer T and Taub E (1999). Constraint-induced movement therapy for focal hand dystonia in musicians. *The Lancet*, **353**(9146), 42.

Cannon W (1915). *Bodily changes in pain, hunger, fear and rage: an account of recent researches into the function of emotional excitement*. Appleton, New York.

Chamagne P (2000). Functional assessment and rehabilitation of musician's focal dystonia. In R Tubiana and PC Amadio, eds, *Medical problems of the instrumentalist musician*, 343–362. Martin Dunitz Ltd, London.

Chen R and Hallett M (1998). Focal dystonia and repetitive motion disorders. *Clinical Orthopaedics and Related Research*, **351**, 102–106.

Chesky KS, Kondraske G and Rubin B (2000). Effect of elastic neck strap on right thumb force and force angle during clarinet performance. *Journal of Occupational and Environmental Medicine*, **42**(8), 775–776.

Choy Y, Fyer AJ and Lipsitz JD (2007). Treatment of specific phobia in adults. *Clinical Psychology Review*, **27**(3), 266–286.

Conrad A and Roth WT (2007). Muscle relaxation therapy for anxiety disorders: it works but how? *Journal of Anxiety Disorders*, **21**(3), 243–264.

Davies C (2002). Musculoskeletal pain from repetitive strain in musicians: insights into an alternative approach. *Medical Problems of Performing Artists*, **17**(1), 42–49.

Dawson WJ, Charness ME, Goode DJ, Lederman RJ and Newmark J (1998). What's in a name? Terminologic issues in performing arts medicine. *Medical Problems of Performing Artists*, **13**(2), 45–50.

Dawson WJ (2002). Upper-extremity problems caused by playing specific instruments. *Medical Problems of Performing Artists*, **17**(3), 135–139.

Dommerholt J (2000). Posture. In R Tubiana and PC Amadio, eds, *Medical problems of the instrumentalist musician*, 399–420. Martin Dunitz Ltd, London.

Dreyer SJ and Boden SD (1999). Natural history of rheumatoid arthritis of the cervical spine. *Clinical Orthopaedics and Related Research*, **366**, 98–106.

Engquist K, Orbaek P and Jakobsson K (2004). Musculoskeletal pain and impact on performance in orchestra musicians and actors. *Medical Problems of Performing Artists*, **19**(2), 55–61.

Fehm L and Schmidt K (2006). Performance anxiety in gifted adolescent musicians. *Journal of Anxiety Disorders*, **20**(1), 98–109.

Fjellman-Wiklund A, Brulin C and Sundelin G. (2003). Physical and psychosocial work-related risk factors associated with neck–shoulder discomfort in male and female music teachers. *Medical Problems of Performing Artists*, **18**(1), 33–41.

Fortune, J. (2007). Performance-related musculoskeletal disorders in tertiary level flute players and relationships with muscle tension, music performance anxiety, musical task complexity and musical ability. Unpublished Masters thesis, Sydney Conservatorium of Music, University of Sydney.

Friedman HS and Silver RC (eds) (2007). *Foundations of health psychology*. Oxford University Press, New York.

Gandevia SC (2001). Spinal and supraspinal factors in human muscle fatigue. *Psychological Reviews*, **81**(4), 1725–1789.

Gar NS, Hudson JL and Rapee RM (2005). Family factors and the development of anxiety disorders. In Hudson JL and Rapee RM, eds, *Psychopathology and the family*, 125–145. Elsevier Science, New York.

Gleitman H, Fridlund AJ and Reisber D (2004). *Psychology*, 6. Norton, New York.

Hagberg M, Christiani D, Courtney TK, Halperin W, Leamon TB and Smith TJ (1997). Conceptual and definitional issues in occupational injury etiology. *American Journal of Industrial Medicine*, **32**, 106–115.

Hanin YL (1986). State-trait anxiety research on sports in the USSR. In CD Spielberger and R Diaz, eds, *Cross-cultural anxiety*, 45–64. Hemisphere Publishing Corp/ Harper and Row Publishers, New York.

Herbert RD (1993). Human strength adaptations-implications for therapy. In J Crosbie and J McConnell, eds, *Key issues in musculoskeletal physiotherapy*, 142–171. Butterworth-Heinemann Ltd, Oxford.

Herring SA and Kibler WB (1998). A framework for rehabilitation. In WB Kibler, SA Herring, JM Press and PA Lee, eds, *Functional rehabilitation of sports and musculoskeletal injuries*, 98–108. Aspen Publishers Inc., Gaithersburg, MD.

Hochberg FH and Hochberg NS (2000). Occupational cramps/focal dystonias. In R Tubiana and PC Amadio, eds, *Medical problems of the instrumentalist musician*, 295–310. Martin Dunitz, London.

Horvath J. (2002). *Playing (less) hurt*. Morris Publishing, Kearney, NE.

Joormann J, Talbot L and Gotlib IH (2007). Biased processing of emotional information in girls at risk for depression. *Journal of Abnormal Psychology*, **116**(1), 135–143.

Kaspersen M and Gotestam KG (2002). A survey of music performance anxiety among Norwegian music students. *European Journal of Psychiatry*, **16**(2), 69–80.

Kember J (1998). The physical therapists contribution. In I Winspur and CB Wynn Parry, eds, *The musician's hand. A clinical guide*, 136–142. Martin Dunitz Ltd, London.

Kendall FP, McCreary EK and Provance PG (1993). *Muscles. Testing and function*, 4th edn. Williams and Wilkins, Baltimore, MD.

Kenny DT (2005). A systematic review of treatment for music performance anxiety. *Anxiety, Stress and Coping*, **18**(3), 183–208.

Kenny DT and Osborne MS (2006). Music performance anxiety: new insights from young musicians. In WF Thompson, ed., *Advances in cognitive psychology*. Retrieved 16 June 2006, from http://www.ac-psych.org.

Kenny DT, Davis P and Oates J (2004). Music performance anxiety and occupational stress amongst opera chorus artists and their relationship with state and trait anxiety and perfectionism. *Journal of Anxiety Disorders*, **18**, 757–777.

Kessler RC, Stang P, Wittchen HU, Stein M and Walters EE (1999). Lifetime comorbidity between social phobia and mood disorders in the US National Comorbidity Survey. *Psychological Medicine*, **29**, 555–567.

Lazarus AA and Abramovitz A. (2004). A multimodal behavioral approach to performance anxiety. *Journal of Clinical Psychology*, **60**, 831–840.

Ma (1986) cited in AG Brandfonbrener (2005). Interview with Yo Yo Ma (parts I and II). *Medical Problems of Performing Artists*, **20**(3), 140–148.

Manchester R (2006). Toward better prevention of injuries among performing artists. *Medical Problems of Performing Artists*, **21**(1), 1–2.

Marieb EN (2001). *Human anatomy and physiology*, 5th edn. Benjamin Cummins, New York.

Markison RE (1998). Adjustment of the musical interface. In I Inspur and C Wynn-Parry, eds, *The musician's hand. A clinical guide*, 149–159. Martin Dunitz, London.

Marr J (2000, October). Commentary: flow, intrinsic motivation, and second generation cognitive science. *The Online Journal of Sport Psychology*, **2**(3). Retrieved 17 May 2006 from http://www.athleticinsight.com/ Vo12Iss3/Commentary_2.htm.

Martens R, Burton D, Vealey R, Bump L and Smith D (1990). The development of the Competitive State Anxiety Inventory-2 (CSAI-2). In R Martens, RS Vealey and D Burton, eds, *Competitive anxiety in sport*, 117–190. Human Kinetics, Champaign, IL.

Melhorn MJ (1998). Cumulative trauma disorders and repetitive strain injuries: the future. *Clinical Orthopaedics and Related Research*, **351**, 107–126.

Murphy WP, Yaruss JS and Quesal RW. (2007). Enhancing treatment for school-age children who stutter I. Reducing negative reactions through desensitization and cognitive restructuring. *Journal of Fluency Disorders*, **32**(2), 121–138.

Nagel JJ. (2004). Performance anxiety theory and treatment: one size does not fit all. *Medical Problems of Performing Artists*, **19**(1), 39–43.

Nash CE, Mickan SM, Del Mar CB and Glasziou PP (2004). Resting injured limbs delays recovery: a systematic review. *The Journal of Family Practice*, **53**(9), 706–712.

Norris R (1993). *The musician's survival manual: a guide to preventing and treating injuries in instrumentalists*. MMB Music Inc, Saint Louis, MO.

Norris RN (2000). Applied ergonomics. In R Tubiana and PC Amadio, eds, *Medical problems of the instrumentalist musician*, 595–613. Martin Dunitz Ltd, London.

Oliveira FTP and Goodman D (2004). Conscious and effortful or effortless and automatic: a practice performance paradox. *Perceptual and Motor Skills*, **99**, 315–324.

Osborne MS, Kenny DT and Holsomback R (2005). Assessment of music performance anxiety in late childhood: a validation study of the Music Performance Anxiety Inventory for Adolescents (MPAI-A). *International Journal of Stress Management*, **12**(4), 312–330.

Pagoto SL, Kozak AT, Spates CR and Spring B (2006). systematic desensitization for an older woman with a severe specific phobia: an application of evidenced-based practice. *Clinical Gerontologist*, **30**(1), 89–98.

Pascarelli EF and Hsu YP (2001). Understanding work-related upper extremity disorders: clinical findings in 485 computer users, musicians, and others. *Journal of Occupational Rehabilitation*, **11**(1), 1–21.

Pope R P, Herbert RD, Kirwan JD and Graham BJ (2000). A randomized trial of pre-exercise stretching for prevention of lower limb injury. *Medicine and Science in Sports and Exercise*, **31**(2), 271–277.

Quarrier NF and Norris RN (2001). Adaptations for trombone performance: ergonomic interventions. *Medical Problems of Performing Artists*, **16**(2), 77–80.

Rauch S and Foa E (2006). Emotional processing theory (EPT) and exposure therapy for PTSD. *Journal of Contemporary Psychotherapy*, **36**(1), 61–65.

Rees CS, McEvoy R and Nathan PR (2005). Relationship between homework completion and outcome in cognitive behaviour therapy. *Cognitive Behaviour Therapy*, **34**(4), 242–247.

Rolland P (1974). *The teaching of action in string playing.* Urbana String Research Associates, Urbana, IL.

Sakai N (2006). Slow-down exercise for the treatment of focal hand dystonia in pianists. *Medical Problems of Performing Artists*, **21**(1), 25–28.

Sanderson WC, DiNardo PA, Rapee RM and Barlow DH (1990). Symptom comorbidity in patients diagnosed with DSM-III-R anxiety disorders. *Journal of Abnormal Psychology*, **99**, 308–312.

Schuele SU and Lederman RJ (2004) Occupational disorders in instrumental musicians. *Medical Problems of Performing Artists*, **19**(3), 123–128.

Scott WA (1997). Overuse injuries. In RE Sallis and F Massimino, eds, *Essentials of sports medicine*, 517–527. Mosby Publishers, Baltimore, MD.

Slade JF, Mahoney JD, Dailinger JE and Baxamusa TH (1999). Wrist and hand injuries in musicians: management and prevention. *The Journal of Musculoskeletal Medicine*, **16**(9), 542.

Spahn C, Ell N and Seidenglanz K (2001). Psychosomatic findings in musician patients at a department of hand surgery. *Medical Problems of Performing Artists*, **16**(4), 144–151.

Sparrow WA and Newell KM (1998). Metabolic energy expenditure and the regulation of movement economy. *Psychonomic Bulletin and Review*, **5**(2), 173–196.

Spinner RJ and Amadio PC (2000). Compression neuropathies of the upper extremities. In R Tubiana and PC Amadio, eds, *Medical problems of the instrumentalist musician*, 273–294. Martin Dunitz Ltd, London.

Sternbach DJ (1995). Musicians: a neglected working population in crisis. In SL Sauter and LR Murphy, eds, *Organizational risk factors for job stress*, 283–302. American Psychological Association, Washington, DC.

Strahan E and Conger AJ (1998). Social anxiety and its effects on performance and perception. *Journal of Anxiety Disorders*, **12**, 293–305.

Tubiana R (2000). Functional anatomy. In R Tubiana and PC Amadio, eds, *Medical problems of the performing instrumentalist*, 1–4. Martin Dunitz Ltd, London.

Tubiana R, Chamagne P and Brockman R (1989). Fundamental positions for instrumental musicians. *Medical Problems of Performing Artists*, **4**(4), 73–76.

Turkington D, Dudley R, Warman DM and Beck AT (2006). Cognitive-behavioral therapy for schizophrenia: a review. *Focus*, **4**, 223–233.

Turner PE and Raglin JS (1991). Anxiety and performance in track and field athletes: a comparison of ZOFR and inverted-U hypothesis. *Medial Science in Sport and Exercise*, **23**, 119.

vande Wiel NMH, Matthys W, Cohen-Kettenis PT, Maassen GH, Lochman JE and van Engeland H (2007). The effectiveness of an experimental treatment when compared to care as usual depends on the type of care as usual. *Behavior Modification*, **31**(3), 298–312.

van Hees OS (1997). Physical exercise as prevention for musculoskeletal problems in musicians. A panacee demasque. *Health and the musician conference proceedings*, A1.20–A1.30. 23–27 March, York, England. British Performing Arts Medicine Trust, London.

van Kemenade JF, van Son M and van Heesch NC (1995). Performance anxiety among professional musicians in symphonic orchestras: a self-report study. *Psychological Reports*, **77**, 555–562.

van Winkel R, Myin-Germeys I, Delespaul P, Peuskens J, De Hert M and van Os J (2006). Premorbid IQ as a predictor for the course of IQ in first onset patients with schizophrenia: a 10-year follow-up study. *Schizophrenia Research*, **88**, 47–54.

Vergara, M and Page A (2002). Relationship between comfort and back posture and mobility in sitting-posture. *Applied Ergonomics*, **33**, 1–8.

Wallace S and Alden L (1997). Social phobia and positive social events: the price of success. *Journal of Abnormal Psychology*, **106**, 416–424.

Wang J (2002). Developing and testing an integrated model of choking in sport. Unpublished PhD dissertation, Victoria University, Melbourne, Australia.

Warrington J, Winspur I and Steinwede D (2002). Upper-extremity problems in musicians related to age. *Medical Problems of Performing Artists*, **17**(3), 131–140.

Wilkinson A (1992). Stretching the truth. A review of the literature on muscle stretching. *Australian Journal of Physiotherapy*, **38**, 283–287.

Willner P (2006). Readiness for cognitive therapy in people with intellectual disabilities. *Journal of Applied Research in Intellectual Disabilities*, **19**(1), 5–16.

Wilson FR (2000). Current controversies on the origin, diagnosis and management of focal dystonia. In R Tubiana and PC Amadio, eds, *Medical problems of the instrumentalist musician*, 311–327. Martin Dunitz Ltd, London.

Wilson GD (2002). *Psychology for performing artists*, 2nd edn. Whurr, London, UK.

Young JA and Pain MD (1999). The zone: evidence of a universal phenomenon for athletes across sports. *The Online Journal of Sport Psychology*, **1**(3). Retrieved 17 May 2006, from http://www.athleticinsight.com/Vol1Iss3/Empirical_Zone.htm.

Yovel I and Safren SA (2007). Measuring homework utility in psychotherapy: cognitive-behavioral therapy for adult attention-deficit hyperactivity disorder as an example. *Cognitive Therapy and Research*, **31**(3), 385–399.

Zaza C (1994). Research-based prevention for musicians. *Medical Problems of Performing Artists*, **9**, 3–6.

Zaza C and Farewell VT (1997). Musicians' playing-related musculoskeletal disorders: an examination of risk factors. *American Journal of Industrial Medicine*, **32**, 292–300.

Zaza C, Fleiszer MS, Main FW and Mechefske C (2000). Beating injury with a different drumstick: a pilot study. *Medical Problems of Performing Artists*, **15**(1), 39–44.

PART 8

Composition and improvisation

Edited by Peter Webster

CHAPTER 37

Making a mark
The psychology of composition

Jonathan Impett

Introduction

Given the central place of creativity as a defining component of the self-image of humanity, it is extraordinary how until recently it has received little attention from psychologists (Albert and Runco 1999). Studies have tended to consider the general case of the generation of new ideas or the process of invention within a particular constrained environment. While both biography and analysis can shed light on the process of composition, musicology has generally been more concerned with the context or fruits of the process. Artistic creativity poses considerable challenges to the experimental psychologist—in gaining access to the creative process itself other than through self-reporting, and in evaluating the quality, significance and uniqueness of work. The formulation of questions concerning an activity which is both cultural and personal naturally tends to reflect current modes of explanation.

There is little agreement on the cultural definition of composition, even within the context of contemporary Western culture. In conventional terms, it may be understood to be an activity bounded by the artefact of the musical work and by the persona of the composer. Discussion of the psychology of composition calls into question fundamental assumptions about the nature and role of musical activity and the musical artefact, and such assumptions must be acknowledged in any investigation. Taking Western masterworks as our sole evidence might be equivalent to understanding architecture only on the basis of the pyramids; objects of wonder but perhaps eccentric to any general case of human behaviour. The modern Western composition could be seen as the distillation of a social activity described by Blacking as 'humanly organized sound' (Blacking 1973). In an economic interpretation, Attali suggests that technology might return composition to its socially distributed state (Attali 1985, pp. 133–148). The cultural environment surrounding such works values them as exceptions, works of unique genius, expressions of individuality. As evidence from which to generalize they are thus to some extent self-invalidating. Biography and autobiography are likewise inseparable from context. The romantic, romanticized or modernist artist is inseparable from his work; Berlioz is an often-cited example. From late Bach to Boulez individual works stand as autobiographical statements, acts of musical self-exploring and self-situating. From at least the late sixteenth century, the advancement of the art has been a conscious obligation on most composers, and must therefore be understood as having substantially informed the relevant processes. Schoenberg's writings are perhaps the clearest expression of this awareness (Schoenberg 1975). In other cultural contexts, the role of the musician may be precisely to practice an art such that it may be transmitted without technical corruption or personal intervention. Guercio (2006) investigates the ways in which an awareness of public biography has fed back into artists' practice.

The concept of the work, the object of composition, has come increasingly into question, particularly in terms of its identity, autonomy, and the intentionalities it may be seen to embody. Goehr (1992) presents a case for the historical contextualizing of the work concept. Davies (2001) proposes a measure of *thickness* of the work to reflect the degree to which its instantiation depends on culturally distributed knowledge. We can identify two characteristics of the activity of composition: a degree of identity between subject and object—composer and composed—and the structuring of music over a temporal scale beyond that of unstructured short-term memory or the doggerel patterning of simple song or dance forms.

Motivation

> I believe that a real composer writes music for no other reason than that it pleases him. Those who compose because they want to please others, and have audiences in mind, are not artists.
>
> Schoenberg (1975, p. 54)

The question of the motivation to compose is likewise beyond the scope of experimental psychology. Where observer, observed and reader inhabit the same cultural milieu this is less problematic; in his view of the artwork as the manifestation of an artist's particular biography and psychological development, Freud is reinforcing the Romantic aesthetic of self-expression native to his own context. He concluded that 'whence it is that the artist derives his creative capacity is not a question for psychology' (Freud 2001a, p. 187). His observations on the relationship between artist, work and public have been more influential. He suggests that the artist is driven to the imagination by dissatisfaction with his reality and returns to reality via the work, which then serves the same function for others (Freud 2001b, p. 224).

Some measure of social empathy is at play, therefore. Heidegger extends the notion of phenomenological reality to one of truth, relating aesthetic success to the ethical behaviour of the artist in respect of his material (Heidegger 1971, pp. 15–86). Badiou's development of this view of artistic behaviour as ethical also in respect of society emphasizes the search for commonality over the assertion of difference, an approach that resonates with theories of creativity discussed below (Badiou 2001). The technical researches of both Schoenberg and Cage could be interpreted in this light; technique mediates

between the banality of the imagination and the aspiration of critical reflection. Freud's insistence on the ludic nature of artistic creativity has been enthusiastically taken up by contemporary critical theorists. The concept of *play* is central to Gadamer's explanation of the ontology of art and of aesthetic experience (Gadamer 1989, pp. 102–171). Lacan's related notion of *jouissance* serves as the basis for his distinction between desire and drive. Following the work of Lacan and Foucault, contemporary critical theory is fundamentally informed by psychoanalysis. Its central topics of the relationships between subject and object, desire and drive, bear directly on the metaphysical and psychological relationship between composer and work and the urge to compose.

> Desire is grounded in its constitutive lack, while drive circulates around a hole, a gap in the order of things … drive is quite literally *the very drive to break the 'all' of continuity in which we are embedded*, to introduce a radical imbalance into it.
>
> Žižek (2006, pp. 61–63)

Psychology and composition

Given the primacy of composition in Western music, the silence of psychology in this respect is deafening. Sloboda (1985, p. 103) observed 'that composition is the least studied and least well understood of all musical processes, and that there is no substantial literature to review'. Brown still notes that 'Although there is growing interest in music cognition, little progress has been made in understanding composition per se' (Brown 2003, p. 2). As psychology has developed through the twentieth century, the authority of earlier psycho-biographical narrative explanations has been called into question. Meanwhile composition has turned consciously to self-reflection as other norms and constraints have dissolved. Already in 1937 Cage suggested that the future principle of the organization of musical sound would be 'man's common ability to think' (Cage 1961, p. 6). In the light of new technologies, Minsky has suggested more recently that art and psychology must inevitably converge (Minsky 1999). Musical expressionism is the stylistic embodiment of unmediated expression in the romantic sense; the conscious embodiment of psychological states. Adorno saw Schönberg's *Erwartung* as heroically confronting the compositional challenge of the dissolution of tonality—by no coincidence a product of the same milieu as psychoanalysis and phenomenology. Subsequent approaches to post-tonal language included Hindemith's *Unterweisung*, based on perceived intervallic tension in melodic and harmonic space (Hindemith 1942, pp. 56–58). Few have attempted to work through the implications of music psychology to derive a set of aesthetic constraints. A notable exception is Lerdahl (1988), for whom only functional tonality satisfies the requirements. Implicit in Huron's theorizing of musical experience in terms of expectation is an understanding of composition as the prediction, management and thus presumably internal modelling of that expectation (Huron 2006, p. 240).

The incapacitating vertigo of the composer faced with infinite possibility is described by Ferneyhough (1995, p. 22). Sloboda suggests that a new dialogue between psychology and the composer can help in reducing this search space (Sloboda 2005, p. 192). The sonic and music–organizational possibilities of new technologies in the late twentieth century and the perception of composition as a potential research activity together informed the shape of institutions such as IRCAM in Paris, incorporating research into the psychology of music; Born (1995) gives an account of the co-evolution of institution and individual compositional practice. Writers such as Roads (1996) and Cook (2001) acknowledge psychoacoustics as an essential part of the electroacoustic composer's necessary knowledge. The close link between compositional technologies and research into psychoacoustics is a strong indicator of the extent to which conventional modes of music-making embody both innate understanding and cultural experience of music psychology. Technological approaches to composition and music-generation have been based on varying degrees of cognitive verisimilitude in the underlying mechanisms. Rowe (2001) presents a broad range of such research, largely developed in imitation of human compositional abilities. Cope's *Experiments in Musical Intelligence* (Cope 2001) generates new compositions within a given style based on the analysis and recombination of individual compositional *signatures*. Hofstadter points out that irrespective of similarity of psychological process, the inability of a culture to distinguish must lead us to question assumptions and understanding (Cope 2001, pp. 33–82).

Theories of creativity

Surely it's premature to ask how great composers write great symphonies before we know how ordinary people think of ordinary tunes. I don't believe there is much difference between ordinary and 'creative' thought. Right now, if asked which seems the more mysterious, I'd have to say the ordinary kind.

Minsky (1985, p. 80)

Study of the general case of creativity begins in earnest as a reaction to the twin myths of romantic aesthetics and mid-twentieth-century information theory. Koestler (1964) was among the first to address the human practice of creativity, to demystify the process. Boden (1990) examines the paradoxes and conceptual difficulties in dealing with such a charged cultural concept. The earlier notion of genius as embodying the distance between conventional experience and that of the great artist—somewhat problematic in psychological terms, in that by definition it cannot be more widely understood—has been revisited. Simonton (1999) proposes an evolutionary explanation; that genius typically explores a wide range of potential behaviours, often in parallel, searching for complexity, novelty and emergent structure.

Most theories of creativity acknowledge that the everyday transmission and reception of ideas is in some sense creative. To varying degrees they incorporate the exploration of conceptual or physical spaces, the drawing of new connections between concepts or spaces, the satisfying of rules or constraints and the solving of problems. Holyoak and Thagard (1995) propose a model of creative thought around the drawing of analogy between different mental spaces within interacting constraints of similarity, structure and purpose. Boden (1990) describes the spontaneous reflexive process of the mind's generation of maps of its own conceptual spaces. In the absence of coherent bodies of data, theories of creativity have been largely informed by the challenges of artificial intelligence. In Copycat, a computational model of analogy-seeking, Hofstader shows how one concept slips into another under different kinds of pressure or attractor, producing the mental fluidity fundamental to creative thought (Hofstadter 1995, pp. 205–267). Gärdenfors' notion of multidimensional *conceptual spaces* avoids the symbolic/connectionist division of computational models (Gärdenfors 2000).

Brown (2003) narrates the composition of Debussy's *Ibéria* as a process of knowledge-based problem-solving. He acknowledges the multidimensionality of the undertaking: 'music historians, music theorists, and cognitive scientists can join forces in trying to understand [how composers make their choices]' (Brown 2003, p. 162). Problem-solving and space-searching models generally rely on some form of heuristic to direct the process. This might be seen as where the craft of composition lies and why it requires such time to develop. Weisberg (1999) examines the relationship between creativity and knowledge through the development of expertise, citing particularly the '10-year rule'

proposed by Hayes (1989) following examination of the creative trajectories of 76 composers. Explanations of this kind also assume some definable end-state. The model of composition proposed by Sloboda (1985, p. 118) takes account of the symbiotic evolution of work and work-definition. Brown's amended version incorporates historical context (Brown 2003, p. 9) (Figure 37.1).

Byrne (2005) shows that rational thought and counterfactual imagination are predicated on common cognitive mechanisms. She describes the probing of possible space by the imagining of alternatives to a given reality and how imagination works by exploring the parameters along which it might be otherwise. This seems a useful model for understanding the selecting of musical material according to its potential in context, as well as its subsequent treatment.

A mechanism of 'conceptual blending' is proposed by Fauconnier and Turner, to model the production of analogical links and inference transfers by mappings between mental spaces. 'Blending … operates on two Input mental spaces to yield a third space, the *blend*. The blend *inherits partial structure* from the input

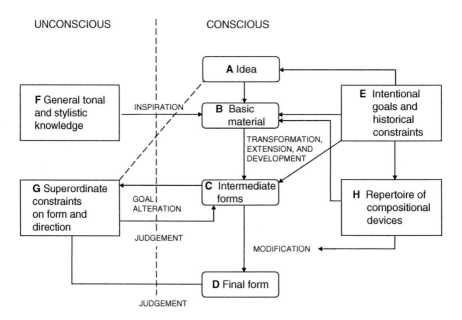

Fig. 37.1 Diagram of typical compositional resources and processes. Brown (2003, p. 9); developed from Sloboda (1985, p. 118).

spaces and *has emergent structure* of its own'
(Fauconnier 1997, p. 149). Blending through
the multimodality, multiple spaces and scales
and potential conflicts of human experience is
achieved in *conceptual integration networks*
(Fauconnier and Turner 2002, pp. 309–353).
Turner describes the integration over time of a
vast perceptual diversity, most clearly embodied
in the activity of the artist, as *compression*
(Turner 206, p. 94). Applying this approach to
music, Zbikowski identifies three fundamental
cognitive mechanisms: categorization, cross-
domain mapping and the use of conceptual
models (Zbikowski 2006, p. 116). Complex cultural and contextual factors can thus be incorporated to account for the emergence of
meaning: 'Compositional strategies … assume
an alliance between syntax and processes of
meaning construction: composers arrange
musical materials with relatively specific expressive or communicative goals in mind' (Zbikowski
2002, p. 138). Specific musical detail derives
from broader strategies through templates of
categories and attribute values (Zbikowski 2002,
pp. 149–153).

Metaphors and models

Psychology and aesthetics are interlinked. The
possibility of the composer having some responsibility to art, music, truth or any higher authority has material implications for the conceptual
model within which composition takes place.
The cosmology of Zarlino, Bach's theology or
the Romantic aesthetics of Wagner in some
respects have equivalent implications. In
acknowledging the limits on understanding the
creative process from sketches, Nottebohm
adduces Goethe's metaphor of a plant, of unity
in diversity, that runs through Romantic
accounts of art and can be presumed to inform
the self-understanding and conceptual models
of composers from Beethoven to Webern
(Webern 1963, p. 40). As mid-twentieth century
composers questioned assumptions about musical language and aesthetics, they sought structuring metaphors in other areas of thought:
natural phenomena (Xenakis), science fiction
(Ligeti), semiotics (Berio), social theory
(Cardew). Lachenmann describes his process
explicitly as a sequence of metaphors: reflection,

instrument-building and the freeing of imagination (Lachenman 2004, p. 45).

The material role of metaphor in thought has
been shown by Lakoff and Johnson:

> Most of our normal conceptual system is
> metaphorically structured; that is, most con-
> cepts are partially understood in terms of
> other concepts … The heart of metaphor is
> inference. Conceptual metaphor allows infer-
> ences in sensory-motor domains … to be
> used to draw inferences about other domains
> (e.g., domains of subjective judgement.
>   Lakoff and Johnson (2003, pp. 56, 244)

They demonstrate how abstract conceptual
thought—which might include musical reasoning—is grounded in metaphors derived from
human physicality and physical context (Lakoff
and Johnson 1999). The reported synesthesia of
Scriabin or Messiaen could be such metaphorical transfer; a case in which both spaces map
onto physical experience. The range of personal,
technical and cultural metaphor used by composers means that their self-reporting requires
sensitive interpretation for use as evidence of
psychological process. The generality of Bahle's
study of 1947, based on the self-reporting of
both living and past composers, illustrates the
difficulty in drawing conclusions. He lists a
range of intra- and extra-musical factors, composing environment, the urge to imitate or
explore and artistic compulsion (Cooper 1990,
pp. 14–15).

If the ability to model certain aspects of the
physical and social world is to some extent
innate (Pinker 1999, pp. 316–333), this can
interact with cultural experience such that a
composer might be able, for example, to model
the performer's physicality and audience's
impression of a particular violin phrase. The
constraints of physical causality are effectively
removed in working with new technologies (Lury
1998), and much contemporary technology-
based creativity is concerned with the search for
structural and conceptual metaphors to focus
unconstrained imagination.

Imagining

What we imagine does not necessarily take on
a concrete form and may remain in a state of

virtuality, whereas invention is not conceivable apart from its actual being worked out.

Stravinsky (1942, p. 53)

Composition is an activity simultaneously of aural and aesthetic imagining, in some kind of feedback relationship. Both physical and artistic percepts are generated as hypotheses. The relative roles of emotional and intellectual elements in the latter are a proper topic for aesthetics, although in brain-science terms emotion and subjectivity are both real and rational (Damasio 1999; Thagard 2006). The compositional behaviour of a particular individual may be characterized by the scope, precision, innovation and relationship of aural and aesthetic imagination.

In many art forms, modes of scaling or reduction retain sufficient salient features of the whole such that the reduced form can be meaningfully understood or manipulated. A sketch for a painting may already display essential stylistic or representational properties while affording compositional reflection. A literary narrative can be outlined in the same language as its full version. Music does not afford the same reduction of scale. There is little invariance; material, surface and 'meaning' are lost. Some established schema—sonata form, for example—might allow the composer to concentrate on appropriate material, development and deviations from norms. Sloboda suggests that the modular process of working simultaneously on different levels of detail is akin to that of architecture (Sloboda 2005, pp. 194–195). Ligeti describes the repeated process of such formal macro planning in his Violin Concerto (Steinitz 2003, p. 335); Berg follows a similar procedure (Hall 1996, p. 21). The composition becomes an autonomous artefact as the composer discovers its nature from multiple perspectives.

In an often-quoted (and doubted) passage of reflection on his own process, Mozart describes imagining a composition as a simultaneity. The act of consciously contemplating a unitary concept takes time. Notation is itself a process of reflection and decision-making, and combined with the time of imagining is unlikely to happen in real time or less. The variables at play here seem to be the degrees of consciousness and assimilation of the processes involved. Following examination of Mozart's sketches, Konrad has concluded that he experimented at the piano and on paper, and that 'he prepared himself consciously for a particular compositional task and sought the working environment necessary for its fulfilment' (Konrad 1992, p. 77).

The relationship between imagined time, musical time as the object of reflection and the experiential time of musical performance is therefore critical to the process of composition; it acts on the temporal plane of memory. Berio describes the process of emergence from the interplay of imagining and memory of 'forms which stir and question memory but at the same time deny it' (Berio 2006, p. 41). A memory-based approach to contemporary composition is proposed by Snyder (2000). Kramer suggests that musical time works not only in a uniform speed and direction, but also non-linearly, retrospectively and in multiple layers (Kramer 1988). Some such principle must be fundamental to composition. Its precise nature is a highly individual question, and closely related to a particular composer's modes of experimentation and representation.

Improvisation

Sloboda (1985, pp. 138–150) suggests that studying improvisation might provide insight into composition. Cultural understandings of improvisation vary; absence of fully prescriptive notation and a degree of ephemerality of the phenomenon are common features. Nettl and Melinda bring ethnomusicological perspectives to bear on 'music created in the course of performance' to investigate the musicians' own understanding of their behaviour (Nettl with Melinda 1998, p. 1). Isolating difficult-to-translate metaphorical descriptions can be misleading; many are technique- or theory-specific. Two have particular resonance, however. Sabah Fahkri describes the development of an ecstatic state through a process of feedback: 'I consider the audience to be me and myself to be the audience' (Racy 1998, p. 96). Jnan Prakash Ghosh describes his role in Hindustani music as 'keeping it going' (Slawek 1998, p. 336), implying an acknowledgment of some autonomy of the musical phenomenon and abstraction of its possibility. In contrast, Boulez dismisses improvisation as irrelevant to composition 'instant imagination misfires more often than it fires; and anyway such freedom has less to do with invention in the proper sense than with the practicalities of invention' (Boulez 1991, p. 32).

Jazz and its successors provide instructive examples of longer-term musical design emerging through the practice of improvisation. Armstrong's *West End Blues* presumably grew out of his own improvisational style, from a continuous, repetitive practice, and having emerged in 1927 remains quite stable through subsequent versions. In Coltrane's solos on *Giant Steps* or *A Love Supreme* we hear the fruit, however spontaneous, of sustained intellectual and technical engagement with his material. Cecil Taylor prefers to communicate his more abstract structures orally: 'That gives the lie to the idea that the only structured music possible is that music which is written. Which is a denial of the whole of human expression' (Spellman 2004, p. 71). The musico-cultural theory and graphical scores of Anthony Braxton demonstrate the role of musical intelligence and imagination in the feedback loop of reflective practice, and the inevitable generation of higher-level structures (Braxton 1985). The technical achievement and musical power of the limit-case work of guitarist Derek Bailey in insisting on an entirely 'non-idiomatic' mode of improvisation is evidence of the irrepressibility of the urge to compose, of the difficulty in suppressing memory, association and imaginative projection (Watson 2004, p. 212). Evan Parker describes his own work as composition through improvisation and points to the impossibility of creativity denying structure, memory and repetition (Parker 1992). As recording technologies evolved from being simply the documentation of a performance, a new situation developed in which compositional exploration may be audibly inscribed. Thus in the recorded activity of composing Miles Davis's *Jack Johnson* or Mick Jagger's *Sympathy for the Devil* we can follow the distribution of musical ideas, the absorption of the input and techniques of others and the pattern of technological intervention (Davis 2005; Godard 2006).

Passages designed to give the impression of successful improvisation are instructive. Presumably improvisation contributed to Beethoven's generation of ideas, for example.

His cadenzas to his own piano concertos could be seen as composed illustrations of his own creative process. Consideration of the cognitive mechanisms of improvisation gives some indication of its relationship to composition. Surveying the skills and components of improvisation, Pressing (2001) proposes a feedback and feedforward problem-solving model based on the generation of and selection from arrays of elements having musical, acoustic and motoric features. Sarath points to time as the essential parameter of difference between composition and improvisation (Sarath 1996). He derives a concept of retensive–protensive temporality from Husserl to describe the relationship of the musical thought of the improviser with the continuously moving present.

Traces

Sketches

A composer's sketches provide a trace of his conscious thought processes. While early sketch studies sought to investigate specific genius rather than composition in general, the field has more recently developed methodologies that afford broader interpretation (Kerman 1982; Brown 2003). Deductions can be made about the chronology of composition and possibly the models and constraints they embody and the problems they address. One might observe the 'harried' nature of Beethoven's writing (Hall 1996, p. 9) or the considered recording of musical thoughts in Webern's sketchbooks. The distribution of ideas on the page can itself reveal patterns of thought (Hall 1996, p. 13); Sloboda notes how Stravinsky uses a single simple idea to generate a variety of material (Sloboda 1985, pp. 108–112). Less certain is any induction as to the precise mental processes of which they are a trace. In reconsidering the discipline in 1982, Kerman observed that 'one could go on to study musical creativity in general, at least in theory' (Kerman 1982, p. 177). In an early case study, Nottebohm points out that Beethoven's sketches demonstrate both top-down and bottom-up approaches; sometimes a movement is repeatedly reformed in its entirety, sometimes a piece of thematic material is worked in different directions. Beethoven's comment that he often works on several compositions simultaneously suggests a mutually reinforcing feedback between projects (Nottebohm 1979, p. 5).

Technology

Modes of representation and the manipulations they afford are essentially a question of technology. So too are issues of dissemination and likely audience; notation, printing and the Internet transform the composer's concepts of self and agency. Banchieri's *Contrapunto alla Mente* (1608) is a parody of the limits of rule-based contrapuntal composition without the use of notation. Luzzaschi and Monteverdi describe the process (Owens 1997, pp. 65–66). The use of the wax tablet to work out points of polyphonic imitation must inform the grain of thought—the relationship between local contrapuntal texture and broader architecture. Changes in paper production through the eighteenth century meant that while we effectively have no sketches by Bach, whose supply of paper had to be approved and accounted for, Beethoven could presume a limitless supply. He could therefore experiment and store freely, reusing, reworking and re-mediating over his whole life—a random access memory allowing the process of composition to be highly distributed through time and contexts. In 1025, Guido d'Arezzo presented his new form of notation as addressing questions of memory. Symbol manipulation lies at the heart of Western composition. The symbolic representation and manipulation afforded by technologies from wax tablet to computer constitute a form of conceptual prosthesis. Virtual, mental quasi-external representations are both more ephemeral and more plastic than their material counterparts. The points at which a current state is externalized constitutes a unique signature in the compositional process. Instruments themselves constitute music computers; the piano is the ideal small-scale calculator for tonal music, with its octave equivalence, registral mapping, unique shapes for keys and scales and consistent but discrete relationships between them.

The multiple and hybrid representational environments of computer-enabled composition generate less transparent traces. Ferneyhough sees the computer as enhancing creative liberty, affording a more immediate and intuitive understanding of a complex compositional situation. 'It can generate a "musical archaeology", accessing and linking vastly different types of material and degrees of evolution from moment to moment' (Ferneyhough 1998). Lyotard describes the conventional modes of memory in the creation of art as *breaching* and *scanning*, to which he adds *anamnesis*—the remembering of the previously unknowable—in the case of technological creativity (Lyotard 1991, p. 48). In his study of digital craft, McCullough (1996, p. 99) describes computational environments as 'dense notational contexts for action'. Technology-informed changes in aesthetic stance also condition the nature of the traces remaining. For some of the late works of Nono, for example, there are copious sketches but no authoritative score. Compositional methodologies as set out in various historical manuals may reflect an understanding of composition which informs any conforming behaviour. They are not identical with an individual's psychological process, however.

Conclusion

Composition is a reflexive, iterative process of inscription. The work, once named as such and externalizable to some degree, passes circularly between inner and outer states. It passes through internal and external representations—mostly partial or compressed, some projected in mental rather than physical space, not all necessary conscious or observable—and phenomenological experience real or imagined. At each state-change the work is re-mediated by the composer, whose decision-making process is conditioned by the full complexity of human experience. This entire activity informs the simultaneous development of the composer's understanding of the particular work in its autonomy, of their own creativity and of music more broadly. Environment (culture, technology) and agents (composer, work) co-evolve at different rates. Important areas of future research include the perception of form, the imagining of music 'off-line' and the process of identifying novelty and potential in that imagining.

Donald (2006) proposes six cognitive principles to art, all fundamental to the activity of composition. They may be paraphrased thus:

1 Composition should be regarded as a specific kind of cognitive engineering, intended to influence the minds of an audience.

2 Composition always takes place in the context of distributed cognition.

3 Composition is constructivist in nature, aimed at the deliberate refinement and elaboration of mental models and world views.

4 Composition is meta-cognitive in nature.

5 Composition is a technology-driven aspect of cognition.

6 The role of the composer, viewed as a component in a distributed cognitive system, is not necessarily fixed.

While the urge to compose—to invent, structure and define sound and musical behaviour—may be to some degree innate, modes of conceiving, representing and realizing are the product of a situated process. Even if some or all of that activity is so well assimilated personally or culturally that it remains hidden from experimental view, it remains a behaviour in respect of an emerging object. That object is an artefact embodying the composer's own simulation of its situated performance. Stravinsky describes the process:

> The very act of putting my work on paper, of, as we say, kneading the dough, is for me inseparable from the pleasure of creation. So far as I am concerned, I cannot separate the spiritual effort from the psychological and physical effort; they confront me on the same level and do not present a hierarchy.
>
> Stravinsky (1942, p. 51)

References

Albert RS and Runco MA (1999). A history of research on creativity. In RJ Sternberg, ed., *Handbook of creativity*, 16–31. Cambridge University Press, Cambridge.

Attali J (1985). *Noise: the political economy of music*, trans B. Massumi. University of Minnesota Press, Minneapolis, MN.

Badiou A (2001). *Ethics: an essay on the understanding of evil*, trans. P. Hallward. Verso, London.

Berio L (2006). *Remembering the future*. Harvard University Press, Cambridge, MA.

Blacking J (1973). *How musical is man?* University of Washington Press, Seattle, WA.

Boden M (1990). *The creative mind: myths and mechanisms*. Weidenfeld and Nicholson, London.

Boulez P (1991). *Stocktakings from an apprenticeship*, trans. S. Walsh. Clarendon Press, Oxford.

Born G (1995). *Rationalising culture*. University of California Press, Berkeley, CA.

Braxton A (1985). *Tri-axium writings*, 3 vols. Synthesis Music, Oakland, CA.

Brown M (2003). *Debussy's Ibéria*. Oxford University Press, Oxford.

Byrne, R (2005). *The rational imagination: how people create alternatives to reality*. MIT Press, Cambridge MA.

Cage J (1961). The future of music: credo. In *Silence*, 3–6. Wesleyan University Press, Hanover, NH.

Cook P (2001). *Music, cognition and computerized sound: an introduction to psychoacoustics*. MIT Press, Cambridge, MA.

Cooper B (1990). *Beethoven and the creative process*. Clarendon Press, Oxford.

Cope D (2001). *Virtual music: computer synthesis of musical style*. MIT Press, Cambridge, MA.

Damasio A (1999). *The feeling of what happens: body and emotion in the making of consciousness*. Harcourt Brace, New York.

Davies S (2001). *Musical works and performances*. Oxford University Press, Oxford.

Davis M (2005). *The complete Jack Johnson sessions* (CD). Sony Records.

Donald M (2006). Art and cognitive evolution. In M Turner, ed., *The artful mind: cognitive science and the riddle of human creativity*, 3–20. Oxford University Press, New York.

Fauconnier G (1997). *Mappings in thought and language*. Cambridge University Press, Cambridge.

Fauconnier G and Turner M (2002). *The way we think: conceptual blending and the mind's hidden complexities*. Basic Books, New York.

Ferneyhough B (1995). *Collected writings*, In J. Boros and R. Toop (eds). Harwood Academic Publishers, Amsterdam.

Ferneyhough B (1998). Talk on Adorno given at Goldsmiths College, London, 21 February 1998. http://www.entretemps.asso.fr/Adorno/Informel/Ferneyhough.htm

Freud S (2001a). *The complete psychological works*, vol. 13. Penguin, London.

Freud S (2001b). *The complete psychological works*, vol. 12. Penguin, London.

Gadamer HG (1989). *Truth and method*, 2nd edn. Continuum, New York.

Gärdenfors P (2000). *Conceptual spaces: the geometry of thought*. MIT Press, Cambridge MA.

Godard JL (2006). *Sympathy for the devil* (DVD). Fremantle Home Entertainment.

Goehr L (1992). *The imaginary museum of musical works*. Oxford University Press, Oxford.

Guercio G (2006). *Art as existence: the artist's monograph and its project*. MIT Press, Cambridge, MA.

Hall P (1996). *A view of Berg's Lulu through the autograph sources*. University of California Press, Berkeley, CA.

Hayes JR (1989). Cognitive processes in creativity. In JA Glover, RR Ronning and CR Reynolds, eds, *Handbook of creativity*, 135–146. New York: Plenum.

Heidegger M (1971). *Poetry, language, thought*, trans. A. Hofstadter. Harper and Row, New York.

Hindemith P (1942). *The craft of music composition*, trans. A. Mendel. Schott, London.

Hofstadter D (1995). *Fluid concepts and creative analogies*. Basic Books, New York.

Holyoak KJ and Thagard P (1995). *Mental leaps: analogy in creative thought*. MIT Press, Cambridge, MA.

Huron D (2006). *Sweet anticipation: music and the psychology of expectation*. MIT Press, Cambridge, MA.

Kerman J (1982). Sketch studies. *19th-Century Music*, **6**(2), 174–180.

Koestler A (1964). *The act of creation*. Hutchinson, London.

Konrad U (1992). *Mozarts Schaffensweise. Studien zu den Werkautographen, Skizzen und Entwürfen*. Vandenhoeck and Ruprecht, Göttingen.

Kramer JD (1988). *The time of music*. Macmillan, New York.

Lachenmann H (2004). Philosophy of composition. In P Dejans, ed., *Identity and difference: essays on music, language and time*, 55–70. Leuven University Press, Leuven.

Lakoff G and Johnson M (1999). *Philosophy in the flesh: the embodied mind and its challenge to Western thought*. Basic Books, New York.

Lakoff G and Johnson M (2003). *Metaphors we live by*, revised edn. Chicago University Press, Chicago, IL.

Lerdahl F (1988). Tonal pitch space. *Music Perception*, **5**(3), 315–335.

Lury C (1998). *Prosthetic culture: photography, memory and identity*. Routledge, London.

Lyotard JF (1991). *The inhuman*, trans. G. Bennington and R. Bowlby. Polity Press, Cambridge.

McCullough M (1996). *Abstracting craft: the practiced digital hand*. MIT Press, Cambridge, MA.

Minsky M (1985). *The society of mind*. Simon and Schuster, New York.

Minsky M (1999). The future merging of art, science and psychology. In T Druckrey, ed., *Arts electronica: facing the future*, 229–233. MIT Press, Cambridge, MA.

Nettl B with Melinda R (eds) (1998). *In the course of performance*. University of Chicago Press, Chicago, IL.

Nottebohm G (1979). *Two Beethoven sketchbooks*, trans J. Katz. Gollancz, London.

Owens JA (1997). *Composers at work: the craft of musical composition 1450–1600*. Oxford University Press, New York.

Parker E (1992). Introduction to *'De Motu' for Buschi Niebergall*. http://www.efi.group.shef.ac.uk/fulltext/demotu.html.

Pinker S (1999). *How the mind works*. Penguin, London.

Pressing J (2001). Improvisation: methods and models. In J Sloboda, ed., *Generative processes in music:the psychology of performance, improvisation, and composition*, 129–178. Oxford University Press, Oxford.

Racy AJ (1998). Improvisation, ecstasy and performance dynamics in arabic music. In B Nettl, R Melinda, eds, *In the course of performance*, 95–112. University of Chicago Press, Chicago, IL.

Roads C (1996). *The computer music tutorial*. MIT Press, Cambridge, MA.

Rowe R (2001). *Machine musicianship*. MIT Press, Cambridge, MA.

Sarath E (1996). A new look at improvisation. *Journal of Music Theory*, **40**(1), 1–38.

Schoenberg A (1975). *Style and idea: selected writings*, L. Stein, (ed.). Faber, London.

Simonton DK (1999). *Origins of genius: Darwinian perspectives on creativity*. Oxford University Press, New York.

Slawek S (1998). Terms, practices and processes of improvisation in Hindustani instrumental music. In B. Nettl, ed., *In the course of performance*, 335–368. University of Chicago Press, Chicago, IL.

Sloboda J (1985). *The musical mind: the cognitive psychology of music*. Oxford University Press, Oxford.

Sloboda J (2005). *Exploring the musical mind*. Oxford University Press, Oxford.

Snyder B (2000). *Music and memory: an introduction*. MIT Press, Cambridge, MA.

Spellman AB (2004). *Four jazz lives*. University of Michigan Press, Ann Arbor, MI.

Steinitz R (2003). *György Ligeti: music of the imagination*. Faber, London.

Stravinsky I (1942). *Poetics of music*. Harvard University Press, Cambridge, MA.

Thagard P (2006). *Hot thought: mechanisms and applications of emotional cognition*. MIT Press, Cambridge, MA.

Turner M (2006). The art of compression. In M Turner, ed., *The artful mind: cognitive science and the riddle of human creativity*, 93–114. Oxford University Press, New York.

Watson B (2004). *Derek Bailey and the story of free improvisation*. Verso, London.

Webern A (1963). *The path to the new music*, trans. L. Black. Theodor Presser, Bryn Mawr, PA.

Weisberg RW (1999). Creativity and knowledge: a challenge to theories. In RJ Sternberg, ed., *Handbook of creativity*, 226–250. Cambridge University Press, Cambridge.

Zbikowski LM (2002). *Conceptualizing music: cognitive structure, theory and analysis*. Oxford University Press, New York.

Zbikowski LM (2006). The cognitive tango. In M Turner, ed., *The artful mind: cognitive science and the riddle of human creativity*, 115–132. Oxford University Press, New York.

Žižek C (2006). *The parallax view*. MIT Press, Cambridge MA.

CHAPTER 38

Musical improvisation

Richard Ashley

Introduction

Musical improvisation is, to many in the Western world, an activity shrouded in mystery. Most listeners are familiar with some genres of music in which improvisation is a commonplace, such as rock and other popular styles, jazz, or perhaps 'ethnic' musics—that is to say, composed or improvised 'traditional' musics falling outside the typical Western canons. Therefore listeners are aware that many musicians can, and routinely do, produce novel musical utterances in real time. The question for most listeners is not 'Can music be improvised?' but rather 'How is improvisation carried out?' With this formulation of the question, musical improvisation becomes a suitable topic for psychological investigation, focusing on cognitive, physical, and interpersonal processes, and on the musical structures on which these processes operate. Viewed in this way, there are parallels that can be seen with regard to processes of verbal production. No one would think it unusual to find native speakers of a language producing new utterances on the spur of the moment; indeed, to find someone without such an ability is the unusual case (as pointed out in Blacking [1976]).

This chapter seeks to bring together the literature on musical improvisation which will be of interest and benefit to those wishing to know more about it from a cognitive perspective. There is currently a modest but growing literature dealing with the psychology of musical improvisation; the curious might compare the number of articles cited herein with those in other chapters of this volume. One major strand of the music–psychological literature will not be dealt with here, namely the use of improvisation in music-therapeutic, clinical, or psychotherapeutic settings. The interested reader is referred to the appropriate sections of this volume for references on those topics.

Constraints on the processes of musical improvisation

Before moving on to a review of some dozens of studies dealing with improvisation, it is helpful to set a minimal theoretical framework for these discussions. The core notion here is that of *constraint*: of the scarcity of resources, in real time, that humans can utilize for making music when they are not following a predetermined plan of action (whether notated or not, as insightfully noted in Baily [1999]). To improvise appropriately in a given musical style—especially if the improviser is concerned with significant, productive interaction with other musicians, and with communicating with an audience—is a kind of tightrope act, where there is always the chance that something will go wrong (the recorded performances of master musicians show that even they make mistakes sometimes). Making music demands considerable resources from people; that is, no doubt, part of why music-making is enjoyable, in that it brings us into some more optimal relationship between our capabilities and our actions, along the lines of Csíkszentmihályi's notion of 'flow' (Csíkszentmihályi 1990, 1996). The use of one's abilities inside the constraints of one's body and its limits in performance, the timing of one's actions with external events, and retrieving and utilizing one's knowledge promptly in improvisation provide a powerful framework for a sense of personal achievement, and is thus a great proving ground for Csíkszentmihályi's concepts of optimal experience and creativity.

What, more precisely, are significant constraints on musical improvisation? We shall consider three here, not closing the door to others. These are: the limits of the body (physical constraints); the limits of time (temporal constraints); the limits of knowledge (cognitive constraints). From these we shall then move into an examination of the psychological literature regarding improvisation.

Constraint 1: the body

Improvisers work with their hands, feet, and voices to make music in the moment. Unlike a composer, who can consider and reconsider at length the different possibilities which a diverse ensemble might provide for the expression of a given musical idea, the improviser is left with only his or her own physical abilities to make the music when needed. The complex relationship of the human body's abilities to real-time music-making has rarely been explored (but see Eric Clarke's *oeuvre* for a stimulating, Gibsonian approach to the issue). In some ways, this can be seen as comparable to processes of speech production and articulatory phonology (Levelt 1989) in language, but is still more complex, in that these musical utterances must typically be articulated in the context of larger-scale structures, like discourse structure in language, and in tight temporal concert with other performers, unlike speech, where the norm is one speaker at a time.

Constraint 2: real time

The proverb says, 'Time and tide wait for no man' ... and, we might add, time waits for no one improvising music. Sometimes the improvising musician is without any other collaborators (many blues recordings fall into this category), and in that case the improviser is free to alter the timing of their performance as they see fit, having no need to to coordinate with other performers. However, in many other situations, the improviser has other musicians with whom they are interacting in the moment and so very close timing constraints apply. These are often

in the range of 1/25th of a second (40 msec or less)—see Iyer (2002, 2004)— and thus are of critical concern, since the margin for error is so slight. Why might this matter? because, as Stravinsky allegedly said, 'Music is the art that defines Man's relationship to Time.' Music provides the fine grid against which our ongoing lives are measured, more finely than with language or with clocks; it is humanity's great measure of time, down to the finest levels we can determine—and our auditory systems can detect the minutest levels of timing, well under 1/1000 of a second.

Constraint 3: limits on what we know

Typically, people can only act on what they know; music is no exception to this rule. For the case of improvisation, the knowledge one uses should be encoded in procedural (know-how-to) rather than declarative (know-about) form. There are several reasons for this, mostly having to do with speed. Declarative knowledge is generally applicable, but slow: it must be interpreted in order to be used. Procedural knowledge, on the other hand, is typically viewed as recoded or 'compiled' into a tighter, more efficient form, from that initially given in its declarative form. Thus, improvisers must have their knowledge encoded in procedural form, to be used quickly enough, but must also make use of the implicit knowledge of musical structure possessed by listeners in order to make their in-the-moment compositions coherent and stylistically appropriate.

Thus, structure, pattern, and bodily engagement emerge as key elements of improvisational technique, and this has been reflected in psychological research into improvisation. This approach attempts to go beyond the limitations of interview and self-report; as Johnson-Laird writes:

> [musicians] can articulate only a limited answer, because the underlying mental processes are largely unconscious. If you ask yourself how you are able to speak a sequence of English sentences that make sense, then you will find that you are consciously aware of only the tip of the process.
>
> Johnson-Laird (2002, p. 417)

making plain why the discipline of psycholinguistics exists as well as the science of music cognition.

Studies on improvisation in jazz

Much of the psychological literature dealing with musical improvisation focuses on jazz improvisation of some kind. The reasons for this are several: some of the researchers involved are themselves jazz musicians; improvisation lies at the heart of jazz, rather than being a more occasional garnishing of precomposed musical structures (as is the case, for example, with guitar solos in many rock songs); and jazz musicians display improvisational skill at a very high level. Since investigations of jazz are centrally placed in psychological studies, we turn now to them.

Where do ideas come from in jazz?

One of the most common popular misconceptions of jazz improvisation is that it involves 'picking notes out of the air' or some similar statement. Jazz musicians themselves know that this is not the case, but have in general done little to explicate the mental and musical processes involved in improvisation. There are notable exceptions, such as Berliner's *Thinking in jazz* (1994), or Monson's *Saying something* (1996), deep ethnomusicological investigations into the workings of jazz improvisation. These studies, which are musicological rather than psychological in nature, provide a rich background for understanding some basics of jazz improvisation. It is a skill which takes thousands of hours of effortful practice to develop; it develops in community rather than with isolated individuals; it is intensely physical in real time; and it involves acquiring and becoming fluent with a kind of musical vocabulary or lexicon of patterns, which form the basis of musical expression the same way words or phrases do in spontaneous production of language.

Improvisation, pitch, and tonality

To many listeners, the facility with which improvising musicians produce the melodies and harmonies they play is something almost magical. How can these notes be found so quickly—and so accurately? Clearly the tones are not selected at random or the results would not be so coherent and compelling. The answers to this question have been sought by researchers in a variety of ways.

The first, and quite well-documented, aspect of pitch organization by improvisers is their use of a set of pre-existing materials which serve as a vocabulary or lexicon from which they can select and on which transformations may be effected. This has long been noted in improvisation outside the Western tradition, for example in Balkan epic song performance (Lord 1960). In the early- to mid-twentieth century, two scholars—Milman Perry and Albert Lord—developed an idea of oral composition in Homeric poetry and in epic bards from the Balkans which has influenced much subsequent thought into the nature of improvisation. This work brought to the fore the notion of formulas as key elements of the oral composer's craft. These formulas can be thought of as recurring turns of phrase, such as 'the rosy fingers of dawn' in the Homeric epics. Researchers into jazz improvisation have adopted this notion using different terms, including 'licks', 'crips', and 'schemas' (Berliner 1994). Building a store of these patterns, which then can be reworked, varied and refined over time, is one of the primary ways in which young improvisers learn their craft and manage the time demands of improvisation.

However, there are deeper organizing principles at work, as well. There is solid evidence that jazz musicians' improvisations obey many of the principles of tonal organization found in the Western art-music tradition, as has been shown in a number of ways. Järvinen (1995) conducted an in-depth analysis of improvised saxophone solos by Charlie Parker. Järvinen's question was: in what ways do 'bebop' jazz improvisations' pitch content reflect the principles of tonal organization that have been found in other, composed repertoires (cf. Krumhansl 1990)? He found that the tonal profile—the prominence of scale degrees relative to the tonic pitch class—of the tones of Parker's solos fit quite well with Krumhansl's results This indicates that the broad statistical properties of tonality serve to guide the improviser at a deep level. This finding is buttressed by other researchers, such as Larson (2002), whose work has long demonstrated that fundamental aspects of tonal organization as shown in melodic and harmonic teleology are shared between jazz and 'classical' music. Another Finnish researcher, Petri Toiviainen (1995), has used computational models of neural networks as a tool for exploring the tonal and rhythmic organization of improvisations, and has demonstrated ways in which the patterns and techniques, such as the improviser's use of centrally important 'target tones', can be simulated with these models, and also the subtle and powerful interplay between pitch and rhythm in improvisation (Järvinen and Toiviainen 2000).

Improvisation, time, and rhythm

Rhythm in its different aspects is the lifeblood of improvisation (Pressing 2002; Iyer 2002). The improviser must be fully in command of rhythm. With regard to jazz, one recurring question is that of 'swing' or 'groove', at varying tempos, especially the extremely fast ones jazz musicians sometimes use. The literature shows (e.g. Friberg and Sundstrom 2002) that improvisers have a very fine control of timing and great accuracy, within the limits of what the body can do. Hence, at very fast tempi, while maintaining an impressively steady beat, the 'swing ratio' of unequal eighth-notes approaches a 1:1 ratio, perhaps because of physical limitations on moving hands and drumsticks.

However, not all improvisations take place under the kind of high real time demands that fast tempo jazz imposes. Ashley (2002) investigated the more small-scale improvisational aspects of master jazz musicians playing the melodies of ballad. These are slow, commonly played songs, and the variations in performance, which are enormously large relative to those found in the Classical tradition, should be considered acts of improvisation rather than simple re-creation and performance nuance. The primary findings of this study were related to performer's responses to musical structures. First, the performers observe the motivic patterning of the melodies, in that musical passages sharing the same basic figures were altered in similar ways, preserving the categorical nature of the

melodies no matter how extreme the differences in timing might be from some original or nominal form of these motives. At a level below this, there were extensive deviations from the nominal rhythms of these materials, either as notated or as performed on prior recordings which served as the model for the improvisers. Above the level of the motive, at the rhythmic level of the phrase, there was a strong tendency for the soloists's expressive deviations to cease at cadence points, thereby anchoring the melody in the larger formal structure through reinforcing cadences. Expressive variation in timing was thus seen as operating on two levels: one structural, where motivic identity is and phrase rhythm is preserved, and one micro-expressive, where individual variation is valued. Micro-timing variations are well-documented throughout the literature on jazz performance, as shown in Iyer (2002) and Collier and Collier (2002) from vastly different literatures and points of view.

Improvisation and the body

Unlike musical composition, which can be mostly construed as a more-or-less purely cognitive undertaking, improvisation is an activity deeply steeped in and connected with the human body. To improvise means that one is producing music, audibly and in real time; this necessarily means either playing an instrument or singing. We approach this topic through the work of the psychologist-turned-ethnomusicologist John Baily, noting that imilar issues are raised, for example, by Sudnow (1993) in his narrative of learning to play the piano. Baily was trained as an experimental psychologist in the area of motor behaviour. When he turned to issues of music performance he found a particularly interesting topic in which to work: issues of performance on a kind of long-necked Afghani lute, the dutâr. This instrument underwent significant changes in its form over a relatively short span of years, and the techniques needed for playing it and the kinds of musical figures which were thereby idiomatic on it were necessarily altered. The study of these issues, and others related to them, led Baily (and his associate Blacking) to reconceptualize the relationship between the body and musical structure. In this 'motor grammar' approach, the sequences of sounds which are typically the object of musical study are not seen as abstract structures which performers then recreate, but are instead understood to be deeply informed and shaped by the physiological processes necessary for their performance (Baily and Blacking 1991). The patterns of sound are the result of motor behaviours, and thus bodily movement can be seen as the ultimate source of musical structures. Baily's work, both on the dutâr (Baily 1985) and on the guitar (Baily and Driver 1992), can be seen as having many parallels to articulatory phonology in linguistics, where the way in which language is shaped as a series of sounds is deeply rooted in the dynamic behaviour of the vocal tract (Browman and Goldstein 1989). It is interesting, and gratifying, to consider speech and music—the two main ways in which humans use sound for communication and for pleasure—as fundamentally connected to the embodied nature of human cognition.

Computational and grammatical models of improvisation

Given the complexity of the issues which have been covered so far, it is no surprise that researchers might seek to tie them together in a more unified model. A trio of scientists serve as examples of the approach to understanding improvisation through compuational modelling: Johnson-Laird, Jeff Pressing and Mark Steedman. We consider each briefly in turn.

Philip Johnson-Laird, who is both a psychologist and an improvising musician, has dealt off and on for years with questions of creativity, touching on jazz improvisation more than once. In his 2002 article, he sets out a computational system which can produce some kinds of jazz-based improvisations (walking bass lines) given a chord progression. The program Johnson-Laird outlines attempts to deal with a primary psychological constraint facing jazz improvisers: limited short-term memory, operating in real time. His intriguing solution is to use the constraints occurring in musical structures as ways of limiting the set of options faced by a player at any given instant, so that the loads on memory

and decision are lessened considerably. From the choices presented in the set of options yielded by the constraint, quite simple and efficient selection mechanisms suffice. This approach is quite different from those based on over-learned pitch-patterns or formulas, and the dialogue between these two viewpoints continues.

Jeff Pressing (1984, 1988, 1998, 2001), a polymath whose musical focus was improvisation, spent years developing a sophisticated, comprehensive approach to musical improvisation which has as the time of this writing no parallel. Its attempt to draw in physiological, cognitive, cultural, and structural dimensions of improvisation is impressive. In Pressing's model, structural and physical representations of improvisational technique are all represented, and work together to inform the musical result. The physical, embodied considerations in improvisation are fundamental to Pressing's thought: he notes 'the historical fact that music, of all art and sport forms, has developed improvisation to the highest degree', due he thinks to the high time resolution of the auditory and motor systems. Pressing's model of improvisation is based on notions of the interaction between the physicality of performance and the materials being performed, and deals in its own way with the notion of constraints (physical or music–structural) as important elements of a control structure for efficient, real-time improvisational behaviours. The model is explained in significant detail in Pressing (1988) and cannot be adequately described in brief terms, but basically generates novel 'utterances' through the production of musical figures ('event clusters') which may then either be continued based on one or more features of the events currently underway, or may be turned in new directions by a process of interruption. It is in part this duality of control structure, which enables both continuity and surprise, which is responsible for the system's quite impressive performance.

Mark Steedman's work has concerned itself with musical structure and its formal representation since his student days. His work, while not properly speaking a model of improvisation, has been very influential in understanding how improvisers might generate new versions of harmonic progressions from simpler underlying prototypes. In Steedman (1984) he proposes a grammar of blues chord progressions which involves the use of typical transformation rules or rewrite rules, allowing a simple progression to be elaborated recursively into much more sophisticated, and yet stylistically appropriate, sequences. Since then he has continued to work on how such a grammar might be best constructed, and Steedman (1996) presents a solution which is more elegant in many ways but presents problems for the reader not already familiar with formal grammars. Steedman's work shows how one of the core issues in jazz improvisation, harmony, can be modelled efficiently for inclusion into a comprehensive model of improvisation.

Improvisation, interaction, and identity

To be an improviser is, most often, to be a member of a community of musicians who share a common purpose, set of skills, and musical vocabulary. Different researchers have pursued this matter in a variety of ways. Some, like the musicologist Ingrid Monson (1996), have focused on the processes of interaction between jazz musicians while they are playing together, finding that the interplay between performers is essential to the nature of the art and to the skills and behaviours of individuals as well as groups. Others, like the communication theorist Keith Sawyer (1999, 2003, 2006) have connected musical improvisation with other collaborative activities, notably in the domain of theatre. Sawyer identifies three main elements of importance: improvisation, collaboration, and emergence. Improvisation, of course, refers to the production of new ideas 'on the spot' rather than recreating already composed ones; collaboration locates creativity not in any individual but in the group as a whole; and emergence, the notion that somehow the 'whole is greater than the sum of its parts,' and has dynamic properties which are hard to predict ahead of time. Seddon (2005) identified six modes of communication between student improvisers, both verbal and non-verbal, and proposes the notion of empathetic attunement and creativity as a key element in successful group improvisation. It is

clear that group process is one of the areas in improvisation research which is ripe for additional study, and the growing field of dynamic systems and complex organization has much to offer in this regard.

Connected to the idea of group activity are the notions of community and the improviser's identity. This topic has produced a few interesting studies (e.g. Duranti and Burrell 2004) but has been most seriously investigated by a pair of researchers, Raymond MacDonald and Graeme Wilson (MacDonald and Wilson 2005, 2006; Wilson and MacDonald 2005). The focus of their research has been the ways in which membership in a community of improvisers serves to define, for the members, both important aspects of their individual 'identities' or self-understandings, and the very concepts they use in understanding what kind of music they see themselves as playing. MacDonald and Wilson make the case that group interviews, rather than interviews with individuals, are the best method for investigating these matters, as issues of identity and cognitive constructs such as the meaning of 'jazz' are in fact developed and shaped by the social group's interactions, which is most clearly seen in group discussions.

Improvisation, children, and music learning

Since the publication of Hargreaves (1986) there has been a significant growth in the research literature surrounding developmental aspects of improvisation. We can only touch on the matter in this chapter but it is clear that improvisation can be a very significant aspect of childrens' musical development and an important avenue of creativity (cf. Webster 1987, 2002). A number of researchers have investigated ways in which children develop as improvisers. Paananen (2007) demonstrated the steady growth of hierarchic concepts in childrens' improvisations from the age of 6 to 11; these hierarchies were reflected in tonal structures as well as in rhythm, metre, and motivic organization. Brophy (2005) undertook a longitudinal study of children from the age of 7 through to the age of 9, recording their pentatonic improvisations on xylophones. His primary interest was in phrase and motivic structure and metre; he found that there was increasing use of motive and antecedent-consequent phrase structure in the first two years of his sample, another sign of increasing sophistication at quite an early age. Kratus (1989) showed that children too young to be skillful in more structured composition (those up to the age of 7) could be productive as improvisors, suggesting that improvisation with younger children would be a good path for music learning. Other research (such as Azzara 1993) has demonstrated that using improvisation as a regular aspect of a fifth-year elementary school music learning curriculum had positive significant transfer to other musical activities and abilities.

Other researchers have looked at the influence of context on children's improvisations. Guilbault (2004) found that 5- and 6-year-olds are sensitive to the accompaniments played while they improvise; when a harmonically oriented accompaniment was provided, the children made more use of tonal function and implied harmony in their improvisations. Young (2003) dealt with 3- and 4-year-olds who were improvising together with an adult partner, and identified social interaction in the form of play to be an important source of children's creative behaviours, resulting in an enriched musical output. Finally, Burnard (1999, 2002) has shown that 12-year-olds engage in quite sophisticated group improvisational behaviours, involving interactions between their bodies, movements, and choices of instruments to facilitate improvisation, and valuing group collaboration and interaction in their music-making.

Conclusions

The value of research into improvisation is clearly demonstrated by the studies mentioned here, and many others as well. Improvisation is not an isolated side issue with regard to human music-making; it connects musical structure, our bodies, and our sense of ourselves as individuals and as members of social units in powerful ways. Much work remains to be done but a strong foundation exists at this time.

References

Ashley R (2002). Do[n't] change a hair for me: the art of jazz rubato. *Music Perception*, **19**(3), 311–332.

Azzara CD (1993). Audiation-based improvisation techniques and elementary instrumental students' music achievement. *Journal of Research in Music Education*, **41**(4), 328–342.

Baily J (1999) Ethnomusicological perspectives on Sawyer's ideas. *Psychology of Music*, **27**(2), 208–211.

Baily J and Blacking J (1991). Some cognitive aspects of motor planning in musical performance. *Psychologica Belgica*, **XXXI**(2), 147–162.

Baily J and Driver P (1992). Spatio-motor thinking in playing folk blues guitar. *World of Music*, **34**(3), 57–71.

Baily J (1985). Music structure and human movement. In P Howell, I Cross and R West, eds, *Musical structure and cognition*, 237–258. Academic Press, London.

Berliner P (1994). *Thinking in jazz: the infinite art of improvisation*. University of Chicago Press, Chicago, IL.

Blacking J (1976). *How musical is man?* University of Washington Press, Seattle, WA.

Brophy TS (2005). A longitudinal study of selected characteristics of children's melodic improvisations. *Journal of Research in Music Education*, **53**(2), 120–133.

Browman CP and Goldstein L (1989). Articulatory gestures as phonological units. *Phonology*, **6**, 201–251.

Burnard P (1999). Bodily intention in children's improvisation and composition. *Psychology of Music*, **27**(2), 159–174.

Burnard P (2002). Investigating children's meaning-making and the emergence of musical interaction in group improvisation. *British Journal of Music Education*, **19**(2), 157–172.

Collier GL and Collier JL (2002). A study of timing in two Louis Armstrong solos. *Music Perception*, **19**(3), 463–483.

Csíkszentmihályi M (1990). *Flow: the psychology of optimal experience*. Harper and Row, New York.

Csíkszentmihályi M (1996). *Creativity: flow and the psychology of discovery and invention*. Harper Perennial, New York.

Duranti A and Burrell K (2004). Jazz improvisation: a search for hidden harmonies and a unique self. *Ricerche di Psicologia*, **27**(3), 71–101.

Friberg A and Sundström A (2002). Swing ratios and ensemble timing in jazz performance: evidence for a common rhythmic pattern. *Music Perception*, **19**(3), 333–349.

Guilbault DM. (2004). The effect of harmonic accompaniment on the tonal achievement and tonal improvisations of children in kindergarten and first grade. *Journal of Research in Music Education*, **52**(1), 64–76.

Hargreaves DJ (1986). *The developmental psychology of music*. Cambridge University Press, New York.

Iyer V (2002). Embodied mind, situated cognition, and expressive microtiming in African-American music. *Music Perception*, **19**(3), 387–414.

Iyer V (2004). Improvisation, temporality and embodied experience. *Journal of Consciousness Studies*, **11**(3–4), 159–173.

Järvinen T (1995). Tonal hierarchies in jazz improvisation. *Music Perception*, **12**(4), 415–437.

Järvinen T and Toiviainen P (2000). The effect of meter on the use of tones in jazz improvisation. *Musicae Scientiae*, **IV**(1), 55–74.

Johnson-Laird PN (2002). How jazz musicians improvise. *Music Perception*, **19**(3), 415–442.

Kratus J (1989). A time analysis of the compositional processes used by children ages 7 to 11. *Journal of Research in Music Education*, **37**(1), 5–20.

Krumhansl C (1990). *Cognitive foundations of musical pitch*. Oxford University Press, Oxford and New York.

Larson S (2002). Musical forces, melodic expectation, and jazz melody. *Music Pereption*, **19**(3), 351–385.

Levelt WJM (1989). *Speaking: from intention to articulation*. MIT Press, Cambridge, MA.

Lord A (1960). *The singer of tales*. Harvard University Press, Cambridge, MA.

MacDonald R and Wilson G (2005). Musical identities of professional jazz musicians: a focus group investigation. *Psychology of Music*, **33**(4), 395–417.

MacDonald RAR and Wilson GB (2006). Constructions of jazz: how jazz musicians present their collaborative musical practice. *Musicae Scientiae*, **10**(1), 59–83.

Monson I (1996). *Saying something: jazz improvisation and interaction*. University of Chicago Press, Chicago, IL.

Paananen PA (2007) Melodic improvisation at the age of 6–11 years: development of pitch and rhythm. *Musicae Scientiae*, **11**(1), 89–119.

Pressing J (1984). Cognitive processes in improvisation. In R Crozier and A Chapman, eds, *Cognitive processes in the perception of art*, 345–363. North Holland, Amsterdam.

Pressing J (1988). Improvisation: methods and models. In J Sloboda, ed., *Generative processes in music*, 129–178. Clarendon, Oxford.

Pressing J (1998). Psychological constaints on improvisational expertise and skill. In B Nettl, ed., *In the course of performance*, 47–67. University of Chicago Press, Chicago, IL.

Pressing J (2001). Improvisation: methods and models. In J Sloboda, ed., *Generative processes in music: the psychology of performance, improvisation, and composition*, 129–178. Clarendon Press/Oxford University Press, New York.

Pressing J (2002). Black Atlantic rhythm: its computational and transcultural foundations. *Music Perception*, **19**(3), 285–310.

Sawyer RK (1999). Improvised conversations: music, collaboration, and development. *Psychology of Music*, **27**(2), 192–205.

Sawyer RK (2003). *Group creativity: music, theater, collaboration*. Lawrence Erlbaum Associates Publishers, Mahwah, NJ.

Sawyer RK (2006). Group creativity: musical performance and collaboration. *Psychology of Music*, **34**(2), 148–165.

Seddon FA (2005). Modes of communication during jazz improvisation. *British Journal of Music Education*, **22**(1), 47–61.

Steedman MJ (1984). A generative grammar for jazz chord sequences. *Music Perception*, **2**, 52–77.

Steedman MJ (1996). The blues and the abstract truth: music and mental models. In A Garnham and J Oakhill, eds, *mental models in cognitive science*, 305–318. Erlbaum, Mahwah, NJ.

Sudnow H (1993). *Ways of the hand*. MIT Press, Cambridge, MA.

Toiviainen P (1995). Modeling the target-note technique of bebop-style jazz improvisation: an artificial neural network approach. *Music Perception*, **12**(4), 398–413.

Webster PR (1987). Conceptual bases for creative thinking in music. In JC Peery, IC Peery and TW Draper, eds, *Music and child development*, 158–174. Springer-Verlag, New York.

Webster PR (2002). Creative thinking in music: advancing a model. In T Sullivan and L Willingham, eds, *Creativity and music education*, 16–33. Canadian Music Educators Association, Edmonton.

Wilson GB and MacDonald RAR (2005) The meaning of the blues: musical identities in talk about jazz. *Qualitative Research in Psychology*, **2**(4), 341–363.

Young S (2003) The interpersonal dimension: a potential source of musical creativity for young children? *Musicae Scientiae, Special Issue*, 175–191.

CHAPTER 39

Children as creative thinkers in music

Focus on composition

Peter R. Webster

T HE study of creative thinking in music involves a complex combination of cognitive and affective variables, often executed at the highest levels of human thinking and feeling. This is such a complicated set of long-term engagements (composition, repeated music listening, or decisions about previously composed music in performance) or 'in the moment' engagements (improvisation and one-time listening), that it becomes quickly apparent why this field has not attracted more music researchers and why many feel the topic is hopelessly impregnable.

There are many reasons for optimism, however, as we are starting a new century of scholarship. The changes in education and the role of music in formal learning demands that we address creative thinking as best we can. The serious study of creative thinking from a psychological perspective is helpful to review as well. This chapter is designed to offer some perspective on these matters and to place in context the growing research literature in music completed by musicians. While it is generally acknowledged that children's creative thinking in music occurs as part of many music experiences such as listening, performance, conducting, and improvising (Reimer 2003), the focus here is on composition.

Education context

Since the beginning of the twentieth century in North America, music educators have seen themselves as largely teachers of music performance, especially in the secondary schools where music study becomes centred on the 'talented' few (Mark 1996, p. 11). Many school systems require music instruction in the elementary and middle school grades for the entire school population with the curriculum often centring on singing, movement activities, and some listening. Attempts to include a wider variety of music experiences, including composition and improvisation at all grade levels, are only now beginning, inspired in part by the National Standards (Consortium of National Arts Education 1994) and arguments from music education philosophers and framers of curriculum (Reimer 2003). The situation in other English-speaking countries such as Australia and England has been qualitatively different. For some time, the emphasis in curriculum has slanted more toward compositional experiences or at least a more balanced approach that has addressed composition together with performance.

The English-language research literature on creative thinking in music for children, therefore, has been influenced in large part by these teaching traditions. Music psychologists interested in children's generative behaviour and unfamiliar with developments in music teaching and learning will find it necessary to understand this context.

One particularly powerful view of learning that has influenced the research is constructivism (Kafai and Resnick 1996). Constructionist thinking is not new to educational theory, with roots that can be traced to Dewey, Piaget, and others. This line of thought has been given a fresh perspective in writings on school reform

(Gardner 1999). The basic goals of constructivism are to place emphasis on creativeness and to motivate learning through activity. Learning is seen as more effective when *situated in activity* rather than received passively. In other words, children learn best when actively involved in creating things and not when asked to only memorize facts for later recall. Such memorization is important of course and must not be eliminated; rather, such learning should be partnered with creative activities that allow students to demonstrate command through action. Each child should be allowed to *construct* their own understanding with the expert help of the teacher. At the heart of these ideas is a shift away from thinking about education as being centred solely in the mind of the teacher to more of a partnership between teacher and student, with the teacher as the major architect of learning. Project-centred learning is celebrated with students solving problems.[1]

Bases in psychological literature

J. Paul Guilford's 1950 keynote address to the American Psychological Association (Guilford 1950) is often cited as the commencement of the modern-day study of creativity. In the address, he noted the lack of attention paid to divergent thinking[2] and called for more systematic study. His work would evolve into the formation of a factor-of-intellect model of human intelligence that celebrated the intersection of product, operations and content (Guilford 1967). His subsequent factor analytic studies brought attention in psychology to a multiple intelligence theory that was meaningful. The specific model proposed came under fire by the research

community due to the problems inherent in factor analysis as an empirical methodology (Sternberg 1999), but the spirit and logic behind Guilford's work lives on in many guises.

Since that time, the growth of formal study of creativity has been slow, at least until most recently. There are two edited volumes published in the last few years that are excellent compilations on the subject of creativity. The first is by Finke *et al.* (1996). The book has 14 chapters aimed at offering a contemporary view of creativity in a cognition context. Topics such as insight, problem-solving, memory, and incubation are included, as well as an interesting opening chapter by the editors on cognitive processes in creative contexts. Attention is also paid to machine intelligence and on connectionism and neural nets.

A more recent collection of writings was published by Cambridge University Press, edited by Sternberg (1999). This volume is perhaps the most comprehensive and definitive, single volume in the field of general creativity and contains 22 chapters written by many notable scholars in the field today. The book is important because it documents the recent upturn in interest among cognitive psychologists in the study of this difficult topic. Sternberg (2006) has also recently completed a retrospective analysis of his own work on creative thinking and it is highly recommended.

There are now major journals in psychology devoted to the topic of creativeness, including the *Journal of Creative Behavior* and the more recent *Thinking Skills and Creativity*. Two books on adult creativity have been written—one by Gardner (1997) and the other by Csikszentmihalyi (1997)—and each applies recent work to the explanation of genius.

Despite these developments, creativity as a construct (or as a set of complicated constructs) has largely been avoided in modern psychology. Sternberg and Lubart (1999) offer six possible reasons:

1 Mystic and spiritual roots of this topic which tends to put off the more scientific community

2 Its pragmatic, commercial nature exploited by those who offer popular accounts of the creative thinking process which are not based on theory and research

---

[1] For an extensive treatment of constructivism and its role in music teaching and learning, see Wiggins *et al.* (2006) and the accompanying response by Webster.

[2] The concepts of 'divergent' and 'convergent' thinking are at the heart of much of my writing and thinking about creativeness. Divergent thinking is simply that kind of thinking for which the result has no single goal and a number of products may result—a kind of personal brainstorming. Convergent thinking is work that focuses on a final result. Creative work involves both kinds of thinking many times and in many complex ways.

3 Early work on the subject that was not theoretically or methodologically central to the field of psychology, and, as such, not respected

4 Problems with definition and criteria that 'put off' the researcher who is looking for easier and perhaps more conceptually understood topics for tenure and promotion committees to understand

5 Approaches that have viewed creativity as an extraordinary part of an ordinary thing so as not to really need separate study, and

6 Unidisciplinary approaches to creativity that have tended to view a part of creativity as the whole phenomenon, trivializing or marginalizing the study (Sternberg 1999, p. 4).

Those researchers in general psychology that have been brave or inspired enough to deconstruct the general creative experience through empirical study have taken the following approaches (Mayer 1999):[3]

♦ *Psychometric*. Assessment work aimed at the creation of tools to measure specific traits or evaluate overall creative ability (Guilford, Torrance, McKinnon)

♦ *Experimental*. Traditional empirical paradigms designed to seek cause and effect relationships (Sternberg and Davidson, Collins and Amabile)

♦ *Biographical*. Studies that use historical data to understand the creative process and creative thinking (Wallace and Gruber, Gardner, Simonton)

♦ *Psychodynamic*. Writings based on clinical evidence and philosophical/psychological speculation about creativeness (Freud, Kris, Kubie)

♦ *Biological*. Data derived from physiological data (Martindale and Hines, Hudspith)

♦ *Computational*. Conceptual work based on mathematical and computer-based models and simulations (Boden, Shank)

♦ *Contextual*. More qualitative work based on the realities of social context (Csikszentmihalyi)

Each approach has strengths and inherent weakness. Selected reading of studies in each approach is highly recommended to gain a sense of the contemporary scene in the general literature before reviewing specific studies in music and music composition with children. In drawing implications for music teaching and learning, this literature helps to bolster the aspects of enabling conditions (both personal and culturally based) and enabling skills (personal competence) that are so critical for creative thought. Much of this literature, too, underscores the vital importance of divergency of thought and imagination in context with more convergent thinking that often involves just plain hard work. The vital role of social context is also apparent from this general literature.

Promising new research for music

When comparing the approaches in the general literature to music, the psychometric, experimental, and contextual approaches from Mayer's listing are noticeable. A more 'descriptive' approach is emerging in music which places emphasis on the content analyses of the creative music experiences themselves. Hickey's review (2002) of creativity research in music and other arts stressed the importance of what she called 'confluence studies' which bring together social/cultural contexts with historical forces, events and trends. These studies, which will be noted below, often focus on the musical decision-making processes and on more personal issues outside of the music itself such as confidence, peer-interaction, and self efficacy.

Over fifteen years ago, I published a review of the literature on creative thinking in music education (Webster 1992). I have continued to maintain an annotated bibliography that attempts to cover the field of music teaching and learning.[4] My organizational model for this

---

[3] A complete review of each approach is not possible here but see Mayer (1999) for a more detailed description of each approach and for references to the scholar's work whose names appear in this listing.

[4] For the most recent annotated bibliography, consult the following website: http://musicalcreativity.com/?cat=3.

literature includes studies organized in three major categories:

1 *Theoretical*, works based on philosophical or psychological arguments as well as review, standards and historical writings;

2 *Practical Application*, literature designed to inform praxis but not derived fundamentally from empirical evidence; and

3 *Empirical*, work from numerical or observational data.

This empirical category is the most complex, with studies that examine teaching strategies, assessment design, technology, relationship between variables in and outside music, and the actual creative experience. Work on collaboration and social context has gained a great deal of ground in the last few years. Work with technology and teaching strategies is growing quickly as well. The early literature model was based on less than 200 writings. A current review of this literature will reveal nearly three times this amount.

There are a number of trends that can be seen in the literature in the last 15 years. Here is a summary of the major developments noted in this new literature in terms of children's composition. Key references are noted to give the reader a start in exploring the body of work. A brief summary of this work follows.

♦ Adoption of the postmodern tendency to question the assumptions made by previous generations and to be concerned more completely with social context and more naturalistic settings and qualitative methodologies in studying data (Burnard 2006).

♦ Empowering children's voices about the composition experience and valuing the meaning that children describe (Barrett 2003; Burnard 2000; Stauffer 2003).

♦ Heighten interest in the young child's work with invented music notation and the child's discussion of the notation as a window to understanding knowledge (Gromko 1994).

♦ New approaches to assessment, including consensual techniques and peer assessment (Byrne *et al.* 2003; Hickey 2001; Hickey and Lipscomb 2006).

♦ Attention to the role of collaboration and group composition (Kaschub 1997; Odam

2000; Miller 2004; Faulkner 2003; Seddon 2006).

♦ Emergent thinking on the pedagogy of composition teaching (Hewitt 2002; Webster 2003; Stephens 2003; Berkley 2004; Strand 2006; Odena and Welch 2007).

♦ New speculation on and experimentation with the role of music technology (Hickey 1997; Nilsson and Folkestad 2005; Crow 2006; Ruthman 2007; Pachet 2006; Burnard 2007).

♦ Models of creative thinking in music from a variety of perspectives (Webster 2002; Burnard and Younker 2002; Hickey 2003; Wiggins 2003; Espeland 2003).

Shift in research paradigm

Burnard (2006) presented an informative retrospective of research approaches as a prelude to a chapter on children's meaning-making as composers. It characterizes a shift from the more 'positivist, large-scale studies aiming to measure creativity in children's composition towards ethnographic, qualitative approaches and to research focusing on the actual site of operations and practice' (p. 111). She argued that, with the development of socially centred theories, the need to study children in more natural settings doing more natural activities is more desirable. She further argued that more attention must be paid to the children's views, perspectives and accounts of process and product. Burnard's accounting of this shift in paradigm is reinforced as one studies many of the most recent research studies on children's composition noted in this chapter; however, it should be noted that more theoretical and positivist approaches continue as researchers seek better answers to assessment, teaching practice, and the description of what children actually produce musically.

Empowering children's voices

A good example of the literature that moves more toward Burnard's characterization is the work honouring the naturally expressed, child perspective on what it means to compose. Barrett (2003) has written eloquently about children's descriptions of composition and the function that it plays in the lives of children.

Of interest is less the musical content itself and more the way children internalize and deal with the request to compose music and the way they make meaning from the experience. It is reasoned that the more we understand this process, the more we understand learning. Burnard (2000) has explored this theme effectively in her examination of how children blend improvisation with composition in the classroom. Stauffer (2003) offered a perspective on identity and voice in her review of several years of compositional data among children using computers to compose music. The accent in her work is on observation of evolving musical thinking with minimal direction from the teacher/researcher.

Invented notation

One window into the minds of children when dealing with music composition is invented notation. Musical drawings offer a means for non-verbal communication of cognitive processing and representation. Gromko (1994) and others such as Barrett (1997) have explored this approach. Typically, children without formal notation understanding are asked to 'notate' their composed work so that others might understand it. After the invented notation is created, children might be asked to tell the researcher what the notation represents. This often leads to a better understanding of what drives or organizes the music composition. Such work leads to a better understanding of how children think in sound and how this changes with age and experience.

New approaches to assessment

Invented notation is one way to deconstruct the complexities of children's composition, but other approaches to assessment of both product and process have been explored. Byrne et al. (2003) have reported positive and significant correlations between levels of optimal experience of Csikszentmihalyi's 'flow' levels and quality of group compositions as measured by creativity ratings. Such work is very tentative to be sure and fraught with difficulties, but such experiments are worthy additions to the literature as a partner to more qualitative work.

Hickey (2001) and Hickey and Lipscomb (2006) have reported some success using the consensual assessment technique made famous by Amabile. This approach is based on a theory that creativeness is best measured by experts in the domain of a field using global approaches and that the articulation of specific criteria is less valid.

Collaboration and group composition

One interesting facet of recent study of children's composition is the effectiveness of collaborative and group composition. Kaschub (1997) profiled the processes of two composition projects, one with six sections of sixth-grade general music students and one with a high school choir. In each case, a composer worked with the groups to create a process cooperatively. The article is rich with examples of how children gained a stronger understanding of music. Seddon (2006) reported success in using composition as a group activity with computer-mediated collaboration over a distance. Similarly positive experiences were reported by Faulkner (2003) in working with group composition involving 6–16-year-olds in a rural school in Iceland; however, his study also identified some causes for concern in terms of group work. Odam (2000) published a critical perspective on group composition as it was implemented in certain schools in England and Wales as part of obligatory Key Stage 3 curriculum; he noted that too many teachers used inappropriate methods and much time was wasted. Miller (2004) contributed an action research study that featured group composition in an elementary school. This study is noteworthy because it was based on a careful review of the literature and featured the story of a teacher who was employing compositional experiences for the first time.

Pedagogy of composition

Of interest to those that teach or are planning to teach, this recent development in the literature deserves special attention. Examples include the work by Hewitt (2002) and Odena and Welch (2007) which demonstrated a direct link between success in teaching composition and past experience with music and compositional thinking. Implications for teacher-preparation programmes seem obvious. Berkley (2004) contributed data on approaching the teaching of composition as a problem-solving activity that should be presented in a positive atmosphere of student autonomy. Stephens (2003) presented several techniques that have been shown to be effective in teaching and stressed the importance of melodic ideas, technique, musical structure, and personal voice. In writing about the judicious use of revision, I have tried to argue for a balance between complete freedom in teacher direction and dominate control (Webster 2003). An extensive survey study by Strand (2006) of music teachers in Indiana revealed no consistent definition of composition and no real consistency in activities that purported to be compositionally based. Much work remains to be done on the preparation of music teachers to lead successful teaching sequences in composition that is inspired by both the more qualitative and quantitative studies described here.

Role of music technology

Advances in music technology have profoundly affected the research and practice of children's compositional engagement. We have already mentioned the work of Seddon and Stauffer in this regard. The case studies by Hickey (1997) of individuals working with computer technology are important models. The work by Nilsson and Folkestad (2005) is yet another example of a set of investigations of how computer-based technology can be used to study the creative process; noteworthy was their desire to study product and process as an organic whole and to do so with a focus on social/process issues together with music content. On the other hand, Crow (2006) provided a more critical perspective on the implementation of certain music technology and fault was found not only with the materials but the techniques that employed them. Ruthman (2006) documented the use of social computing software applications and online collaboration techniques which promise to make a major advancement in music teaching. Pachet (2006) provided a more pessimistic view of common hardware and software applications and favoured interactive, reflexive music systems. One such system, The Continuator-I, developed at the Sony Computer Science Laboratories in France, allows the user to perform gestures on a music keyboard with an answer returned in such a way that a musical dialogue can be established. Implications for this system in encouraging and studying creative thinking in music are great.

One of the most interesting contributions to the literature concerning the nexus of technology and creative thinking in music is from Burnard (2007). She provided a set of theoretical constructs for the consideration of technology as a pedagogic change agent.

Models of creative thinking

Finally, model building related to children's creative thinking in music continues to flourish. My own model (Webster 2002) has been newly revised based on much of the literature cited here. The model argues for a central process of staged thinking with music materials that represent the interplay of divergent and convergent processes—all informed by enabling skills and conditions. The work by Burnard and Younker (2002) on the pathways that children follow in the creative process is supportive of this model and extends it in fascinating ways. Espeland (2003) has contributed a model for compositional process that features personal and compositional actions in the context of school. Hickey (2003) has offered a componential model based in part on the work of Amabile; it stresses the critical role of social and intrinsic motivation and the nature of instructional set. Inspired by her own extensive teaching and the recent socially based literature on learning, Wiggins (2003) has provided a powerful 'frame' for understanding creative process for individuals and groups. Embedded in the frame is a carefully conceived interplay between teacher and student that stresses a safe and rich environment and a shared understanding of culture, curriculum, and compositional problem.

Conclusion

This chapter has taken a decidedly 'teaching and learning' approach in summarizing the many studies on creative thinking in music. This has been purposeful on my part because some of the best work in this field is done by researchers interested in the developing minds of children and the best way to educate them in this rich and complex century. Chapters such as this are difficult to write as much good work is not mentioned. The hope is that this sampling of recent studies may convince the reader to delve deeper into this topic, design and execute research, and apply the ideas in practice.

References

Barrett M (2007). Invented notations: a view of young children's musical thinking. *Research Studies in Music Education*, **8**, 2–14.

Barrett M (2003). Freedom and constraints: constructing musical worlds through the dialogue of compositions. In M Hickey, ed., *Why and how to teach music composition: a new horizon for music education*, 3–31. MENC, Reston, VA.

Berkley R (2004). Teaching composing as creative problem solving: conceptualising composing pedagogy. *British Journal of Music Education*, **21**(3), 239–264.

Burnard P (2000). Examining experiential differences between improvisation and composition in children's music-making. *British Journal of Music Education*, **17**(3), 227–245.

Burnard P (2006). Understanding children's meaning-making as composers. In I Deliège and G Wiggins eds, *Musical creativity*, 111–133. Psychology Press, New York.

Burnard P (2007). Reframing creativity and technology: promoting pedagogic change in music education. *Journal of Music, Technology and Education*, **1**(1), 37–55.

Burnard P and Younker B (2002). Mapping pathways: fostering creativity in composition. *Music Education Research*, **4**(2), 245–261.

Byrne C, MacDonald R and Carlton L (2003). Assessing creativity in musical compositions: flow as an assessment tool. *British Journal of Music Education*, **20**(3), 277–290.

Csikszentmihalyi M (1997). *Creativity: flow and the psychology of discovery and invention*. Harper Collins, New York.

Crow B (2006). Musical creativity and the new technology. *Music Education Research*, **8**(1), 121–130.

Espeland M (2003). The African drum: the compositional process as discourse and interaction in a school context. In M Hickey, ed., *Why and how to teach music composition: a new horizon for music education*, 167–192. MENC, Reston, VA.

Faulkner R (2003). Group composing: pupil perceptions from a social psychological study. *Music Education Research*, **5**(2), 101–124.

Finke R Ward T and Smith S (1996). *Creative cognition: theory, research, and applications*. MIT Press, Cambridge, MA.

Gardner H (1997). *Extraordinary minds: portraits of exceptional individuals and an examination of our extraordinariness*. Basic Books, New York.

Gardner H (1999). *The disciplined mind: what all students should understand*. Simon and Schuster, New York.

Gromko J (1994). Children's invented notations as measures of musical understanding. *Psychology of Music*, **22**(2), 136–147.

Guilford J (1950). Creativity. *American Psychologist*, **5**, 444–454.

Guilford J (1967). *The nature of human intelligence*. McGraw-Hill, New York.

Hewitt A (2002). A comparative analysis of process and product with specialist and generalist pre-service teachers involved in a group composition activity. *Music Education Research*, **4**(1), 25–36.

Hickey M (1997). The computer as a tool in creative music-making. *Research Studies in Music Education*, **8**(1), 56–70.

Hickey M (2001) An application of Amabile's consensual assessment technique for rating the creativity of children's musical compositions. *Journal of Research in Music Education*, **49**(3), 234–244.

Hickey M (2002). Creativity research in music, visual art, theatre, and dance. In R Colwell and C Richardson, eds, *The new handbook of research on music teaching and learning*, 398–415. Oxford University Press, New York.

Hickey M (2003). Creative thinking in the context of music composition. In M Hickey, ed., *Why and how to teach music composition: a new horizon for music education*, 31–53. MENC, Reston, VA.

Hickey M and Lipscomb S (2006). How different is good? How good is different? The assessment of children's creative musical thinking. In I Deliège and G Wiggins, eds, *Musical creativity*, 97–110. Psychology Press, New York.

Kaschub M, (1997). A comparison of two composer-guided large group composition projects. *Research Studies in Music Education*, **8**, 15–28.

Kafai Y and Resnick M (eds) (1996). *Constructionism in practice: designing, thinking, and learning in a digital world*. Lawrence Erlbaum, Mahwah, NJ.

Mark M (1996). *Contemporary music education*, 3rd edn. Schirmer Books, New York.

Mayer R (1999). Fifty years of creativity research. In R Sternberg, ed., *Handbook of creativity*, 449–460. Cambridge University Press, New York.

Miller B (2004). Designing compositional tasks for elementary music classrooms. *Research Studies in Music Education*, **22**, 59–71.

Consortium of National Arts Education, (1994). *National Standards for Arts Education*. MENC, Reston, VA.

Nilsson B and Folkestad G (2005). Children's practice of computer-based composition. *Music Education Research*, **7**(1), 21–38.

Odam G (2000). Teaching composing in secondary schools: the creative dream. *British Journal of Music Education*, **17**(2), 109–128.

Odena O and Welch G (2007). The influence of teachers' backgrounds on their perceptions of musical creativity: a qualitative study with secondary school music teachers. *Research Studies in Music Education*, **28**, 71–82.

Pachet F (2006). Enhancing individual creativity with interactive musical reflexive systems. In I Deliège and G Wiggins, eds, *Musical creativity*, 359–375. Psychology Press, New York.

Reimer B (2003). *A philosophy of music education: advancing the vision*, 3rd edn. Prentice Hall, Upper Saddle River, NJ.

Ruthman A (2007). Strategies for supporting music learning through online collaborative technologies. In J Finney and P Burnard, eds, *Music education with digital technology*, 131–141. Continuum, London.

Seddon F (2006). Collaborative computer-mediated music composition in cyberspace. *British Journal of Music Education*, **23**(3), 273–284.

Stauffer S (2003). Identity and voice in young composers. In M Hickey, ed., *Why and how to teach music composition: a new horizon for music education*, 91–112. MENC, Reston, VA.

Stephens J (2003). Imagination in education: strategies and models in the teaching and assessment of composition. In M Hickey, ed., *Why and how to teach music composition: a new horizon for music education*, 113–140. MENC, Reston, VA.

Sternberg R and Lubart T, (1999) The concept of creativity: prospects and paradigms. In R Sternberg, ed., *Handbook of creativity*, 3–15. Cambridge University Press, New York.

Sternberg R (1999). *Handbook of creativity*. Cambridge University Press, New York.

Sternberg R (2006). Creating a vision of creativity: the first 25 years. *Psychology of Aesthetics, Creativity, and the Arts*, **S**(1), 2–12.

Strand K (2006). Survey of Indiana music teachers on using composition in the classroom. *Journal of Research in Music Education*, **54**(6), 154–167.

Webster P (1992). Research on creative thinking in music: the assessment literature. In R Colwell, ed., *Handbook of research on music teaching and learning*, 266–279. Schirmer Books, New York.

Webster P (2002). Creative thinking in music: advancing a model. In T Sullivan and L Willingham, eds, *Creativity and music education*, 16–33. Canadian Music Educators' Association, Edmonton, AB.

Webster P (2003). What do you mean, 'Make my music different?' Encouraging revision and extension in children's music composition. In M Hickey, ed., *Why and how to teach music composition: a new horizon for music education*, 55–65. MENC, Reston, VA.

Wiggins J (2003). A frame for understanding children's compositional processes. (M Hickey, ed.), *Why and how to teach music composition: a new horizon for music education*, 141–167. MENC, Reston, VA.

Wiggins J, Blair D, Ruthman A and Shively J, (2006). Constructivism. In E Wing, ed., *Mountain lake reader—Spring 2006*, 82–93. Middle Tennessee State University, Murfreesboro, TN.

PART 9

The role of music in everyday life

Edited by John Sloboda

CHAPTER 40

Choosing to hear music

Motivation, process, and effect

John Sloboda, Alexandra Lamont and Alinka Greasley

Introduction

A substantial amount of music listening in contemporary Western society is deliberately chosen. This chapter reviews what is known about the psychology of self-chosen exposure to musical performances of others (recorded or live).

The cultural contexts studied in this research are characterized by three broad trends. First is the growing prevalence of 'musical consumers' (i.e. people who do not participate in musical events as performers, or rarely do so). Second is the increasing availability of recorded music of all genres and periods (through methods of production, marketing and distribution—especially Internet-based). Finally, the increasing miniaturization, portability, and flexibility of music delivery systems (e.g. iPods) means that the choice to hear specific music can be exercised in more and more situations. This has led to fundamental changes in the ways in which people use music (Liebowitz 2004).

These trends present a paradox. Although musical engagement is increasingly passive, because it is not linked to performance skill or participation, music use has never provided more opportunities for active agency. The choice of what music to listen to, when, and how has proliferated.

We organize the research reviewed here by the functional niche that the music is chosen to be part of. Music often accompanies some non-musical activity, chosen to enhance that activity in some way by affecting a psychological state which impacts on desired outcomes. In these contexts the music may not be the primary focus of attention or concern—the focus is rather on its effects.

Six main niches appear in the literature. These are:

1 travel (e.g. driving a car, walking, using public transport);

2 physical work (everyday routines like washing, cleaning, cooking, and other forms of manual labour);

3 brain work (e.g. private study, reading, writing, and other forms of thinking);

4 body work (e.g. exercise, yoga, relaxation, pain management);

5 emotional work (e.g. mood management, reminiscence, presentation of identity); and

6 attendance at live music performance events as an audience member.

Within these niches, we also identify four recurring functions of self-chosen music use. *Distraction* is a way of engaging unallocated attention and reducing boredom. *Energizing* is a means of maintaining arousal and task attention. In *entrainment*, the task movements are timed to coincide with the rhythmic pulses of the music, giving the task or activity elements of a dance. Finally, *meaning enhancement* is where the music draws out and adds to the significance of the task or activity in some way. Evidence for these comes predominantly from qualitative and ethnographic research, where music listeners are asked to talk or write freely about their music uses (e.g. DeNora 2000; Sloboda 1999; Sloboda *et al.* 2001), but we also present experimental findings as appropriate.

Travel

Most everyday travel is made alone (for instance, to work). Music is chosen to accompany travel more consistently than in almost any other setting. This is made possible through mobile sound delivery systems that can accompany the traveller. Around 90 per cent of travel episodes are accompanied by self-chosen music (North *et al.* 2004; Sloboda *et al.* 2001; Stutts *et al.* 2001).

Driving a car

Driving is a highly skilled task, requiring constant vigilance, which—if not appropriately applied—can result in death or serious injury. Dibben and Williamson (2007) review evidence that in-car music can decrease driving performance through its distracting and masking qualities: music makes it more difficult to attend to the key visual and auditory signals that must be constantly monitored to avoid accidents (e.g. engine noise, external warning signals). An additional accident-related distractor is adjusting controls on in-car audio-systems, thus taking attention off the road (Stutts *et al.* 2001).

Music while driving generally enhances performance through its capacity to assist with achieving or maintaining appropriate levels of arousal and concentration. Long and boring drives (e.g. on rural highways) promote drowsiness. Use of a sound system has been found to reduce accidents in such situations (Cummings *et al.* 2001), although the drowsiness-reducing effect is most marked in the first 30 minutes of driving, and drivers believe that music reduces their drowsiness more than it actually does as measured by EEG (Reyner and Horne 1998).

Some studies have looked at the effects of music on driver behaviour, often in simulated driving environments (e.g. Beh and Hirst 1999; Brodsky 2002; Turner *et al.* 1996). The benefits of music on reaction times and avoidance of hazards are found to depend on the nature, speed, and intensity of the music. Whilst music enhances reaction times to signals in the centre of vision, high levels of music-induced or situation-induced arousal can narrow the field of attention, causing people to drive faster and decreasing their driving safety.

Are drivers aware of the potentially deleterious effects of the music they choose to drive to? A survey of 2473 UK drivers by Dibben and Williamson (2007) showed that most drivers (87 per cent) listen to the same music while driving as at home. When asked about the effect of music in the car, many (62 per cent) cited music's capacity to soothe them, making them calmer and more relaxed. Rather fewer (around 25 per cent) claimed that music helped them concentrate whilst driving. The safest drivers (as indicated by having retained their no-claims insurance discount) were most likely to prefer silence while driving.

In sum, drivers listen to music in their cars for primarily motivational and enjoyment reasons. They do not typically self-consciously design an auditory environment designed to minimize accidents, but rather listen to the music they like in general in the car.

On public transport

Around 60 per cent of journeys on UK public transport involve listening to chosen music via portable sound systems (North *et al.* 2004). Selecting reasons for listening in this context, respondents noted that 85 per cent of music listening episodes 'helped to pass the time', and 73 per cent chose 'I enjoyed it'. However, only 21 per cent of music-listening episodes helped participants concentrate/think. This confirms that, in general, music listening on public transport is used to enhance (or distract from) a routine, even boring, low-demand experience.

One obvious consequence of private music listening via headphones is that the music isolates the listener from other people (Bull 2001). This choice may thus allow music to mask unwanted noise or conversation, or to function as a defence mechanism against the anxiety-provoking elements of being in close proximity with strangers.

Physical work

Domestic chores (such as washing, cooking, cleaning, gardening) are the most prevalent everyday physical tasks. These simple and often-repeated tasks have low interest and attentional demands, and music is a very frequent accompaniment.

'Singing while you work' has been a core activity in cultures over time and space (e.g. Gioia 2006). Music is frequently described as an accompaniment to mundane (mainly solitary and domestic) everyday activities (Sloboda 1999), and North *et al.* (2004) found that self-chosen music accompanied housework on 90 per cent of occasions.

Qualitative ethnographic evidence suggests that all four functions of music use—distracting, energizing, entrainment, and meaning enhancement—arise in relation to this activity (DeNora 2000; Sloboda *et al.* 2001). The following example highlights how music energizes, entrains and adds meaning to the routine of cleaning (from Greasley and Lamont 2006):

> I've got a CD that I **always** clean my house to, which is Swing When You're Winning by Robbie Williams [laughs]… it just kinda makes it a bit easier, a spoonful of sugar I suppose helps the medicine go down, and it's just, it's lively as well, most of it is quite lively and if you're hoovering, it's yeah, you can dance around to it while you're doing it.
>
> (Female 26 years old)

The interviewee later noted that she was 'not a massive Robbie Williams fan'. This exemplifies the functionality of the chosen music. Individuals choose music in conjunction with concurrent tasks and activities to help them achieve goals (see also DeNora 2000; Hargreaves and North 1999; Sloboda 1992, 1999).

Brain work

Desk work in occupational settings

Technological advances mean that individual workers can increasingly make self-directed decisions about whether and how to listen to music. In an office environment, Lesiuk (2005) provided a selection of CDs for individual use via headphones over a 2-week period. Music was found to improve a number of work-related measures, including overall mood: those who listened to music for more time had a more positive mood (see also Oldham *et al.* 1995).

Haake and Dibben (2006) surveyed employees' personal use of music in a variety of office settings. They found a high degree of music listening at work from their volunteers (80 per cent reported listening at work, for an average of 36 per cent of total working time). Respondents tended to listen to music while doing routine solitary tasks, word processing, web-surfing and emailing. They tended not to listen during tasks involving interaction with colleagues. Considering the functions of music listening, respondents cited task-related functions (improving concentration and focus, or blocking out unwanted noise) and more general positive effects (reducing stress, contributing to well-being and improving the perceived quality of the working environment). Some respondents suggested that music stimulated positive social interaction between colleagues by providing a talking point. Finally, particularly for those undertaking low-demand tasks, music was a way of relieving boredom. In common with other studies (e.g. Sloboda 1999) the main disadvantages of music in the workplace related to the involuntary overhearing of music chosen by others. Another problem raised was the difficulty of attracting a colleague's attention when they were wearing headphones.

Private study

Very often children undertake homework in a room where a TV or radio is playing. Pool and colleagues (2003) found that background music from TV or radio had no significant effect on homework performance or duration. In contrast, soap operas caused a significant decline in performance, probably as their explicit narrative and verbal content caused cognitive interference with the task. Beentjes and van der Voort (1997) found 64 per cent of Dutch children claimed to play pop music 'often' or 'always' while doing writing assignments for homework. Most children claimed that this benefited their performance, although these results can imply that if there must be background media, music is less disruptive than spoken media.

Music is frequently used by adults as an accompaniment to private study at home (as recently confirmed for university students by Kotsopoulou and Hallam [2006]). However, there appears to be no systematic published research on the use of music for adult private study.

Body work

Music has the capacity to alter bodily processes, such as physiological states and behavioural movements (see Chapter 11 this volume) and coordination and motivational levels (Chapter 44 this volume), and is used to accompany activities such as exercise, relaxation, and pain management. Below we review studies exploring factors that influence people's choices of music to accompany such activities.

Exercise, yoga and relaxation

The key issue in the choice of music to accompany physical activities such as exercise or relaxation is the appropriateness of the music for the activity, and the functions of energizing and entrainment are central. Most experimental research uses experimenter-selected music (e.g. North and Hargreaves 1996, 2000), although some include a limited choice within this; one recent study surveyed the preferred music of their population before selecting music for use in their experiment (Karageorghis *et al.* 2006). Results indicate that choice and preference is affected by the appropriateness of the arousal potential of the music for the activity. For example, people prefer listening to high arousal music during exercise and low arousal music during relaxation (North and Hargreaves 2000), and faster music is preferred for higher intensity exercise (Karageorghis *et al.* 2006). Studies with restricted music choices also show that the perceived appropriateness of the music for the exercise affects liking (North and Hargreaves 1996), and over the long term this might affect independent choices made in real-life settings.

Belcher and DeNora (1999; see also DeNora 2000) explored the function of entrainment in relation to music and exercise in some detail. Using ethnographical methods (including in-depth interviews, questionnaires, and observation), weekly aerobics sessions were studied over a year. They found that beats per minute was one important feature of music choice for different exercise settings. Successful entrainment was partly influenced by participants' perceptions of the music. Valued sessions had music

which varied in rhythm, lyrics, melodies and orchestration, facilitating appropriate levels of energy, motivation and endurance for the aerobics routines. Despite evidence for a consistent relationship between features of music (especially tempo) and exercise settings, there has been virtually no research looking at wholly self-chosen music that accompanies body work activities like exercise and relaxation.

Pain management

As music is held to have active and structuring properties on and for the body (DeNora 2000), it has been explored as a tool for pain management. Studies have examined the effects of music on pain perception and management in both clinical and experimental settings (Good 1996; Mitchell and MacDonald 2006; Mitchell *et al.* 2006). Beneficial effects of repeated music listening over a week have been found for chronic pain sufferers in terms of higher levels of perceived control over the pain and lower levels of reported pain, depression and disability (Siedliecki and Good 2006).

Experimental studies show that choosing from a range of experimenter-selected music is more beneficial than listening to entirely experimenter-chosen music (Siedliecki and Good 2006), but listening to one's own preferred music has the most significant effect on pain (Mitchell and MacDonald 2006; Mitchell *et al.* 2006). Survey research illustrates that chronic pain sufferers regularly listen to music (75 per cent of the sample in Mitchell *et al.* 2007) and are also aware of music's potential for attention diversion and relaxation. Music which is entirely under the listener's control can thus be a very effective tool in pain management for a number of different reasons, including attention diversion and perceived control over the situation (Mitchell *et al.* 2007).

Emotional work

Having evaluated the use of music in relation to non-musical tasks and goals, we next consider some more intrinsic outcomes of music listening by focusing on the use of music to manage mood, self, and emotions.

Reminiscence

A common function of self-chosen music listening is reminiscence (reminding oneself of past events), which is particularly common in older adults (Juslin and Laukka 2004). Sloboda (1999) found that adult participants who were asked to recall early memories involving music were able to report detailed and highly emotional memories despite the considerable time which had elapsed. Many adults use their musical autobiographies to reconstruct their life story (DeNora 2000; Greasley and Lamont 2006), illustrating that music is intertwined in the construction of autobiographical narrative.

Mood management

Listeners also regularly report mood management as a common function of self-chosen music listening, as indicated from surveys (Laukka 2007; Sloboda 1999) and qualitative studies (DeNora 2000; Greasley and Lamont 2006; Hays and Minichiello 2005). Unsurprisingly, given that people choose to listen to music that they like and that makes them feel good, they predominantly experience positive emotions as a consequence of music listening (Juslin and Laukka 2004). Individuals have considerable awareness of how they can use music for personal functions such as mood management. Batt-Rawden and DeNora (2005) describe this practical knowledge as 'lay' therapeutic practice, which, they note, is often subsumed by other goals or tasks rather than an independent act of behaviour (see earlier sections).

There are some differences in this awareness between individuals. For example, Sloboda (1999) found that women's free responses relating to mood were more detailed and articulate, and North et al. (2000) found adolescent girls to be more concerned than boys with how music could aid their emotional needs. Greasley and Lamont (2006) show that less musically engaged listeners seem less aware of the range of emotional functions that music has, while more engaged listeners have this 'lay' practice at their fingertips. For example, one male respondent noted:

> There's a different mood attached to all of them, there's a different feeling attached to all

of them, um, I know every single one of them inside out, so I know what I want and where it'll be and I always have a choice.

Research itself can also stimulate the process of self-reflection, making listeners more aware of the emotional potential of music listening in everyday settings. In an innovative participatory study, Batt-Rawden and DeNora (2005) explored links between music listening, well-being and health. Participants reported the process of listening, choosing, and responding to different CDs to be therapeutic in its own right, sometimes heightening awareness of how and what to listen to for purposes of self-care.

Presentation or confirmation of social identity

As well as using music for reminiscence and emotional self-regulation, music can also be used in the presentation or confirmation of identity. Preferences for particular types of music may carry a message to others regarding a range of attitudes and values (Zillmann and Gan 1997; Rentfrow and Gosling 2006; North and Hargreaves 2007). Adolescents' music preferences in particular have been shown to reinforce both how they see themselves and how they are seen by others (Tarrant et al. 2001). Listeners are also aware of the messages they may send by expressing particular musical preferences. Finnäs (1989) found marked differences between the music preferences young people stated publicly and those that they privately endorsed. Young adults also believe music preferences reveal information about their personal qualities (Rentfrow and Gosling 2003). In subscribing to a music taste culture, people are often associating with a particular lifestyle and wider set of values (Russell 1997). (For a more detailed account of musical identity, see Chapter 43 this volume).

Attending live events

Despite the technological advancements in availability of recordings and media portability mentioned at the outset, attending live music events is still popular. For example, the Arts Council of England reports that around 10 per cent of the population attend classical concerts in a year, while 36–39 per cent attend any live musical event (cited in Riley and Laing 2006; see also DCMS 2006). However, despite the sustained popularity of attending live musical events, this facet of everyday musical experience has received very little research attention.

Motivations for attending live musical events

Socio-economic factors have long been recognized as influential in determining patterns of arts attendance. While most people report enjoyment and seeing a specific performer or event as their primary motivations for attending arts events (DCMS 2006; Pitts 2005a), it seems that more people would attend classical concerts if tickets were free of charge (Knight Foundation 2002). Moreover, in the US, only 4 per cent of the population regularly attend live events out of 27 per cent 'potential' classical music consumers (Brown and Bare 2003). This suggests an economic barrier (absolute or perceived) to concert-going amongst the less affluent.

Economic approaches to culture provide complex analyses of how people choose to spend their leisure time. Linder (1970) suggested that economic growth leads to *less* time spent on culture, since the opportunity cost of attending a concert rises alongside wages. However, increased income leads those people who choose to engage in cultural activities to do so through relatively goods-intensive experiences such as CD buying rather than time-intensive experiences such as concert attending (Ekelund and Ritenour 1999). Bourdieu's (1984) sociological concept of cultural capital explains why certain social groups engage in particular kinds of cultural behaviour, relating patterns of cultural consumption to sociological variables such as class and gender. Considering music concert attendance, classical music concert audiences are typically professionals with higher incomes, while folk music attendees are typically middle- and lower-class (DiMaggio and Useem 1978; Pegg 1984).

These large-scale approaches (see also North and Hargreaves 2007) are useful in informing us of high-level social factors influencing patterns of engagement, and powerfully demonstrate that many people decide that classical music in particular is 'not for them'. However, they tell us little from a psychological perspective about motivations for attending live events or the experiences that audiences have at such events, and there has been very little research directly addressing these questions.

In her exploration of audience participation at a chamber music festival, Pitts (2005a) provided some insight into why, having chosen to attend the festival, audiences selected particular concerts within it. Reasons broadly related to musical preferences (for example, avoidance of vocal concerts), the performers, and the audience's familiarity or unfamiliarity with the music (for example, many deliberately chose concerts with some unfamiliar elements). Reasons for not selecting a concert related mainly to musical preference and familiarity, especially relating to over-familiarity with certain works. While Pitts' research emphasizes musical factors that influence participation and attendance at events, non-musical factors like the mood of the listener and the physical environment (e.g. traffic noise, uncomfortable seating) also affect listeners' predicted enjoyment of concerts (Thompson 2007). This might also influence audiences' choice to attend a particular event. The reasons for attending live events are thus complex and extend well beyond the content of the programme or the star performer.

What kinds of experiences do concert-goers have?

The expressive and emotional effects that a performer or group can have on a single listener are now well understood (e.g. Juslin 2001; Davidson 2005), but much less is known about the experiences of a group of listeners at real musical events.

Some research has focused on the retrospective nature of the listener's experience at live events. Gabrielsson and Lindstrom-Wik (2003) found around 75 per cent of strong experiences related to music arose in listening rather than performing situations, and a similar proportion in live rather than recorded experiences. Free written descriptions show that these experiences are diverse in nature, encompassing physical reactions, perception, cognition, feeling and emotion, existential and transcendental aspects and personal and social aspects. A recent UK study (Lamont, in preparation) indicated that 54 per cent of university students' strongest experiences of music were at pop or rock festivals and concerts and 27 per cent related to live classical events, while less than 20 per cent of the strong experiences resulted from listening to recorded music.

Less research has focused directly on the live performance situation as it occurs. Pitts (2005a) reported informal conversations with audience members at a chamber music festival, although her analysis focused mainly on retrospective accounts provided by audiences through written and interview methods. Using a more structured yet highly ecologically valid method, Thompson (2006) asked a concert audience to rate their experience, enjoyment and emotional response to the performance. Listeners were able to differentiate between the quality of the performance and their own affective responses. Moreover, their enjoyment of the event was better predicted by their own degree of emotional engagement than the perceived quality of the performance, although much variance was left unexplained. Thompson's research highlights some important questions for further research, including the importance of looking at both musical and non-musical factors (see also Thompson 2007).

Is attending a live event different to listening to recorded music?

Little research has directly considered the relationship of live experiences in comparison with listening to recorded music. Gabrielsson and Lindstrom-Wik (2003) did not present analysis of the differences between live and recorded experiences, although Lamont's (in preparation) study highlights some striking differences:

> Listening to them [Radiohead] on CD is one thing, but when thousands of people surround you, singing to every word like you, the atmosphere electric, there's no other feeling as strong, or intense, as that.

Thus concert attending provides a greater sense of community than solitary listening (see also Bogucki *et al.* 2005), and for the popular music audience, concerts complement rather than duplicate the experience of listening to pre-recorded music. Similar responses were found from some classical music festival attendees who suggest that CDs complement the live listening situation (Pitts 2005a). However, other audience members reported avoiding recordings of pieces they had experienced live, noting that 'nothing can replicate what we have experienced this evening' (Pitts 2005b, p. 99). This selective approach to listening to recordings may be more common amongst classical music listeners, although more research is required.

In summary, the live performance situation and the audience's response to it are only beginning to be understood from a psychological perspective. Biographical retrospective data highlights that the live performance situation can have a substantial impact on individuals' lives, and research undertaken closer to the time of experiencing the event emphasizes the importance of emotional engagement with the experience. Future research will need to continue to explore this complex but highly significant aspect of music listening in everyday life.

Conclusions

There is an idealized view of music listening which is implicit in much of the traditional music appreciation literature (see, for instance, Cook 1998). This places 'pure art music' as an object for the reverent attention of the ideal listener, silent, still, totally focused on the music and its aesthetic or spiritual value.

The psychological research presented here paints a much more varied picture, where the surrounding contexts of music not only intrude on the act of hearing, but in many cases shape and control the very purpose, nature, and effect of that hearing. Music may, indeed, be listened to with total silent attentiveness, but for many people this appears to be the exception rather than the norm. Instead, music is more often the chosen accompaniment to all sorts of activities which have no direct connection to music, and could mainly be accomplished without music being present at all. Far from requiring reverent attention, much music experience could be described as background—like the soundtrack of a film, never defining of the focus of attention, yet psychologically powerful nonetheless.

Two areas of research are ripe for development. One is a fuller characterization of the factors which shift music experiences from the periphery to the centre. Under what conditions does the urge to hear and re-hear specific music become a dominant one, and what kind of changes in thought and feeling come about as one becomes very familiar with a piece of music, through choice? To put it another way, how does music move between 'background' and 'foreground' in a person's everyday life? A second, related question, is the extent to which individuals develop expertise in music choice, in the sense of selecting specific pieces of music with the reliably fulfilled intention of achieving certain psychological outcomes (just as taking an analgesic is done to reliably ease pain). Are some people more expert in their self-chosen administration of musical 'doses' than others, and what makes them more expert? Placing the study of self-chosen music listening within a theoretical framework that acknowledges the high degree of agency involved may well be an important next step in advancing understanding a phenomenon which, despite its ubiquity, still proves elusive to characterize.

References

Batt-Rawden K and DeNora T (2005). Music and informal learning in everyday life. *Music Education Research*, 7, 289–304.

Beentjes JW J and van der Voort THA (1997). The impact of background media on homework performance: students' perceptions and experimental findings. In P Winterhoff-Spurk and THA van der Voort, eds, *New horizons in media psychology: research co-operation and projects in Europe*, pp 175–189. Westdeutscher Verlag, Wiesbaden.

Beh HC and Hirst R (1999) Performance on driving-related tasks during music. Ergonomics, 42, 1087–1098.

Belcher S and DeNora T (1999). Music is part of the equipment that makes your body hard! *eXercise (Publication of the National Governing Body for Exercise and Fitness in England)*, 5, 4–5.

Bogucki Duncan N and Fox MA (2005). Computer–aided music distribution: the future of selection, retrieval and transmission. *First Monday*, 10(4), http://firstmonday.org/issues/issue10_4/duncan/index.html.

Bourdieu P (1984). Distinction: a social critique of the judgement of taste. Routledge, London.

Brodsky W (2002) The effects of music tempo on simulated driving performance and vehicular control. *Transportation Research Part F*, 4, 219–241.

Brown AS and Bare J (2003). *Bridging the gap: orchestras and classical music listeners* (Issues Brief No. 2.) John S. and James L. Knight Foundation, Miami, FL.

Bull M (2001). The world according to sound: investigating the world of Walkman users. *New Media Society*, 3, 179–197.

Cook N (1998). *Music: a very short introduction*. Oxford University Press, Oxford.

Cummings R, Kopesell TD, Moffat JM and Rivara FP (2001). Drowsiness, counter-measures to drowsiness, and the risk of a motor vehicle crash. *Injury Prevention*, 7, 194–199.

Davidson JW (2005). Bodily communication in musical performance. In D Miell, RAR MacDonald and DJ Hargreaves, eds, *Musical communication*, 215–237. Oxford University Press, Oxford.

DeNora T (2000). *Music in everyday life*. Cambridge University Press, Cambridge.

DCMS (Department for Media, Culture and Sport) (2006). *Taking part: the national survey of culture, leisure and sport*. Statistical release: Department for Culture, Media and Sport. http://ww.culture.gov.uk/global/research/taking_part_survey/survey_outputs.htm.

Dibben N and Williamson VJ (2007). An exploratory survey of in-vehicle music listening. *Psychology of Music*, 35(4), 571–589.

DiMaggio P and Useem M (1978). Social class and arts consumption: the origins and consequences of class differences in exposure to the arts in America. *Theory and Society*, 5, 141–161.

Ekelund RB Jr and Ritenour S (1999). An exploration of the Beckerian theory of time costs: symphony concert demand. *The American Journal of Economics and Sociology*, http://www.findarticles.com/p/articles/mi_m0254/is_4_58/ai_58496764/pg_1.

Finnäs L (1989). A comparison between young people's privately and publicly expressed musical preferences. *Psychology of Music*, 17, 132–145.

Gabrielsson A and Linström Wik S (2003). Strong experiences related to music: a descriptive system. *Musicae Scientiae*, VII(2), 157–217.

Gioia T (2006). *Work songs*. Duke University Press, Durham, NC.

Good M (1996). Effects of relaxation and music on post-operative pain: a review. *Journal of Advanced Nursing*, 24, 905–914.

Greasley AE and Lamont A (2006). Music preference in adulthood: why do we like the music we do? In M Baroni, AR Addessi, R Caterina and M Costa, eds, *Proceedings of the 9th international conference on music perception and cognition*, 960–966. University of Bologna, Bologna, Italy.

Haake AB and Dibben NJ (2006). Music-listening practices in workplace settings in the UK. In M. Baroni, AR Addessi, R Caterina and M Costa, eds, *Proceedings of the 9th international conference on music perception and cognition*, p. 1094. University of Bologna, Bologna, Italy.

Hargreaves DJ and North AC (1999). The functions of music in everyday life: redefining the social in music psychology. *Psychology of Music*, **27**, 71–83.

Hays T and Minichiello V (2005). The meaning of music in the lives of older people: a qualitative study. *Psychology of Music*, **33**, 437–451.

Juslin PN (2001). Communicating emotion in music performance: a review and a theoretical framework. In PN Juslin, JA Sloboda, eds, *Music and emotion: theory and research*, 309–337. Oxford University Press, Oxford.

Juslin PN and Laukka P (2004). Expression, perception and induction of musical emotions: a review and a questionnaire study of everyday listening. *Journal of New Music Research*, **33**, 217–238.

Karageorghis CI Jones L and Low DC (2006). Relationship between exercise, heart rate and music tempo preference. *Research Quarterly for Exercise and Sport*, **77**(2), 240–244.

Knight Foundation (2002). *Classical music consumer segmentation study: how Americans relate to classical music and their local orchestras*. John S. and James L. Knight Foundation, Miami, FL.

Kotsopoulou A and Hallam S (2006). Age differences in listening to music while studying. In M Baroni, AR Addessi, R Caterina and M Costa eds, *Proceedings of the 9th international conference on music perception and cognition*, University of Bologna, Bologna, Italy.

Lamont A (in preparation). University students' musical biographies and strong emotional experiences of music.

Laukka P (2007). Uses of music and psychological well-being among the elderly. *Journal of Happiness Studies*, **8**, 215–241.

Lesiuk T (2005). The effect of music listening on work performance. *Psychology of Music*, **33**(2), 173–191.

Liebowitz S (2004). Will MP3 downloads annihilate the record industry? The evidence so far. *Advances in the Study of Entrepreneurship, Innovation, and Economic Growth*, **V**(15), 229–260.

Linder S (1970). *The harried leisure class*. Columbia University Press, New York.

Mitchell LA and MacDonald RAR (2006). An experimental investigation of the effects of preferred and relaxing music listening on pain perception. *Journal of Music Therapy*, **XLIII**(4), 295–316.

Mitchell LA, MacDonald RAR, Knussen C and Serpell MG (2007). A survey investigation of the effects of music listening on chronic pain. *Psychology of Music*, **35**(1), 39–59.

Mitchell LA, MacDonald RAR and Brodie EE (2006). A comparison of the effects of preferred music, arithmetic and humour on cold pressor pain. *European Journal of Pain*, **10**, 343–351.

North AC and Hargreaves DJ (1996). Responses to music in aerobic exercise and yogic relaxation classes. *British Journal of Psychology*, **87**, 535–547.

North AC and Hargreaves DJ (2000). Musical preferences during and after relaxation and exercise. *American Journal of Psychology*, **113**, 43–67.

North AC and Hargreaves DJ (2007). Lifestyle correlates of musical preference: 1. Relationships, living arrangements, beliefs, and crime. *Psychology of Music*, **35**(1), 58–87.

North AC, Hargreaves DJ and Hargreaves JJ (2004). Uses of music in everyday life. *Music Perception*, **22**, 41–77.

North AC, Hargreaves DJ and O'Neill SA, (2000). The importance of music to adolescents. *British Journal of Educational Psychology*, **70**, 255–272.

Oldham G, Cummings A, Mischel L, Schmidtke J and Zhou J (1995). Listen while you work? Quasi-experimental relations between personal-stereo headset use and employee work responses. *Journal of Applied Psychology*, **80**(5), 547–564.

Pegg C (1984). Factors affecting the musical choices of audiences in East Suffolk, England. In R Middleton and D Horn, eds, *Popular music 4: performers and audiences*, 51–73. Cambridge University Press, Cambridge.

Pitts S (2005a). What makes an audience? Investigating the roles and experiences of listeners at a chamber music festival. *Music and Letters*, **86**(2), 257–269.

Pitts S (2005b). *Valuing musical participation*. Ashgate, Aldershot.

Pool MM, Koolstra CM and van der Voort THA (2003). The impact of background radio and television on high school students' homework performance, *Journal of Communication*, **53**(1), 74.

Rentfrow PJ and Gosling SD (2003). The do re mi's of everyday life. The structure and personality correlates of music preferences. *Journal of Personality and Social Psychology*, **84**(6), 1236–1256.

Rentfrow PJ and Gosling SD (2006). Message in a ballad: the role of musical preferences in interpersonal perception. *Psychological Science*, **17**(3), 236–242.

Reyner LA and Horne JA (1998). Evaluation of 'in-car' countermeasures to sleepiness: cold air and radio. *Sleep*, **21**(1), 46–50.

Riley M and Laing D (2006). *The value of jazz in Britain*. Arts Council England/Jazz Services, London.

Russell PA (1997). Musical tastes and society. In DJ Hargreaves and AC North, eds, *The social psychology of music*, 161–187. Oxford University Press, Oxford.

Siedliecki SL and Good M (2006). Effect of music on power, pain, depression and disability. *Journal of Advanced Nursing*, **54**(5), 553–562.

Sloboda JA (1992). Empirical studies of emotional response to music. In M Riess-Jones and S Holleran, eds, *Cognitive bases of musical communication*, 33–46. American Psychological Association, Washington, DC.

Sloboda JA (1999). Everyday uses of music listening: a preliminary study. In SW Yi, ed., *Music, mind and science*, 354–369. Western Music Institute, Seoul.

Sloboda JA, O'Neill SA and Ivaldi A (2001). Functions of music in everyday life: an exploratory study using the Experience Sampling Method. *Musicae Scientiae*, **V**, 9–32.

Stutts JC, Reinfurt DW, Staplin L and Rodgman EA (2001) *The role of driver distraction in traffic crashes*. Report prepared for the AAA foundation for traffic safety,

Washington, DC. www.aaafoundation.org/projects/index.cfm?button=distraction (consulted 14 August 2006).

Tarrant M, North AC and Hargreaves DJ (2001). Social categorisation, self-esteem, and the musical preferences of male adolescents. *Journal of Social Psychology*, **141**(5), 565–581.

Thompson S (2006). Audience responses to a live orchestral concert. *Musicae Scientiae*, **X**(2), 215–244.

Thompson S (2007). Determinants of listeners' enjoyment of a performance. Psychology of Music, 35(1), 20–36.

Turner ML, Fernandez JE and Nelson K (1996). The effect of music amplitude on the reaction to unexpected visual events. *Journal of General Psychology*, **123**, 51–62.

Zillmann D and Gan S (1997). Musical taste in adolescence. In DJ Hargreaves and AC North, eds, *The social psychology of music*, 161–187. Oxford University Press, Oxford.

CHAPTER 41

Music in performance arts
Film, theatre and dance

Annabel J. Cohen

Introduction

Music in performance arts: music that is not alone

Music is rarely alone (Cook 1998). Throughout civilization, it has typically been performed in conjunction with dance, poetic text, theatre, and, more recently, film and television (Cohen 1999). This chapter considers the psychology of music in the contexts of performance arts, in particular the arts of the moving image, drama, and dance. Research in the psychology of music far exceeds psychological research in any of the other arts. Within music psychology, research on the role of music in film and television constitutes a small but vibrant subdomain (e.g., Cohen 1994; Lipscomb 2008). The growing research on the psychology of film music reveals that the role of music in the context of other performance arts is amenable to psychological investigation. Similar progress can be envisioned for a psychology of music in theatre and dance where foundations are fortunately beginning to emerge (e.g., for dance Grove *et al.* 2005; for opera Boerner 2004). The present chapter may help to further set the stage for such work.

Nomenclature

The psychology of music usually focuses on the listener, but in fact visual and kinaesthetic senses usually play a role, be it watching the motion of the performer, sensing the ambiance of the venue, or tapping one's foot to a beat. Music for film, video, theatre and dance more obviously requires not only a *listener* but also a *viewer*. For participatory dance, a *mover* sensitive to kinaesthetic information, that is bodily motion, must also be considered. In the present chapter, the term *audience* refers to the generic member of an audience. Thus the statement *the mind of the audience* refers to the mind of a typical member of the group attending a performance (notwithstanding individual differences).

Music as part of a multimedia experience

The following section begins with a review of the role of music in film and television, taking a historical approach and considering the recent research in the field of music psychology. Next we will consider the role of music in dramatic contexts and finally dance performance and participatory social dance.

Moving images and the psychology of music

The art of moving images began in the early twentieth century just after the beginnings of experimental psychology which originated only a few decades earlier, and, like film, owed its progress to twentieth century technologies. Hugo Münsterberg of Harvard University was the first psychologist to take film seriously.

As indicated in his book *The Photoplay*, published in 1916, he believed that of all the arts, film was most like music from a structural and psychological standpoint, although theatre and photography more strongly resembled film on the surface than did music. Münsterberg also noted the value of music in film for relieving tension, maintaining interest, providing comfort, reinforcing emotion, and contributing to the aesthetic experience. Of course his views applied only to silent film as he predated the talking film. Although there is no psychological research on the role of music in the original silent film context, the conditions of the silent film (i.e., without dialogue and sound effects) simplify psychological studies of the role of music in film, and several researchers have taken advantage of this to study effects of music on interpretation, beginning with Marshall and Cohen (1988).

Marshall and Cohen (1988) asked whether two contrasting examples of background music would alter observers' attitudes toward characters in a short (2-minute) animation. The animation featured two triangles and a circle and had been used in social psychology research by Heider and Simmel (1944), who showed that typically viewers ascribe personality traits to these geometric 'characters' in systematic ways. For example, the larger triangle was regarded as a bully. Using semantic differential judgements (bipolar adjectives scales such as fast–slow, strong–weak), Marshall and Cohen showed that the ratings of the film overall and of the individual characters differed under the two types of music. For example, the rated activity of the small triangle was greater for one than for the other of the two types of music. Further examples of the role of music on the interpretation of silent film have been shown in studies of sense of closure (Thompson *et al.* 1994), the perceived aggressiveness–friendliness of wolves (Bolivar *et al.* 1994), and realistic clips of ambiguous human interactions (Bullerjahn and Güldenring 1994; Cohen 1993; Shevy 2007; Tan *et al.* 2007).

It was assumed that the advent of the talking film in 1927 would drive music for film into obsolescence. However, surprisingly, films without music were found lacking (Kalinak 1992, p. 45; Kracauer 1960, p. 138), and a new industry for recorded music for the talking film replaced the old industry of live musical accompaniment for the silent film. The movie industry soon recognized the importance of the music soundtrack. Recently, Simonton (2007) analysed the relation between success of over 400 award-winning films (as measured by ticket sales, awards, and critic ratings) and success (as indicated by awards) of film songs and film scores. He sampled data from seven professional organizations which give annual awards for film including film music, either best score or song or both, for example, the Academy of Motion Picture Arts and Sciences (Oscars), the British Academy of Film and TV Arts (BAFTAs), and the Online Film Critics Society. Success of score, but not film song, was positively correlated with receipt of the best picture award. The positive influence of the film score was as high as that for visual effects (e.g., cinematography, costumes, etc.) and for technical aspects, though all of these were less effective than dramatic components (e.g., best actor). Simonton (2007) suggested that a successful score contributes to the film narrative without drawing attention to itself, while a successful song may actually disrupt the narrative.

Tan and colleagues (2008) compared the effects of background and foreground music. In their study, a 1.25 minute action sequence from Spielberg's *Minority Report* (2002) was paired with three soundtracks: (1) the original soundtrack which belonged to the shopping mall environment of the action, (2) the same soundtrack presented as a background score, and (3) a second soundtrack presented as background score. There were 245 participants who completed rating scales following the presentation of each condition. Background music as compared to foreground music in a film led to different interpretations with respect to characters' emotions, relationship between characters, and mood of the scene. The study is the first to show that different specific effects of the music arise depending on whether the music is part of the foreground drama (known as the *diegesis*), or part of the background (*non-diegesis*).

Music in a film is typically non-diegetic, having no basis in the reality of the story (cf. Gorbman 1987). This non-diegetic function of music raises an important question for the psychology of music. How does the audience use this musical information and why does it add value to a film, as suggested by Simonton's (2007) correlational study of award-winning films and

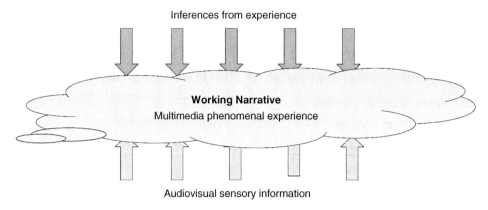

Fig. 41.1 Sensory and cognitive sources of information that contribute to the audience's creation of the experience of an arts performance

as consistent with the experience of most film-goers? The answer arises by considering that the audience does not aim to record all of the information impinging on the eye and ear. Rather, the audience seeks sufficient information to support engagement and entertainment, making use of two sources of information: sensory information arising from the real world presentation and past experience residing in long-term memory (see Figure 41.1). The audience is constantly synthesizing a story, a working narrative, derived jointly from sensory information and hypotheses or expectations based on long-term memory. According to this model, then, the audience takes what is needed from music and discards or ignores the rest. Given the capacity limitations of the mind (Miller 1956), including in multimedia settings (Fisch 2000; Mayer 2005; Sweller 2005), the audience has really no other choice. This approach is basic to Cohen's Congruence–Association Model of music in multimedia contexts, to be described later.

Film information other than music, such as the film's visual images, speech or sound effects, have been regarded as less effective than music in communicating emotional meaning (cf. discussion of music as the most efficient code for emotional expression in film by film-music theorist Kalinak [1992, p. 87]). The actual sounds of the music used to convey emotion are irrelevant to the story and consequently to the audience. Thus, acoustical information from the music can be discarded as far as engagement in film is considered. The sound of the music may be registered but not as an essential component of the story.

The integration of film and music within the constraints of mental capacity may also be viewed from the perspective of two analytic processes (Cohen 2005; Marshall and Cohen 1988). The first focuses on the *structural* aspects of the media: how patterns of information change in time and space (for example, rhythms of loudness and pitch, visual movement, visual intensity, colour, and contour). Marshall and Cohen (1988) argued that the temporal congruence of musical and visual patterns directed attention to specific elements of animation, and thus visual attention patterns could differ as a function of the particular pattern of music–visual congruency.

Several researchers have explored structural congruency of music and film. Lipscomb (2005) showed influences of temporal audiovisual alignment on judged effectiveness of simple visual animations. Kendall (2005, 2008) defined specific iconic archetypal forms (e.g., arch and ramp) which apply in both musical and spatial domains and has noted that judged congruence of visual and auditory versions of these forms is higher for some forms (e.g. arch) than others. Kim and Iwamiya (2008) examined the effect of formal congruency between sound patterns and animated text (Telops) using materials from television programmes as well as computer synthesis. They distinguished two kinds of formal congruency: similarity in temporal accent pattern and similarity in other changes (e.g., augmentation). In a related follow-up study, Iwamiya (2008) noted that increased formal congruency led to increased subjective congruency and as well influenced the evaluation (goodness) of the visual form. On a larger scale, musicologist Kulezić-Wilson (2005) has recently explored the notion of the musicality of the structure of film, with specific emphasis on temporality, rhythm and kinesis. She analysed two recent films (Jim Jarmusch's *Dead Man* and Darren Aronofsky's *Pi*) focusing on the opposing aesthetic choices of the shot and the cut, and this work begs for psychological research to test the human sensitivity to the structures described. Cohen (2002) noted the rondo-like structure of *The Red Violin* and suggested comparable music and film research to explore its cognitive and aesthetic effects.

The second aspect of film and music for analysis is *meaning*. Earlier in this section, studies of film music were referred to that showed the effect of music on interpretation of a film, film characters or depicted world. The music can also lead to the feeling of emotions, which is an aspect of meaning that can often be best measured physiologically. Thayer and Levenson (1983) showed that background film scores were successful in both reducing and increasing electrodermal (skin conductance) responses to a stressful film. Baumgartner *et al.* (2006) have shown that classical music (as compared to no music) enhanced the emotional meaning of and physiological response (skin conductance, heart rate, respiration, and EEG) to emotional visual images taken from the International Affective Picture System (IAPS). Related work has been reported by Spreckelmeyer *et al.* (2006) who measured brain evoked potentials (ERP) to brief (350–550 ms) presentations of happy or sad emotional IAPS scenes and happy or sad single tones sung by trained opera singers. Participants focused on either the visual or auditory information and were required to rate the emotional meaning. Influence of integration of the two modalities was seen in ERP waves as early as 150 ms. The brain-wave recordings were more sensitive than were the ratings of the emotional valence. The visual scenes had a greater influence on the judgements while focusing on the audio than did the audio stimuli while focusing on the visual modality. These studies pave the way to research with actual video (as opposed to pictorial) and music materials so as to reveal the underlying music–video integration process.

The research suggests that integration occurs quickly and that the brain treats the emotional meaning of visual and auditory material similarly, with sensory (audio or visual) dominance likely depending on the relative salience of the materials.

Marshall and Cohen (1988) proposed the Congruence–Associationist model to accommodate the two analytic processes for structure and meaning, arguing that structural congruencies direct attention to particular elements of a film scene, and that the associations (meaning) from the music are then ascribed to this direction of attention. In light of research on comprehension in other fields (e.g., Kintsch 1998, for text comprehension), Cohen (2001) expanded the model to emphasize the audience's narrative purpose in viewing a media presentation. She proposed that the audience is constantly engaged in generating a *working narrative*, a story of the unfolding drama. The working narrative is the audience's experience of a film. Cues from music as well as from the other sources of information contribute to the working narrative. The second expansion of the model accommodated a notion of the influential French film theorist Christian Metz. Metz gave prominence to music as one of five channels relevant to the experience of film: text, visual scenes, speech, sound effects (noise), and music (described by film theorist Stam 2000). The Congruence–Associationist model thus included these five channels as seen in Figure 41.2.

Marilyn Boltz (2004) conducted research on the role of music in television, and interpreted her results with respect to the Congruence–Associationist Model which she referred to as the C-A Model (to be referred to hereafter as CAM). In Boltz'study, 72 participants were presented with short (approximately 4 min) audiovisual television clips for which the music was presented as either mood congruent or incongruent. They were asked to attend to the audio track, the video track, or to both tracks. Subsequently, they were tested for their memory of the visual film clips and the music excerpts. Performance in the mood-congruent condition was superior to that of the incongruent condition. Performance in the incongruent condition was good for the attended audio or visual medium but did not extend to the unintended

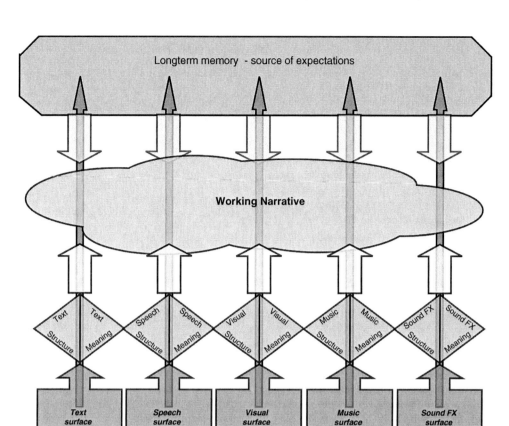

Fig. 41.2 Congruence–Associationist framework for understanding film-music communication (see text for explanation).

medium as it did when the mood of the music and video clip coincided. According to Boltz, congruence in mood of the music and film elicited a search for similar structural properties in the music and film, and the success of the search led to jointly encoding the music and visual material and an integrated music–video memory. Thus, memory for music information would mean memory for the visual information. However, without mood congruencies, attention to the entire music visual complex suffers as the focus is on only one of the modalities (as per instructions in the experiment) and attention is not automatically directed to the other modality which conveys incongruent meaning.

Arguing that an effective working narrative leads to audience absorption or involvement in the film, our laboratory has aimed to determine the role of music in engaging the audience in the film, a phenomenon with which most moviegoers can identify. Two procedures were developed. One is a direct method in which the audience is asked to rate their level of absorption in a film clip presented under different conditions of music. Cohen *et al.* (2005) have shown higher absorption in the presence versus absence of music in short excerpts of several types of genre (e.g., animation, soap opera, drama). As predicted, more realistic genres (such as news) did not show the effect, although the relation between impact of music on absorption and realism of the genre was non-linear, no doubt a result of numerous variables arising from the specific examples chosen. Cohen *et al.* (2006), also explored the relative contributions of the three audio channels–sound effects, dialogue, and music–on self-rated absorption using two contrasting 1-minute clips (from *Witness* and *Day of the Jackal*) presented with only one type of auditory background. Heightened absorption in the presence of music, as opposed to speech and sound effects, was noted for the *Witness* clip that used music which had originally accompanied it in the film.

The second methodology for studying the role of music on absorption in film is less direct, and is based on the rationale that higher absorption (arising from a more compelling working narrative) will increase the difficulty of detecting extraneous information. Cohen *et al.* (2008) have tested this idea using the Canadian National Film Board 'silent' film *The Railrodder* (1965) (starring Buster Keaton; original music composed by the eminent Eldon Rathburn). There were 72 participants assigned to one of three music background conditions (original, inappropriate, no music). While watching the 20-minute film, they responded with a key-press when an 'X' appeared in a random location of the computer screen on 20 occasions. The film was presented twice. Consistent with the hypothesis, the original music, as compared to no music, led to slower response time. On the second presentation, the original music also led to slower responses than inappropriate music. Individual scores on the Tellegen (1982) Absorption Scale correlated negatively with hit rate, validating the detection task as a measure of absorption.

The paradigms that have been developed for studying music perception and cognition in the context of film have thus begun to reveal the effects of music on meaning, memory, structural judgments, physiological variables, and absorption (involvement). The Congruence–Associationist model has been proposed to accommodate these data and suggest testable hypotheses. All of this may be useful in addressing the role of music in other performance art forms of theatre and dance.

Theatre

The role of music in opera, musical theatre, and other dramatic genres has received little attention from researchers in music psychology, in contrast to that which has focused on film and video. Part of the reason for this arises from the live nature of theatre, which makes replication of experimental conditions difficult. Nevertheless, many questions raised by music in theatrical contexts in fact could be studied.

Opera is among the most ambitious and complex of the performance art forms. It entails an orchestral score, soloists, ensemble, libretto, sets, dance, as well as epic dramatic themes. How the mind integrates and appreciates such rich information should be of great interest to psychologists in general and to music psychology in particular.

In an analysis of several indicators of success of an opera (e.g., performance and recording frequency) Simonton (2000) found that the music is aesthetically more critical to opera than is the libretto. Gregory (1998) conducted a study of opera music in which listeners showed the changes in the strength of their emotional response to a selection of opera arias by moving a mouse whose position indicated high or low emotion on a computer screen. They also completed emotional adjective checklists. Consistency among listeners was shown, and higher emotion was elicited by voice than by the orchestra alone. Similar studies with video recording or in a live situation beg to be conducted.

Boerner (2004) proposed a hierarchical componential framework of performance quality in opera, emphasizing a distinction between the musical and staging aspects. The audience is viewed as judging the congruence of musical and staging dimension, congruence within these separate dimensions (the relation between soloists, choir, and orchestra), congruence within the individual components (relation among soloists). The author admits the concept congruence here, based on Adorno, is vague and in need of operationalism. A questionnaire study of audience assessment of live opera (Verdi's *La forz del destino*) supported Boerner's componential model, but suggested that staging contributed more to the judgments than did the music (Boerner *et al.* 2008). While this seems paradoxical, particularly in the face of Simonton's evidence for the importance of the music in opera, the authors suggest that high quality of the music is assumed by the audience, while the quality and type of staging is more variable and thus gains greater conscious attention. The authors note the importance of further related research that would explore different operas and control for individual differences.

It would also be of interest to apply this methodology to musical theatre, which bears similarities to opera yet has notable differences which might be regarded in terms of reduced cognitive load (e.g., use of popular musical style and native language). Music is also occasionally found in dramatic works. For example, Mendelssohn composed music specifically for Shakespeare's *A Midsummer Night's Dream*. Frankly, however, the psychology of music knows little about the role of music in musical theatre and in drama, and the field is wide open to exploration on the more microanalytic level using paradigms from film-music research or at the level of audience appreciation as recently developed for opera.

Dance

With the advent of film and video recorders, progress in dance research seems more secure than in the past, now that dance performances and choreography can be preserved. Jordan (2000, p. 102) however emphasizes that no single source of information about dance provides an adequate basis for research, as each form of representation highlights some aspects at the expense of others. Notation systems for dance, such as Labanotation and Benesh, have both selective and subjective components.

With few exceptions, classical ballet entails dancing to music. Choreographers have varied in the significance they attach to the structure of the music and the function of ballet in representing this structure. The Russian choreographer Fedor Lopukhov (1886–1973) influenced the development of dance as a non-narrative art form (cf. Jordan 2002) which gave full importance to the structure of music. Lopukhov prescribed matching dance to music on the dimensions of emotional climaxes, curve, colour, and key changes. Major and minor keys were to be treated differently, 'en dehors' and 'en dedans' respectively. Lopukhov was an influence on Ballanchine, who danced in one of Lopukhov's famous works, 'Dance Symphony' (Jordan 2002, p. 3). Contemporaneous with these two eminent choreographers is Jacques-Dalcroze, the Swiss pedagogue who shared the basic principle of the structural similarities of music and human motion. He believed that the best way to understand and learn about music was to experience the elements of music with the body. His curriculum, known as Dalcroze Eurhythmics, has been taught to generations of young people worldwide. Recent attention has been directed to Dalcroze from the perspectives of psychology, developmental education, and African musical pedagogy respectively (Seitz 2005; Juntunen and Hyvönen 2004; Phuthego 2005) supporting the significance of Dalcroze' ideas, and implying the need for empirical research that will validate intuitions about the connections between bodily motion and musical understanding.

A pioneering psychological study of the interaction between music and dance is provided by Krumhansl and Schenk (1997) who used a film of Balanchine's choreography of Mozart's Divertimento No. 15 to test whether dance could represent the structural and expressive qualities of music. Three groups of participants were asked to watch the choreography alone, listen to the music without seeing the dance, or watch the dance and listen to the music simultaneously. All three groups then rated the tension and emotion throughout the piece as well as indicated the beginnings and endings of phrases. Results showed agreement among all three groups and additivity of the information from the separate channels of music and dance: the response in the 'music and dance' condition could be predicted as a combination of the responses to the 'music only' and 'dance only' conditions. The generality of these results to other works of dance would be worth exploring in view of the fact that the particular work chosen by Ballanchine was one in which the choreography was treated with great sensitivity to music-theoretic structural parallels.

Mitchell and Gallaher (2001) examined the ability to detect a 'match' between a piece of music and its intended choreography. The musical pieces were by John Cage, Peter Gabriel, and David Lanz, and the dances were choreographed and performed by a university-level dance educator. Participants were presented with a piece of choreography in silence followed by three selections of music. They were then asked to choose the musical selection that best matched the choreography. The reverse condition, in which the music was presented followed by three examples of dance, was also tested. Participants were also presented with a piece of choreography paired with a piece of music, either intended or not intended to go with it. In both the sequential and simultaneous test format Mitchell and Gallaher's results show consistently high ratings for perceiving a 'match' between a piece of music and choreography intended to go with it. Participants' answers to a questionnaire indicated that their matches were influenced by similar characteristics perceived in the media, 'including emotion, fluidity, an African or Middle Eastern quality, and temporal characteristics such as rhythm and pace'. The results indicated that memory for dance was sufficient to enable judgements of congruence with musical excerpts presented later, and that the basis for judged music–dance congruence generalized across participants in the study and was multidimensional.

Based on both the work of Mitchell and Gallaher (2001) and that of a dance theorist, Fogelsanger and Afanador (2006) propose four parallels between music and dance that may contribute to a sense of congruency:

1 matching or intertwining pulse or rhythm

2 alignment of coincident structural temporal aspects other than pulse

3 analogous cross-modal qualities

4 complementary referents.

It is notable that the first two items refer to structural characteristics, while the latter refer to associations or meanings, which echoes a distinction made earlier between structure and meaning in the discussion of film and music. Dance can represent structure for its own sake (e.g., choreography of George Ballanchine) and be independent of typical narrative plot but can also tell a story through pantomime and other symbolic movement, such as the story of *Coppelia, les Sylphides, the Nutcracker*, or a *Midsummers Night's Dream*.

As such the proposal of Folgelsanger and Afanador (2006) fits within the CAM framework and is amenable to psychological test, for example, to determine whether in fact these parallel aspects of music and dance lead to perceived congruency, and whether some dimensions of congruency are more salient than others. While it is appreciated that music–dance structural congruence is hardly a universal choregraphic

goal, it is still important to know what congruencies are discernable by an audience and what impact they have on appreciation. In regard to audience appreciation of choreography, Renee Glass completed a doctoral thesis which developed a qualitative and quantitative questionnaire (Audience Response Tool, ART) to determine audience responses to contemporary dance. The dances she examined entailed sound effects but not music in the traditional sense, but the tool in theory could be applied to dances in which music played a role.

Ivar Hagendoorn (2004) has recently proposed that the experience of watching dance creates pleasure for us through the fulfilling and undermining of our expectations. Viewers of a dancer to some extent sense the dancer's movement as if they were doing it themselves. Hagendoorn's proposal of a neurobiological system for a kinaesthetic response to dance aligns with recent evidence for mirror neurons which respond equally to an action carried out by the organism or simply from viewing such action (Rizzolatti and Craighero 2004). However, other research on biological motion detection by Troje (2002) accounts for perception of biological motion without having to call into play mirror neurons. Brown *et al.* (2006) in a unique if not extraordinary positron emission tomography (PET)-scan study of experienced dancers of tango localized a portion of the brain known as the cerebellar vermis that enables entrainment of dance steps to music as opposed to self-paced movement.

Whereas classical ballet and modern dance are performance art for the stage, social dance is an avenue open to and taken by most individuals by their adolescence or early adulthood. In spite of both the prevalence of social dance as an aspect of human behaviour and the reliance on music for this activity, there has been almost no attention of music psychology directed to the social dance situation. Music in the context of social dance in a sense legitimates patterns of human interaction that might seem ridiculous or embarrassing otherwise. Music is at least one of the components in social settings that allows people to behave differently than they otherwise would. The permission-giving power of music may result from effects of music that engage more emotional as opposed to analytic processing

(Niedenthal *et al.* 1999). Cross (2007, p 660) has suggested that

> music's powers of entrainment, together with its 'floating intentionality', fit it for use as a medium for communicative interactions in which meanings are under-determined to the extent that participants are free to develop their own interpretations of the significance of their own, and others', contribution to the collective musical behaviour.

Concluding comments: future research, trans-art congruencies, and lifespan experience

Because music occurs frequently in the context of other arts, a model of music perception and cognition must take these other domains into account. The next decades may well see research programmes on the promising frontiers of the psychology of opera, musical theatre, and dance that will match the recent research activity of the psychology of music and the moving image.

The psychology of music and the moving image may also do well to take note of recent research in opera and dance which aims at a global understanding of what the audience appreciates.

For all of the performance contexts for music, a recurrent concept is that of congruence: congruence between music structures and structure within the visual or kinaesthetic dimensions, congruence of meaning, and congruence that refers to the gestalt or sense of the whole. Thus, questions remain about the perceptual and cognitive responses elicited by these similarities between the music, visual, and kinaesthetic domains, and the temporal course of any integration processes.

Yet another aspect that will need attention is that of the role of individual experience of the audience member and when in the life course this experience occurs. A final diagram is therefore offered to reflect both the chronometric and synchronic dimensions of a general model of the audience engaged in music and the performance arts (Figure 41.3). This model, though very abstract, conceptualizes the mind of the audience as actively engaged in performances in

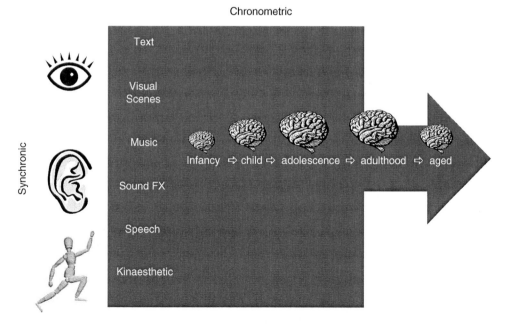

Fig. 41.3 The Congruence–Associationist Model (CAM) in a developmental context. The kinaesthetic sense has been added to accommodate its significance as referred to in the text.

the arts and affected by such engagement in different ways across the lifespan.

Author note and acknowledgements

The Social Sciences and Humanities Research Council is acknowledged for its support of the author's program of research in the psychology of film music.

References

Baumgartner T, Esslen M and Jäncke L (2006). From emotion perception to emotion experience: emotions evoked by pictures and classical music. *International Journal of Psychophysiology*, **60**, 34–43.

Boerner S (2004). Artistic quality in an opera company: toward the development of a concept. *Nonprofit Management and Leadership*, **14**, 425–436.

Boerner S, Neuhoff H, Renz S and Moser V (2008). Evaluation of music theatre: empirical results on content and structure of the audience's quality judgment. *Empirical Studies of the Arts*, **26**, 15–35.

Bolivar VJ, Cohen AJ and Fentress JC (1994). Semantic and formal congruency in music and motion pictures: effects on the interpretation of visual action. *Psychomusicology*, **13**, 28–59.

Boltz M (2004). The cognitive processing of film and musical soundtracks. *Memory and Cognition*, **32**, 1194–1205.

Brown S, Martinez MJ and Parsons LM (2006). The neural basis of human dance. *Cerebral Cortex*, **16**, 1157–1167.

Bullerjahn C and Güldenring M (1994). An empirical investigation of effects of film music using qualitative content analysis. *Psychomusicology*, **13**, 99–118.

Cohen AJ (1993). Associationism and musical soundtrack phenomena. *Contemporary Music Review*, **9**, 163–178.

Cohen AJ (ed) (1994). The psychology of film music. Special volume, *Psychomusicology*, **13**, 1–165.

Cohen AJ (1999). The functions of music in multimedia: a cognitive approach. In SW Yi, ed., *Music, mind, and science*, 53–69. Seoul National University Press, Seoul, Korea.

Cohen AJ (2001). Music as a source of emotion in film. In PN Juslin, JA Sloboda, eds, *Music and emotion*, 249–272. Oxford University Press, Oxford.

Cohen AJ (2002). Music cognition and the cognitive psychology of film structure. *Canadian Psychology*, **43**, 215–232.

Cohen AJ (2005). How music influences the interpretation of film and video: approaches from experimental psychology. In RA Kendall and RW Savage, eds, *Selected reports in ethnomusicology: special issue in systematic musicology*, **12**, 15–36.

Cohen AJ, Macmillan KA and Drew R (2005). The role of music on absorption in film and video: effects of genre. Poster presented at Neuroscience and Music II. Leipzig.

Cohen AJ, MacMillan KA and Drew R (2006). The role of music, sound effects and speech on absorption in a film: the congruence–associationist model of media cognition. *Canadian Acoustics*, **34**, 40–41.

Cohen AJ and Siau, Y-M (2008). The Narrative Role of Music in Multimedia Presentations: The Congruence-Association Model (CAM) of Music and Multimedia. In K. Miyazaki, M. Adachi, Y. Hiraga, Y. Nakajima and M. Tsuzaki (eds), Proceedings of the 10th International Conference on Music Perception & Cognition (ICMPC10), August 2008, Sapporo Japan. Adelaide: Causal Productions. CD-ROM.

Cook N (1998). *Analysing musical multimedia*. Clarendon Press, Oxford.

Cross I (2007). *Music and cognitive evolution*. In RIM Dunbar, L Barrett, eds, *Oxford handbook of evolutionary psychology*, 649–667. Oxford University Press, Oxford.

Fisch SM (2000). A capacity model of children's comprehension of educational content on television. *Media Psychology*, **2**, 63–91.

Fogelsanger A and Afanador K (2006). Parameters of perception: vision, audition, and twentieth-century music an d dance. 38th Congress on Research in Dance, Tempe, Arizona.

Gorbman C (1987). *Unheard melodies: narrative film music*. Indiana University Press, Bloomington, IL.

Gregory AH (1998). Tracking the emotional response to operatic arias. In SW Yi, ed., *Fifth ICMPC Proceedings*, 265–270. Seoul National University, Seoul.

Grove R, Stevens C and McKechnie S (eds) (2005). *Thinking in four dimensions: creativity and cognition in contemporary dance*. Melbourne University Press, Melbourne, AU.

Hagendoorn I (2004). Some speculative hypotheses about the nature and perception of dance and choreography. *Journal of Consciousness Studies*, **11**, 79–110.

Heider F & Simmel M (1944). An experimental study of apparent behavior. *American Journal of Psychology*, **57**, 243–259.

Iwamiya S (2008). Subjective congruence between moving picture and sound. Paper submitted to S Lipscomb (organizer-invited session) Experiencing musical multimedia: empirical investigations of cross-modal perception and cognition organized by S Lipscomb for the 10th International Conference on Music Perception and Cognition, Hokkaido, Japan.

Jordan S (2000). *Moving music: dialogues with music in twentieth-century ballet*. Dance Books, London.

Jordan, S (2002) *Writings on Ballet and Music, Fedor Lopukhov, Studies in Dance History*, Madison, Wisconsin: University of Wisconsin Press.

Juntunen M-L and Hyvönen L (2004), Embodiment in musical knowing: How body movement facilitates learning with Dalcroze Eurythmics, *British Journal of Music Education* 21 (2), 199–214.

Kalinak K (1992). *Settling the score*. University of Wisconsin Press, Madison, WI.

Kendall RA (2005). Empirical approaches to musical meaning. In RA Kendall and R Savage (eds). *Selected Reports in Ethnomusicology*, **12**, 69–102.

Kendall R (2008). Stratification of musical and visual structures ii: visual and pitch contours. Paper submitted to S Lipscomb (organizer-invited session) Experiencing musical multimedia: empirical investigations of cross-modal perception and cognition organized by S Lipscomb for the 10th International Conference on Music Perception and Cognition, Hokkaido, Japan.

Kim K-H and Iwamiya S-I (2008). Formal congruency between telop patterns and sounds effects. *Music Perception*, **25**, 429–448.

Kintsch W (1998). *Comprehension: a paradigm for cognition*. Cambridge University Press, Cambridge.

Kracauer S (1960). *Theory of film: the redemption of physical reality*. Oxford University Press, Oxford.

Krumhansl CL and DL Schenck (1997). Can dance reflect the structural and expressive qualities of music? A perceptual experiment on Balanchine's choreography of Mozart's Divertimento No. 15. *Musicae Scientiae*, **1**, 63–85.

Kulezić-Wilson D (2005). Composing on screen: the musicality of film. Unpublished Dissertation. Faculty of Art, Design and Humanities of the University of Ulster.

Lipscomb S (2005). The perception of audio-visual composites: accent structure alignment of simple stimuli. *Selected Reports in Ethnomusicology*, **12**, 37–67.

Lipscomb S (2008). (Organizer-invited session) Experiencing musical multimedia: empirical investigations of cross-modal perception and cognition. 10th International Conference on Music Perception and Cognition, Hokkaido, Japan.

Marshall S and Cohen AJ (1988). Effects of musical soundtracks on attitudes to geometric figures. *Music Perception*, **6**, 95–112.

Mayer RE (2005). Cognitive theory of multimedia learning. In R. E. Mayer (ed.) *Cambridge handbook of multimedia learning* (31-48). New York, NY: Cambridge.

Miller GA (1956). The magical number seven plus or minus two: Some limits on our capacity for processing information. *Psychological Review*, **63**, 81–97.

Mitchell RW and MC Gallaher (2001). Embodying music: matching music and dance in memory. *Music Perception*, **19**, 65–85.

Münsterberg H (1916/1970). *The photoplay: a psychological study*. Arno, New York.

Niedenthal PM, Halberstadt JB and Innes-Ker AH (1999). Emotional response categorization. *Psychological Review*, **106**, 337–361.

Phuthego M (2005). Teaching and learning African music and Jaques-Dalcroze's eurhythmics. *International Journal of Music Eduction*, **23**, 239–248.

Rizzolatti G and Craighero I (2004). The mirror-neuron system. *Annual Review of Neuroscience*, **27**, 169–92.

Seitz J (2005) Dalcroze, the body, movement and musicality. *Psychology of Music*, **33**, 419–435.

Shevy M (2007). The mood of rock music affects evaluation of video elements differing in valence and dominance. *Psychomusicology*, **19**(2), 57–78.

Simonton DK (2000). The music or the words? Or how important is the libretto for an opera's aesthetic success? *Empirical Studies of the Arts*, **18**, 105–118.

Simonton DK (2007). Film music: are award-winning scores and songs heard in successful motion pictures? *Psychology of Aesthetics, Creativity, and the Arts*, **1**(2), 53–60.

Spreckelmeyer K, Kutas M and Urbach T (2006). Combined perception of emotion in pictures and musical sounds. *Brain Research*, **1070**, 160–170.

Stam R (2000). *Film theory: an introduction*. Blackwell, Malden, MA.

Sweller J (2005). Implications of cognitive load theory for multimedia learning. In RE Mayer, ed., *Cambridge handbook of multimedia learning*, 19–30. Cambridge University Press, New York.

Tan S-L, Spackman MP and Bezdek MA (2007). Viewers' interpretation of film characters' emotions: effects of presenting film music before or after a character is shown. *Music Perception*, **25**, 135–152.

Tan S-L, Spackman MP and Wakefield EM (2008). Source of film music (diegetic or non-diegetic) affects viewers' interpretation of film. In Miyazali et al. (eds.), Proceedings of the 10th International Conference on Music Perception & Cognition (ICMPC10), August 2008, Sapporo, Japan. Adelaide: Causal Productions. CD-Rom.

Tellegen A (1982). *Brief manual for the Differential Personality Questionnaire*. Unpublished manuscript, University of Minnesota, Minneapolis.

Thayer JF and Levenson R (1983). Effects of music on psychophysiological responses to a stressful film. *Psychomusicology*, **3**, 44–54.

Thompson WF, Russo FA and Sinclair D (1994). Effects of underscoring on the perception of closure in filmed events. *Psychomusicology*, **13**, 9–27.

Troje NF (2002). Decomposing biological motion: a framework for analysis and synthesis of human gait patterns. *Journal of Vision*, **2**, 371–387.

CHAPTER 42

Peak experiences in music

John Whaley, John Sloboda and Alf Gabrielsson

Introduction

Many people experience intensely positive affective states in response to music. The intensity of these experiences often brings about a sense of transcendence and transformation, and their relative rarity makes them greatly prized in the minds and lives of the individuals experiencing them. People tend to retain vivid memories of such experiences many years after they have occurred, and they are often cited as a major reason for continued involvement with music (to increase the chances of such an experience occurring again: see e.g. Sloboda [2005]). Yet these are 'everyday' experiences in the sense that they seem to require no special context in which to occur. They may occur in the home, while travelling, in places of work or study, or in the more specialized contexts of concert hall or place of worship. They may be triggered by any genre of music, and during both listening and performance. Peak experiences also seem to require no specific musical training or expertise; they have been described by young and old, by the learned and the musically unlettered. Moreover, these experiences are not conjured by acts of will or intention—they usually come unannounced and unexpected—and thus cannot be the subject of skill acquisition or pedagogy.

Maslow (1959) was one of the first to formalize the study of what he called Peak Experiences, or 'moments of highest happiness and fulfilment' (1999, p. 85), and 'a spurt in which the powers of the person come together in a particularly efficient and intensely enjoyable way'

(1999, p. 106). Maslow spent many years studying peak experiences, and his findings laid the groundwork upon which all peak literature is built. While his investigations were not limited to musical triggers, he discovered very early that 'the two easiest ways of getting peak experiences [are] through music and sex' (1976, p. 169), and it is upon the former that this chapter is based.

What follows highlights research on the peak experience, emphasizing literature focusing on music-specific peaks. After outlining four studies fundamental to the study of peaks in music, a section will discuss precursors to peaks and proposed differences between those who have achieved peaks and those who have not. A section on the cognitive, perceptual, emotional, and physical phenomena associated with peak experiences will then be followed by an investigation on the after-effects of peaks. Next, a section discussing methodologies for the investigation of musical peak experiences highlights the possibilities and difficulties of this work. Finally, a brief section summarizes the contents of the chapter and looks towards the future of research in this field.

Fundamental peak experience in music literature

Four studies represent the empirical backbone of the study of the musical peak experience. As these will be heavily referenced in each subsequent section, a brief description here of their methods and findings is helpful.

Maslow coined the term 'peak experience' after analysing 190 written and 80 oral responses, having asked participants for descriptions of

the most wonderful experience of your life; happiest moments, ecstatic moments, moments of rapture, perhaps from being in love, or from listening to music, or suddenly 'being hit' by a book or painting, or from some great creative moment.

(1999, p. 83)

The contents of the experiences were individually unique, and in reporting his findings the author 'added together all the partial responses to make a "perfect" composite syndrome' (1999, p. 83). Beyond arguing that music is a reliable trigger of peak experiences, Maslow describes many of the phenomena experienced both during and after the peak, and asserts that: the peak experience is a self-validating, self-justifying moment with its own intrinsic value. It fills an individual with a sense of wonder and awe. Peaks are never negative, unpleasant, or evil, and cause a characteristic disorientation of time and space as well as a loss of fear, anxiety, doubts, and inhibitions. Frequently eliciting sudden feelings of happiness and well-being, peaks also bring about a heightened sense of an individual's physical and 'existential' state of being, a sort of positive hyper self-awareness. After a peak the individual may experience a number of effects, including a more positive view of the self, other people, and the world, various therapeutic effects (both physical and mental), even a sense that life itself is worth living.

In an effort to analyse art-specific peaks, Panzarella (1980) gathered reports of an 'intense joyous experience of listening to music or looking at visual art' (p. 71) from a pool largely composed of musicians and visual artists. Roughly half of responses were music-related. Content analysis revealed 11 response categories that were factored into four major dimensions of the experience: renewal ecstasy, motor-sensory ecstasy, withdrawal ecstasy, and fusion-emotional ecstasy: renewal ecstasy concerned a new or altered perception of the world and a desire to engage further with the artistic medium. Any physical elements like tears, changed heart rhythms, chills, or quasi-physical elements like a floating sensation were categorized as motor-sensory ecstasy. Withdrawal ecstasy involved a perceptual narrowing, during which there was a sense that everything disappeared except the object (i.e. music or art) and that the object was in perfect focus. Finally, fusion-emotion ecstasy referred to a 'fusion' with the medium, like a sense that the music or painting merged and became 'one' with the individual. Panzarella (1980) also argues that the peak experience has three distinct 'temporal stages', beginning with 'cognitive responses and loss of self; climaxing with continued loss of self and motor responses; and subsiding with emotional responses, [and] self-transformations' (p. 69). Various precursors and aftereffects of the 'joyous experience' are also reported.

Ecstasy was also a central theme in an earlier study by Laski (1961), who collected 63 incidents of 'transcendent ecstasy'. Triggers of such experiences included childbirth, sex, art, beauty, science, and religion, though the author concludes that 'of all the more common triggers to ecstasy, music would be the most rewarding to study in any attempt to find a relation between the qualities of the triggers and the effects produced' (p. 190). The contents of these episodes were collapsed into four categories: feelings of loss (e.g. sense of time, space, self, sorrow), feelings of gain (e.g. joy, salvation, perfection, unity with music or mankind, knowledge), feelings of ineffability (the experience eludes description or analysis), and quasi-physical feelings (e.g. peace, pain, light, heat).

To date, the most comprehensive attempt to understand exceptional experiences with music is the Strong Experiences of Music (SEM) project conducted by Gabrielsson and Lindström Wik (1993, 2000, 2003). This project makes use of over 1000 free descriptions of strong experiences in connection with music, collected and content-analysed over more than 10 years. Participants were asked, in as much detail as they could, to describe 'the strongest, most intense experience of music that [they had] ever had' (2003, p. 163). The resulting wealth of data culminated in the Strong Experiences of Music Descriptive System (SEM-DS), which lists the most common attributes of strong experiences in music and includes seven categories: general characteristics, physical reactions, perception, cognition, feeling/emotion, existential/transcendental, and personal/social. These attributes, which will be further discussed on p. 455–7 of this chapter, provide significant insight into the nature of the strong experience, what occurs *during* the experience. Various other publications using SEM data discuss other aspects of the experience, including therapeutic after-effects (Gabrielsson and Lindström 1995), emotions (Gabrielsson 2001), experiences reported by old people (Gabrielsson 2002), and musical triggers (Gabrielsson 2006).

A note about nomenclature is necessary. Maslow's (1999) peak experience, Laski's (1961) ecstasy, Panzarella's (1980) joyous experience, and Gabrielsson and Lindström-Wik's (2003) strong experience are not identical concepts. For instance, peak experiences are, by definition, positive, whereas some strong experiences are negative. In addition, one could argue for a separation between *exceptional* experiences (like strong, ecstatic, or joyous) and true *peak experiences* which, thanks to Maslow, have a slightly more stringent definition.

Recognizing these inherent problems, we focus this chapter on 'peak experience in music' for two reasons: First, the term peak experience is a recognized term within the broad psychological literature. A term such as joyous experience is not in common use. Second, although there are negative experiences triggered by music, we would argue that positive experience is the most frequent and prototypical case, from which negative experiences may be considered a deviation, or a special case. However, we do not intend to restrict this discussion to any single, strictly defined term. We recognize the overlap amongst these terms, and accept the fact that no single term or definition fully captures the experience discussed here, be it peak, strong, optimal, ecstatic, or otherwise.

Precursors and predictors of the peak experience

Maslow (1976) concluded that 'any experience of real excellence, of real perfection. ... tends to produce a peak experience', but immediately and frustratingly added 'though not always' (p. 17). Peak experience literature is full of such qualifications, and has shown mixed results with

regard to the demographic, situational, and musical differences between those who have achieved peaks (henceforth referred to as 'peakers') and those who have not ('non-peakers').

Maslow stated that only the self-actualized, i.e. those who had achieved the highest level of his hierarchy of needs (1943), were capable of enjoying a peak experience, as it was a 'momentary intensification of their general tendency to apprehend reality more directly and clearly' (1999, p. 19). Lacking a strict definition of self-actualization, subsequent research identified some general personality characteristics of peakers which include openness, tender-mindedness, flexibility, an experimental nature, an interest in creative work and a holistic, interpersonal, and emotional approach (Masluk 1999; Mathes 1982; McClain and Andrews 1969; Paffard 1970). Peakers appear to display a general willingness to explore and experience states of consciousness differing from their usual states of being and are 'open' in the broadest sense of the word (Masluk 1999).

Within music-specific peak literature, Panzarella (1980) discovered only minor, insignificant personality differences between peakers and non-peakers and argues that 'peak experiences represent an unusual mode of functioning for the individual rather than an intensification of the person's usual mode of functioning' (p. 85).

Research has also shown mixed results with regard to the predictive power of demographic differences between peakers and non-peakers. Studies comparing the peak reports of various demographic sample groups have shown that despite significant differences between groups' age, gender, education, race, and religion, there are no significant differences observed in their descriptions of peak experiences (Allen *et al.* 1964; Gordon 1985; Yeagle *et al.* 1989; Lanier *et al.* 1996). Nevertheless, some older studies found significant differences in peak descriptions between Caucasians and blacks (Mathis and McClain 1968), non-psychotics and psychotics (Margoshes and Litt 1966), and low and high verbal abilities (McClain and Andrews 1969).

Research on where a musical peak experience is most likely to occur has shown a few tendencies, though the situational unpredictability remains similar to that of personality and demographic differences. Having collected a sample of experiences with music during childhood, one study found that peak experiences were most likely to occur during relaxed, informal music listening, while surrounded by positive social and environmental factors (like friends and family), and in casual non-evaluative surroundings, like listening to the radio (Sloboda 2005). Although this finding is confirmed by other studies (e.g. Gabrielsson and Lindström Wik 2003), research has yet to systematically examine the peak-inducing power of various settings. With regard to music performance, Gabrielsson and Lindström Wik (2003) found that, despite the large number of musicians in their sample, over 80 per cent of all SEM were in music listening. A survey of performing musicians revealed a wide variety of circumstantial factors in performance-specific peak experiences, including perception and involvement with audience, relationships among band members, and connection with music being performed (Boyd and George-Warren 1992).

With regard to musical genre, Maslow found that classical music, specifically 'the great classics' (1976, p. 170) were the most reliable trigger of peak experiences. Panzarella (1980) and Laski (1961) also list 'serious/classical music' as the primary peak-inducing music in their work, though each include descriptions of experiences induced by rock, folk, jazz, and other previously less well-represented genres. A recent analysis of Gabrielsson's (2006) SEM data produced 15 separate categories/genres, which included all varieties of classical, folk, and popular pieces. This analysis also revealed significant demographic differences between participants and their triggers, where older participants were more likely to list classical music and younger participants more likely to list popular music.

Do peak-producing musical works have structural or sonic features that predict their ability to evoke peaks? Very little research has been undertaken on this topic. In analysing the capacity of music to evoke 'chills' (one physical component of some peak experiences), Sloboda (1991) discovered that certain musical devices were statistically associated with the precise temporal location of a chill. These devices,

including appoggiaturas and syncopations, all seem to involve violations of listener expectancy. His findings confirm those of Gabrielsson (2006) in that the responses collected were not specific to any one musical genre, and were found in a wide range of genres.

The nature of the peak experience

I was filled by a special feeling that the music began to take command of my body. I was charged in a way. A tremendous feeling of harmony which made me really enjoy the music, and I found it difficult to stand still ... the mystery and power really gripped me. I was filled by an enormous warmth and heat. I really swallowed all the notes that were streaming out in the air, not a single note, effect or sequence missed my hungry ears. I was captivated by each of the instruments and what they had to offer me. Nothing else existed!

Gabrielsson and Lindström Wik
(2003, p. 166)

The research literature contains much data, exemplified by excerpt above, about the nature of the peak experience drawn from retrospective accounts of how it felt *while* it was happening. Such accounts demonstrate key features of the peak: their positivity, their powerfulness, rarity, non-voluntary nature, and some emotional, physical, perceptual, and cognitive correlates (Gabrielsson and Lindström-Wik 2003; Maslow 1976). In short, the peak is the antithesis of mundane, it goes beyond the everyday, and is not easily forgotten. The peak has even been called indescribable, and many find their expressive palate insufficient to properly elucidate the experience (Thorne 1963; McClain and Andrews 1969). Peaks are somewhat unpredictable; they are non-volitional and cannot be 'generated' (Maslow 1976).

Verbal reports provide insights into the subjective content of a peak experience, what happens during it, and what it feels like. There is no single element a peak experience *must* contain—rather there exists a diverse set of elements, each of which could be said to be indicative or typical. Gabrielsson and Linstrom Wik (2003) categorize these elements into a three-level hierarchy, the top and most general of which includes seven categories: general characteristics, physical reactions, perceptions, cognitions, feelings/emotions, existential/transcendental and personal/social aspects. These categories are proposed as capturing the most common elements of the experience.

The following excerpt, taken from Gabrielsson and Lindström (1993, p. 123), is from a woman's description of how she experienced Tchaikovsky's Symphony No. 6, *Pathétique*, when she listened to it for the first time. Note the various elements—physical, perceptual, cognitive, emotional, transcendental and personal/social—in her description:

I have had similar [strong] experiences of other music but none so terribly deep as *Pathétique*. In certain passages it evokes sobs, and I feel totally crushed. My listening is fully concentrated, the rest of the world disappears in a way, and I become merged with the music or the music with me, it fills me completely. I also get physical reactions, wet eyes, a breathing that gets sobbing in certain passages, a feeling of crying in my throat and chest. Trying to find words for the emotion themselves, I would like to use words as crushed, shaken, tragedy, maybe death, absorption, but also tenderness, longing, desire in vain, a will to live, prayer. The whole experience also has the character of a total standstill, a kind of meditative rest, a last definite and absolute end, after which nothing else can follow.

After the experience I am sort of 'gone'—the people in the foyer and their murmur are at a distance, like a stage set rather than something real. I have a hard time trying to talk to them, to 'get started' and to 'return' to the ordinary reality. The most difficult part is to talk about the music experience itself, it is possible only after a while, when it has faded out a little. One of my concert friends is very sensitive to classical music and he too can have wet eyes. It has happened several times that we are just standing there, shaking our heads and looking down on the floor. Nobody finds any words, one cannot add anything to what the music already has told.

Descriptions like these testify to both the uniquely powerful nature of the strong experience and its ability to include many experiential elements in a single moment. This woman's experience is not only physical ('wet eyes ... breathing.... sobbing'), emotional ('tenderness, longing'), or perceptual ('the rest of the world disappears, and I become merged with the music'), but *all* of these, and more. It is these unique but overlapping elements that Gabrielsson and Lindström Wik's (2003) SEM-DS attempts to categorize, and in what follows these categories will be elaborated with reference to other research studies where available.

Physical reactions during the peak experience may include such physiological responses as chills/thrills, tears, changes in breathing, heart rate, and body temperature. Beyond internal physical manifestations, overt actions range from closing of the eyes to singing, shouting, jumping or dancing around. Contrarily, some people experience total physical immobility, or a sudden desire to be alone. Finally, included with physical reactions are a set of quasi-physical reactions, like a sense that the body has been dissolved into the music or merged with it, or that the body has actually transcended time or space, an out-of-body experience.

Some of the physical reactions which typically accompany peaks also occur in the context of emotional reactions to music which are less intense. This is particularly true of chills/thrills (e.g. Konecni et al. 2006; Panksepp 1995; Sloboda 1991). These are phenomena such as pilo-erection, 'shivers down the spine', tears and lump in the throat. These phenomena are ubiquitous—in some people they can occur several times a day, or even several times within the same piece of music. On their own they may be of rather little lasting significance, but when accompanied by other psychological experiences may become part of a memorable and significant peak.

Perceptual phenomena during peaks may include auditory, visual, tactile, kinaesthetic, synaesthetic, intensified/multimodal perception, and musical perception–cognition elements. The auditory–musical perception may be accompanied by strong visual impressions, tension or relaxation of the muscles, or simply an intensified sense of perception, among others. Performers, like listeners, frequently describe a perceptual sense of being 'embedded' in the sound (Boyd and George-Warren 1992).

The cognitive category includes elements like changed attitude, a changed experience of situation, body and mind, time and space, or wholeness, a loss of control, a changed attitude to music, a connection to old associations, memories, and thoughts, cognitive imagery, and musical cognition–emotion. Cognitive elements may relate to some of the more lasting effects of the experience (further discussed in the next section) when, for example, an individual achieves a new understanding of some element in their life, like a relationship or their appreciation of the art.

Emotional elements include strong/intense emotions, both positive and negative emotions, and mixed emotions. Positive emotions predominate, especially joy and happiness, while typical low arousal feelings include a sense of peace and calm, and high arousal feelings include rapture and euphoria. In addition to the prototypical positive emotions, there are examples of negative emotions such as loneliness, sadness, anxiety, or even anger during the experience. Typically such negative feelings are related to various personal and other circumstances rather than to the music itself. Mixed emotions often result from the mix of positive affect and the negative social or personal circumstances, such as hearing music that reminds one of a lost loved one. For the majority of people, however, peaks are accompanied by unusually intense positive emotions.

Existential and transcendental aspects include, among other things, reflections on human life and existence, cosmic experience, experience of other worlds, religious visions, and encounters with the divine. While these items are easily categorized and listed, their experiential impact and post-experience implications can be immense. Many, for example, describe their peak experience as having resulted in a better understanding of the human condition, or offered a glimpse at God, Heaven, or similar 'other worldly' elements.

Finally, personal and social aspects include elements such as feeling liberated, uplifted or cleansed, getting new insights, hope, power and increased self-esteem, and further various therapeutic effects.

Effects of the peak experience

Maslow (1999) likened the peak to a 'personally defined Heaven from which the person then returns to earth. Desirable after-effects of such an experience, some universal and some individual, are … very probable' (pp. 110–111) and discovered that some 'after-effects may be permanent, [though] the high moment itself is not' (p. 14). His analysis of peak reports revealed seven broad categories of after effects, not all of which result from every experience. These categories are supported by a later peak experience literature (Frick 1982; Lanier *et al.* 1996; Warmoth 1965).

In relation to music, Panzarella (1980) reported that 90 per cent of participants attributed long-lasting, often permanent, effects to their peaks. Through his analysis, he derived a list that closely resembles Maslow's (1999) and includes:

1 General appreciation of music or visual art

2 Altering of self-appreciation

3 Altering of relationships with other people

4 Altering of attitudes toward life or world in general

5 Increased aesthetic sensitivity

6 Enhanced perception of everyday reality

7 Long-lasting mood effects.

The first element, 'general appreciation of music or visual art', is notably absent from previous lists of after-effects, including Maslow's (1999). Participants in this study who achieved joyous experiences through either art or music emerged with a renewed appreciation for the medium. A similar study found that participants reported a desire to continue pursuing music either as a hobby or profession, and a desire to continue listening and engaging with music (Gabrielsson and Lindström Wik 2003).

Gabrielsson and Lindström (1995) document the ability of strong experiences to elicit positive therapeutic effects. Having analysed hundreds of SEM reports, the authors mention therapeutic implications including: relief from physical pain, grief, and depression, a release of personal and social barriers, increased self-confidence and sense of one's ego, even a total reorientation of one's attitude and value system. This report, the most specific and thorough of its kind, provides substantial music-specific evidence of one of Maslow's original effects.

A final after-effect that warrants discussion is the desire to continue pursuing peaks. Research has shown that peak experiences in music, particularly in early childhood, have long-lasting effects on the likelihood of engagement with music (Sloboda 2005). Having collected descriptions of experiences with music before age ten, Sloboda (2005) found that positive experiences early in life were likely to spur continued involvement in music or, in other words, continued peak-seeking behaviour. Similar behaviour has been observed in adult music performers, who demonstrate a desire to repeat the strong feelings they experience while performing, so much so that a survey of pop and rock musicians uncovered a tendency to turn to drugs to induce the same feelings (Boyd and George-Warren 1992). Interestingly, veteran skydivers showed similar peak-seeking rationale for their continued desire to engage in their work (Lipscombe 1999), which suggests that peaks are of great consequence to the continued pursuit of both professions.

Despite the preceding evidence in support of Maslow's (1999) list of after-effects, there is a significant methodological pitfall in peak research, namely the attempt to measure an effect without a baseline. As a result of the unpredictability of the peak, it is hard to establish any independent, pre-peak data. Thus when a study discovers a 'more positive view' or an 'altered perception', these are derived from retrospective comparisons provided in the narratives of participants. One method for overcoming this limitation would be testing a large number of people who all attend the same musical event, monitoring experience before, during, and after. This would permit statistical comparison of pre and post-experience scores among peakers. This approach is currently being pursued by two of the current authors.

In conclusion, existing research provides evidence that music-related peak experiences have meaningful after-effects, and that most people who experience peaks report such effects (Ebersole 1972). The fact that reports in Gabrielsson and Lindström Wik (2003) contain all of Maslow's (1999) and Panzarella's (1980)

after effects further supports this conclusion. The effects of the musical peak experience, it seems, do not end after the fleeting moment, but carry on in the lives of the peaker.

Methodology

The majority of the music-related peak experience literature is based on what Sloboda (2005) calls the 'autobiographical memory technique', which he finds both 'rich and workable'(p. 188). Relying on participants' memories for these significant moments, researchers using this technique simply ask participants to produce narratives about experiences with music. The prompt can be as simple as asking participants to describe 'the ... most intense experience of music that you have ever had' (Gabrielsson and Lindström Wik 2003, p. 163), or more generic like that used by Maslow (1999), who asked participants to describe 'the most wonderful experience of [their lives]'(p. 83). Variations on these prompts are found in numerous articles (Laski 1961; Panzarella 1980; Lanier *et al.* 1996; Minassian *et al* 2003; Sloboda 2005).

The autobiographical memory technique is not, however, without its methodological limitations. There is some doubt about participants' ability to recall specific details about an experience, particularly when recall is many years after the episode. There are also disclosure issues, as strong verbal and expressive skills are critical to describing the experience (Thorne 1963; McClain and Andrews 1969). This could mean that many potential peakers, including children, are expressively incapable of describing their peak experiences. Finally, the qualitative methods of this technique afford somewhat limited quantitative analyses.

As a response to the latter, peak experience researchers have developed hybrid methodologies which combine the autobiographical memory technique with a set of quantitative methods. After asking participants to freely 'describe one incident in your life characterized by highest happiness', the Experience Questionnaire (Privette 1983, 1984; Privette and Bundrick 1987) presents a series of 42 Likert-scale questions and five scaled descriptions of the peak experience, to which participants rate their agreement. Reliability of this technique is well within reasonable limits (Privette and Sherry 1986), and the quantitative data produced permits more aggressive statistical analyses.

This method has been successfully applied to music-specific experiences. Participants in Gabrielsson and Lindström Wik (2003) not only produced free descriptions of their strong experiences but also rated how well their reactions corresponded with a large set of statements on strong experiences with music. Across participants, statements indicating positive feelings and other salient characteristics in SEM (e.g. absorption, confirmation, transcendence) received high ratings, whereas statements indicating negative feelings received low ratings. Factor analysis revealed up to 14 factors accounting for 64 per cent of the total variance. Most of these factors corresponded to (and thus confirmed) various categories in the SEM-DS, though there were also factors revealing co-occurrence of different categories (e.g, one factor included transcendent state, perfection, peace and happiness, healing experience), which may be difficult using solely content analysis of free descriptions. Notable, however, is the fact that these 14 factors fail to account for over one-third of the total variance—a testament to the extremely multifaceted character of SEM. Nevertheless, using these hybrid qualitative/quantitative methods, this study is able to collect bias-free, ecologically valid narratives and use quantitative techniques to test for the presence of correlated elements. For further discussion, see Gabrielsson and Lindström Wik (2003, p. 186 onwards).

Despite the benefits of these newer techniques, the ability to derive sound conclusions from qualitative data should not be underestimated. In his autobiographical memory research, for instance, Sloboda (2005) coded qualitative statements for the presence or absence of certain situational elements. These included internal significance (where the significance of the event was attributed to some factor internal to the music—such as a particular sound event or quality) and external significance (where the significance was attributed to some factor external to the music—such as the social context). Analysis showed a statistically significant relationship between internal and external significance. There were no cases of

internal significance when the external significance was negative. This qualitative data thus clearly reveals something about the necessary conditions for a peak.

In sum, the study of musical peak experience poses substantial methodological challenges which require empirical ingenuity to overcome. Progress is likely to be furthered by a broader combination of qualitative and quantitative methods. Such progress should never blind us, however, to the fact that a full appreciation of peak experiences requires us to keep hold of the uniqueness and unrepeatability of each individual experience. Such uniqueness is not 'irrelevant noise' to be filtered out of analyses, but is a core component of what makes these experiences what they are.

Conclusions

Musical peak experiences are a significant component of the lives of many people. They are powerful, valued, have lasting effects, and—for some—are a reason for continued engagement with music. They involve elements of life that could be described as transcendent, transformational, even spiritual. Indeed, it is perhaps no coincidence that music has been such an essential part of many religious traditions and rituals, aimed at encouraging various states of 'uplift', be they contemplative or ecstatic (e.g. Becker 2001). Nonetheless, psychology rightly and necessarily concentrates on the inner characteristics of such experiences rather than their wider social and cultural meanings.

The research reviewed in this chapter shows that, despite significant methodological difficulties and a relatively small literature, a number of facts about the musical peak experience are known with some certainty:

1 Not all individuals are equally prone to peak experiences. Some elements of personality (specifically flexibility and openness) seem to encourage these experiences. On the other hand, demographic factors such as age, gender, and education seem to be of little importance.

2 All types and genres of music can engender peaks, though perception of aesthetic value seems important.

3 Many different settings and environmental circumstances can be found in descriptions of peaks, including both formal and informal music listening and performance.

4 Peaks contain strong and distinctive perceptual, cognitive, physical, and emotional components which make them highly salient to the person experiencing them.

5 Peaks are often remembered, and ascribed causal significance for various after-effects, long after their occurrence.

Relative to other areas of music psychology (e.g. cognition/perception, developmental topics), the study of peaks has not attracted as large a body of research. As a result, the topic has not benefited to the full extent from recent methodological developments in the field, for instance, the use of multivariate statistical methods, or innovative experience-sampling methods. With such methods, it should be possible to make progress on some of the unanswered questions in the field, such as whether there are distinct syndromes within the larger phenomenon, and whether specific enabling conditions can be more precisely characterized, thus potentially helping people to find their way more reliably to these high-value and life-enhancing experiences.

References

Allen RM, Haput TD and Jones RW (1964). Analysis of peak experiences reported by college students. *Journal of Clinical Psychology*, **20**, 207–212.

Becker J (2001). Anthropological perspectives on music and emotion. In PN Juslin, JA Sloboda, eds, *Music and emotion: theory and research*, 135–160. Oxford University Press, Oxford.

Boyd J and George-Warren H (1992). *Musicians in tune: seventy-five contemporary musicians discuss the creative process*. Simon and Schuster, New York.

Ebersole P (1972). Effects and classification of peak experience. *Psychological Reports*, **30**, 631–635.

Frick WB (1982). Conceptual foundations of self-actualization: a contribution to motivation theory. *Journal of Humanistic Psychology*, **22**, 33–52.

Gabrielsson A (2001). Emotions in strong experiences with music. In PA Juslin, JA Sloboda, eds), *Music and emotion: theory and research*, 431–449. Oxford University Press, Oxford.

Gabrielsson A (2002). Old people's remembrance of strong experiences related to music. *Psychomusicology*, **18**, 103–122.

Gabrielson A (2006). Strong experiences elicited by music—what music? In P Locher, C Martindale and L Dorfman, eds, *New directions in aesthetics, creativity and the arts*, 251–267. Baywood Publishing, New York.

Gabrielsson A and Lindström S (1993). On strong experiences of music. *Jahrbuch der Deutschen Gesellschaft für Musikpsychologie*, 10, 118–139.

Gabrielsson A and Lindström S (1995). Can strong experiences of music have therapeutic implications? In R Steinberg, ed., *Music and the mind machine. The psychophysiology and psychopathology of the sense of music*, 195–202. Springer-Verlag, Berlin.

Gabrielsson A and Lindström Wik S (2000). Strong experiences of and with music. In D Greer, ed., *Musicology and sister disciplines: past, present and future*, 100–108. Oxford University Press, Oxford.

Gabrielsson A and Lindström Wik S (2003). Strong experiences related to music: a descriptive system. *Musicae Scientiae*, 7(2), 157–217.

Gordon RD (1985). Dimensions of peak communication experiences: an exploratory study. *Psychological Reports*, **57**, 824–826.

Konecni VJ, Wanic RA and Brown A (2007). Emotional and aesthetic antecedents and consequences of music-induced thrills. *American Journal of Psychology*, **120**, 619–643.

Lanier LS, Privette G, Vodanovich S and Bundrick CM (1996). Peak experiences: lasting consequences and breadth of occurrences among realtors, artists, and a comparison group. *Journal of Social Behavior and Personality*, **11**(4), 781–791.

Laski M (1961). *Ecstasy: a study of some secular and religious experiences*. Cresset Press, London.

Lipscombe N (1999). The relevance of the peak experience to continued skydiving participation: a qualitative approach to assessing motivations. *Leisure Studies*, **18**(4), 267–288.

Margoshes A and Litt S (1966). Vivid experience: peak and nadir. *Journal of Clinical Psychology*, **22**, 175.

Maslow AH (1943). A theory of human motivation. *Psychological Review*, **50**, 370–396.

Maslow AH (1959). Cognition of being in the peak experience. *Journal of Genetic Psychology*, **94**, 43–66.

Maslow AH (1976). *The farther reaches of human nature*. Penguin Books, New York.

Maslow AH, (1999). *Toward a psychology of being*, 3rd edn. John Wiley and Sons, Princeton, NJ.

Masluk TJ (1999). Reports of peak and other experiences during a neuro-technology-based training program. *Journal of the American Society for Psychical Research*, **93**, 1–98.

Mathes EW (1982) Peak experience tendencies: scale development and theory testing. *Journal of Humanistic Psychology*, **22**(3), 92–108.

Mathis WJ and McClain EW (1968). Peak experiences of white and Negro college students. *Journal of Clinical Psychology*, **24**, 318–319.

McClain EW and Andrews HB (1969). Some personality correlates of peak experiences: a study in self-actualization. *Journal of Clinical Psychology*, **25**(1), 36–38.

Minassian C, Gayford C and Sloboda JA (2003). Optimal experience in music performance: a survey of young musicians. Papers presented at a meeting of the society for education, music, and psychology research. London, March 2003.

Panksepp J (1995). The emotional sources of 'chills' induced by music. *Music Perception*, **13**, 171–207.

Panzarella R (1980). The phenomenology of aesthetic peak experiences. *Journal of Humanistic Psychology*, **20**(1), 69–85.

Paffard MK (1970). Creativity and peak experiences. *British Journal of Educational Psychology*, **40**, 283–290.

Privette G (1983). Peak experience, peak performance, and flow: a comparative analysis of positive human experiences. *Journal of Personality and Social Psychology*, **45**(6), 1361–1368.

Privette G (1984). *Experience questionnaire*. The University of West Florida, Pensacola, FL.

Privette G and Bundrick CM (1987). Measurement of experience: construct and content validity of the experience questionnaire, *Perceptual and Motor Skills*, **65**(1), 415–332.

Privette G and Sherry D (1986). Reliability and readability of questionnaire: peak performance and peak experience. *Psychological Reports*, **58**, 491–494.

Sloboda JA (1991). Musical structure and emotional response: some empirical findings. *Psychology of Music*, **19**(2), 110–120.

Sloboda JA (2005). Music as a language. In Sloboda JA, *Exploring the Musical Mind*, 175–189. Oxford University Press, Oxford.

Thorne FC (1963). The clinical use of peak and nadir experience reports. *Journal of Clinical Psychology*, **19**, 248–50.

Warmoth A (1965). The peak experience and the life history. *Journal of HumanisticPsychology*, **3**, 86–91.

Yeagle E, Privette G and Dunham F (1989). Highest happiness: an analysis of artists' peak experience. *Psychological Reports*, **65**, 523–530.

CHAPTER 43

Musical identities

Raymond MacDonald, David J. Hargreaves and Dorothy Miell

Introduction

Many chapters within this Handbook have highlighted just how important music is for us all, and the extent to which music is ever-present within modern society. This ubiquitous aspect of music signals many features about how we as humans respond to music and highlights the universal importance of musical communication. Indeed, the notion that we all respond emotionally to music is not a vague utopian ideal, but the conclusion drawn by an increasing number of academic researchers interested in researching the foundations of musical behaviour (Juslin and Sloboda 2001; Trevarthen 2002). We suggest, given the importance of music within our lives, that it influences how we see ourselves and how we relate to the world around us. In short, we contend that music crucially influences our identity.

This chapter presents a number of key themes relating to the concept of musical identities. We provide a definition of identity, with a discussion of why identity is a timely topic for consideration. Also presented is a specific definition of musical identities, and we implicate music as an important feature of personal identity. We then move on and consider a number of specific research examples to shed further light upon the importance of musical identities. We present an overview of a series of studies investigating musical identities of jazz musicians. These highlight the utility of qualitative techniques, and in particular focus group and semi-structured interview methods, for understanding how professional musicians construct their identities in relation to both their musical activities and wider psychological and cultural issues. The chapter looks next at how theories of motivation and the self can help to explain some of the behavioural aspects of musical identities. We provide evidence that children's self-concepts, and in particular their levels of confidence (both of which are related to musical identities), can influence the rate of musical development and musical achievement, drawing briefly on a study which compares the views of pupils, parents and teachers about what it is to be 'good at music'.

Defining identities

Our contention is that music is not only important for us all, but that it plays a fundamental role in the development, negotiation and maintenance of our personal identities (MacDonald et al. 2002; Roe 1999; Stålhammar 2006). Any individual involved in musical activities (i.e. both listening and performing) develops aspects of personal identity that are inextricably linked to these musical behaviours. Moreover, for young people at least, it seems that music may play an absolutely fundamental role in the development and maintenance of identity: a number of researchers have provided evidence to suggest that music is the most important recreational activity in which young people engage (Zillman and Gan 1997; Roe 1999). In terms of signalling to the world fundamental aspects about a young person's sense of self, music is often used as a kind of 'badge of identity' (Tarrant et al. 2002; MacDonald and Miell 2000). Furthermore, there is growing evidence that music remains a fundamental part of our identity across the life span (Applegate and Potter 2002; Carlton 2006).

Turning to identity research at a more general level, Anthony Giddens asserts that identity, within contemporary society, is the most important issue with which humans must engage (Giddens 1991). We all have to make choices about our lives; from mundane questions about what to wear when we get up in the morning, to life-changing decisions about family, friendships and career paths. A key point here is that in earlier times, when traditional social order with clearly defined roles gave much more specific guidance regarding our life choices, these decisions were much easier to make and in some ways made for us. However, we now have many more options open to us and we have to make these decisions, what Giddens calls 'identity work', in a much more individualized and detailed manner. As Giddens states:

> What to do? How to act? Who to be? These are focal questions for everyone living in circumstances of late modernity—and ones which, on some level or another, all of us answer, either discursively or through day-to-day social behaviour.
>
> (1991, p. 70)

Consequently, identity research is now established as a multidisciplinary field, taking place in a wide variety of academic contexts, to such an extent that there exists a international organization called *The Society for Research on Identity Formation*, and a related journal, *Identity*, whose aim is 'to provide a forum for identity theorists and researchers around the globe to share their ideas and findings regarding the problems and prospects of human self-definition'. We find identity research not only in all branches of the arts and humanities, but also within the much more positivistic worlds of medicine and science. No single discipline has exclusive rights to identity research, nor can each identity research project be informed by all current thinking on identity (MacDonald *et al.* 2004). Of course, each research project will highlight different facets of identity processes and, in many cases, may involve differing definitions of identity. For example, the studies of jazz musicians outlined below utilize a discursive definition of identity, and emphasize how language shapes and constructs our sense of self, whereas the motivational theories presented later on in the chapter take a more social cognitive approach to the self. While there is no agreed definition of identity,

researchers generally emphasize aspects that relate to how individuals construct themselves in relation to one or more phenomena. There is also an acknowledgement that each of us has many identities relating to the different roles we adopt (mother, musician, friend, colleague etc.). These identities are not discrete, will often merge and are constantly being negotiated and evolving. Identity is currently a very topical research issue for academics from many disciplines, perhaps because it is a fundamental issue for individuals worldwide in this period of postmodernity.

Musical identities

Moving on to the specific domain of music, we contend that music plays an important role in the negotiation, construction and maintenance of identities. For example, an individual who is a keen Bob Dylan fan will maintain a sense of self that is influenced by this liking for Bob Dylan: many of his friends may also be Bob Dylan fans, and his choice of clothes and political beliefs may be influenced by his taste in music. His linguistic devices may be influenced by his musical tastes, and in conversation he may choose to signal these musical tastes as a marker of his individuality. Thus, music plays a central role in this individual's identity. Zillman and Gan (1997), Tarrant *et al.* (2002), and DeNora (2000) all investigate the role that music plays in identity construction and maintenance. Zillman and Gan (1997) provide evidence to suggest that music is the primary leisure activity and, in terms of identity construction, the most important recreational activity undertaken young people. Tarrant *et al.* (2002) highlight the importance that shared musical tastes have in forming and maintaining friendship groups. This demonstrates how music can be an important marker of identity and now young people in particular want to have musical tastes in common with their friends. De Nora (2000) takes a sociological perspective in demonstrating how enmeshed music is within everyday life, and quite clearly draws a direct link between the importance of music and the construction of the self.

Individuals who are involved in music-making (be that as a professional opera singer or an occasional singer in the bath tub) develop an identity that is crucially influenced by these activities. For example, a young child going to piano lessons for the first time may be praised by her parents for practising and, over a period of time, sees her piano playing as one of many important activities in which she is engaged. Thus, when talking about her routine and weekly activities to friends and family her view of herself as a piano player influences how she talks and thinks about herself: as such, she develops an identity as a musician in the broadest sense of the word.

Another important point to note is that the identity of being a musician is a socially and culturally defined concept. We don't acquire the label 'musician' simply by attaining advanced technical skills. By this we mean that viewing ourselves as musical is not directly linked to the levels of technical ability or knowledge that we have. Similarly, there is no legal control over who can or can not call themselves musicians. It appears that whether or not we view ourselves as 'musicians' or 'musical' is crucially influenced by our social and cultural surroundings and by the ways in which we relate to people around us (Green 2002). The notion of being a musician is influenced by certain non-musical factors, which involves what we have termed *identity paradoxes*. Lamont (2002) highlights how the school setting plays a role in a child's developing musical identity by taking a detailed look at the music education environment, and demonstrating how the organization of lessons within a school has a crucial effect upon a child developing musical identity. Borthwick and Davidson (2002), on the other hand, look at more informal family environments, and how communication within the family influences children's developing sense of musicality. Specifically, these authors show how one sibling adopts the identity of *musician* while other siblings, who may be musically experienced, view themselves as not musical in comparison to this sibling. O'Neill (2002) investigates how young people learn to view themselves as musicians and uses a qualitative social constructionist approach to investigate the relationship between a young person's sense of musicality and wider social influences.

Gender issues are also important to take into consideration when thinking about how musical identities develop and are maintained. A number of researchers have highlighted how cultural expectations and hegemonic influences affect the developing musical identities of males and females differently, both in terms of musical tastes and participation (Dibben 2002; Green 1997; McClary 1991; O'Neill 1997a; Welch 2006). For example, Dibben (2002) and McClary (1991) discuss how women are underrepresented within the professional music world and Green (1997) provides evidence to support the notion that hegemonic masculine identities facilitate the development of a composer's identity. This may help explain why there are proportionally far fewer women, in comparison to men, working as composers within Western classical music. O'Neill (1997a) shows how gender stereotypes influence musical instrument choices made by boys and girls while Welch (2006) points out that the exclusion of women from cathedral choirs dates back to AD 597.

Crucially, all of the work highlighted above demonstrates how environmental and wider cultural influences are brought to bear on self-perceptions of musicianship and musical tastes. In particular, this work also demonstrates how essentially non-musical variables fulfill fundamental roles in an individual's sense of developing musical identity.

Identities in jazz

One particular approach to studying musical identities is to consider how musicians talk about their musical lives. This approach was utilized in series of studies that investigated how jazz musicians construct, maintain and negotiate their musical identities in a variety of different contexts (Wilson and MacDonald 2005; MacDonald and Wilson 2005, 2006). This approach is presented as an exemplar of how research into musical identities can be conducted from a qualitative perspective. The key methodological points are that this research can utilize both focus group and interview methodology. Additionally, the data can be analysed using a range of theoretical perspectives including thematic analysis, interpretative phenomenological analysis, discourse analysis and narrative analysis. The jazz context provides a particular useful and timely way to study identity. On the one hand the performance of this music represents a unique form of collaborative creativity (Sawyer 1992; Meadows 2003; Berliner 1994). Secondly, while there is a growing literature investigating the particular psychological and musical processes of jazz music (Cooke and Horne 2002), there is a need for research to focus upon the social aspects of identity maintenance, and in particular the multifaceted ways in which the collaborative context of jazz performance influences these identity projects (Sawyer 2003).

The first study utilized a thematic analysis of focus group data to investigate how jazz musicians talked about improvisation (Wilson and MacDonald 2005). What emerged from focus group data was a negotiated social construct rooted in the understanding of the participants themselves and an excellent method for investigating musical identities. From the analysis two main themes were identified. The first theme was termed 'Jazz is'. While there was considerable debate around the topic of what jazz music is, the discussions centred around: *improvising and composing; swing elements of jazz* and *collective processes involved in jazz playing*. Improvisation was seen as a stronger expectation in jazz than in other forms of music, and was discussed both as the elaboration of a tune and as a looser form of collective creativity. *Swing*, the maintenance of a common and consistent pulse of a particular quality, was widely seen as a central yet intangible quality in the collaboration of musicians playing jazz. A perceived tension between collective and individual creativity, such as that identified by Sawyer (1992), also emerged in the accounts presented, however; achieving the requisite collective interaction was voiced as more important than individual goals of self-expression. Individual and collective creativity were often viewed as existing in balance with each other in jazz. Social interaction therefore becomes extremely important in its execution. The second broad theme that emerged from the data was termed 'Jazz life is' and related to wider social and cultural issues pertaining how jazz musicians live. Within this category discussion centred around: *social context, professional context, being in a group* and *self and others*. These four themes gave detailed accounts of what the participants reported as being the key features of a jazz musician's life style.

This focus group analysis presented a thematic account highlighting the importance of shared understandings and practices in musical, social and cultural terms and features of identity for these participants. This thematic analysis coded what participants said into descriptive categories, and this is a common approach within qualitative studies of musical identity (e.g. Monson 1996). However, discourse analysis seeks to move beyond the categorical grouping of thematic content analysis to investigate structural features in discourse and to explore how particular speech acts perform a range of functions for a speaker and move beyond a thematic account (Edwards and Potter 1992).

With this issue in mind we examined discursive features of dialogue between jazz practitioners during the focus group interviews to reveal the relationship between the construction of specific meanings for the music and musicians and the negotiation of musical identities (Wilson and MacDonald 2005). This paper reported three key elements of identity work from a discursive analytic position: interpretative repertoires for jazz; the resolution of uncertainties created in handling these repertoires within the conversation; and ways in which the data are characterized by the focus group context. Two distinct interpretative repertoires (cf. Gilbert and Mulkay 1984) were employed in these data, which we termed the 'expert' and the 'naïve'. These were used flexibly to support participants' claims to identity as jazz musicians, while positioning others as separate from this identity. In the expert repertoire, jazz was accounted for as music produced by groups of individuals whose hard-won knowledge and skills gave them a particular insight into the music. In the 'naïve' repertoire participants emphasized the ineffable and soulful aspects of jazz music that were seen as being beyond complete comprehension.

The two papers discussed above give accounts of focus group data analyses and suggested a number of themes and features that we wished to follow up outwith the group context. In particular, we wanted to gather the views of both male and female practitioners (all focus group participants had been men) who were not previously known to the interviewer (both researchers had known the focus group participants personally and professionally). A series of ten individual in-depth interviews with professional jazz musicians in London was therefore conducted to provide rich data on individual identities, social contexts, and the experience of improvising (MacDonald and Wilson 2006). The findings highlighted how identity as a jazz musician was negotiated with other individual identities. For example, the relationship between gendered identities and identity as a jazz musician was examined as an instance of how conflict between these identities may allow hegemonic influences to operate.

In summary, these three papers highlight the importance of talking about music in terms of negotiating the constantly evolving musical identities of professional musicians. For these participants, musical identities were implicated as central to identity construction across a range of social situations. In the next section we move from analysing talk about music to investigating how motivation is related to musical participation and musical identities.

Musical identity and motivation

In our earlier discussion we cited the example of a young child, going to piano lessons for the first time, who gradually develops a view of herself as a pianist, or more generally as a musician. This development can be encouraged by praise from her parents and wider family about practising, or about particular musical achievements, and by talking to her friends and schoolmates about her progress. The positive feedback that she gets from these significant others in her social world will play an important role in her developing identity as a musician, and will thereby motivate her to higher levels of practice and achievement, which in turn will lead to further strengthening of the 'musician' role: and so a 'virtuous cycle' can develop in which growing levels of musical achievement and musical identity are interdependent. In other words, children's motivation to succeed in music is inextricably linked with aspects of their musical identity: the ways in which they think about their own abilities have a direct influence upon their motivation to engage in activities which develop those

abilities, and vice versa. It therefore makes sense to consider how theories of motivation and the self can explain some of the effects of musical identities.

Motivation to learn in music is the topic of Chapter 27 in this volume, by Susan Hallam, and we refer the reader to that chapter: our distinctive emphasis in this section is on how musical identities give rise to certain aspects of motivation. An extensive body of theory and research has been conducted on motivation for educational attainment more generally—in subjects such as mathematics and reading—and this also has been applied to motivation in music learning by O'Neill and McPherson (2002), Hallam (2002) and Austin et al. (2006).

Self-theories form a central part of the theoretical models of educational and musical motivation which have emerged in recent decades, and Austin et al. (2006) illustrate this point very clearly in proposing a process model of motivation which is based on the work of Connell (1990). The model has four components—the *self system* (e.g. perceptions, beliefs, thoughts, emotions); the *social system* (e.g. teachers, peers, siblings); *actions* (e.g. motivated behaviours including learning and self-regulation); and *outcomes* (e.g. learning, achievements). Each of these four components is seen to have a reciprocal causal relationship with each of the others, such that the motivational system develops and changes as learning proceeds, and as new challenges are sought by the learner. Hallam (Chapter 27) goes further than this, proposing a wide-ranging model of musical motivation which sees 'malleable aspects of the personality and self-concept' feeding, along with various environmental influences, into motivation, interaction with the cognitive characteristics of the individual, and with the different cognitive processes involved.

Most writers in this area agree that expectancy –value theory (e.g., Eccles et al. 1983; Pintrich and Schunk 2002) is the most well established and useful theoretical approach, and models based on this approach have three main components. These are *value* components—the extent to which learners view a particular task, activity or domain as being important, and as being of value to them: *expectancy* components—learners' beliefs about their abilities to succeed in the activity: and *affective* components, namely how learners feel about themselves in relation to the activity. Thus, our young pianist's motivation to progress to higher levels will depend on the extent to which she sees playing the piano as being important in her life, and in having future benefits and pay-offs: on whether or not she perceives she is capable of achieving higher levels of success; and on whether or not she simply enjoys playing the piano in relation to all her other interests and activities.

Eccles *et al.* (1983) proposed that there are four main aspects of the value component, namely its *attainment value* (the importance to the individual of success in the task); its *utility value* (its perceived usefulness to the individual); its *intrinsic interest* (the absorption in and enjoyment of the activity for its own sake); and its *perceived cost* (the loss of time spent on other activities as a result of engagement in musical activities, and the consequent loss of interest in them. Many parents, including the present authors, have faced the 'Saturday morning dilemma'—school sports team or band/or chestra?!). The third of these aspects raises the important distinction between intrinsic and extrinsic motivation: the former is evident when interest in an activity is natural, unforced and high, and the latter occurs when external rewards and punishments (such as praise and criticism) are involved.

Amabile's (1996) social psychological theory of creativity emphasizes the importance of intrinsic motivation, proposing that 'the intrinsically motivated state is conducive to creativity, whereas the extrinsically motivated state is detrimental' (p. 107). The *perceived cost* of engaging in an activity may involve both intrinsic and extrinsic motivation: children may decide that the time and work involved in practising an instrument is not worth the effort, for example, and consciously decide to give up in favour of other pursuits (e.g. Eccles *et al.* 1998). It is also worth pointing out that external rewards do not always lead to improvements in performance: if intrinsic motivation is already high, rewards can have the effect of undermining performance rather than of improving it.

The decision to either persist in music, or to give up, is clearly interdependent with the second, *expectancy* component of the expectancy–value model, which refers to learners' beliefs in their own ability to succeed on the task, and this is what Bandura (1997) calls *self-efficacy*. Learners' prior view of their own potential ability to succeed on a task—their competency beliefs—can be an important determinant of their actual performance on that task, and this leads to some further conceptual distinctions. Dweck (2000) suggests that people differ in the extent to which they display *mastery-oriented* as distinct from *helpless* behaviour, which in turn relates to their *locus of control*. Learners with an *internal* locus of control are likely to display mastery-oriented patterns of behaviour, for example in trying to persist with a task even when they meet difficulties or setbacks. Those with an *external* locus of control, however, feel that circumstances are beyond their own control, and may display helpless patterns of behaviour. In Chapter 27, Hallam draws on these concepts in describing how learners' competency beliefs can be an important determinant not only of whether they engage in that task as well as of their actual performance on that task.

O'Neill (1997b) investigated the longer term effects of these motivational patterns on children who were about to begin instrumental tuition by giving them problem-solving tasks which were arranged such that they were bound to fail. She found that those who displayed mastery-oriented behaviour after failing on the task made more progress after one year of instrumental music lessons than those who initially displayed helpless behaviour. This result leads us to a more general consideration of the third component of expectancy–value theory, namely the *affective* component: people's beliefs about and reactions to success and failure can be explained in terms of attribution theory (e.g. Weiner 1985, 1992). According to this, people attribute their success or failure on a task to four main factors: *ability* ('I am good/poor at this task'): *effort* ('I practised hard/insufficiently'); *task difficulty* ('this particular task was easy/difficult'); and *luck* ('I had a lucky/unlucky day'). The first and second of these are internal in the sense that they are under the control of the learner, and the third and fourth are subject to external influences.

These theoretical analyses of educational motivation, along with Hallam's discussion in Chapter 27, reveal some of the mechanisms by which musical achievement and development can be determined by musical identities. We referred earlier to a hypothetical 'virtuous cycle' according to which increasing levels of musical achievement give rise to higher levels of musical self-esteem, and vice versa; children who feel that they are competent musicians are likely to achieve higher levels of success than those who do not, as are those who find music intrinsically interesting, and value it positively (Eccles *et al.* 1983). This can work in both directions, of course: some children may get the idea that they are 'unmusical', perhaps because of an unwitting remark by a teacher, parent or another pupil, and this perception could correspondingly lead on to a downward spiral of not trying, therefore becoming less able, therefore trying even less, and so on.

The *content* of musical ability self-perceptions were investigated as part of a series of studies conducted within the Curriculum Development Project in the Arts and Music Monitoring Programme, sponsored by the Qualifications and Curriculum Authority (QCA) in England. Hargreaves and colleagues (2004) compared the views of pupils, parents and teachers about 'what it is to be good at music' along with parallel questions about art and design, dance, and drama, from the points of view of pupils, teachers and parents. Focus groups of pupils and parents, and individual teachers, were asked to discuss three questions: (a) what does it mean to be good at music (what does it involve)?; (b) can one 'be good at' some aspects of music and not others?; and (c) how can one get better at music, and how would others know whether or not this had occurred?

Performing, and knowledge about music, were both seen as especially important aspects, particularly by pupils and teachers. Music was seen as comprising a range of different skills and capacities, including non-musical skills such as learning quickly, leading a group, and having confidence. Teachers tended to emphasize the requirements of the English National Curriculum, and to conceive their views of musical ability and achievement in those terms. Parents tended to focus on skills and activities

which are visible, notably those involving public performance. All three groups' responses suggested that music is no longer seen as a special talent which individuals either do or do not possess, and that it is perfectly possible to be good at some parts of it and not others. Qualifications and exams assumed lesser importance than might have been expected, and pupils' views were no less detailed and insightful than those of teachers and parents.

The pupils' views were explored in detail in a more recent report by Lamont *et al.* (2007) on a focus group investigation of 134 8–14-year-olds' understandings of what it means to be a musician, and of the differences between their descriptions of musicians in general with their own self-concepts as musicians. The results clearly showed that they defined musicians in terms of playing a musical instrument, making up music, and that closely related to this were being a singer, and being a music teacher. These children also emphasized effort, practice and hard work as being important characteristics of musicians. Their beliefs about themselves as musicians were more varied, however, and were more likely to include factors beyond their control (such as musical ability, and critical periods in their lives). There was a general acknowledgment of the role and importance of music in society, and of the possibility of music as a career and leisure choice. The motivation to be active and to succeed in music seems to be closely bound up with the development of positive musical identity.

Conclusions

In summary, recent developments within the psychology of music advocate a theoretically eclectic position for academics endeavouring to develop our understanding of the psychology of music (Miell *et al.* 2005). Much of the earlier research utilized a predominately quantitative empirical epistemology which focused on isolating discrete variables and was less concerned with the wider social and cultural influences on music perception (Hargreaves and North 1997; MacDonald *et al.* 2002). However, a more multidisciplinary and pluralistic position is entirely in keeping with postmodern research priorities within the wider academic community, and so researchers interested in investigating musical identities including psychologists, music therapists, musicologists, music educationalists and others, can adopt quite different theoretical stances on the research processes. The current situation within musical identity research reflects these multidisciplinary features, and we find research that is empirical (using both qualitative and quantitative approaches), and review based.

In this chapter we have focused on key themes and approaches within musical identities research. We have highlighted these issues with examples from published material and from our own current research, and in doing so have concentrated on two broad areas: jazz identities and motivations and identity. These two areas highlight the pluralistic manner in which researchers are currently investigating musical identities. In particular the section above on jazz identities highlights how the way in which musicians talk about their musical experiences helps to construct their musical identities. Related to these observations, the section on motivation draws together recent thinking in this area to highlight the importance of motivational aspects of musical development and also how self-perceptions influence the development of music skills and, through these, the development of musical identities. This chapter highlights the crucial role of wider cultural and social variables in determining not only the extent to which we view ourselves as musical or not, but also the extent to which we engage in musical activities (both listening and playing).

Musical identities are an important consideration for researchers interested in the psychology of music, not least because we all have musical identities, but also because identity 'work' is a fundamental psychological process in which we all engage. This identity work can take the form of musicians reflecting on their own practice and how this practice is related to their lifestyle, or it can be how children view their own sense of musical skill and development. In short, we are suggesting that talking about music and, through this, developing and negotiating musical identities, influence our engagement with music in important ways.

References

Applegate C and Potter P (2002). *Music and German national identity*. University of Chicago Press, Chicago, IL.

Austin J, Renwick J, and McPherson GE (2006). Developing motivation. In G. E. McPherson (ed), *The child as musician: A handbook of musical development*, 213–238. Oxford: Oxford University Press.

Bandura A (1997). *Self-efficacy: the exercise of control*. W.H. Freeman, New York.

Becker H (2000). The etiquette of improvisation. *Mind, Culture, and Activity*, 7(3), 171–176.

Berliner P (1994). *Thinking in jazz: the infinite art of improvisation*. University of Chicago Press, Chicago, IL.

Borthwick SJ and Davidson JW (2002). Personal identity and music: a family perspective. In RAR MacDonald, DJ Hargreaves and D Miell, eds, *Musical identities*, 60–79. Oxford University Press, Oxford.

Carlton (2006) A qualitative analysis of everyday uses of preferred music across the life span. Paper presented at ICMPC 9, Bologna, Italy, August 2006.

Connell JP (1990). Context, self and action: A motivational analysis of self-system processes across the life-span. In D. Cicchetti & M. Beeghly (eds) *The self in transition: Infancy to childhood*, 61–97. Chicago: University of Chicago Press.

Cooke M and Horne D (2002). *The Cambridge companion to jazz*. Cambridge University Press, Cambridge.

DeNora T (2000). *Music in everyday life*. Cambridge University Press, Cambridge.

Dibben N (2002). Gender identity and music. In RAR MacDonald, DJ Hargreaves and D Miell, eds, *Musical identities*, 117–134. Oxford University Press, Oxford.

Dweck CS (2000). *Self-theories: their role in motivation, personality and development*. Psychology Press, Hove, Sussex.

Eccles JS, Adler TF, Futterman R, Goff SB, Kaczala CM, Meece JL and Midgley C (1983). Expectancy, values, and academic behaviours. In JT Spence, ed., *Achievement and achievement motives: psychological and sociological approaches*, 75–146. W.H. Freeman, San Francisco.

Eccles JS, Wigfield A and Scheinfele U. (1998). Motivation to succeed. In W Damon and N Eisenberg, eds, *Handbook of child psychology: vol 4. Social, emotional and personality development*, 5th edn, 215–225. Wiley, New York.

Edwards D and Potter J (1992). *Discursive psychology*. Sage, London.

Giddens A (1991). *Modernity and self-identity. Self and society in the late modern age*. Polity Press, Cambridge.

Gilbert N and Mulkay (1984). *Opening Pandora's box: a sociological analysis of scientists' discourse*. Cambridge University Press, Cambridge.

Green L (1997) *Music, gender, education*. Cambridge University Press, Cambridge.

Green L (2002) *How popular musicians learn*. Ashgate, Aldershot.

Hallam, S (2002). *Musical Motivation: Towards a Model Synthesising the Research Music Eduction Research*, **4**(2), 225–244.

Hargreaves DJ, Lamont A, Marshall N and Tarrant M (2004). What is 'being good at music'? *NAME (National Association of Music Educators) Magazine*, **13**, 4–7.

Hargreaves DJ & North AC (eds) (1997). *The social psychology of music*. Oxford: Oxford University Press.

Juslin PN and Sloboda JA (eds) (2001). *Music and emotion: theory and research*. Oxford University Press, New York.

Lamont A (2002). Musical identities and the school environment. In RAR MacDonald, DJ Hargreaves and D Miell, eds), *Musical identities*, 49–55. Oxford University Press, Oxford.

Lamont A, Hargreaves DJ, Marshall N and Tarrant M. (2007). *Musical identities at school*. (Submitted).

MacDonald RAR and Miell D (2000). Creativity and music education: the impact of social variables. *International Journal of Music Education*, **36**, 58–68.

MacDonald RAR and Wilson GB (2006). Constructions of jazz: how jazz musicians present their collaborative musical practice. *Musicae Scientiae*, **10**(1), 59–85.

MacDonald RAR and Wilson GB (2005). The musical identities of professional jazz musicians: a focus group investigation. *Psychology of Music*, **33**(4), 395–419.

MacDonald RAR, Hargreaves DJ and Miell D (2004). The sounds of ideologies clashing. *Action, Criticism and Theory for Music Education*, **3**(1), 3–9. http://www.siue.edu/MUSIC/ACTPAPERS/v3/EditorResponse04.pdf.

MacDonald RAR, Hargreaves DJ and Miell D (eds) (2002). *Musical identities*. Oxford University Press, Oxford.

McClary S (1991) *Feminine endings: music, gender and sexuality*. University of Minnesota Press, Minneapolis, MN.

Meadows ES (2003) *Bebop to cool: context, ideology*, and musical identity. Greenwood, Westport CT.

Miell D, MacDonald RAR and Hargreaves DJ (eds) (2005). *Musical communication*. Oxford University Press, Oxford.

Monson I (1996). *Saying something: jazz improvisation and interaction*. University of Chicago, Chicago, IL.

O'Neill S (1997a) Gender and music. In D J Hargreaves and AC North, eds, *The social psychology of music*, 46–60. Oxford University Press, Oxford.

O'Neill S (1997b). The role of practice in children's early musical performance achievement. In H Jørgensen and AC Lehmann, eds, *Does practice make perfect? Current theory and research on instrumental practice*, 53 Norges Musikhøgskole, Oslo.

O'Neill S (2002) The self-identity of young musicians. In RAR MacDonald, DJ Hargreaves and D Miell, eds), *Musical identities*, 79–97. Oxford University Press, Oxford.

O'Neill S and McPherson GE (2002). Motivation. In R Parncutt & GE McPherson, eds, *The science and psychology of musical performance: Creative strategies for music teaching and learning*, 31–46. Oxford: Oxford University Press

Pintrich PR and Schunk DH, (2002). *Motivation in education: theory, research, and applications*, 2nd edn. Merrill, Upper Saddle River, NJ.

Roe K (1999) Music and identity among European youth: music as communication. Soundscape.info, *Journal on Media Culture*, **2**, http://www.icce.rug.nl/~soundscapes/HEADER/colophon.shtml.

Sawyer K (1992). Improvisational creativity: an analysis of jazz performance. *Creativity Research Journal*, **5**(3), 253–263.

Sawyer RK (2003) *Group creativity: music*. Erlbaum, Theater, Collaboration, Mahwah, NJ.

Stålhammar B, (2006) *Musical identities and music education*. Shaker Verlag, Aachen.

Tarrant M, North AC and Hargreaves DJ (2002). Youth identity and music. RAR MacDonald, DJ Hargreaves and D Miell, eds), *Musical identities*, 134–150. Oxford University Press, Oxford.

Trevarthen C (2002) Origins of musical identity: evidence from infancy for musical social awareness. In RAR MacDonald, DJ Hargreaves and DE Miell, eds, *Musical identities*, 22–46. Oxford University, Oxford.

Weiner B (1985). An attributional theory perspective of achievement motivation and emotion. *Psychological Review*, **92**, 548–573.

Weiner B (1992). *Human motivation: metaphors, theories, and research*. Sage, Newbury Park, CA.

Welch G (2006) Singing and vocal development. In GE McPherson, ed., *The child as musician: a handbook of music development*, 311–331. Oxford University Press, Oxford.

Wilson GB and MacDonald RAR (2005). The meaning of the blues: musical identities in talk about jazz. *Qualitative Research in Psychology*, **2**, 341–363.

Zillman D and Gan S (1997) Musical taste in adolescence. In DJ Hargreaves and AC North, eds, *The social psychology of music*, 161–188. Oxford University Press, Oxford.

CHAPTER 44

The effects of music in community and educational settings

Susan Hallam and Raymond MacDonald

Introduction

It has been recognized through the ages that music can have a very powerful influence on our emotions, moods and behaviour. In recent years technology has led to easy access to music listening, and individuals and organizations have taken advantage of this to utilize music to influence how we feel and act in many areas of our lives (see Chapters 40 and 45). Young people in particular spend a great deal of time playing music and often use it to accompany their studying. Alongside the increase in and ease of music listening, there has been an acknowledgement that there are wider benefits to active engagement with music beyond those emanating from its value as an art form. In the Western world, the latter part of twentieth century saw a huge growth in opportunities for making music within formal educational settings and more recently, through what is termed 'community music', playing, teaching and learning music outside of formal education (Elliot 2004). Research assessing the impact of such engagement has been used by music educators and community musicians to support the continued funding of such activities by policy makers.

In this chapter we will review the literature which has explored the ways that music may have benefits beyond those associated with our enjoyment of active engagement or listening in community and educational settings. We will outline developments in community music, consider research which has assessed its impact, explore the way that music has been used to attain educational aims beyond those relating to music education itself, and consider issues and findings relating to the use of background music when studying.

The impact of active engagement with making music in community and educational settings

In general, individuals actively engage with making music because they enjoy it, although where it is a compulsory element of the school curriculum this may not be the case. In recent years, perhaps in part because of the need to justify the place of music in the school curriculum and the continuance of funding for informal community music-making opportunities, there has been an increasing focus on the wider benefits of active engagement in music.

The impact of music in the community

Over the past 15 years there has been an explosion of interest in music making outside of formal educational settings. Much of this has come to be termed 'Community Music' and it is now an established area of research and practice with a dedicated journal, *The International Journal of*

Community Music and a commission of The International Society for Music Education. Veblen (2004) presented an overview of the many different ways in which community music is practiced around the world which highlighted the key concern of community music practitioners to increase access to music-making for all members of the public. The growing recognition of community music as an important musical activity is very much in keeping with current ideas of multidisciplinary practices that signal the integration of social, educational, medical, and therapeutic practices and thinking (Ruud 2004).

The growth of community education has in part been an acknowledgement that every human being has a social and biological guarantee of musicianship (Trevarthen 2002; MacDonald *et al.* 2002) and evidence that everybody, regardless of social, educational, psychological or medical aspects can communicate through music (Elliot 2004; Ansdell and Pavlicevic 2004; Miell *et al.* 2005). Musical skill develops through opportunities for musical engagement in childhood, adolescence and early adulthood, the influence of family, school and wider cultural factors being crucial in the individual's developing musicality (Borthwick and Davidson 2002; Lamont 2002; MacPherson in press; see also Chapters 22, 27, 28, and 29). Adult participation in community music is an extension of active music-making in childhood (e.g. Conda 1997), the pattern of engagement changing over the life course, diminishing in the middle years and increasing in retirement (Larson 1983), life-changing events sometimes providing an impetus for re-engagement (Conda 1997). The reasons for adults' participation in music have been grouped into three main categories: personal motivations (self-expression, recreation, self-improvement, and use of leisure time); musical motivations (love of music, performing for oneself and others, learning more about music); and social motivations (meeting new people, being with friends, and having a sense of belonging). No single reason consistently emerges as the most important (Coffman 2002). Hinkle (1988) suggests a further category—spirituality.

There is a growing body of evidence that involvement in music-making in community contexts has positive psychological or social benefits for the participants (Davidson 2004). While it is important to distinguish community music from music therapy (see Chapters 46 and 47), much has been written about the parallels and contrasts between community music-making, music education and music therapy. In particular Ansdell and Pavlicevic's edited text *Community music therapy* (2004) outlines how recent advances in community music-making and music therapy can facilitate a greater cross-fertilization of ideas between these areas of practice. Ockelford (2000) also discusses the need for greater communication between practitioners and researchers involved in music education and music therapy in order to develop our knowledge of the kinds of effects music may have.

The benefits of adult participation in music, in a professional or amateur capacity, are many and varied. Choral singing seems to have positive emotional, social, physical, and creative outcomes (Beck *et al.* 2000) which may also be spiritual (Clift and Hancox 2001). Bailey and Davidson (2002), researching members of choirs for homeless men and middle class participants, found that group singing and performance even at low levels of musicality yielded considerable emotional, social and cognitive benefits to participants. The emotional effects were similar regardless of training or socio-economic status, but interpersonal and cognitive components had different meanings for marginalized and middle-class singers. The marginalized individuals appeared to embrace all aspects of the group singing experience, while the middle class choristers were inhibited by prevalent social expectations of musicianship. Social and musical components appear to contribute equally to commitment to and enjoyment of membership of amateur operatic societies, the musical and acting components providing challenge, achievement, and opportunity to escape temporarily the frustrations of everyday living (Pitts 2004).

Community music interventions can provide senior citizens with a venue to make friends and encourage participation in intergenerational music activities between children, teenagers, and senior citizens, all of which have considerable social value (Bowers 1998; Darrow *et al.* 1994).

Music, through community education programmes, can also help adults move toward socio-political transformation (Kaltoft 1990). Engaging with music has a range of positive personal and social outcomes which do not seem to diminish with age. In older people music assists in developing self-identity, connecting with others, maintaining well-being, and experiencing and expressing spirituality, providing ways for people to maintain positive esteem, feel competent, independent, and avoid feelings of isolation or loneliness (Hays and Minichiello 2005). Although older adults require more time to encode and select information and have slower reaction times these can be minimized through task familiarity, sufficient structuring of information and regular exercise (Cavanaugh 1997). Primary mental abilities decline with age but higher-order mental activities do not, and adults may maintain or even increase mental abilities in areas of expertise including music (Pieters 1996).

There are direct health benefits for active musical participation. Choral performance increases secretory immunoglobulin A and reduces cortisol levels of professional (Beck *et al.* 2000) and amateur (Kreutz *et al.* 2004) choristers before and after singing. Playing the piano exercises the heart as much as a brisk walk (Parr 1985) and music-making contributes to perceived good health, quality of life, and mental well-being (Coffman and Adamek 1999; Vanderark *et al.* 1983).

Community music-making for adults with learning difficulties can facilitate both musical and psychological developments. MacDonald and colleagues (1999) reported that 12 weeks of community-based music workshops focused on playing a Javanese gamelan produced significant improvements in musical ability, communication skills and self-perception of musical ability. The improvement in communication skills may be linked to development in joint attention (O'Donnell *et al.* 1999). This is defined as a shared focus of attention on the same object by two individuals and is similar to the concept of 'shared social reality' (Nameera *et al.* 2007). MacDonald and Miell (2002) highlighted various ways in which community music-making was perceived by participants with special needs to be of benefit to them. The participants provided detailed accounts of how involvement was empowering and indicated that other people's expectations of their abilities changed positively. Important for them was that the music-making they were involved in was perceived to be of a professional standard. Other research has shown how improvisation workshops, percussion workshops, instrumental lessons, and singing workshops delivered to a variety of groups of adults with dementia, and adolescents with mental health disorders, can have beneficial effects on particular aspects of cognitive function (De Simone and MacDonald 2007).

The wider benefits of music in formal education

The impact of active engagement with music in the classroom is usually explained through transfer effects (see Chapter 23), the emphasis frequently being on intellectual rather than personal and social outcomes, although there has been some research considering the latter. One strand of research has focused on the impact of different types of music tuition, e.g. Dalcroze, Orff, Kodaly, while others have explored the way that music can be used to directly enhance learning materials.

Effects of particular teaching approaches

Over time, there has been considerable interest in the impact of the Kodaly method of teaching music on children's intellectual development. Positive effects have been found on temporal and spatial abilities (Hurwtiz *et al.* 1975), reading and arithmetic (Gardiner *et al.* 1996) and IQ (Schellenberg 2004), while activities involving music and movement have been found to have a positive impact on a range of outcomes including delayed development (Moore 1984) and motor performance (Zachopoulou *et al.* 2004) in comparison with controls (see also Chapter 23).

The role of music in enhancing language and literacy skills

Some researchers have focused on the impact of more general musical activities on language and literacy skills (e.g. McCarthy 1985). Using rhyme, rhythm and repetition has been shown to facilitate the learning of vocabulary (Baechtold and Algier 1986), particularly in remedial readers (Newsom 1979), and has subsequently led to improvement in reading, comprehension, attitudes and motivation. Musical activities have also been shown to assist in developing second language learning in children (e.g. Kennedy and Scott 2005) and in improving memory for a range of other materials including multiplication tables (Clauson and Thaut 1997), and stories (e.g. Allen and Butler 1996).

The direct impact of the use of music to improve literacy through the use of songs and singing has not been clearly demonstrated (e.g. Ebisutani *et al.* 1991), although music lessons designed to develop auditory, visual and motor skills have benefited reading (Douglas and Willats 1994), as have studies aimed at improving rhythmic skills (Long 2007), and there is evidence that there is a relationship between phonemic awareness, simply reading ability and pitch discrimination (e.g. Anvari *et al.* 2002). Early skill with music might enhance reading acquisition to the extent that reading depends on the same basic auditory analysis skills.

Social and personal learning outcomes

In formal education, increasing the number of classroom music lessons has been shown to have a positive impact on social behaviour. In a large-scale European study, children receiving additional music lessons demonstrated increased social cohesion within class, greater self-reliance, better social adjustment and more positive attitudes. These effects were particularly marked in low ability, disaffected pupils (Spychiger *et al.* 1993). In the UK, Harland and colleagues (2000) showed that the most frequent overall influences of engagement with music on pupils were related to their personal and social development, in particular confidence and self-esteem.

Music has also been used to change problem behaviours in particular groups of students. DeCarlo (2001) used rap music, with some success, with young urban African American adolescents with behaviour problems to promote the development of appropriate social skills related to morality, identity, judgement, decision-making, anger management, impulse control, and crime and punishment. Also in the USA, after school music programmes have been

shown to be especially beneficial for reducing the likelihood of disaffection in at-risk children (e.g. Otterbourg 2000).

The impact of background music in educational settings

Issues in studying the impact of background music

There are a number of methodological and theoretical issues which have bedevilled research exploring the impact of background music on learning and behaviour in educational settings: finding robust ways of categorizing the nature of the music itself; considering how to systematically measure its impact; and how to take account of individual differences in response.

Early research tended to ignore the characteristics of the particular music being played, assuming that all music would have a similar impact. More recent research has attempted to address this issue by differentiating music on the basis of genre, its perceived potential to stimulate or relax, whether it is vocal or instrumental, and in relation to its cognitive complexity. While all of these approaches have some merit, none have been able to capture the complexity of music as it occurs in real time. This particularly applies to Western classical music with its frequent changes of mood, tempo, timbre, complexity, and volume.

The second key methodological issue relates to the way that impact is assessed. A range of methods has been adopted including physiological and neurological measures, observation of behaviour, assessment of task performance, and the use of rating scales. However, the relationships between outcomes assessed by these various measures are complex. While arousing music tends to lead to an increase in a variety of physiological responses in children (e.g. Furman 1978) this is not always the case with adults. For instance, Iwanaga and colleagues (1996) found that university students reported increased excitation when listening to the Sacrifice Dance from the Rite of Spring but their heart rate and respiration rates did not change, although calming effects reported accompanying listening to Satie's Gymnopedie No. 1 were matched with a decrease in heart rate and respiration. Favourite music, whether stimulating or relaxing, also tends to lower subjective tension without necessarily having a similar impact on physiological responses (Iwanaga and Moroki 1999).

The third methodological issue relates to the subjective aspects of music perception. Individuals respond to the same music in very different ways, depending on their musical preferences and their individual characteristics. The structural features of the music (e.g. tempo, modality, instrumentation, genre); cultural factors (aspects of our environment including tonality and the way that musical associations are culturally shaped and learned); and associative factors (personal and subjective meanings we place on a particular piece of music depending on our musical experiences) all play a part in our responses to music. Where associative factors come into play, the structural and cultural aspects of the music are superseded by the personal and associative aspects (see Figure 44.1). Preference may therefore render very different types of music *functionally equivalent*. For example, the music which young people may chose to play while studying may differ widely but lead to similar physiological effects.

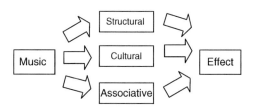

Fig. 44.1 Influences on music perception.

Explanations for the differential impact of background music include those invoking music's ability to affect arousal and mood, interfere with processing, and reduce distraction. The Yerkes–Dodson law provides one explanation stating that the arousal level of the individual increases performance up to an optimal level beyond which over-arousal leads to deterioration. This occurs more quickly when the task to be performed is complex or under-learned.

Completing a simple task requires a higher level of arousal for concentration to be maintained, complex tasks require lower arousal levels (Konecni and Sargent-Pollock 1976). Personality factors are also implicated in optimal arousal levels. Introverts have higher resting levels of arousal than extroverts and are more susceptible to over arousal. Closely related to arousal theories are those related to mood and emotions, there being considerable evidence that music can affect mood (e.g. Niedenthal and Setterland 1994) and alertness (Sousou 1997).

An alternative explanation for the impact of background music is that it reduces the cognitive processing capacity available for other material. Concentrated listening to music requires cognitive effort for processing, analysis and extracting meaning (Berlyne 1971). Listening to complex, arousal-evoking music may therefore reduce the attentional space available for task performance (e.g. Broadbent 1971). However, when people play background music they do not attend to both the music and the task simultaneously. Attention switches between the two (Madsen 1987). Depending on their interest, their focus may be greater on the task or the music. A further complication is the role of meta-cognition—participants being aware that the music is interfering with task performance and consciously adopting strategies to prevent this. This may explain age-related differences in the actual and perceived impact of music on performance (Kaniel and Aram 1998; Kotsopoulou and Hallam 2006).

The impact of background music on behaviour and task performance

Research on background music in educational contexts has explored the impact on children at different ages, with special educational needs, and undertaking a range of different tasks. For instance, in young children there is evidence that arousing music increases activity (Reiber 1965) and interactive play (Gunsberg 1991), while in older children calming music can enhance reported altruistic behaviour (Hallam *et al.* 2002). Calming music has also been found to have a positive impact on the behaviour of children with emotional and behavioural difficulties, reducing their stress and anxiety in a variety of settings (Hallam and Price 1998; Savan 1998). Sedative music can result in a greater increase in activity level in children with learning difficulties than stimulating music, the latter replacing the children's need for activity and self-stimulation. These differences in response mean that music interventions aimed at changing behaviour need to be tailored to the requirements of specific groups of children (Reardon and Bell 1970).

Much of the research on the impact of background music has lacked a clear theoretical basis for predicting outcomes, and findings often appear to be contradictory. For instance, in research relating to memorization, when music has been played concurrently with material to be remembered aurally it has not facilitated memory (Furnman 1978), paired associate recall (Myers 1979), or phonological short-term memory (Salame and Baddeley 1989), but when recall is of written sentences presented visually primary-aged children perform better when calming music is playing as opposed to silence (Hallam *et al.* 2002). Music may interfere with aural presentation and recall because of shared cognitive structures reducing processing capacity. Written presentation does not interfere in this way so arousal effects come into play. Similarly, where background music has words it may have a greater negative impact on reading comprehension and other literacy tasks (Martin *et al.* 1988).

Much of the research exploring the impact on tasks in other domains, for instance, mathematics, can be explained through the impact of music on arousal levels (e.g. Mayfield and Moss 1989), although other factors may also be important, for instance, the extent to which learners are used to working with music playing in the background (e.g. Etaugh and Michal 1975), the familiarity of the particular music being played (Hilliard and Tolin 1979), or whether the music is vocal or instrumental (Donlan 1976). Well-learned skills are less affected by high levels of arousal than those requiring creativity or high levels of concentration (Hallam and Godwin 2000) and older students may also be better able to adopt strategies which minimize the negative impact of the music on task outcomes (Kotsopoulou and Hallam 2006). Overall, the impact of background music on performance on

any particular task depends on many interacting factors.

A framework for future research

Figure 44.2 sets out a model of possible contributory factors including the nature of the music itself: its genre; whether it is stimulating or relaxing; its complexity; whether it is familiar; liked; and has been selected by the individual listening to it or imposed by others. The model suggests that the effects of music are mediated by the characteristics of the individual; their age, ability; personality; meta-cognitive skills; musical expertise; familiarity with the music being played; and the frequency with which they normally listen to music when they are studying. The current emotional arousal and mood state of the individual may also be influenced by individual characteristics and recent life events. Individual characteristics also have a direct effect on learning outcomes and a further indirect effect through meta-cognitive activity. The environment within which the activity is taking place may also be important, for instance, whether the individual is alone, in a familiar place, whether there are other distractions. The characteristics of the task, for instance, the nature of the processing required, its difficulty, whether it is perceived as interesting or boring will also play a part. Currently little research takes account of these factors.

Issues for future research

Many similar factors are important in relation to assessing the impact of active music-making as in assessing the impact of background music, for instance, taking account of the characteristics of the individual, the nature of the music itself, and the context within which the activity takes place. However, there are important differences. Crucially, when making music the focus is the musical task, which of itself may be rewarding. In addition, playing background music to support non-musical task completion has an immediate, time-limited impact restricted to that task which is unlikely to bring about long-term change in the individual. In contrast, active engagement with music making may have a longer-term impact on the individual's

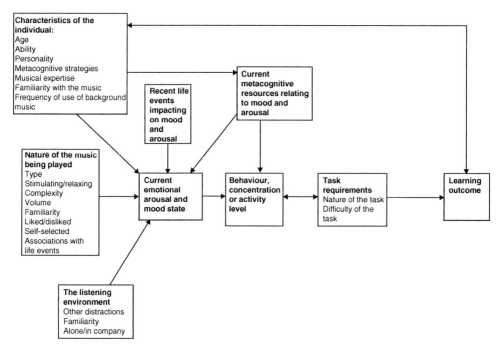

Fig. 44.2 Model of the effects of background music and learning (derived from Hallam and Goodwin 2000).

intellectual, personal, social and spiritual development. A range of different issues therefore need to be considered by researchers including:

♦ over what timescale does the impact occur?

♦ how long is it maintained?

♦ does participation have to be voluntary for there to be a positive impact?

♦ to what extent is the musical activity as opposed to any concurrent social activity important in determining the impact?

Conclusions

In the modern world all kinds of music are available to most people 24 hours a day. It pervades our everyday lives and influences our behaviour. Children are exposed to it at home and in the wider community. In contrast to this, in schools, music is rarely used to enhance behaviour and subsequently learning, although it can have powerful effects and create an environment which is more conducive to on-task behaviour. It may be that educators feel that it is inappropriate to use music in this way or that it may

interfere with the learning of some students, even though it may benefit others. Music can also support learning in other subjects through transfer effects and the way in which it can provide additional cues for remembering. This may be particularly beneficial for young children.

There are now more opportunities than ever before for all sections of society to engage in organized music-making through the growth of community music interventions around the world including signing groups for older adults, percussion workshops for disadvantaged young people, gamelan groups for individuals with special needs, and song-writing classes. There is growing evidence to suggest that these community music interventions not only help people develop musical skills but that they also are psychologically beneficial in a variety of ways.

However, there is a need for more systematic research in community and formal education contexts which establishes the conditions under which music can enhance a variety of learning, intellectual, personal, and social outcomes. Such research would be invaluable in helping to develop our knowledge of the processes and outcomes of music listening and participation, increasing our understanding of the ways in which music impacts on learning and behaviour, and enabling us to guide musicians working in education and the community as to how to maximize the positive benefits.

References

Allen BA and Butler L (1996). The effects of music and movement opportunity on the analogical reasoning performance of African American and white school children: a preliminary study. *Journal of Black Psychology*, **22**, 316–328.

Anvari SH and Trainor LJ, Woodside J and Levy BA, (2002). Relations among musical skills, phonological processing and early reading ability in preschool children. *Journal of Experimental Child Psychology*, **83**, 111–130.

Ansdell G and Pavlicevic M (2004). *Community music therapy*. Jessica Kingsley, London.

Baechtold S. and Algier A (1986). Teaching college students vocabulary with rhyme, rhythm and ritzy characters. *Journal of Reading*, **30**, 240–253.

Bailey BA and Davidson JW (2002). Adaptive characteristics of group singing: perceptions from members of a choir for homeless men. *Musicae Scientiae*, **6**, 221–256.

Beck R, Cesario T, Yousefi S and Enamoto H (2000). Choral singing, performance perception and immune system changes in salivary immunoglobulin and cortisol. *Music Perception*, **18**, 87–106.

Berlyne DE (1971). *Aesthetics and psychobiology*. New York, Appleton-Century Crofts.

Borthwick SJ and Davidson JW (2002). Personal identity and music: a family perspective. In R MacDonald, D Miell and DJ Hargreaves, eds, *Musical identities*, 60–78. Oxford University Press, Oxford.

Bowers J (1998). Effects of an intergenerational choir for community-based seniors and college students on age-related attitudes. *Journal of Music Therapy*, **35**, 2–18.

Broadbent D (1971). *Decision and stress*. Academic Press, London.

Cavanaugh JC (1997). *Adult development and aging*, 3rd edn. Brooks/Cole, Pacific Grove, CA.

Clauson DW and Thaut MH (1997). Music as a mnemonic device for children with learning disabilities. *Canadian Journal of Music Therapy*, **5**, 55–66.

Clift S and Hancox G (2001). The perceived benefits of singing: findings from preliminary surveys of a university college choral society. *The Journal of the Royal Society for the Promotion of Health*, **121**, 248–256.

Coffman DD (2002). Adult education. In R Colwell and C Richardson, eds, *The new handbook of research on music teaching and learning*, 199–209. Oxford University Press, Oxford.

Coffman DD and Adamek M (1999). The contribution of wind band participation to quality of life of senior adult band members. *Dialogue in Instrumental Music Education*, **20**, 25–34.

Conda JM (1997). The late bloomers piano club: a case study of a group in progress. Unpublished Doctoral Dissertation, University of Oklahoma, 1997. Dissertation Abstracts International, 58, 409A.

Darrow AA, Johnson CM and Ollenberger T (1994). The effect of participation in an intergenerational choir on teens' and older persons' cross-age attitudes. *Journal of Music Therapy*, **31**, 119–134.

Davidson JW (2004). What social psychology of music offers music therapy. In G Ansdell and M Pavlicevic, eds, *Community music therapy*, 47–68. Jessica Kingsley, London

DeCarlo A (2001). Rap therapy? An innovative approach to groupwork with urban adolescents. *Journal of Intergroup Relations*, **27**, 40–48.

De Simone J and MacDonald RAR (2007). An investigation of the effects of a structured music programme on cognition in the treatment of patients with dementia. Paper presented at The 7th European Music Therapy Congress, Eindhoven, August 2007.

Donlan D (1976) The effect of four types of music on spontaneous writings of high school students. *Research in the Teaching of English*, **10**, 116–126.

Douglas S and Willats P (1994). The relationship between musical ability and literacy skills. *Journal of Research in Reading*, **17**, 99–107.

Ebisutani K, Donlan D and Siebers E (1991). The effects of music on reading, oral language, and writing abilities: a review of literature. ERIC database document 333 356.

Etaugh C and Michal D (1975). Effects on reading comprehension or preferred music and frequency of studying to music. *Perceptual and Motor Skills*, **41**, 553–554.

Elliott D (2004). Editorial. *The International Journal of Community Music*, **1**, 1.

Furman CE (1978). The effect of musical stimuli on the brainwave production of children. *Journal of Music Therapy*, **15**, 108–117.

Gardiner MF, Fox A, Knowles F and Jeffrey D (1996). Learning improved by arts training. *Nature*, **381**, 284.

Gunsberg AS (1991). Play as improvisation: the benefits of music for developmentally delayed young children's social play. *Early Child Development and Care*, **66**, 85–91.

Hallam S and Godwin C (2000). The effects of background music on primary school pupils' performance on a writing task. Paper presented at the annual conference of the British Educational Research Association, University of Wales, Cardiff, 7–9 September, 2000.

Hallam S and Price J (1998). Can the use of background music improve the behaviour and academic performance of children with emotional and behavioural difficulties? *British Journal of Special Education*, **25**, 87–90.

Hallam S, Price J and Katsarou K (2002). The effects of background music on primary school pupils' task performance. *Educational Studies*, **28**, 111–122.

Harland J, Kinder K, Lord P, Stott A, Schagen I and Haynes J (2000). *Arts education in secondary schools: effects and effectiveness*. NFER/The Arts Council of England, RSA, London.

Hays T and Minichiello V (2005). The meaning of music in the lives of older people: a qualitative study. *Psychology of Music*, 33, 437–452.

Hilliard OM and Tolin A (1979). Effect of familiarity with background music on performance of simple and difficult reading comprehension tasks. *Perceptual and Motor Skills*, 49, 713–714.

Hinkle LB (1988). The meaning of choral experience to the adult membership of the German singing societies comprising the United Singers Federation of Pennsylvania. Unpublished doctoral dissertation, Pennsylvania State University, 1987. Dissertation Abstracts International, 48, 2568A.

Hurwitz I, Wolff PH, Bortnick BD and Kokas K (1975). Non-musical effects of the Kodaly music curriculum in primary grade children. *Journal of Learning Disabilities*, 8, 45–52.

Iwanaga M and Moroki Y (1999). Subjective and physiological responses to music stimuli controlled over activity and preference. *Journal of Music Therapy*, xxxvi, 26–38.

Iwanaga M, Ikeda M and Iwaki T (1996). The effects of repetitive exposure to music on subjective and physiological responses. *Journal of Music Therapy*, xxxiii, 219–230.

Kaltoft G (1990). Music and emancipatory learning in three community education programs. *Dissertation Abstracts International*, 51(7), 2239A. (UMI No. AAT90–33861.).

Kaniel S and Aram D (1998). Influence of task difficulty and background music on working memory activity: developmental considerations. *Alberta Journal of Educational Research*, 44, 342–345.

Kennedy R and Scott A (2005). A pilot study: the effects of music therapy interventions on middle school students' ESL skills. *Journal of Music Therapy*, 42, 244–261.

Konecni VJ and Sargent-Pollock D (1976). Choice between melodies differing in complexity under divided-attention conditions. *Journal of Experimental Psychology: Human Perception and Performance*, 2, 347–356.

Kotsopoulou A and Hallam S (2006). Age differences in listening to music while studying. In M Baroni, AR Addessi, R Caterina and M Costa, eds, *Proceedings of the 9th International Conference on Music Perception and Cognition*. University of Bologna, 22–26 August 2006. Available at: http://www.icmpc2006.org.

Kreutz G, Bongard S, Rohrmann S, Hodapp V and Grebe D (2004). Effects of choir singing or listening on secretory immunoglobulin A, cortisol, and emotional state. *Journal of Behavioural Medicine*, 27, 623–635.

Lamont A (2002). Musical identities and the school environment. In RAR MacDonald, DJ Hargreaves, D Miell, eds, *Musical identities*, 49–55. Oxford University Press, Oxford.

Larson P (1983). An exploratory study of lifelong musical interest and activity: case studies of twelve retired adults. Unpublished Doctoral dissertation, Temple University, 1982. Dissertation Abstracts International, 44, 100A.

Long M (2007). The effect of a music intervention on the temporal organisation of reacing skills. Unpublished PhD Thesis, Institute of Education, University of London.

MacDonald RAR, JB Davies and O'Donnell PJ (1999). Structured music workshops for individuals with learning difficulty: an empirical investigation. *Journal of Applied Research in Intellectual Disabilities*, 12, 225–241.

MacDonald RAR, Hargreaves DJ and Miell D (eds) (2002). *Musical identities*. Oxford University Press, Oxford.

MacDonald RAR and Miell D (2002). Music for individuals with special needs: a catalyst for developments in identity, communication and musical ability. In RAR MacDonald, DJ Hargreaves and DE Miell, eds, *Musical identities*, 163–179. Oxford University, Oxford.

Madsen CK (1987). Background music: competition for focus of attention. In CK Madsen, CA Prickett, eds, *Applications of research in music behaviour*, 315–325. The University of Alabama Press, Tucaloosa, AL.

Martin RC, Wogalter MS and Forlano JG (1988). Reading comprehension in the presence of unattended speech and music. *Journal of Memory and Language*, 27, 382–398.

Mayfield C and Moss S (1989). Effect of music tempo on task performance. *Psychological Reports*, 65, 1283–1290.

McCarthy WG (1985). Promoting language development through music. *Academic Therapy*, 21, 237–242.

McPherson GE (in press). The role of parents in children's musical development. *Psychology of Music*

Miell D, MacDonald RAR and Hargreaves DJ (eds) (2005). *Musical communication*. Oxford University Press, Oxford.

Moore J (1984). Rhythm and movement: an objective analysis of their association with music aptitude. *Dissertation Abstracts International*, 45, 1328 A.

Myers EG (1979) The effect of music on retention in a paired-associate task with EMR children. *Journal of Music Therapy*, 16, 190–198.

Nameera A, Morton A and Gernsbacher R (2007). Joint attention and vocabulary development: a critical look. *Language and Linguistics Compass*, 1, 195–207.

Newsom SD (1979). Rock 'n' roll 'n' reading. *Journal of Reading*, 22, 726–730.

Niedenthal PM and Setterland MB (1994). Emotion congruence in perception. *Personality and Social Psychology Bulletin*, 20, 401–411.

Ockelford A (2000). Music in the education of children with severe or profound difficulties: issues in current UK provision, a new conceptual framework and proposals for research. *Psychology of Music*, 28, 197–218.

O'Donnell PJ, MacDonald RAR and Davies JB (1999). Video analysis of the effects of structured music workshops for individuals with learning difficulties. In D Erdonmez and RR Pratt, eds, *Music therapy and music medicine: expanding horizons*, 219–228. MMB Music, Saint Louis, MO.

Otterbourg SD (2000). *How the arts can enhance after-school programs*. National Endowment for the Arts (ERIC Document Reproduction Service No ED446829), Washington, DC.

Parr SM (1985). The effects of graduated exercise at the piano on the pianist's cardiac output, forearm blood flow, heart rate, and blood pressure. *Dissertation Abstracts International*, **46**(6), 1436A. (UMI No. AAT85–18673.).

Pieters JM (1996). Psychology of adult education. In AC Tuijnman, ed., *International encyclopedia of adult education and training*, 2nd edn, 150–158. Elsevier Science, New York.

Pitts SE (2004). Everybody wants to be Pavarotti: the experience of music for performers and audience at a Gilbert and Sullivan festival. *Journal of the Royal Musical Association*, **129**, 149–167.

Reardon DM and Bell G (1970). Effects of sedative and stimulative music on activity levels of severely retarded boys. *American Journal of Mental Deficiency*, **75**, 156–159.

Reiber M (1965). The effect of music on the level of activity of children. *Psychonomic Science*, **3**, 325–326.

Ruud E (2004). Introduction: the ripple effect. In G Ansdell, M Pavlicevic, eds, *Community music therapy*, i–vi. Jessica Kingsley, London.

Salame P and Baddeley A (1989). Effects of background music on phonological short term memory.

The Quarterly Journal of Experimental Psychology, **41**, 107–122.

Savan A (1998). A study of the effect of background music on the behaviour and physiological responses of children with special educational needs. *The Psychology of Education Review*, **22**, 32–36.

Schellenberg EG (2004). Music lessons enhance IQ. *Psychological Science*, **15**, 511–514.

Sousou SD (1997). Effects of melody and lyrics on mood and memory. *Perceptual and Motor Skills*, **85**, 31–40.

Spychiger M, Patry J, Lauper G, Zimmermann E and Weber E (1993). Does more music teaching lead to a better social climate? In R Olechowski and G Svik, eds, *Experimental research in teaching and learning*, 322–336. Peter Lang, Bern.

Trevarthen C (2002). Origins of musical identity: evidence from infancy for musical social awareness. In RAR MacDonald, DJ Hargreaves and DE Miell, eds, *Musical identities*, 22–46. Oxford University Press, Oxford.

Vanderark SD, Newman I and Bell S (1983). The effects of music participation on quality of life in the elderly. *Music Therapy*, **3**, 71–81.

Veblen KK (2004). The many ways of community music. *The International Journal of Community Music*, **1**, 8–16.

Zachopoulou E, Tsapakidou A and Derri V (2004). The effects of a developmentally appropriate music and movement program on motor performance. *Early Childhood Research Quarterly*, **19**, 631–642.

CHAPTER 45

Music and consumer behaviour

Adrian C. North and David J. Hargreaves

THE past 20 years has seen a massive increase in research on the effects of music on consumers in both retail and commercial leisure settings such as restaurants, hotels, bars, gyms, and the like. There are at least two reasons for this, namely an increasing interest among music psychologists in social psychological factors and the application of findings to practice (North and Hargreaves 2008), and an increasing interest among consumer psychologists (and people in cognate disciplines) in how aspects of the service environment can influence customers. Indeed, the quantity of research has reached such a level that North and Hargreaves (2008) were able to devote an extended chapter to a detailed review, and Garlin and Owen (2006) were able to conduct a meta-analysis based on only a portion of the number of studies published. Garlin and Owen's analysis showed 'small-to-moderate, yet quite robust effects in terms of background music and the dependents: value returns, behaviour duration and affective response' (p. 755): North and Hargreaves' (2008) review concurred. Indeed in addition to our extended chapter on the subject in *The social and applied psychology of music*, we have been invited to contribute chapters to edited volumes on four separate occasions over recent years (North and Hargreaves 1997, 2005, 2006; North *et al.* 2002) which suggests that, if nothing else, the field has become a recognized part of the psychology of music.

Given the recency of these other reviews it would be a wasted opportunity to merely reiterate the same arguments here. Instead we have opted to take this opportunity to focus solely on our own research on the subject that has been carried out over the past decade. Each of these studies has had its own particular theoretical perspective of course, but as a whole our research in this area has had a broader ambition, namely to begin mapping out the *range* of influences that music might have. In short, the question we have asked is 'What effects can music have on consumers?'

There is both a theoretical and a practical motivation behind this question. From a theoretical perspective, the existing research points to three psychological processes that underlie many effects. The first of these processes concerns the effect of music on physiological arousal. As we shall see shortly, several studies have argued that faster music speeds up customer activity, and explain this by referring to (now fairly antiquated) evidence from experimental aesthetics concerning how factors such as musical tempo might increase activity in the autonomic nervous system. The second process concerns the ability of music to prime certain thoughts. Several specific variations of the theory have been proposed (e.g. Hansen and Hansen 1990; Martindale and Moore 1989; North *et al.* 2004), but all of them describe how hearing a piece of music can activate several related ideas that are either expressed directly or indirectly in the music and lyrics or expressed indirectly as a result of shared cultural understanding of the meaning of the music in question. For example, hearing the *Sergeant Pepper* album by The Beatles primes thoughts related to 'love' as a result of not just those lyrics that directly address the subject, but also because, on a cultural level, we associate the album with the 'flower power' movement of the late 1960s. Finally, the research suggests that the emotional effects of music can also influence consumers. There are many specific manifestations of this approach, although most involve some aspect of emotional response to music having a subsequent influence on the processing of commercially relevant information.

Of course three of the key explanations evoked by over a century of experimental psychology have also concerned arousal-based effects, priming effects, and the impact of emotion on behaviour. For example, classic research on skilled performance (e.g. Yerkes and Dodson 1908) has focused on how the arousal and information-processing load evoked by a stimulus can mediate performance across numerous domains. Similarly one of the central tenets of social cognition is that each new stimulus is processed in the light of stimuli encountered previously, such that responses to the latter prime responses to the former. Furthermore, large sections of social psychology (e.g. prosocial behaviour, environmental psychology) have considered the impact of emotional states on the ways in which people behave in everyday situations. Since arousal-, priming-, and emotion-based effects have such fundamental relevance to a range of human behaviours and can all result from hearing music, it seems reasonable to make the starting assumption that arousal-, priming-, and emotion-based effects of music might influence a broad range of consumer behaviours.

It also makes practical sense to map out the range of influences of music on consumer behaviour. In short, a store manager may use a certain type of music because they have read reports suggesting that it increases the speed with which customers shop. However, the music could be extremely counter-productive from a commercial standpoint if it nonetheless decreases customers' propensity to spend money, distracts their attention from special offers, makes the store feel crowded, or annoys customers so much that they decide to leave, to name but a few of the possible unintended outcomes. In short, the store manager can only use music optimally if they understand *all* the effects that a

given piece of music will have. In particular, the commercial world should be interested in purely theoretical research, as we have long-subscribed to the maxim that 'There is nothing so practical as a good theory': in a commercial context, this means that if a store manager understands how music has the effects that it does, then they can control those effects and use them to their best advantage. A theoretical and a practical understanding of the effects of music in commercial environments go hand in hand with one another.

We begin the chapter with a brief overview of two particular effects of music that have received a considerable amount of attention. From here we go on to use our own research to illustrate the many other commercially relevant processes that can be influenced by music.

Speed of activity and time perception

Two particular topics have dominated research on music and consumer behaviour. These are the effect of music on the speed with which customers behave, and the impact of music on time perception.

Several studies indicate that the speed of customer activity is related positively to the tempo and volume of background music. Many researchers have drawn on the findings of research on experimental aesthetics from the 1960s and 1970s (e.g. Berlyne 1971) which argued that louder or faster music lead to greater levels of physiological arousal, whereas slower or quieter music lead to correspondingly lower levels of physiological arousal. For example, Milliman (1982) found that slow music led to customers in a supermarket shopping 15 per cent more slowly than when fast music was played. Furthermore, customers in the slow music condition also spent around 33 per cent more money, and this is probably because the act of shopping more slowly also gave customers more opportunity to browse a range of products. Smith and Curnow (1966) produced similar results when they manipulated musical volume rather than tempo in a supermarket. Similarly Milliman (1986) studied 1392 groups of restaurant customers over 8 weekends.

Slow music led to customers eating more slowly, completing their meal in 56 minutes on average compared to 45 minutes when fast music was played. This also affected spending. Customers in the slow music condition, who ate more slowly, ending up spending more money on drinks ($30.47 vs $21.62 in the fast music condition). Roballey *et al.* (1985) adopted a dependent variable that is surely unique in the entirety of published psychology, namely bites per minute, finding that fast music in a cafeteria led to 4.40 bites per minute whereas slow music led to only 3.83 bites per minute.

Effects such as these highlight a theme that we will return to several times in this chapter, namely that almost all uses of music in commercial environments reflect a trade-off in which practitioners must decide what type of music they want to use in order to achieve what specific commercial gain. In this case, there is a clear trade-off between the speed of customer activity and spending. For example, if someone is the manager of a café then on Saturday lunchtime all the tables will be full. It is consequently in their interest to play fast music, free up some tables, and therefore maximize profit. If it is Tuesday morning and the café is quite empty then it makes more sense to play slower music in the hope that Milliman's (1986) findings would be replicated and customers would spend more money on drinks.

The second topic that has received considerable research attention has concerned the possible impact of music on time perception. There are numerous, slightly differing, explanations of this effect. However, common to many is the notion, drawn from mainstream research on time perception, that the perception of the passage of time is related to the amount of information encoded during the period in question. This explanation states that the mind invokes an heuristic to the effect that 'if more has happened then more time must have passed'. Research using this approach has, for example, suggested that louder music should therefore lead to the perception of more time having passed. Louder music imposes a greater information-processing load, 'tricks' people into believing that more has happened, and therefore leads to the perception that more time has passed (e.g. Kellaris and Altsech 1992). Another version of this argument

reasons that if music imposes a greater processing load on the listener (i.e. by being loud, fast, or complex) then this distracts attention from an internal cognitive timer that monitors the passage of time. Other research has gone on from here and related time perception to whether people like the music they hear. This research employs the intuitive notion that people pay more attention to stimuli that they like. So if somebody likes music that they hear then they pay more attention to it. Because they pay more attention to it, the music imposes a greater information processing load, and so liked music leads to the perception that more time has passed (e.g. Kellaris and Mantel 1994). Although there is evidence to support the arguments set out here, unfortunately this neat theorizing has not led to consistently neat findings. If correct, however, this line of reasoning again implies the existence of another trade-off for practitioners. Followed through to the logical conclusion, research on time perception implies that if a business aims solely to reduce the amount of time that people think they have been waiting for then it might be better to play music that the customers don't like! Alternately, disliked music will nonetheless annoy customers of course, so if perceptions of service quality are more important than waiting time customers should hear music that they like.

The range of effects of music

In 1996 we began a series of studies that have aimed to outline the range of consumer behaviours that might be influenced by music. The remainder of this chapter is devoted to an overview of seven of these influences.

Visiting

North and Hargreaves (1996a) used an emotion-based approach to investigate whether music could influence where people went. We set up an 'advice stall' in an on-campus cafeteria. In effect, the stall was a couple of tables pushed together on which were leaflets offering advice on a range of typical student welfare issues such as safe sex, recommended maximum levels of alcohol consumption, how to find good housing, and similar issues. From the stall we played pop music of three levels of complexity. Melodic complexity is the extent to which the music is erratic, varied, and difficult to predict. Several lab-based studies in experimental aesthetics (see Berlyne 1971) have shown that moderately complex music seems to be liked most: music of low and high complexity tends to be unpopular.

We measured the impact of the music on the number of people visiting the stall. 'Visiting' was measured in two ways. First, diners in the cafeteria were asked to complete a questionnaire asking them to state how likely they were to visit the stall. Measured this way, people's propensity to visit the advice stall was not influenced by the music. However, a behavioural measure of visiting produced a very different conclusion. On the floor, about one metre from the stall, were a series of small stickers that marked the boundary of an 'approach zone'. Someone was counted as having visited the stall if they put one foot inside this zone and took another step towards the stall. When moderately complex pop music was played then 10.71 people visited the stall every 10 minutes, and this represented significantly more people than when no music (4.01 people) and high complexity pop music (3.67 people) was played.

This has several implications. First, people were predisposed to visit the physical source of liked music. This suggests strongly that playing liked music, in a shop for instance, would encourage people to enter the premises, or could attract people to areas of the premises that they tend not to visit otherwise (e.g. the point farthest from the door or upstairs). Second, the effect of the no music condition relative to the moderate and high complexity pop was interesting. The 'right' music was better at attracting people to the stall than was playing nothing: the 'wrong' music was worse than playing nothing. In short, the real question facing practitioners is not 'Should I play music or not?' but rather 'What is the right kind of music to play?': music that is liked is commercially 'better' than no music, whereas music that is disliked is commercially 'worse' than no music. Again, practitioners face a decision. If a manager is not confident that customers will like the music that is played then they should turn it off: if they are confident that customers

will like the music then this should bestow a considerable commercial advantage. Third, these findings show that complexity is one of the variables that allows managers to determine what the 'right' kind of music is: laws of musical preference derived from the lab can be applied in commercial premises to produce music that customers like. Indeed, when completing the questionnaire diners were asked to say how much they liked the music (see North and Hargreaves 1996b), with data showing that moderately complex music was most popular. Diners' answers to the questionnaire also showed however that the more they disliked the music so the more noticeable it became: if a business plays the 'right' kind of music then it will get no thanks, but if it plays the 'wrong' kind of music then everyone will notice! This probably goes a long way to explaining the negative stereotype that the general public holds concerning piped music.

Arousal-based goals

North and Hargreaves (2000) adopted an arousal-based approach to investigate further what the 'right' kind of music might be for commercial premises. As noted earlier, research on experimental aesthetics has argued that people like moderately complex music the most. Researchers such as Berlyne (1971; see also e.g. North and Hargreaves 1996c) have argued that this is because moderately complex music brings about a moderate level of arousal in the autonomic nervous system: Berlyne's theory says that high complexity music brings about too much arousal, and low complexity music brings about too little arousal. Berlyne's theory also argues that factors other than complexity can also cause music to have arousal-evoking properties. For example, louder or faster music is claimed to bring about more arousal than quieter or slower music.

However, if Berlyne's theory is correct and people always use musical complexity, tempo, and volume to bring about a state of moderate arousal, then why do gyms and nightclubs play music that is loud, fast, and otherwise designed apparently to increase an already very *high* level of arousal? According to Berlyne's theory, this music ought to be disliked. Indeed, North and

Hargreaves (1996d) found that when people were asked to imagine themselves in a nightclub then they claimed that they would want to hear arousing music, which suggests that this type of music is not simply being foisted upon an ungrateful public but is instead what people want to hear. In short, there is a problem when attempting to apply Berlyne's theory to common practice in commercial premises.

North and Hargreaves (2000) investigated this by using an experimental simulation of a gym and also a relaxing situation. In our first experiment we asked people to ride an exercise bike or lie down and relax. *After* doing these tasks, people could choose between a loud, fast (i.e. arousing) piece of music or a slow, quiet (i.e. much less arousing) version of the same piece. Consistent with Berlyne's theory, people who had just finished exercising chose to listen to the slow, quiet music that would reduce the level of arousal brought about by cycling to a moderate level: people who had just finished relaxing chose to listen to the fast, loud music that would raise their level of arousal from the low level brought about by relaxation back up to a moderate level. However, in the second experiment we asked people to choose between the two types of music *while* they either exercised or relaxed. This time we got the opposite pattern of results. People who were cycling chose to listen to loud, fast music that would further increase their level of arousal: people who were relaxing chose slow, quiet music that would further reduce their level of arousal. In other words, although most of the time (e.g. when sitting in a café at lunchtime) people like moderately arousing music, we sometimes choose to put ourselves in a state of very high or very low arousal and, under these circumstances, we use music to help achieve these arousal-based goals. In particular, people in gyms and nightclubs want to be in a state of high arousal and loud, fast music can help them to achieve this goal: people in hotels, health spas, or on long-haul flights want to be in a state of low arousal, and would want access to slow, quiet music that helps to achieve this goal.

Store image and purchasing

North and Hargreaves (1998) used a priming-based approach to investigate the effect of music on the atmosphere or 'image' of a store and also actual purchasing. We returned to the same café that we used in our 'visiting' study. Rather than focus on complexity, this time we played different musical styles. Over four days we played pop music, classical music, easy listening music (that was modelled on the 'sweeping strings' stereotype of piped music), and no music. Customers were asked to complete a questionnaire. First they were given a list of 14 items on sale in the café such as a can of Diet Coke and a slice of vegetarian pizza. Customers had to say the *maximum* that they would be prepared to spend on each item in turn. They also had to rate the atmosphere in the café according to 20 different adjectives.

Different musical styles gave rise to very different 'atmospheres'. Pop music led to the perception that the café was lively and youthful, classical music led to the perception that the café was upmarket and sophisticated, whereas the stereotypical piped music led to the perception that the café was downmarket. This is quite interesting in its own right. However, where store atmosphere really seemed to make itself felt was in customers' statements of how much they were prepared to spend in the café. When no music was played, customers were prepared to spend a total of £14.30 on the 14 items. When stereotypical piped music was played, customers were prepared to spend a total of £14.51 on the 14 items. However, when pop music was played (which made the café seem lively and youthful), customers were then prepared to spend £16.61 on the 14 items. Furthermore, when classical music was played (which made the café seem upmarket and sophisticated) then customers were prepared to spend £17.23 on precisely the same items in precisely the same place. Remember also that the customers were exclusively students who would prefer pop music over classical music: although the effect of pop music on the amount that customers were prepared to spend can probably be attributed to liking for that music, the greater effect of classical music cannot be. Rather it seems that customers were tapping in to the atmosphere portrayed by the music and acting accordingly. To put it bluntly, the upmarket and sophisticated atmosphere promoted by classical seemed to prime customers to feel more affluent.

This idea of using music to predispose people to behave in a particular way has been referred to sometimes as 'musical fit', and has been studied by several researchers over the past few years. For example, Areni and Kim (1993) played classical music and pop music in a wine cellar. They found that although the two different types of music did not lead to customers buying any more wine, classical music led to customers buying more *expensive* wine, and they argue that this was because the classical music primed customers to feel more affluent and act accordingly. This notion of musical fit was the subject of a follow-up study that we carried out. North *et al.*'s (2003) study was carried out in a restaurant in the town of Market Bosworth in Leicestershire. Classical music, pop music, and no music were played over three weeks, and customers' spending seemed to be influenced by the apparent effects of musical fit. When classical music was played, customers spent £32.52 on average, whereas when pop music was played customers spent £29.46, and when no music was played customers spent £29.73. Since the restaurant management, quite understandably, did not want us to approach customers we were unable to measure their degree of liking for the music and rule this out as an explanation for the results. However, in apparent support for the 'musical fit' explanation of diners' spending, the positive effects of classical music on spending were particularly strong in the case of starters and coffee; in other words, items that it is possible for customers to avoid while nonetheless being able to tell themselves that they had 'eaten out'. Did they spend more on starters and coffee because the classical music made them feel more affluent?

Product choice

North and colleagues (1997, 1999a) also used a priming-based approach to investigate another aspect of musical fit, namely product choice. We used an aisle-end display in a local supermarket that featured several French and German wines. Each shelf on the display featured one type of French wine and one type of German wine, with the two wines on that shelf representing a similar degree of 'dryness' and being of very similar price. In other words, the main

distinction between the two types of wine on each shelf (at least for non-connoisseurs) was arguably the country of origin. On the top shelf of the display was a small tape player. On alternate days this played either French or German music. Note that this manipulation of the music did not require customers to know that for example, Debussy was French or that Beethoven was German. Rather the manipulation went for the lowest common denominator such that 'French music' featured accordions heavily (as well as other stereotypically 'French' features), whereas the 'German music' featured an oompah band performance of songs concerning, among other issues, the pleasures of drinking white wine on the Rhein. The display was in view of the checkouts, and we sat behind these, next to a taxi phone, with carrier bags full of shopping to create the impression that we were normal customers waiting for our taxi to arrive. In reality we were observing the number of bottles of wine sold.

The results were consistent with the notion of musical fit. When French music was played then French wine outsold German by five bottles to one. When German music was played then German wine outsold French by two bottles to one. We investigated this further using a questionnaire. Once customers left the wines section (and entered the frozen pizza aisle!) they were approached by a researcher who asked them to state whether the type of wine they had bought had been influenced by the music that was playing. The sales data showed that they ought to answer that it had been. Unfortunately only 44 customers agreed to answer this question. However, although the sales data indicated that wine choices had been influenced by the music, only one customer was prepared to admit this on the questionnaire.

Findings such as these have obvious implications. First and most obviously they suggest that musical fit can influence product choice as well as spending. Second, the difference between actual wine sales and responses to the questionnaire could be taken as implying that customers were in some way unaware of the effect of musical fit on their behaviour. If this were so, it would of course have serious ethical implications (and indeed one national newspaper headline at the time claimed that psychologists had discovered a way of making consumers buy things that they didn't want). We suspect strongly, however, that a far more mundane explanation is correct. We noted earlier that the music played from our display was crass. Consequently we find it hard to believe that, when asked midway through a shopping trip, people would be prepared to say that 'in effect, yes, all it took to get me to buy French wine was a bit of music played from a tinny speaker': they had a far stronger motivation to tell the researcher, in effect, that 'no, I was not influenced, and I can assure you that I always buy this type of wine'. Instead the music probably worked in just the same way as an advert placed by the entrance, advertising the fact that French (or German) products were on sale and raising their salience. Indeed we would actually go a step further than this and argue that the effects of musical fit will probably occur only under conditions where customers are otherwise undecided about which course of action to take. For example, if the supermarket study had replaced wines with cars, then it seems almost inconceivable that music could have affected people choosing between buying a Renault and a Volkswagen (although this does of course remain to be shown by data). When other information is available to demonstrate which of the available options is best, or when people otherwise have a very strong motivation to think about the options in detail, we expect that musical fit would become a relatively unimportant factor in their decision-making. Balanced against this of course is the fact that consumers do make many decisions on the spur of the moment with little thought: a shopper may have pasta on their shopping list but no firm opinion about which of two brands is best, and be even less inclined to stand in the supermarket for a few moments and think about it. There is tremendous scope for the application of musical fit.

Musical 'fit' in advertising

If musical fit does operate by raising the salience of ideas related to the music, then this greater salience ought to have implications for memory. North et al. (2004) studied musical fit in radio advertising. We reasoned that if music in the

adverts 'fitted' with the advertised product then, by raising the salience of the product, the music should help people to remember it. We prepared radio adverts for five brands, an online bank, a people carrier, a bathroom cleaner, a chocolate bar, and an energy (i.e. high-sugar) drink. On top of the voiceover in each advert we played music that either did or did not fit with the characteristics of each brand. After hearing the adverts, people were asked to read a short story before then being asked to recall what they had heard. Recall was indeed higher when the adverts had featured music that 'fitted' the advertised product. This is consistent with the notion that musical fit had primed listeners' thought processes, such that this priming aided recall. Rather less profoundly, these results show that musical fit also operates in the context of advertising. Also, if musical fit improves memory by raising the salience of certain ideas or causing a greater degree of thought, then it may also be the case that very low levels of congruity between music and product achieve the same effect: people would be expected to try to resolve the extreme incongruity between music and product, and the greater amount of thought devoted subsequently to the product may also have the effect of improving memory for it.

Music on-hold

Several other studies have considered time-related effects of music. North et al. (1999b) investigated a simple question, namely whether on-hold phone music should work. The research was set up to look into two competing hypotheses. On the one hand, as described earlier, the research on time perception indicates that liked music should lead to longer time duration estimates. This means that hearing liked music while waiting on hold ought to produce longer estimated waiting times and an increased propensity to hang up. On the other hand, an emotion-based approach led us to reason that if callers like the music they hear while on-hold then they ought to be more inclined to stay on the line: if North and Hargreaves (1996a) showed that that liked music could attract people to an advice stall then why shouldn't liked music attract people to a phone line? Alternately, another emotion-based possibility was that liking for the music was less relevant than the potential ability of music to simply calm callers down and counteract their irritation at being kept waiting.

To test these ideas we placed an advert in our local newspaper. This asked people to call a phone number in order to take part in a survey. When people called we automatically put them on hold. While waiting they heard one of three things. Some people heard 'liked music' which we operationalised as excerpts of three songs by The Beatles, namely *Yesterday*, *Eleanor Rigby*, and *Hey Jude*. Other people heard the 'weapon of choice' of most on-hold phone systems, namely pan-pipe music, which in this case featured cover versions of the same excerpts of the three Beatles' songs. A final group of people heard nothing at all apart from a brief, repeating spoken message encouraging them to keep waiting. At no point in the experiment did we actually answer to the phone: instead we simply timed how long people waited for before they lost patience and hung up.

The spoken message led to callers waiting, on average, for 197.76 seconds; and the original songs by The Beatles led to callers waiting for 229.50 seconds. However, the most successful condition was the pan-pipe cover versions, which led to callers waiting for an average of 257.28 seconds. Indeed, the success of the pan-pipes is best illustrated by pointing out that, in order to keep the line clear for new callers, we automatically cut people off once they had waited for 300 seconds. Given that some people hung up the moment they realized they had been put on hold, the average waiting time for the pan-pipe condition indicates in effect that we simply couldn't get rid of people in this condition!

In an attempt to explain the success of the pan-pipes (and arrange to pay people for their trouble) we used caller identification to call people back. Callers were asked to rate our telephone service on several dimensions. The Beatles and the pan-pipes conditions were liked as much as one another, and so liking for the music could not explain the effects of the pan-pipes on waiting time. However, when people were asked to rate the phone service according to five adjectives only one, 'peaceful', gave rise to significant differences between the conditions,

with the pan-pipe condition receiving the highest ratings. In short, on-hold phone music can persuade people to wait for longer than can a spoken message, but it is important that this music should reduce stress and irritation in order to be successful.

Priming store image

Much of the research reviewed above highlights the importance of using music to control the impression that customers have of a particular set of commercial premises. This then raises the issue of how precisely music influences these impressions, and this was investigated by North *et al.* (2000). We studied music in a bank branch and a local bar. In the city centre bar we played classical music, pop music, and no music over nine days. Customers rated the extent to which the bar could be described in terms of 11 different adjectives. Factor analysis of these ratings indicated that the adjectives fell into three factors, namely 'dynamic/upbeat', 'cerebral', and 'aggressive/downmarket'. The bank study played classical music, easy listening music, and no music over three weeks. Customers rated the extent to which the bank could be described in terms of 20 different adjectives, and a factor analysis showed that these adjectives fell into four factors that were remarkably similar to those in response to the bar, namely 'dynamic/upbeat', 'dignified', 'assertive/aggressive', and 'inspirational'. In both the bar and the bank, different musical styles gave rise to different scores on these factors. More simply, any attempt to use music to control the impression that customers form of commercial premises should focus primarily on the factors described here, since these subsume many of the other, more fine-grained responses that customers might have.

Conclusions

The findings reviewed here provide initial positive signs that music can have a wide range of positive commercial benefits. Music can influence the places that customers go to, customers' ability to achieve a desired level of arousal, the atmosphere of commercial premises, the amount that customers are prepared to spend, the amount they actually spend, the products they buy, their memory for advertising, and the amount of time they wait on hold. In addition to research by other academics on time perception and the impact of musical tempo and volume on the speed of customer behaviour, our own studies described here begin to map out the range of effects that music might have on consumers. Furthermore, the 10 effects described here seem to be based on fundamental psychological processes concerning arousal, priming, and the effects of emotions on behaviour, such that they may represent only the beginning of a list rather than a final definitive account.

Furthermore the research described here highlights an important issue for practitioners. If music can have many different effects it is important to prioritize those that correspond best with the business' marketing goals. Following from this, there can be no single 'right' type of music that is a universal commercial panacea, and the real issue is how to select music that addresses the most important marketing goals and does not hamper others. The specific answer to the question 'What music should my business play?' involves consideration of the psychological effects of music that are known to exist, the importance of various marketing goals, the musical preference of the customers (or at least careful steps to avoid annoying customers), along with numerous practical constraints such as budget or the need to install appropriate equipment.

Note also that we say that the evidence here provides only 'initial signs' of a positive effect of music because of the obvious difficulty of devising a detailed model of the process and testing all the possible aspects of this. The typical customer is engaged in a complex decision-making task, weighing up at least two competing alternative products along numerous cognitive and social psychological dimensions (e.g. a consideration of price vs benefit, product quality, relevance to self-concept, prevailing fashions etc.). Furthermore, some of these dimensions will only have become salient very recently, whereas others have been evaluated in detail over extended periods of time (as a result of prior experience of the products, advertising, or the opinions of friends, to name just three). At the same time, the customer will be managing several competing attentional demands (e.g. the presence of others, other time pressures etc.). As if understanding this were not complicated enough, music itself of course varies along numerous dimensions, all of which affect a customer in some way, with some of these effects being complementary and others less so. Devising an explanation of how all these factors interact is a daunting task, but at least work has begun on the basic building blocks, namely an outline of the various effects of music on consumers.

References

Areni CS and kim D (1993). The influence of background music on shopping behavior: classical versus top-forty music in a wine store. *Advances in Consumer Research*, **20**, 336–340.

Berlyne DE (1971). *Aesthetics and psychobiology*. Appleton-Century-Crofts, New York.

Garlin FV and Owen K (2006). Setting the tone with the tune: a meta-analytic review of the effects of background music in retail settings. *Journal of Business Research*, **59**, 755–764.

Hansen CH and Hansen RD (1990). Rock music videos and antisocial behavior. *Basic and Applied Social Psychology*, **11**, 357–369.

Kellaris JJ and Altsech MB (1992). The experience of time as a function of musical loudness and gender of listener. *Advances in Consumer Research*, **19**, 725–729.

Kellaris JJ and Mantel SP (1994). The influence of mood and gender on consumers' time perceptions. *Advances in Consumer Research*, **21**, 514–518.

Martindale C and Moore K (1989). Relationship of musical preference to collative, ecological, and psychophysical variables. *Music Perception*, **6**, 431–455.

Milliman RE (1982). Using background music to affect the behavior of supermarket shoppers. *Journal of Marketing*, **46**, 86–91.

Milliman RE (1986). The influence of background music on the behavior of restaurant patrons. *Journal of Consumer Research*, **13**, 286–289.

North AC and Hargreaves DJ (2008). *The social and applied psychology of music*. Oxford University Press, Oxford.

North AC and Hargreaves DJ (1996a). The effects of music on responses to a dining area. *Journal of Environmental Psychology*, **16**, 55–64.

North AC and Hargreaves DJ (1996b). Responses to music in a dining area. *Journal of Applied Social Psychology*, **24**, 491–501.

North AC and Hargreaves DJ (1996c). Responses to music in aerobic exercise and yogic relaxation classes. *British Journal of Psychology*, **87**, 535–547.

North AC and Hargreaves DJ (1996d). Situational influences on reported musical preference. *Psychomusicology*, **15**, 30–45.

North AC and Hargreaves DJ (1997). Music and consumer behaviour. In DJ Hargreaves and AC North, eds, *The social psychology of music*, 268–289. Oxford University Press, Oxford.

North AC and Hargreaves DJ (1998). The effect of music on atmosphere and purchase intentions in a cafeteria. *Journal of Applied Social Psychology*, **28**, 2254–2273.

North AC and Hargreaves DJ, (2000). Musical preference during and after relaxation and exercise. *American Journal of Psychology*, **113**, 43–67.

North AC and Hargreaves DJ (2005). Musical communication in commercial contexts. In D Miell R MacDonald and DJ Hargreaves, eds, *Musical communication*, 405–422. Oxford University Press, Oxford.

North AC and Hargreaves DJ (2006). Music in business environments. In S Brown and U Volgsten, eds, *Music and manipulation: on the social uses and social control of music*, 103–125. Berghahn, Oxford.

North AC, Hargreaves DJ and McKendrick J (1997). In-store music affects product choice. *Nature*, **390**, 132.

North AC, Hargreaves DJ and McKendrick J (1999a). The effect of music on in-store wine selections. *Journal of Applied Psychology*, **84**, 271–276.

North AC, Hargreaves DJ and McKendrick J (1999b). Music and on-hold waiting time. *British Journal of Psychology*, **90**, 161–164.

North AC, Hargreaves DJ and McKendrick J (2000). The effects of music on atmosphere and purchase intentions in a bank and a bar. *Journal of Applied Social Psychology*, **30**, 1504–1522.

North AC, Hargreaves DJ, MacKenzie L and Law R (2004). The effects of musical and voice 'fit' on responses to adverts. *Journal of Applied Social Psychology*, **34**, 1675–1708.

North AC, Hargreaves DJ and Tarrant M (2002). Social psychology and music education. In RJ Colwell and CP Richardson, eds, *The new handbook of research on music teaching and learning*, 604–625. Oxford University Press, New York.

North AC, Shilcock A and Hargreaves DJ (2003). The effect of musical style on restaurant customers' spending. *Environment and Behavior*, **35**, 712–718.

Roballey TC, McGreevy C, Rongo RR, Schwantes ML, Steger PJ, Wininger MA and Gardner EB. (1985). The effect of music on eating behavior. *Bulletin of the Psychonomic Society*, **23**, 221–222.

Smith PC and Curnow R (1966). 'Arousal hypothesis' and the effects of music on purchasing behavior. *Journal of Applied Psychology*, **50**, 255–256.

Weyant JM (1978). Effects of mood states, costs, and benefits on helping. *Journal of Personality and Social Psychology*, **36**, 1169–1176.

Yerkes RM and Dodson JD (1908). The relation of strength of stimulus to rapidity of habit-formation. *Journal of Comparative Neurological Psychology*, **18**, 459–482.

PART 10

Music Therapy

Edited by Michael Thaut

CHAPTER 46

Processes of music therapy

Clinical and scientific rationales and models

Shannon de l' Etoile

> To apprehend music as an essential form of human behavior is to make more secure the foundations of music in therapy. Music therapy has long needed such a platform for its theoretical constructs, one that would be in accord with biological as well as psychological concepts.
>
> Gaston 1968

Introduction

These groundbreaking words clarified the need for a theoretical basis for music therapy practice; however, decades later, a consistent theory has yet to be recognized. The problem may stem from poorly organized research that has little relevance to clinical practice, thus limiting its applicability (Aigen 1991; Asmus and Gilbert 1981; Gfeller 1995; Nicholas and Gilbert 1980; Wheeler 1983). Furthermore, music therapists have traditionally borrowed research paradigms from other disciplines, such as psychology or the biological sciences (Aigen 1991). While such efforts might have initially helped the profession to gain recognition in scientific or academic settings, they do not clarify the unique role of music in changing human behaviour. Consequently, these external paradigms may not be appropriate for guiding music therapy practice.

To explore this idea, Gfeller (1987) conducted a content analysis of 243 articles published in the *Journal of Music Therapy (JMT)* between 1964 and 1985 that related to theory or practice in music therapy. Her results revealed that no single theory or philosophy appeared to be prominent in music therapy practice. Rather, 48 per cent of the articles utilized various theories in psychology, including psychoanalytic (11 per cent), behavioural (26 per cent) or other prominent schools (11 per cent), including cognitive, humanistic and developmental theories.

Without a common theory, music therapists may struggle to produce consistent clinical outcomes and to communicate effectively with other health care professionals (Scovel and Gardstrom 2002). A unified theory may best emerge from a review of previous theories. While it would not be within the purview of this chapter to review all theories ever applied in music therapy practice, Gfeller's research (1987) provides a logical point of reference. Based on her findings, this chapter will review behavioural, psychoanalytic and humanistic music therapy. This discussion will culminate in the presentation of two newly developed theories that demonstrate a mutually beneficial relationship between research and clinical practice.

Behavioural music therapy

Behaviourism grew out of B.F. Skinner's work, which dominated the practice of psychology between 1920 and the middle of the twentieth century (Scovel and Gardstrom 2002). Skinner claimed that learning happens when events are paired with consequences. Originally, behaviourism emphasized the study of objective behaviour of individuals while interacting with the environment and relied on experimental methods, thus minimizing a focus on mental processes or emotions.

Since its inception, behaviourism has evolved and become less mechanistic in its current clinical applications. Contemporary behaviour therapy offers three basic approaches, starting with operant conditioning, in which behaviour is a function of its consequences (Standley et al. 2004). A second approach is classical conditioning, which involves manipulation of the environment to alter cognitive processes. More recently, social learning theory has emerged as another approach that incorporates strategies from social, personality and developmental psychology, such as vicarious learning and self-regulation (Standley et al. 2004).

Behavioural music therapy was most prominent during the 1960s and 1970s; peaked from 1976–1978, and slightly declined after that time (Gfeller 1987; Standley et al. 2004). Results from a more recent content analysis of the JMT (Gregory 2002) further indicate that behaviourism was emphasized in the literature during the 1970s and 1980s, and continued throughout the 1990s. The approach has most often been reported with children in educational settings, but has also been used with a variety of other clinical populations, including premature infants, adults with developmental disabilities and older adults with Alzheimer's disease (Standley et al. 2004).

A behavioural music therapist manipulates musical stimuli to facilitate a change in the client's observable, measurable behaviour (Scovel and Gardstrom 2002). A well-known behavioural approach is Applied Behaviour Analysis (ABA), which utilizes principles of operant conditioning. With ABA, the therapist first establishes a baseline of the client's behaviour, implements a strategy for change, and then documents the client's response (Brownell 2002; Hanser 1995). Another common application of behavioural music therapy is the use of music as contingent reinforcement. The opportunity to play a favourite instrument, for example, could reinforce a desired behaviour (Scovel and Gardstrom 2002).

Standley (1996) conducted a meta-analysis of 98 studies that used music as a contingent reinforcer for educational and therapeutic behaviours. Results indicated that contingent music is more effective than other, non-musical contingent reinforcers, and is more effective than continuous music at facilitating positive changes in behaviour. While Standley's findings provide strong evidence of music's effectiveness as a contingent reinforcer, other researchers may disagree. In an earlier study by Wolfe and Hom (1993), typically developing preschool-age children participated in a number of musical and non-musical interventions designed to help them learn phone numbers. Results revealed that the contingent use of music (i.e., being able to play a preferred musical instrument) was not effective in helping the children to memorize the numbers. Rather, the children were most successful at learning during the intervention involving singing the phone numbers to the melodies of familiar songs.

These contrasting findings may cast some doubt on the behaviourism's appropriateness as a comprehensive theory to explain music's therapeutic mechanism. The fact that contingent music is not consistently effective points to the idea that the behavioural principle of contingency is not the agent of change. Rather, the clients' behaviour is likely to change due to their response to the perceived, inherent value of the music. Understanding the reward value of music should then become the central focus of both research and therapy.

To explain further, while behaviourism has benefited the music therapy profession, the theory does not explain how music is functioning to change behaviour. For example, certain behavioural principles are necessary and effective in a number of therapeutic settings, including the use of contingent reinforcement (musical or otherwise), adherence to group rules and the ability to self-regulate. These constructs; however, may be applied in any therapeutic situation (musical or otherwise) and may have little to do with the music itself. Furthermore, within schools of psychology, clinical applications of behaviourism tend to fall under the 'psychotherapy' heading. While music therapy certainly does address many psychotherapeutic goals, it can also focus on other clinical needs, such as language development or gait training, which clearly would be misplaced under the psychotherapy heading. Aligning music therapy strictly with behaviourism could potentially be an inaccurate and restrictive manoeuvre.

While behavioural research approaches (i.e., single subject and multiple baseline designs) can effectively identify treatment outcomes, they must be substantiated by a scientific understanding of how the music is functioning within the design. Critical questions remain unanswered, such as: *why* does the behaviour change only when the music is present? Is the music rewarding due to timbre, style, familiarity, tempo, or pitch range? Does simple pattern repetition provide an appropriate level of sensory stimulation that the client finds innately rewarding?

Music therapists should not operate from blind assumptions about how the music is functioning. As Gfeller (1987) states, recognizing music as an effective reinforcement in behavioural therapy may not adequately explain music's influence on human behaviour. Rather, the therapist's application of music must be based on an extensive and systematic examination of the involved musical elements (i.e., novelty, complexity, redundancy, etc.), and the ways that these elements interact with the individual and the environment (Gfeller 1987). Without this knowledge, generalization of techniques will be limited at best. In summary, despite its widespread usage and demonstrated efficacy, behavioural music therapy does not offer a complete theoretical explanation for practice and research in music therapy.

Psychoanalytic music therapy

Psychoanalysis is based on the work of Sigmund Freud, whose groundbreaking ideas transformed the practice of psychotherapy during the early twentieth century (Scovel and Gardstrom 2002). More contemporary adaptations of Freud's ideas have since been developed by Alfred Adler, Carl Jung, Erik Erikson, Melanie Klein, and others (Hadley 2002; Scovel and Gardstrom 2002). Freud claimed that people function at various levels of awareness, including unconscious, preconscious and conscious. For some individuals, unresolved emotional conflicts may reside in the unconscious and thus create personality abnormalities. Consequently, the personality must be reconstructed to achieve optimum health. According to Freud, repressed unconscious material must be brought into the client's awareness and then processed through the experiences of transference and countertransference (Bruscia 1998a; Scovel and Gardstrom 2002). Common psychoanalytic techniques include free association, dream analysis and interpretation.

To avoid confusion, various terms may be used interchangeably with psychoanalytic psychotherapy, including 'psychodynamic psychotherapy' and 'insight-oriented psychotherapy' (Isenberg-Grzeda *et al.* 2004). For the purposes of this chapter, all of these terms pertain to clinical techniques that have evolved from Freud's classical psychoanalytic technique.

Gfeller's (1987) content analysis of the *JMT* showed that from 1964 to 1984, 11 per cent of the articles published were linked to psychoanalytic theory. In addition, psychoanalytic theory dominated the *JMT* within its first six months of publication before declining in the mid 1970s. In psychoanalytic music therapy, music experiences may be used to supplement or replace traditional verbal psychoanalysis (Bruscia 1998a). The music therapist creates experiences to stimulate thoughts and feelings related to the client's past and present life, thus eliciting repressed unconscious material. One of the most common techniques used in psychoanalytic music therapy is vocal and/or instrumental improvisation between therapist and client (Bruscia 1998a). Improvisation gives the client the opportunity to engage in free expression of all thoughts, feelings and sensations; thus, a musical free association.

Mary Priestley and colleagues expanded these fundamental ideas in the 1970s by establishing the Analytical Music Therapy (AMT) approach, which combines musical improvisation with movement and verbal processing (Scovel and Gardstrom 2002). In AMT, therapist and patient improvise together, and subsequently use psychoanalytic techniques to determine what happened or what they were thinking about during the improvisation (Eschen 2002). According to Priestley, improvised music essentially provides a gateway to the unconscious, as it allows for non-verbal expression of unconscious processes (Hadley 2002). The therapist works as a non-directive partner with the patient and maintains an openness to the processes of transference and countertransference (Eschen 2002). Transference occurs when the client projects unfinished emotional business onto the therapist or the music, while countertransference pertains to the therapist's emotional response to the patient (Priestley 1975). The technique is most often used with patients in psychiatric settings and in other areas of health care. While AMT has not gained strong acceptance in the United States, it is widely practised in Europe.

Another common technique in psychoanalytic music therapy is imaging to music, which is often achieved through the Bonny Method of Guided Imagery and Music (GIM) (Scovel and Gardstrom 2002). With this technique, the therapist provides carefully sequenced classical music selections to help the client achieve altered states of consciousness. In these altered states, repressed emotional themes may emerge through imagery, which can be processed with the therapist through verbal dialogue (Bonny 1994).

While AMT and GIM offer guidelines for how a clinician should proceed during a therapy session, psychoanalytic music therapy does not typically utilize specific techniques (Isenberg-Grzeda et al. 2004). Rather, the clinician will use any number of strategies, such as vocal or instrumental improvisation, songwriting, lyric analysis or imaging to music, based on his understanding of the therapeutic process as it unfolds. While this flexibility might seem appealing initially, the lack of consistent, standardized techniques can hinder general understanding and application of the theory.

Furthermore, some disagreement exists among psychoanalytic clinicians regarding the

agent of change in the therapeutic process: is it the musical experience, the verbal exchange, or the combination of the two? (Isenberg-Grzeda et al. 2004). The fact that at least part of the technique's success depends on the nature of the relationship between patient and therapist also raises some concerns, as this highly subjective variable is not easily replicated, generalized or measured. Additionally, much of the explanation for the therapeutic mechanism in psychoanalytic music therapy seems to result from the therapist's *interpretation* of the client's behaviour (i.e., the meaning of the instrument that the client selects, the way that the instrument is played, recurring themes within melodic and rhythmic patterns, etc.). This interpretation is also subject to bias, including the clinician's level of training and amount of clinical experience.

The subjective nature of psychoanalytic music therapy also does not lend itself well to empirical examination. Consequently, most of the research conducted in this area has been qualitative with some documentation of treatment effects published via case studies (e.g., Bruscia 1991). Certainly qualitative research can guide clinical practice and inform subsequent quantitative investigation. Additionally, a recent proliferation of literature on psychoanalytic music therapy indicates a growing interest in this application and belief in its efficacy (Isenberg-Grzeda et al. 2004). Overall, however, little empirical evidence exists pertaining to the effectiveness of psychoanalytic music therapy or its direct generalizability to other clients and settings. This lack of data limits the theory's growth as well as its acceptance and recognition within the medical community.

Another issue regarding psychoanalytic music therapy pertains to music's ability to elicit unconscious material, as well as to create opportunities for transference and countertransference. These processes are considered fundamental to the client's experience in psychoanalysis, yet the theory lacks a scientific description of the precise way in which music facilitates these events. If a therapist does not understand how a technique works, he will be restricted in his ability to use it effectively and risks using the technique inappropriately.

Like behavioural music therapy, the psycho-analytic approach is considered a psychothera-peutic modality. Limiting music therapy to this one application may be detrimental to the pro-fession's growth and viability. Even casual observation reveals that musical experiences can improve numerous skills outside the psycho-therapeutic realm, such as short-term memory, or movement accuracy. Despite the many clients who have benefited from this approach, psychoanalytic music therapy does not offer standardized techniques, nor does it provide a scientific explanation for music's therapeutic mechanism. For these reasons, psychoanalytic music therapy does not provide a comprehen-sive theory for clinical practice and research.

Humanistic music therapy

In the 1960s and 1970s, therapists developed alternatives to the behavioural and psychoana-lytic approaches, thus producing several new theories with a humanistic approach, including existential therapy (Viktor Frankl, Rollo May), person-centred therapy (Carl Rogers) and Gestalt therapy (Fritz Perls) (Corey 2005). While each approach includes unique tenets and techniques, all humanistic approaches share common elements, including a respect for the client's experience and a belief in the client's ability to make constructive choices (Corey 2005). Perhaps at the heart of the humanistic movement is the concept that each human being has an innate potential that can be actualized and through which one can find meaning.

Abraham Maslow was one of the earliest and most influential proponents of the humanistic movement (Scovel and Gardstrom 2002). He described a hierarchy of human needs, ranging from biological requirements to self-actualization, or the need to move toward wholeness and ful-fillment. Mental disorders result when one fails to progress through the hierarchy, thus inhibit-ing the ability to find meaning and be responsible for oneself and others. By providing uncondi-tional acceptance and maintaining a focus on the here-and-now, the humanistic therapist helps the client to identify and address factors that are blocking his self-actualization and to take greater responsibility for his choices and actions.

In her content analysis of the *JMT* from 1964–1984, Gfeller (1987) discovered that 11 per cent of the articles pertained to theories borrowed from various schools of psychology, including humanistic, and that these articles were most prominent after 1970. The humanistic music therapist uses music to identify the client's needs and facilitate the process of self-actualization (Scovel and Gardstrom 2002). A variety of methods may be used, ranging from active (i.e., improvisation) to receptive (i.e., listening) (Bruscia 1998b).

One of the most well-known approaches within humanistic music therapy is Creative Music Therapy (CMT), developed by Paul Nordoff and Clive Robbins (Aigen *et al.* 2004; Scovel and Gardstrom 2002). Both Nordoff and Robbins were drawn to Maslow's humanistic concepts, which they adopted and integrated with the ongoing development of their approach in the 1970s (Robbins 1993). In particular, they appreciated Maslow's emphasis on developing a client's strengths and potentials, rather than focusing on his deficiencies (Aigen *et al.* 2004).

With CMT, the clinician uses vocal and/or instrumental improvisation to encourage growth of the client's inner creative drive, thus accessing unknown developmental potentials that are blocked due to disability (Nordoff and Robbins 1977; Robbins 1993). Through the improvisation, the therapist can describe the client's personality, match the client's mood, mirror the client's facial expression or physical bearing, as well as imitate sounds that the client is making (Aigen *et al.*, 2004). Consequently, a client should experience increased emotional awareness as well as improved personality organization, and be able to interact with the environment in a more meaningful way (Nordoff and Robbins 1977; Turry 1998). CMT has been used primarily with children who have cognitive and motor deficits, and also adults in medical, psychiatric and geriatric settings (Andsell 1995; Scovel and Gardstrom 2002).

CMT does not prescribe a format or proce-dural sequence for the improvisations (Aigen *et al.* 2004). Rather, the therapist matches and enhances the client's emotions from moment to moment and the process is one of trial and error. A wide spectrum of beliefs exists among CMT clinicians regarding application of the technique and whether or not it should be combined with various modes of psychotherapy. Some practitioners are more interpretive regarding client behaviour, and others are more music-centred, believing that interpretation can distort the musical interaction (Aigen *et al.* 2004; Turry 1998). Ultimately, CMT stems from a music-centred philosophy, in that music functions as the primary agent of change and offers unique therapeutic benefits that cannot be achieved verbally.

Similar to psychoanalytic music therapy, the humanistic approach is highly subjective, and thus difficult to examine using traditional scientific methods. Consequently, most research in humanistic music therapy has been qualitative, using the case study format (Aigen *et al.* 2004; Aigen 1995, 1998). To document treatment outcome, CMT clinicians typically do not collect data pertaining to specific target behaviours (Aigen *et al.* 2004). Rather, sessions are recorded and then reviewed in an extensive process known as indexing, which identifies ongoing changes in the client as well as in the music.

The humanistic approach has benefited the music therapy profession in several ways. Philosophically, a belief in the client's ability to change and grow should underlie any effective approach to treatment. Musically, the CMT focus on the aesthetic quality of the music and artistic acumen of the therapist certainly elevates standards of professional competence. Despite these benefits, the humanistic approach offers no consistent, standardized techniques, as would be expected of a therapeutic intervention in a medical setting. Data collection within CMT, albeit extensive, appears to focus more on musical outcomes as opposed to functional outcomes that may translate to improved behaviour beyond the therapy session.

Additionally, humanistic music therapy lacks a scientific explanation for how music functions as the agent of change. For instance, how does music access the inner creative drive? How does music facilitate personality organization, or improved perceptual processes? While client responses are evident from behavioural observation, a thorough understanding of music therapy's effect must include scientific knowledge of internal processes. Without this information, a clinician is essentially 'reinventing the wheel' in every therapy session, and will struggle to produce reliable outcomes. These issues undermine the strength of humanistic music therapy as an all-encompassing paradigm for the profession.

Paradigm shift: from social science to neuroscience

The above theories reveal that music therapy practice has been based largely on a social science framework; that is, music has been valued for its ability to facilitate emotional expression and social integration (Thaut 2005). While these musical effects continue to have merit in contemporary practice, more recent evidence has prompted the profession toward a paradigm shift. Since the early 1990s, the advent of modern research techniques in cognitive neuroscience, such as brain imaging, brain-wave recordings and kinematic motion analysis, have provided a greater understanding of the neural processes involved in the perception and production of music. These data collection methods provide an understanding of how music 'works' in a therapy session. With this knowledge, music therapists can operate from a scientific framework and produce stronger, more specific outcomes than general well-being. Consequently, music therapy has evolved from a social science model to a neuroscience model of clinical practice and research.

This evolution has resulted in the formation of a new theory for research and clinical practice, known as Neurologic Music Therapy (NMT) (Clair and Pasiali 2004; Thaut 2005). NMT techniques address cognitive, sensory, and motor dysfunction resulting from disease of the human nervous system. Such techniques are designed to produce functional outcomes and are evidence-based, drawing from scientific data in basic and clinical research. Furthermore, while NMT techniques should be modified to meet each patient's unique needs, they are standardized in terminology and application, thus enhancing communication and clinical efficacy among music therapists and with other health care providers. Specific details regarding NMT techniques are provided elsewhere in this volume. The purpose of this chapter is to elucidate the theoretical components of the NMT model.

The Rational-Scientific Mediating Model

NMT theory is founded in a neuroscience model of music perception, known as the Rational-Scientific Mediating Model (R-SMM), which explains how music functions as a mediating stimulus (Clair and Pasiali 2004; Thaut 2000, 2005). To explain further, aesthetic stimuli such as music typically evoke two sequential responses (Berlyne 1971). The initial response produces some type of feedback or internal stimulation in the recipient. This response joins with the stimulation coming directly from the music, thus producing a mediating response that determines what the recipient will do. Consequently, overt behaviour results from the stimulation coming from the music itself, as well as the stimulation arising from one's initial reactions to the music. Mikiten (1996) eloquently describes how a mediating response to music produces a desirable outcome:

> It is hard to frame a hypothesis and conduct research into how playing a certain song makes a cancer patient 'feel' better. Further, different songs affect patients differently. However, it does make sense to hypothesize that sound structures are detected by brain structures involved in memory. The act of recognition by brain circuits triggers endorphin release that modulates the brain structures responsible for pain. This point of view facilitates the design of hypotheses for experimental verification.
>
> Mitiken (1996, p. 21)

The mediating response in this case is recognition of sound structures and subsequent endorphin release. With knowledge of these internal processes, the music therapist understands how the intervention works and can apply it most effectively. The R-SMM explains how music functions to elicit a mediating response that eventually produces a desired, overt, behavioural response. Understanding of the mediating response is based on scientific evidence and not on speculation inferred from behavioural observations.

The R-SMM provides a framework for exploring and understanding mediating responses to music within the domains of affect, cognition and sensorimotor processes (Clair and Pasiali 2004; Thaut 2000, 2005). The model is rooted in the idea that the scientific basis for music therapy is found in the neurological, physiological and psychological foundations of music perception and production. Application of the R-SMM proceeds in the following four steps:

1 Musical response models: research in music therapy must begin with a solid understanding of musical behaviour, including its neurological, physiological and psychological components. At this step, the researcher might ask, how do humans perceive, produce or respond to music? What systems of the body, underlying neural pathways or perceptual processes are involved?

2 Non-musical parallel models: research at this level examines processes in non-musical brain and behaviour function. Through comparative analysis with step 1, this step establishes a meaningful link between musical behaviour and non-musical behaviour. A parallel process between musical and non-musical functioning must be established, before suggesting that music can influence non-musical behaviour.

3 Mediating models: if a parallel process has been identified at step 2, the researcher can move forward by examining or conducting research to explore the influence of music on non-musical brain and behaviour function. Mediating research does not involve investigation of long-term treatment effects; rather, it explores music's immediate effect on both typical and clinical populations. Results clarify the scientific mechanisms of music's effect on behaviour, or mediating response, thus providing the foundation for clinical research.

4 Clinical research models: when positive mediating effects have been established at step 3, the researcher can design and implement a clinical protocol examining the long-term, therapeutic effects of music. The focus at this level is on lasting functional behaviour change and carry-over after treatment.

As an example of the R-SMM, a researcher may explore music therapy for memory deficits in children with learning disabilities. In Step 1, musical response models, the researcher gathers evidence regarding how music is memorized. In perusing the literature, he may discover that when learning music, Gestalt laws of perceptual grouping are commonly used to combine similar musical elements, thus reducing the memory load and allowing for more effective storage and recall of musical information. In Step 2, non-musical parallel models, the researcher explores how non-musical information is typically memorized, and looks for any shared strategies with memory for music. Examination of previous literature reveals that when memorizing visual or textual information (i.e., lists of words or phone numbers), Gestalt laws of perception are also utilized to group items based on similar features, thus facilitating efficient storage and recall.

With this parallel process established, the researcher can proceed to Step 3, mediating models. Here the researcher examines the effect of the musical behaviour (i.e., memory strategies for music) on the non-musical behaviour (i.e., memory strategies for textual information). The mediating response is the innate human tendency to perceive order and groupings in music stimuli. Perceptual grouping then provides a framework or vehicle for organizing and rehearsing the new information, thus leading to improved storage and recall.

The researcher might first implement his idea with a typical population, such as teaching a new phone number to preschool-age children by singing it to the melody of a familiar song. If positive results are obtained, then the researcher may apply the technique to children with memory deficits due to learning disabilities. Promising evidence at this stage would logically support systematic research at step 4, clinical research models. The researcher could then design a long-term treatment study, investigating the effect of a musical mnemonic device as a memory strategy for children with learning disabilities.

The Transformational Design Model

The R-SMM provides clear guidelines for conducting research regarding music's therapeutic effects. A supplemental model is needed; however, to assist the clinician in translating research findings from the R-SMM into everyday practice (Thaut 2005). The Transformational Design Model (TDM) meets this need by providing a systematic, step-by-step approach to designing, implementing and evaluating clinical interventions (Clair and Pasiali 2004; Thaut 2000, 2005). The five steps of the TDM include:

1 Diagnostic and functional assessment of the patient

2 Development of therapeutic goals and objectives

3 Design of functional, non-musical therapeutic exercises and stimuli

4 Translation of step 3 into functional therapeutic music experiences

5 Transfer of therapeutic learning to functional, non-musical, real world applications.

Steps 1, 2, 3 and 5 of the TDM are common to all therapeutic disciplines (Thaut 2000, 2005). Step 1 involves a diagnostic and etiological assessment of the client which leads to Step 2, establishment of functional goals with corresponding measurable objectives. This information informs Step 3, the design of therapeutic exercises and activities to address the goals and objectives. A critical component of Step 3 is designing such exercises according to the functional behaviours of the patient and not on musical considerations. This approach to treatment planning ensures a functional outcome, not a musical outcome, and enhances collaborative efforts with other disciplines, thus producing more specific and meaningful treatment outcomes.

Step 4 makes the TDM unique to neurologic music therapy practice. Here the music therapist translates the functional and therapeutic exercises from Step 3 into musical experiences that are isomorphic; that is, they share the same functional structure (Thaut 2000, 2005). For example, if a patient has recently experienced a right hemisphere stroke, he may have weakness in his left arm and hand, including difficulty with independent finger movement. The functional exercise in this case would be repetitive movement of the affected arm, hand and fingers, for an appropriate duration of time and at an adequate pace, in order to increase range of motion and to increase strength and endurance. The musical translation of this functional exercise could consist of playing simple fingering exercises on the piano, while being guided by the therapist's accompaniment which determines tempo, frequency and duration of movement, in addition to providing aesthetic motivation.

To ensure the isomorphic nature of the therapeutic music experience (TME), three types of logic must be incorporated (Thaut 2005):

1 Functional logic: the TME must serve as a musical analogue of the non-musical experience. Furthermore, the TME must give the client multiple or sustained opportunities to practice the non-musical behaviour. By incorporating functional logic, the therapist can facilitate positive changes in a functional behaviour that the client will utilize in everyday life.

2 Musical logic: the musical component of the TME must meet the aesthetic and artistic principles of good musical forms. To explain further, the music must be aesthetically pleasing, whether it is provided in active (i.e., improvisation) or receptive (i.e., listening) forms. Regardless of complexity, only with optimal musical patterns can the beneficial effects of music be manifest.

3 Scientific logic: the most effective TME will draw from the scientific evidence established using the R-SMM. Whenever possible, the music therapist must design TMEs based on a solid understanding of the parallel process between musical and non-musical experiences in order to elicit a mediating response to influence behaviour. By utilizing the research evidence, the therapist need not reinvent the wheel in each therapy session, and can instead, select the most appropriate technique from a validated taxonomy of strategies.

Summary

The R-SMM and the TDM give music therapists two critical tools for research and clinical practice. The R-SMM integrates the understanding of musical and non-musical behaviours into a framework for effective therapy and rehabilitation (Thaut 2005). Its dynamic and open-ended nature allows for incorporation of future research efforts to continuously establish new evidence and rationales for the music's therapeutic effects. Meanwhile, the TDM provides a practical guide for music therapists to create goal-oriented interventions based on scientific evidence. Together, the models offer an approach to research and practice based on an understanding of how music influences behaviour to produce functional outcomes. Clinicians cannot assume that music magically or automatically brings about a desired change in behaviour. Rather, interventions must be founded in empirical knowledge of the internal processes and mechanisms at work during musical experiences.

By providing a scientific understanding of music's influence on behaviours in all domains of functioning, as well as standardized techniques, NMT addresses the profession's needs. Simultaneously, NMT fulfills Gaston's original appeal for a theory that incorporates both biological and psychological constructs. Furthermore, NMT provides an approach to practice and research that is unique to the music therapy profession and not borrowed from other disciplines. As a theoretical foundation, NMT will secure the profession's acceptance, credibility and future viability as a valid therapeutic modality.

References

Aigen K (1991). The roots of music therapy: towards an indigenous research paradigm. *Dissertation Abstracts International*, **52**(6), 1933A. (University Microfilms No. DEY91–34717.)

Aigen K (1995). Cognitive and affective processes in music therapy with individuals with developmental delays: a preliminary model for contemporary Nordoff–Robbins practice. *Music Therapy*, **13**, 13–45.

Aigen K (1998). *Paths of development in Nordoff–Robbins music therapy*. Barcelona, Phoenixville, PA.

Aigen K Miller CK, Kim Y, Pasiali V, Kwak EM and Tague DB (2004). Nordoff–Robbins music therapy. In AA Darrow, ed., *Introduction to approaches in music therapy*, 63–77. American Music Therapy Association, Silver Spring, MD.

Andsell G (1995). *Music for life: aspects of creative music therapy with adult clients*. Jessica Kingsley, London.

Asmus EP and Gilbert JP (1981). A client-centered model of therapeutic intervention. *Journal of Music Therapy*, **18**, 41–51.

Berlyne DE (1971). Perception. In DE Berlyne, ed. *Aesthetics and psychobiology*, 96–114 Meredith Corporation, New York.

Bonny H (1994). Twenty-one years later: a GIM update. *Music Therapy Perspectives*, **12**, 70–74.

Brownell MD (2002). Musically adapted social stories to modify behaviors in students with autism: four case studies. *Journal of Music Therapy*, **39**, 117–144.

Brusica K (1991). *Case studies in music therapy*. Barcelona, Phoenixville, PA.

Bruscia K (1998a). An introduction to music psychotherapy. In K Bruscia, ed., *The dynamics of music psychotherapy*, 1–15 Barcelona, Gilsum, NH.

Bruscia K (1998b). *Defining music therapy*. Barcelona, Gilsum NH.

Clair AA and Pasiali V (2004). Neurologic music therapy. In AA Darrow, ed., *Introduction to approached in music therapy*, 143–158. American Music Therapy Association, Silver Spring, MD.

Corey G (2005). Person-centered therapy. In G Corey, ed. *Theory and practice of counseling and psychotherapy*, 7th edn, 162–189. Brooks/Cole–Thomson Learning, Belmont, CA.

Eschen JT (2002). Analytical music therapy—introduction. In JT Eschen, ed., *Analytical music therapy*, 17–33. Jessica Kingsley Publishers, London.

Gaston ET (1968). Man and music. In ET Gaston, ed., *Music in therapy*, 7–29. Macmillan Publishing, New York.

Gfeller KE (1987). Music therapy theory and practice as reflected in research literature. *Journal of Music Therapy*, **24**, 178–194.

Gfeller KE (1995). Status of music therapy research. In BL Wheeler, ed., *Music therapy research: quantitative and qualitative perspectives*, 29–63. Barcelona Publishers, Phoenixville, PA.

Gregory D (2002). Four decades of music therapy behavioral research designs: a content analysis of *Journal of Music Therapy* articles. *Journal of Music Therapy*, **39**, 56–71.

Hadley S (2002). Theoretical bases of analytical music therapy. In JT Eschen, ed., *Analytical music therapy*, 34–48. Jessica Kingsley Publishers, London.

Hanser SB (1995). Applied behavior analysis. In BL Wheeler, ed., *Music therapy research: quantitative and qualitative perspectives*, 149–164. Barcelona Publishers, Phoenixville, PA.

Isenberg-Grzeda C, Goldberg F and Dvorkin JM (2004). Psychodynamic approach to music therapy. In AA Darrow, ed., *Introduction to approaches in music therapy*, 79–101. American Music Therapy Association, Silver Spring, MD.

Mikiten T (1996). A method for research in music medicine. In RR Pratt and R Spintge, eds, *Musicmedicine*, Vol. 2, 14–23. MMB Music, St. Louis, MO.

Nicholas MJ and Gilbert JP (1980). Research in music therapy: a survey of music therapists' attitudes and knowledge. *Journal of Music Therapy*, **17**, 207–213.

Nordoff P and Robbins C (1977). *Creative music therapy*. John Day, New York.

Priestley M (1975). *Music therapy in action*. MMB Music, St. Louis, MO.

Robbins C (1993). The creative processes are universal. In M Heal and T Wigram, eds, *Music therapy in health and education*, 7–25. Jessica Kingsley, London.

Scovel MA and Gardstrom SC (2002). Music therapy within the context of psychotherapeutic models. In RF Unkefer and MH Thaut, eds, *Music therapy in the treatment of adults with mental disorders: theoretical bases and clinical interventions*, 2nd edn, 117–132. MMB Music, St. Louis, MO.

Standley JM (1996). A meta-analysis on the effects of music as reinforcement for education/therapy objectives. *Journal of Research in Music Education*, **44**, 105–133.

Standley JM, Johnson CM, Robb SL, Brownell MD and Kim SH (2004). Behavioral approach to music therapy. In AA Darrow, ed., *Introduction to approaches in music therapy*, 103–123. American Music Therapy Association, Silver Spring, MD.

Thaut MH (2000). *A scientific model of music in therapy and medicine*. IMR Press, San Antonio, TX.

Thaut MH (2005). Music in therapy and medicine: from social science to neuroscience. In MH Thaut, ed. *Rhythm, music and the brain: scientific foundations and clinical applications*, 113–136. Taylor and Francis Group, New York.

Turry A (1998). Transference and countertransference in Nordoff-Robbins music therapy. In K Bruscia, ed., *The dynamics of music psychotherapy*, 161–212. Barcelona, Gilsum, NH.

Wheeler BL (1983). Prologue. *Music Therapy*, **3**, 2–3.

Wolf DE and Hom C (1993). Use of melodies as structural prompts for learning and retention of sequential verbal information by preschool students. *Journal of Music Therapy*, **30**, 100–118.

CHAPTER 47

Clinical practice in music therapy

Corene Hurt-Thaut

Introduction

What is music therapy?

Music therapy is a health care profession in which music is used as a therapeutic medium to address developmental, adaptive, and rehabilitative goals in the areas of psychosocial, cognitive, and sensorimotor behaviour of individuals with disabilities. A music therapist designs therapeutic music interventions which address the client's functional goals and are adapted to the client's functional level. Over 5000 music therapist are employed throughout the United States, serving a wide range of clients, including the elderly, developmentally disabled adults and children, mental health populations, physically disabled, school-aged children, early childhood, substance abuse, sensory impaired, neurologically impaired, and terminally ill (AMTA 2006).

There are three critical components when considering the use of music in therapy: musical creativity and proficiency, scientific logic, and therapeutic logic. First, the music used in therapy must come from a trained professional who has a high quality of understanding of music theory, history, and performance. Therefore, a music therapist background involves extensive training in music, including proficiency in voice, guitar, and piano. Second, in order to use music as a therapeutic tool, a therapist must understand the scientific foundations of the influence of music on functional changes in non-musical brain and behaviour functions. Although course work at different universities varies considerably, music therapist are exposed to, and in some

cases, take extensive course work in the sciences in order to gain an understanding of anatomy and physiology, neuroanatomy, biology, and psychological functions. Thirdly, in order to use music in therapy, music interventions must make sense therapeutically. It is essential for music therapist to be trained in group and individual counselling skills, therapeutic design, and selection of music interventions based on functional goals and objectives.

The music therapy treatment process

Music therapists typically work in conjunction with a team of professionals including physicians, nurses, social workers, physical therapist, occupational therapist, and speech therapist. A music therapist must receive a referral or request for music therapy services, upon which they are responsible for completing an assessment, developing a treatment plan including goals and objectives, documenting the progress of a client throughout treatment, evaluating progress toward goals and objectives, and developing a termination plan for their clients.

Referrals typically come from the physician in a hospital setting, but in other settings they may come from the psychologist, another therapist, teachers, parents, social workers, and even from the client themselves.

Once a referral is received, the therapist must do an assessment, of the person's strengths, needs and problems, including information about the client's medical history, cognition, social abilities, physical abilities, vocational or educational background, emotional status, communication skills, family, and leisure skills. A music therapy assessment is typically non-musical in nature, and designed to identify whether a client is appropriate for music therapy and then assist the music therapist in treatment selection based on need areas.

Once an assessment has determined the strength and need areas, a treatment plan can be established. The treatment plan identifies the goals and objectives that will be addressed with the client during treatment. The goal identifies and area that is in need of improvement (e.g. to improve fine motor skills). The objective identifies the specific parameters of the behaviour that the client needs to accomplish, the criterion and qualifiers for that behaviour, and the target date of achievement.

Documentation of treatment progress is essential not only to monitor the quality, cost effectiveness, and efficiency of treatment, but also as a means to communicate with other members of the treatment team and to justify charges to insurance companies. Documentation requirements and formats vary greatly depending on the type of facility that a therapist is working at.

Once a client has met their treatment goals, or is recommended for discharge, the music therapist must complete a final evaluation of treatment. This evaluation includes a review of the entire music therapy process, from the initial goals and objectives to the final progress made toward them.

The history of music therapy

The profession of music therapy was established in the United States in 1950, as a result of work being done with patients in veterans' hospitals following the Second World War. Music was being used with returning soldiers to boost the morale, and help with the rehabilitation of physical, social and emotional health. However, evidence of the powerful value of music has been documented for thousands of years in all cultures. David played the harp to sooth Saul; in Egypt, certain songs were legally ordained in the education of youth to promote virtue and morality; Pythagoras directed certain mental

disorders to be treated by music; Xenocrates cured maniacs by melodious sounds, and Asclepiades conquered deafness with a trumpet (Davis *et al.* 1999). Music therapy has grown substantially in the research and clinical knowledge since 1950, and today is recognized in the medical community as a solid, thriving profession.

Application of music therapy to clinical populations

Music therapy in psychiatric populations

During the early development of music therapy, most therapists were working with psychiatric populations. Although the use of music in therapy has become much more diverse since then, mental health accounts for 21 per cent of the populations served by music therapist (AMTA 2006). Treatment most often addresses thought disorders, mood disorders, personality disorders and anxiety disorders.

Wheeler (1983) classified the treatment of adults with mental disorders into three levels: (1) supportive music therapy as an activity therapy: (2) insight music therapy with re-educative goals, and (3) insight music therapy with reconstructive goals. Each level of classification requires a higher degree of insight and participation from the client.

On the level of supportive music therapy, the therapist main goals are to promote mood-lifting stimulation and healthy behaviours. Music therapy experiences at this level require active involvement and awareness of the here and now.

On the level of insight and process-oriented music therapy with re-educative goals, the client is now at a higher level of insight and is ready to reflect and process interpersonal relationships and emotions with a greater level of verbal participation. A client at this level is well oriented to reality, demonstrates appropriate interaction skills and is ready to focus on conscious conflicts and associated unhealthy defence mechanisms.

The last level of intervention involves reconstructive, analytically and catharsis-oriented music therapy. At this level, the music therapy interventions are used to uncover and process subconscious conflicts resulting from past traumatic situations. Therapist working at this level require advanced training in psychotherapeutic techniques.

In addition to different levels of treatment, music therapy clinical practice with mental disorders is guided within the framework of several different psychotherapeutic models. The therapist typically chooses different treatment approaches based on the needs of a particular client or the philosophy of a treatment facility. Some of the most frequently used models include: psychodynamic, cognitive, humanistic/existential, cognitive neuropsychiatric, biomedical, behavioural, and holistic.

Interventions

A wide range of music therapy programmes and techniques are currently used in the treatment of mental disorders, including music performance, music psychotherapy, music and movement, music combined with other expressive arts, recreational music, and music for relaxation.

Music performance addresses goal areas such as affective self-expression, identification of feelings, appropriate outlet for negative feeling processes, reality testing, retraining auditory and perceptual skills and memory function, executive functions, motivation, self-esteem, and socialization. Music therapy techniques may be process- or product-oriented, depending on the therapeutic goal, and often include instrumental group improvisation, instrumental and vocal performance ensembles, group singing therapy, individual instrumental or vocal instruction, and individual music improvisation (Unkefer and Thaut 2002).

Music psychotherapy implements music therapy techniques such as supportive, interactive, and catalytic music groups and individual therapy. A supportive music group would address goals in the areas of identification and expression of feeling responses, expanding range of expressiveness, appropriate outlets for negative feelings, reality focus, task-oriented activities, attention-focusing activities and social participations. An intervention may involve guided music listening techniques to focus attention, provide theme-centred structure for verbal interaction, and evoke feeling responses or alter feeling states. In an interactive music group or individual therapy, the main goal areas become focused on the identification and expression of one's own feelings, problem-solving, awareness of one's own behaviours, and facilitation of behaviour changes (Unkefer and Thaut 2002). Music therapy interventions may frequently consist of guided music listening which leads to discussion of lyric content, mood of the music, and relevance of the music to the client's personal life. The catalytic music group encourages the the client to become more aware of feelings, thoughts, and experiences that have previously been repressed, through music therapy interventions such as guided listening techniques, guided imagery and music (GIM), and psychodrama.

Music and Movement can be used on many different levels in order to address a variety of goals ranging from awareness and expression of feelings and emotions, to social interaction and physical exercise. *Movement awareness* is a technique which encourages clients to move and express themselves on a non-threatening level through beginning music and movement exercises in a group setting. Another technique called *Movement exploration* uses elements of music and movement to help the client develop a repertoire of body movements as they improve their body image and begin to feel competent in moving effectively. *Movement interaction* is a technique which uses music and movement to provide the opportunity to experience social and emotional concepts in a non-verbal modality. At this level of movement, the focus is on the client and the client's relationship to others. *Expressive movement* is a technique using music and movement to help a client become aware of feelings and emotions that relate to their personal functioning and coping skills in daily life. Musical themes are used to encourage the experience and expression of feeling concepts such a love, loss, grief, depression, social isolation and withdrawal, interpersonal conflict, hope, and joy. *Dance* is another form of music and movement which uses prestructured dance forms, steps, and styles with music to encourage social interaction, self-confidence, and recreational skills. *Music and exercise* can be used with any age group and level of movement ability to address strength, endurance, muscle tone, flexibility, agility, body control, vital capacity, and cardiovascular efficiency. Music becomes not only a motivator for movement, but also provides a rhythmic structure to pace and cue movement patterns (Thaut 2002).

Music combined with other expressive arts is frequently used in the treatment of mental disorders as a multisensory external stimulus to provide pleasant and motivating reality experiences. The technique *music and fine arts* integrates music with other mediums such as drawing, drama and sculpting in order to allow for expression of feelings and emotions. *Music and writing* pairs music with writing such as poetry or prose, which also provides experiences for expression of feelings and cognitive responses. Both of these techniques can be used in a group or individual setting.

Recreational music programmes can address goals such as non-threatening reality orientation, involvement in goal-directed activity, completion of task, and social participation. Music therapy interventions may include music games, recreational music, music appreciation awareness, and leisure-time skill development.

Music and relaxation programmes can be very effective at providing an outlet for negative feeling processes, providing feedback and support for movement control, pairing physical exercise with relaxation, increasing frustration tolerance, promoting coping skills, and focusing attention in a structured and calming environment. Numerous music therapy techniques are currently used for relaxation. *Music and progressive muscle relaxation training* pairs relaxing music with the relaxing and tensing of different muscle groups, in order to help a client discriminate between relaxation and tension responses. *Music for surface relaxation* allows a client's preferred music to provide a temporary respite from anxiety-provoking or stressful situations. *Music imagery* encourages a client to explore altered states of consciousness for the purpose of allowing imagery, symbols, and latent feelings to surface from the inner self. *Music-centred relaxation* is a technique which uses music to divert a client's attention from states of psychological and physical tension.

Through this technique the client's focus on the music helps them gain a safe, pleasant perceptual experience.

Future direction

Currently, music therapy practice in mental health has primarily been based on borrowed theories from other disciplines. Thaut (2002) purposed that a major mechanism of the therapeutic effectiveness is embedded in music's unique ability to access affective/motivational systems in the brain. Therefore, a theoretical paradigm of music therapy in psychiatry must integrate musical response models in music perception and music cognition with the understanding of music's influence on non-musical human behaviour, psychologically and neurobiologically, and with concepts of behavioural learning and therapeutic change (Gaston 1968, Thaut 2000).

Research in psychology and the neurosciences has increasingly pointed to the important relationship between affect and cognition. According to Izard *et al.* (1984), emotions are an essential part of cognitive processing. He stated that emotion is the main force for motivation, and motivation is and essential force that drives behaviour and cognition. Rachman (1981) also believed that emotions accompany all cognition, but emotional reactions occur before cognitive processing. The associative network theory purposed by Bower (1981) states that the human memory can be compared to an associative network of events and emotions. In this network, events are considered to be memory units that become associated with certain emotional states experienced while the event is occurring. Thus, when memory units feed in to our emotional state they become attached. Therefore, during cognitive learning, people associate emotion with certain elements of environmental context. These three theories are important in establishing the relationship between mood, behaviour, and cognition.

Other research has compared the effects of musical and non-musical mood-induction techniques. Studies by Clark (1983), Sutherland (1982), Teasdale and Spencer (1984), and Thaut and de L'Etoile (1993) have shown music induction techniques to produce stronger and longer lasting results than other non-musical techniques in affect modification.

Nielzen and Cesarec (1982) and Steinberg *et al.* (1985), compared the emotional experience of music in normal and psychiatric subjects. Findings of their studies indicated that music communicated the same emotional experience to both normal and psychiatric groups.

Martin *et al.* (1988) and Eifert *et al.* (1988) examined affect modification through music. Martin looked at the relationship between the intensity of a headache and mood, finding that a positive change in affect decreased the intensity of headaches while the negative change in affect increased headache intensity. Eifert, when looking at affect modification through evaluative conditioning with music, identified that liked and disliked music provided strong positive and negative conditioning, respectively.

A cognition–affect model in neuropsychiatric music therapy, based on scientific mechanisms relating the perceptual experience in music to brain and behaviour, could lead to meaningful therapeutic applications within an understanding of the biological basis and the role of affect–cognition processes in mental disorders (Halligan and David 2001).

Music therapy with children

Music therapy addresses three goal areas in order to increase cognitive, motor, social, communicative, musical and emotional functioning in disabled children: (a) educational, (b) rehabilitative, and (c) developmental (Thaut1999). A music therapist works closely with the interdisciplinary treatment team and must be familiar with developmental, psychological, and medical information that pertains to each disability in order to address these goals appropriately. Music therapists work with children, ranging from early childhood to school-aged. Diagnosis can include autism, cerebral palsy, developmental delays, burn injuries, traumatic brain injury, and other neurological impairments.

Educational goals focus on the academic development of a child. These goals may address social, cognitive, or physical skills. Examples of this may be using a musical mnemonic to teach a child his phone number and address, practicing learning colours and shapes by filling in the blanks of a song, doing creative movement to music, or practicing social skills while participating in a group instrumental playing experience.

Rehabilitative goals work toward restoration or compensatory strategies to improve movement, respiration, posture and sensory perception. For example, using rhythmic auditory stimulation to address gait in a 10-year-old who has developmentally already learned to walk, but recently suffered a traumatic brain injury which has left him with ataxic gait.

Developmental goals strive toward enhancing the normal development of a child by providing normal social, emotional, and sensorimotor experiences through music. Musical experiences are used to submerge the child in normal recreational and leisure experiences that meet the child on their existing functional level. For example, teaching a child how to play a musical instrument, using adaptive equipment, in order for the child to play in the school orchestra.

Interventions

Motor function

Music therapy offers a variety of musical interventions and experiences to address motor function in disabled children. The possibilities are limitless for creatively challenging children to reach, balance, stretch, and utilize their upper and lower extremities in functional movements. Musical instruments can provide a specific target for the children to aim towards, defining the parameters of the desired movement. The music therapist uses the music to help facilitate the client's participation while simplifying and readily adapting to the functional level of the child. Simple, repetitive melodies, familiar or not, have been most successful with children. The music therapist's ability to distil the lyrics to an appropriate vocabulary level, or simply create their own, more appropriate musical compositions, leads to much more effective interaction with children of all functional levels.

Communication skills

Music therapy can play a large role in the development and rehabilitation of both verbal and non-verbal communication skills in children. Music therapist can address disorders such as apraxia; fluency disorders such as stuttering and cluttering; aphasia; and voice disorders which may result in abnormal pitch, loudness, timbre, breath control, or prosody of speech. Goals in the area of speech and communication address issues such as functional and spontaneous speech, speech comprehension, motor control and coordination essential for articulation, fluency of speech, vocal production and sequencing of speech sounds, and rate and intelligibility. When working with children it is especially important to be aware of their developmental stage when choosing an intervention that would best address their current needs. Developmental Speech and Language Training Through Music (DSLM) is one neurologic music therapy technique which uses developmentally appropriate musical materials and experiences to enhance speech and language development through singing, chanting, playing musical instruments, and combining music, speech and movement.

Cognitive learning

Several music therapy interventions are used to address cognitive learning in children in order to aid in memory, attention, and executive function skills. Musical mnemonics can be an organizational tool, using grouping or chunking through melodic and rhythmic patterns to assist in text recall with children. Many studies have looked at the relationship between music and the performance of autistic children on cognitive tasks such as attention (Kostka 1993), auditory processing (Heaton *et al.* 1988, 2001), affective perception (Heaton *et al.*1999), improvisation (Hermelin *et al.* 1989), local and global processing of music (Mottron *et al.* 2000), auditory discrimination (McGovern *et al.* 1991), and learning and retention of information (Wolfe 1993).

Emotional and social development

Children with disabilities have the same need for healthy emotional and social development and opportunities to express their feelings as do normal children. Because of the experiences of their disabilities, these children may actually have an increased need to cope with feelings such as grief, depression, or loneliness (Thaut 1999). On the other hand, they may also be withdrawn socially, causing them to miss out on the support systems that develop through peer relationships. A combination of a lack of ability to participate in some of the more traditional channels to express emotions and a decreased social support system can become a real dilemma for these children.

Music therapy interventions can provide an effective medium to create rewarding social and emotional experiences for children. In addition to working on physical, sensory, cognitive or speech goals, music can also help to increase self-esteem and provide an outlet for emotional expression through success-oriented experiences at any level of functioning. Music can also be used in a group setting to provide opportunities for peer interaction and support. Learning how to enjoy the recreational use of music or even developing a lifelong musical skill such as playing an instrument are also important in the overall strategy to normalize the life of a disabled child.

Music therapy in neurological rehabilitation

Neurological rehabilitation is an area in music therapy that is strongly substantiated by the basic science and clinical research coming from scientists in and out of the field of music therapy since the mid-1990s. Advanced training is strongly recommended when working with this population due to the knowledge of neuroanatomy, brain pathology, and medical terminology, that is required by the therapist. A wide variety of techniques are used to address motor control, cognition, and psychosocial behaviour with neurological disorders such as stroke, Parkinson's disease, Huntington's disease, traumatic brain injury, multiple sclerosis, and spinal cord injuries.

Interventions

The following intervention are based on neurologic music therapy (NMT), a research-based system of standardized clinical techniques for sensorimotor training, speech and language training, and cognitive training. NMT is used in neurologic rehabilitation, neuropaediatric therapy, neurogeriatric therapy, and neurodevelopmental therapy. It is based on the Rational

Scientific Mediating Model (R-SMM), a neuroscience model of music perception and production and the influence of music on functional changes in non-musical brain and behaviour function (Thaut 2005).

Sensorimotor rehabilitation

Music therapy offers a variety of musical interventions and experiences to address motor skills in neurological rehabilitation. Common goals that are addressed include gait and mobility, strength and endurance, coordination, balance and posture and range of motion. These goals are addressed through techniques such a: Rhythmic Auditory Stimulation (RAS), Patterned Sensory Enhancement (PSE), and Therapeutic Instrumental Music Performance (TIMP).

Rhythmic auditory stimulation (RAS) is a neurologic technique used to facilitate the rehabilitation of movements that are intrinsically biologically rhythmical, most importantly gait. RAS uses the physiological effects of auditory rhythm on the motor system to improve the control of movement in rehabilitation of functional, stable and adaptive gait patterns in patients with significant gait deficits due to neurological impairment. RAS can be used in two different ways: (1) as an immediate entrainment stimulus providing rhythmic cues during movement, and (2) as a facilitating stimulus for training in order to achieve more functional gait patterns.

Patterned sensory enhancement (PSE) is a technique which uses the rhythmic, melodic, harmonic and dynamic–acoustical elements of music to provide temporal, spatial, and force cues for movements which reflect functional exercises and activities of daily living. PSE is broader in application than RAS, because it is (a) applied to movements that are not rhythmical by nature (e.g., most arm and hand movements, functional movement sequences such as dressing or sit-to-stand transfers) and (b) it provides more than just temporal cues. PSE uses musical patterns to assemble single, discrete motions (e.g., arm and hand movements during reaching and grasping), into functional movement patterns and sequences. PSE cues movements temporally, spatially, and dynamically during training exercises (Thaut et al. 1991).

Therapeutic instrumental music performance (TIMP) is the playing of musical instruments in order to exercise and stimulate functional movement patterns. Appropriate musical instruments are selected in a therapeutically meaningful way in order to emphasize range of motion, endurance, strength, functional hand movements, finger dexterity, and limb coordination (Elliot 1982, Clark and Chadwick 1980). During TIMP, instruments are not typically played in the traditional manner, but are placed in different locations to facilitate practice of the desired functional movements.

Speech rehabilitation

Music therapy can play a large role in the development and rehabilitation of both verbal and nonverbal communication skills. Techniques in music therapy can be used to address disorders such as apraxia; fluency disorders such as stuttering and cluttering; aphasia; and voice disorders which may result in abnormal pitch, loudness, timbre, breath control, or prosody of speech. Goals in the area of speech and communication address issues such as functional and spontaneous speech, speech comprehension, motor control and coordination essential for articulation, fluency of speech, vocal production and sequencing of speech sounds, and rate and intelligibility.

The following eight techniques address speech disorders, based on the current research in this area:

1 Melodic intonation therapy (MIT) is a treatment technique developed for expressive aphasia rehabilitation which utilizes a patient's unimpaired ability to sing, to facilitate spontaneous and voluntary speech through sung and chanted melodies which resemble natural speech intonation patterns (Sparks et al. 1974). When using MIT with aphasia, the emphasis is in increasing the linguistic or semantic aspects of verbal utterances.

2 Speech stimulation (STIM) is the use of musical materials such as songs, rhymes, chants, and musical phrases simulating prosodic speech gestures to stimulate non-propositional speech. STIM uses completion or initiation of over learned familiar song lyrics, association of words with familiar tunes, or musical phrases to elicit

functional speech responses (Basso *et al.* 1979). For example, spontaneous completion of familiar sentences is stimulated through familiar tunes or obvious melodic phrases (e.g., 'You are my'…, or 'How are you …?').

3 Rhythmic speech cuing (RSC) is the use of rhythmic cuing to control the initiation and rate of speech thru cuing and pacing. The therapist may use the client's hand, a drum, or possibly a metronome to prime speech patterns or pace the rate of speech. This technique can be useful to facilitate motor planning for an apraxic patient, cue muscular coordination for dysarthria, or assist in pacing with fluency disorders.

4 Vocal intonation therapy (VIT) is the use of intoned phrases simulating the prosody, inflection, and pacing of normal speech. This is done through vocal exercises which train all aspects of voice control including: inflection, pitch, breath control, timbre, and dynamics. An example would be to sing a five-note scale and gradually move the starting pitch up or down by half steps with a child who has a limited pitch range in their normal speaking voice. This exercise could be further expanded by adding a functional sentence i.e., 'Let's go out and play.'

5 Therapeutic singing (TS) is a technique which involves the unspecified use of singing activities to facilitate initiation, development, and articulation in speech and language as well as to increase functions of the respiratory apparatus. Therapeutic singing can be used with a variety of neurological or developmental speech and language dysfunctions (Glover *et al.* 1996; Jackson *et al.* 1997).

6 Oral motor and respiratory exercises (OMREX) involves the use of musical materials and exercises, mainly through sound vocalization and wind instrument playing, to enhance articulatory control and respiratory strength and function of the speech apparatus. This technique would be used with such populations as developmental disorders, dysarthria, and muscular dystrophy (Hass and Distenfield 1986).

7 Developmental Speech and Language Training Through Music (DSLM) is the specific use of developmentally appropriate musical materials and experiences to enhance speech and language development through singing, chanting, playing musical instruments, and combining music, speech, and movement.

8 Symbolic communication training through music (SYCOM) is the use of musical performance exercises using structured instrumental or vocal improvisation to train communication behaviour, language pragmatics, appropriate speech gestures, emotional communication in non-verbal language systems, that is sensory structured, has strong affective saliency, and can simulate communication structures in social interaction patterns in real time.

Cognitive rehabilitation

Several music therapy interventions have been developed to address cognitive learning, based on research evidence providing clinical support in the role of music to aid in memory, attention, and executive function training. Three areas are addressed in cognitive training techniques: auditory attention and perception training, memory training, and executive function training.

1 Musical sensory orientation training (MSOT) is the use of music, presented live or recorded, to stimulate arousal and recovery of wake states and facilitate meaningful responsiveness and orientation to time, place, and person. In more advanced recovery of developmental stages, training would involve active engagement in simple musical exercises to increase vigilance and train basic attention maintenance with emphasis on quantity rather than quality of response (Ogata 1995).

2 Musical neglect training (MNT) involves active performance exercises on musical instruments, which are structured in time, tempo, and rhythm, with an appropriate spatial configuration of instruments to focus attention to neglected or unattended visual field. It may also involve receptive music listening to stimulate hemispheric brain arousal while engaging in exercises addressing visual neglect or inattention (Hommel *et al.* 1990; Frasinetti *et al.* 2002; Anderson and Phelps 2001).

3 Auditory perception training (APT) is the use of musical exercises to discriminate and identify different components of sound, such as time, tempo, duration, pitch, timbre, and rhythmic patterns, as well as speech sounds. Integration of different sensory modalities such as visual, tactile, and kinaesthetic input are used during active musical exercises such as playing from symbolic or graphic notion, using tactile sound transmission, or integrating movement to music (Bettison 1996; Gfeller *et al.* 1997; Heaton *et al.* 1988).

4 Musical attention control training (MACT) involves structured active or receptive musical exercises, using pre-composed performance or improvisation, in which musical elements cue different musical responses in order to practice sustained, selective, divided, and alternating attention functions (Thaut 2005).

5 Musical mnemonics training (MMT) is the use of musical exercises to address various memory encoding and decoding/recall functions. Immediate recall of sounds or sung words using musical stimuli may be used to address echoic functions. Musical stimuli may be used as a mnemonic device or memory template in a song, rhyme, chant, or to facilitate learning of nonmusical information by sequencing and organizing the information in temporally structured patterns or chunks (Deutsch 1982; Gfeller 1983; Wallace 1994; Claussen and Thaut 1997; Maeller 1996).

6 Associative mood and memory training (AMMT) involves musical mood induction techniques to instate (a) a mood-congruent mood state to facilitate memory recall, or (b) to access associative mood and memory function through inducing a positive emotional state in the learning and recall process (Bower 1981; Dolan 2002).

7 Musical executive function training (MEFT) is the use of improvisation and composition exercises in a group or individually to practice executive function skills such as organization, problem-solving, decision-making, reasoning, and comprehension, within a social context that provides important therapeutic elements such as performance products in real time, temporal structure, creative

process, affective content, sensory structure, and social interaction patterns (Dolan 2002).

Music therapy in the geriatric population

Due to advances in research and increased medical knowledge, the life expectancy of the average American has continues to grow, resulting in an estimated 21 per cent of the population over the age of 65 by 2030. The growing number of elderly has forced an increased interest in the unique challenges associated with aging, particularly among health care professionals.

Music therapy has demonstrated great success with the geriatric population, and is currently used in hospitals, nursing homes, assisted living facilities, psychiatric settings, adult day care, and wellness programmes, in order to address cognitive, sensorimotor, and psychosocial skills. A vast range of both rehabilitative and adaptive goals are addressed through music therapy techniques, including increasing upper and lower extremity range of motion, strength and endurance, and mobility; increasing independence in activities of daily living; improving attention, long- and short-term memory and executive functions; increasing reality orientation; improving verbal and non-verbal communication skills; decreasing agitation and wandering; promoting relaxation; leisure skill training; increasing social interaction and participation; and enhancing reminiscence.

Interventions

Numerous music therapy interventions are used with the geriatric population to help validate or orient them to their environment. Reality orientation through music can help a disoriented client remember information pertaining to where they are and why, what day it is, and what their schedule will be.

Validation therapy may also be used with a late stage Alzheimer's or dementia patient who is unable to orient to current information, but is perhaps living in a memory of the past. With this technique, the music therapist's role is to meet the patient where they are at, and try to listen and validate their point of view.

Reminiscence in a group or individual setting can be a powerful structural tool in therapy to help clients remember past events and experiences in their life. Music can effectively set the mood for a discussion, stimulate or validate past memories, and create a theme for dialogue. Reminiscence also promotes social interaction, participation and positive sense of self.

Leisure skill reintegration or training can be another effective use of music in therapy. Many elderly people no longer participate in past leisure interest due to lack of motivation, or decreased physical or cognitive functioning. Reintegrating a client into a past interest or teaching them a new skill can provide opportunities for self-expression, intellectual stimulation, and social integration. A music therapist may teach a client compensatory strategies in order to play a musical instrument that they once played, or utilize their past musical knowledge to teach them a new instrument which is more suited to their current level of functioning. Another form of leisure integration may involve assisting a client in finding community resources in order to pursue their leisure interest (ie. singing in a church choir or attending a performance).

Intergenerational music programmes are frequently integrated in residential care facilities for older adults. Music can be an excellent tool to promote interaction between generations through movement, instrument playing, singing, and performance experiences.

Elderly people frequently experience decrease activity levels due to difficulty with mobility, lack of motivation or even lack of transportation. Research has shown that exercise is an important factor in promoting health and wellbeing. Lack of exercise can contribute to heart disease, decreased energy levels, and increased risk of falls in the elderly. Music paired with exercise in a group setting can be an effective tool to help motivate, improve coordination and timing of movement patterns, and increase endurance, as well as promote socialization.

Summary and future directions

The field of music therapy has grown substantially since it was founded in 1950. The advances in research and medical knowledge continue to help explain the therapeutic effects of music on behaviour based on scientific evidence; providing the framework to systematically and creatively transform musical responses into therapeutic responses.

When looking at the use of music in therapy for mental disorders, Thaut (2002) purposed that a major mechanism of the therapeutic effectiveness is embedded in music's unique ability to access affective/motivational systems in the brain. Research in psychology and the neurosciences has increasingly pointed to the important relationship between affect and cognition. Halligan and David (2001), addressed the movement toward a cognition–affect model in neuropsychiatric music therapy, leading to meaningful therapeutic applications within an understanding of the biological basis and the role of affect–cognition processes in mental disorders.

In addition to working on physical, sensory, cognitive and speech goals, music therapy interventions can also help to increase self-esteem and provide an outlet for emotional expression. Music can be used in an individual or group setting to provide and teach overall strategies to normalize the life of a disabled child.

The use of music in therapy in neurological rehabilitation continues to grow, as scientific models provide evidence which explains the therapeutic effects of music on behaviour. Based on the evidence provided in the areas of cognition, speech and language, and motor behaviours, a taxonomy of music therapy techniques can be used to select applications of music in therapy that have predictable therapeutic outcome and benefits for this population.

In 2006, geriatrics accounted for about 15 per cent of the populations served by music therapist. As the elderly population continues to grow, the demand for music therapy will also grow.

Research has shown that music can be a very effective tool in the treatment of the elderly. Interventions such as reality orientation, reminiscence, leisure skill reintegration and training, intergenerational music programmes, and music and exercise, have been implemented with excellent success with this populations.

In the past 15 years, new approaches to scientific research based on a neuroscience model of music perception and production and the influence of music on functional changes in non-musical brain and behaviour functions, have helped begin to answer the questions that need to be addressed in order for future growth of scientific and medical acceptance of music therapy. In many areas of motor control, cognition, and affective behaviour, research clearly explains the therapeutic effect of music on behaviour based on scientific evidence, therefore providing the framework to systematically and creatively transform music into therapy.

References

AMTA (2006). *AMTA member sourcebook*. AMTA, Silver Springs, MD

Anderson AK and Phelps EA (2001). Lesions of the human amygdale impair enhanced perception of emotionally salient events. *Nature*, **411**, 305–309.

Basso A, Capitani E and Vigndo LS (1979). The influence of rehabilitation on language skills in aphasic patients. *Archives of Neurology*, **36**, 190–196.

Bettison S (1996). The long-term effects of auditory training on children with autism. *Journal of Autism and Developmental Disorders*, **26**, 361–375.

Bower GH (1981). Mood and memory. *American Psychologist*, **36**(2), 129–148.

Clark C and Chadwick D (1980).*Clinically adapted instruments for the multiply handicapped*. Magnamusic-Baton, St. Louis, MO.

Clark DM (1983). On the induction of depressed mood in the laboratory; evaluation of the Velten and musical procedures. *Advances in Behavior Research and Therapy*, **5**, 27–49.

Claussen DW and Thaut MH (1997). Music as a mnemonic device for children with learning disabilities. *Canadian Journal of Music Therapy*, **5**, 55–56.

Davis, WB, Gfeller, KE and Thaut MH (eds) (1999). *An introduction to music therapy, theory and practice*. Boston: McGraw-Hill.

Deutsch D (1982). Organizational processes in music. M Clynes, ed., Music, *mind and brain*, 119–131. Plenum Press, New York.

Dolan RJ (2002). Emotion, cognition, and behavior. *Science*, **298**, 1191–1194.

Eifert G, Craill L, Carey E and O'Connor C (1988). Affect modification through evaluative conditioning with music. *Behavior Research and Therapy*, **26**, 321–330.

Elliott B (1982). *Guide to the selection of musical instruments with respect to physical ability and disability*. MMB Music, Inc., Saint Louis, MO.

Frasinetti F, Pavani F and Ladavos E (2002). Acoustical vision of neglected stimuli: interaction among spatially convergent audio-visual imputs in neglect patients. *Journal of Cognitive Neuroscience*, **14**, 62–69.

Gaston ET (ed.) (1968). *Music in therapy*. Macmillan, New York.

Gfeller K, Woodworth G, Robin DA, Witt S and Knutson JF (1997) Perception of rhythmic and sequential pitch patterns by normally hearing adults and adult cochlear implant users. *Ear and Hearing*, **18**, 252–260.

Gfeller KE (1983). Musical mnemonics as an aid to retention with normal and learning disabled students. *Journal of Music Therapy*, **20**, 179–189.

Glover H, Kalinowski J, Rastatter M and Stuart A (1996) Effect of instruction to sing on stuttering frequency at normal and fast rates. *Perceptual and Motor Skills*, **83**, 511–522.

Haas F, Distenfeld S and Axen K (1986). Effects of perceived music rhythm on repiratory patterns. *Journal of Applied Physiology*, **61**, 1185–1191.

Halligan PW and David AS (2001). Cognitive neuropsychiatry; towards a scientific psychopathology. *Nature Reviews Neuroscience*, **2**, 209–214.

Heaton P, Hermelin B and Pring L (1988). Autism and pitch processing: a precursor for savant musical ability? *Music Perception*, **15**, 291–305.

Heaton P, Hermilin B and Pring L (1999). Can children with autistic spectrum disorders perceive affect in music? An experimental investigation. *Psychological Medicine*, **29**(6), 1405–1410.

Heaton P, Pring L and Hermelin B (2001). Musical processing in high functioning children with autism. *Annals of the New York Academy of Sciences*, **930**, 443–444.

Hermelin B, O'Connor N, Lee S and Treffert D (1989). Intelligence and musical improvisation. *Psychological Medicine*, **19**(2), 447–457.

Hommel M, Peres B, Pollak P, Memin B *et al.* (1990). Effects of passive tactile and auditory stimuli on left visual neglect. *Archives of Neurology*, **47**, 573–576.

Izard C, Dagan J and Zajonc RB (eds) (1984). *Emotions, cognition, and behavior*. Cambridge University Press, New York.

Jackson SA, Treharne DA and Boucher J (1997). Rhythm and language in children with moderate learning difficulties. *European Journal of Disorders of Communication*, **32**, 99–108.

Kostka M (1993). A comparison of selected behaviors of a student with autism in special education and regular music class. *Music Therapy Perspectives*, **11**, 57–60.

Maeller DH (1996). Rehearsal strategies and verbal working memory in multiple sclerosis. Unpublished master thesis, Colorado State University.

Martin P, Nathan P, Milech D and Van Kappel M (1988). The relationship between headaches and mood. *Behavior Research and Therapy*, **26**, 353–356.

McGovern RF, Berka C, Languis ML and Chapman D (1991). Detection of deficits in temporal pattern discrimination using the Seashore rhythm test in young children with reading impairments. *Journal of Learning Disabilities*, **24**, 58–62.

Mottron L, Peretz I and Menard E (2000). Local and global processing of music in high-functioning persons with autism: beyond central coherence. *Journal of Child Psychology and Psychiatry*, **41**(8), 1057–1065.

Nielzen S and Cesarec Z (1982). Emotional experience of music by psychiatric patients compared with normal subjects. *Acta Psychiatrica Scandinavica*, **65**, 450–460.

Ogata D (1995). Human EEG responses to classical music and simulated white noise: effects of a musical loudness component on consciousness. *Perceptual and Motor Skills*, **80**, 779–790.

Rachman S (1981). The primacy of affect: some theoretical implications. *Behavior Research and Therapy*, **19**, 279–290.

Sparks RW, Helm N and Albert M (1974). Aphasia rehabilitation resulting from melodic intonation therapy. *Cortex*, **10**, 313–316.

Steinberg R, Raith L, Rossnagl G and Eben E (1985). Music psychopathology; III. Musical expression and psychiatric disease. *Psychopathology*, **18**, 274–285.

Sutherland G, Newman B and Rachman S (1982). Experimental investigations of the relations between mood and intrusive, unwanted cognitions. *British Journal of Medical Psychology*, **55**, 127–138.

Teasdale and Spencer (1984). Induced mood and estimate of past success. *British Journal of Clinical Psychology*, **23**, 149–150.

Thaut MH (1999). Music therapy for children with physical disabilities. In WB Davis, KE Gfeller and MH Thaut, eds, *An introduction to music therapy, theory and practice*, 148–162. McGraw-Hill, Boston, MA.

Thaut MH (2000). *A scientific model of music in therapy and medicine*. MMB Music Inc., Saint Louis, MO.

Thaut MH (2002). Toward a cognitive-affective model in neuropsychiatric music therapy. In RF Unkefer and MH Thaut, eds, *Music therapy in the treatment of adults with mental disorders: theoretical bases and clinical interventions*, 86–99. MMB Music Inc., Missouri, MO.

Thaut MH and De L'Etoille SK (1993). The effect of music on mood-state dependent recall. *Journal of Music Therapy*, **30**, 70–80.

Thaut MH, Schleiffers S and Davis WB (1991). Analysis of EMG activity in biceps and triceps muscle in a gross motor task under the influence of auditory rhythm. *Journal of Music Therapy*, **28**, 64–88.

Thaut MM (2005). *Rhythm, music and the brain*. Taylor and Francis Group, Abingdon, UK.

Unkefer RF and Thaut MH (2002). *Music therapy in the treatment of adults with mental disorders: theoretical bases and clinical interventions*. MMB Music Inc., Missouri, MO.

Wallace WT (1994). Memory for music: effect of melody on recall of text. *Journal of Experimental Psychology: Learning, Memory, Cognition*, **20**, 1471–1485.

Wheeler B (1983). A psychotherapeutic classification of music therapy practices: a continuum of procedures. *Music Therapy Perspectives*, **1**, 8–16.

Wolfe DE and Hom C (1993). Use of melodies as structural prompts for learning and retention of sequential verbal information by preschool students. *Journal of Music Therapy*, **30**, 100–118.

CHAPTER 48

Research and evaluation in music therapy

Barbara L. Wheeler

RESEARCH has been an integral part of music therapy since the inception of the National Association for Music Therapy (NAMT) in 1950. The first of the original six objectives of NAMT was 'to encourage and report research projects' (Gilliland 1952, p. v). Gfeller (1995) states:

> Research activities were included immediately in the publications of this fledgling organization. *Music Therapy 1951* (Gilliland 1952), the first Book of Proceedings of NAMT, included a small offering of research abstracts by music therapists and a bibliography of pertinent research from fields such as psychology and physiology. This bibliography was no doubt intended to raise professional awareness of and competence in scientific research. Each subsequent Book of Proceedings (*Music Therapy 1952–1962*) included a section entitled Research, which contained not only abstracts but also philosophical addresses by music therapists, psychologists, and physicians espousing the need for scientific experiments to justify music therapy.
>
> Gfeller (1995, p. 38)

Research was also included prominently in the Certificate of Incorporation of the American Association for Music Therapy (AAMT), founded in 1971, including:

- To stimulate, guide, and direct research of music therapists nationally.

- To publish the results of such research in scientific papers and in professional journals and to authorize publication of the results of such research by other educational institutions without compensation payable to the corporation. ...

- To furnish grants in aid to investigators who propose to undertake study and research in the field of music therapy.

- To promote the exchange of information among the various individuals and institutions engaged in the practice and research of music therapy nationally (Dena Condron, personal communication, 27 January 1993, in Gfeller 1995, pp. 41–42).

The Bylaws of the American Music Therapy Association (AMTA), formed when NAMT and AAMT unified in 1998, include this statement: 'The Association serves as the primary organizational agency for the advancement of education, clinical practice, research, and ethical standards in the music therapy profession' (AMTA 2005b, p. 11). Research was adopted as a strategic priority by the AMTA Board of Directors in 2005, including the development of an operational plan that:

> (a) addresses the direction of research in support of evidence-based music therapy practice and improved workforce demand; and, (b) recognizes and incorporates, where necessary, federal, state and other entity requirements

Table 48.1 Refereed journals in music therapy published in English*

Journal	Country of publication	First year of issue
Journal of Music Therapy (JMT)	US	1964
Canadian Journal of Music Therapy (CAM)	Canada	1973
Music Therapy: Journal of the American Association for Music Therapy (MT)	US	1981(–96)
Music Therapy Perspectives (MTP)	US	1982
British Journal of Music Therapy (BJMT)[†]	UK	1987
Australian Journal of Music Therapy (AJMT)	Australia	1990
Nordic Journal of Music Therapy (NJMT)	Norway	1992
Annual Journal of the New Zealand Society for Music Therapy (NZ)	New Zealand	1994

*This list does not include the many creative arts therapy journals and bulletins published internationally nor online publications in music therapy. *The South African Journal of Music Therapy*, no longer in publication, was not consulted.
[†]Until 1994, this was titled the *Journal of British Music Therapy*.
From Edwards, J. (2005). Developments and issues in music therapy research. In B. L. Wheeler (ed.), *Music Therapy Research*, 2nd edn. Barcelona, Gilsum, NH. Reprinted with permission.

for evidence-driven research as it relates to practice policy and reimbursement.

Hairston (2005, p. 8)

The AMTA Professional Competencies (AMTA 2003) include:

- Interpret information in the professional research literature;
- Determine if conclusions drawn in a study are supported by the results;
- Demonstrate basic knowledge of the purpose and methodology of historical, quantitative, and qualitative research;
- Perform a data-based literature search;
- Apply selected research findings to clinical practice.

NAMT began publication of the *Journal of Music Therapy* in 1964. This journal has served as an important venue for disseminating music therapy research in the United States and internationally. Other publications that include some research are *Music Therapy: Journal of the American Association for Music Therapy* (published from 1981 to 1996) and *Music Therapy Perspectives*.

Music therapy research has, of course, not been limited to the United States. Edwards (2005) summarizes the refereed journals in music therapy in Table 48.1. This shows the remarkable growth in the number of publications, growing from one in 1970 to two in 1980 and six in 1990 and continuing to the present.

Numerous analyses of the music therapy literature have been done (see Edwards 2005 for a summary). Several analyses (Brooks 2003; Edwards 2005; Gregory 2002) illuminate recent changes in the focus of music therapy research.

Brooks (2003) examined 1521 articles from nine music therapy journals over a 37-year period. She tallied the numbers of research articles classified as quantitative, qualitative, clinical, historical, philosophical/theoretical, and professional.[1] The number of articles published in each of these journals is, of course, related to the length of time that the journal has been

[1] Since the focus of this chapter is music therapy research, clinical and professional articles are not included in this summary, although they were part of Brooks' (2003) analysis.

published and the number of issues a year. Brooks found quantitative research articles to be the predominant category across all journals, with 542 articles. She found 55 historical articles and 136 philosophical/theoretical articles.

Of course, only a portion of music therapy research is published in journals for which music therapy is the primary focus. Many music therapy studies are found in medical publications, including those devoted to nursing, rehabilitation, and neuropsychology. Music therapists also publish in special education, psychology, and psychotherapy publications journals and books and in other interdisciplinary areas. Systematic music therapy reviews are also conducted and published as part of the Cochrane reviews (see http://www.cochrane.org/reviews/index.htm).

Examples of music therapy research

Music therapy research is approached from various perspectives and thus employs a number of methodologies. The value and use of quantitative and qualitative research has been debated by music therapists (Aigen 1995; Bruscia 1995a; Wheeler 1995). Questions about when each is appropriate and whether and/or when they can be combined are of interest.

One of the considerations when thinking of the differences between quantitative and qualitative research is the purpose of the research. Research conducted within a positivistic paradigm is concerned with cause and effect and uses the natural science model of discovery, while research conducted within a non-positivistic paradigm aims to increase understanding of people's multiple constructions of reality. These are very different positions and goals. The distinctions between quantitative and qualitative research thus go far beyond the type of data with which they deal to encompass differences in philosophy, research interests, and methodology. These different purposes should be kept in mind in the discussion that follows.

Bruscia (2005) suggests that there are three broad topical areas of music therapy research: discipline, profession, and foundational. Much of the discussion that follows will be organized around these three broad topical areas. Because

music therapy is an applied discipline, most music therapy research is related to clinical or translational research (National Advisory Mental Health Council 2000; Nunes *et al.* 2002), although some research may be more strictly clinical than others.

Discipline research, according to Bruscia (2005), 'includes all those studies that examine the myriad facets of music therapy practice. As such, it deals with clinical topics such as assessment, treatment, and evaluation' (p. 81), areas that are at the heart of music therapy. The AMTA definition of music therapy, 'the clinical and evidence-based use of music interventions to accomplish individualized goals within a therapeutic relationship by a credentialed professional who has completed an approved music therapy program' (AMTA 2005a), points to the importance of data and research for providing evidence-based interventions.

Profession research includes

studies that deal with music therapists and what they do collectively to establish and promote music therapy as a healthcare service. It deals with psychological, socioeconomic, political, legal, and educational aspects of music therapy as an organized profession.

Bruscia (2005, p. 81)

Bruscia suggests that topics of profession music therapy research include employment practices, music therapists (characteristics, attitudes, etc.), professional education and training, professional standards, legislation and public relations, and history and culture.

Foundational research includes

all those studies that relate partially but not completely to the discipline or profession of music therapy. It deals with topics that emanate from related fields (for example, psychology, music, medicine, education) but have important implications for music therapy.

Bruscia (2005, p. 81)

Because music therapy is an interdisciplinary endeavor, topics in these related areas are important. Bruscia says, 'Such research can be considered foundational because the findings often provide empirical or theoretical support for practices, principles, or constructs used in music therapy, but, strictly speaking, were not originally focused on music therapy matters' (p. 81).

Some foundational research is basic research (Borg and Gall 1989) in that it is done primarily to increase knowledge without necessarily having in mind an application of the research findings, but much of it is applied research in areas other than music therapy. Foundational research may study either the discipline or the profession of music therapy.

This section will consider quantitative and qualitative music therapy research.

Quantitative research

As research is so important to music therapy, it is not surprising that it covers a number of topics. With increased reliance on evidence-based practice,[2] the amount and quality of the research that is available has increased in importance.

One way of making sense of a large number of research studies is through a review. Dileo (2005) suggests that there are two primary types of reviews, qualitative and systematic. A qualitative review involves a narrative presentation of relevant literature, while a systematic review 'involves the application of scientific strategies, in ways that limit bias, to the assembly, critical appraisal, and synthesis of all relevant studies that address a specific clinical question' (Cook et al. 1997, p. 376). Quantitative systematic reviews use statistical techniques to combine or evaluate studies, while qualitative systematic reviews summarize studies but do not combine them statistically.

The Cochrane Database of Systematic Reviews (http://www.cochrane.org) includes numerous reviews of various healthcare interventions. While the results of Cochrane reviews of some medical areas (e.g., drug trials) are accepted with little controversy, there is considerable discussion of their applicability to some clinical areas,[3] as well as the implications of their exclusion of certain ways of knowing.[4] Cochrane

reviews have been done of music therapy for people with dementia (Vink et al. 2003/2006), autistic spectrum disorder (Gold et al. 2006), and schizophrenia (Gold et al. 2005), and music for pain relief (Cepeda et al. 2006).

Some systematic reviews are meta-analyses, in which the researcher combines the numerical results of studies with various research methods and findings and looks for consistencies among these findings (meta-analyses are also often used in Cochrane reviews). The researcher who performs a meta-analysis calculates a standard effect size for each study, giving an indication of the size and variability of the phenomenon under investigation and allowing the studies to then be compared among themselves across all measures and variables. Although concerns have been raised about several aspects of meta-analyses (Bailar 1997; Eysenck 1994; Naylor 1988), meta-analysis is generally considered to be a useful technique for discerning patterns among disparate studies and reaching conclusions. Meta-analyses in music therapy have been done of the following populations and types of treatment: medical and dental treatment (Standley 1986, 2000), medical treatment (Dileo and Bradt 2005), medical treatment of paediatric patients (Standley and Whipple 2003), premature infants in neonatal intensive care units (NICU) (Standley 2002), dementia (Koger et al. 1999), children and adolescents with autism (Whipple 2004), children and adolescents with psychopathology (Gold et al. 2004), symptoms of psychosis (Silverman 2003), neurologic rehabilitation of upper and lower limbs (Chandra 2005), and stress reduction (Pelletier 2004).

In general, meta-analyses have shown quite positive results for music therapy while the Cochrane reviews, which tend to have more stringent requirements for inclusion of studies and thus generally include far fewer studies, have been less positive. Some results from meta-analyses and Cochrane reviews are discussed below.

Discipline research

Research and results will be reviewed for autistic spectrum disorders, neurological disorders, and medical problems of children and adults. These are a few of the areas in which music therapy research exists.

---

[2] Evidence-based practice (EBP) refers to 'integrating individual clinical expertise with the best available external clinical evidence from systematic research' (Sackett et al. 1996, p.71). It is also referred to as evidence-based medicine (EBM).
[3] See Hömberg's (2005) discussion which asks, 'How far can principles of EBM practice be applied to training techniques in neurological rehabilitation?' (p. 3).
[4] Morse (2006) discusses the implications of the lack of acceptance of qualitative research in the evidence-based movement.

Autistic spectrum disorder

There is a great deal of clinical literature on music therapy with children with autistic spectrum disorders (see Alvin and Warwick 1991; Nordoff and Robbins 2007) but much less research. Two systematic analyses of music therapy research with autism have been done. Whipple (2004) analysed 12 dependent variables from nine quantitative studies that compared music to no-music conditions during treatment of children and adolescents with autism and concluded that all music interventions, regardless of purpose or implementation, have been effective. A Cochrane review by Gold *et al.* (2006) of all randomized controlled trials or controlled clinical trials that compared music therapy or music therapy added to standard care to placebo therapy, no treatment, or standard care included three small studies. It found music therapy to be superior to placebo therapy with respect to verbal and gestural skills, but without significant effects on behavioural problems. It is clear that additional research on music therapy and autism is needed.

Neurological disorders

A large amount of empirical research has been done on music therapy with neurological problems, including people who have had cerebral vascular accidents (CVA, stroke), traumatic brain injuries (TBI), Parkinson's disease, and cerebral palsy. Many of the studies in this area have been of Neurologic Music Therapy (NMT), a model developed at the Center for Biomedical Research in Music at Colorado State University (http://www.colostate.edu/depts/cbrm/) and based in findings from empirical research that have demonstrated the effects of music on sensorimotor training as well as on speech and language training and cognitive training. As a model that integrates scientific research into the biological effects of music with parallel models of non-music therapy treatment (Thaut 2005), it tries to build a systematic path from basic science research to various stages of translational and clinical research. NMT has been accepted as a proven effective intervention for this population. One of the methods of NMT, Rhythmic Auditory Stimulation (RAS), is listed as one of 10 higher-level evidence-based motor therapies

in a critical review of this area (Hömberg 2005). Chandra's (2005) meta-analysis on neurologic rehabilitation of upper and lower limbs, including many NMT techniques, provided evidence for the effectiveness of these procedures.

Medical problems

Meta-analyses have provided important information on the effectiveness of music and music therapy in medicine. Standley did the first of these in 1986 and has updated them several times. In the most recent meta-analysis (2000), she found an overall average effect size (ES) of 0.84 for music versus non-music conditions in all of the 92 studies and 232 dependent variables that were included. When including only the primary dependent variables of the 92 studies, she found an average ES of 1.17 and an average ES of 1.40 in the studies that utilized patients' preferred music. Both are considered large effect sizes (Cohen 1977).

Standley and Whipple (2003) did a meta-analysis of empirical research studies that contrasted music versus no music conditions during medical treatment of paediatric patients. They found a medium effect size (Cohen 1977) in an analysis of 29 studies, indicating that including music is better than not including music in paediatric medical treatment. Standley (2002) also performed a meta-analysis of 10 research studies on the effectiveness of music with premature infants in neonatal intensive care units. She concluded that music has significantly positive effects that remain consistent across a number of variables.

Most recently, Dileo and Bradt (2005) completed a meta-analysis of 184 studies involving music in medical treatment. They included only studies that had a no-music control group and only those dependent variables for which two or more study results were available, and included 47 dependent variables. Effects of music and music therapy were reported for each dependent variable, grouped according to 11 medical specialty areas: premature infants, fetal responses to music, paediatric, obstetrics/gynaecology, cardiology/intensive care, oncology and terminal illness, general hospital, surgery, rehabilitation, dementia, and dentistry. Nearly all showed statistically significant effect sizes, although with a lack of consistency across studies.

Profession research

Profession research topics to be presented here include ethical issues and employment practices, a sample of the topics for which music therapy research exists. The studies analysing music therapy research trends, discussed earlier, are also examples of profession research. To this author's knowledge, no meta-analyses or systematic reviews of the quantitative profession music therapy literature have been done.

Ethical issues

Most of the research on ethical issues in music therapy has been done by Dileo and her colleagues and has included a broad range of topics. Dileo (2000) wrote a textbook on music therapy ethics, built on her research and that of others, that makes the study of ethics in music therapy accessible to students and others.

Employment practices

Employment practices of music therapists have been investigated periodically for many years, primarily through surveys. These surveys focus on several areas.

Some surveys are of the clinical practice of music therapists. Recent surveys have been of music therapists in specific settings, including school settings (Smith and Hairston 1999), correctional psychiatry (Codding 2002), and private practice (Silverman and Hairston 2005); of music therapy methods in the treatment of early elementary school children with ADHD (Jackson 2003); and of the collaboration and consultation of music therapists (Register 2002). A comparative analysis of surveys focused on hospice administrators' knowledge of music therapy (Hilliard 2004).

Other surveys have focused on the educational process, including clinical training. Maranto and Bruscia (1988) conducted separate surveys of music therapy educators, music therapy clinical training supervisors, music therapy clinicians, and university catalogues to gather information on a number of areas. Jensen and McKinney (1990) studied university curricula by studying the catalogues to compare the requirements in music therapy and related areas with the curricular requirements of NAMT. Groene and Pembrook (2000) surveyed collegiate faculty for their views of new knowledge and skills needed, competency-based assessment, and clinical training practices and potential changes.

Some surveys sought music therapists' opinions of the usefulness of their educational and clinical training for their later work as music therapists. These include surveys on the perceptions of the quality of collegiate training by Gault (1978) and of the relationship of applied music requirements to clinical practice by Cohen *et al.* (1997).

Some surveys were of the tasks and competencies required of music therapists. Some of these have been done and are done on a regular basis by the music therapy organizations and by the Certification Board for Music Therapists (CBMT) and the results are often published in their professional newsletters and other publications, while others have been done by individuals.

Several surveys of professional practices of music therapists have been conducted in the United Kingdom. Hills *et al.* (2000) used the Maslach Burnout Inventory to study how burnout varied among people working in multidisciplinary teams and those who worked independently. Stewart (2000) surveyed UK music therapists to assess personal qualities of music therapists, working models, support networks, and job satisfaction.

Foundational research

Many studies that are done in disciplines outside of music therapy, with no direct relationship to music, can be foundational to music therapy. In addition, much of the content of the psychology of music that is presented in this book, when it is research-based, can be foundational to music therapy. An overview of types of research in the psychology of music, psychology, music, medicine, and education that can be foundational to music therapy will be given here, although it is beyond the scope of this chapter to provide specific examples.

Psychology of music

Studies of the perception and cognition of music would be included as foundational to music therapy. Similarly, studies of people's responses to music, including physiological, behavioural, emotional, cognitive, and aesthetic, would be in this area, as would studies of the neural processing of music. Many other topics in the psychology of music could also be included.

Music

Research on various types of music can also be foundational to music therapy. An analysis of a particular piece of music as done by a musicologist might be useful for a music therapist to use to enhance the understanding of music used in music therapy.

Psychology

The same areas that were listed as possible foundational studies for the psychology of music, but without application to music, could begin this section. Thus, we include perception and cognition; physiological, behavioural, emotional, cognitive, and aesthetic responses; and research on neural processing of stimuli. We might also add studies of personality and of the social behaviour of humans. Any area of psychological research can potentially be foundational to music therapy.

Medicine

Research on medical areas is foundational to music therapists who work in those specialties. Examples include research on medical areas such as cancer, cardiac problems, respiratory problems, neurological disorders, and so forth, and issues surrounding medical care such as pain, pre-surgical anxiety, and family support.

Education

Both regular education and special education can be foundational to music therapy. Development and teaching methods are among the areas that may be relevant from education research. Examples of special education research that is foundational to music therapy includes research on the assessment, needs, and education of children who are enrolled in special education classes and on the benefits of inclusion or of children's responses to children with special needs who are in their classes.

Qualitative research

Qualitative research generally has a different focus than does quantitative research, and the assumptions that underlie it are different. As stated earlier, a general goal of qualitative research is to increase understanding of people's multiple constructions of reality. The purpose of qualitative research is often to lead to a deeper understanding of the music therapy process. Qualitative research goes beyond the use of qualitative data to reflect the beliefs of its followers

> that not all that is important can be reduced to measurements [and] it is essential to take into account the interaction between the researcher and the participant(s) being studied. Findings cannot be generalized beyond the context in which they are discovered, and values are inherent in and central to any investigation.
>
> Wheeler (2005b, p. 13)

Although qualitative research is newer in most disciplines than is quantitative research, its regular use in music therapy began in the 1980s and has grown greatly in the last few decades. A recent book on music therapy research (Wheeler 2005a) includes 12 chapters on types of qualitative research, reflecting the growth of this type of research.

Discipline research

Qualitative discipline research in music therapy focuses on understanding the client and therapy better. This improved understanding of therapy is important for understanding the music therapy process. A number of studies in this area examine the therapy process and thus contribute to understanding music therapy. Some of these, selected to give an overview of some of the research in this area, are shared here. No attempt is made to summarize their 'results', as results have a different meaning in qualitative research, and a summary of any of the findings would not do justice to the research.

One of the early music therapy qualitative studies led to a theory of a field of play as underlying the improvisational music therapy process (Kenny 1989, 2006). In 'A suspiciously cheerful lady', Aasgaard (2000), looked at what happened to a song after it was composed. Aigen (1997) studied a group of adolescents over a year, including videotaping and analysing the sessions and interviewing the therapists about the sessions and, in a separate study (Aigen 2002) examined the music therapy process of a young adult with a developmental disability. Gardstrom (2004) and Skewes (2001) studied adolescents in improvisationally based music therapy groups, while Langenberg and her colleagues (Langenberg *et al.* 1993, 1995) developed a set of research procedures to study psychoanalytically informed music therapy.

Several studies have looked at aspects of the music therapist's experience or interaction in the music therapy process; some studies look at both therapists' and clients' experiences. Because the focus of these studies is on the therapy, they are considered examples of discipline research. Bruscia (1995b) examined several modes of consciousness in Guided Imagery and Music (GIM), Forinash (1992) examined therapists' experience of clinical improvisation, Amir (1993, 1996) examined meaningful moments in music therapy, Grocke (1999) studied pivotal moments in GIM, and Comeau (2004) studied music therapists' experiences of being effective and ineffective. Wheeler (1999) looked at her experience of pleasure when working with children with multiple severe disabilities.

Profession research

The only completed profession qualitative research study of which the author is aware is an investigation of students' experiences during music therapy practice (Wheeler 2002).

Foundational research

Foundational research can be found in many related disciplines. It has a long history in anthropology; more recent extensive applications in education, psychology, and nursing; and has been used for research in numerous other disciplines, many of which can potentially be useful as foundations for music therapy.

One study that was done by a music therapist but could be considered foundational is Racette's (2004) study of the experience of listening to music when upset. Ferrara's (1984) 'Phenomenology as a tool for musical analysis', a study and set of research methods that focused on music but influenced music therapy research, served as the basis for adaptations of phenomenological research methods to music therapy (Forinash and Gonzalez 1989; Ruud 1987).

Other types of research

Additional types of research make important contributions to the music therapy literature. These are listed in a recent book on music therapy research (Wheeler 2005a) as music research, philosophical inquiry, and historical research, with an additional chapter that focuses on developing theory. Examples of these types of music therapy research are available in the literature.

Summary

Music therapy research is an integral part of music therapy and has been since the beginning of the US music therapy associations. Numerous journals, both in music therapy and related disciplines, include music therapy research. Quantitative, qualitative, and other types of research are important in music therapy, each fulfilling different purposes.

References

Aasgaard T (2000). 'A suspiciously cheerful lady': a study of a song's life in the paediatric oncology ward, and beyond. *British Journal of Music Therapy*, **14**, 70–82.

Aigen K (1995). Principles of qualitative research. In BL Wheeler, ed., *Music therapy research: quantitative and qualitative perspectives*, 283–311. Barcelona, Gilsum, NH.

Aigen K (1997). *Here we are in music: one year with an adolescent creative music therapy group*. MMB, St. Louis, MO.

Aigen K (2002). *Playin' in the band: a qualitative study of popular music styles as clinical improvisation*. Barcelona, Gilsum, NH.

Alvin J and Warwick A (1991). *Music therapy for the autistic child*, 2nd edn. Oxford University Press, Oxford.

Amir D (1993). Moments of insight in the music therapy experience. *Music Therapy*, **12**, 85–100.

Amir D (1996). Experiencing music therapy: meaningful moments in the music therapy process. In M Langenberg, K Aigen and J Frommer, eds, *Qualitative music therapy research: beginning dialogues*, 109–130. Barcelona, Gilsum, NH.

AMTA (American Music Therapy Association) (2003). *AMTA professional competencies*. Available from http://www.musictherapy.org/competencies.html (Accessed 18 July 2006).

AMTA (American Music Therapy Association)(2005a). *Frequently asked questions about music therapy*. Available from:http://www.musictherapy.org/faqs.html#WHAT_IS_MUSIC_THERAPY (Accessed 18 July 2006).

AMTA (American Music Therapy Association) (2005b). *AMTA bylaws*. Available at: http://www.musictherapy.org/membersonly/official/bylaws.html (Accessed 18 July 2006).

Bailar JC (1997). The promise and problems of meta-analysis. *The New England Journal of Medicine*, **337**(8), 559–561.

Borg WR and Gall MD (1989). *Educational research: an introduction*, 5th edn. Longman, White Plains, NY.

Brooks D (2003). A history of music therapy journal articles published in the English language. *Journal of Music Therapy*, **40**, 151–168.

Bruscia KE (1995a). Differences between quantitative and qualitative research paradigms: implications for music therapy. In BL Wheeler, ed., *Music therapy research: quantitative and qualitative perspectives*, 65–76. Barcelona, Gilsum, NH.

Bruscia KE (1995b). Modes of consciousness in Guided Imagery and Music (GIM): a therapist's experience of the guiding process. In CB Kenny, ed., *Listening, playing, creating: essays on the power of sound*, 165–197. State University of New York Press, Albany, NY.

Bruscia KE (2005). Research topics and questions in music therapy. In BL Wheeler, ed., *Music therapy research*, 2nd edn, 81–93. Barcelona, Gilsum, NH.

Cepeda MS, Carr DB, Lau J and Alvarez H (2006). Music for pain relief [Cochrane Review]. *The Cochrane Library*, 2, no pagination. John Wiley and Sons, Chichester.

Chandra P (2005). The effect of sound stimuli on neurologic rehabilitation of upper and lower limbs: a meta analysis. Unpublished master's thesis, Florida State University, Tallahassee, FL. Available at: http://etd.lib.fsu.edu/theses/available/etd-07112005–131201/ (Accessed 8 January 2007).

Codding PA (2002). A comprehensive survey of music therapists practicing in correctional psychiatry: demographics, conditions of employment, service provision, assessment, therapeutic objectives, and related values of the therapist. *Music Therapy Perspectives*, **20**, 56–68.

Cohen J (1977). *Statistical power analysis for the behavioral sciences*, 2nd edn. Academic Press, New York.

Cohen NS, Hadsell NA and Williams SL (1997). The perceived quality of applied music requirements in the vocational practices of professional music therapists. *Music Therapy Perspectives*, **15**, 67–72.

Comeau P (2004). A phenomenological investigation of being effective as a music therapist. In B Abrams, ed., *Qualitative inquiries in music therapy*, Vol. 1, 19–36. Barcelona, Gilsum, NH.

Cook DJ, Mulrow CD and Haynes RB (1997). Systematic reviews: synthesis of best evidence for clinical decisions. *Annals of Internal Medicine*, **126**, 376–380.

Dileo C (2000). *Ethical thinking in music therapy*. Jeffrey Books, Cherry Hill, NJ.

Dileo C (2005). Reviewing the literature. In BL Wheeler, ed., *Music therapy research*, 2nd edn, 105–111. Barcelona, Gilsum, NH.

Dileo C and Bradt J (eds) (2005). *Music therapy and medicine: a meta-analysis of the literature according to medical specialty*. Jeffrey Books, Cherry Hill, NJ.

Edwards J (2005). Developments and issues in music therapy research. In BL Wheeler, ed., *Music therapy research*, 2nd edn, 20–32. Barcelona, Gilsum, NH.

Eysenck HJ (1994). Systematic reviews: meta-analysis and its problems. *British Medical Journal*, **309**, 789–792.

Ferrara L (1984). Phenomenology as a tool for musical analysis. *The Musical Quarterly*, **7**, 355–373.

Forinash M (1992). A phenomenological analysis of Nordoff-Robbins approach to music therapy: the lived experience of clinical improvisation. *Music Therapy*, **11**, 120–141.

Forinash M and Gonzalez D (1989). A phenomenological perspective of music therapy. *Music Therapy*, **9**, 35–46.

Gardstrom SC (2004). An investigation of meaning in clinical music improvisation with troubled adolescents. In B Abrams, ed., *Qualitative inquiries in music therapy*, Vol. 1, 77–160. Barcelona, Gilsum, NH.

Gault AW (1978). An assessment of the effectiveness of clinical training in collegiate music therapy curricula. *Journal of Music Therapy*, **15**, 36–39.

Gfeller K (1995). The status of music therapy research. In BL Wheeler, ed., *Music therapy research: quantitative and qualitative perspectives*, 29–63. Barcelona, Gilsum, NH.

Gilliland E (1952). The development of music therapy as a profession. In E Gilliland, ed., *Music therapy 1951*, v–xvi. North Shore Printers, Waukegan, IL.

Gold C, Heldal TO, Dahle T and Wigram T (2005). Music therapy for schizophrenia and schizophrenia-like illnesses [Cochrane Review]. *The Cochrane Library*, **2**, no pagination. John Wiley and Sons, Chichester.

Gold C, Voracek M and Wigram T (2004). Effects of music therapy for children and adolescents with psychopathology: a meta-analysis. *Journal of Child Psychology and Psychiatry and Allied Disciplines*, **45**, 1054–1063.

Gold C, Wigram T and Elefant C (2006) Music therapy for autistic spectrum disorder [Cochrane Review]. *The Cochrane Library*, **2**, no pagination. John Wiley and Sons, Chichester.

Gregory D (2002). Four decades of music therapy behavioral research designs: a content analysis of *Journal of Music Therapy* articles. *Journal of Music Therapy*, **39**, 56–71.

Grocke DE (1999). A phenomenological study of pivotal moments in Guided Imagery and Music therapy. Unpublished doctoral dissertation, University of Melbourne, Melbourne, Australia. Available at http://www.musictherapyworld.net.

Groene RW and Pembrook RG (2000). Curricular issues in music therapy: a survey of collegiate faculty. *Music Therapy Perspectives*, **18**, 92–102.

Hairston M (2005) Presidential perspectives. In American Music Therapy Association, *Music Therapy Matters*, **8**(3and4), 8. Available at: http://www.musictherapy.org/membersonly/news/MTM8(3).pdf (Retrieved 18 July 2006).

Hilliard RE (2004). Hospice administrators' knowledge of music therapy: a comparative analysis of surveys. *Music Therapy Perspectives*, **22**, 104–108.

Hills B, Norman I and Forster L (2000). A study of burnout and multidisciplinary team—working amongst professional music therapists. *British Journal of Music Therapy*, **14**(1), 32–40.

Hömberg V (2005). Evidence-based medicine in neurological rehabilitation—a critical review. *Acta Neurochirurgica Supplement*, **93**, 3–14.

Jackson NA (2003). A survey of music therapy methods and their role in the treatment of early elementary school children with ADHD. *Journal of Music Therapy*, **40**, 302–323.

Jensen KL and Mckinney CH (1990). Undergraduate music therapy education and training: current status and proposals for the future. *Journal of Music Therapy*, **26**, 158–178.

Kenny CB (1989). *The field of play: a guide for the theory and practice of music therapy*. Ridgeview, Atascadero, CA.

Kenny C (2006). *Music and life in the field of play: an anthology*. Barcelona, Gilsum, NH.

Koger SM, Chapin K and Brotons M (1999). Is music therapy an effective intervention for dementia? A meta-analytic review of the literature. *Journal of Music Therapy*, **36**, 2–15.

Langenberg M, Frommer J and Tress W (1993). A qualitative approach to analytical music therapy. *Music Therapy*, **12**, 59–84.

Langenberg M, Frommer J and Tress W (1995). From isolation to bonding: a music therapy case study of a patient with chronic migraines. *The Arts in Psychotherapy*, **22**, 87–101.

Maranto C Dileo, and Bruscia K (1988). *Methods of teaching and training the music therapist*. Temple University, Philadelphia, PA.

Morse JM (2006). The politics of evidence. *Qualitative Health Research*, **16**, 395–404.

National Advisory Mental Health Council (2000). *Translating behavioral science into action: Report of the National Advisory Mental Health Council Behavioral Science Workgroup*. National Institute of Mental Health, Bethesda, MD.

Naylor CD (1988). Two cheers for meta-analysis: problems and opportunities in aggregating results of clinical trials. *Canadian Medical Association Journal*, **138**, 891–895.

Nordoff P and Robbins C (2007). *Creative music therapy: a guide to fostering clinical musicianship*, 2nd edn, revised and expanded. Barcelona, Gilsum, NH.

Nunes EV, Carroll KM and Bickel WK (2002). Clinical and translational research: introduction to the special issue. *Experimental and clinical psychopharmacology*, **10**, 155–158.

Pelletier CL (2004). The effect of music on decreasing arousal due to stress: a meta-analysis. *Journal of Music Therapy*, **41**, 192–214.

Racette K (2004). A phenomenological analysis of the experience of listening to music when upset. In B Abrams, ed., *Qualitative inquiries in music therapy*, Vol. 1, 1–18. Barcelona, Gilsum, NH.

Register D (2002). Collaboration and consultation: a survey of board certified music therapists. *Journal of Music Therapy*, **39**, 305–321.

Ruud E (1987). Musikk som kommunikasjon og samhandling [Music as communication and interaction]. Institutt for musikk og teate. Unpublished doctoral dissertation, Oslo University, Oslo Norway.

Sackett DL, Rosenberg WMC, Gray JAM, Haynes RB and Richardson WD (1996). Evidence-based medicine: what it is and what it isn't. *British Medical Journal*, **312**(7023), 71–72.

Silverman MJ (2003). The influence of music on the symptoms of schizophrenia: a meta-analysis. *Journal of Music Therapy*, **40**, 27–40.

Silverman MJ and Hairston MJ (2005). A descriptive study of private practice in music therapy. *Journal of Music Therapy*, **42**, 262–271.

Skewes K (2001). The experience of group music therapy for six bereaved adolescents. Unpublished doctoral dissertation, University of Melbourne, Melbourne, Australia. Available at: http://www. musictherapyworld.net.

Smith DS and Hairston MJ (1999). Music therapy in school settings: current practice. *Journal of Music Therapy*, **36**, 274–292.

Standley J (1986). Music research in medical/dental treatment: meta-analysis and clinical implications. *Journal of Music Therapy*, **23**, 56–122.

Standley JM (2000). Music research in medical treatment. In *Effectiveness of music therapy procedures: documentation of research and clinical practice*, 3rd edn, 1–64. American Music Therapy Association, Silver Spring, MD.

Standley JM (2002). A meta-analysis of the efficacy of music therapy for premature infants. *Journal of Paediatric Nursing*, **17**(2), 107–113.

Standley JM and Whipple J (2003). Music therapy for premature infants in the neonatal intensive care unit: HEALTH and developmental benefits. In SL Robb, ed., *Music therapy in paediatric healthcare: research and evidence-based practice*, 1–30. American Music Therapy Association, Silver Spring, MD.

Stewart D (2000). The state of the UK music therapy profession: personal qualities, working models, support networks and job satisfaction. *British Journal of Music Therapy*, **14**(1), 13–31.

Thaut MH (2005). *Rhythm, music, and the brain: scientific foundations and clinical applications*. Routledge, New York.

Vink AC, Birks JS, Bruinsma MS and Scholten RJS (2003/2006). Music therapy for people with dementia [Cochrane Review]. *The Cochrane Library*, 1, no pagination. John Wiley and Sons, Chichester.

Wheeler BL (ed.) (1995). *Music therapy research: quantitative and qualitative perspectives*. Barcelona, Gilsum, NH.

Wheeler BL (1999). Experiencing pleasure in working with severely disabled children. *Journal of Music Therapy*, **36**, 56–80.

Wheeler BL (2002). Experiences and concerns of students during music therapy practica. *Journal of Music Therapy*, **39**, 274–304.

Wheeler BL (ed.) (2005a). *Music therapy research*, 2nd edn. Barcelona, Gilsum, NH.

Wheeler BL (2005b). Overview of music therapy research. In BL Wheeler, ed., *Music therapy research*, 2nd edn, 3–19. Barcelona, Gilsum, NH.

Whipple J (2004). Music in intervention for children and adolescents with autism: a meta-analysis. *Journal of Music Therapy*, **41**, 90–106.

CHAPTER 49

Music therapy in medical and neurological rehabilitation settings

Anne Kathrin Leins, Ralph Spintge and Michael Thaut

S INCE the 1990s treatment models for the functional use of music in specific clinical pictures were developed under the label 'musicmedicine' or 'medical music therapy'. The new understanding of the biological basis of music and the influence of music on non-musical behaviour and brain function has led to a redefinition of music and its working mechanisms as a therapeutic tool.

Focus so far has been on the theoretically founded application of music in pain therapy and neurological rehabilitation, while the term 'neurological rehabilitation' is not understood in the narrow sense that its semantic meaning might imply. It applies not only to the actual restoration of function, e.g. post-stroke or traumatic brain injury, but also to degenerative illnesses and disorders such as Alzheimer's or Parkinson's disease (Thaut 2005).

Music therapy in neurological rehabilitation settings

Introduction

Research of the last 20 years on neuroplasticity and cortical reorganization has led to the development of innovative, neuroscientifically founded treatment models for neurologic rehabilitation. Music as a complex, temporally structured 'sound language' arouses the human brain on a sensory, motor, perceptive–cognitive and emotional level simultaneously and stimulates and integrates neuronal pathways in a music-specific way.

This stimulation can enhance and modify behaviour, processing and perception processes by specific and well-directed use in therapeutic approaches, which are based on active training (Thaut 2005).

The therapeutic application of music to cognitive, sensory and motor dysfunctions due to neurologic disease of the human nervous system has been subsumed under the term 'neurologic music therapy (NMT)'.

NMT encompasses a wide variety of standardized treatment techniques which are evidence-based on scientific and clinical research and directed toward functional non-musical therapeutic goals.

Clinical applications of NMT are subdivided into three domains of rehabilitation:

◆ sensorimotor rehabilitation,

◆ speech and language rehabilitation and

◆ cognitive rehabilitation.

In each domain NMT can be applied to treat patients within different clinical fields and disciplines, such as inpatient and outpatient neurologic rehabilitation, neurogeriatrics, neuropaediatrics and neurodevelopmental therapies. Depending on the patient's needs, therapeutic goals are directed towards functional rehabilitative, developmental or adaptive efforts.

Clinical outcome studies

Clinical research provides evidence that NMT training has a positive effect on relevant outcome criteria. Focus of research so far has been

NMT in motor rehabilitation. In several studies it has shown to significantly improve gait and other movement parameters (e.g. upper extremity function) in hemiparetic motor rehabilitation (cf. Luft *et al.* 2004; Schauer and Mauritz 2003; Thaut *et al.* 1993, 1997, 2002, 2007; Whitall *et al.* 2000) as well as gait training in Parkinson's disease (cf. Bernatzky *et al.* 2004; Del Olmo and Cudeiro 2003; Howe *et al.* 2003; Lim *et al.* 2005; McIntosh *et al.* 1997; Morris *et al.* 2004; Pacchetti *et al.* 2000; Rochester *et al.* 2005; Thaut *et al.* 1996;).

A smaller number of studies has found positive results also in cerebral palsy (Malherbe 1992; Thaut *et al.* 1998), traumatic brain injury (Hurt *et al.* 1998; Kenyon and Thaut 2000) and developmental disabilities (Robertson *et al.* 2002a, b). NMT in gait rehabilitation can be used as a self-contained training protocol but its principles of rhythmic cuing and temporal regulation can also be integrated into other intervention methods.

Research efforts on the effect of rhythm on motor facilitation started with the evaluation of the effect of rhythmic cuing on stride and muscle activation patterns through use of electromyography (EMG) in the gait of healthy individuals (Thaut *et al.* 1992). Improvement in stride symmetry and EMG patterns, particularly the amplitude variability in muscle contractions across the stride cycle, was observed (Thaut *et al.* 1992). Based on these results the immediate effect of rhythm on gait ability in stroke patients was explored (Thaut *et al.* 1993). Results of this study showed that most patients were clearly able to synchronize their step times to the rhythm. In the course of synchronizing gait movements to the rhythm, stride time symmetry and stride length symmetry improved significantly, as did weight-bearing time on the paretic side. Stride time variability decreased to a significant degree. Subjects also showed a more balanced muscular activation pattern on EMG between the paretic and non-paretic leg, and EMG patterns on the paretic side became significantly more consistent.

In order to evaluate the long-term use of NMT in gait rehabilitation, a two-armed parallel group design was used comparing the NMT-method 'rhythmic auditory stimulation' (RAS) (for details see Thaut 2005) to conventional physical therapy gait training (Thaut *et al.* 1997a). Results demonstrated a statistically significant superiority of the RAS-group compared to the physiotherapy group with regard to the kinematic parameters gait velocity and stride length. This positive outcome has been undermined in a multicentre study (Thaut *et al.* 2007). Thaut *et al.* (2007) found a significant superiority of the RAS-group as compared to the physiotherapy group concerning gait velocity, stride length and frequency.

The immediate effect of RAS on repetitive flexion–extension–reaching movements of the paretic arm in hemiparetic stroke patients was the subject of another study (Thaut *et al.* 1998b). Results revealed immediate improved performance with RAS.

As to Parkinson's disease (PD) patients, results of an initial study revealed that patients could synchronize their step patterns to auditory rhythm even when not taking medication and this effect produced significant improvements in mean gait velocity, cadence and stride length over walking without RAS. Based on this data, it was shown in a controlled study design that PD patients profit from a music-based 3-week home-based walking programme of 30 minutes each day (Thaut *et al.* 1996a) and that the therapeutic effect lasts for 3–4 weeks (Mc Intosh *et al.* 1998).

Data on the differential use of metronome vs rhythmic–auditory stimulation in a music context are not consistent. Thaut *et al.* (1997a) have provided evidence in an experimental setting that the temporal synchronization of a sensorimotor task is more precise with rhythmically accentuated musical stimulation than with metronome clicks in healthy subjects. In relation to the improvement of the quality of gait in Parkinson's disease patients, Enzensberger *et al.* (1997), however, found a superiority of metronome stimulation as compared to stimulation by rhythmically accentuated music.

In the course of the development of innovative methods of rhythmical auditory stimulation in neurologic motor rehabilitation, the therapeutic use of music was also applied to speech and language training. Thaut *et al.* (2001) provided evidence for a significant improvement of PD patients with dysarthria as to intelligibility after 'rhythmic speech cuing' (see Thaut 2005). There is also empirical evidence for 'melodic intonation therapy' with patients suffering from Broca aphasia (Sparks and Holland 1976).

NMT techniques in motor therapy have found their way into the corpus of scientific medical survey literature (cf. Adler and Ahlskog 2000; Hömberg 2005; Hummelsheim 1999; Jeffrey and Gould 1995).

As to the application of music in the therapy of cognitive functions—focusing on memory and attention training—a number of studies have been published within the last years (cf. Chan *et al.* 1998; Claussen and Thaut 1997; Foster and Valentine 2001; Haslam and Cook 2002; Knox and Jutai 1996; Ma *et al.* 2001). These studies broaden the evidence-base for NMT as a therapeutic technique in the rehabilitation of neurologic diseases.

Neuroscientific foundation of NMT: a working model

Thaut (2005) suggests a preliminary working model of specific mechanisms of music as a rehabilitative stimulus. The aim is to summarize evidence as a step toward a clearer understanding of the biomedical properties embedded in music perception. He advises that these mechanisms cannot be considered as working linearly in a mutually exclusive manner.

Thaut (2005) identifies four such mechanisms or underlying rationales for biomedical application of music and rhythm:

1 *Rhythmic stimulation and entrainment.* Rhythmic stimulation has profound effects as coordinative sensory input to entrain timing functions (cf. Paltsev and Elner 1967; Rossignol and Melvill 1976; Thaut *et al.* 1999; Thaut 2003), especially in motor control and speech. Rhythm provides temporal structure through metrical organization, predictability and patterning. Rhythm regulates physiological and behavioural functions via entrainment mechanisms (cf. Aschersleben and Prinz 1995; Molinari *et al.* 2003; Stephan *et al.* 2002, 2003; Tecchio *et al.* 2000; Thaut and Schauer 1997b; Thaut *et al.* 1998e). Rhythmic entrainment provides immediate time regulation but can also be accessed to enhance long-term training effects. Temporal regulation not only affects timing issues but also provides templates for optimization of spatial and force dynamics (cf. Thaut *et al.* 1996).

2 *Patterned information processing.* Timing is a key component in neural information processing in regard to perception and learning (cf. Galaretta and Hestrin 2001). Rhythm and synchronization are critical parameters in this processing, creating temporal structure in neural network activation (cf. Ikegaya *et al.* 2004; Fries *et al.* 2001). Time cues in the objects and stimuli of perception and learning themselves may be important facilitators to enhance the underlying physiology of temporal pattern formation, thus enhancing critical aspects of cognitive processes (cf. Lee and Blake 1999). Music is a very complex temporal stimulus. In all dimensions of its temporal architecture—from the spectral patterns of its psychoacoustical foundations to the most complex compositional principles of rhythm and polyphony—we find pattern structures of timing and synchronization embedded as building principles (see Kenyon and Thaut 2003; Thaut 1998c). Research suggests that music can uniquely engage the brain as a language of time (cf. Buonomano and Merzenich 1995), providing temporal structure to enhance learning and perception, especially in the areas of cognition, language and motor learning (Thaut 2005).

3 *Differential neurological processing.* The neuroanatomy and neurophysiology of music processing show shared, parallel and distinct neural processing systems for non-musical functions (Thaut 2005). For example, speech and singing are mediated by different neural networks (Patel 2003). Music regulates attention and arousal in the brain in a complex, bilaterally distributed fashion (Coull *et al.* 2004). Learning verbal material through song accesses different neural network configurations than learning through verbal presentation (Thaut and Peterson 2003). Auditory rhythm is a powerful sensory cue that can regulate motor timing and coordination in the presence of a deficient internal timing system in the brain. These are examples of how music can be used as an alternative modality to access functions or provide alternative transmission routes for information processing in the brain.

4 *Affective–aesthetic response: arousal, motivation, emotion.* Music communicates emotion

and meaning through the perception of its intrinsic symbol structure of musical elements as well as through emotional responses that have become connected to it through an associative learning process (cf. Berlyne 1971; Juslin and Sloboda 2001; Meyer 1956). Many theories of the meaning of music see the primary purpose of music as expressing and representing emotions and feelings. Regardless of its precise nature, music is a powerful stimulus that induces emotions (cf. Juslin and Sloboda 2001). As such, it has a strong influence on affective states. Arousal, motivation and emotions have important regulatory functions in behaviour organization, behaviour change and learning. Attention, perception, memory, executive function, physical response and learning can be effectively influenced and enhanced by appropriate affective states (cf. Thaut 2005).

Summary

Neurologic music therapy encompasses evidence-based methods of the functional application of music in the rehabilitation of neurologic disorders.

One of the most widely implemented clinical areas is its application in sensorimotor therapy, focusing on gait training. These methods are based on neurophysiological and neuroanatomic research on auditory–motor synchronization. It has been demonstrated that rhythm can serve as an anticipatory and continuous time reference onto which the movement is mapped within a stable temporal template. Furthermore, a clinical research basis is rapidly developing in the application of neurologic music therapy in speech/language rehabilitation and cognitive rehabilitation.

Music therapy and pain therapy

Introduction

Meta-analyses (Bunt 1997; Standley 1986) underline the effectiveness of music therapy in acute pain. Dileo (2003) finds small to medium effect sizes in children and medium to large effect sizes in adult pain management. A Cochrane review (Cepeda et al. 2006) on music for pain relief finds that listening to music reduces pain intensity levels and opioid requirements, but

evaluates the overall magnitude of the benefits as small. Spintge (cf. 2000) has provided extensive evidence on the effectiveness of music therapy in pain management an on its psychophysiological effects.

There is anecdotal evidence for the use of both receptive and active music therapy in pediatric pain management, but research studies in this field are scarce. Bradt (2001) finds music therapy to be effective in postoperative pain management of orthopaedic paediatric patients. Results of a pilot study from Barrera et al. (2002) reveal that interactive music therapy is effective in reducing anxiety and pain of hospitalized children with cancer. Earlier studies of music therapy during medical invasive procedures provide inconsistent results (cf. Arts et al. 1994; Fowler-Kerry and Lander 1987). It seems that with children interactive music therapy approaches during painful medical invasive procedures are preferable to the use of receptive music therapy, because the use of headphones during these procedures may enhance feelings of insecurity.

Music therapy is also applied effectively in chronic pain therapy (Chesky et al. 1997; Hillecke 2005; Leins 2006; Müller-Busch 1997; Nickel et al. 2005; Rider 1985, 1987; Sedei-Godley 1987; Shorr 1993). It is usually administered within an interdisciplinary framework and aims at improving pain sensation, but also coping with pain and comorbid disorders.

Concepts and effects of anxioalgolytic music against acute pain and stress in medical settings

Musical stimuli alleviating psychophysiological responses to stress and pain are comprised as anxioalgolytic music (AAM) (Spintge 1983). Medico-functional applications of AAM include, for instance, perioperative stress in surgery and dental care, anaesthesia and pain medicine, intensive care, behavioural disorders, obstetrical care, geriatrics, neurological and psychological motor dysfunctions, and palliative care (Avancini et al. 2003, 2005; Droh and Spintge 1987; Leins 2006; Pratt and Spintge 1996, Spintge 1998, 2000, 2007; Spintge et al. 1999; Spintge and Droh 1991, 1992). The psychophysical condition of a patient in such situations is characterized by emotional distress, anxiety, and, very often, pain (spintge 1991). The traditional

Fig. 49.1 Circulus vitiosus of pain.

medical interventions, using analgesics and sedatives, for example, often fall short when drugs prove insufficient or reduce the ability of a patient to cooperate. In the following we focus upon acute pain and stress.

The so-called circulus vitiousus of stress and pain (Figure 49.1) describes the psychophysiological situation. Conscious perception, self-esteem, and subjective feeling are as significantly impaired as the central nervous (neurovegetative) regulation of cardiovascular and cardio-respiratory systems. Hormonal control, motor control, sensory and perceptive information processing are disturbed.

Over the course of 30 years in more than 160 000 patients, the routine application of AAM demonstrates that music, as the most intense emotional means of communication, has its special significance as part of a multimodal treatment regime. In this instance, multimodal means to consider illness as a holistic phenomenon, demanding a therapeutic approach, which includes emotional, psychological, social and biological (somatic) aspects (see the so-called biopsychosocial model of pain and the definition of health as given by the WHO).

At present medico-functional music research has identified several target areas for AAM, as explained in Table 49.1. Musical rhythm is an especially effective structural parameter (Koepchen *et al.* 1992; Spintge 1996).

Within a multimodal treatment regime of both acute and chronic distress and pain, music can be used both as a complementary and therapeutic

means itself, with impacts upon different levels of neurophysiological processing of pain and stress.

On the one hand, the influence of music (a very complex stimulus) on consciousness is very powerful compared to other environmental stimuli. Averse stimuli are less or even no longer perceived and processed 'under music'. On the other hand, subcortical centres of pain-processing and emotional control, such as the limbic system, are directly influenced. In addition, descending pain-inhibiting structures of the central nervous system are activated in the same way as Melzack and Wall (1965) describe in their (adapted version of the) gate-control-theory. Also, the new concept of neuroplasticity explains the genetical re-programming of dorsal root nerve cells that have been sensitized against pain input before (Zieglgaensberger 1998). These concepts force us to reconsider the role of so-called complementary therapies in general, because we find that the genome of nerve cells can be reprogrammed, thereby changing their functional capacities. Furthermore, the continuous input of similar stimuli for instance through a piece of music enhances this reprogramming.

Another target area for the influence of music upon pain perception lies in musicogenic muscle detonization. Proprioception from skeletal muscles influences emotional state as well as pain perception, and vice versa (David 1985; Gellhorn *et al.* 1964; Simons 1988).

Also, there is a direct pain-decreasing impact of music on reticular formation and thalamus in the central nervous system (Avanzini *et al.* 2003, 2005; David 1985). This process reduces the sensitivity of other areas in the brain to incoming pain signals as well as decreasing the release of stress hormones and catecholamines.

Last, but not least, subjective perception of ongoing, pain-accompanying vegetative activation can be changed through the parallel input of external musical stimuli. By listening to music a situation can be re-construed as being less threatening and less stressful and painful.

Research findings lead to what we call the 'missing link concept' of rhythmicity as a bridge between AAM on one side and physiology and medicine on the other side (Spintge 1996).

Music stimuli are processed through interdependent mechanisms that are as yet not fully understood, by themselves or together. It is clear, however, that the aggregate of all the mechanisms involved is responsible for the observable psychophysiological effects of AAM music.

Through methodological and technical effort and with the help of up-to-date central nervous system (CNS) monitoring equipment such as functional magnetic resonance imaging (fMRI) and positron emission tomography (PET), it is possible, however, to scientifically correlate quantitatively and qualitatively physiological parameters and subjective measures with the structure of medico-functional music stimuli (cf. Avanzini *et al.* 2003, 2005; Hodges *et al.* 2005; Sergent 1993).

The practical relevance of all these findings and concepts expresses itself in many ways (see Table 49.1) and leads for instance to improved motor coordination in rehabilitation programmes for low back pain, Parkinson's disease, stroke, etc. (McIntosh *et al.* 1996; Thaut 1997, 2003).

Music therapy with chronic pain patients

In earlier studies predominantly receptive music therapy approaches are used (Chesky *et al.* 1997; Rider 1985, 1987; Sedei-Godley 1987; Shorr 1993) but within the last ten years active music therapy approaches with chronic pain patients have gained more attention (Hillecke 2005; Leins 2006; Müller-Busch 1997).

Müller-Busch (1997) proved the effectiveness of music therapy for patients with muscle-related pain. Hillecke (2005) found significant effects in the pre-post-comparison and the

Table 49.1 Music in pain therapy - psychophysiological effects and treatment outcome

System/Parameter	Reaction
cardiovascular	decrease of heartrate decrease of arterial bloodpressure anti arrhythmic
respiration	decrease of respiratory minute-volume decrease of oxygen-consumption synchronisation/harmonisation of rhythm
inner secretion & metabolism	reduced release of: catecholamines ACTH Cortisol Prolactin β-Endorphin decrease in basal metabolic rate sleep induction
immune system	psychomeuronal modulation of neuroendocrine receptors for catecholamines, endorphins, substance P, dopamine leading to: rise in IgA-salive-levels rise in T-cell activity relief of inflammatory pain
external secreation & excretion	reduced salivation and perspiration
reception & perception	rise in pain tolerance
motor control	reduced restlessness reduced muscle tonus muscle spasms dissolved psychomotor facilitation
drug consumption	50% to 100% reduced premedication
hospital treatment period	reduced: premature infants intensive care: 3 days surgery in the elderly: 1 day

group comparison condition in a sample of chronic pain patients. Music therapy enhanced effectiveness in a clinically significant way in pain and psychological measures.

Leins (2006) investigated the effectiveness of music therapy with children with migraine headache in a randomized, placebo-controlled, three-armed parallel group design. A specific music therapy concept has been developed (Nickel *et al.* 2002) which takes particular developmental stages of children into account and integrates the patients family. It focuses on the re-establishment of well-being and on coping with pain and pain-inducing situations/emotions through specific music therapeutic interventions. After therapy and in the follow-up measure the music therapy condition showed a significant placebo superiority with regard to relative reduction of headache frequency (Leins 2006).

Summary

Music therapy is widely applied in pain therapy. Meta-analyses underline the effectiveness of music therapy in acute pain of adult pain patients. Research focuses on clinical outcome, but also investigates possible underlying mechanisms such as the psychophysiological effects of music. There is large anecdotal evidence for the use of receptive but also active music therapy in paediatric pain management, research studies in this field are however scarce. Music therapy is also applied effectively in chronic pain therapy. It is usually administered within an interdisciplinary framework and aims at improving pain sensation, but also coping with pain and comorbid disorders.

References

Adler H and Ahlskog J (2000). *Parkinson's disease and movement disorders.* Humana Press, Totawa, NJ.

Arts SE, Abu-Saad HH, Champion GD, Crawford MR, Fisher RJ, Juniper KH and Ziegler JB (1994). Age-related response to lidocaine-prilocaine (EMLA) emulsion and effect of music distraction on the pain of intravenous cannulation. *Pediatrics*, **93**, 797–801.

Aschersleben G and Prinz W (1995). Synchronizing actions with events: the role of sensory information. *Perception and Psychophysics*, **57**, 305–317.

Avanzini G, Faienza C, Minciacchi D, Lopez L and Majno M (2003). The neurosciences and music. *Annals of the New York Academy of Sciences*, **999**, whole issue.

Avanzini G, Lopez L, Koelsch S and Majno M (2005). The neurosciences and music vol 2. From perception to performance. *Annals of the New York Academy of Sciences*, **1060**, whole issue.

Barrera ME, Rykov MH and Doyle SL (2002). The effects of interactive music therapy on hospitalized children with cancer: a pilot study. *Psycho-Oncology*, **11**, 379–388.

Berlyne DE (1971). *Aesthetics and psychobiology.* Appleton, Century and Crofts, New York.

Bernatzky G, Bernatzky P, Hesse HP, Staffen W and Ladurner G (2004). Stimulating music increases motor coordination in patients afflicted by Morbus Parkinson. *Neuroscience Letters*, **361**, 4–8.

Bradt J (2001). The effect of music entrainment on postoperative pain perception in pediatric patients. Dissertation submitted to the Temple University Graduate Board.

Bunt L (1997). Clinical and therapeutic uses of music. In DJ Hargraeves and AC North, eds, *The social psychology of music*, 249–267. Oxford University Press, New York.

Buonomano DV and Merzenich MM (1995). Temporal information transformed into a spatial code by a neural network with realistic properties. *Science*, **267**, 1028–1030.

Cepeda MS, Carr DB, Lau J and Alvarez H (2006). Music for pain relief. *The Cochrane Database Systematic Reviews*, **2**.

Chan AS, Ho YC and Cheung MC (1998). Music training improves verbal memory. *Nature*, **396**, 128.

Chesky KS, Russel J, Lopez Y and Kondraske GV (1997). Fibromyalgia tender point pain: a double-blind, placebo-controlled pilot study of music vibration using the music vibration table. *Journal of Musculosceletal Pain*, **5**, 33–42.

Claussen D and Thaut MH (1997). Music as a mnemonic device for children with learning disabilities. *Canadian Journal of Music Therapy*, **5**, 55–66.

Coull JT, Vidal F, Nazarian B and Macar F (2004). Functional anatomy of the attentional modulation of time estimation. *Science*, **303**, 1506–1508.

David E (1985). Clickevozierte Potentiale während der Darbietung unterschiedlicher Musikprogramme am Menschen. In R Spintge, R Droh, Eds, *Music in medicine*, 61–86. Editiones Roche, Grenzach.

Del Olmo MF and Cudeiro J (2003). A simple procedure using auditory stimuli to improve movement in Parkinson's disease: a pilot study. *Neurology and Clinical Neurophysiology*, **2**, 1–7.

Dileo C (2003). A meta-analysis of the literature in medical music therapy and MusicMedicine with an agenda for future research. *Abstractband des VIII. Symposium for Music in Medicine of the International Society of Music in Medicine* (ISMM), 100–101.

Droh R and Spintge R (1987). *Musik in der Medizin* (Music in medicine). Heidelberg-New York: Springer.

Enzensberger W, Oberländer U and Stecker K (1997). Metronomtherapie bei Parkinson Patienten. *Nervenarzt*, **12**, 972–977.

Foster N and Valentine E (2001). The effect of auditory stimulation on autobiographical recall in dementia. *Experimental Aging Research*, **27**, 215–228.

Fowler-Kerry S and Lander JR (1987). Management of injection pain in children. *Pain*, **30**, 169–175.

Fries P, Reynolds JH, Rorie AE and Desimone R (2001). Modulation of oscillatory neuronal synchronization by selective visual attention. *Science*, **291**, 1560–1563.

Galaretta M and Hestrin S (2001). Spike transmission and synchrony detection in networks of GABAergic interneurons. *Science*, **291**, 1560–1563.

Gellhorn E (1964). Motion and Emotion. *Psychological Review*, **71**, 457–472.

Gembris H (1997). Psychovegetative Zustände des Musikhörens. *Zeitschrift für Musikpädagogik*, **2**, 59–65.

Haslam C and Cook M (2002). Striking a chord with amnesic patients: evidence that song facilitates memory. *Neurocase*, **8**, 453–465.

Hillecke TK (2005). *Heidelberger Musiktherapiemanual: Chronischer, nicht maligner Schmerz.* uni-edition, Berlin.

Hodges DA, Hairston WD and Burdette J (2005). Aspects of multisensory perception: the integration of visual and auditory information in musical experiences. *Annals of the New York Academy of Science*, **1060**, 175–185.

Hömberg V (2005). Evidence-based medicine in neurological rehabilitation—a critical review. *Acta Neurochir Suppl*, **93**, 3–14.

Howe TE, Lovgreen B, Cody FW, Ashton VJ, Oldham JA, (2003). Auditory cues can modify the gait of persons with early-stage Parkinson's disease: a method for enhancing Parkinsonian walking performance? *Clinical Rehabilitation*, **17**(4), 363–367.

Hummelsheim H (1999). Rationales for improving motor function. *Current Opinion in Neurology*, **12**(12), 697–701.

Hurt CP, Rice RR, McIntosh GC and Thaut MH (1998). Rhythmic auditory stimulation in gait training for patients with traumatic brain injury. *Journal of Music Therapy*, **35**(4), 228–241.

Ikegaya Y, Aaron G, Cossart R, Aronov D, Lampl I, Ferster D and Yuste R (2004). Synfire chains and cortical songs: temporal modules of cortical activity. *Science*, **302**, 559–564.

Jeffrey DR and Gould DC (1995). Rehabilitation of the stroke patient. *Current Opinion in Neurology*, **8**, 62–28.

Juslin PN and Sloboda JA (2001). *Music and emotion: Theory and research.* Oxford: Oxford University Press.

Kenyon GP and Thaut MH (2000). A measure of kinematic limb instability modulation by rhythmic auditory stimulation. *Journal of Biomechanics*, **33**, 1319–1323.

Kenyon GP and Thaut MH (2003). Rhythm-driven optimization of motor control. *Recent Research and Developments in Biomechanics*, **1**, 29–47.

Knox R and Jutai J (1996). Music-based rehabilitation of attention following brain injury. *Canadian Journal of Rehabilitation*, **9**, 169–181.

Koepchen HP, Droh R, Spintge R Abel HH, Kluessendorf D and Koralewski E (1992). Rhythmicity and music in medicine. In R Spintge and R Droh, Eds, *MusicMedicine*, 39–70. MMB, Saint Louis, MO.

Lee SH and Blake R (1999). Visual form created solely from temporal structure. *Science*, **284**, 1165–1167.

Leins AK (2006). *Heidelberger Musiktherapiemanual: Migräne bei Kindern* (Heidelberg Music Therapy Manual: Migraine in Children). uni-edition, Berlin.

Lim I, Van Wegen E, de Goede C, Deutekom M, Nieuwboer A, Willems A and Jones D (2005). Effects of external rhythmical cueing on gait in patients with Parkinson's disease. *Clinical Rehabilitation*, **19**(7), 695–713.

Luft AR, McCombe-Waller S, Whitall J, Forrester LW, Macko R, Sorkin JD, Schulz JB, Goldberg AP and Hanley DF (2004). Repetitive bilateral arm training and motor cortex activation in chronic stroke: a randomized controlled trial. *JAMA*, **292**(15), 1853–1861.

Ma Y, Nagler J, Lee M and Cabrera I (2001). Impact of music therapy on the communication skills of toddlers with pervasive developmental disorder. *Annals of the New York Academy of Sciences*, **930**, 445–447.

Malherbe V, Breniere Y and Bril B (1992). How do cerebral palsied children with hemiplegia control their gait? In M Woollacott and F Horak, eds, *Posture and Control Mechanisms, vol 2*, 102–105. University of Oregon Books, Eugene, OR.

McIntosh GC, Brown SH, Rice RR and Thaut MH (1997). Rhythmic auditory-motor facilitation of gait patterns in patients with Parkinson's disease. *Journal of Neurology, Neurosurgery, and Psychiatry*, **62**, 122–126.

McIntosh GC, Rice RR, Hurt CP and Thaut MH (1998). Long-term training effects of rhythmic auditory stimulation on gait in patients with Parkinsonian's disease. *Movement Disorders*, **13**(2), 212.

McIntosh GC, Thaut MM and Rice RR (1996) Rhythmic auditory stimulation as an entrainment and therapy technique: effects on gait of stroke and Parkinson's patients. In RR Pratt, R Spintge, eds, *MusicMedicine*, 145–152. MMB, Saint Louis, MO.

Melzack R and Wall P (1965). Pain mechanisms. *Science*, **150**, 971–979.

Meyer LB (1956). *Emotion and meaning in music.* The University of Chicago Press, Chicago, IL.

Molinari M, Leggio MM, De Martin M, Cerasa A and Thaut MH (2003). Neurobiology of rhythmic motor entrainment. *Ann NY Acad Sci*, **999**, 313–321.

Morris GS, Suteerawattananon M, Etnyre BR, Jankovic J and Protas EJ (2004). Effects of visual and auditory cues on gait in individuals with Parkinson's disease. *Journal of the Neurological Sciences*, **219**, 63–69.

Müller-Busch C (1997). *Schmerz und Musik— Musiktherapie bei Patienten mit chronischen Schmerzen.* Gustav Fischer, Stuttgart.

Nickel AK, Hillecke T, Argstatter H and Bolay HV (2005). Outcome research in music therapy—a step on the long road to an evidence-based treatment. *Annals of the New York Academy of Science*, **1060**, 283–293.

Nickel AK, Hillecke TK, Oelkers R, Resch F and Bolay HV (2002). Musiktherapie mit Kindern mit Migräne. *Psychotherapeut*, **47**, 285–290.

Pacchetti C, Mancini F, Aglieri R, Fundaro C, Martignoni E and Nappi G (2000). Active music therapy in Parkinson's disease: an integrative method for motor and emotional rehabilitation. *Psychosomatic Medicine*, **62**(3), 386–393.

Paltsev YI and Elner AM (1967). Change in the functional state of the segmental apparatus of the spinal cord under the influence of sound stimuli and its role in voluntary movement. *Biophysics*, **12**, 1219–1226.

Patel AD (2003). Language, music, syntax and the brain. *Nature Neuroscience*, **6**(7), 674–681.

Pratt RR and Spintge R (1996). *MusicMedicine* vol. 2. MMB, Saint Louis, MO.

Rider MS (1985). Entrainment mechanisms are involved in pain reduction, muscle relaxation, and music-mediated imagery. *Journal of Music Therapy*, **22**, 183–192.

Rider MS (1987). Treating chronic disease and pain with music-mediated imagery. *Arts in Psychotherapy*, **14**, 113–120.

Robertson SD, Chua R, Maraj BK, Kao JC and Weeks DJ (2002a). Bimanual coordination dynamics in adults with Down syndrome. *Motor Control*, **6**, 388–407.

Robertson SD, Van Gemmert AW and Maraj BK (2002b). Auditory information is beneficial for adults with down syndrome in a continuous bimanual task. *Acta Psychologica*, **110**, 213–229.

Rochester L, Hetherington V, Jones D, Nieuwboer A, Willems AM, Kwakkel G and Van Wegen E (2005). The effect of external rhythmic cues (auditory and visual) on walking during a functional task in homes of people with Parkinson's disease. *Archives of Physical Medicine and Rehabilitation*, **86**(5), 999–1006.

Rossignol S and Melvill J (1976). Audio-spinal influence in man studied by the h-reflex and its possible role on rhythmic movements synchronized to sound. *Electroencephalography and Clinical Neurophysiology*, **41**, 83–92.

Schauer M and Mauritz KH (2003). Musical motor feedback (MMF) in walking hemiparetic stroke patients: randomized trials of gait improvement. *Clinical Rehabilitation*, **17**, 713–722.

Sedei-Godley CA (1987). The use of music therapy in pain clinics. *Music Therapy Perspectives*, **4**, 24–28.

Sergent J (1993). Mapping the musician's brain. *Human Brain Mapping*, **1**, 20–38.

Shorr JA (1993). Music and pattern change in chronic pain. *Advances in Nursing Science*, **15**, 27–36.

Simons DG (1988). Myofascial pain syndromes of head, neck and low back. In R Dubner, GF Gebhart and MR Bond, Eds, *Pain research and clinical management*, 186–200. Blackwell, New York.

Juslin PN and Sloboda JA (2001). *Music and emotion: theory and research*. Oxford University Press, Oxford.

Sparks RW and Holland AL (1976). Melodic intonation therapy for aphasia. *Journal of Speech and Hearing Disorders*, **41**, 287–297.

Spintge R (1983). Psychophysiologische Operations-Fitness mit und ohne anxiolytische Musik (Psychophysiological fitness for surgery with, without anxiolytic music). In R Droh and R Spintge Eds, *Angst, Schmerz, Musik in der Anaesthesie* (Anxiety, pain, music in anesthesia), 77–88. Editiones Roche, Grenzach.

Spintge R (1991). The neurophysiology of emotion and its therapeutic applications in music therapy and MusicMedicine. In C Maranto,ed., *Applications of music in medicine*, 59–72. National Association for Music Therapy, Washington, DC.

Spintge R (2000). Musik in Anaesthesie und Schmerztherapie. (Music in anaesthesia and pain therapy). *Anaesthesie Intensivtherapie Notfallmedizin Schmerztherapie AINS*, 254–261.

Spintge R (2007). MusikMedizinische Forschung Heute und Morgen (Musicmedicine research today, tomorrow). In H.-H Decker-Voigt, ed., *Lexikon Musiktherapie* (Encyclopedia of music therapy), 37–42. Hogreve, Stuttgart.

Spintge R and Droh R (1987). *Music in medicine*. Springer, Heidelberg–New York.

Spintge R and Droh R (1991). Ergonomic approach to treatment of patient's perioperative stress. *Canadian Anesthetist Society Journal*, **35**(3), 104–106.

Spintge R, Besser-Siegmund C, Hodges DA, Nichols C and Schlaefke M (1999). *Schlafstörungen* [Sleep disorders]. Polymedia, Hamburg.

Spintge R. (1996). Physiology, mathematics, music, and medicine: definitions and concepts for research. In RR Pratt, R Spintge, Eds, *MusicMedicine*, 3–13. MMB, Saint Louis, MO.

Spintge R. (1998a). *Verspannungsschmerz* (Myofascial pain). Polymedia, Hamburg.

Standley JM (1986). Music research in medical/dental treatment: meta-analysis and clinical applications. *Journal of Music Therapy*, **23**, 56–122.

Stephan KM, Thaut MH, Wunderlich G, Schicks W, Tellmann L, Herzog H, McIntosh GC, Seitz RJ and Hömberg V (2003). Distinct cerebro-cerebellar circuits underlie temporal adjustment of motor behavior. *Proc Soc Neurosci*, **462**, 8.

Stephan KM, Thaut MH, Wunderlich G, Schicks W, Tian B, Tellmann L, Schmitz T, Herzog H, McIntosh GC, Seitz RJ and Hömberg V (2002). Conscious and subconscious sensorimotor synchronization— prefrontal cortex and the influence of awareness. *NeuroImage*, **15**, 345–352.

Tecchio F, Salustri C, Thaut MH, Pasqualetti P and Rossigni PM (2000). Conscious and preconscious adaptations to rhythmic auditory stimuli: a magnetoencephalographic study of human brain responses. *Exp Brain Res*, **135**, 222–230.

Thaut MH (1996c). Physiological and motor responses to music stimuli. In RF Unkefer, ed., *Music therapy in the treatment of adults with mental disorders: theoretical basis and clinical interventions*, 33–49. Schirmer Books, New York.

Thaut MH (2003). Neural basis of rhythmic timing networks in the human brain. *Annals of the New York Academy of Sciences*, **999**, 364.

Thaut MH (2005). *Rhythm, music, and the brain*. Routledge, New York.

Thaut MH and Peterson DA (2003). A role of theta and alpha synchronization in verbal learning with a musical template. *Proceedings of the Society for Neuroscience*, **194**, 21.

Thaut MH and Schauer ML (1997b). Weakly coupled oscillators in rhythmic motor synchronization. *Proc Soc Neurosci*, **298**, 20.

Thaut MH, Hoemberg V, Kenyon G and Hurt CP (1998b). Rhythmic entrainment of hemiparetic arm movements in stroke patients. *Proceedings of the Society for Neuroscience*, **653**, 7.

Thaut MH, Hurt CP, Dragan D and McIntosh GC (1998a). Rhythmic entrainment of gait patterns in children with cerebral palsy. *Developmental Medicine and Child Neurology*, **40**(78), 15.

Thaut MH, Kenyon GP, Hurt CP, McIntosh GC and Hömberg V (2002). Kinematic optimization of spatiotemporal patterns in paretic arm training with stroke patients. *Neuropsychologia*, **40**, 1073–1081.

Thaut MH, Kenyon GP, Schauer ML and McIntosh GC (1999a). The connection between rhythmicity and brain function. *IEEE Engineering in Medicine and Biology*, **18**, 101–108.

Thaut MH, McIntosh GC and Rice RR (1997a). Rhythmic facilitation of gait training in hemiparetic stroke rehabilitation. *Journal of Neurological Sciences*, **151**, 207–121.

Thaut MH, McIntosh GC, McIntosh KW and Hömberg V (2001). Auditory rhythmicity enhances movement and speech motor control in patients with Parkinson's disease. *Functional Neurology*, **16**, 163–172.

Thaut MH, McIntosh GC, Rice RR and Prassas SG (1992). Effect of auditory rhythmic cueing on temporal stride parameters and EMG patterns in normal gait. *J Neurol Rehab*, **6**, 185–190.

Thaut MH, McIntosh GC, Rice RR and Prassas SG (1993). The effect of auditory rhythmic cuing on stride and EMG patterns in hemiparetic gait of stroke patients. *Journal of Neurologic Rehabilitation*, **7**, 9–16.

Thaut MH, McIntosh GC, Rice RR, Miller RA, Rathburn J and Brault JM (1996a). Rhythmic auditory stimulation in gait training with Parkinson's disease patients. *Movement Disorders*, **11**, 193–200.

Thaut MH, Miller RA and Schauer LM (1998c). Multiple synchronization strategies in rhythmic sensorimotor tasks. Phase vs. period correction. *Biological Cybernetics*, **73**, 241–250.

Thaut M, Leins AK, Rice R, Argstatter H, Kenyon GP, McIntosh GC, Bolay HV and Fetter M (2007). Rhythmic Auditory Stimulation improves gait more than NDT/Bobath training in near-ambulatory patients early post stroke: a single-blind, randomized trial. *Neurorehabilitation and Neural Repair (NNR)*, 5, American Society of Neurorehabilitation, online DOI 10.1177/1545968307300523.

Whitall J, McCombe WS, Waller S, Silver KH and Macko RF (2000). Repetitive bilateral arm training with rhythmic auditory cueing improves motor function in chronic hemiparetic stroke. *Stroke*, **31**(10), 2390–2395.

Zieglgänsberger W and Schadrack J (1998). Neuronal plasticity and pain signalling in the central nervous system. *Acta Anaesthesiologica Scandinavica*, **42**, 9–10.

PART 11

Conceptual frameworks, research methods and future directions

Edited by Susan Hallam, Ian Cross and Michael Thaut

CHAPTER 50

Beyond music psychology

Adam Ockelford

LTHOUGH music psychology in the latter part of the twentieth century was dominated by the principles of cognitive–psychological thinking, these never completely drove nor, indeed, constrained this domain of research: even in 1970s, 80s and 90s, before the explosion of activity related to music and the cognitive sciences that has characterized the early years of the twenty-first century, music psychology did not function as a tightly defined academic discipline operating within a single, clear-cut epistemological framework. One can speculate as to the reasons why this should have been so. Partly, no doubt, different views as to what constituted valid music–psychological 'evidence' arose as a consequence of the heterogeneous and constantly evolving nature of musicological discourse, which provided a starting point for some who were seeking to adopt a psychological approach. The lack of an homogenous depth to the corpus of music–psychological research may be attributable to the relatively few participants who were active in the area, and their diverse disciplinary and institutional locations. Also, the field may have attracted visitors whose concerns lay primarily at the periphery of mainstream music–psychological work because they could find no other home for their theoretical or empirical endeavours. Finally, the very interdisciplinary nature of music psychology itself meant that as a conceptual territory it had extensive borders that offered many opportunities for intellectual interlopers to cross.

It is notable that the first journal to be devoted exclusively to the subject (*Psychology of Music*,

which dates from 1973)[1] was founded by the (then) Society for Research in Psychology of Music *and Music Education*,[2] conferring on the publication a multidisciplinary focus that it has maintained ever since. Today, the stated aim of *Psychology of Music* is to 'increase scientific understanding of all psychological aspects of music and music education', a desideratum which 'includes studies on listening, performing, creating, memorizing, analysing, learning and teaching as well as applied social, developmental, attitudinal and therapeutic studies'.[3] This breadth of intention is fully reflected in the journal's content. Of the 471 papers published between 1973 and the first half of 2007, an informal classification suggests that only 207 (44 per cent) can reasonably be defined as falling within the realm of cognitive psychology (including the measurement of musical abilities, the perception of musical sounds, the cognition of musical structures, learning, memory and the development of music-related skills). Sixty papers (12.5 per cent) are concerned with issues pertaining to performing (including improvisation and performance anxiety). Notwithstanding the journal's stated aims, only 55 articles (11.5 per cent) relate directly to music education, although a further

[1] Until that time publication was solely in mainstream psychology journals.
[2] Italics added; from 2003 known as 'SEMPRE'—the Society for Education, Music and Psychology Research.
[3] From the journal's 'aims and scope', *Psychology of Music*, **35**(2), 2007.

15 (3 per cent) investigate the use and potential effect of music in wider educational or developmental contexts. Fifty-four (11.5 per cent) explore aesthetics or affective response to music in one form or another. Thirteen articles (3 per cent) are primarily ethnomusicological in content. Eleven (2.5 per cent) engage with issues of epistemology or methodology (matters to which we shall return). Eight (1.5 per cent) involve research in music therapy. Seven (1.5 per cent) have a music–theoretical focus. The remaining 41 (9 per cent) are not readily categorizable, by virtue of small numbers or idiosyncratic content—ranging from the philosophy of melody to a consideration of the potential relevance of music to extra-terrestrials!

Music Perception, which first appeared in 1983 under the editorship of Diana Deutsch at the University of California, while having cognitive–psychological research as its primary focus, was always more explicit than *Psychology of Music* about its wide-ranging academic purview, which has changed little over the last quarter of a century. Today, *Music Perception* is overtly interdisciplinary in nature, with an editorial policy that seeks to publish 'theoretical and empirical papers, methodological articles and critical reviews concerning the study of music', incorporating articles from a broad range of disciplines, including 'psychology, psychophysics, neuroscience, music theory, acoustics, artificial intelligence, linguistics, philosophy, anthropology and cognitive science'.[4] Similarly, *Musicae Scientiae*, the journal of the European Society for the Cognitive Sciences of Music (ESCOM), which first appeared in 1997, is interdisciplinary in nature too, although cognitive psychology is, once again, the predominant strand in its fabric. *Musicae Scientiae* accepts 'empirical, theoretical and critical articles directed at increasing understanding of how music is perceived, represented and generated'. Consideration is given to any 'systematic work within the domains of psychology, philosophy, aesthetics, music analysis, historic musicology, cognitive science,

education, artificial intelligence, modelling and neuropsychology'[5, 6]

The broad church espoused by the three specialist journals currently active in the field of music psychology is reflected in the conferences and seminars organized by its proponents. Chief among these, the International Conference of Music Perception and Cognition (ICMPC), which was first staged in 1989, and since 1992 has occurred biennially, attracts a remarkable breadth of contributions.[7] For example, ICMPC 9, which was held in Bologna in 2006, called for presentations on the following topics: pitch and tonal perception; rhythm, metre, and timing; aesthetic perception and response; computational models; timbre and orchestration; emotion in music; memory and music; neuroscience; development; education; music, meaning, and language; performance and composition; the singing voice; acoustics and psychoacoustics; the social psychology of music; cognitive musicology; and music therapy. These were realized in some 526 papers, posters, workshops and symposia (a fivefold growth over the 17 years since ICMPC 1).

Surely (it could be argued), such eclecticism is unreservedly a good thing, presumably resulting in a rich cross-fertilization of ideas and approaches, yielding new, broad-based research that is rooted in a range of epistemologies and utilizing a variety of methodologies? Actually the position turns out to be much more complicated than this: as we shall see, conceptual cross-pollination often proves to be difficult to pull off; and where some see epistemological hybridization as a strength, others are wary of diluting the relative purity of purpose and procedure characteristic of a single discipline.

Given such issues, it is hardly surprising that the manner in which music psychology could

---

[4] From 'Information for authors', *Music Perception*, **24**(4), 2007.

[5] From 'Information for authors', *Musicae Scientiae*, **11**(1), 2007.
[6] The interdisciplinary output of *Psychology of Music, Music Perception* and *Musicae Scientiae* contrasts with that of the fourth specialist publication in the field, *Psychomusicology*, which, styling itself as a 'journal of music cognition', first appeared in the US in 1981 and continued to appear until 1997. Throughout these 16 years, *Psychomusicology* adhered closely to its initial editorial brief.
[7] See http://www.icmpc.org/organisation.html#history for a brief history of the ICMPC series.

and should relate to its sister disciplines has exercised a number of those working in these fields over the years. An early and perhaps inevitable tension that emerged in *Psychology of Music*, which was articulated by John Sloboda (then editor) in his 'open letter' of 1986,[8] was between music psychology and music education. In particular (to make explicit what was implicit in Sloboda's statement), one could sense a certain discomfort in his having to consider for publication certain music *education* research within the context of a music *psychology* journal, with its rather different perceptions of what constituted an appropriate level of rigour and objectivity. With their distinct epistemologies, could the two disciplines every work together productively? Was the latter ever likely to be of value to the former? A number of responses to Sloboda's letter were made, including one by David Hargreaves,[9] who, in looking back over the first decade of *Psychology of Music*'s output, acknowledged that 'Contributions tend to be *either* psychological *or* educational, and those which combine theoretical and practical concerns tend to be few and far between.' He concluded that 'the end result is something of a shotgun wedding'. Hargreaves suggested that the most fruitful way forward might lie in the *developmental* psychology of music, an area to which he gave a focus and impetus in the mid-1980s, and which has flourished ever since—particularly in relation to the early years (see, for example, Deliège and Sloboda 1996; the special issue of *Musicae Scientiae* 1999/2000; McPherson 2006) and, more recently, special educational needs (for example, Pring and Ockelford 2005; Ockelford *et al.* 2006; Ockelford 2008). Beyond developmental psychology, in the 1990s, a number of new fronts opened up between music psychologists and educationists in what has proved to be a highly fruitful union (Parncutt and McPherson 2002; Williamon 2004). For example, research of relevance to those learning to perform has been undertaken in the areas of practice and the acquisition of expertise (Hallam 1995, 2001; Jørgensen 2004); memorization (Ginsborg 2007); sight-reading

(Lehmann and McArthur 2002; Thompson and Lehmann 2004) and improvisation (Kenny and Gellrich 2002).

Returning, for a moment, to the 1980s, further contributions followed in *Psychology of Music* on other interdisciplinary issues, including the report of a seminar held at The City University, London, in 1987 concerning the relationship between music therapy and music psychology (whose discussants were Leslie Bunt, Ian Cross, Eric Clarke and Sarah Hoskyns).[10] With echoes of the perennial quantitative/qualitative dichotomy, key elements in the debate were the relevance to therapy of what was measurable in psychological terms, and, conversely, the psychological status of the inferences that therapists were content to accept as admissible evidence. It was agreed that what mattered was whether the insights so gained—which, ideally, should be couched within a theoretical framework—were relevant and interesting rather than ultimately 'provable'. The long-term impact thinking such as this can be felt today in collected editions such as *Microanalysis in Music Therapy* edited by Thomas Wosch and Tony Wigram (2007). Here, as Barbara Wheeler notes in the Foreword (p. 11), the common thread linking the contributions is a new-found rigour in analysing therapy sessions, involving the study of 'specific responses and experiences and precise musical and behavioral responses and interactions' (see also Ockelford 2008).

During the 1990s, comparable interdisciplinary discourse rumbled on in other areas too, leading, for example, to Elizabeth Tolbert's (2001) exploration of the evolution of musical meaning through an attempt to bridge ethnomusicological and psychological approaches (between which she considered there had been little rapprochement up to that time). In particular, she pointed to differing perspectives on the relative importance of individual as opposed to collective meaning, and divergent views as to the significance of universal rather than culturally embedded musical processes and structures.

Arguably the interface about which there has been most vociferous debate in recent years,

[8] *Psychology of Music*, **14**(2), 144–145.
[9] *Psychology of Music*, **14**(2), 83–96.

[10] *Psychology of Music*, **16**(1), 62–70.

however, is that between music psychology and music *theory* (as it is generally known in the US) or music *analysis* (the term most widely used in the UK). Why the contention? Perhaps because proponents from the two camps feel that they have an equal claim over a common territory: an understanding of how music 'works'. Their aims, though, are quite different, and this appears to be where the difficulties arise. Writing in 1989, Eric Clarke put it like this:

> Broadly speaking, the aim of musicologists and composers in tackling issues of musical structure can be characterized as the attempt to formulate theories of the structural relations within and between musical works, and their origins, development and effectiveness as formal devices. A correspondingly brief summary of the aim of psychologists of music is the development of theories of the mental processing of musical events, or the relationship between the listener, performer or composer and the musical environment. In a number of respects these aims are quite complementary, but the different disciplines that they represent come into conflict in the way in which they describe their material, and in what they extract and evaluate as significant findings.
>
> Clarke (1989, pp. 1–2)

At times this conflict has become quite heated. In his 'Fortenotes' that appeared in *Music Analysis*, 17(2) (a tribute volume to the Yale music theorist Allen Forte, who introduced 'pitch-class set analysis' to musicology in his seminal book *The structure of atonal music* [1973]), Jonathan Dunsby satirizes music psychologists as would-be enforcers of an imaginary law which dictates that musicological validity necessarily equates to perceptibility:

> I cannot be alone in having taught, *StrAMly* [*The structure of atonal music*], surreptitiously, 'hunt the hexachord'. That's the way you make a set complex work, asking a student to interrogate whether that embarrassing challenger-set really mattered so much and could not perhaps be excluded as a feature of the music, or whether there were not many more lurking hexachords that s/he had heard/seen (I am almost tempted to add '/played', but

presumably in this forum I can write shielded from the Perception Police).

> Dunsby (1998, p. 179)

In order to understand how academic discourse on music could have become so polarized, one has to appreciate that groups within the music-theoretical community had felt themselves under attack from music psychologists who had shown, for example, that the perception of octave equivalence in pitch sequences—a 'given' in the composition of serial music and pitch-class set analysis—was by no means a 'given' to the musical ear operating in the absence of a score (Deustch and Boulanger 1984),[11] and that the measures of similarity between pitch-class sets as developed by Robert Morris (1979–1980)—measures that lay at the heart of this music-theoretical enterprise—did not accord with similarity judgements made aurally.[12]

However, the traffic was not all one way. Still on the subject of differing perceptions of similarity, in 1994, Nicholas Cook launched a scathing attack on Rita Wolpert's (1990) research, in which musicians and 'non-musicians' (so-called) were asked, among other things, to compare a tune and accompaniment played (a) on a different instrument and (b) on the same instrument as the original, but with the accompaniment transposed down a fifth. The musicians consistently chose option (a)—for them, playing the accompaniment in the wrong key made a bigger difference than playing the music on a different instrument—whereas the non-musicians almost exclusively opted for (b): for them, the identity of the instrument outweighed any changes they noticed in the accompaniment. According to Wolpert, these findings show that musicians do not listen in the same way as non-musicians: their choice of instrumentation over correct harmonic accompaniment 'suggests a profound overestimation of what most listeners hear'. As Cook points out, though, this is a far-fetched conclusion: what Wolpert's experiment actually reveals is that listeners with different backgrounds respond in different ways to questions

---

[11] See also the psychologically inspired critique of serialism by Fred Lerdahl (1992).
[12] Cheryl Bruner (1984).

as to whether one musical extract is more or less like another (1994, p. 68).[13]

These two examples bring sharply into focus just how different the aims and values of music psychology and music theory continued to be in the years that followed Eric Clarke's (1989) exhortation to researchers to seek to establish a rapport between them.[14] In 2003, David Temperley summarized the ongoing division thus:

> music psychology tends to focus on how people typically hear (or play or compose) pieces, tending towards generalities or commonalities; whereas music theory and analysis usually seek to discover what listeners could (or should) hear, and bear largely on specific compositions.[15]

In similar vein, in reviewing Kevin Korsyn's *Decentering Music* of 2003, Elizabeth Margulis (2005) wrote:

> Music cognition tends to explore those aspects of musical experience that are relatively robust and shared across large populations (betraying a dependence on what Korsyn sees as the problematic construct of 'normalcy'), rather than those that are unique and more amenable to the committed introspection of a single listener. … Music analysts who rely on introspection as a methodology might manifest a commitment to music as an individual experience, constructed as fully by the listener as by the composer and performer. This vision elevates the specialist, and promotes the importance of training. Researchers who rely on empirical methodologies might reveal a commitment to music as more of a shared experience, with invariant features that characterize the hearing of a neophyte as much as a person with decades of training.
>
> Margulis (2005, pp. 334–335)

Joshua Mailman (2007), in his review of Adam Ockelford's *Repetition in music: theoretical*

and metatheoretical perspectives (2005a) refers to the music-cognitive approach as 'populist', as opposed to the 'progressive' tack taken by theorists and analysts, which seeks to extend the boundaries of musical understanding, rather than defining what may be 'typical' or 'usual'. Mailman cites Joseph Dubiel (1999) in support:

> The crucial condition for any increase in musical knowledge is to keep yourself ready to be struck by aspects of sound that you weren't listening for. [This means that] the value of analyses will ultimately be their value as ear-openers.
>
> (p. 274)

In accordance with this sentiment, Mailman takes Ockelford to task for his critique of David Lewin's analysis of the opening of the development section of Mozart's Symphony No. 40, K. 550, which had appeared in Lewin's landmark text *Generalized musical intervals and transformations* (1987)—a mathematically based theory of musical structure. The passage in question, Lewin had observed, can be interpreted as a chain of retrograde inversions (RICH); see Figure 50.1.

However, the ontological status of this pattern is unclear. As Ockelford (2005a, p. 99) asserts: 'There is no evidence that Mozart conceived the passage in this way, nor that listeners perceive it so, nor even that analysts typically construe the sequence as being structured thus,[16] although there are precedents.'[17] Ockelford hypothesizes that listeners would be more likely to make sense of the passage by (subconsciously) modelling its structure as a series of transpositions: a more direct interpretation than Lewin's, which requires less cognitive manipulation of the musical information that is available.

Mailman, however, considers Ockelford's approach to the passage to be 'too narrowly conceived' (op. cit, p. 369), contending that he

> overlooks what we gain from Lewin's discovery of RICH in Mozart's symphony: when we notice RICHs in Webern's 12-tone works, we

---

[13] Ironically, Cook himself comes in for comparable methodological criticism in relation to his foray into experimental psychology which investigated the perception of large-scale tonal closure (1987); see Gjerdingen (1999).

[14] In 'Mind the gap'—see note 10.

[15] Personal communication to Adam Ockelford, cited in Ockelford (2005b).

[16] See, for example, Saint-Fox (1947), Dearling (1982) and Abert (1990).

[17] For instance, Keller (1966, p. 97).

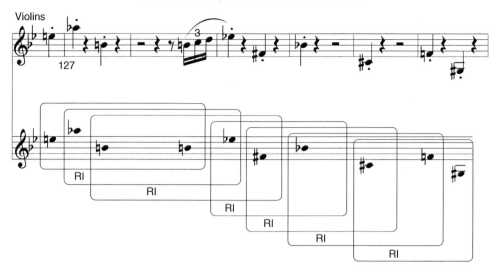

Fig. 50.1 'RICH' in Mozart, K. 550 (after Lewin 1987, p. 230).

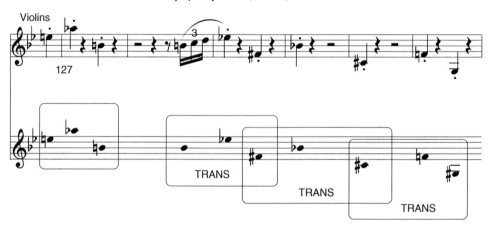

Fig. 50.2 More straightforward interpretation of the structure of the passage as a series of transpositions (after Ockelford, 2005a, p. 102).

can relate these conceptually to the RICHs in Mozart—a lucrative inter-repertoire link ... Abstractions like RICH push beyond the everyday experience of repertoire that the 'populist' approach often assumes.

However, as Ockelford points out, in a conceptual thread that weaves its way through *Repetition in music*, there is a serious problem with this line of thinking. To understand why, let us first take a step back to the theory that

lies at the heart of the volume: namely, that all internal musical structure relies ultimately on repetition, in one manifestation or another. For example, as Sloboda noted in his first book *The musical mind: the cognitive psychology of music* (1985), for music perception to 'get off the ground', there is a need for a framework of discrete and re-identifiable locations in pitch and perceived time, without which the dialectics of tension/resolution and motion/rest could not exist (pp. 154 and 259). That is to say, in order for our perceptual and cognitive processing abilities not to be overwhelmed, composers have to work within tight constraints, whereby the number of different categories of pitch, interval, and the time between the onsets of successive notes is limited. This means that a high degree of 'background' repetition is inevitable in any piece. Furthermore, while the burden of the musical message tends to be conveyed by characteristic combinations of pitch and rhythm, further background restrictions typically apply to other qualities of perceived sound too, such as timbre and loudness. These almost invariably fulfil a secondary role as 'carriers' of the principal stream of information, and as a consequence tend towards coherence based on uniformity or incremental change—features which, once more, are founded on repetition.[18] Hence, behind the creation of every work lie constraints that mean that many musical events, and the relationships between them, will be the same, regardless of the subsequent choices of the composer. A key issue, therefore, for those trying to fathom how we make sense of musical structures is not so much about the discovery of sameness and similarity per se, but of analysing the *significance of commonality in different contexts*.

To give an idea of the scale of this issue, take, for example, Chopin's Prelude in B minor, Op. 28, No. 6, which comprises 403 separate notes that are played on the piano, typically within a period of two to three minutes. If one considers the relationships between (any) pairs of pitches the same as being of potential structural significance, then the analyst is faced with around 13 000 candidates. If it is the relationships between pairs of *intervals* the same that are thought to be of possible structural relevance, then she or he would have 500 *million* to choose from. And this is in just one domain: pitch.

Arresting statistics, one might think, but of no possible musicological value, since they ignore two key factors in the creation of musical structure: the sequence of events and their associated rhythm. Yet that is exactly what Allen Forte's set theory, alluded to above, does. The theory was originally intended to offer a mechanism

through which the structure of the atonal music of Schoenberg, Webern and Berg and other composers written at the beginning of the twentieth century could be explained systematically. In undertaking set-theoretical analysis, one makes the initial assumption that all pitches and intervals (unlike those in tonal music) are potentially equal in structural terms. Hence the immediate analytical challenge posed is one of scale: how to reduce the available data to manageable proportions. To tackle this problem, a process of reduction was devised that borrowed a number of concepts from Schoenberg's 'serial' compositional procedures. This holds that one set of pitches can be regarded as equivalent to another, irrespective of transposition or inversion, the octave in which values are realized, whether or not they are repeated and, additionally, the order in which they occur. Ferreting out equivalent sets (as the citation from Dunsby above indicates) is fundamental to this type of analysis. But how is it to be done? Although some sets can be isolated as units 'by conventional means, such as a rhythmically distinct melodic figure' (Forte 1973, p. 83), such techniques do not necessarily 'adequately reveal structural components', since methods of segmentation may be 'concealed' (ibid.). In order to uncover the hidden organization of pitch, Forte recommends a procedure termed 'imbrication': 'the systematic (sequential) extraction of subcomponents of some configuration'— that is, listing all the pitch-class sets contained within a passage in the hope that this will reveal relationships that were not otherwise apparent.[19]

While it is conceivable that such a process may uncover pitch structures of musical interest that listening alone would have failed to detect (and which may inform subsequent audition), there remain a number of problems with this technique. For example, sets may not have been apparent in the first instance for the very good reason that they could not be extracted perceptually from large and complex aggregations of notes—and how, therefore, could they *ever* be structurally relevant to any listener, novice or expert? Again, the scale of the enterprise presents a huge problem. Take, for example, Schoenberg's

---

[18] See, for example, Boulez (1963/71, p. 37); Erickson (1975, p. 12).

[19] See, for example, John Roeder's (1988) analysis of Webern's Piece for Cello and Piano, Op. 11, No. 3.

Three Piano Pieces, Op. 11, No. 1—one of the first atonal works to be composed. The opening 4½ bars comprise 24 events in the form of a right-hand melody supported with discrete chords and traces of counterpoint, together lasting no more than 10 seconds. Forte (1981) undertakes an analysis, in which he identifies 14 different pitch-class sets, occurring in total 28 times. However, by adopting a systematic approach, using Forte's recommended technique of imbrication, it becomes apparent that all of the 208 possible pitch-class sets are actually present! These occur with mind-numbing frequency: for example, there are 262 appearances of 3-note sets, 884 4-note sets, 3152 5-note sets and (preliminary analysis suggests) over 10 000 6-note sets. How is the analyst ever to make sense of these data? Presumably by reverting to the musical intuitions that were abandoned in the first place in the interests of scientific rigour!

Although analysis of this type occupies only one region in the broad domain of music theory—arguably in an area that is furthest away in epistemological and methodological terms from music psychology—the issues of perceptibility and relevance for different groups of listeners apply to other music-theoretical approaches too. For example, Heinrich Schenker's multilayered analyses, which are based on the notion that, in the context of tonal music, some pitches and harmonies can structurally 'prolong' others, are not contentious in music-psychological terms when the prolongations are relatively near to the musical 'surface' and last only a few seconds.[20] However, Schenker's own application of this principle deep into the structural foundations of a piece, whereby it is asserted that single chords may in some sense control events lasting many minutes, has found no empirical support (see note 13). Unlike much pitch-class set analysis, however, it is conceivable, particularly for those with 'absolute pitch', that pieces *could* be heard as Schenker analyses them—as long-term prolongations of the tonic and dominant chords—if expert listeners chose to do so.

The same applies to other music-analytical approaches too. Take, for example, Rudolph Réti's modus operandi, as set out in *The thematic process in music* (1951), through which he seeks to unearth (typically) 'hidden' motivic relationships that he claims exist within and between the movements of pieces, subconsciously unifying them in the ears of listeners. Again, despite the feeling that Réti may be confusing the 'background' repetition that, as we have seen, is inevitable in any comprehensible piece of music, with the 'foreground' that a composer may choose to overlay upon it, it is conceivable for expert listeners to hear music in line with Réti's analyses if they elect to do so.

Where do approaches such as this leave the relationship between music psychology and music theory? Let us return to Eric Clarke's proposed 'rapport' of 1989, which, he suggests, could be achieved by developing a kind of description that recognizes the mutual relationship between a perceiver and his or her environment.

> The aim of such an approach would be to describe musical events for a particular kind of perceiver [ranging, we may surmise, in Mailman's terminology, from a 'populist' listener to a 'progressive' theorist], taking account of the stimulus material, the perceptual systems that exist, and the cultural systems within which evaluations of musical function are made. This is in essence an argument for an ecological description, since it proposes that while there is an indefinite number of possible descriptions of the same state of affairs from a variety of different perspectives, and at a number of different levels, the kind of description that is of primary interest to us will be at a level, and of a breadth appropriate to human beings, their musical artifacts and activities, and the natural and cultural environment within which they are situated.
>
> Clarke (1989, p. 12)

Ockelford (2005b) proposes a way in which such a description could be modelled. He suggests that all potential music–structural relationships[21] can be considered to exist on a continuum with

---

[20] As the recent empirical work of Isabel Martinez shows (The cognitive reality of prolongational structures in tonal music, unpublished Ph.D. dissertation, University of Roehampton, 2007.)

[21] That is, in terms of Ockelford's 'zygonic' theory, between events the same, where one could conceivably be deemed to derive from the other.

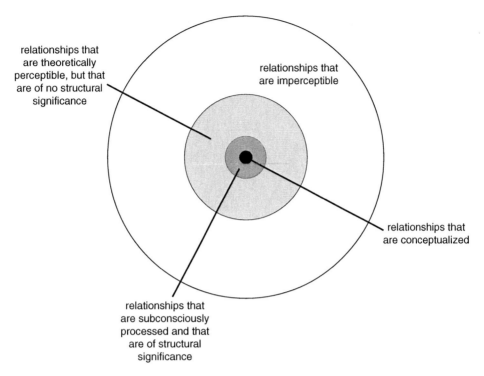

relationships that
are theoretically
perceptible, but that
are of no structural
significance

relationships that
are imperceptible

relationships that
are conceptualized

relationships that
are subconsciously
processed and that
are of structural
significance

Fig. 50.3 Representation through different shading of a set of potentially structural relationships as they are hypothesized to exist in relation to mental processing.

three distinct sectors: those that are (1) imperceptible or non-cognizable; (2) perceptible but of no direct significance to musical structure (arising, for example, by chance, as a result of 'background' repetition); and (3) subconsciously processed and of direct relevance to the cognition of structure. Inevitably, the boundaries between these sectors are fuzzy, since which potential relationships actually become reified in cognition, and the significance of these, is, as Clarke's ecological standpoint indicates, liable to vary from listener to listener, and even with the same listener on different occasions. However, where a given relationship is likely to reside on the continuum can in broad terms be predicted in relation to cognitive constraints and preferences that could be empirically tested (Ockelford 2002). A fourth condition—structural relationships that are consciously processed/conceptualized (by composers and theorists or analysts, for example)—is subject to even greater variation, having the potential to be overlaid anywhere on the other three regions.

This model can be represented graphically as shown in Figure 50.3. In order to interpret the diagram correctly, one has to imagine an exponential growth in the number of potential relationships as one moves outwards from the centre. Using the model, it is possible to capture visually the epistemological issues raised above and clarify some of the misunderstandings that are reported—a necessary step in seeking to resolve them.

First, we will use the model to depict the case of a listener relatively familiar with a piece and its broader stylistic context, though not approaching matters with a mindset to conceptualize what is being heard (an example of Mailman's 'populist' perceiver). Intuitively, the music makes sense to the person concerned, and so we can surmise that he or she must be processing structural relationships subconsciously—a situation represented in Scenario A (shown in Figure 50.4). Turning next to Margulis's neophyte, one could imagine that she or he would pick up on rather fewer structural relationships,

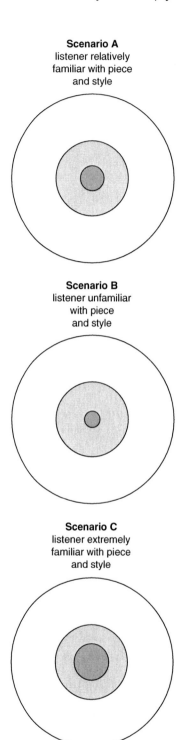

Scenario A
listener relatively
familiar with piece
and style

Scenario B
listener unfamiliar
with piece
and style

Scenario C
listener extremely
familiar with piece
and style

Fig. 50.4 Varying state of relationships
hypothesized to exist in different scenarios
pertaining to listening.

though still presumably enough for the music to be recognizable as abstract patterns in sound that in this case convey a certain, rather limited, meaning. This is depicted in Scenario B. Notice that Sector 1 is diminished in size. Conversely, the situation with an expert listener, who is attending to piece without conceptualizing what is heard, may be illustrated with a somewhat larger Sector 1: Scenario C. It is important to appreciate that in Scenarios A, B and C, the processing of musical structure can occur within the absence of description or analysis of the organization that is present—indeed, without the listener having had any formal musical education—the recognition of perceived sonic patterns and the ascription of meanings to them being enabled purely through repeated exposure.

Naturally, when composers, performers or listeners, whether functioning as psychologists, theorists, educators, therapists or others, consciously *think about* music—or ask others to—the situation changes. Take, for example, Wolpert's experiment, mentioned above. Her results show that the musicians in her experiment were able to conceptualize structural relationships in the domains of pitch and perceived time that they would otherwise have been likely to hear subconsciously. Hence, the situation arose that is depicted in Scenario D (see Figure 50.5). However, it appears that Wolpert's so-called non-musicians, when required to effect the same comparisons, were drawn by the nature of the question they were asked: to conceptualize *different* perceptible relationships, this time in the domain of timbre, that are not generally considered by musicians to be 'structural' (rather, residing in the musical 'background'). Hence we have Scenario E. Clearly, both Scenarios D and E have a certain intrinsic validity (since they both represent sets of empirical findings), but the situations they model are quite different, and the danger occurs when the two are subjected to a common interpretational framework.

We move next to the scenarios engendered by the music analyses that have been discussed, beginning with Forte's account of Schoenberg's Op. 11, No. 1. Now it may be that some of the relationships between pitch-class sets of three notes, which we can assume would pass the great majority of listeners by unnoticed (and which

Scenario D
the conceptualization of
structural relationships
by musicians

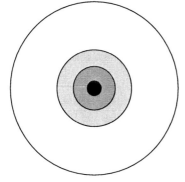

Scenario F
status of relationships identified
in Forte's set-theoretical analysis

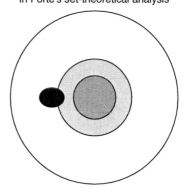

Scenario E
the conceptualization of
relationships that are typically
regarded as non-structural by
'nonmusicians'

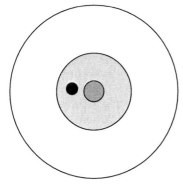

Scenario E
status of relationships
identified in Réti's
motivic analysis

Fig. 50.6 Interpretation and representation of Forte's and Réti's styles of analysis.

Fig. 50.5 Interpretation and representation of Wolpert's findings (1990).

would therefore in most circumstances be deemed structurally non-essential), could be perceived with practice, although there are others that would appear to be inaudible, no matter how well-prepared the listener were to be: for example, when the analysis decrees that a pitch within a four-note chord should be heard as functioning in three different four-note sets simultaneously. Hence it seems that Forte's analysis spans Sectors 2 and 3—see Scenario F (in Figure 50.6). Réti's analyses, on the other hand, would on the whole be perceptible once they have been drawn to listeners attention: hence Scenario G. However, these arguably

imbue the regular warp and the weft of the musical fabric with significance over and above the melodic and harmonic patterns that composers have woven through it, and they have failed to gain acceptance among musicologists or musicians.

A similar situation holds in relation to Mailman's critique of Ockelford's assessment of Lewin's late-Mozart analysis, which is discussed above. In terms of the three-sector model, Lewin's approach, using the transformation 'RICH', conceptualizes relationships that would typically be in Sector 2, whereas it is possible to assign the same musical structure to transpositional relationships, which exist in Sector 1. To return to Mailman's argument, however, if we are ever to *expand* Sector 1—to be 'progressive', which he sees as a crucial part of music theorists' role—then we need to push out the boundaries beyond those which the ear would otherwise determine unassisted. That is, there is virtue in consciously seeking to claim structural territory from Sector 2. The implication is that conceptualization may affect perception and, in effect, a migratory effect is possible, whereby relationships that were once in Sector 2 metaphorically shift to Sector 1. Within limits, this seems reasonable enough. The author can recall such an experience, when, having become acquainted with Schoenberg's analysis of Brahms's fourth symphony, motivic relationships became apparent that were subsequently embedded in listening experiences (1947/75, pp. 405–408). However, this is a long way from saying that much set-theoretical analysis could ever have intrinsically *musical* relevance, no matter now practised the listener. As we have seen, because all music is supersaturated with repetition, any piece contains a virtually infinite number of potential patterns, which will be of varying degrees of interest, no doubt, according to one's point of view, but the majority of these should not be intellectually conflated with *musical* structure. Rather, they exist as a by-product of the way that music is put together in order for it to be comprehensible. It is surely at this point that the music psychology's relationship with music theory reaches a boundary (and arguably where music theory itself becomes something rather different).

Summary

In summary, then, music psychology overlaps with a number of other disciplines, including music education, therapy, ethnomusicology, and music theory and analysis. There are tensions in each case, but, as the citations above have indicated, benefits too for those who are prepared to explore with an open mind. Ultimately, however, music psychology cannot be extended beyond the boundaries of its epistemological box, always granted that the sides are flexible and subject to change: indeed, such movement is likely to come about through the influence of adjacent disciplines. This has been shown, for example, in the groundbreaking work of Aaron Williamon and his colleagues at the Royal College of Music in London—the first UK conservatoire to establish a music–psychological research centre, which has aimed to support students in improving their performance skills and managing the high levels of stress that are often induced by performing in public. In terms of the common space occupied by elements of music psychology and music theory, further developments may well mean having to accept that the initial research questions and the *evaluation* of data may well be guided by musical intuitions, but that the gathering and *analysis* of data should be rigorous and undertaken with a 'scientific' detachment. Two decades on from Clarke's appeal to 'Mind the gap', there is now a greater clarity as to what this conceptual intersection might look like, how it might function, and even what it should be called: 'empirical musicology'. According to Honing (2006), empirical musicology, which now has its own journal (*Empirical Musicology Review*) 'grew out of a desire to ground theories on empirical observation and to construct theories on the basis of the analysis and interpretation of such observations'. And as Cook and Clarke put it in the introduction to their book *Empirical musicology: aims, methods, prospects* (2004), 'Empirical musicology. can be thought of as musicology that embodies a principled awareness of both the potential to engage with large bodies of relevant data, and the appropriate methods for achieving this' (p. 5). Hence one senses that in this sphere of activity the influence of music psychology may be keenly felt in the next decade.

References

Abert H (1990). *W.A. Mozart: Zweiter Teil*, 1783–1791. Breitkopf and Härtel Musikverlag, Leipzig.

Boulez P (1963/71). *Boulez on music today*, trans. S Bradshaw and RR Bennett. Faber and Faber, London.

Bruner C (1984). The perception of contemporary pitch structures. *Music Perception*, **2**(1), 25–39.

Clarke (1989). Mind the gap: formal structures and psychological processes in music. *Contemporary Music Review*, 3, 1–13.

Cook N (1987). The perception of large-scale tonal closure. *Music Perception*, 5(2), 197–206.

Cook N (1994). Perception: a perspective from music theory. In R Aiello, J Sloboda, eds, *Musical perceptions*, 64–95. Oxford University Press, Oxford.

Cook N and Clarke E (eds) (2004). *Empirical musicology: aims, methods, prospects.* Oxford University Press, Oxford.

Dearling R (1982). *The music of Wolfgang Amadeus Mozart.* Associated University Presses, East Brunswick, NJ.

Deliège I and Sloboda J (1996). *Musical beginnings: origins and development of musical competence.* Oxford University Press, Oxford.

Deutsch D and Boulanger R (1984). Octave equivalence and the immediate recall of pitch sequences. *Music Perception,* **2**(1), 41–51.

Dubiel J (1999). Composer, theorist, composer/theorist. In N Cook and M Everist, eds, *Rethinking music,* 262–283. Oxford University Press, Oxford.

Dunsby J (1998). Fortenotes. *Music Analysis,* **17**, 171–181.

Erickson R. (1975). *Sound structure in music.* University of California Press, Berkeley, CA.

Forte A (1973). *The structure of atonal music.* Yale University Press, New Haven, CT.

Forte A (1981). The magical kaleidoscope: Schoenberg's first atonal masterwork, Op. 11, No. 1. *Journal of the Arnold Schoenberg Institute,* **5**, 127–168.

Ginsborg J (2007). Strategies for memorizing music. In A Williamon, ed., *Musical excellence: strategies and techniques to enhance performance,* 123–141. Oxford University Press, Oxford.

Gjerdingen R (1999). An experimental music theory? In N Cook and M Everist, eds, *Rethinking music,* 161–170. Oxford University Press, Oxford.

Hallam S (1995). Professional musicians' orientations to practice: implications for teaching. *British Journal of Music Education,* **12**(1), 3–19.

Hallam S (2001). The development of expertise in young musicians: strategy use, knowledge acquisition and individual diversity. *Music Education Research,* **3**(1), 7–23.

Honing H (2006). On the growing role of observation, formalization and experimental method in musicology. *Empirical Musicology Review,* **1**(1), 2–6.

Jørgensen H (2004). Strategies for individual practice. In A Williamon, ed., *Musical excellence: strategies and techniques to enhance performance,* 85–103. Oxford University Press, Oxford.

Keller H (1966). Wolfgang Amadeus Mozart. In R Simpson, ed., *The symphony: volume one,* 50–103. Penguin Books Ltd, Harmondsworth, Middlesex.

Kenny B and Gellrich M (2002). Improvisation. In R Parncutt, G McPherson, eds, *The science and psychology of music performance: creative strategies for teaching and learning,* 117–134. Oxford University Press, Oxford.

Korsyn K (2003). *Decentering music: a critique of contemporary musical research.* Oxford University Press, New York.

Lehmann A and McArthur V (2002). Sightreading. In R Parncutt, G McPherson, eds, *The science and psychology of music performance: creative strategies for teaching and learning,* 135–150. Oxford University Press, Oxford.

Lerdahl F (1992). Cognitive constraints on compositional systems. *Contemporary Music Review,* **6**(2), 97–121.

Lewin D (1987). *Generalized intervals and transformations.* Yale University Press, New Haven, CT.

Mailman J (2007). Review article. *Psychology of Music,* **35**(2), 363–375.

Margulis E (2005). Review of the book *Decentering music. Psychology of Music,* **33**(3), 331–337.

McPherson G (2006). ed. *The child as musician: a handbook of musical development.* Oxford University Press, Oxford.

Morris R (1979–1980). A similarity index for pitch-class set. *Perspectives of New Music,* **18**, 445–460.

Ockelford A (2002). The magical number two, plus or minus one: some limitations on our capacity for processing musical information, *Musicae Scientiae,* **6**, 177–215.

Ockelford A (2005a). *Repetition in music: theoretical and metatheoretical perspectives.* Ashgate, London.

Ockelford A (2005b). Relating musical structure and content to aesthetic response: a model and analysis of Beethoven's Piano Sonata, Op. 110. *Journal of the Royal Musical Association,* **130**(1), 74–118.

Ockelford A (2008). *Music for children and young people with complex needs.* Oxford University Press, Oxford.

Ockelford A, Pring L, Welch G and Treffert D (2006). *Focus on music: exploring the musical interests and abilities of blind and partially-sighted children with septo-optic dysplasia.* Institute of Education, London.

Parncutt R and McPherson G (eds) (2002). *The science and psychology of music performance: creative strategies for teaching and learning.* Oxford University Press, Oxford.

Pring L and Ockelford A (2005). Children with septo-optic dysplasia—musical interests, abilities and provision: the results of a parental survey, *British Journal of Visual Impairment,* **23**(2), 58–66.

Réti R (1951). *The thematic process in music.* Greenwood Press, Westport, CT.

Roeder J (1988). A declarative model of atonal analysis. *Music Perception,* **6**(1), 21–34.

Sloboda J (1985). *The musical mind: the cognitive psychology of music.* Clarendon Press, Oxford.

Saint-Fox G de (1947). *The symphonies of Mozart,* trans. L Orrey. Dennis Dobson Ltd, London.

Schoenberg A (1947/75). Brahms the progressive. In L Stein, Ed., *Style and idea: selected writings of Arnold Schoenberg,* 398–448. University of California Press, Berkeley, CA.

Thompson S and Lehmann A (2004). Strategies for sight-reading and improvising music. In A Williamon, ed., *Musical excellence: strategies and techniques to enhance performance,* 143–159. Oxford University Press, Oxford.

Tolbert E (2001). Music and meaning: an evolutionary` story. *Psychology of Music,* **29**(1), 84–94.

Williamon A (ed.) (2004). *Musical excellence: strategies and techniques to enhance performance.* Oxford University Press, Oxford.

Wolpert R (1990). Recognition of melody, harmonic accompaniment, and instrumentation: musicians vs. non-musicians. *Music Perception,* **8**, 95–105.

Wosch T and Wigram T (2007). *Microanalysis in music therapy: methods, techniques and applications for clinicians, researchers, educators and students.* Jessica Kingsley, London.

CHAPTER 51

History and research

Michael Thaut

THIS chapter will provide an introductory synopsis of the history of research developments and research themes in music psychology from its inception in the nineteenth century until the early twenty-first century. The synopsis has to be broad to fit into the limitations of a book chapter, but a broader approach also offers the advantage to lay out more clearly discernible lines of evolution of large research themes over time. That is of particular interest in music psychology as it is a research-based field with an intrinsically inter- or multidisciplinary character. A bibliography of books rather than a reference list of specific papers should provide the appropriate data support for this synopsis.

Psychology of music as a new and independent scientific discipline started its development in the middle of the nineteenth century. It was a component part of the arrival of psychology as a new discipline studying human behaviour through observation, measurement, and testing using scientific methods (experiments, hypotheses, statistics). Previously, the scholarly discourse about music as an artistic and human phenomenon was mostly dominated by philosophy and—perhaps surprisingly to the modern reader—the discourses in the early natural sciences. The first work that is usually associated with the original impetus for studies in the psychology of music was Helmholtz' book *On the sensation of tones as a physiological basis for the theory of music* (Die Lehre von den Tonempfindungen als physiologische Grundlage fuer die Theorie der Musik, 1863), a primarily physiological study on tone perception. Helmholtz was a physician, physiologist, and physicist whose landmark work on sensory perception (visual and auditory) refuted at that time the still dominating schools of Naturphilosophie (natural philosophy), a

speculative way of thinking and interpreting the physical world. Helmholtz was an empiricist and a very influential scientific thinker of his times. Interestingly, Wilhelm Wundt—who is considered with William James to be one of the founders of modern experimental psychology—was for a while a student in Helmholtz' laboratories in Berlin.

It is important to remember some of the beginnings of the psychology of music, in order to understand the fundamental and extraordinarily radical change and determination of the future directions in studying music that was brought on by this new discipline. Only a few decades earlier, the German philosopher Schopenhauer had called music the purest incarnation of the human will, the embodiment and expression of human feelings (sadness, joy, love) in their abstract interpretation as metaphysical ideas. Even while a new experimental science of music as human behaviour emerged, contemporary philosophers such as Nietzsche still interpreted music philosophically, for example, as transcending reality, redemptive to the human condition, and either destructive (Dionysiac) or idealizing (Apollonic) reality and dissolving individuality to become one with the governing forces of the universe.

The new psychology of music diverged quickly from such centuries-old traditions of philosophical interpretation of music as human behaviour. The physicist Carl Stumpf was in 1883 the first to utilize modern scientific methodologies (experimental testing, hypotheses, statistical analysis) applied to investigations of musical–psychological phenomena—in his particular case to perceptions of consonance and dissonance—in his publication *Tonpsychologie* (Psychology of Tones) and other works.

The early and foundational works in psychology of music were mostly driven by experimental investigations into sound perception, linking psychology and psychophysics—or specifically psychoacoustics in regard to music—to understanding human responses to music. Interestingly, psychoacoustics remains to this day an important part of research agendas and teaching curricula in psychology of music. Carl Seashore, who in many ways is considered the primary pioneer in American psychology of music, developed the first objective test of musical aptitude in 1919, conceptually it was strongly connected to the psychophysical origins of the psychology of music. He designed a test, consisting of acoustical stimulus pairs, for which the test subject had to decide if both stimuli were same or different. The test items measured, e.g., differences in the perception of pitch, timbre, duration, or rhythmic pattern structure. Test items were produced by tone generators to avoid bias and influence for the test subjects on test performance through differences in musical exposure and familiarity. Seashore's ideas were rigorously scientific and revolutionary for his times: however, in many follow-up studies his test showed fairly low predictive power for future musical success and achievement in people. Seashore's ideas were so rigorously perception-based in psychophysics that his test is nowadays still considered an objective measure of acoustical acuity, but not a good measure of the more complex nature of musical abilities. Interestingly, the rhythm section of the Seashore test has survived and continues to show its validity as part of a neuropsychological assessment test for brain injuries (Halstead–Reitan), testing in all probability abstract auditory temporal perception as a measure of cognitive-perceptual functioning in an injured brain.

In the 1920s and 30s, a new focus entered the original research focus of psychology of music. This shift is often referred to as a shift from a psychology of tone to a more analytical and penetrating psychology of 'music', emphasizing the comprehensive perception and evaluation of complex pattern structures of melody, harmony, form, and rhythm as constituent building blocks of the language of music. Ernst Kurth's work *Musikpsychologie* (1931) is often cited as one of the first works to proceed with this new shift. This new shift was well supported experimentally and theoretically by the emergence of a new direction in the psychology of perception, the new school of Gestalt perception which holds—in basic tenet—that the sum of individual parts in a complex pattern structure assume a new perceptual quality as a 'whole' that is different from simply viewing a stimulus pattern as collection of individual parts. One of the simplest experiments to illustrate this concept was based on the so-called phi phenomenon or phenomenon of apparent movement. The rapid alteration of blinking lights being turned on and off periodically and in sequence creates the optical illusion of light moving back and forth along a line from point to point. Musical forms follow a complex architecture of sound patterns, assembled in rule-based systems, and acoustically and perceptually organized in five dimensions simultaneously and sequentially: rhythm/time—pitch/melody/polyphony—space—timbre—loudness. It is an interesting observation, that music is the only sensory language code that proceeds sequentially and simultaneously at the same time within its rhythm–polyphony dimensions and thus presents unique challenges to complexity thinking in the perception/cognition of information processing. Contrarily, verbal language, for example, only proceeds in sequentiality. A large amount of research has followed and continues to follow this direction of investigating experimentally complex music perception, following gestalt principles of perception. The vitality of this field shows the continued benefits of this approach, also in light of modern brain research within the models of cognitive neuroscience. We will return to this subject again later in this chapter.

Roughly in tandem with the emergence of Gestalt psychology and its extensions on the study of music perception, a third strand of research became subject of new investigations: the affective response to music. Verbal responses to quantify and categorize affective responses to music appeared in the early twentieth century as a new study focus, differentiating affective responses into studies of emotional responses, mood states, and perceived feeling states.. One of the first and widely used such verbal tests was Hevner's Adjective Circle (1936), a checklist of adjectives characterizing and categorizing subjective feeling responses to music. Researchers tried to find useful categories in music that would allow them to study potential links how musical variables would influence affective responses. Among the first categorizations of music al variables were consonance vs dissonance and minor vs major modes. Soon other variables were examined, such as tempo, pitch, and variations in melody, harmony, and rhythm, frequently subcategorized under descriptors like sedative or stimulative music. Other variables investigated included repetition, familiarity, and various investigations into the function of musical taste. Many leading music psychologists of the first half of the twentieth century, such s Farnsworth, Hevner, Schoen, and Seashore, engaged in studies of the affective response in music. An impressive array of data demonstrated overwhelming evidence that music can evoke deep and complex affective responses, but direct linear cause–effect linkages between music variables and specific affective responses were difficult to pinpoint. Predictive power in such studies remained very low. Data showed on the contrary that affective responses to music were often highly idiosyncratic to individual listeners and their musical enculturation as well as to the specific conditions in which the listening and testing took place, e.g., mood states or arousal needs the subjects brought into the listening condition. Studies of the affective response in music were also complicated by the difficulties in the general psychological studies of affect, mood, and emotion to conceptualize affective states. Two theoretical approaches have dominated and continue to shape such discussion: a categorical approach to defining emotional states, using a limited number of emotion states, such as happiness, anger, disgust, surprise, sadness, etc. A second school of thinking is often called a dimensional approach in which emotion states are not categorically defined but emotions occur only within two or more dimensions, such as levels of perceived pleasure and levels of perceived intensity. A dimensional approach has obviously had more attraction to music research as music is void of connotative semantic meaning, and therefore a dimensional response to affect in music would bypass the dilemma of exact verbal descriptors of felt emotion in music

and definitions of what musical variables are associated with exactly what categorical states in affect and emotion. However, dimensional approaches have the disadvantage for emotion research in music that the determination of affective states remains somewhat diffuse, and causal or predictive linkage with musical variables is difficult to conceptualize. Not until the second half of the twentieth century did several new landmark theories in aesthetics—influential for re-approaching affective response research in music—move this area of research in psychology of music decidedly forward.

In conjunction with studying verbal responses in affective responses to music, a very active line of physiological investigations emerged in this particular area, holding with the original impetus of the new psychology of music to study perception objectively as close to the human nervous system as possible. The research into the affective response to music as a physiological response spanned almost the full circle of the twentieth century, until it was superseded by breakthrough developments in brain research technology that allowed researchers to study brain responses *in vivo* under complex affective and cognitive stimulus conditions that began to include music at a very early stage of using these new technologies.

Prior to this new development, starting in the first years of the twentieth century, a huge amount literature begin to be amassed for the next 70 to 80 years, studying mostly physiological responses of the autonomic nervous system such as cardiac (heart rate), respiratory function, vascular changes (blood pressure), or galvanic skin response (GSR: changes in electrical skin conductance). This research showed many fascinating insights into the reactivity and sensitivity of physiological responses to music. The research has shown unequivocally that music elicits physiological changes that are indicative of changes in the perception and interpretation of the music by the listener. However, after those basic insights the data picture quickly became more complicated. Changes in physiological responses to musical stimuli did not seem to follow clear linear relationships with characteristics and changes in musical variables. For example, slower tempi in music do not always show slower heart rates, higher loudness levels or brighter timbres do not consistently create increases in vascular constriction or other measures. To create better interpretations of the physiology, studies quickly went to design paradigms combining verbal responses with physiological measures. Also in such a two-pronged assessment approach, simple cause–effect relationships remained elusive. For example, studies have shown that increases in self-reported relaxation measures may coexist with increases in physiological measures, e.g., accelerated heart rates.

Data seemed to suggest that the physiological response per se appears contentless, i.e., similar changes in heart rate or GSR can be associated with very different interpretations as to behavioural meaning. Secondly, the data suggested that interpretations of musical pieces or changes in musical elements (e.g., tempo) are highly idiosyncratic and contingent upon a listener's complex personal interpretation system. Therefore, in later developments many studies began to move away from music that was pre-selected or pre-categorized by the researcher to musical stimuli that—often self-selected by the experimental participants—could be very different in structure, style, and genre but had consistent meanings across listeners. In addition to recognizing complex idiosyncratic response models that made generalized investigations and interpretations of responses in physiology and verbal reports to pre-categorized music styles almost meaningless, further insight came from arousal theories that pointed out that changes in physiological reactions are highly dependent in their meaning and interpretations on existing arousal states preceding the stimulus-elicited changes. For example, temporary boosts to high arousal may be perceived as pleasant inductors and precursors of subsequent relaxation (the gym effect). In states of low arousal, moderate boosts of arousal (e.g., increases in heart rates) may be perceived as pleasant and relaxing.

Considerable breakthroughs in aesthetic theory began to influence psychology of music research in the second half of the twentieth century. Two highly influential theories—that still continue to influence most new developments in theories of meaning and music—were proposed respectively by Leonard Meyer in the 1950s and Daniel Berlyne in the 1960s and 70s.

Meyer proposed a model mechanism how music elicits meaningful affective responses in the music recipient—be it performer or listener. Based on Dewey's conflict theory of emotion which states that emotional responses are triggered when a tendency to respond is inhibited, expectations are built in music through compositional schemes that are continuously delayed, inhibited, and resolved—creating a complexly woven sound architecture based on building musical structures of anticipation–tension–resolution. In the interplay between the build-up of anticipation, the interjection of tension, and the creation of resolutions, the suspense evokes arousal—especially during the tension phase, i.e., the temporary inhibition of expectations—accompanied by a search for resolutions that is subsequently resolved within the musical structure. The resolution may then serve dialectically as the next springboard to renew the sequence of events since the resolution sets up a new set of expectations. The stronger the build-up of suspense or tension, the stronger will be the arousal build-up, and consequently the stronger will be the emotional release upon resolution. In order to have an appropriately structured experience, the music must have a well-balanced mixture of elements of novelty or uncertainty and redundancy or certainty in order to build meaningful tension-release schemes. Meyer's model, which was initially a purely theoretical proposal, has received considerable empirical support and is at the basis of many newer aesthetic models using tension–release mechanisms to explain musical meaning and affective experience in music elicited by the perception of music structures. Proponents of this view are usually called absolute expressionists because they believe that although musical meaning is communicated intrinsically through the perception of musical elements, i.e., the syntax of music, the perception of the melodic, rhythmic, and harmonic patterns and structures of the music can evoke meaningful affective experiences, however, not in the categorical semantic sense of emotion as previously discussed. Meyer's model constituted significant progress in explanatory accounts of understanding the nature and causation of meaning in music, including affective responses. His model and later models, connected to him, have received a slow but steady appreciation in the cognitive neuroscience of music, influencing study designs and hypothesis development for assessing brain responses to music.

Berlyne was the main proponent of another new development in aesthetic theory which is still highly relevant for modern brain research in music and aesthetic theories in the psychology of music. Berlyne founded the movement of 'experimental aesthetics' which was in many ways ahead of its time. He laid out a framework for how the perception of elements and patterns in artworks contain arousal-inducing attributes that constitute physiological arousal as the basis for affective–aesthetic behaviour in art perception. Berlyne—whose views on how we respond and how we perceive artworks was clearly influenced by gestalt theories of perception—showed at least in principle how artworks can have a profound effect on brain and behaviour by linking perceptual and arousal processes that are intrinsic to the human brain. At the time, his physiological elaborations on how aesthetically ordered visual and sound patterns in the visual arts and music have unique arousal-inducing properties that—when perceived as 'Good Gestalts'—create meaningful and affectively rich perceptual experiences, did not have the benefit of new research models and deeper knowledge of human brain function in cognitive neuroscience. However, his basic framework has been not so much rejected but simply vastly expanded by modern human brain imaging and neurophysiology. Berlyne was perhaps the first scholar in music psychology close to suggesting a basis for a new biological aesthetics that includes music as a biological core function of the human brain. We will come back to this point later.

In the last 25 years of the twentieth century, music psychology underwent its most fundamental change with the advent of brain imaging as an entirely new technology of studying the human *in vivo*, involved in complex cognitive operations. Up that point, human brain research could learn much from animal models in regard to motor system function or the neuroanatomy of various perceptual systems, but higher cognitive functions could only be diffusely approximated through animal brain research. Other techniques had major limitations in creating large samples, establishing testable hypotheses, or studying brain processes during complex cognitive tasks. For example, posthumous brain research from persons who had known and

well described behavioural dysfunctions, research with persons who had undergone well-defined neurosurgical interventions (e.g., split brain surgery), or dichotic listening tests linking ear preference with hemispheric preference in perceptual processing, all had helped contribute knowledge on cognitive brain function and were widely used in music research, but could never accomplish what the development of comprehensive knowledge on brain function measuring a human brain *in vivo* could deliver.

The two most prevalent brain imaging techniques, positron emission tomography (PET) and functional magnetic resonance imaging (fMRI), allowed unprecedented access to studying the brain basis of human cognition and helped establish a new field of scientific inquiry, appropriately referred to as cognitive neuroscience. Cognitive neuroscience in many ways has begun to change psychology as a mostly behaviourally based research discipline. Interestingly, music became rather quickly—even in the pioneer stages of these new technologies—a subject of immediate interest, and music studies are among some of the first human brain imaging studies carried out. The cognitive neuroscience of music is now an integral part music psychology, its research efforts and the knowledge base of the biology underlying music behaviour. Brain imaging has profoundly altered the traditional nature of research in music psychology.

Initially, research paradigms using brain imaging in music were relatively basic and looked for simple contrasts. For example, typical early studies compared listening to music vs listening to a narrated text, or compared musical responses of professional musicians vs non-musicians. Based on such baseline designs, some of the early findings focused on differential hemispheric activations in music compared to non-musical tasks, where the right hemisphere seemed particularly involved in music processing compared to the left brain hemisphere. Such findings created a certain amount of publicity and notoriety in considering that the right hemisphere may be the site of artistic abilities in the brain. As research designs became more sophisticated and more complex designs investigated specific musical responses, such notions turned out to be highly oversimplified. Music as a complex sound language that engages multiple processing systems in the brain in the area of perceptual, motor, and cognitive functions, actually turned out to be a stimulus that is best characterized by very complex activations patterns in highly distributed patterns across the whole brain on cortical and subcortical levels. The brain imaging research of the past 20 years has evolved in roughly four categories: music perception—broader cognitive processes, e.g., regarding emotional saliency—music learning and plasticity—biomedical applications of music.

In music perception, a wide array of studies have investigated the functional neuroanatamy of music perception (and production) relative to specific musical elements or specific production tasks. Perception of smaller elements such as pitch, harmony, rhythm, timbre, and perception of larger pattern elements such as melodies or scales, vs full musical excerpts, and other structural components of music have been studied in respect to underlying brain function. Additionally, aspects of music production such as motor control in instrumental and vocal (singing vs speech) performance have been extensively studied. Investigations into rhythm perception and rhythm production—especially issues in rhythmic sensorimotor synchronization—have received particular attention in brain imaging research as an important component aspect of music perception.

Broader aspects of music responses—for example more interpretative responses in regard to meaning and emotional saliency—have been studied less to date than more structural music perception questions. However, recent attempts are beginning to make up for this noticeable lag. Imaging studies in regard to emotion and music may still face age-old challenges in regard to the previously discussed difficulties in appropriate conceptualizations and theoretical underpinnings of meaning and emotional behaviour in music. Also, brain research into the meaning and emotion in music must be based on solid theoretical foundations in aesthetic theory and may require more intense and integrative collaborative efforts between musicologists, music psychologists, and cognitive neuroscientists in the future. However, a very important and fertile field for future research seems wide open in this area.

New findings in the neurobiology of learning have motivated considerable efforts in musical brain imaging. The discovery that experience, learning, and training can drive brain plasticity—i.e., changes in the neural organization and connectivity of the brain—led to a number of studies investigating brain plasticity induced by music learning and music training. The evidence shows impressively that music changes the brain and that certain areas, e.g., motor areas involved in instrumental training (keyboard, violin, etc.) or visuospatial and cognitive areas trained through intense music training can become enlarged and preferentially activated via the establishment of new and well-developed neural circuits. There is a broader impact implied by many of these studies because changes in brain plasticity through music learning—especially if they involve brain areas that also mediate critical non-musical cognitive and perceptual functions—may suggest that music learning can confer a wider cognitive benefit to general non-musical cognition and intellectual functions. Such notions have considerable importance for all forms of music training as well as the role of music education in public education.

Finally, since the early 1990s a combination of brain imaging and clinical behavioural studies has investigated the biomedical effect of music in a neurorehabilitation environment, where music is used as a therapeutic stimulus to retrain motor, language, and cognitive function in persons with brain injuries and neurological disorders, such as stroke, Parkinson's disease, traumatic brain injury, dementia, cerebral palsy, and other dysfunctions of the human nervous system. Studies have shown impressively that music is an effective sensory language to facilitate the recovery of neurologic function when used in a therapeutic context that emphasizes learning and training models to re-educate the brain via mechanisms of brain plasticity. In that respect, the new neuroscience research in music has led to a fairly radical reformulation of concepts and principles for the role of music in therapy and medicine, away from traditional social science-based concepts of music therapy—traditionally emphasizing notions of well-being and cultural values in relationship building and human interaction—to neuroscience-based models, emphasizing music as a language that can actively address the rehabilitation of perception, cognition, and motor function.

Brain imaging has brought about enormous changes in research directions and virtually re-invented the cognitive science of music embedded in music psychology form its early origins. However, as a technique it has several serious limitations that need to be kept in mind when assessing its importance. Interestingly these limitations are particularly relevant in music research. The current techniques in neuroimaging provide a detailed look at brain activation based on topography, i.e., maps of highly developed spatial resolution. Brain imaging creates maps of brain activity, measured over a relatively long period of recording time in the second range (e.g., 20–30 secs). In other words, the time resolution—i.e., when something happens rather than where—has limits in assessing with exactitude the timing of brain activations. This is important in music research because music is physically based on vibration patterns of air molecules, and as such the perception of sound is based on time parameters of vibrating objects. Music is a temporally based sensory language and brain activations in music perception must respond to information processing in the range of milliseconds (or below). To that end, the auditory system which processes music is a highly sensitive system in regard to speed and precision in responding to very small fluctuations in temporal changes in the vibrations patterns that constitute sound. Thus, neuroimaging can make important contributions to the mapping of music perception and musical responses but can only add limited information to the temporal aspects of music processing in the brain.

For this reason, two other techniques measuring brain activations—one new and one older—have received considerable attention in music research, providing an excellent complement to brain imaging via PET or fMRI. The techniques are called electroencephalography (EEG) and magnetoencephalography (MEG). Their respective mechanisms of signal recording are somewhat different although they record the same brain signal. EEG records brain waves—usually via sensors attached to the scalp—by detecting the electrical currents that are emitted by the electrochemical potentials of neurons during their firing activity. MEG records the same electrochemical signal but measures it by the measuring the magnetic field created by the electrochemical signal. EEG is a technique going back at least 50 years that was developed initially to detect any abnormalities in the patterns of neuronal firing activity which occur in an oscillatory 'rhythmic' fashion: hence the somewhat misleading term brain 'waves' was created. Data recordings and analysis of brain rhythms have become exceedingly more detailed and complex, so that EEG research has experienced a very fruitful renaissance. EEG measures have very high temporal resolution down to 1 millisecond—however, they have poor spatial precision because surface sensors receive and record signals from widely distributed neuron ensembles and exact spatial determination of the source of the signals is not possible. MEG has a major advantage over EEG because a technique called dipole analysis in the magnetic field allow the creation of fairly good spatial locators for the brain signal source. Both EEG and MEG can record brain activity associated with a certain behavioural task with high accuracy of timing of the signal processing in the brain. In music, EEG and MEG can be used to study the time course of music perception across different brain areas in millisecond ranges which give an excellent picture of the brain's temporal processing of music. In conjunction with PET or fMRI imaging, a very complete spatial and temporal map of music processing in the brain can be established. However, combining techniques requires complex equipment interfaces that are not easy to carry out technologically.

One of the most innovative current approaches to studying music perception is to compare music perception on analogue variables to verbal language. The comparison makes sense in many ways as both music and verbal language are auditory-based communication systems, hold vital function in human society, and have several systems of structural organization in parallel, such as phonological sound category systems and syntactical rule systems. There are also some obvious differences, of course. For instance, both systems have pitch and timbre as sound categories, but in music pitch is the primary categorical system to organize sounds into musical patterns, whereas in verbal language timbre is a primary organizer of speech sounds (vowels, consonants). One of the most critical differences lies in the absence of semantics in music, whereas linguistic semantics is a critical component of verbal language. The semantic meaning of a word is the reference to objects or experiences in reality and to the mental representations of such reality. Semantic meaning is referential, making propositions about reality. Those are fairly philosophical concepts that show how deeply linguistics is embedded in concepts of mind and thought. Musical statements or communication symbols—melodic motifs, rhythmic phrases, harmonic sequences—are non-semantic in the sense that they only refer to themselves within the rules of the musical syntax used. That brings up another important point for consideration. Both music and verbal language can be said to be based on rules of how structures of sounds or words are constructed, via linguistic grammar or compositional grammar (in music). Both grammars are generative in that they have rules that can generate and predict meaningful 'correct' statements in many combinatorial ways in a given language. They also have, however, decisive differences. Violations of linguistic grammar can be determined to be incorrect and rendering statements meaningless. Violations of musical 'grammar' rules are soft and not absolute. Violations of musical grammar are common and often deliberate in order to discover new musically meaningful 'grammars'. Therefore, direct comparisons between musical syntax violations and linguistic syntax violations are not entirely possible and reveal little about shared or parallel brain processing for different language systems. However, carefully constructed comparisons between analogue language processes in music and linguistics have been recently attempted in brain imaging, and can yield insight not only into music-specific cognitive brain processes but also into aspects of cognitive processing systems in the brain that may operate cross-modally for different 'language' systems.

A new model may push investigations in music research one step further within the language model. Instead of investigating music in comparison to verbal language, a new model may investigate music as an autonomous biological language of the brain in relationship to other verbal and non-verbal language systems. In this model, the brain is considered a multiple language generator. The brain generates and operates in multiple languages of thought. Thoughts as mental representations occur in verbal language form but also other forms of languages in non-verbal systems come easily to mind, e.g., the language of quantities and size expressed through numbers. The arts and music would be a specific case within the languages of images and percepts. Music as a language is based on the ability to think in sound, to perceive relationships between sounds and to generate rules to build sound events into complex sound scapes. The whole architecture of music as such would then be considered based on the ability of complex non-verbal temporal auditory thinking, which is by definition a deeply cognitive process. Human beings are clearly born with that ability, just as they are born with a biologically innate knowledge of verbal language. It is of great interest in this matter to study pre-historic artworks which show figurines and paintings of highly modern design, shape, and with highly evolved aesthetic qualities of abstraction and symbolism. We find artifacts like that dated 70 000 or more years old—tens of thousands of years before the first emergence of written documents for word languages and basic numerical concepts. Artefacts of musical instruments can currently be dated as far back as 35–45 000 years. Recent brain investigations regarding music processing show interestingly many areas involved that are also involved in complex linguistic (verbal language) processing and other cognitive functions. These findings may provide support for a 'music as a language' model within a comprehensive model of multiple brain languages.

Modern psychology of music has engaged in other areas of investigation and analysis besides the ones discussed so far. Social communication in regard to cultural values, uses, and function of music have always been an important aspect of research in music psychology. Music psychology and music anthropology have interacted in studies of music perception as well as historical roles of music in human culture. Music education and music therapy often consider psychology of music as a foundational field of study for their disciplines, and music psychology has indeed contributed important knowledge to such those fields. However, it is probably fair to say that the majority of research effort in music psychology has not been in applied or translational research for educational, developmental, or therapeutic purposes. However, such applied or translational focus may become one of many new future directions in the psychology of music.

Bibliography

Avanzini G, Faienza C, Minciacchi D, Lopez L and Majno M (eds) (2003). *The neurosciences and music.* New York Academy of Sciences, New York.

Avanzini G, Lopez L, Koelsch S and Majno M (eds) (2005). *The neurosciences and music II.* New York Academy of Sciences, New York.

Berlyne DE (1971). *Aesthetics and psychobiology.* Appleton Century Crofts, New York.

Bregman A (1990). *Auditory scene analysis: the perceptual organization of sound.* MIT Press, Cambridge, MA.

Clynes M (ed.) (1982). *Music, mind, and brain: the neuropsychology of music.* Plenum Press, London, New York.

Cook PR (ed.) (1999). *Music, cognition, and computerized sound: an introduction to psychoacoustics.* MIT Press, Cambridge, MA.

Critchley M and Henson RA (1977). *Music and the brain: studies in the neurology of music.* CC Thomas, Springfield IL.

Deutsch D (1999). *The psychology of music.* Academic Press, New York.

Dowling WJ and Harwood DL (1986). *Music cognition.* Academic Press, New York.

Fauconnier G and Turner M (2002). *The way we think.* Perseus Basic Books, New York.

Galaburda AM, Kosslyn SM and Christen Y (eds) (2002). *The languages of the brain.* Harvard University Press, Cambridge, MA, London.

Hodges DA (ed) (1999). *Handbook of music psychology.* IMR Press, San Antonio, TX.

Jackendoff R (2002). *Foundations of language.* Oxford University Press, Oxford.

Juslin PN and Sloboda JA (eds) (2001). *Music and emotion: theory and research.* Oxford University Press, Oxford.

Lundin RW (1967). *An objective psychology of music.* The Ronald Press Company, New York.

Merriam AP (1964). *The anthropology of music.* Northwestern University Press, Evanston IL.

Meyer LB (1956). *Emotion and meaning in music.* University of Chicago Press, Chicago, IL.

Miell D, MacDonald R and Hargreaves DJ (2005). *Musical communication.* Oxford University Press, Oxford.

Pierce JR (1992). *The science of musical sound.* WH Freeman, New York.

Patel AD (2008). *Music, language, and the brain.* Oxford University Press, Oxford, New York.

Radocy RE and Boyle JD (1979). *Psychological foundations of musical behavior.* Charles C Thomas, Springfield IL.

Riess Jones M and Holleran S (eds) (1990). *Cognitive bases of musical communication.* American Psychological Association, Washington, DC.

Sefarine ML (1988). *Music as cognition.* Columbia University Press, New York.

Sethares WA (2007). *Rhythm and transforms.* Springer, London.

Shaw-Miller S (2002). *Visible deeds of music: art and music from Wagner to Cage.* Yale University Press, New Haven, CT.

Snyder B (2000). *Music and memory.* MIT Press, Cambridge, MA.

Thaut MH (2005). *Rhythm, music, and the brain.* Routledge, New York, London.

Wallin NL, Merker B and Brown S (2000). *The origins of music.* MIT Press, Cambridge, MA.

Zatorre RJ and Peretz I (eds) (2001). *The biological foundations of music.* New York Academy of Sciences, New York.

CHAPTER 52

Where now?

Susan Hallam, Ian Cross and Michael Thaut

THE purpose of this chapter is to draw together emerging themes from across all sections of the book. The themes identified are not exhaustive but capture broad trends, ideas, issues and questions which have resonance across the whole of music psychology. The themes are not mutually exclusive. There is overlap between them. Each theme has implications for many areas of music psychology. The first theme concerns the power of music, the second the way that modern technology has enhanced music's influence through increasing access and enabling individuals to listen to the music of their choice at any time or place. Subsequent themes relate to our understanding of basic perceptual and cognitive processes, and music as language, communication and interaction. A key issue is the need to take greater account of culture and context, with more research being undertaken in non-Western cultures. The chapter concludes with a consideration of methodological advances and the need for those from different disciplines with an interest in music psychology to work more closely together.

The power of music

Music has a multiplicity of functions which operate at several levels: that of the individual, the social group and society in general. In relation to each of these music can have a very powerful impact influencing behaviour, emotions, and moods in a variety of settings frequently without our conscious awareness (see Chapters 11–15 and 40–45). The exceptional power of music may be related to it being able to stimulate us aurally, visually, intellectually, emotionally and physically, simultaneously.

Background music selected by others and music accompanying visual images and verbal messages can have a very immediate impact through its power to invoke associations and change moods and arousal levels. This has led to its use in a variety of leisure, commercial and employment settings (see Chapters 40, 41 and 45). The ever-growing body of research in this area has made considerable progress in understanding the nature of the relationships between musical stimuli and behaviour but there is still much work to do to establish the particular conditions, contexts and musical characteristics which lead to specific outcomes and to identify those characteristics of the individual which may ameliorate the impact. We also need to establish the factors that are important in determining negative responses to music.

Concentrated engagement with music, usually through listening, can evoke peak emotional experiences which can have permanent and powerful therapeutic effects enhancing relationships, attitudes, general appreciation of art or music, aesthetic sensitivity and perception of everyday reality (see Chapter 42). To understand these powerful responses better we need to be able to identify the specific conditions, individual and contextual, which pertain at the time. There is also a growing body of evidence of the longer-term effects which active engagement with music in educational, community, therapeutic and medical contexts can have on health, well-being and intellectual development (see Chapters 23, 44, 46–49). Traditionally, active engagement with music and music therapy, informed by cultural values and social science models, has been assigned a rather global and diffuse role in bringing about long-term change in behaviour, relying on concepts of well-being, social relationship building and the development of transferable skills. Recent developments in the neurobiology of music have enabled more concrete evidence about what music can achieve. By studying the brain basis of musical behaviour and learning, it has become clear how music learning reciprocally effects changes in the brain (Chapters 16 and 18). The concept of neuroplasticity applied to musical learning in relation to the initial education of the brain and re-educating the injured brain (Chapters 17, 18, 23, 46–49) has created the conditions for new scientific research on the effects of music in educational, medical, therapeutic, and rehabilitation settings that can be transferred and generalized to a wide range of non-musical functions, for instance, motor and speech training and cognitive functions such as memory, attention, and executive functions. In music therapy and medicine much promising research has been accumulated and has begun to be translated into practice (Chapters 46–49). In educational and community contexts progress is slower (see Chapters 23 and 44), but overall these developments will continue to present a powerful research agenda in the future, creating a new form of neurologically and evidence-based music research in education, medicine and related disciplines, and therapy for the twenty-first century.

Music also has a powerful impact on social interactions, the identities individuals create for themselves, the social groups with which they engage, and the meanings that they construct and experience in and through music (see Chapters 1–4, 27 and 43). A limitation of research to date is that most has been undertaken within Western musical cultures. Its validity needs to be tested within other musical contexts and cultures to explore whether similar phenomena occur elsewhere. Other relatively neglected issues relate to the extent to which identification with particular musical genres determines behaviour beyond the musical. For instance, with regard to engendering violent, antisocial or rebellious behaviour, are particular musical genres preferred because they reflect already existing behavioural tendencies, or does the music itself encourage particular behaviours? We also need to explore the relationships between the extent, quality and antecedents of the individual's involvement

with music and their identification with particular genres, taking account of the experiences of individuals for whom music is relatively unimportant. Understanding why some individuals do not engage with music may shed light on a range of issues relating to musical ability, musical preferences and motivation.

The impact of technology

Technological advances in the twentieth century changed the ways in which music could be experienced. They not only made music more accessible but made it possible for each individual to select the music that they wished to listen to in any combination of genres in any environment. People now use music to meet a range of psychological needs: as a distraction, to focus attention or energize, to manipulate moods, and to work through emotional issues (see Chapter 40). Music plays a key role in people's lives as they travel, and engage in domestic and social activities in the home and community, and at leisure. Considerable progress has been made in identifying the ways in which music is used at the individual level, but we know little about how it is selected for particular purposes, or how successful this process is. The way that music impacts on and is used in our daily lives will clearly continue to be a major focus of research in the future.

The easy availability of music and its commodification challenges earlier idealized conceptions of music listening as a concentrated process with a focus on the spiritual or aesthetic. Currently, we lack knowledge about different approaches to listening, and the way that music used as background moves from the periphery to the centre of attention. This is an area for future development.

Technology has not only led to the increased availability of music but also its globalization and commercialization. These changes will inevitably have impacted on those involved in the creation and performance of music. As yet we know relatively little about this. Research which explored the nature of the work of professional performers and composers in the twenty-first century and the impact of this on learning, motivation and performance would have major implications for the future training of musicians (see Chapters 30–38).

Understanding of basic perceptual and cognitive processes

Although there now exists a considerable body of empirical research on music perception and cognition, many 'primitive' perceptual processes are not yet known in sufficient detail to allow us to feel that we fully understand the processes of music perception and cognition (see Chapters 5–10). Many fundamental aspects of musical sound are not yet well enough understood in terms of their physics in order for us to be confident that we can develop predictive theories about how we experience such sounds. For example, the ways in which our perception of a violin's sound may be shaped by the pattern of the radiation of sound from the instrument is constrained by the fact that, as yet, there exists no complete physical account of how the instrument's structure, and mode and physical context of performance, might shape that pattern of radiation. The nature of the factors that influence how we hear sounds as having particular timbral qualities is not wholly clear (see Chapter 7), nor do we know how judgements about sound quality relate to issues of attention and memory (see Chapter 10). These are all questions for future research.

There is also the question of the contribution to music perception and cognition of sensory modalities other than the auditory (see Chapter 3). Several researchers have theorized and explored ways in which music perception and cognition appear to involve cross-domain mappings between the auditory attributes of music and features of other domains of human experience (visual, haptic, motional, etc., as well as cognitively higher-order constructs such as body-image schemas). At present, it is not clear how integral these cross-domain mappings might be for our experience of music and there is immense scope for future exploration.

Music and language/music as language

Recently, there has been a regeneration of interest in the relationship between music and language as communicative systems, and as manifesting common properties as representation systems within the brain. The parallel and shared components between these two auditorily based systems of communication and mental representation offer new opportunities for research and early findings are promising, with notions of generativity, syntax and grammar suggested as accounting for the processes involved in the experience of musical structures (see Chapters 6 and 19). The extent to which syntactical aspects of music can be regarded as being of the same order—in terms of scope and complexity—as syntax in language is still unclear, as is the nature of the factors that enable complex serial structures to be perceived and remembered in both language and music. If music can be conceived of and perceived as though it conforms to grammatical principles, what types of grammar are entailed, and do these constitute 'true' grammars of the type that form foci of linguistic research, or are they more constrained in their scope and power? If the grammars of music and language were to be found to be closely comparable, the question then arises of how music can be differentiated from language as a domain of human thought and behaviour (see Chapters 1–4). There is also the issue of how different musical practices have arisen in different cultures.

This research agenda may be strengthened by studying music—within a broader concept of all the arts—as an autonomous language itself, i.e., a representation of thought in non-verbal aesthetic images and percepts. Such conceptualization may create new and productive insights into music as an innate biological language of the brain, its origins, its role and function in the cognitive and intellectual development of the human brain, and its unique contributions to the complexity of human brain function—not as an enriching cultural phenomenon, but as a core modality of human cognition.

Music as communication and interaction

A key emerging theme is that of music as communication. Advances in technology have enabled more detailed consideration of the assessment and modelling of performance processes providing new insights into performance practices, communication issues relating to playing from memory, the role of movement, collaboration between performers and issues relating to performance anxiety and the medical problems that can arise from a lengthy career in the music profession (see Chapters 30–36). This research has focused almost exclusively on Western classical music, and we know little about these issues as they relate to other genres and musical cultures.

There is also a dearth of research on the way that audiences participate in the communicative process. The relationship between music in the individual mind and music as an interactive behaviour is not well understood, we know little about how our private musical cognitions relate to our public musical interactions. Musical performance may appear as the exercise of individual musical skills, but equally as the outcome of joint musical endeavour. To date we have few insights regarding the way in which the musical behaviours of others, our perceptions of those behaviours, and our conceptions of the mental processes that we infer as underlying them, contribute to the experience of music as performance or as interaction. While some empirical research has begun to explore these issues and to develop theories of music cognition in interaction (see Chapters 1, 4, 34 and 38), the vast majority of research has focused on individual music cognitions and perceptions. Exploration of capacities that are likely to be central to interactive musicality, such as that for entrainment (see Chapters 4 and 8) is in its infancy, and questions of how such capacities relate to broader human capacities for complex social communicative interaction have barely been addressed. Indeed, the question of whether or not at least some types of musical judgement may be exercised as social and interactive behaviours rather than being evidenced in acts of individual judgement (as much music sociology would suggest) remain to be explored, as does the problem of how such situations might be investigated scientifically.

The interface between the biological and cultural

An ongoing issue is the relationship between what is biologically determined at the species or individual level and what is determined by the cultural environment in which the individual develops. Are aspects of the human capacity for music found in the behavioural and mental capacities of any non-human animal species (see Chapter 1)? If so, are those human capacities interpretable as evolutionarily homologous to those of non-human species (which would indicate common evolutionary descent), or are they best construed as analogous (likely to have arisen because of similar selection pressures)? Answers to these questions would greatly advance our understanding of the significance of music as a human faculty, and require to be pursued by music psychologists in collaboration with ethnologists, geneticists, and evolutionary biologists and psychologists. Investigations of the 'social mind' and the 'social brain' are now major foci for cognitive and neuroscientific investigation, in part precipitated by the realization that the complexity of human sociality is one of the principal defining characteristics that appears to differentiate us from other species. Behavioural research has focused on issues such as theory of mind, social reasoning, and decision-making, and has often adverted to evolutionary approaches in seeking explanations for the scope of, and the constraints on, human social behaviours. Neuroscientific research has also begun to turn its attention to these and other aspects of human social capacities, and exploration of the place of music in human social capacities must be a primary focus for future research.

There are also unresolved issues relating to the propensity for individual differences in musical ability (see Chapter 24). Advances in research on genetics, to date, have had little impact on the debate. Few human behaviours or traits have been traced to specific gene pairs and it is likely that those who exhibit musical skills are drawing on a range of different gene combinations, which exert an influence on physical make-up in addition to cognitive and emotional development. Interactive rather than additive models of the relationship between the environment and genetic inheritance are now generally accepted. These interactions begin in the womb and continue throughout the lifespan (see Chapters 20–22).

Developing empirical methodologies are making it increasingly possible to carry out methodologically sound investigations relating to the prenatal period. As our understanding of prenatal influences increases we need to be able to relate these to postnatal behaviour. Cross-cultural longitudinal research following individuals from birth would enable us to identify those factors which contribute to the development of different musical skills in particular contexts. This would enable us to explore how children acquire musicality in non-Western, particularly traditional cultures and establish the factors which are common across cultures in child rearing and other social practices which encourage the acquisition of musical skills (see Chapters 20–22 and 28 and 29). While the family plays an important role in the early stages of engagement with music in Western cultures, this may not be the case elsewhere. Cultural influences on families, for instance the extent to which music is valued in the subculture to which the family belongs and the nature of the value placed on music in society, may be important, for instance, whether it is viewed as related to religion, as entertainment, as a form of protest, or as a way of life. Cross-cultural research would also enable us to establish if what we know about practice and performance applies equally to all cultures and musical genres (see Chapters 25 and 30–36). Currently there is little research on learning, practice, memorization processes, and performance outside the Western classical tradition. Realistically, longitudinal cross-cultural research is unlikely to be funded (though highly desirable) but it would be possible to undertake cross-cultural, cross-sectional research which would offer some insights. This would elaborate our knowledge of the impact of different cultural and familial traditions on perception, learning, cognition, and responses to music. The research would need to acknowledge that musical potential manifests itself in a range of different ways, creating further challenges for researchers in developing appropriate methodologies for exploring the processes of learning, assessing change, and attempting to identify the contribution of particular environmental influences. A number of systemic interactive models have been developed which would assist this process (see Chapters 26–29).

While existing research has made a major contribution to understanding the way in which specialist musical skills are acquired in a Western musical context, there still remain a number of key questions. For instance, how important is the child's choice of instrument in determining motivation and the level of expertise attained? To what extent do opportunities to engage in a wide range of musical activities contribute to the development of expertise as opposed to deliberate practice on a single instrument? To what extent do other factors, apart from those relating to musical expertise, contribute to success in the music profession (see Chapters 24–29)? There is also a developing research agenda in relation to amateur engagement with music. With the population in the Western world having more time for leisure and living longer, more people are developing musical skills as a hobby. We know relatively little about the factors that contribute to individuals returning to or taking up musical activities in later life, whether their motivation is musical, social or a combination of these, and how it is sustained.

The processes of composition and improvisation are situated within particular musical contexts which have their own conventions and rules. Existing research has largely taken place within a Western context, with a focus on professional musicians or the activities of young people working within the school curriculum (see Chapters 37–39). The relative lack of research in non-Western cultures means that we do not know whether the approaches and strategies identified in expert and novice composers and improvisers are specific to Western musical contexts or whether they have relevance elsewhere. We also know relatively little about the long-term development of composers and the way that their thinking, skills and careers change over time and may differ between genres. For instance, has the increasing commercialization of music had an impact on their working practices and output? The other ongoing challenge for research in this area relates to assessment and developing ways of judging the relative value or creativity of particular compositions or improvisations.

The majority of music cognition research has been laboratory-based, using Western-encultured listeners and Western–generally common-practice period–musical materials. While these studies, with the tight controls and replicable methodologies required by a scientific approach, have yielded many insights into music in mind, very few studies have managed to investigate non-Western musical perceptions with the same degree of rigour. In some ways this is not surprising; the exigencies of conducting empirical research in field contexts are not particularly consonant with the need to be able to control experimental variables and exclude those that cannot be controlled. Nevertheless, it is vital that future research should aim to investigate the ways in which non-Western musical perceptions and cognitions are aligned with, or differ from, those of the Western participants from whom our current knowledge is principally derived, ideally by using means that will enable the exploration of a wide range of emic perceptions and conceptions.

Methodological limitations and advances

All research is limited by the methodologies available to it, and music psychology is no exception. A wide range of approaches and methodologies have been adopted across the field in attempts to develop our understanding of musical practices and processes many of which are unavailable to conscious awareness. There has been much reliance on self-report (interviews, diaries, rating scales), either concurrent or retrospective, and experiments or observations the outcomes of which are used to infer musical processes. The advent of *in vivo* brain imaging technology in the field of cognitive neuroscience has emerged as a new force complementing existing methods, enabling the integration of behavioural research designs in psychology with concomitant studies into the functional neuroanatomy underlying these cognitive behaviour functions (see Chapter 51). An important and highly fruitful trend is likely to be the fusing of many areas of research. We see the beginnings of this already, for instance, when more and more sophisticated and musicologically sound behavioural studies in the perception of musical structure are combined with investigations into the underlying neurobiology of music. Advances in technology and the use of innovative experimental methods might

also enable exploration and comparison of the brain states of participants in musical interaction, which could greatly illuminate the dynamics of music as social process.

Collaboration in research

Emerging throughout the book are issues relating to the need for collaboration between those working in different disciplines. The historic synopsis of research developments in music psychology illustrates the high degree of diversity as well as the unique dynamics of forming interdisciplinary research agendas that have continuously driven the field forward in a number of different directions (see Chapters 50 and 51). Music psychology has never presented itself as a uniform field of investigation and research goals. Various influences from different fields have converged on a scientific study of music and shaped the research, including aesthetics, cognitive psychology, physics, physiology, social sciences, anthropology, and most recently, cognitive neuroscience. Music psychology also overlaps with a number of other disciplines, including music education, therapy, ethnomusicology, and music theory and analysis. To further our understanding in many areas of work greater collaboration is required. For instance, in developing understanding of musical learning and development, music psychologists need to join forces with researchers in music education and with ethnomusicologists, as the types of information, theory and research practice that the questions demand require that developmental theories of music be elaborated and tested in a wide range of ethnographic contexts.

A continual multidisciplinary integration of and collaboration with musicology, i.e., music theorists, composers, and historians, into scientific research agendas where musicologists, musicians, psychologists, and other sciences work shoulder to shoulder in equal partnerships would also greatly benefit music psychology. For instance, there is much research by both musicologists and psychologists on expressive performance, particularly rubato. However, these two strands of work rarely make reference to each other. Yet both seek to explain and describe musical behaviours and cross-fertilization of methodologies and knowledge would aid a deeper understanding.

In relation to developing our understanding of the perceptual and cognitive processes in music, it is essential for music psychologists to collaborate closely with engineers, physicists, psychoacousticians, linguists, and others in order to develop the field. This is necessary not only to ensure that theory and experiment in music psychology is informed and guided by well-founded understandings of physical and psychoacoustical facts and processes, but also to make clear to those with whom we are collaborating the ways in which the complexities of the questions raised by music perception and cognition may be informative in the development of their own disciplines.

There would also be benefits in closer collaboration with researchers working in relation to other art forms. The study of creativity in performance, improvisation and composition would benefit from collaboration with those working in the visual arts, drama and dance. This would enable communalities and differences to be identified and shared issues, for instance in relation to assessment, to be better understood.

Endnote

Music psychology does not function as a tightly defined academic discipline operating within a single, focused epistemological framework. It is interdisciplinary. This has led to contributions from a wide range of related fields, although from time to time there are tensions between them. While some may argue that the interdicsplinary nature of music psychology is a weakness leading to a lack of focus, there have been clear benefits to the quantity and quality of research generated when compared with the other visual and performing arts. From this perspective interdisciplinarity is a cause for celebration.

Index

Please note that page references to Figures or Tables are in *italic* print